GLC
DETAILING FOR BUILDING CONSTRUCTION

GLC DETAILING FOR BUILDING CONSTRUCTION

A Designers' Manual of
over 350 Standard Details

The Architectural Press Ltd : London

First published in Great Britain by
The Architectural Press Ltd : London 1980

ISBN : 0 85139 233 4 (cloth)
ISBN : 0 85139 234 2 (paper)

© Department of Architecture and Civic Design
of the Greater London Council 1980

All rights reserved. No part of this publication may be reproduced, stored in a retrieval system, or transmitted, in any form or by any means, electronic, mechanical, recording or otherwise, for publication purposes, without the prior permission of the publishers. Such permission, if granted, is subject to a fee depending on the nature of the use.

No guarantee is given that any detail shown in this book will be suitable for a particular use, and any detail similar to, or based upon those shown, should not be used without expert advice as to suitability.

Printed in Great Britain by
Biddles Limited, Guildford

Foreword

by Malcolme Gordon Technical Policy Architect GLC Department of Architecture and Civic Design

Standard details have been used in the GLC since its inception in 1965 and were produced by the three main branches of the Architects Department (Education, Housing, and Special Works) for their own work. With the creation of a Technical Policy Branch—later Division—in 1971, the responsibility for Standard Drawings was centralized.

As the bulk of the Architect's Departments work in the 1970s was housing, the majority of details were created with housing in mind, but many of the details have been used on non-housing projects. A conscious decision was originally taken that Standard Details would rarely cover the external envelope of buildings, in order to give Architects freedom of expression; more recently, however, as the Department's housing policy has changed and the emphasis has been on providing low rise houses with gardens, Standard Details of the external envelope have been produced under the heading of 'Good Practice Details' which is a complementary volume to the present edition (see note on cover). The obvious drawback of using Standard Drawings on a large scale is that if they turn out to be defective in any way the defect will be multiplied many times over. The Group producing Standard Details therefore carries a very heavy responsibility in ensuring that as far as is humanly possible they reflect good building practice.

The creation of a Standard Detail must of necessity take longer to produce than an individual detail for a particular job, as an involved process of discussions has to be conducted. Notwithstanding this extra time element, a recent cost exercise showed that if a Standard Drawing could be used 'cold' 3 times it paid for itself and any further use was all profit. This is merely a typical example, but over the years the saving in GLC Architects' time has been considerable. The raison d'etre of Standard Drawings is to provide consistently good detailing which all members of the team including the Clerk of Works, Contractor and materials supplier can immediately recognize and use with confidence.

The task of updating to take account of new legislation, new materials and new technology is of course never-ending. The drawings produced in this edition cannot be regarded as definitive, and some have been overtaken by changing GLC policy. They represent the product of the latest experience and benefits of feedback facilities, but at the same time are intended to be used only as a guide.*

*It should be noted that the various Guidance Notes are reproduced here in the form in which they are issued to GLC Architects.

External Works

Contents

Guidance notes

Pedestrian pavings

Drawings

Standard drawings show the most commonly used materials for pedestrian pavings, steps, and non-structural changes of level.

Foundations

Thick hardcore or lean mix concrete are shown as alternative foundations under a number of pavings. Lean mix concrete is preferable if the pavings:

1 may be subjected to occasional light vehicular traffic;
2 are to be laid on poor quality or made up ground; or
3 are small units (bricks, setts, etc) to be laid in large areas where irregular settlement would lead to ponding.

In connection with the above, reports from site indicate cases of pedestrian pavings being ruined by the unauthorised use of vehicles. Care should be taken at design stage to discourage this practice by separating the two areas wherever possible or by the erection of natural or artificial barriers.

Bricks

Bricks for steps and paving should be non-absorbent and frost resistant. Not all stocks are suitable, and job architects should consult Materials Information Group. The brick chosen should be specified on the job layout drawing and/or Preambles clause G6.

Bricks and cobbles have been known to be used as missiles on some housing estates. It is left to the architect's discretion whether they should be used where no supervision of any kind is available. Cobble hazards are exactly what the name implies and should not be used for pedestrian traffic.

Mortars

Generally, the use of sulphate resistant cement is

not justified on these details, but the mortar specified on drawing D5142 'External steps—brick' has been chosen to provide the best resistance to frost, and sulphates leaching from the bricks.

Falls

Normally recommended falls are:

BS Paving Slabs	1:30 maximum, 1:72 minimum
Bricks	1:60 minimum
Bituminous surfaces	1:40 cross falls, 1:200 long fall, 1:60 maximum on playgrounds

Rise and Going of Stairs

External steps require easier gradients than internal stairs conforming to traditional arithmetical formula. The following familiar examples may be useful as a guide:

1 Shell Building, podium opposite County Hall (GLC) North Block entrance, 275mm going × 138mm rise.

2 County Hall (GLC) main entrance, risers vary, but opposite the opening doors 392mm going × 137mm rise.

Mowing Strips and Splash Strips

Drawing D5148 shows a selection of mowing and splash strips intended for use round the perimeters of buildings, against fences and against boundary walls to enable the use of mechanical lawn mowers on grass areas, or to prevent the disfiguring of wall surfaces when flower beds are placed close against the building.

Drainage: Inspection Chambers

General

The drainage details have been prepared in consultation with the GLC Civil Engineer's Division, but are applicable to any type of building.

The Civil Engineer's Division offers either a full consultancy service or an advisory service where GLC architects wish to carry out drainage design themselves.

Element (50) indicates services, including drainage outside the building up to outside face of building.

Terminology In domestic or 'building drainage', access to drains for inspecting, testing or clearance of obstruction is by means of an inspection chamber. (The term 'manhole' applies to main drainage works for means of access to sewers).

A standard inspection chamber schedule is available in the form of a melinex print, where the additional information, eg invert levels, cover levels and types, etc, should be filled in according to the details of the drainage layout.

Types of Inspection Chambers

Precast Concrete On larger schemes it is usually more economical to use pre-formed inspection chambers and two types are available:

1 circular, as detailed;

2 rectangular.

Brick Where so requested by the local authority, eg some Inner London Boroughs, or where there is a limited number of inspection chambers, it may be more convenient to construct them in brickwork, in accordance with recommendations of CP 301:1971.

Plastics The present range of plastic inspection chambers and components are more suited to shallow depths (approximately 900mm from cover to invert level). This limits their use to situations such as housing developments, where they may be sited at constant shallow depths to receive drain branches from houses, with a connection from each inspection chamber to a 'collector drain'.

Cast Iron Covers for use with Inspection Chambers, Petrol Interceptors Etc.

Covers are divided into three groups for purposes

of Departmental Standard Drawings. They are:

1 Heavy Duty (for use in areas subject to heavy commercial vehicles). BS 497 Grade A or approved alternative.
2 Medium Duty (for use in areas subject to light vehicular traffic only). BS 497 Grade B or approved alternative.
3 Light Duty (for use in non-vehicular areas). BS 497 Grade C or approved alternative.

The key reference used for these groups is 'H', 'M' and 'L' respectively. This primary letter is followed by a number indicating a specific size and type of cover (see below). Where securing screws are required the letter 'S' should be suffixed to the key reference.

All covers and frames should conform to the requirements of the local authority involved.

Where non BS covers are used the Architect/ Engineer must ensure their suitability with regards to loading.

Drawings showing covers and frames for a particular range of inspection chambers have been rationalized to those sizes of covers most commonly used. Where a cover other than those shown is required it should be specified in the Inspection Chamber Schedule, and if necessary shown on a supplementary drawing.

Schedule of Covers and Frames with Key References*

Heavy Duty
BS 497, 495 × 520mm nominal single triangular — H1
BS 497, 558mm diameter nominal double triangular — H2
Non BS rectangular cover 750 × 600mm nominal — H3
Non BS rectangular cover 750 × 750mm nominal — H4
Non BS rectangular cover 900 × 600mm nominal — H5

Medium Duty
BS 497, 600 × 450mm nominal solid top — M1
Non BS cover size 600 × 600mm nominal solid top — M2
BS 497, 600 × 450mm nominal recessed top — M3
Non BS cover size 600 × 600mm nominal recessed top — M4
Non BS cover size 750 × 600mm nominal recessed top — M5
Non BS cover size 900 × 600mm nominal recessed top — M6
Non BS cover size 750 × 600mm nominal solid top — M7
Non BS cover size 900 × 600mm nominal solid top — M8

Light Duty
BS 497, 600 × 450mm nominal solid top — L1
BS 497, 600 × 450mm nominal solid top — L2
Messrs Broad's 'Broadstel' No. 347 range or similar 600 × 450mm nom — L3
Messrs Broad's 'Broadstel' No 347 range or similar 600 × 600mm nom — L4
BS 497, 600 × 450mm nominal recessed top — L5
BS 497, 600 × 600mm nominal recessed top — L6
Non BS cover size 750 × 600mm nominal solid top — L7
Non BS cover size 750 × 750mm nominal solid top — L8
Non BS cover size 900 × 600mm nominal solid top — L9
Messrs Broad's 'Broadstel' No 347 range or similar 750 × 600mm nom — L11
Messrs Broad's 'Broadstel' No 347 range or similar 750 × 750mm nom — L12
Messrs Broad's 'Broadstel' No 347 range or similar 900 × 600mm nom — L13
Non BS cover size 750 × 600mm nominal recessed top — L14
Non BS cover size 750 × 750mm nominal recessed top — L15
Non BS cover size 900 × 600mm nominal recessed top — L16

* All dimensions quoted are nominal clear opening.

Drainage: Dual Trenches

Where sewer and drain runs are parallel and in close proximity to each other the pipeline may be constructed in a dual trench, provided the following conditions are strictly observed.

The situation where the minimum dimension between the centre lines of adjacent sewers occurs is shown in figure **1.**

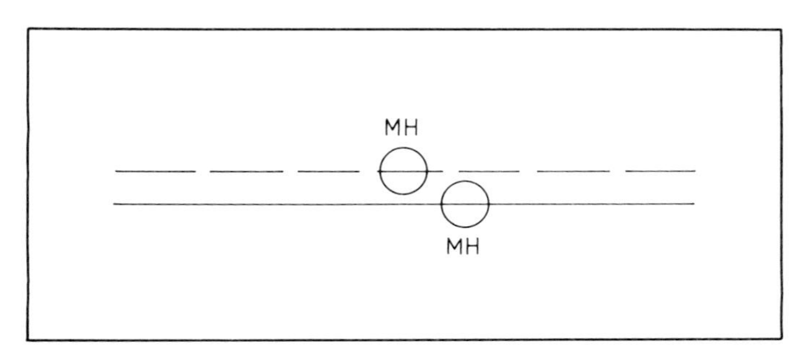

1 *Situation where minimum dimension between centre lines of adjacent sewers occurs.*

Dual manholes will not be permitted because:

1 Upper pipe must be in cast iron with hatchbox access. The hatchbox cover may be left off causing cross pollution between the two drains and/or overloading.

2 Some London Boroughs do not permit hatchboxes in dual manholes for the reason given, therefore two dual manholes must be provided giving independent access to each of the pipelines. This practice is expensive.

3 Dual manholes are necessarily much larger than single manholes, therefore more expensive.

Dimensional parameters are given in figure **2.**

Construction details are given in figure **3.**

Trench widths Bd_A and Bd_B are given in Table I. Where BS precast concrete circular manholes are used, see table II and figure **2** for the required spacing X between the two adjacent sewers.

The use of dual trenches impose additional loads on the pipelines not allowed for in the Pipe Selection Tables, therefore any Contractor wishing to adopt the dual trench method of construction must submit his pipe loading calculations to the Architect for approval.

In phasing construction, the lower pipeline must be completed, tested and the subtrench containing it completely backfilled before commencement of work on the upper pipeline, This is to prevent the possible collapse of the upper trench bed into the sub trench.

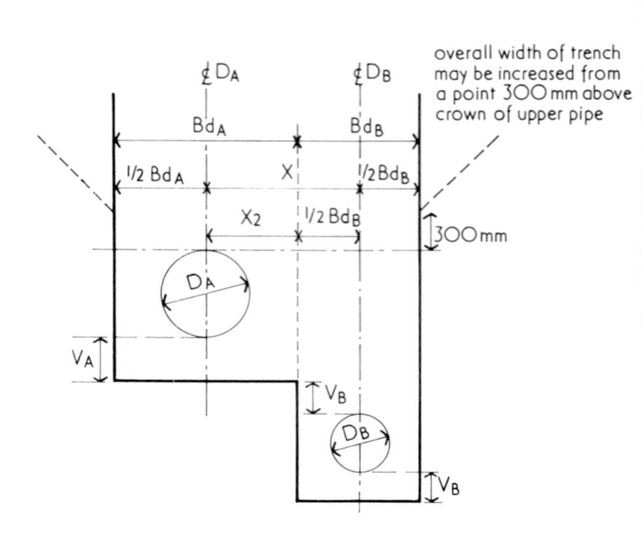

Bd_A = trench width for upper pipe

Bd_B = trench width for lower pipe

D_A = upper pipe

D_B = lower pipe

$V_A = \frac{D_A}{4}$ or 150 mm whichever is greater

$V_B = \frac{D_B}{4}$ or 150 mm whichever is greater

X_2 minimum $= \frac{Bd_A}{2}$

X minimum = the largest dimension given by equations (i) and (ii)

(i) where manhole is on upper pipeline

$X \text{ min} = M + \frac{Bd_B}{2}$

(ii) where manhole is on lower pipeline

$X \text{ min} = M + \frac{Bd_A}{2}$

where M = distance between the centre line of manhole channel and the external surface of manhole wall

2 *Dimensional parameters for dual trenches. Where BS precast concrete circular manholes are used, and the centre line of the main channel is on a diameter of a manhole, dimension X between the centre lines of two adjacent sewers/drains in a dual trench is given in table II.*

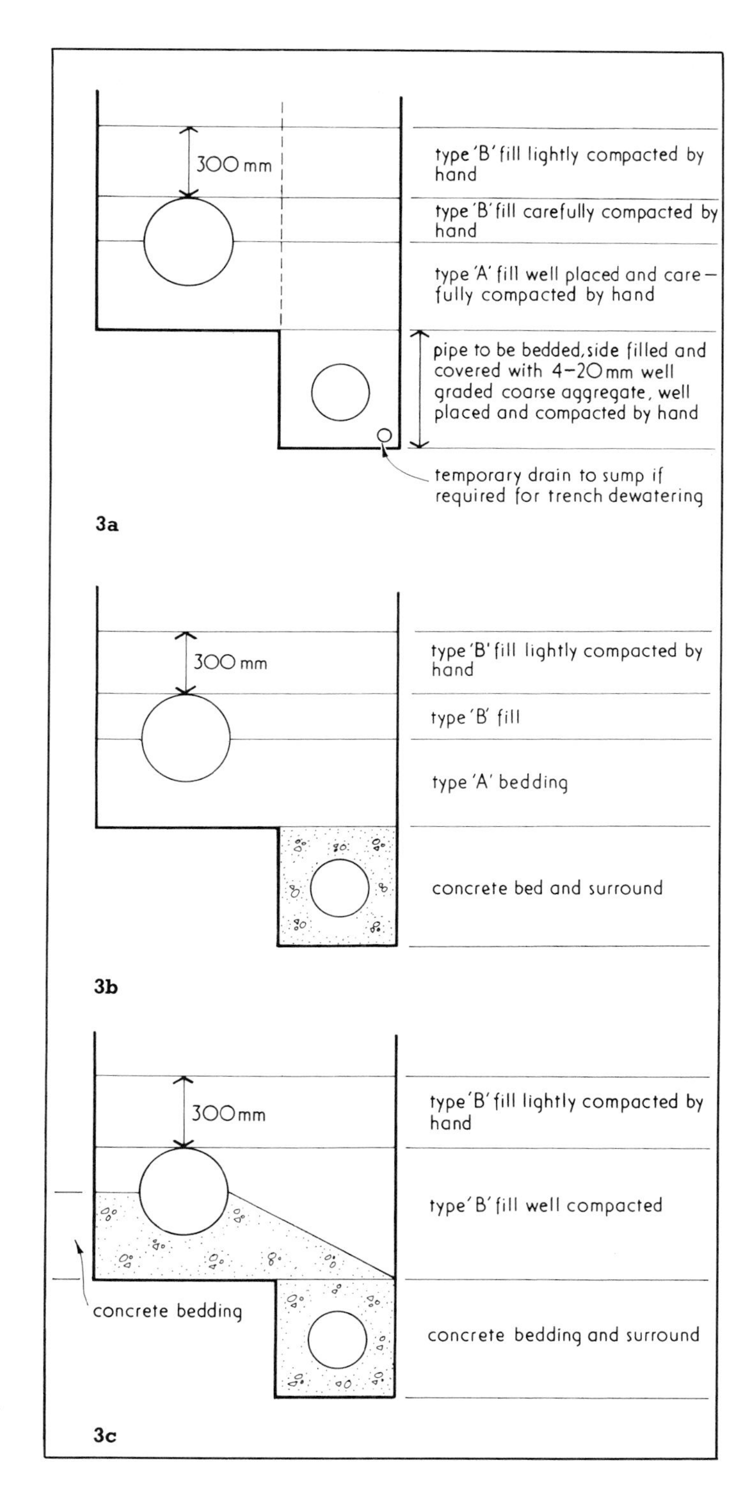

3 *Constructional details for dual trenches.*

Class A and B bedding refer to the classification given in the National Building Studies, Special Report 37 Loading Charts for the Design of Buried Rigid Pipes.

Type A bedding material: granular material, ideally broken stone or gravel, but other similar uniform material available locally may be used, eg crushed concrete. Material to pass 13-25 mm sieve according to pipe size, and be retained on a 4 mm sieve.

Type B fill material: selected uniform readily compactible material – free from tree roots, vegetable matter, building rubbish, frozen soil and excluding clay lumps retained on a 75 mm sieve and stones retained on a 25 mm sieve.

Table I Trench widths Bd, to be used when calculating dimension X (see figure 2). If trench sheeting is used, add 150mm to the trench widths shown below.

Nominal pipe diameter (mm)	**Trench width Bd_A or Bd_B** (mm)
100	500
150	600
225	680
300	760
375	890
450	1000
525	1130
600	1250
675	1380
750	1500
825	1630
900	1750
975	1870
1050	2000
1125	2120
1200	2250
1350	2500
1500	2650
1650	2800
1800	2950
2000	3150

Table II Minimum dimension 'X' between centre lines of sewers in dual trenches, for precast concrete ring manholes. Applies only to manholes placed symmetrically over sewer.

Nominal pipe bore (mm)	**Manhole diameter** (nominal), mm							
	900	1050	1200	1350	1500	1800	2100	2400
	Minimum dimension between centre lines of pipes							
100	930	1010	1100	1190	1270	1420	1570	1730
150	990	1060	1150	1240	1320	1470	1620	1780
225	1030	1100	1190	1280	1360	1510	1660	1820
300	1070	1140	1230	1320	1400	1550	1700	1860
375	1140	1210	1300	1390	1470	1620	1770	1930
450	1190	1270	1350	1440	1520	1670	1830	1980
525	1250	1330	1410	1500	1580	1730	1890	2040
600	1310	1390	1470	1560	1640	1790	1950	2100
675	1380	1460	1540	1630	1710	1860	2020	2170
750	1440	1520	1600	1690	1770	1920	2080	2230
825	1500	1580	1660	1750	1820	1980	2140	2290
900	1560	1640	1720	1810	1880	2040	2200	2350
975	1620	1700	1780	1870	1940	2100	2260	2410
1050	1690	1770	1850	1940	2010	2170	2330	2480
1125	1750	1830	1910	2000	2070	2230	2390	2540
1200	1810	1890	1970	2060	2130	2290	2450	2600
1350	1940	2020	2100	2190	2260	2420	2580	2730
1500	2010	2090	2170	2260	2330	2490	2650	2800
1650	2080	2160	2240	2330	2400	2560	2720	2870
1800	2160	2240	2320	2410	2480	2640	2800	2950
2000	2260	2340	2420	2510	2680	2740	2900	3050

1 Site signs

3141 Estate sign—illuminated (layout)
3140 Estate sign—illuminated (construction)
3143 Dwelling block name sign—illuminated
3120 Employers sign board—type A and B
3121 Employers sign board—type C
3124 Employers sign board—layout—type A and B
3125 Employers sign board—layout—type C

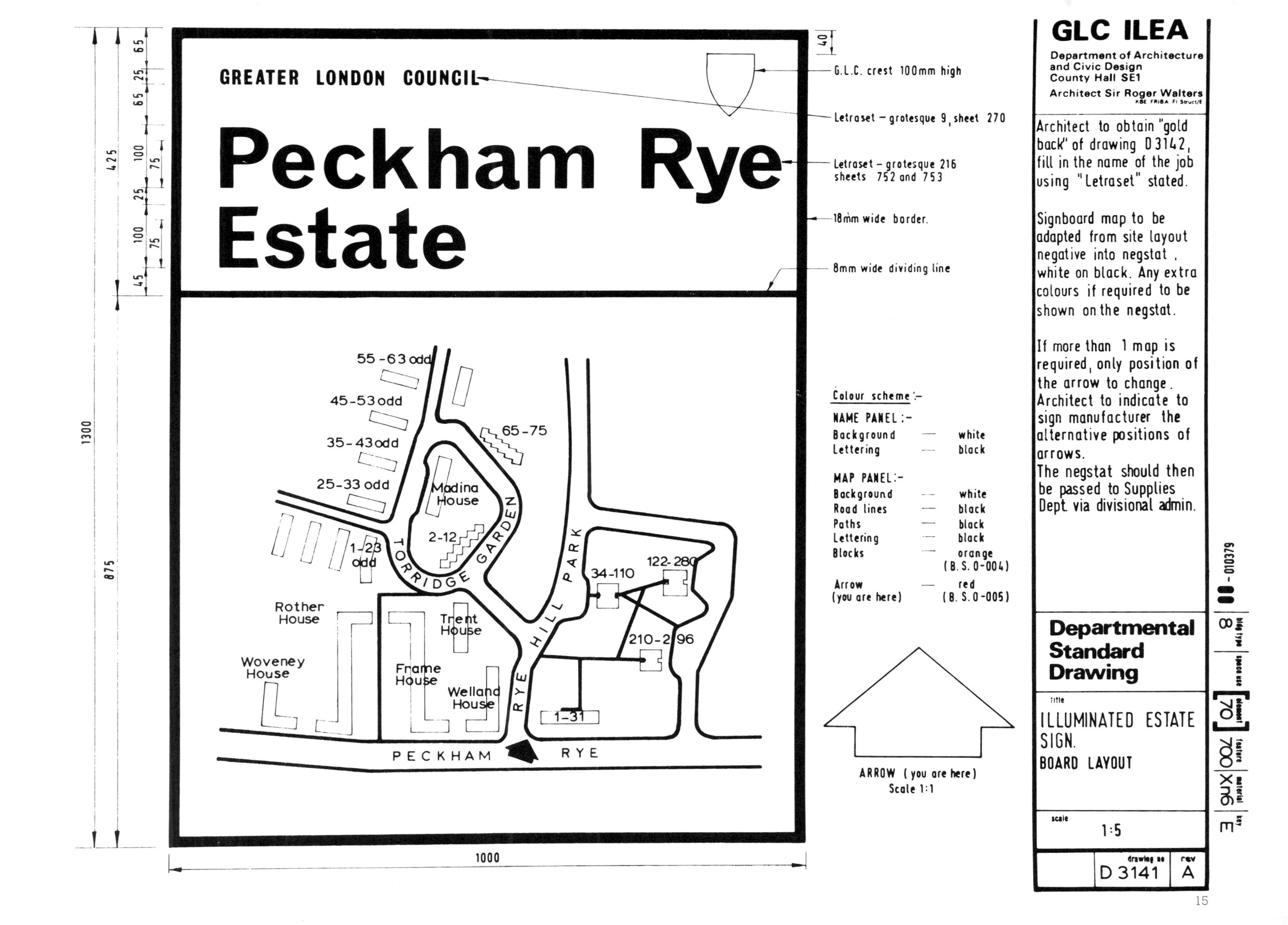

GREATER LONDON COUNCIL
Peckham Rye Estate
55-63 odd
45-53 odd
35-43 odd
25-33 odd
65-75
Madina House
2-12
1-23 odd
TORRIDGE GARDEN
RYE HILL PARK
34-110
122-280
210-296
1-31
Rother House
Woveney House
Trent House
Frame House
Welland House
PECKHAM RYE
G.L.C. crest 100mm high
Letraset – grotesque 9, sheet 270
Letraset – grotesque 216 sheets 752 and 753
18mm wide border.
8mm wide dividing line
Colour scheme:–
NAME PANEL:–
Background — white
Lettering — black
MAP PANEL:–
Background — white
Road lines — black
Paths — black
Lettering — black
Blocks — orange (B.S. 0-004)
Arrow (you are here) — red (B.S. 0-005)
ARROW (you are here)
Scale 1:1
1300
875
425
1000
GLC ILEA
Department of Architecture and Civic Design
County Hall SE1
Architect Sir Roger Walters
Architect to obtain "gold back" of drawing D3142, fill in the name of the job using "Letraset" stated.
Signboard map to be adapted from site layout negative into negstat, white on black. Any extra colours if required to be shown on the negstat.
If more than 1 map is required, only position of the arrow to change. Architect to indicate to sign manufacturer the alternative positions of arrows.
The negstat should then be passed to Supplies Dept. via divisional admin.
Departmental Standard Drawing
title
ILLUMINATED ESTATE SIGN.
BOARD LAYOUT
scale
1:5
drawing no
D 3141
rev
A
00-010379
8 [70] 700 Xn6 E

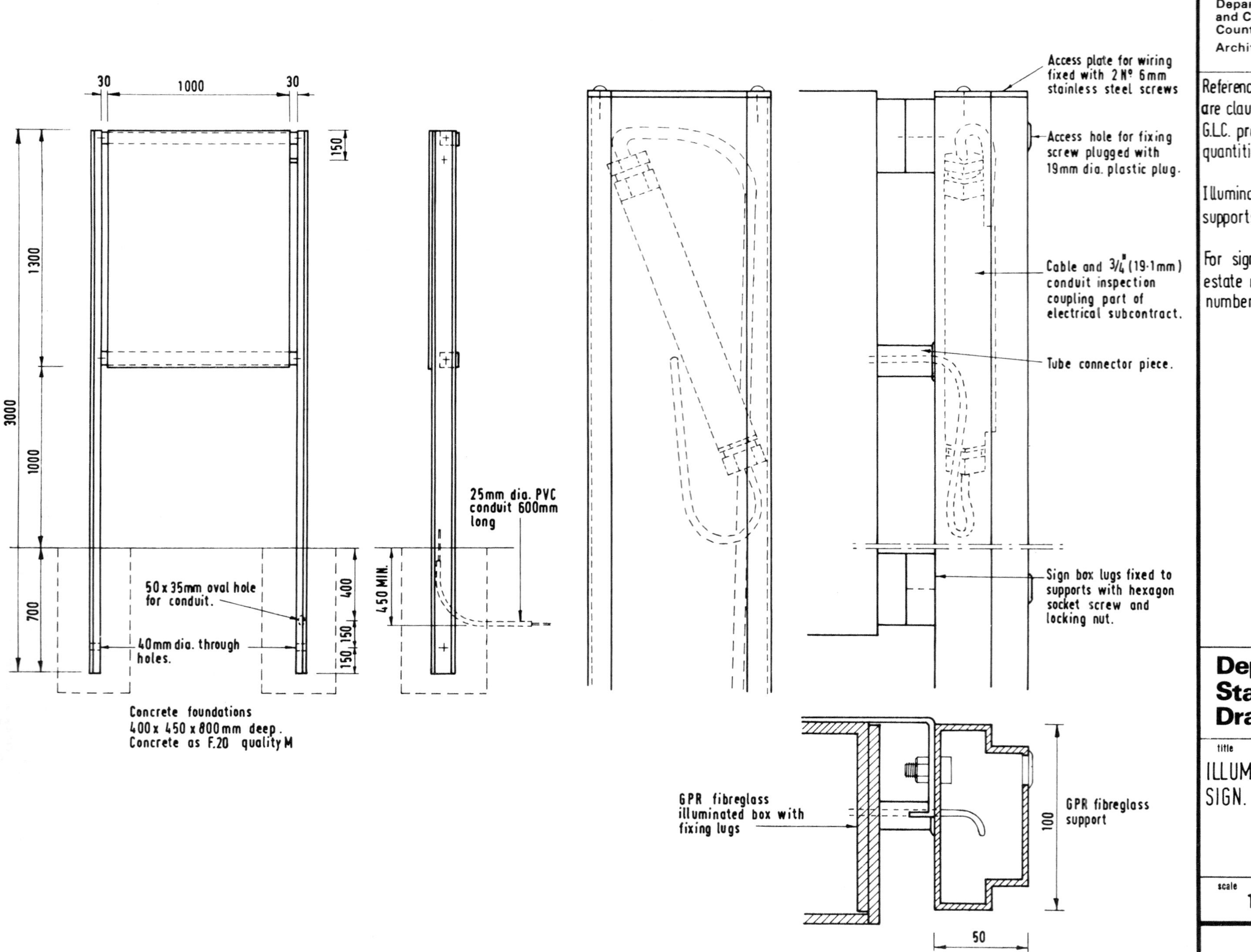

GLC ILEA

Department of Architecture and Civic Design
County Hall SE1
Architect Sir Roger Walters KBE FRIBA FI StructE

References following notes are clause numbers from G.L.C. preambles to bills of quantities.

Illuminated sign box and supports by the employer.

For signboard lettering and estate map see drawing number [70] D 3142.

Departmental Standard Drawing

title
ILLUMINATED ESTATE SIGN.

scale
1 : 20 and 1 : 2

drawing no
D3140 A

bldg type	space use	element	feature	material	key
8		[70]	700	Xn6	E

0-010379

PARK HOUSE

SAMPLE OF LETTERING (NOT TO SCALE)

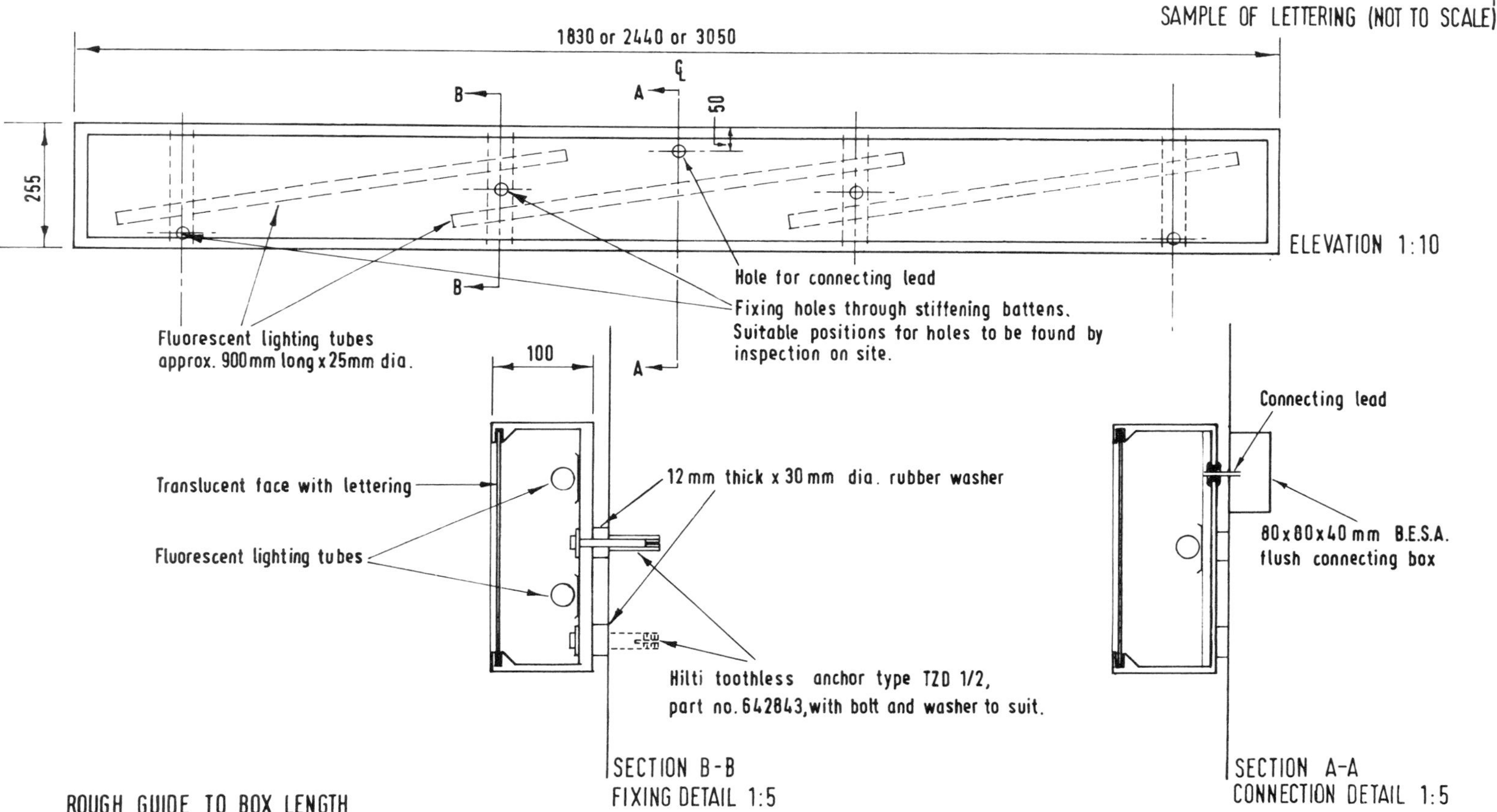

ROUGH GUIDE TO BOX LENGTH

Key Code	Length of box	Number of letters
F	3050mm	15-17 letters
G	2440mm	12-14 letters
H	1830 mm	9-11 letters

GLC ILEA

Department of Architecture and Civic Design
County Hall SE1 7PB
Architect Sir Roger Walters
KBE ARIBA FI Struct/E

References following notes are clause numbers from G.L.C. preambles to bills of quantities

Box and fixings supplied by employer.

Box to be mounted at first floor slab level.

Box available in three lengths:- 1830, 2440 and 3050 mm. The length used depends upon the number of letters in the name.

The lettering used is M.O.T. type lettering, 150 mm high capitals.

The position of the fluorescent tubes varies depending on the length of the box.

Stiffening battens - which are laminated into back of box - also provide fixing base for tube clips.

Departmental Standard Drawing

title
ILLUMINATED BLOCK NAME SIGN

scale
1:5 and 1:10

drawing no D3143 rev

bldg type | space use | element [70] | feature 700 | material Xn8 | key as matrix

010379

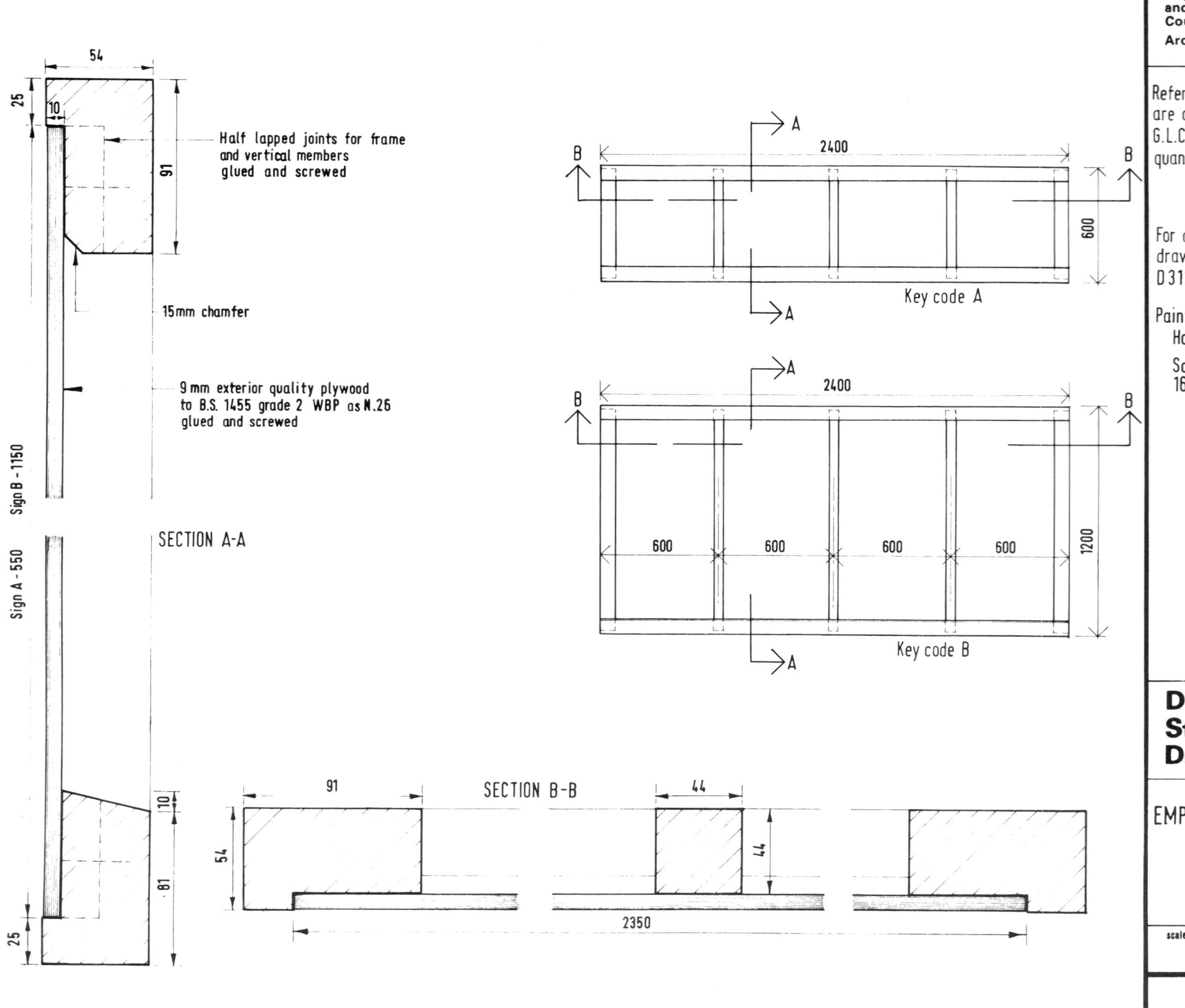

GLC ILEA

Department of Architecture
and Civic Design
County Hall SE1
Architect Sir Roger Walters
KBE FRIBA FI StructE

References following notes are clause numbers from G.L.C. preambles to bills of quantities.

For details of lettering see drawing numbers D 3122 D 3124

Painting as:
Housing ref. 55 and 56
Schools and General ref. 161 and 162

Departmental Standard Drawing

EMPLOYERS SIGN BOARD
CONSTRUCTION
TYPE A & B

scale 1:2 and 1:20

drawing no D3120

00-010379 | bldg type | space use | element [- -] | feature 905 | material Xi2 | key | as drawing

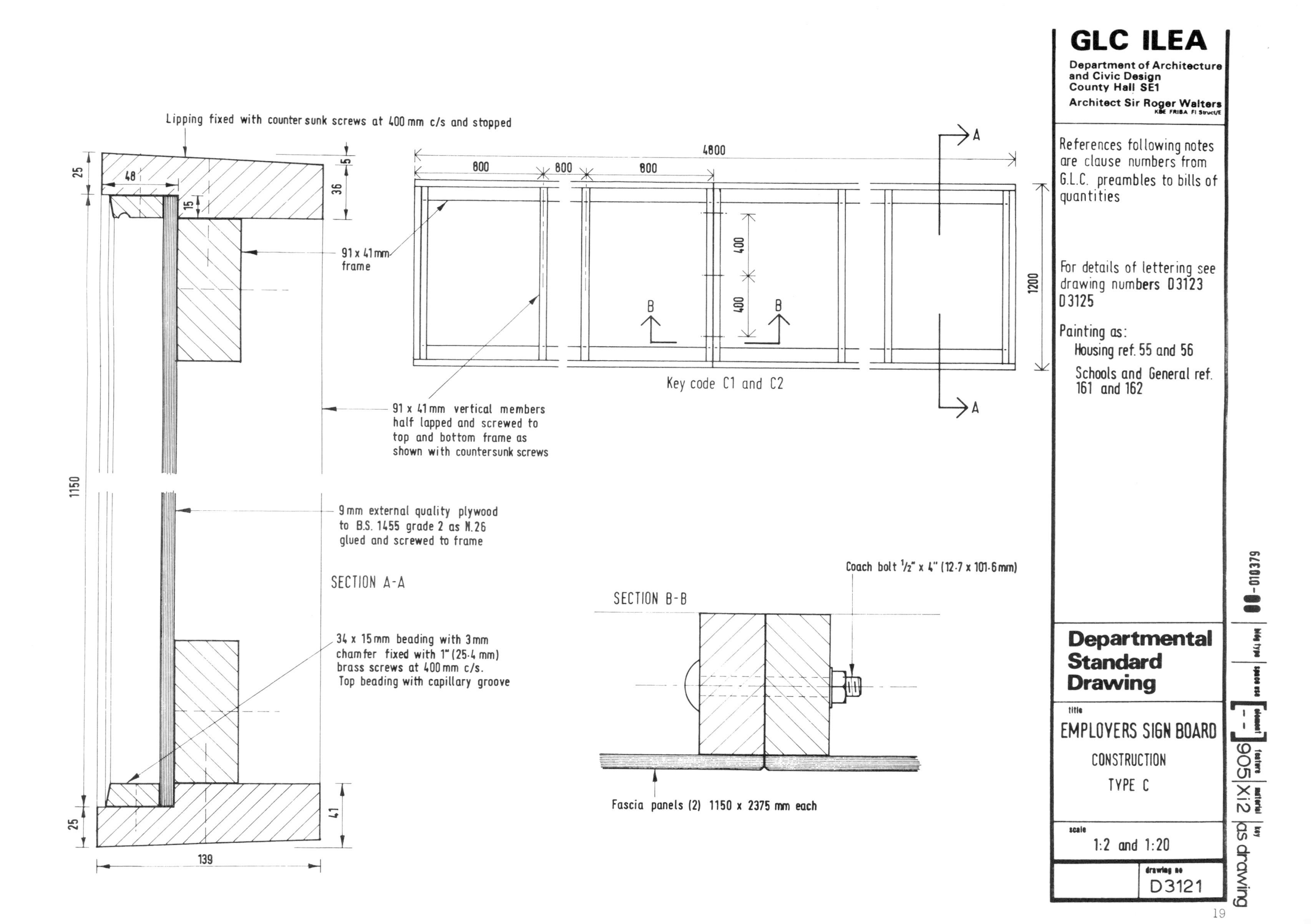

GLC ILEA
Department of Architecture and Civic Design
County Hall SE1
Architect Sir Roger Walters KBE FRIBA FI StructE
Lipping fixed with counter sunk screws at 400 mm c/s and stopped
25
48
5
36
15
91 x 41 mm frame
91 x 41 mm vertical members half lapped and screwed to top and bottom frame as shown with countersunk screws
1150
9 mm external quality plywood to B.S. 1455 grade 2 as N.26 glued and screwed to frame
SECTION A-A
34 x 15 mm beading with 3 mm chamfer fixed with 1" (25·4 mm) brass screws at 400 mm c/s. Top beading with capillary groove
41
25
139
4800
800
800
800
400
400
B
B
A
A
1200
Key code C1 and C2
SECTION B-B
Coach bolt 1/2" x 4" (12·7 x 101·6 mm)
Fascia panels (2) 1150 x 2375 mm each
References following notes are clause numbers from G.L.C. preambles to bills of quantities
For details of lettering see drawing numbers D3123 D3125
Painting as:
Housing ref. 55 and 56
Schools and General ref. 161 and 162
Departmental Standard Drawing
title
EMPLOYERS SIGN BOARD
CONSTRUCTION
TYPE C
scale
1:2 and 1:20
drawing no
D3121
00-010379
bldg type
space use
element
feature
material
key
[- -] 905 Xi2 as drawing

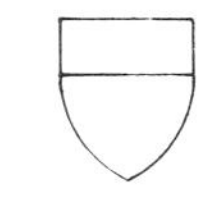

Barnardo Gardens
157 NEW HOMES

Key code A

Key code B

GLC ILEA

Department of Architecture
and Civic Design
County Hall SE1
Architect Sir Roger Walters
KBE FRIBA FI StructE

Architect to obtain 'gold back' of drawing no. D3122 fill in the name of the job using 'Letraset' as follows

Sign A:
road name - no. 373
no. of homes - no. 374

Sign B:
road name - nos. 370, 371
no. of homes - no. 372

then issue to general contractor

Departmental Standard Drawing

title
EMPLOYERS SIGN BOARD
TITLE LAYOUT EXAMPLE
TYPE A & B
(FOR G.L.C. CONTRACTS)

scale
1:10

drawing no
D3124

00-010379 | [--] | 905 | X12 | as drawing

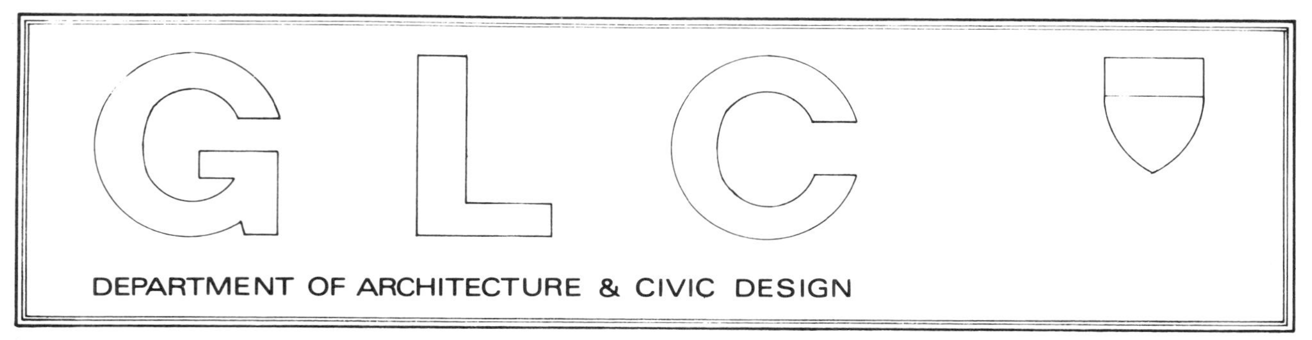

Key code C1

Stewart's Road

450 NEW HOMES

Key code C2

GLC ILEA

Department of Architecture and Civic Design
County Hall SE1
Architect Sir Roger Walters KBE FRIBA FI StructE

Architect to obtain 'gold back' of drawing no. D3123 fill in the name of the job using 'Letraset' as follows

road name - nos. 370 371
no. of homes - no. 372

then issue to general contractor

Departmental Standard Drawing

title

EMPLOYERS SIGN BOARD
TITLE LAYOUT EXAMPLE
TYPE C
(FOR G.L.C. CONTRACTS)

scale

1:20

drawing no

D3125

00-010379 | bldg type | space use | element [- -] | feature 905 | material Xi2 | key as drawing

2
Gallows gate

3118 Gallows gate—5.2m wide
3119 Gallows gate—traffic sign
3203 Gallows gate—traffic sign
4048 Gallows gate—5.2m wide—details ; Sheet 1, 2, 3
4049 Gallows gate—5.2m wide—details ; Sheet 1, 2, 3, 4

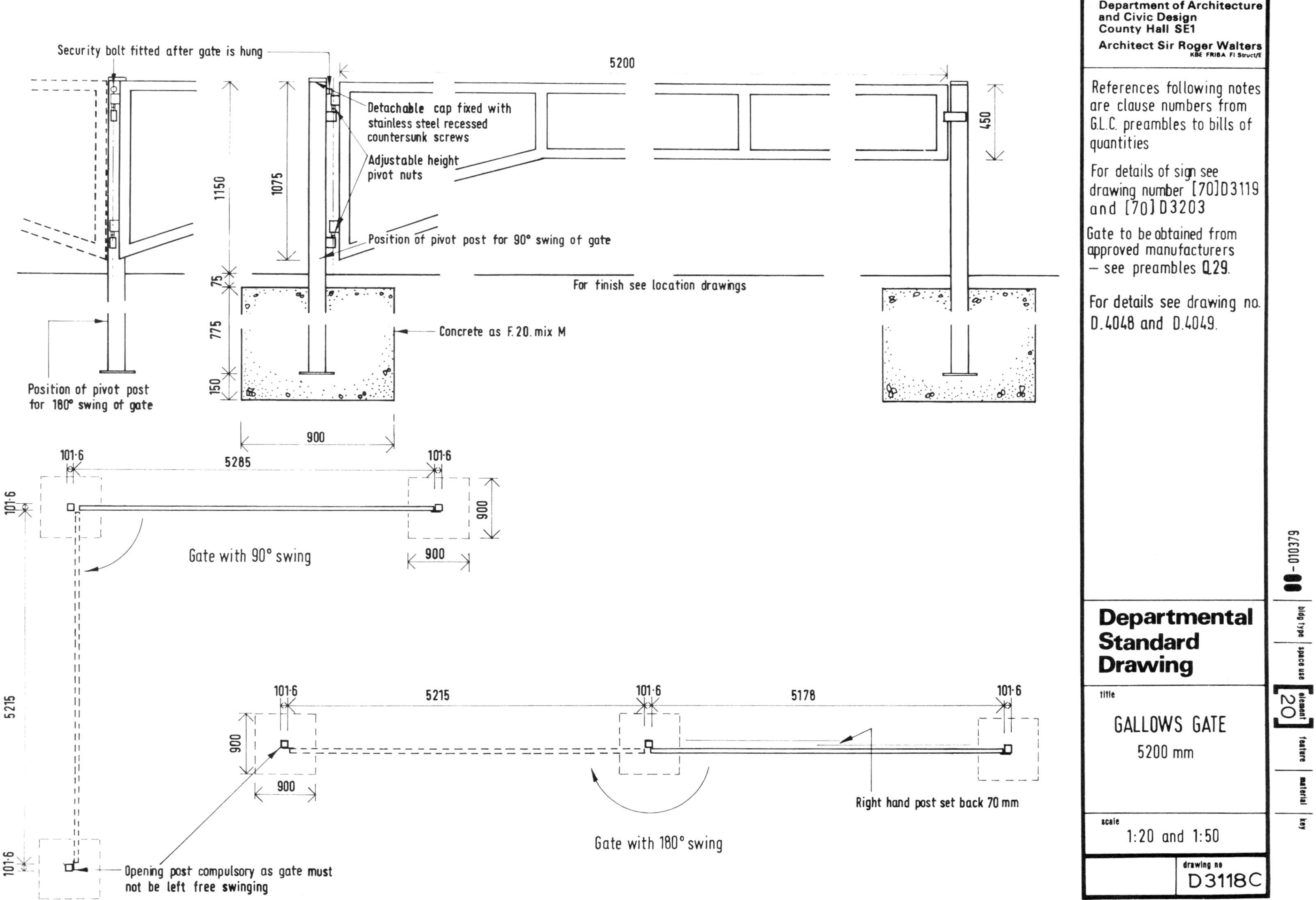
Security bolt fitted after gate is hung
5200
Detachable cap fixed with stainless steel recessed countersunk screws
Adjustable height pivot nuts
Position of pivot post for 90° swing of gate
450
1150
1075
75
775
150
For finish see location drawings
Concrete as F.20. mix M
Position of pivot post for 180° swing of gate
900
101·6
5285
101·6
101·6
900
Gate with 90° swing
900
5215
101·6
101·6
5215
101·6
5178
101·6
900
900
Right hand post set back 70 mm
Gate with 180° swing
Opening post compulsory as gate must not be left free swinging
GLC ILEA
Department of Architecture and Civic Design
County Hall SE1
Architect Sir Roger Walters
KBE FRIBA FI StructE
References following notes are clause numbers from G.L.C. preambles to bills of quantities
For details of sign see drawing number [70]D3119 and [70] D3203
Gate to be obtained from approved manufacturers – see preambles Q29.
For details see drawing no. D.4048 and D.4049.
Departmental Standard Drawing
title
GALLOWS GATE
5200 mm
scale
1:20 and 1:50
drawing no
D3118C
bldg type
space use
element
[20]
feature
material
key

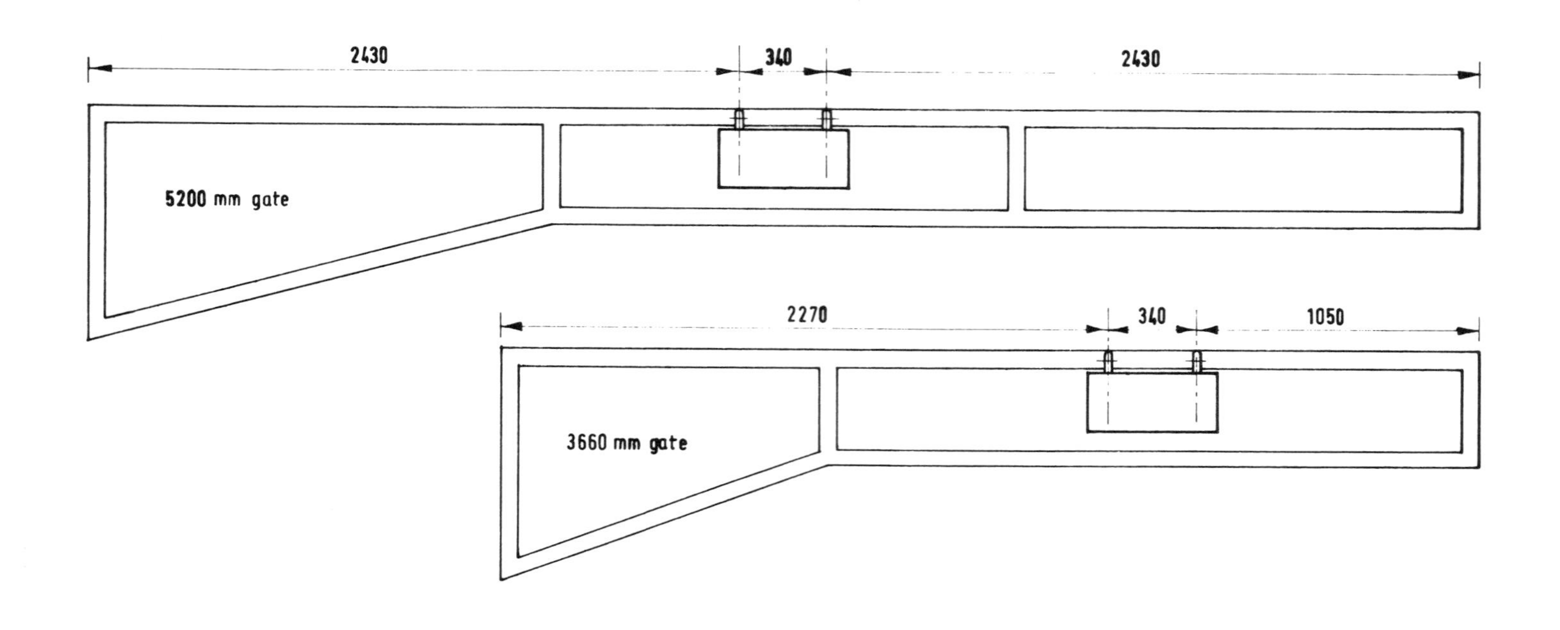

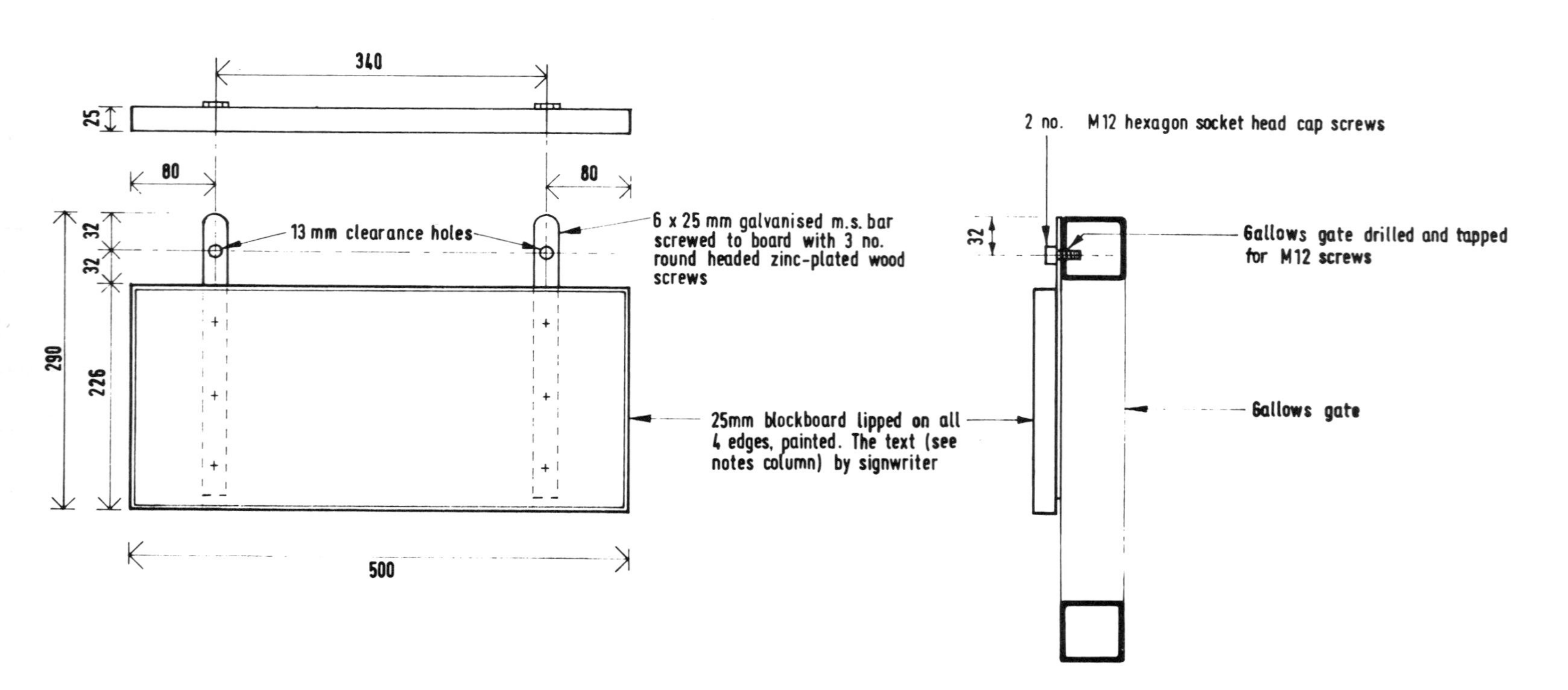

GLC ILEA

Department of Architecture and Civic Design
County Hall SE1
Architect Sir Roger Walters KBE FRIBA FI Struct/E

References following notes are clause numbers from G.L.C. preambles to bills of quantities

To be read in conjunction with drawing numbers [20] D3117 D3118 and [70] D3203

Sign reads:

KEEP CLEAR
for Fire Brigade & Ambulances
Gates Open 8 a.m. to 5 p.m.

Departmental Standard Drawing

title

TRAFFIC SIGN

GALLOWS GATE FIXING

scale

1:5 and 1:20

drawing no	rev
D3119	B

00 - 010379

[70]

GLC ILEA

Department of Architecture
and Civic Design
County Hall SE1 7PB
Architect Sir Roger Walters
KBE ARIBA FI Struct/E

References following notes are clause numbers from G.L.C. preambles to bills of quantities

"KEEP CLEAR" to be in Helvetica Bold

"for Fire Brigade & Ambulances" to be in Helvetica Light

"Gates open 8a.m. to 5pm" to be in Helvetica Light

Lettering in white

Background colour B.S.4800/1972 10.A.11 (grey)

G.L.C. crest transfer to be obtained from T.I.G.

This drawing to be read in conjunction with drawings [70] D 3119 and [20] D 3117 and [20] D 3118

Departmental Standard Drawing

title
TRAFFIC SIGN
FOR GALLOWS GATE
PAINTING INSTRUCTIONS

scale
1:2

drawing no
D3203

rev

00 - 010379

bldg type | space use | element [70] | feature | material | key

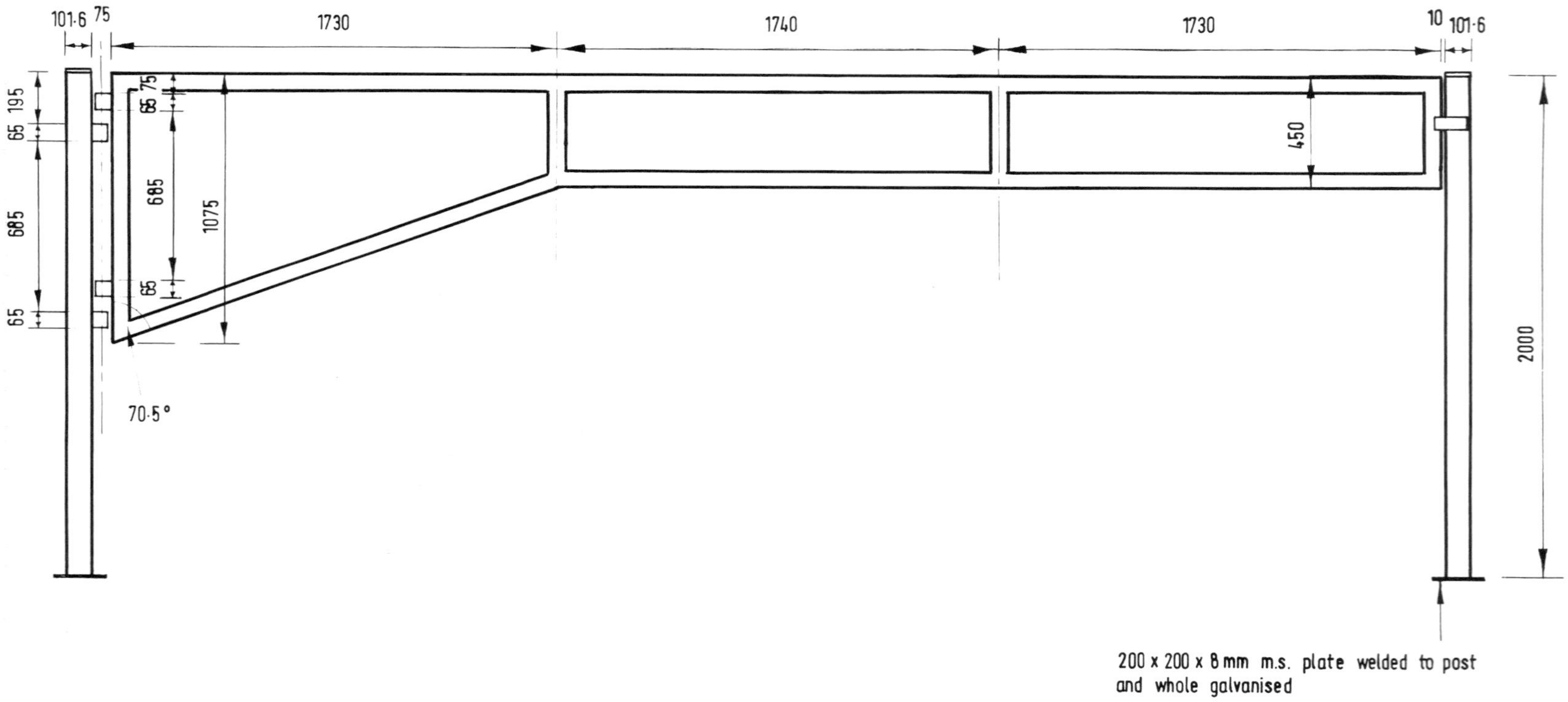

GLC ILEA

Department of Architecture and Civic Design
County Hall SE1 7PB
Architect F B Pooley C B E

References following notes are clause numbers from G.L.C. preambles to bills of quantities

Gate slam lock opened by F.B.1. & F.B.2. to be obtained from:

ALBERT MARSTON & CO. LTD.
WELLINGTON WORKS
NEACHELLS LANE
STAFFS.

.... by manufacturer - plus number of keys as billed.

2 locks required for each gate.

All parts to be hot dipped galvanised as Q.14 after fabrication.

Welding to be 5mm fillet welds around the full profile of the members to be joined and sealing welds on flush edges, except for lock, where 3mm fillet welds to be used. Welding to be as B.S. 5135. Welds <u>must not</u> be ground flat.

See also drg. Nos. [20] D.3118 & D.4049

200 x 200 x 8 mm m.s. plate welded to post and whole galvanised

70.5°

Departmental Standard Drawing

title

5200mm GALLOWS GATE DETAILS

scale

1:20

Sheet 1 | drawing no D.4048 | rev A

010379 -

bldg type | space use | element [20] | feature | material | key

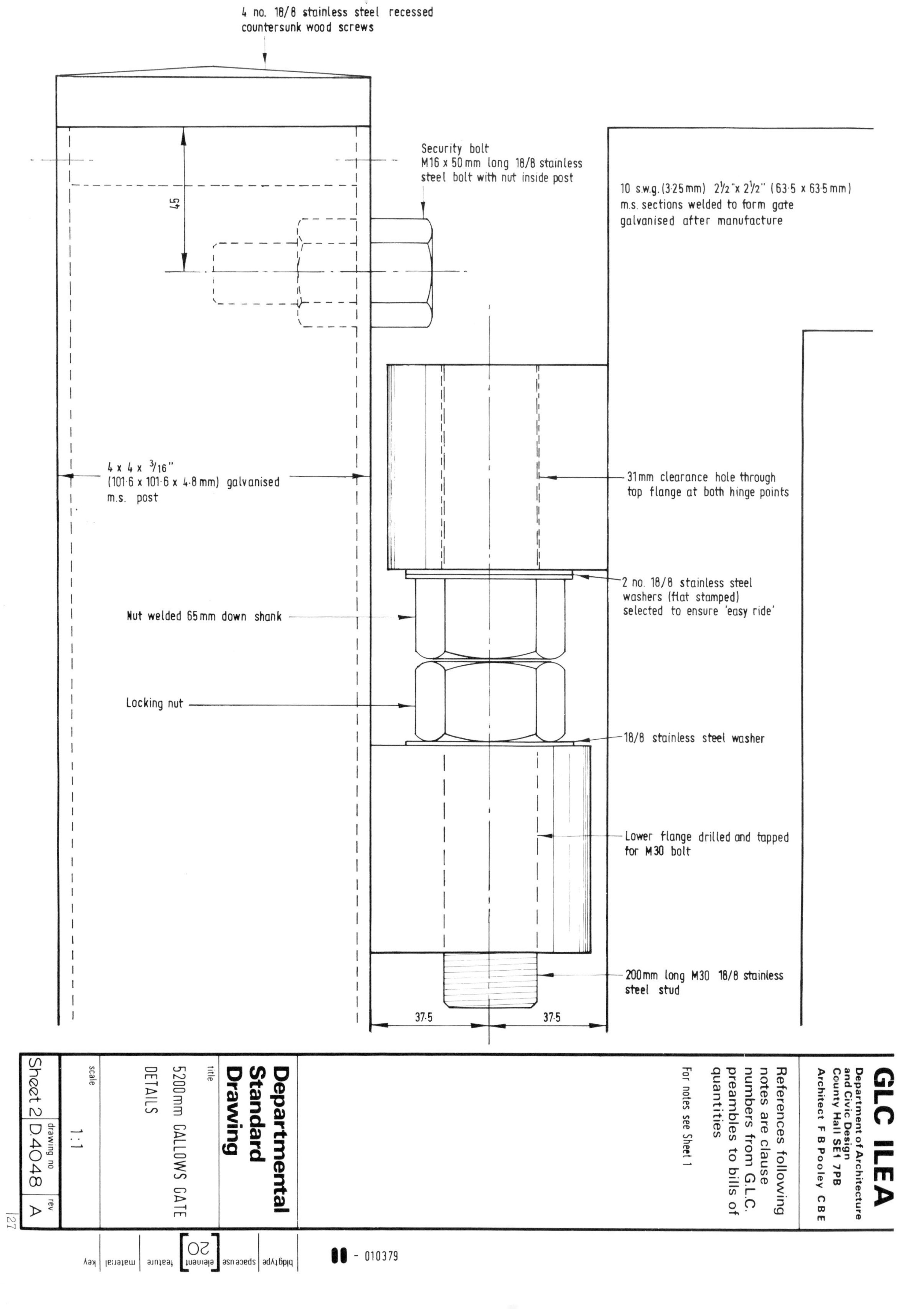
4 no. 18/8 stainless steel recessed countersunk wood screws
45
Security bolt M16 x 50 mm long 18/8 stainless steel bolt with nut inside post
10 s.w.g. (3·25 mm) 2½" x 2½" (63·5 x 63·5 mm) m.s. sections welded to form gate galvanised after manufacture
4 x 4 x 3/16" (101·6 x 101·6 x 4·8 mm) galvanised m.s. post
31mm clearance hole through top flange at both hinge points
2 no. 18/8 stainless steel washers (flat stamped) selected to ensure 'easy ride'
Nut welded 65 mm down shank
Locking nut
18/8 stainless steel washer
Lower flange drilled and tapped for M30 bolt
200mm long M30 18/8 stainless steel stud
37·5
37·5
GLC ILEA
Department of Architecture and Civic Design
County Hall SE1 7PB
Architect F B Pooley C B E
References following notes are clause numbers from G.L.C. preambles to bills of quantities
For notes see Sheet 1
Departmental Standard Drawing
title
5200mm GALLOWS GATE DETAILS
scale
1:1
Sheet 2
drawing no
D.4048
rev
A
bldgtype
spaceuse
element
20
feature
material
key
00 - 010379

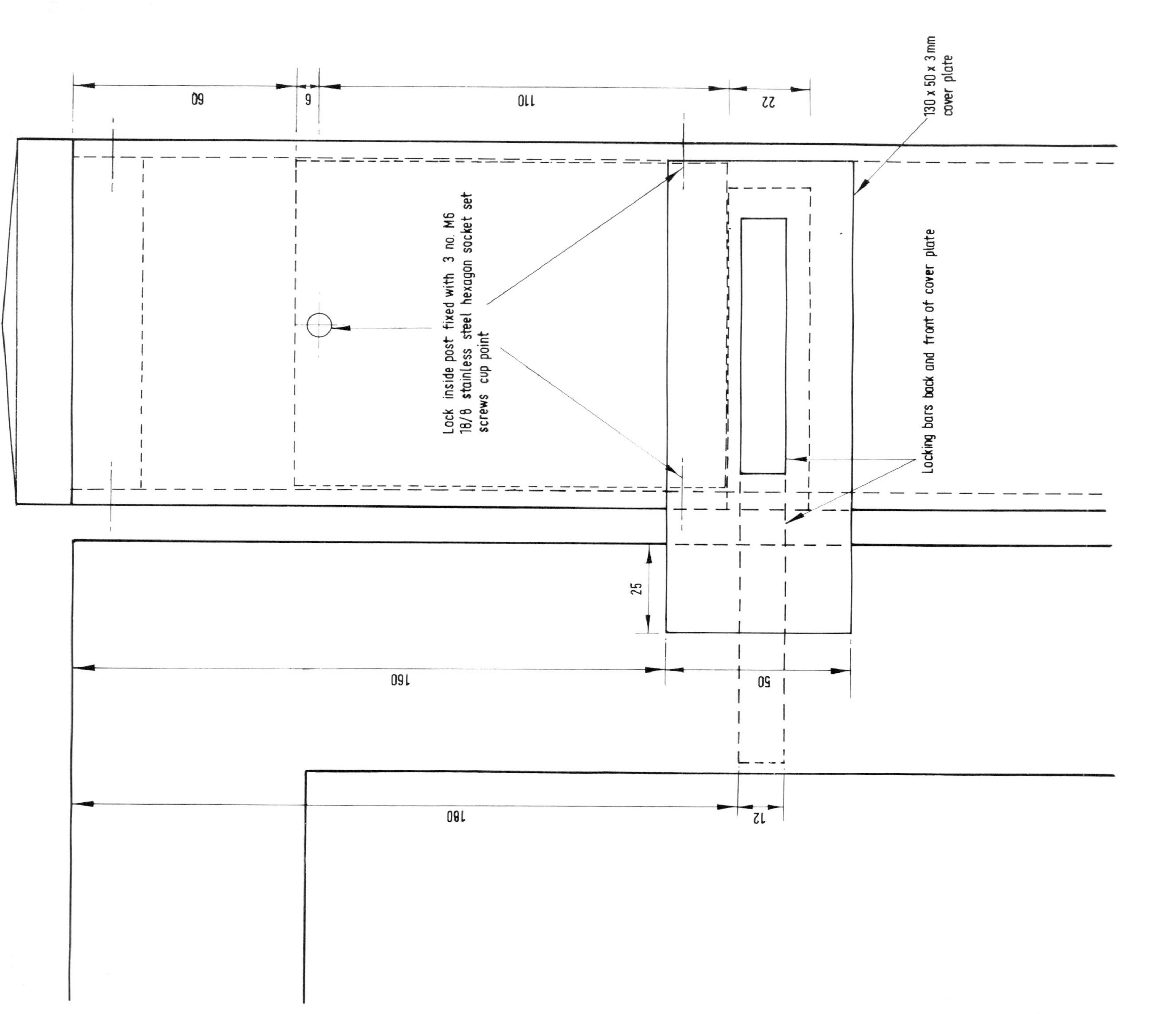

GLC ILEA

Department of Architecture and Civic Design
County Hall SE1 7PB
Architect F B Pooley CBE

References following notes are clause numbers from G.L.C. preambles to bills of quantities

For notes see Sheet 1

Departmental Standard Drawing

title

5200mm GALLOWS GATE DETAILS

scale

1:1

	drawing no	rev
Sheet 3	D.4048	A

bldg type | spaceuse | element [20] | feature | material | key

010376

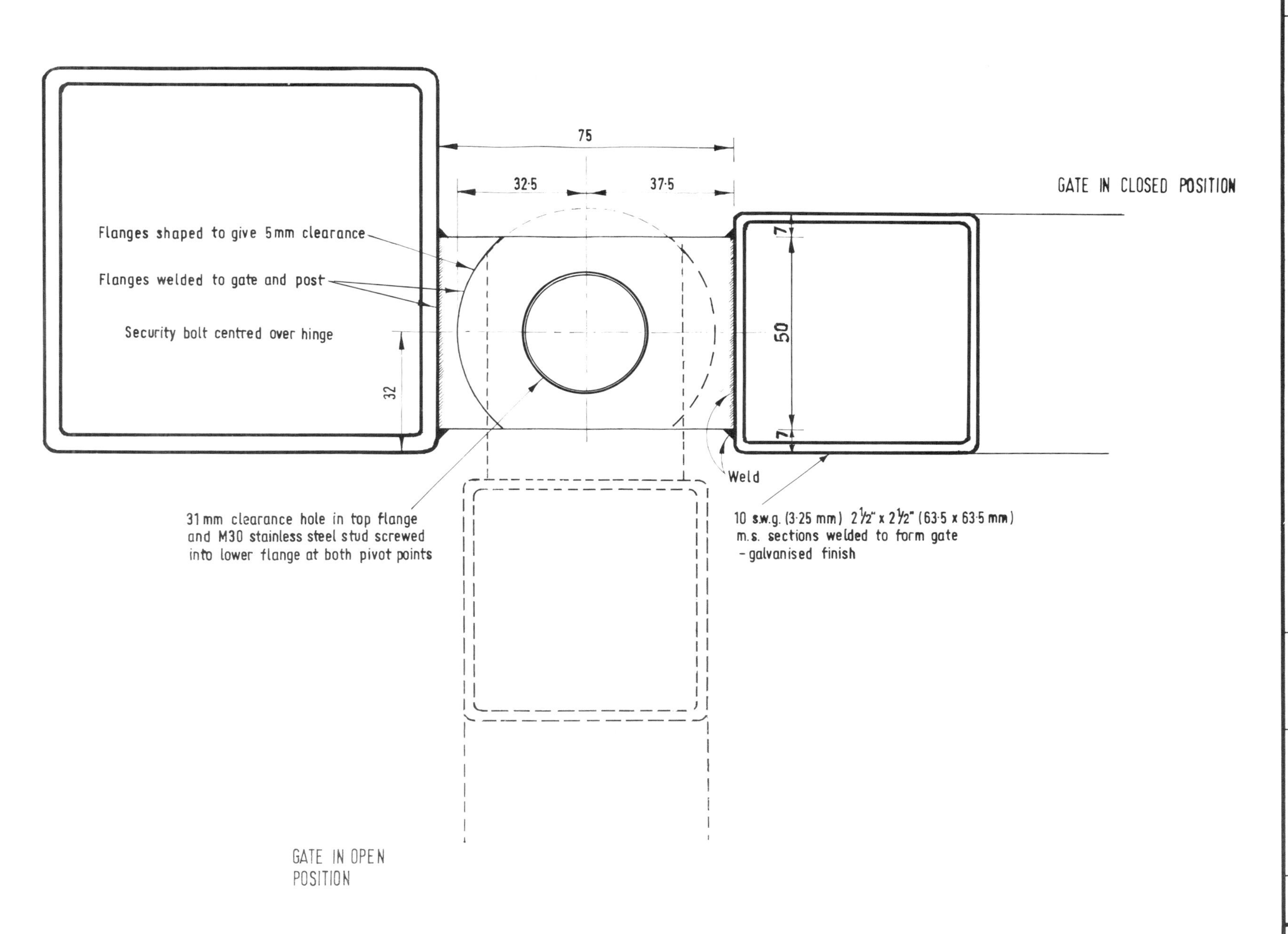

GLC ILEA

Department of Architecture and Civic Design
County Hall SE1 7PB
Architect F B Pooley CBE

References following notes are clause numbers from G.L.C. preambles to bills of quantities

1. All parts to be hot dipped galvanised as Q.14 after fabrication.
2. Welding to be 5mm fillet welds around the full profile of the members to be joined and sealing welds on flush edges, except for lock, where 3mm fillet welds to be used. Welding to be as B.S. 5135. Welds must not be ground flat.
3. See also drg. Nos. [20] D.3118 & D.4048

010379

Departmental Standard Drawing

bldg type	space use	element	feature	material	key
		[20]			

title

5200mm GALLOWS GATE DETAILS

scale

1:1

	drawing no	rev
Sheet 1	D.4049	A

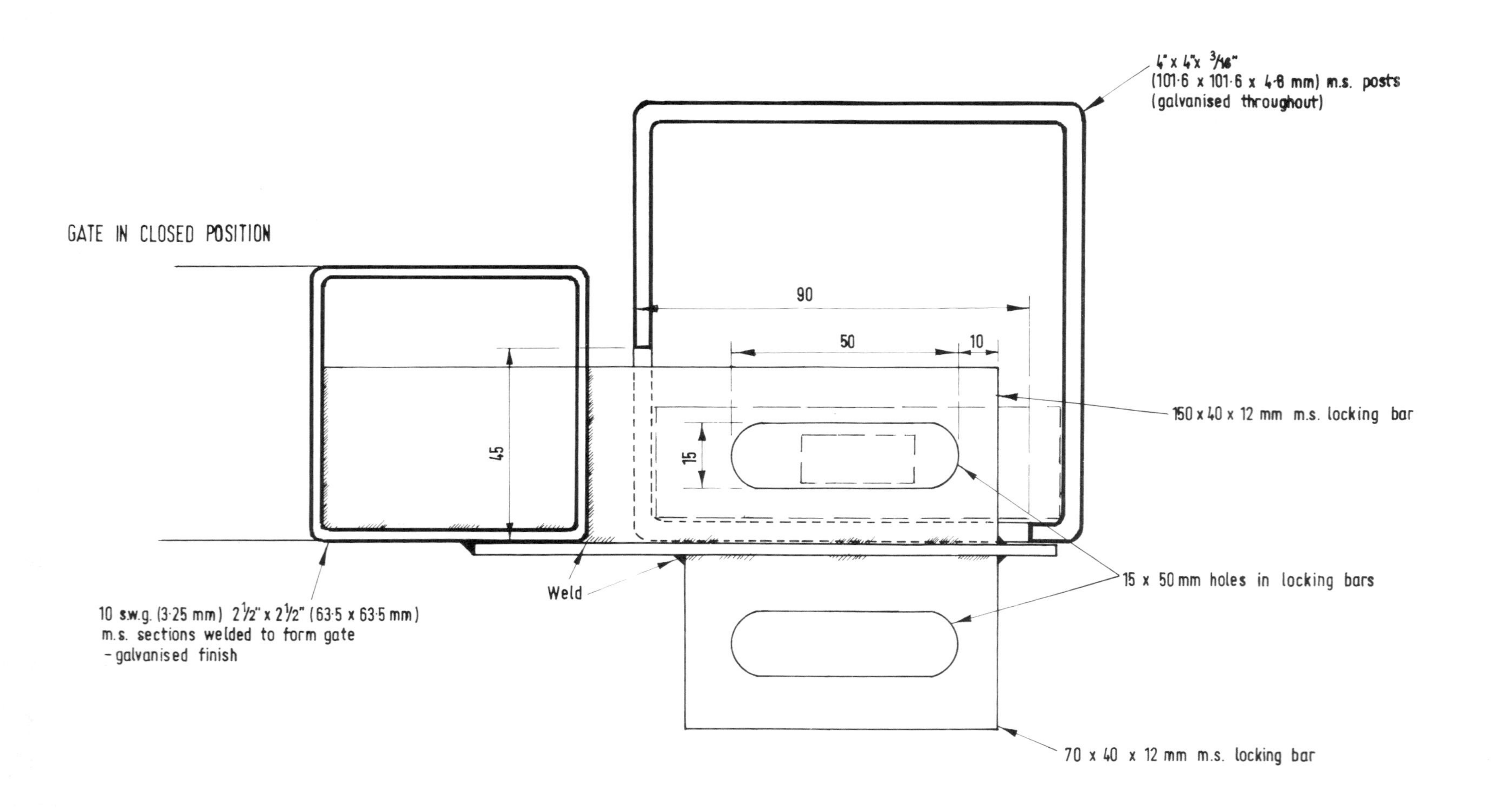

GLC ILEA

Department of Architecture and Civic Design
County Hall SE1 7PB
Architect F B Pooley CBE

References following notes are clause numbers from G.L.C. preambles to bills of quantities

For notes see Sheet 1

010379 -

Departmental Standard Drawing

title

5200mm GALLOWS GATE DETAILS

bldg type | space use | element 20 | feature | material | key

scale 1:1

Sheet 2 | drawing no D.4049 | rev A

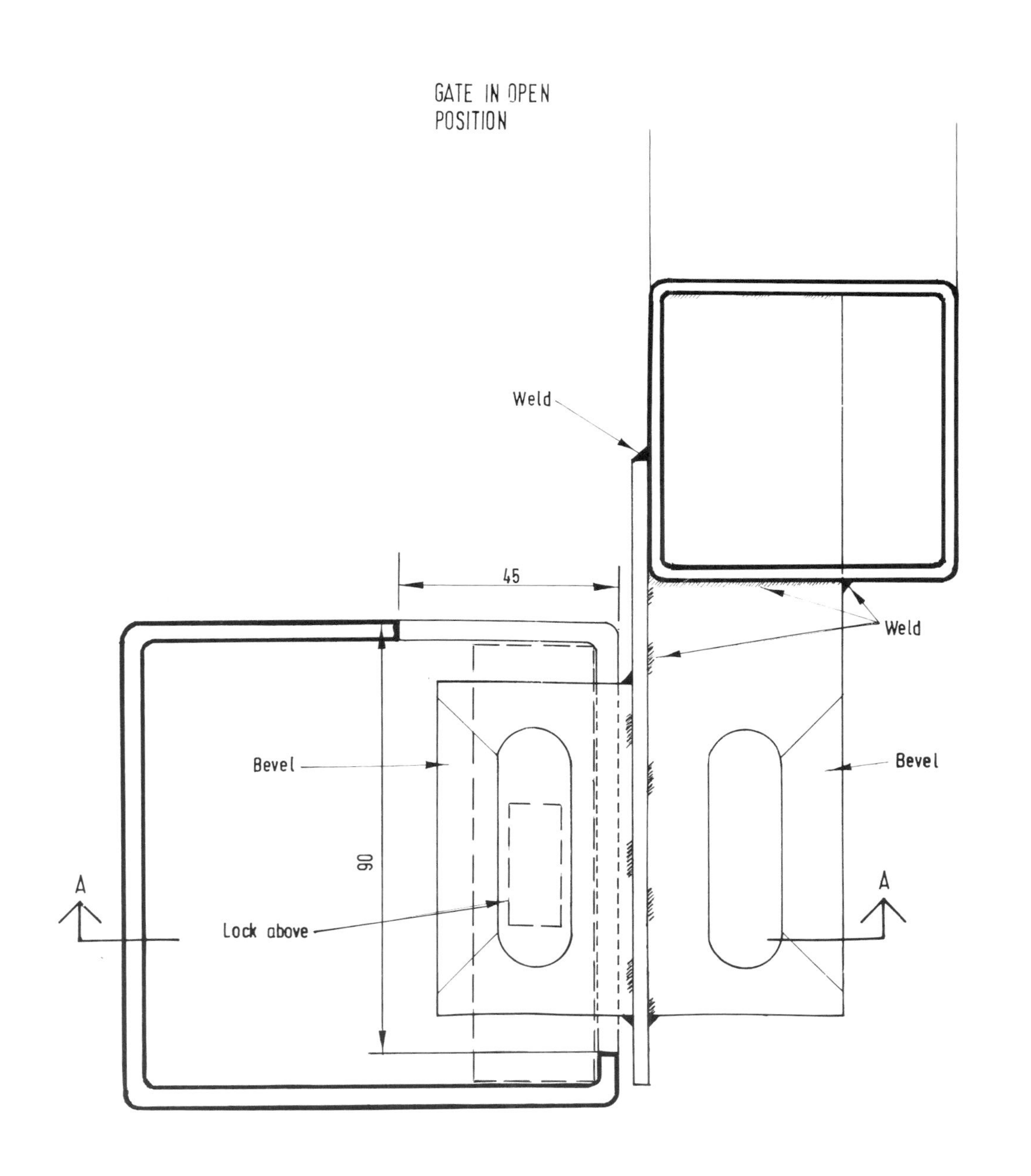

GLC ILEA

Department of Architecture
and Civic Design
County Hall SE1 7PB
Architect F B Pooley C B E

References following notes are clause numbers from G.L.C. preambles to bills of quantities

For notes see Sheet 1

Departmental Standard Drawing

title

5200mm GALLOWS GATE DETAILS

scale 1:1

Sheet 3 | drawing no D.4049 | rev A

bldgtype | spaceuse | element [20] | feature | material | key

00 - 010379

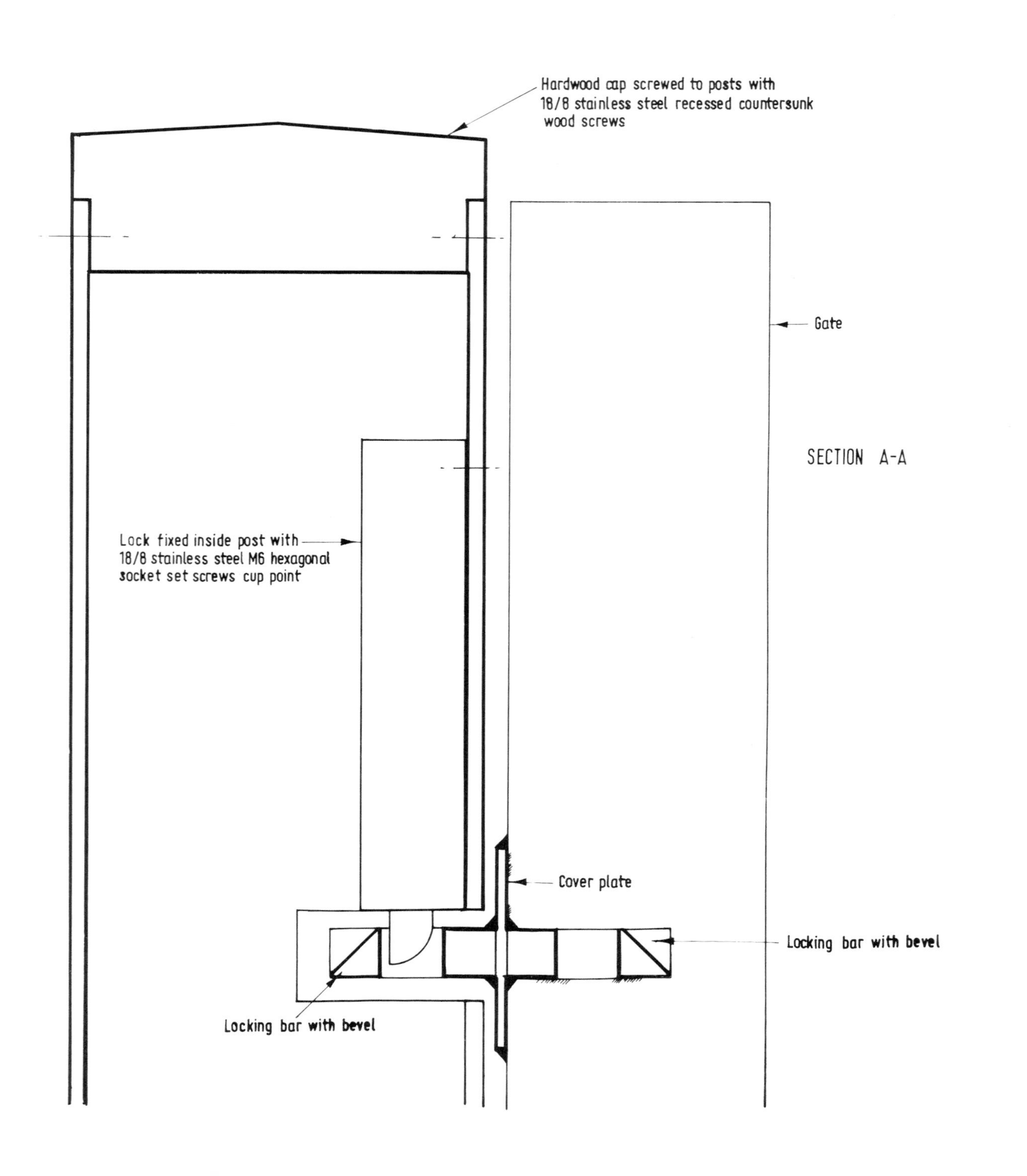

GLC ILEA

Department of Architecture and Civic Design
County Hall SE1 7PB
Architect F B Pooley CBE

References following notes are clause numbers from G.L.C. preambles to bills of quantities

For notes see Sheet 1

Departmental Standard Drawing

title

5200mm GALLOWS GATE DETAILS

scale

1:1

	drawing no	rev
Sheet 4	D.4049	A

bldg type | space use | element 20 | feature | material | key

010379 -

3
Metal fencing and gates

5167 MS Fence—horizontal flat top
4056 MS Fence—horizontal flat top (details)
5162 MS Fence—bow tops
4055 MS Fence—bow tops (details)
2010 MS Double gates range
2011 MS Single gate range
2012 MS Double gates over kerb swing range
2013 MS Domestic gates range
5339 MS Double gates—horizontal flat top-hung on MS posts
5341 MS Double gates—horizontal flat top-hung on brick piers
5197 MS Double gates—horizontal flat top—3m wide
5169 MS Double gates—horizontal flat top—4.4m wide
5199 MS Double gates—horizontal flat top—5m wide
5171 MS Single gate—horizontal flat top
5194 MS Single gate with top panel
5196 MS Single gate with middle panel
5212 MS Double gates with top panel—3m wide
5214 MS Double gates with top panel—5m wide
5166 MS Single gate—bow tops
5164 MS Double gates—bow tops 4.4m wide
4036 MS Single gate—horizontal flat top—details
4039 MS Double gates—details
4041 MS Single gate—bow top—details
4042 MS Double gates—bow top—details
4043 MS Double gates over kerb swing—details
4044 MS Double gates over kerb swing—details
4057 MS Double gates—details
4058 MS Double gates—details
4074 MS Double gates—details
4075 MS Double gates—details
5172 Tubular steel shin rail

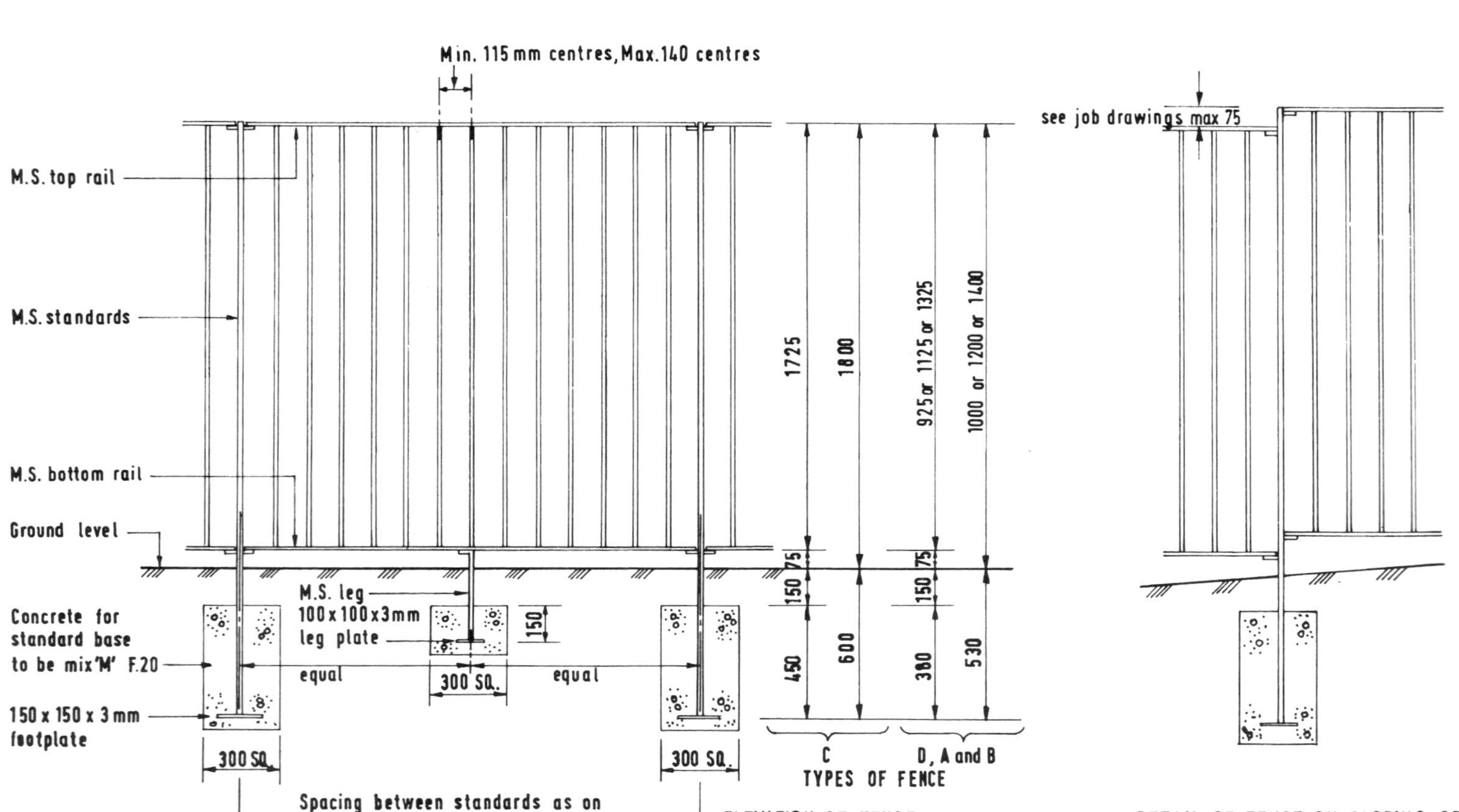

HEIGHT OF FENCE ABOVE G.L. (mm)	M.S. STANDARDS (mm)	M.S. VERTICALS AT APPROX. 128mm c/c	HORIZONTAL M.S. FLAT (mm)	M.S. LUGS (mm)	TYPE OF GROUND	KEY
1000	50 x 20	12 x 12	50 x 10	50 x 10 x 40	LEVEL	D 21
					SLOPING	D 22
1200	50 x 20	12 x 12	50 x 10	50 x 10 x 40	LEVEL	A 21
					SLOPING	A 22
1400	50 x 20	16 x 16	50 x 10	50 x 10 x 40	LEVEL	B 21
					SLOPING	B 22
1800	50 x 20	19 x 19	50 x 10	50 x 10 x 40	LEVEL	C 21
					SLOPING	C 22

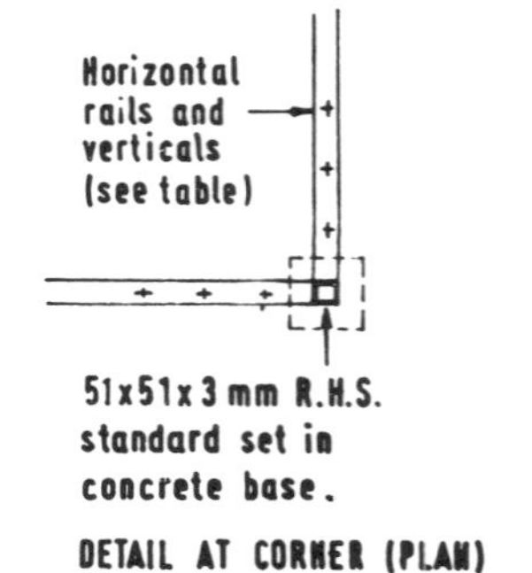

DETAIL AT CORNER (PLAN)

GLC ILEA

Department of Architecture and Civic Design
County Hall SE1
Architect Sir Roger Walters KBE FRIBA FI StructE

References following notes are clause numbers from G.L.C. preambles to bills of quantities.

All metal parts to be hot dipped galvanised as Q.14.

This drawing is to be read in conjunction with job drawings.

For full size manufacturing details see drawing number [20] D 4056.

For metal fences see B.S.1722 part 9.

Departmental Standard Drawing

title

MILD STEEL FENCE
1000, 1200, 1400 and 1800 mm HIGH.

scale 1:20

drawing no D5167 rev B

[20] 86 Xh2 as matrix

00-010379

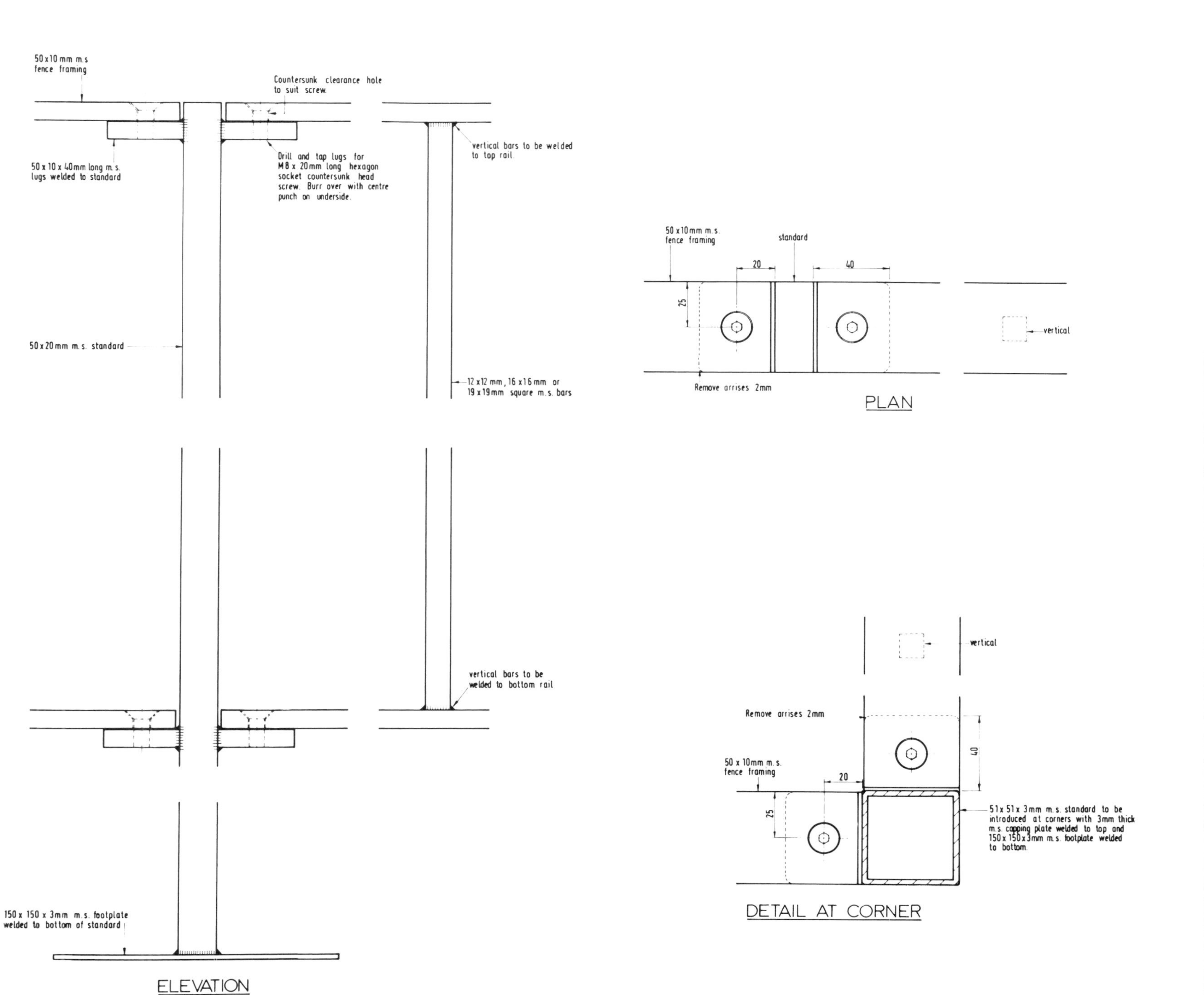

GLC ILEA

Department of Architecture
and Civic Design
County Hall SE1
Architect Sir Roger Walters
KBE FRIBA FI Struct E

ALL METAL PARTS TO BE HOT DIPPED GALVANISED AS Q.14.

THIS DRAWING IS TO BE READ IN CONJUNCTION WITH DRAWING NUMBER [20] D5167B

WELDING TO BE 5mm FILLET WELDS (UNLESS STATED OTHERWISE) AROUND THE FULL PROFILE OF THE MEMBERS BEING JOINED AND SEALING WELDS ON FLUSH EDGES. WELDING TO BE AS B.S. 5135. WELDS <u>MUST NOT</u> BE GROUND FLAT

Departmental Standard Drawing

title
MILD STEEL FENCE 1200, 1400, 1800mm HIGH WITH HORIZONTAL FLAT TOPS

scale
FULL SIZE

drawing no. D4056 rev. B

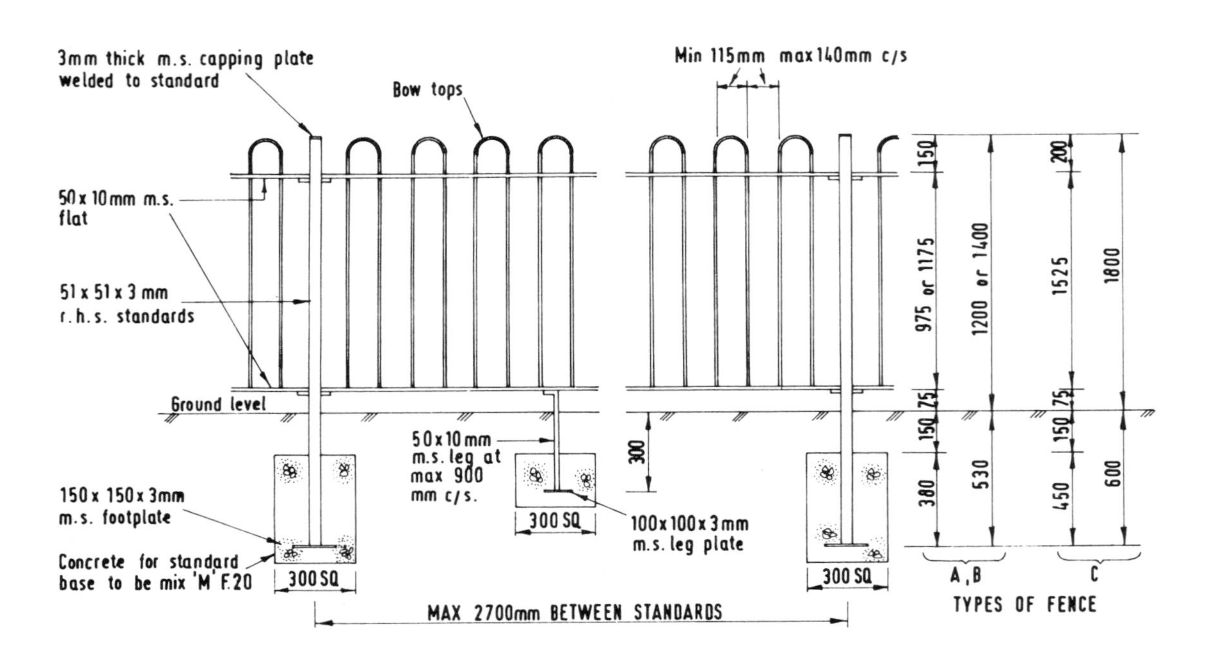

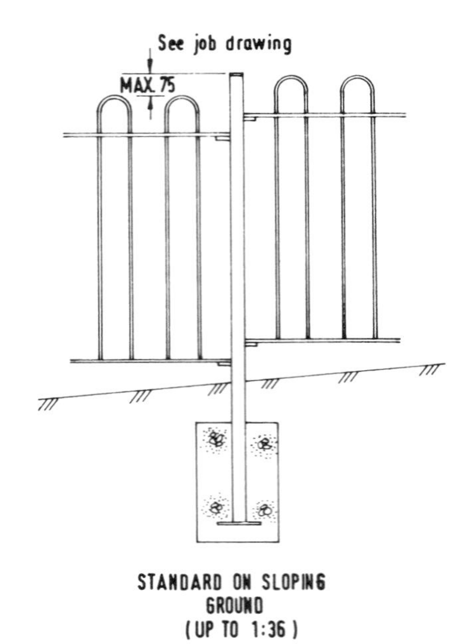

GLC ILEA

Department of Architecture and Civic Design
County Hall SE1
Architect Sir Roger Walters
KBE FRIBA FI StructE

References following notes are clause numbers from G.L.C. preambles to bills of quantities.

All metal parts to be hot dipped galvanised as Q.14.

This drawing is to be read in conjunction with job drawings.

For full size manufacturing details see drawing number [20] D 4055.

For metal fences see B.S. 1722 part 9.

HEIGHT OF FENCE ABOVE GROUND LEVEL (mm)	DIAMETER OF VERTICALS (mm)	HEIGHT OF TOPS (mm)	TYPE OF GROUND	KEY CODE
1200	13	150	LEVEL	A11
			SLOPING	A12
1400	13	150	LEVEL	B11
			SLOPING	B12
1800	19	200	LEVEL	C11
			SLOPING	C12

Departmental Standard Drawing

title

MILD STEEL FENCE
1200, 1400, 1800 mm HIGH

scale 1 : 20

drawing no D5162

00-010379

[20 860 Xh2 as matrix

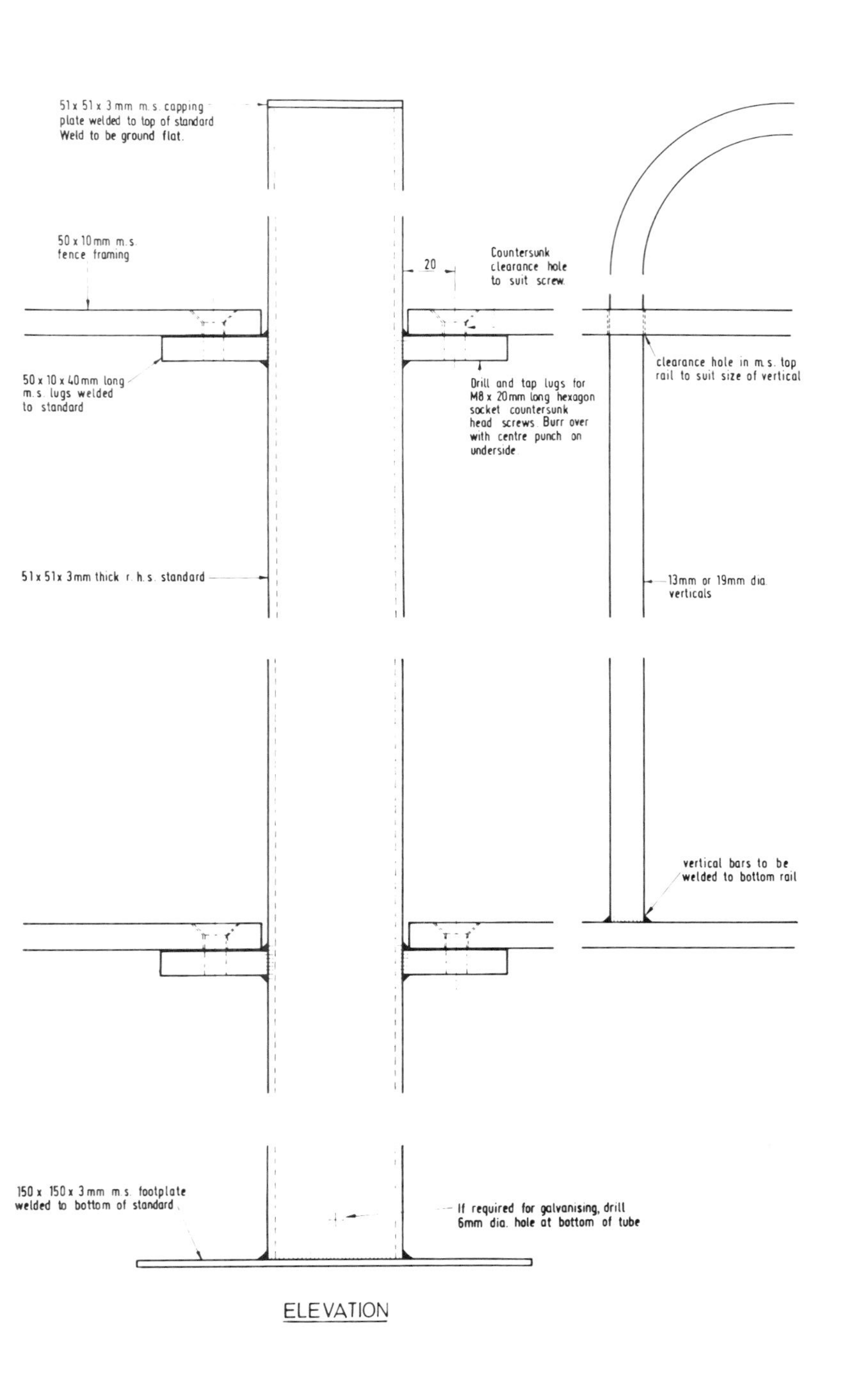

ELEVATION

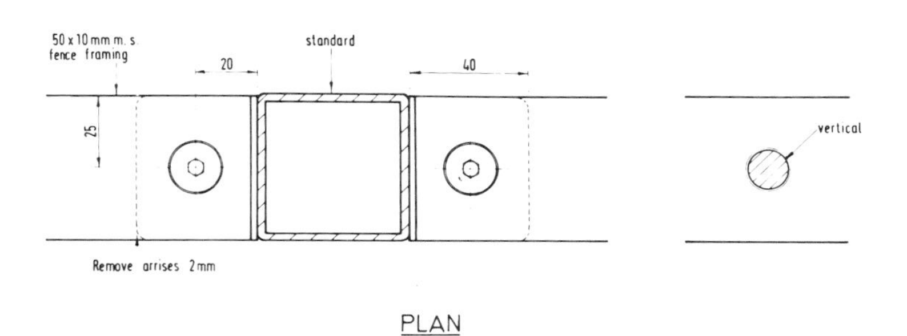

PLAN

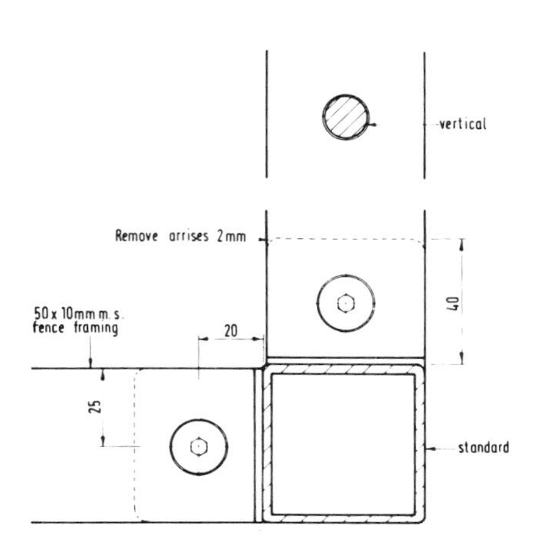

DETAIL AT CORNER

GLC ILEA

Department of Architecture and Civic Design
County Hall SE1
Architect Sir Roger Walters
KBE FRIBA F.Struct.E

ALL METAL PARTS TO BE HOT DIPPED GALVANISED AS Q14.

THIS DRAWING IS TO BE READ IN CONJUNCTION WITH DRAWING NUMBER [20] D5162

WELDING TO BE 5mm FILLET WELDS (UNLESS STATED OTHERWISE) AROUND THE FULL PROFILE OF THE MEMBERS BEING JOINED AND SEALING WELDS ON FLUSH EDGES. WELDING TO BE AS B.S. 5135. WELDS MUST NOT BE GROUND FLAT.

Departmental Standard Drawing

title

MILD STEEL FENCE
1200, 1400, 1800 mm HIGH
WITH BOW TOPS

scale

FULL SIZE

drawing no	rev
D 4055	A

bldg type | space use | element [20] | feature 860 | material Xh2 | key

	3000mm WIDE	4000mm WIDE	5000mm WIDE
1200mm HIGH	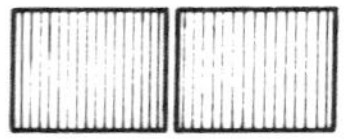 For details see drawing number D5197	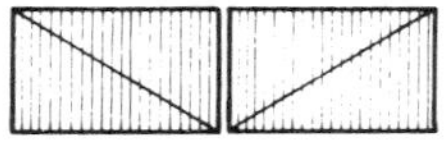 For details see drawing number D5198	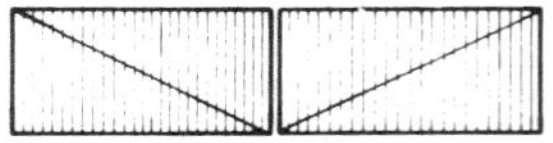 For details see drawing number D5199
	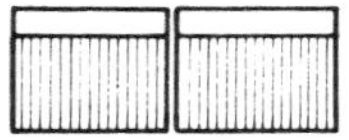 For details see drawing number D5212	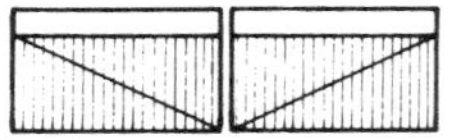 For details see drawing number D5213	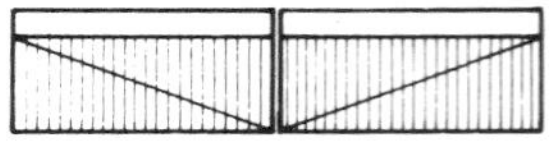 For details see drawing number D5214
	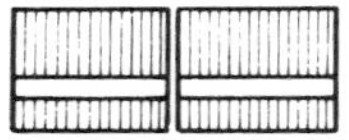 For details see drawing number D5215	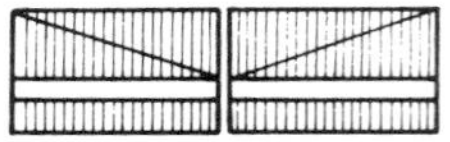 For details see drawing number D5216	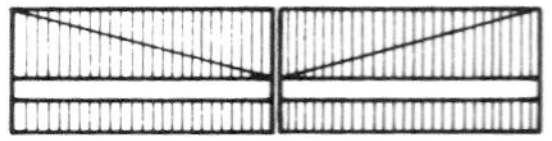 For details see drawing number D5217
1800mm HIGH	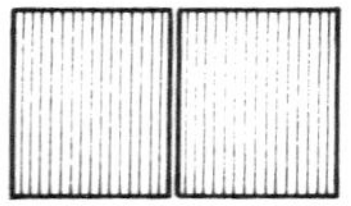 For details see drawing number D5197	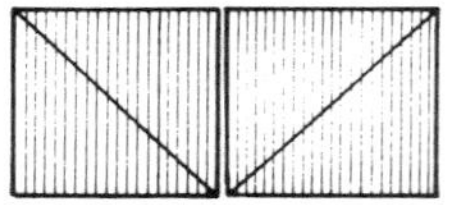 For details see drawing number D5198	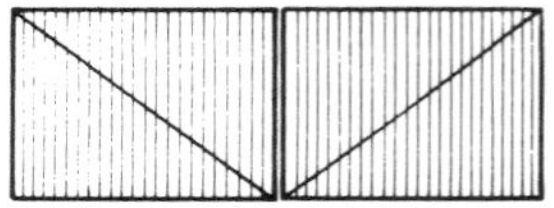 For details see drawing number D5199
	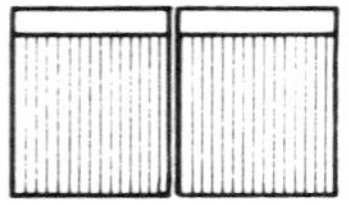 For details see drawing number D5212	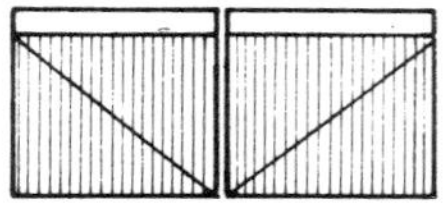 For details see drawing number D5213	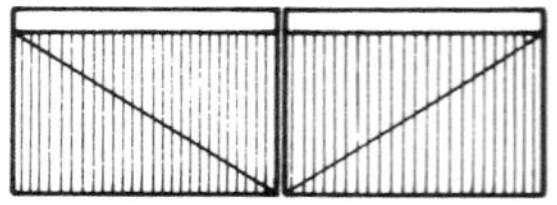 For details see drawing number D5214
	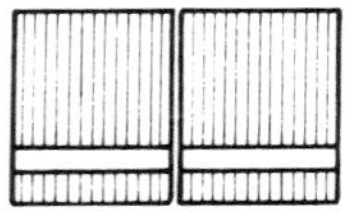 For details see drawing number D5215	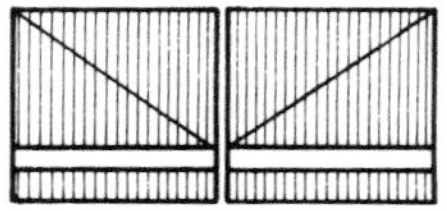 For details see drawing number D5216	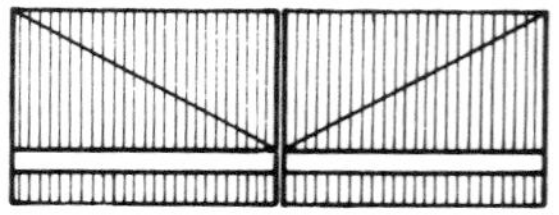 For details see drawing number D5217

GLC ILEA
Department of Architecture and Civic Design
County Hall SE1
Architect Sir Roger Walters KBE FRIBA FI StructE

References following notes are clause numbers from G.L.C. preambles to bills of quantities.

For full size manufacturing details see drawing numbers
[20] D4057 - Horizontal flat top.
[20] D4058 - Top infill panel.
[20] D4059 - Middle infill panel.
[20] D4039 - Common catch and bolt details.

ONLY THOSE GATES SHOWN WITHIN HEAVY LINED BOXES ARE DETAILED IN THIS BOOK.

Departmental Standard Drawing

title
MILD STEEL DOUBLE GATES.
RANGE OF GATES.

scale 1:100

drawing no D2010

bldg type 7 | space use | element [20] | feature 860 | material Xh2 | key

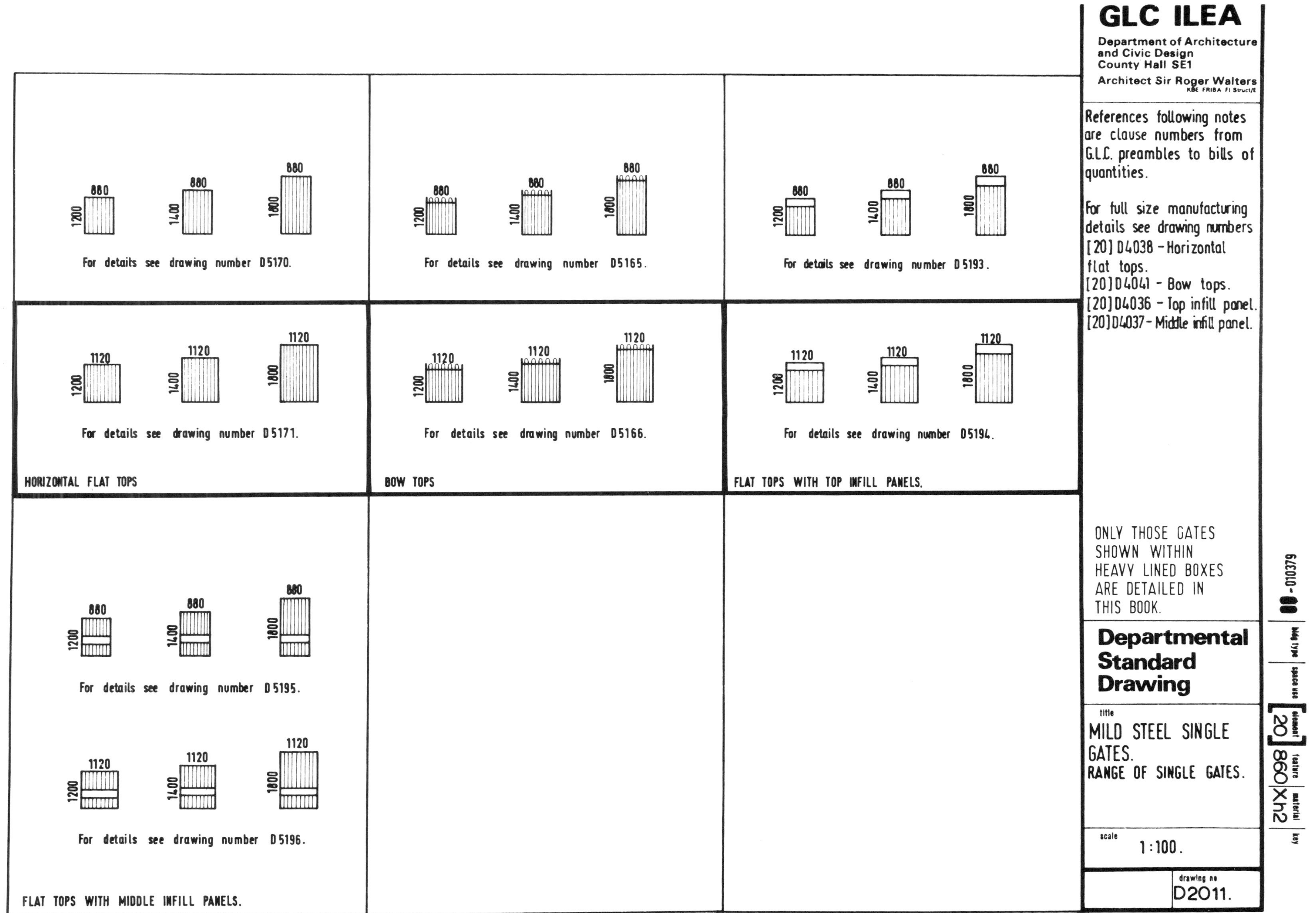
GLC ILEA
Department of Architecture and Civic Design
County Hall SE1
Architect Sir Roger Walters
KBE FRIBA FI StructE
References following notes are clause numbers from G.L.C. preambles to bills of quantities.
For full size manufacturing details see drawing numbers
[20] D4038 - Horizontal flat tops.
[20] D4041 - Bow tops.
[20] D4036 - Top infill panel.
[20] D4037 - Middle infill panel.
880
1120
1200
1400
1800
For details see drawing number D5170.
For details see drawing number D5165.
For details see drawing number D5193.
For details see drawing number D5171.
For details see drawing number D5166.
For details see drawing number D5194.
HORIZONTAL FLAT TOPS
BOW TOPS
FLAT TOPS WITH TOP INFILL PANELS.
For details see drawing number D5195.
For details see drawing number D5196.
FLAT TOPS WITH MIDDLE INFILL PANELS.
ONLY THOSE GATES SHOWN WITHIN HEAVY LINED BOXES ARE DETAILED IN THIS BOOK.
Departmental Standard Drawing
title
MILD STEEL SINGLE GATES.
RANGE OF SINGLE GATES.
scale
1:100.
drawing no
D2011.
[20] 860 Xh2
bldg type
space use
element
feature
material
key

GLC ILEA

Department of Architecture and Civic Design
County Hall SE1
Architect Sir Roger Walters KBE FRIBA FIStructE

	3800 mm WIDE	4400 mm WIDE	3800 mm WIDE	4400 mm WIDE
1200 mm HIGH	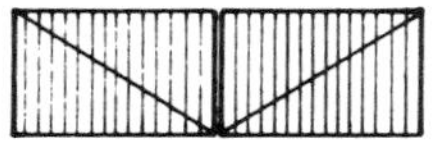 For details see drawing no. D5168	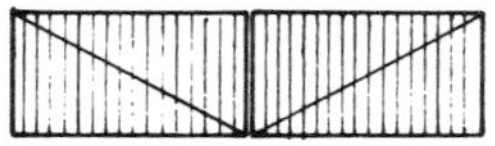 For details see drawing no. D5169	 For details see drawing no. D5163	 For details see drawing no. D5164
1400 mm HIGH	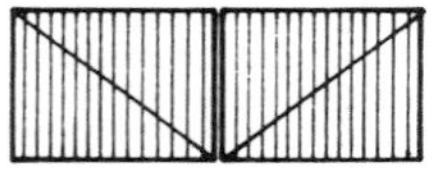 For details see drawing no. D5168	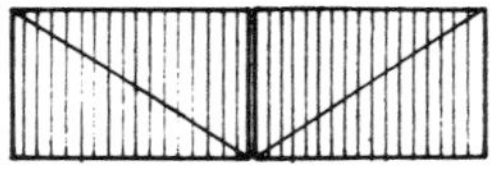 For details see drawing no. D5169	 For details see drawing no. D5163	 For details see drawing no. D5164
1800 mm HIGH	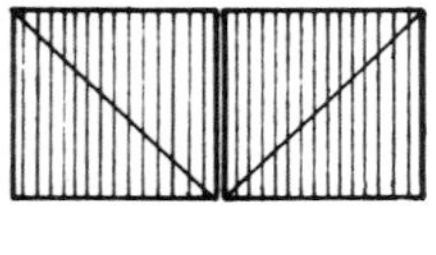 For details see drawing no. D5168	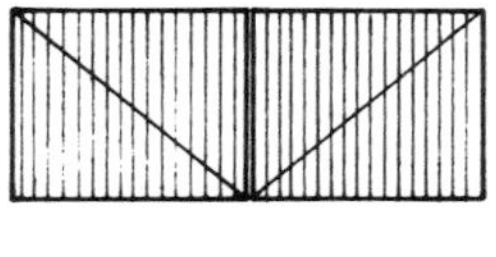 For details see drawing no. D5169	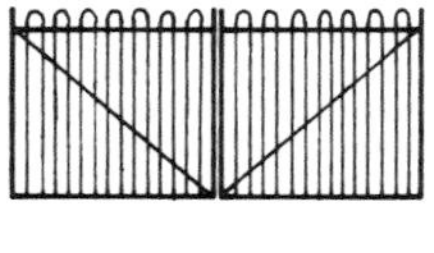 For details see drawing no. D5163	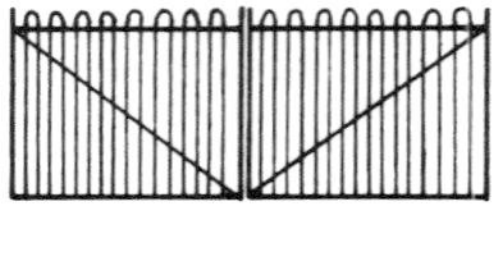 For details see drawing no. D5164

References following notes are clause numbers from G.L.C. preambles to bills of quantities

For full size manufacturing details see drawing numbers :-

[20] D4043 - Horizontal flat tops
[20] D4042 - Bow tops
[20] D4044 - Common catch and bolt details

ONLY THOSE GATES SHOWN WITHIN HEAVY LINED BOXES ARE DETAILED IN THIS BOOK.

Departmental Standard Drawing

title
MILD STEEL DOUBLE GATES
RANGE OF GATES
OVER KERB SWING

scale 1:100

drawing no D2012

bldg type | space use | element [20] | feature 860 | material Xh2 | key

01 - 010379

	1000 mm WIDE		2400 mm WIDE	
1000 mm HIGH — BRICK PIERS	 For details see drawing number D 5340. For manufacturing details see D4073.		 For details see drawing number D5341. For manufacturing details see D4074, D4075.	
1000 mm HIGH — STEEL POSTS	 For details see drawing number D5338. For manufacturing details see D4038.		 For details see drawing number D5339. For manufacturing details see D4074, D4075.	

GLC ILEA

Department of Architecture and Civic Design
County Hall SE1 7PB
Architect Sir Roger Walters KBE ARIBA FI Struct/E

References following notes are clause numbers from G.L.C. preambles to bills of quantities

ONLY THOSE GATES SHOWN WITHIN HEAVY LINED BOXES ARE DETAILED IN THIS BOOK.

Departmental Standard Drawing

title
MILD STEEL SINGLE AND DOUBLE GATES FOR DOMESTIC USE.
RANGE OF GATES.

scale 1:50.

drawing no D2013 | rev

bldg type | space use | element [20] | feature 860 | material Xh2 | key

00 - 010379

8 N° 12 x 12mm verticals at approx. 123 mm c/c

3 mm capping plate welded to top of standard

76·2 x 76·2 x 4mm m.s. gate standard

50 x 10mm gate framing m.s. flat.

Gate catch

2400

65 | 1128 | 14 | 1128 | 65

80

775

1000

60

75

150

380

Ground level

Bolts

Concrete base as F.20 mix M

150 x 150 x 5mm m.s. foot plate

350 x 250 x 150mm deep concrete base as F20 mix M

300 SQ.

ELEVATION

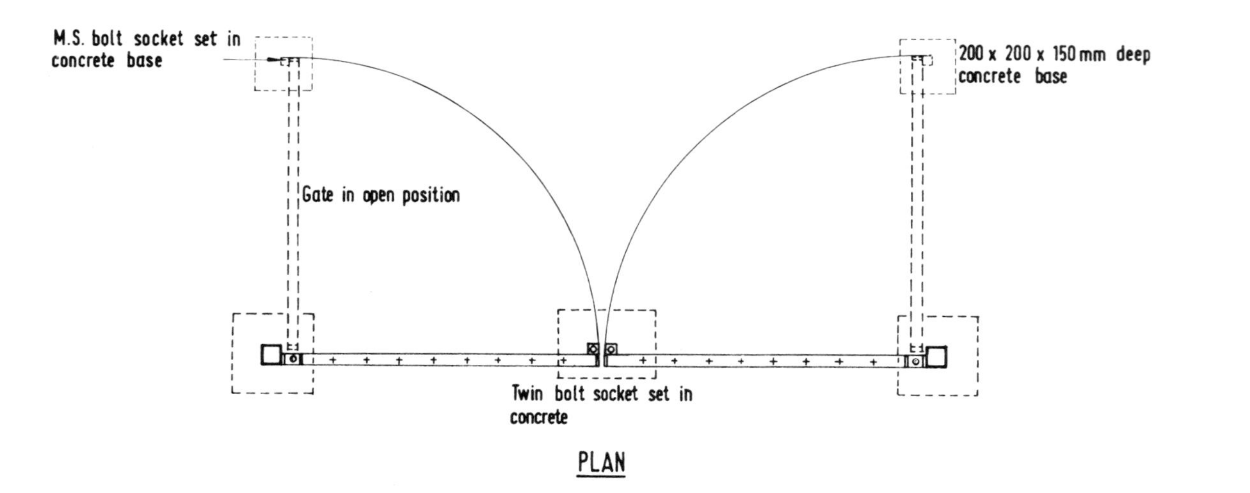

GLC ILEA

Department of Architecture and Civic Design
County Hall SE1 7PB
Architect Sir Roger Walters
KBE ARIBA FI Struct/E

References following notes are clause numbers from G.L.C. preambles to bills of quantities

All metal parts to be hot dipped galvanised as Q.14.

This drg. is to be read in conjunction with job drgs.

For fencing details see drawing number [20]D5167.

For full size manufacturing details see drawing numbers [20] D4074 and D4075.

Foundation design is based on ground bearing capacity of not less than 50kN/m²

Departmental Standard Drawing

title

M.S. DOUBLE GATES.
WITH HORIZONTAL FLAT TOPS.
2400mm WIDE, 1000mm HIGH.
FOR DOMESTIC USE ONLY.

scale 1: 20.

drawing no D5339

rev

bldg type	space use	element	feature	material	key
		[20]	860	Xh2	D2A

00 - 010379

8 N° 12 x 12 mm verticals at approx. 123 mm c/c.

2420
75 1128 14 1128 75

Gate catch

Gate framing 50 x 10mm m.s. flat.

50 x 5 x 300mm long m.s. L shaped ties, welded to 50 x 10 x 925mm long m.s. flat, built into brickwork.

60 775 60 225 675 1000

Bolts

75

Ground level

300MIN.

350 x 250 x 150mm deep concrete base as F20 mix M.

Concrete as F20 mix K or O

225 150

ELEVATION

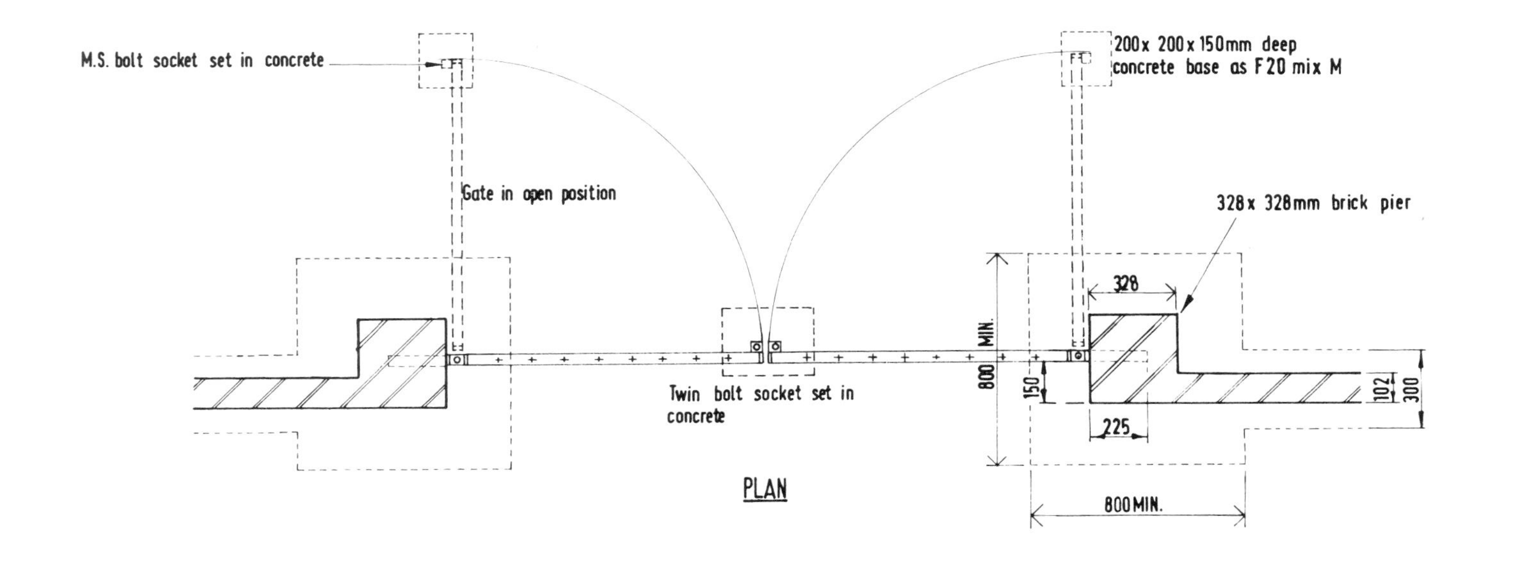

GLC ILEA

Department of Architecture and Civic Design
County Hall SE1 7PB
Architect Sir Roger Walters
KBE ARIBA FI Struct/E

References following notes are clause numbers from G.L.C. preambles to bills of quantities

All metal parts to be hot dipped galvanised as Q.14.

This drg is to be read in conjunction with job drgs.

For full size manufacturing details see drawing numbers [20] D4074 and D4075.

Bricks to have a minimum crushing strength of 10·5 N/mm²

Ground bearing capacity to have min. value of 50 kN/m²

If required, brick pier can be used as free standing.

Departmental Standard Drawing

title

M.S. DOUBLE GATES.
WITH BRICK PIERS.
2400mm WIDE, 1000mm HIGH.
FOR DOMESTIC USE ONLY.

scale 1:20.

drawing no D5341 rev

bldg type | space use | element | feature | material | key
[20] 860 Xh2 D6A.

010379

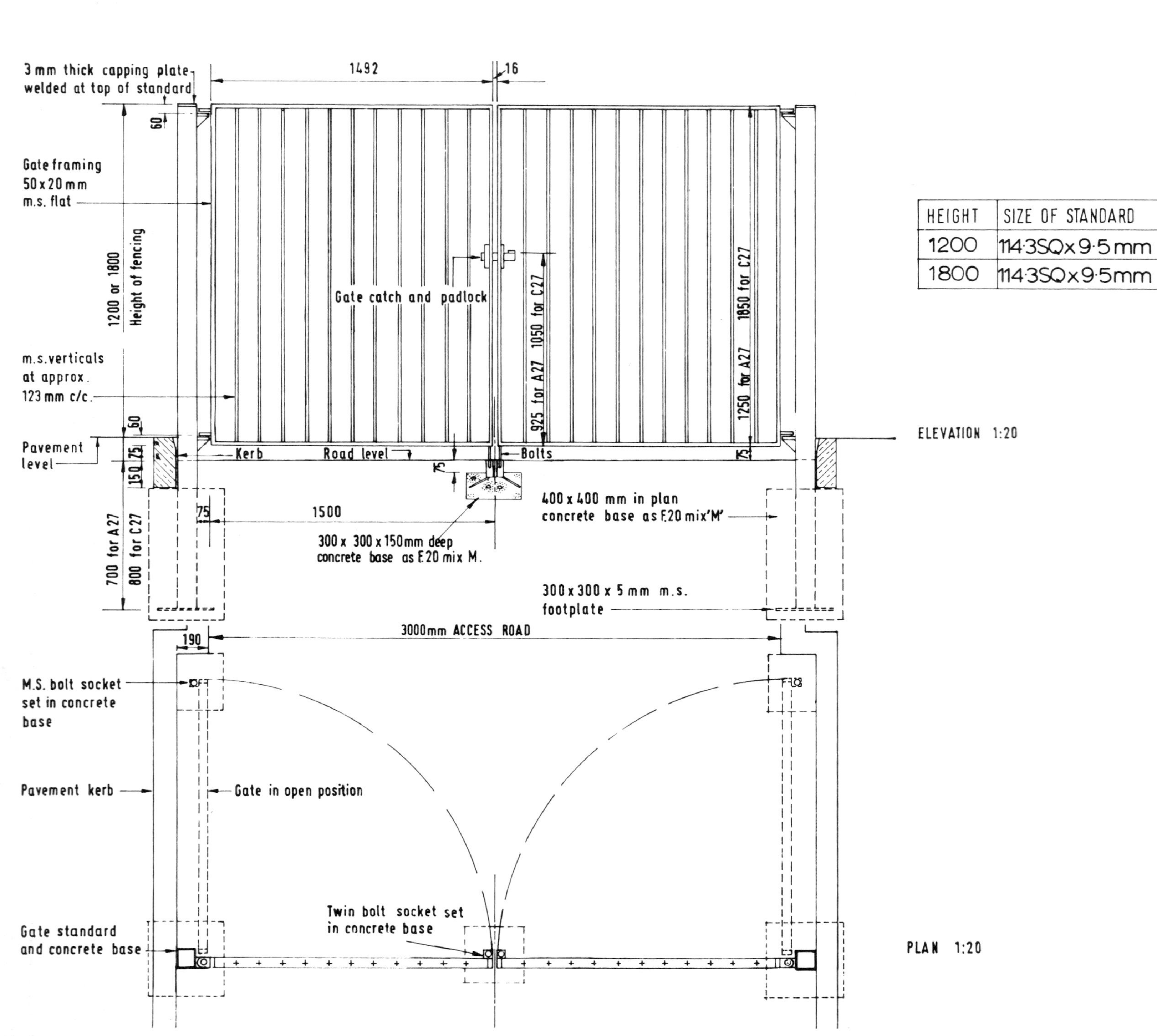

ELEVATION 1:20

PLAN 1:20

HEIGHT	SIZE OF STANDARD	KEY
1200	114·3SQ x 9·5 mm	A27
1800	114·3SQ x 9·5mm	C27

GLC ILEA

Department of Architecture and Civic Design
County Hall SE1
Architect Sir Roger Walters KBE FRIBA FI StructE

References following notes are clause numbers from G.L.C. preambles to bills of quantities.

All metal parts to be hot dipped galvanised as Q.14.

Steel standards to comply with requirements of Q.8.

For full size details see (20)D4057 and (20)D4039.

For paving and kerb details see job drawings.

Ground bearing capacity to have min. value of $50 kN/m^2$

Departmental Standard Drawing

title

DOUBLE GATES
WITH HORIZONTAL FLAT TOPS
3,000 mm WIDE GATE SET

scale

1:20

drawing no

D5197

(20) 860 Xh2 as matrix

00-010379

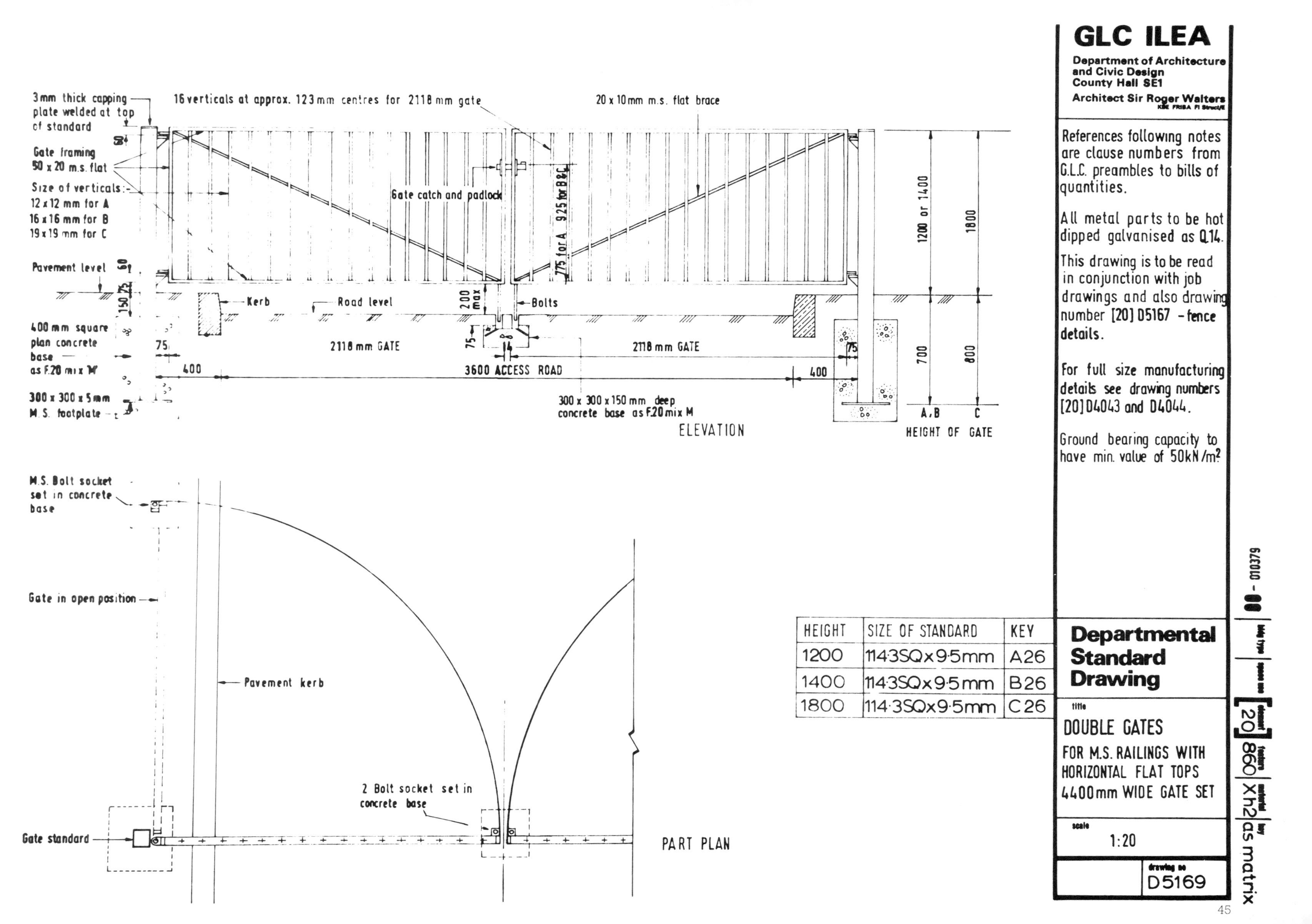

HEIGHT	SIZE OF STANDARD	KEY
1200	114·3SQx9·5mm	A26
1400	114·3SQx9·5mm	B26
1800	114·3SQx9·5mm	C26

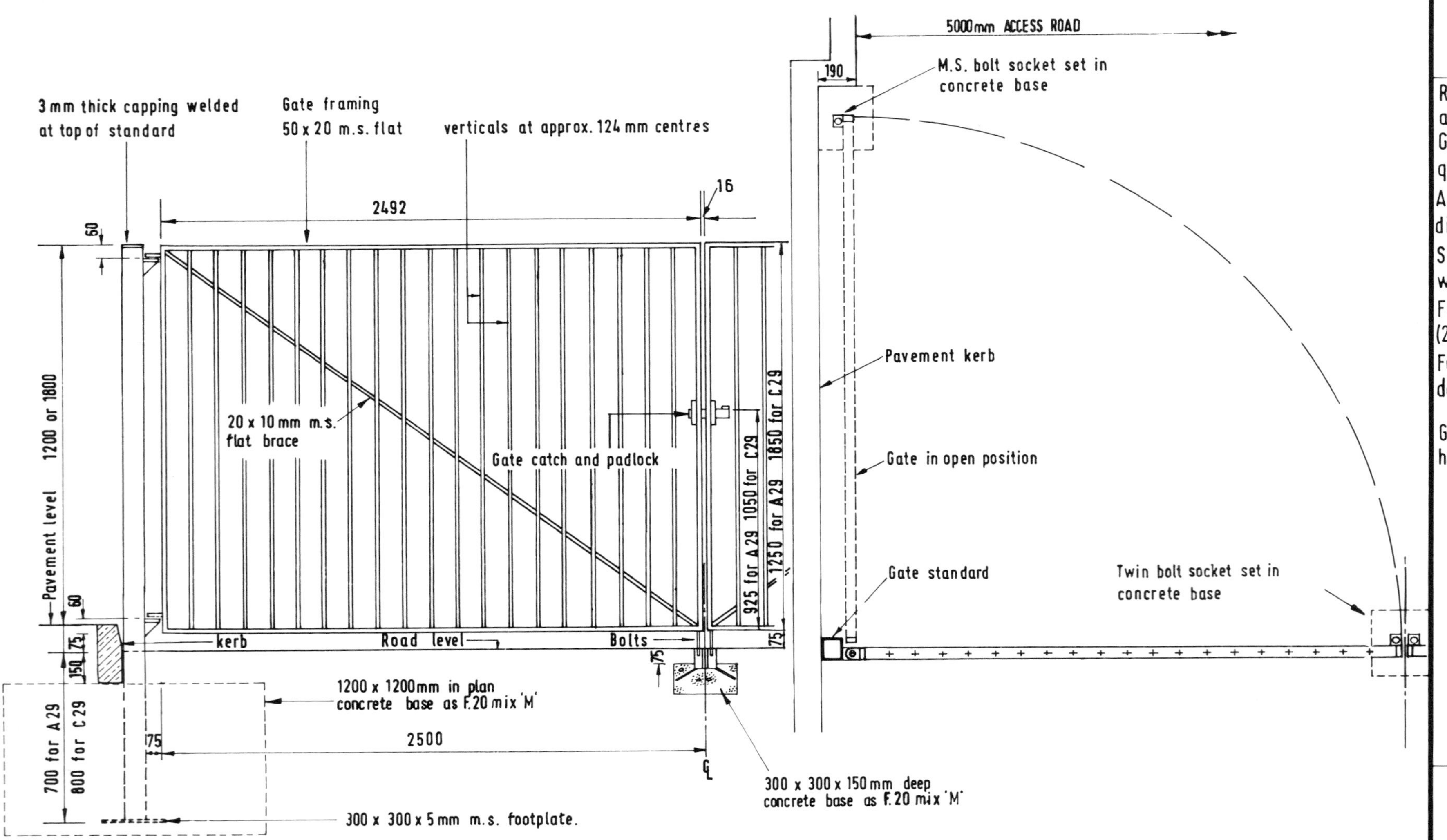

HEIGHT	SIZE OF STANDARD	KEY
1200	114·3SQ x 9·5mm	A29
1800	114·3SQ x 9·5mm	C29

GLC ILEA

Department of Architecture and Civic Design
County Hall SE1
Architect Sir Roger Walters KBE FRIBA FI Struct E

References following notes are clause numbers from G.L.C. preambles to bills of quantities.

All metal parts to be hot dipped galvanised as Q.14.

Steel standards to comply with requirements of Q.8.

For full size details see (20)D4057 and (20)D4039

For paving and kerb details see job drawings.

Ground bearing capacity to have min. value of 50kN/m².

Departmental Standard Drawing

title
DOUBLE GATES
WITH HORIZONTAL FLAT TOPS
5000 mm WIDE GATE SET

scale 1:20

drawing no D5199

[20] 860 Xh2 as matrix

010379

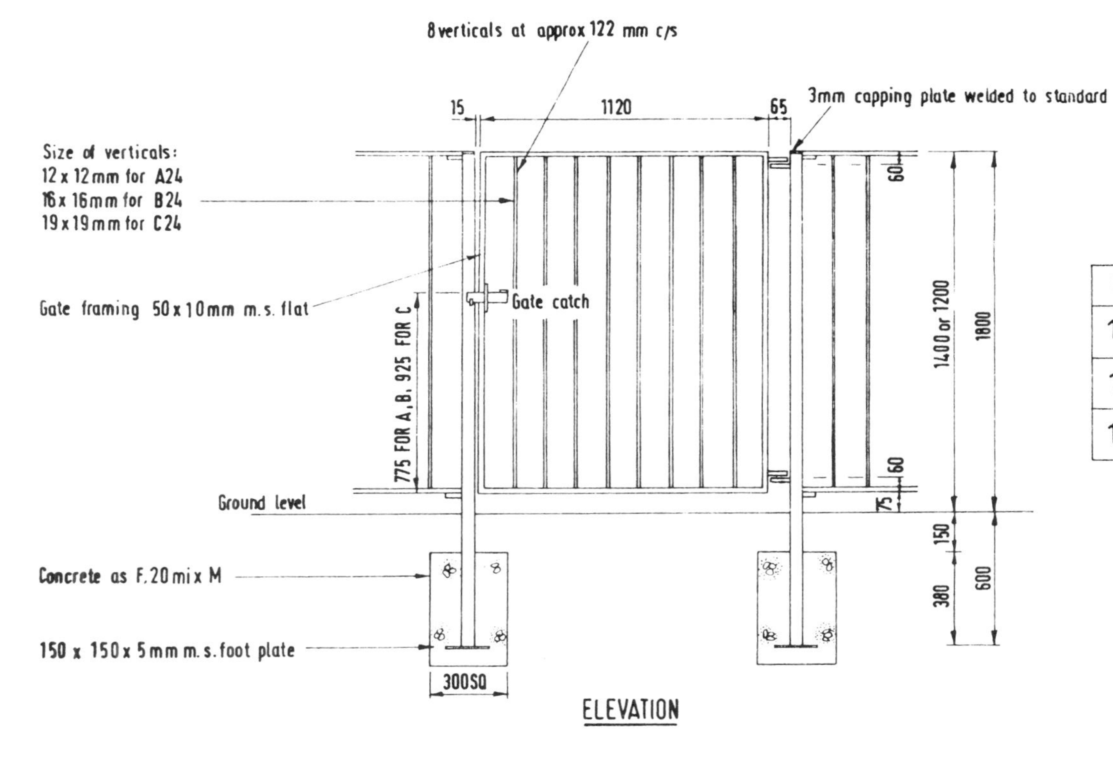

HEIGHT	SIZE OF STANDARD	KEY CODE
1200	76·2SQ x 4mm	A24
1400	76·2SQ x 4mm	B24
1800	76·2SQ x 4mm	C24

GLC ILEA

Department of Architecture and Civic Design
County Hall SE1
Architect Sir Roger Walters
KBE FRIBA FI StructE

References following notes are clause numbers from G.L.C. preambles to bills of quantities.

All metal parts to be hot dipped galvanised as Q.14.

This drawing is to be read in conjunction with job drawings and also drawing number [20] D5167 – fence details.

For full size manufacturing details see drawing number [20] D4038.

Departmental Standard Drawing

title
SINGLE GATES
FOR MILD STEEL RAILINGS WITH HORIZONTAL FLAT TOPS 1200mm WIDE GATE SET.

scale 1 : 20

drawing no D5171

00 - 010379 | unit type | space use | element [20] | feature 860 | material Xh2 | key | as matrix

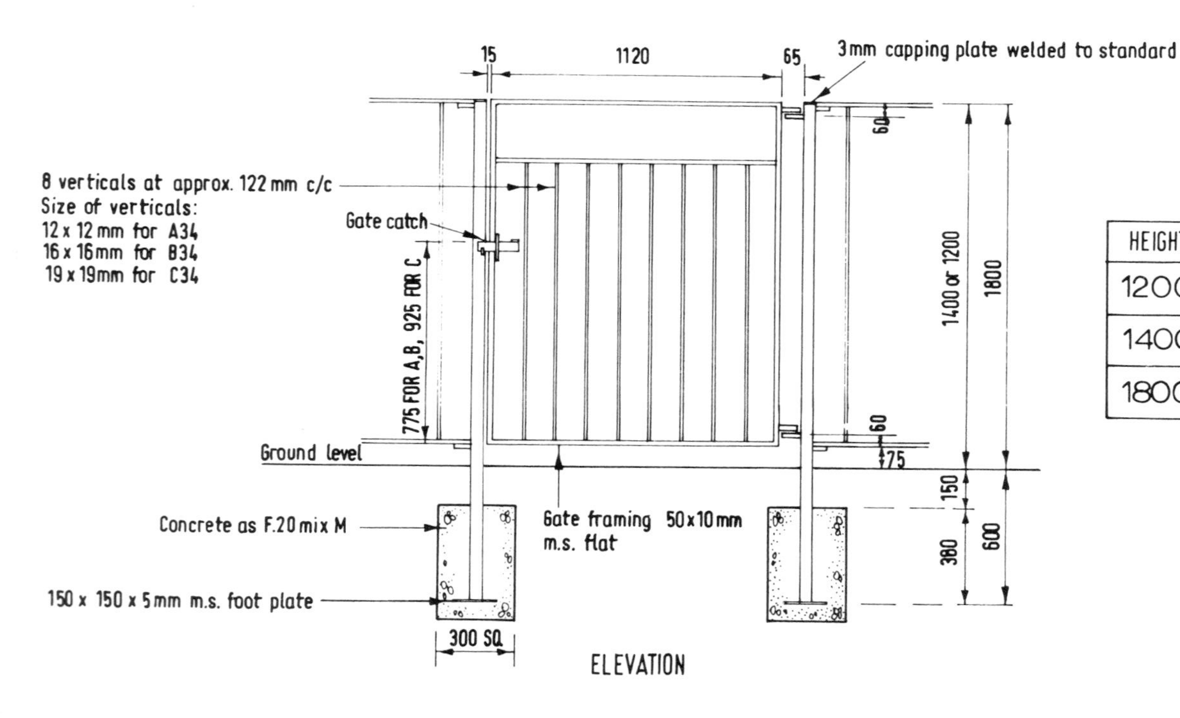

ELEVATION

HEIGHT	SIZE OF STANDARD	KEY CODE
1200	76·2SQ x 4mm	A34
1400	76·2SQ x 4mm	B34
1800	76·2SQ x4mm	C34

GLC ILEA

Department of Architecture and Civic Design
County Hall SE1
Architect Sir Roger Walters KBE FRIBA FI StructE

References following notes are clause numbers from G.L.C. preambles to bills of quantities

All metal parts to be hot dipped galvanised as Q.14.

To be read in conjunction with job drawings and drawing nos. [20] D5167, [20] D4036

Departmental Standard Drawing

title

SINGLE GATES WITH TOP PANEL
FOR MILD STEEL RAILINGS WITH HORIZONTAL FLAT TOPS 1200 mm WIDE GATE SET

scale 1:20

drawing no D5194

00-010379

[20] 860 Xh2 as matrix

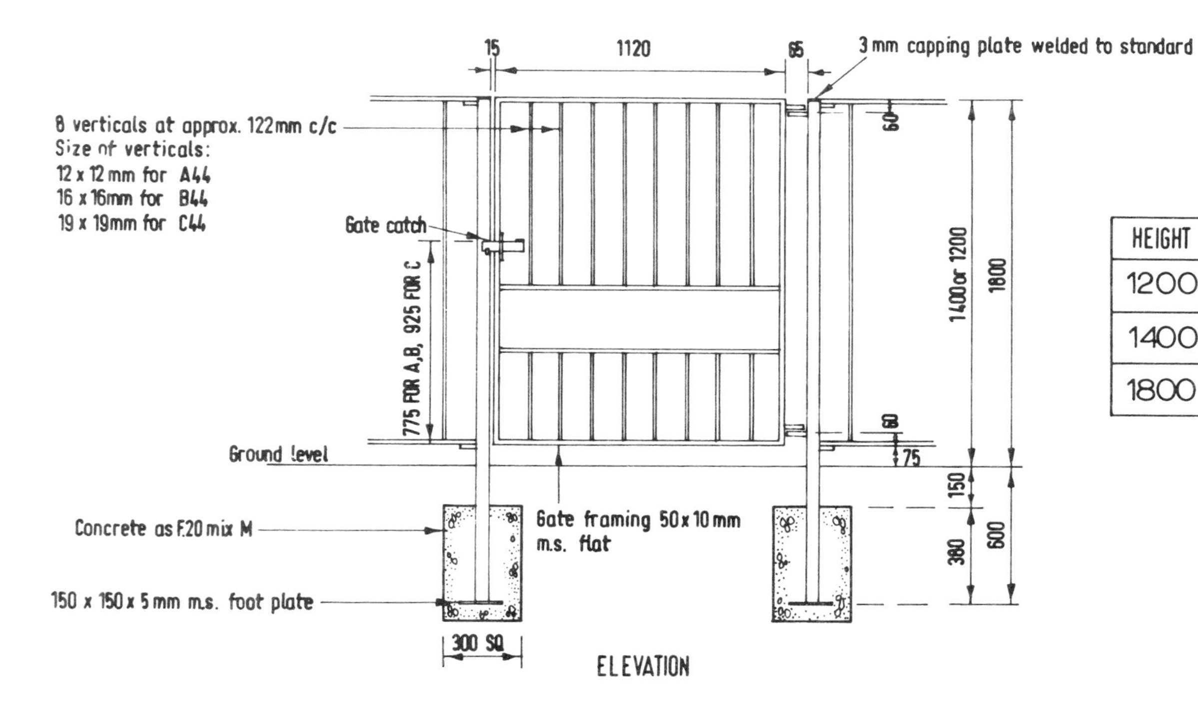

HEIGHT	SIZE OF STANDARD	KEY CODE
1200	76·2SQ x 4mm	A44
1400	76·2SQ x 4mm	B44
1800	76·2SQ x 4mm	C44

GLC ILEA

Department of Architecture and Civic Design
County Hall SE1
Architect Sir Roger Walters KBE FRIBA FI StructE

References following notes are clause numbers from G.L.C. preambles to bills of quantities

All metal parts to be hot dipped galvanised as Q.14.

To be read in conjunction with job drawings and drawing nos. [20] 5167, [20] D4037

Departmental Standard Drawing

title

SINGLE GATES WITH MIDDLE PANEL
FOR MILD STEEL RAILINGS WITH HORIZONTAL FLAT TOPS 1200mm WIDE GATE SET

scale 1:20

drawing no D5196

[20] 860 Xh2 as matrix

00 - 010379

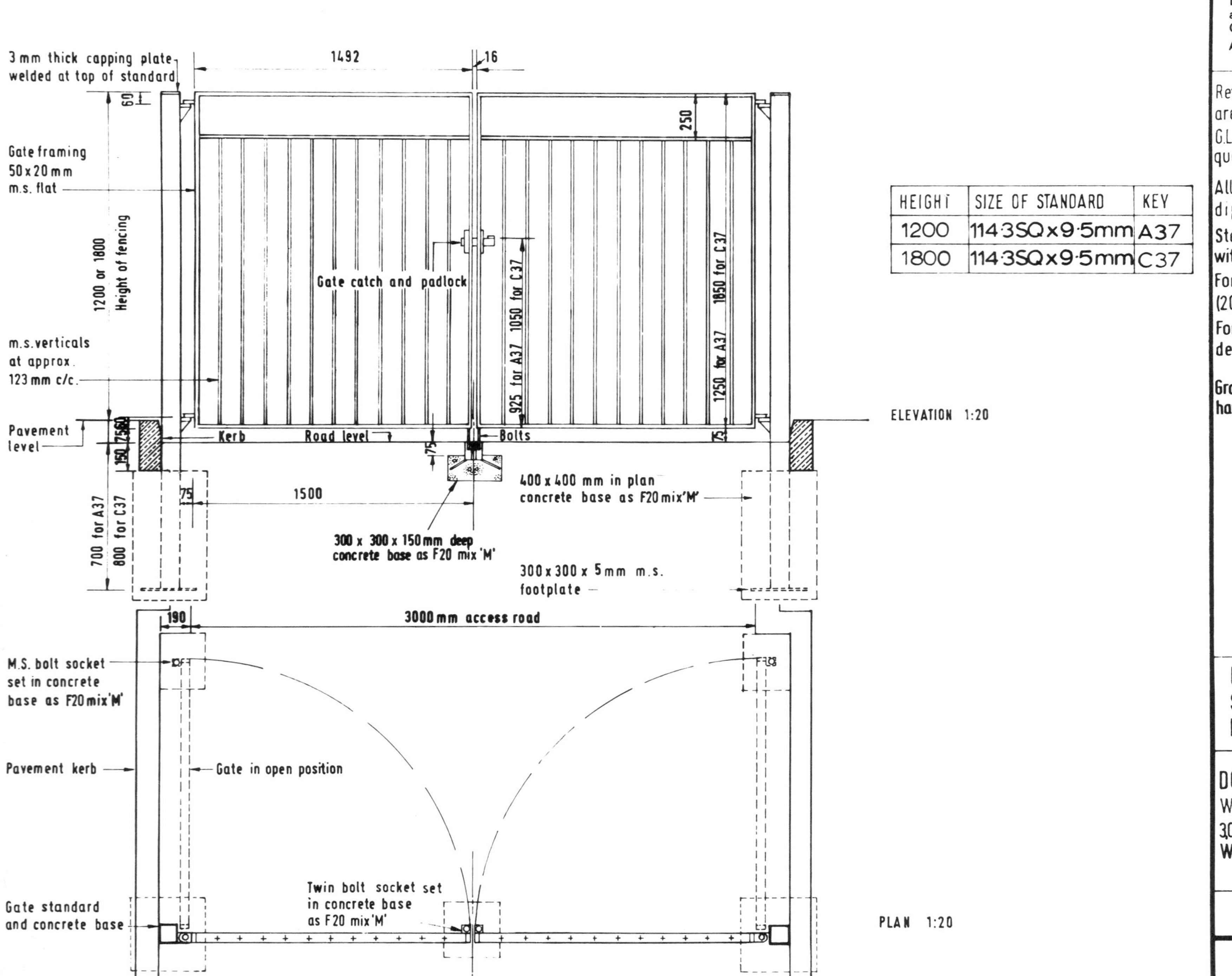

HEIGHT	SIZE OF STANDARD	KEY
1200	114·3SQ x 9·5mm	A37
1800	114·3SQ x 9·5mm	C37

GLC ILEA

Department of Architecture and Civic Design
County Hall SE1
Architect Sir Roger Walters KBE FRIBA FI StructE

References following notes are clause numbers from G.L.C. preambles to bills of quantities.

All metal parts to be hot dipped galvanised as Q.14.

Steel standards to comply with requirements of Q.8.

For full size details see (20)D4058 and (20)D4039

For paving and kerb details see job drawings.

Ground bearing capacity to have min. value of $50 kN/m^2$

Departmental Standard Drawing

title

DOUBLE GATES
WITH HORIZONTAL FLAT TOPS
3,000 mm WIDE GATE SET
WITH PANEL AT TOP

scale 1:20

drawing no D5212

bldg type | space use | element [20] | feature 860 | material Xh2 | key as matrix

010379

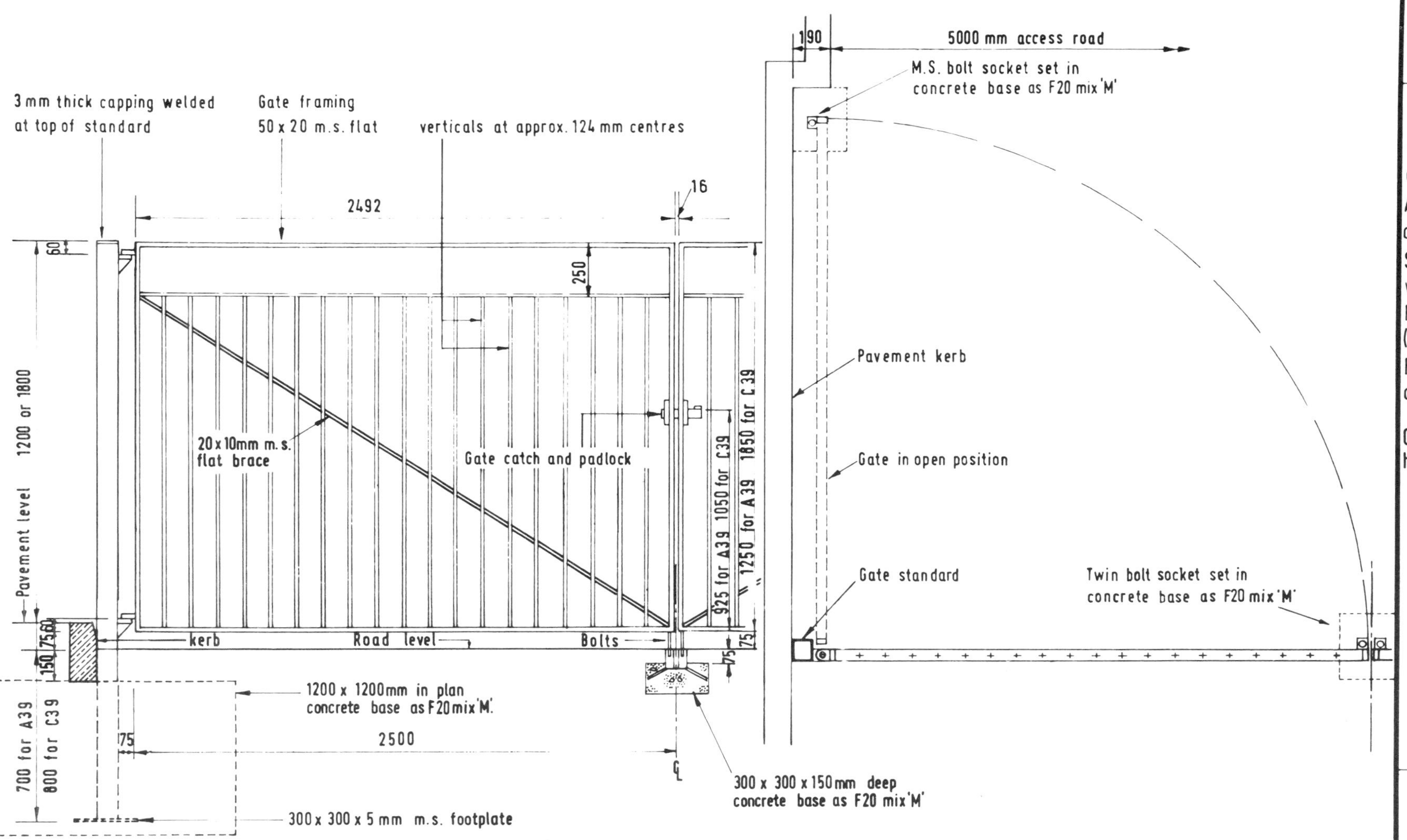

HEIGHT	SIZE OF STANDARD	KEY
1200	114·3SQ x 9·5 mm	A39
1800	114·3SQ x 9·5 mm	C39

GLC ILEA

Department of Architecture and Civic Design
County Hall SE1
Architect Sir Roger Walters KBE FRIBA FI Struct E

References following notes are clause numbers from G.L.C. preambles to bills of quantities.

All metal parts to be hot dipped galvanised as Q.14.

Steel standards to comply with requirements of Q.8..

For full size details see (20)D4058 and (20)D4039

For paving and kerb details see job drawings.

Ground bearing capacity to have min. value of 50kN/m²

Departmental Standard Drawing

title

DOUBLE GATES

WITH HORIZONTAL FLAT TOPS 5,000 mm WIDE GATE SET WITH PANEL AT TOP

scale 1:20

drawing no D5214

00 - 01037 | bldg type | space use | element [20] | feature 860 | material Xh2 | key as matrix

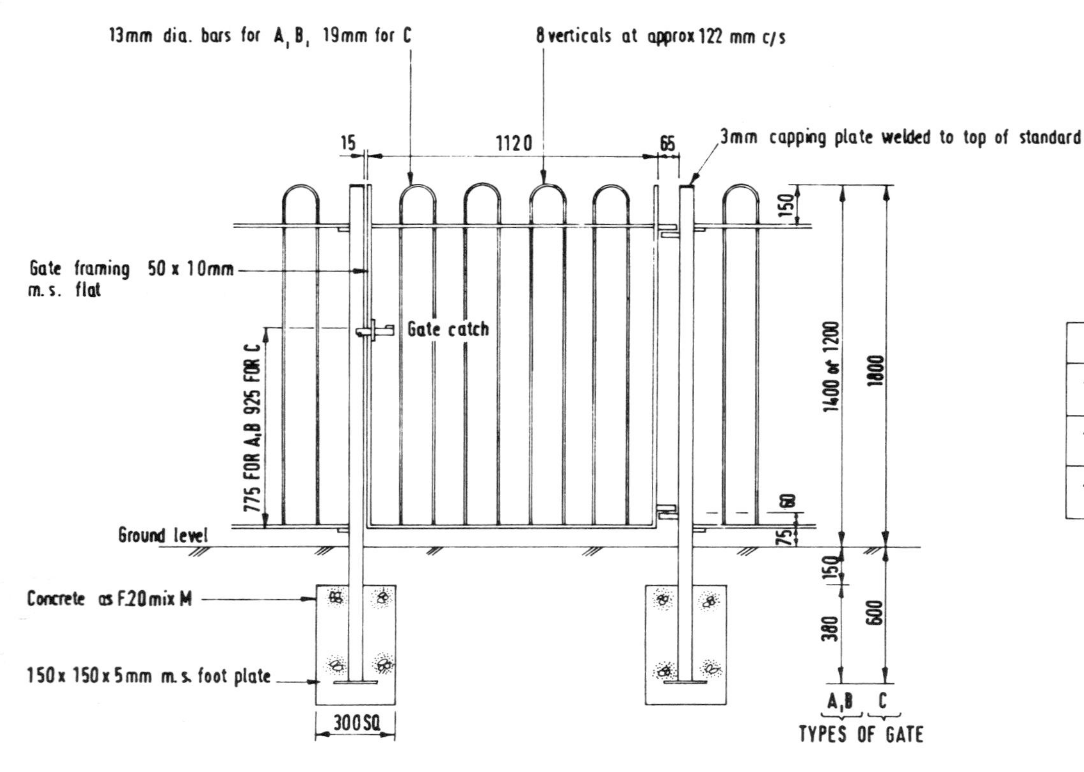

HEIGHT	SIZE OF STANDARD	KEY CODE
1200	76·2SQ x 4mm	A 14
1400	76·2SQ x 4mm	B 14
1800	76·2SQ x 4mm	C 14

GLC ILEA

Department of Architecture and Civic Design
County Hall SE1
Architect Sir Roger Walters KBE FRIBA FI StructE

References following notes are clause numbers from G.L.C. preambles to bills of quantities.

All metal parts to be hot dipped galvanised as Q.14.

This drawing is to be read in conjunction with job drawings and also drawing number [20] D5162 - fence details.

For full size manufacturing details see drawing number [20] D4041.

Departmental Standard Drawing

title
SINGLE GATES
FOR MILD STEEL RAILINGS
WITH BOW TOPS.
1200mm WIDE GATE SET.

scale
1 : 20

drawing no
D5166

010379 - 00 bldg type | space use | [20] element | 860 feature | Xh2 material | as matrix key

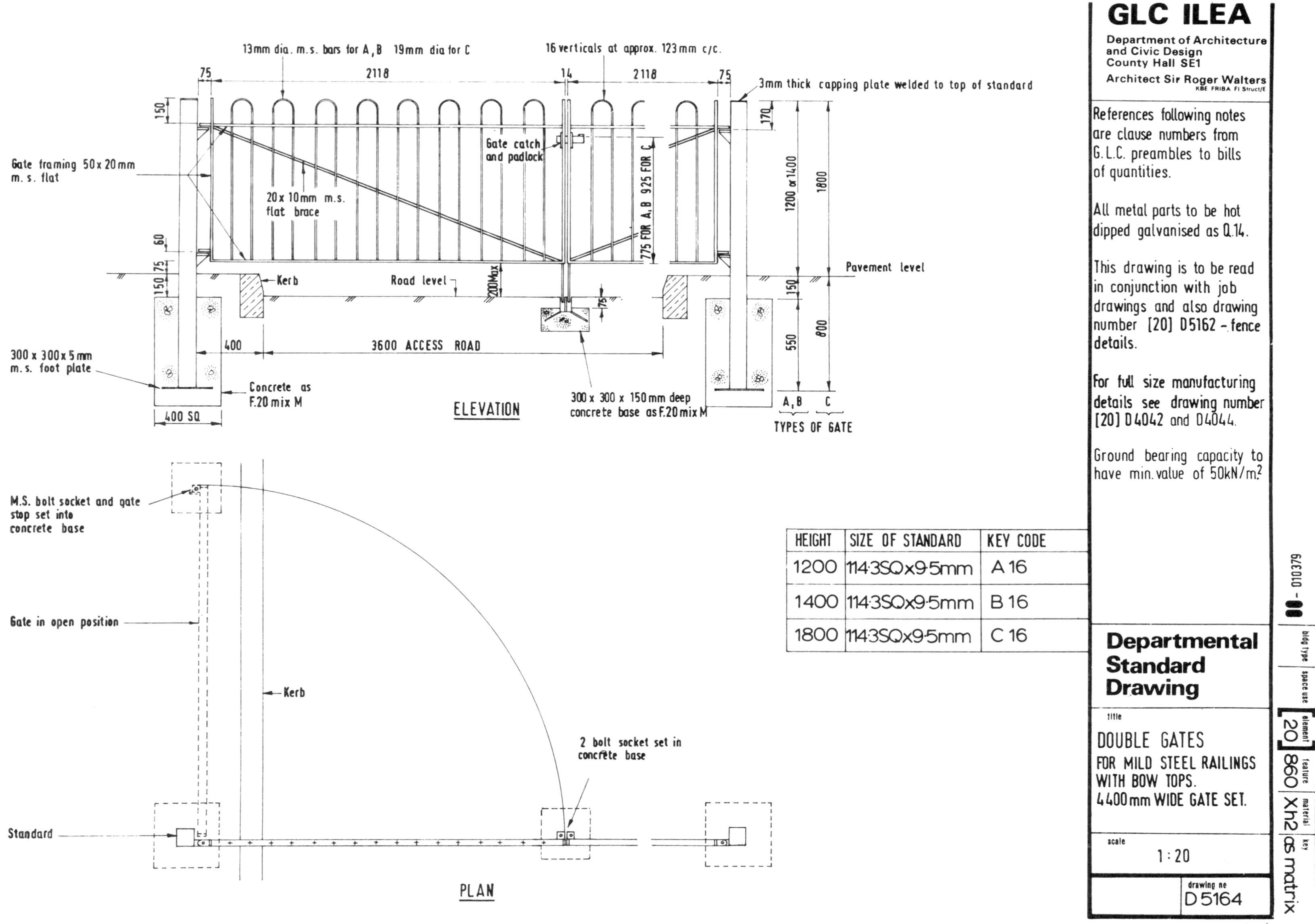
GLC ILEA
Department of Architecture and Civic Design
County Hall SE1
Architect Sir Roger Walters KBE FRIBA FI Struct/E
References following notes are clause numbers from G.L.C. preambles to bills of quantities.
All metal parts to be hot dipped galvanised as Q.14.
This drawing is to be read in conjunction with job drawings and also drawing number [20] D5162 - fence details.
For full size manufacturing details see drawing number [20] D4042 and D4044.
Ground bearing capacity to have min. value of 50kN/m²
13mm dia. m.s. bars for A, B 19mm dia for C
16 verticals at approx. 123mm c/c.
3mm thick capping plate welded to top of standard
Gate framing 50x20mm m.s. flat
20x10mm m.s. flat brace
Gate catch and padlock
775 FOR A, B 925 FOR C
1200 or 1400
1800
Pavement level
Kerb
Road level
200Max
3600 ACCESS ROAD
300 x 300 x 5mm m.s. foot plate
Concrete as F.20 mix M
400 SQ
ELEVATION
300 x 300 x 150mm deep concrete base as F.20 mix M
TYPES OF GATE
M.S. bolt socket and gate stop set into concrete base
Gate in open position
Kerb
2 bolt socket set in concrete base
Standard
PLAN
HEIGHT	SIZE OF STANDARD	KEY CODE
1200	114·3SQx9·5mm	A 16
1400	114·3SQx9·5mm	B 16
1800	114·3SQx9·5mm	C 16
Departmental Standard Drawing
title
DOUBLE GATES
FOR MILD STEEL RAILINGS WITH BOW TOPS.
4400mm WIDE GATE SET.
scale 1:20
drawing no D5164
010379
[20] 860 Xh2 as matrix

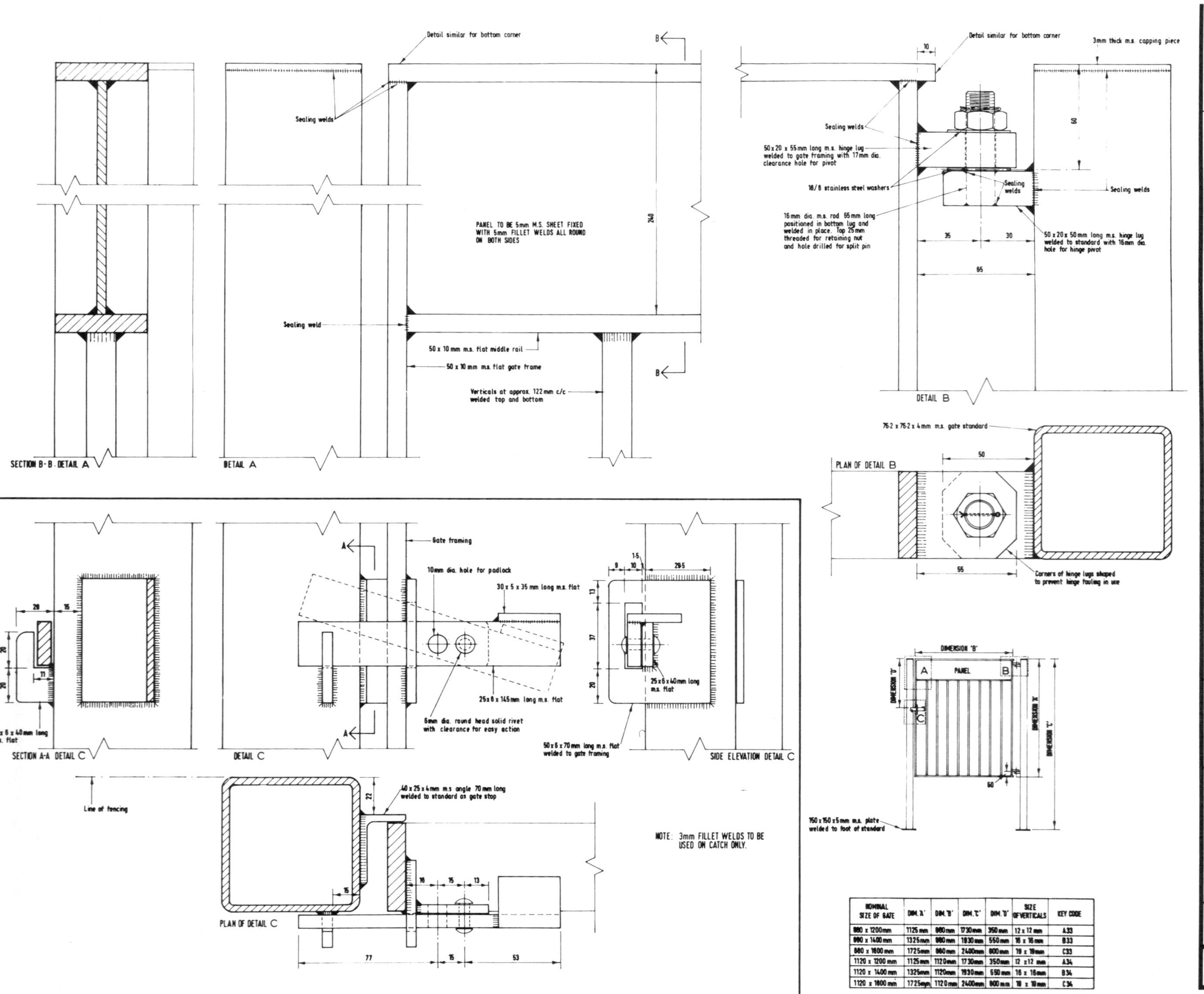

NOMINAL SIZE OF GATE	DIM. 'A'	DIM. 'B'	DIM. 'C'	DIM. 'D'	SIZE OF VERTICALS	KEY CODE
880 x 1200mm	1125 mm	880mm	1730mm	350mm	12 x 12 mm	A33
880 x 1400mm	1325mm	880mm	1930mm	550mm	16 x 16mm	B33
880 x 1800mm	1725mm	880mm	2400mm	800mm	19 x 19mm	C33
1120 x 1200 mm	1125mm	1120mm	1730mm	350mm	12 x 12 mm	A34
1120 x 1400 mm	1325mm	1120mm	1930mm	550mm	16 x 16mm	B34
1120 x 1800 mm	1725mm	1120mm	2400mm	800mm	18 x 18mm	C34

GLC ILEA

Department of Architecture and Civic Design
County Hall SE1
Architect Sir Roger Walters
KBE FRIBA FI Struct E

All metal parts to be hot dipped galvanised as Q.14 after fabrication.

Welding to be 5mm fillet welds (unless stated otherwise) around the full profile of the members being joined and sealing welds on flush edges. Welding to be as BS 5135 Welds must not be ground flat.

This drawing to be read handed when necessary.

Departmental Standard Drawing

title
MILD STEEL SINGLE GATE

CONSTRUCTION DETAILS

GATE WITH HORIZONTAL FLAT TOP AND TOP PANEL

scale
1:1 & 1:20

drawing no. D4036 | rev. B

bldg type | space uses | element 20 | feature 860 | material Xh2 | key as matrix

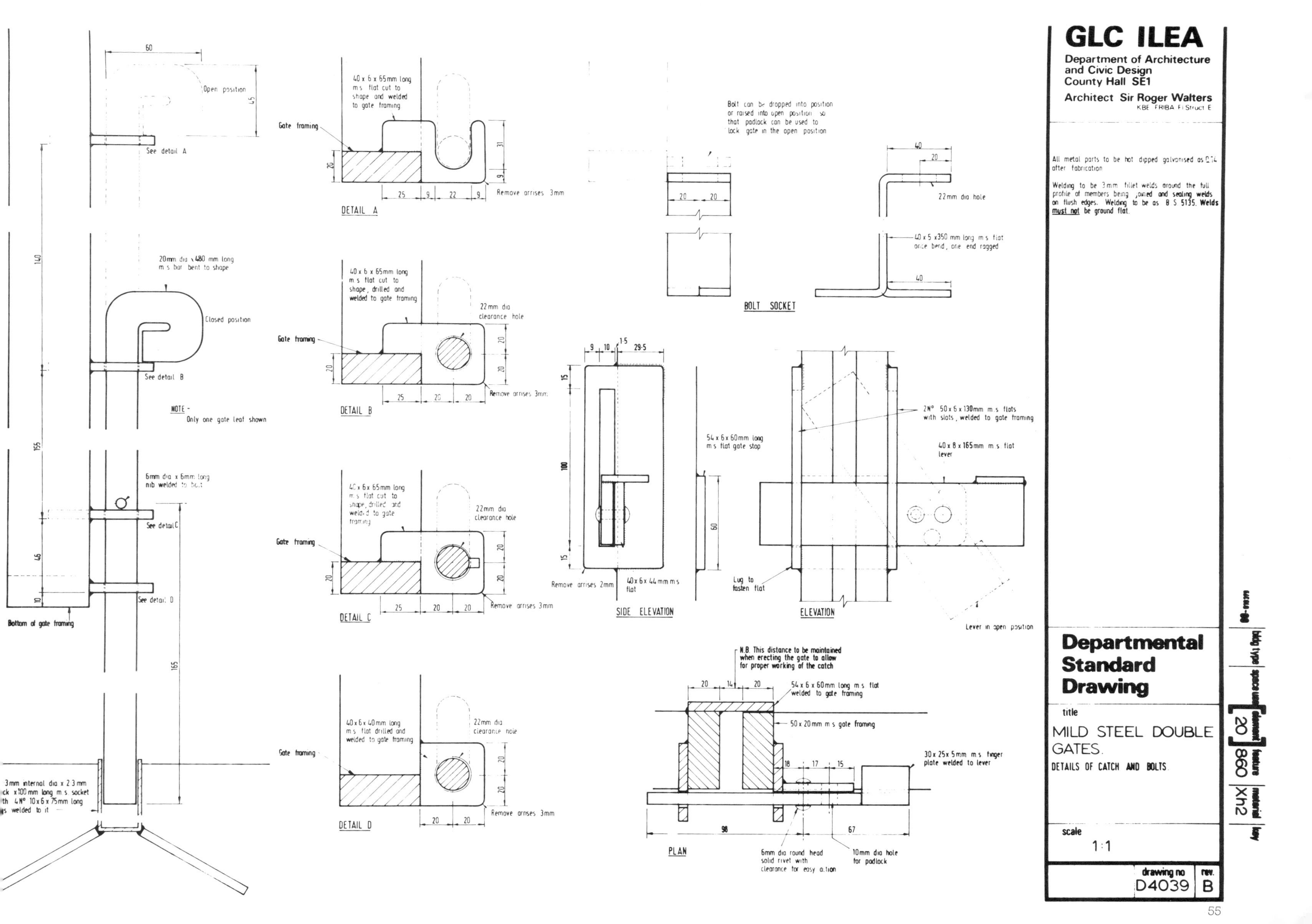
GLC ILEA
Department of Architecture and Civic Design
County Hall SE1
Architect Sir Roger Walters
KBE FRIBA FI Struct E
All metal parts to be hot dipped galvanised as 0.14 after fabrication
Welding to be 3mm fillet welds around the full profile of members being jointed and sealing welds on flush edges. Welding to be as B S 5135. Welds must not be ground flat.
Departmental Standard Drawing
title
MILD STEEL DOUBLE GATES.
DETAILS OF CATCH AND BOLTS.
scale
1:1
drawing no
D4039
rev.
B
bldg type
space used
element
20
feature
860
material
Xh2
key
Open position
See detail A
20mm dia x 480 mm long m s bar bent to shape
Closed position
See detail B
NOTE -
Only one gate leaf shown
6mm dia x 6mm long nib welded to bolt
See detail C
See detail D
Bottom of gate framing
3mm internal dia x 2.3mm thick x 100mm long m s socket with 4N° 10x6x75mm long lugs welded to it
40 x 6 x 65mm long m s flat cut to shape and welded to gate framing
Gate framing
Remove arrises 3mm
DETAIL A
40 x 6 x 65mm long m s flat cut to shape, drilled and welded to gate framing
22mm dia clearance hole
DETAIL B
DETAIL C
40 x 6 x 40mm long m s flat drilled and welded to gate framing
DETAIL D
Bolt can be dropped into position or raised into open position so that padlock can be used to lock gate in the open position
22mm dia hole
40 x 5 x 350 mm long m s flat once bend, one end ragged
BOLT SOCKET
Remove arrises 2mm
40 x 6 x 44mm m s flat
SIDE ELEVATION
54 x 6 x 60mm long m s flat gate stop
Lug to fasten flat
2N° 50 x 6 x 130mm m s flats with slots, welded to gate framing
40 x 8 x 165mm m s flat lever
ELEVATION
Lever in open position
N.B. This distance to be maintained when erecting the gate to allow for proper working of the catch
54 x 6 x 60mm long m s flat welded to gate framing
50 x 20mm m s gate framing
30 x 25 x 5mm m s finger plate welded to lever
PLAN
6mm dia round head solid rivet with clearance for easy action
10mm dia hole for padlock

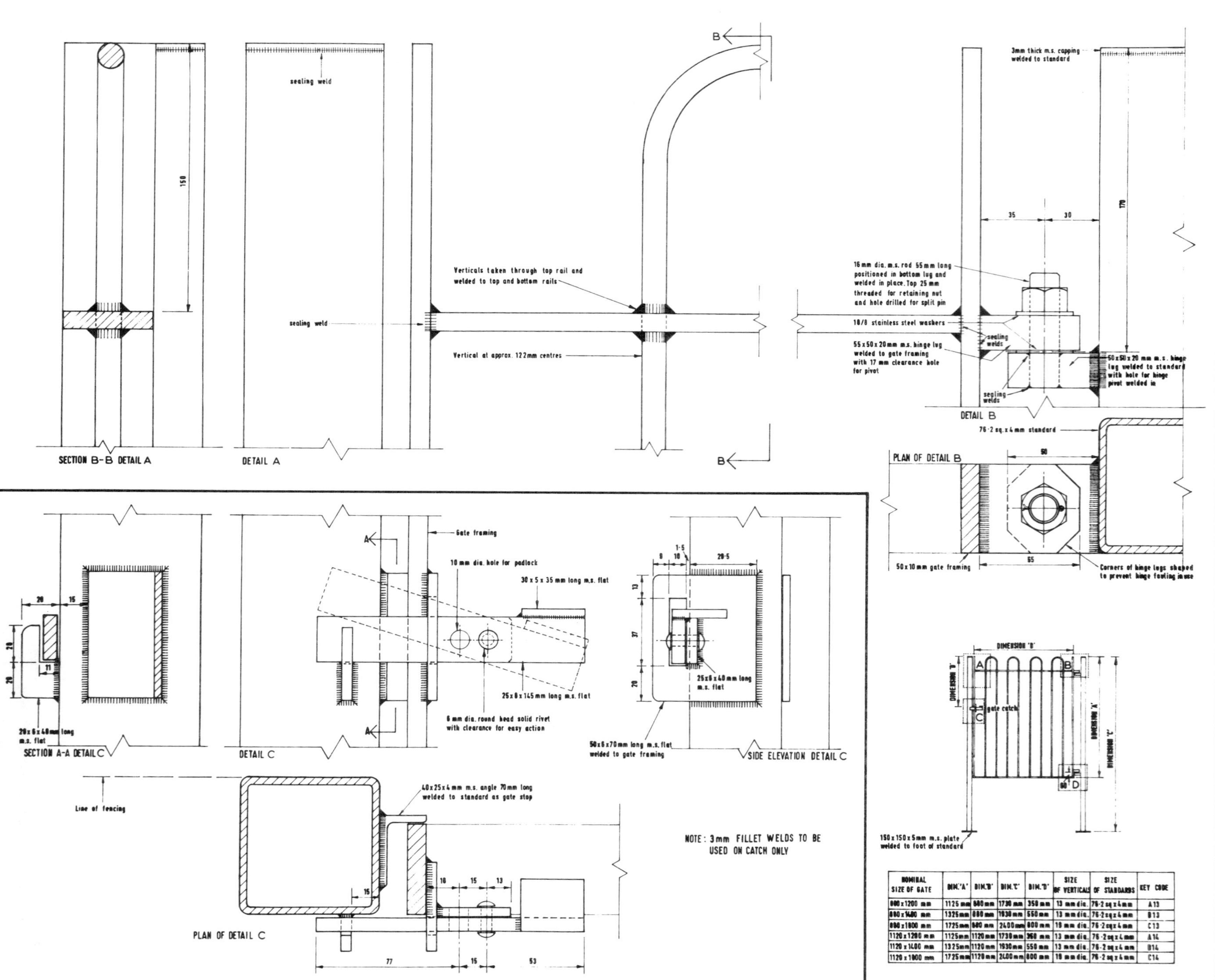

NOMINAL SIZE OF GATE	DIM.'A'	DIM.'B'	DIM.'C'	DIM.'D'	SIZE OF VERTICALS	SIZE OF STANDARDS	KEY CODE
880x1200 mm	1125 mm	880mm	1730 mm	350 mm	13 mm dia.	76·2 sq x 4mm	A13
880x1400 mm	1325mm	880 mm	1930 mm	550 mm	13 mm dia.	76·2 sq x 4mm	B13
880x1800 mm	1725mm	880 mm	2400mm	800 mm	19 mm dia.	76·2 sq x 4mm	C13
1120x1200 mm	1125mm	1120mm	1730mm	350 mm	13 mm dia.	76·2 sq x 4mm	A14
1120 x 1400 mm	1325mm	1120 mm	1930mm	550 mm	13 mm dia.	76·2 sq x 4mm	B14
1120 x 1800 mm	1725mm	1120mm	2400mm	800 mm	19 mm dia.	76·2 sq x 4mm	C14

GLC ILEA

Department of Architecture and Civic Design
County Hall SE1
Architect Sir Roger Walters
KBE FRIBA FI Struct E

All metal parts to be hot dipped galvanised as Q.14 after fabrication.

Welding to be 5mm fillet welds (unless stated otherwise) around the full profile of the members being joined and sealing welds on flush edges. Welding to be as B.S. 5135. Welds must not be ground flat.

This drawing to be read handed when necessary.

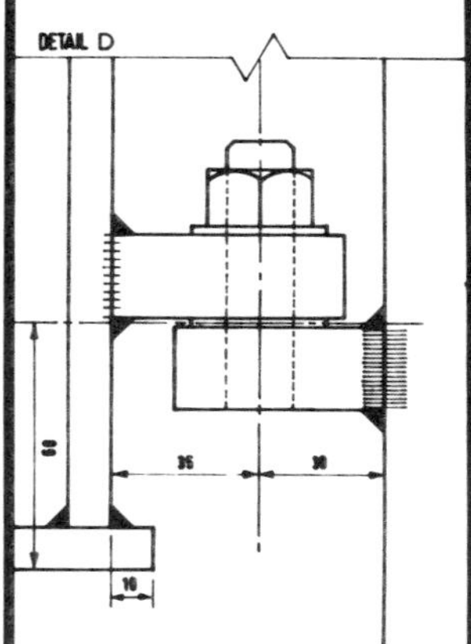

Departmental Standard Drawing

title
MILD STEEL SINGLE GATE
WITH BOW TOPS
CONSTRUCTION DETAILS

scale 1:1 & 1:20

drawing no. D4041 | rev. C

20 | 860 | Xh2 | as matrix

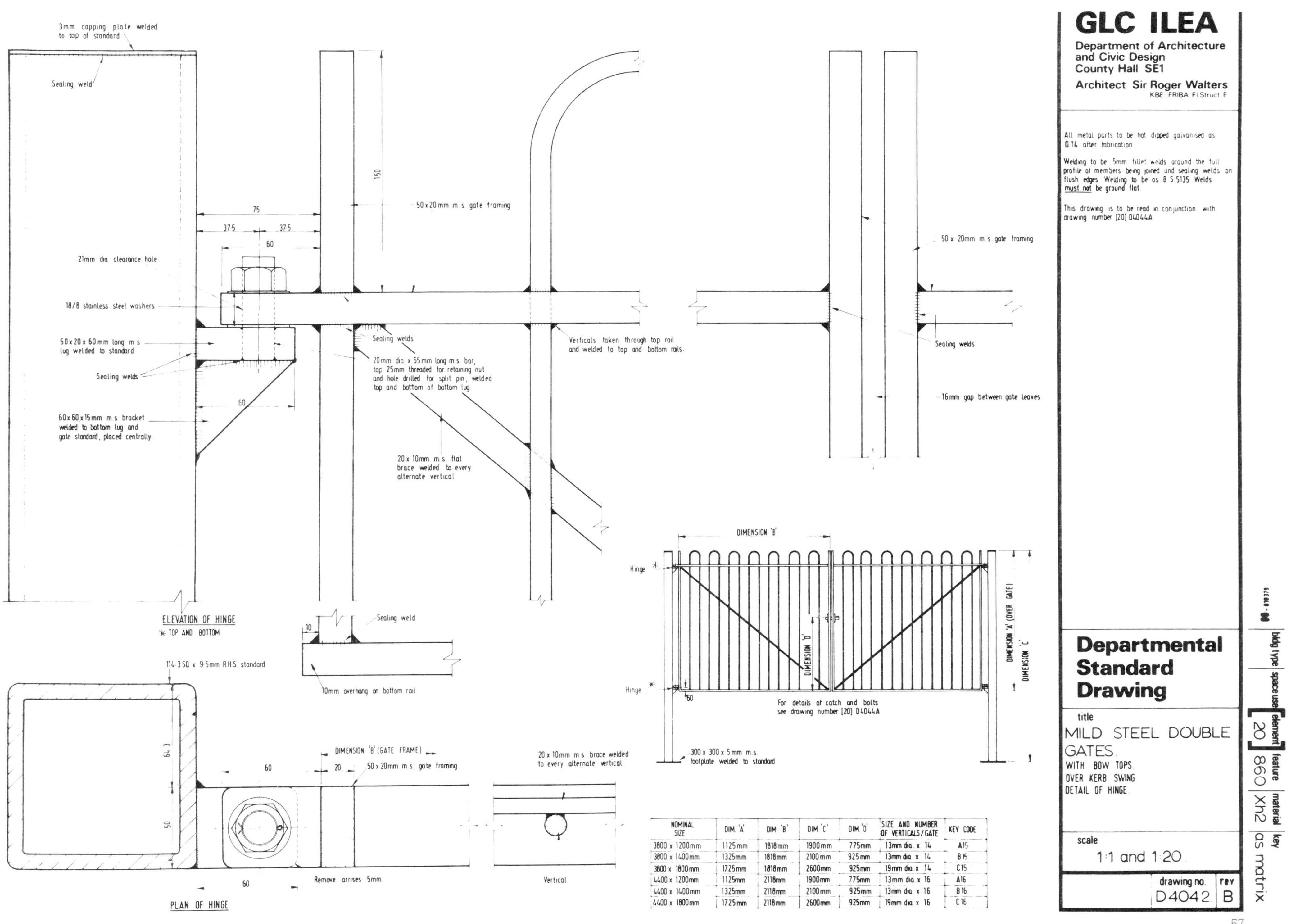

NOMINAL SIZE	DIM. 'A'	DIM 'B'	DIM 'C'	DIM 'D'	SIZE AND NUMBER OF VERTICALS / GATE	KEY CODE
3800 x 1200mm	1125mm	1818mm	1900mm	775mm	13mm dia. x 14	A15
3800 x 1400mm	1325mm	1818mm	2100mm	925mm	13mm dia. x 14	B15
3800 x 1800mm	1725mm	1818mm	2600mm	925mm	19mm dia. x 14	C15
4400 x 1200mm	1125mm	2118mm	1900mm	775mm	13mm dia. x 16	A16
4400 x 1400mm	1325mm	2118mm	2100mm	925mm	13mm dia. x 16	B16
4400 x 1800mm	1725mm	2118mm	2600mm	925mm	19mm dia. x 16	C16

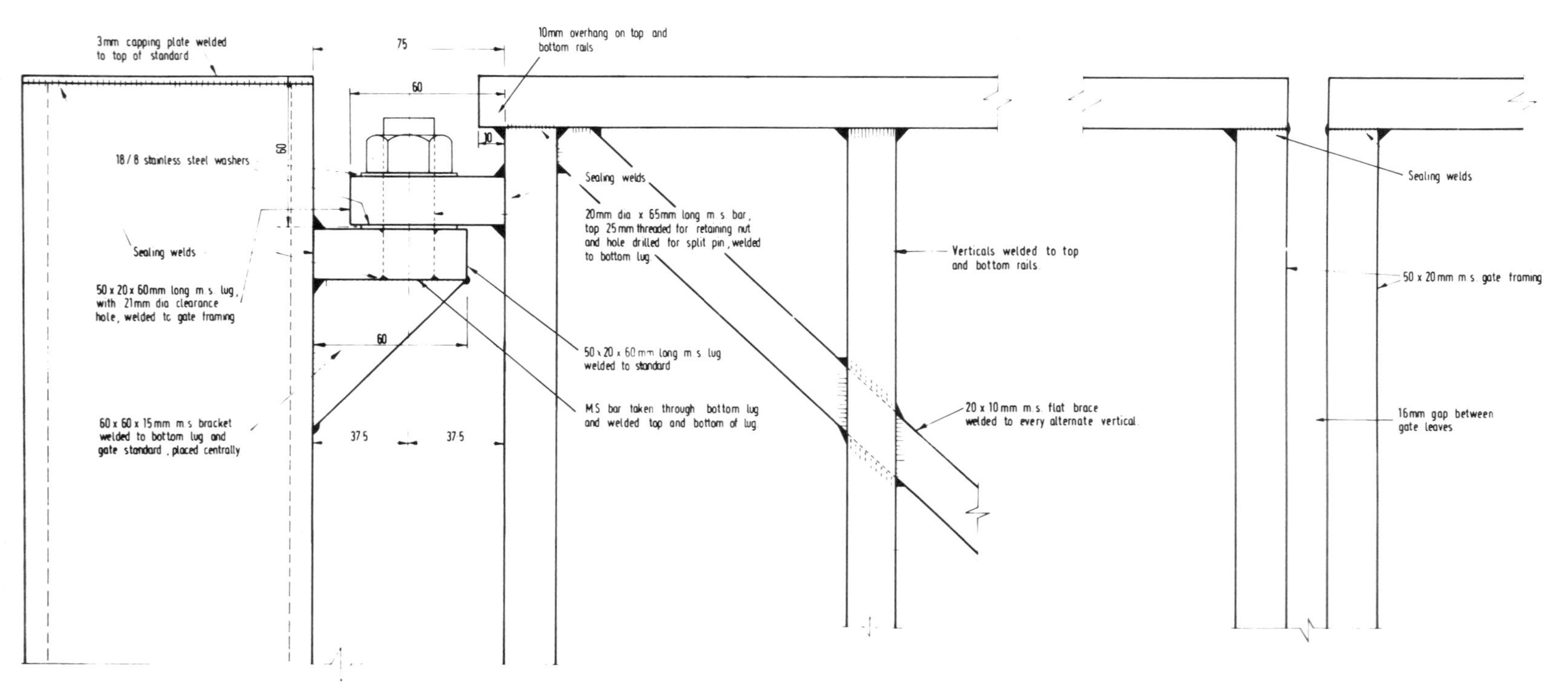

ELEVATION OF HINGE * TOP AND BOTTOM

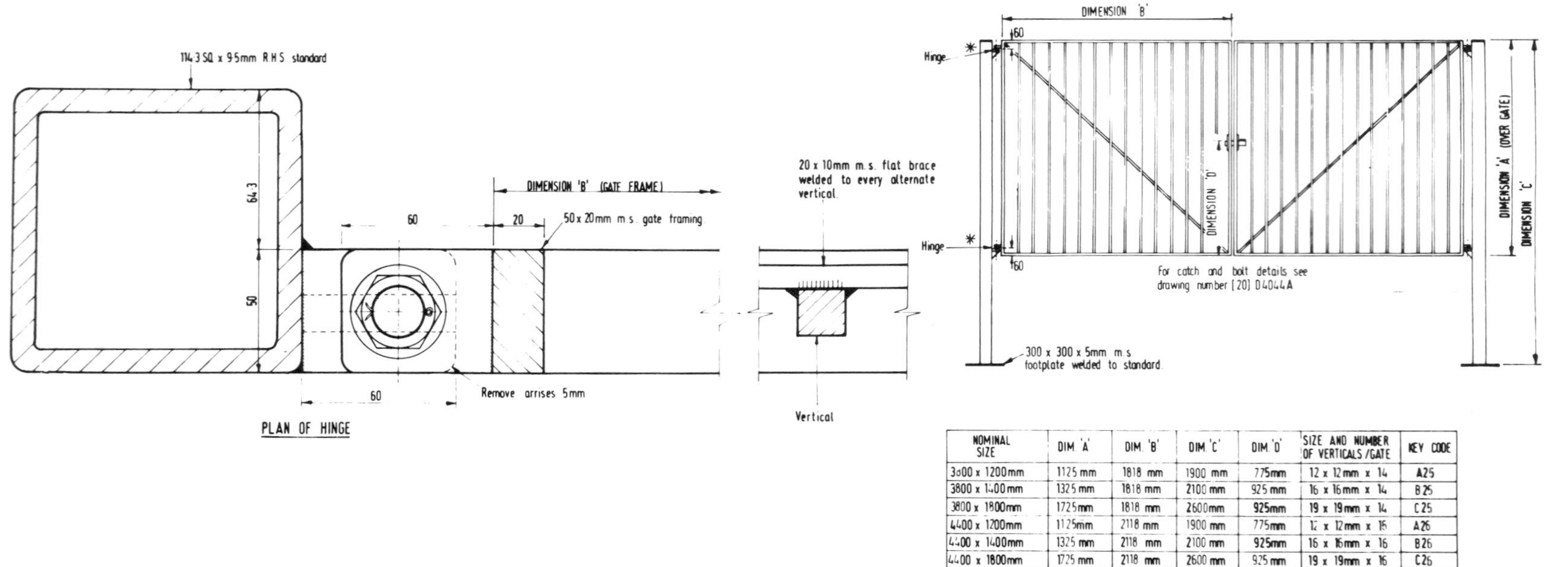

NOMINAL SIZE	DIM. 'A'	DIM. 'B'	DIM. 'C'	DIM. 'D'	SIZE AND NUMBER OF VERTICALS/GATE	KEY CODE
3800 x 1200mm	1125 mm	1818 mm	1900 mm	775mm	12 x 12mm x 14	A25
3800 x 1400mm	1325 mm	1818 mm	2100 mm	925 mm	16 x 16mm x 14	B25
3800 x 1800mm	1725mm	1818 mm	2600mm	925mm	19 x 19mm x 14	C25
4400 x 1200mm	1125mm	2118 mm	1900 mm	775mm	12 x 12mm x 16	A26
4400 x 1400mm	1325 mm	2118 mm	2100 mm	925mm	16 x 16mm x 16	B26
4400 x 1800mm	1725 mm	2118 mm	2600 mm	925 mm	19 x 19mm x 16	C26

GLC ILEA

Department of Architecture and Civic Design
County Hall SE1
Architect Sir Roger Walters
KBE FRIBA FI Struct E

All metal parts to be hot dipped galvanised as Q.14 after fabrication.

Welding to be 5mm fillet welds around the full profile of the members being joined and sealing welds on flush edges. Welding to be as B.S. 5135. Welds must not be ground flat.

This drawing is to be read in conjunction with drawing number [20] D4044A

Departmental Standard Drawing

title

MILD STEEL DOUBLE GATES.

DETAIL OF HINGE.
OVER KERB SWING

scale

1:1 and 1:20.

drawing no. D4043 rev. A

98-01679

bldg type | space use | element [20] | feature 860 | material Xh2 | key as matrix

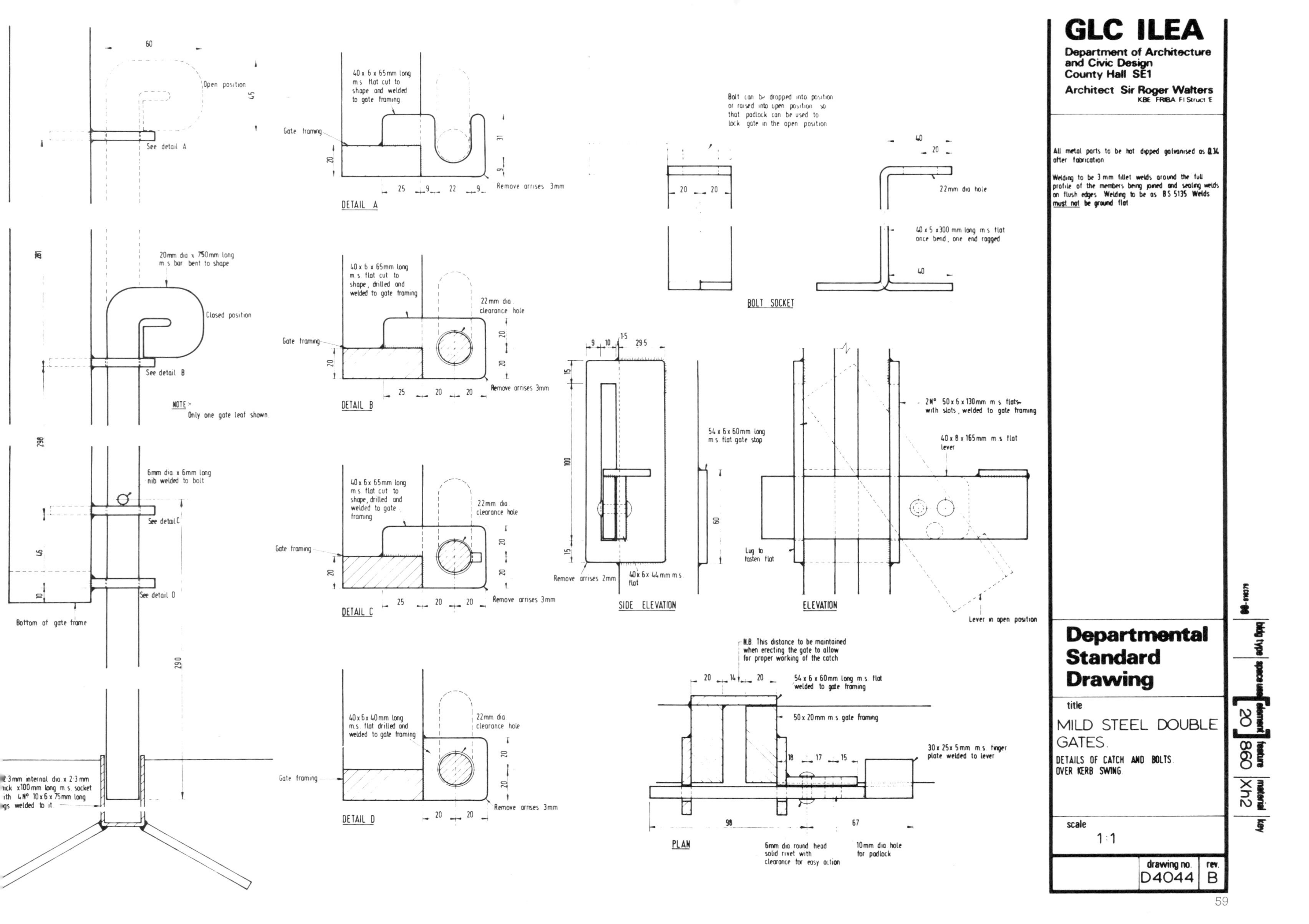
GLC ILEA
Department of Architecture and Civic Design
County Hall SE1
Architect Sir Roger Walters KBE FRIBA FI Struct E
All metal parts to be hot dipped galvanised as B.14 after fabrication
Welding to be 3mm fillet welds around the full profile of the members being joined and sealing welds on flush edges. Welding to be as BS 5135. Welds must not be ground flat
Departmental Standard Drawing
title
MILD STEEL DOUBLE GATES.
DETAILS OF CATCH AND BOLTS. OVER KERB SWING.
scale
1:1
drawing no. D4044
rev. B
20 860 Xh2
DETAIL A
DETAIL B
DETAIL C
DETAIL D
BOLT SOCKET
SIDE ELEVATION
ELEVATION
PLAN
Open position
See detail A
Closed position
See detail B
See detail C
See detail D
20mm dia x 750mm long m.s. bar bent to shape
6mm dia x 6mm long nib welded to bolt
NOTE - Only one gate leaf shown.
Bottom of gate frame
Gate framing
Remove arrises 3mm
22mm dia clearance hole
40 x 6 x 65mm long m.s. flat cut to shape and welded to gate framing
40 x 6 x 40mm long m.s. flat drilled and welded to gate framing
Bolt can be dropped into position or raised into open position so that padlock can be used to lock gate in the open position
22mm dia hole
40 x 5 x 300 mm long m.s. flat once bent, one end ragged
54 x 6 x 60mm long m.s. flat gate stop
2N° 50 x 6 x 130mm m.s. flats with slots, welded to gate framing
40 x 8 x 165mm m.s. flat lever
Lug to fasten flat
Lever in open position
Remove arrises 2mm
40 x 6 x 44mm m.s. flat
N.B. This distance to be maintained when erecting the gate to allow for proper working of the catch
54 x 6 x 60mm long m.s. flat welded to gate framing
50 x 20mm m.s. gate framing
30 x 25 x 5mm m.s. finger plate welded to lever
6mm dia round head solid rivet with clearance for easy action
10mm dia hole for padlock

GLC ILEA

Department of Architecture
and Civic Design
County Hall SE1

Architect Sir Roger Walters
KBE FRIBA FI Struct E

All metal parts to be hot dipped galvanised as Q.14 after fabrication.

Welding to be 5mm fillet welds around the full profile of the members being joined and sealing welds on flush edges. Welding to be as B.S.5135. Welds must not be ground flat.

This drawing is to be read in conjunction with drawing number [20] D4039A

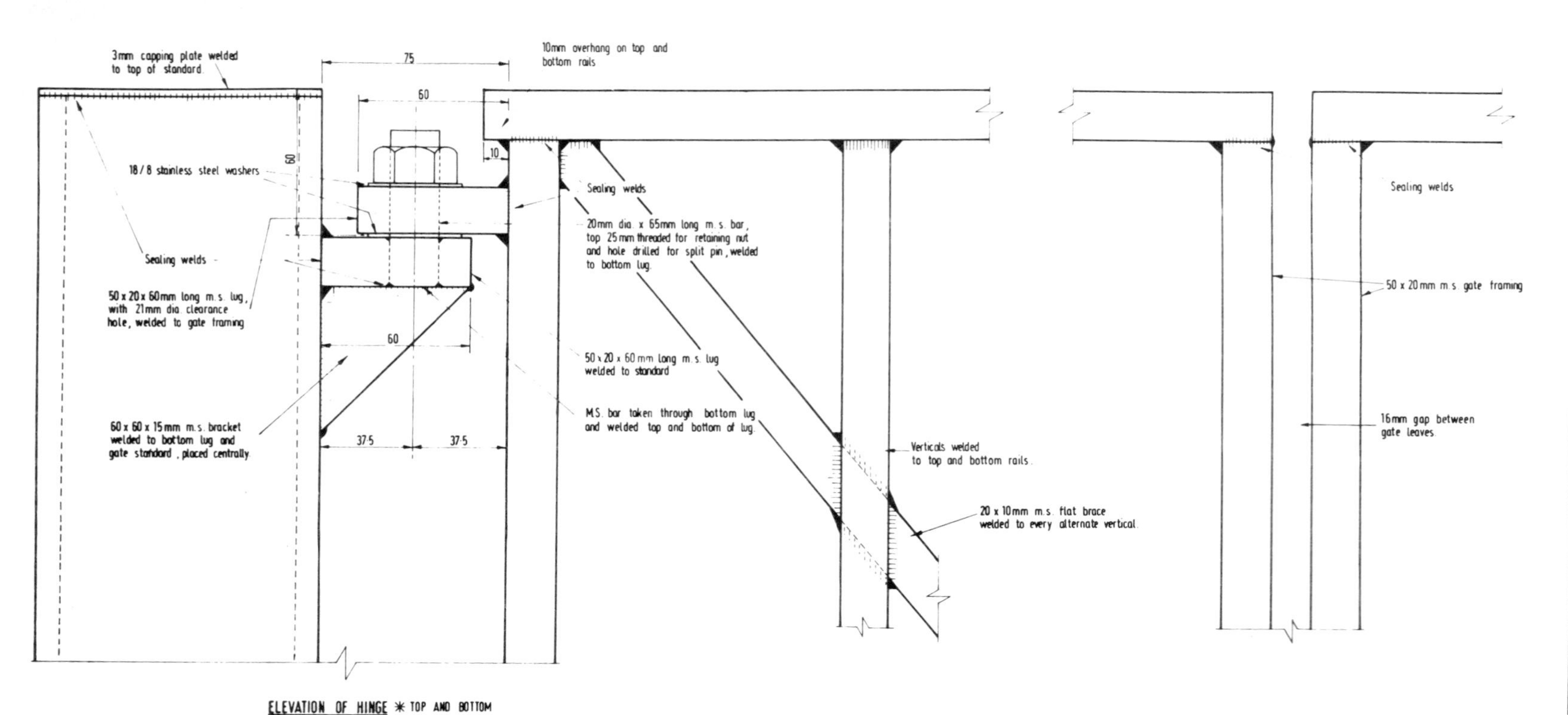

ELEVATION OF HINGE * TOP AND BOTTOM

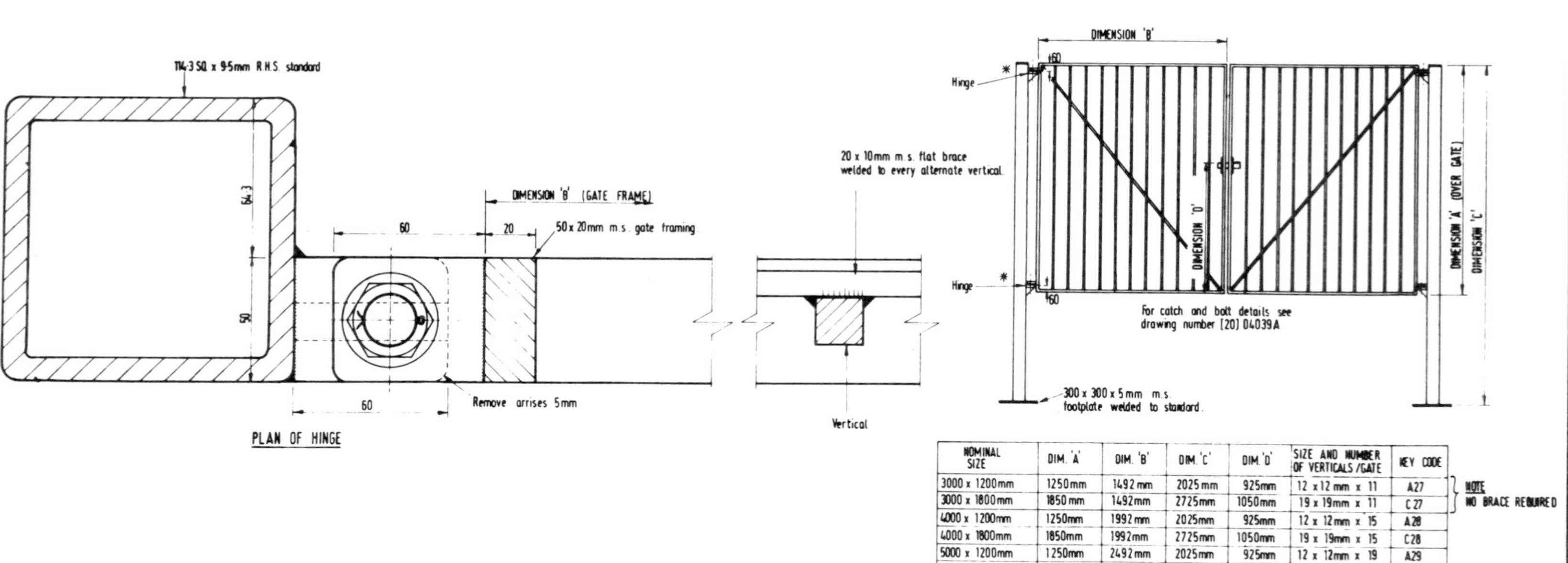

PLAN OF HINGE

NOMINAL SIZE	DIM. 'A'	DIM. 'B'	DIM. 'C'	DIM. 'D'	SIZE AND NUMBER OF VERTICALS /GATE	KEY CODE
3000 x 1200mm	1250mm	1492mm	2025mm	925mm	12 x 12mm x 11	A27
3000 x 1800mm	1850mm	1492mm	2725mm	1050mm	19 x 19mm x 11	C27
4000 x 1200mm	1250mm	1992mm	2025mm	925mm	12 x 12mm x 15	A28
4000 x 1800mm	1850mm	1992mm	2725mm	1050mm	19 x 19mm x 15	C28
5000 x 1200mm	1250mm	2492mm	2025mm	925mm	12 x 12mm x 19	A29
5000 x 1800mm	1850mm	2492mm	2725mm	1050mm	19 x 19mm x 19	C29

NOTE (A27, C27): NO BRACE REQUIRED

Departmental Standard Drawing

title

MILD STEEL DOUBLE GATES

DETAIL OF HINGE.

scale

1:1 and 1:20.

drawing no. D4057 rev. A

bldg type | space used | element [20] | feature 860 | material Xh2 | key as matrix

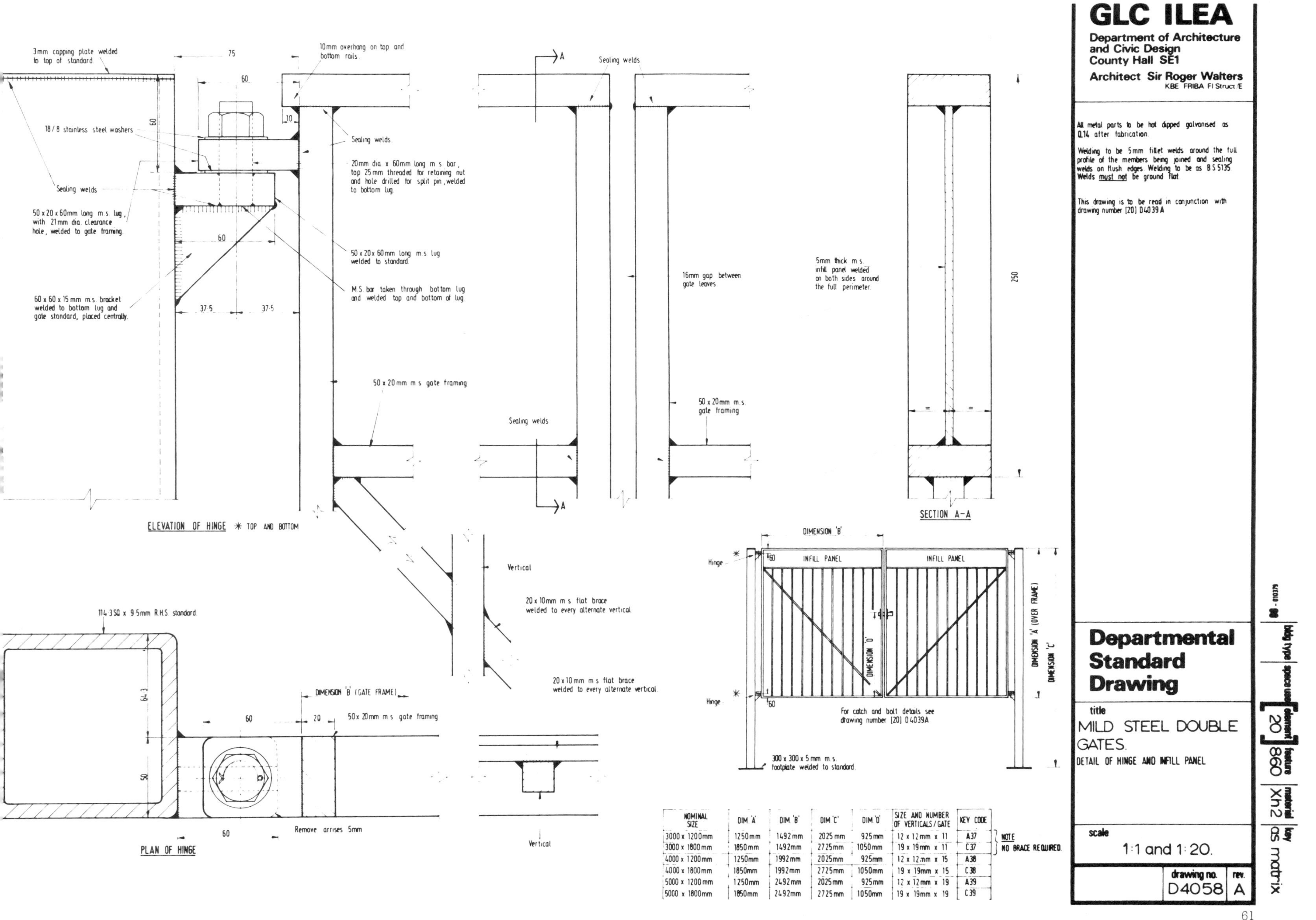

NOMINAL SIZE	DIM 'A'	DIM 'B'	DIM 'C'	DIM 'D'	SIZE AND NUMBER OF VERTICALS / GATE	KEY CODE
3000 x 1200mm	1250mm	1492mm	2025mm	925mm	12 x 12mm x 11	A37
3000 x 1800mm	1850mm	1492mm	2725mm	1050mm	19 x 19mm x 11	C37
4000 x 1200mm	1250mm	1992mm	2025mm	925mm	12 x 12mm x 15	A38
4000 x 1800mm	1850mm	1992mm	2725mm	1050mm	19 x 19mm x 15	C38
5000 x 1200mm	1250mm	2492mm	2025mm	925mm	12 x 12mm x 19	A39
5000 x 1800mm	1850mm	2492mm	2725mm	1050mm	19 x 19mm x 19	C39

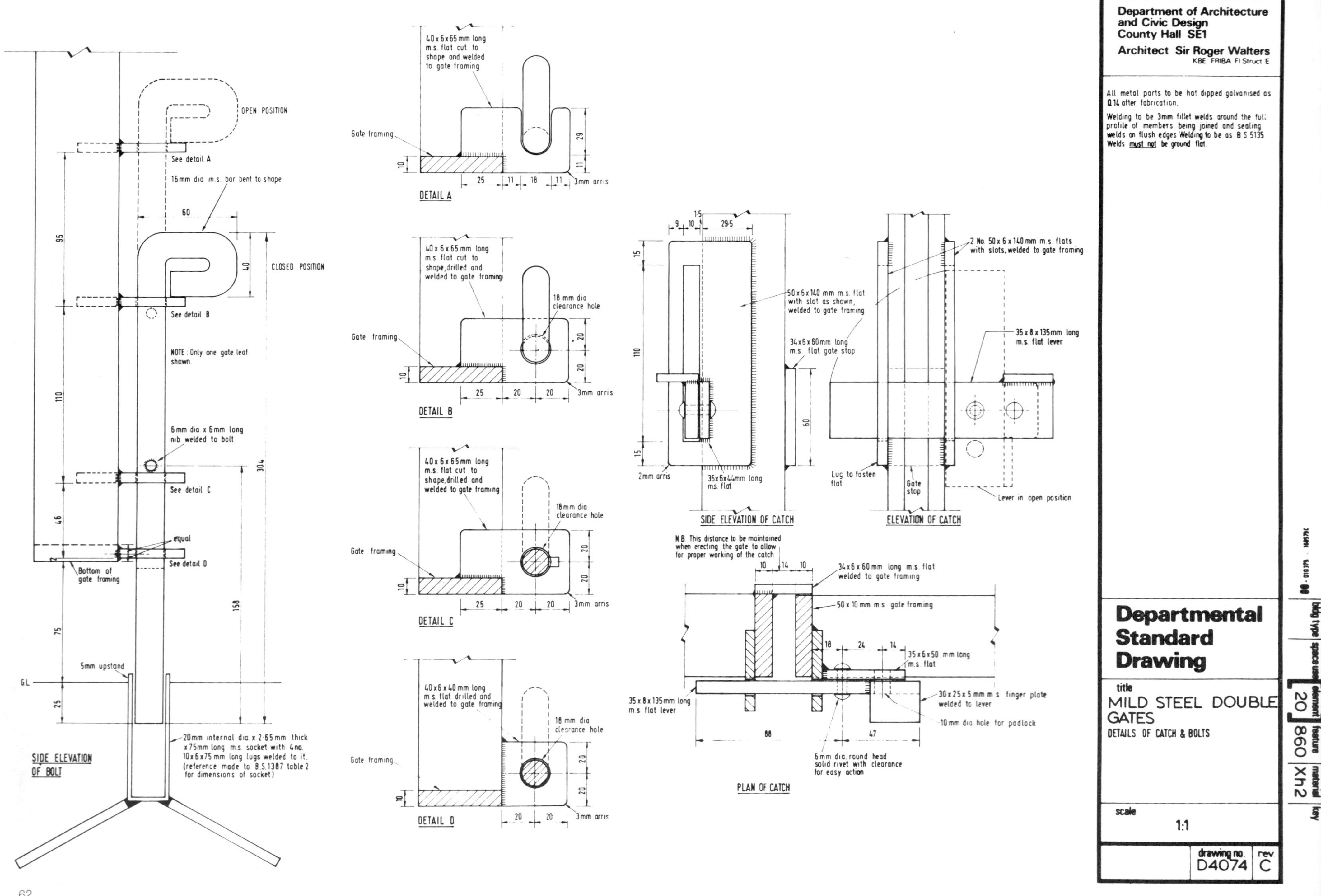
GLC ILEA
Department of Architecture and Civic Design
County Hall SE1
Architect Sir Roger Walters
KBE FRIBA FI Struct E
All metal parts to be hot dipped galvanised as Q.14 after fabrication.
Welding to be 3mm fillet welds around the full profile of members being joined and sealing welds on flush edges. Welding to be as B.S. 5135. Welds must not be ground flat.
Departmental Standard Drawing
title
MILD STEEL DOUBLE GATES
DETAILS OF CATCH & BOLTS
scale
1:1
drawing no.
D4074
rev
C
SIDE ELEVATION OF BOLT
OPEN POSITION
CLOSED POSITION
See detail A
See detail B
See detail C
See detail D
16mm dia. m.s. bar bent to shape
NOTE: Only one gate leaf shown.
6mm dia. x 6mm long nib welded to bolt
Bottom of gate framing
5mm upstand
GL
20mm internal dia. x 2·65mm thick x 75mm long m.s. socket with 4no. 10x6x75mm long lugs welded to it. (reference made to B.S.1387 table 2 for dimensions of socket)
DETAIL A
40 x 6 x 65mm long m.s. flat cut to shape and welded to gate framing
Gate framing
3mm arris
DETAIL B
40 x 6 x 65mm long m.s. flat cut to shape, drilled and welded to gate framing
18 mm dia. clearance hole
DETAIL C
40 x 6 x 65mm long m.s. flat cut to shape, drilled and welded to gate framing
18mm dia. clearance hole
DETAIL D
40 x 6 x 40mm long m.s. flat drilled and welded to gate framing
18 mm dia. clearance hole
SIDE ELEVATION OF CATCH
50 x 6 x 140 mm m.s. flat with slot as shown, welded to gate framing
34 x 6 x 60mm long m.s. flat gate stop
35 x 6 x 44mm long m.s. flat
2mm arris
ELEVATION OF CATCH
2 No. 50 x 6 x 140mm m.s. flats with slots, welded to gate framing
35 x 8 x 135mm long m.s. flat lever
Lug to fasten flat
Gate stop
Lever in open position
N.B. This distance to be maintained when erecting the gate to allow for proper working of the catch
34 x 6 x 60mm long m.s. flat welded to gate framing
50 x 10 mm m.s. gate framing
35 x 6 x 50 mm long m.s. flat
35 x 8 x 135mm long m.s. flat lever
30 x 25 x 5 mm m.s. finger plate welded to lever
10mm dia. hole for padlock
6mm dia. round head solid rivet with clearance for easy action
PLAN OF CATCH
bldg type
space use
element
feature
material
key
(20)
860
Xh2

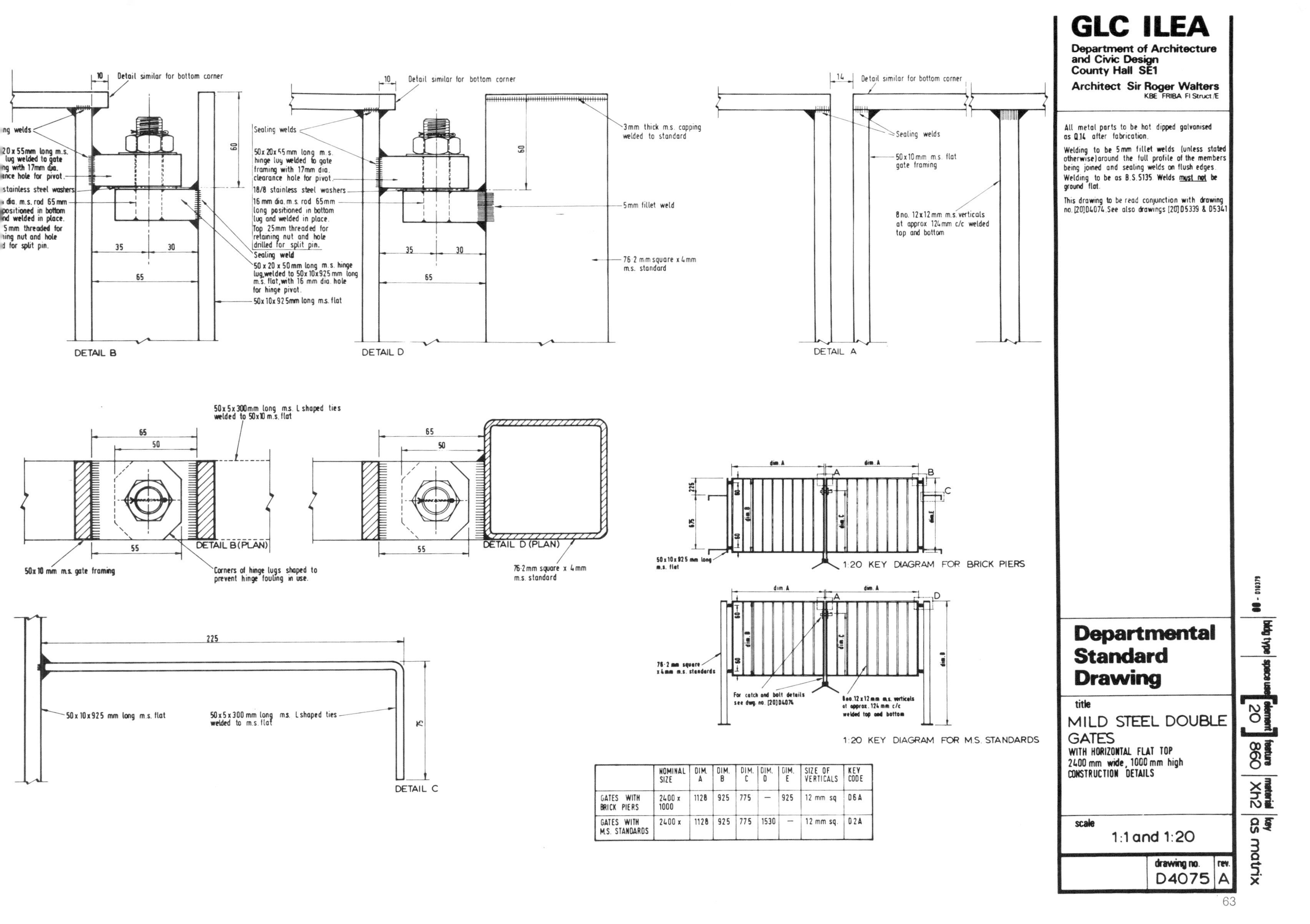

	NOMINAL SIZE	DIM. A	DIM. B	DIM. C	DIM. D	DIM. E	SIZE OF VERTICALS	KEY CODE
GATES WITH BRICK PIERS	2400 x 1000	1128	925	775	—	925	12 mm sq	D6A
GATES WITH M.S. STANDARDS	2400 x	1128	925	775	1530	—	12 mm sq.	D2A

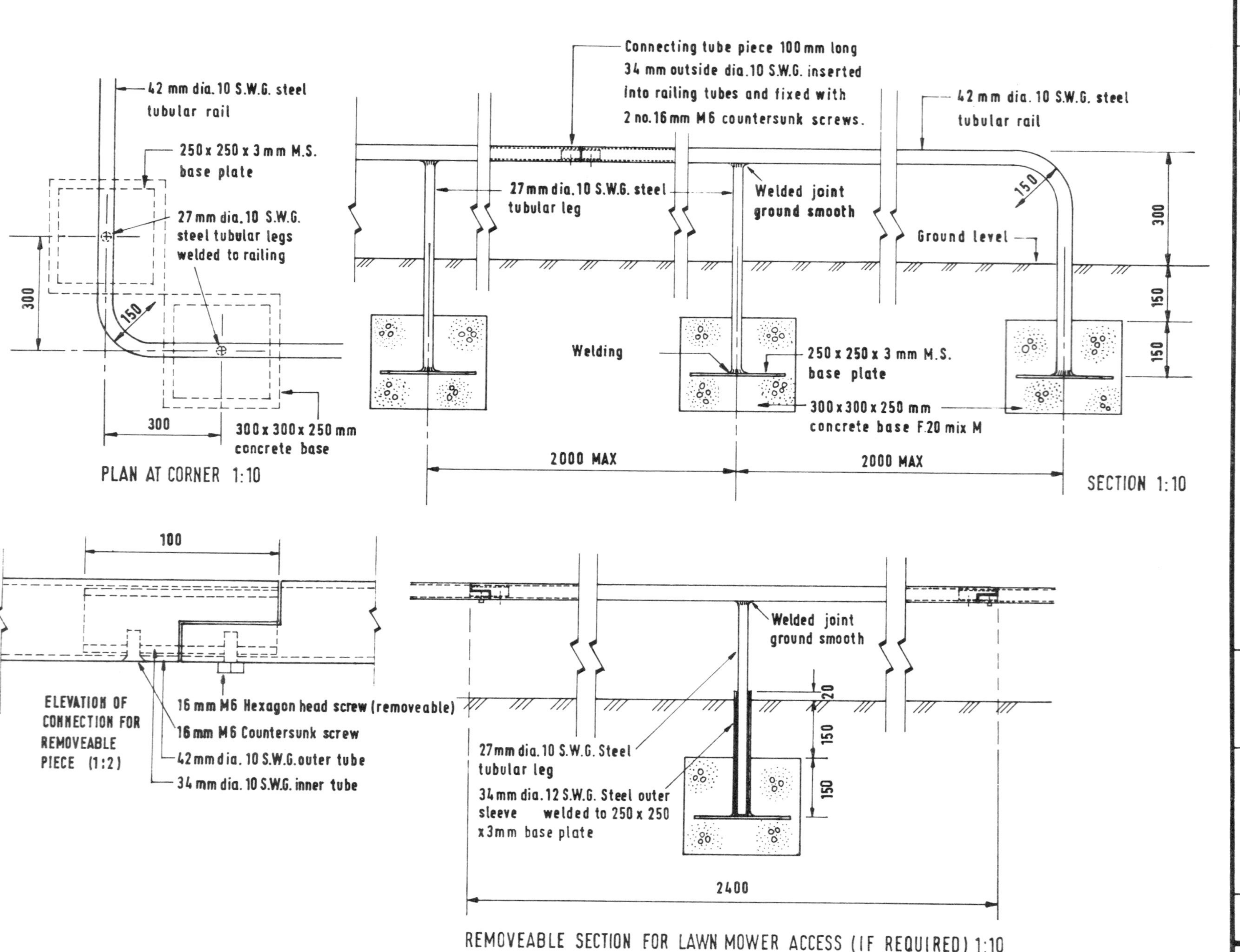

GLC ILEA

Department of Architecture and Civic Design
County Hall SE1

Architect Sir Roger Walters KBE FRIBA FI StructE

References following notes are clause numbers from G.L.C. preambles to bills of quantities

All metal parts to be galvanised as Q.14.

This drawing to be read in conjunction with job drawings

Tube to be as Q.8.

Welding to be as Q.34.

Departmental Standard Drawing

title

TUBULAR STEEL SHIN RAIL

scale

1:10 & 1:2

drawing no

D5172

6/E0139-00

bldg type | space use | element 20 | feature 860 | material Xh2 | key B31

4 Chain link fencing and gates

5153 Chain link fence with concrete posts
5154 Chain link fence with steel posts
5155 Chain link fence with steel posts 3m high
5185 Chain link fence with steel posts 3m high—for schools
5186 Chain link fence with steel post—3m high—details
5210 Chain link fence with steel post—4.5m high
5211 Chain link fence with steel post—4.5m high—details
5188 Chain link fence double gates
5189 Chain link fence single gate
4031 Chain link fence double gates—details
4032 Chain link fence single gate—details
4034 Chain link fence double gates—details
4035 Chain link fence double gates—details

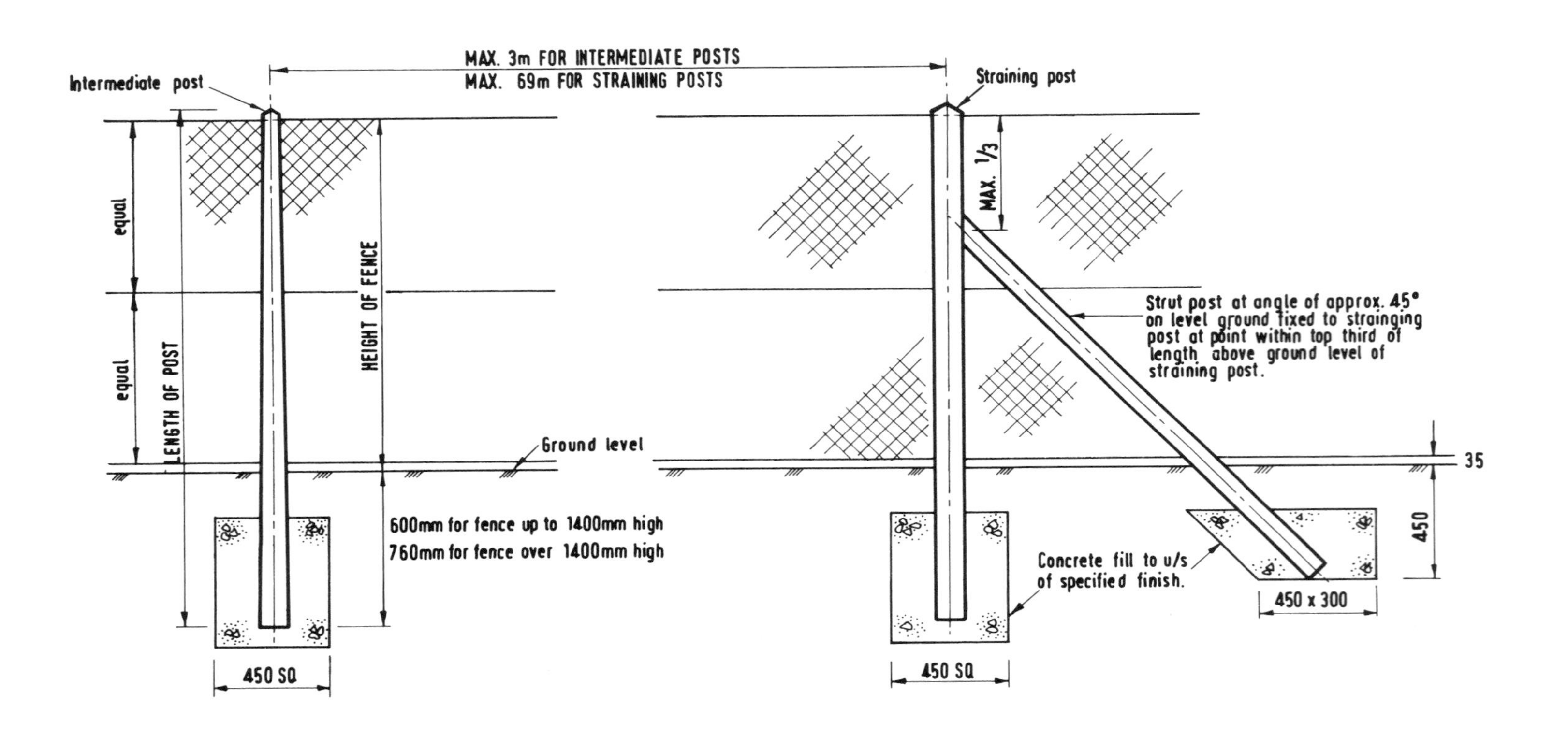

HEIGHT OF FENCE	CONCRETE POSTS			CONCRETE POST HEADS		
	INTERMEDIATE	STRAINING	STRUTS	ROUNDED	PYRAMIDAL	WEATHERED
1200	1870 125x125	1870 125x125	1870 100x75	1A	1B	1C
1400	2070 125x125	2070 125x125	1980 100x75	2A	2B	2C
1800	2630 125x125	2630 125x125	2590 100x85	3A	3B	3C

KEY CODE

NOTES:-

Straing posts shall be provided at all ends, corners, at changes of direction and at intervals not exceeding 69m on straight length of fence.

Intermediate posts shall be tapered to 75 x 75mm at top.

Chain link fence wire to comply with grade A, B. S. 4102. Galvanised or finished with plastic coating — size of mesh to be 50mm.

Galvanised wire — 3mm dia.
Plastic coated, core – 3mm dia (4mm dia. overall)

GLC ILEA

Department of Architecture and Civic Design
County Hall SE1
Architect Sir Roger Walters KBE FRIBA FI StructE

References following notes are clause numbers from G.L.C. preambles to bills of quantities.

This drawing is to be read in conjunction with job drgs.

All metal parts to be galvanised.

Concrete for posts base to be F.20. mix M.

For chain link fences see B.S. 1722 part 1 and 10.

For details of paving finishes see drg. number D5148.[40]

Departmental Standard Drawing

title

CHAIN LINK FENCE. WITH CONCRETE POSTS. TO B.S. 1722 PARTS 1 & 10.

scale 1:20.

drawing no D5153 rev C

00-010379

[20] 860 Jh2 as matrix

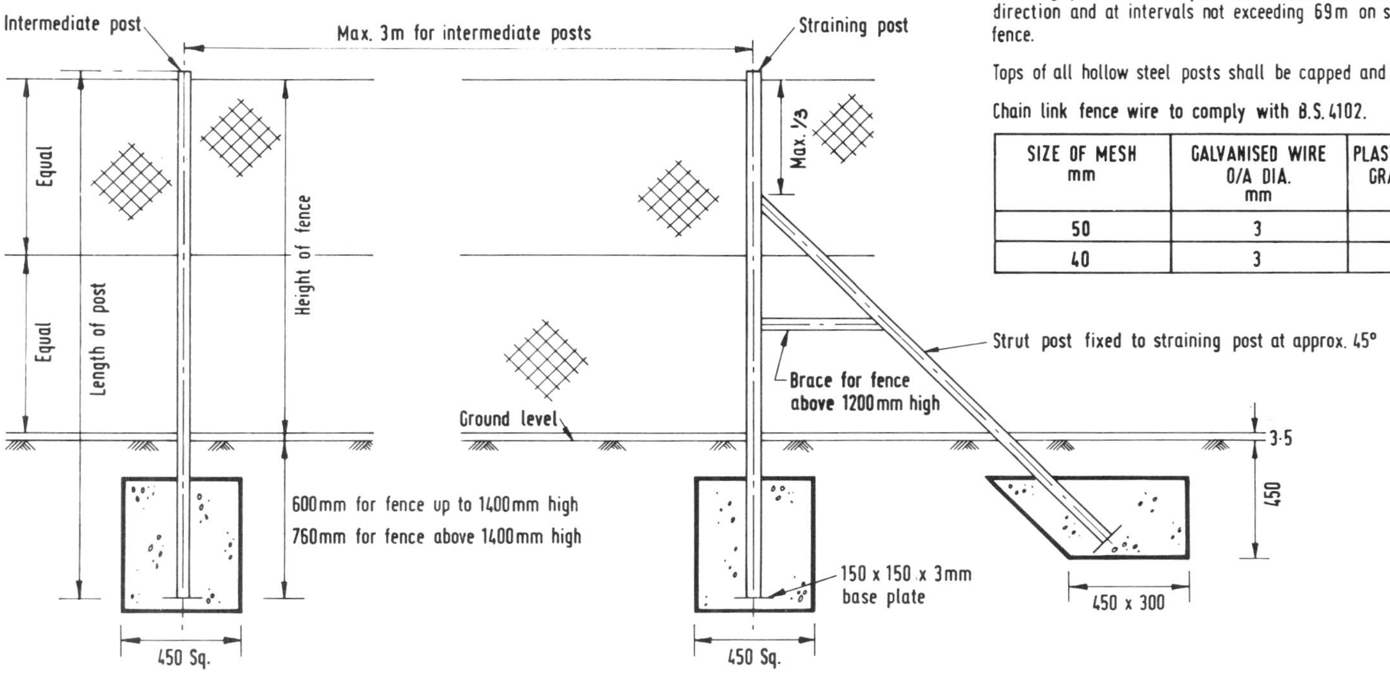

Intermediate post

Max. 3m for intermediate posts

Straining post

Equal

Equal

Length of post

Height of fence

Max. 1/3

Ground level

Brace for fence above 1200mm high

Strut post fixed to straining post at approx. 45°

3·5

450

600mm for fence up to 1400mm high

760mm for fence above 1400mm high

150 x 150 x 3mm base plate

450 Sq.

450 Sq.

450 x 300

NOTES:-

Straining posts shall be provided at all ends, corners, at changes of direction and at intervals not exceeding 69m on straight length of fence.

Tops of all hollow steel posts shall be capped and sealed

Chain link fence wire to comply with B.S. 4102.

SIZE OF MESH mm	GALVANISED WIRE O/A DIA. mm	PLASTIC COATED WIRE GRADE 'A' O/A DIA. mm
50	3	4
40	3	3·55

HEIGHT OF FENCE	LENGTH OF STEEL POSTS	ROLLED STEEL ANGLES					CIRCULAR HOLLOW SECTIONS					RECTANGULAR HOLLOW SECTIONS				
		INTERMED.	STRAINING	STRUTS	BRACES	KEY	INTERMED.	STRAINING	STRUTS	BRACES	KEY	INTERMED.	STRAINING	STRUTS	BRACES	KEY
1200	1800	40 x 40 x5	50x50 x6	40 x 40 x5	-	1D	33·7 DIA. x2·6	48·3 DIA. x3·2	33·7 DIA. x3·2	-	1E	40 x 40 x2·6	50 x 50 x3·2	40 x 40 x2·6	-	1F
1400	2000	45 x 45 x5	60x60 x6	45 x 45 x5	30 x 30 x5	2D	42·4 DIA. x2·6	60·3 DIA. x3·2	42·4 DIA. x3·2	42·4 DIA. x2·6	2E	40 x 40 x2·6	50 x 50 x3·2	40 x 40 x2·6	30 x 30 x2·0	2F
1800	2600	45 x 45 x5	60x60 x6	45 x 45 x5	30 x 30 x5	3D	42·4 DIA. x2·6	60·3 DIA. x3·2	42·4 DIA. x3·2	42·4 DIA. x2·6	3E	40 x 40 x2·6	50 x 50 x3·2	40 x 40 x2·6	30 x 30 x2·0	3F

GLC ILEA

Department of Architecture and Civic Design
County Hall SE1 7PB
Architect F B Pooley CBE

References following notes are clause numbers from G.L.C. preambles to bills of quantities

To be read in conjunction with job drawings

All metal parts to be galvanised

Concrete for post bases to be as F20, mix M

For chain link fences see B.S. 1722 parts 1 and 10

For details of paving finishes see drawing [40] D.5148

Departmental Standard Drawing

title

CHAIN LINK FENCE WITH STEEL POSTS.
TO B.S. 1722 PARTS 1 & 10.

scale
1 : 20

drawing no D.5154 | rev F

010379 - 020879F

bldg type | space use | element [20] | feature 860 | material Jh2 | key as matrix

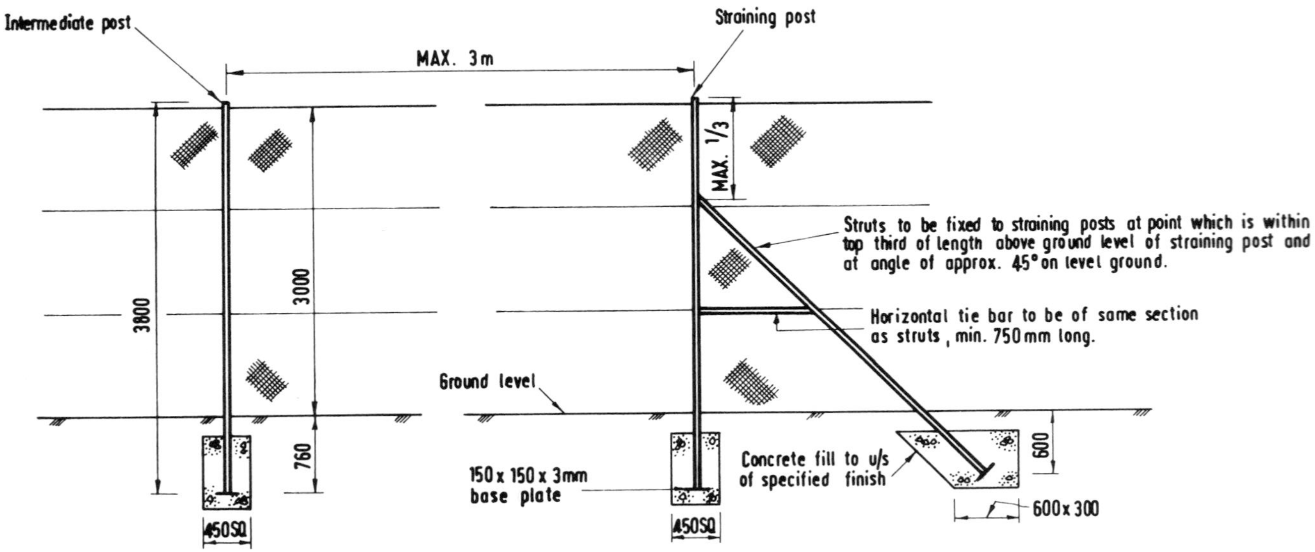

Intermediate post

Straining post

MAX. 3m

MAX. 1/3

3800

3000

760

Struts to be fixed to straining posts at point which is within top third of length above ground level of straining post and at angle of approx. 45° on level ground.

Horizontal tie bar to be of same section as struts, min. 750mm long.

Ground level

600

150 x 150 x 3mm base plate

Concrete fill to u/s of specified finish

600 x 300

450SQ

450SQ

TYPE OF POSTS	SECTIONS			KEY
	INTERMEDIATE	STRAINING	STRUTS & BRACES	
ROLLED STEEL ANGLE	50x50 x6	60x60 x8	45x45 x5	4D
CIRCULAR HOLLOW SECTION	48·30 x3·2	60·30 x4·0	48·30 x3·2	4E
RECTANGULAR HOLLOW SECTION	40 SQ x4·0	50 SQ x4·0	40 SQ x4·0	4F

NOTES:-

Straining posts shall be provided at all end, corners, at changes of direction and at intervals not exceeding 66m on straight length of fence.

Chain link fence wire to comply with grade Ä B.S.4102 and to be finished with plastic coating and to be of super weight pattern and mesh to be 50mm.

GLC ILEA

Department of Architecture and Civic Design
County Hall SE1
Architect Sir Roger Walters
KBE FRIBA FI StructE

References following notes are clause numbers from G.L.C. preambles to bills of quantities

This drawing is to be read in conjunction with job drgs.

All metal parts to be galvanised.

Concrete for post base to be F.20 mix M.

For chain link fences see B.S. 1722 part 1 and 10.

For details of paving finishes see drg. number D5148 [40]

Departmental Standard Drawing

title

CHAIN LINK FENCE.
3000mm HIGH.
TO B.S. 1722 PARTS
1 & 10.

scale

1:50

drawing no D5155 rev B

[20] 860 Jh2 as matrix

010379

Maximum distance between intermediates to be 3 metres.

Straining posts shall be provided at all ends, corners, changes of direction and at intervals not exceeding 36 metres in a straight length of fence.

Chain link fence wire to comply with B.S. 4102, grade A galvanised or grade A plastic coated. Size of mesh to be 40mm. Galvanised wire 3·00 mm dia., plastic coated 2·50mm dia. core (3·55mm overall).

Chain link fixed to line wires with wire clamps (hog-rings) at 300mm c/c.

Line wires to be 5mm dia. 7 strand galvanised.

Straining eye bolts, nuts and washers to be as "Nicholls & Clarke" catalogue no. BC. 1885 8" x 5/16".

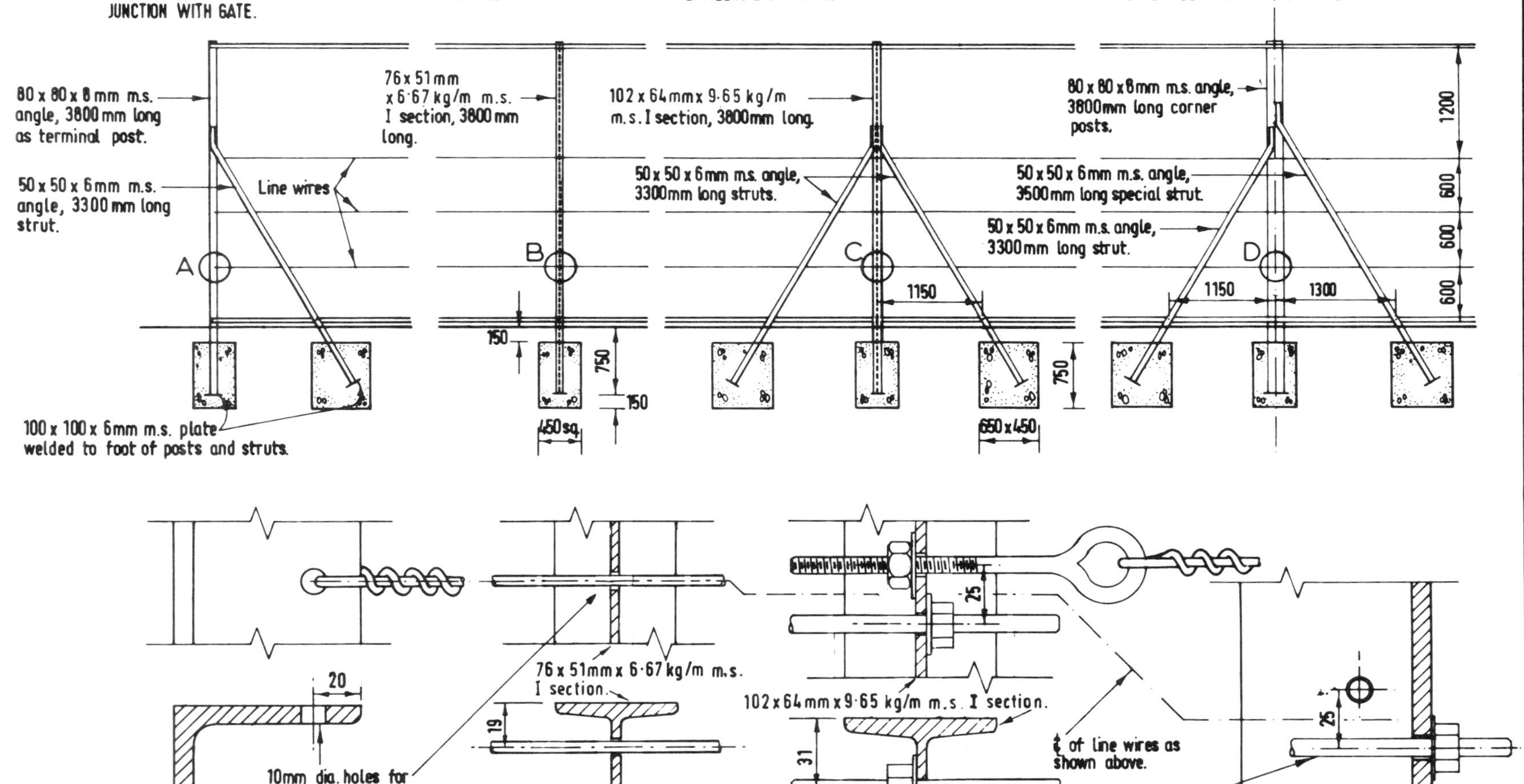

Detail A

Detail B

Detail C

Detail D
Drillings for internal and external corners

GLC ILEA

Department of Architecture and Civic Design
County Hall SE1 7PB
Architect Sir Roger Walters KBE ARIBA FI Struct/E

References following notes are clause numbers from G.L.C. preambles to bills of quantities

To be read in conjunction with drg. no. [20] D5186 and job drawings.

Concrete at base of posts as F20 mix M.

For details of paving finishes see drg. no. [40] D5148.

For chain link fences see B.S. 1722 pts. 1 and 10.

Departmental Standard Drawing

title
3000mm HIGH CHAIN LINK FENCE
LAYOUT AND FIXING DETAILS M.S. 'I' SECTION POSTS

scale 1:50 & 1:2

drawing no D5185 | rev A

bldg type 7 | space use | element [20] | feature 860 | material Jh2 | key 4G

0-01039

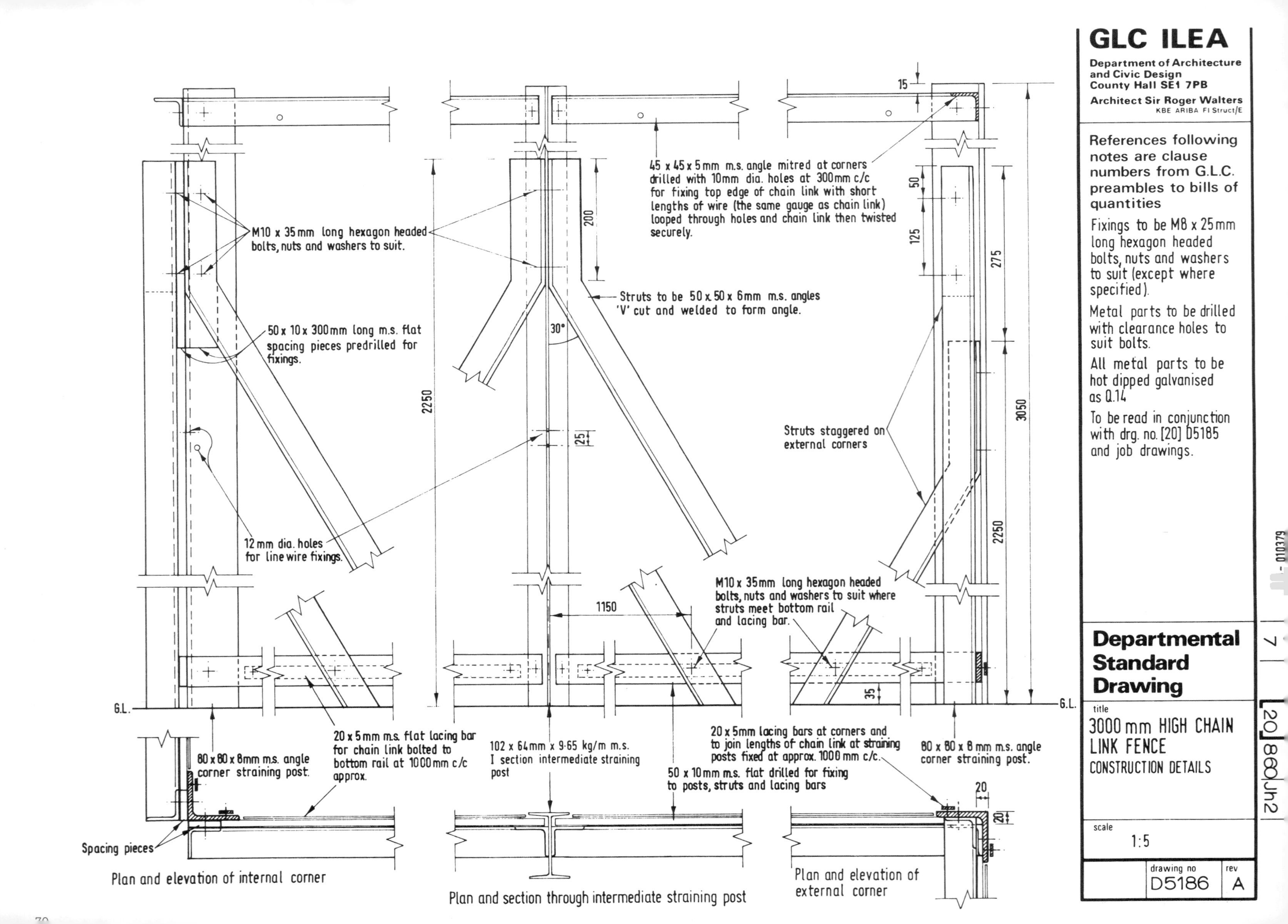
GLC ILEA
Department of Architecture and Civic Design
County Hall SE1 7PB
Architect Sir Roger Walters
KBE ARIBA FI Struct/E
References following notes are clause numbers from G.L.C. preambles to bills of quantities
Fixings to be M8 x 25mm long hexagon headed bolts, nuts and washers to suit (except where specified).
Metal parts to be drilled with clearance holes to suit bolts.
All metal parts to be hot dipped galvanised as Q.14
To be read in conjunction with drg. no. [20] D5185 and job drawings.
Departmental Standard Drawing
7
[20] 860 Jh2
title
3000 mm HIGH CHAIN LINK FENCE
CONSTRUCTION DETAILS
scale
1:5
drawing no
D5186
rev
A
M10 x 35mm long hexagon headed bolts, nuts and washers to suit.
50 x 10 x 300mm long m.s. flat spacing pieces predrilled for fixings.
12mm dia. holes for line wire fixings.
45 x 45 x 5mm m.s. angle mitred at corners drilled with 10mm dia. holes at 300mm c/c for fixing top edge of chain link with short lengths of wire (the same gauge as chain link) looped through holes and chain link then twisted securely.
Struts to be 50 x 50 x 6mm m.s. angles 'V' cut and welded to form angle.
30°
200
2250
25
1150
15
50
125
275
3050
2250
35
20
20
Struts staggered on external corners
M10 x 35mm long hexagon headed bolts, nuts and washers to suit where struts meet bottom rail and lacing bar.
G.L.
G.L.
80 x 80 x 8mm m.s. angle corner straining post.
20 x 5mm m.s. flat lacing bar for chain link bolted to bottom rail at 1000mm c/c approx.
102 x 64mm x 9·65 kg/m m.s. I section intermediate straining post
20 x 5mm lacing bars at corners and to join lengths of chain link at straining posts fixed at approx. 1000 mm c/c.
50 x 10mm m.s. flat drilled for fixing to posts, struts and lacing bars
80 x 80 x 8 mm m.s. angle corner straining post.
Spacing pieces
Plan and elevation of internal corner
Plan and section through intermediate straining post
Plan and elevation of external corner
010379

Maximum distance between intermediates to be 3 metres.

Straining posts shall be provided at all ends, corners, changes of direction and at intervals not exceeding 36 metres in a straight length of fence.

Chain link fence wire to comply with B.S. 4102, grade A galvanised or grade A plastic coated. Size of mesh to be 40mm. Galvanised wire 3·0mm dia., plastic coated 2·5mm dia. core (3·55mm overall).

Chain link fixed to line wires with wire clamps (hog-rings) at 300mm c/c.

Line wires to be 5mm dia. 7 strand galvanised.

Straining eye bolts, nuts and washers to be as "Nicholls & Clarke" catalogue no. BC.1885 8" x 5/16".

GLC ILEA

Department of Architecture and Civic Design
County Hall SE1 7PB
Architect Sir Roger Walters KBE ARIBA FI Struct/E

References following notes are clause numbers from G.L.C. preambles to bills of quantities

To be read in conjunction with drawing number [20] D 5211 and job drgs.

Concrete at base of posts as F20 mix M.

For details of paving finishes see drg. no. [40] D5148.

For chain link fences see B.S. 1722 pts 1 and 10.

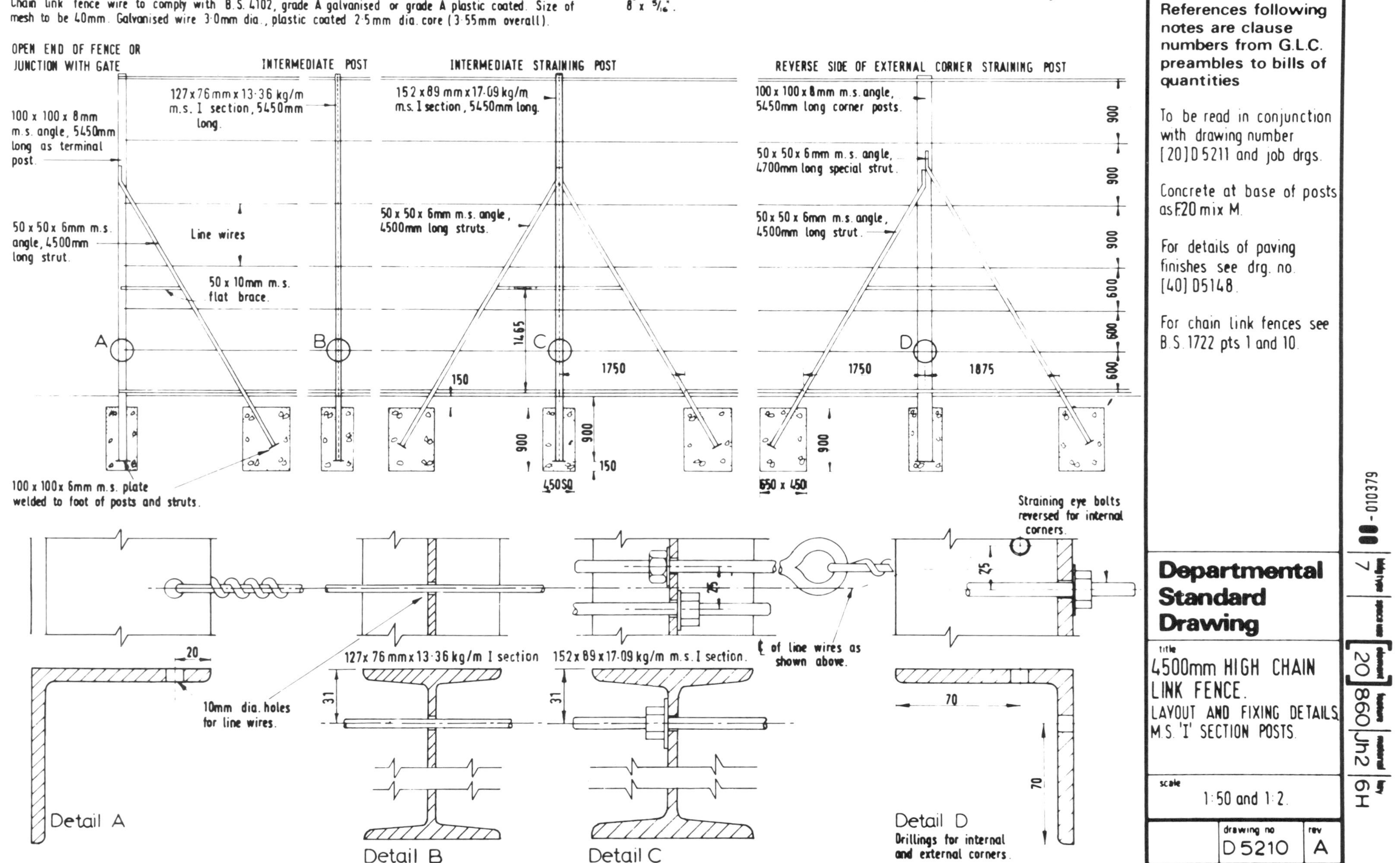

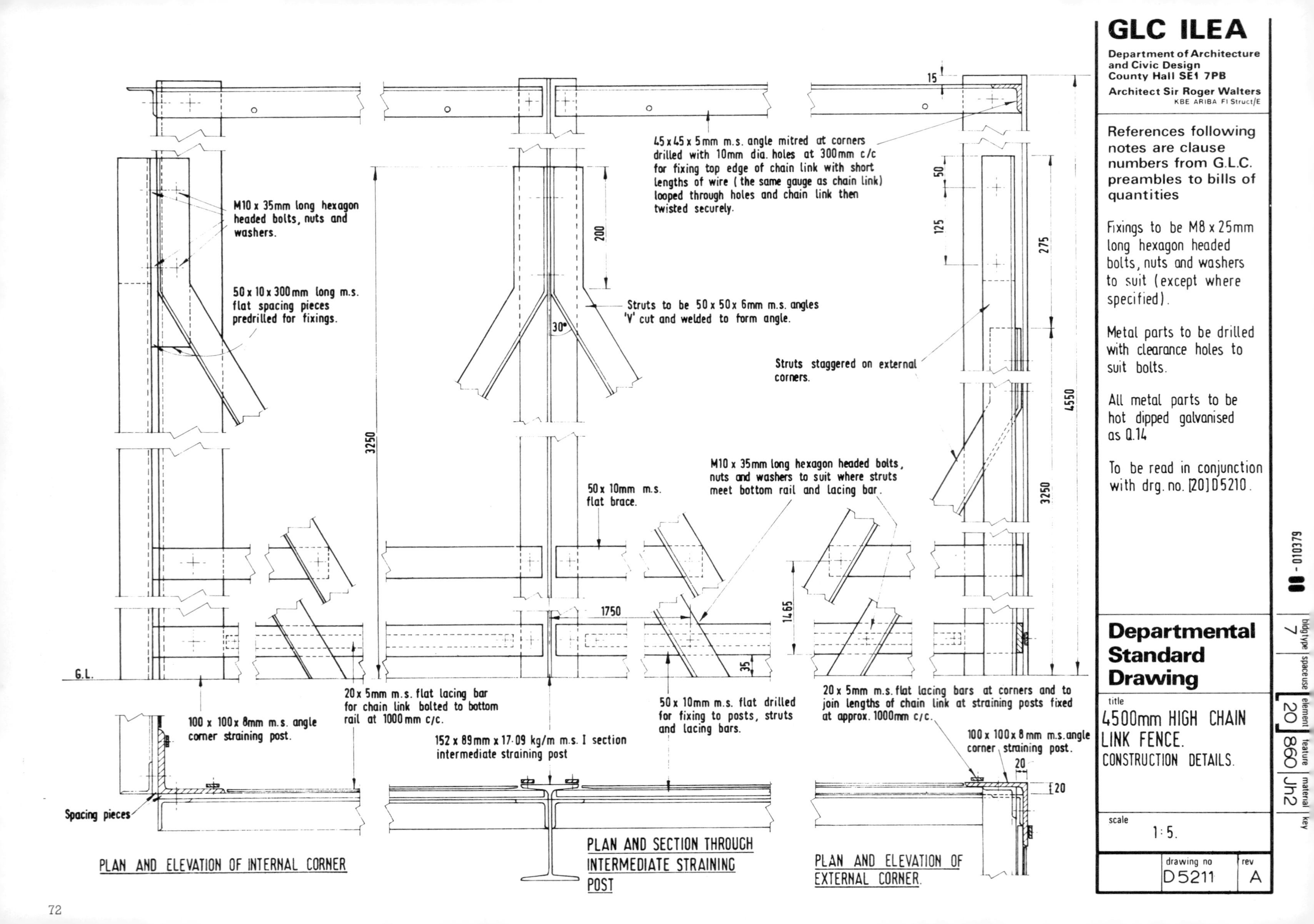
GLC ILEA
Department of Architecture and Civic Design
County Hall SE1 7PB
Architect Sir Roger Walters
KBE ARIBA FI Struct/E
References following notes are clause numbers from G.L.C. preambles to bills of quantities
Fixings to be M8 x 25mm long hexagon headed bolts, nuts and washers to suit (except where specified).
Metal parts to be drilled with clearance holes to suit bolts.
All metal parts to be hot dipped galvanised as Q.14
To be read in conjunction with drg. no. [20] D5210.
Departmental Standard Drawing
title
4500mm HIGH CHAIN LINK FENCE.
CONSTRUCTION DETAILS.
scale
1:5.
drawing no
D5211
rev
A
bldg type 7
space use
element [20]
feature 860
material Jh2
key
010379
M10 x 35mm long hexagon headed bolts, nuts and washers.
50 x 10 x 300mm long m.s. flat spacing pieces predrilled for fixings.
45 x 45 x 5mm m.s. angle mitred at corners drilled with 10mm dia. holes at 300mm c/c for fixing top edge of chain link with short lengths of wire (the same gauge as chain link) looped through holes and chain link then twisted securely.
Struts to be 50 x 50 x 6mm m.s. angles 'V' cut and welded to form angle.
30°
200
3250
Struts staggered on external corners.
15
50
125
275
4550
3250
M10 x 35mm long hexagon headed bolts, nuts and washers to suit where struts meet bottom rail and lacing bar.
50 x 10mm m.s. flat brace.
1750
1465
35
G.L.
100 x 100 x 8mm m.s. angle corner straining post.
20 x 5mm m.s. flat lacing bar for chain link bolted to bottom rail at 1000mm c/c.
152 x 89mm x 17·09 kg/m m.s. I section intermediate straining post
50 x 10mm m.s. flat drilled for fixing to posts, struts and lacing bars.
20 x 5mm m.s. flat lacing bars at corners and to join lengths of chain link at straining posts fixed at approx. 1000mm c/c.
100 x 100 x 8mm m.s. angle corner straining post.
20
20
Spacing pieces
PLAN AND ELEVATION OF INTERNAL CORNER
PLAN AND SECTION THROUGH INTERMEDIATE STRAINING POST
PLAN AND ELEVATION OF EXTERNAL CORNER.

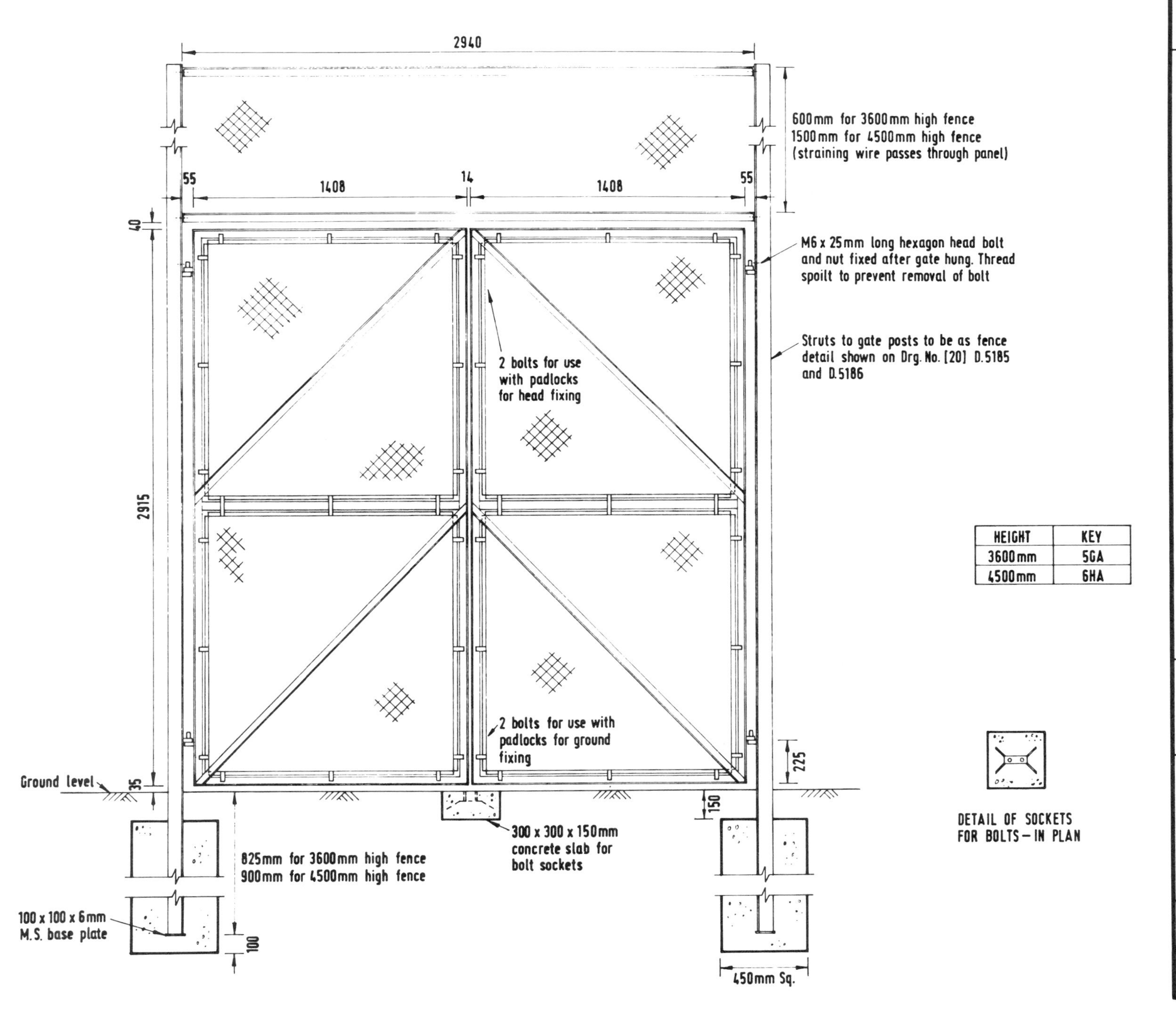

GLC ILEA

Department of Architecture and Civic Design
County Hall SE1 7PB
Architect F B Pooley CBE

References following notes are clause numbers from G.L.C. preambles to bills of quantities

This drawing is to be read in conjunction with job drawings and drawing Nos.
[20] D.5136 & D.5137 (3600mm high)
[20] D.5210 & D.5211 (4500mm high)

For full size manufacturing details see drawing Nos. [20] D.4031 & D.4034

Concrete to be as F.20 mix M

All metal parts to be hot dipped galvanised as Q.14

08-010379A 011179B

Departmental Standard Drawing

title

CHAIN LINK FENCE — DOUBLE GATES
3600mm AND 4500mm HIGH FENCING

scale 1 : 20

drawing no D.5188 | rev B

bldg type | space use | element [20] | feature | material | key

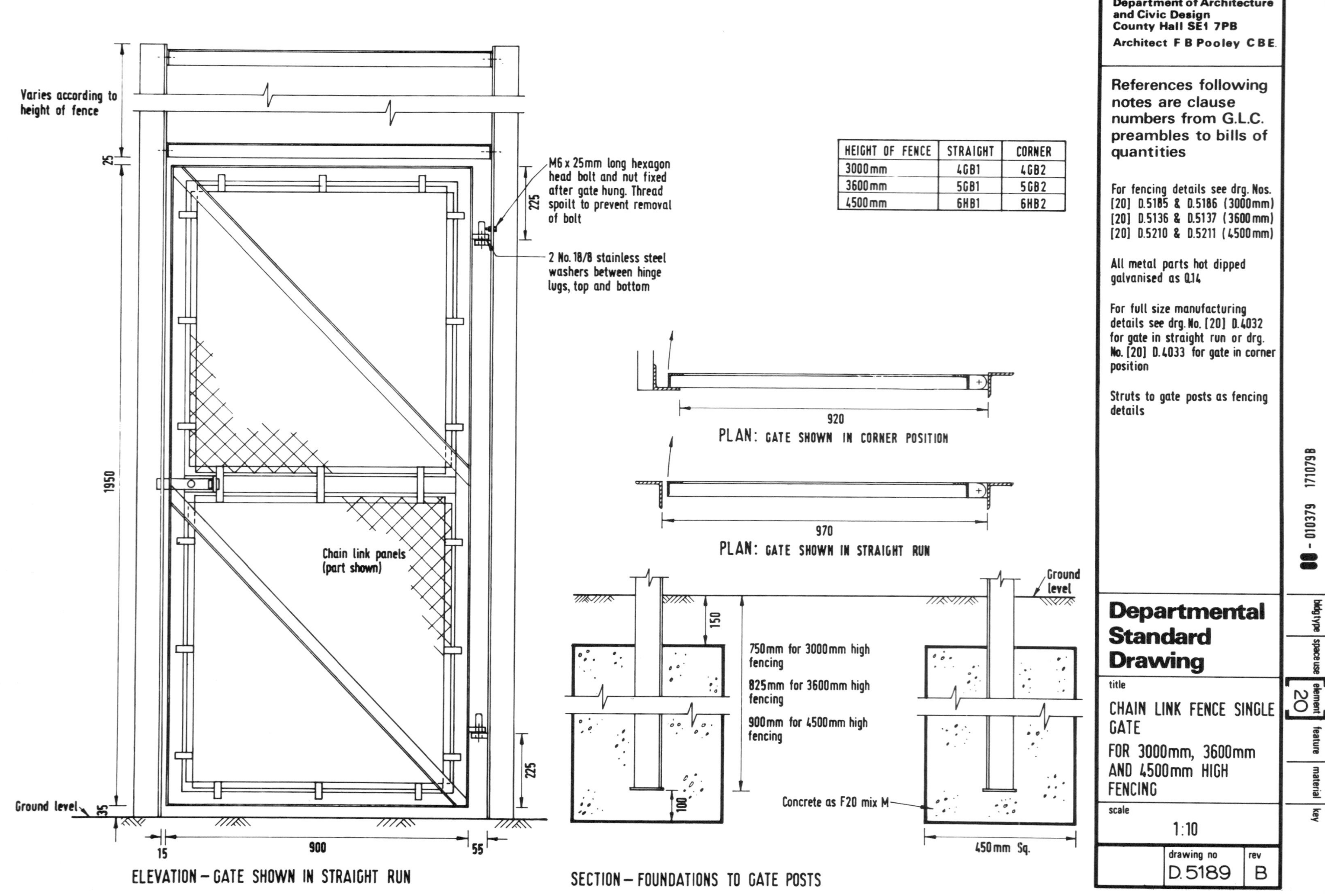

GLC ILEA
Department of Architecture and Civic Design
County Hall SE1 7PB
Architect F B Pooley C B E
References following notes are clause numbers from G.L.C. preambles to bills of quantities
For fencing details see drg. Nos. [20] D.5185 & D.5186 (3000mm) [20] D.5136 & D.5137 (3600mm) [20] D.5210 & D.5211 (4500mm)
All metal parts hot dipped galvanised as Q14
For full size manufacturing details see drg. No. [20] D.4032 for gate in straight run or drg. No. [20] D.4033 for gate in corner position
Struts to gate posts as fencing details
Departmental Standard Drawing
title
CHAIN LINK FENCE SINGLE GATE
FOR 3000mm, 3600mm AND 4500mm HIGH FENCING
scale
1:10
drawing no
D.5189
rev
B
bldg type
spaceuse
element
[20]
feature
material
key
00 - 010379 1710798
HEIGHT OF FENCE | STRAIGHT | CORNER
3000mm | 4GB1 | 4GB2
3600mm | 5GB1 | 5GB2
4500mm | 6HB1 | 6HB2
Varies according to height of fence
25
1950
35
Ground level
M6 x 25mm long hexagon head bolt and nut fixed after gate hung. Thread spoilt to prevent removal of bolt
225
2 No. 18/8 stainless steel washers between hinge lugs, top and bottom
Chain link panels (part shown)
225
15
900
55
ELEVATION – GATE SHOWN IN STRAIGHT RUN
920
PLAN: GATE SHOWN IN CORNER POSITION
970
PLAN: GATE SHOWN IN STRAIGHT RUN
Ground level
150
750mm for 3000mm high fencing
825mm for 3600mm high fencing
900mm for 4500mm high fencing
100
Concrete as F20 mix M
450mm Sq.
SECTION – FOUNDATIONS TO GATE POSTS

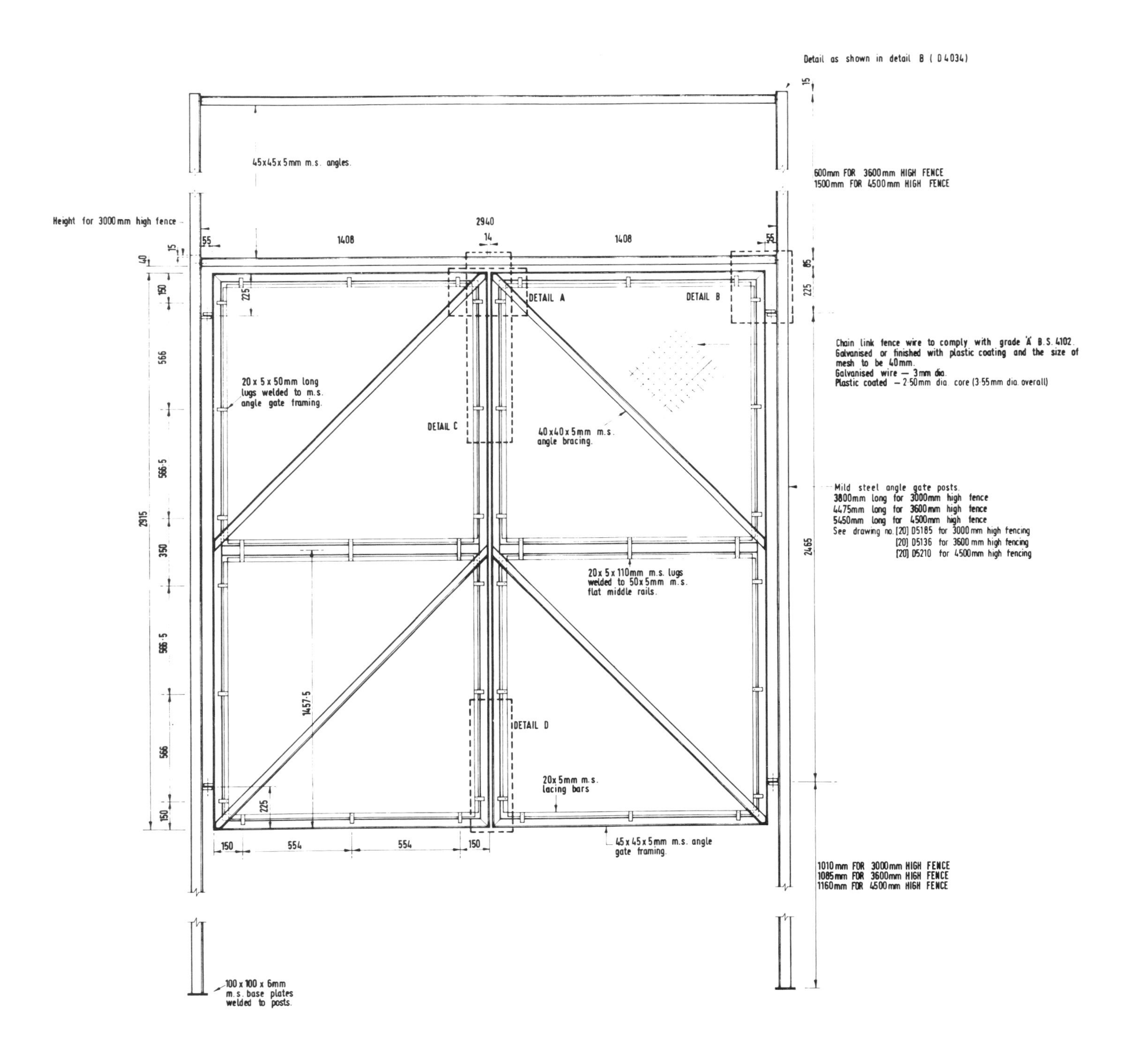

GLC ILEA

Department of Architecture and Civic Design
County Hall SE1

Architect Sir Roger Walters
KBE FRIBA FI Struct/E

For details A,B,C,D — see drawing numbers [20] D4034, D4035.

All metal parts to be hot dipped galvanised after fabrication.

All welding to be continuous all round joints and achieve maximum penetration.

Chain link wire for gate panels to comply with grade A B.S. 4102. Galvanised or finished with plastic coating (as specified by architect). Size of mesh 40mm.
Galvanised wire type to be 3mm dia.
Plastic coated type to have 2·50mm dia. core (3·55mm dia. overall).

Departmental Standard Drawing

title
CHAIN LINK FENCE DOUBLE GATES FOR 3000, 3600, 4500mm HIGH FENCING.

scale 1:10.

drawing no	rev
D 4031.	A

bldg type	space use	element	feature	material	key
7		[20]	860	Jh2	

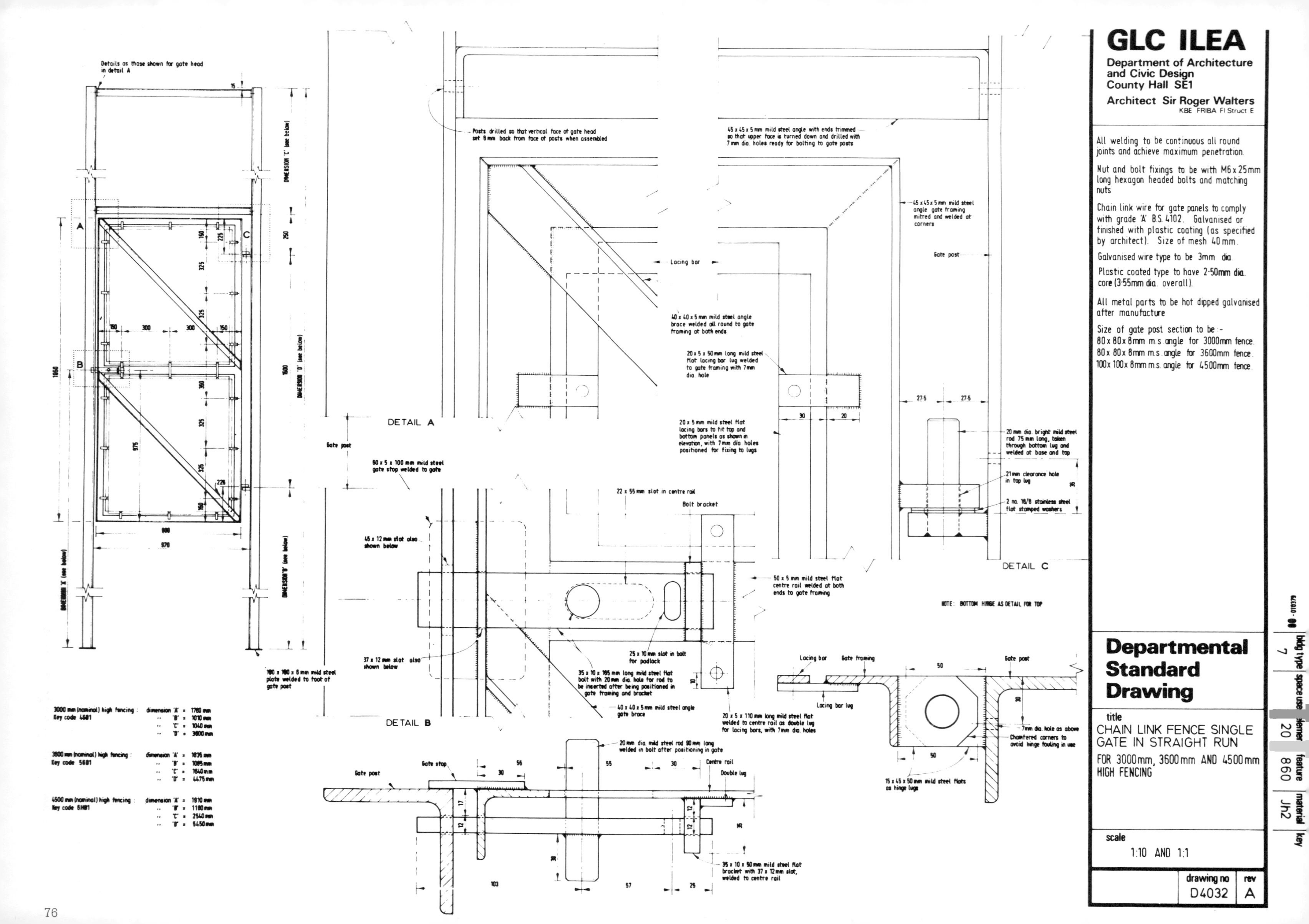
GLC ILEA
Department of Architecture and Civic Design
County Hall SE1
Architect Sir Roger Walters
KBE FRIBA FI Struct E
All welding to be continuous all round joints and achieve maximum penetration.
Nut and bolt fixings to be with M6 x 25mm long hexagon headed bolts and matching nuts
Chain link wire for gate panels to comply with grade 'A' B.S. 4102. Galvanised or finished with plastic coating (as specified by architect). Size of mesh 40mm.
Galvanised wire type to be 3mm dia.
Plastic coated type to have 2·50mm dia. core (3·55mm dia. overall).
All metal parts to be hot dipped galvanised after manufacture
Size of gate post section to be :-
80 x 80 x 8mm m.s. angle for 3000mm fence.
80 x 80 x 8mm m.s. angle for 3600mm fence.
100 x 100 x 8mm m.s. angle for 4500mm fence.
Departmental Standard Drawing
title
CHAIN LINK FENCE SINGLE GATE IN STRAIGHT RUN
FOR 3000mm, 3600mm AND 4500mm HIGH FENCING
scale
1:10 AND 1:1
drawing no
D4032
rev
A
bldg type 7
spaceuse
element 20
feature 860
material
key Jh2
Details as those shown for gate head in detail A
DIMENSION 'C' (see below)
DIMENSION 'D' (see below)
DIMENSION 'B' (see below)
DIMENSION 'A' (see below)
A
B
C
100 x 100 x 8 mm mild steel plate welded to foot of gate post
3000 mm (nominal) high fencing : Key code 4681 dimension 'A' = 1780 mm 'B' = 1010 mm 'C' = 1040 mm 'D' = 3800 mm
3600 mm (nominal) high fencing : Key code 5681 dimension 'A' = 1835 mm 'B' = 1085 mm 'C' = 1640 mm 'D' = 4475 mm
4500 mm (nominal) high fencing : Key code 6H81 dimension 'A' = 1910 mm 'B' = 1180 mm 'C' = 2540 mm 'D' = 5450 mm
Posts drilled so that vertical face of gate head set 8 mm back from face of posts when assembled
45 x 45 x 5 mm mild steel angle with ends trimmed so that upper face is turned down and drilled with 7 mm dia. holes ready for bolting to gate posts
45 x 45 x 5 mm mild steel angle gate framing mitred and welded at corners
Gate post
Lacing bar
40 x 40 x 5 mm mild steel angle brace welded all round to gate framing at both ends
20 x 5 x 50 mm long mild steel flat lacing bar lug welded to gate framing with 7 mm dia. hole
20 x 5 mm mild steel flat lacing bars to fit top and bottom panels as shown in elevation, with 7mm dia. holes positioned for fixing to lugs
DETAIL A
80 x 5 x 100 mm mild steel gate stop welded to gate
20 mm dia. bright mild steel rod 75 mm long, taken through bottom lug and welded at base and top
21 mm clearance hole in top lug
2 no. 18/8 stainless steel flat stamped washers
DETAIL C
NOTE: BOTTOM HINGE AS DETAIL FOR TOP
22 x 55 mm slot in centre rail
Bolt bracket
45 x 12 mm slot also shown below
50 x 5 mm mild steel flat centre rail welded at both ends to gate framing
37 x 12 mm slot also shown below
25 x 10 mm slot in bolt for padlock
35 x 10 x 185 mm long mild steel flat bolt with 20 mm dia. hole for rod to be inserted after being positioned in gate framing and bracket
40 x 40 x 5 mm mild steel angle gate brace
20 x 5 x 110 mm long mild steel flat welded to centre rail as double lug for lacing bars, with 7mm dia. holes
DETAIL B
Lacing bar
Gate framing
Lacing bar lug
7mm dia. hole as above
Chamfered corners to avoid hinge fouling in use
15 x 45 x 50 mm mild steel flats as hinge lugs
20 mm dia. mild steel rod 80 mm long welded in bolt after positioning in gate
Gate stop
Centre rail
Double lug
35 x 10 x 50 mm mild steel flat bracket with 37 x 12 mm slot, welded to centre rail

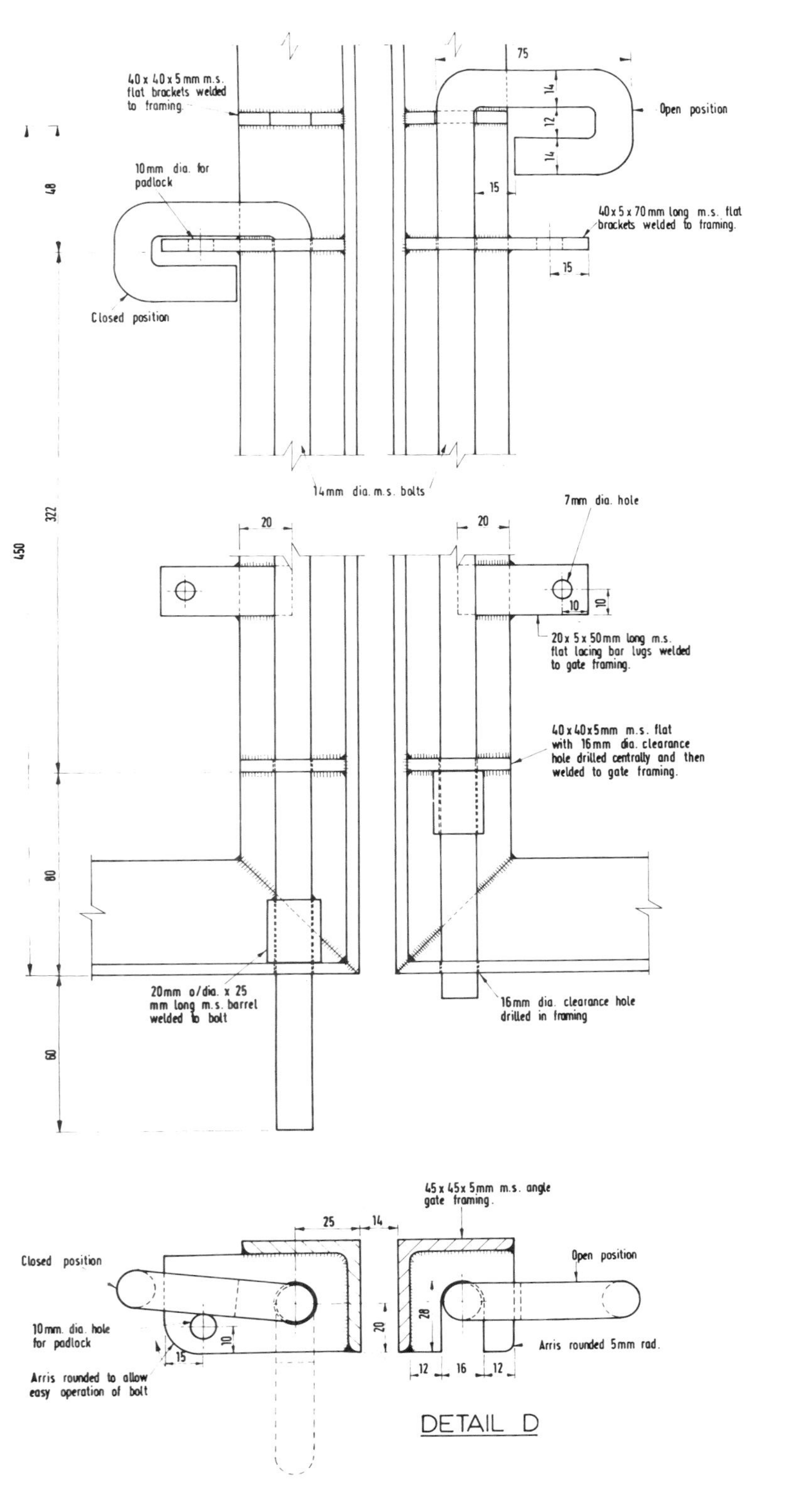

40 x 40 x 5 mm m.s. flat brackets welded to framing
75
Open position
14
12
14
10mm dia. for padlock
15
40 x 5 x 70 mm long m.s. flat brackets welded to framing
15
Closed position
48
322
450
80
60
14mm dia. m.s. bolts
20
20
7mm dia. hole
10
10
20 x 5 x 50mm long m.s. flat lacing bar lugs welded to gate framing
40 x 40 x 5mm m.s. flat with 16mm dia. clearance hole drilled centrally and then welded to gate framing
20mm o/dia. x 25 mm long m.s. barrel welded to bolt
16mm dia. clearance hole drilled in framing
45 x 45 x 5mm m.s. angle gate framing
25
14
Closed position
Open position
10mm dia. hole for padlock
Arris rounded to allow easy operation of bolt
15
10
20
28
12
16
12
Arris rounded 5mm rad.
DETAIL D

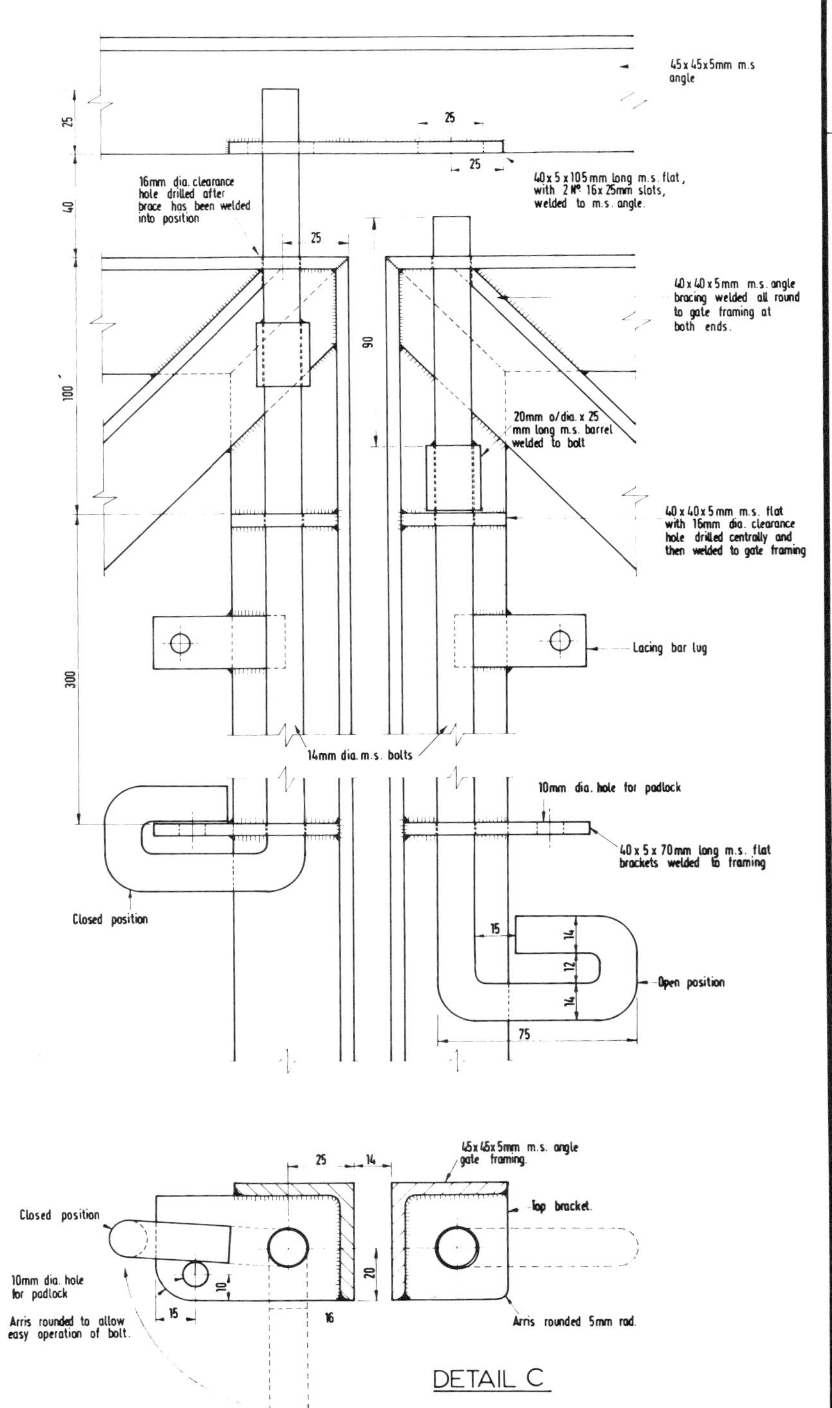

45 x 45 x 5mm m.s angle
25
25
25
40 x 5 x 105 mm long m.s. flat, with 2 No 16 x 25mm slots, welded to m.s. angle.
16mm dia. clearance hole drilled after brace has been welded into position
25
40
100
90
300
40 x 40 x 5mm m.s. angle bracing welded all round to gate framing at both ends.
20mm o/dia. x 25 mm long m.s. barrel welded to bolt
40 x 40 x 5 mm m.s. flat with 16mm dia. clearance hole drilled centrally and then welded to gate framing
Lacing bar lug
14mm dia. m.s. bolts
10mm dia. hole for padlock
40 x 5 x 70mm long m.s. flat brackets welded to framing
Closed position
15
14
12
14
Open position
75
25
14
45 x 45 x 5mm m.s. angle gate framing.
Closed position
Top bracket.
10mm dia. hole for padlock
10
20
15
16
Arris rounded to allow easy operation of bolt.
Arris rounded 5mm rad.
DETAIL C

GLC ILEA
Department of Architecture and Civic Design
County Hall SE1
Architect Sir Roger Walters
KBE FRIBA FI Struct E
This drawing is to be read in conjunction with drawing numbers [20] D4031A and D4035B
Welding to be 5mm fillet welds (unless stated otherwise) around the full profile of the members being joined and sealing welds on flush edges. Welding to be as B S 5135 Welds must not be ground flat
Departmental Standard Drawing
title
CHAIN LINK FENCE DOUBLE GATES FOR 3000, 3600, 4500mm HIGH FENCING. FULL SIZE DETAILS.
scale
1:1
drawing no.
D4034
rev
A
bldg type
7
space use
element
[20]
feature
860
material
Jh2
key

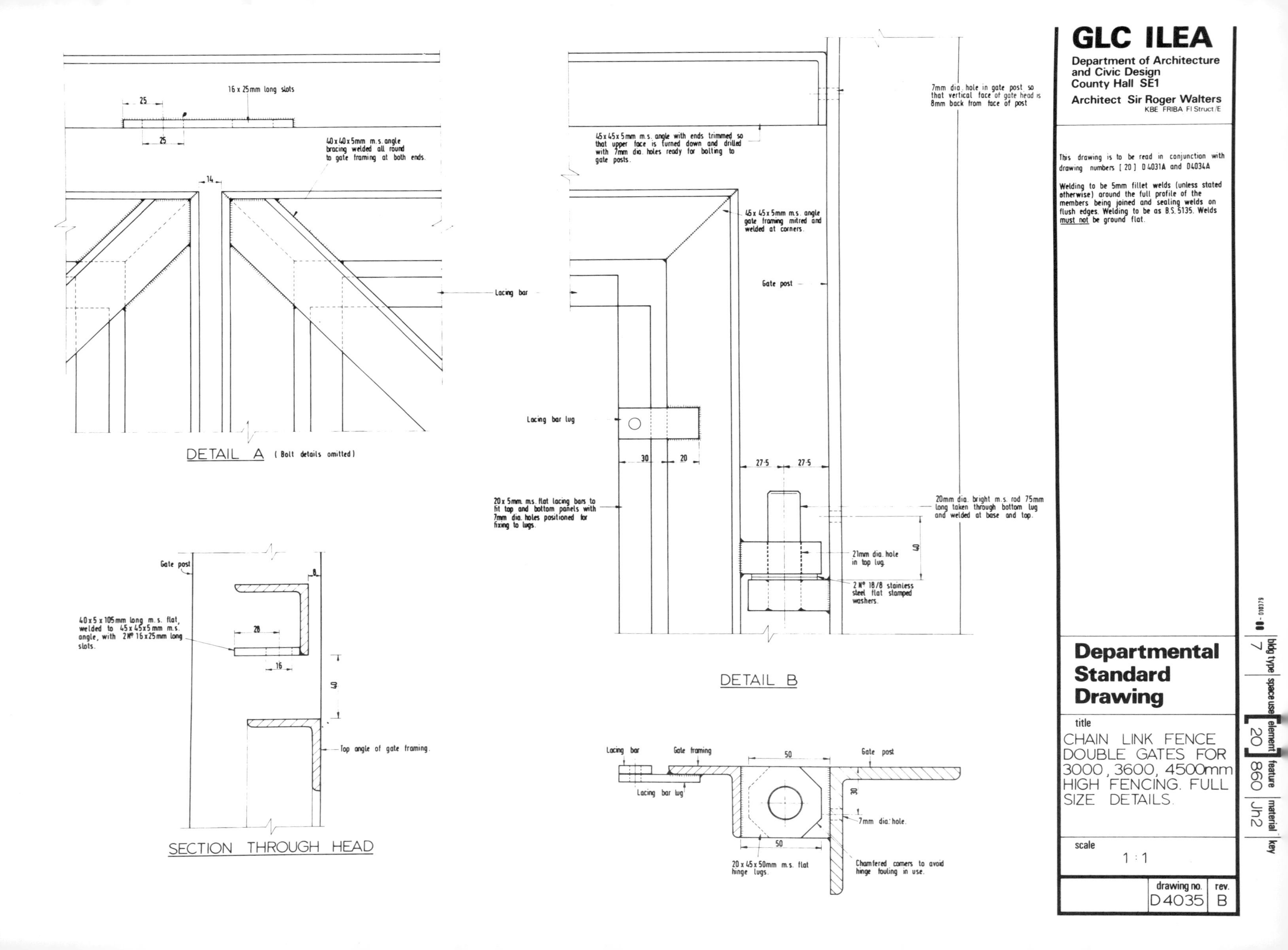

16 x 25mm long slots
25
25
40 x 40 x 5mm m.s. angle bracing welded all round to gate framing at both ends.
14
Lacing bar
DETAIL A (Bolt details omitted)
45 x 45 x 5mm m.s. angle with ends trimmed so that upper face is turned down and drilled with 7mm dia. holes ready for bolting to gate posts.
7mm dia. hole in gate post so that vertical face of gate head is 8mm back from face of post
45 x 45 x 5mm m.s. angle gate framing mitred and welded at corners.
Gate post
Lacing bar lug
30
20
27·5
27·5
20 x 5mm m.s. flat lacing bars to fit top and bottom panels with 7mm dia. holes positioned for fixing to lugs.
20mm dia. bright m.s. rod 75mm long taken through bottom lug and welded at base and top.
21mm dia. hole in top lug.
40
2 N° 18/8 stainless steel flat stamped washers.
DETAIL B
Gate post
8
40 x 5 x 105mm long m.s. flat, welded to 45 x 45 x 5mm m.s. angle, with 2 N° 16 x 25mm long slots.
28
16
40
Top angle of gate framing
SECTION THROUGH HEAD
Lacing bar
Gate framing
50
Gate post
Lacing bar lug
30
7mm dia. hole.
50
20 x 45 x 50mm m.s. flat hinge lugs.
Chamfered corners to avoid hinge fouling in use.
GLC ILEA
Department of Architecture and Civic Design
County Hall SE1
Architect Sir Roger Walters
KBE FRIBA FI Struct E
This drawing is to be read in conjunction with drawing numbers [20] D4031A and D4034A
Welding to be 5mm fillet welds (unless stated otherwise) around the full profile of the members being joined and sealing welds on flush edges. Welding to be as B.S. 5135. Welds must not be ground flat.
Departmental Standard Drawing
title
CHAIN LINK FENCE DOUBLE GATES FOR 3000, 3600, 4500mm HIGH FENCING. FULL SIZE DETAILS.
scale
1 : 1
drawing no.
D4035
rev.
B
bldg type
7
space use
element
[20]
feature
860
material
Jh2
key

5 Timber fencing and gates

5173 Close-boarded fence—softwood
5175 Open slatted fence—softwood
5176 Horizontal slatted fence—softwood
5177 Horizontal double slatted fence—softwood
5178 Post and rail fence—low level—softwood
5190 Close-boarded fence (for schools)
5191 Timber single gate—1.8m and 1.2m high
5192 Timber double gates—1.8m and 1.2m high
5336 Timber single gate with brick piers
5337 Timber double gates with brick piers

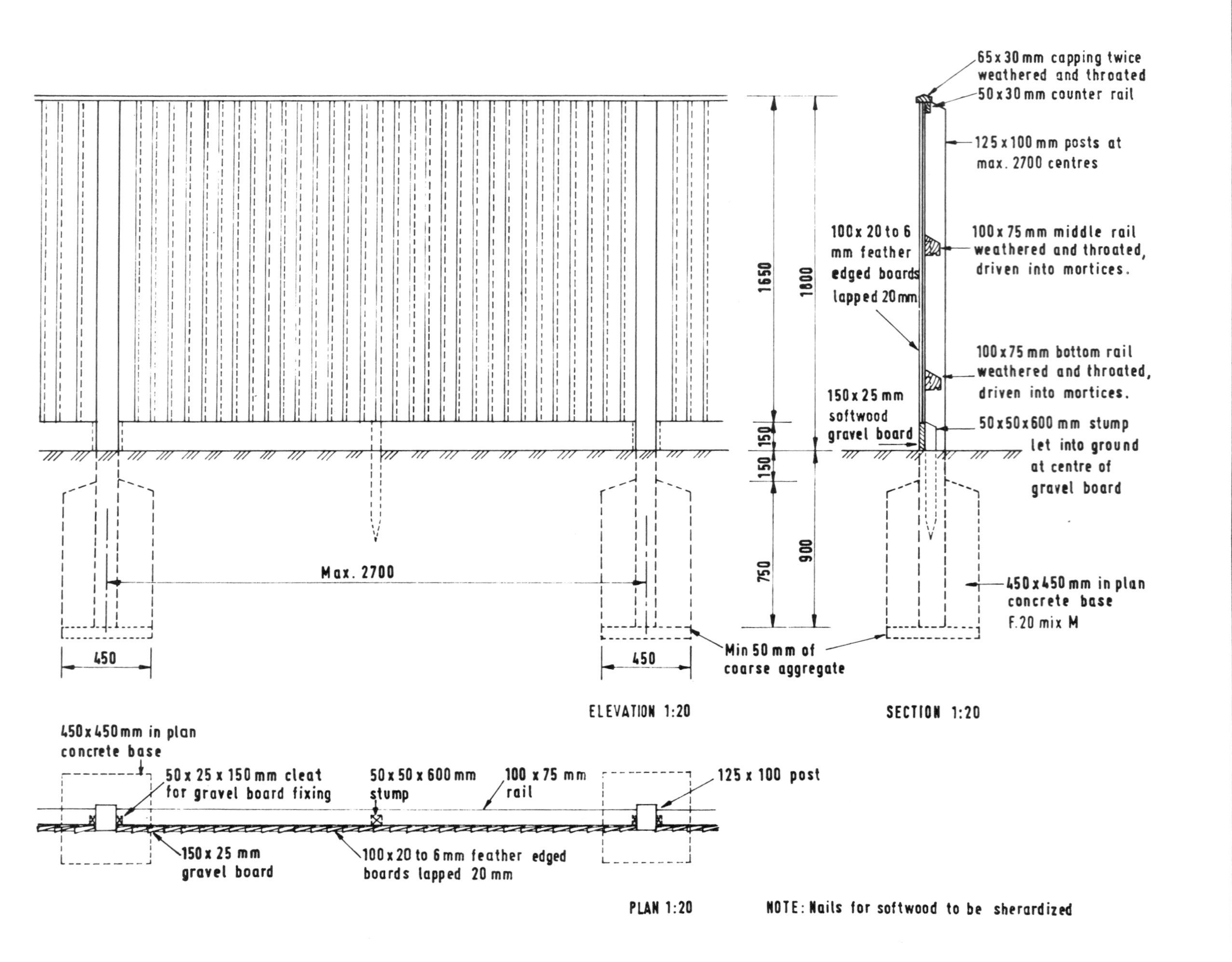

GLC ILEA

Department of Architecture and Civic Design
County Hall SE1
Architect Sir Roger Walters KBE FRIBA FI StructE

References following notes are clause numbers from G.L.C. preambles to bills of quantities

This drawing to be read in conjunction with relevant job drawings.

Timber and treatment to comply with B.S.1722 and with G.L.C. preambles to bills of quantities V.39, V.40 or X.5.

For type and method of treatment see job specification.

Departmental Standard Drawing

title
CLOSE - BOARDED FENCE (SOFTWOOD)

scale
1:20

drawing no
D5173

00 - 010379 | bldg type | space use | element [20] | feature 860 | material Hi2 | key A

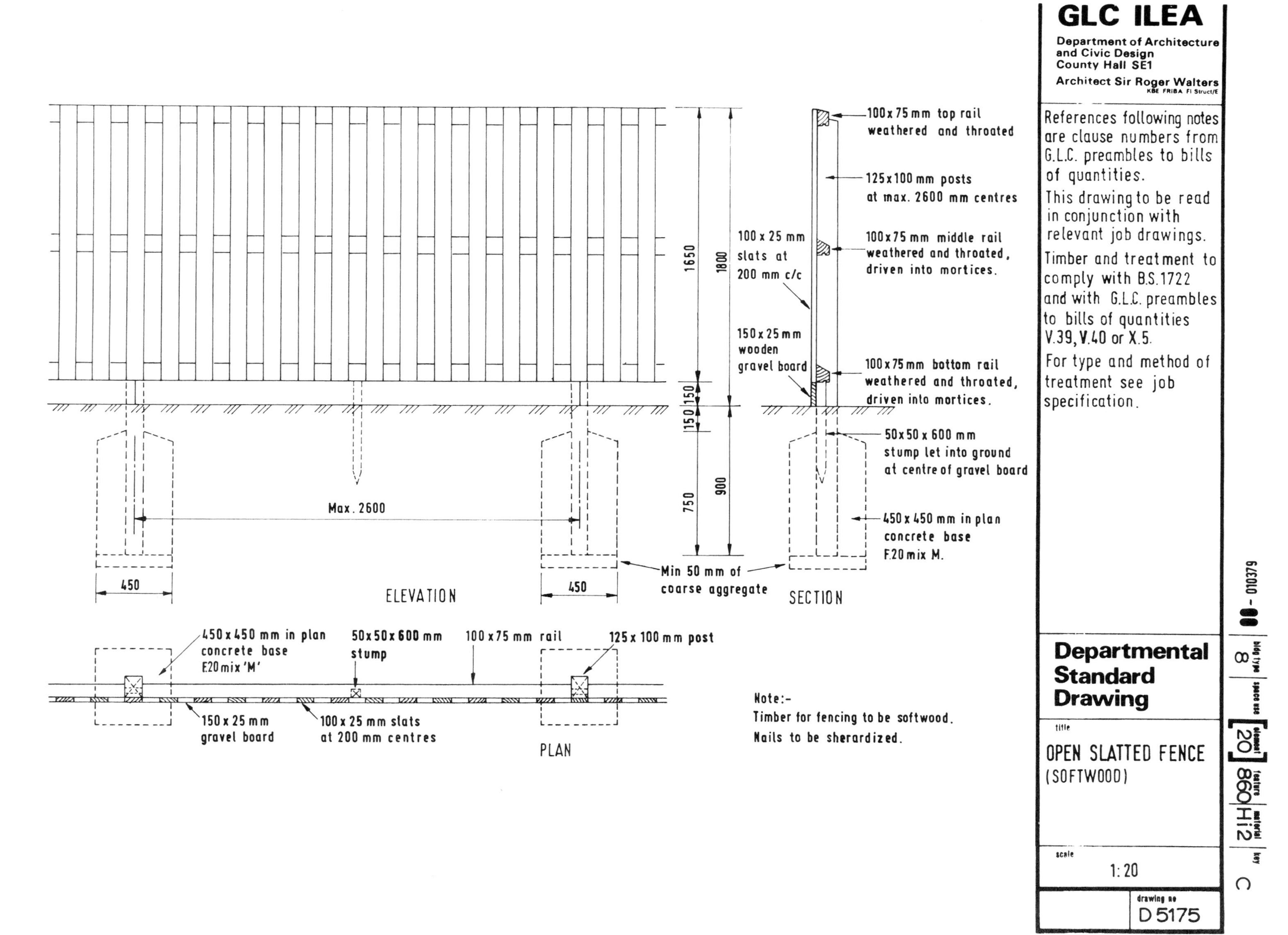
GLC ILEA
Department of Architecture and Civic Design
County Hall SE1
Architect Sir Roger Walters
KBE FRIBA FI StructE
References following notes are clause numbers from G.L.C. preambles to bills of quantities.
This drawing to be read in conjunction with relevant job drawings.
Timber and treatment to comply with B.S.1722 and with G.L.C. preambles to bills of quantities V.39, V.40 or X.5.
For type and method of treatment see job specification.
100 x 75 mm top rail weathered and throated
125 x 100 mm posts at max. 2600 mm centres
100 x 25 mm slats at 200 mm c/c
100 x 75 mm middle rail weathered and throated, driven into mortices.
150 x 25 mm wooden gravel board
100 x 75 mm bottom rail weathered and throated, driven into mortices.
50 x 50 x 600 mm stump let into ground at centre of gravel board
450 x 450 mm in plan concrete base F.20 mix M.
Min 50 mm of coarse aggregate
1650
1800
150
150
750
900
Max. 2600
450
450
ELEVATION
SECTION
450 x 450 mm in plan concrete base F.20 mix 'M'
50 x 50 x 600 mm stump
100 x 75 mm rail
125 x 100 mm post
150 x 25 mm gravel board
100 x 25 mm slats at 200 mm centres
PLAN
Note:-
Timber for fencing to be softwood.
Nails to be sherardized.
Departmental Standard Drawing
title
OPEN SLATTED FENCE (SOFTWOOD)
scale
1:20
drawing no
D 5175
010379
bldg type 8
space use
element [20]
feature 860
material Hi2
key
C

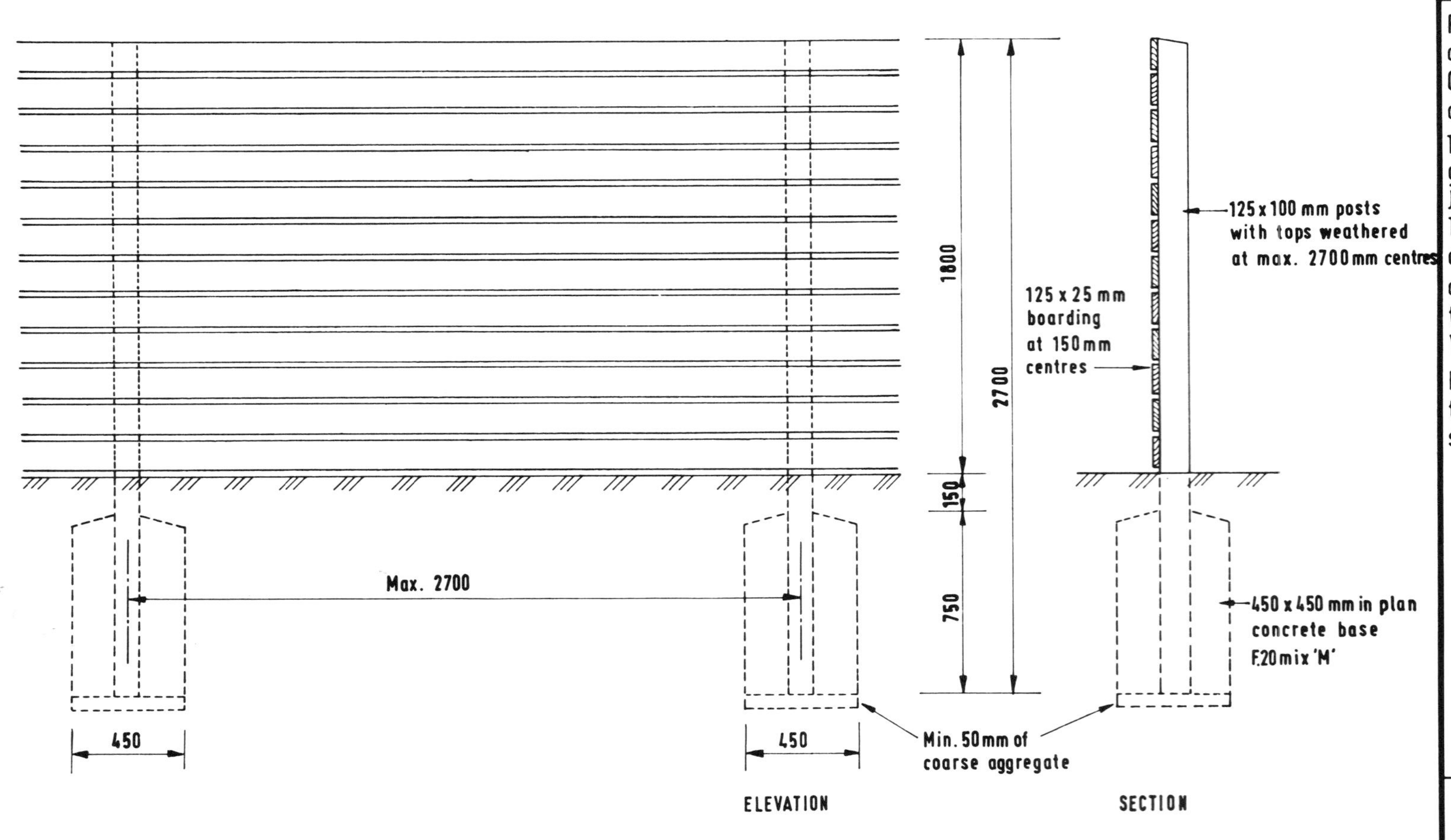

Note:-
Timber for fencing to be softwood.
Nails to be sherardised.

GLC ILEA

Department of Architecture
and Civic Design
County Hall SE1
Architect Sir Roger Walters
KBE FRIBA FI StructE

References following notes are clause numbers from G.L.C. preambles to bills of quantities.

This drawing to be read in conjunction with relevant job drawings.

Timber and treatment to comply with B.S.1722 and with G.L.C. preambles to bills of quantities V.39 V.40 or X.5.

For type and method of treatment see job specification.

Departmental Standard Drawing

title

HORIZONTAL SLATTED FENCE (SOFTWOOD)

scale

1:20

drawing no

D5176

8 | 20 | 860 | Hi2 | D

GLC ILEA
Department of Architecture and Civic Design
County Hall SE1
Architect Sir Roger Walters KBE FRIBA FI StructE

References following notes are clause numbers from G.L.C. preambles to bills of quantities.
This drawing to be read in conjunction with relevant job drawings.
Timber and treatment to comply with B.S. 1722 and with G.L.C. preambles to bills of quantities V.39, V.40 or X.5.
For type and method of treatment see job specification.

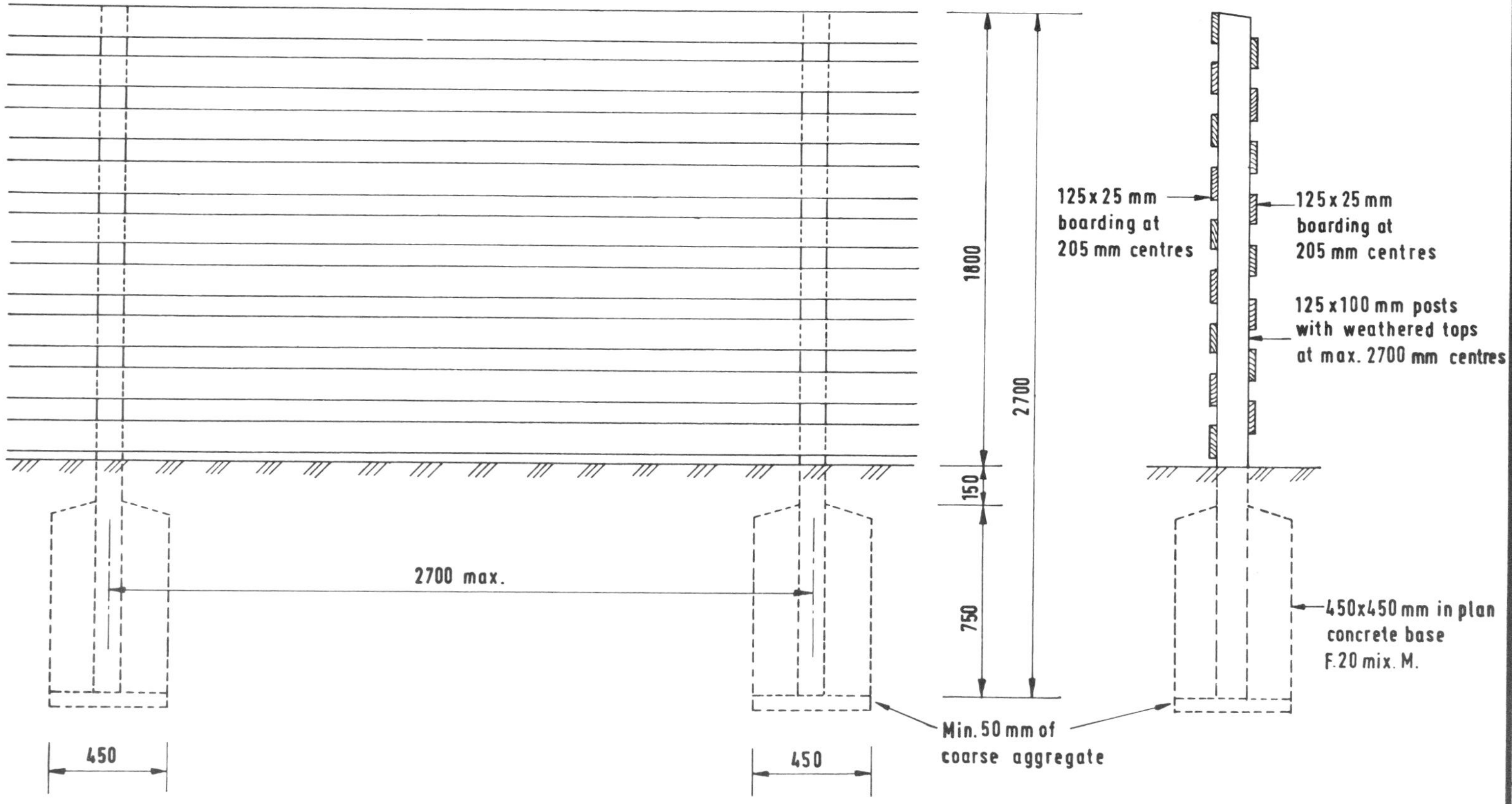

125 x 25 mm boarding at 205 mm centres

125 x 25 mm boarding at 205 mm centres

125 x 100 mm posts with weathered tops at max. 2700 mm centres

1800

2700

150

750

2700 max.

450x450 mm in plan concrete base F.20 mix. M.

Min. 50 mm of coarse aggregate

450

450

ELEVATION

SECTION

Note:-
Timber for fencing to be softwood
Nails to be sherardized

Departmental Standard Drawing

title
HORIZONTAL DOUBLE SLATTED FENCE (SOFTWOOD)

scale
1:20

drawing no
D 5177

bldg type 8 | space use | element [20] | feature 860 | material Hi2 | key E

00 - 010379

GLC ILEA

Department of Architecture and Civic Design
County Hall SE1
Architect Sir Roger Walters KBE FRIBA FI StructE

References following notes are clause numbers from G.L.C. preambles to bills of quantities

This drawing to be read in conjunction with relevant job drawings.

Timber and treatment to comply with B.S.1722 and with G.L.C. preambles to bills of quantities V.39 V.40 or X.5.

For type and method of treatment see job specification.

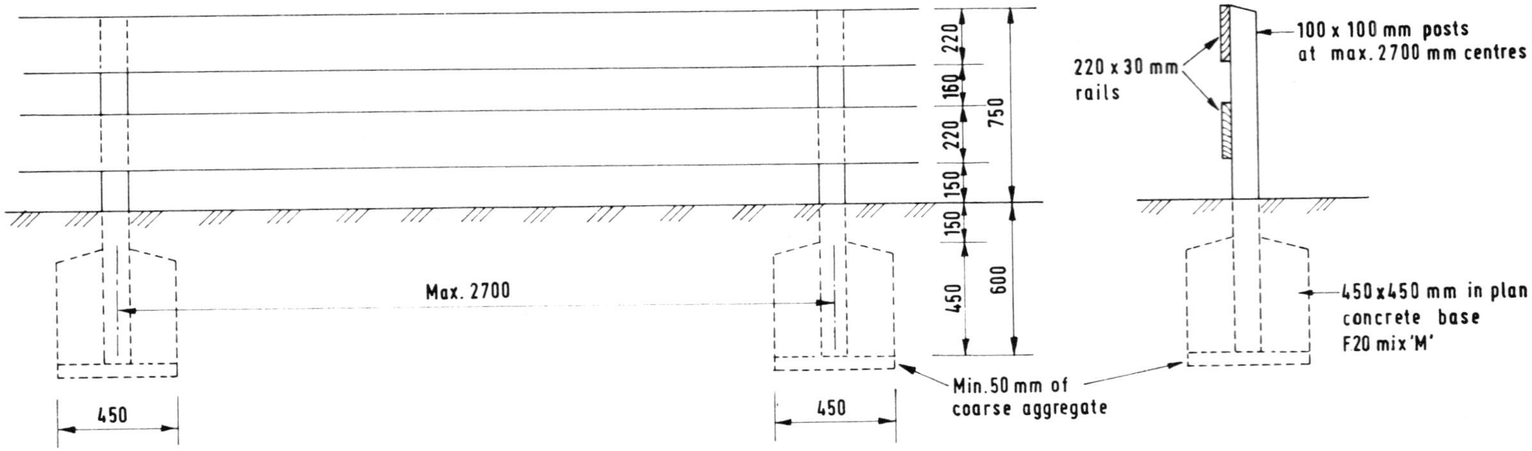

220 x 30 mm rails

100 x 100 mm posts at max. 2700 mm centres

220

160

220

150

150

450

750

600

Max. 2700

450

450

450x450 mm in plan concrete base F20 mix 'M'

Min. 50 mm of coarse aggregate

ELEVATION

SECTION

Note:-

Timber for fencing to be softwood

Nails to be sherardised

Departmental Standard Drawing

title

POST AND RAILS FENCE (SOFTWOOD)

scale

1:20

drawing no

D 5178

8 | (20) 860 | Hi2 | F

010379

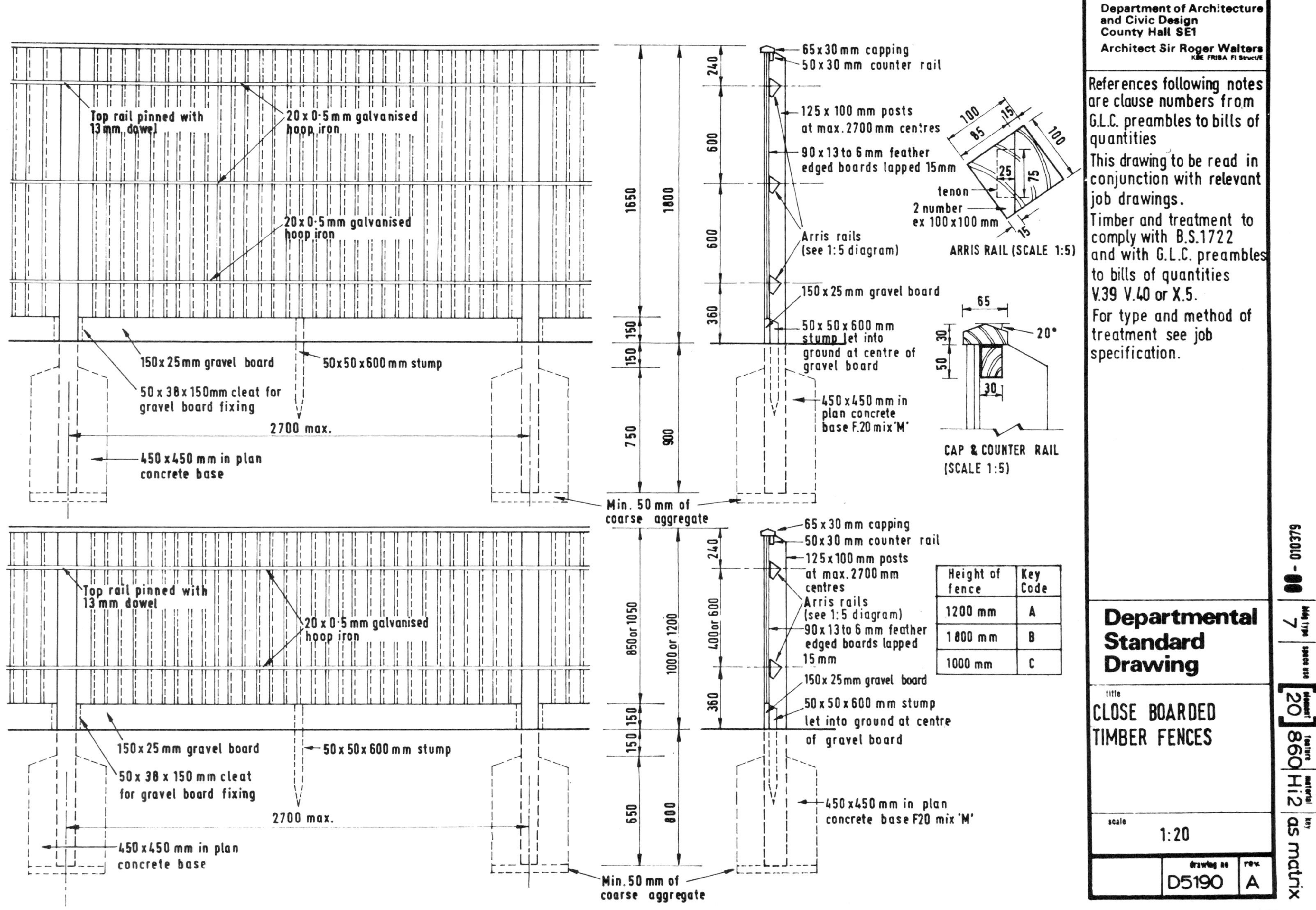

Height of fence	Key Code
1200 mm	A
1800 mm	B
1000 mm	C

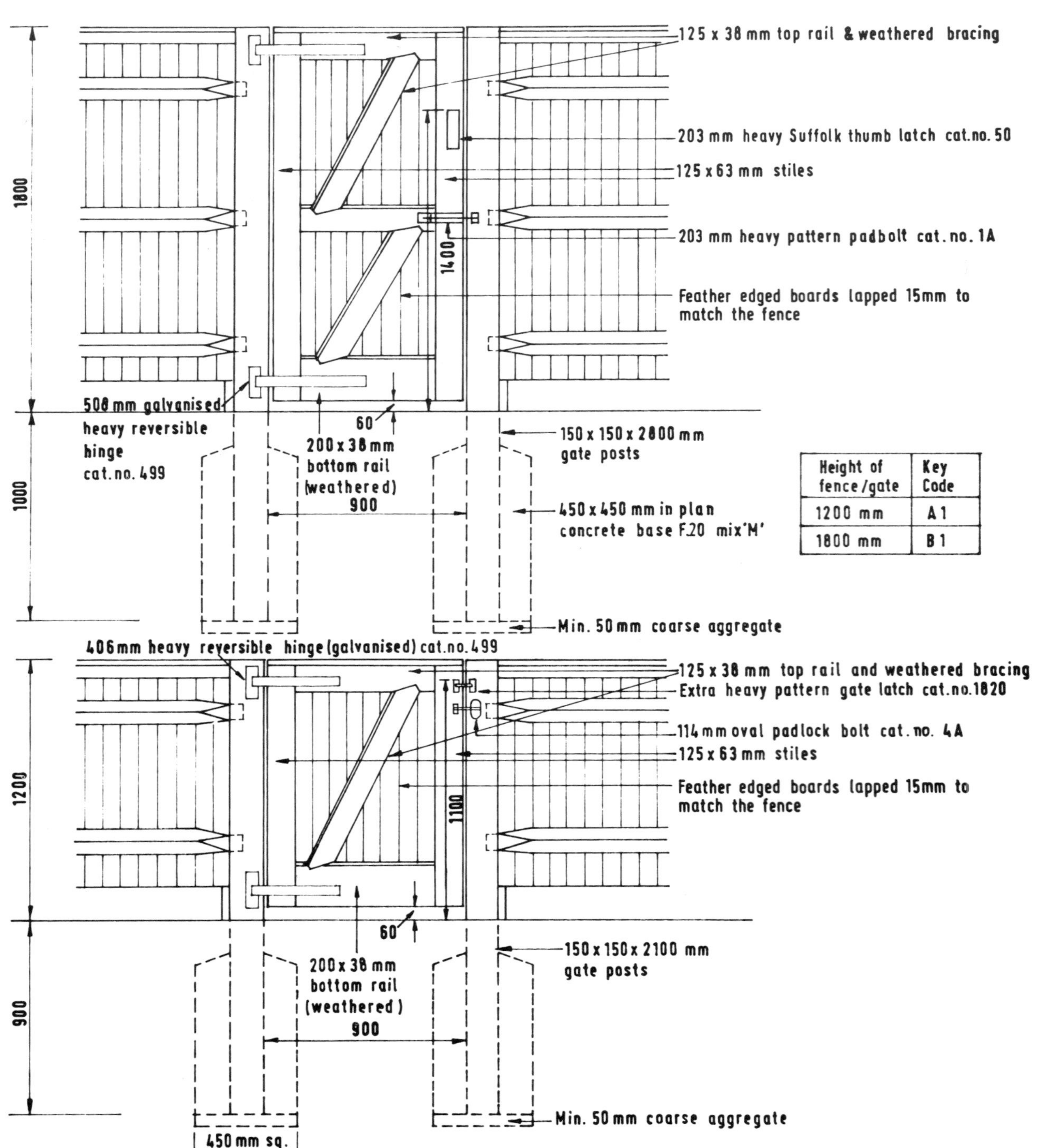

Height of fence/gate	Key Code
1200 mm	A1
1800 mm	B1

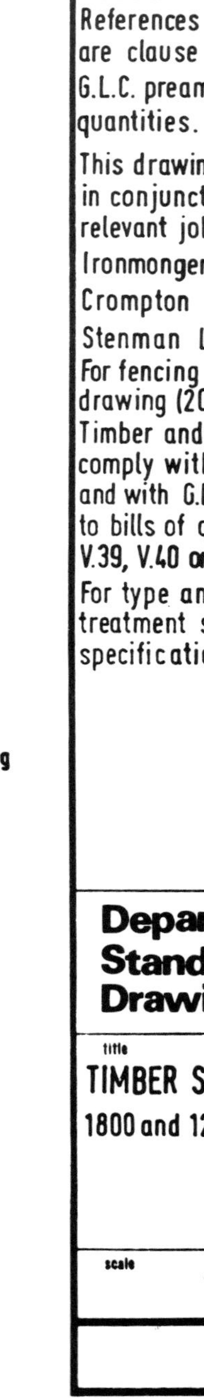

References following notes are clause numbers from G.L.C. preambles to bills of quantities.

This drawing to be read in conjunction with relevant job drawings

Ironmongery items by Crompton Nettlefold Stenman Ltd.

For fencing details see drawing (20) D5190.

Timber and treatment to comply with B.S.1722 and with G.L.C. preambles to bills of quantities V.39, V.40 or X.5.

For type and method of treatment see job specification.

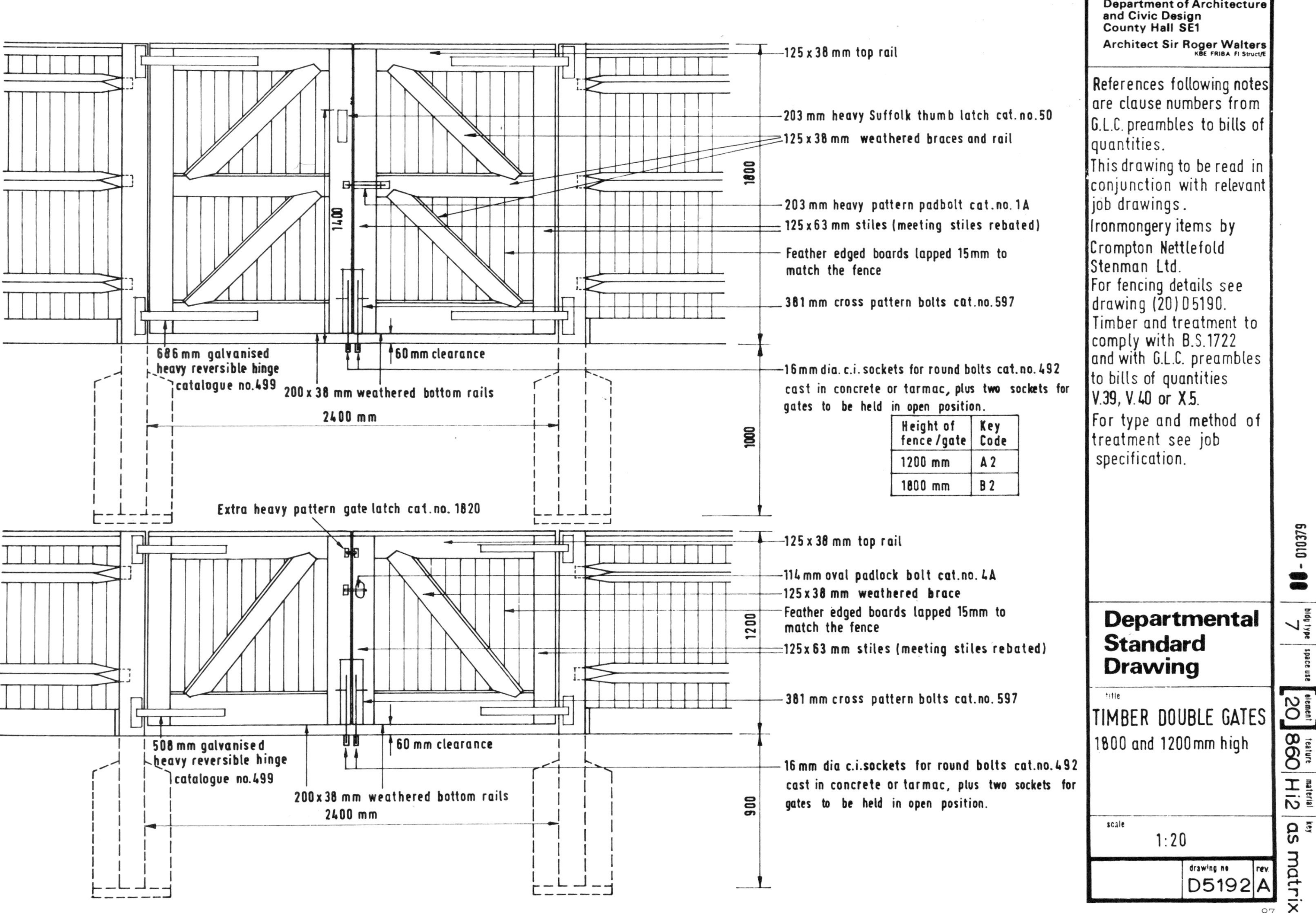

Height of fence / gate	Key Code
1200 mm	A 2
1800 mm	B 2

GLC ILEA

Department of Architecture and Civic Design
County Hall SE1
Architect Sir Roger Walters
KBE FRIBA FI StructE

References following notes are clause numbers from G.L.C. preambles to bills of quantities.
This drawing to be read in conjunction with relevant job drawings.
Ironmongery items by Crompton Nettlefold Stenman Ltd.
For fencing details see drawing (20) D5190.
Timber and treatment to comply with B.S. 1722 and with G.L.C. preambles to bills of quantities V.39, V.40 or X.5.
For type and method of treatment see job specification.

Departmental Standard Drawing

title
TIMBER DOUBLE GATES
1800 and 1200 mm high

scale
1:20

drawing no D5192 rev. A

bldg type 7 | space use | element [20] | feature 860 | material Hi2 | key as matrix

0010 - 9/79

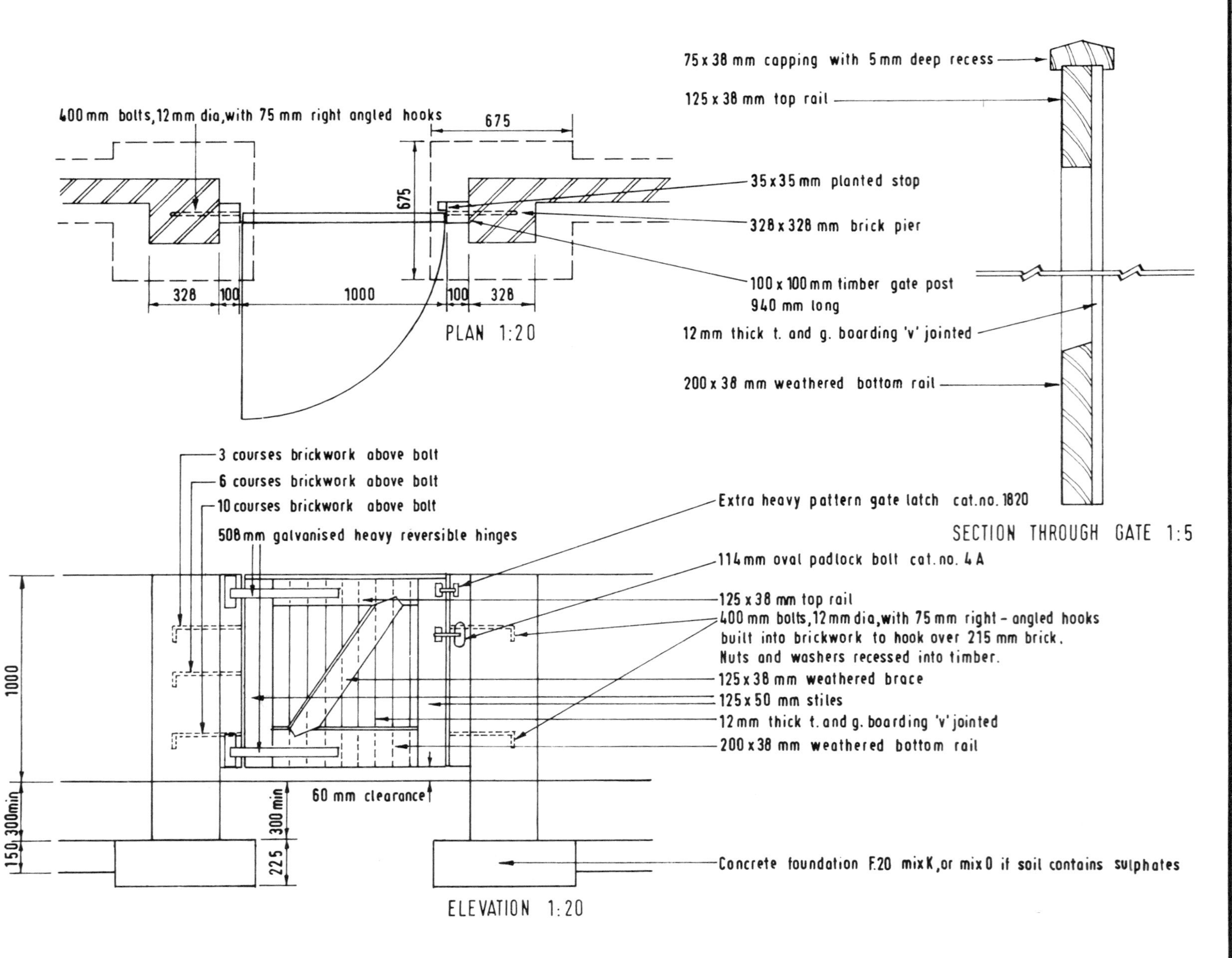

GLC ILEA

Department of Architecture
and Civic Design
County Hall SE1 7PB
Architect Sir Roger Walters
KBE ARIBA FI Struct/E

References following notes are clause numbers from G.L.C. preambles to bills of quantities

Ironmongery items by Crompton Nettlefold Stenman Ltd.

For timber and treatment see job specification

Departmental Standard Drawing

title

TIMBER SINGLE GATE
1000 mm high and 1000 mm wide
BETWEEN BRICK PIERS
DOMESTIC USE ONLY

scale

1:20 & 1:5

drawing no	rev
D5336	

20 860 Hi2 C3

010379

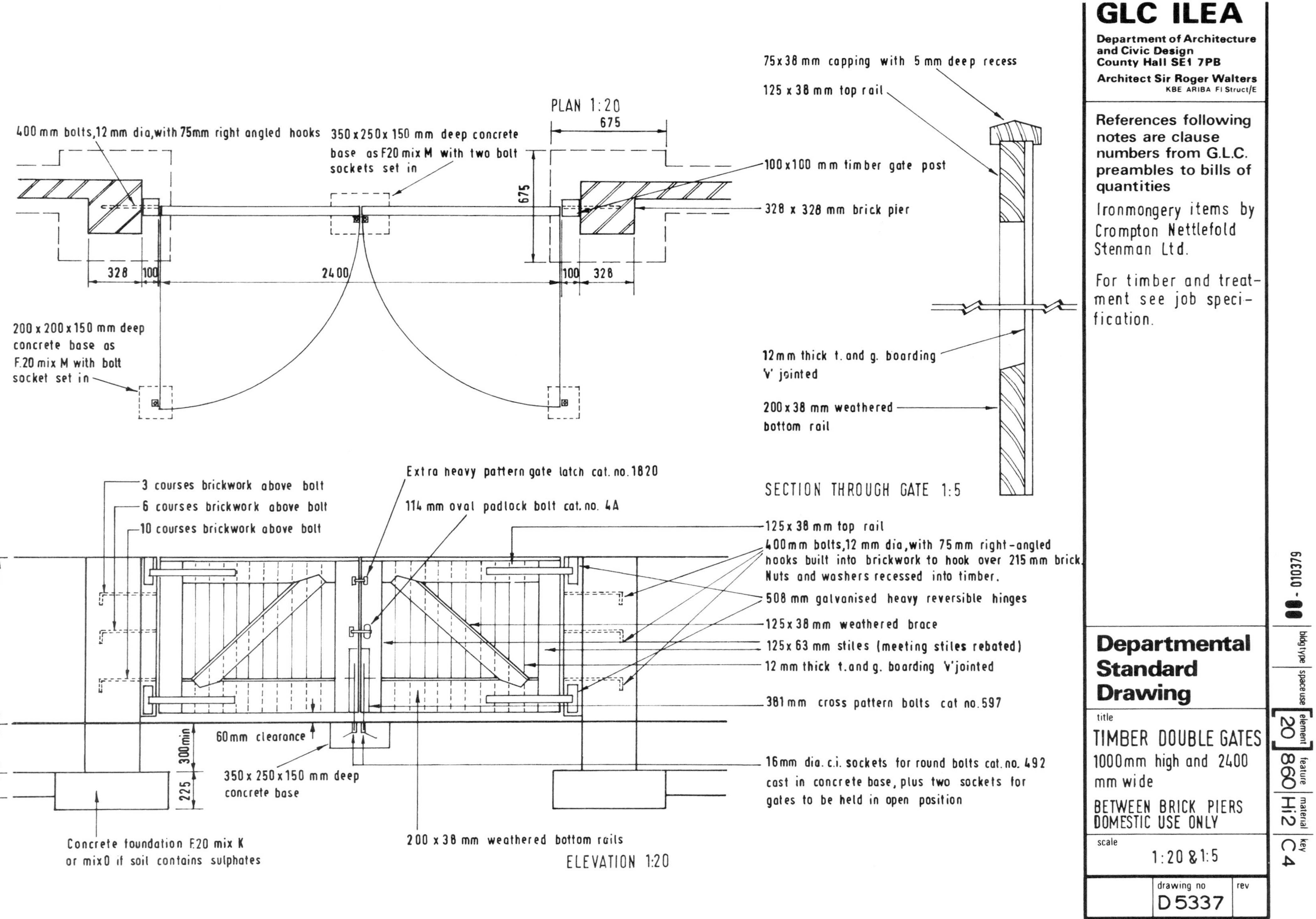
GLC ILEA
Department of Architecture and Civic Design
County Hall SE1 7PB
Architect Sir Roger Walters KBE ARIBA FI Struct/E
References following notes are clause numbers from G.L.C. preambles to bills of quantities
Ironmongery items by Crompton Nettlefold Stenman Ltd.
For timber and treatment see job specification.
PLAN 1:20
675
400 mm bolts, 12 mm dia, with 75mm right angled hooks
350 x 250 x 150 mm deep concrete base as F20 mix M with two bolt sockets set in
328
100
2400
200 x 200 x 150 mm deep concrete base as F.20 mix M with bolt socket set in
75 x 38 mm capping with 5 mm deep recess
125 x 38 mm top rail
100 x 100 mm timber gate post
328 x 328 mm brick pier
12 mm thick t. and g. boarding 'V' jointed
200 x 38 mm weathered bottom rail
SECTION THROUGH GATE 1:5
3 courses brickwork above bolt
6 courses brickwork above bolt
10 courses brickwork above bolt
Extra heavy pattern gate latch cat. no. 1820
114 mm oval padlock bolt cat. no. 4A
125 x 38 mm top rail
400 mm bolts, 12 mm dia, with 75 mm right-angled hooks built into brickwork to hook over 215 mm brick. Nuts and washers recessed into timber.
508 mm galvanised heavy reversible hinges
125 x 38 mm weathered brace
125 x 63 mm stiles (meeting stiles rebated)
12 mm thick t. and g. boarding 'V' jointed
381 mm cross pattern bolts cat no. 597
1000
300 min
150
225
60 mm clearance
350 x 250 x 150 mm deep concrete base
16 mm dia. c.i. sockets for round bolts cat. no. 492 cast in concrete base, plus two sockets for gates to be held in open position
Concrete foundation F.20 mix K or mix 0 if soil contains sulphates
200 x 38 mm weathered bottom rails
ELEVATION 1:20
Departmental Standard Drawing
title
TIMBER DOUBLE GATES
1000mm high and 2400 mm wide
BETWEEN BRICK PIERS DOMESTIC USE ONLY
scale
1:20 & 1:5
drawing no
D 5337
rev
bldg type
space use
element
20
feature
860
material
Hi2
key
C4
010379

6 Pavings, bollards and tree pits

5140 Paved bank
5141 Steps—paving slabs
5142 Steps—bricks
5143 Paving—cobble hazard
5144 Paving—concrete paving flags
5145 Paving—brick
5146 Paving—tar macadam—cold asphalt
5147 Paving—tar macadam—bituminous grit
5148 Paving—cultivated areas
5112 Metal bollard with padlock
5138 Tree pit—details
5139 Tree pit—details

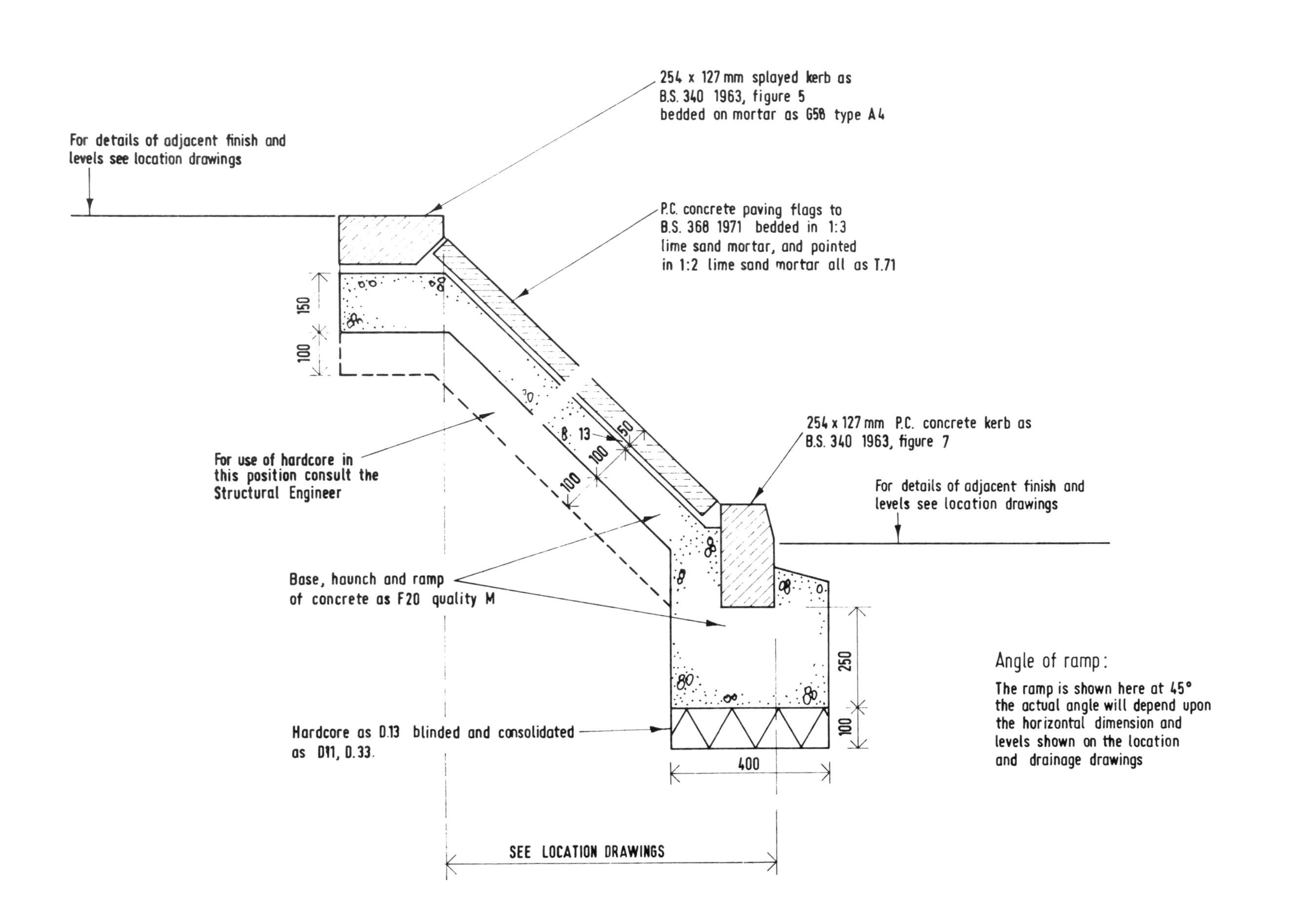

Angle of ramp:

The ramp is shown here at 45°
the actual angle will depend upon
the horizontal dimension and
levels shown on the location
and drainage drawings

GLC ILEA

Department of Architecture and Civic Design
County Hall SE1
Architect Sir Roger Walters
KBE FRIBA FI StructE

References following notes are clause numbers from G.L.C. preambles to bills of quantities

This drawing to be read in conjunction with location and drainage drawings

Departmental Standard Drawing

title
PAVED BANK.
PAVED CHANGE OF LEVEL

scale
1:10

drawing no
D5140 C

010379 - 310579 C

bldg type | space use | [element 40] | feature 365 | material Xf2 | key A

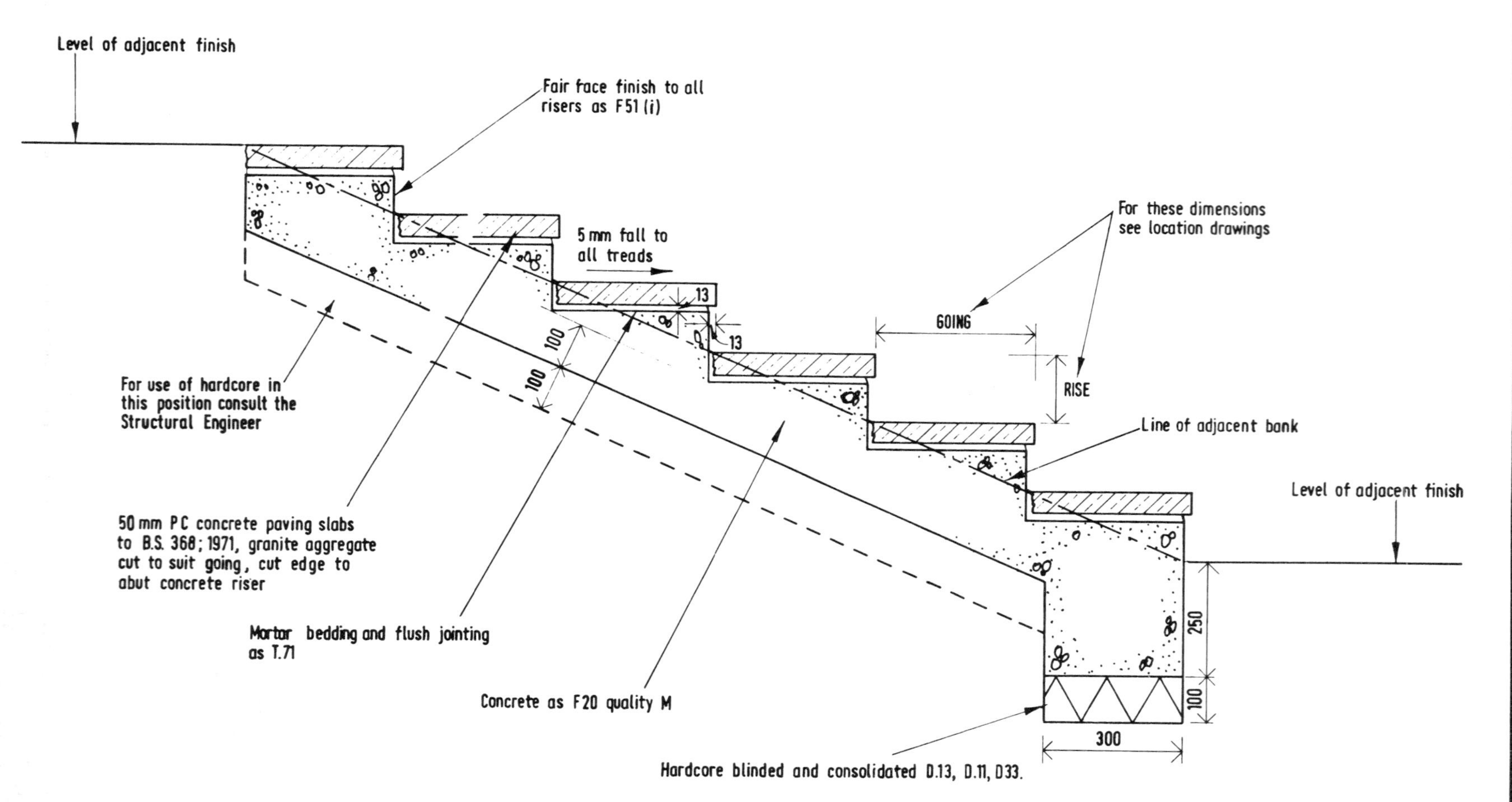

GLC ILEA

Department of Architecture and Civic Design
County Hall SE1
Architect Sir Roger Walters KBE FRIBA FI StructE

References following notes are clause numbers from G.L.C. preambles to bills of quantities

This drawing to be read in conjunction with location and drainage drawings

Departmental Standard Drawing

title
STEPS
B.S. PAVING SLABS FINISH

scale
1:10

drawing no
D5141 A

00 - 010379

bldg type | space use | element [40] | feature 361 | material Xf2 | key A

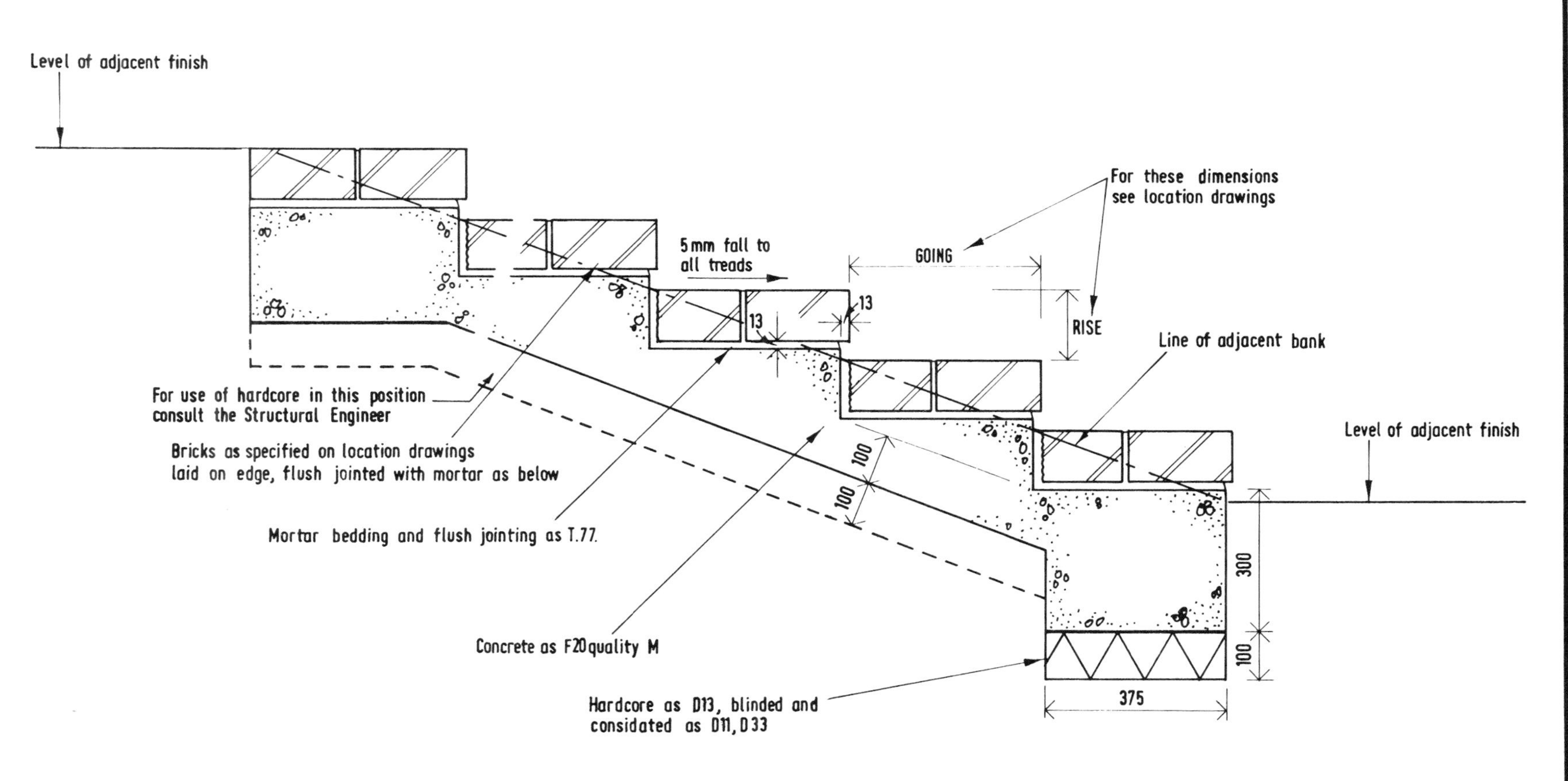

GLC ILEA

Department of Architecture and Civic Design
County Hall SE1
Architect Sir Roger Walters KBE FRIBA FI StructE

References following notes are clause numbers from G.L.C. preambles to bills of quantities

This drawing to be read in conjunction with location and drainage drawings

Departmental Standard Drawing

title

STEPS
BRICK FINISH

scale 1:10

drawing no D5142.B

bldg type | space use | element [40] | feature 361 | material Fg2 | key A

00379

Precast concrete edging slabs 203 x 900 x 50 mm
to B.S. 340 1963 figure 11, square edge
bedded and haunched in mortar as G58 mix A4
Grouted in lime sand mortar 1:2

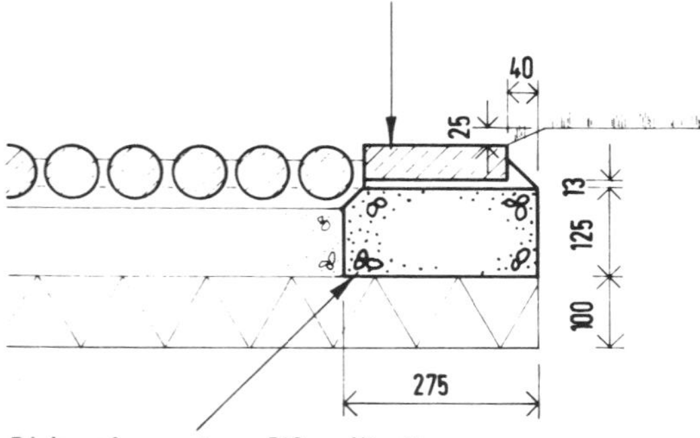

Edging of concrete as F20 quality M
on hardcore and formation as below

EDGING TO GRASSED AREA
With 203 mm slab — KEY: 1

Precast concrete paving slabs 450 x 600 x 50 mm
to B.S. 368 1971 as T.71

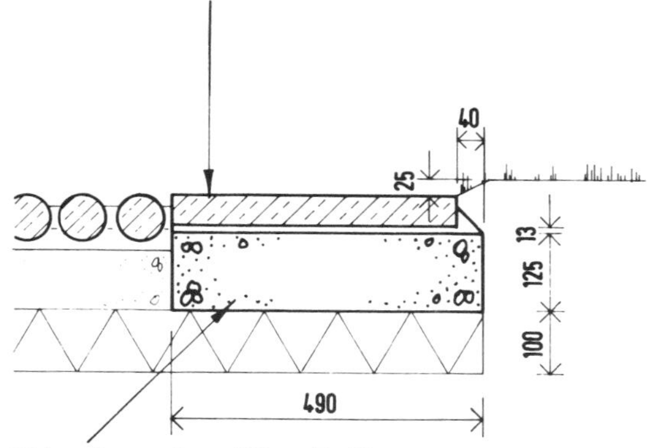

Edging of concrete as F20 quality M
on hardcore and formation as below

EDGING TO GRASSED AREA
With 450 mm slab — KEY: 2

Precast concrete paving slabs 450 x 600 x 50 mm
to B.S. 368 1971 as T.71

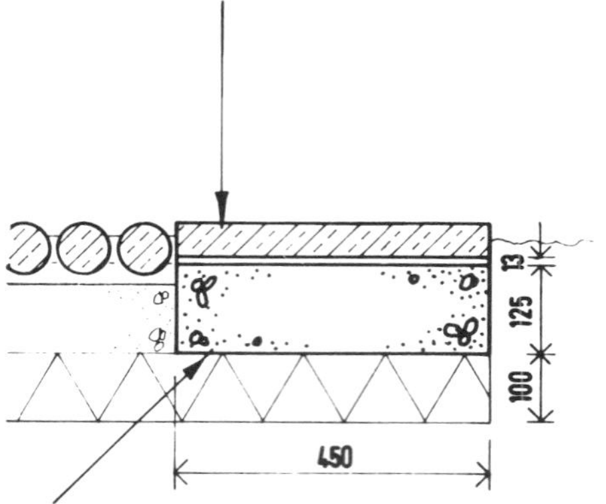

Edging of concrete as F20 quality M
on hardcore and formation as below

EDGING TO CULTIVATED AREA — KEY: 3

Flint cobbles 70 - 83 mm dia. placed upright in mortar as G58 mix A4
gaps to be filled to 2/3 cobble height with same mortar mix, dry as T.78
All watered with a fine rose. Surface of cobbles to be left clean.

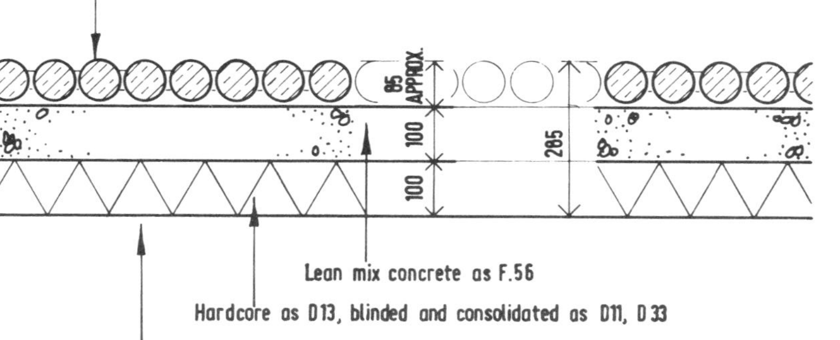

Lean mix concrete as F.56

Hardcore as D13, blinded and consolidated as D11, D33

Formation consolidated as D 32.

GENERAL CONSTRUCTION - KEY: A

GLC ILEA

Department of Architecture and Civic Design
County Hall SE1
Architect Sir Roger Walters KBE FRIBA FI StructE

References following notes are clause numbers from G.L.C. preambles to bills of quantities

This drawing to be read in conjunction with location and drainage drawings

Departmental Standard Drawing

title
PAVINGS
COBBLE HAZARD

scale
1:10

drawing no
D5143

010379
bldg type | space use | element [40] | feature 325 | material Fe3 | key as drawing

Edging of concrete as F20 quality M

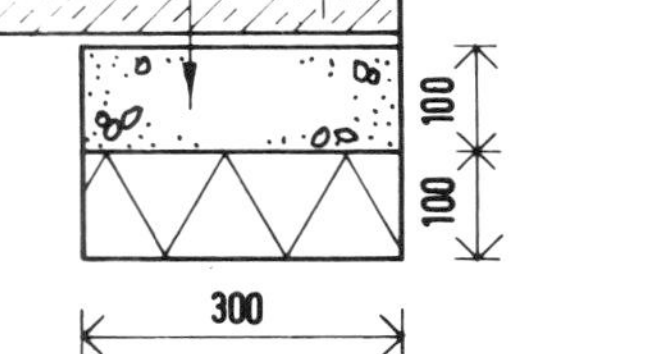

300

EDGE TO GRASSED AREA – KEY: 1

Edging of concrete as F20 quality M

125
100
300

EDGE TO CULTIVATED AREA – KEY: 2

50 mm precast concrete paving slabs
bedded and grouted as T.71

Hardcore as D13 blinded as D11
compacted as D33

13 50
100 OR 150
163 OR 213

Formation consolidated as D 32

GENERAL CONSTRUCTION HARDCORE BASE

100 mm hardcore base KEY: A

150 mm hardcore base KEY: B

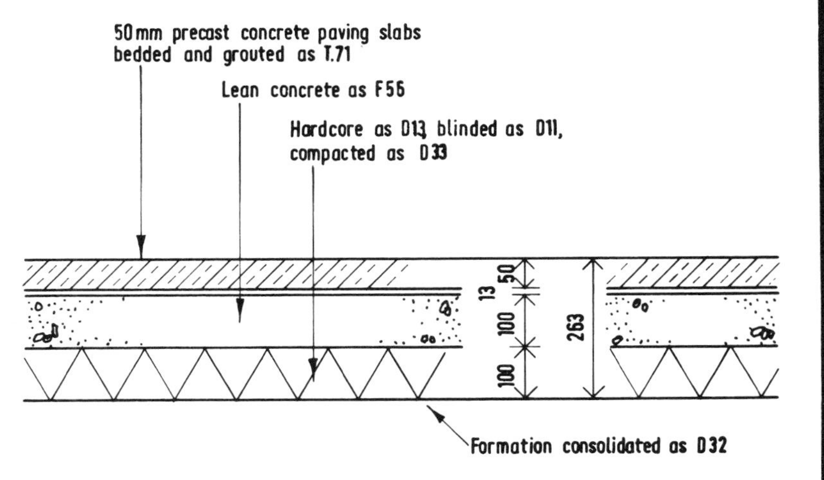

GENERAL CONSTRUCTION CONCRETE BASE – KEY: C

GLC ILEA

**Department of Architecture
and Civic Design
County Hall SE1**

Architect Sir Roger Walters
KBE FRIBA FI StructE

References following notes are clause numbers from G.L.C. preambles to bills of quantities

This drawing to be read in conjunction with location and drainage drawings

Departmental Standard Drawing

title

PAVINGS

B.S. PRECAST CONCRETE PAVING FLAGS

scale

1:10

drawing no

D5144

00 - 010379

bldg type | space use | element [40] | feature 325 | material Xf2 | key as drawing

GLC ILEA

Department of Architecture and Civic Design
County Hall SE1
Architect Sir Roger Walters KBE FRIBA FI StructE

Brick paving laid to pattern as shown on plan, on 50mm approx. hoggin, and similar central infill.

1462·5 (Brick dim.)

562·5 (Brick dim.)

38

900 or 600

200

1100

Tree pit excavated by builder

Existing subsoil cleaned and broken by builder as D.17.

SECTION

NB. Under no circumstances is the top of the rootball to be cut or damaged. Should the top of the planted rootball be too high for this detail to be built as shown, any variation or remedial work must be agreed with the Architect's and Parks Department's representatives on site.

For details of adjacent finishes see job layout drawing.

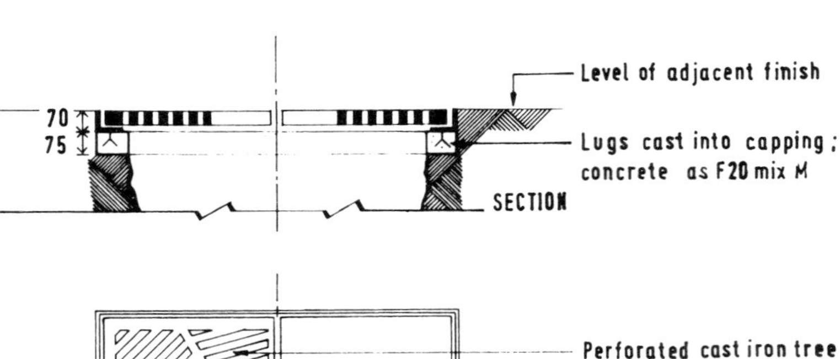

Perforated cast iron tree grid in two sections (pattern only partly shown)

and cast iron angle frame with anchoring lugs

1200 sq overall frame

PLAN CAST IRON TREE GRID

Finish as shown on site layout drawing brought up to and neatly finished around opening for tree.

150

SECTION

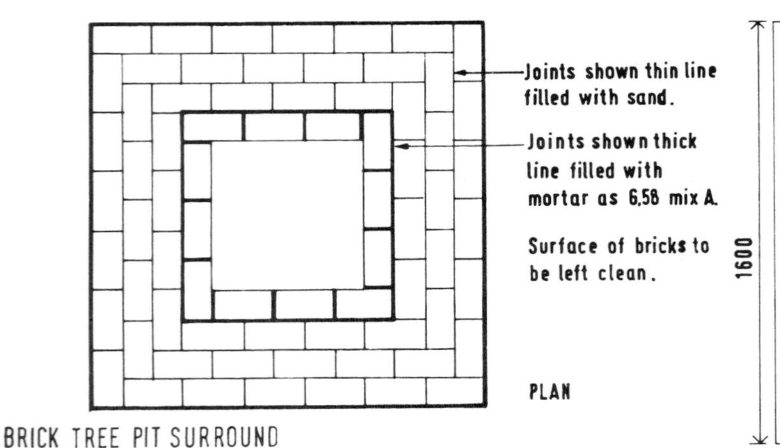

BRICK TREE PIT SURROUND

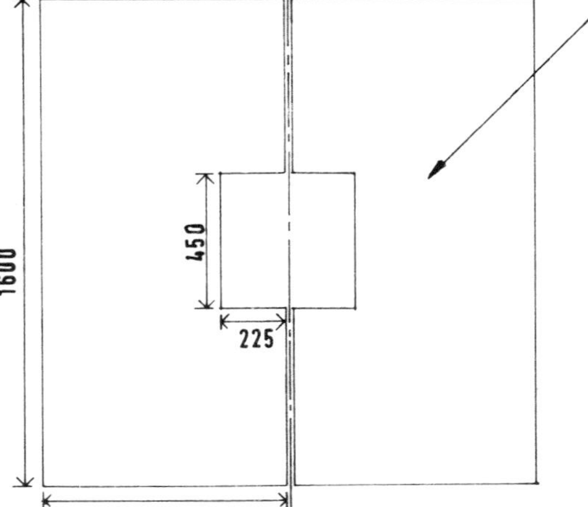

Precast (by builder) concrete tree pit cover in two halves.

Concrete - "no fines":
1 part cement
6 parts 10-20 mm aggregate

Reinforcement: 1 layer steel mesh as B.S.4483:1969, ref A 142, laid centrally, and finishing 60 mm from any edge.

N.B:-

Final placement of cover slabs and finish over to take place after soiling and planting. Perforated slabs or open joint construction recommended to facilitate water penetration.

PLAN CONCRETE TREE PIT COVER

References following notes are clause numbers from G.L.C. preambles to bills of quantities.

This drawing to be read in conjunction with site layout/drainage drawing

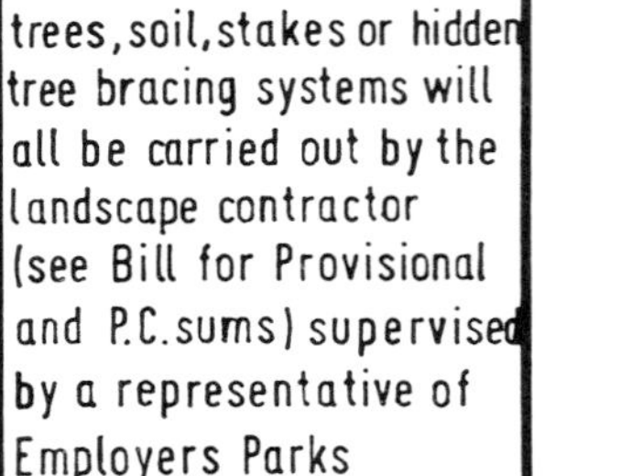

Soiling and planting to these treepits, including supply and fixing of trees, soil, stakes or hidden tree bracing systems will all be carried out by the landscape contractor (see Bill for Provisional and P.C. sums) supervised by a representative of Employers Parks Department: see also clause D.8.

Departmental Standard Drawing

title
TREE PITS
PLAIN EXCAVATION WITH COVERS OR BRICK PAVING TOPPING

scale 1:20

drawing no D5139

00-010379

bldg type | space use | element 40 | feature 329 | material | key as drawing

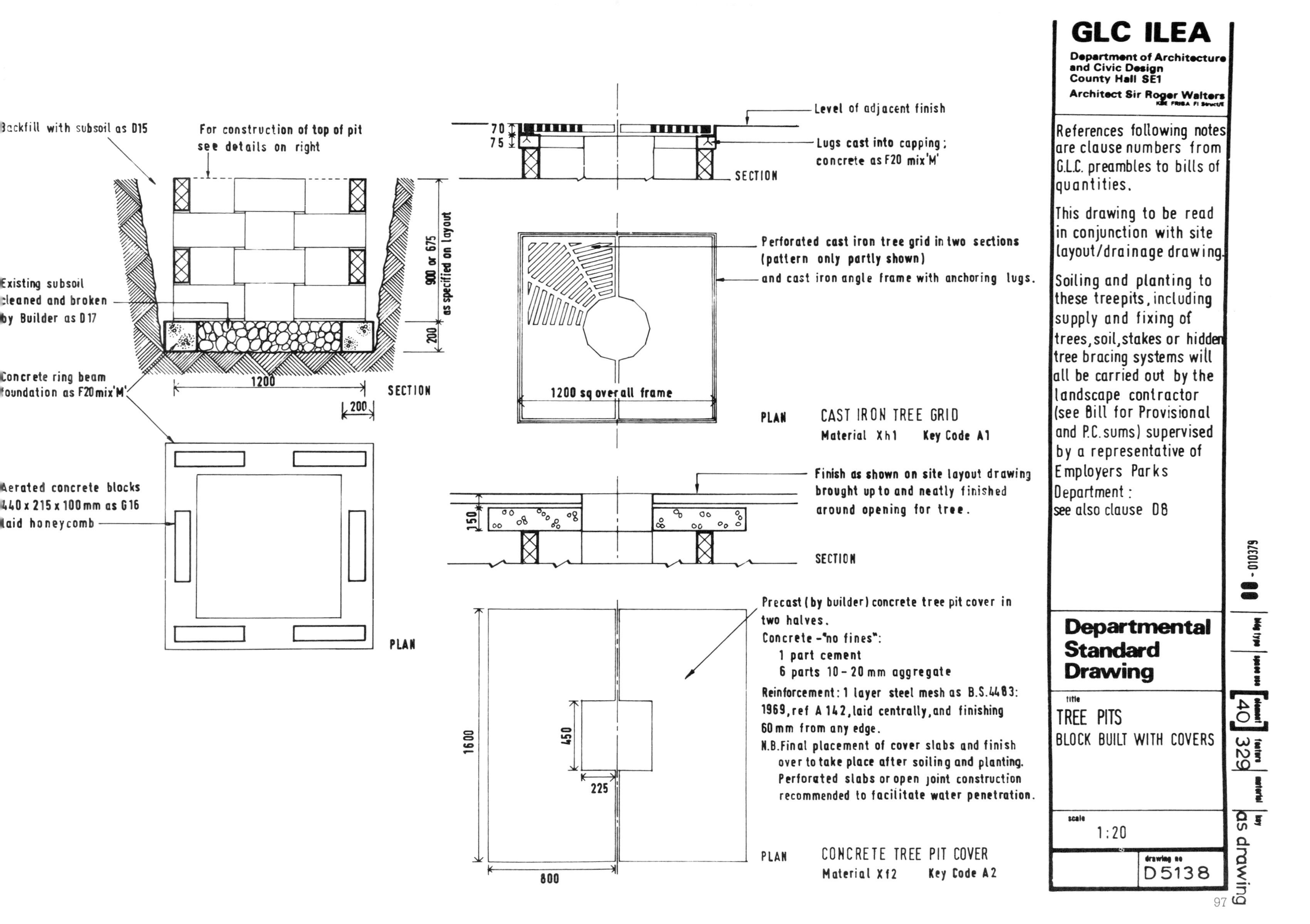
GLC ILEA
Department of Architecture and Civic Design
County Hall SE1
Architect Sir Roger Walters
Backfill with subsoil as D15
For construction of top of pit see details on right
Existing subsoil cleaned and broken by Builder as D17
Concrete ring beam foundation as F20 mix 'M'
900 or 675 as specified on layout
200
1200
200
SECTION
Aerated concrete blocks 440 x 215 x 100 mm as G16 laid honeycomb
PLAN
Level of adjacent finish
70
75
Lugs cast into capping; concrete as F20 mix 'M'
SECTION
Perforated cast iron tree grid in two sections (pattern only partly shown) and cast iron angle frame with anchoring lugs.
1200 sq overall frame
PLAN
CAST IRON TREE GRID
Material Xh1 Key Code A1
Finish as shown on site layout drawing brought up to and neatly finished around opening for tree.
150
SECTION
Precast (by builder) concrete tree pit cover in two halves.
Concrete - "no fines":
1 part cement
6 parts 10 - 20 mm aggregate
Reinforcement: 1 layer steel mesh as B.S.4483: 1969, ref A 142, laid centrally, and finishing 60 mm from any edge.
N.B. Final placement of cover slabs and finish over to take place after soiling and planting. Perforated slabs or open joint construction recommended to facilitate water penetration.
1600
450
225
800
PLAN
CONCRETE TREE PIT COVER
Material Xf2 Key Code A2
References following notes are clause numbers from G.L.C. preambles to bills of quantities.
This drawing to be read in conjunction with site layout/drainage drawing.
Soiling and planting to these treepits, including supply and fixing of trees, soil, stakes or hidden tree bracing systems will all be carried out by the landscape contractor (see Bill for Provisional and P.C. sums) supervised by a representative of Employers Parks Department:
see also clause D8
Departmental Standard Drawing
title
TREE PITS
BLOCK BUILT WITH COVERS
scale
1:20
drawing no
D5138
010379
[40] 329
as drawing

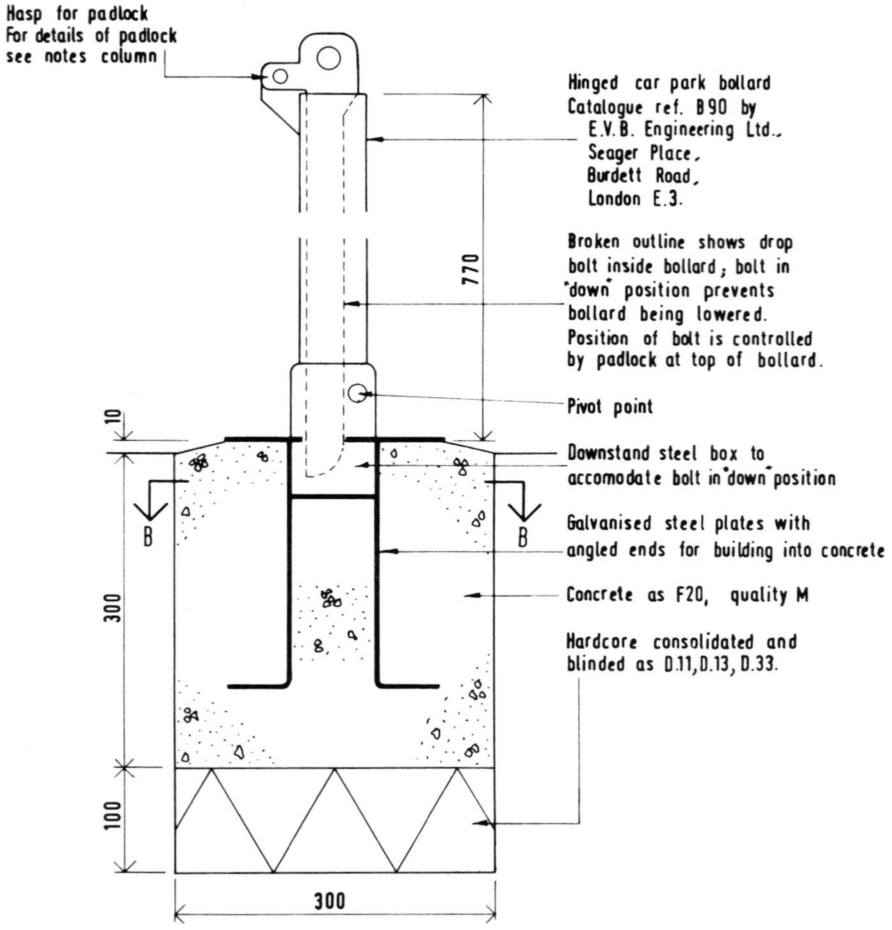

Hasp for padlock
For details of padlock
see notes column

Hinged car park bollard
Catalogue ref. B90 by
E.V.B. Engineering Ltd.,
Seager Place,
Burdett Road,
London E.3.

Broken outline shows drop bolt inside bollard; bolt in "down" position prevents bollard being lowered.
Position of bolt is controlled by padlock at top of bollard.

Pivot point

Downstand steel box to accomodate bolt in "down" position

Galvanised steel plates with angled ends for building into concrete

Concrete as F20, quality M

Hardcore consolidated and blinded as D.11, D.13, D.33.

770
10
300
100
300
B B

SECTION A–A (Post in elevation)

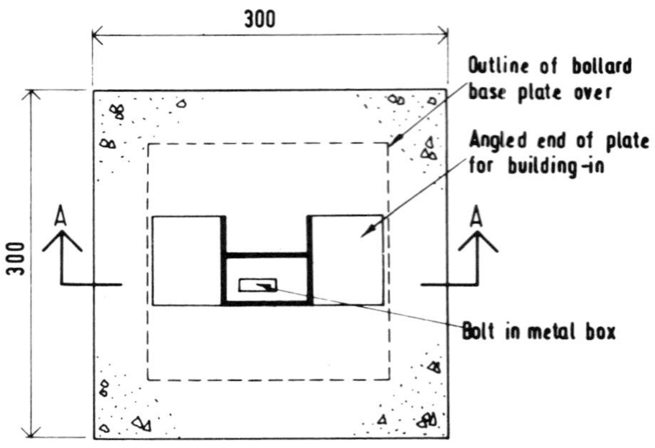

300
300
A A

Outline of bollard base plate over

Angled end of plate for building-in

Bolt in metal box

PLAN AT B–B

GLC ILEA

Department of Architecture and Civic Design
County Hall SE1
Architect Sir Roger Walters
KBE FRIBA FI StructE

References following notes are clause numbers from G.L.C. preambles to bills of quantities.

This drawing is to be read in conjunction with site layout/drainage drawing.

Padlocks:-

(a). Tenants car parking spaces:- padlock to be supplied by tenant.

(b). Fire brigade access:- employer to supply 2" (50mm) Speltre 2-lever padlock with brass cover to keyhole stamped F.B. to pass Fire Brigade key. 1 Nº per bollard and 2 Nº keys per estate.

Departmental Standard Drawing

title

BOLLARDS
FIXING DETAILS

scale
1:5

drawing no
D5112

70 | 865 | Xh2 | A

00 - 010379

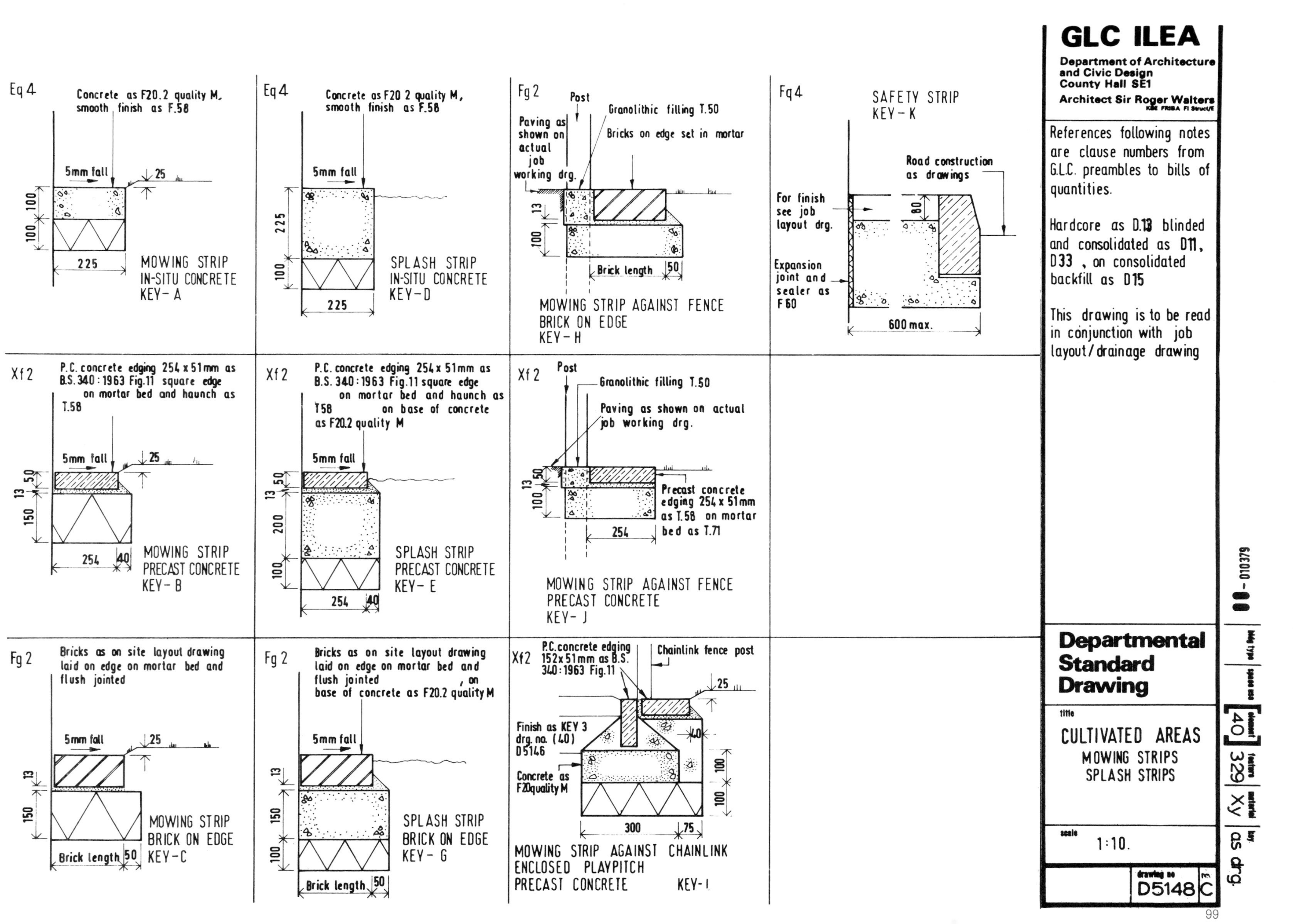
GLC ILEA
Department of Architecture and Civic Design
County Hall SE1
Architect Sir Roger Walters KBE FRIBA FI StructE
References following notes are clause numbers from G.L.C. preambles to bills of quantities.
Hardcore as D13 blinded and consolidated as D11, D33, on consolidated backfill as D15
This drawing is to be read in conjunction with job layout/drainage drawing
Eq 4
Concrete as F20.2 quality M, smooth finish as F.58
5mm fall
25
100
100
225
MOWING STRIP
IN-SITU CONCRETE
KEY- A
Eq 4
Concrete as F20.2 quality M, smooth finish as F.58
5mm fall
225
100
225
SPLASH STRIP
IN-SITU CONCRETE
KEY- D
Fg 2
Post
Granolithic filling T.50
Paving as shown on actual job working drg.
Bricks on edge set in mortar
13
100
Brick length
50
MOWING STRIP AGAINST FENCE
BRICK ON EDGE
KEY – H
Fq 4
SAFETY STRIP
KEY – K
Road construction as drawings
For finish see job layout drg.
80
Expansion joint and sealer as F60
600 max.
Xf 2
P.C. concrete edging 254 x 51mm as B.S. 340 : 1963 Fig.11 square edge on mortar bed and haunch as T.58
5mm fall
25
50
13
150
254
40
MOWING STRIP
PRECAST CONCRETE
KEY- B
Xf 2
P.C. concrete edging 254 x 51mm as B.S. 340 : 1963 Fig.11 square edge on mortar bed and haunch as T58 on base of concrete as F20.2 quality M
5mm fall
13
50
200
100
254
40
SPLASH STRIP
PRECAST CONCRETE
KEY- E
Xf 2
Post
Granolithic filling T.50
Paving as shown on actual job working drg.
13
50
100
Precast concrete edging 254 x 51mm as T.58 on mortar bed as T.71
254
MOWING STRIP AGAINST FENCE
PRECAST CONCRETE
KEY- J
Fg 2
Bricks as on site layout drawing laid on edge on mortar bed and flush jointed
5mm fall
25
13
150
Brick length
50
MOWING STRIP
BRICK ON EDGE
KEY – C
Fg 2
Bricks as on site layout drawing laid on edge on mortar bed and flush jointed , on base of concrete as F20.2 quality M
5mm fall
13
150
100
Brick length
50
SPLASH STRIP
BRICK ON EDGE
KEY – G
Xf2
P.C. concrete edging 152 x 51mm as B.S. 340 : 1963 Fig.11
Chainlink fence post
25
Finish as KEY 3 drg. no. (40) D5146
40
Concrete as F20 quality M
100
100
300
75
MOWING STRIP AGAINST CHAINLINK
ENCLOSED PLAYPITCH
PRECAST CONCRETE
KEY- I
Departmental Standard Drawing
title
CULTIVATED AREAS
MOWING STRIPS
SPLASH STRIPS
scale
1:10.
drawing no
D5148
C
40
329
Xy
as drg.

125 x 32 mm soft wood board twice fixed with 50 mm galvanised clout nails to 38 x 38 x 450 mm shaped soft wood pegs set at 1250 mm c/c
2 no. pegs at junction of boards. Boards mitred at changes of direction. All treated with creosote before use including brush treating cut ends

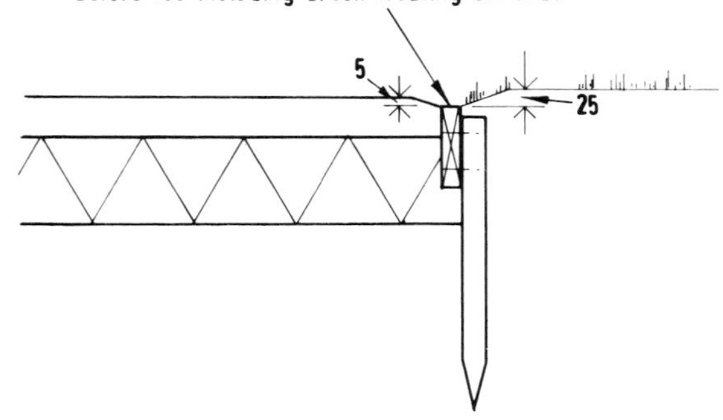

SOFT WOOD BOARD EDGING TO GRASSED AREA – KEY 4

Precast concrete edging as B.S. 340 1963 figure 11 square edged as T.58

5
25
100
100
40 152 40
232

Base and haunching in concrete as F20 quality M on hardcore and formation as below

HORIZONTAL PRECAST CONCRETE EDGING TO GRASSED AREA – KEY 5

152 x 51 mm precast concrete edging

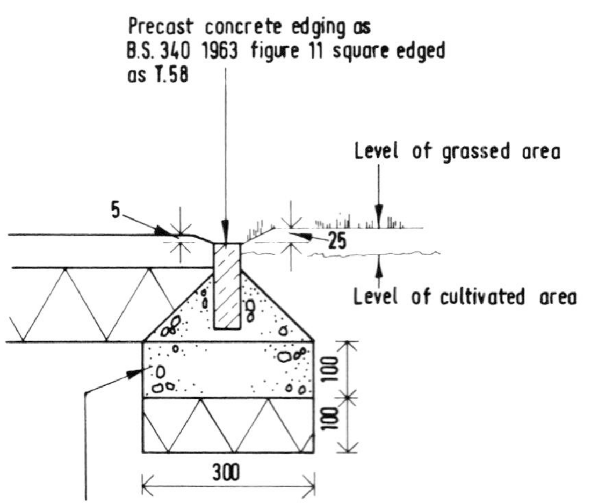

Base and haunching in concrete as F20 quality M on hardcore and formation as below

VERTICAL PRECAST CONCRETE EDGING TO GRASSED OR CULTIVATED AREA – KEY 6

152 x 51 mm precast concrete edging

64 mm tar paving in 2 courses with bituminous grit finish supplied and laid by nominated subcontractor (Employers scheduled tar paving contractor)

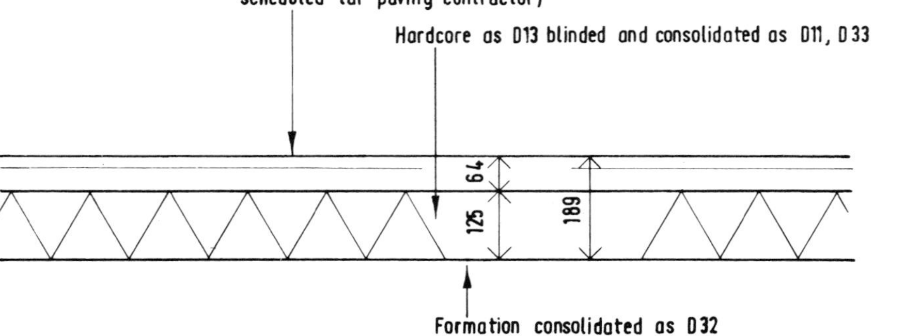

GENERAL CONSTRUCTION – KEY B

GLC ILEA
Department of Architecture and Civic Design
County Hall SE1
Architect Sir Roger Walters KBE FRIBA FI StructE

References following notes are clause numbers from G.L.C. preambles to bills of quantities

This drawing to be read in conjunction with location and drainage drawings

Departmental Standard Drawing

title

PAVINGS

64 mm TAR MACADAM BITUMINOUS GRIT FINISH

scale

1:10

drawing no

D5147

[40] 325 Ps5 as drawing

0 - 010379

GLC ILEA
Department of Architecture and Civic Design
County Hall SE1
Architect Sir Roger Walters KBE FRIBA FI StructE

References following notes are clause numbers from G.L.C. preambles to bills of quantities

This drawing to be read in conjunction with location and drainage drawings

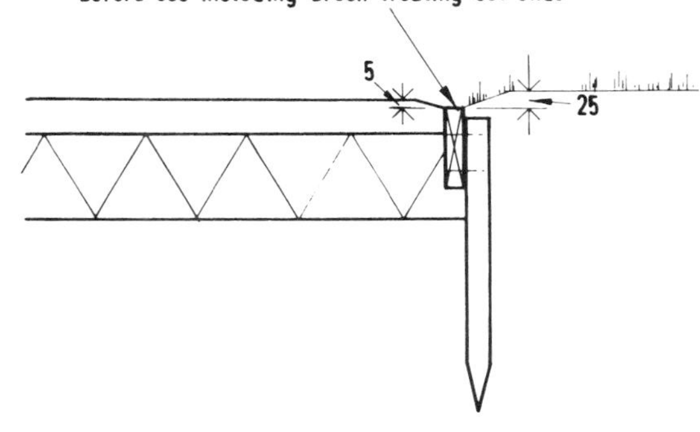

SOFT WOOD BOARD EDGING TO GRASSED AREA – KEY 1

Precast concrete edging as B.S. 340 1963 figure 11 square edged as T.58

5

25

100

100

40 152 40

232

Base and haunching in concrete as F20 quality M on hardcore and formation as below

HORIZONTAL PRECAST CONCRETE EDGING TO GRASSED AREA – KEY 2

152 x 51 mm precast concrete edging

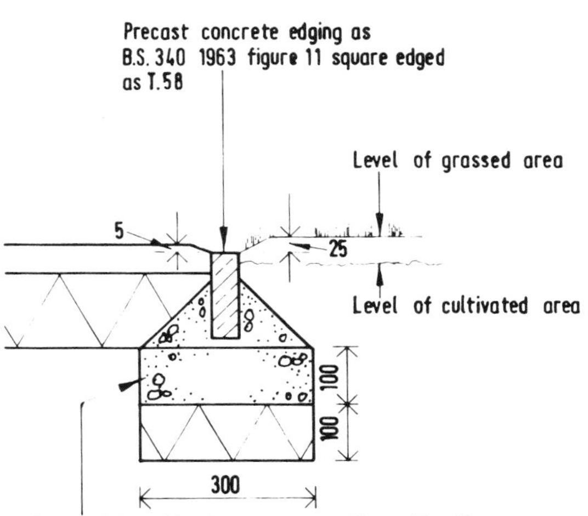

Base and haunching in concrete as F20 quality M on hardcore and formation as below

VERTICAL PRECAST CONCRETE EDGING TO GRASSED OR CULTIVATED AREA – KEY 3

152 x 51 mm precast concrete edging

61 mm tar paving in 2 courses with cold asphalt finish supplied and laid by nominated subcontractor (Employers scheduled tar paving contractor)

Hardcore as D13 blinded and consolidated as D11, D:33.

61

125

186

Formation consolidated as D32

GENERAL CONSTRUCTION – KEY A

Departmental Standard Drawing

title

PAVINGS

61 mm TAR MACADAM COLD ASPHALT FINISH

scale 1:10

drawing no D5146

00 - 010379 | bldg type | space use | element [40] | feature 325 | material Ps5 | key as drawing

GLC ILEA

Department of Architecture and Civic Design
County Hall SE1
Architect Sir Roger Walters KBE FRIBA FI StructE

References following notes are clause numbers from G.L.C. preambles to bills of quantities

This drawing to be read in conjunction with location and drainage drawings

Edge formed in concrete as F20 type M
Brick headers on edge
25
75
100
100
300
300

EDGE TO GRASSED AREA - KEY : 1

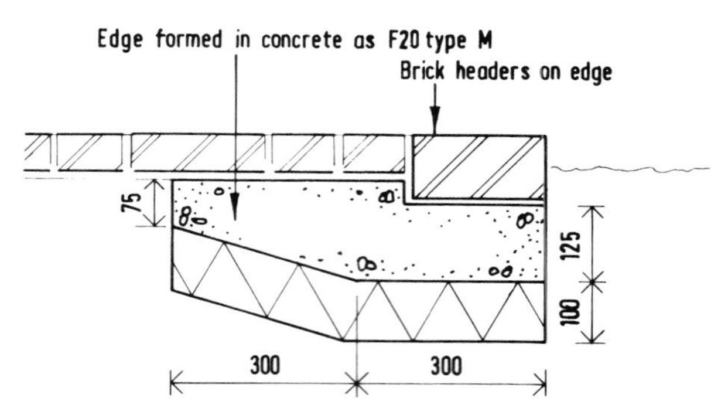

EDGE TO CULTIVATED AREA - KEY: 2

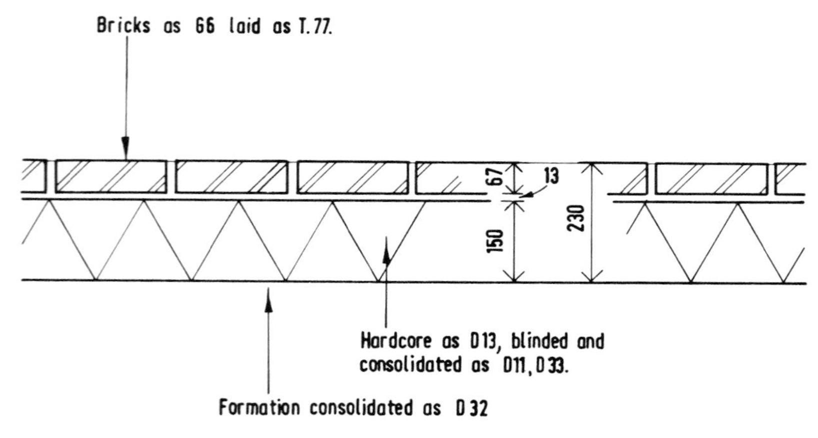

GENERAL CONSTRUCTION HARDCORE BASE - KEY: A

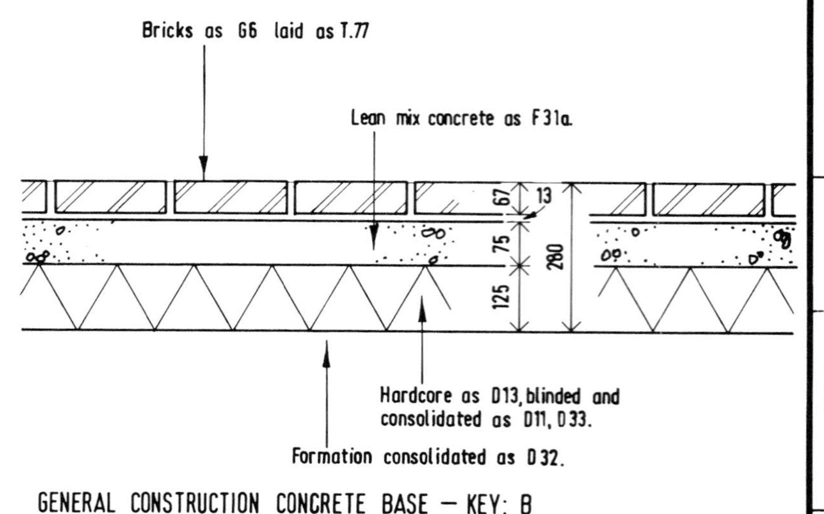

GENERAL CONSTRUCTION CONCRETE BASE — KEY: B

Departmental Standard Drawing

title
PAVINGS
BRICK

scale
1:10

drawing no
D5145

[40]325|Fg2| as drawing

010379

7
Play spaces and ball games areas

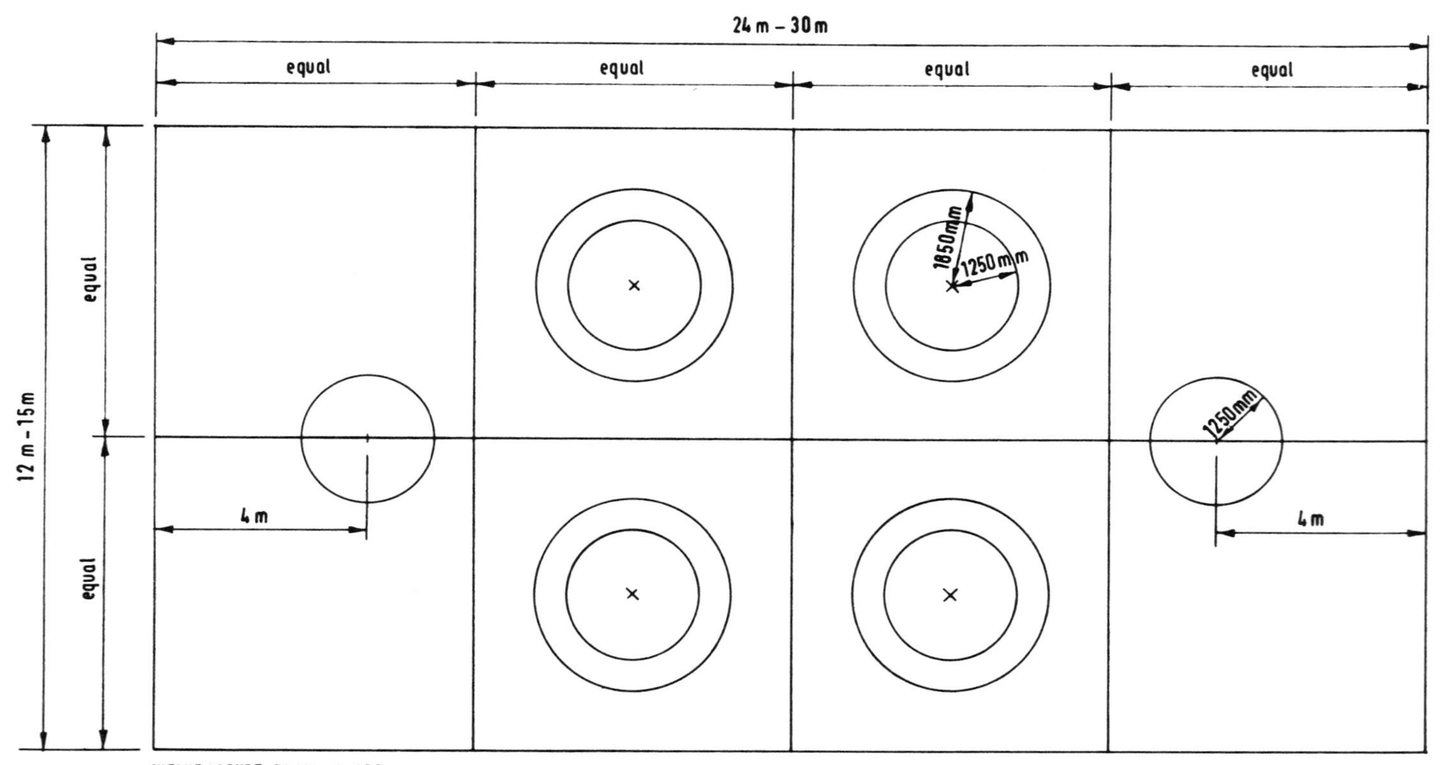

INFANT COURT PLAN 1:100

NOTES :

Court markings should be 1metre clearance minimum from all walls or obstructions

Lines to be 50 mm wide in white.

Dimensions are to inside of lines

Circles to be 2·5 m dia. and 3·7 m dia. lines to be in yellow.

Marking paint to be spirit resin type as V55

See architects note regarding overall dimensions

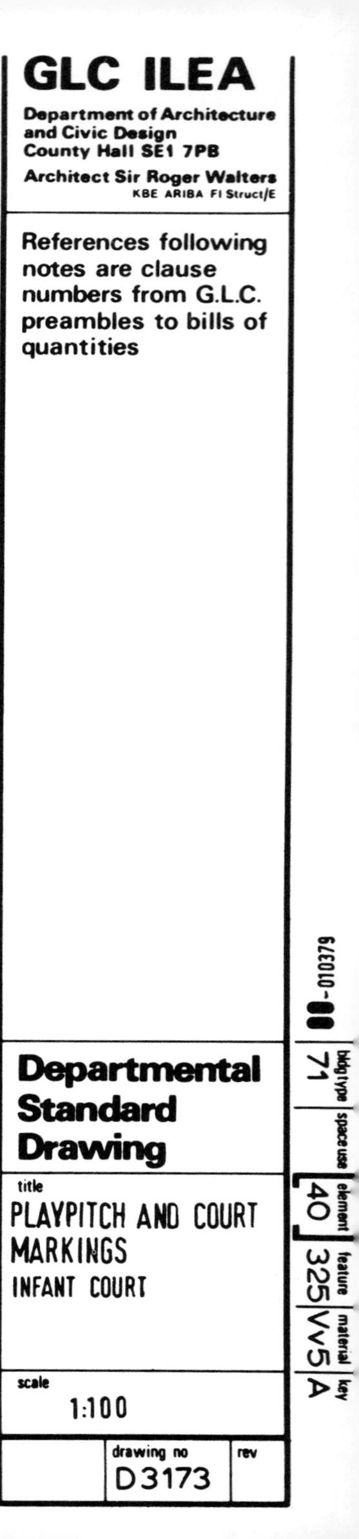

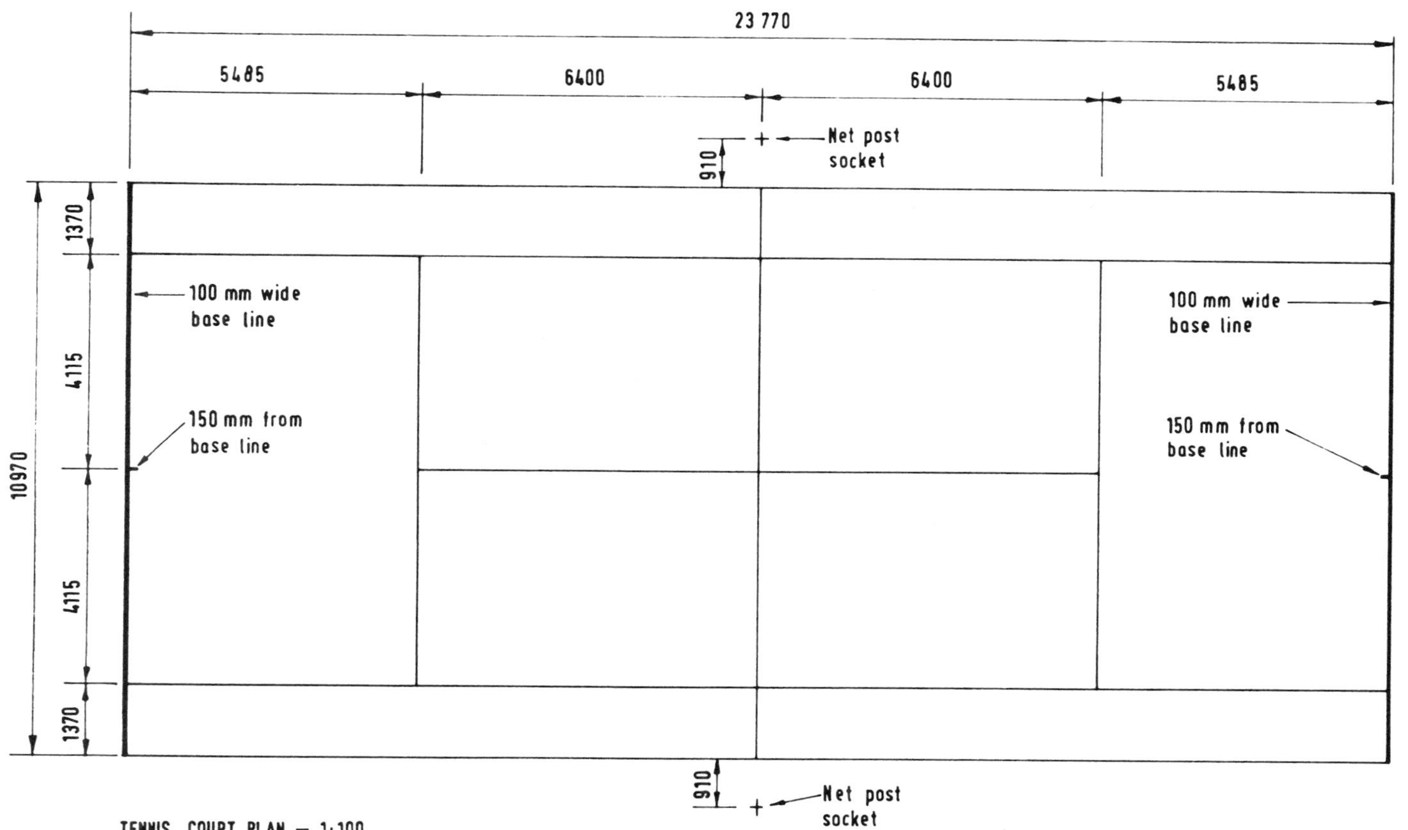

TENNIS COURT PLAN — 1:100

NOTES:

Court markings should be minimum 3 metres clear at ends and 2 metres clear at sides from any walls or obstructions.

Base lines to be 100 mm wide, other lines 50 mm wide, all in white.

Dimensions shown to outside of lines.

Marking paint to be spirit resin type as V55

GLC ILEA

Department of Architecture and Civic Design
County Hall SE1 7PB
Architect Sir Roger Walters
KBE ARIBA FI Struct/E

References following notes are clause numbers from G.L.C. preambles to bills of quantities

010379

Departmental Standard Drawing

title
PLAYPITCH AND COURT MARKINGS
TENNIS COURTS

scale
1:100

drawing no D3174

rev

bldg type	space use	element	feature	material	key
71		40	325	Vv5	B

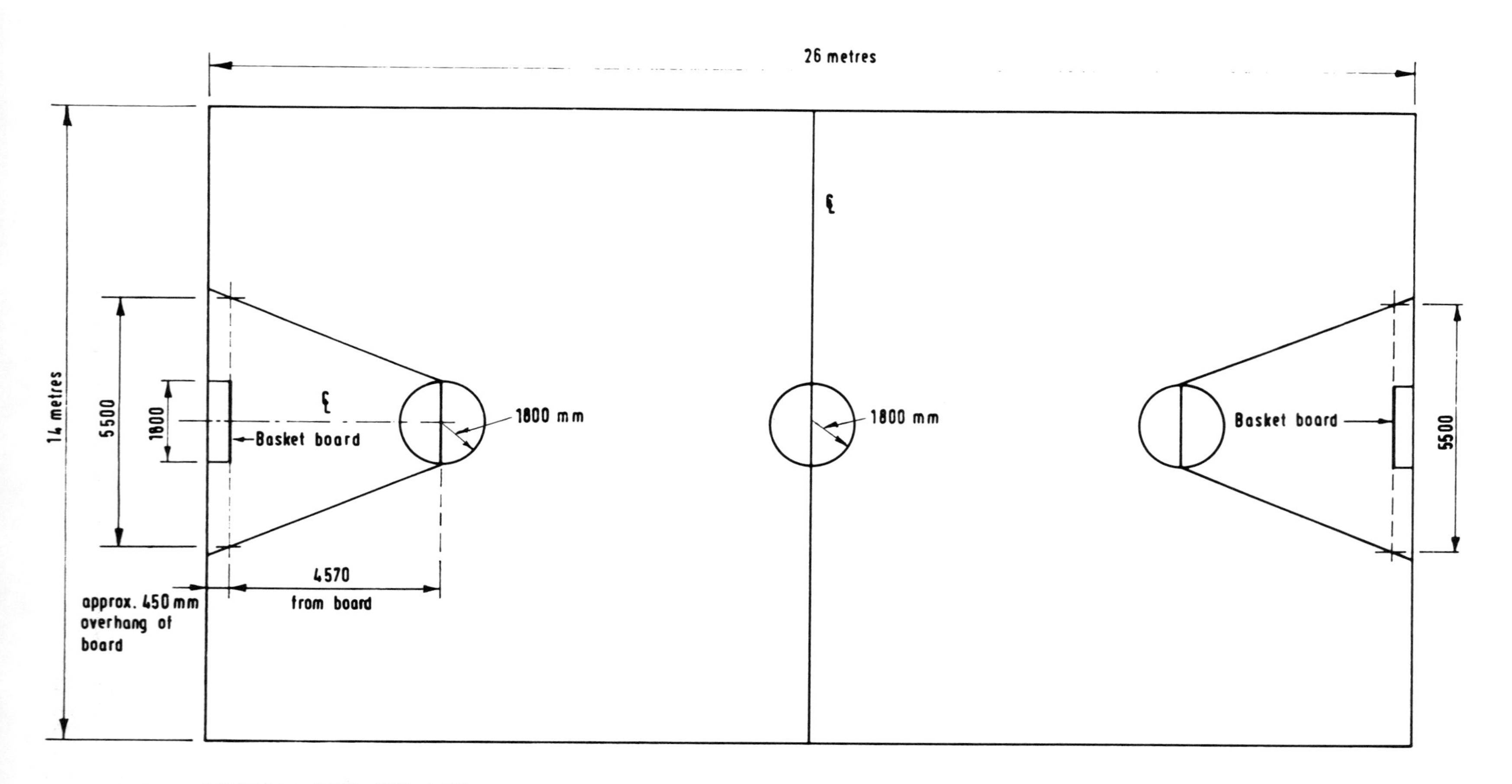

BASKET BALL COURT – PLAN 1:100

NOTES:

Court markings – min. 1 metre clear from all walls or obstructions.

Lines to be 50 mm wide in white. Dimensions are to inside of lines.

Marking paint to be spirit resin type as V.55

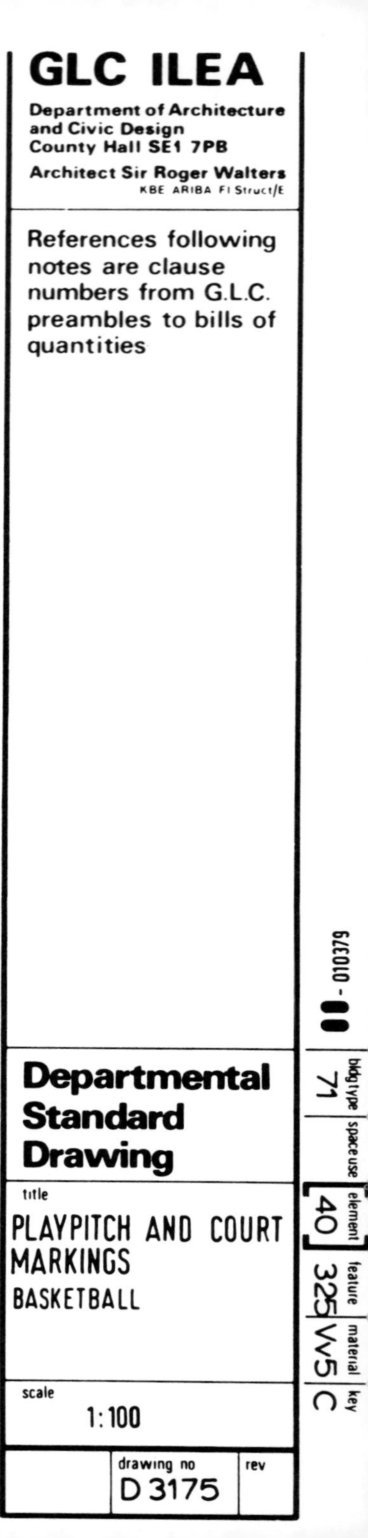

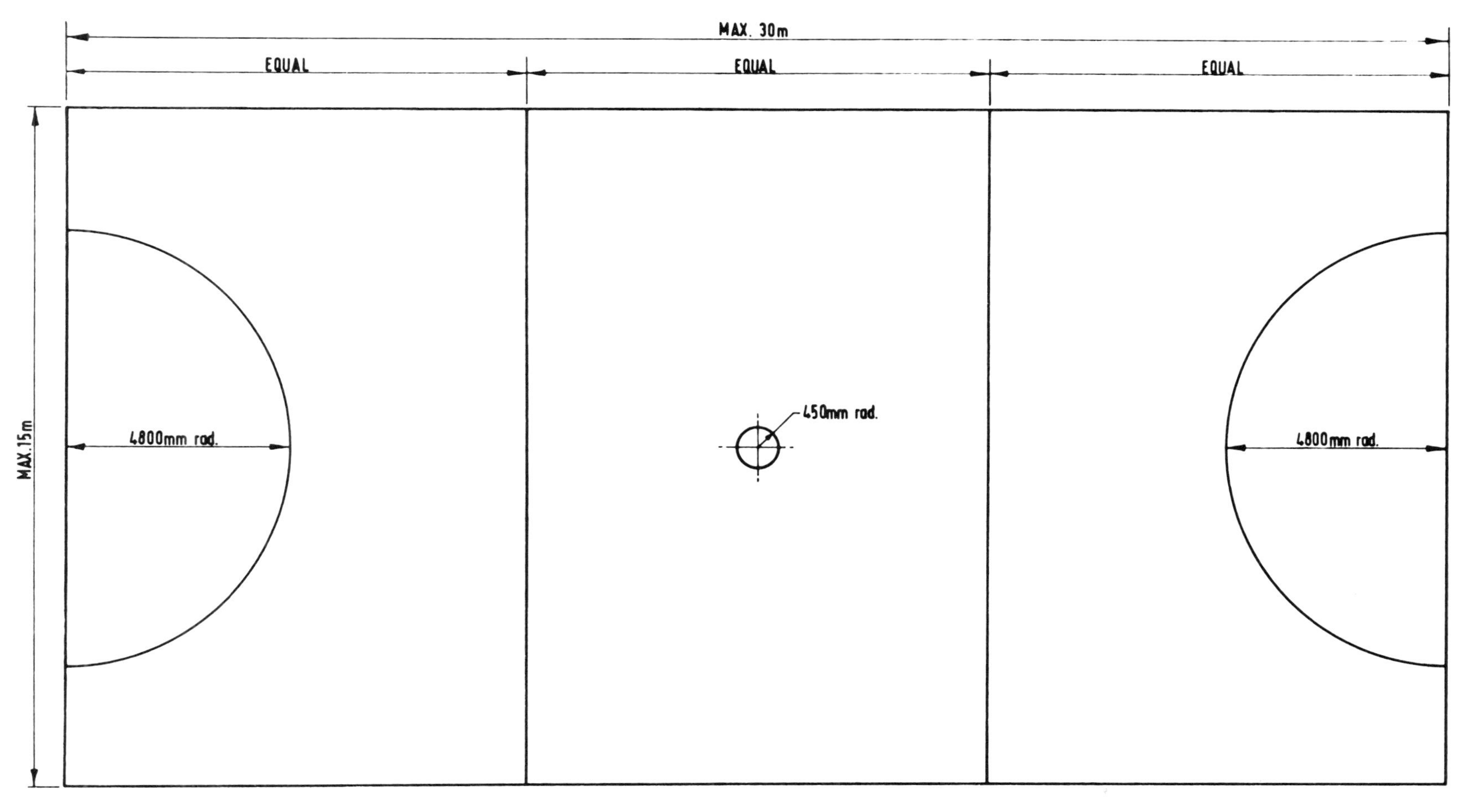

NETBALL COURT PLAN

NOTES :-

Court markings — min. 1000mm clear from all walls or obstructions.

Lines to be 50mm wide in white, inside dimensions.

Marking paint to be spirit resin type as V.55

GLC ILEA

Department of Architecture and Civic Design
County Hall SE1 7PB

Architect Sir Roger Walters
KBE ARIBA FI Struct/E

References following notes are clause numbers from G.L.C. preambles to bills of quantities

Departmental Standard Drawing

title
PLAYPITCH AND COURT MARKINGS.
NETBALL COURT.

scale
1 : 100.

drawing no D3176

rev

bldg type 71 | space use | element [40] | feature 325 | material Vv5 | key D

010379

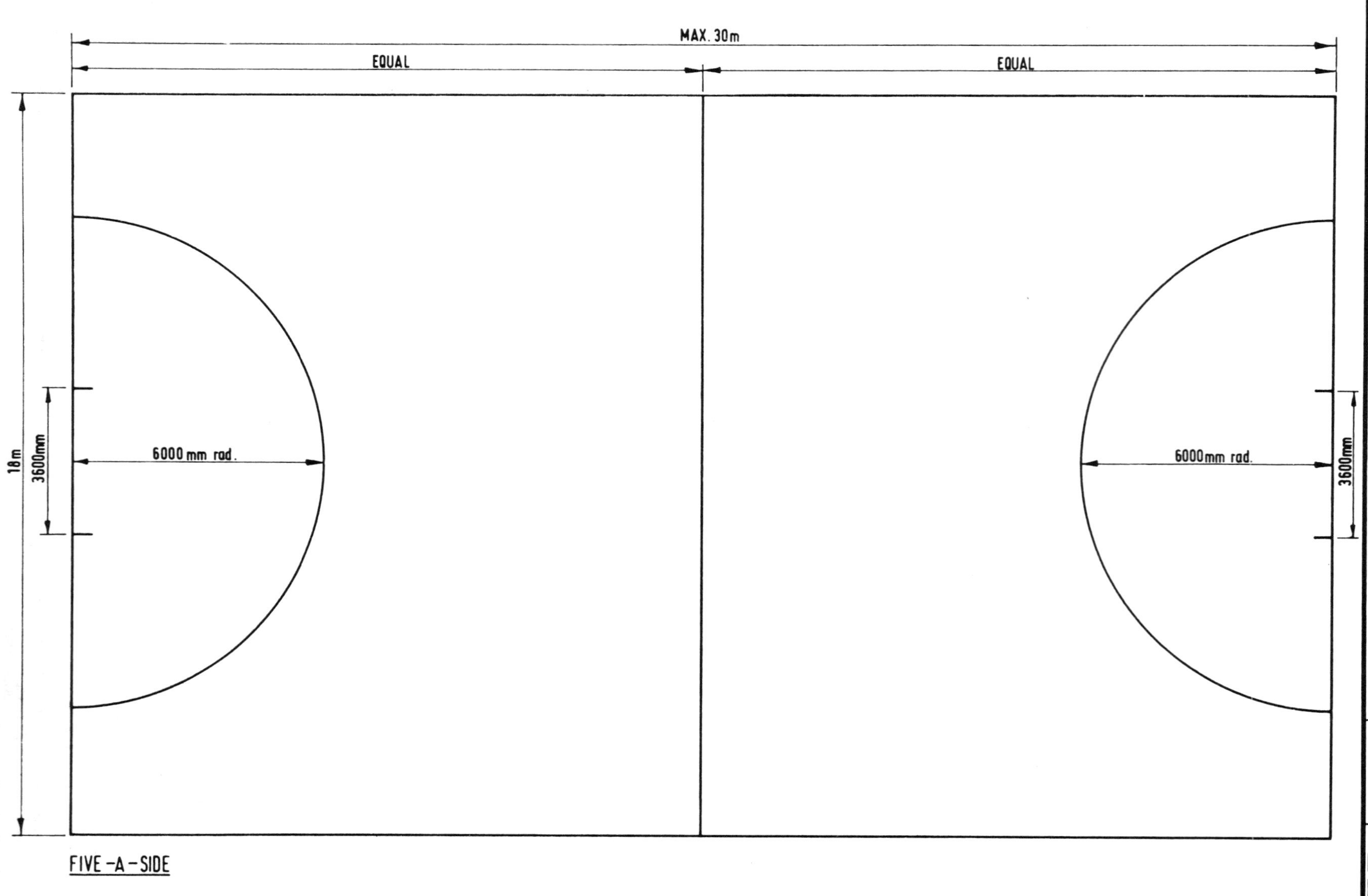

NOTES:-

Court markings – min. 1000mm clear from all walls or obstructions.

Lines to be 50mm wide in white, inside dimensions.

Marking paint to be spirit resin type as V.55

GLC ILEA

Department of Architecture and Civic Design
County Hall SE1 7PB
Architect Sir Roger Walters
KBE ARIBA FI Struct/E

References following notes are clause numbers from G.L.C. preambles to bills of quantities

Departmental Standard Drawing

title
PLAYPITCH AND COURT MARKINGS.
FIVE-A-SIDE.

scale
1:100.

drawing no
D 3177

rev

bldg type: 71 | space use: | element: [40] | feature: 325 | material: Vv5 | key: E

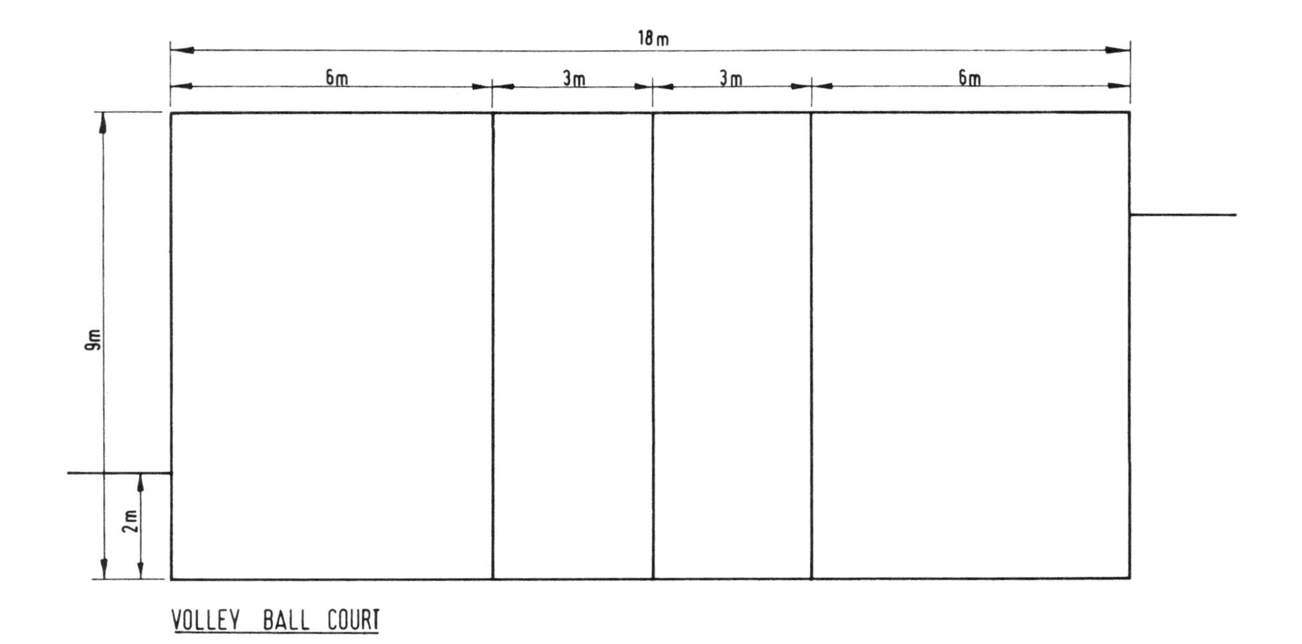

VOLLEY BALL COURT

NOTES:-

Court markings – min. 1000mm clear of all walls or obstructions.

Lines to be 50mm wide in white, inside dimensions.

Marking paint to be spirit resin type as V.55

GLC ILEA

Department of Architecture and Civic Design
County Hall SE1 7PB
Architect Sir Roger Walters
KBE ARIBA FI Struct/E

References following notes are clause numbers from G.L.C. preambles to bills of quantities

Departmental Standard Drawing

title
PLAYPITCH AND COURT MARKINGS.
VOLLEY BALL COURT.

scale
1:100.

drawing no D 3178 | rev

bldg type 71 | space use | element [40] | feature 325 | material Vv5 | key F

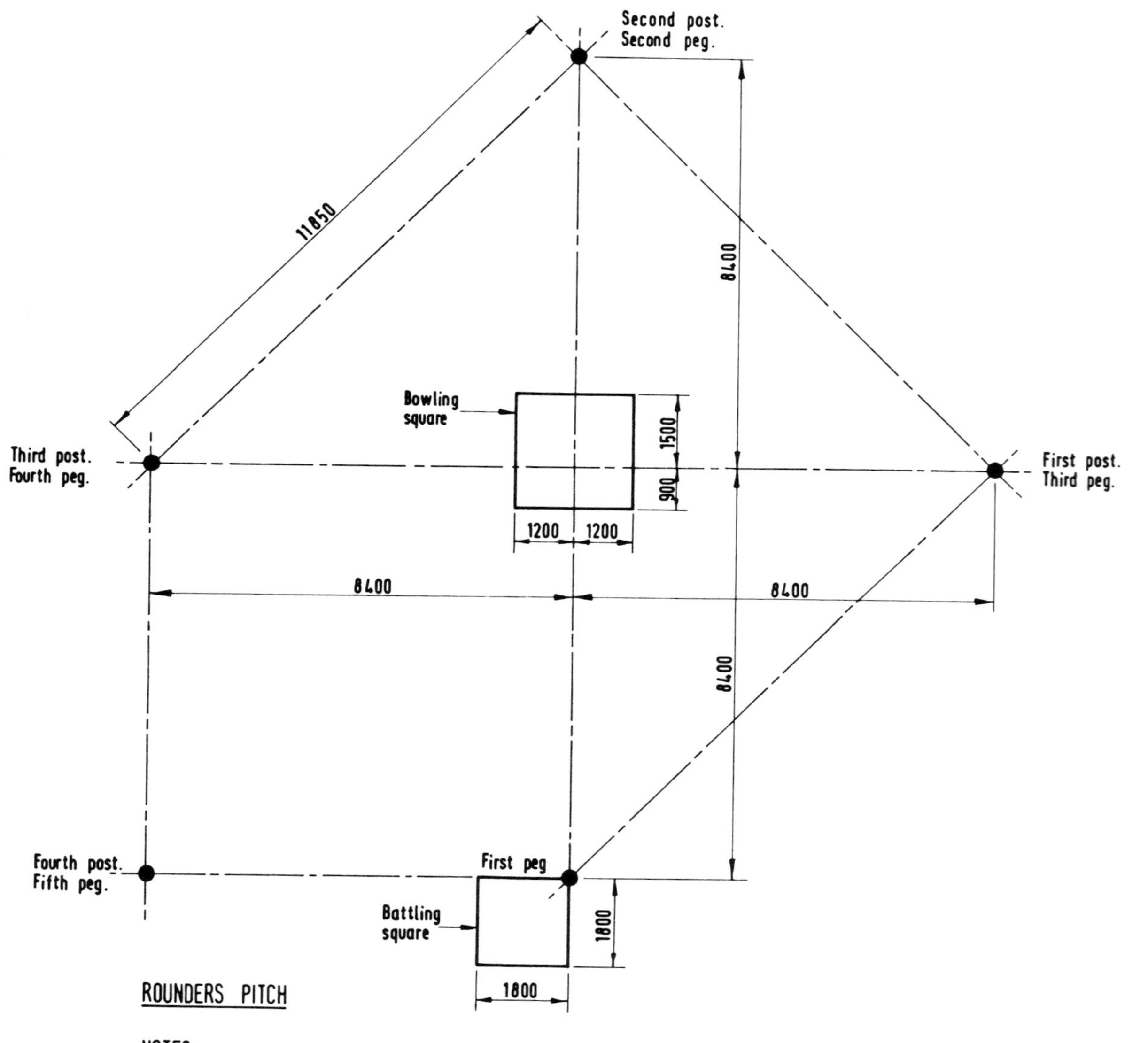

NOTES:-

Pitch markings — min. 1000mm clear of all walls or obstructions.

Lines to be 50mm wide in white, inside dimensions.

Marking paint to be spirit resin type as V.55

GLC ILEA

Department of Architecture and Civic Design
County Hall SE1 7PB
Architect Sir Roger Walters
KBE ARIBA FI Struct/E

References following notes are clause numbers from G.L.C. preambles to bills of quantities

Departmental Standard Drawing

title
PLAYPITCH AND COURT MARKINGS.
ROUNDERS PITCH.

scale
1:100.

drawing no
D 3179

rev

bldg type 71 | spaceuse | element [40] | feature 325 | material Vv5 | key G

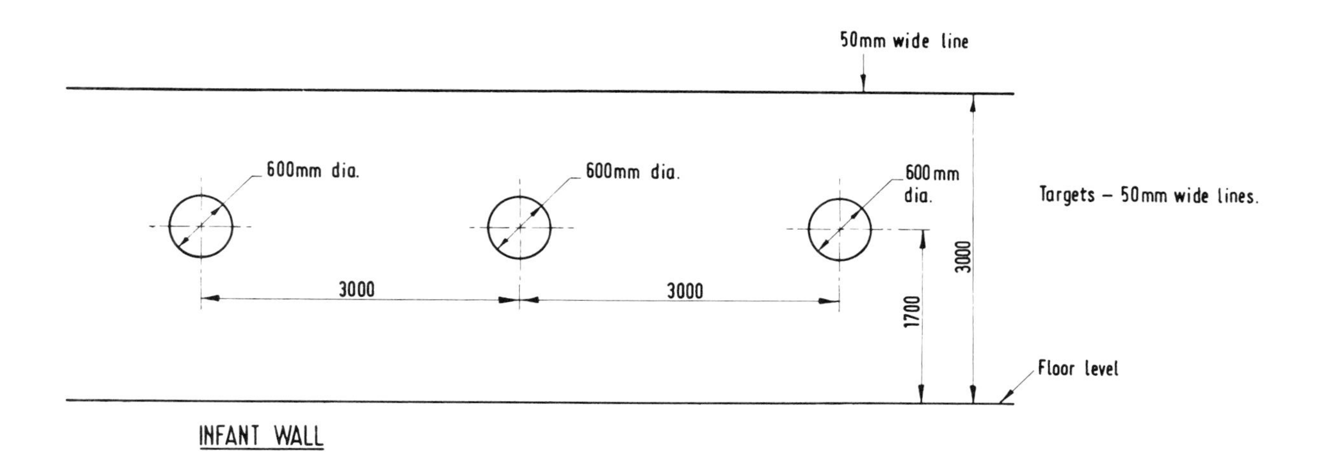

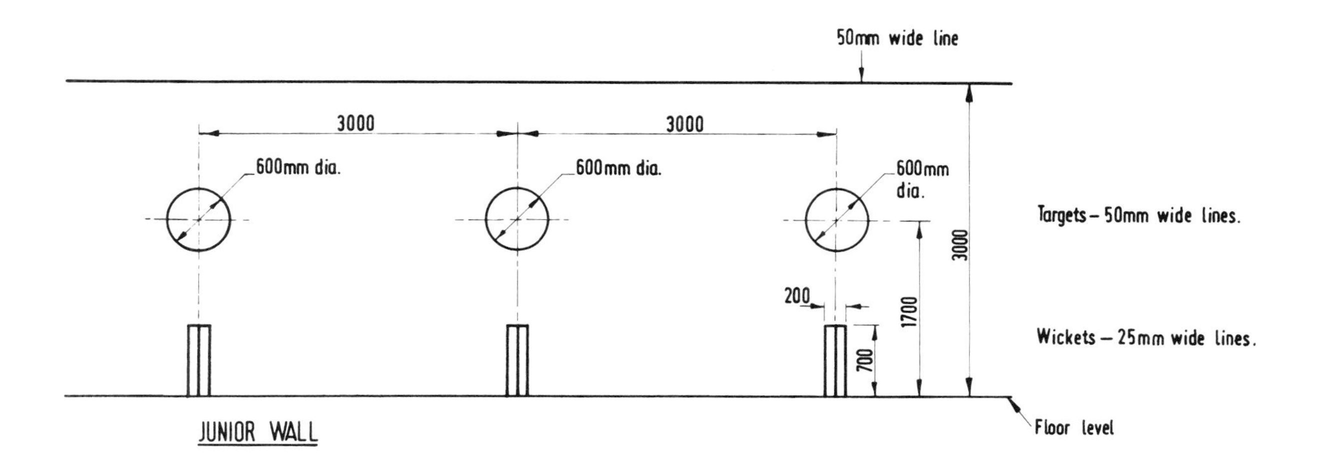

NOTES :–

Lines to be white with dimensions to outside of lines.

Marking paint to be spirit resin type as V.55.

GLC ILEA

Department of Architecture and Civic Design
County Hall SE1 7PB
Architect Sir Roger Walters
KBE ARIBA FI Struct/E

References following notes are clause numbers from G.L.C. preambles to bills of quantities

Departmental Standard Drawing

title
PLAYPITCH AND COURT MARKINGS.
INFANT WALL AND JUNIOR WALL.

scale 1: 50.

drawing no D3180 | rev

bldg type 71 | space use | element [40] | feature 325 | material Vv5 | key H

00 - 10379

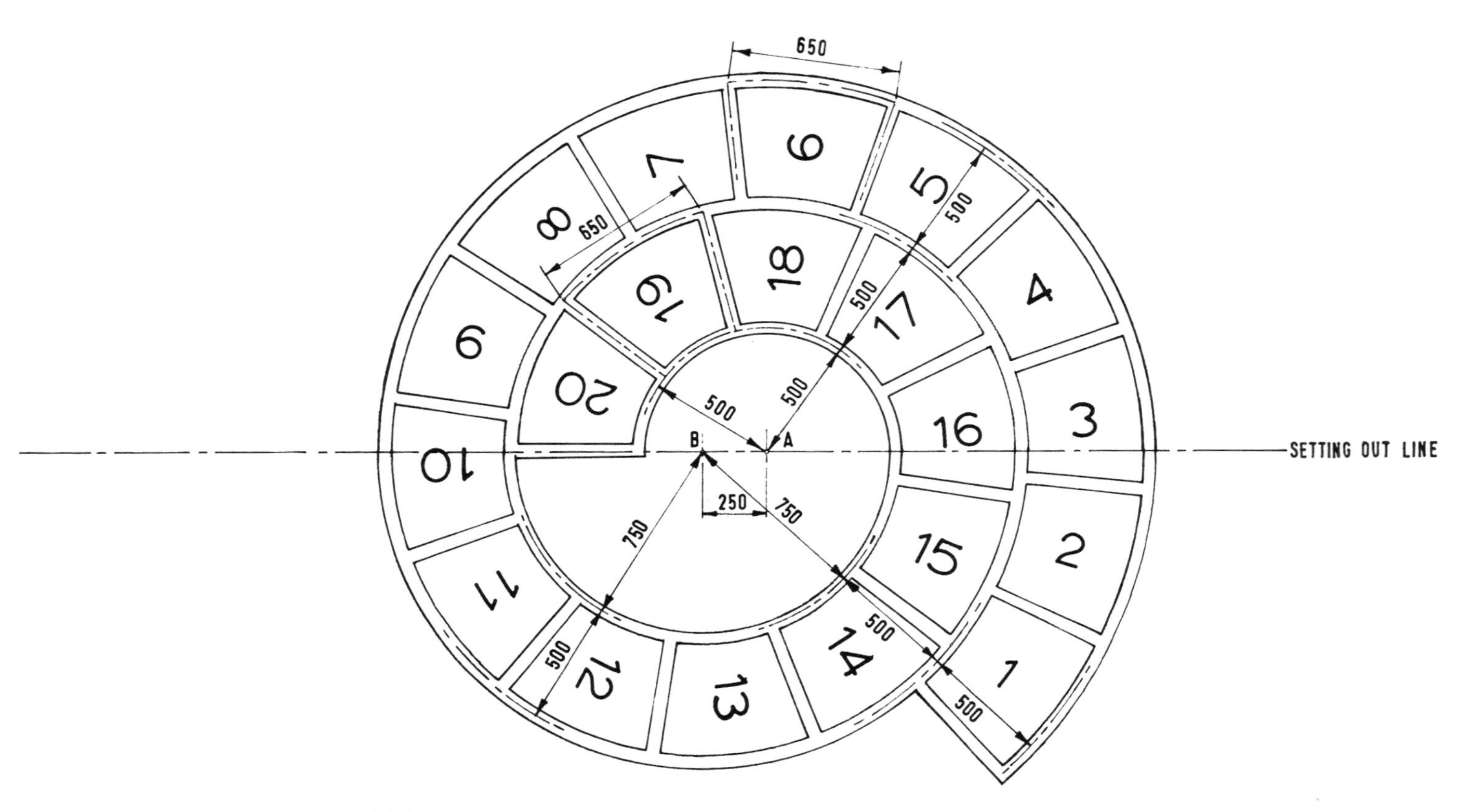

INFANT SPIRAL HOPSCOTCH PLAN 1:20

NOTES:

All markings should be at least 1 metre clear of all walls or obstructions.

For semi-circles above setting-out line use centre point "A."

For semi-circles below setting-out line use centre point "B."

All segments to be equal on outside perimeter, i.e. 650 mm.

All lines to be 50 mm wide in white.

Numbering should be 200 mm high. Numbering shown is not to scale.

GLC ILEA

Department of Architecture and Civic Design
County Hall SE1 7PB
Architect Sir Roger Walters
KBE ARIBA FI Struct/E

References following notes are clause numbers from G.L.C. preambles to bills of quantities

Departmental Standard Drawing

title

PLAYPITCH AND COURT MARKINGS

INFANT SPIRAL HOPSCOTCH

scale

1:20

drawing no	rev
D3181	

71 | 40 | 325 | Vv5 | J

010379

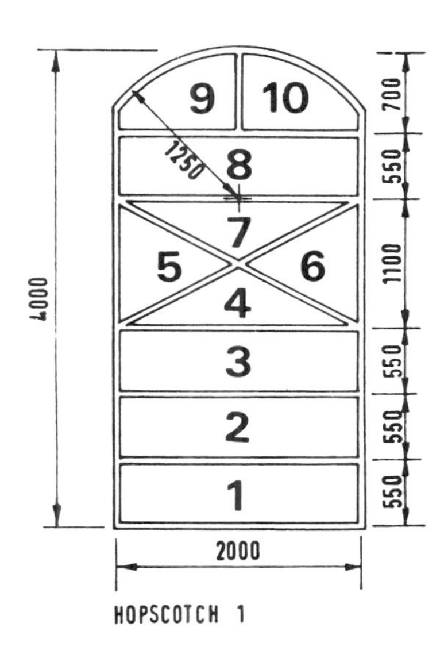

HOPSCOTCH 1

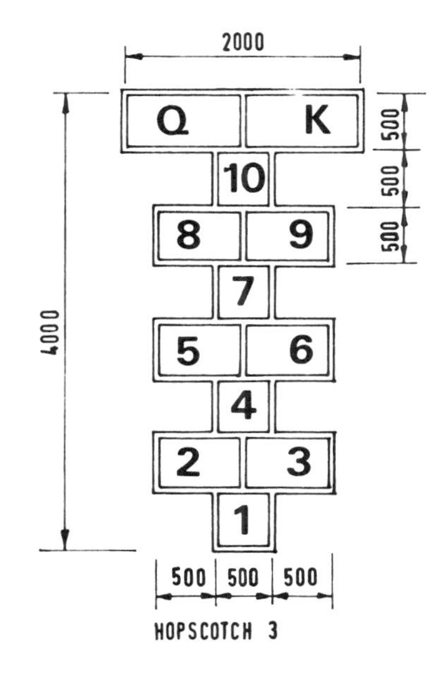

HOPSCOTCH 3

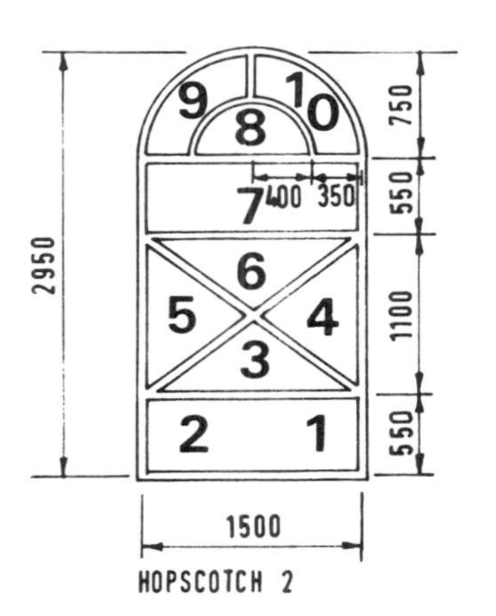

HOPSCOTCH 2

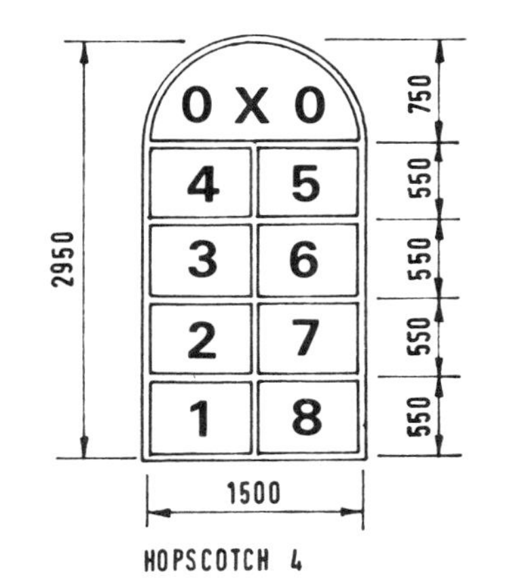

HOPSCOTCH 4

NOTES :

Floor markings for juniors and infants should be a minimum of 1 metre clear of all walls or obstructions.

Dimensions indicate centre lines.

All lines to be 50 mm wide in white.

Marking paint to be spirit resin type as V.55.

Numbering to be 250 mm high.

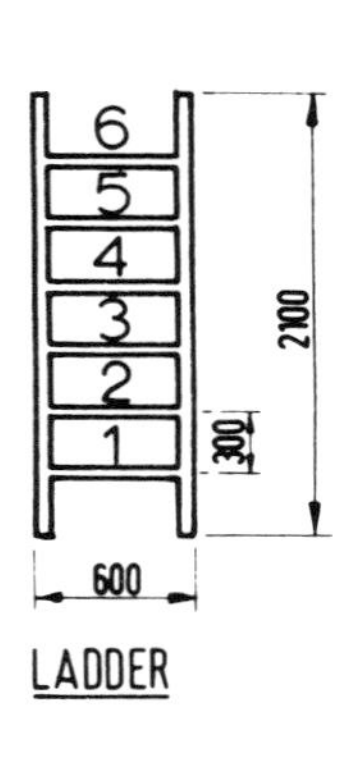

LADDER

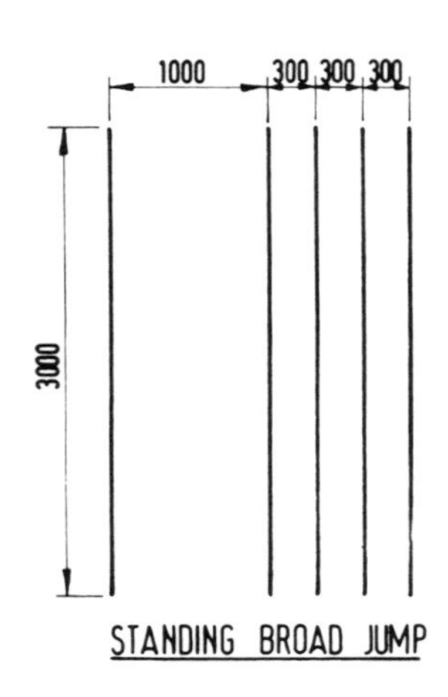

STANDING BROAD JUMP

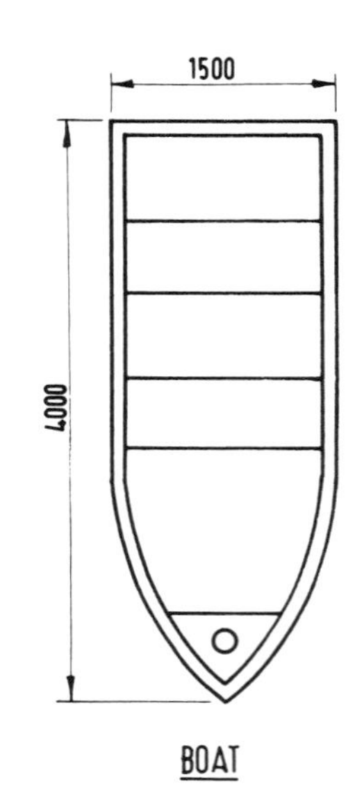

BOAT

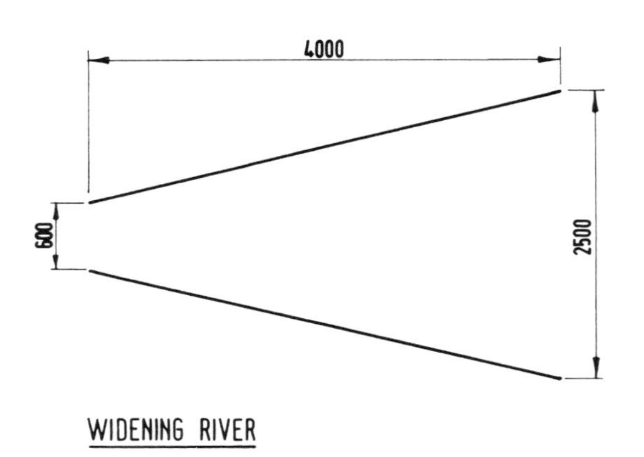

WIDENING RIVER

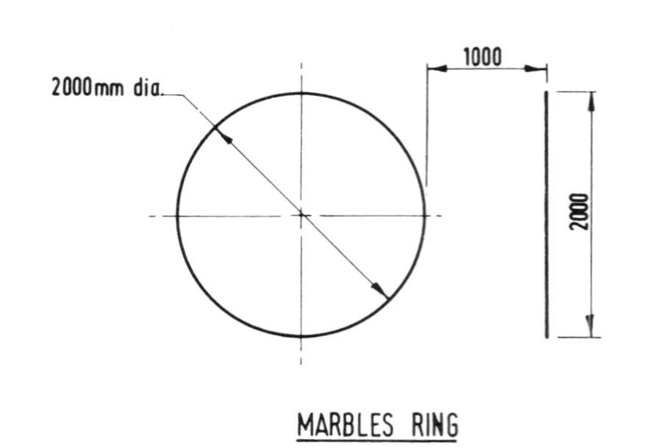

MARBLES RING

NOTES:–

Markings – min. 1000mm clear of all walls or obstructions.

Lines to be 50mm wide in white, inside dimensions.

Marking paint to be spirit resin type as V.55

GLC ILEA

Department of Architecture and Civic Design
County Hall SE1 7PB
Architect Sir Roger Walters KBE ARIBA FI Struct/E

References following notes are clause numbers from G.L.C. preambles to bills of quantities

Departmental Standard Drawing

title
PLAYPITCH AND COURT MARKINGS.
JUNIOR AND INFANTS GAME MARKINGS.

scale
1 : 50.

drawing no
D3183

rev

40 | 325 | Vv5 | L

71

00-010379

8 Seats

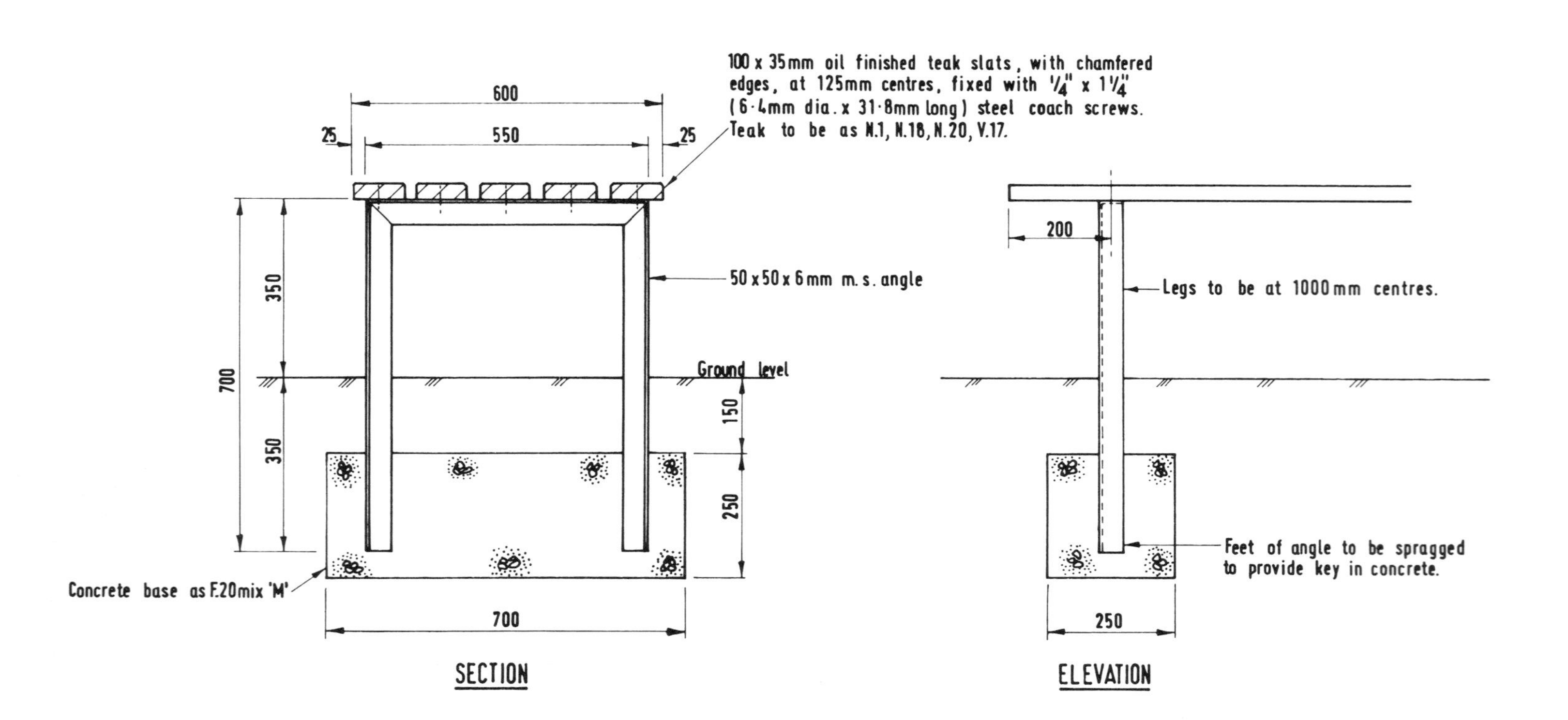

LENGTH	NUMBER OF LEGS	KEY
1400	2	1A
2400	3	2A
3400	4	3A

GLC ILEA

Department of Architecture and Civic Design
County Hall SE1
Architect Sir Roger Walters
KBE FRIBA FI StructE

References following notes are clause numbers from G.L.C. preambles to bills of quantities.

This drawing is to be read in conjunction with job drawings.

All metal parts to be hot dipped galvanised as Q.14 and painted with hard gloss paint (above G.L.), black bituminous paint (below G.L.) as tables of painting and decorating reference.

Steel parts to be as Q.8

Departmental Standard Drawing

title
EXTERNAL FURNITURE
SEAT TYPE 'A'

scale
1 : 10

drawing no
D5180

70 | 708 | Xi3 | as matrix

010379

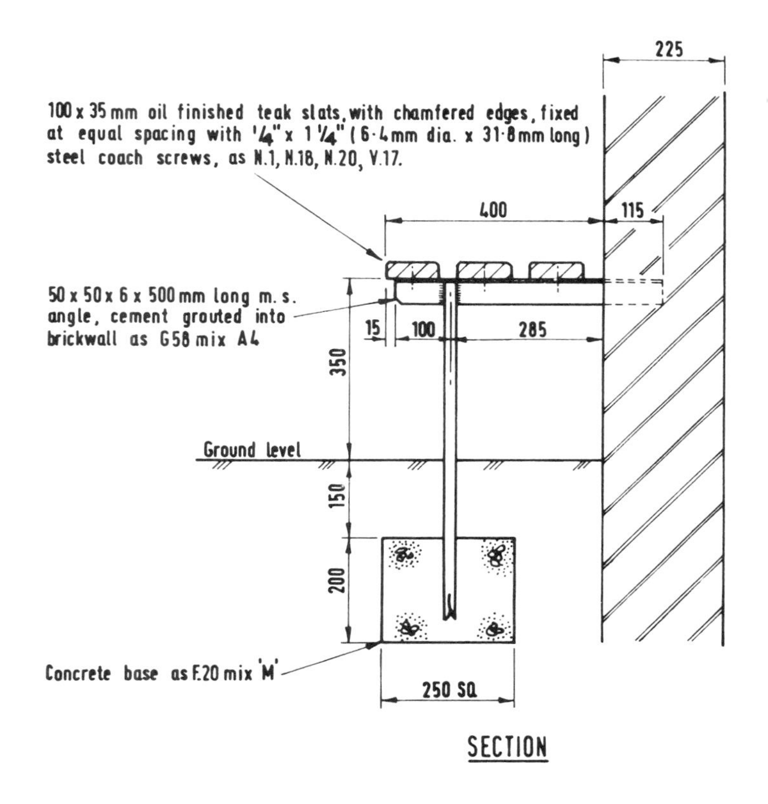

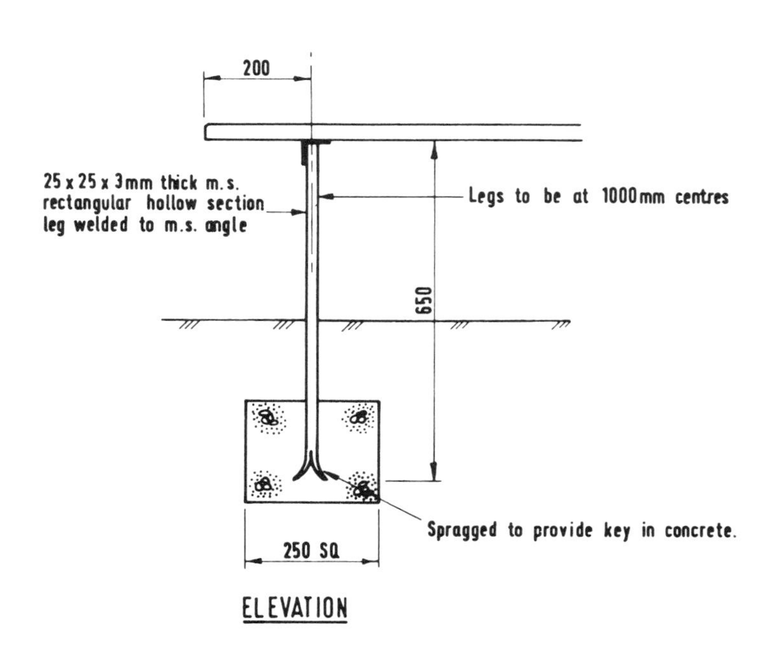

LENGTH	NUMBER OF LEGS	KEY
1400	2	1B
2400	3	2B
3400	4	3B

GLC ILEA

Department of Architecture and Civic Design
County Hall SE1
Architect Sir Roger Walters KBE FRIBA FI Struct/E

References following notes are clause numbers from G.L.C. preambles to bills of quanties.

This drawing is to be read in conjunction with job drawings.

All metal parts to be hot dipped galvanised as Q.14. and painted with hard gloss paint (above G.L.), black bituminous paint (below G.L.) as tables of painting and decorating reference.

Steel parts to be as Q.8.

Departmental Standard Drawing

title
EXTERNAL FURNITURE
SEAT TYPE 'B'.

scale 1:10

drawing no D5181

bldg type | space use | element [70] | feature 708 | material Xi3 | key

cs matrix

00 - 010379

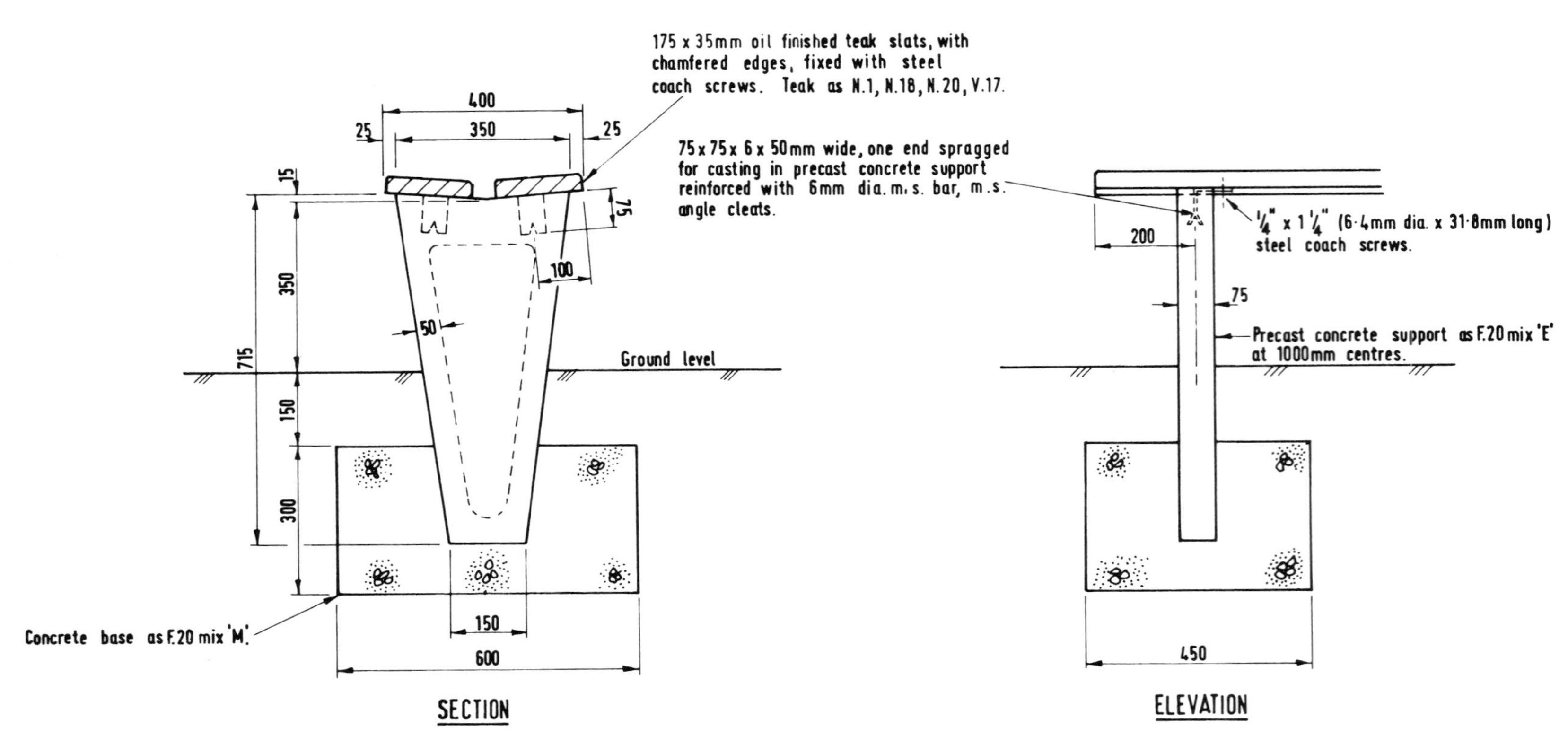

LENGTH	NUMBER OF SUPPORTS	KEY
1400	2	1C
2400	3	2C
3400	4	3C

GLC ILEA

Department of Architecture and Civic Design
County Hall SE1
Architect Sir Roger Walters KBE FRIBA FI StructE

References following notes are clause numbers from G.L.C. preambles to bills of quantities.

This drawing is to read in conjunction with job drawings.

All metal parts to be hot dipped galvanised as Q.14. and painted with hard gloss paint as tables of painting and decorating reference.

Steel parts to be as Q.8.

Departmental Standard Drawing

title

EXTERNAL FURNITURE
SEAT TYPE 'C'

scale

1 : 10

drawing no

D5182

70 708 Xi3 as matrix

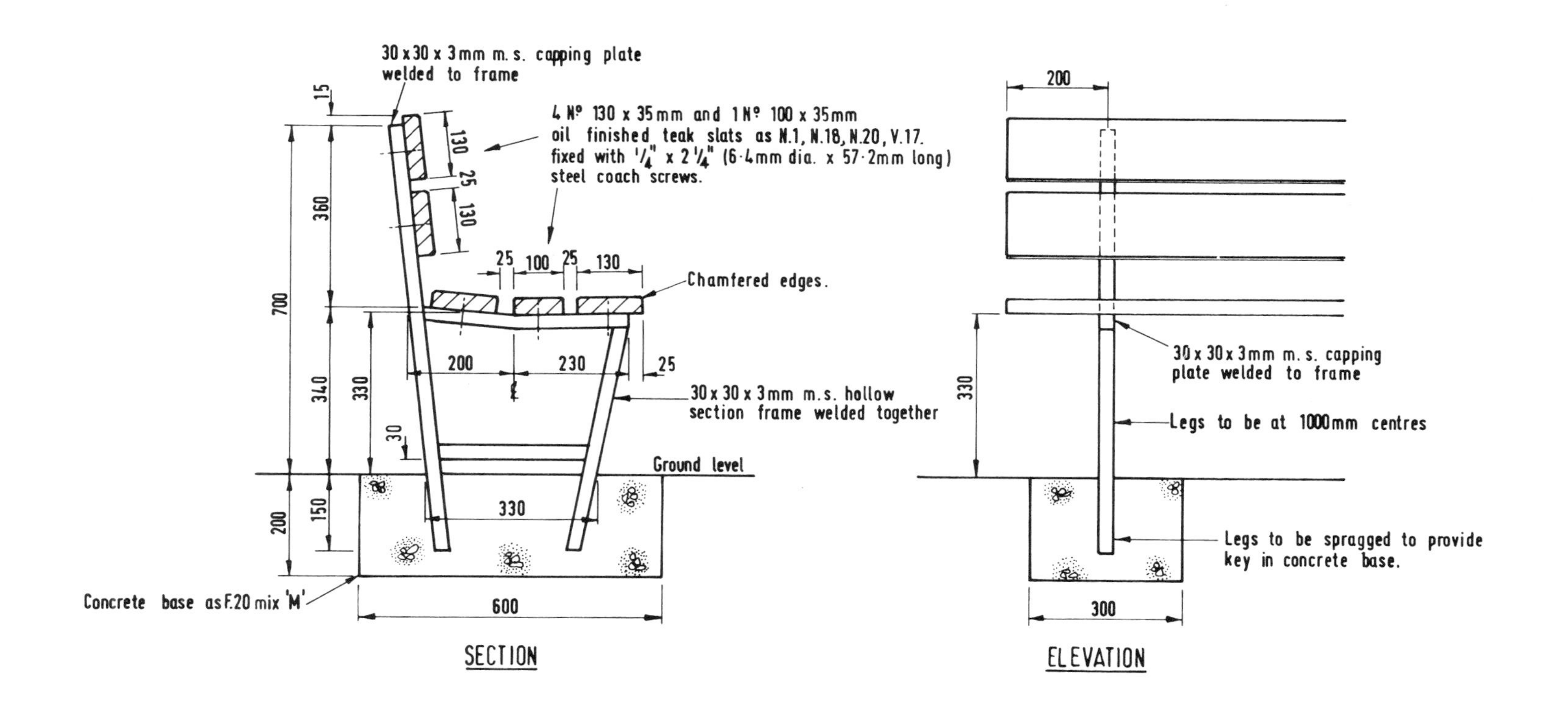

LENGTH	NUMBER OF LEGS	KEY
1400	2	1D
2400	3	2D
3400	4	3D

GLC ILEA

Department of Architecture and Civic Design
County Hall SE1
Architect Sir Roger Walters
KBE FRIBA FI StructE

References following notes are clause numbers from G.L.C. preambles to bills of quantities.

This drawing is to be read in conjunction with job drawings.

All metal parts to be hot dipped galvanised as Q.14. and painted with hard gloss paint (above G.L.), black bituminous paint (below G.L.) as tables of painting and decorating references.

Steel parts to be as Q.8.

Departmental Standard Drawing

title

EXTERNAL FURNITURE
SEAT TYPE 'D'

scale

1 : 10

drawing no

D5183

00 - 010379

bldg type | space use | element [70] | feature 708 | material Xi3 | key as matrix

9 Garages

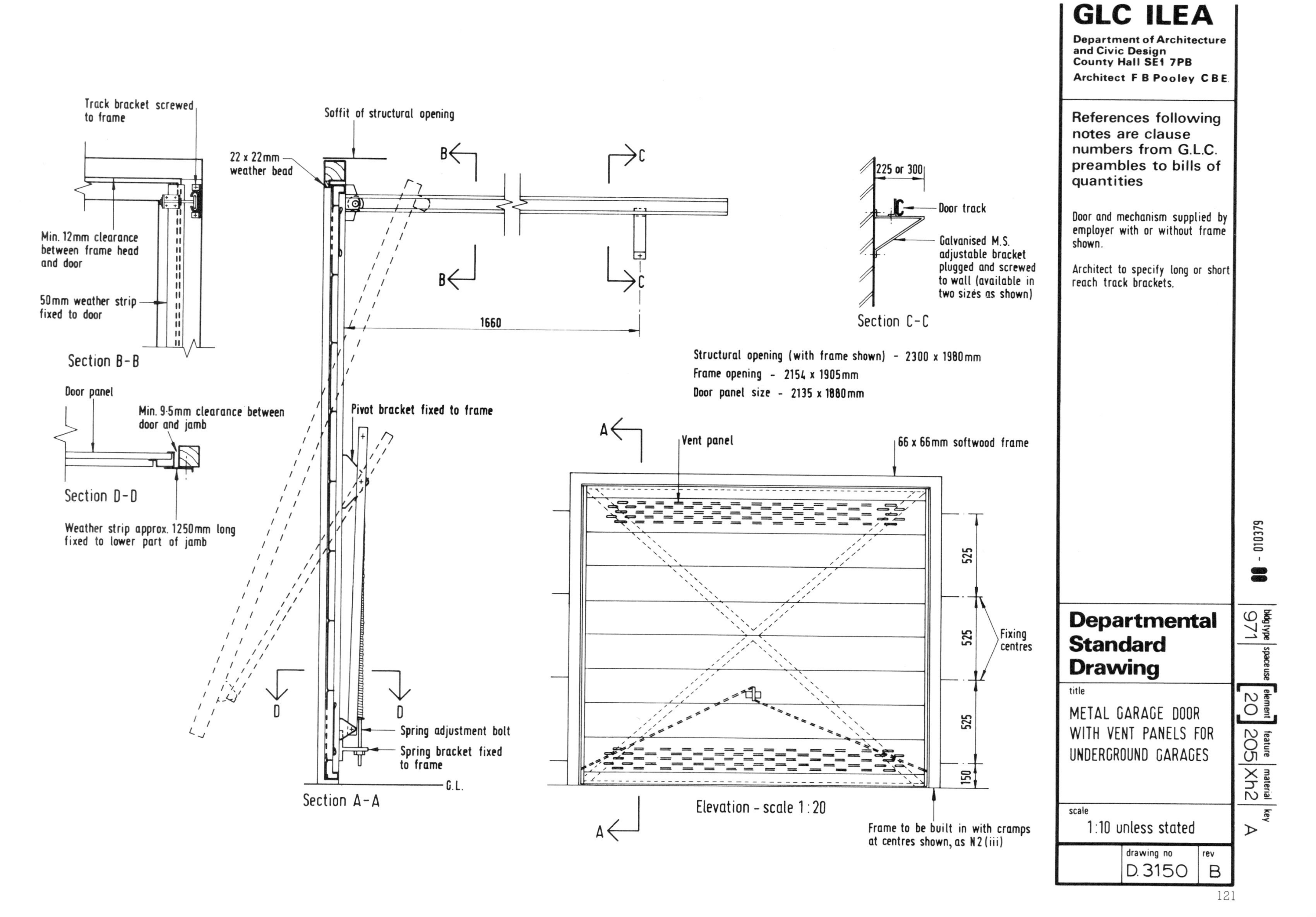
GLC ILEA
Department of Architecture and Civic Design
County Hall SE1 7PB
Architect F B Pooley CBE
References following notes are clause numbers from G.L.C. preambles to bills of quantities
Door and mechanism supplied by employer with or without frame shown.
Architect to specify long or short reach track brackets.
Track bracket screwed to frame
Min. 12mm clearance between frame head and door
50mm weather strip fixed to door
Section B-B
Door panel
Min. 9·5mm clearance between door and jamb
Section D-D
Weather strip approx. 1250mm long fixed to lower part of jamb
Soffit of structural opening
22 x 22mm weather bead
1660
Pivot bracket fixed to frame
Spring adjustment bolt
Spring bracket fixed to frame
G.L.
Section A-A
225 or 300
Door track
Galvanised M.S. adjustable bracket plugged and screwed to wall (available in two sizes as shown)
Section C-C
Structural opening (with frame shown) - 2300 x 1980mm
Frame opening - 2154 x 1905mm
Door panel size - 2135 x 1880mm
Vent panel
66 x 66mm softwood frame
525
525
525
150
Fixing centres
Elevation - scale 1:20
Frame to be built in with cramps at centres shown, as N2(iii)
Departmental Standard Drawing
title
METAL GARAGE DOOR WITH VENT PANELS FOR UNDERGROUND GARAGES
scale
1:10 unless stated
drawing no
D.3150
rev
B
bldg type 971
space use
element 20
feature 205
material Xh2
key A
010379

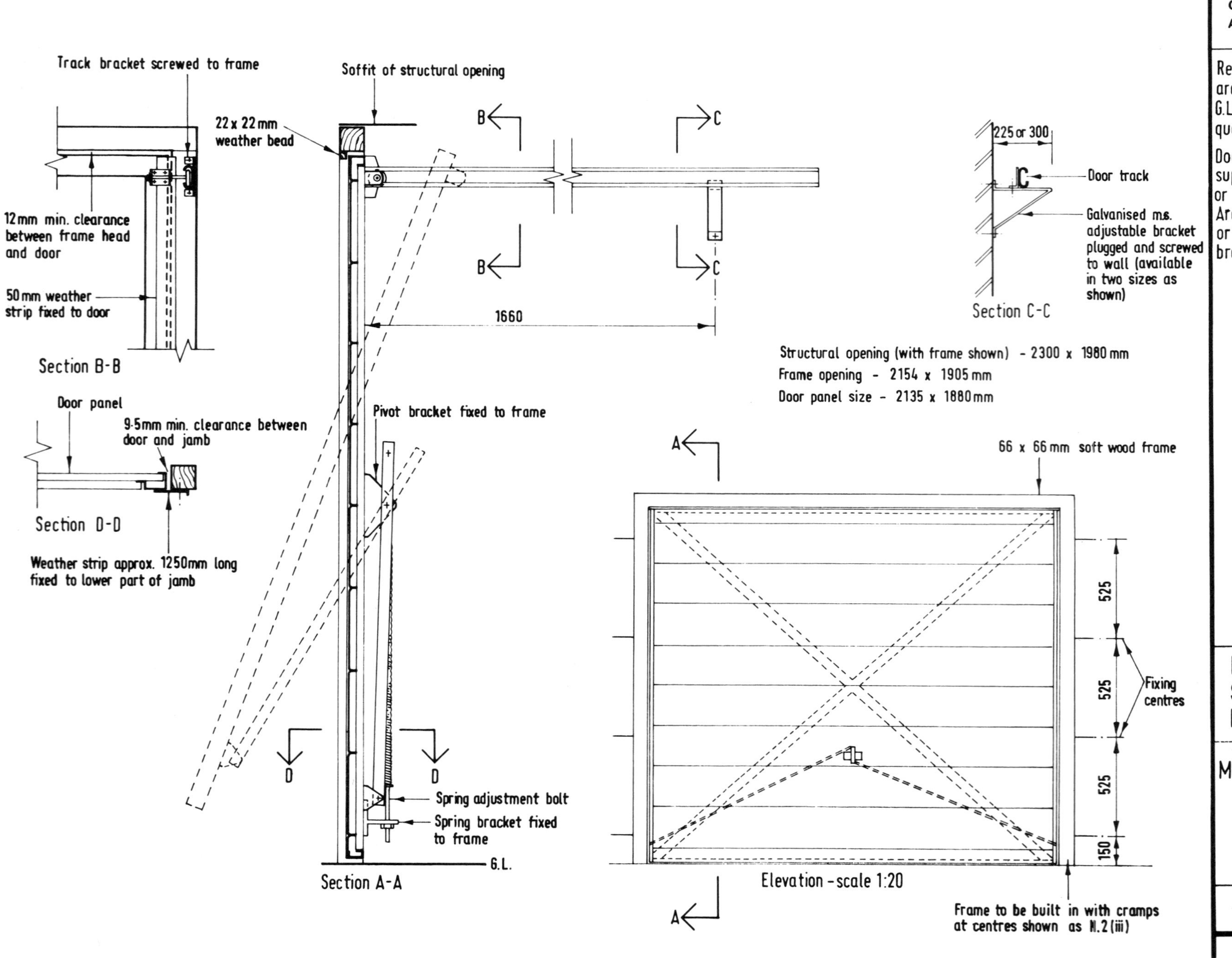

GLC ILEA

Department of Architecture and Civic Design
County Hall SE1
Architect Sir Roger Walters
KBE FRIBA FI StructE

References following notes are clause numbers from G.L.C. preambles to bills of quantities

Door and mechanism supplied by employer with or without frame shown. Architect to specify long or short reach track brackets

Departmental Standard Drawing

title
METAL GARAGE DOOR

scale
1:10 unless stated

drawing no D3151 | rev C

971 | (20) | 205 | Xh2 | B

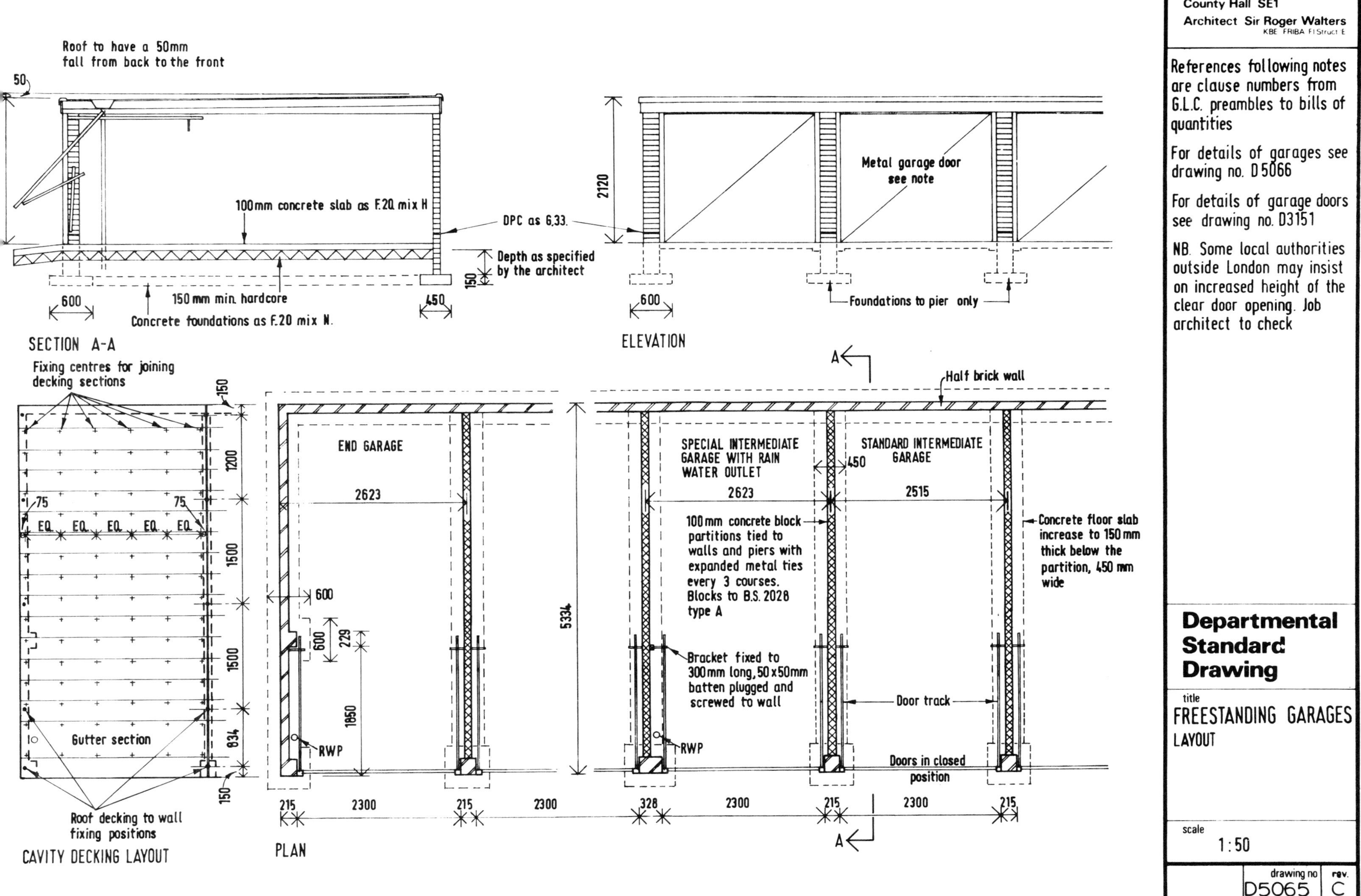
GLC ILEA
Department of Architecture and Civic Design
County Hall SE1
Architect Sir Roger Walters KBE FRIBA FIStructE
References following notes are clause numbers from G.L.C. preambles to bills of quantities
For details of garages see drawing no. D5066
For details of garage doors see drawing no. D3151
NB. Some local authorities outside London may insist on increased height of the clear door opening. Job architect to check
Departmental Standard Drawing
title
FREESTANDING GARAGES
LAYOUT
scale
1:50
drawing no
D5065
rev.
C
bldg type 971
space use
element 20
feature 218
material
key
170579 C
010379
Roof to have a 50mm fall from back to the front
50
100mm concrete slab as F.20 mix H
DPC as 6.33.
Depth as specified by the architect
150
150 mm min. hardcore
Concrete foundations as F.20 mix N.
600
450
SECTION A-A
2120
Metal garage door see note
Foundations to pier only
600
ELEVATION
Fixing centres for joining decking sections
150
1200
75
75
EQ.
EQ.
EQ.
EQ.
EQ.
1500
1500
834
150
Gutter section
Roof decking to wall fixing positions
CAVITY DECKING LAYOUT
A
Half brick wall
END GARAGE
SPECIAL INTERMEDIATE GARAGE WITH RAIN WATER OUTLET
STANDARD INTERMEDIATE GARAGE
450
2623
2623
2515
100mm concrete block partitions tied to walls and piers with expanded metal ties every 3 courses. Blocks to B.S. 2028 type A
Concrete floor slab increase to 150mm thick below the partition, 450 mm wide
600
600
229
1850
5334
Bracket fixed to 300mm long, 50x50mm batten plugged and screwed to wall
Door track
RWP
RWP
Doors in closed position
215
2300
215
2300
328
2300
215
2300
215
A
PLAN

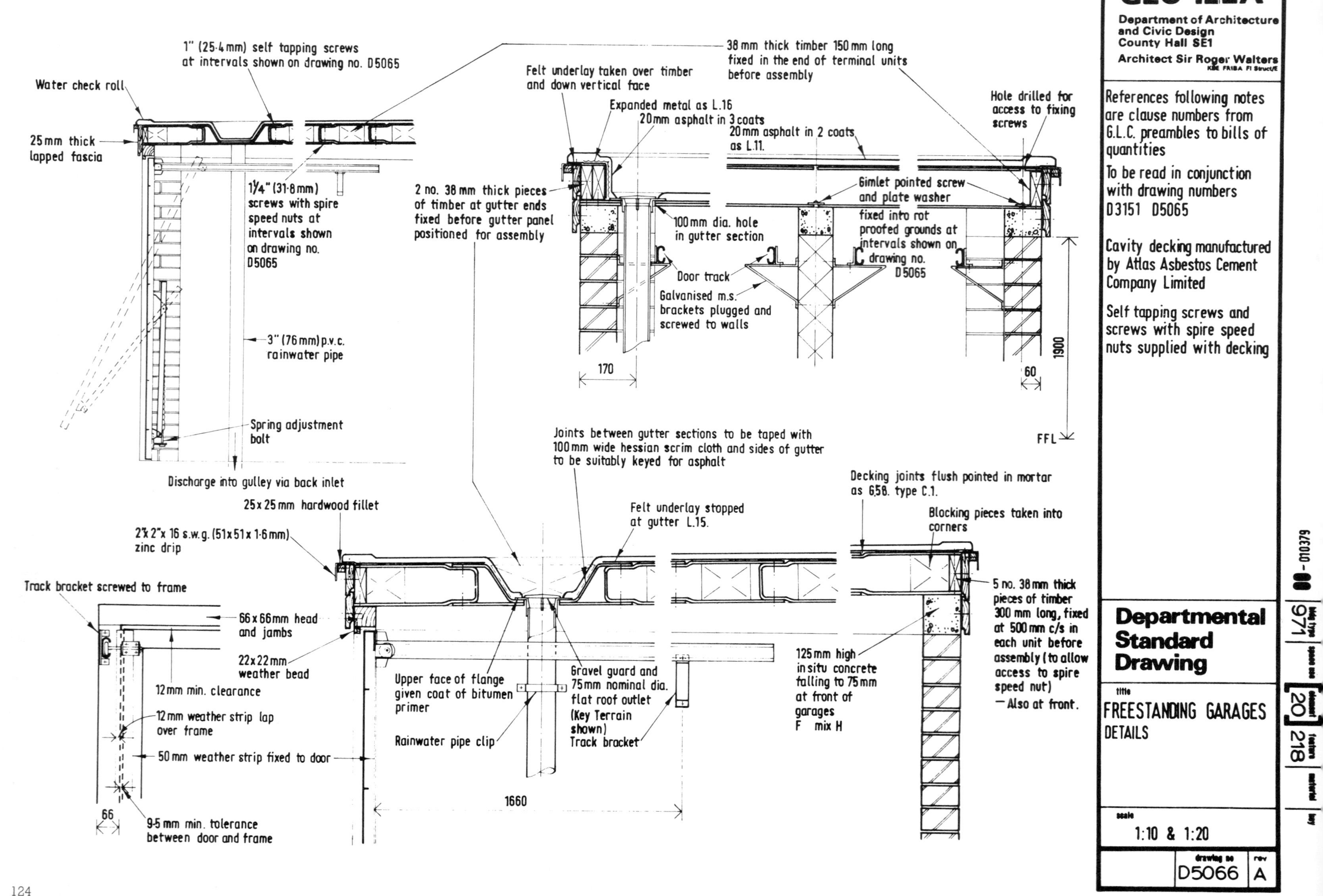
GLC ILEA
Department of Architecture and Civic Design
County Hall SE1
Architect Sir Roger Walters
References following notes are clause numbers from G.L.C. preambles to bills of quantities
To be read in conjunction with drawing numbers D3151 D5065
Cavity decking manufactured by Atlas Asbestos Cement Company Limited
Self tapping screws and screws with spire speed nuts supplied with decking
Departmental Standard Drawing
title
FREESTANDING GARAGES
DETAILS
scale
1:10 & 1:20
drawing no
D5066
rev
A
971
20
218
Water check roll
1" (25·4 mm) self tapping screws at intervals shown on drawing no. D5065
25 mm thick lapped fascia
1¼" (31·8 mm) screws with spire speed nuts at intervals shown on drawing no. D5065
3" (76 mm) p.v.c. rainwater pipe
Spring adjustment bolt
Discharge into gulley via back inlet
2 no. 38 mm thick pieces of timber at gutter ends fixed before gutter panel positioned for assembly
Felt underlay taken over timber and down vertical face
Expanded metal as L.16
20mm asphalt in 3 coats
38 mm thick timber 150 mm long fixed in the end of terminal units before assembly
20 mm asphalt in 2 coats as L.11.
Hole drilled for access to fixing screws
Gimlet pointed screw and plate washer fixed into rot proofed grounds at intervals shown on drawing no. D5065
100 mm dia. hole in gutter section
Door track
Galvanised m.s. brackets plugged and screwed to walls
170
60
1900
FFL
Joints between gutter sections to be taped with 100 mm wide hessian scrim cloth and sides of gutter to be suitably keyed for asphalt
Decking joints flush pointed in mortar as 6.58. type C.1.
Felt underlay stopped at gutter L.15.
Blocking pieces taken into corners
25 x 25 mm hardwood fillet
2" x 2" x 16 s.w.g. (51 x 51 x 1·6 mm) zinc drip
Track bracket screwed to frame
66 x 66 mm head and jambs
22 x 22 mm weather bead
12 mm min. clearance
12 mm weather strip lap over frame
50 mm weather strip fixed to door
66
9·5 mm min. tolerance between door and frame
Upper face of flange given coat of bitumen primer
Rainwater pipe clip
Gravel guard and 75 mm nominal dia. flat roof outlet (Key Terrain shown)
Track bracket
1660
125 mm high in situ concrete falling to 75 mm at front of garages F mix H
5 no. 38 mm thick pieces of timber 300 mm long, fixed at 500 mm c/s in each unit before assembly (to allow access to spire speed nut)
— Also at front.

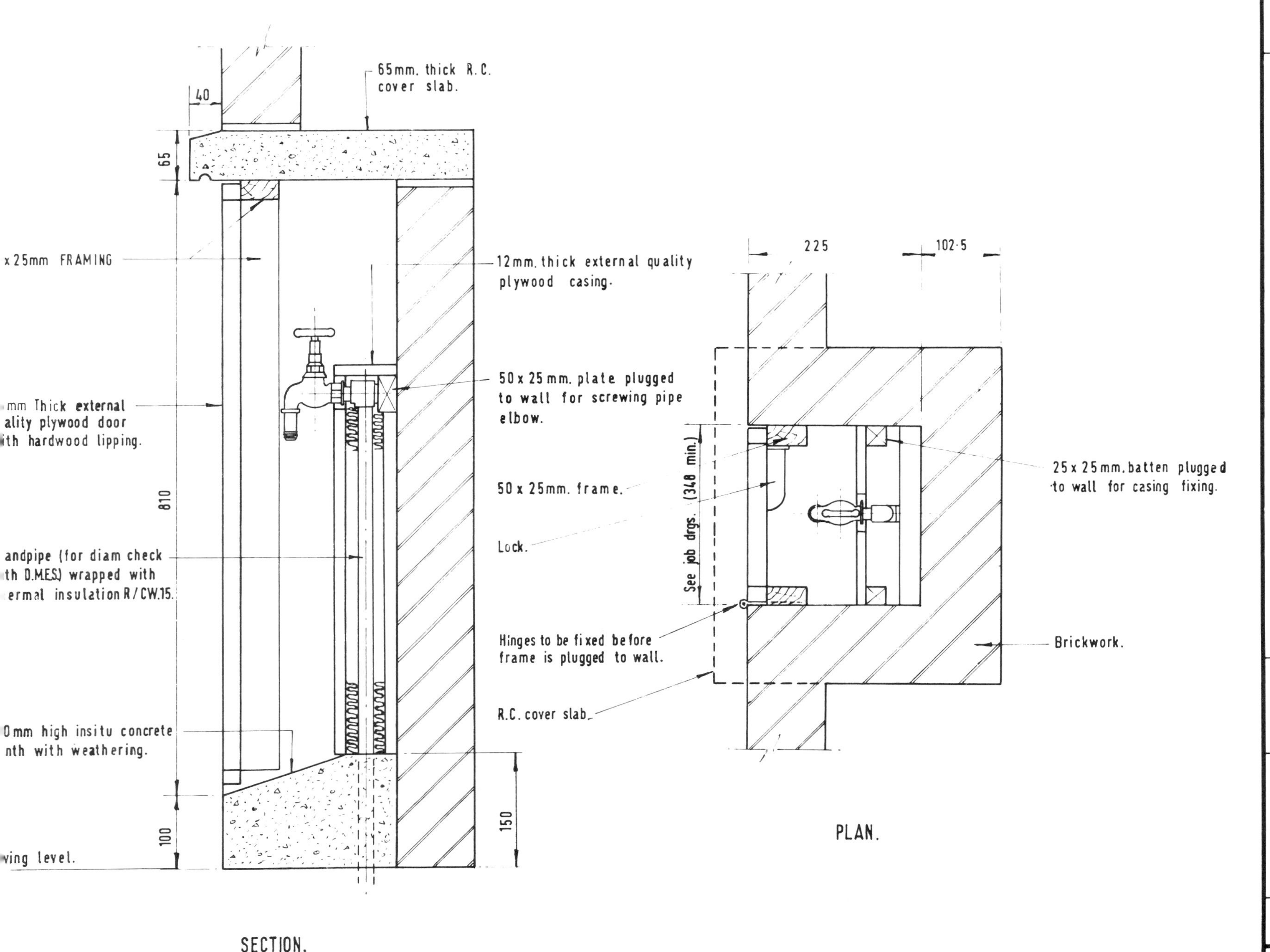

GLC ILEA

Department of Architecture
and Civic Design
County Hall SE1 7PB
Architect Sir Roger Walters
KBE ARIBA FI Struct/E

References following notes are clause numbers from G.L.C. preambles to bills of quantities

IRONMONGERY.

(1). Pair of steel cranked hinges as item 143

(2). Steel rim night latch as item 39. N° of keys to be specified by job architect.

8— | bldg type | space use | 20 | element | 218 | feature | material | key

010379

Departmental Standard Drawing

title

STANDPIPE HOUSING
for
CAR WASHING, ETC.

scale 1 : 5

drawing no D.5068. | rev B.

10 Drainage

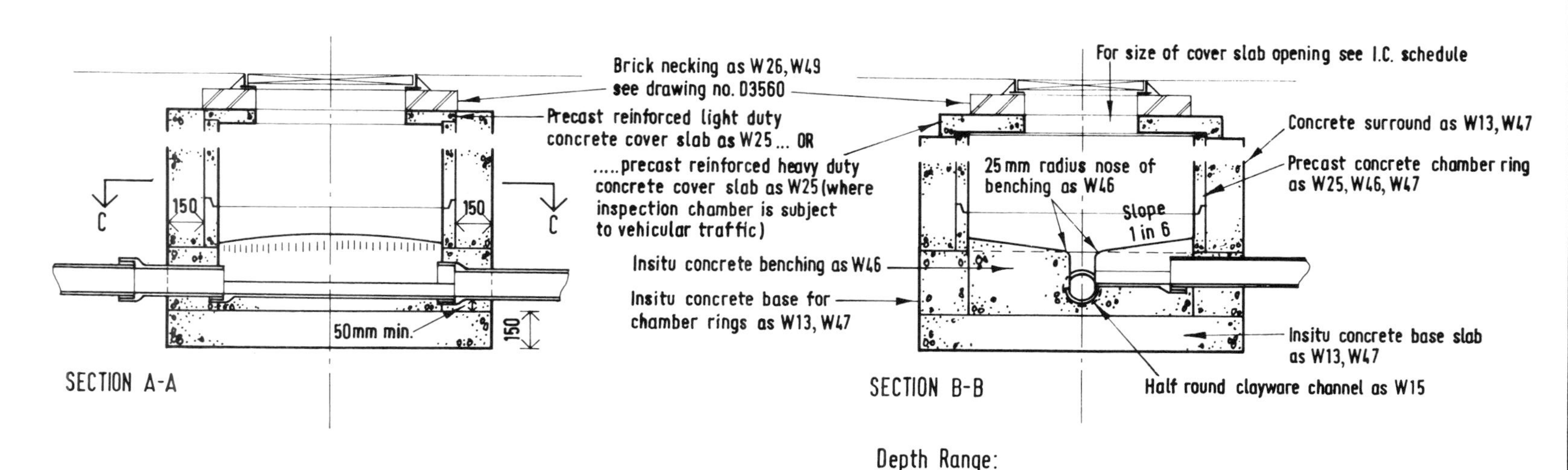

Depth Range:

Up to 900mm between cover level and invert level.

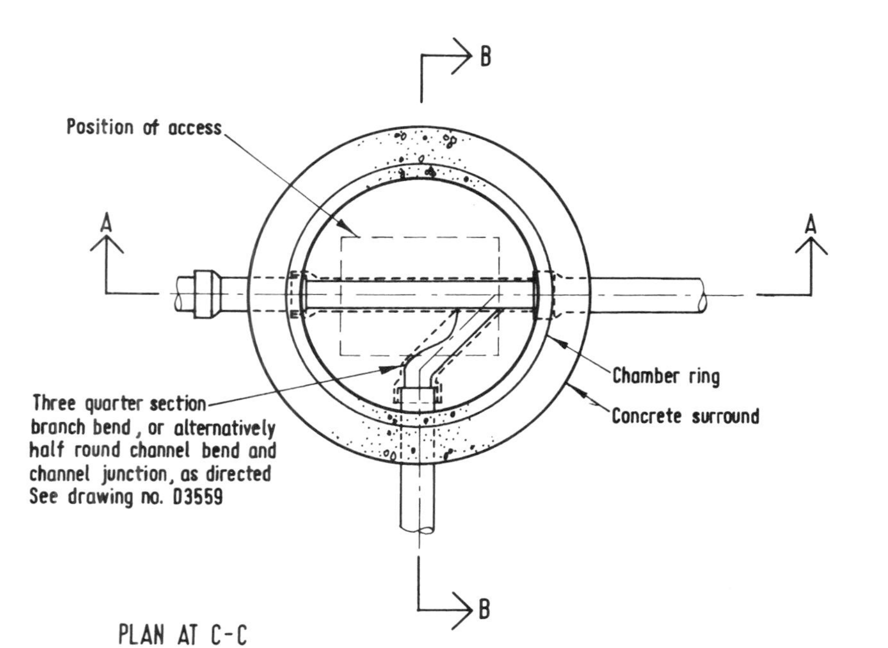

CONCRETE MIX	CHAMBER DIAMETER	LIGHT DUTY SLAB	HEAVY DUTY SLAB
NORMAL	750 mm	BA1A	BA2A
	900 mm	BA1B	BA2B
	1050 mm	BA1C	BA2C
SULPHATE RESISTANT	750 mm	BB1A	BB2A
	900 mm	BB1B	BB2B
	1050 mm	BB1C	BB2C

Suggested minimum inspection chamber diameters:

(i) With not more than 1 branch per side 750 mm

(ii) With not more than 2 branches per side 900 mm

(iii) With not more than 3 branches per side 1050 mm

GLC ILEA

Department of Architecture
and Civic Design
County Hall SE1
Architect Sir Roger Walters
KBE FRIBA FI Struct/E

References following notes are clause numbers from G.L.C. preambles to bills of quantities

For details of covers and frames of type to suit location of inspection chamber see drawing number D3560

For channel details see drawing no. D3559

Departmental Standard Drawing

title

INSPECTION CHAMBER
SHALLOW (EXTERNAL)
PRECAST CONCRETE (CIRCULAR)
WITH CONCRETE SURROUND
(UP TO 900mm BETWEEN
COVER LEVEL AND INVERT)

scale 1:20

drawing no D3550

bldg type | space use | element [50] | feature 826 | material Xf2 | key as matrix

010379

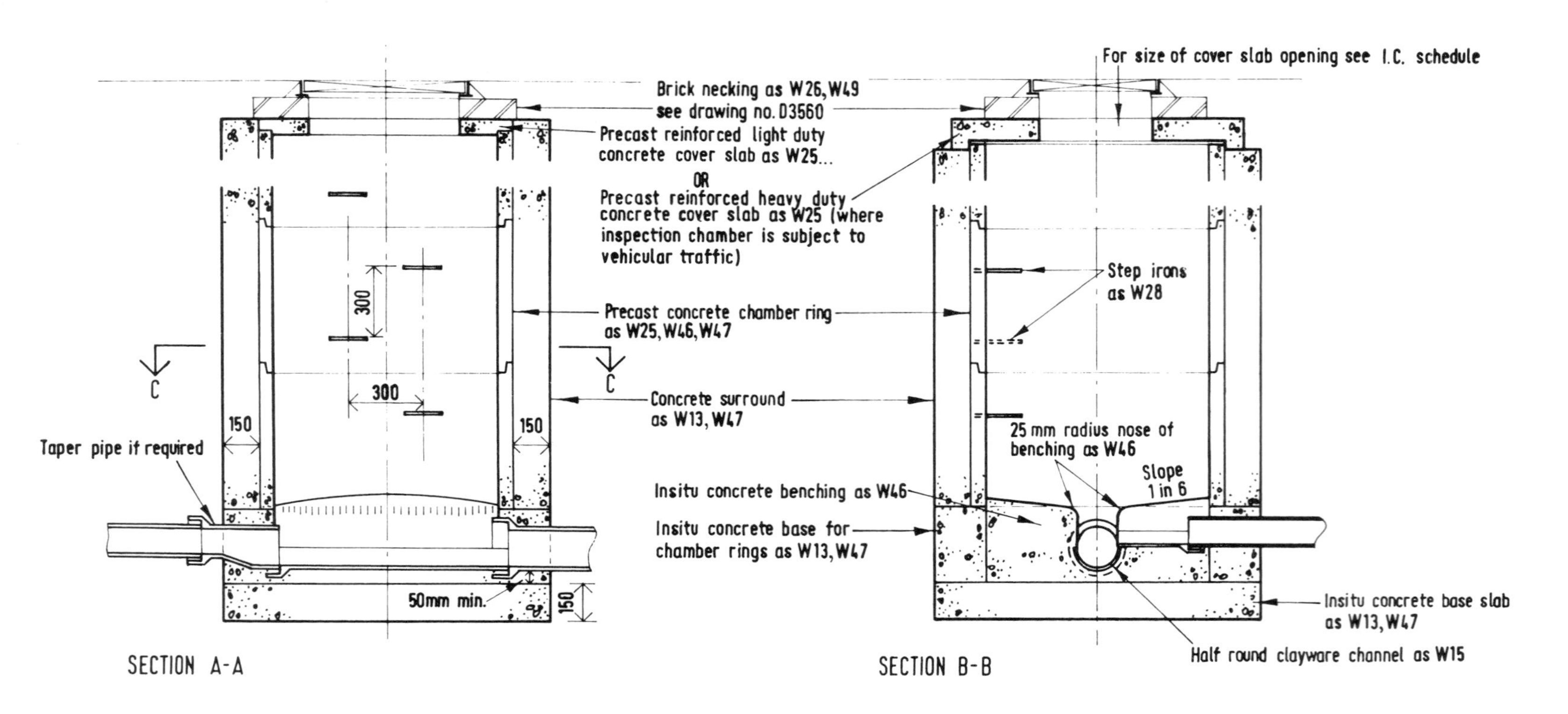

Depth Range:

900 to 1850 mm between cover level and invert level

B

Position of access

A

A

Three quarter section branch bend, or alternatively half round channel bend and channel junction, as directed

See drawing no. D3559

Chamber ring

Concrete surround

B

PLAN AT C-C

CONCRETE MIX	CHAMBER DIAMETER	LIGHT DUTY SLAB	HEAVY DUTY SLAB
NORMAL	900 mm	BA1D	BA2D
	1050 mm	BA1E	BA2E
SULPHATE RESISTANT	900 mm	BB1D	BB2D
	1050 mm	BB1E	BB2E

Suggested minimum inspection chamber diameters:

(i) With not more than 2 branches per side 900 mm

(ii) With not more than 3 branches per side 1050 mm

GLC ILEA

Department of Architecture and Civic Design
County Hall SE1
Architect Sir Roger Walters KBE FRIBA FI StructE

References following notes are clause numbers from G.L.C. preambles to bills of quantities

For details of covers and frames of type to suit location of inspection chamber see drawing number D3560

For channel details see drawing no. D3559

Departmental Standard Drawing

title

INSPECTION CHAMBER
AVERAGE DEPTH (EXTERNAL)
PRECAST CONCRETE (CIRCULAR)
WITH CONCRETE SURROUND
(900 TO 1850mm BETWEEN COVER LEVEL AND INVERT)

scale

1:20

drawing no

D3552

bldg type | space use | element (50) | feature 826 | material Xf2 | key as matrix

010379

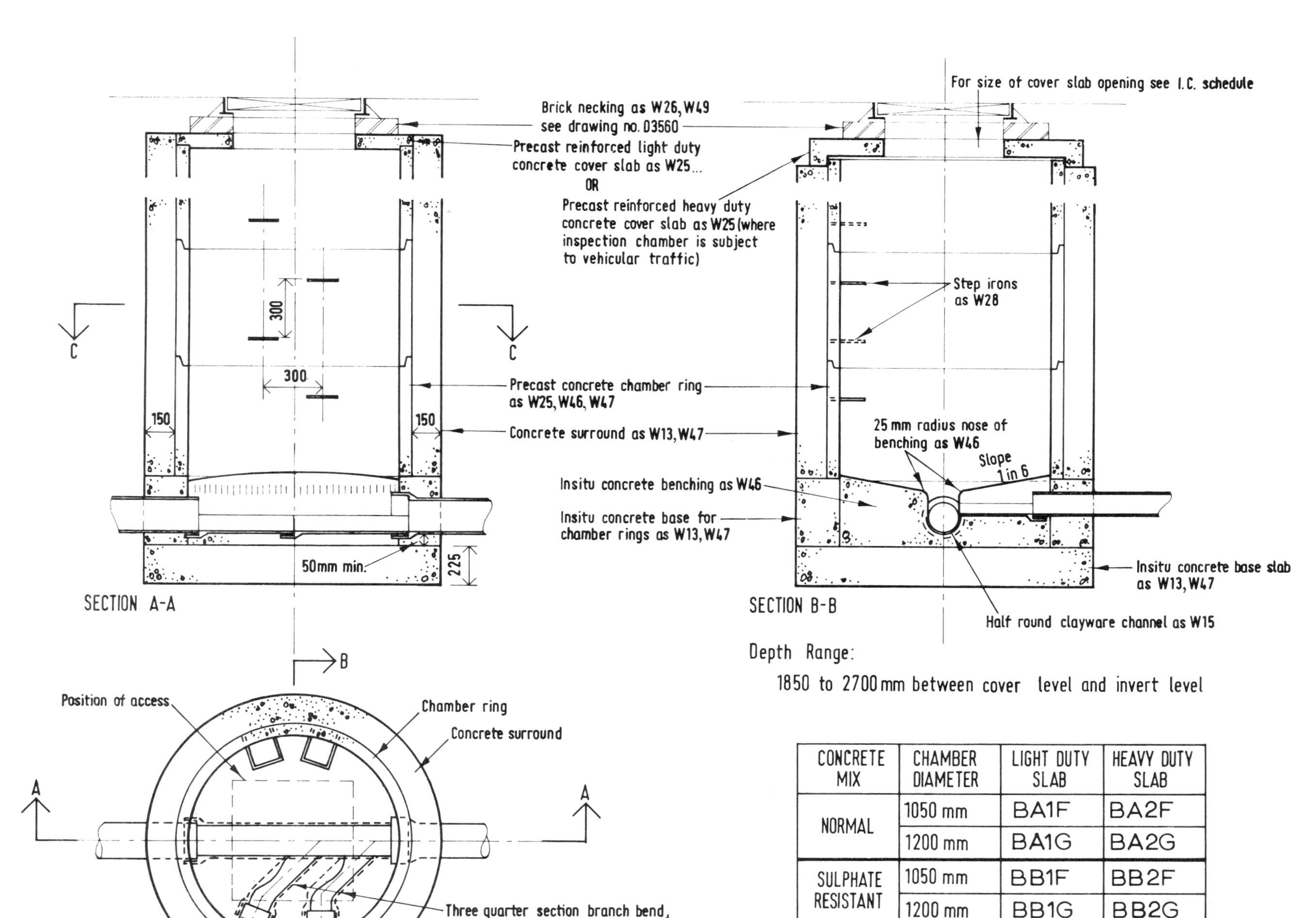

CONCRETE MIX	CHAMBER DIAMETER	LIGHT DUTY SLAB	HEAVY DUTY SLAB
NORMAL	1050 mm	BA1F	BA2F
	1200 mm	BA1G	BA2G
SULPHATE RESISTANT	1050 mm	BB1F	BB2F
	1200 mm	BB1G	BB2G

Suggested inspection chamber diameters:

(i) With not more than 3 branches per side — 1050 mm

(ii) As alternative to above, as per local authority requirements — 1200 mm

GLC ILEA

Department of Architecture and Civic Design
County Hall SE1
Architect Sir Roger Walters KBE FRIBA FI StructE

References following notes are clause numbers from G.L.C. preambles to bills of quantities

For details of covers and frames of type to suit location of inspection chamber see drawing number D3560

For channel details see drawing no. D3559

Departmental Standard Drawing

title

INSPECTION CHAMBER
DEEP (EXTERNAL)
PRECAST CONCRETE (CIRCULAR)
WITH CONCRETE SURROUND
(1850 TO 2700mm BETWEEN COVER LEVEL AND INVERT)

scale 1:20

drawing no D3554

bldg type | space use | element [50] | feature 826 | material Xf2 | key as matrix

GLC ILEA
Department of Architecture
and Civic Design
County Hall SE1
Architect Sir Roger Walters
KBE FRIBA FI StructE

References following notes are clause numbers from G.L.C. preambles to bills of quantities

This drawing shows alternative details for backdrops and should be read in conjunction with I.C. schedule

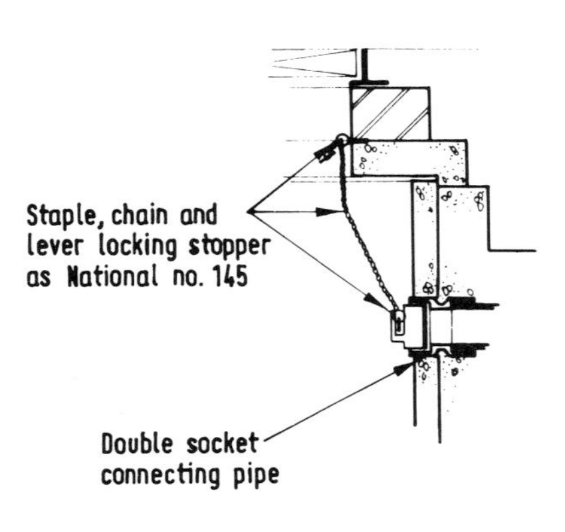

ACCESS STOPPER DETAIL – KEY 1
(Where required)

Hole made in precast concrete ring to accept pipe

90° tumbling bay junction

150

150

Pipe bedded as drainage details

150mm concrete surround to pipe as W13, W47

One quarter bend

Channels as inspection chamber detail drawings

90° VERTICAL BACKDROP
DETAIL – KEY A

Hole made in precast concrete ring to accept pipe

45° tumbling bay junction

150

150

Pipe bedded as drainage details

150mm concrete surround to pipe as W13, W47

One eighth bend

Channels as inspection chamber detail drawings

45° RAMPED BACKDROP
DETAIL – KEY B

Backdrops shown on branch, but details similar when on main run.

This drawing is for information on backdrops only and details of inspection chamber are referred to in the I.C. schedule

Departmental Standard Drawing

title

PRECAST CONCRETE (CIRCULAR) INSPECTION CHAMBERS

ALTERNATIVE BACKDROP DETAILS (EXTERNAL USE)

scale

1:20

drawing no

D3558

(50) 826 | Xf2 | as drawing

GLC ILEA

Department of Architecture
and Civic Design
County Hall SE1
Architect Sir Roger Walters
KBE FRIBA FI StructE

This drawing shows alternative details for I.C. channels and should be read in conjunction with I.C. schedule

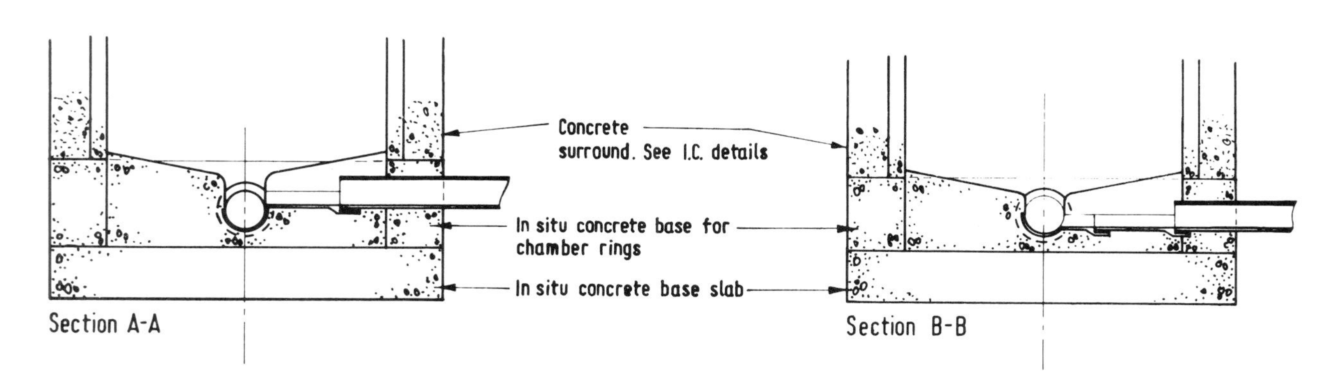

Angle(s) of branch drain entry to I.C. achieved by using three quarter section branch bends from National 104 range. (Note limitation on angle)

Angle(s) of branch drain entry to I.C. achieved by using half section channel junctions from National range of oblique junctions with half section channel bends from National 81 - 91 (inclusive) range. (Note limitation on angle)

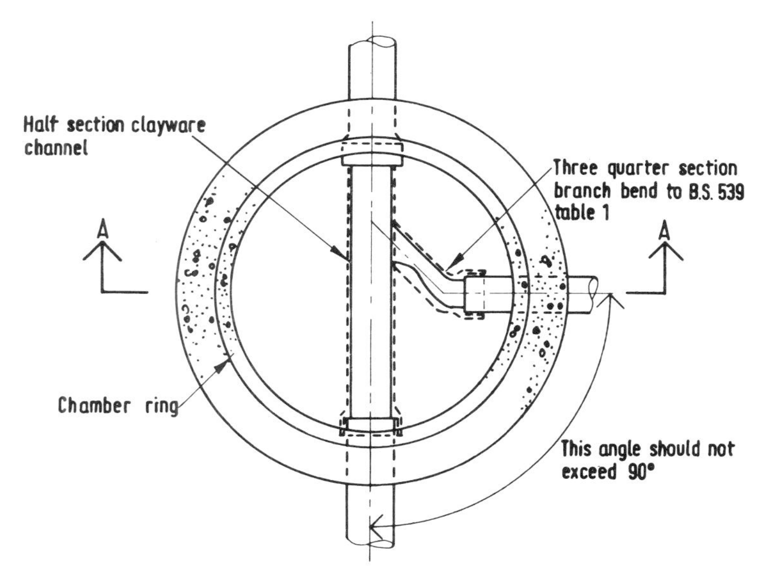

Half section clayware channel with three quarter section branch bend
KEY 1

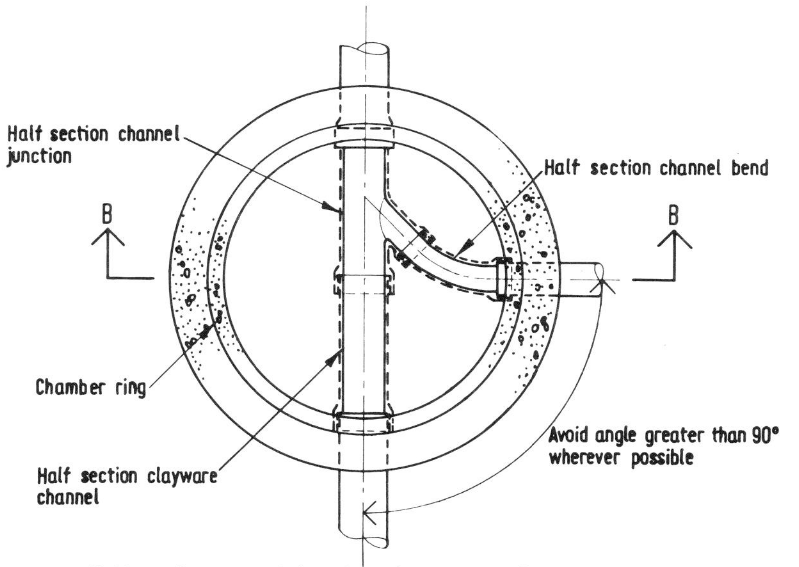

Half section channel junction with half section channel bend
KEY 2

Main half section channels shown straight, but curved channels will also be specified for some situations.

Departmental Standard Drawing

title
PRECAST CONCRETE (CIRCULAR) INSPECTION CHAMBERS
ALTERNATIVE CHANNEL DETAILS (EXTERNAL USE)

scale 1:20

drawing no D3559.A.

(A) 16078 - 010379

bldg type | space use | [50] element | 826 feature | Xf2 material | as drawing key

- Inspection chamber covers in vehicular pavings
  not subject to heavy commercial vehicles

A) where cover is not required to match surrounding finish

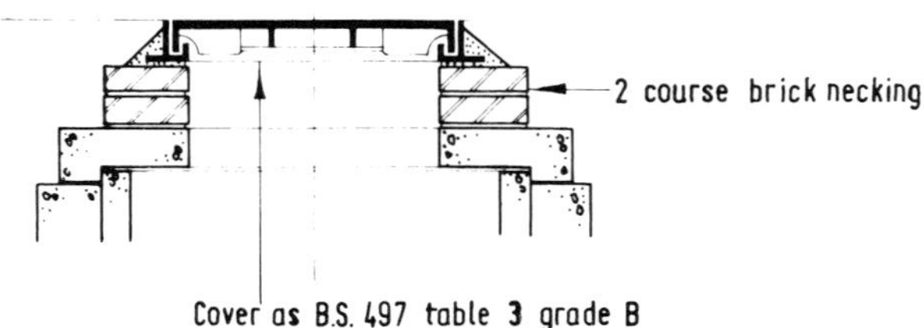

Cover as B.S. 497 table 3 grade B
medium duty, solid top 600 x 450 mm nominal. KEY M1
600 x 600 mm nominal. KEY M2

B) where cover is required to match surrounding finish

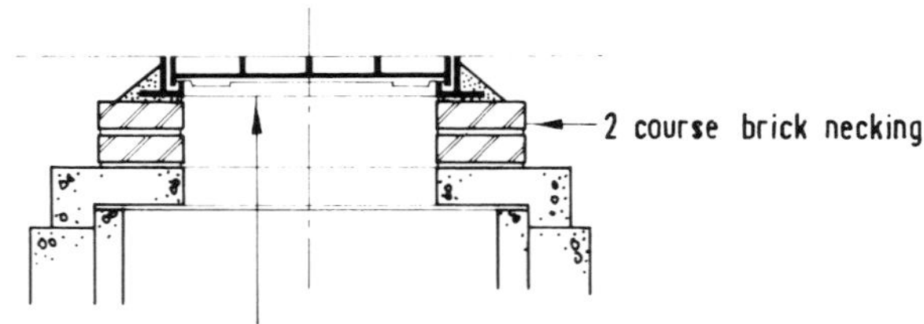

Cover as B.S. 497 table 3 grade B
medium duty, recessed cover 600 x 450 mm nominal. KEY M3
600 x 600 mm nominal. KEY M4

- Inspection chamber covers in carriageways subject
  to fast moving traffic

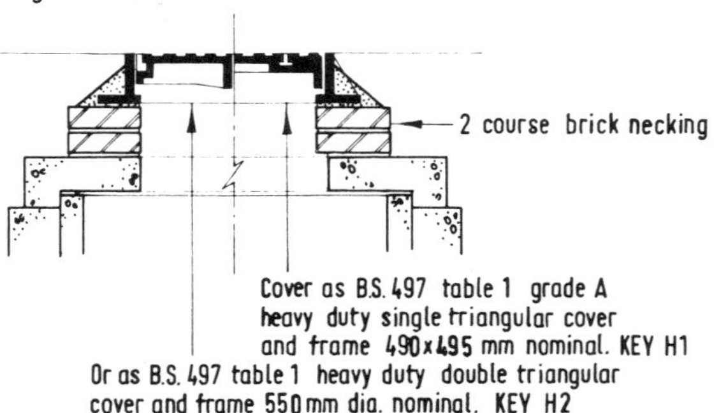

Cover as B.S. 497 table 1 grade A
heavy duty single triangular cover
and frame 490 x 495 mm nominal. KEY H1
Or as B.S. 497 table 1 heavy duty double triangular
cover and frame 550 mm dia. nominal. KEY H2

- Inspection chamber covers in grassed or planted areas,
  also pedestrian pavings where cover is not required to
  match surrounding finish

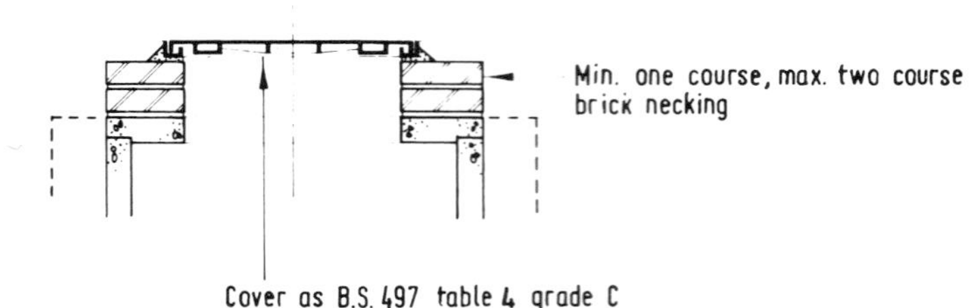

Cover as B.S. 497 table 4 grade C
light duty cover and frame 600 x 450 mm nominal. KEY L1
600 x 600 mm nominal. KEY L2

- Inspection chamber covers in pedestrian pavings where
  cover is required to match surrounding finish

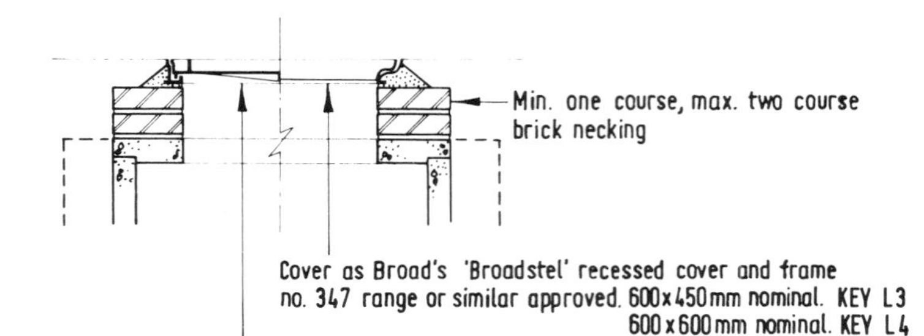

Cover as Broad's 'Broadstel' recessed cover and frame
no. 347 range or similar approved. 600 x 450 mm nominal. KEY L3
600 x 600 mm nominal. KEY L4

Or as B.S. 497 table 4 grade C
light duty recessed cover and frame. 600 x 450 mm nominal. KEY L5
600 x 600 mm nominal. KEY L6

Where securing screws are required add suffix 'S' to key reference

INSPECTION CHAMBER INTERNAL DIAMETER	SIZE OF HOLE IN PRECAST CONCRETE SLAB — GENERAL AVAILABILITY			
	610 x 457mm	610 x 610mm	560mm DIA.	600mm DIA.
750 mm	X		X	
900 mm	X	X	X	X
1050 mm	X	X	X	X
1200 mm	X	X	X	X

GLC ILEA
Department of Architecture and Civic Design
County Hall SE1
Architect Sir Roger Walters KBE FRIBA FI StructE

Cover sizes of light and medium duty related to size and depth of I.C. (see I.C. Schedule)

Heavy duty covers shall conform to local authority requirements

Additional alternatives may be required at local authority's request

Departmental Standard Drawing

title
METAL COVERS AND FRAMES, AND R.C. COVER SLABS
FOR PRECAST CONCRETE CIRCULAR INSPECTION CHAMBERS (EXTERNAL USE)

scale
1:20

drawing no
D3560A.

171178 A - 010379

50 826 Xf2 as drawing

SECTION A-A

50mm min.

150

C

C

SECTION B-B

For size of clear opening and details of cover see I.C. schedule. (Nominal 750 x 600 mm cover on 787·5 x 787·5 mm chamber shown)

Maximum 3 course corbelling not to exceed 45 mm projection per course

25mm radius nose of benching as W46

Slope 1 in 6

Brickwork as W26, W46, W48

In situ concrete benching as W46

Insitu concrete base slab as W13, W48

Half round clayware channel as W15

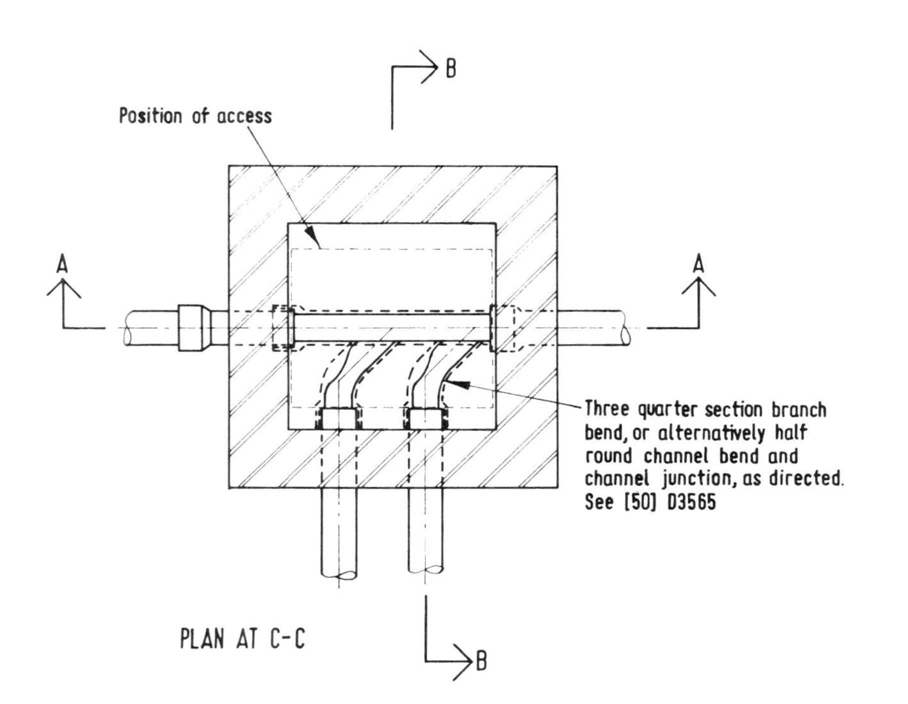

PLAN AT C-C

Depth Range:

Up to 900 mm between cover level and invert level

CONCRETE AND MORTAR MIX	INTERNAL DIMENSIONS OF CHAMBER	KEY CODE
NORMAL	675 x 450 mm	EAOA
	787·5 x 787·5 mm	EAOB
	1012·5 x 787·5 mm	EAOC
SULPHATE RESISTANT	675 x 450 mm	EBOA
	787·5 x 787·5 mm	EBOB
	1012·5 x 787·5 mm	EBOC

Suggested minimum inspection chamber dimensions:

(i) With not more than 1 side branch at depths less than 750mm, with main channel off centre if necessary	675 x 450 mm
(ii) With not more than 2 no. 100mm branches per side, or turning I.C's. at major changes of direction	787·5 x 787·5 mm
(iii) With not more than 3 no. 100 mm branches per side	1012·5 x 787·5 mm

Note: As an alternative to (ii) for I.C. with not more than 2 no. 100 mm branches per side, see [50] D3577

GLC ILEA

Department of Architecture and Civic Design
County Hall SE1
Architect Sir Roger Walters KBE FRIBA FI StructE

References following notes are clause numbers from G.L.C. preambles to bills of quantities

For details of covers and frames of type to suit location of inspection chamber see [50] D3566

For channel details see [50] D3565

Departmental Standard Drawing

title

INSPECTION CHAMBER
SHALLOW (EXTERNAL)
BRICK WITH CORBELLING
(UP TO 900mm BETWEEN COVER LEVEL AND INVERT)

scale 1:20

drawing no D3561

bldg type | space use | element [50] | feature 826 | material Fg2 | key as matrix

00 - 010379

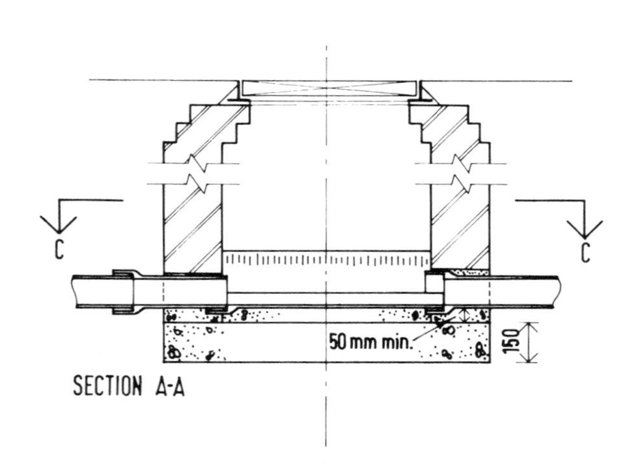

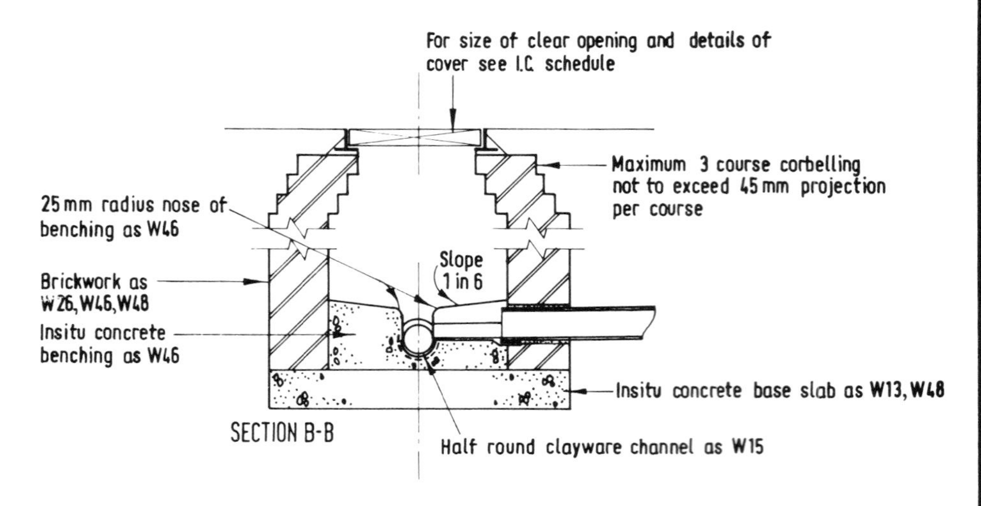

Depth Range:

Up to 900 mm between cover level and invert level

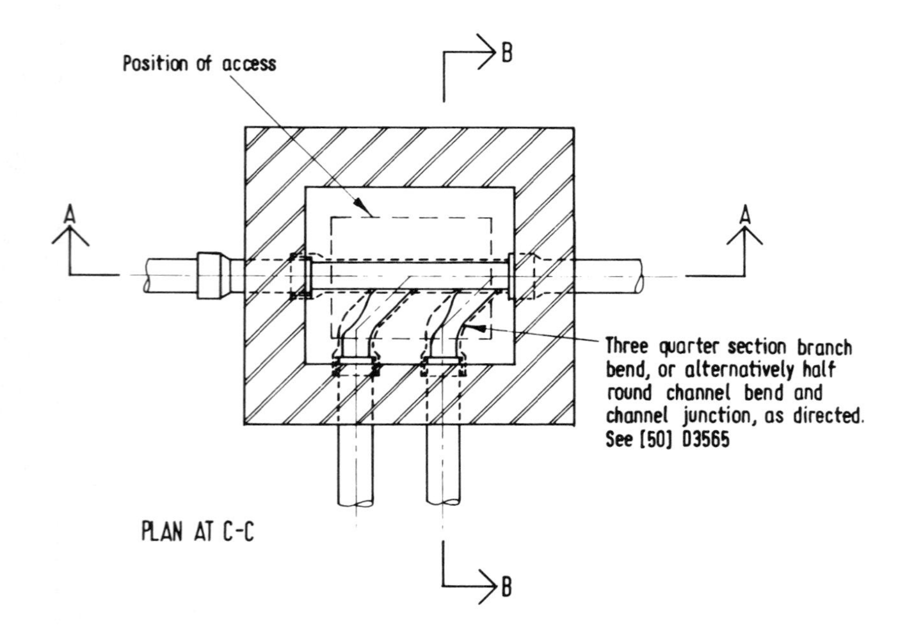

INTERNAL DIMENSIONS OF CHAMBER	CONCRETE AND MORTAR MIX	KEY CODE
787·5 x 675 mm	NORMAL	EAOD
MAXIMUM 2 No. 100 mm BRANCHES PER SIDE	SULPHATE RESISTANT	EBOD

Note: Internal dimensions of I.C. (nearest brick sizes) are marginally below C.P. 301: 1971 requirements

GLC ILEA

Department of Architecture and Civic Design
County Hall SE1
Architect Sir Roger Walters KBE FRIBA FI StructE

References following notes are clause numbers from G.L.C. preambles to bills of quantities

For details of covers and frames of type to suit location of inspection chamber see [50] D3566

For channel details see [50] D3565

Departmental Standard Drawing

title

INSPECTION CHAMBER
SHALLOW (EXTERNAL)
BRICK WITH CORBELLING
787·5 x 675 mm

scale 1:20

drawing no D3577

50 | 826 | Fg2 | as matrix

08 - 010379

GLC ILEA

Department of Architecture
and Civic Design
County Hall SE1
Architect Sir Roger Walters
KBE FRIBA FI StructE

References following notes are clause numbers from G.L.C. preambles to bills of quantities

For details of covers and frames of type to suit location of inspection chamber see [50] D3567

For channel details see [50] D3565

Insitu concrete cover slab where not subject to vehicular loading reinforced with 8 mm mild steel bars at 150 mm centres both ways

Insitu concrete cover slab where subject to vehicular loading reinforced with 12 mm mild steel bars at 150 mm centres both ways

100

200

40 mm from underside of slab to m.s. bars

C

C

50mm min.

150

SECTION A-A

For details of covers see [50] D3567

Brick necking as W26, W49 see [50] D3567

Concrete cover slab to be 1:2:4 mix

25mm radius nose of benching

Brickwork as W26, W46, W48

Insitu concrete benching as W46

Insitu concrete base slab as W13, W48

Half round clayware channel as W15

SECTION B-B

Depth Range:

Up to 900 mm between cover level and invert level

CONCRETE AND MORTAR MIX	INTERNAL DIMENSIONS OF CHAMBER	LIGHT DUTY SLAB	HEAVY DUTY SLAB
NORMAL	787·5 x 787·5 mm	EA1B	EA2B
	1012·5 x 787·5 mm	EA1C	EA2C
	1350 x 787·5 mm	EA1E	EA2E
SULPHATE RESISTANT	787·5 x 787·5 mm	EB1B	EB2B
	1012·5 x 787·5 mm	EB1C	EB2C
	1350 x 787·5 mm	EB1E	EB2E

Suggested minimum inspection chamber dimensions:

(i) With not more than 2 no. 100 mm branches per side, or turning I.C's. at major changes of direction — 787·5 x 787·5 mm

(ii) With not more than 3 no. 100mm branches per side — 1012·5 x 787·5 mm

(iii) With not more than 4 no. 100mm branches per side — 1350 x 787·5 mm

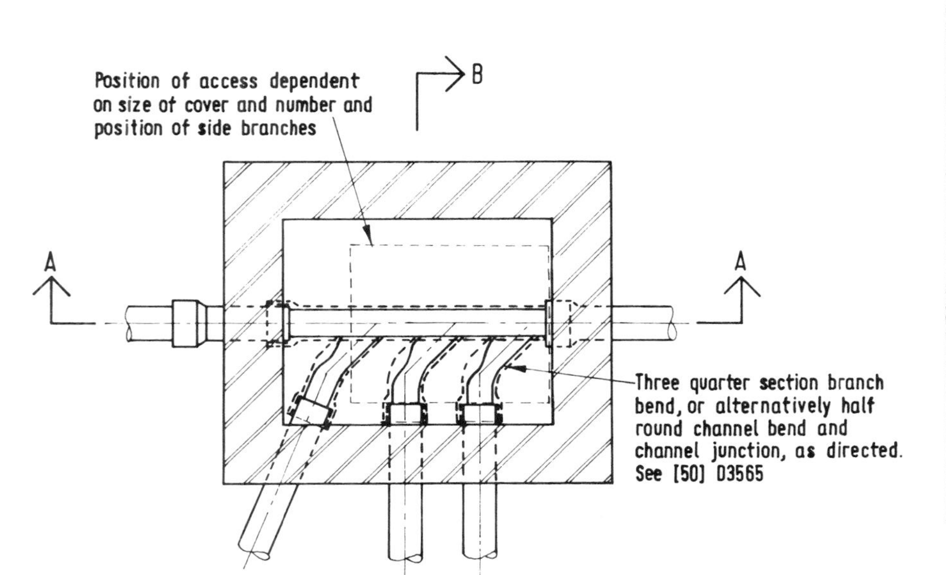

PLAN AT C-C

B

Departmental Standard Drawing

title

INSPECTION CHAMBER SHALLOW (EXTERNAL) BRICK WITH CONCRETE COVER SLAB (UP TO 900 mm BETWEEN COVER LEVEL AND INVERT)

scale 1:20

drawing no D3562

bldg type | space use | element [50] | feature 826 | material Fg2 | key as matrix

Department of Architecture and Civic Design
County Hall SE1
Architect Sir Roger Walters KBE FRIBA FI Struct/E

References following notes are clause numbers from G.L.C. preambles to bills of quantities

For details of covers and frames of type to suit location of inspection chamber see [50] D3567

For channel details see [50] D3565

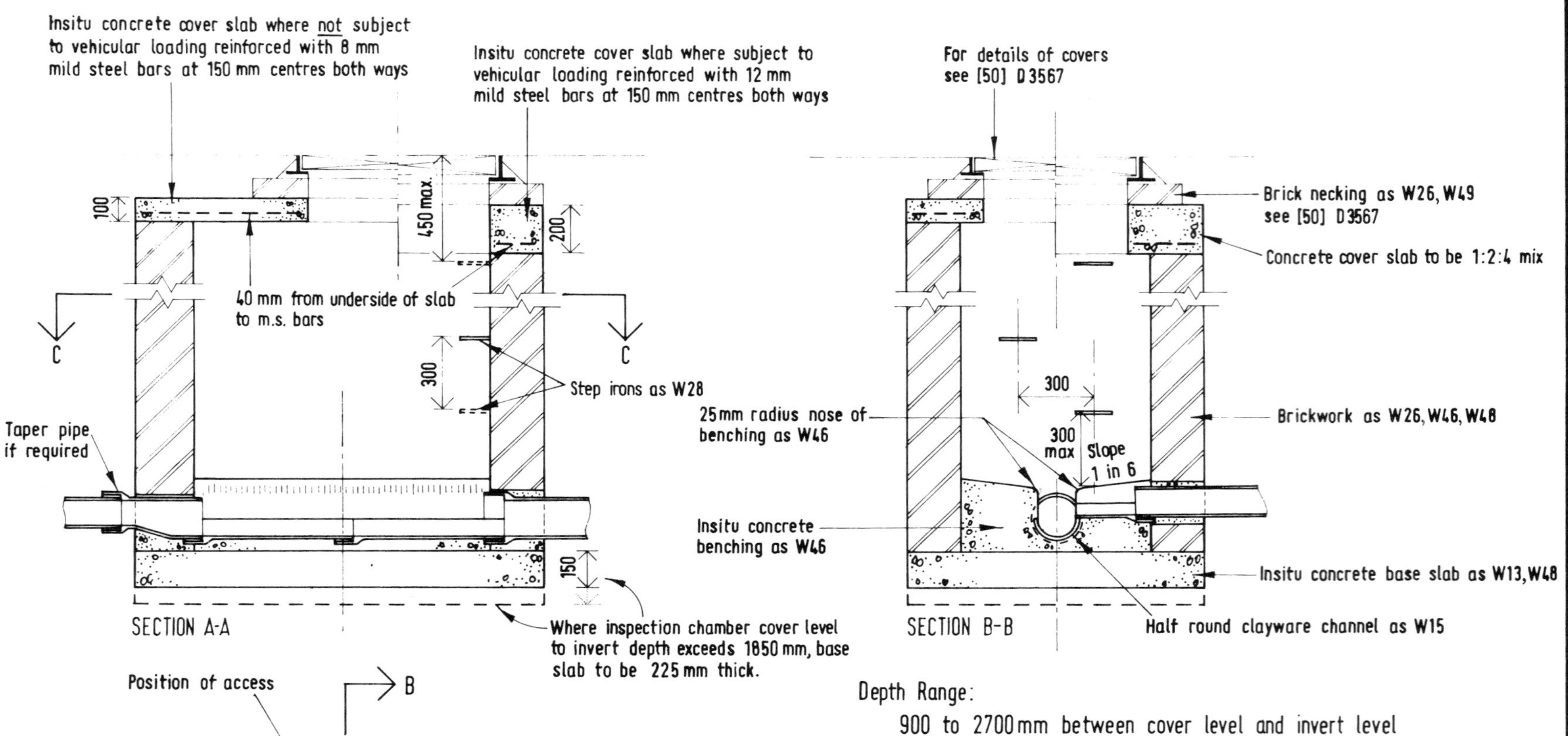

Depth Range:

900 to 2700mm between cover level and invert level

CONCRETE AND MORTAR MIX	INTERNAL DIMENSIONS OF CHAMBER	LIGHT DUTY SLAB	HEAVY DUTY SLAB
NORMAL	1237·5 x 787·5mm	EA1F	EA2F
	1350 x 787·5 mm	EA1G	EA2G
SULPHATE RESISTANT	1237·5 x 787·5 mm	EB1F	EB2F
	1350 x 787·5 mm	EB1G	EB2G

Suggested minimum inspection chamber dimensions:

(i) With not more than 3 no. 100mm branches per side 1237·5 x 787·5 mm

(ii) With not more than 4 no. 100mm branches per side 1350 x 787·5 mm

Departmental Standard Drawing

title

INSPECTION CHAMBER
AVERAGE/DEEP (EXTERNAL) BRICK WITH CONCRETE COVER SLAB (900 TO 2700 mm BETWEEN COVER LEVEL AND INVERT)

scale 1:20

drawing no D3563

bldg type | space use | element [50] | feature 826 | material Fg2 | key as matrix

Main half section channels shown straight, but curved channels will also be specified for some situations

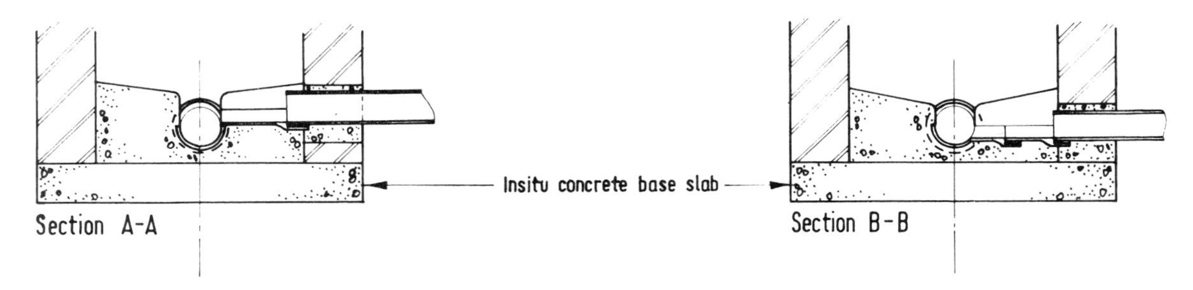

Angle(s) of branch drain entry to I.C. achieved by using three quarter section branch bends from National 104 range (Note limitation on angle)

Angle(s) of branch drain entry to I.C. achieved by using half section channel junctions from National range of oblique junctions with half section channel bends from National 81 - 91 (inclusive) range. (Note limitation on angle)

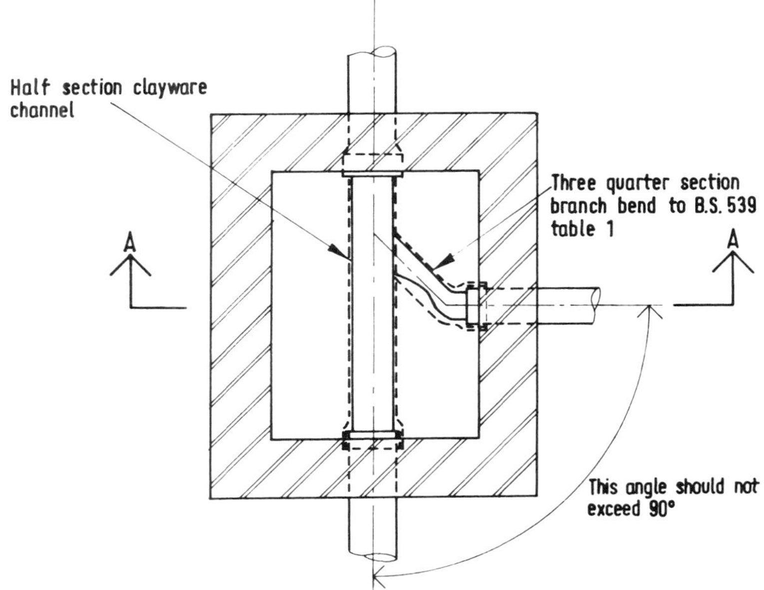

Half section clayware channel with three quarter section branch bend
KEY 1

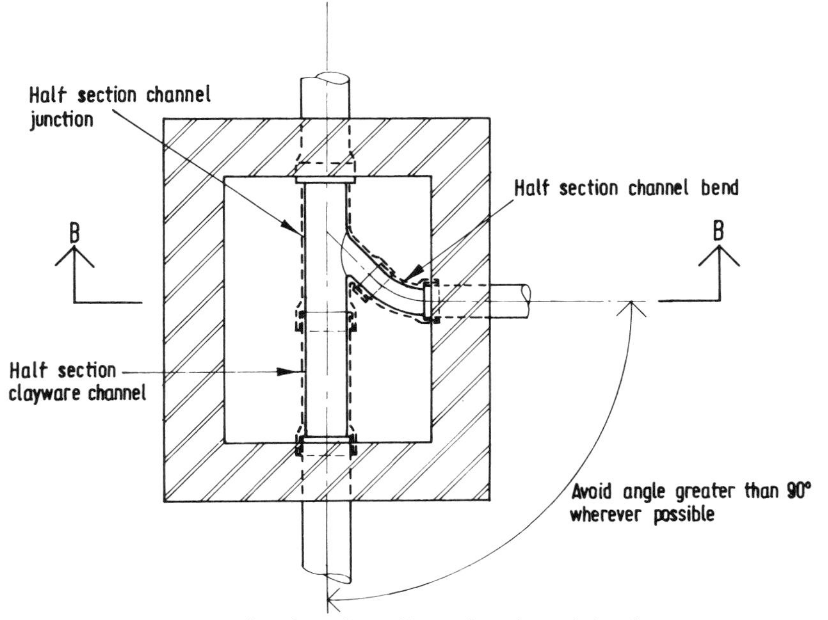

Half section channel junction with half section channel bend
KEY 2

GLC ILEA

Department of Architecture and Civic Design
County Hall SE1
Architect Sir Roger Walters KBE FRIBA FI StructE

This drawing shows alternative details for I.C. channels and should be read in conjunction with I.C. schedule

Departmental Standard Drawing

title
BRICK INSPECTION CHAMBERS
ALTERNATIVE CHANNEL DETAILS (EXTERNAL USE)

scale 1:20

drawing no D3565

bldg type | space use | element [50] | feature 826 | material Fg2 | key as drawing

00 - 010379

- Inspection chamber covers in vehicular pavings not subject to heavy commercial vehicles

A) where cover is not required to match surrounding finish

Cover as B.S. 497 table 5 grade B
medium duty, solid top 600 x 450 mm nominal. KEY M1
Or non B.S. cover sizes 750 x 600 mm nominal. KEY M7
900 x 600 mm nominal. KEY M8

B) where cover is required to match surrounding finish

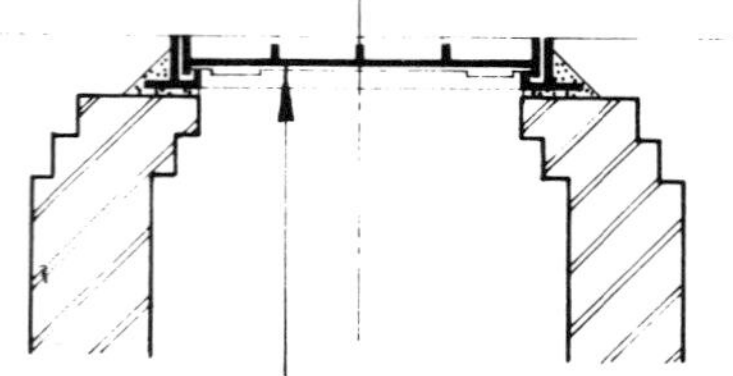

Cover as B.S. 497 table 5 grade B
medium duty, recessed cover 600 x 450 mm nominal. KEY M3
Or non B.S. cover sizes 750 x 600 mm nominal. KEY M5
900 x 600 mm nominal. KEY M6

- Inspection chamber covers in carriageways subject to fast moving traffic

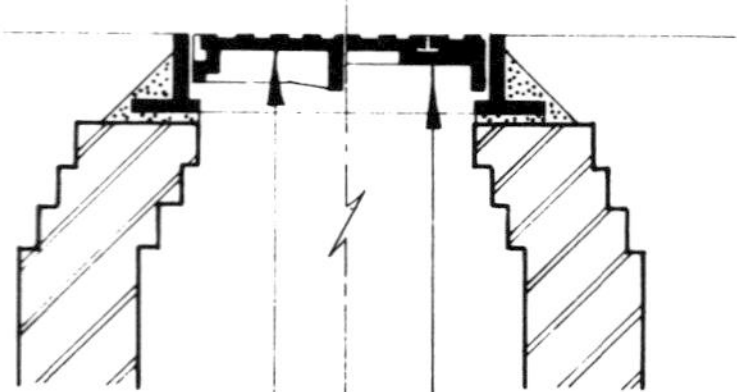

Cover as B.S. 497 table 2 grade A
heavy duty single triangular cover
and frame 495 x 520 mm nominal. KEY H1
Cover as B.S. 497 table 1 grade A heavy duty double triangular
cover and frame 558 mm dia. nominal. KEY H2
Or non B.S. rectangular covers 750 x 600 mm nominal. KEY H3
750 x 750 mm nominal. KEY H4
900 x 600 mm nominal. KEY H5

- Inspection chamber covers in grassed or planted areas, also pedestrian pavings where cover is not required to match surrounding finish

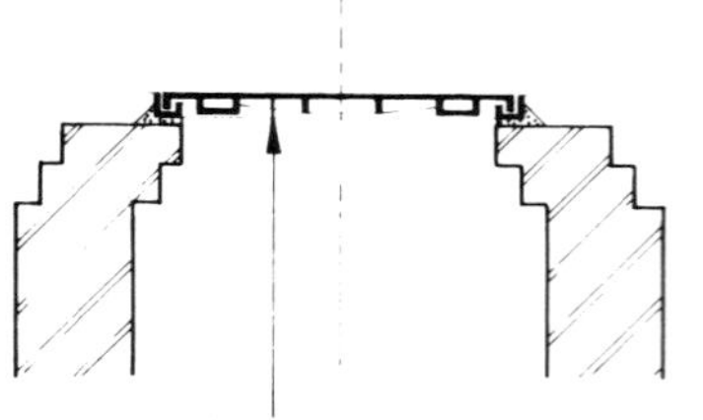

Cover as B.S. 497 table 6 grade C
light duty cover and frame 600 x 450 mm nominal. KEY L1
600 x 600 mm nominal. KEY L2
Or non B.S. cover sizes 750 x 600 mm nominal. KEY L7
750 x 750 mm nominal. KEY L8
900 x 600 mm nominal. KEY L9

- Inspection chamber covers in pedestrian pavings where cover is required to match surrounding finish

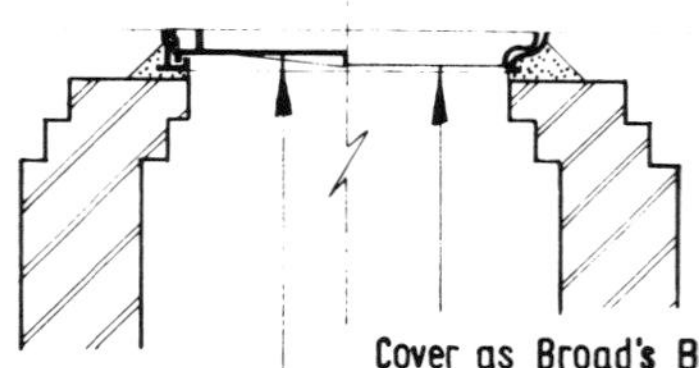

Cover as Broad's Broadstel recessed cover and frame
no. 347 range or similar approved. 600 x 450 mm nominal. KEY L3
750 x 600 mm nominal. KEY L11
750 x 750 mm nominal. KEY L12
900 x 600 mm nominal. KEY L13

Cover as B.S. 497 table 8 grade C
light duty recessed cover and frame. 600 x 450 mm nominal KEY L5
600 x 600 mm nominal KEY L6
Or non B.S. cover sizes 750 x 600 mm nominal. KEY L14
750 x 750 mm nominal. KEY L15
900 x 600 mm nominal. KEY L16

Where securing screws are required add suffix 'S' to key reference

INSPECTION CHAMBER DIMENSIONS	SUITABLE COVER SIZES (NOMINAL)				
	To B.S. 497		Non B.S. sizes (Where larger opening required to conform with C.P. 301 recommendations)		
675 x 450 mm	600 x 450 mm	495 x 520 mm	———	———	———
787·5 x 675 mm	600 x 450 mm 600 x 600 mm	495 x 520 mm 558 mm dia.	750 x 600 mm	———	———
787·5 x 787·5 mm	600 x 600 mm	558 mm dia.	750 x 600 mm	750 x 750 mm	———
1012·5 x 787·5 mm	———	———	750 x 600 mm	750 x 750 mm	900 x 600 mm

GLC ILEA
Department of Architecture and Civic Design
County Hall SE1
Architect Sir Roger Walters KBE FRIBA FI StructE

Cover sizes of light and medium duty related to size of inspection chamber (see I.C. schedule)

Heavy duty covers shall conform to local authority requirements

Additional alternatives may be required at local authority's request

Departmental Standard Drawing

title
COVERS AND FRAMES
FOR BRICK INSPECTION CHAMBERS WITH CORBELLING
(EXTERNAL USE)

scale 1:20

drawing no D3566

bldg type | space use | element | feature | material | key
[50] 826 Fg2 as drawing

010379 - 00

- Inspection chamber covers in vehicular pavings not subject to heavy commercial vehicles

A) where cover is not required to match surrounding finish

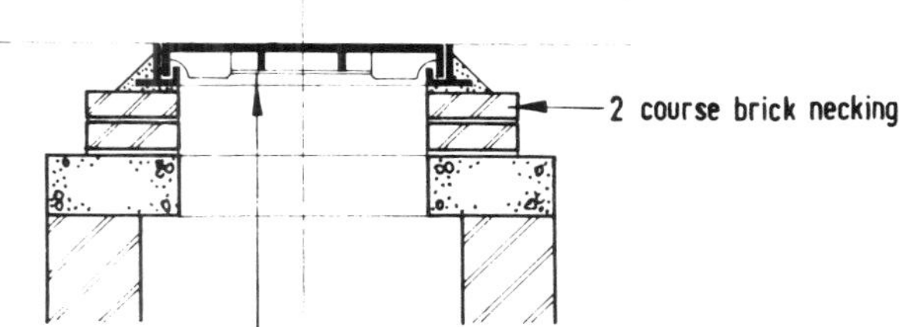

Cover as B.S. 497 table 3 grade B
medium duty, solid top 600 x 450 mm nominal KEY M1
Or non B.S. cover sizes 750 x 600 mm nominal. KEY M7
900 x 600 mm nominal. KEY M8

B) where cover is required to match surrounding finish

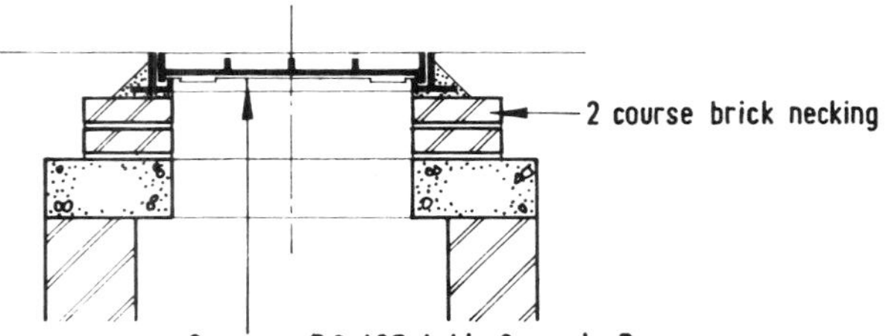

Cover as B.S. 497 table 3 grade B
medium duty, recessed cover 600 x 450 mm nominal KEY M3
Or non B.S. cover sizes 750 x 600 mm nominal. KEY M5
900 x 600 mm nominal. KEY M6

- Inspection chamber covers in carriageways subject to fast moving traffic

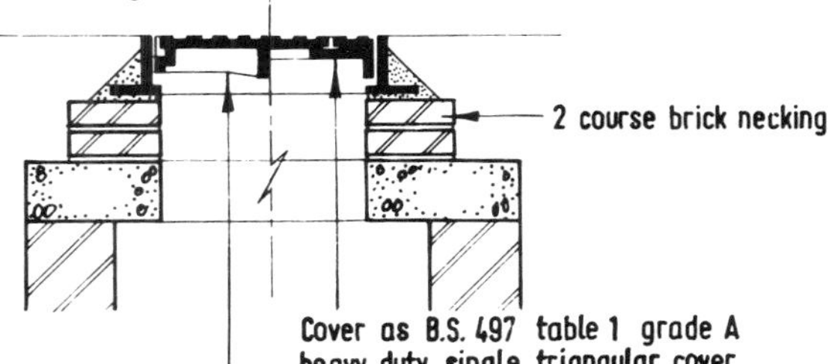

Cover as B.S. 497 table 1 grade A
heavy duty single triangular cover
and frame 490 x 495 mm nominal KEY H1
Cover as B.S. 497 table 1 grade A heavy duty double triangular
cover and frame 550 mm dia. nominal KEY H2
Or non B.S. rectangular covers 750 x 600 mm nominal. KEY H3
750 x 750 mm nominal. KEY H4
900 x 600 mm nominal. KEY H5

- Inspection chamber covers in grassed or planted areas, also pedestrian pavings where cover is not required to match surrounding finish

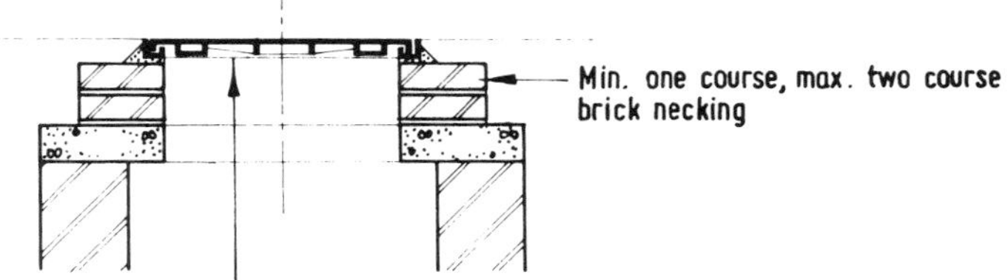

Cover as B.S. 497 table 4 grade C
light duty cover and frame 600 x 600 mm nominal KEY L2
Or non B.S. cover sizes 750 x 600 mm nominal. KEY L7
750 x 750 mm nominal. KEY L8
900 x 600 mm nominal. KEY L9

- Inspection chamber covers in pedestrian pavings where cover is required to match surrounding finish

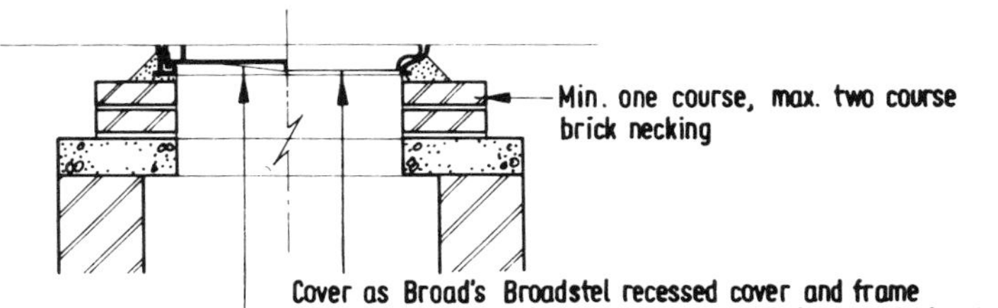

Cover as Broad's Broadstel recessed cover and frame
no. 347 range or similar approved. 750 x 750 mm nominal KEY L12
900 x 600 mm nominal KEY L13
Cover as B.S. 497 table 4 grade C
light duty recessed cover and frame. 600 x 600 mm nominal KEY L6
Or non B.S. cover sizes 750 x 600 mm nominal. KEY L14
750 x 750 mm nominal. KEY L15
900 x 600 mm nominal. KEY L16

Where securing screws are required add suffix 'S' to key reference

INSPECTION CHAMBER DIMENSIONS	SUITABLE COVER SIZES (NOMINAL)						
	To B.S. 497				Non B.S. sizes (Where larger opening required to conform with C.P. 301 recommendations)		
787·5 x 787·5 mm	600 x 450 mm	600 x 600 mm	490 x 495 mm	550 mm dia.	750 x 600 mm	——	——
1012·5 x 787·5 mm	600 x 450 mm	600 x 600 mm	490 x 495 mm	550 mm dia.	750 x 600 mm	750 x 750 mm	900 x 600 mm
1237·5 x 787·5 mm	600 x 450 mm	600 x 600 mm	490 x 495 mm	550 mm dia.	900 x 600 mm	——	——
1350 x 787·5 mm	600 x 450 mm	600 x 600 mm	490 x 495 mm	550 mm dia.	900 x 600 mm	——	——

GLC ILEA
Department of Architecture and Civic Design
County Hall SE1
Architect Sir Roger Walters KBE FRIBA FI StructE

Cover sizes of light and medium duty related to size and depth of I.C. (see I.C. schedule)

Heavy duty covers shall conform to local authority requirements

Additional alternatives may be required at local authority's request

Cover slab opening to suit cover and frame

171178 A 00 - 010379

Departmental Standard Drawing

title
COVERS AND FRAMES
FOR BRICK INSPECTION CHAMBERS WITH CONCRETE COVER SLAB
(EXTERNAL USE)

scale 1:20

drawing no D3567.A.

bldg type | space use | element [50] | feature 826 | material Fg2 | key as drawing

GLC ILEA

Department of Architecture
and Civic Design
County Hall SE1
Architect Sir Roger Walters
KBE FRIBA FI StructE

References following notes are clause numbers from G.L.C. preambles to bills of quantities

This drawing shows alternative details for backdrops and should be read in conjunction with I.C. schedule

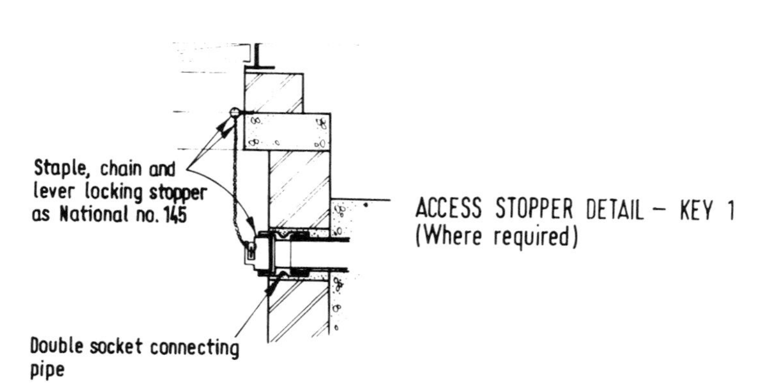

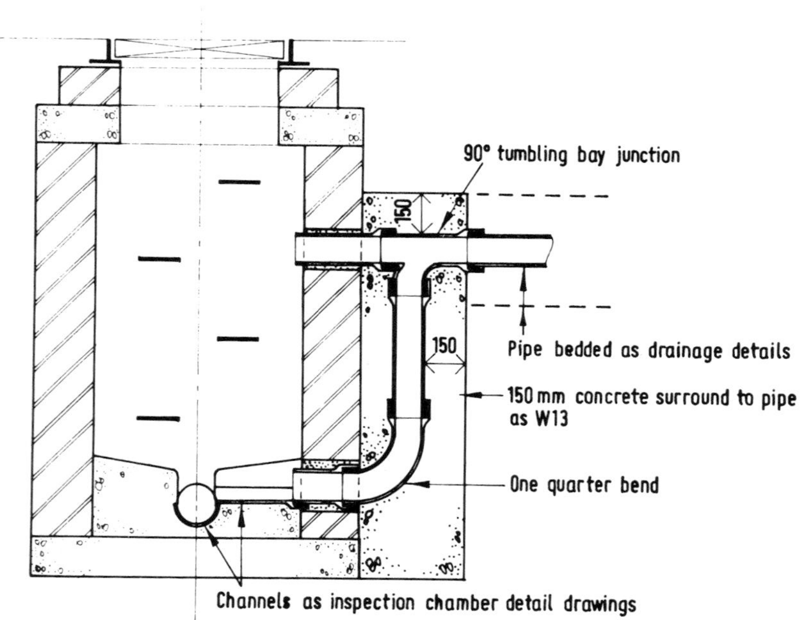

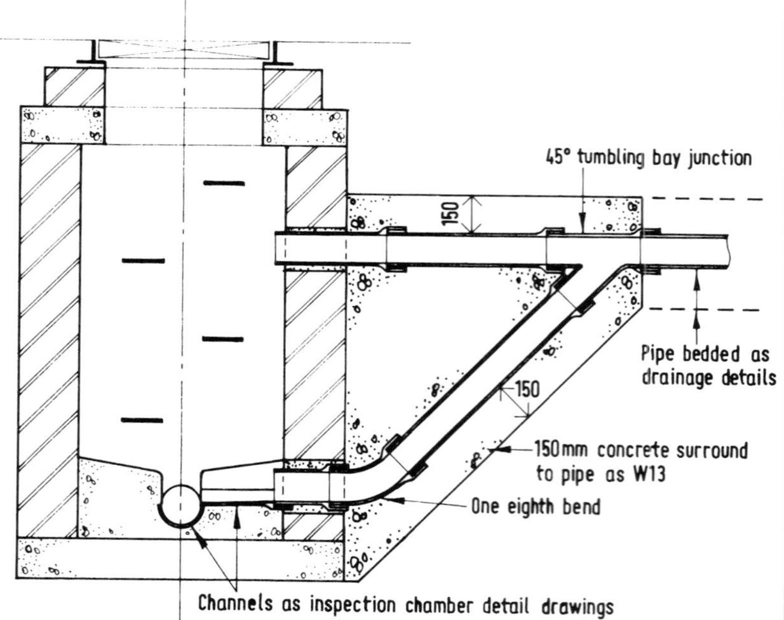

Backdrops shown on branch, but details similar when on main run.

This drawing is for information on backdrops only and details of inspection chamber are referred to in the I.C. schedule

Departmental Standard Drawing

title
BRICK INSPECTION CHAMBERS
ALTERNATIVE BACKDROP DETAILS (EXTERNAL USE)

scale 1:20

drawing no D3568

bldg type | space use | element [50] | feature 826 | material Fg2 | key as drawing

010379

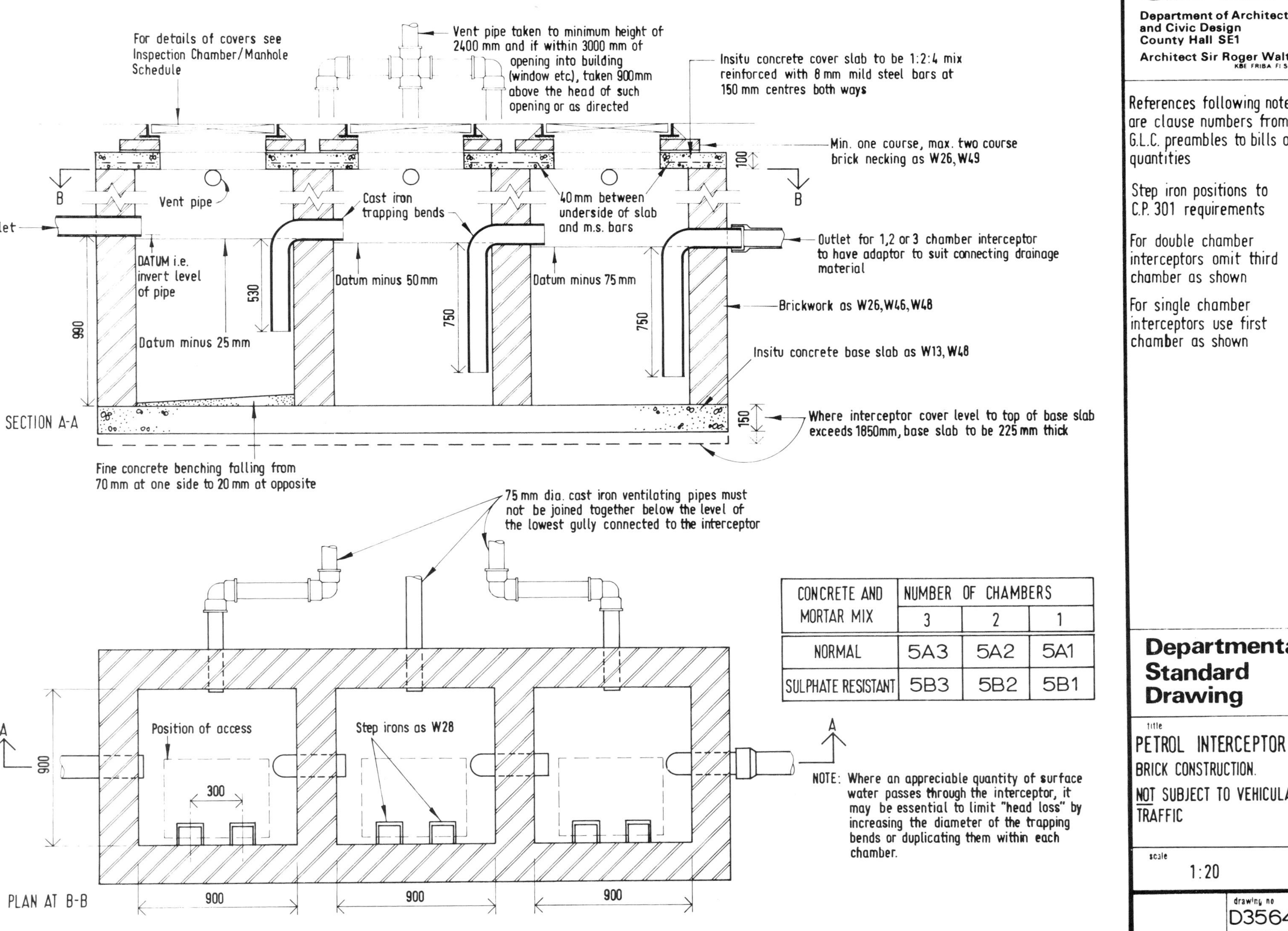

CONCRETE AND MORTAR MIX	NUMBER OF CHAMBERS		
	3	2	1
NORMAL	5A3	5A2	5A1
SULPHATE RESISTANT	5B3	5B2	5B1

00 - 010379

[50] 826 Fg2 as matrix

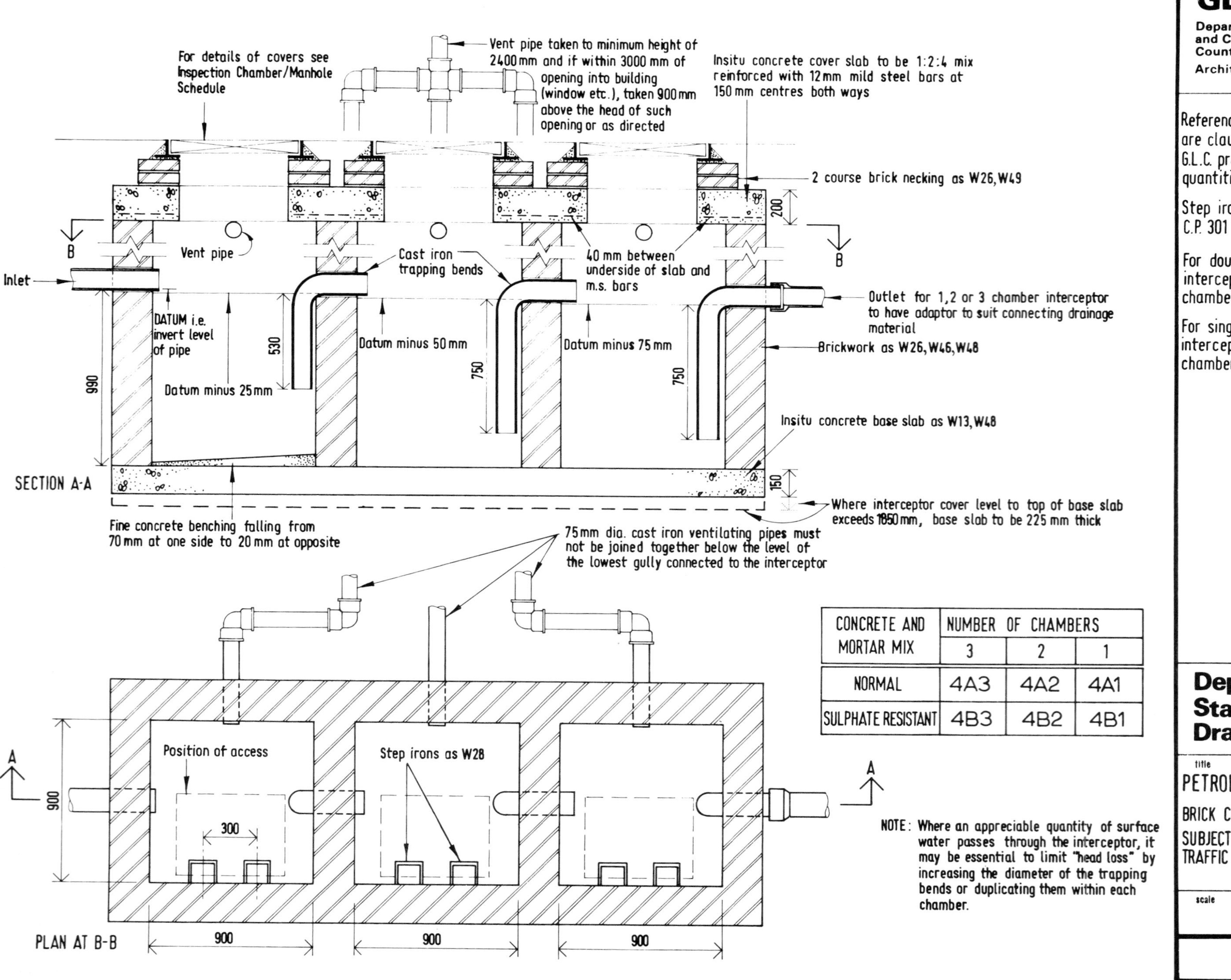

CONCRETE AND MORTAR MIX	NUMBER OF CHAMBERS		
	3	2	1
NORMAL	4A3	4A2	4A1
SULPHATE RESISTANT	4B3	4B2	4B1

NOTE: Where an appreciable quantity of surface water passes through the interceptor, it may be essential to limit "head loss" by increasing the diameter of the trapping bends or duplicating them within each chamber.

GLC ILEA

Department of Architecture and Civic Design
County Hall SE1
Architect Sir Roger Walters KBE FRIBA FI StructE

References following notes are clause numbers from G.L.C. preambles to bills of quantities

Step iron positions to C.P. 301 requirements

For double chamber interceptors omit third chamber as shown

For single chamber interceptors use first chamber as shown

Departmental Standard Drawing

title
PETROL INTERCEPTOR
BRICK CONSTRUCTION.
SUBJECT TO VEHICULAR TRAFFIC

scale
1:20

drawing no
D3569

50 826 Fg2 as matrix

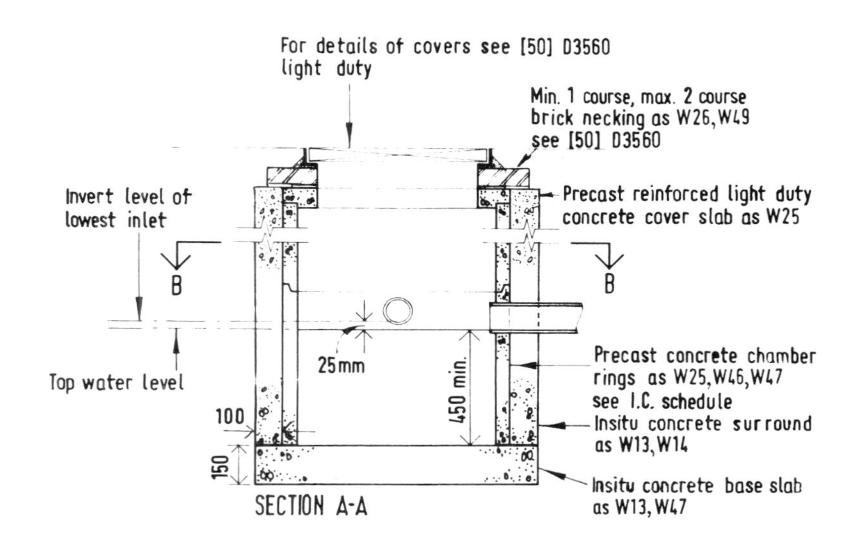

CATCH PITS
NOT SUBJECT TO VEHICULAR TRAFFIC

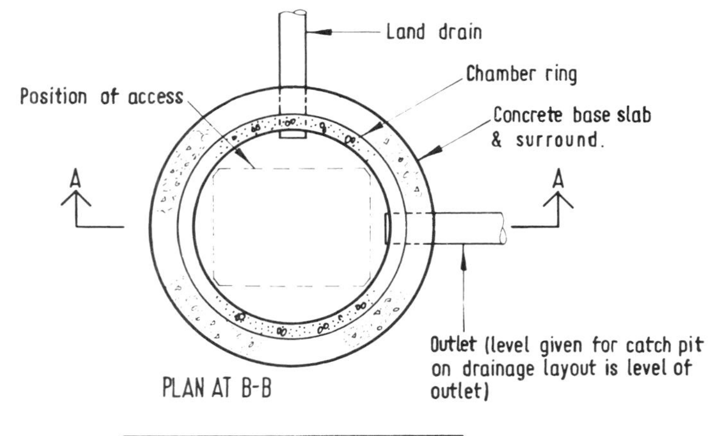

CONCRETE	KEY
NORMAL	6A1
SULPHATE RESISTANT	6B1

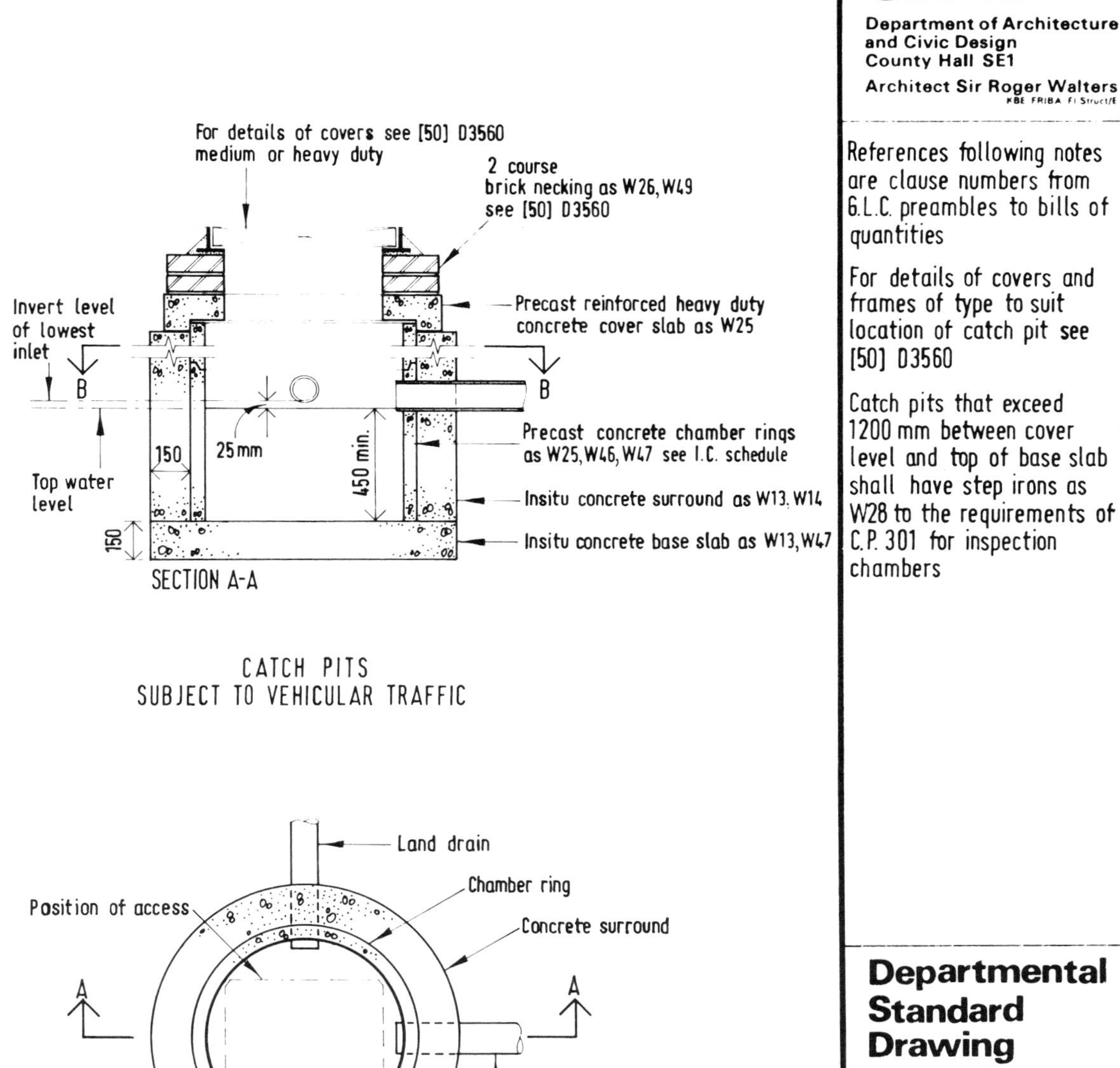

CONCRETE	KEY
NORMAL	6A2
SULPHATE RESISTANT	6B2

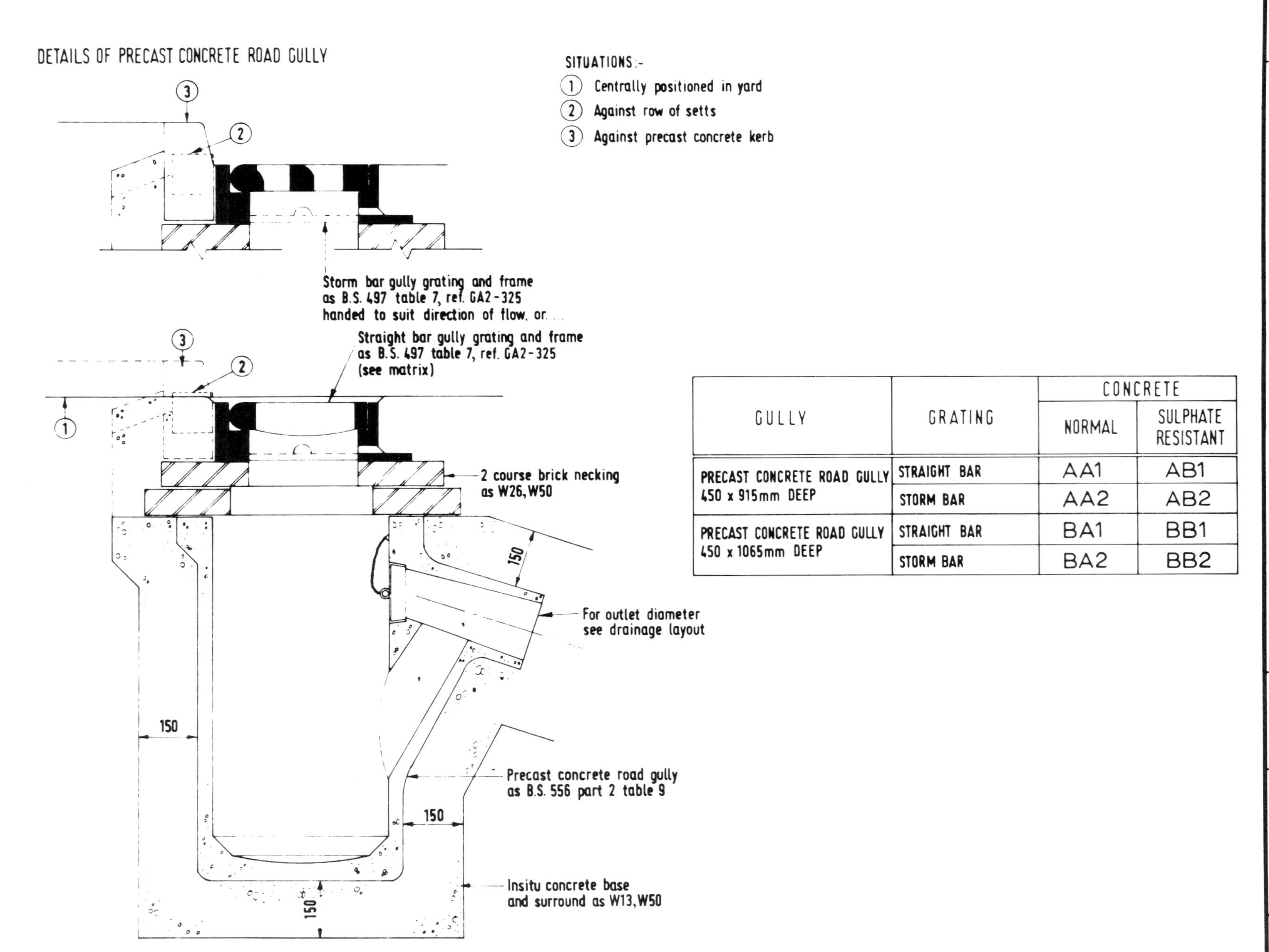

GULLY	GRATING	CONCRETE	
		NORMAL	SULPHATE RESISTANT
PRECAST CONCRETE ROAD GULLY 450 x 915mm DEEP	STRAIGHT BAR	AA1	AB1
	STORM BAR	AA2	AB2
PRECAST CONCRETE ROAD GULLY 450 x 1065mm DEEP	STRAIGHT BAR	BA1	BB1
	STORM BAR	BA2	BB2

GLC ILEA

Department of Architecture and Civic Design
County Hall SE1 7PB
Architect Sir Roger Walters KBE ARIBA FI Struct/E

References following notes are clause numbers from G.L.C. preambles to bills of quantities

This detail is not applicable for basement or other covered garages and parking areas.

Departmental Standard Drawing

title
GULLIES
FOR DRAINING GARAGE YARDS AND PARKING AREAS (PRECAST CONCRETE)

scale
1:10

drawing no D3578 rev B

[50] 823 Xf2 as matrix

171178 B

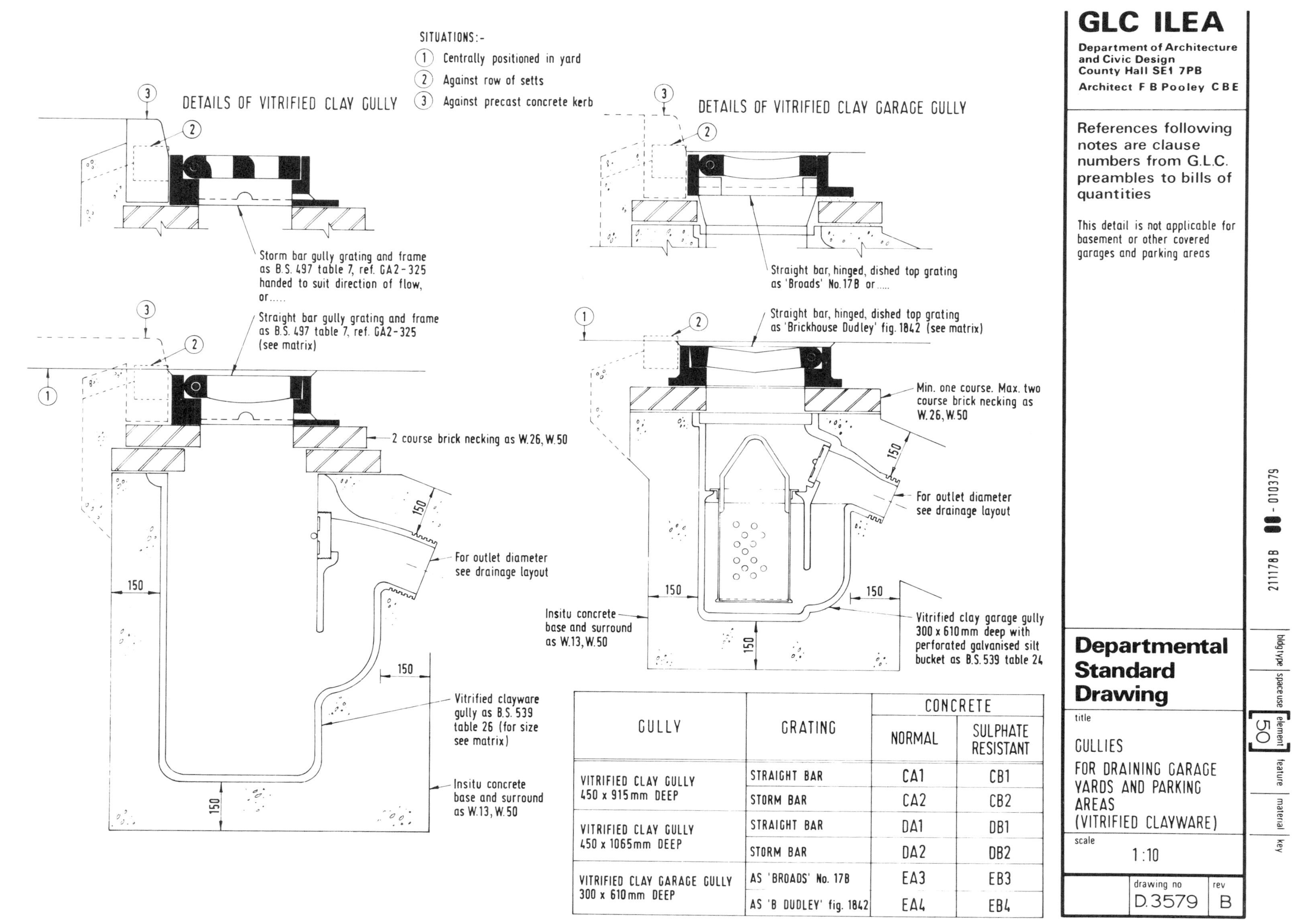

GULLY	GRATING	CONCRETE	
		NORMAL	SULPHATE RESISTANT
VITRIFIED CLAY GULLY 450 x 915mm DEEP	STRAIGHT BAR	CA1	CB1
	STORM BAR	CA2	CB2
VITRIFIED CLAY GULLY 450 x 1065mm DEEP	STRAIGHT BAR	DA1	DB1
	STORM BAR	DA2	DB2
VITRIFIED CLAY GARAGE GULLY 300 x 610mm DEEP	AS 'BROADS' No. 17B	EA3	EB3
	AS 'B DUDLEY' fig. 1842	EA4	EB4

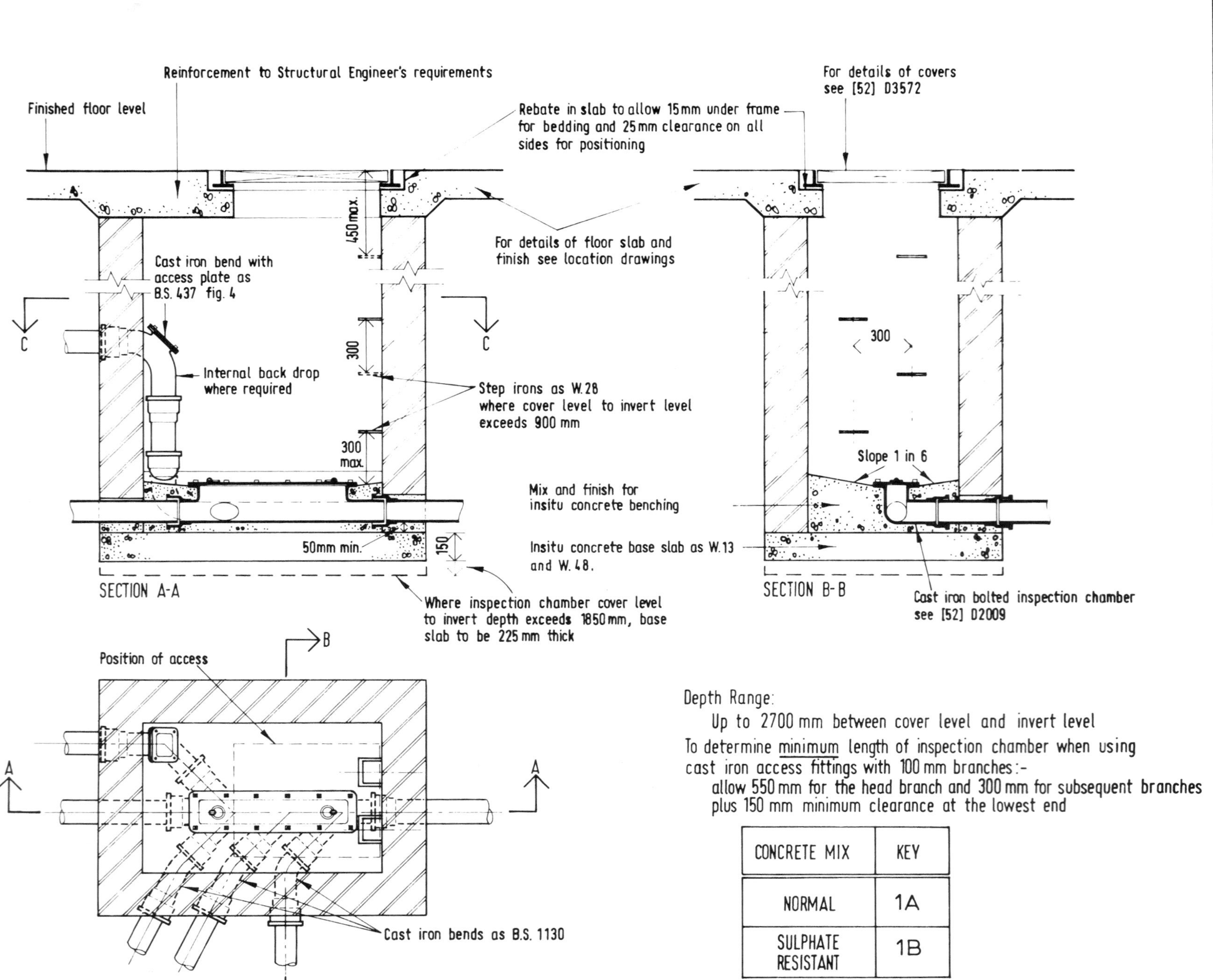

Depth Range:

Up to 2700 mm between cover level and invert level

To determine minimum length of inspection chamber when using cast iron access fittings with 100 mm branches:-

allow 550 mm for the head branch and 300 mm for subsequent branches plus 150 mm minimum clearance at the lowest end

CONCRETE MIX	KEY
NORMAL	1A
SULPHATE RESISTANT	1B

For dimensions of chamber see I.C. schedule

GLC ILEA

Department of Architecture and Civic Design
County Hall SE1
Architect Sir Roger Walters KBE FRIBA FI StructE

References following notes are clause numbers from G.L.C. preambles to bills of quantities

Internal back drops when specified in I.C. schedule only

All as clauses W.26, W.46, W.48.

Departmental Standard Drawing

title

INSPECTION CHAMBER

BRICK WITH C.I. BOLTED ACCESS.

INTEGRAL COVER SLAB

scale 1:20

drawing no D3570

[52] 826|Fg2 | as matrix

010379

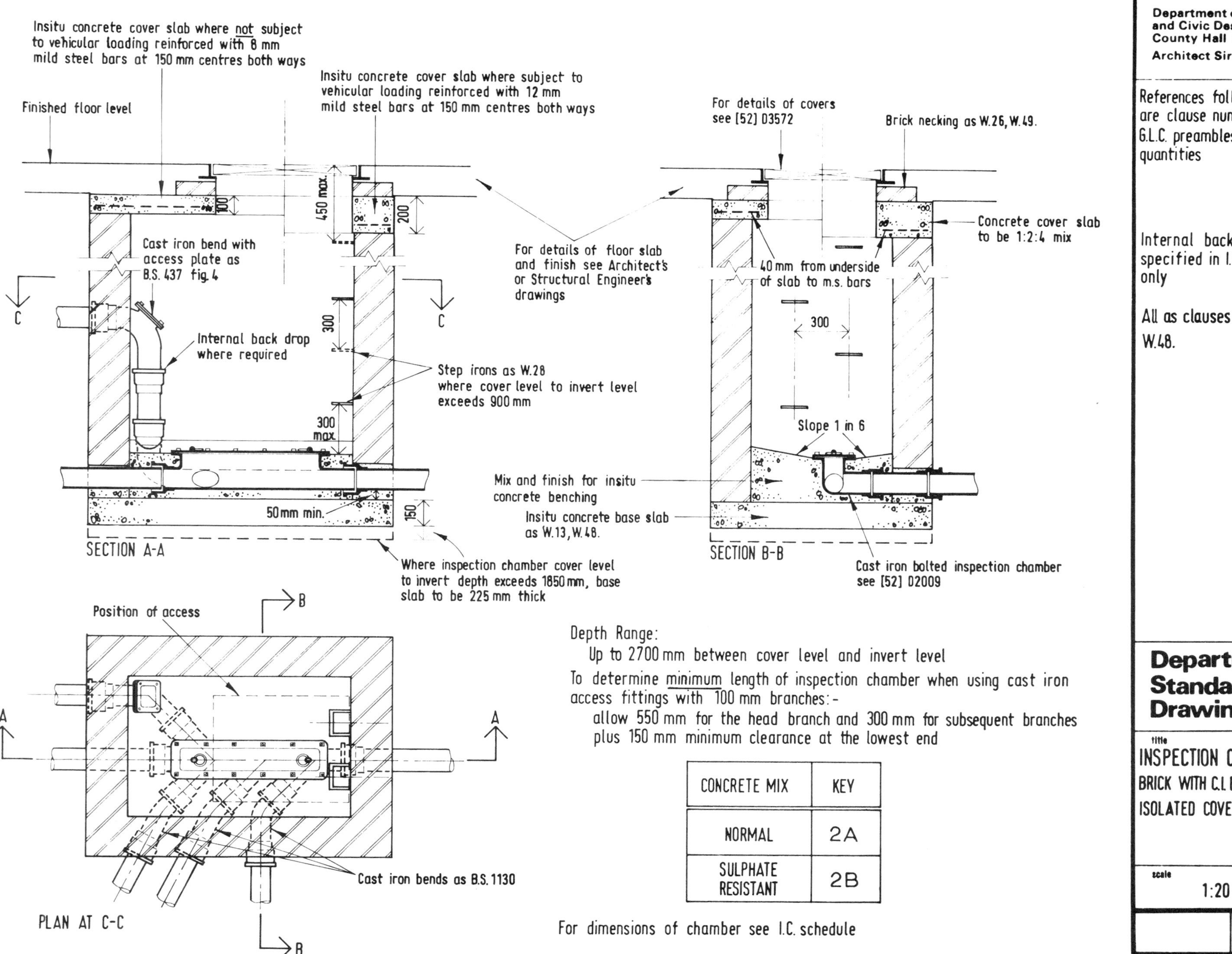

Depth Range:
Up to 2700 mm between cover level and invert level

To determine minimum length of inspection chamber when using cast iron access fittings with 100 mm branches:-
allow 550 mm for the head branch and 300 mm for subsequent branches plus 150 mm minimum clearance at the lowest end

CONCRETE MIX	KEY
NORMAL	2A
SULPHATE RESISTANT	2B

For dimensions of chamber see I.C. schedule

GLC ILEA

Department of Architecture and Civic Design
County Hall SE1
Architect Sir Roger Walters KBE FRIBA FI StructE

References following notes are clause numbers from G.L.C. preambles to bills of quantities

Internal back drops when specified in I.C. schedule only

All as clauses W.26, W.46, W.48.

Departmental Standard Drawing

title
INSPECTION CHAMBER
BRICK WITH C.I. BOLTED ACCESS
ISOLATED COVER SLAB

scale 1:20

drawing no D3571

00-010379

[52] 826 Fg2 as matrix

● Inspection chamber covers subject to light vehicular traffic

A) where cover is not required to match surrounding finish

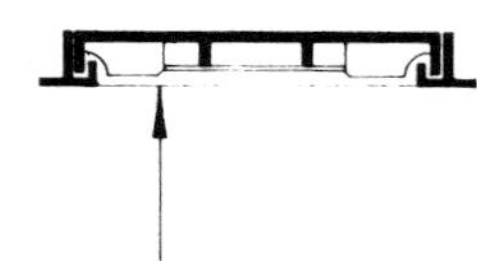

Cover as B.S. 497 table 3 grade B
medium duty, solid top 600 x 450 mm nominal KEY M1

Or non B.S. cover sizes 750 x 600 mm nominal KEY M7
900 x 600 mm nominal KEY M8

B) where cover is required to match surrounding finish

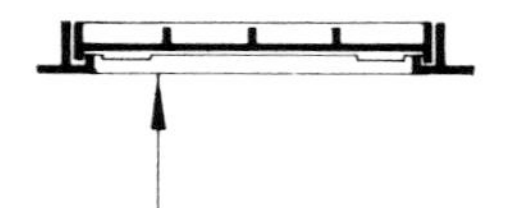

Cover as B.S. 497 table 3 grade B
medium duty, recessed cover 600 x 450 mm nominal KEY M3

Or non B.S. cover sizes 750 x 600 mm nominal KEY M5
900 x 600 mm nominal KEY M6

● Inspection chamber covers subject to heavy vehicular traffic

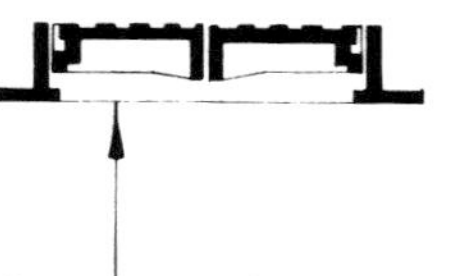

Cover as B.S. 497 table 1 grade A heavy duty
double triangular cover and frame 550 mm dia. nominal KEY H2

Or non B.S. rectangular covers 750 x 600 mm nominal KEY H3
750 x 750 mm nominal KEY H4
900 x 600 mm nominal KEY H5

● Inspection chamber covers subject to pedestrian traffic only

A) where cover is not required to match surrounding finish

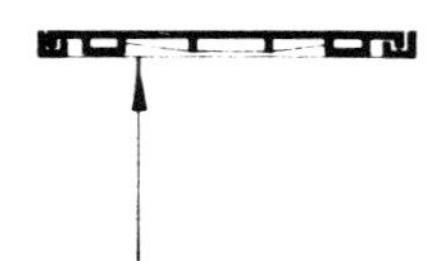

Cover as B.S. 497 table 4 grade C
light duty cover and frame 600 x 600 mm nominal KEY L2

Or non B.S. cover sizes 750 x 600 mm nominal KEY L7
750 x 750 mm nominal KEY L8
900 x 600 mm nominal KEY L9

B) where cover is required to match surrounding finish

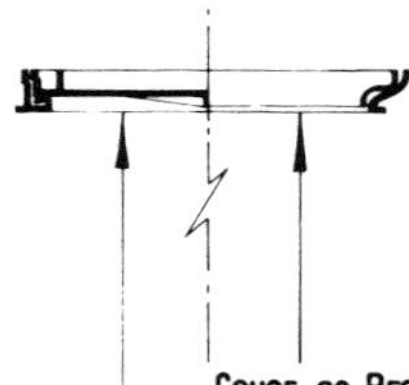

Cover as Broad's Broadstel recessed cover and frame
no. 347 range or similar approved. 750 x 750 mm nominal KEY L12
900 x 600 mm nominal KEY L13

Cover as B.S. 497 table 4 grade C
light duty recessed cover and frame. 600 x 600 mm nominal KEY L6

Or non B.S. cover sizes 750 x 600 mm nominal KEY L14
750 x 750 mm nominal KEY L15
900 x 600 mm nominal KEY L16

Where securing screws are required add suffix 'S' to key reference

Cover sizes to C.P. 301 requirements

GLC ILEA
Department of Architecture
and Civic Design
County Hall SE1
Architect Sir Roger Walters
KBE FRIBA FI StructE

Cover sizes of light and medium duty related to size and depth of I.C. (see I.C. schedule)

Heavy duty covers shall conform to local authority requirements

Additional alternatives may be required at local authority's request

Cover slab opening to suit cover and frame

Departmental Standard Drawing

title
COVERS AND FRAMES
FOR BRICK INSPECTION CHAMBERS WITH C.I. BOLTED ACCESS FITTINGS
(INTERNAL USE)

scale 1:20

drawing no D3572.A.

52 826 Fg2 as drawing

010379

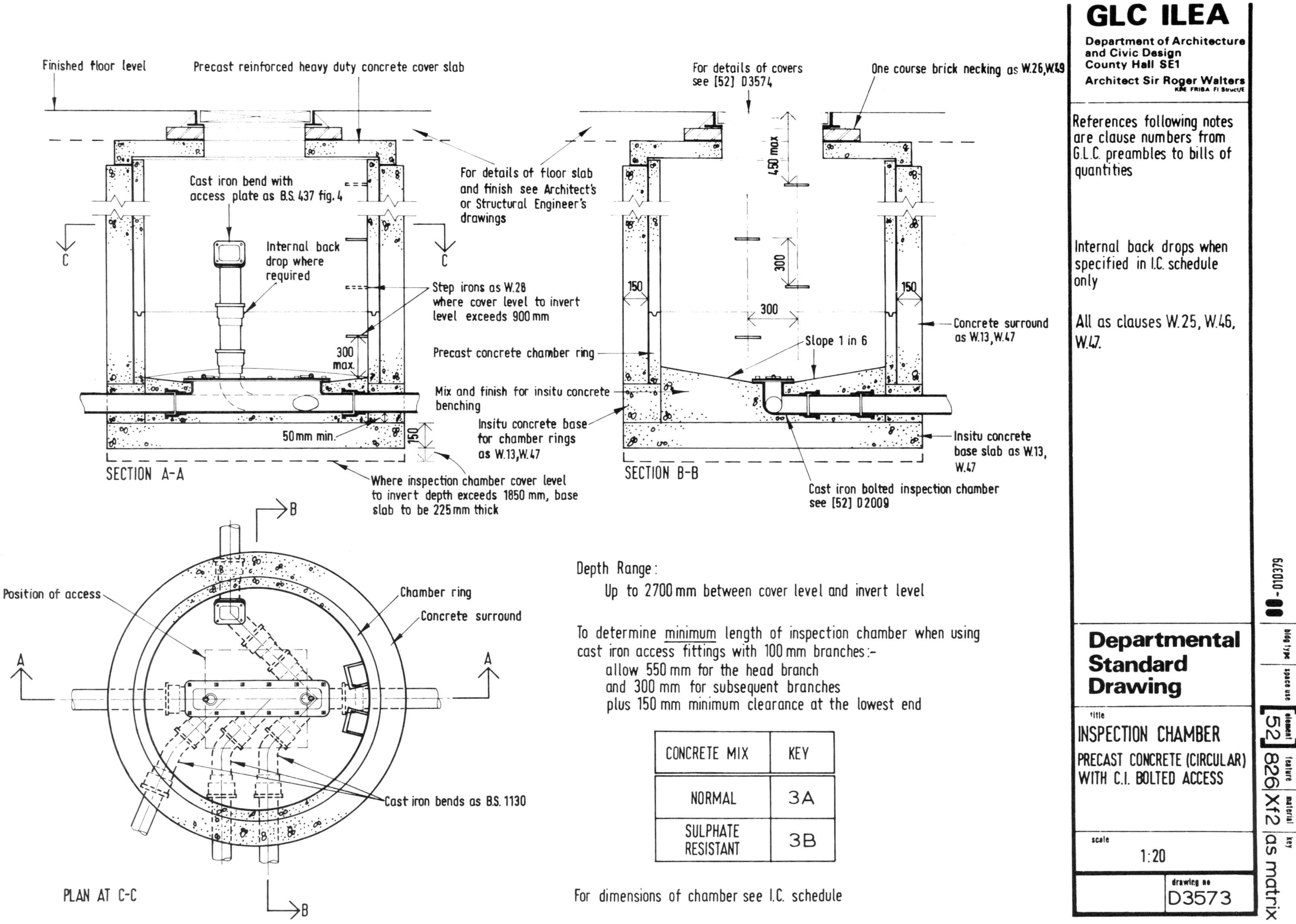

Depth Range:

Up to 2700 mm between cover level and invert level

To determine minimum length of inspection chamber when using cast iron access fittings with 100 mm branches:-

allow 550 mm for the head branch
and 300 mm for subsequent branches
plus 150 mm minimum clearance at the lowest end

CONCRETE MIX	KEY
NORMAL	3A
SULPHATE RESISTANT	3B

For dimensions of chamber see I.C. schedule

● Inspection chamber covers subject to light vehicular traffic

A) where cover is not required to match surrounding finish

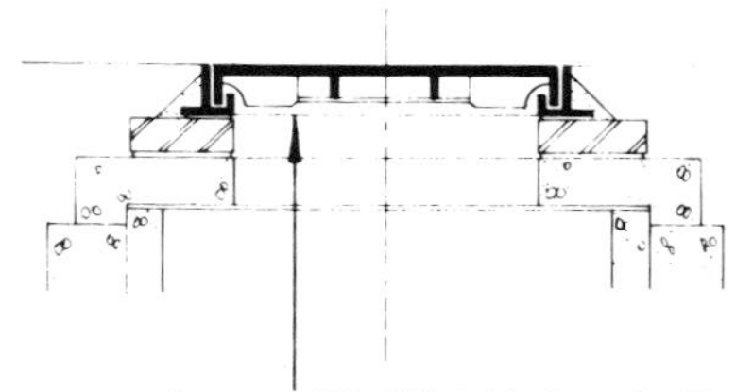

Cover as B.S. 497 table 3 grade B
medium duty, solid top 600 x 450 mm nominal. KEY M1
600 x 600 mm nominal. KEY M2

B) where cover is required to match surrounding finish

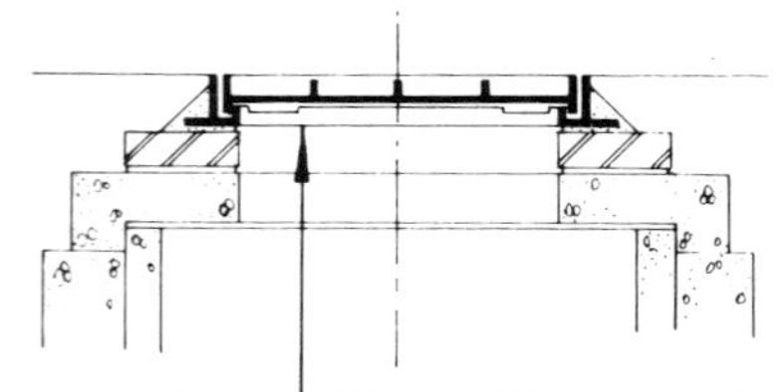

Cover as B.S. 497 table 3 grade B
medium duty, recessed cover 600 x 450 mm nominal. KEY M3
600 x 600 mm nominal. KEY M4

● Inspection chamber covers subject to heavy vehicular traffic

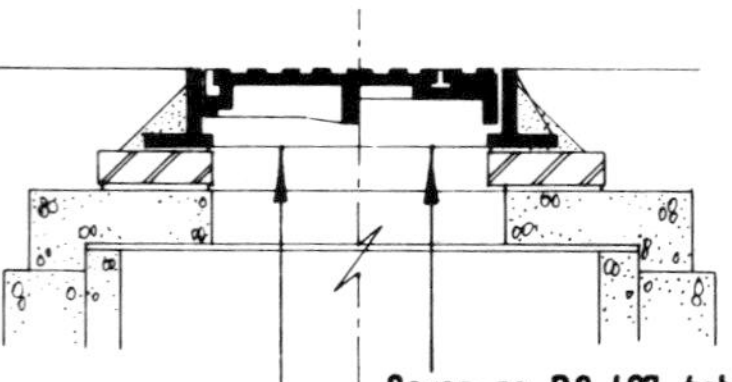

Cover as B.S. 497 table 1 grade A
heavy duty single triangular cover
and frame 490 x 495 mm nominal. KEY H1

Or as B.S. 497 table 1 grade A heavy duty
double triangular cover and frame 550 mm dia. nominal. KEY H2

● Inspection chamber covers subject to pedestrian traffic only

A) where cover is not required to match surrounding finish

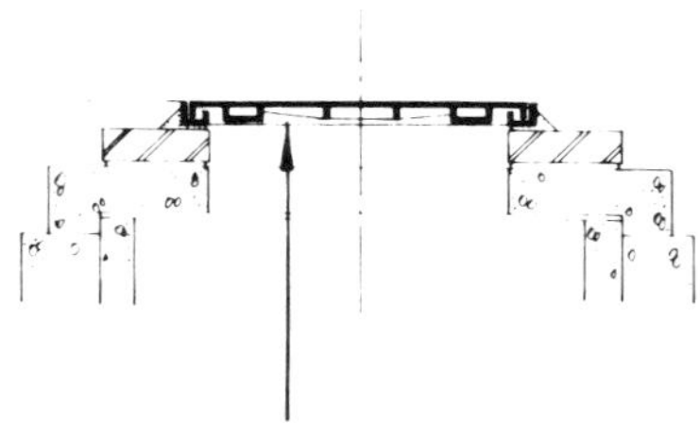

Cover as B.S. 497 table 4 grade C
light duty cover and frame 600 x 450 mm nominal. KEY L1
600 x 600 mm nominal. KEY L2

B) where cover is required to match surrounding finish

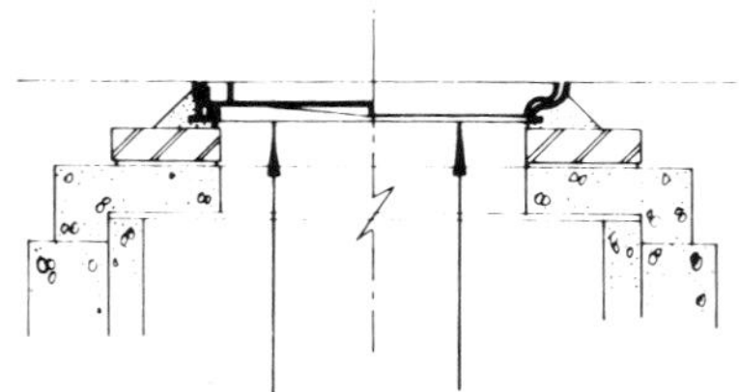

Cover as Broad's 'Broadstel' recessed cover and frame
no. 347 range or similar approved. 600 x 450 mm nominal. KEY L3
600 x 600 mm nominal. KEY L4

Or as B.S. 497 table 4 grade C
light duty recessed cover and frame 600 x 450 mm nominal. KEY L5
600 x 600 mm nominal. KEY L6

Where securing screws are required add suffix 'S' to key reference

INSPECTION CHAMBER INTERNAL DIAMETER	SIZE OF HOLE IN PRECAST CONCRETE SLAB — GENERAL AVAILABILITY			
	610 x 457 mm	610 x 610 mm	560 mm DIA.	600 mm DIA.
750 mm	X		X	
900 mm AND OVER	X	X	X	X

GLC ILEA

Department of Architecture and Civic Design
County Hall SE1
Architect Sir Roger Walters KBE FRIBA FI StructE

Cover sizes of light and medium duty related to size and depth of I.C. (see I.C. Schedule)

Heavy duty covers shall conform to local authority requirements

Additional alternatives may be required at local authority's request

Departmental Standard Drawing

title
COVERS AND FRAMES
FOR PRECAST CONCRETE CIRCULAR INSPECTION CHAMBERS WITH C.I. BOLTED ACCESS FITTINGS (INTERNAL USE)

scale 1:20

drawing no D3574.A.

00-00379 | 52 | 826 | Xf2 | as drawing

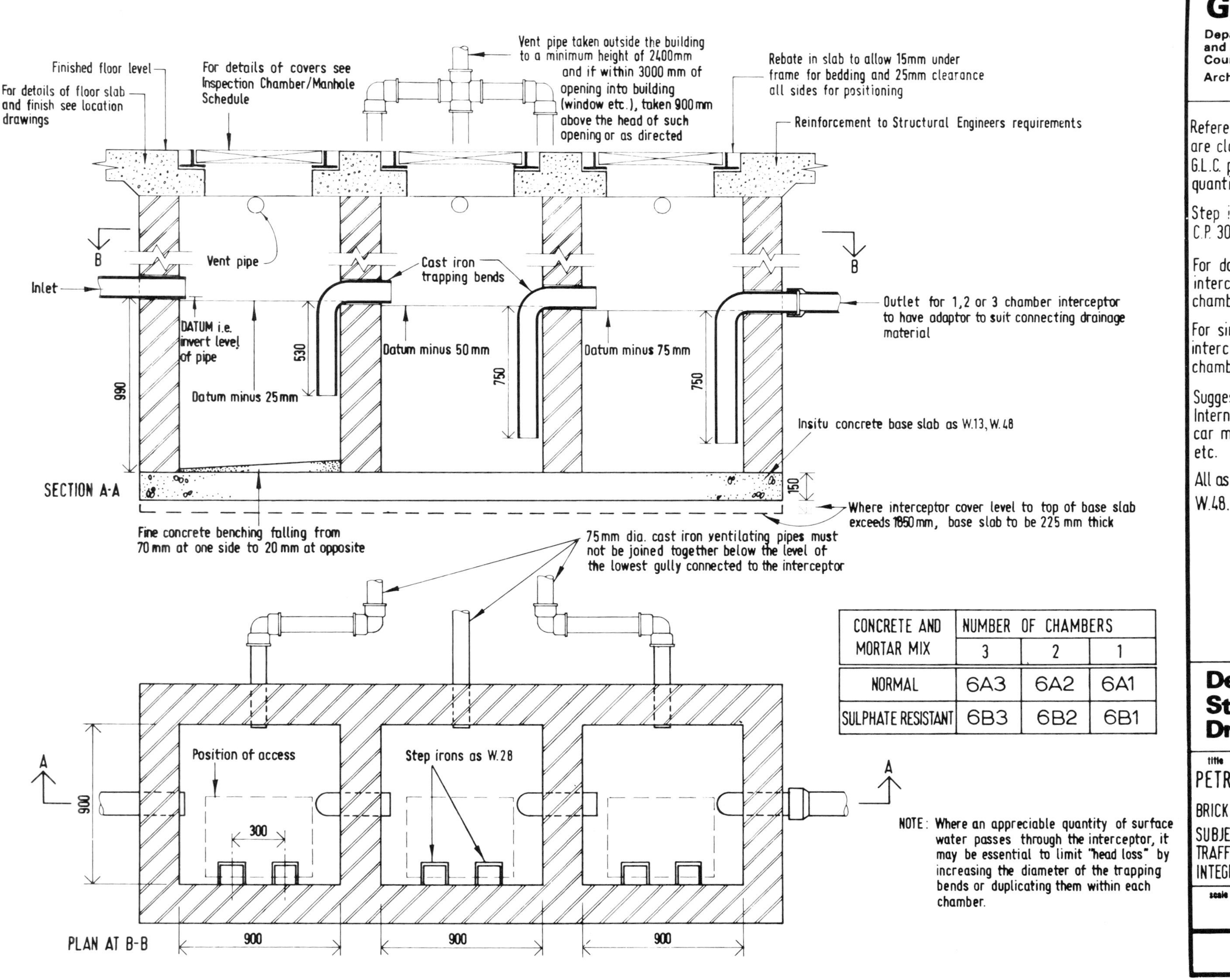

CONCRETE AND MORTAR MIX	NUMBER OF CHAMBERS		
	3	2	1
NORMAL	6A3	6A2	6A1
SULPHATE RESISTANT	6B3	6B2	6B1

NOTE: Where an appreciable quantity of surface water passes through the interceptor, it may be essential to limit "head loss" by increasing the diameter of the trapping bends or duplicating them within each chamber.

GLC ILEA

Department of Architecture and Civic Design
County Hall SE1
Architect Sir Roger Walters KBE FRIBA FI StructE

References following notes are clause numbers from G.L.C. preambles to bills of quantities

Step iron positions to C.P. 301 requirements

For double chamber interceptors omit third chamber as shown

For single chamber interceptors use first chamber as shown

Suggested use:
Internally in large garages, car maintenance workshops etc.

All as clauses W.26, W.46, W.48.

Departmental Standard Drawing

title
PETROL INTERCEPTOR
BRICK CONSTRUCTION.
SUBJECT TO VEHICULAR TRAFFIC
INTEGRAL COVER SLAB

scale
1:20

drawing no
D3576

010379 - 00 | bldg type | space use | element [52] | feature 826 | Fg2 material | key as matrix

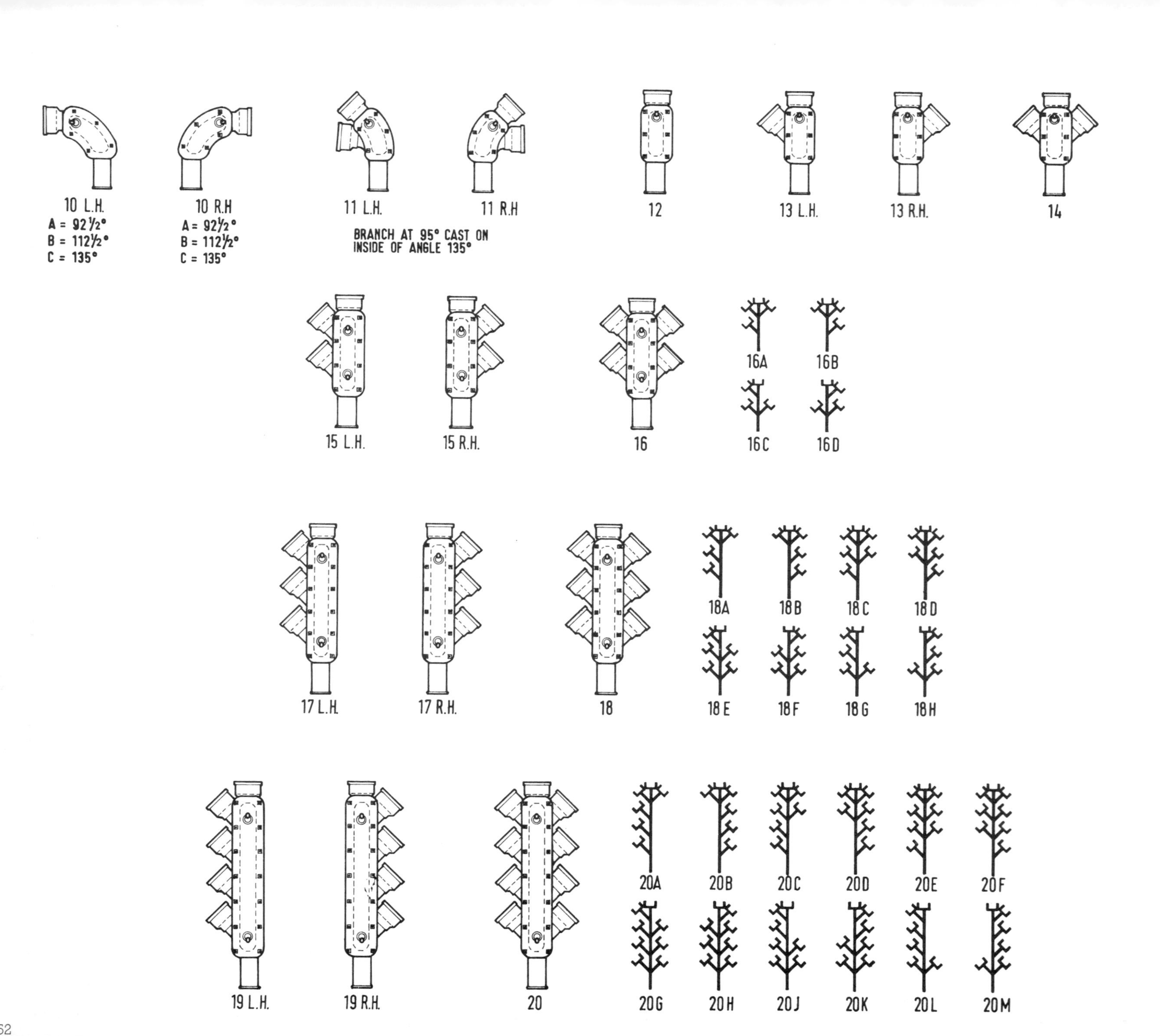

GLC ILEA

Department of Architecture and Civic Design
County Hall SE1
Architect Sir Roger Walters

Fittings numbered in accordance with B.S. 1130

Departmental Standard Drawing

title

INSPECTION CHAMBERS

RANGE OF CAST IRON BOLTED INSPECTION FITTINGS (INTERNAL USE)

scale

NOT TO SCALE

drawing no

D2009

00-010379

element 52 | feature 826 | material Xh1 | key as drawing

INSPECTION CHAMBER										COVER DETAILS				
NO.	SIZE	COVER LEVEL	DRAIN SIZE	INVERT LEVEL	DEPTH	INSPECTION CHAMBER DETAILS		CHANNEL DETAILS		TYPE	CLEAR OPENING	DETAIL DRWG. REFERENCE		REMARKS
						Drwg. no.	Key	Drwg. no.	Key			Drwg. no.	Key	
	'D' SERIES DRAWING NUMBERS ARE DEPARTMENTAL STANDARD DRAWINGS													
	For details of 'back drops' see drg. no. D3558 key A (for precast concrete inspection chambers) and drg. no. D3568 key A (for brick inspection chambers) unless stated otherwise.													
9/2	1237·5 x 787·5	62·170	150	60·615	1·555	D 3563	EA1F	D 3565	1	B.S. 497 TABLE 6/C	600 x 600	D 3567	L2	
9/4	1237·5 x 787·5	62·170	150	60·745	1·425	D 3563	EA1F	D 3565	1	B.S. 497 TABLE 6/C	600 x 600	D 3567	L2	
9/6	1350 x 787·5	62·170	150	60·870	1·300	D 3563	EA16	D 3565	1	B.S. 497 TABLE 6/C	600 x 600	D 3567	L2	
9/8	1237·5 x 787·5	62·170	150	60·995	1·175	D 3563	EA1F	D 3565	1	B.S. 497 TABLE 6/C	600 x 600	D 3567	L2	
9/10	1237·5 x 787·5	62·170	150	61·125	1·045	D 3563	EA2F	D 3565	1	B.S. 497 TABLE 6/C	600 x 600	D 3567	L2	
9/12	1350 x 787·5	62·170	150	61·250	0·920	D 3563	EA26	D 3565	1	"BROADS" Nº 129D	750 x 600	D 3567	M7	
9/14	1012·5 x 787·5	62·320	100	61·495	0·825	D 3570	1A	D 2009	15 RH	"BROADS" Nº 347	900 x 600	D 3572	L13	
9/16	1012·5 x 1012·5	62·250	150	60·750	1·500	(JOB DRAWING NOS. AS APPLICABLE)				"BROADS" Nº 129 D	750 x 600	D 3567	M7	
8/1	1050	61·500	150	59·590	1·910	D 3554	BA1F	D 3559	1	B.S. 497 TABLE 6/C	600 x 600	D 3560	L2	
8/3	1050	62·000	150	59·850	2·150	D 3554	BA1F	D 3559	2	B.S. 497 TABLE 6/C	600 x 600	D 3560	L2	
8/5	900	62·000	100	60·535	1·465	D 3552	BA1D	D 3559	1	B.S. 497 TABLE 6/C	600 x 600	D 3560	L6	
8/7	900	62·630	100	61·035	1·595	D 3552	BA1D	D 3559	1	B.S. 497 TABLE 6/C	600 x 600	D 3560	L2	
8/9	900	62·000	100	60·465	1·535	D 3552	BA2D	D 3559	1	B.S. 497 TABLE 2/A	495 x 520	D 3560	H1	
8/11	900	62·750	100	61·600	1·150	D 3552	BA2D	D 3559	1	B.S. 497 TABLE 2/A	495 x 520	D 3560	H1	
8/13	900	63·000	100	62·000	1·000	D 3552	BA1D	D 3559	1	B.S. 497 TABLE 6/C	600 x 600	D 3560	L2	
8/15	750	63·000	100	61·900	1·100	D 3575	6A1	—	—	B.S. 497 TABLE 6/C	600 x 450	D 3560	L1	CATCH PIT
8/17	1050	62·500	100	60·000	2·500	D 3554	BA1F	D 3559	2	B.S. 497 TABLE 6/C	600 x 600	D 3560	L2	BACK DROP

GLC ILEA

Department of Architecture and Civic Design
County Hall SE1 7PB
Architect Sir Roger Walters KBE FRIBA FIStructE

drawn | checked | date

telephone 01-633

Blank melinex copies are available.

revisions | date

01-00379

job
example

bldg type | space use | element [5-] | feature 826 | material | key

title
INSPECTION CHAMBER SCHEDULE

ref. drawing no

sheet no

job no | drawing no D6002 A

Superstructure Details

Contents

1 Timber flat roofs

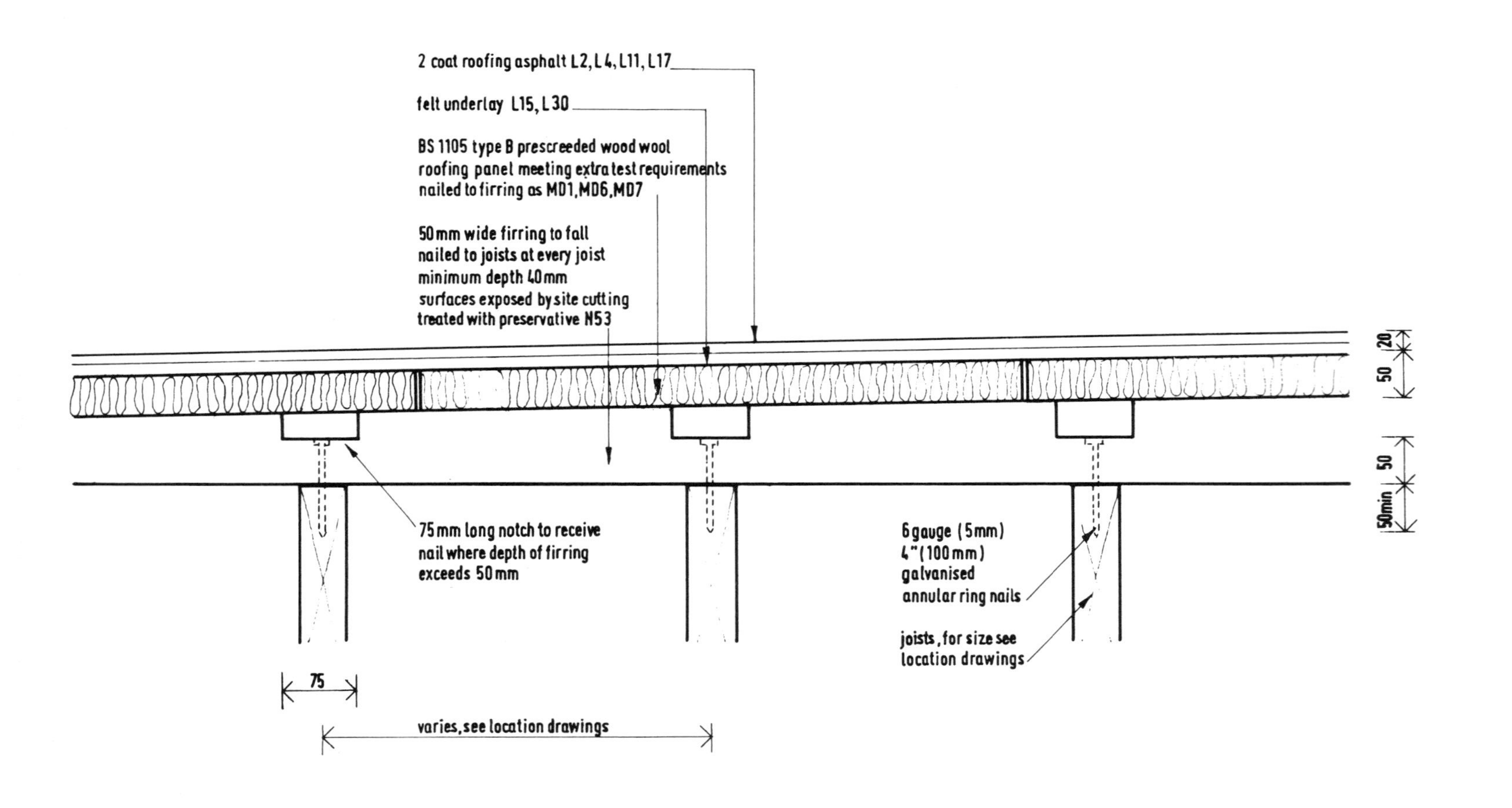
2 coat roofing asphalt L2, L4, L11, L17
felt underlay L15, L30
BS 1105 type B prescreeded wood wool roofing panel meeting extra test requirements nailed to firring as MD1, MD6, MD7
50 mm wide firring to fall nailed to joists at every joist minimum depth 40 mm surfaces exposed by site cutting treated with preservative N53
20
50
50
50min
75 mm long notch to receive nail where depth of firring exceeds 50 mm
6 gauge (5mm) 4" (100 mm) galvanised annular ring nails
joists, for size see location drawings
75
varies, see location drawings

GLC ILEA
Department of Architecture and Civic Design
County Hall SE1
Architect Sir Roger Walters
KBE FRIBA FI Struct E
References following notes are clause numbers from GLC preambles to bills of quantities
Departmental Standard Drawing
title
ROOF FINISH
TIMBER ROOF
FIRRING ACROSS JOISTS
scale
1:5
drawing no
D 5020A
010379
bldg type
space use
element
47
feature
141
material
Ps4
key
B1

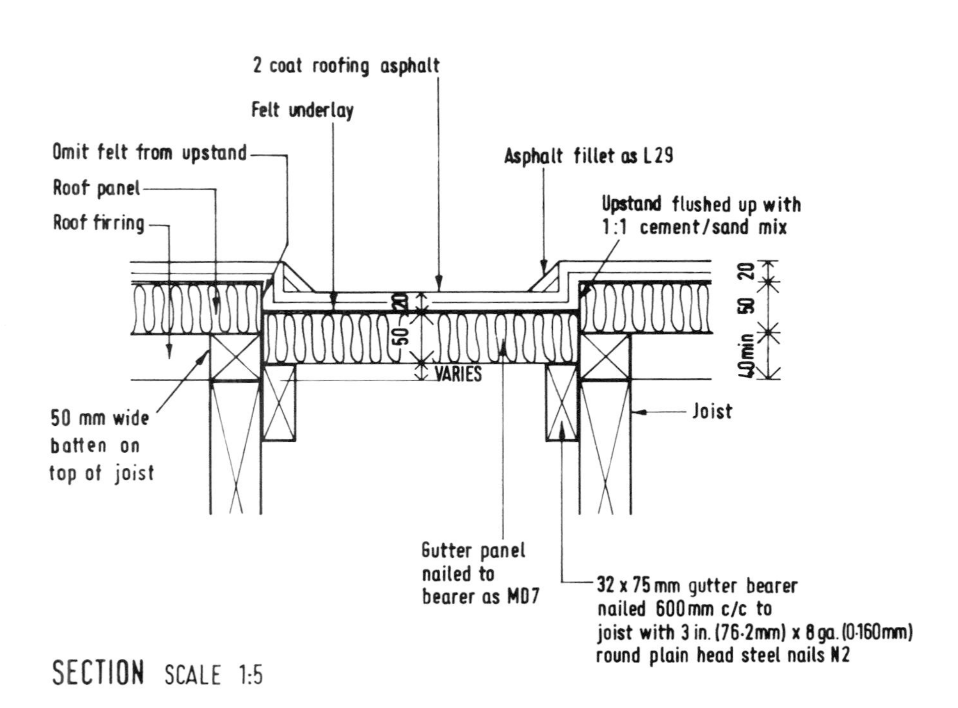

SECTION SCALE 1:5

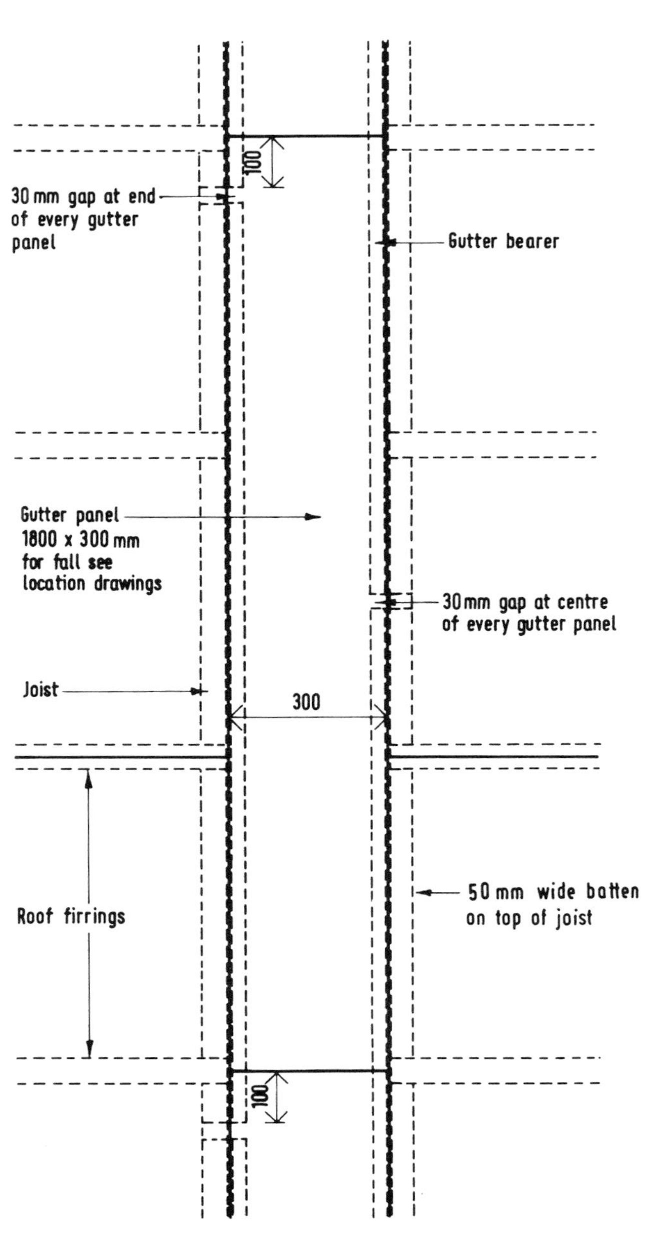

PLAN SCALE 1:10 ASPHALT AND FELT UNDERLAY OMITTED

GLC ILEA

Department of Architecture
and Civic Design
County Hall SE1
Architect Sir Roger Walters
KBE FRIBA FI Struct E

References following notes are clause numbers from G.L.C. preambles to bills of quantities

For full description of roof finish see drawing number D5020

Departmental Standard Drawing

title

300mm GUTTER

TIMBER ROOF
FIRRINGS ACROSS JOISTS

scale 1:5 1:10

drawing no D5021 rev A

bldg type | space use | element [47] | feature 141 | material Ps4 | key B2

00 - 010379

GLC ILEA
Department of Architecture and Civic Design
County Hall SE1
Architect. Sir Roger Walters

References following notes are clause numbers from G.L.C. preambles to bills of quantities

For full description of roof finish see drawing number D 5020

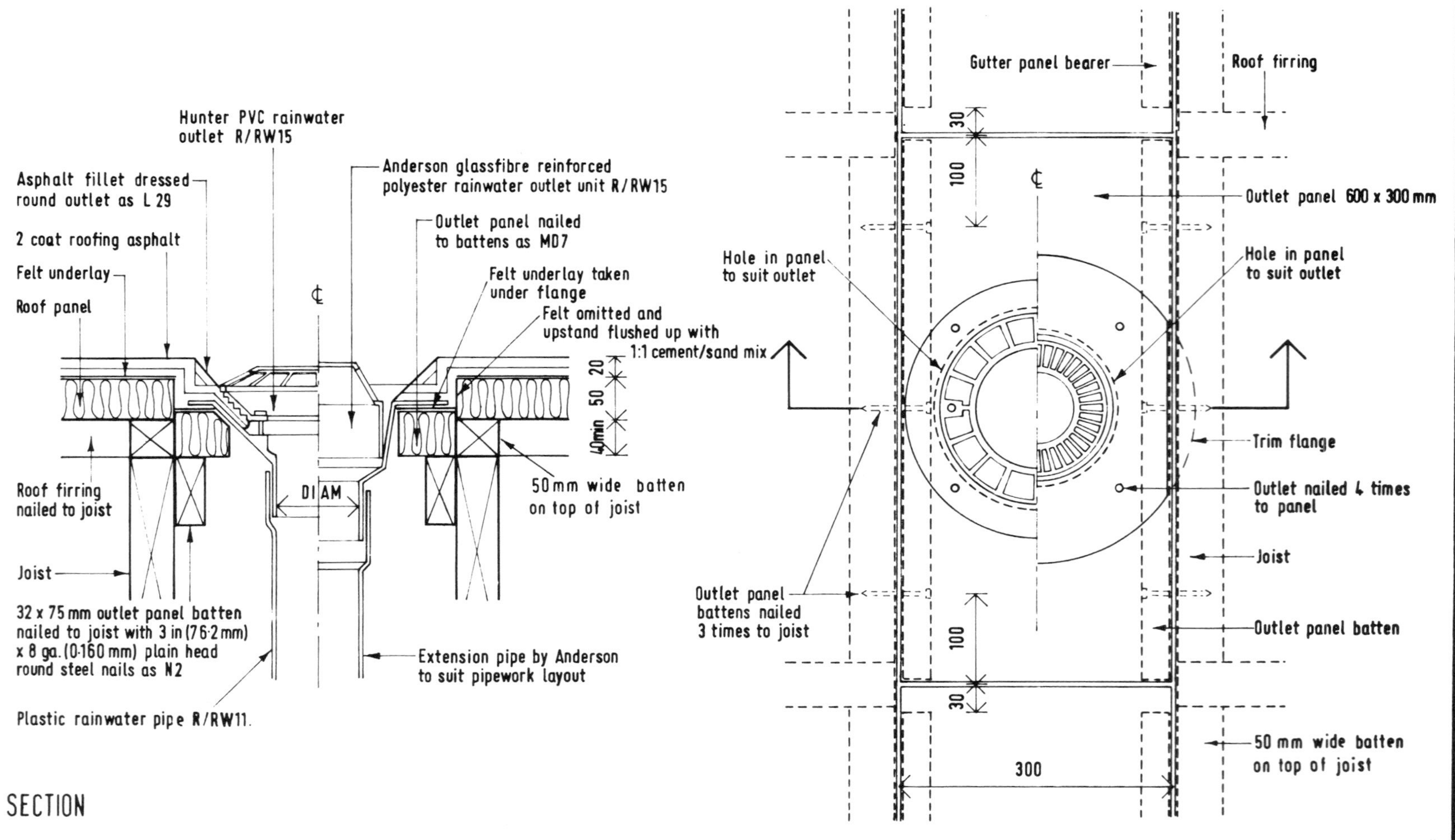

NOM DIAM	KEY - ANDERSON	KEY - HUNTER
2 in (50·8 mm)	B1A	
2½ in (63·5 mm)	B1B	
3 in (76·2 mm)	B1C	B1C
4 in (104·1 mm)	B1D	B1D
6 in (153·4 mm)	B1E	

NOTE:
The metric equivalent of the Hunter 3" outlet is 75mm and the 4" outlet 102mm

Departmental Standard Drawing

title

RAINWATER OUTLET

TIMBER ROOF FIRRINGS ACROSS JOISTS

scale 1:5

drawing no D5022 | rev A

bldg type | space use | element | feature | material | key
52 | 186 | Xn6 | as matrix

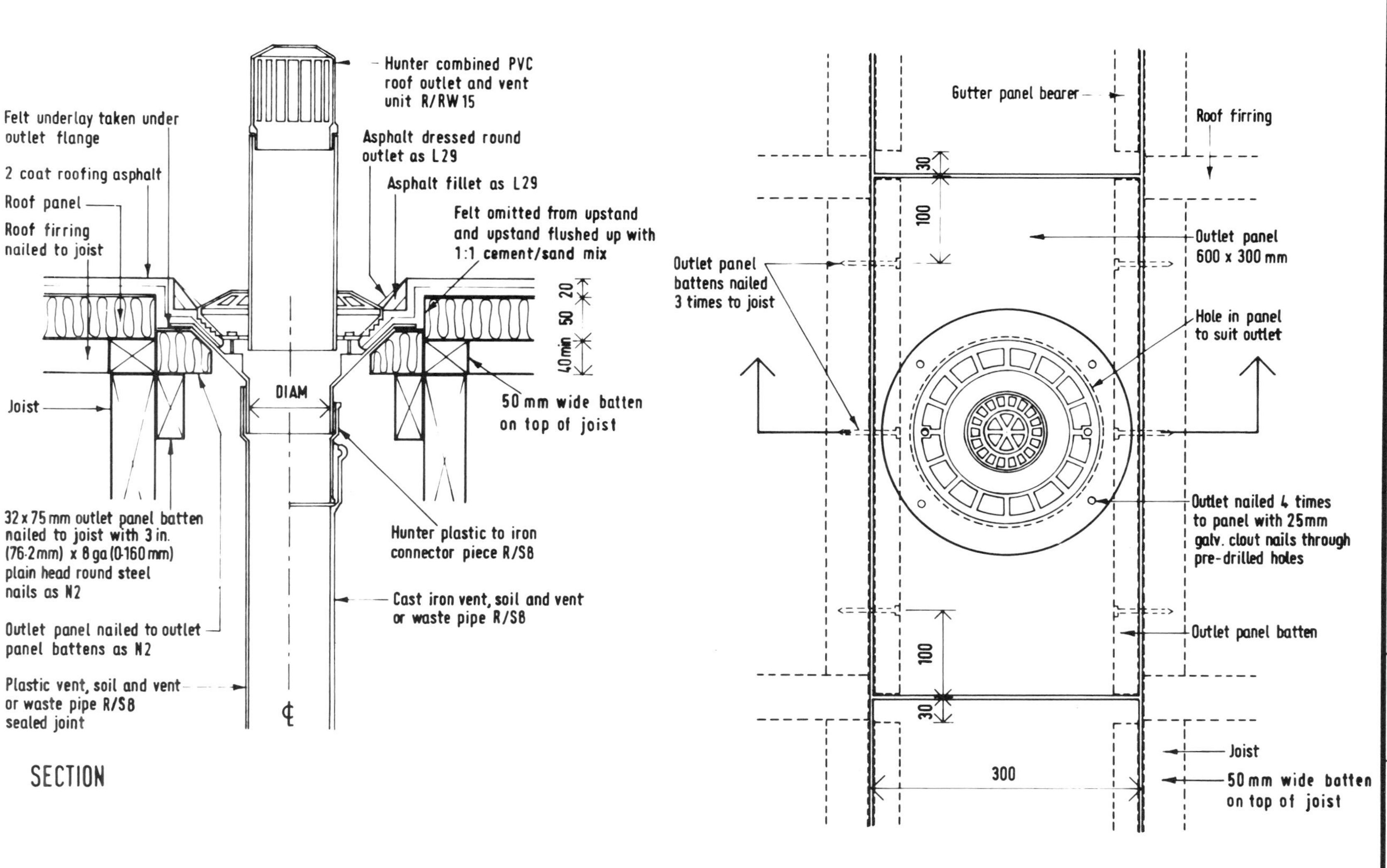

DIAM	KEY
3 IN (75 mm)	B2 A
4 IN (102 mm)	B2 B

GLC ILEA

Department of Architecture and Civic Design
County Hall SE1
Architect Sir Roger Walters KBE FRIBA F Struct E

References following notes are clause numbers from G.L.C. preambles to bills of quantities

For full description of roof finish see drawing number D5020

Departmental Standard Drawing

title
VENTILATING RAINWATER OUTLET

TIMBER ROOF FIRRINGS ACROSS JOISTS

scale 1:5

drawing no D5023 | rev A

00-010379

bldg type | space use | element [52] | feature 186 | material Xn6 | key as matrix

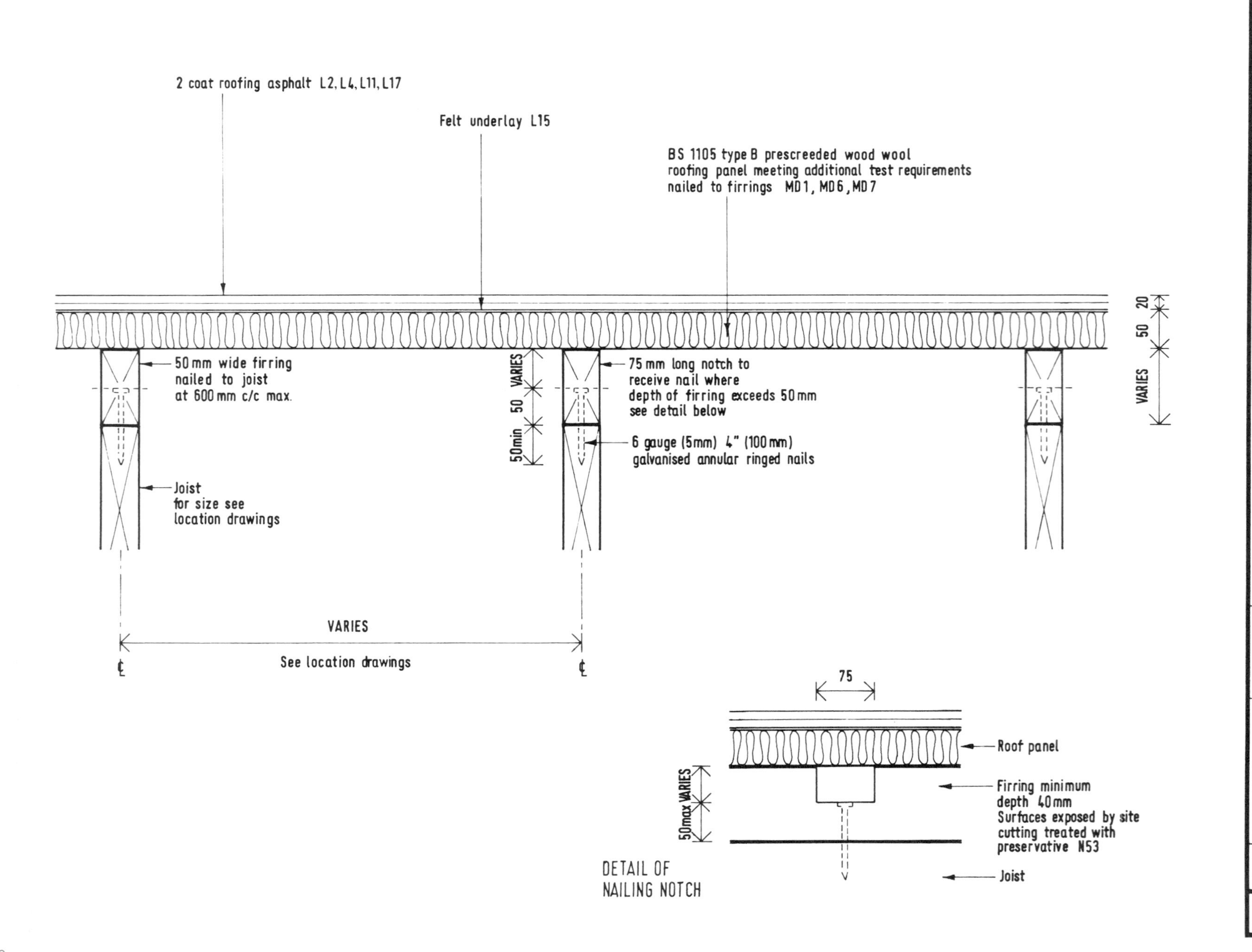

GLC ILEA

Department of Architecture and Civic Design
County Hall SE1

Architect Sir Roger Walters
KBE FRIBA FI Struct/E

References following notes are clause numbers from G.L.C. preambles to bills of quantities

Departmental Standard Drawing

title ROOF FINISH

TIMBER ROOF
FIRRINGS ALONG JOISTS

scale 1:5

drawing no D5040A

Dwg type | space use | element 47 | feature 141 | material Ps4 | key C1

010379

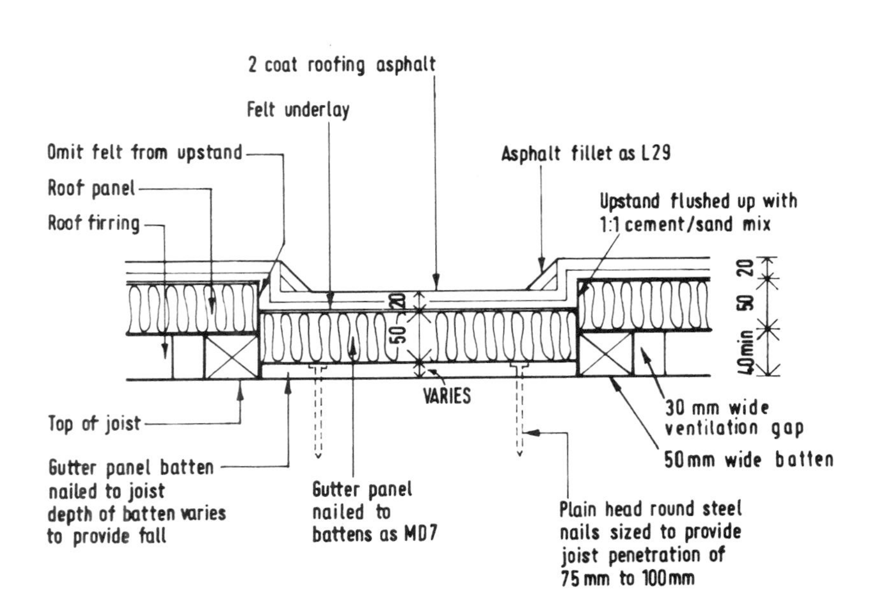

SECTION SCALE 1:5

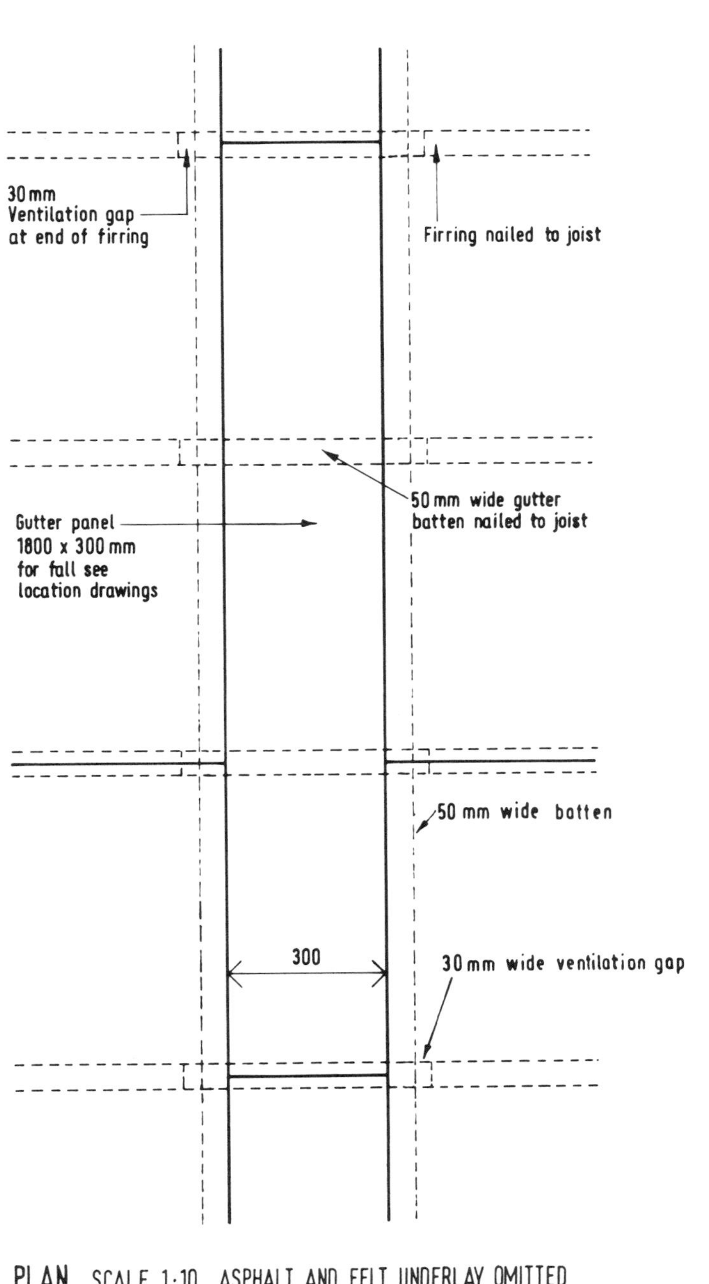

PLAN SCALE 1:10 ASPHALT AND FELT UNDERLAY OMITTED

GLC ILEA

Department of Architecture and Civic Design
County Hall SE1
Architect Sir Roger Walters KBE FRIBA FIStructE

References following notes are clause numbers from G.L.C. preambles to bills of quantities

For full description of roof finish see drawing number D5040

Departmental Standard Drawing

title
300mm GUTTER

TIMBER ROOF
FIRRINGS ALONG JOISTS

scale 1:5 1:10

drawing no D5041 rev A

bldg type | space use | element [47] | feature 141 | material Ps4 | key C2

010379

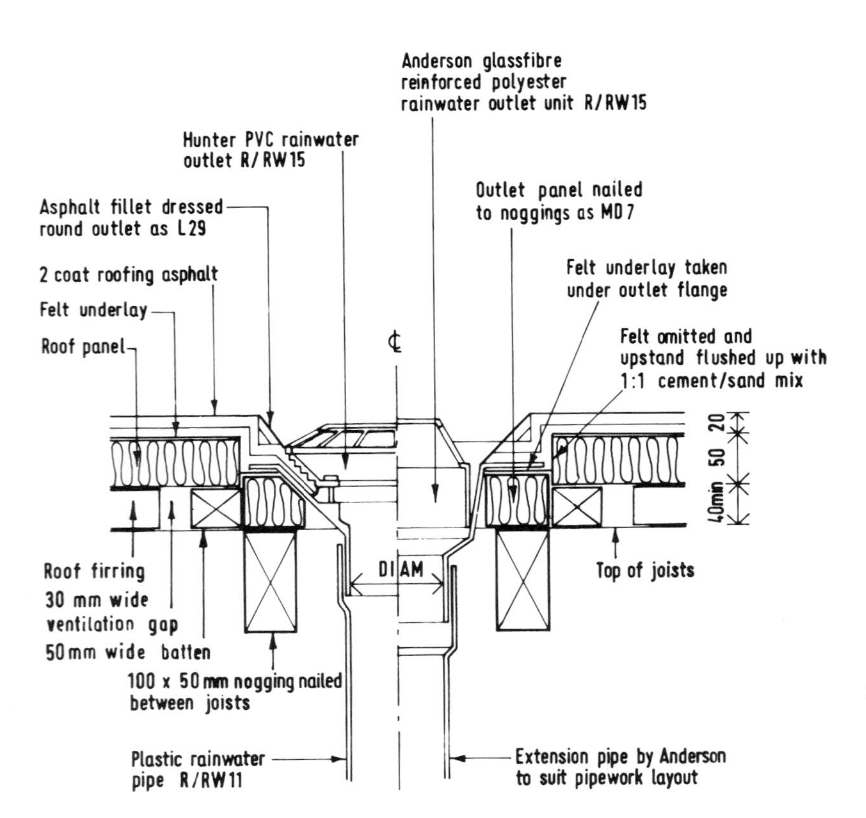

SECTION

Gutter panel

Roof firring nailed to joist

℄

Outlet panel 600 x 300 mm

Hole in panel to suit outlet

Hole in panel to suit outlet

Trim flange

Outlet nailed to outlet panel

30mm ventilation gap

Nogging nailed between joists

300

50 mm wide batten across top of joist

PLAN ASPHALT AND FELT UNDERLAY OMITTED

NOM DIAM	KEY - ANDERSON	KEY - HUNTER
2 in (50·8 mm)	C1A	
2½in (63·5 mm)	C1B	
3 in (76·2 mm)	C1C	C1C
4 in (104·1 mm)	C1D	C1D
6 in (153·4 mm)	C1E	

NOTE:
The metric equivalent of the Hunter 3" outlet is 75mm and the 4" outlet 102mm

GLC ILEA
Department of Architecture and Civic Design
County Hall SE1
Architect Sir Roger Walters

References following notes are clause numbers from G.L.C. preambles to bills of quantities

For full description of roof finish see drawing number D5040

Departmental Standard Drawing

title
RAINWATER OUTLET

TIMBER ROOF
FIRRINGS ALONG JOISTS

scale 1:5

drawing no D5042 rev A

[52] 186 Xn6 as matrix

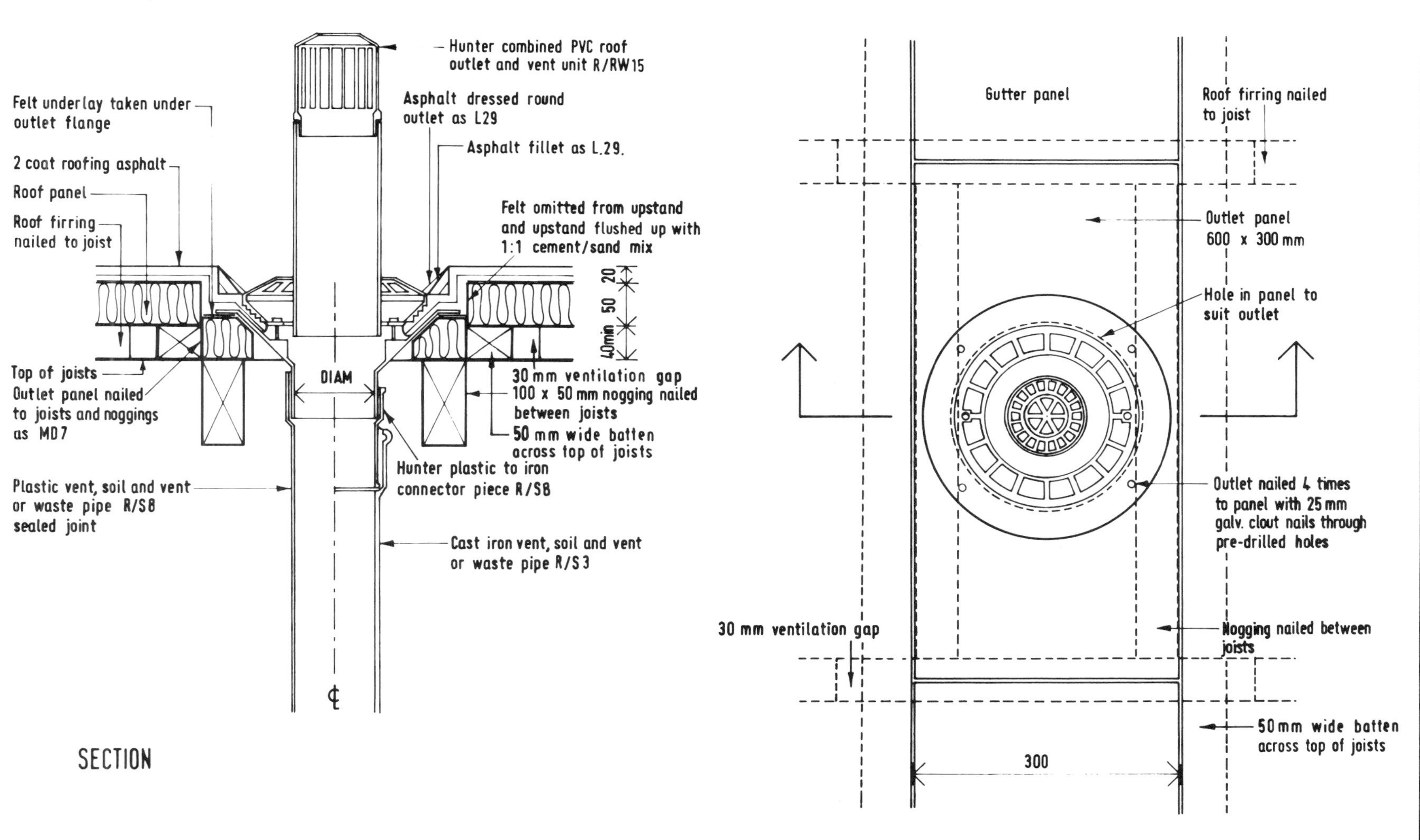

DIAM	KEY
3 IN (75 mm)	C2A
4 IN (102 mm)	C2B

GLC ILEA

Department of Architecture and Civic Design
County Hall SE1
Architect Sir Roger Walters KBE FRIBA F Struct E

References following notes are clause numbers from G.L.C. preambles to bills of quantities

For full description of roof finish see drawing number D 5040

Departmental Standard Drawing

title
VENTILATING RAINWATER OUTLET

TIMBER ROOF FIRRINGS ALONG JOISTS

scale 1:5

drawing no D 5043 rev A

bldg type | space use | element [52] | feature 186 | material Xn6 | key as matrix

-010379

GLC ILEA

Department of Architecture
and Civic Design
County Hall SE1 7PB
Architect Sir Roger Walters
KBE ARIBA FI StructE

References following notes are clause numbers from G.L.C. preambles to bills of quantities

For full description of roof finish see drawing numbers D5020 or D5040

Prevailing wind direction

Diagram showing location of Vaporvents. The arrows indicate the movement of air to the base of the vents within the roof void. The vents should be spaced at 6 metre centres. This diagram applies only where it is not possible to use wall vents. On small roofs a minimum of 4 vents should be used.

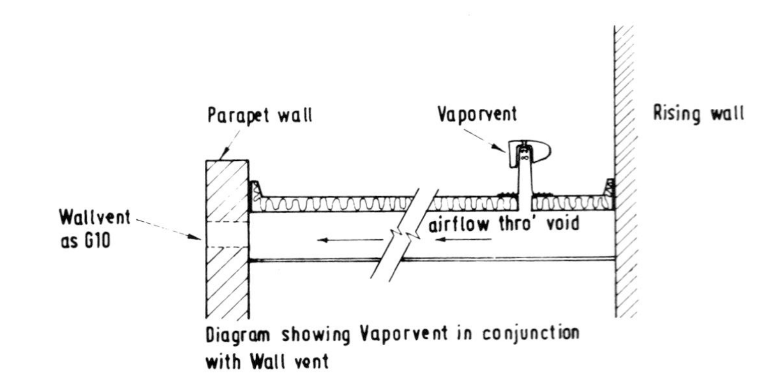

Diagram showing Vaporvent in conjunction with Wall vent

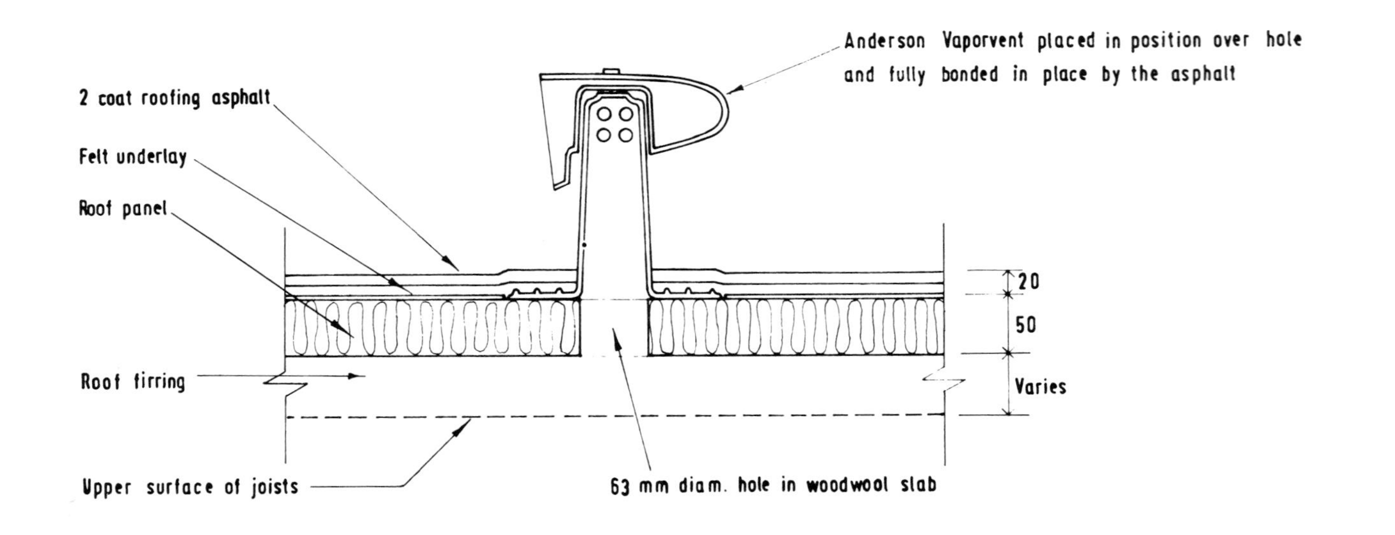

Departmental Standard Drawing

title
VAPORVENT

TIMBER ROOF

scale
1:5

drawing no	rev
D5070	B

47

010379

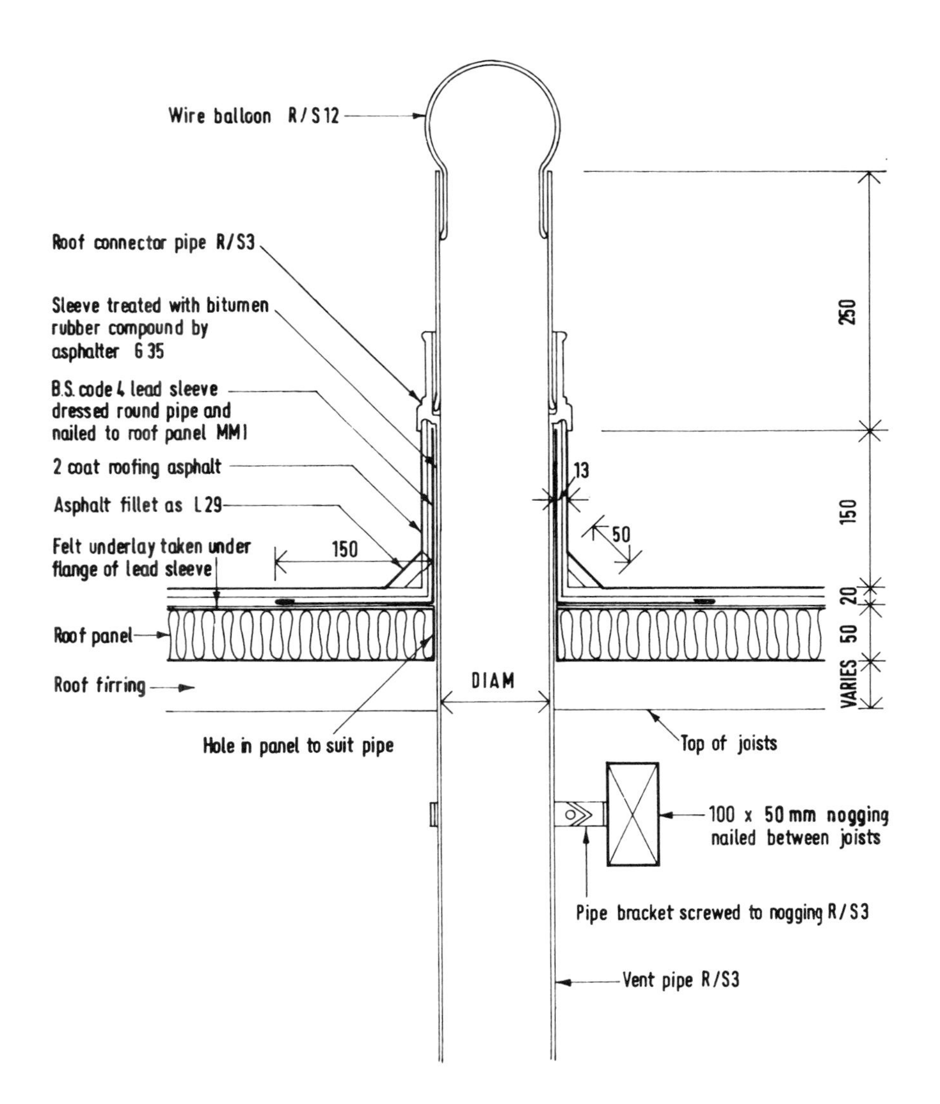

DIAM	KEY
2 in (50·8mm)	B1A
2½ in (63·5mm)	B1B
3 in (76·2mm)	B1C
3½ in (88·9mm)	B1D
4 in (101·6mm)	B1E
5 in (127·0mm)	B1F
6 in (152·4mm)	B1G

GLC ILEA

Department of Architecture and Civic Design
County Hall SE1
Architect Sir Roger Walters

References following notes are clause numbers from G.L.C. preambles to bills of quantities.

For full description of roof finish see drawing number D5020 or D5040

Departmental Standard Drawing

title
CAST IRON VENT PIPE

TIMBER ROOF

scale 1:5

drawing no D5060

bldg type | space use | element [52] | feature 470 | material Xh1 | key as matrix

00 - 010379

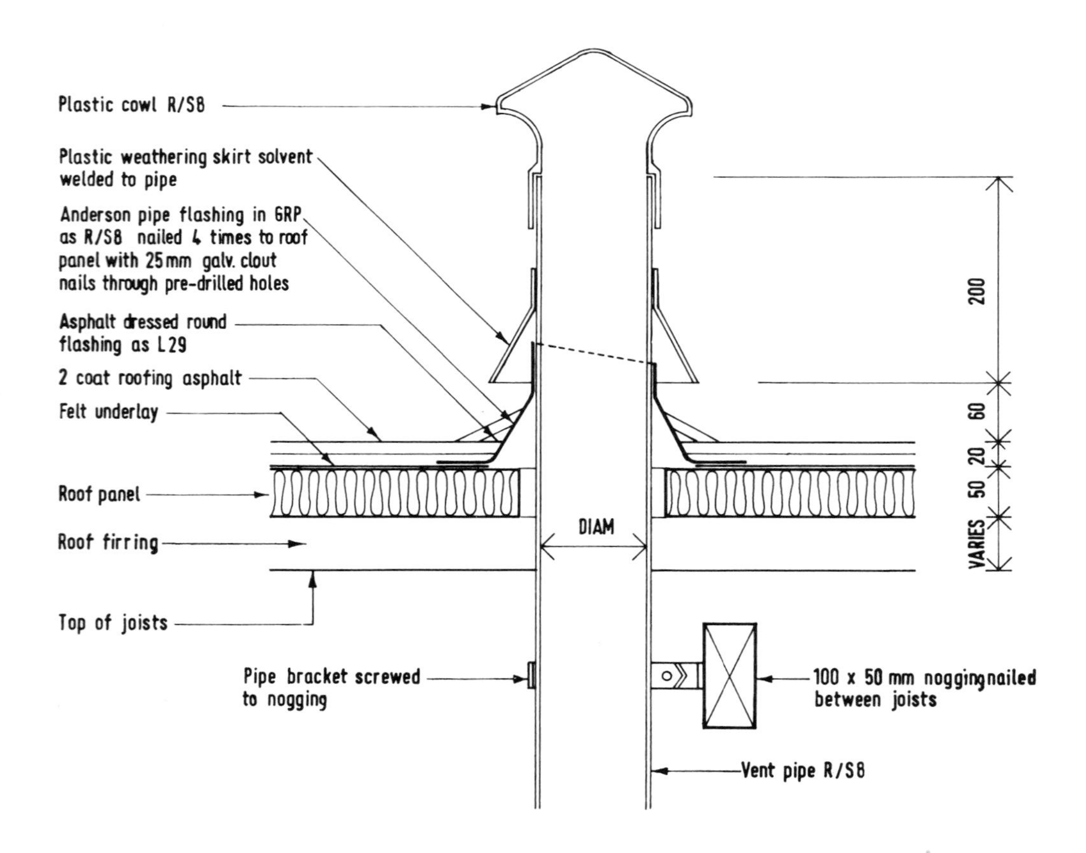

DIAM	KEY
3 IN (75mm)	B1A
4 IN (100mm)	B1B

GLC ILEA

Department of Architecture and Civic Design
County Hall SE1
Architect Sir Roger Walters
KBE FRIBA FI Struct E

References following notes are clause numbers from G.L.C. preambles to bills of quantities

For full description of roof finish see drawing number D5020 or D5040

Departmental Standard Drawing

title
PLASTIC VENT PIPE

TIMBER ROOF

scale
1:5

drawing no
D5061A

[52] 470 Xn6 as matrix

Outlet to be min. 600mm above any obstruction within 1525mm.

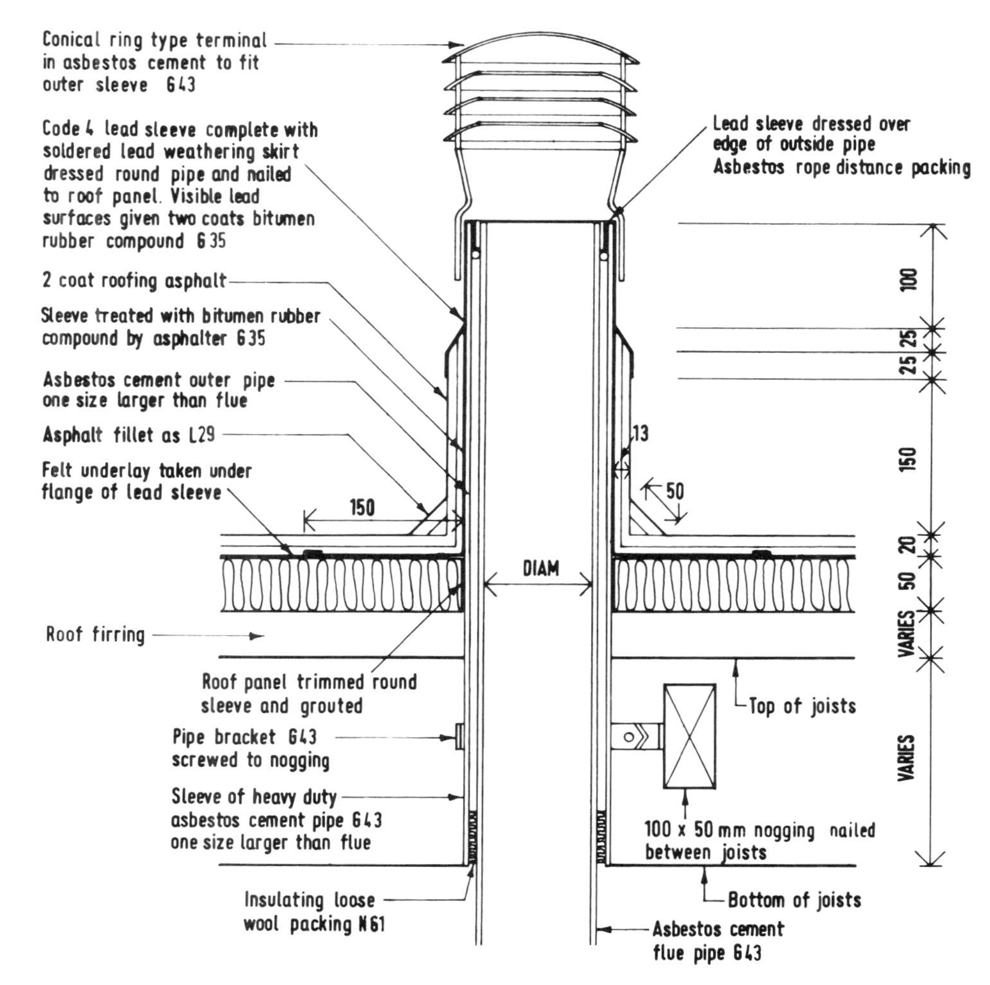

Unless appliance compartment is immediately below pipe outlet, pipe enclosure to achieve 1 hour fire resistance to satisfaction of district surveyor

DIAM	KEY
3 IN (76 mm)	B A
4 IN (102 mm)	B B
5 IN (127 mm)	B C

GLC ILEA

Department of Architecture and Civic Design
County Hall SE1
Architect Sir Roger Walters
KBE FRIBA FIStructE

References following notes are clause numbers from G.L.C. preambles to bills of quantities

For full description of roof finish see drawing number [47] D5020 or D5040.

Departmental Standard Drawing

title
ASBESTOS CEMENT FLUE

TIMBER ROOF

scale 1:5

drawing no D5063 rev. C

00-010379

bldg type | space use | element [27] | feature 614 | material Xf6 | key as matrix

GLC ILEA

Department of Architecture
and Civic Design
County Hall SE1 7PB

Architect Sir Roger Walters
KBE ARIBA FI Struct/E

References following notes are clause numbers from G.L.C. preambles to bills of quantities

To be read in conjunction with [52]D5022,D5023, D5042,D5043.

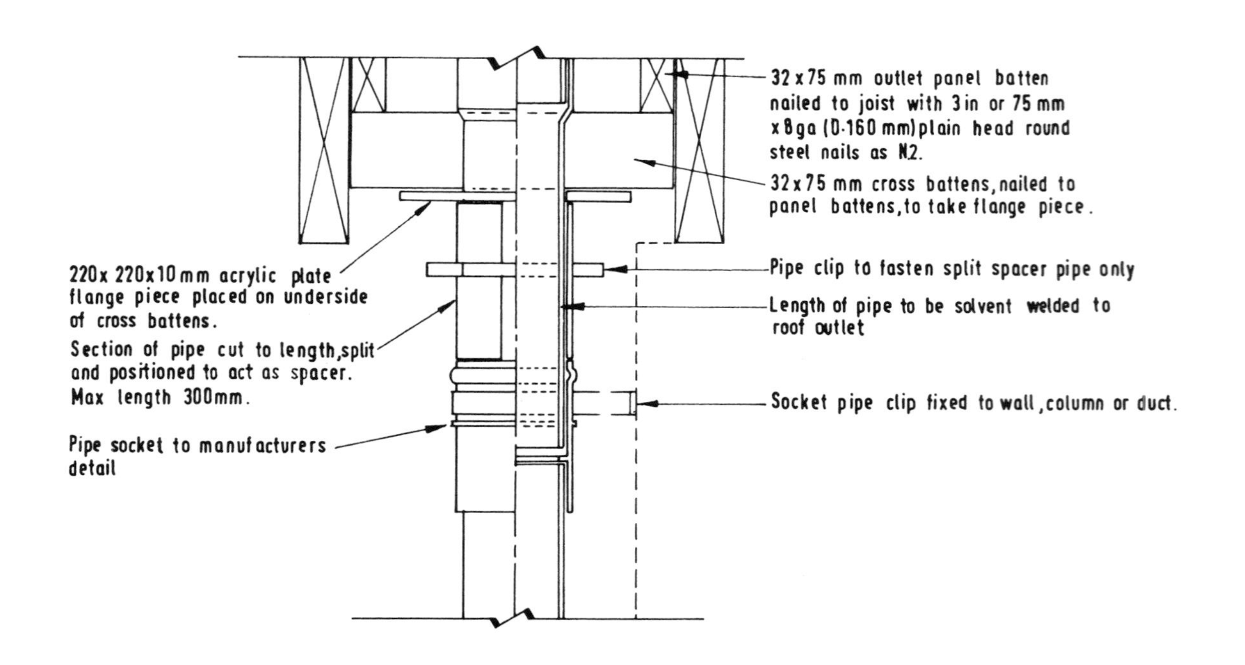

KEY	HOLE IN ACRYLIC FLANGE
B3C	For 75mm pipe
B3D	For 100mm pipe

N.B. When ordering acrylic flange piece it should be stressed that hole to be close fitting to outside diameter of R.W.P. or stack.

Departmental Standard Drawing

title

PIPE FIXING DETAIL
RAINWATER OUTLET

TIMBER ROOF

scale

1:5

drawing no D5219 | rev

[52] 186 Rn6 as matrix

00-010379

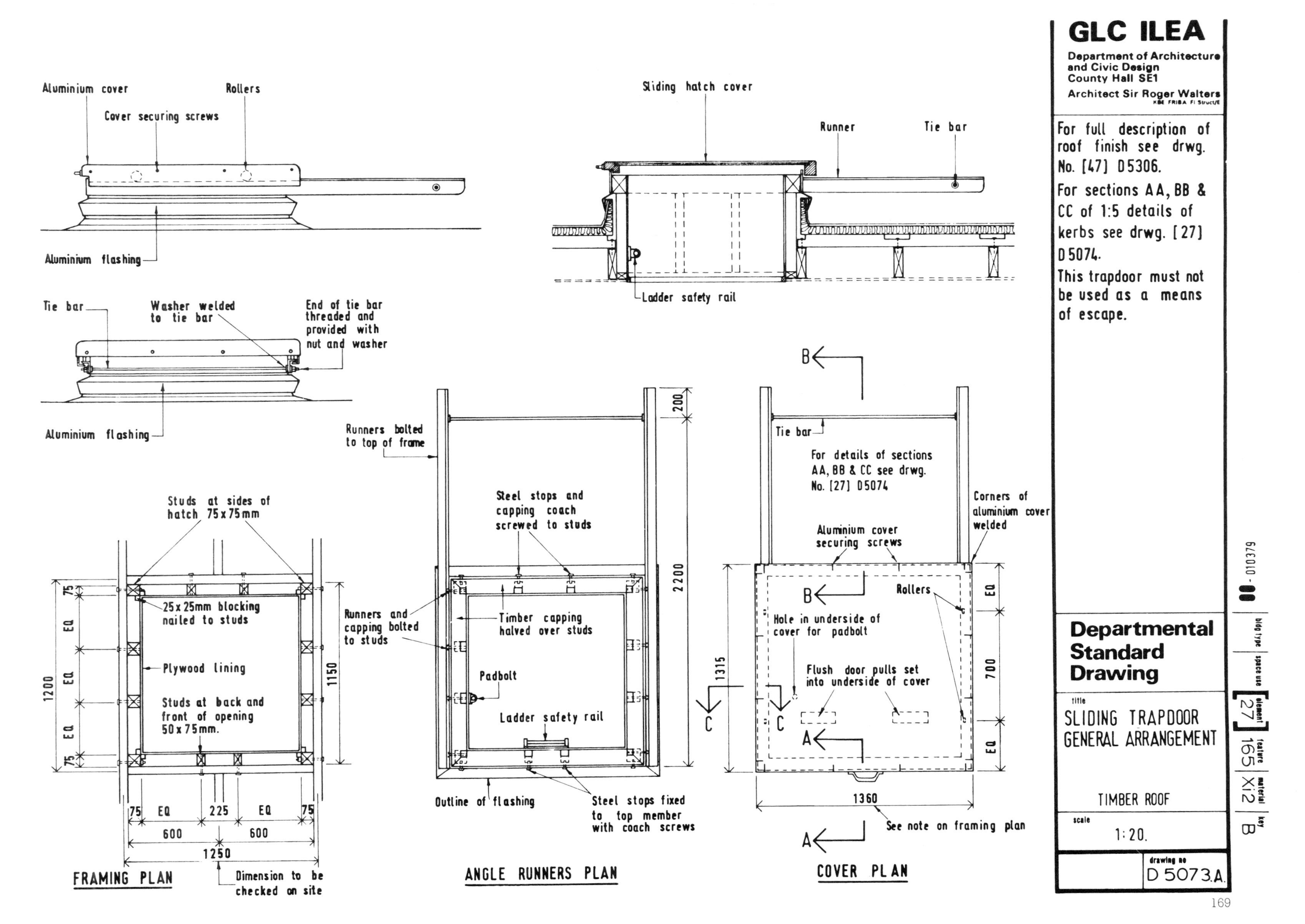
GLC ILEA
Department of Architecture and Civic Design
County Hall SE1
Architect Sir Roger Walters KBE FRIBA FI StructE
For full description of roof finish see drwg. No. [47] D5306.
For sections AA, BB & CC of 1:5 details of kerbs see drwg. [27] D5074.
This trapdoor must not be used as a means of escape.
Aluminium cover
Rollers
Cover securing screws
Aluminium flashing
Tie bar
Washer welded to tie bar
End of tie bar threaded and provided with nut and washer
Aluminium flashing
Sliding hatch cover
Runner
Tie bar
Ladder safety rail
Runners bolted to top of frame
Tie bar
For details of sections AA, BB & CC see drwg. No. [27] D5074
Corners of aluminium cover welded
Studs at sides of hatch 75 x 75 mm
Steel stops and capping coach screwed to studs
Aluminium cover securing screws
Rollers
25 x 25mm blocking nailed to studs
Runners and capping bolted to studs
Timber capping halved over studs
Hole in underside of cover for padbolt
Plywood lining
Padbolt
Flush door pulls set into underside of cover
Studs at back and front of opening 50 x 75mm.
Ladder safety rail
Outline of flashing
Steel stops fixed to top member with coach screws
See note on framing plan
Dimension to be checked on site
1200
1150
1250
600
600
225
75
EQ
200
2200
1315
1360
700
B
C
A
FRAMING PLAN
ANGLE RUNNERS PLAN
COVER PLAN
Departmental Standard Drawing
title
SLIDING TRAPDOOR GENERAL ARRANGEMENT
TIMBER ROOF
scale
1:20.
drawing no
D 5073.A
010379
bldg type
space use
element [27]
feature 165
material Xi2
key B

Bow handle

97 x 60 mm

32

150 x 5mm steel stops fixed on both sides with 101·6 x 9·6mm coach screws. Four per side.

100 x 125mm top member.

10mm water and boilproof plywood.

Standard flashing MF and XCMF.

50 x 75mm studs.

Depth of firrings and joist varies. Dimension to be checked on site prior to manufacture.

Ladder safety rail fixed to studs with 50·8 x 9·6mm coach screws.

50 x 75mm bottom member

1150

SECTION AA

Cover of softwood frame treated as N53. 3 sheets water and boil proof plywood bonded together to form panel, fixed to frame with wood screws. The whole covered with 1·6mm aluminium sheet condition 4, as MM2 welded at corners and fixed with wood screws and plastic washer. Four per side.

25

365

Cantilevered angle runner.

30mm rad.

25mm dia. steel tie bar with a washer welded to it. Tie bar threaded and secured with nut and washer.

Firring on all four sides.

12·7 mm [½"] bolt. [Any discrepancy between size of frame and clear distance between joist to be packed with washers]

Joist [for size see location drawing]

Ceiling as location drawing.

SECTION BB

65 x 50 x 5 mm steel angle screwed to frame

Roller.

Pad bolt and padlock

38

80 x 60 x 6 mm steel angle with welded on 20 x 5 mm steel guide for roller.

20

50

VARIES

VARIES

75 x 75mm studs.

46 x 15mm softwood trim.

Trimmer or joist [see location drawing]

1150

Dimension to be checked on site prior to manufacture.

SECTION CC

GLC ILEA
Department of Architecture and Civic Design
County Hall SE1
Architect Sir Roger Walters KBE FRIBA FI Struct/E

References following notes are clause numbers from G.L.C. preambles to bills of quantities.

For full description of roof finish see drg. number D 5306

For full description of flashing sections see drg. number D 2100.

All steel parts to be galvanised after fabrication as Q.14.

Ironmongery set 0.

For detail of door see drawing number D 3152

To be read in conjunction drawing number D 5073

Departmental Standard Drawing

title
SLIDING TRAPDOOR DETAILS

TIMBER ROOF

scale 1:5

drawing no D5074 rev A

010379

bldg type | space use | element 27 | feature 165 | material Xi2 | key B

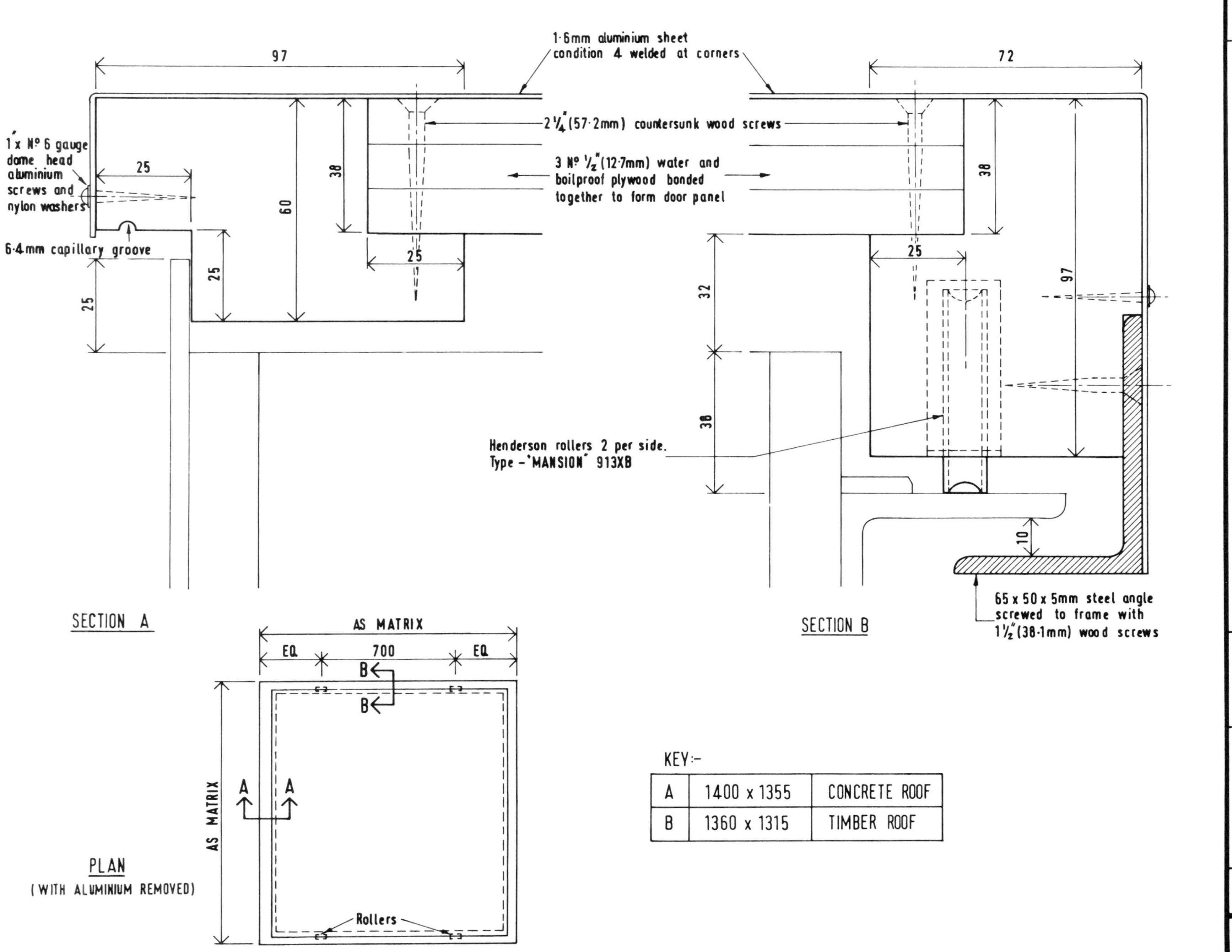

KEY:-

A	1400 x 1355	CONCRETE ROOF
B	1360 x 1315	TIMBER ROOF

GLC ILEA

Department of Architecture
and Civic Design
County Hall SE1
Architect Sir Roger Walters
KBE FRIBA FI StructE

References following notes are clause numbers from G.L.C. preambles to bills of quantities.

This trapdoor must not be used as a means of escape.

Departmental Standard Drawing

title

SLIDING TRAPDOOR

DOOR CONSTRUCTION

scale

1:1 and 1:20

drawing no

D 3152A

010379 - 00

bldg type | space use | element [27] | feature 165 | material Xi2 | key as matrix

2 Party and separating walls

GLC ILEA
Department of Architecture and Civic Design
County Hall SE1 7PB
Architect Sir Roger Walters KBE ARIBA FI Struct/E

References following notes are clause numbers from G.L.C. preambles to bills of quantities

For full description of roof finish see drawing number [47] D5040.

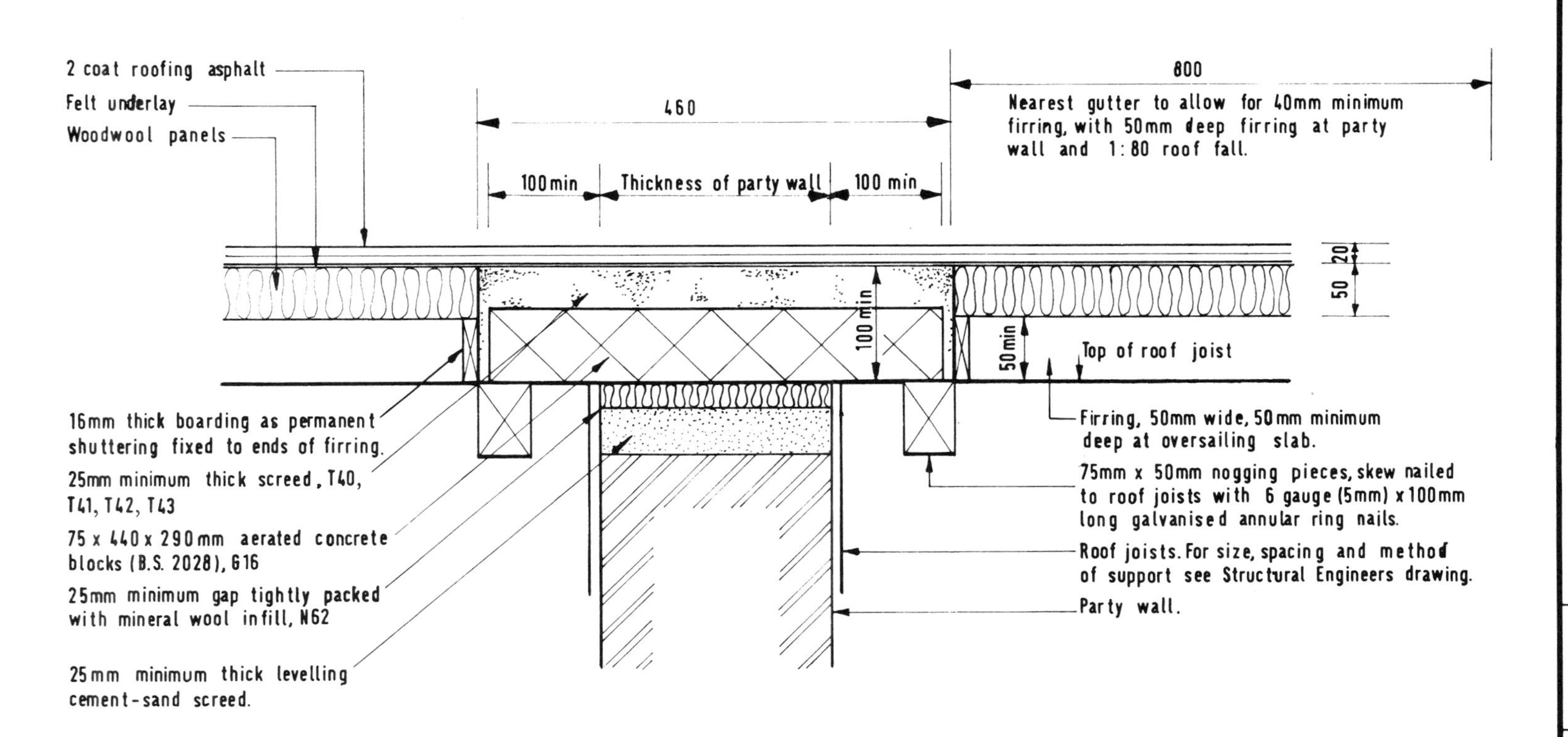

TIMBER JOISTS AT RIGHT ANGLES TO PARTY WALL

FIRRING ALONG JOISTS, MINIMUM 50mm DEEP.

FOR GUTTER SEE DRAWING NUMBER [47] D 5041 AND FOR RAINWATER OUTLET SEE DRAWING NUMBER [47] 5042.

LONDON BUILDING BYLAWS (Bylaw 11·02 Domestic Buildings).

Departmental Standard Drawing

title

ROOF DETAIL AT PARTY WALL.
(LONDON BUILDING BYLAWS)

scale 1:5

drawing no D 5220 | rev

bldg type | space use | element [47] | feature 348 | material Ps4 | key C1C

0010379 - 00

GLC ILEA

Department of Architecture and Civic Design
County Hall SE1 7PB
Architect Sir Roger Walters
KBE ARIBA FI Struct/E

References following notes are clause numbers from G.L.C. preambles to bills of quantities

For full description of roof finish see drawing number [47] D5040.

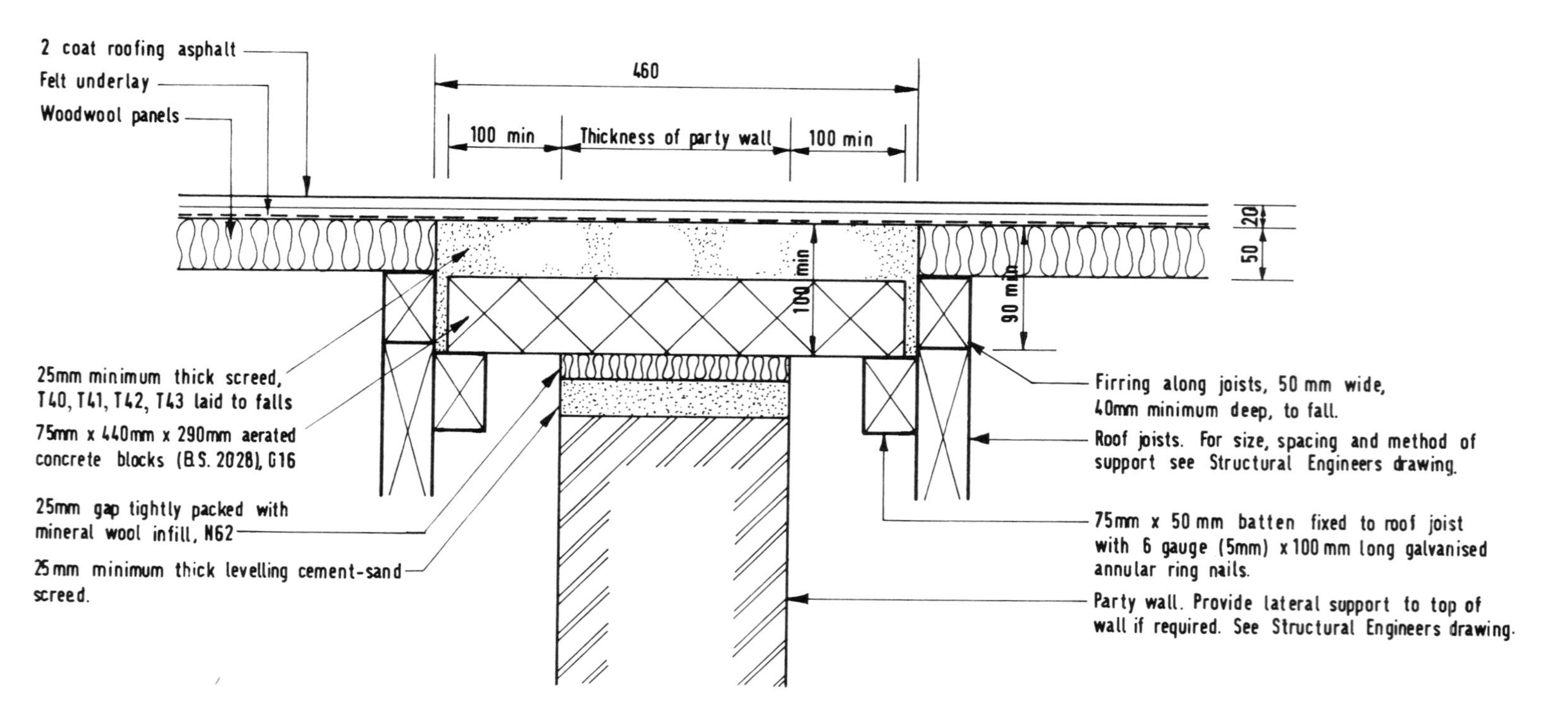

TIMBER JOISTS PARALLEL TO PARTY WALL.
FIRRING ALONG JOISTS, MINIMUM 40 mm DEEP.
LONDON BUILDING BYLAWS. (Bylaw 11·02 Domestic Buildings).

title
ROOF DETAIL AT PARTY WALL. (LONDON BUILDING BYLAWS).

scale
1 : 5

drawing no
D5226

rev

bldg type | space use | element | feature | material | key
[47] 348 Ps4 C1F

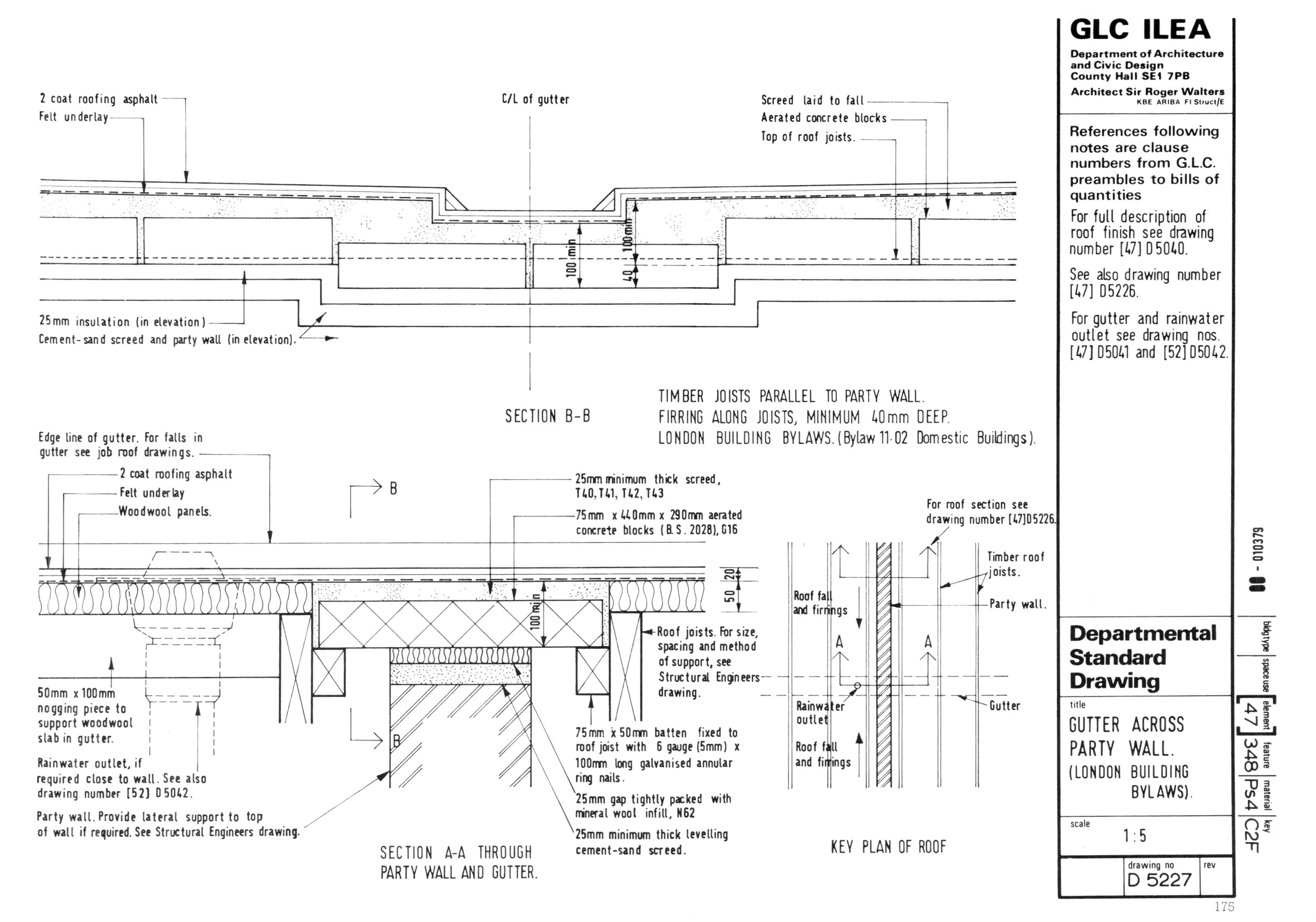
GLC ILEA
Department of Architecture and Civic Design
County Hall SE1 7PB
Architect Sir Roger Walters KBE ARIBA FI Struct/E
References following notes are clause numbers from G.L.C. preambles to bills of quantities
For full description of roof finish see drawing number [47] D5040.
See also drawing number [47] D5226.
For gutter and rainwater outlet see drawing nos. [47] D5041 and [52] D5042.
2 coat roofing asphalt
Felt underlay
C/L of gutter
Screed laid to fall
Aerated concrete blocks
Top of roof joists.
100 min
100 min
40
25mm insulation (in elevation)
Cement-sand screed and party wall (in elevation).
SECTION B-B
TIMBER JOISTS PARALLEL TO PARTY WALL.
FIRRING ALONG JOISTS, MINIMUM 40mm DEEP.
LONDON BUILDING BYLAWS. (Bylaw 11·02 Domestic Buildings).
Edge line of gutter. For falls in gutter see job roof drawings.
2 coat roofing asphalt
Felt underlay
Woodwool panels.
B
25mm minimum thick screed, T40, T41, T42, T43
75mm x 440mm x 290mm aerated concrete blocks (B.S. 2028), G16
20
50
100 min
Roof joists. For size, spacing and method of support, see Structural Engineers drawing.
50mm x 100mm nogging piece to support woodwool slab in gutter.
Rainwater outlet, if required close to wall. See also drawing number [52] D5042.
Party wall. Provide lateral support to top of wall if required. See Structural Engineers drawing.
B
75mm x 50mm batten fixed to roof joist with 6 gauge (5mm) x 100mm long galvanised annular ring nails.
25mm gap tightly packed with mineral wool infill, N62
25mm minimum thick levelling cement-sand screed.
SECTION A-A THROUGH PARTY WALL AND GUTTER.
For roof section see drawing number [47] D5226.
Timber roof joists.
Party wall.
Roof fall and firrings
A
A
Rainwater outlet
Roof fall and firings
Gutter
KEY PLAN OF ROOF
Departmental Standard Drawing
title
GUTTER ACROSS PARTY WALL. (LONDON BUILDING BYLAWS).
scale 1:5
drawing no D 5227
rev
bldg type
space use
element [47]
feature 348
material Ps4
key C2F
0 - 00379

GLC ILEA

Department of Architecture and Civic Design
County Hall SE1 7PB
Architect Sir Roger Walters KBE ARIBA FI Struct/E

References following notes are clause numbers from G.L.C. preambles to bills of quantities

For full description of roof finish see drawing number [47] D 5020.

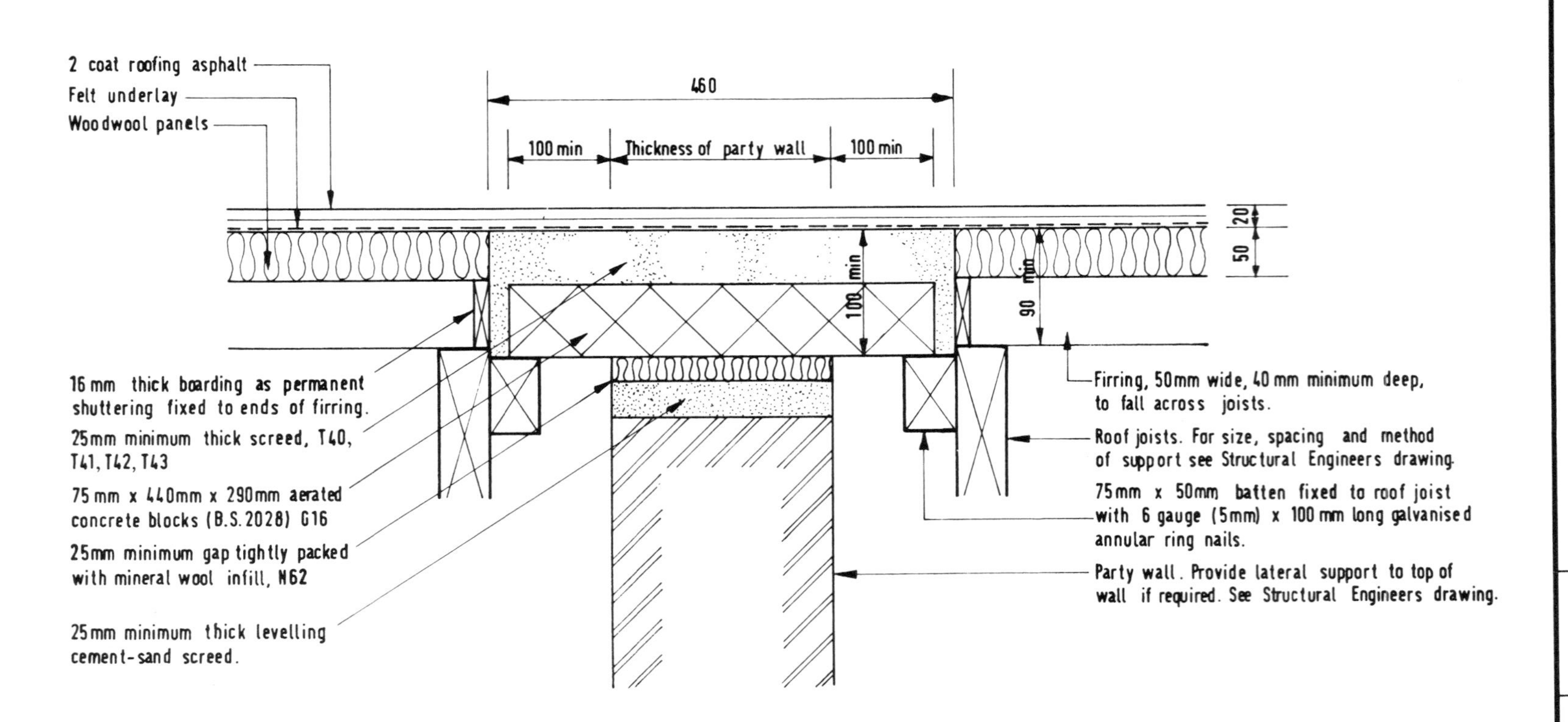

TIMBER JOISTS PARALLEL TO PARTY WALL.
FIRRING ACROSS JOISTS, MINIMUM 40mm DEEP.
THIS DETAIL CAN BE USED WITH SLOPING TOP OF PARTY WALL.
LONDON BUILDING BYLAWS. (Bylaw 11·02 Domestic Buildings).

Departmental Standard Drawing

title
ROOF DETAIL AT PARTY WALL. (LONDON BUILDING BYLAWS).

scale
1 : 5

drawing no
D 5225

rev

[47] 348 | Ps4 | B1F

01037

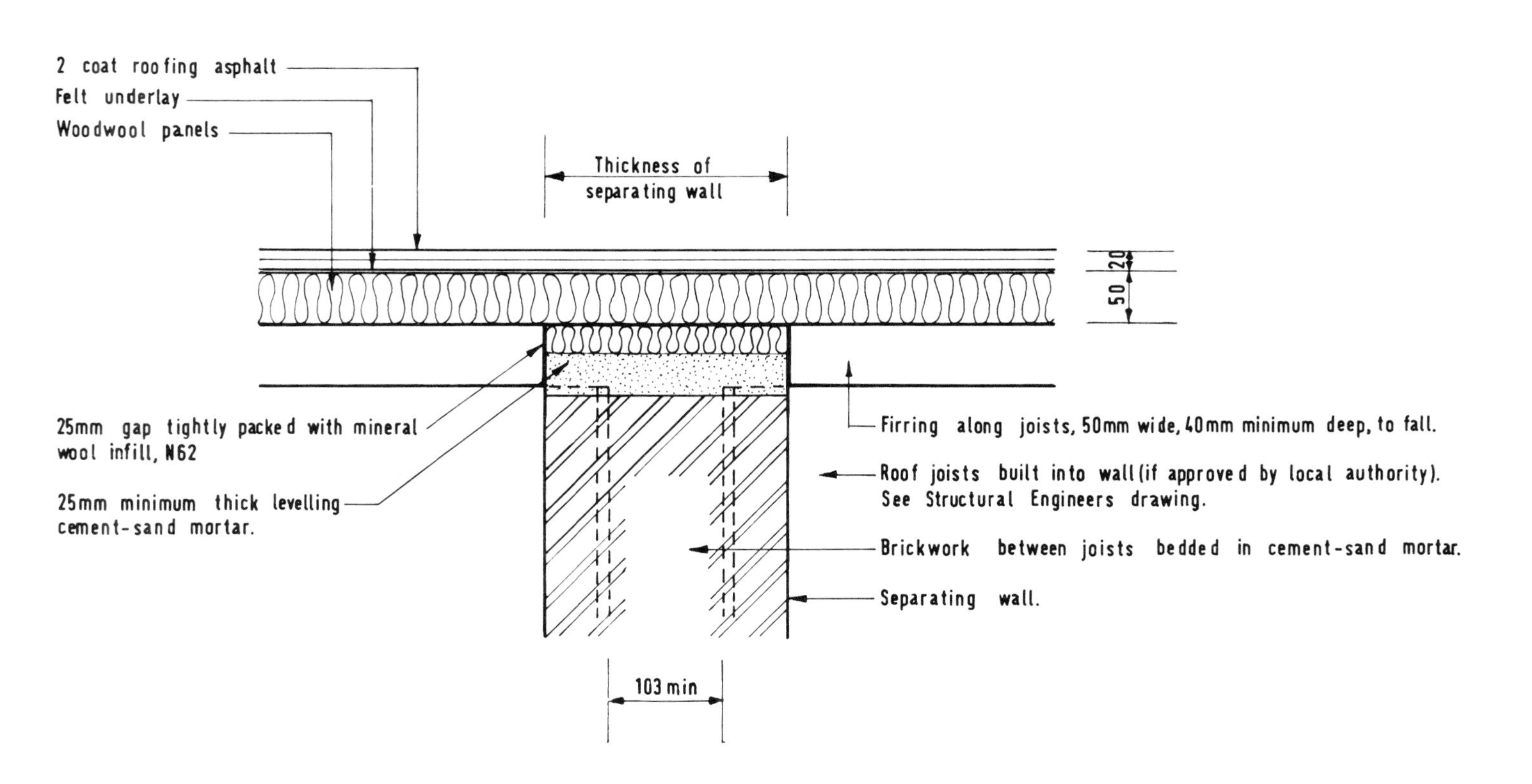

TIMBER JOISTS AT RIGHT ANGLES TO SEPARATING WALL
FIRRING TO FALL ALONG JOISTS, MINIMUM 40mm DEEP.
BUILDING REGULATIONS.

GLC ILEA

Department of Architecture and Civic Design
County Hall SE1 7PB
Architect Sir Roger Walters
KBE ARIBA FI Struct/E

References following notes are clause numbers from G.L.C. preambles to bills of quantities

For full description of roof finish see drawing number [47] D 5040.

010379

Departmental Standard Drawing

title
ROOF FINISH AT SEPARATING WALL. (BUILDING REGULATIONS).

bldg type | space use | element [47] | feature 348 | material Ps4 | key C1A

scale 1:5

drawing no D 5231 | rev

GLC ILEA

Department of Architecture
and Civic Design
County Hall SE1 7PB

Architect Sir Roger Walters
KBE ARIBA FI Struct/E

References following notes are clause numbers from G.L.C. preambles to bills of quantities

For full description of roof finish see drawing number [47] D5040.

See also drawing number [47] D5231.

For gutter and rainwater outlet see drawing nos. [47] D5041 and [52] D5042.

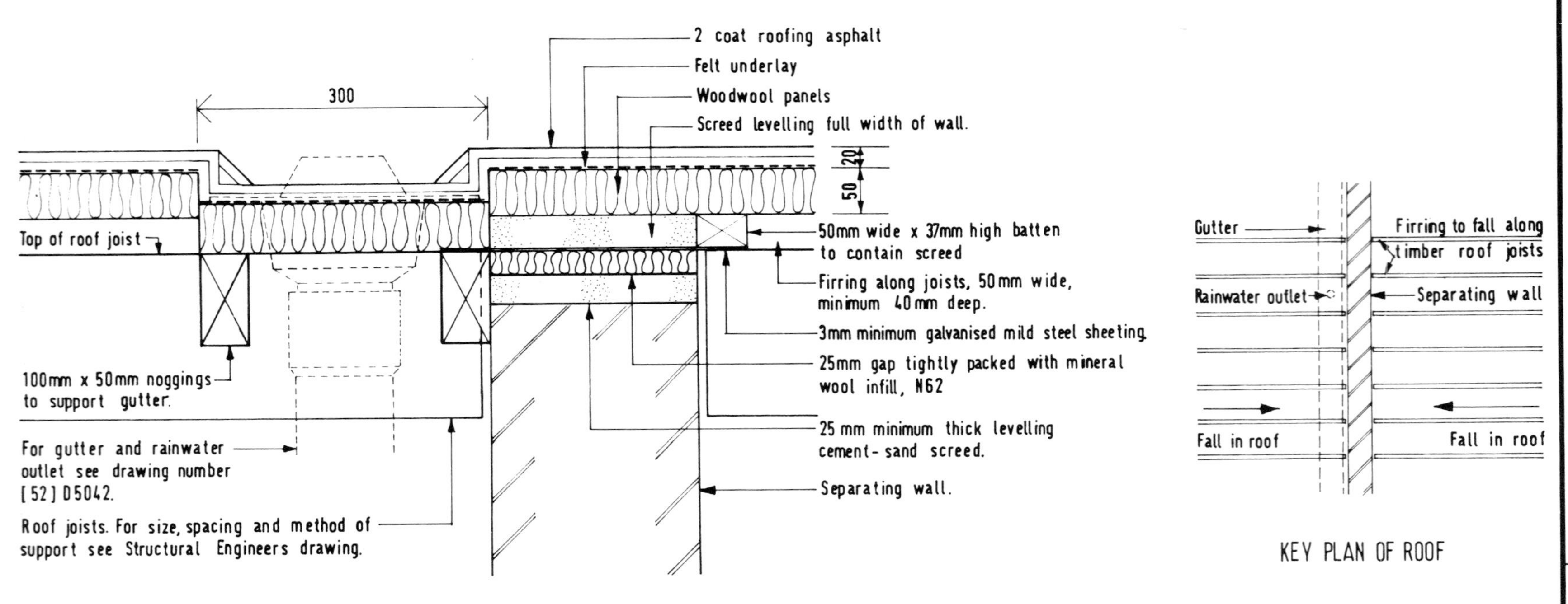

SECTION THROUGH SEPARATING WALL AND GUTTER

TIMBER JOISTS AT RIGHT ANGLES TO SEPARATING WALL.
FIRRING TO FALL ALONG JOISTS, MINIMUM 40mm DEEP.
BUILDING REGULATIONS.

Departmental Standard Drawing

title
GUTTER ALONG SEPARATING WALL. (BUILDING REGULATIONS).

scale
1:5

drawing no	rev
D 5232	

47 J 348 | Ps4 | C2A

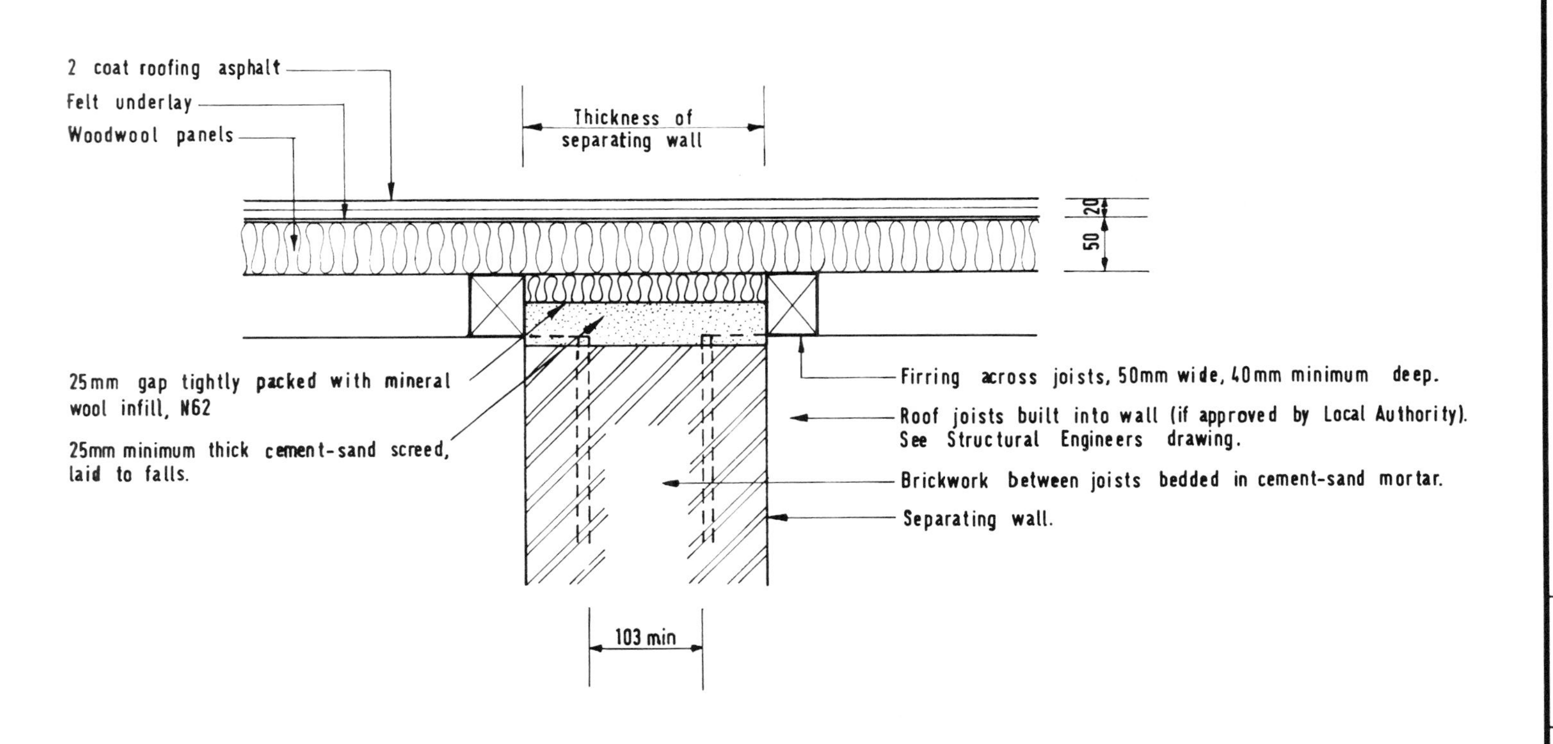

TIMBER JOISTS AT RIGHT ANGLES TO SEPARATING WALL.
FIRRING TO FALL ACROSS JOISTS, MINIMUM 40mm DEEP.
BUILDING REGULATIONS.

GLC ILEA

Department of Architecture and Civic Design
County Hall SE1 7PB
Architect Sir Roger Walters KBE ARIBA FI Struct/E

References following notes are clause numbers from G.L.C. preambles to bills of quantities

For full description of roof finish see drawing number [47] D5020.

Departmental Standard Drawing

title
ROOF FINISH AT SEPARATING WALL.
(BUILDING REGULATIONS).

scale 1:5

drawing no D5233 | rev

bldg type | space use | element [47] | feature 348 | material Ps4 | key B1A

010379

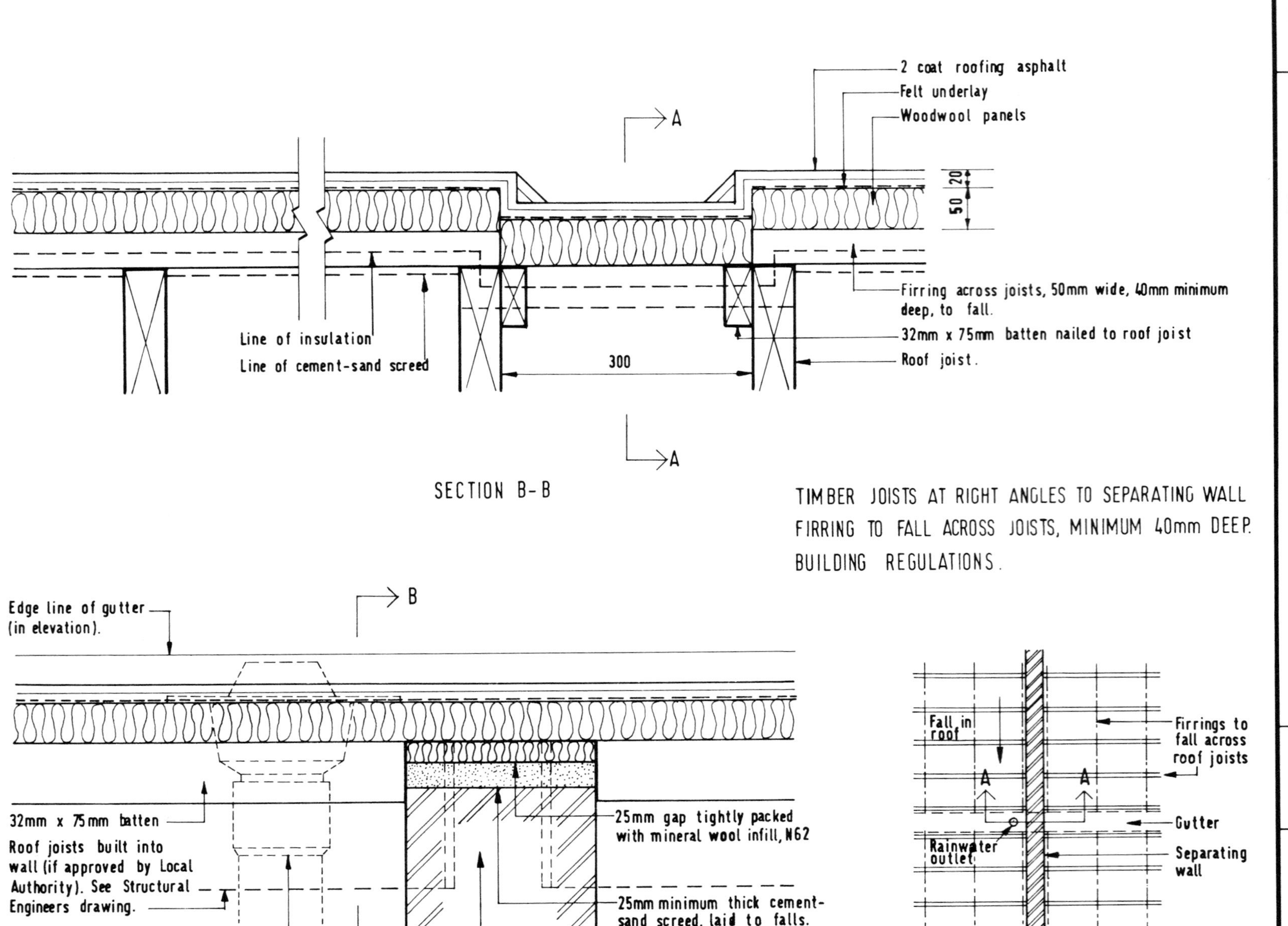

GLC ILEA

Department of Architecture and Civic Design
County Hall SE1 7PB
Architect Sir Roger Walters
KBE ARIBA FI Struct/E

References following notes are clause numbers from G.L.C. preambles to bills of quantities

For full description of roof finish see drawing number [47] D5020.

See also drawing number [47] D5233.

For gutter and rainwater outlet see drawing nos. [47] D5021 and [52] D5022.

Departmental Standard Drawing

title
GUTTER ACROSS SEPARATING WALL. (BUILDING REGULATIONS).

scale
1:5

drawing no	rev
D5234	

47 348 Ps4 B2A

010379 - 00

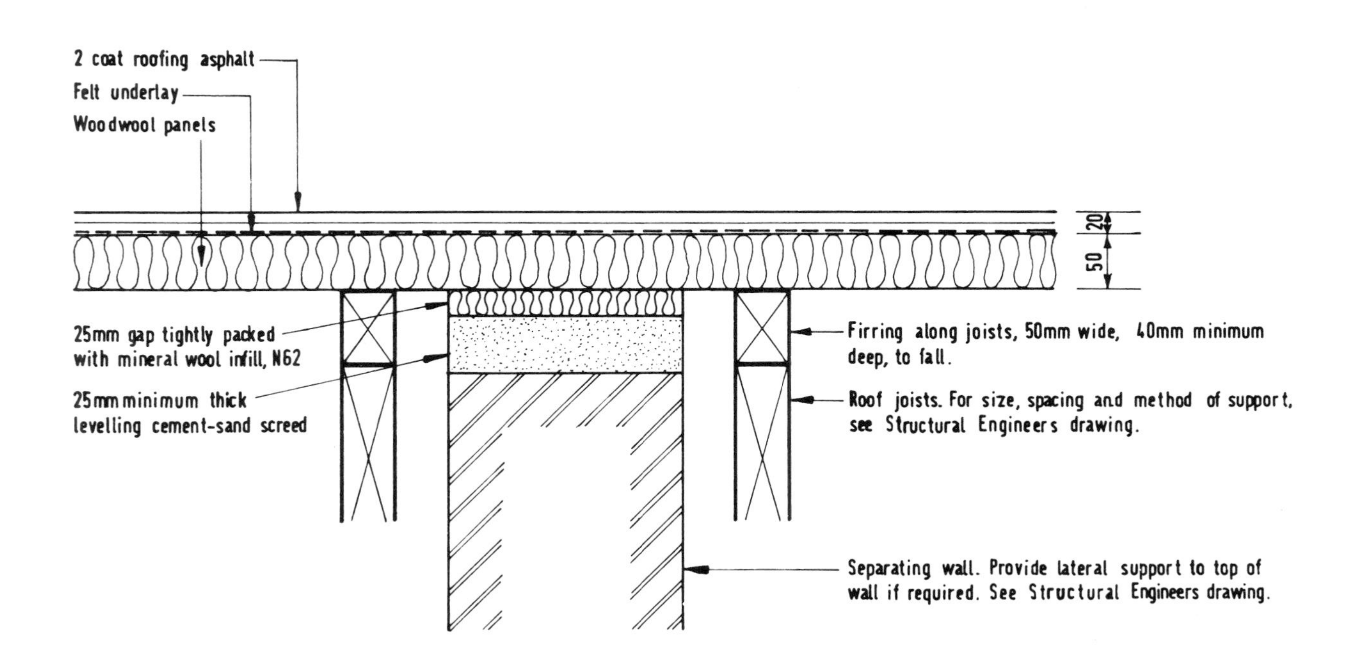

TIMBER JOISTS PARALLEL TO SEPARATING WALL.
FIRRING TO FALL ALONG JOISTS, MINIMUM 40mm DEEP.
BUILDING REGULATIONS.

GLC ILEA

Department of Architecture and Civic Design
County Hall SE1 7PB
Architect Sir Roger Walters
KBE ARIBA FI Struct/E

References following notes are clause numbers from G.L.C. preambles to bills of quantities

For full description of roof finish see drawing number [47] D5040.

Departmental Standard Drawing

title
ROOF FINISH AT SEPARATING WALL. (BUILDING REGULATIONS).

scale 1:5

drawing no D 5236 | rev

bldg type | space use | element [47] | feature 348 | material Ps4 | key C1D

0 - 0103/9

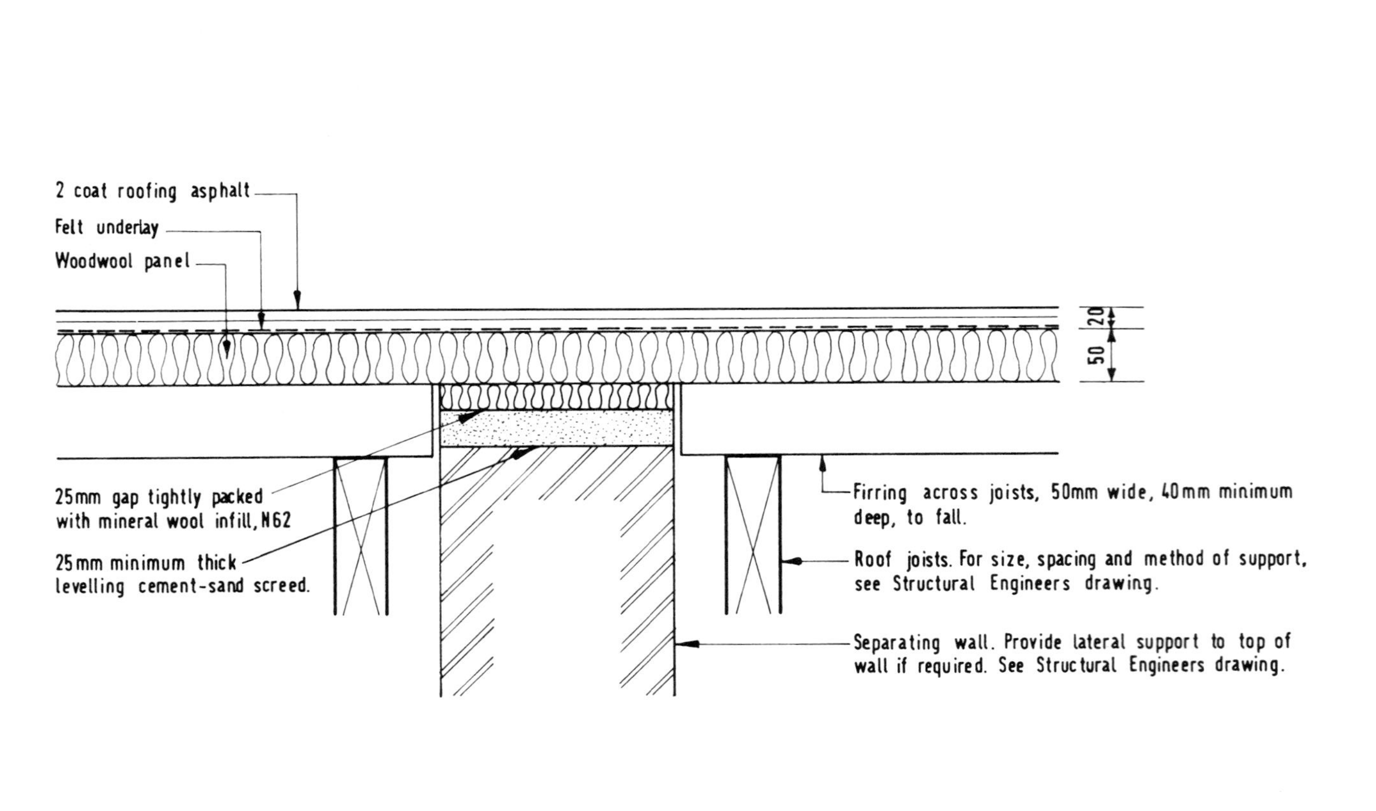

TIMBER JOISTS PARALLEL TO PARTY WALL
FIRRING TO FALL ACROSS JOISTS, MINIMUM 40mm DEEP.
BUILDING REGULATIONS.

GLC ILEA

Department of Architecture and Civic Design
County Hall SE1 7PB
Architect Sir Roger Walters
KBE ARIBA FI Struct/E

References following notes are clause numbers from G.L.C. preambles to bills of quantities

For full description of roof finish see drawing number [47] D5020.

Departmental Standard Drawing

title
ROOF FINISH AT SEPARATING WALL (BUILDING REGULATIONS).

scale 1:5

drawing no D5235 | rev

[47] 348 Ps4 B1D

010379

3
Concrete flat roofs and balconies

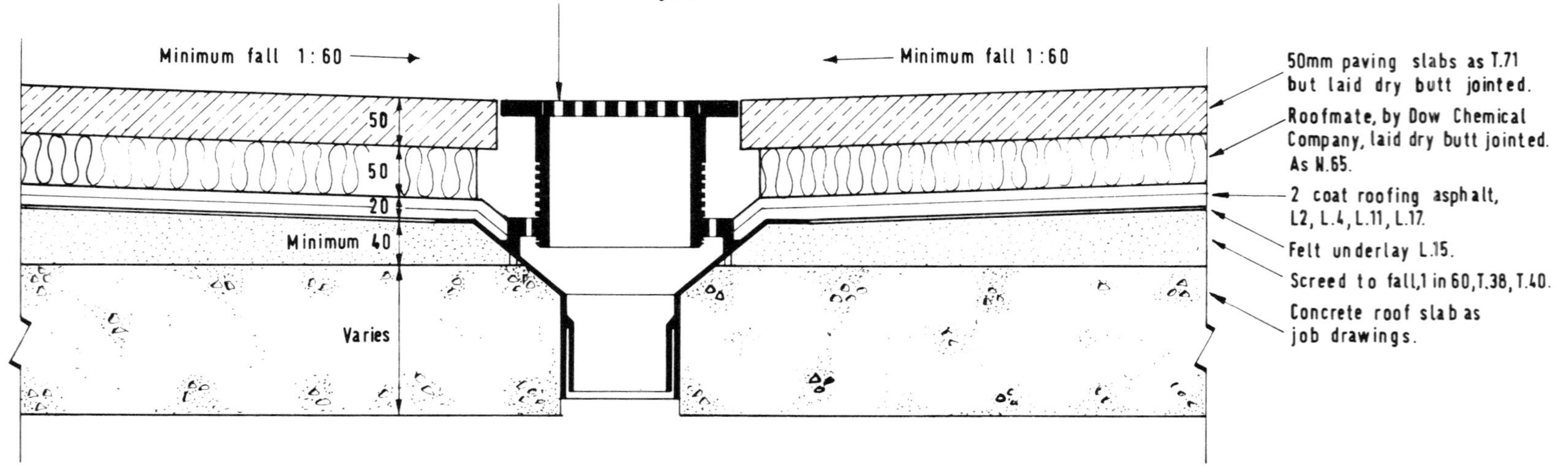

GLC ILEA

Department of Architecture and Civic Design
County Hall SE1 7PB
Architect Sir Roger Walters
KBE ARIBA FI Struct/E

References following notes are clause numbers from G.L.C. preambles to bills of quantities

THERMAL INSULATION
to requirements of Parts F or FF of Building Regulations.

Departmental Standard Drawing

title

RAINWATER OUTLET
INVERTED INSULATING
ROOFING SYSTEM.

scale

1: 5

drawing no

D 5330

rev

[52] 186 Xn6 F1D

010379

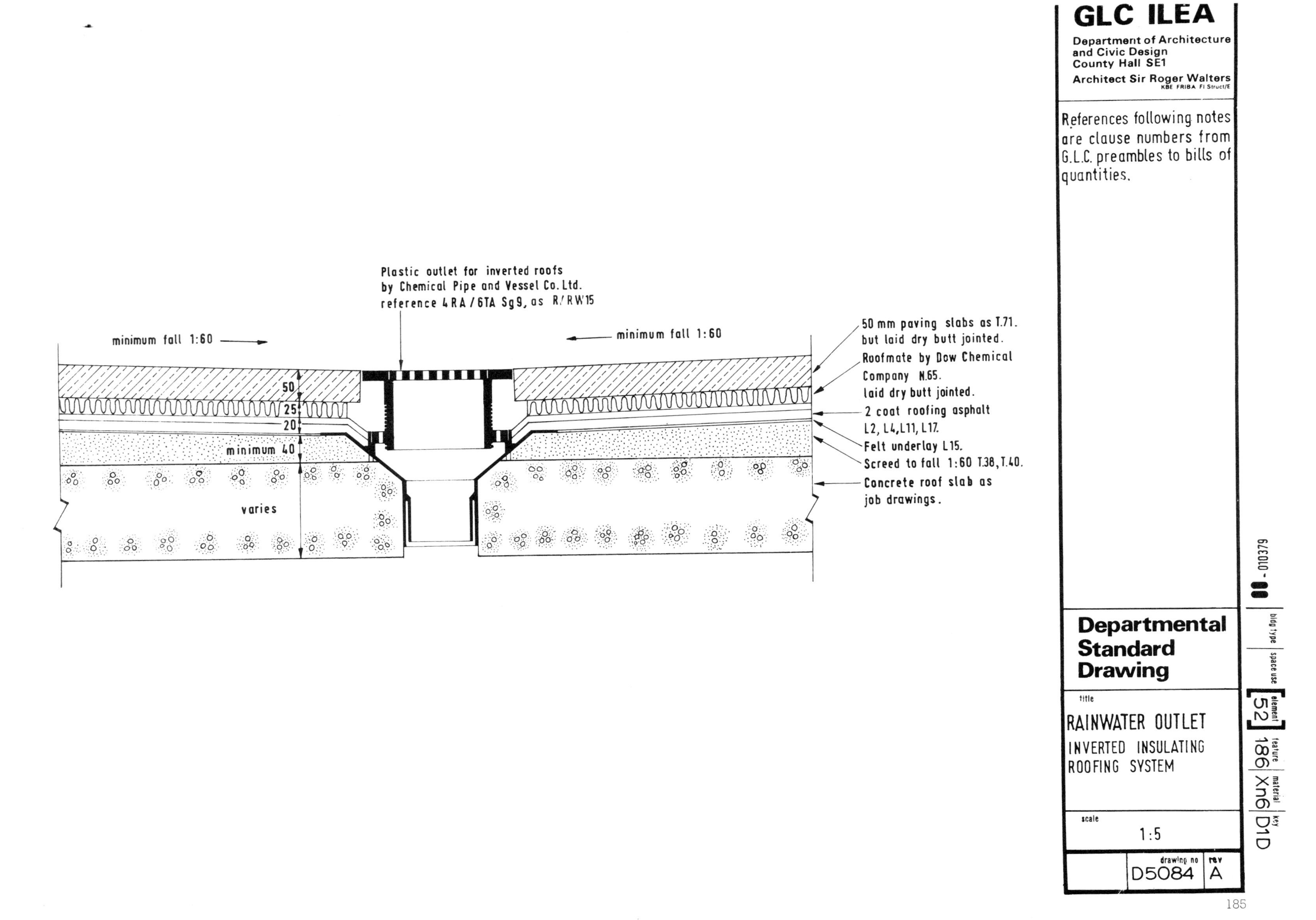
GLC ILEA
Department of Architecture and Civic Design
County Hall SE1
Architect Sir Roger Walters
KBE FRIBA FI StructE
References following notes are clause numbers from G.L.C. preambles to bills of quantities.
Plastic outlet for inverted roofs by Chemical Pipe and Vessel Co. Ltd. reference 4RA/6TA Sg9, as R/RW15
minimum fall 1:60
minimum fall 1:60
50 mm paving slabs as T.71. but laid dry butt jointed.
Roofmate by Dow Chemical Company N.65. laid dry butt jointed.
2 coat roofing asphalt L2, L4, L11, L17.
Felt underlay L15.
Screed to fall 1:60 T.38, T.40.
Concrete roof slab as job drawings.
50
25
20
minimum 40
varies
Departmental Standard Drawing
title
RAINWATER OUTLET
INVERTED INSULATING ROOFING SYSTEM
scale
1:5
drawing no
D5084
rev
A
bldg type
space use
element
[52]
feature
186
material
Xn6
key
D1D
00 - 01029

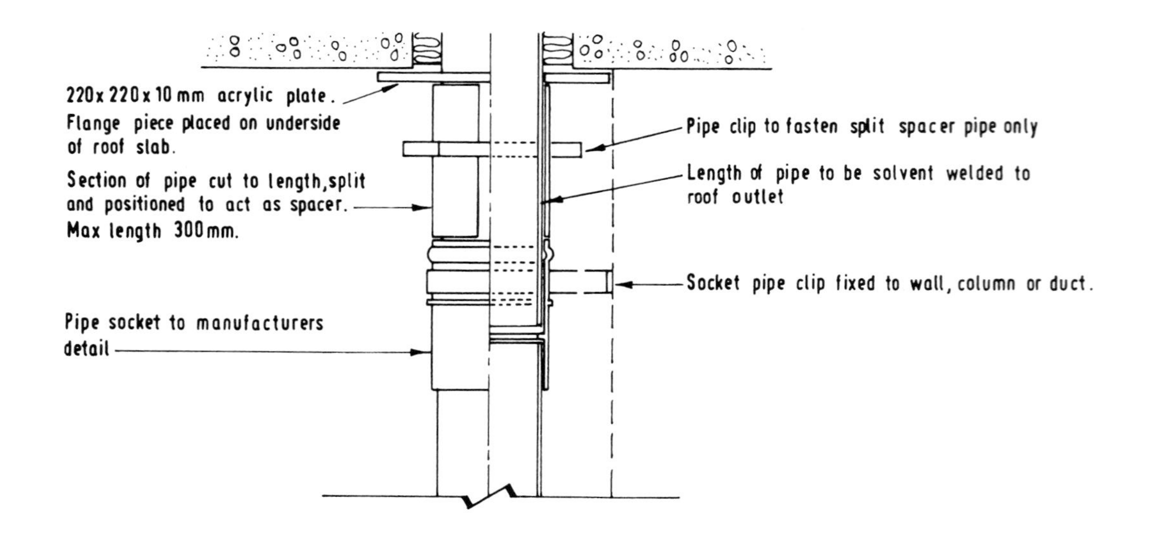

KEY	HOLE IN ACRYLIC FLANGE
A3C	For 75mm pipe
A3D	For 100mm pipe

N.B. When ordering acrylic flange piece it should be stressed that hole to be close fitting to outside diameter of R.W.P. or stack.

GLC ILEA

Department of Architecture and Civic Design
County Hall SE1 7PB
Architect Sir Roger Walters KBE ARIBA FI Struct/E

References following notes are clause numbers from G.L.C. preambles to bills of quantities

To be read in conjunction with [52] D 5319 and D 5320

Departmental Standard Drawing

title
PIPE FIXING DETAIL
RAINWATER OUTLET

CONCRETE ROOF

scale 1:5

drawing no D5218 rev A

bldg type | space use | element [52] | feature 186 | material Rn6 | key as matrix

010379

GLC ILEA
Department of Architecture
and Civic Design
County Hall SE1 7PB
Architect Sir Roger Walters
KBE ARIBA FI Struct/E

References following notes are clause numbers from G.L.C. preambles to bills of quantities

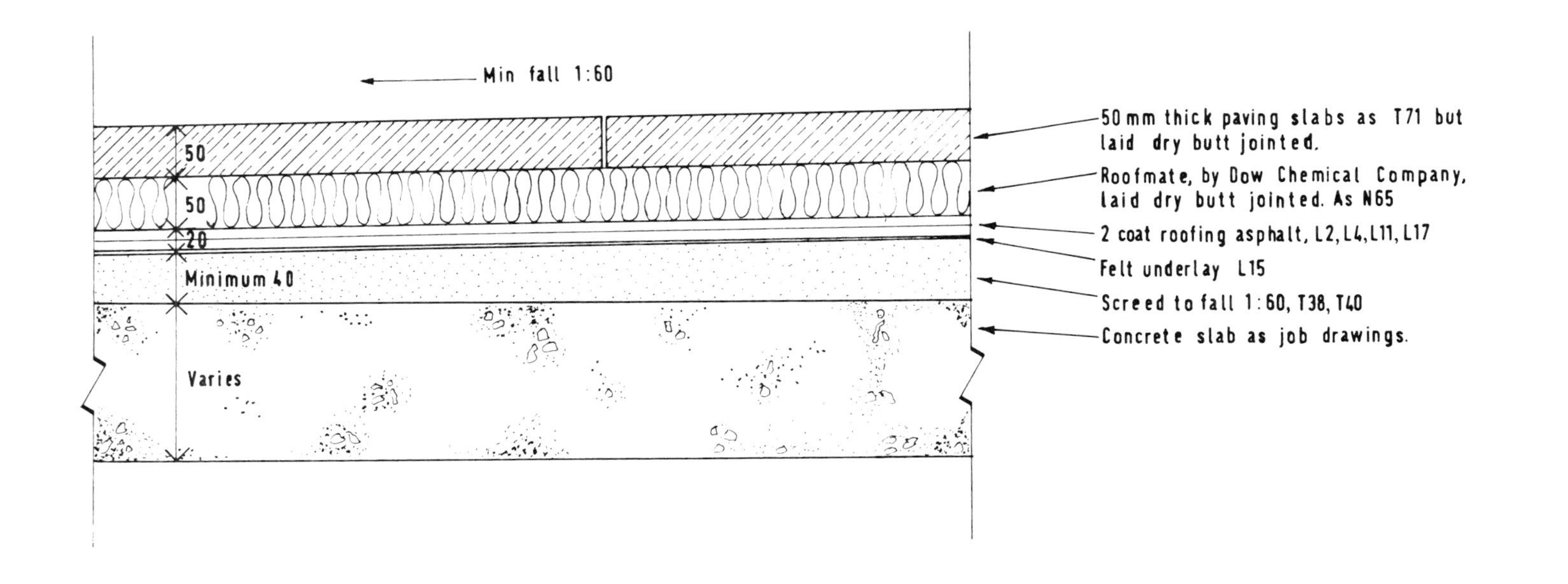

THERMAL INSULATION to requirements of Parts F or FF of Building Regulations.

Departmental Standard Drawing

title

BALCONY FINISH
INVERTED INSULATING ROOFING SYSTEM

scale 1 : 5

drawing no D5331

rev

bldg type	space use	element	feature	material	key
		[43]	233	Ps4	F1

00 - 01039

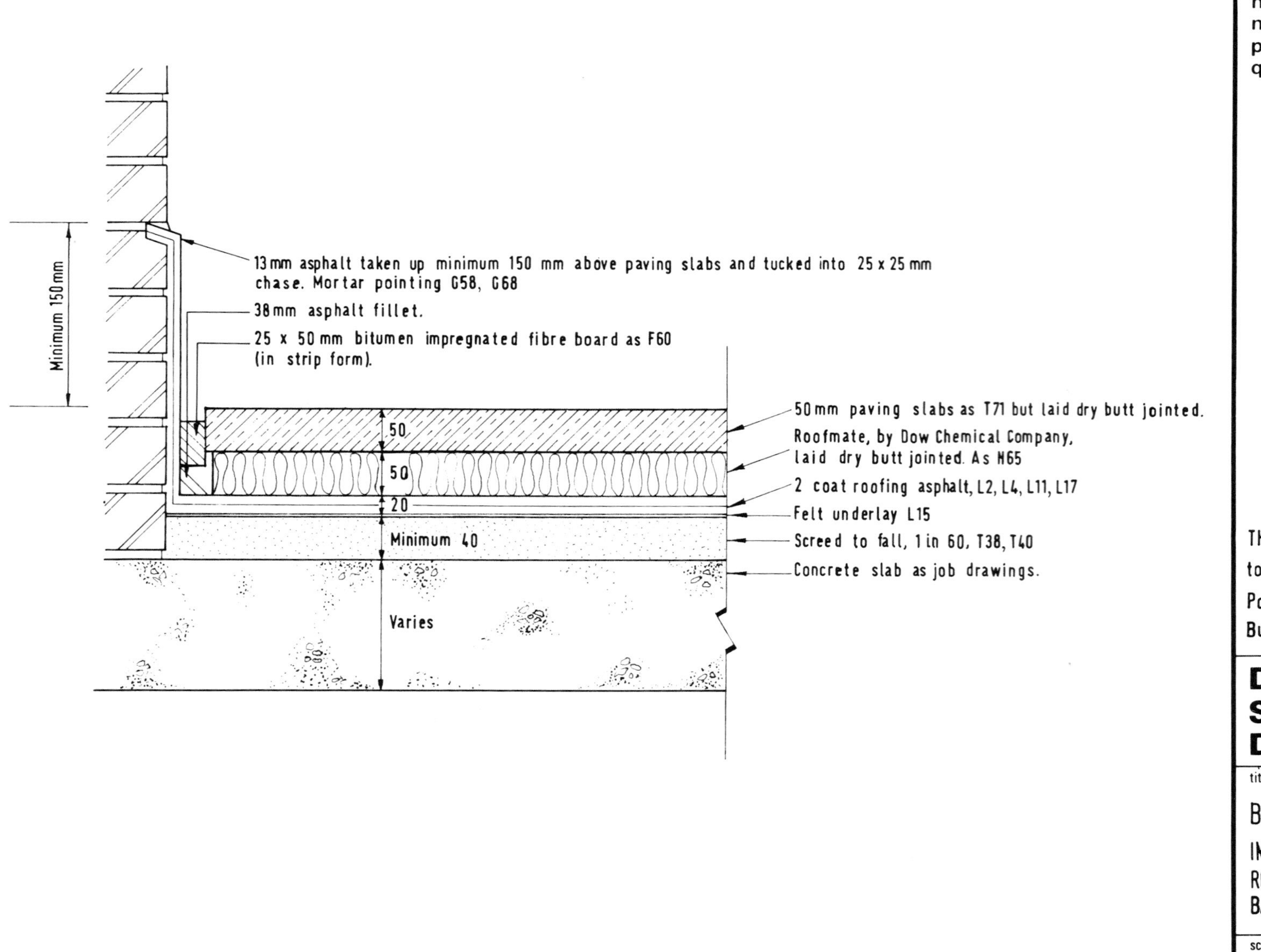

GLC ILEA

Department of Architecture and Civic Design
County Hall SE1 7PB
Architect Sir Roger Walters
KBE ARIBA FI Struct/E

References following notes are clause numbers from G.L.C. preambles to bills of quantities

THERMAL INSULATION to requirements of Parts F or FF of Building Regulations.

Departmental Standard Drawing

title
BRICK ABUTMENT
INVERTED INSULATING ROOFING SYSTEM BALCONY DECK

scale
1:5

drawing no	rev
D5332	A

bldg type	space use	element	feature	material	key
		43	233	Ps4	F2

040679A
010379 -

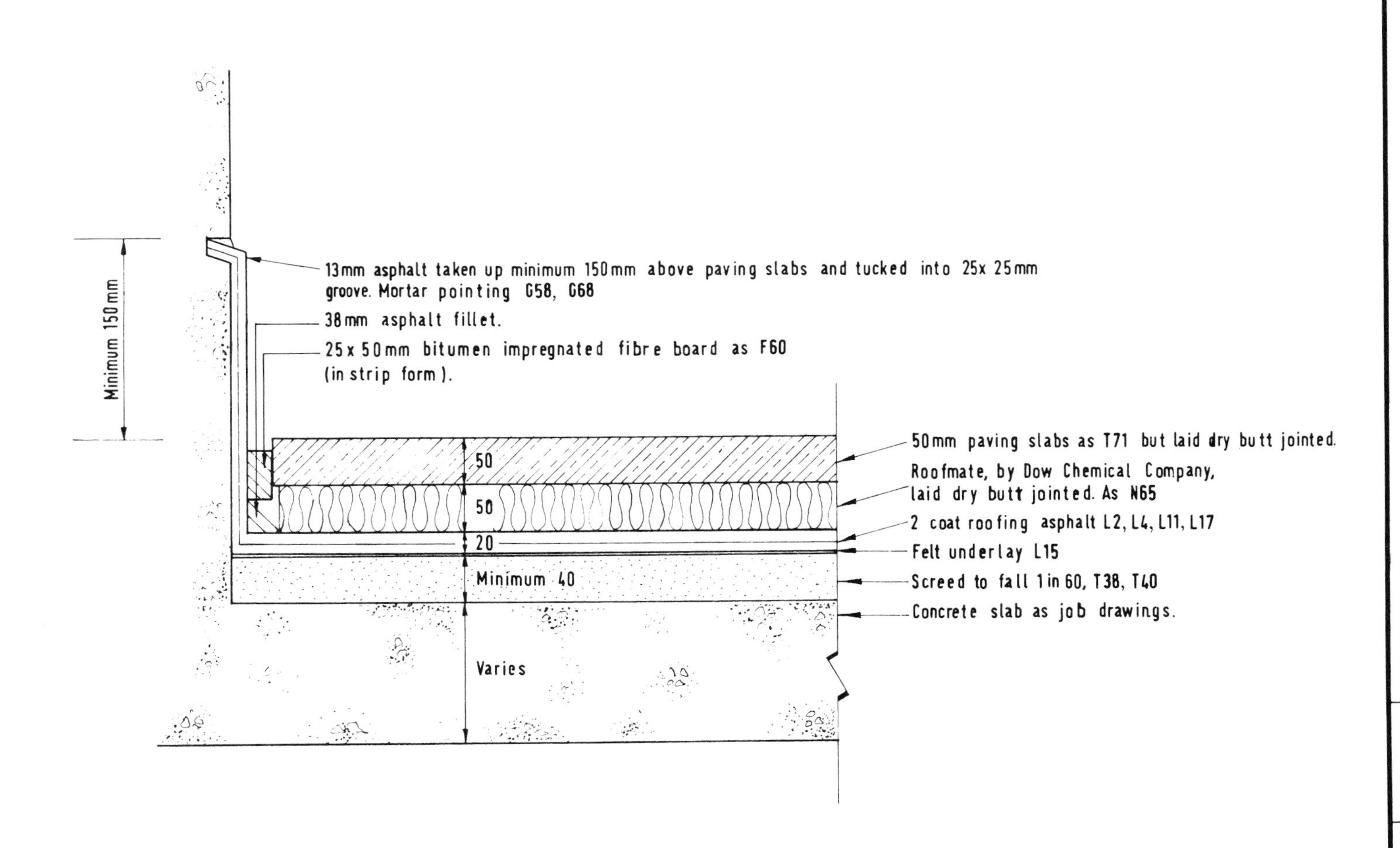

GLC ILEA

Department of Architecture
and Civic Design
County Hall SE1 7PB
Architect Sir Roger Walters
KBE ARIBA FI Struct/E

References following notes are clause numbers from G.L.C. preambles to bills of quantities

THERMAL INSULATION to requirements of Parts F or FF of Building Regulations.

Departmental Standard Drawing

title

CONCRETE ABUTMENT
INVERTED INSULATING ROOFING SYSTEM
BALCONY DECK.

scale 1:5

drawing no D5333 rev A

bldgtype | spaceuse | element [43] | feature 233 | material Ps4 | key F3

010379 - 010679A

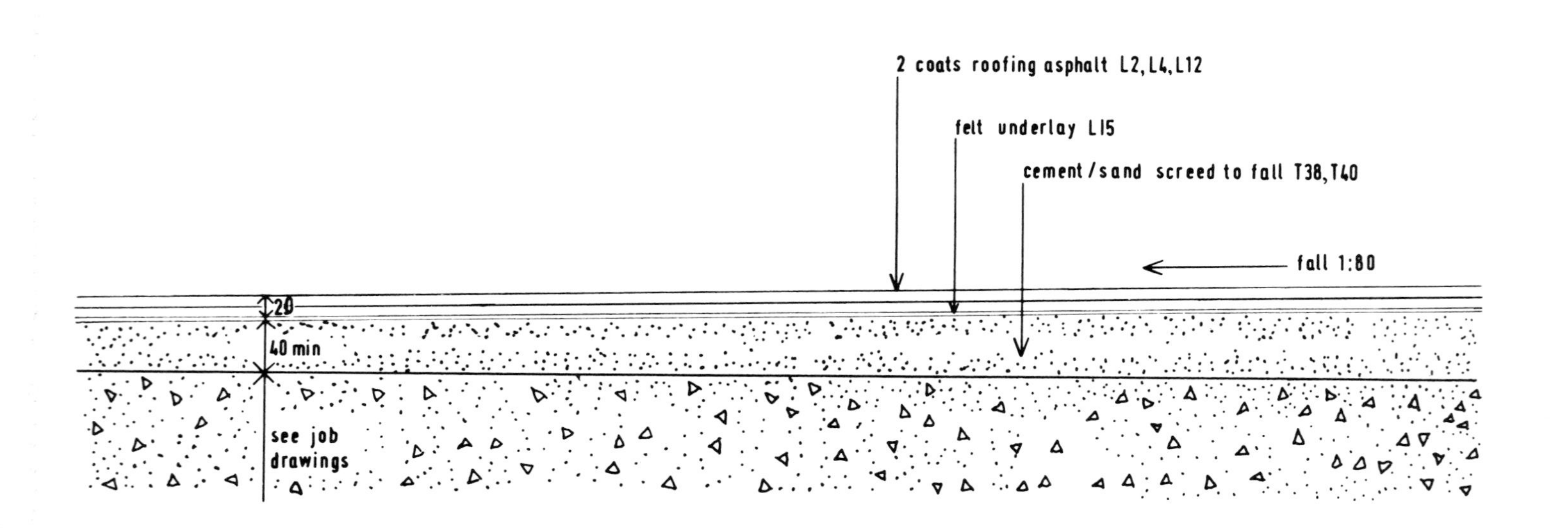

GLC ILEA

Department of Architecture and Civic Design
County Hall SE1
Architect Sir Roger Walters KBE FRIBA FI Struct/E

References following notes are clause numbers from GLC preambles to bills of quantities

Departmental Standard Drawing

title

CANTILEVERED BALCONY FINISH FOR LIGHT TRAFFIC

scale

1:5

drawing no D5026 | rev B

bldg type | space use | element [43] | feature 233 | material Ps4 | key A1

08 - 010379

GLC ILEA

Department of Architecture and Civic Design
County Hall SE1
Architect Sir Roger Walters
KBE FRIBA FI StructE

References following notes are clause numbers from GLC preambles to bills of quantities

For full description of the balcony finish see drg. no. [43] D5026

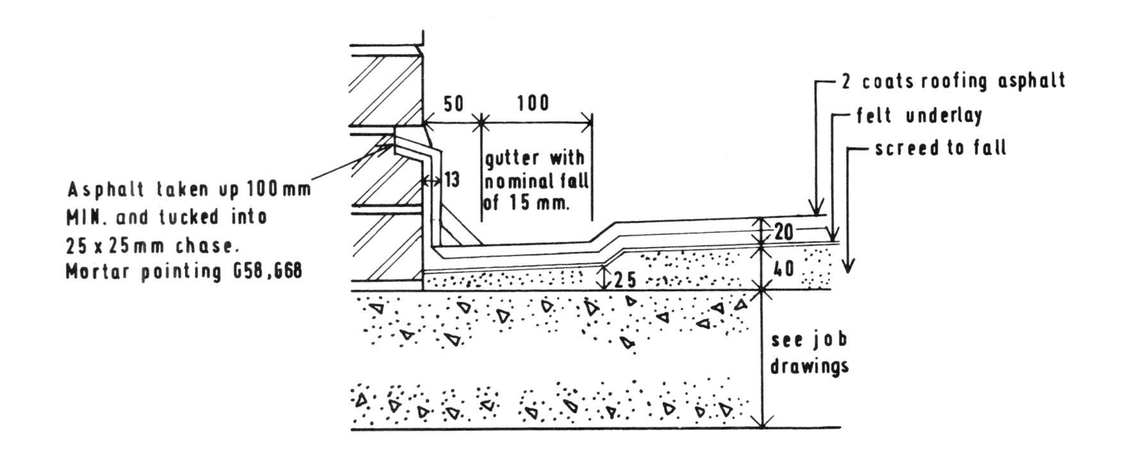

010379 - 00

Departmental Standard Drawing

title
CANTILEVERED BALCONY FINISH FOR LIGHT TRAFFIC BRICK ABUTMENT

scale 1:5

bldg type	space use	element	feature	material	key
		[43]	233	Ps4	A2

drawing no	rev
D5027	B

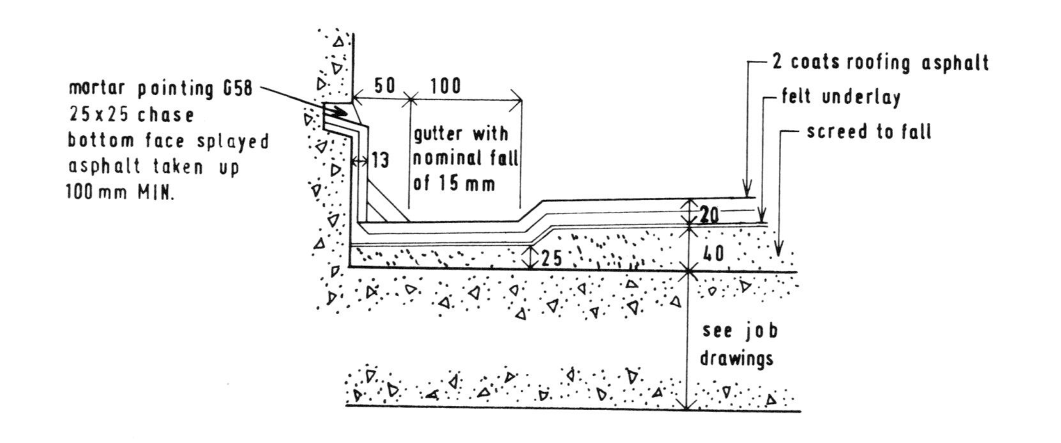

GLC ILEA

Department of Architecture and Civic Design
County Hall SE1
Architect Sir Roger Walters KBE FRIBA FI Struct/E

References following notes are clause numbers from GLC preambles to bills of quantities

For full description of the balcony finish see drg. no. [43] D5026

Departmental Standard Drawing

title

CANTILEVERED BALCONY FINISH FOR LIGHT TRAFFIC CONCRETE ABUTMENT

scale 1:5

drawing no D5028 rev B

[43] 233 Ps4 A3

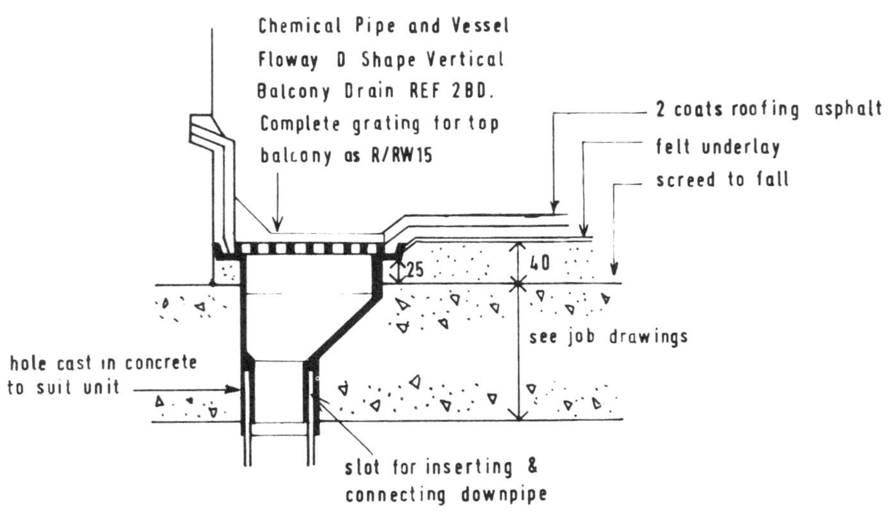

DETAIL AT TOP BALCONY KEY A1A

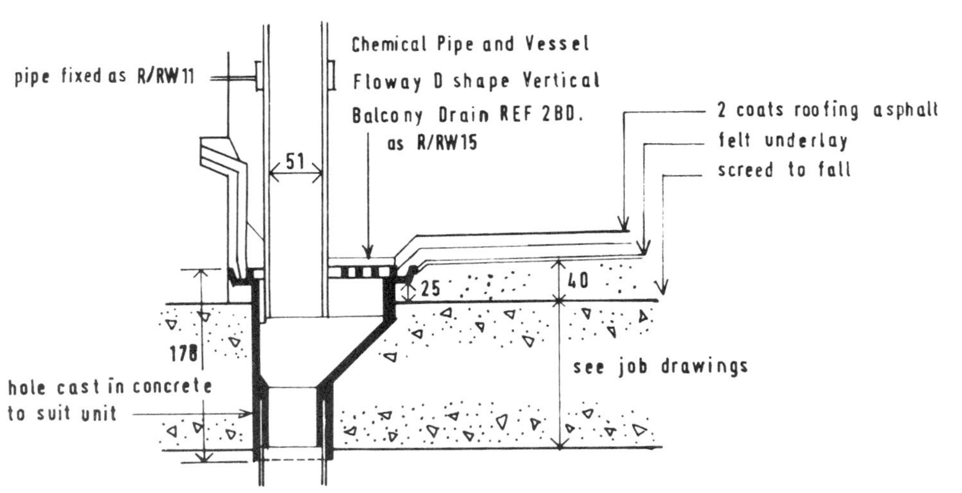

DETAIL AT INTERMEDIATE BALCONY KEY A2A

GLC ILEA

Department of Architecture and Civic Design
County Hall SE1
Architect Sir Roger Walters

References following notes are clause numbers from GLC preambles to bills of quantities

For full description of balcony finish see drg. [43] D5026

Departmental Standard Drawing

title
RAINWATER OUTLET CANTILEVERED BALCONY FOR LIGHT TRAFFIC

scale 1:5

drawing no D5030 rev C

010379-00 | bldg type | space no | element [52] | feature 221 | material Xn6 | key as drawing

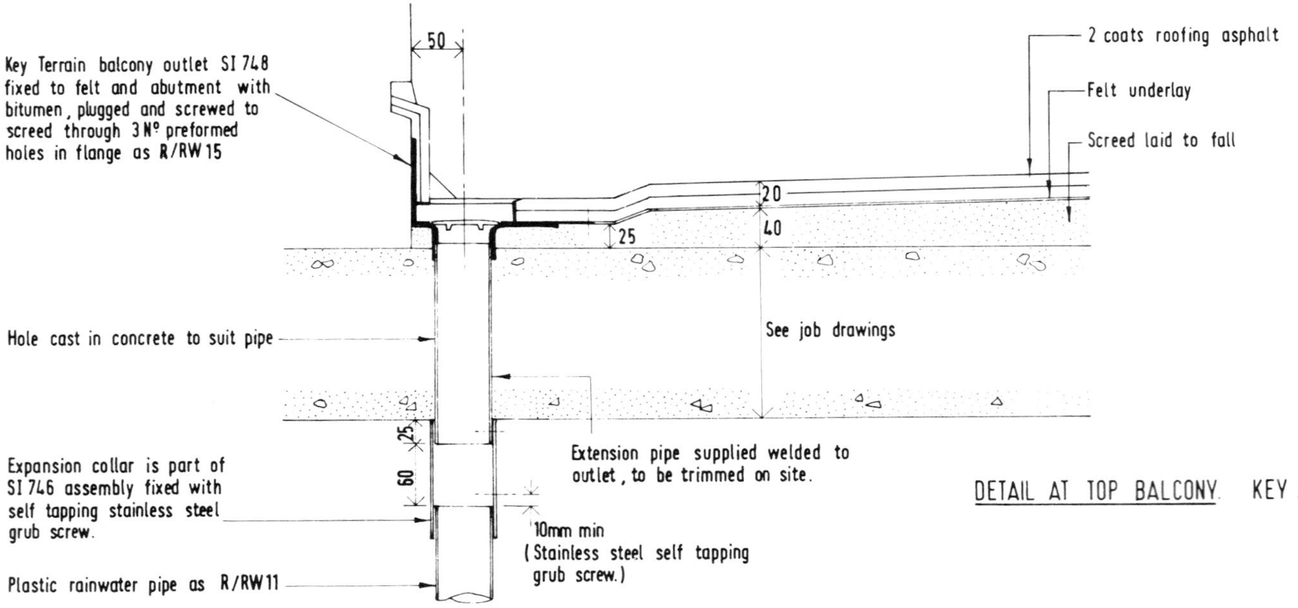

GLC ILEA

Department of Architecture
and Civic Design
County Hall SE1 7PB
Architect Sir Roger Walters
KBE ARIBA FI Struct/E

References following notes are clause numbers from G.L.C. preambles to bills of quantities

For full description of balcony finish see drawing number [43] D5026.

Key Terrain balcony outlet SI 748 fixed to felt and abutment with bitumen, plugged and screwed to screed through 3 Nº preformed holes in flange as R/RW15

50

2 coats roofing asphalt

Felt underlay

Screed laid to fall

20

25

40

Hole cast in concrete to suit pipe

See job drawings

25

60

Expansion collar is part of SI 746 assembly fixed with self tapping stainless steel grub screw.

Extension pipe supplied welded to outlet, to be trimmed on site.

10mm min
(Stainless steel self tapping grub screw.)

Plastic rainwater pipe as R/RW11

DETAIL AT TOP BALCONY. KEY A1A.

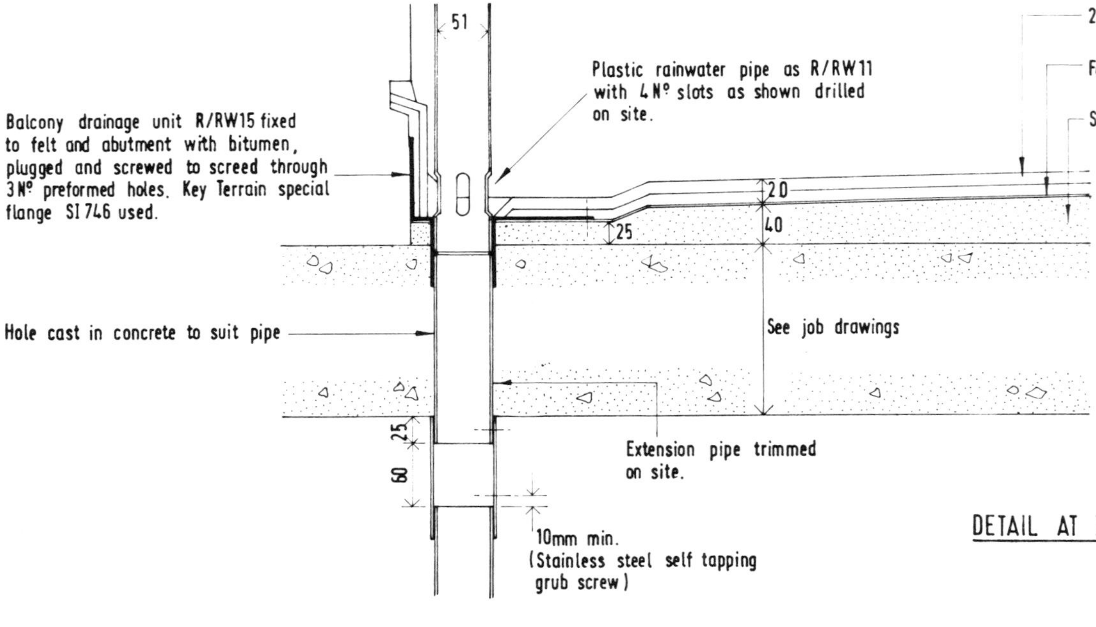

51

2 coats roofing asphalt

Plastic rainwater pipe as R/RW11 with 4 Nº slots as shown drilled on site.

Felt underlay

Balcony drainage unit R/RW15 fixed to felt and abutment with bitumen, plugged and screwed to screed through 3 Nº preformed holes. Key Terrain special flange SI 746 used.

Screed laid to fall.

20

25

40

Hole cast in concrete to suit pipe

See job drawings

25

60

Extension pipe trimmed on site.

10mm min.
(Stainless steel self tapping grub screw)

DETAIL AT INTERMEDIATE BALCONY. KEY A2A

Departmental Standard Drawing

title

RAINWATER OUTLET
CANTILEVERED BALCONY
FOR LIGHT TRAFFIC.

scale 1:5.

drawing no: D5031 rev C

[52] 221 Xn6 as drawing

010379

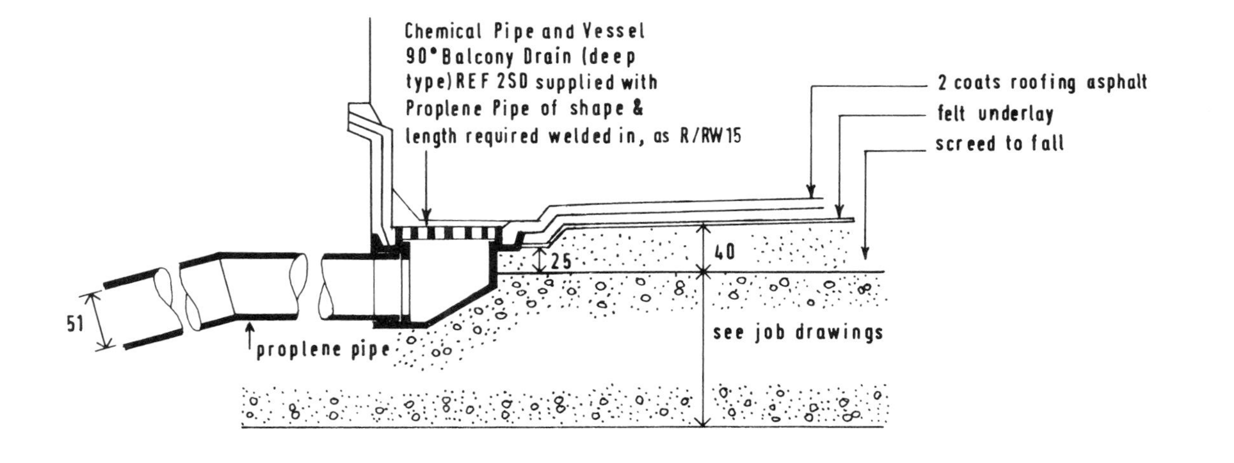

GLC ILEA

Department of Architecture
and Civic Design
County Hall SE1
Architect Sir Roger Walters
KBE FRIBA FI StructE

References following notes are clause numbers from GLC preambles to bills of quantities

For full description of the balcony finish see drg. [43] D5026.

Departmental Standard Drawing

title
RAINWATER OUTLET
CANTILEVERED BALCONY
FOR LIGHT TRAFFIC

scale
1:5

drawing no	rev
D5033	C

bldg type | space use | element [52] | feature 221 | material Xn6 | key A1B

00-03379

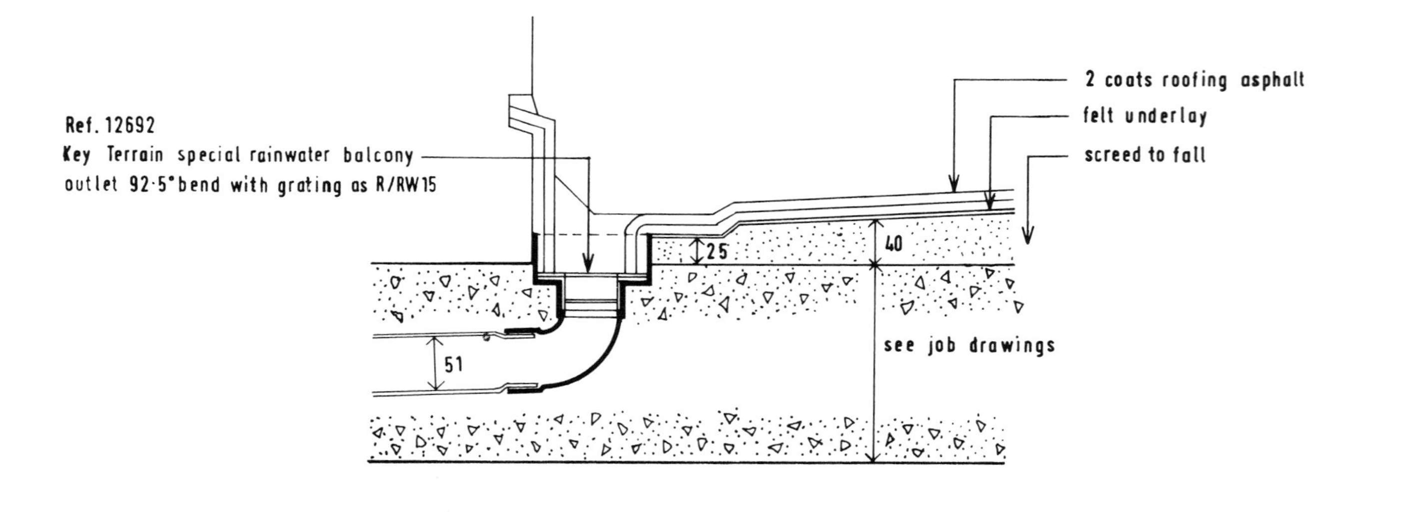

GLC ILEA

Department of Architecture
and Civic Design
County Hall SE1
Architect Sir Roger Walters
KBE FRIBA FI StructE

References following notes are clause numbers from GLC preambles to bills of quantities

For full description of the balcony finish see drg. [43] D5026.

Departmental Standard Drawing

title
RAINWATER OUTLET
CANTILEVERED BALCONY
FOR LIGHT TRAFFIC

scale
1:5

drawing no D5046
rev. C

00 - 010379

[52] 221 Xn6 A1B

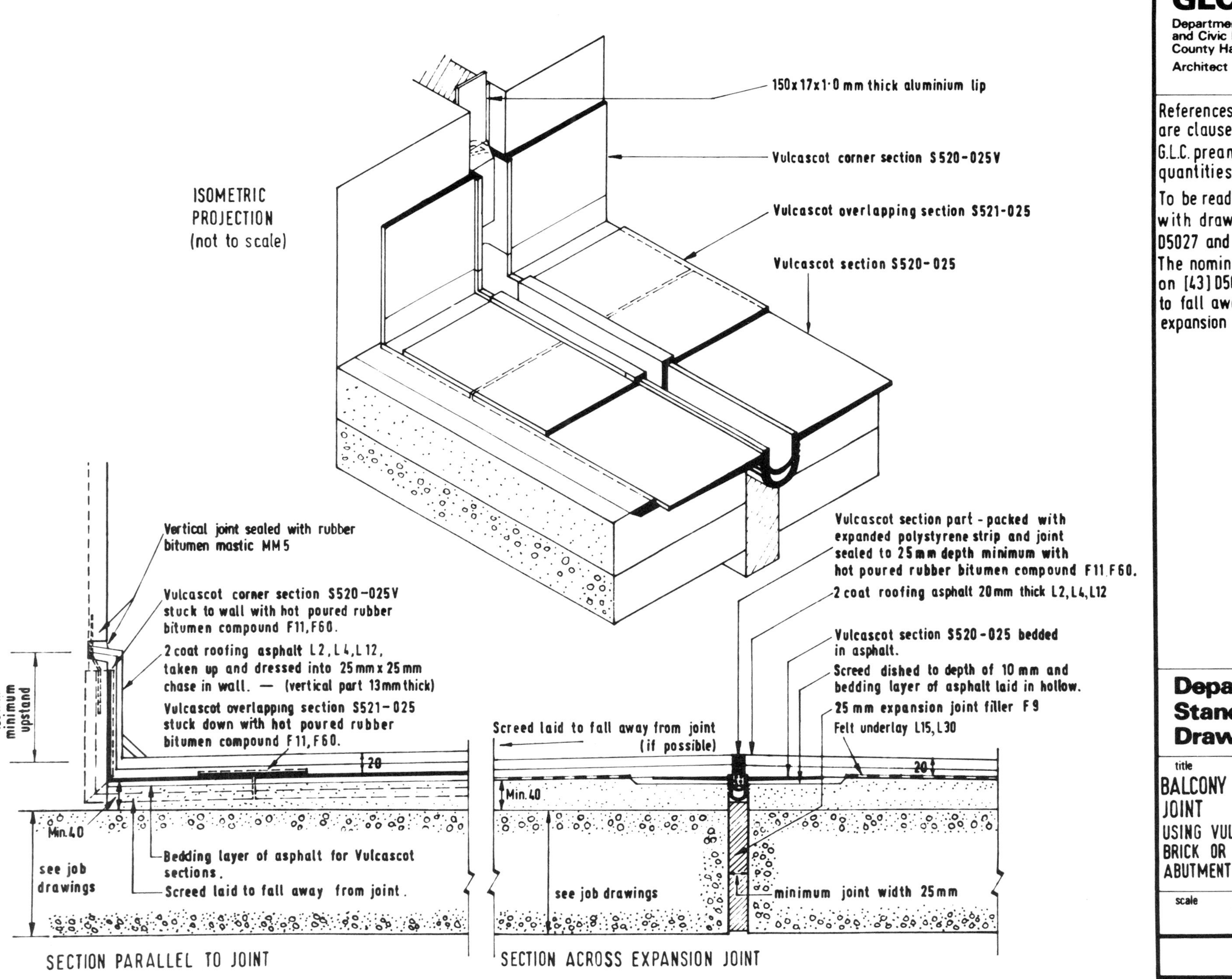

GLC ILEA

Department of Architecture and Civic Design
County Hall SE1
Architect Sir Roger Walters
KBE FRIBA FI Struct E

References following notes are clause numbers from G.L.C. preambles to bills of quantities.

To be read in conjunction with drawings [43] D5026, D5027 and D5028.

The nominal gutter shown on [43] D5027 and D5028 to fall away from the expansion joint.

C:17/5/78 1307 79 0510790

Departmental Standard Drawing

title
BALCONY EXPANSION JOINT
USING VULCASCOT SECTIONS
BRICK OR CONCRETE ABUTMENT

bldg type	space use	element	feature	material	key
		[43]	233	Ps4	A21

scale 1:5

drawing no. D5093 rev. D

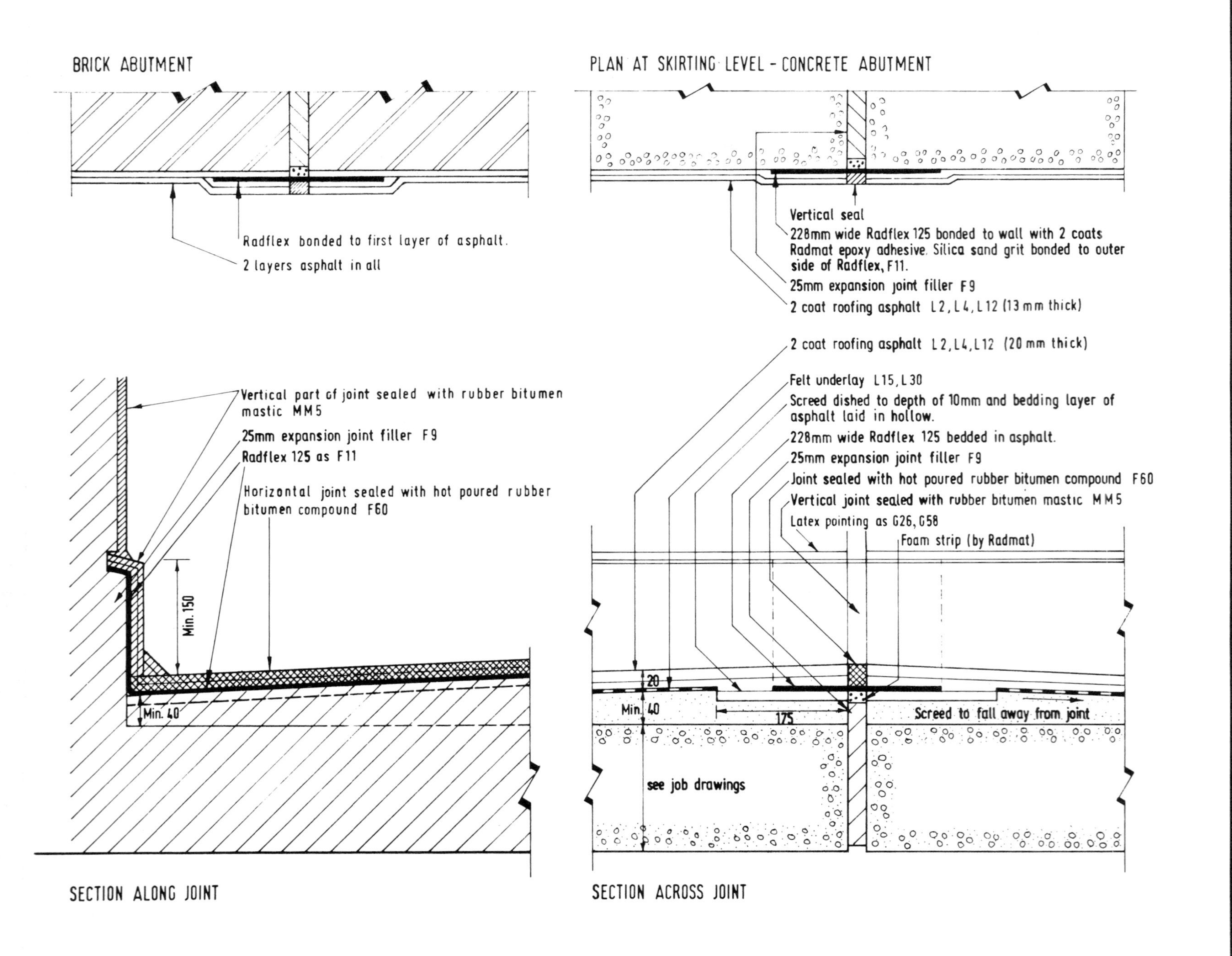

GLC ILEA

Department of Architecture and Civic Design
County Hall SE1 7PB
Architect Sir Roger Walters
KBE ARIBA FI Struct/E

References following notes are clause numbers from G.L.C. preambles to bills of quantities

To be read in conjunction with drawings [43] D5026, D5027 and D5028.

The nominal gutter shown on [43] D5027 and D5028 to fall away from joint.

A:17/5/78 090879 B: 100979

Departmental Standard Drawing

title
BALCONY EXPANSION JOINT USING RADFLEX 125 WITH ASPHALT BED BRICK OR CONCRETE ABUTMENT.

scale
1 : 5

drawing no D5276 | rev B

[43] 233 | Ps4 | A04

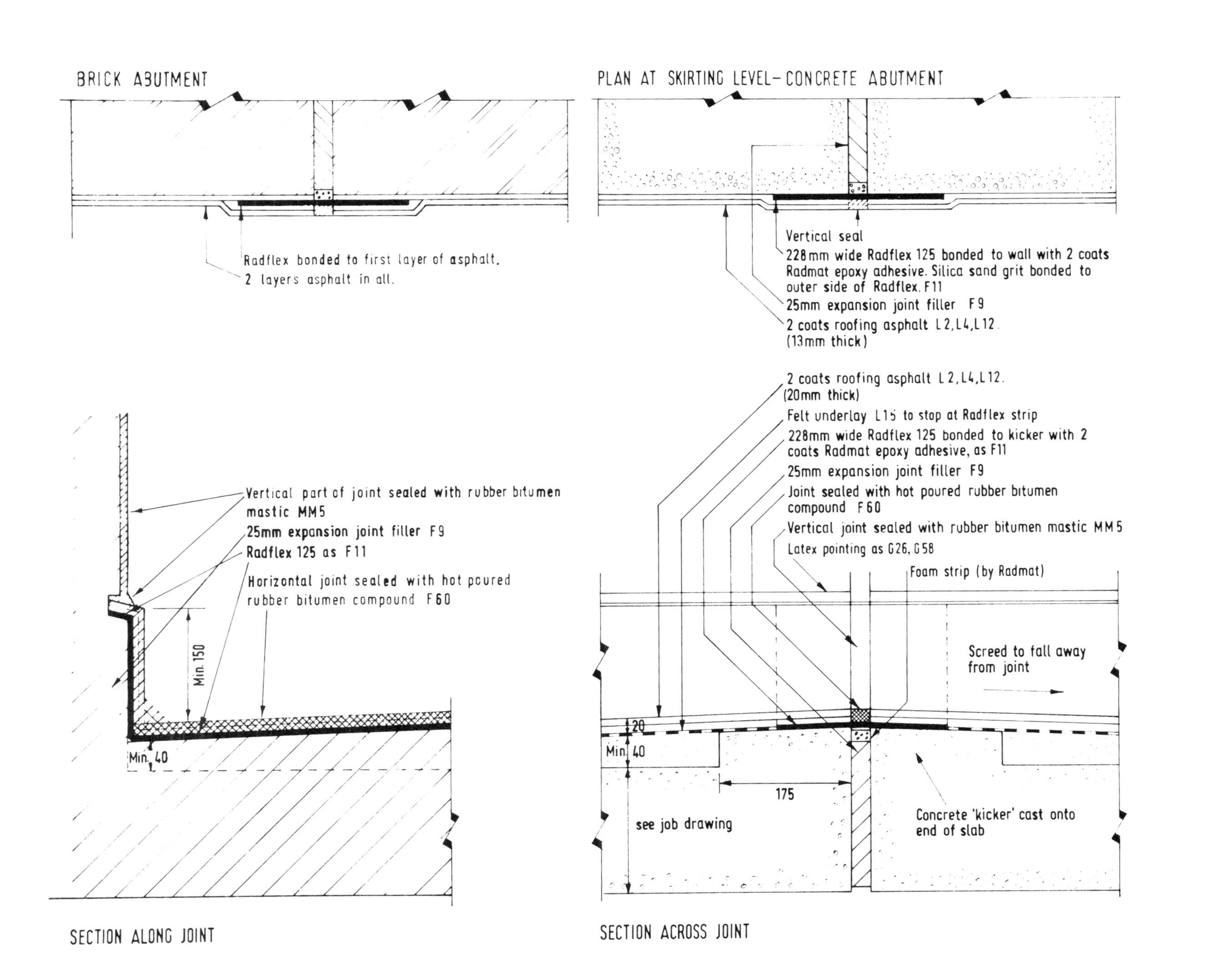

GLC ILEA

Department of Architecture and Civic Design
County Hall SE1 7PB
Architect Sir Roger Walters KBE ARIBA FI Struct/E

References following notes are clause numbers from G.L.C. preambles to bills of quantities

To be read in conjunction with drawings [43] D5026, D5027 and D5028.

The nominal gutter shown on drawings [43] D5027 and D5028 to fall away from joint.

A: 17/5/78 140879 B 040979

Departmental Standard Drawing

title
BALCONY EXPANSION JOINT
USING RADFLEX 125 WITH CONCRETE KICKER BRICK OR CONCRETE ABUTMENT.

scale 1:5

drawing no D5278 | rev B

bldg type | space use | element [43] | feature 233 | material Ps4 | key A05

4 External doors

2064 Normal flush inward opening with threshold
2065 Normal framed inward opening with threshold
2062 FR flush inward opening with threshold
2063 FR framed inward opening with threshold
2070 Normal flush outward opening with threshold
2071 Normal framed outward opening with threshold
2072 FR flush outward opening with threshold
2073 FR framed outward opening with threshold
2066 Normal flush inward opening mobility dwelling
2067 Normal framed inward opening mobility dwelling
2068 FR flush inward opening mobility dwelling
2069 FR framed inward opening mobility dwelling
2074 Normal flush outward opening without threshold
2075 Normal framed outward opening without threshold
2076 FR flush outward opening without threshold
2077 FR framed outward opening without threshold
3270 Normal/FR inward opening with threshold no fanlight doorset details
3274 Normal inward opening with threshold with fanlight doorset details
3271 FR inward opening with threshold with fanlight doorset details
3280 Normal/FR outward opening with threshold no fanlight doorset details
3281 Normal outward opening with threshold with fanlight doorset details
3283 FR outward opening with threshold with fanlight doorset details
3276 Normal/FR inward opening without fanlight mobility dwelling doorset details
3277 Normal inward opening with fanlight mobility dwelling doorset details
3279 FR inward opening with fanlight mobility dwelling doorset details
3286 Normal/FR outward opening without fanlight without threshold doorset details
3287 Normal outward opening with fanlight without threshold doorset details
3288 FR outward opening with fanlight without threshold doorset details
3278 Normal framed inward opening with threshold/mobility dwelling door details
3272 FR framed inward opening with threshold/ mobility dwelling door details
3284 Normal framed outward opening without threshold door details
3285 FR framed outward opening without threshold door details
3275 Normal flush door glass panel and beads
3282 FR flush door glass panel and beads
3273 External doors ironmongery
3029 Postal plate details
5069 Bonaire ventilator window or door fanlight
3172 Emergency exit lock details

WITHOUT FANLIGHT.

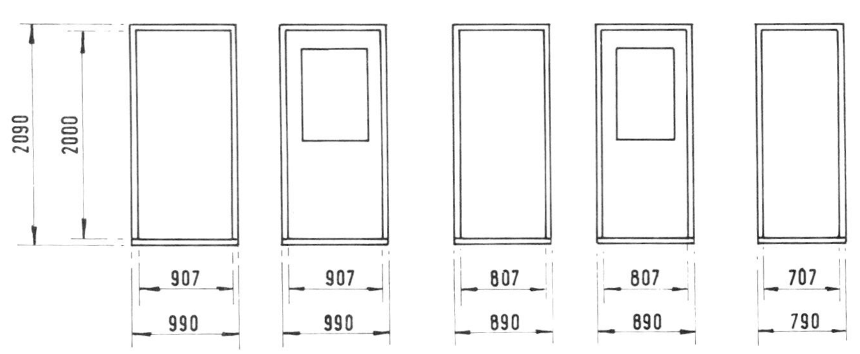

FRAME DEPTH (mm)	FRAME & DOOR DETAILS. DRG Nº
91	D.3270

NOTE: Job architects to specify the following on the door schedule:

a. Frame and door details drg no. from table.

b. Height, width and depth of door frame.

c. Height, width, thickness and facing of door.

d. Door glass panel and beads (990, 890 and 1790 doorsets only) if required; see D.3275.

WITH FANLIGHT.

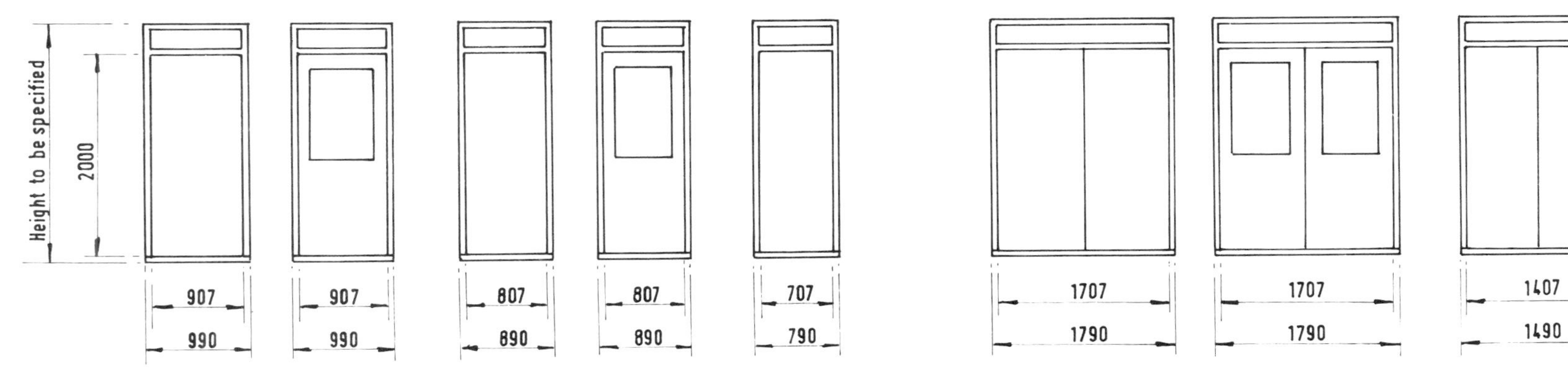

FRAME DEPTH (mm)	FRAME & DOOR DETAILS DRG Nº
91	D.3274

NOTE: Job architects to specify the following on the door schedule:

a. Frame and door details drg no. from table.

b. Height, width and depth of door frame.

c. Fanlight panel (see doorset detail drawing)

d. Height, width, thickness and facing of door.

e. Door glass panel and beads (990 890 and 1790 doorsets only) if required see D.3275

GLC ILEA

Department of Architecture
and Civic Design
County Hall SE1 7PB
Architect F B Pooley CBE

References following notes are clause numbers from G.L.C. preambles to bills of quantities

All doors are 44mm thick and faced with external quality ply.

For reference to relevant building-in details see notes on doorset detail. D.3270 or D.3274

All dimensions are work sizes.

Structural openings as shown on working drawings.

Departmental Standard Drawing

title

EXTERNAL NORMAL FLUSH DOORSET RANGE.
INWARD OPENING.
WITH THRESHOLD.

scale 1 : 50

	drawing no	rev
GP	D.2064	

00 - 210779

bldg type | space use | element [21] | feature | material | key

WITHOUT FANLIGHT.

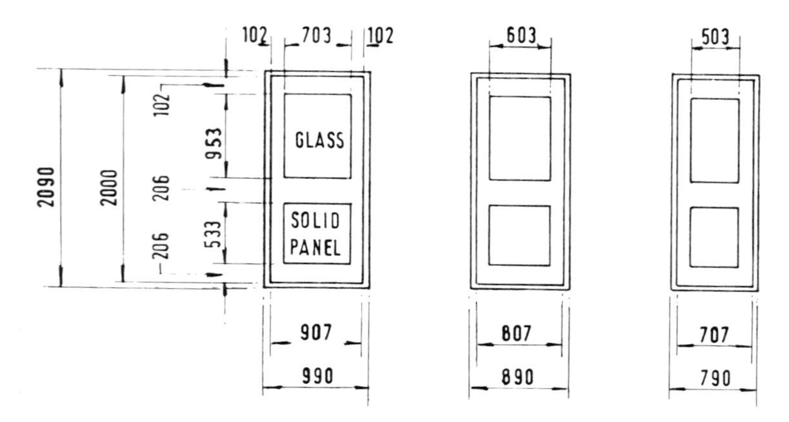

Width of glazed panels for doors with rebated meeting stiles

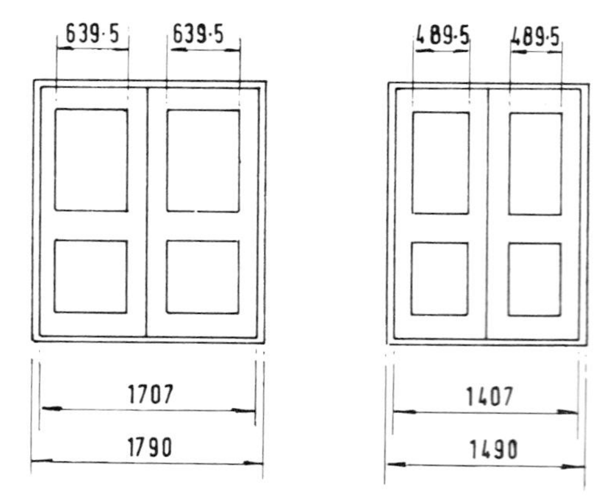

FRAME DEPTH. (mm)	FRAME DETAILS	DOOR DETAILS
	DRG Nº	DRG. Nº
91	D. 3270	D.3278

NOTE:

Job architect to specify the following on the door schedule:

a. Frame and door details drg nos. from table.
b. Height, width and depth of door frame.
c. Height, width and thickness of door.
d. Door glass panels and beads as D.3278.

WITH FANLIGHT.

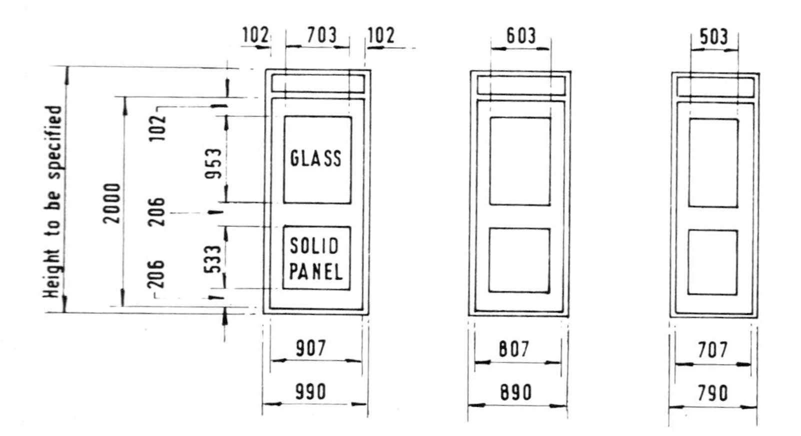

Width of glazed panels for doors with rebated meeting stiles.

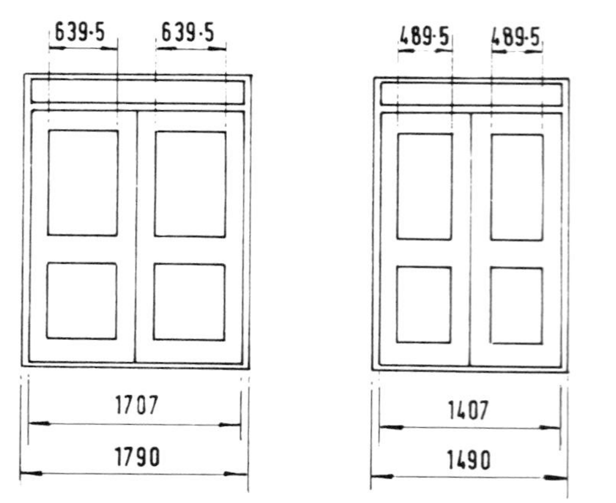

FRAME DEPTH (mm)	FRAME DETAILS	DOOR DETAILS.
	DRG Nº	DRG Nº
91	D. 3274	D. 3278

NOTE:

Job architect to specify the following on the door schedule:

a. Frame and door details drg nos. from table.
b. Height, width and depth of door frame.
c. Fanlight panel (see doorset detail drawing)
d. Height, width and thickness of door.
e. Door glass panels and beads as D.3278.

GLC ILEA

Department of Architecture and Civic Design
County Hall SE1 7PB
Architect Sir Roger Walters
KBE ARIBA FI Struct/E

References following notes are clause numbers from G.L.C. preambles to bills of quantities

All doors are 44mm thick.

For reference to relevant building-in details see notes on doorset detail: D. 3270 or D.3278

All dimensions are work sizes.

Structural openings as shown on working drawings.

161078 ■■ 010379

bldg type | space use | element [21] | feature | material | key

Departmental Standard Drawing

title

EXTERNAL NORMAL FRAMED DOORSET RANGE.

INWARD OPENING. WITH THRESHOLD.

scale 1 : 50

GP · drawing no D. 2065. rev

WITHOUT FANLIGHT.

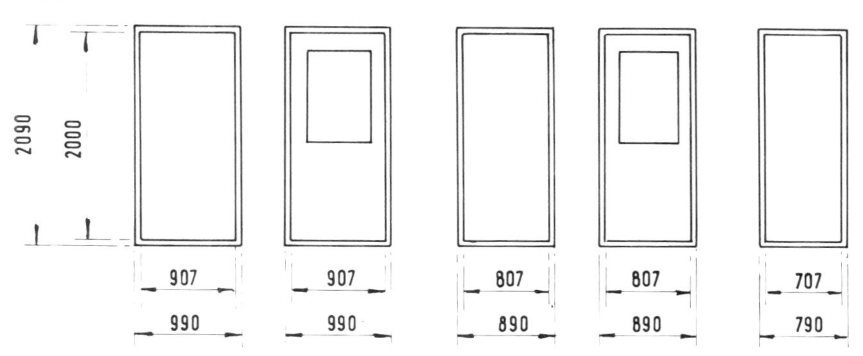

1707
1790
1707
1790
1407
1490

FRAME DEPTH (mm)	FRAME & DOOR DETAILS DRG N°
91	D.3270

NOTE: Job architects to specify the following on the door schedule:

a. Frame and door details drg no. from table.
b. Height, width and depth of door frame.
c. Height, width, thickness and facing of door.
d. Door glass panel and beads (990, 890 and 1790 doorsets only) if required; see D.3272

WITH FANLIGHT.

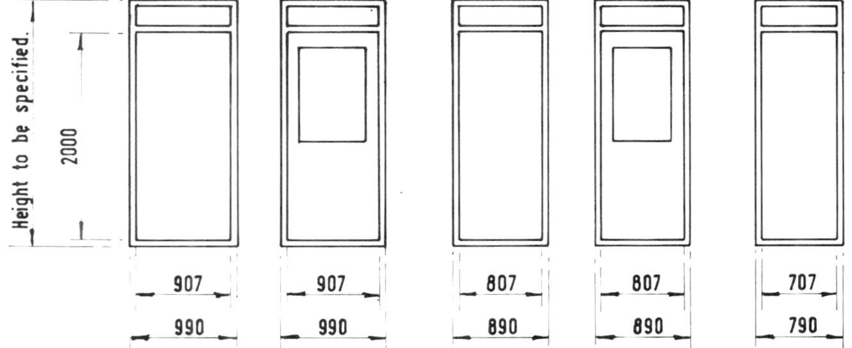

1707
1790
1707
1790
1407
1490

FRAME DEPTH (mm)	FRAME & DOOR DETAILS DRG N°
91	D.3271

NOTE: Job architects to specify the following on the door schedule:

a. Frame and door details drg no. from table.
b. Height, width and depth of door frame.
c. Fanlight panel (see doorset detail drawing.)
d. Height, width, thickness and facing of door.
e. Door glass panel and beads (990, 890 and 1790 doorsets only) if required; see D.3272

GLC ILEA

Department of Architecture and Civic Design
County Hall SE1 7PB
Architect F B Pooley CBE

References following notes are clause numbers from G.L.C. preambles to bills of quantities

All doors are 44mm thick and faced with external quality ply.

For relevant building in details see notes on doorset detail D.3270, D.3271.

All dimensions are work sizes.

Structural openings as shown on working drawings.

Departmental Standard Drawing

title
EXTERNAL ½ HR FIRE FLUSH DOORSET RANGE.
INWARD OPENING.
WITH THRESHOLD.

scale 1 : 50

GP | drawing no D.2062 | rev

00 - 010379

bldg type | space use | element [21] | feature | material | key

WITHOUT FANLIGHT.

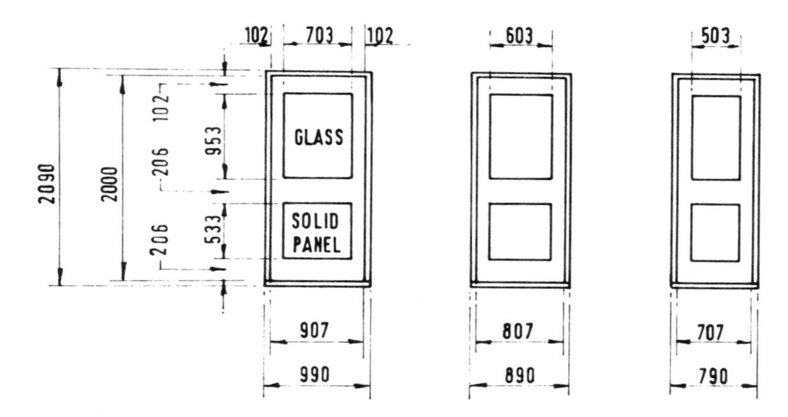

Widths of glazed panels for doors with rebated meeting stiles.

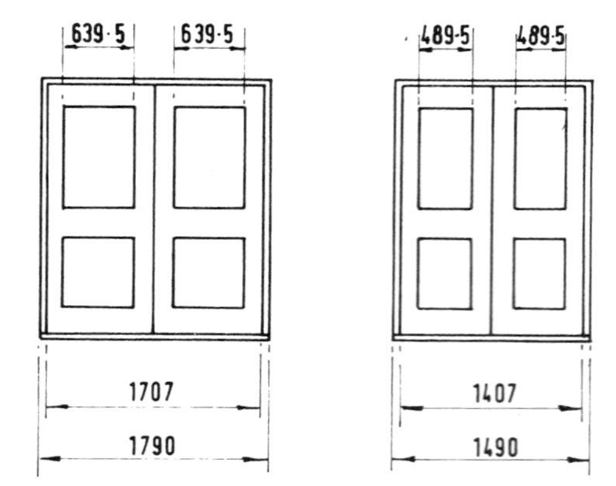

FRAME DEPTH (mm)	FRAME DETAILS	DOOR DETAILS
	DRG. N°	DRG. N°
91	D.3270	D.3272

NOTE: Job architect to specify the following on the door schedule:

a. Frame and door details drg nos. from table.
b. Height, width and depth of door frame.
c. Height, width and thickness of door.
d. Door panels and beads as D.3272.

WITH FANLIGHT.

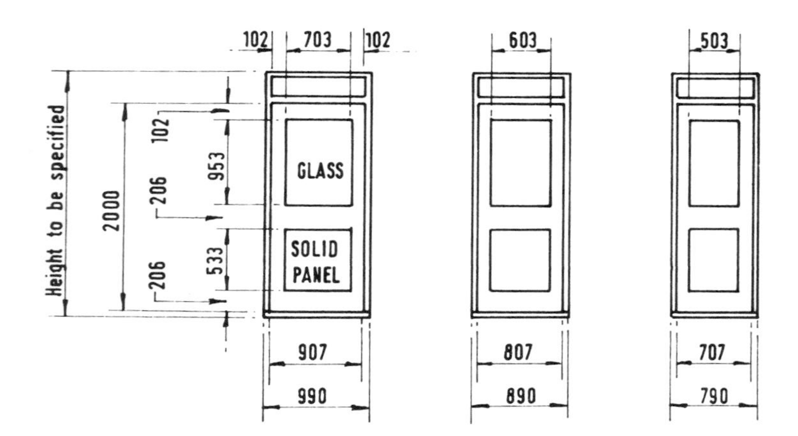

Widths of glazed panels for doors with rebated meeting stiles.

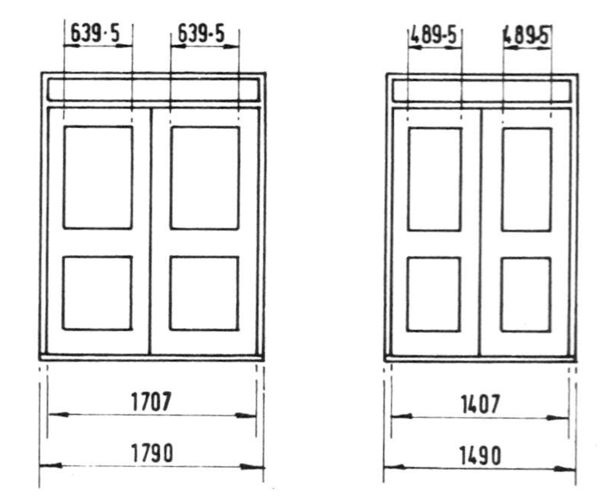

FRAME DEPTH (mm)	FRAME DETAILS	DOOR DETAILS
	DRG N°	DRG N°
91	D.3271	D.3272

NOTE: Job architect to specify the following on the door schedule:

a. Frame and door details drg nos. from table.
b. Height, width and depth of door frame.
c. Fanlight panel (see doorset detail drawing).
d. Height, width and thickness of door.
e. Door panels and beads as D.3272.

GLC ILEA

Department of Architecture and Civic Design
County Hall SE1 7PB
Architect F B Pooley CBE

References following notes are clause numbers from G.L.C. preambles to bills of quantities

All doors are 44mm thick.

For reference to relevant building-in details see notes on doorset detail D.3270 or D.3271.

All dimensions are work sizes.

Structural openings as shown on working drawings.

00 - 100779

Departmental Standard Drawing

bldg type | space use | element (21) | feature | material | key

title

EXTERNAL 1/2 HR FIRE FRAMED DOORSET RANGE, INWARD OPENING WITH THRESHOLD.

scale 1 : 50

GP | drawing no D.2063 | rev

WITHOUT FANLIGHT.

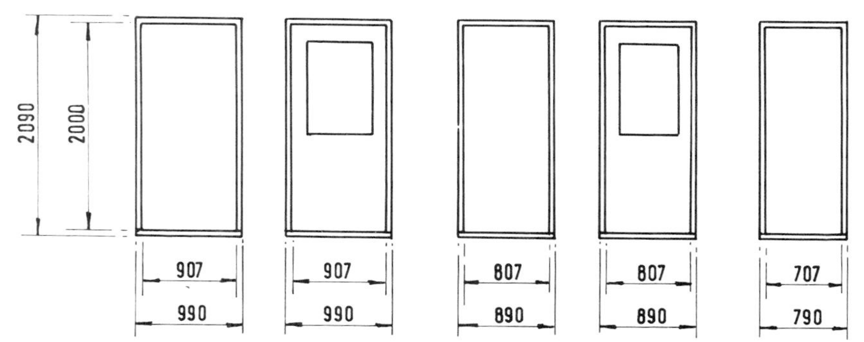

1707
1790
1707
1790
1407
1490

FRAME DEPTH (mm)	FRAME & DOOR DETAILS. DRG Nº
91	D.3280.

NOTE: Job architects to specify the following on the door schedule:

a. Frame and door details drg no from table.
b. Height, width and depth of door frame.
c. Height, width, thickness and facing of door.
d. Door glass panel and beads (990, 890 and 1790 doorsets only) if required; see D.3275.

WITH FANLIGHT.

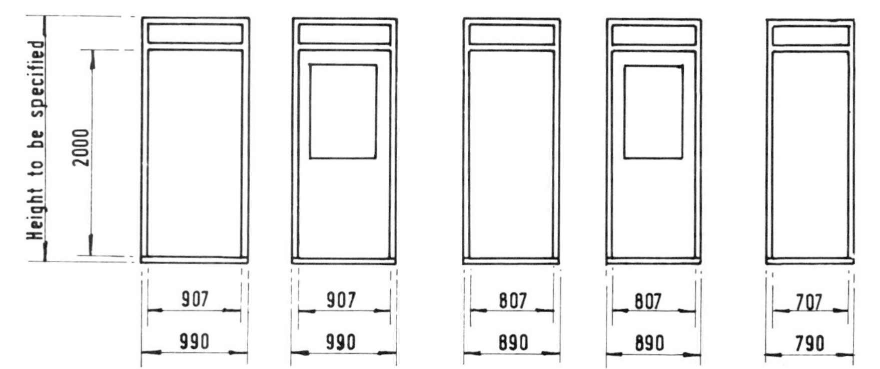

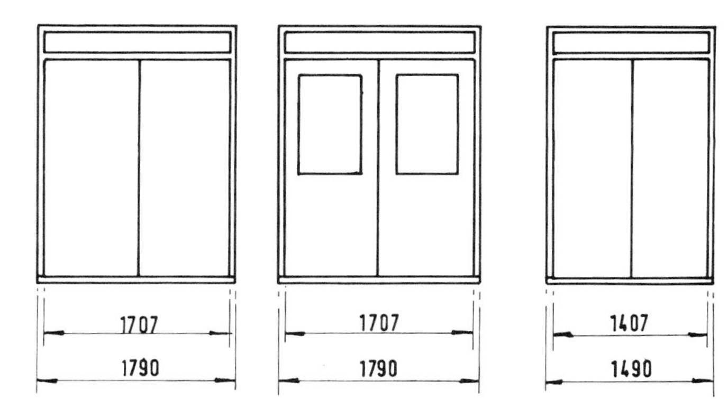

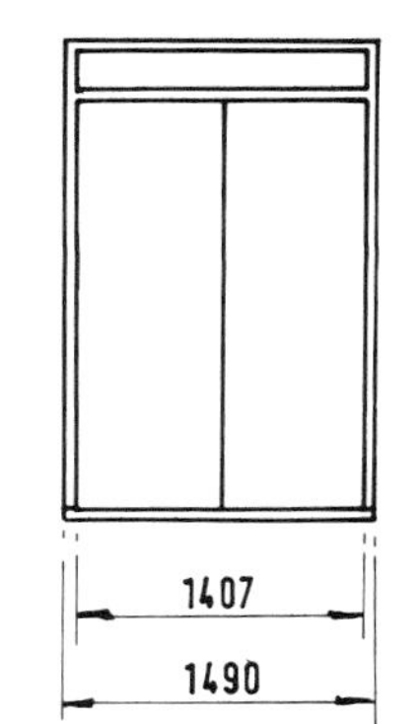

FRAME DEPTH (mm)	FRAME & DOOR DETAILS. DRG Nº
91	D.3281.

NOTE: Job architects to specify the following on the door schedule:

a. Frame and door details drg no from table.
b. Height, width and depth of door frame.
c. Fanlight panel (see doorset detail drawing).
d. Height, width, thickness and facing of door.
e. Door glass panel and beads (990, 890 and 1790 doorsets only) if required; see D.3275.

GLC ILEA

Department of Architecture and Civic Design
County Hall SE1 7PB
Architect F B Pooley C B E

References following notes are clause numbers from G.L.C. preambles to bills of quantities

All doors are 44mm thick and faced with external quality ply.

For reference to relevant building-in details see notes on doorset detail D.3280 or D.3281

All dimensions are work sizes.

Structural openings as shown on working drawings.

08 - 291079

Departmental Standard Drawing

title
EXTERNAL NORMAL FLUSH DOORSET RANGE.
OUTWARD OPENING WITH THRESHOLD.

scale 1 : 50

bldgtype | spaceuse | element | feature 21 | material | key

GP | drawing no D.2070 | rev

WITHOUT FANLIGHT.

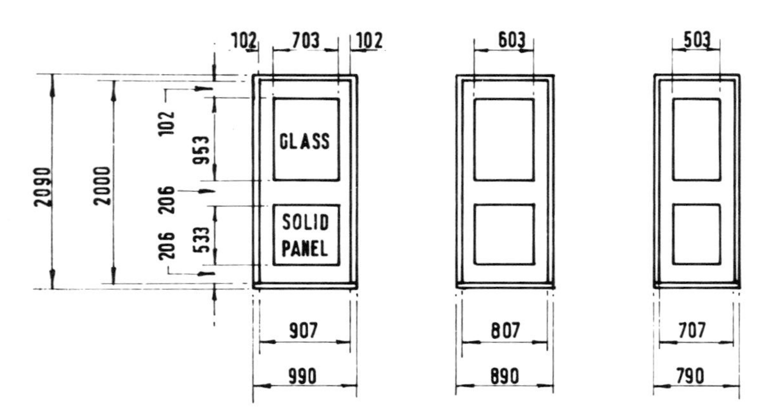

Width of glazed panels for doors with rebated meeting stiles.

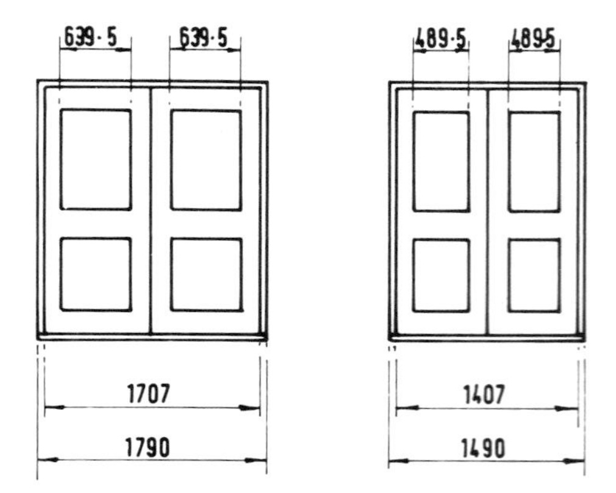

FRAME DEPTH (mm)	FRAME DETAILS.	DOOR DETAILS.
	DRG N°	DRG N°
91	D.3280	D.3284

NOTE: Job architect to specify the following on the door schedule:

a. Frame and door details drg no from table.
b. Height, width and depth of door frame.
c. Height, width and thickness of door.
d. Door glass panels and beads as D.3284.

WITH FANLIGHT.

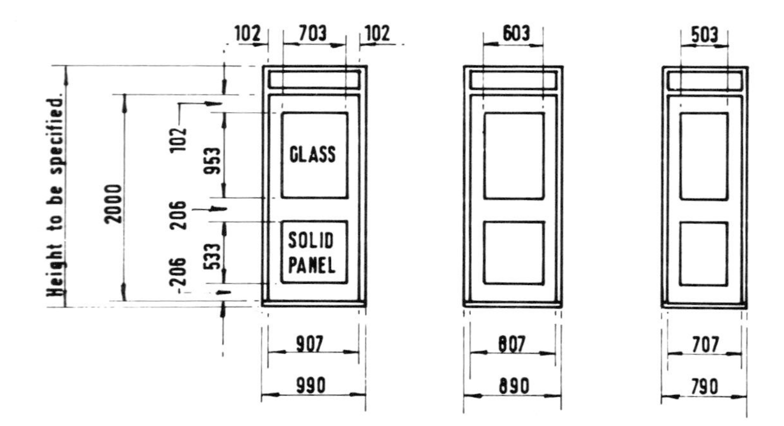

Width of glazed panels for doors with rebated meeting stiles.

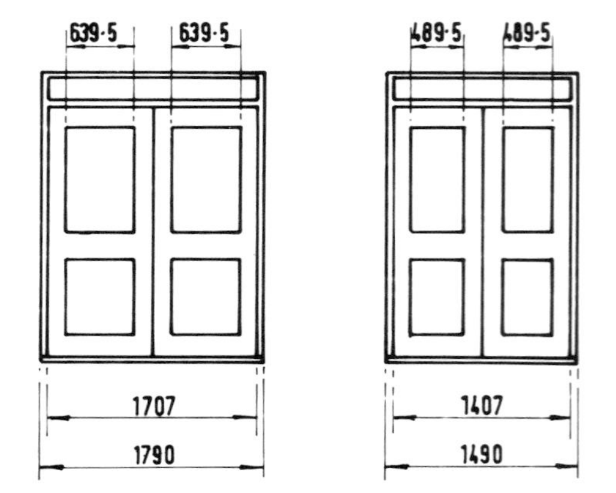

FRAME DEPTH (mm)	FRAME DETAILS.	DOOR DETAILS.
	DRG N°	DRG N°
91	D.3281.	D.3284

NOTE: Job architect to specify the following on the door schedule:

a. Frame and door details drg nos from table.
b. Height, width and depth of door frame.
c. Fanlight panel (see doorset detail drawing.)
d. Height, width and thickness of door.
e. Door glass panels and beads as D.3284.

GLC ILEA

Department of Architecture and Civic Design
County Hall SE1 7PB
Architect F B Pooley CBE

References following notes are clause numbers from G.L.C. preambles to bills of quantities

All doors are 44 mm thick.

For reference to relevant building in details see notes on doorset detail D.3280 or D.3281.

All dimensions are work sizes.

Structural openings as shown on working drawings.

Departmental Standard Drawing

title
EXTERNAL NORMAL FRAMED DOORSET RANGE.
OUTWARD OPENING.
WITH THRESHOLD.

scale 1 : 50

GP | drawing no D. 2071. | rev

bldgtype | spaceuse | element 21 | feature | material | key

061179

WITHOUT FANLIGHT.

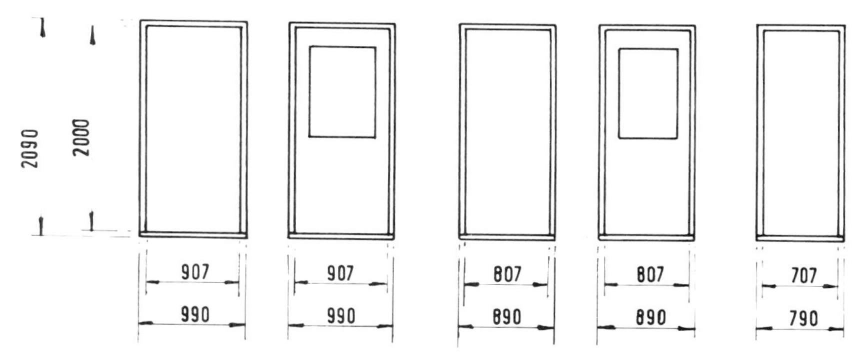

FRAME DEPTH (mm)	FRAME & DOOR DETAILS. DRG N°
91	D. 3280

NOTE: Job architects to specify the following on the door schedule:

a. Frame and door details drg no from table.
b. Height, width and depth of door frame.
c. Height, width, thickness and facing of door.
d. Door glass panel and beads (990, 890 and 1790 doorsets only) if required; see D.3282

WITH FANLIGHT.

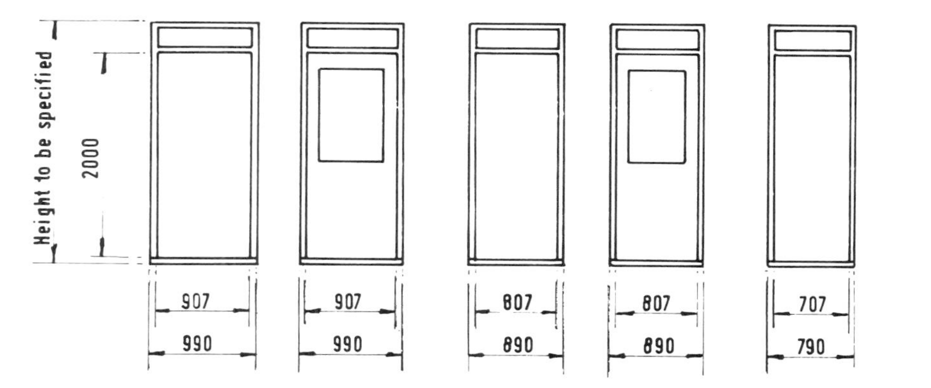

FRAME DEPTH (mm)	FRAME & DOOR DETAILS DRG N°
91	D.3283.

NOTE: Job architects to specify the following on the door schedule:

a. Frame and door details drg no from table.
b. Height, width and depth of door frame.
c. Fanlight panel (see doorset detail drawing.)
d. Height, width, thickness and facing of door.
e. Door glass panel and beads (990 890 and 1790 doorsets only) if required; see D.3282.

GLC ILEA
Department of Architecture and Civic Design
County Hall SE1 7PB
Architect F B Pooley C B E

References following notes are clause numbers from G.L.C. preambles to bills of quantities

All doors are 44mm thick and faced with external quality ply.

For reference to relevant building-in details see notes on doorset detail D.3280 or D.3283.

All dimensions are work sizes.

Structural openings as shown on working drawings.

311079.

bldg type | space use | element 21 | feature | material | key

Departmental Standard Drawing

title
EXTERNAL 1/2 HR FIRE FLUSH DOORSET RANGE.
OUTWARD OPENING.
WITH THRESHOLD.

scale 1 : 50

GP | drawing no D. 2072 | rev

WITHOUT FANLIGHT.

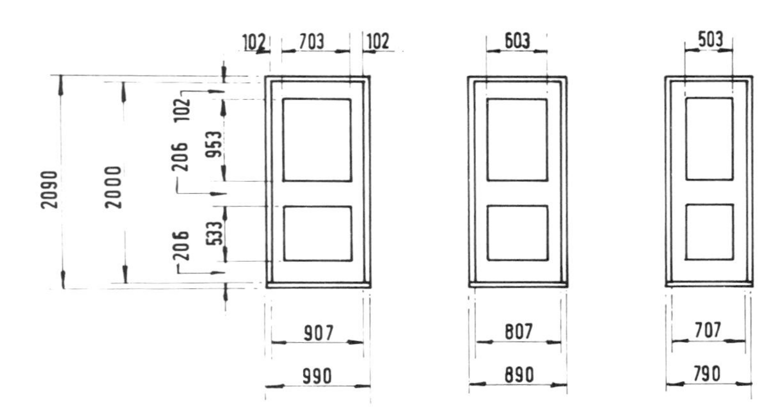

Width of glazed panels for doors with rebated meeting stiles.

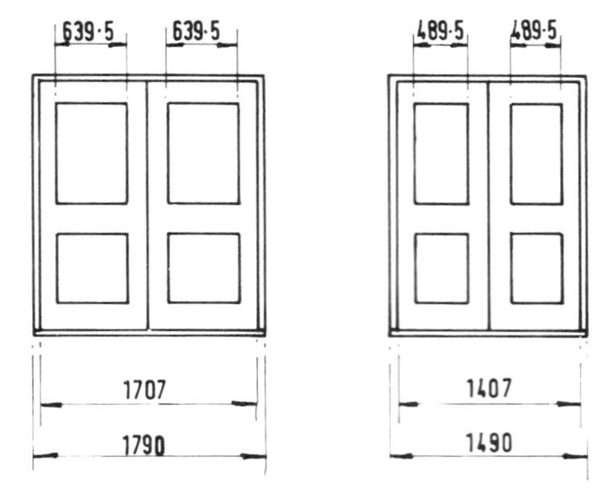

FRAME DEPTH (mm)	FRAME DETAILS	DOOR DETAILS.
	DRG N°	DRG N°
91	D.3280	D.3285.

NOTE: Job architect to specify the following on the door schedule:

a. Frame and door details drg nos from table.
b. Height, width and depth of door frame.
c. Height, width and thickness of door.
d. Door glass panels and beads as D.3285

WITH FANLIGHT.

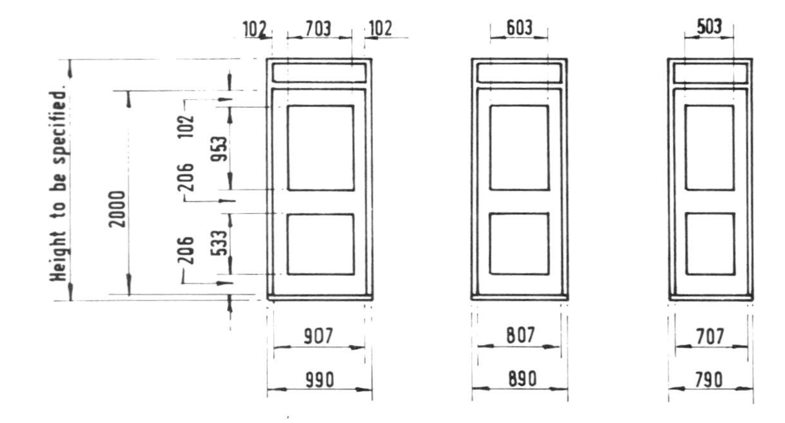

Width of glazed panels for doors with rebated meeting stiles.

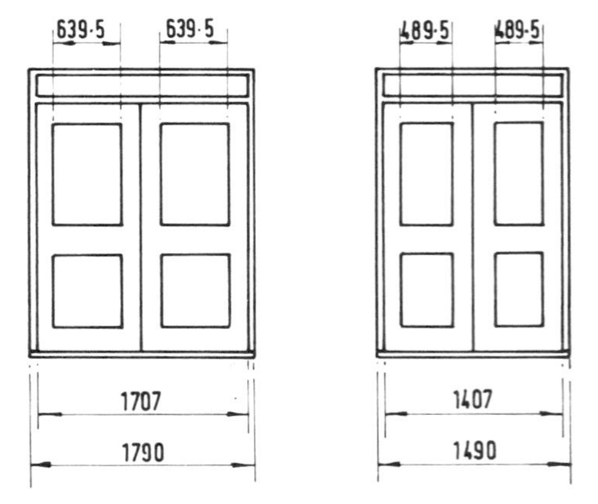

FRAME DEPTH (mm)	FRAME DETAILS	DOOR DETAILS.
	DRG N°	DRG N°
91	D.3283	D.3285.

NOTE: Job architect to specify the following on the door schedule:

a. Frame and door details drg nos from table.
b. Height, width and depth of door frame.
c. Fanlight panel (see doorset detail drawing)
d. Height, width and thickness of door.
e. Door glass panels and beads as D.3285.

GLC ILEA

Department of Architecture and Civic Design
County Hall SE1 7PB
Architect F B Pooley CBE

References following notes are clause numbers from G.L.C. preambles to bills of quantities

All doors are 44mm thick.

For reference to relevant building-in details see notes on doorset detail D.3280 or D.3283.

All dimensions are work sizes.

Structural openings as shown on working drawings.

Departmental Standard Drawing

title

EXTERNAL 1/2 HOUR FIRE FRAMED DOORSET RANGE.

OUTWARD OPENING.

WITH THRESHOLD.

scale 1 : 50.

GP | drawing no D. 2073 | rev

00 - 071179

21

WITHOUT FANLIGHT.

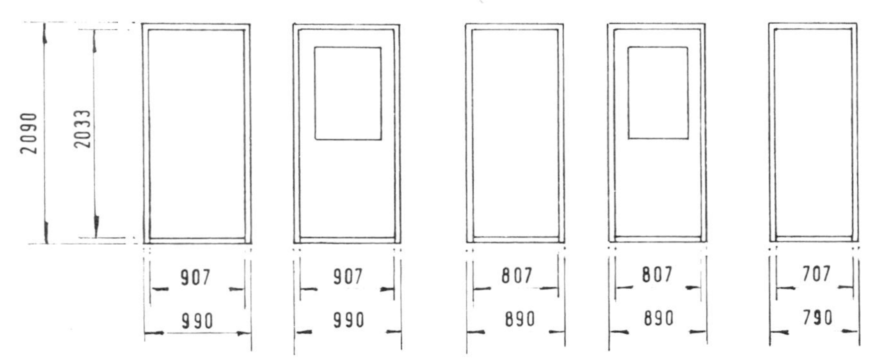

FRAME DEPTH. (mm)	FRAME & DOOR DETAILS. DRG Nº
91	D. 3276.

NOTE: Job architects to specify the following on the door schedule:

a. Frame and door details drg no. from table.
b. Height, width and depth of door frame.
c. Height, width, thickness and facing of door.
d. Door glass panel and beads (990, 890 and 1790 doorsets only) if required; see D. 3275.

WITH FANLIGHT.

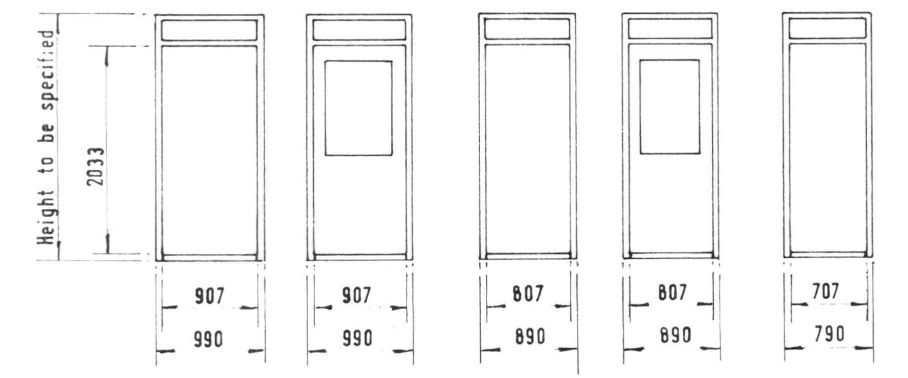

FRAME DEPTH (mm)	FRAME & DOOR DETAILS DRG.Nº
91	D. 3277.

NOTE: Job architects to specify the following on the door schedule:

a. Frame and door details drg no. from table.
b. Height, width and depth of door frame.
c. Fanlight panel (see doorset detail drawing.)
d. Height, width, thickness and facing of door.
e. Door glass panel and beads (990, 890 and 1790 doorsets only) if required; see D. 3275.

GLC ILEA

Department of Architecture and Civic Design
County Hall SE1 7PB
Architect Sir Roger Walters
KBE ARIBA FI Struct/E

References following notes are clause numbers from G.L.C. preambles to bills of quantities

All doors are 44mm thick and faced with external quality ply.

For reference to relevant building-in details see notes on doorset detail: D. 3276, D. 3277.

All dimensions are work sizes.

Structural openings as shown on working drawings.

310778 ●● - 010379

Departmental Standard Drawing

title

EXTERNAL NORMAL FLUSH DOORSET RANGE.

INWARD OPENING. - MOBILITY DWELLING.

scale 1 : 50

	drawing no	rev
GP	D. 2066.	

bldg type | space use | element [21] | feature | material | key

WITHOUT FANLIGHT

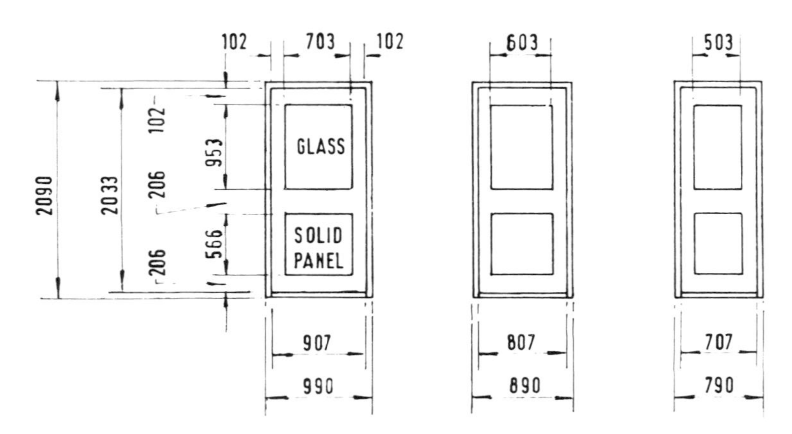

FRAME DEPTH (mm)	FRAME DETAILS.	DOOR DETAILS
	DRG. N°	DRG. N°
91	D. 3276.	D. 3278.

Width of glazed panels for doors with rebated meeting stiles

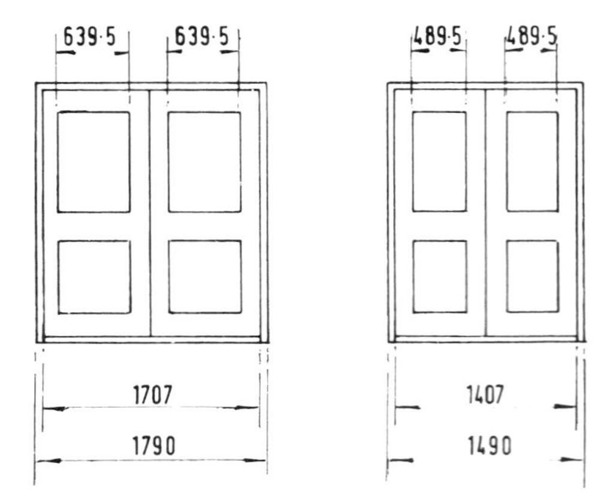

NOTE: Job architect to specify the following on the door schedule:

a. Frame and door details drg no. from table.
b. Height, width and depth of door frame.
c. Height, width and thickness of door.
d. Door glass panels, solid panels and beads see D.3278.

WITH FANLIGHT.

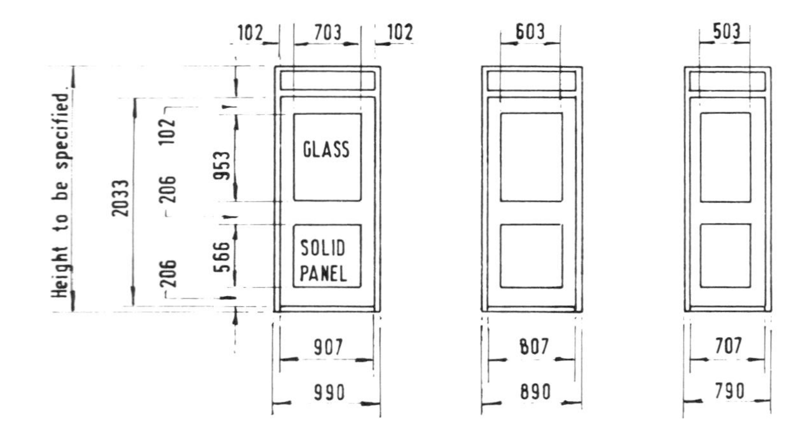

FRAME DEPTH (mm)	FRAME DETAILS	DOOR DETAILS
	DRG N°	DRG N°
91	D. 3277	D. 3278

Width of glazed panels for doors with rebated meeting stiles.

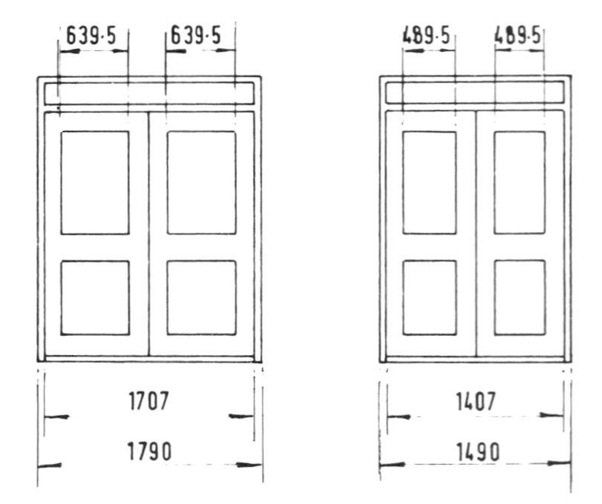

NOTE: Job architect to specify the following on the door schedule:

a. Frame and door details drg no. from table.
b. Height, width and depth of door frame.
c. Fanlight panel (see doorset detail drawing.
d. Height, width and thickness of door.
e. Door glass panels solid panels and beads see D.3278.

GLC ILEA
Department of Architecture and Civic Design
County Hall SE1 7PB
Architect Sir Roger Walters
KBE ARIBA FI Struct/E

References following notes are clause numbers from G.L.C. preambles to bills of quantities

All doors are 44mm thick.

For reference to relevant building in details see notes on doorset detail D. 3276 or D. 3277.

All dimensions are work sizes.

Structural openings as shown on working drawings.

Departmental Standard Drawing

title

EXTERNAL NORMAL FRAMED DOORSET RANGE.
INWARD OPENING MOBILITY DWELLING.

scale 1 : 50.

	drawing no	rev
GP	D.2067	

040878 - 010379

21

WITHOUT FANLIGHT.

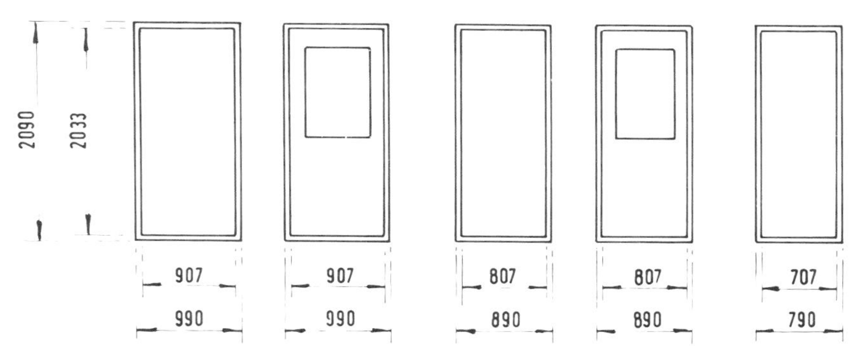

707
790
1707
1790
1707
1790
1407
1490

FRAME DEPTH (mm)	FRAME & DOOR DETAILS DRG N°
91	D.3276

NOTE: Job architects to specify the following on the door schedule:

a. Frame and door details drg no. from table.
b. Height, width and depth of door frame.
c. Height, width, thickness and facing of door.
d. Door glass panel and beads (990, 890 and 1790 doorsets only) if required see D.3275

WITH FANLIGHT.

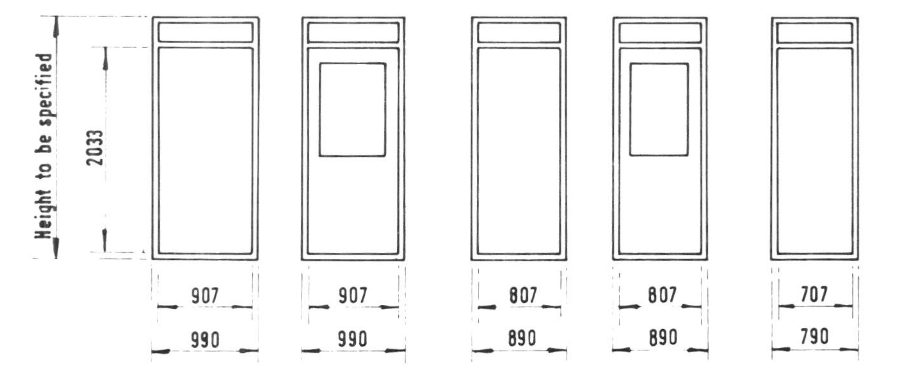

707
790
1707
1790
1707
1790
1407
1490

FRAME DEPTH (mm)	FRAME & DOOR DETAILS DRG N°
91	D.3279

NOTE: Job architects to specify the following on the door schedule:

a. Frame and door details drg no. from table.
b. Height, width and depth of door frame.
c. Fanlight panel (see doorset detail drawing)
d. Height, width, thickness and facing of door.
e. Door glass panel and beads (990, 890 and 1790 doorsets only) if required; see D.3275.

GLC ILEA

Department of Architecture and Civic Design
County Hall SE1 7PB
Architect F B Pooley CBE

References following notes are clause numbers from G.L.C. preambles to bills of quantities

All doors are 44mm thick and faced with external quality ply.

For reference to relevant building-in details see notes on doorset detail D.3276 or D.3279.

All dimensions are work sizes

Structural openings as shown on working drawings.

Departmental Standard Drawing

title
EXTERNAL 1/2 HR FIRE FLUSH DOORSET RANGE.
INWARD OPENING.
MOBILITY DWELLING.

scale 1 : 50

GP | drawing no D.2068 | rev

bldg type | space use | element [21] | feature | material | key

00 - 020879

WITHOUT FANLIGHT.

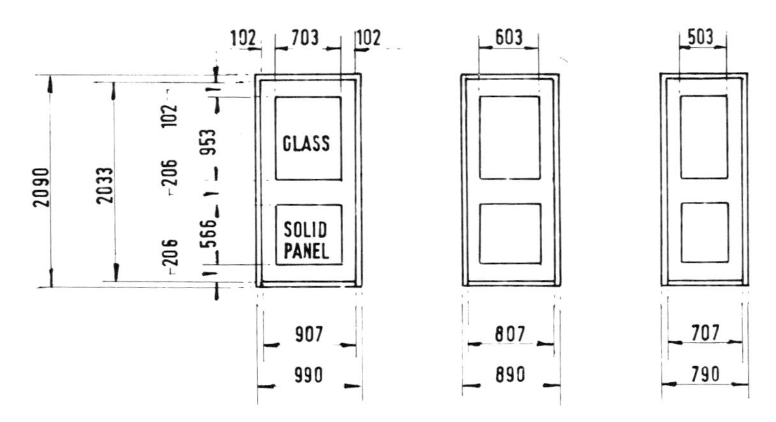

FRAME DEPTH (mm)	FRAME DETAILS	DOOR DETAILS
	DRG Nº	DRG Nº
91	D.3276	D.3272

Width of glazed panels for doors with rebated meeting stiles.

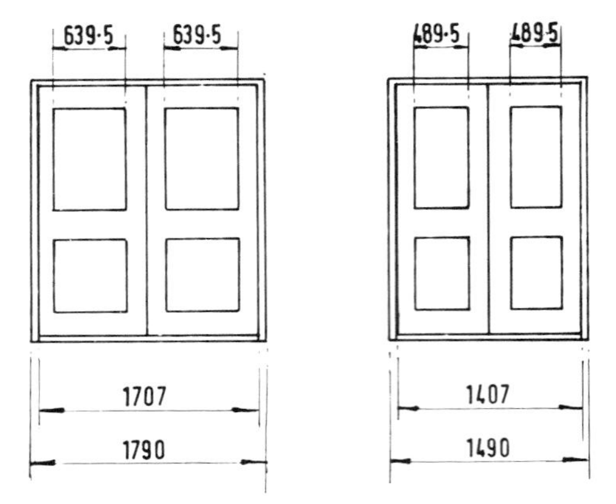

NOTE: Job architects to specify the following on the door schedule:

a. Frame and door details drg no. from table.
b. Height, width and depth of door frame.
c. Height, width and thickness of door.
d. Door glass panels, solid panels and beads see D.3275.

WITH FANLIGHT.

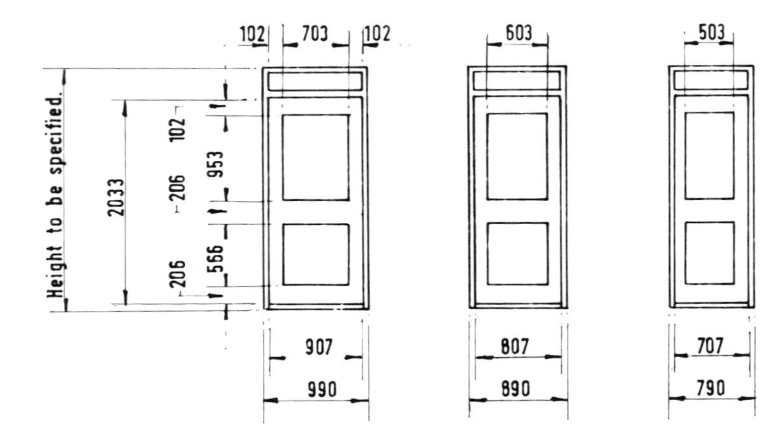

FRAME DEPTH (mm)	FRAME DETAILS	DOOR DETAILS
	DRG Nº	DRG Nº
91	D.3277	D.3272

Width of glazed panels for doors with rebated meeting stiles.

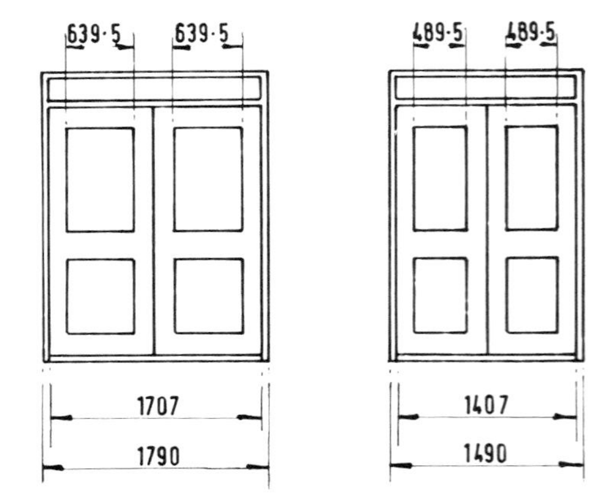

NOTE: Job architects to specify the following on the door schedule:

a. Frame and door details drg no. from table.
b. Height, width and depth of door frame.
c. Fanlight panel (see doorset detail drawing.)
d. Height, width and thickness of door.
e. Door glass panels, solid panels and beads see D.3275.

GLC ILEA

Department of Architecture and Civic Design
County Hall SE1 7PB
Architect F B Pooley CBE

References following notes are clause numbers from G.L.C. preambles to bills of quantities

All doors are 44mm thick.

For reference to relevant building-in details see notes on doorset detail D.3276 or D.3279

All dimensions are work sizes.

Structural openings as shown on working drawings.

Departmental Standard Drawing

title

EXTERNAL 1/2 HR FIRE FRAMED DOORSET RANGE.
INWARD OPENING.
MOBILITY DWELLING.

scale 1 : 50

GP | drawing no D.2069 | rev

[21]

GLC ILEA

Department of Architecture and Civic Design
County Hall SE1 7PB
Architect F B Pooley CBE

References following notes are clause numbers from G.L.C. preambles to bills of quantities

All doors are 44mm thick and faced with external quality ply.

For reference to relevant building-in details see notes on doorset detail D.3286 or D.3287.

All dimensions are work sizes.

Structural openings as shown on working drawings.

WITHOUT FANLIGHT.

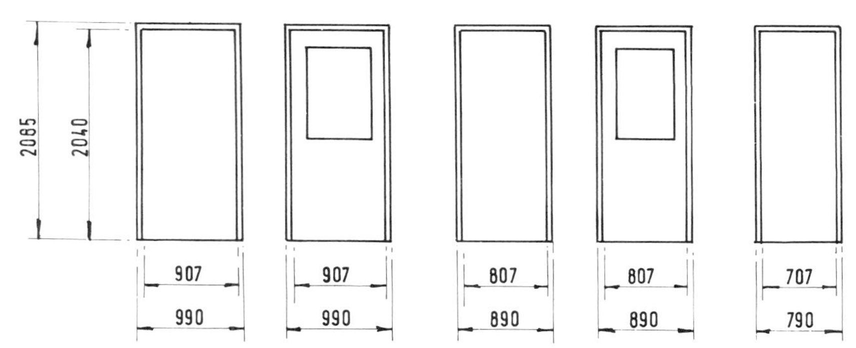

1707 / 1790 1707 / 1790 1407 / 1490

FRAME DEPTH (mm)	FRAME & DOOR DETAILS. DRG Nº
91	D. 3286

NOTE: Job architect to specify the following on the door schedule:

a. Frame and door details drg no from table.
b. Height, width and depth of door frame.
c. Height, width, thickness and facing of door.
d. Door glass panel and beads (990, 890 and 1790 doorsets only) if required, see D.3275.

WITH FANLIGHT.

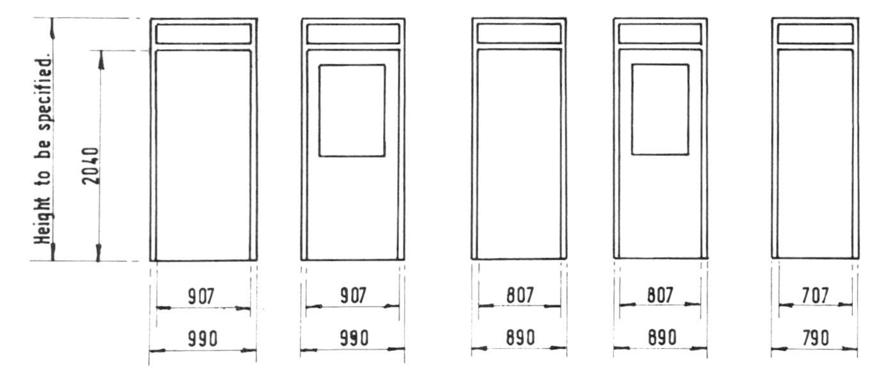

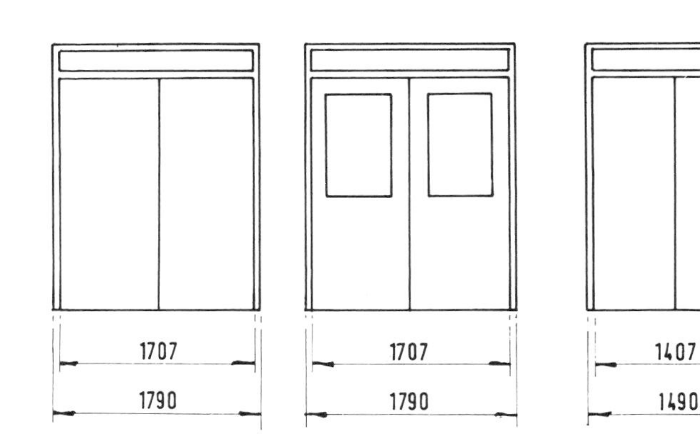

FRAME DEPTH (mm)	FRAME & DOOR DETAILS. DRG Nº
91	D. 3287

NOTE: Job architect to specify the following on the door schedule:

a. Frame and door details drg no from table:
b. Height, width and depth of door frame.
c. Fanlight panel (see doorset detail drawing)
d. Height, width, thickness and facing of door.
e. Door glass panel and beads (990, 890 and 1790 doorsets only) if required, see D.3275.

08L060 - ■■

Departmental Standard Drawing

bldg type | space use | element [21] | feature | material | key

title

EXTERNAL NORMAL FLUSH DOORSET RANGE.

OUTWARD OPENING WITHOUT THRESHOLD

scale 1 : 50

GP | drawing no D.2074 | rev

GLC ILEA
Department of Architecture and Civic Design
County Hall SE1 7PB
Architect F B Pooley CBE

References following notes are clause numbers from G.L.C. preambles to bills of quantities

All doors are 44mm thick.

For reference to relevant building-in details see notes on doorset detail D.3286 or D.3287.

All dimensions are work sizes.

Structural openings as shown on working drawings.

WITHOUT FANLIGHT.

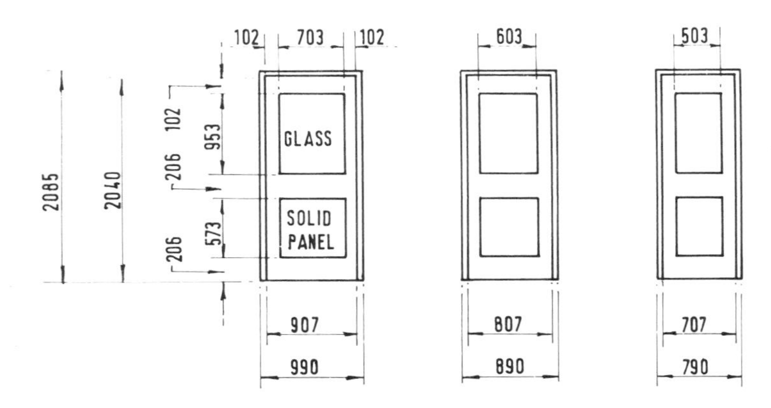

Width of glazed panels for doors with rebated meeting stiles.

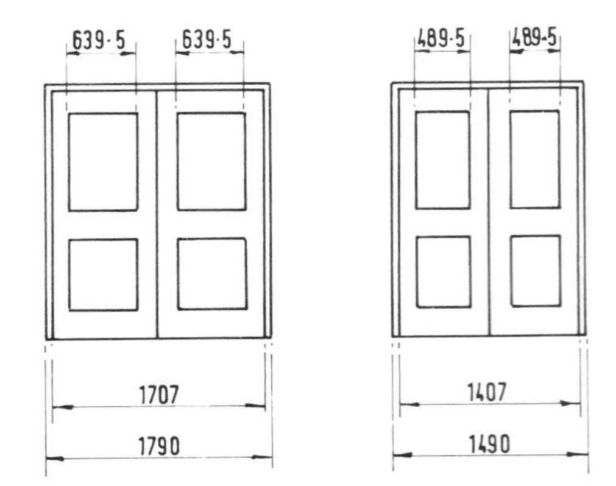

FRAME DEPTH. (mm)	FRAME DETAILS	DOOR DETAILS.
	DRG N°	DRG N°
91	D.3286	D.3284

NOTE: Job architect to specify the following on the door schedule:

a. Frame and door details drg no from table.
b. Height, width and depth of door frame.
c. Height, width and thickness of door.
d. Door glass panels and beads as D.3284.

WITH FANLIGHT.

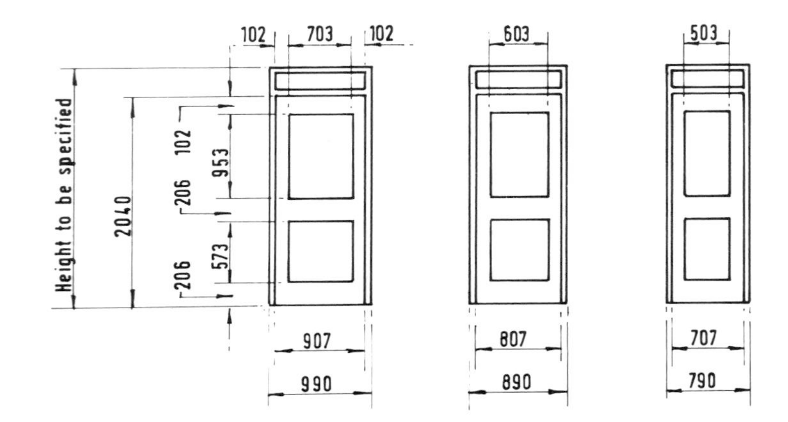

Width of glazed panels for doors with rebated meeting stiles.

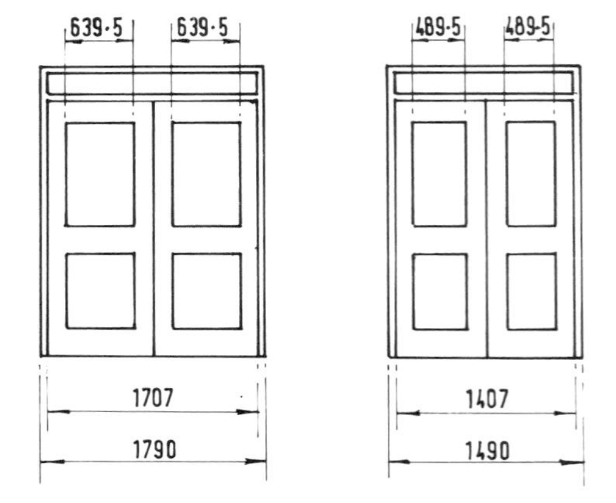

FRAME DEPTH (mm)	FRAME DETAILS	DOOR DETAILS.
	DRG N°	DRG N°
91	D.3287	D.3284

NOTE: Job architect to specify the following on the door schedule:

a. Frame and door details drg no from table.
b. Height, width and depth of door frame.
c. Fanlight panel (see doorset detail drawing)
d. Height, width and thickness of door.
e. Door glass panels and beads as D.3284.

Departmental Standard Drawing

title
EXTERNAL NORMAL FRAMED DOORSET RANGE.
OUTWARD OPENING.
WITHOUT THRESHOLD.

scale 1 : 50

	drawing no	rev
GP	D. 2075	

(21)

090180

WITHOUT FANLIGHT.

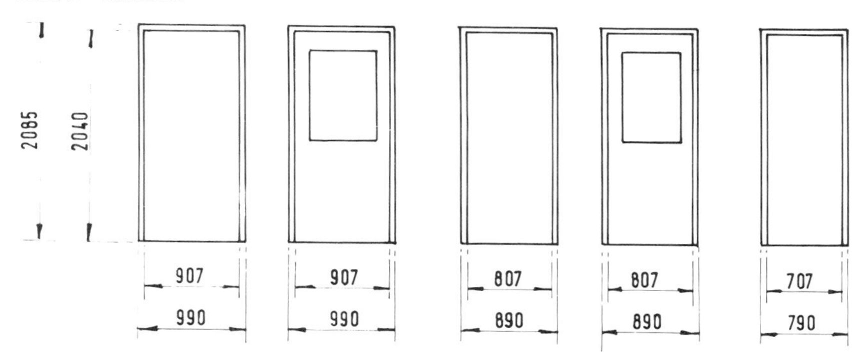

FRAME DEPTH (mm)	FRAME & DOOR DETAILS. DRG N°
91	D.3286

NOTE: Job architect to specify the following on the door schedule:

a. Frame and door details drg no from table.
b. Height, width and depth of door frame.
c. Height, width, thickness and facing of door.
d. Door glass panel and beads (990, 890 and 1790 doorsets only) if required, see D.3282.

WITH FANLIGHT.

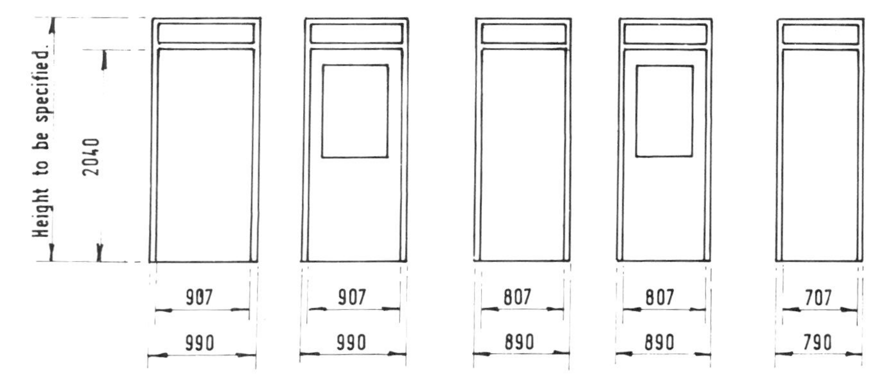

FRAME DEPTH (mm)	FRAME & DOOR DETAILS DRG N°
91	D.3288

NOTE: Job architect to specify the following on the door schedule:

a. Frame and door details drg no from table.
b. Height, width and depth of door frame.
c. Fanlight panel (see doorset detail drawing)
d. Height, width, thickness and facing of door.
e. Door glass panel and beads (990, 890 and 1790 doorsets only) if required, see D.3282.

GLC ILEA
Department of Architecture and Civic Design
County Hall SE1 7PB
Architect F B Pooley CBE

References following notes are clause numbers from G.L.C. preambles to bills of quantities

All doors are 44mm thick and faced with external quality ply.

For reference to relevant building-in details see notes on doorset detail D.3286 or D.3288.

All dimensions are work sizes.

Structural openings as shown on working drawings.

100180 - ■■

bldg type | space use | [element] | feature 21 | material | key

Departmental Standard Drawing

title
EXTERNAL 1/2 HR FIRE FLUSH DOORSET RANGE.
OUTWARD OPENING
WITHOUT THRESHOLD

scale
1 : 50

	drawing no	rev
GP	D.2076	

WITHOUT FANLIGHT.

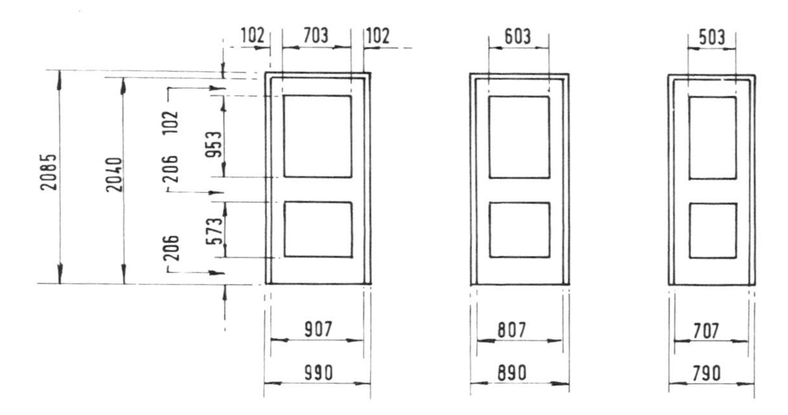

FRAME DEPTH (mm)	FRAME DETAILS.	DOOR DETAILS.
	DRG N°	DRG N°
91	D.3286	D.3285

Width of glazed panels for doors with rebated meeting stiles.

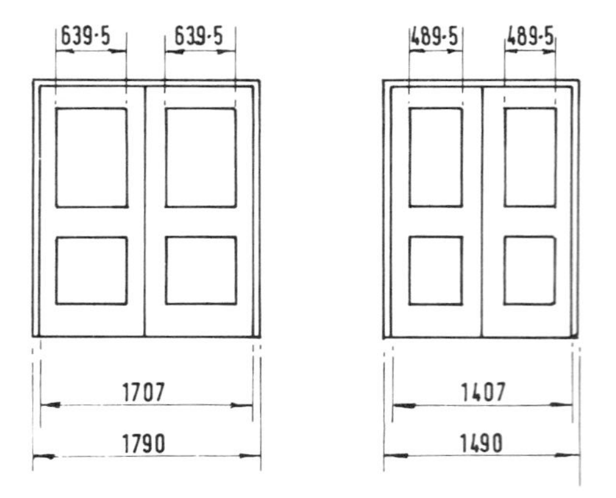

NOTE: Job architect to specify the following on the door schedule:

a. Frame and door details drg no from table.
b. Height, width and depth of door frame.
c. Height, width and thickness of door.
d. Door glass panels and beads as D.3285.

WITH FANLIGHT.

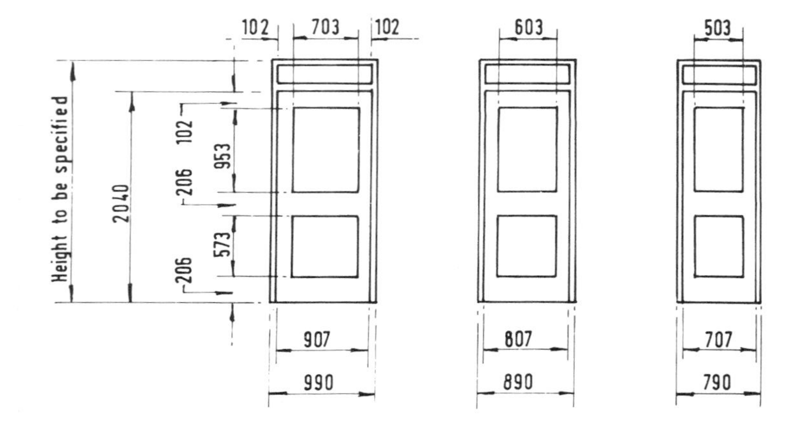

FRAME DEPTH (mm)	FRAME DETAILS	DOOR DETAILS
	DRG N°	DRG N°
91	D.3287	D.3285

Width of glazed panels for doors with rebated meeting stiles.

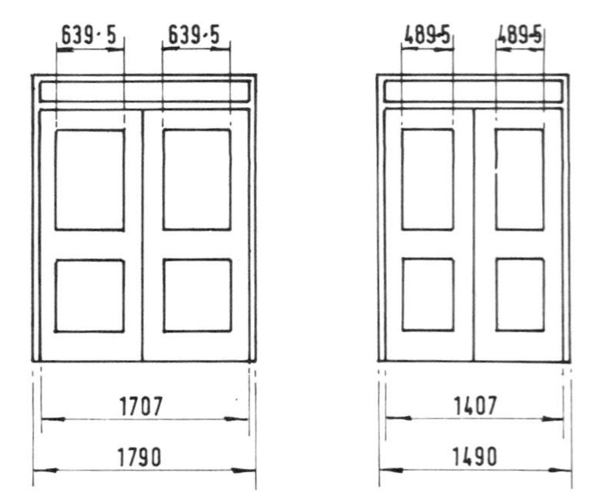

NOTE: Job architect to specify the following on the door schedule:

a. Frame and door details drg no from table.
b. Height, width and depth of door frame.
c. Fanlight panel (see doorset detail drawing)
d. Height, width and thickness of door.
e. Door glass panels and beads as D.3285.

GLC ILEA

Department of Architecture and Civic Design
County Hall SE1 7PB
Architect F B Pooley CBE

References following notes are clause numbers from G.L.C. preambles to bills of quantities

All doors are 44mm thick.

For reference to relevant building-in details see notes on doorset detail D.3286 or D.3287.

All dimensions are work sizes.

Structural openings as shown on working drawings.

Departmental Standard Drawing

title

EXTERNAL 1/2 HOUR FIRE FRAMED DOORSET RANGE

OUTWARD OPENING WITHOUT THRESHOLD.

scale 1 : 50

	drawing no	rev
GP	D.2077	

21

100180

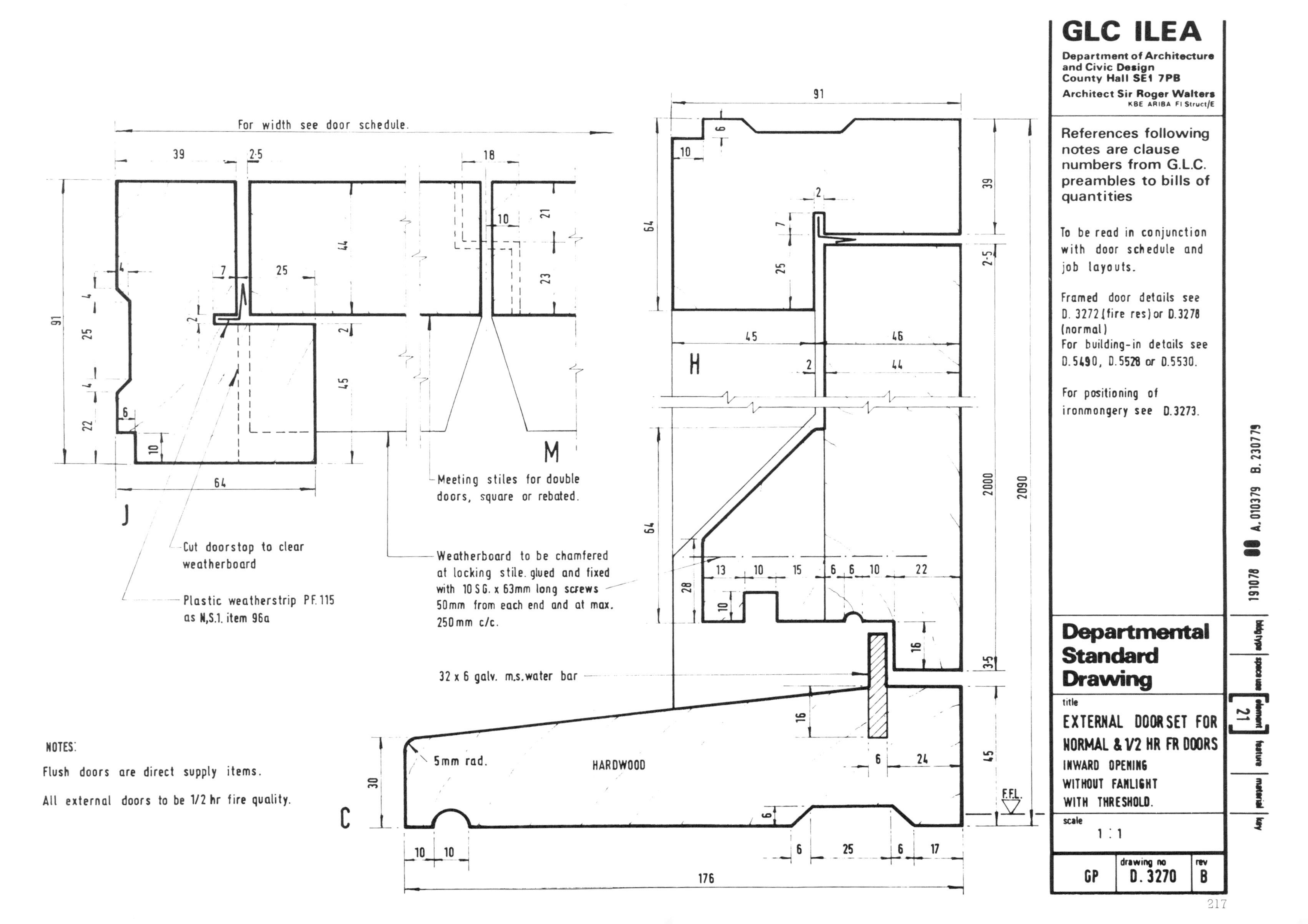

GLC ILEA
Department of Architecture and Civic Design
County Hall SE1 7PB
Architect Sir Roger Walters
KBE ARIBA FI Struct/E
References following notes are clause numbers from G.L.C. preambles to bills of quantities
To be read in conjunction with door schedule and job layouts.
Framed door details see D. 3272 (fire res) or D.3278 (normal)
For building-in details see D.5490, D.5528 or D.5530.
For positioning of ironmongery see D.3273.
Departmental Standard Drawing
title
EXTERNAL DOORSET FOR NORMAL & 1/2 HR FR DOORS
INWARD OPENING
WITHOUT FANLIGHT
WITH THRESHOLD.
scale
1 : 1
GP
drawing no
D. 3270
rev
B
191078 A. 010379 B. 230779
bldg type
space use
element
21
feature
material
key
For width see door schedule.
J
M
H
C
Meeting stiles for double doors, square or rebated.
Cut doorstop to clear weatherboard
Plastic weatherstrip PF. 115 as N.S.1. item 96a
Weatherboard to be chamfered at locking stile. glued and fixed with 10 S G. x 63mm long screws 50mm from each end and at max. 250mm c/c.
32 x 6 galv. m.s. water bar
5mm rad.
HARDWOOD
F.F.L.
NOTES:
Flush doors are direct supply items.
All external doors to be 1/2 hr fire quality.

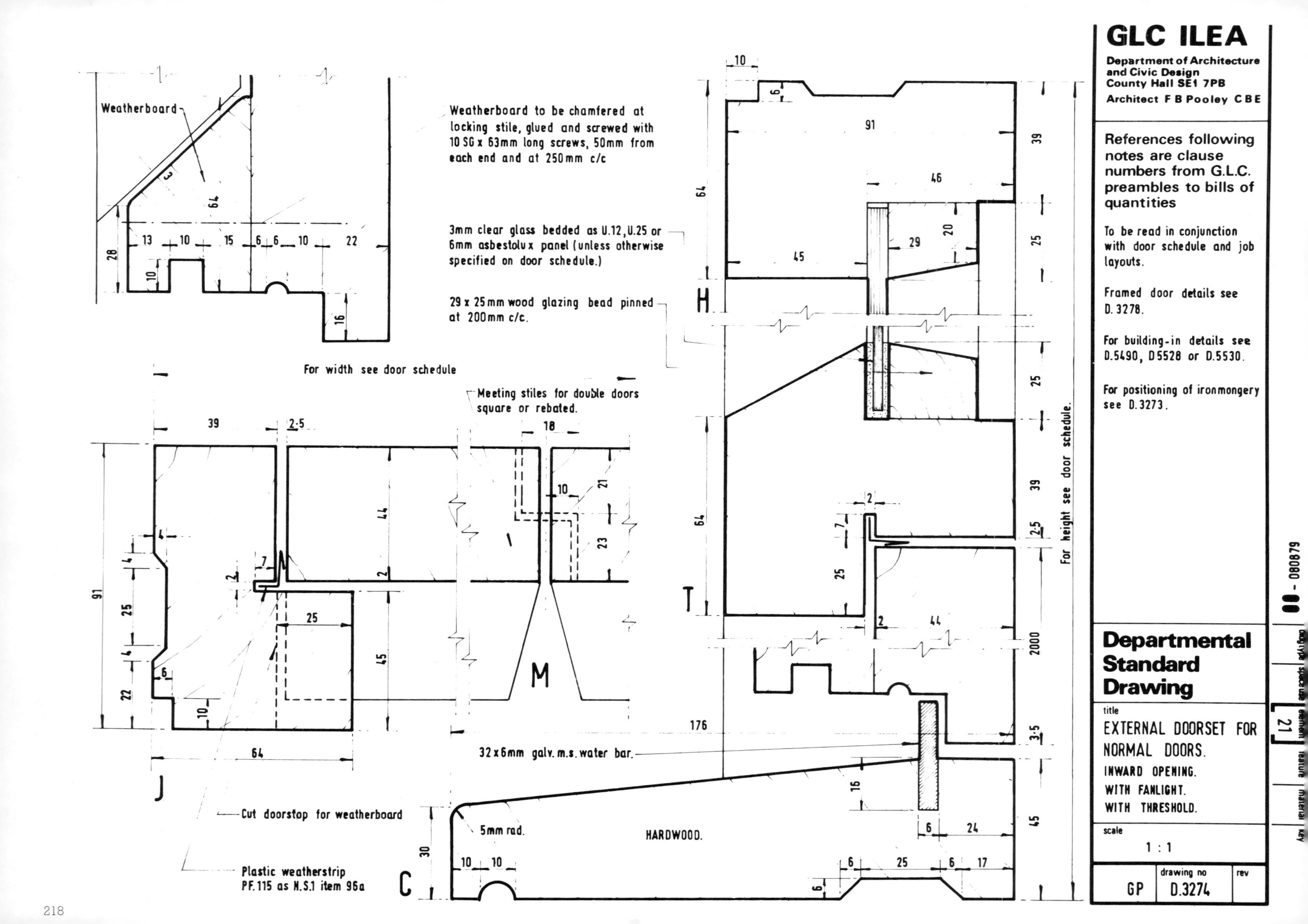

GLC ILEA
Department of Architecture and Civic Design
County Hall SE1 7PB
Architect F B Pooley CBE
References following notes are clause numbers from G.L.C. preambles to bills of quantities
To be read in conjunction with door schedule and job layouts.
Framed door details see D. 3278.
For building-in details see D.5490, D5528 or D.5530.
For positioning of ironmongery see D.3273.
Departmental Standard Drawing
title
EXTERNAL DOORSET FOR NORMAL DOORS.
INWARD OPENING.
WITH FANLIGHT.
WITH THRESHOLD.
scale
1 : 1
drawing no
GP D.3274
rev
Weatherboard
Weatherboard to be chamfered at locking stile, glued and screwed with 10 SG x 63mm long screws, 50mm from each end and at 250mm c/c
3mm clear glass bedded as U.12, U.25 or 6mm asbestolux panel (unless otherwise specified on door schedule.)
29 x 25mm wood glazing bead pinned at 200mm c/c.
For width see door schedule
Meeting stiles for double doors square or rebated.
For height see door schedule.
32 x 6mm galv. m.s. water bar.
Cut doorstop for weatherboard
Plastic weatherstrip PF.115 as N.S.1 item 96a
5mm rad.
HARDWOOD.
H
T
J
M
C

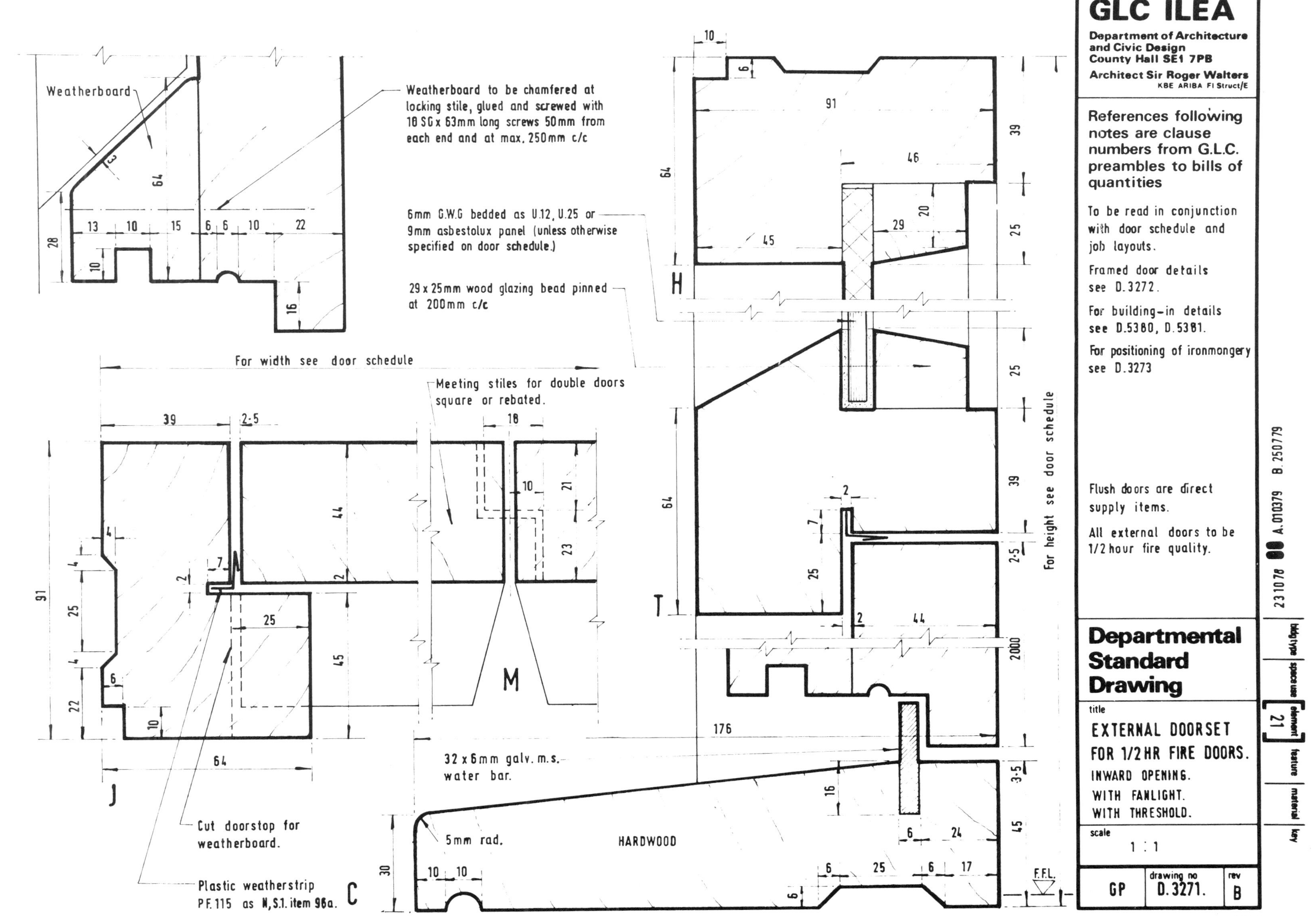
GLC ILEA
Department of Architecture
and Civic Design
County Hall SE1 7PB
Architect Sir Roger Walters
KBE ARIBA FI Struct/E
References following notes are clause numbers from G.L.C. preambles to bills of quantities
To be read in conjunction with door schedule and job layouts.
Framed door details see D.3272.
For building-in details see D.5380, D.5381.
For positioning of ironmongery see D.3273
Flush doors are direct supply items.
All external doors to be 1/2 hour fire quality.
Departmental Standard Drawing
title
EXTERNAL DOORSET FOR 1/2 HR FIRE DOORS.
INWARD OPENING.
WITH FANLIGHT.
WITH THRESHOLD.
scale
1 : 1
GP
drawing no
D.3271.
rev
B
231078 A.010379 B.250779
bldg type
space use
element
21
feature
material
key
Weatherboard
Weatherboard to be chamfered at locking stile, glued and screwed with 10 SG x 63mm long screws 50mm from each end and at max. 250mm c/c
6mm G.W.G bedded as U.12, U.25 or 9mm asbestolux panel (unless otherwise specified on door schedule.)
29 x 25mm wood glazing bead pinned at 200mm c/c
For width see door schedule
Meeting stiles for double doors square or rebated.
For height see door schedule
32 x 6mm galv. m.s. water bar.
5mm rad.
HARDWOOD
Cut doorstop for weatherboard.
Plastic weatherstrip PF.115 as N,S.1. item 96a.
F.F.L.
H
T
M
J
C
2000
176

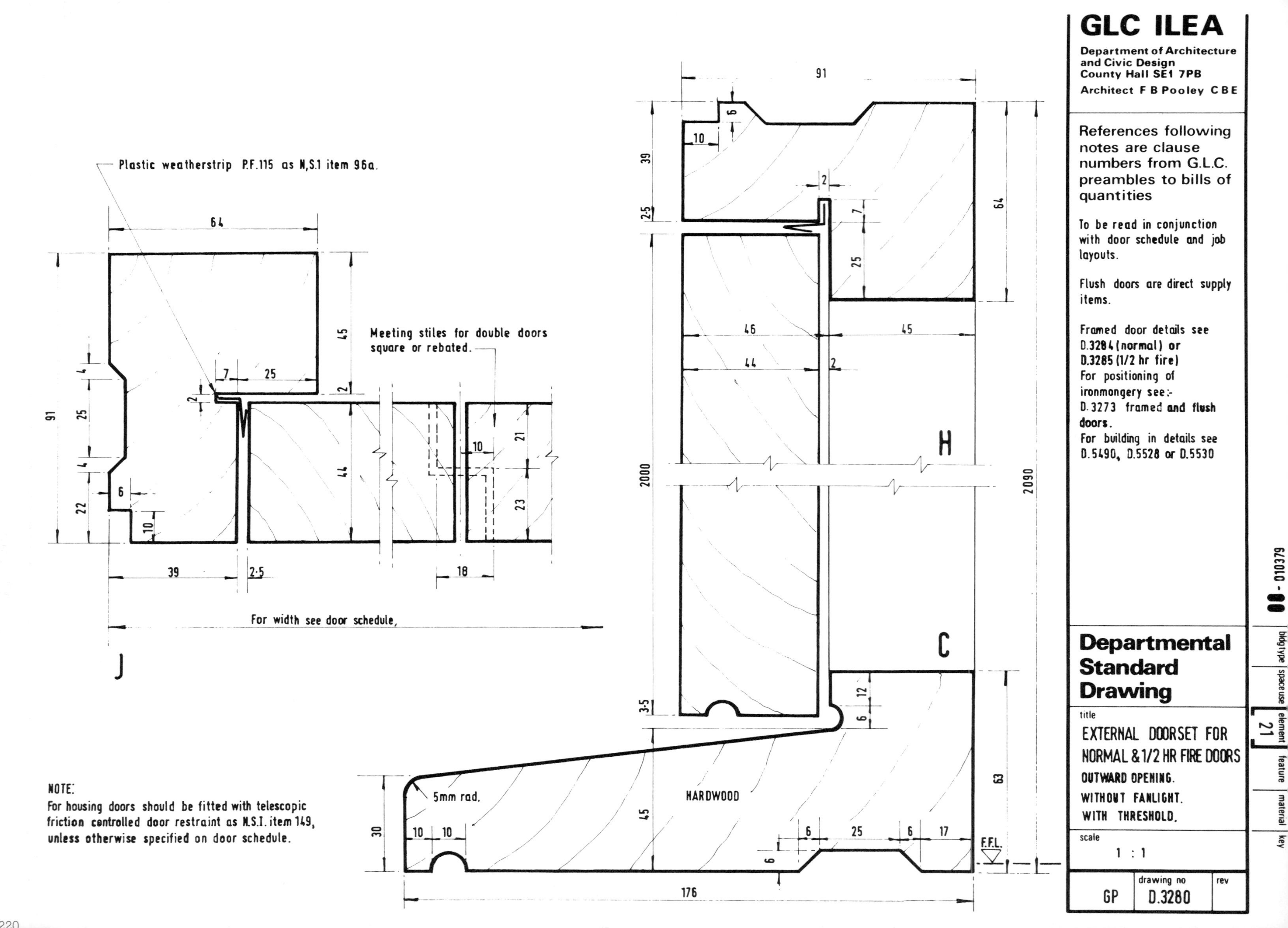
GLC ILEA
Department of Architecture and Civic Design
County Hall SE1 7PB
Architect F B Pooley CBE
References following notes are clause numbers from G.L.C. preambles to bills of quantities
To be read in conjunction with door schedule and job layouts.
Flush doors are direct supply items.
Framed door details see D.3284 (normal) or D.3285 (1/2 hr fire)
For positioning of ironmongery see:-
D.3273 framed and flush doors.
For building in details see D.5490, D.5528 or D.5530
Departmental Standard Drawing
title
EXTERNAL DOORSET FOR NORMAL & 1/2 HR FIRE DOORS
OUTWARD OPENING.
WITHOUT FANLIGHT.
WITH THRESHOLD.
scale
1 : 1
drawing no
GP
D.3280
rev
bldg type
space use
element
21
feature
material
key
010379
Plastic weatherstrip P.F.115 as N,S.1 item 96a.
Meeting stiles for double doors square or rebated.
For width see door schedule,
J
H
C
HARDWOOD
5mm rad.
F.F.L.
NOTE:
For housing doors should be fitted with telescopic friction controlled door restraint as N.S.I. item 149, unless otherwise specified on door schedule.

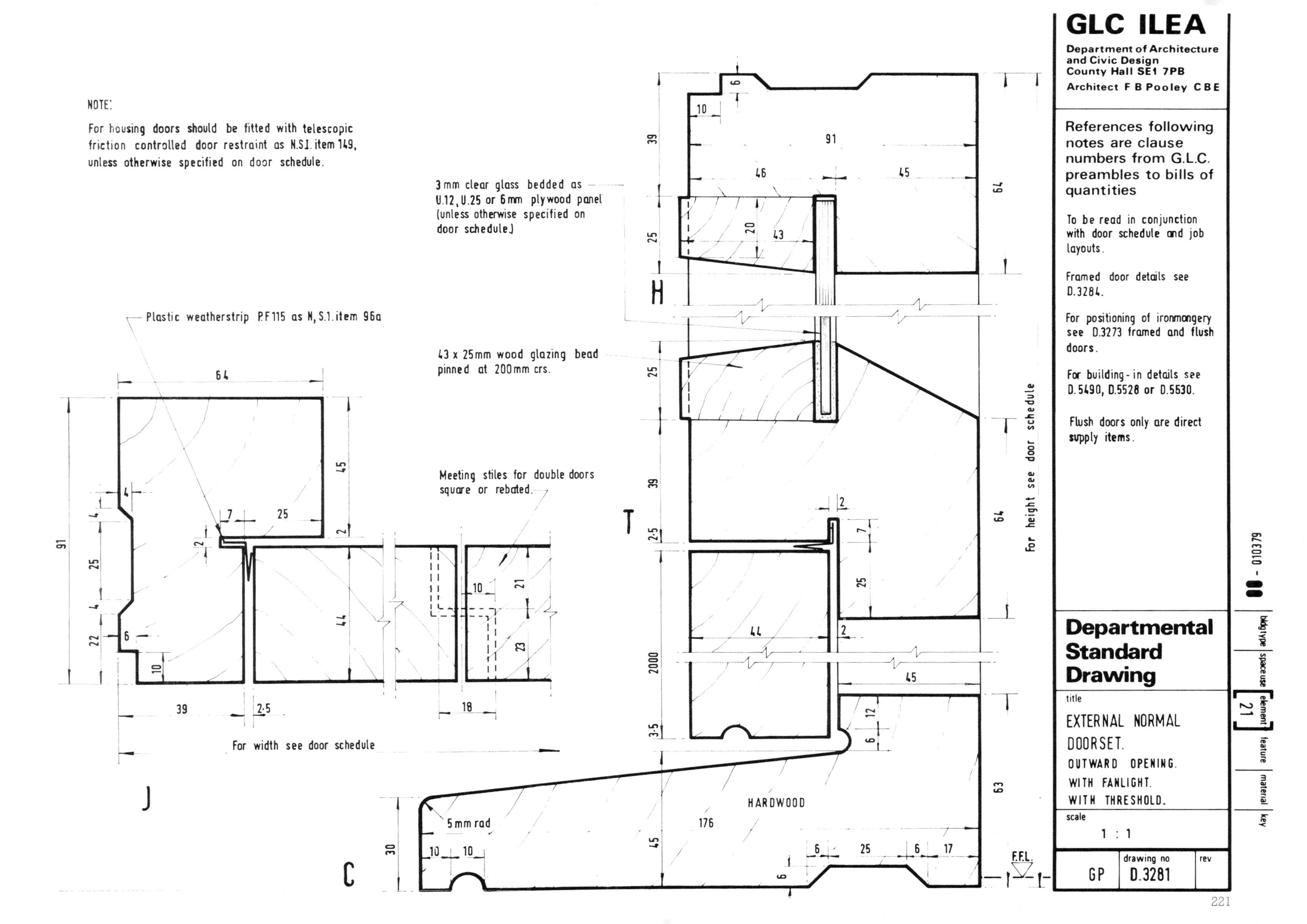
GLC ILEA
Department of Architecture and Civic Design
County Hall SE1 7PB
Architect F B Pooley CBE
References following notes are clause numbers from G.L.C. preambles to bills of quantities
To be read in conjunction with door schedule and job layouts.
Framed door details see D.3284.
For positioning of ironmongery see D.3273 framed and flush doors.
For building-in details see D.5490, D.5528 or D.5630.
Flush doors only are direct supply items.
Departmental Standard Drawing
title
EXTERNAL NORMAL DOORSET.
OUTWARD OPENING.
WITH FANLIGHT.
WITH THRESHOLD.
scale
1 : 1
GP
drawing no
D.3281
rev
NOTE:
For housing doors should be fitted with telescopic friction controlled door restraint as N.S.I. item 149, unless otherwise specified on door schedule.
3mm clear glass bedded as U.12, U.25 or 6mm plywood panel (unless otherwise specified on door schedule.)
Plastic weatherstrip P.F 115 as N.S.I. item 96a
43 x 25mm wood glazing bead pinned at 200mm crs.
Meeting stiles for double doors square or rebated.
For width see door schedule
For height see door schedule
HARDWOOD
5mm rad
F.F.L.
H
T
J
C
010379
bldg type
space use
element
21
feature
material
key

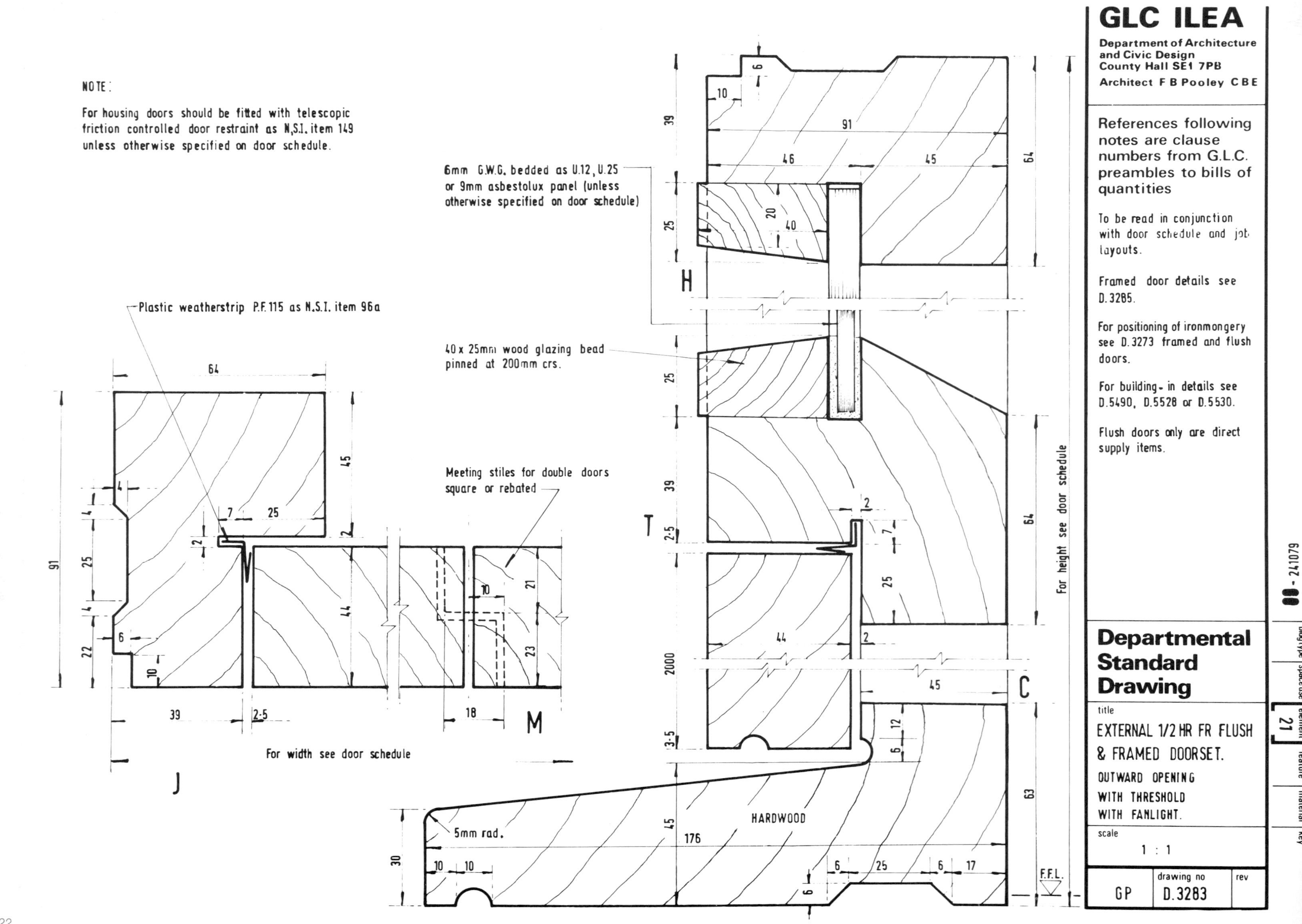
GLC ILEA
Department of Architecture and Civic Design
County Hall SE1 7PB
Architect F B Pooley CBE
References following notes are clause numbers from G.L.C. preambles to bills of quantities
To be read in conjunction with door schedule and job layouts.
Framed door details see D.3285.
For positioning of ironmongery see D.3273 framed and flush doors.
For building-in details see D.5490, D.5528 or D.5530.
Flush doors only are direct supply items.
Departmental Standard Drawing
title
EXTERNAL 1/2 HR FR FLUSH & FRAMED DOORSET.
OUTWARD OPENING
WITH THRESHOLD
WITH FANLIGHT.
scale
1 : 1
GP
drawing no
D.3283
rev
NOTE:
For housing doors should be fitted with telescopic friction controlled door restraint as N.S.I. item 149 unless otherwise specified on door schedule.
6mm G.W.G. bedded as U.12, U.25 or 9mm asbestolux panel (unless otherwise specified on door schedule)
Plastic weatherstrip P.F. 115 as N.S.I. item 96a
40 x 25mm wood glazing bead pinned at 200mm crs.
Meeting stiles for double doors square or rebated
For width see door schedule
For height see door schedule
HARDWOOD
5mm rad.
F.F.L.
H
T
C
J
M

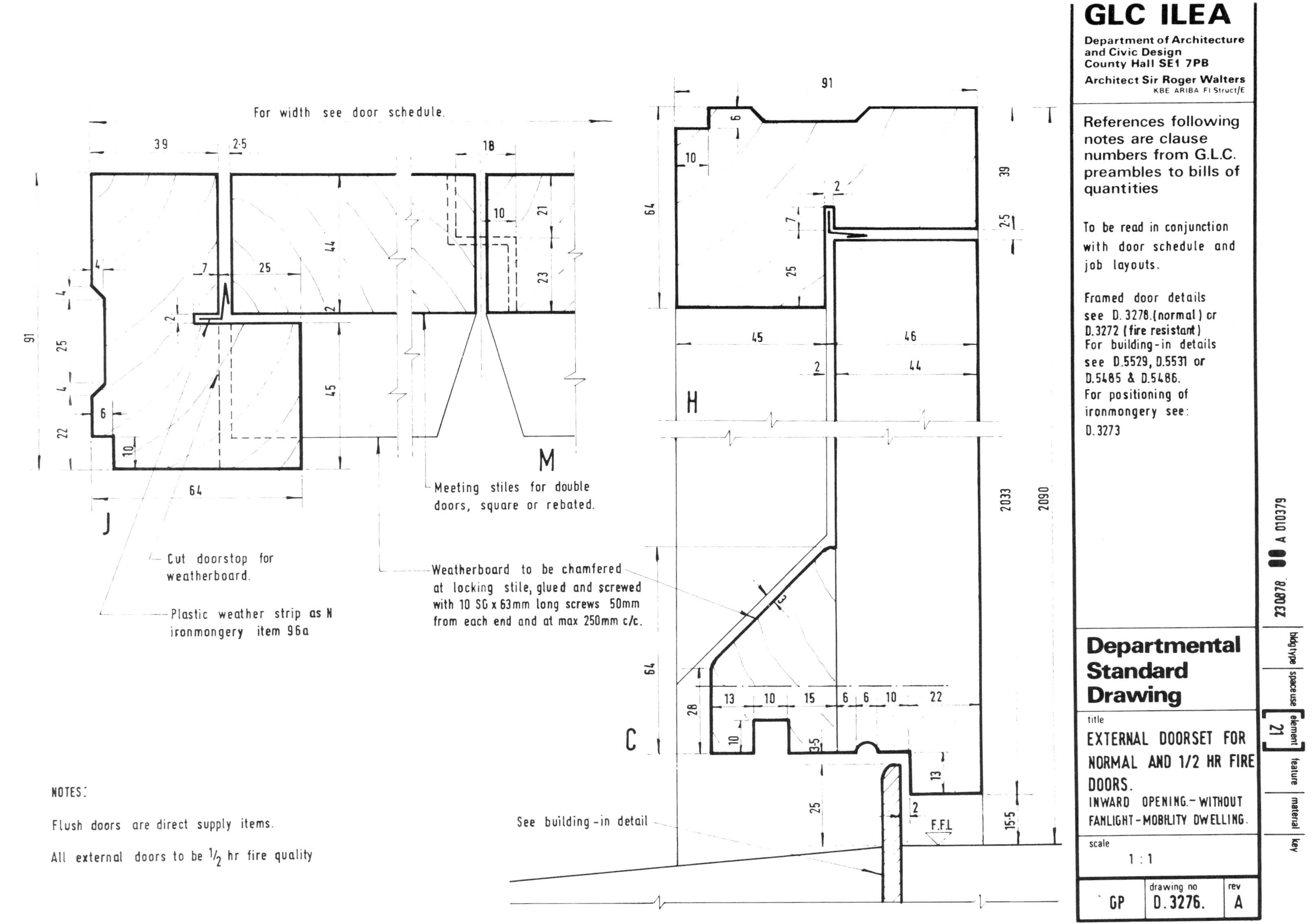
GLC ILEA
Department of Architecture and Civic Design
County Hall SE1 7PB
Architect Sir Roger Walters KBE ARIBA FI Struct/E
References following notes are clause numbers from G.L.C. preambles to bills of quantities
To be read in conjunction with door schedule and job layouts.
Framed door details see D. 3278.(normal) or D.3272 (fire resistant)
For building-in details see D.5529, D.5531 or D.5485 & D.5486.
For positioning of ironmongery see: D.3273
Departmental Standard Drawing
title
EXTERNAL DOORSET FOR NORMAL AND 1/2 HR FIRE DOORS.
INWARD OPENING.- WITHOUT FANLIGHT - MOBILITY DWELLING.
scale 1 : 1
GP
drawing no D.3276.
rev A
230878 A 010379
bldg type | space use | element 21 | feature | material | key
For width see door schedule.
Meeting stiles for double doors, square or rebated.
Cut doorstop for weatherboard.
Plastic weather strip as N ironmongery item 96a
Weatherboard to be chamfered at locking stile, glued and screwed with 10 SG x 63mm long screws 50mm from each end and at max 250mm c/c.
See building-in detail
F.F.L.
J
M
H
C
NOTES:
Flush doors are direct supply items.
All external doors to be 1/2 hr fire quality

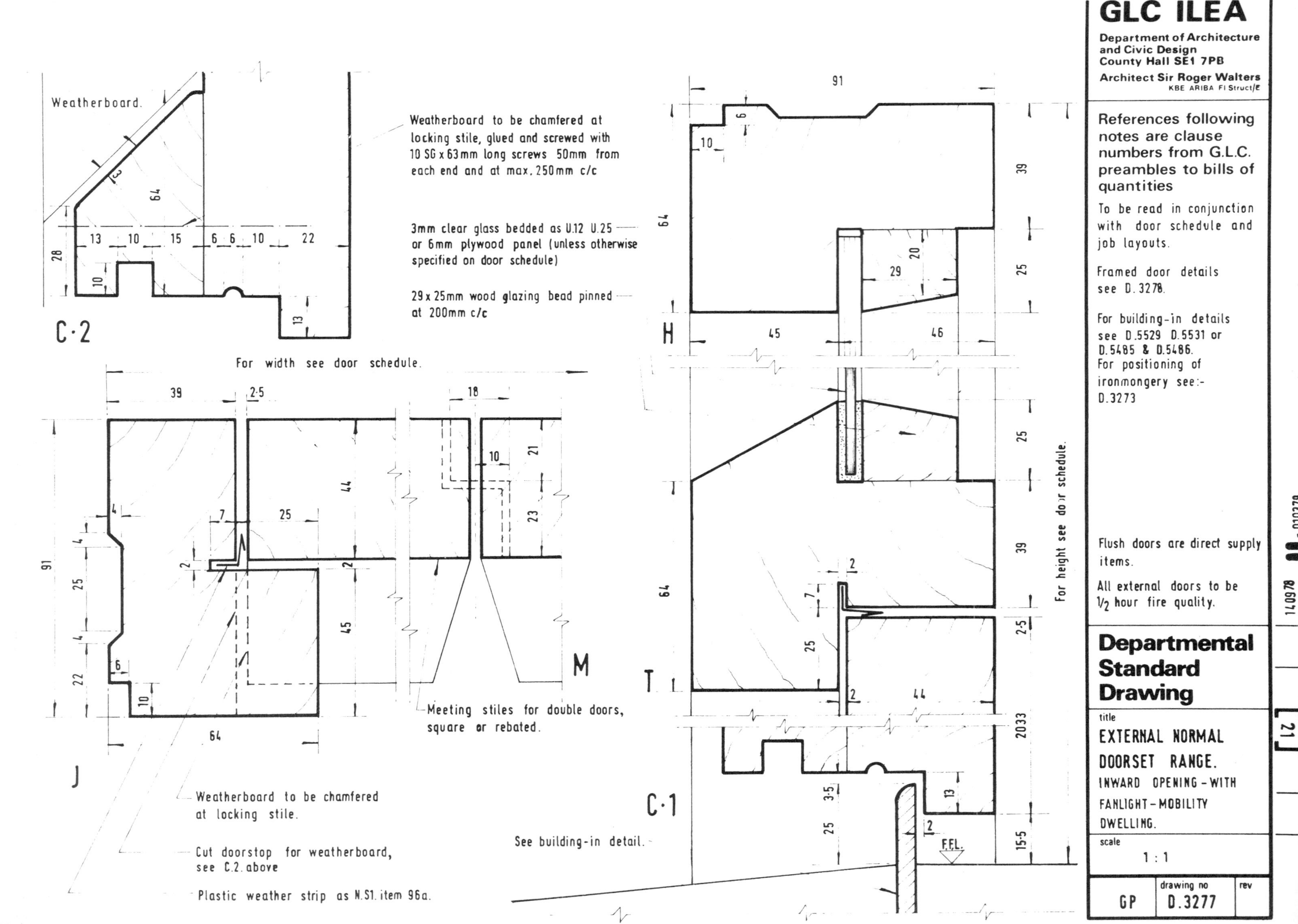
GLC ILEA
Department of Architecture and Civic Design
County Hall SE1 7PB
Architect Sir Roger Walters KBE ARIBA FI Struct/E
References following notes are clause numbers from G.L.C. preambles to bills of quantities
To be read in conjunction with door schedule and job layouts.
Framed door details see D.3278.
For building-in details see D.5529 D.5531 or D.5485 & D.5486.
For positioning of ironmongery see:- D.3273
Flush doors are direct supply items.
All external doors to be 1/2 hour fire quality.
Departmental Standard Drawing
title
EXTERNAL NORMAL DOORSET RANGE.
INWARD OPENING - WITH FANLIGHT - MOBILITY DWELLING.
scale
1 : 1
GP
drawing no
D.3277
rev
21
Weatherboard.
Weatherboard to be chamfered at locking stile, glued and screwed with 10 SG x 63mm long screws 50mm from each end and at max. 250mm c/c
3mm clear glass bedded as U.12 U.25 or 6mm plywood panel (unless otherwise specified on door schedule)
29 x 25mm wood glazing bead pinned at 200mm c/c
C·2
For width see door schedule.
Meeting stiles for double doors, square or rebated.
M
J
Weatherboard to be chamfered at locking stile.
Cut doorstop for weatherboard, see C.2. above
Plastic weather strip as N.S1. item 96a.
See building-in detail.
C·1
H
T
F.F.L.
For height see door schedule.

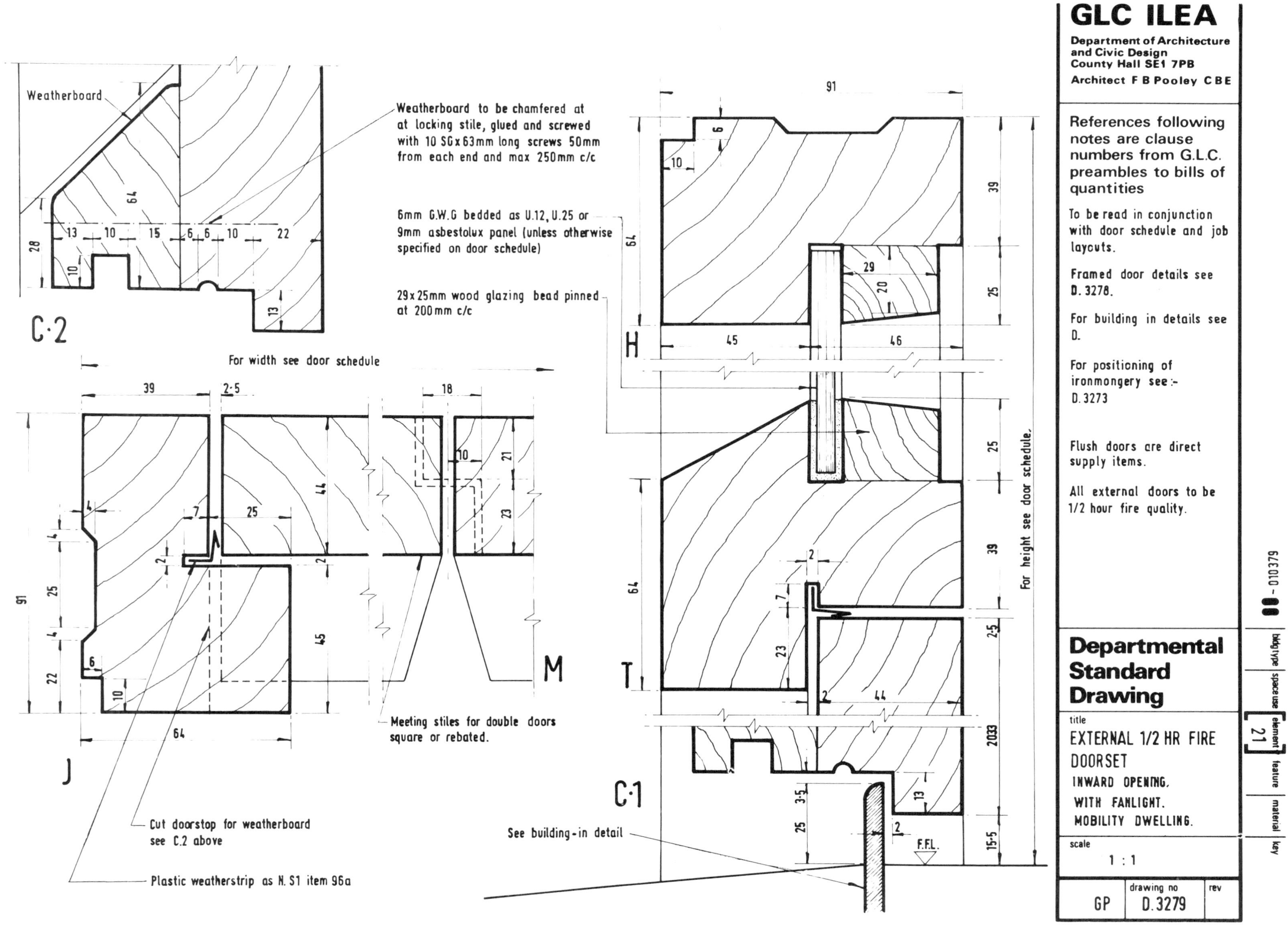

GLC ILEA
Department of Architecture and Civic Design
County Hall SE1 7PB
Architect F B Pooley CBE
References following notes are clause numbers from G.L.C. preambles to bills of quantities
To be read in conjunction with door schedule and job layouts.
Framed door details see D.3278.
For building in details see D.
For positioning of ironmongery see:- D.3273
Flush doors are direct supply items.
All external doors to be 1/2 hour fire quality.
Departmental Standard Drawing
title
EXTERNAL 1/2 HR FIRE DOORSET
INWARD OPENING.
WITH FANLIGHT.
MOBILITY DWELLING.
scale
1 : 1
GP
drawing no
D.3279
rev
Weatherboard
Weatherboard to be chamfered at at locking stile, glued and screwed with 10 SG x 63mm long screws 50mm from each end and max 250mm c/c
6mm G.W.G bedded as U.12, U.25 or 9mm asbestolux panel (unless otherwise specified on door schedule)
29x25mm wood glazing bead pinned at 200mm c/c
C·2
For width see door schedule
H
T
C·1
J
M
Meeting stiles for double doors square or rebated.
Cut doorstop for weatherboard see C.2 above
Plastic weatherstrip as N.S1 item 96a
See building-in detail
For height see door schedule.
F.F.L.

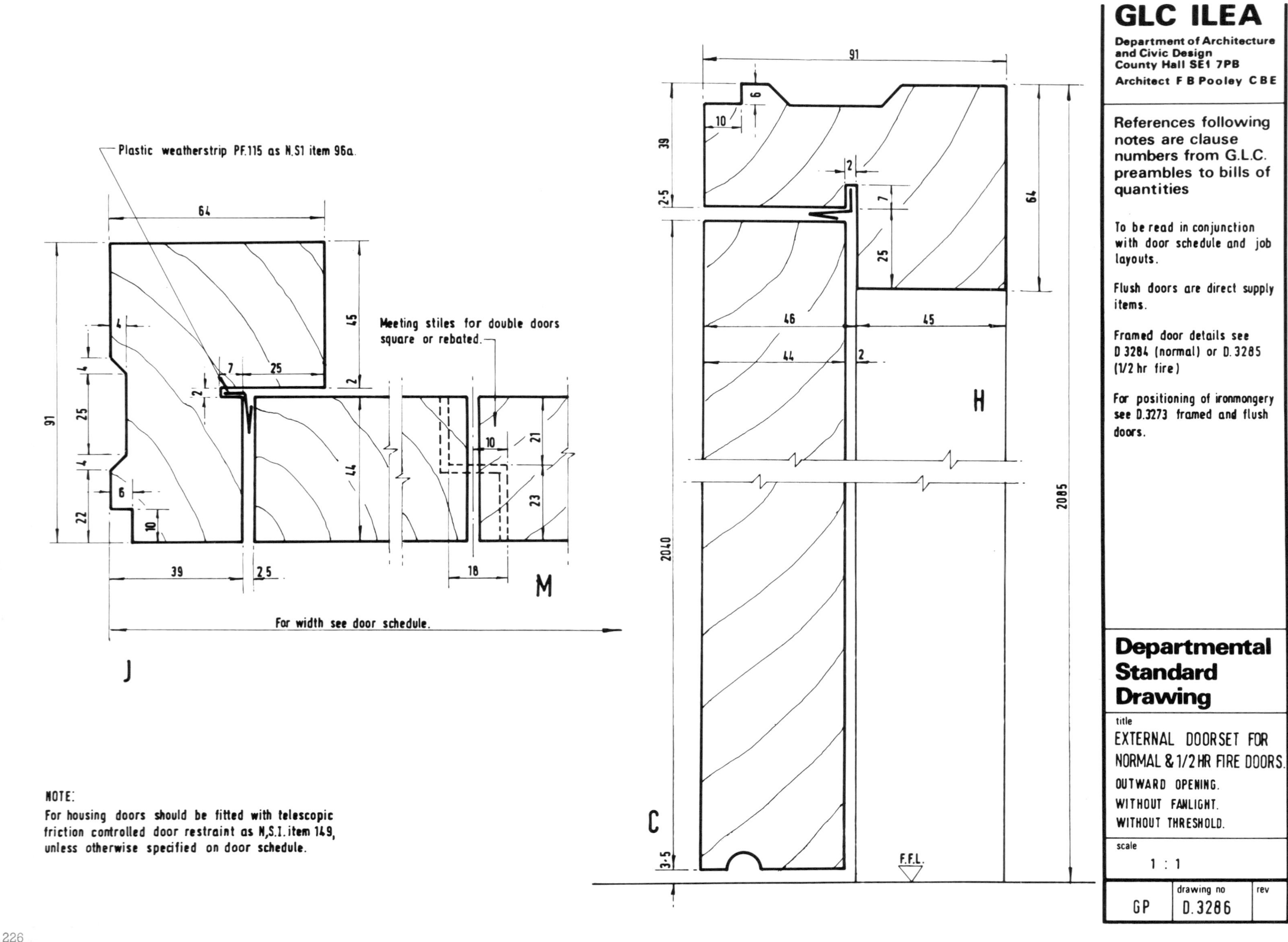
GLC ILEA
Department of Architecture and Civic Design
County Hall SE1 7PB
Architect F B Pooley CBE
References following notes are clause numbers from G.L.C. preambles to bills of quantities
To be read in conjunction with door schedule and job layouts.
Flush doors are direct supply items.
Framed door details see D 3284 (normal) or D. 3285 (1/2 hr fire)
For positioning of ironmongery see D.3273 framed and flush doors.
Departmental Standard Drawing
title
EXTERNAL DOORSET FOR NORMAL & 1/2 HR FIRE DOORS.
OUTWARD OPENING.
WITHOUT FANLIGHT.
WITHOUT THRESHOLD.
scale
1 : 1
drawing no
rev
GP
D.3286
Plastic weatherstrip PF.115 as N.S1 item 96a.
Meeting stiles for double doors square or rebated.
For width see door schedule.
F.F.L.
J
M
H
C
NOTE:
For housing doors should be fitted with telescopic friction controlled door restraint as N.S.I. item 149, unless otherwise specified on door schedule.

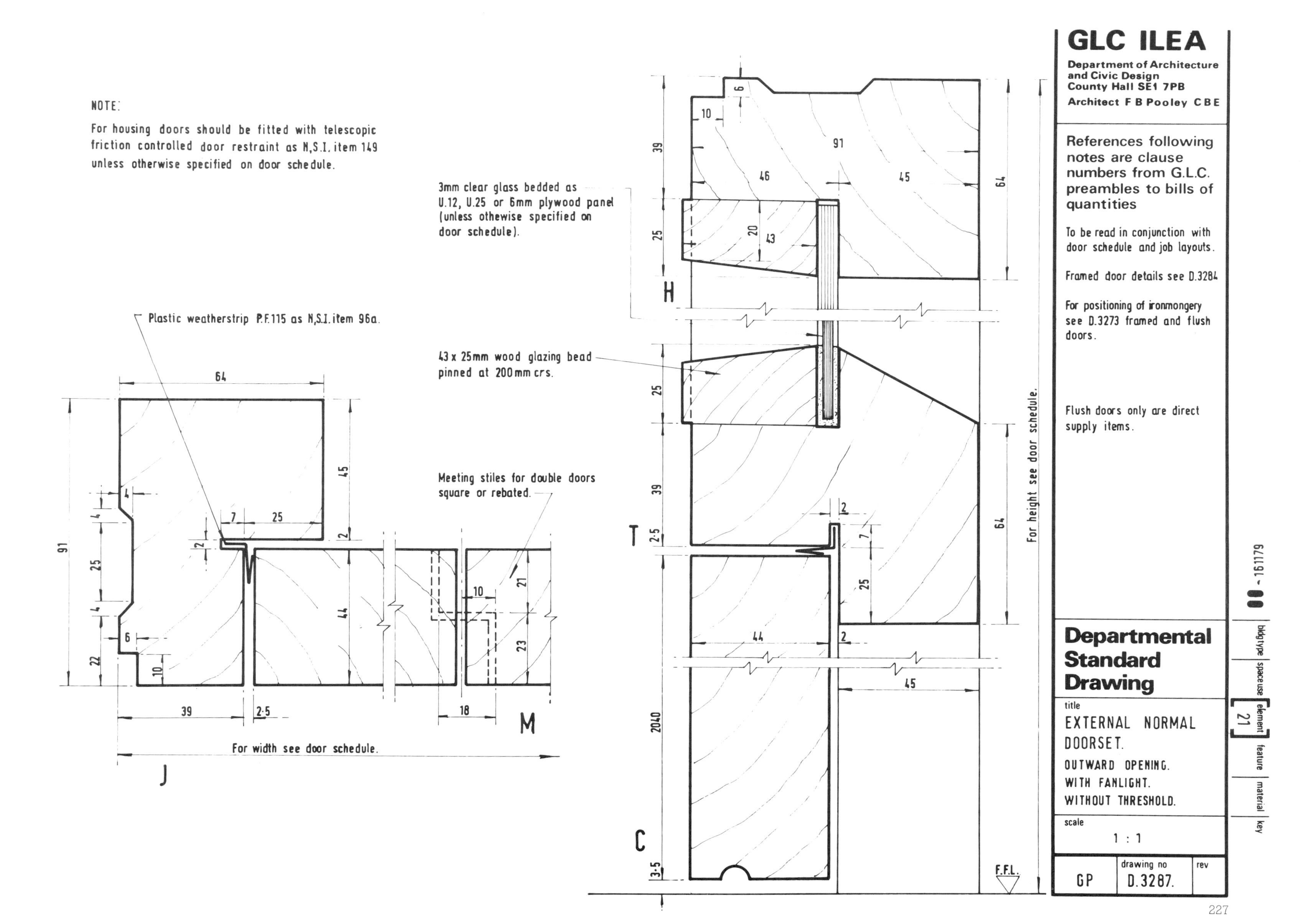
NOTE:
For housing doors should be fitted with telescopic friction controlled door restraint as N.S.I. item 149 unless otherwise specified on door schedule.
3mm clear glass bedded as U.12, U.25 or 6mm plywood panel (unless othewise specified on door schedule).
Plastic weatherstrip P.F.115 as N.S.I. item 96a.
43 x 25mm wood glazing bead pinned at 200mm crs.
Meeting stiles for double doors square or rebated.
For width see door schedule.
For height see door schedule.
F.F.L.
H
T
C
J
M
GLC ILEA
Department of Architecture and Civic Design
County Hall SE1 7PB
Architect F B Pooley CBE
References following notes are clause numbers from G.L.C. preambles to bills of quantities
To be read in conjunction with door schedule and job layouts.
Framed door details see D.3284
For positioning of ironmongery see D.3273 framed and flush doors.
Flush doors only are direct supply items.
Departmental Standard Drawing
title
EXTERNAL NORMAL DOORSET.
OUTWARD OPENING.
WITH FANLIGHT.
WITHOUT THRESHOLD.
scale
1 : 1
GP
drawing no
D.3287.
rev
bldgtype
space use
element
21
feature
material
key
161179

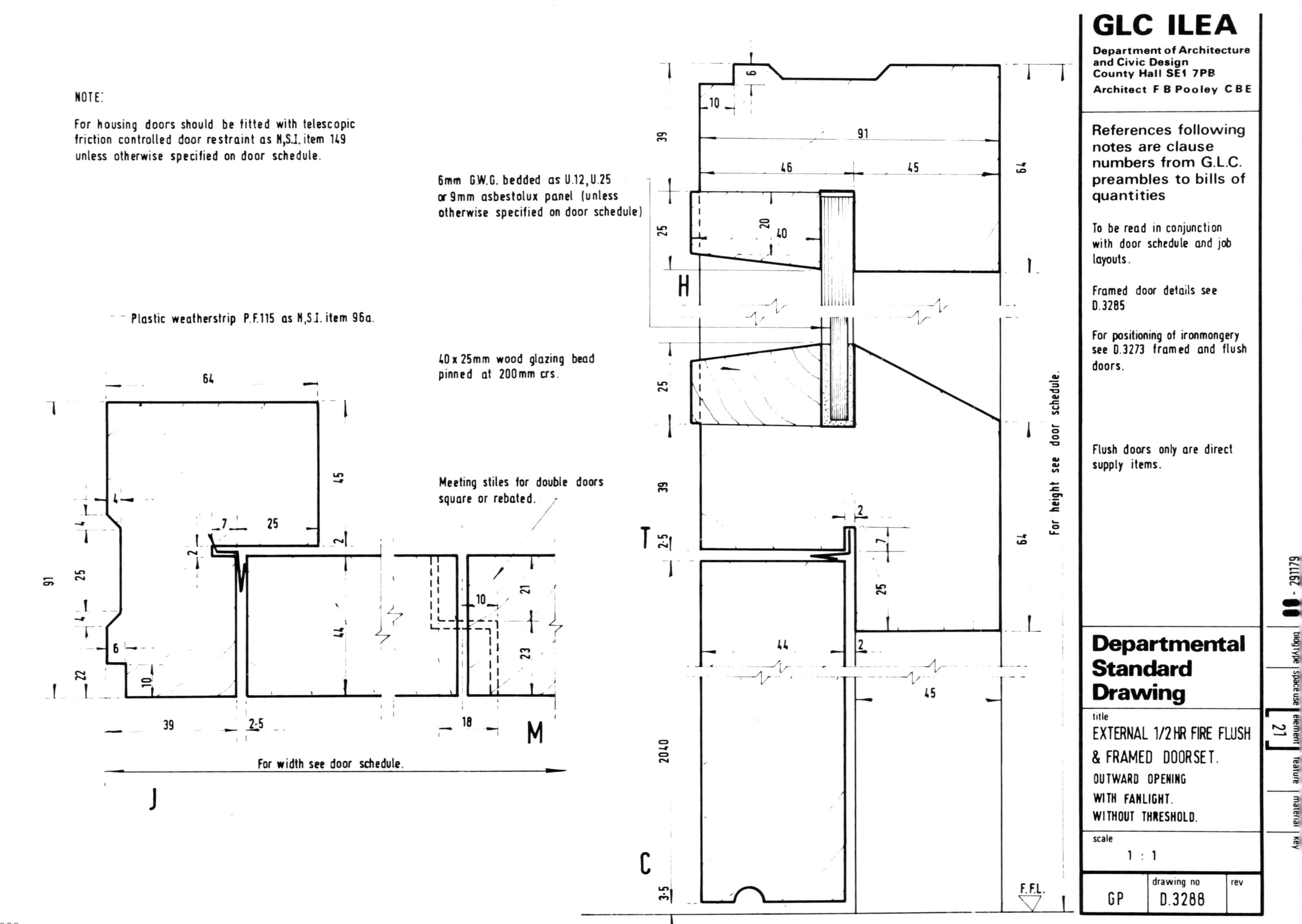

NOTE:
For housing doors should be fitted with telescopic friction controlled door restraint as N.S.I. item 149 unless otherwise specified on door schedule.
6mm G.W.G. bedded as U.12, U.25 or 9mm asbestolux panel (unless otherwise specified on door schedule)
Plastic weatherstrip P.F.115 as N.S.I. item 96a.
40 x 25mm wood glazing bead pinned at 200mm crs.
Meeting stiles for double doors square or rebated.
For width see door schedule.
For height see door schedule.
F.F.L.
H
T
C
J
M
GLC ILEA
Department of Architecture and Civic Design
County Hall SE1 7PB
Architect F B Pooley CBE
References following notes are clause numbers from G.L.C. preambles to bills of quantities
To be read in conjunction with door schedule and job layouts.
Framed door details see D.3285
For positioning of ironmongery see D.3273 framed and flush doors.
Flush doors only are direct supply items.
Departmental Standard Drawing
title
EXTERNAL 1/2 HR FIRE FLUSH & FRAMED DOORSET.
OUTWARD OPENING
WITH FANLIGHT.
WITHOUT THRESHOLD.
scale
1 : 1
GP
drawing no
D.3288
rev
291179
bldg type
space use
element
21
feature
material
key

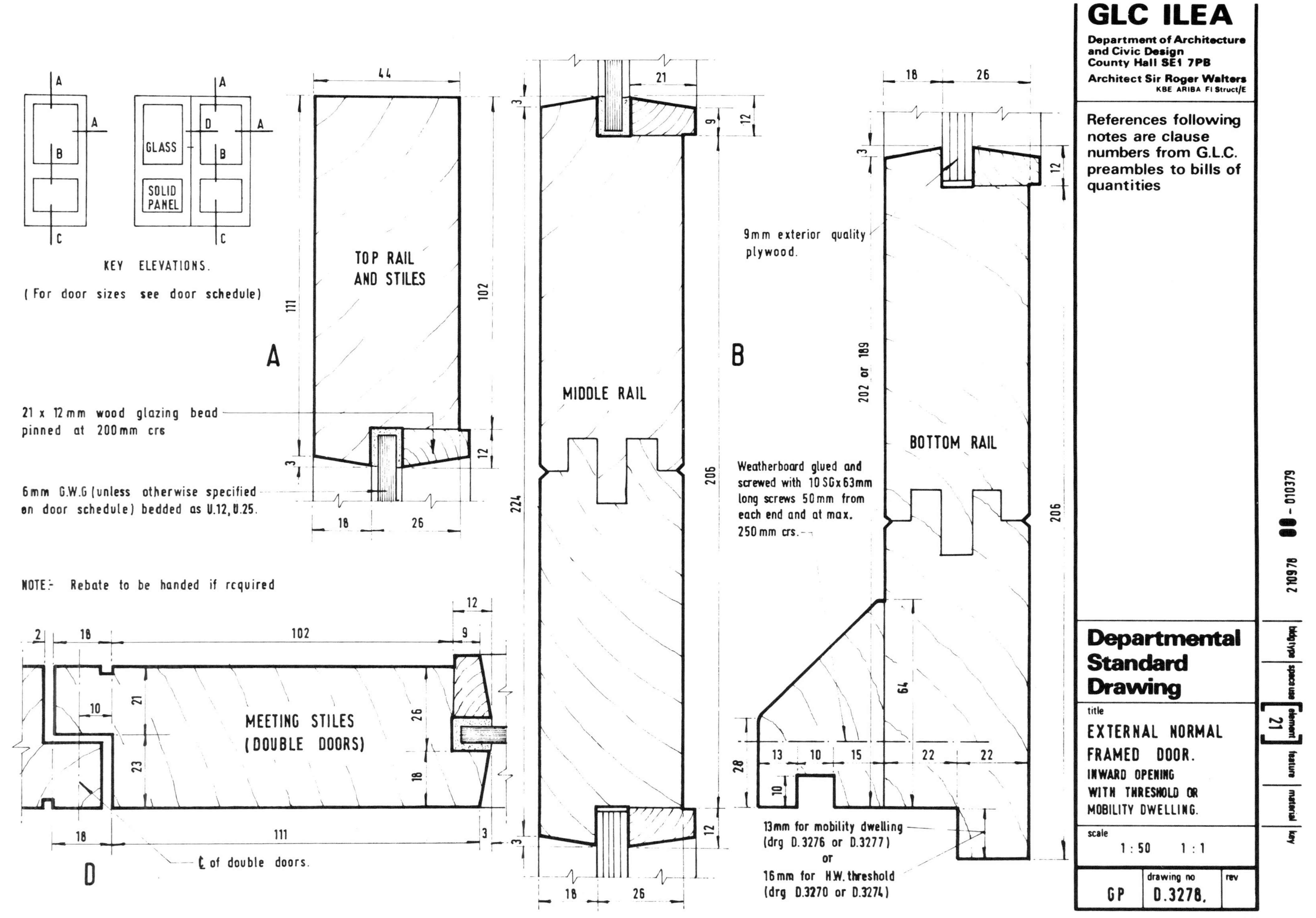
GLC ILEA
Department of Architecture and Civic Design
County Hall SE1 7PB
Architect Sir Roger Walters
KBE ARIBA FI Struct/E
References following notes are clause numbers from G.L.C. preambles to bills of quantities
KEY ELEVATIONS.
(For door sizes see door schedule)
GLASS
SOLID PANEL
TOP RAIL AND STILES
A
B
D
MIDDLE RAIL
BOTTOM RAIL
21 x 12 mm wood glazing bead pinned at 200 mm crs
6 mm G.W.G (unless otherwise specified on door schedule) bedded as U.12, U.25.
NOTE:- Rebate to be handed if required
MEETING STILES (DOUBLE DOORS)
℄ of double doors.
9mm exterior quality plywood.
Weatherboard glued and screwed with 10 SG x 63mm long screws 50mm from each end and at max. 250mm crs.
13mm for mobility dwelling (drg D.3276 or D.3277)
or
16mm for H.W. threshold (drg D.3270 or D.3274)
202 or 189
Departmental Standard Drawing
title
EXTERNAL NORMAL FRAMED DOOR.
INWARD OPENING WITH THRESHOLD OR MOBILITY DWELLING.
scale
1 : 50 1 : 1
GP
drawing no
D.3278.
rev
210978
010379
bldg type
space use
element
21
feature
material
key

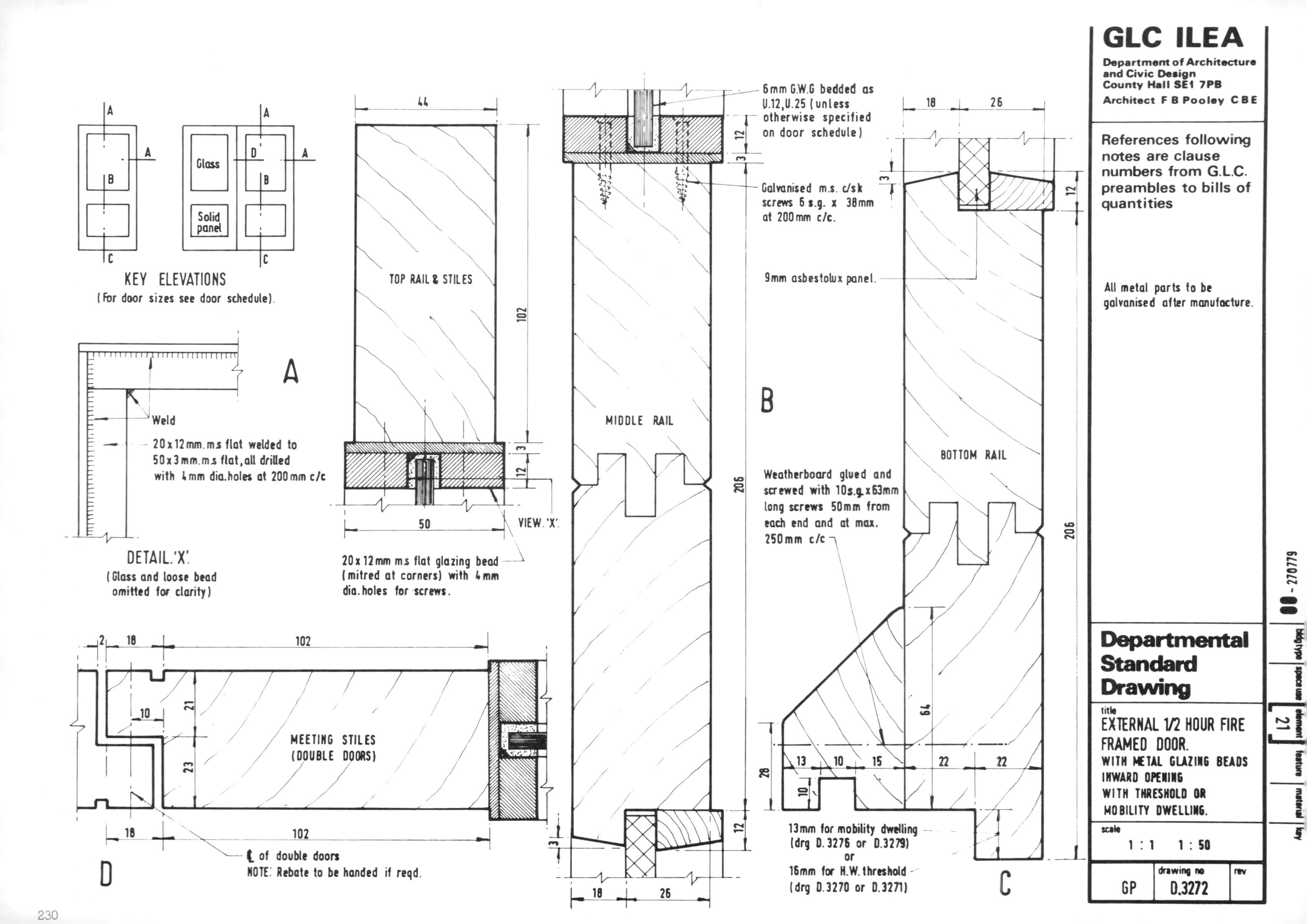
GLC ILEA
Department of Architecture and Civic Design
County Hall SE1 7PB
Architect F B Pooley CBE
References following notes are clause numbers from G.L.C. preambles to bills of quantities
All metal parts to be galvanised after manufacture.
KEY ELEVATIONS
(For door sizes see door schedule).
Glass
Solid panel
DETAIL 'X'.
(Glass and loose bead omitted for clarity)
Weld
20 x 12 mm. m.s flat welded to 50 x 3 mm. m.s flat, all drilled with 4 mm dia. holes at 200 mm c/c
TOP RAIL & STILES
VIEW 'X'.
20 x 12 mm m.s flat glazing bead (mitred at corners) with 4 mm dia. holes for screws.
MIDDLE RAIL
6 mm G.W.G bedded as U.12, U.25 (unless otherwise specified on door schedule)
Galvanised m.s. c/sk screws 6 s.g. x 38 mm at 200 mm c/c.
9 mm asbestolux panel.
BOTTOM RAIL
Weatherboard glued and screwed with 10 s.g. x 63 mm long screws 50 mm from each end and at max. 250 mm c/c
13 mm for mobility dwelling (drg D.3276 or D.3279)
or
16 mm for H.W. threshold (drg D.3270 or D.3271)
MEETING STILES (DOUBLE DOORS)
℄ of double doors
NOTE: Rebate to be handed if reqd.
Departmental Standard Drawing
title
EXTERNAL 1/2 HOUR FIRE FRAMED DOOR.
WITH METAL GLAZING BEADS
INWARD OPENING
WITH THRESHOLD OR MOBILITY DWELLING.
scale
1 : 1 1 : 50
GP
drawing no
D.3272
rev
bldg type
space use
element
feature
material
key
21
- 270779

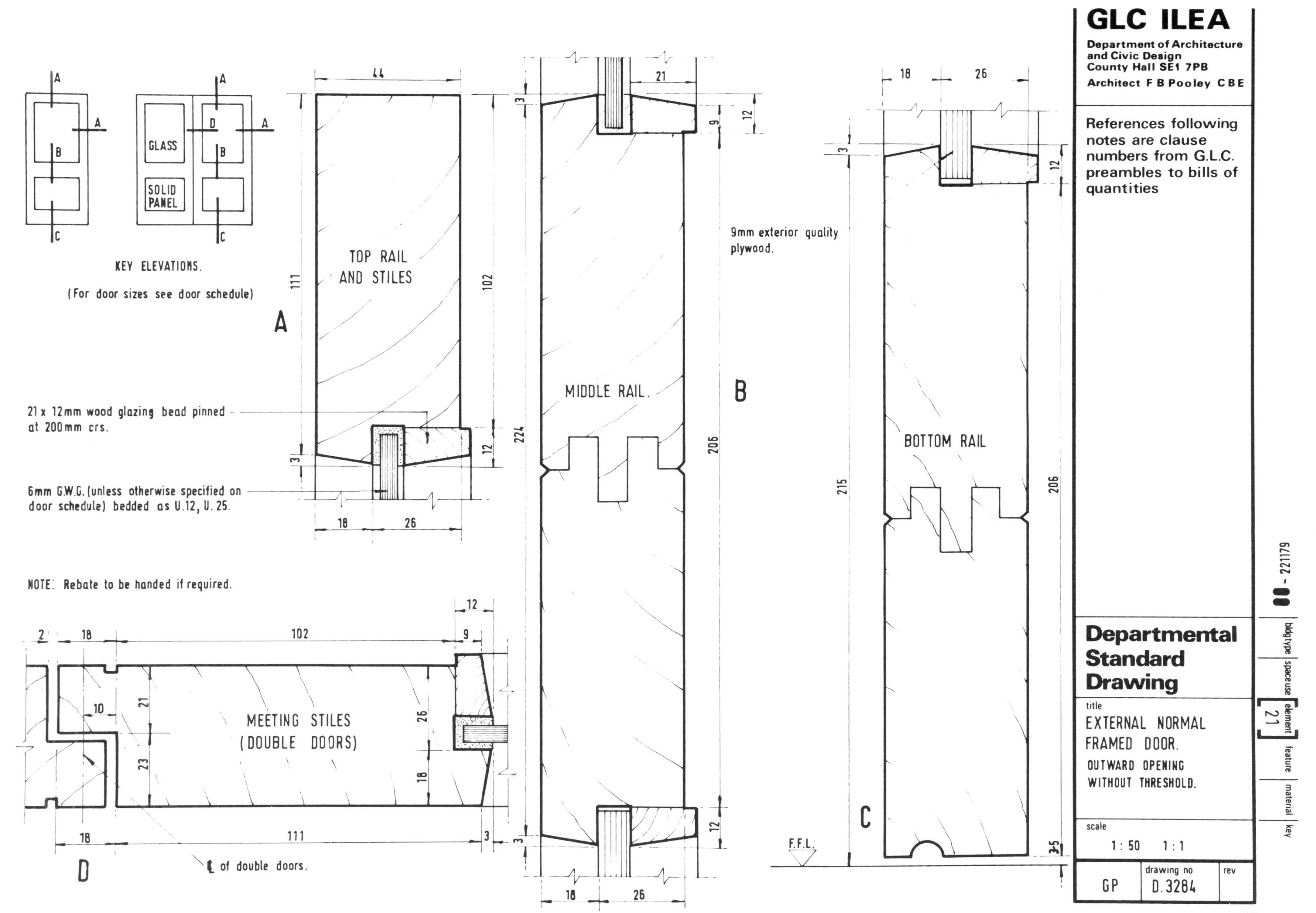
GLC ILEA
Department of Architecture and Civic Design
County Hall SE1 7PB
Architect F B Pooley CBE
References following notes are clause numbers from G.L.C. preambles to bills of quantities
KEY ELEVATIONS.
(For door sizes see door schedule)
GLASS
SOLID PANEL
TOP RAIL AND STILES
A
MIDDLE RAIL.
B
BOTTOM RAIL
C
9mm exterior quality plywood.
21 x 12mm wood glazing bead pinned at 200mm crs.
6mm G.W.G. (unless otherwise specified on door schedule) bedded as U.12, U.25.
NOTE: Rebate to be handed if required.
MEETING STILES (DOUBLE DOORS)
D
℄ of double doors.
F.F.L.
Departmental Standard Drawing
title
EXTERNAL NORMAL FRAMED DOOR.
OUTWARD OPENING WITHOUT THRESHOLD.
scale
1 : 50 1 : 1
GP
drawing no
D.3284
rev
221179
bldg type
space use
element
21
feature
material
key

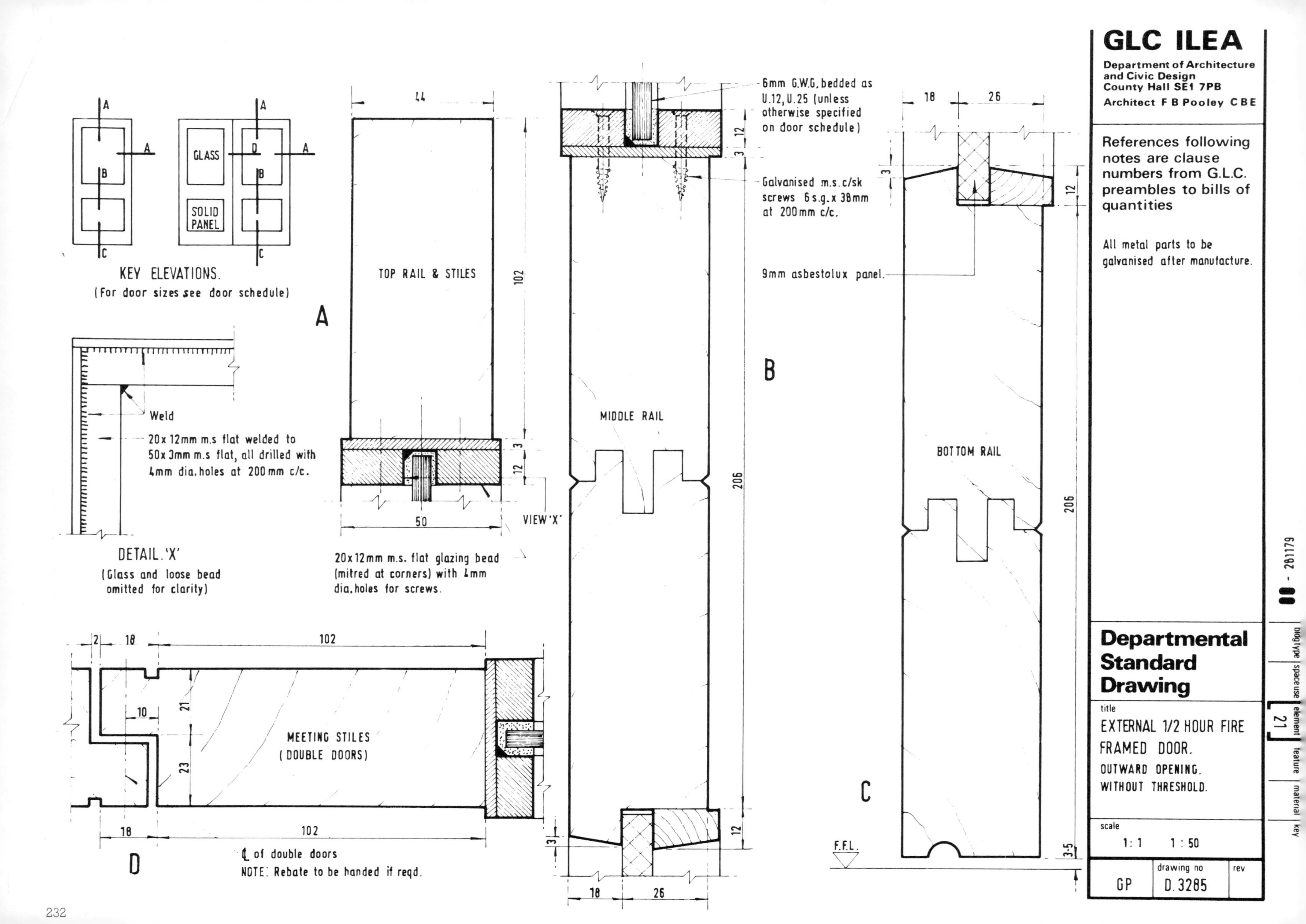
GLC ILEA
Department of Architecture and Civic Design
County Hall SE1 7PB
Architect F B Pooley CBE
References following notes are clause numbers from G.L.C. preambles to bills of quantities
All metal parts to be galvanised after manufacture.
KEY ELEVATIONS.
(For door sizes see door schedule)
GLASS
SOLID PANEL
A
B
C
D
TOP RAIL & STILES
MIDDLE RAIL
BOTTOM RAIL
MEETING STILES
(DOUBLE DOORS)
6mm G.W.G. bedded as U.12, U.25 (unless otherwise specified on door schedule)
Galvanised m.s. c/sk screws 6 s.g. x 38mm at 200mm c/c.
9mm asbestolux panel.
Weld
20x12mm m.s flat welded to 50x3mm m.s flat, all drilled with 4mm dia. holes at 200mm c/c.
DETAIL. 'X'
(Glass and loose bead omitted for clarity)
VIEW 'X'
20x12mm m.s. flat glazing bead (mitred at corners) with 4mm dia. holes for screws.
℄ of double doors
NOTE: Rebate to be handed if reqd.
F.F.L.
Departmental Standard Drawing
title
EXTERNAL 1/2 HOUR FIRE FRAMED DOOR.
OUTWARD OPENING.
WITHOUT THRESHOLD.
scale
1:1 1:50
GP
drawing no
D.3285
rev
bldg type
space use
element
21
feature
material
key
281179

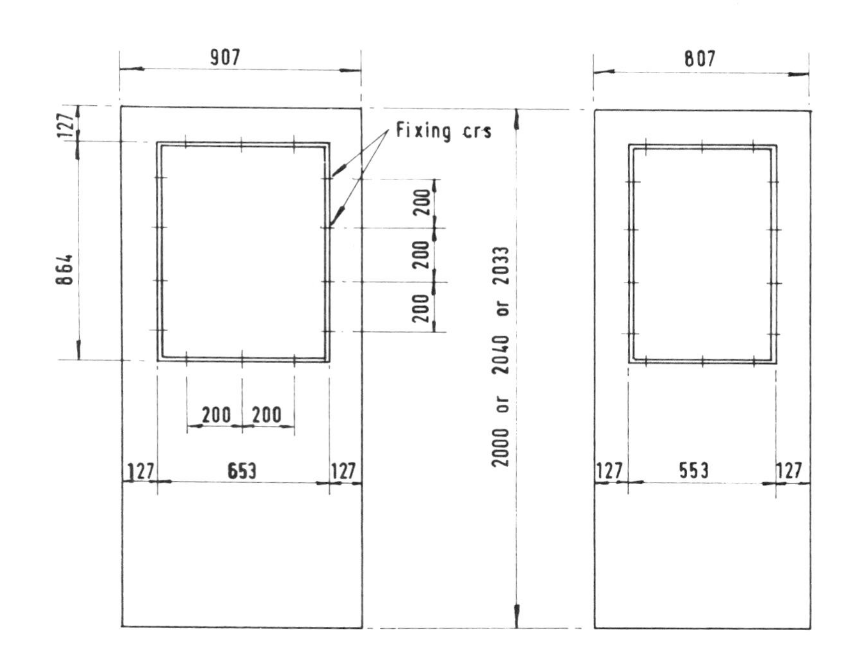

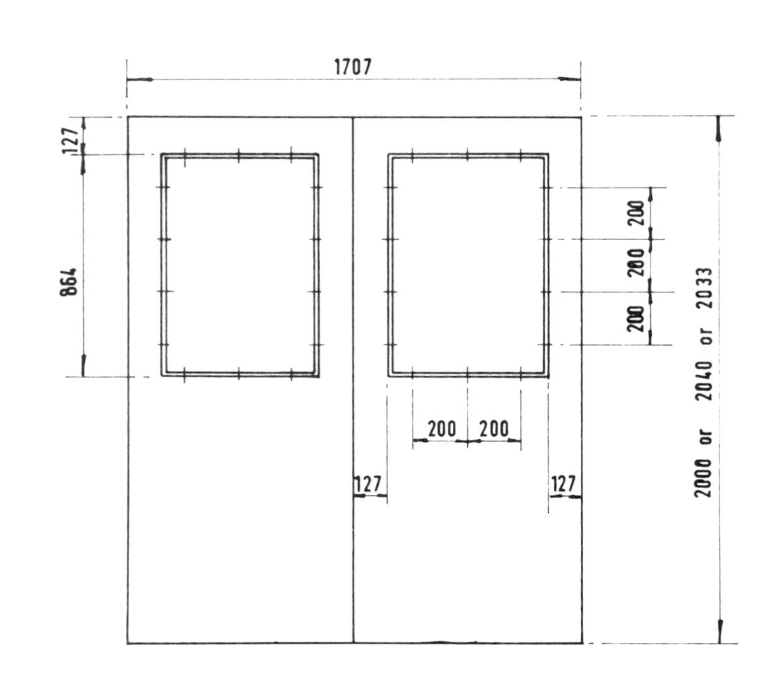

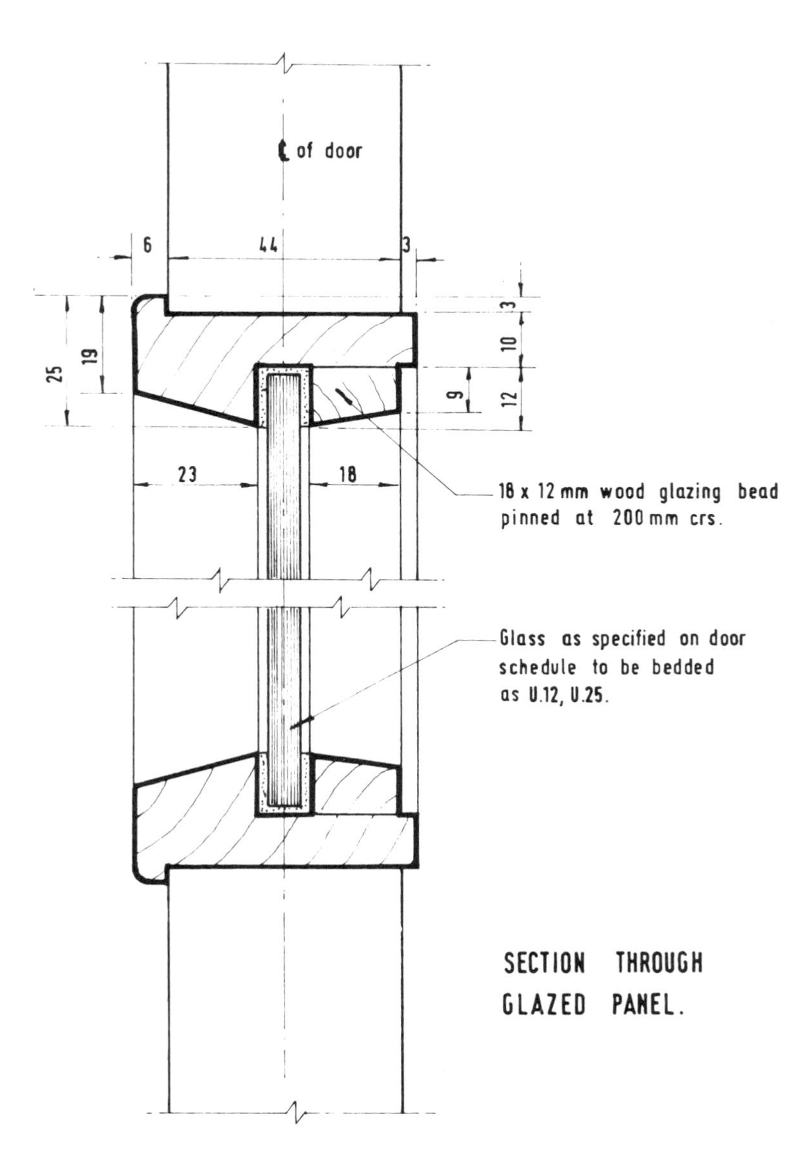

SECTION THROUGH GLAZED PANEL.

GLC ILEA

Department of Architecture and Civic Design
County Hall SE1 7PB
Architect Sir Roger Walters
KBE ARIBA FI Struct/E

References following notes are clause numbers from G.L.C. preambles to bills of quantities

Departmental Standard Drawing

title
EXTERNAL NORMAL FLUSH DOORS.
DETAILS OF DOOR GLASS PANELS AND BEADS.

scale
1 : 20 1 : 1.

	drawing no	rev
GP	D. 3275.	

220878 00-010379

bldg type	space use	element	feature	material	key
		[21]			

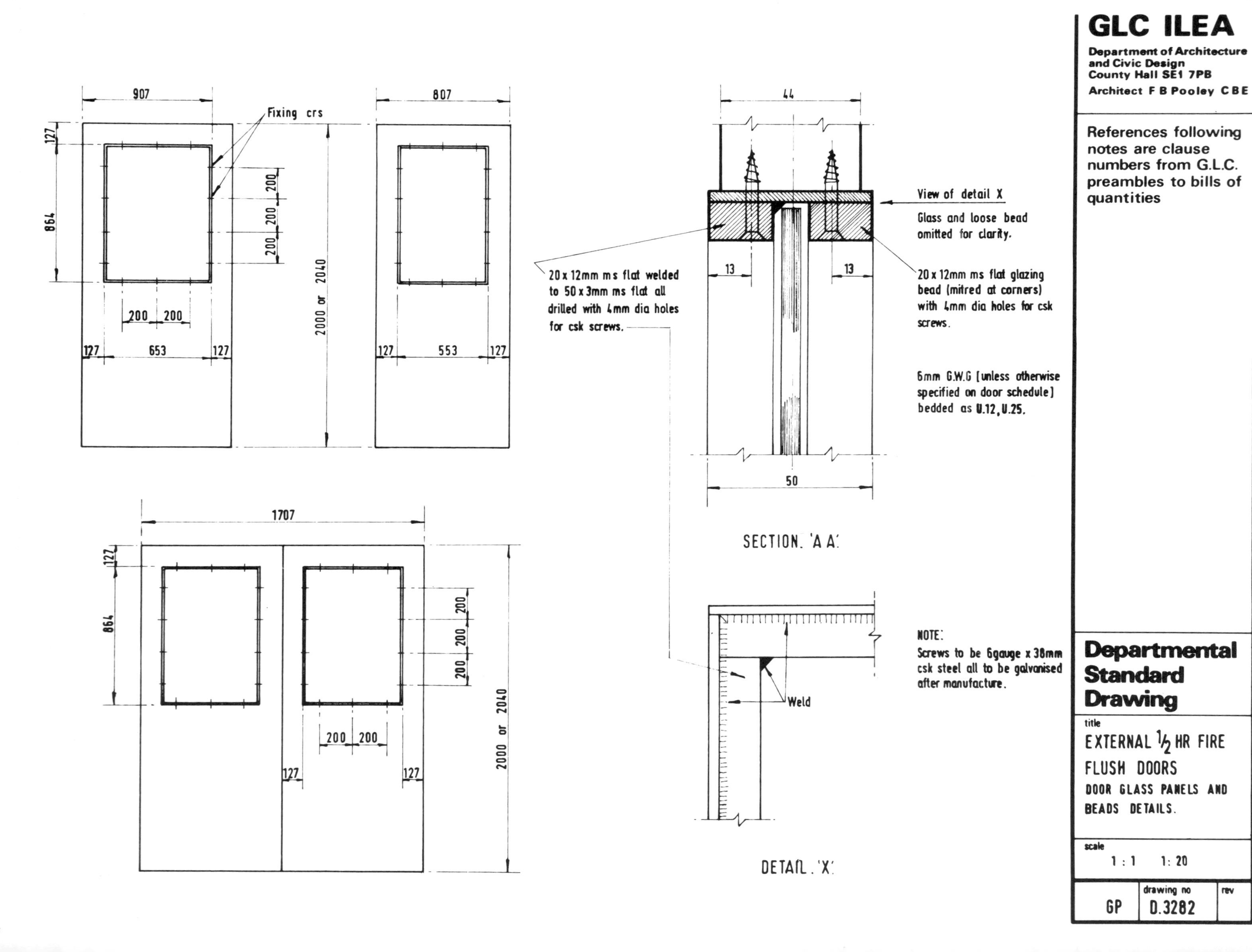

GLC ILEA
Department of Architecture and Civic Design
County Hall SE1 7PB
Architect F B Pooley CBE
References following notes are clause numbers from G.L.C. preambles to bills of quantities
907
807
Fixing crs
127
864
200
200
200
2000 or 2040
200 200
127 653 127
127 553 127
1707
44
View of detail X
Glass and loose bead omitted for clarity.
20 x 12mm ms flat welded to 50 x 3mm ms flat all drilled with 4mm dia holes for csk screws.
13
13
20 x 12mm ms flat glazing bead (mitred at corners) with 4mm dia holes for csk screws.
6mm G.W.G (unless otherwise specified on door schedule) bedded as U.12, U.25.
50
SECTION. 'A A'
NOTE:
Screws to be 6gauge x 38mm csk steel all to be galvanised after manufacture.
Weld
DETAIL. 'X'
Departmental Standard Drawing
title
EXTERNAL ½ HR FIRE FLUSH DOORS
DOOR GLASS PANELS AND BEADS DETAILS.
scale
1 : 1 1: 20
drawing no
rev
GP
D.3282
21
00 - 010379

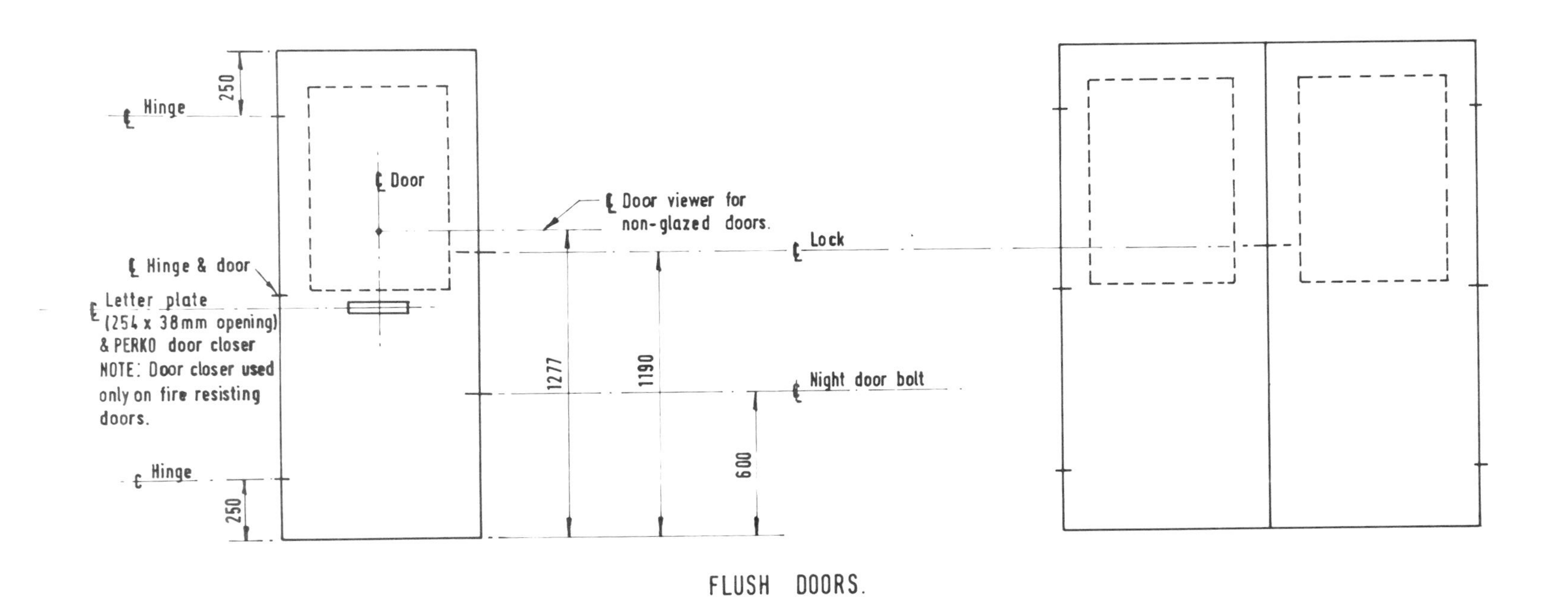

FLUSH DOORS.

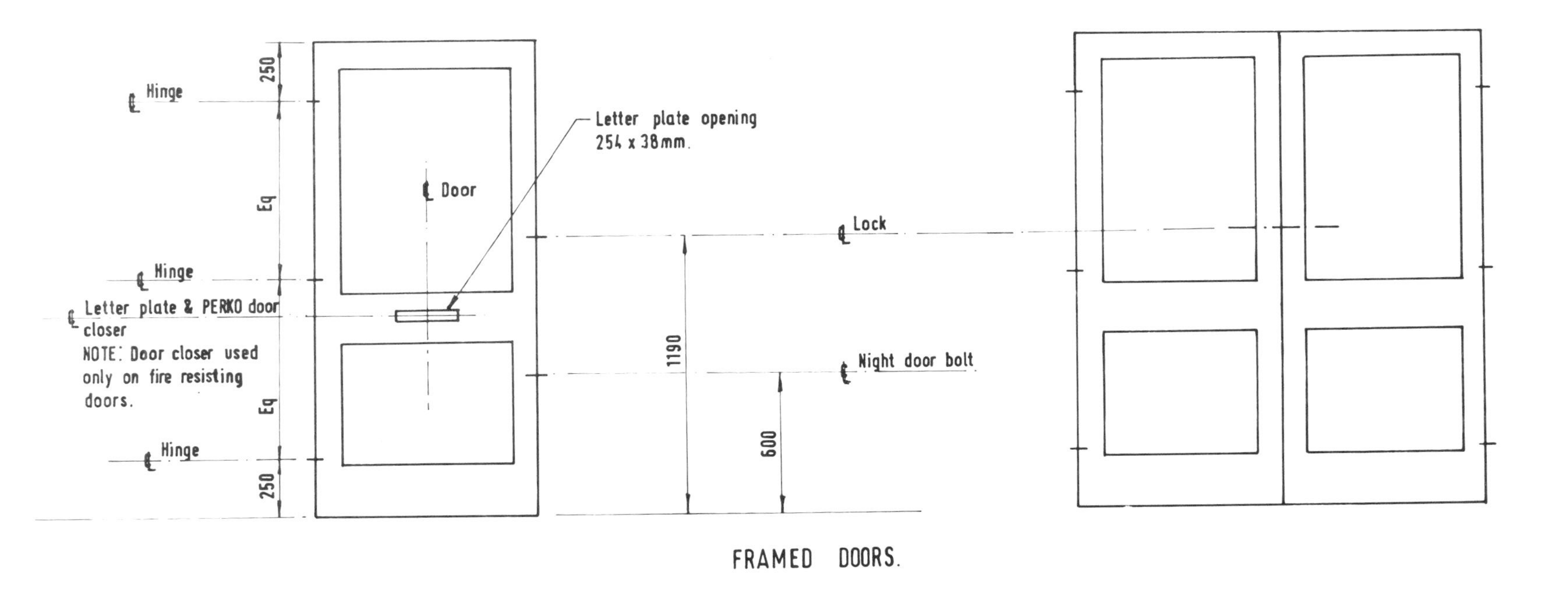

FRAMED DOORS.

GLC ILEA
Department of Architecture and Civic Design
County Hall SE1 7PB
Architect F B Pooley CBE

References following notes are clause numbers from G.L.C. preambles to bills of quantities

Bolts on double doors to be fixed according to type and architects instructions.

For postal plate details see D.3029.

Additional items of ironmongery if required to be fixed according to architects instructions.

Departmental Standard Drawing

title
EXTERNAL DOORS
IRONMONGERY.

scale 1 : 20

GP | drawing no D.3273 | rev

00 - 010379

bldg type | space use | element [21] | feature | material | key

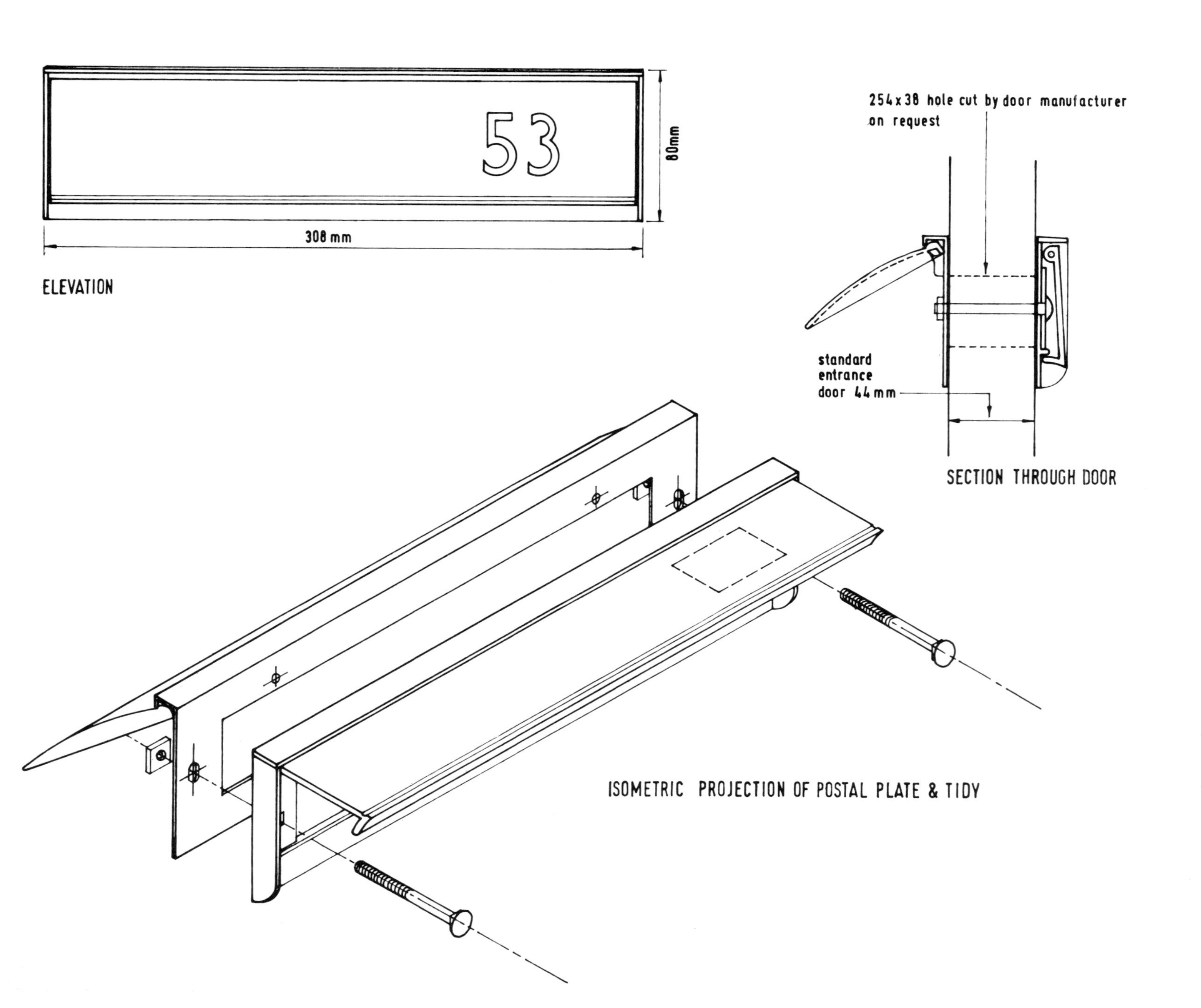

GLC ILEA

Department of Architecture
and Civic Design
County Hall SE1

Architect Sir Roger Walters
KBE FRIBA FI Struct E

References following notes are clause numbers from G.L.C. preambles to bills of quantities.

Ironmongery N.S.I. item 93a

For position of postal plate in door see D.3273.

Departmental Standard Drawing

title

STANDARD POSTAL PLATE FOR HOUSING

scale

1:2

drawing no

D 3029A

8 | 21 | 204 | Xi2

00 - 010379

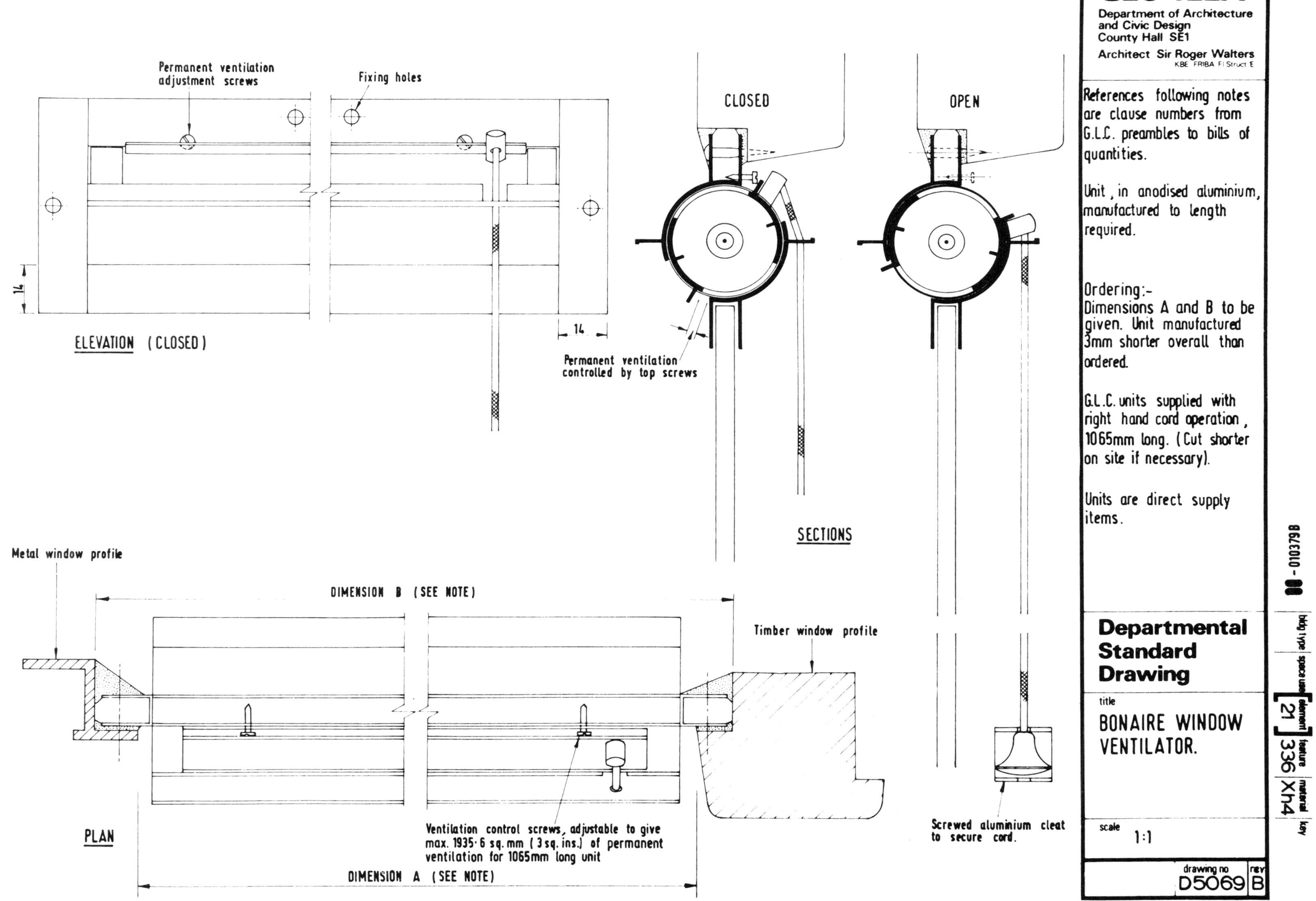
Permanent ventilation
adjustment screws
Fixing holes
14
14
ELEVATION (CLOSED)
CLOSED
OPEN
Permanent ventilation
controlled by top screws
SECTIONS
Metal window profile
DIMENSION B (SEE NOTE)
Timber window profile
PLAN
Ventilation control screws, adjustable to give
max. 1935·6 sq. mm (3 sq. ins.) of permanent
ventilation for 1065mm long unit
DIMENSION A (SEE NOTE)
Screwed aluminium cleat
to secure cord.
GLC ILEA
Department of Architecture
and Civic Design
County Hall SE1
Architect Sir Roger Walters
KBE FRIBA FIStructE
References following notes
are clause numbers from
G.L.C. preambles to bills of
quantities.
Unit, in anodised aluminium,
manufactured to length
required.
Ordering:-
Dimensions A and B to be
given. Unit manufactured
3mm shorter overall than
ordered.
G.L.C. units supplied with
right hand cord operation,
1065mm long. (Cut shorter
on site if necessary).
Units are direct supply
items.
Departmental
Standard
Drawing
title
BONAIRE WINDOW
VENTILATOR.
scale
1:1
drawing no
D5069
rev
B
0103798
bldg type
space use
element
21
feature
336
material
Xh4
key

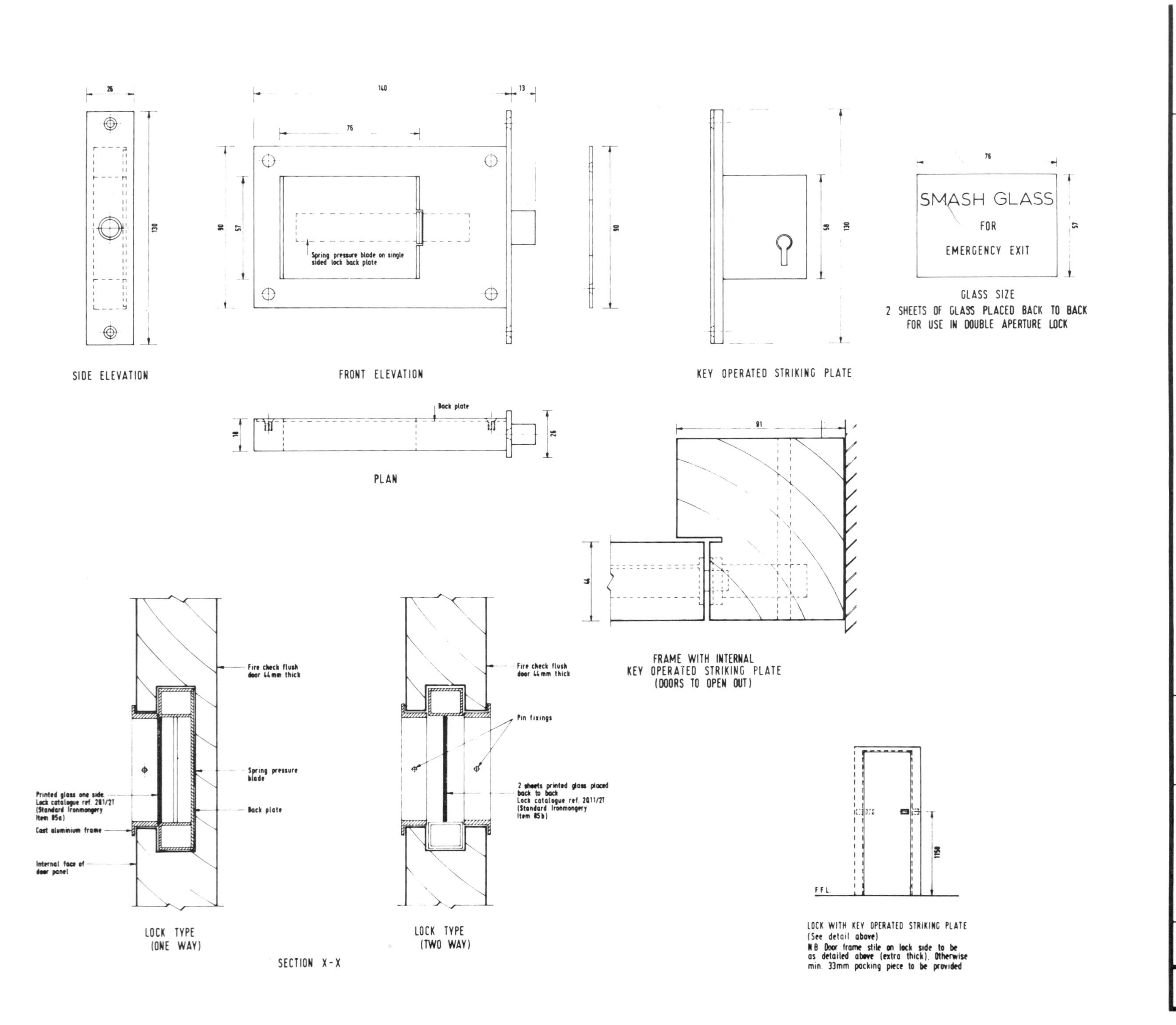

GLC ILEA

Department of Architecture
and Civic Design
County Hall SE1

Architect Sir Roger Walters
KBE FRIBA FI Struct E

References following notes are clause numbers from G.L.C preambles to bills of quantities

Lock supplied with printed glass, frame and key operated striking plate

Where access required (for window cleaning, etc) tenant to be issued with key

Departmental Standard Drawing

title

EMERGENCY EXIT
LOCK DETAILS

scale

1 : 1

drawing no	rev.
D3172	C

[21] 204 Xh2

Internal Details

Contents

1 Internal doors

2051 Normal flush door range
2053 Normal flush door with threshold range
2054 FR flush door with threshold range
2061 FR flush door range
3251 Normal, flush, no fanlight, details
3252 Normal, flush, with fanlight, details
3253 Normal, flush, OP sanitary spaces, without fanlight
3254 Normal, flush, OP sanitary spaces, with fanlight
3247 Normal, flush, with threshold, no fanlight details
3248 Normal, flush, with threshold, with fanlight details
3249 Normal, flush, OP sanitary spaces, with threshold, no fanlight, details
3250 Normal, flush, OP sanitary spaces, with threshold, with fanlight, details
3255 Normal, flush, glazed panel details
3261 FR flush, no fanlight details
3262 FR flush, with fanlight details
3266 FR flush, with threshold, no fanlight details
3267 FR flush, with threshold, with fanlight details
3263 FR flush glazing beads details
3010 OP sanitary space, door pivot, detail
5110 Vents for bathroom doors
3264 Flush door ironmongery position
5370 Normal jamb details 50mm partition
5371 Normal head details 50 and 75mm partitions
5372 Normal jamb details 75mm partition
5373 Normal jamb details solid walls
5374 Normal head details solid walls
5365 Normal and FR cill details 50 and 75mm partitions
5363 FR jamb details 50mm partition
5364 FR head details 50mm partition
5366 FR jamb details 75mm partition
5367 FR head details 75mm partition
5368 FR jamb details solid walls
5369 FR head details solid walls
6010 Door schedule

WITHOUT FANLIGHT.

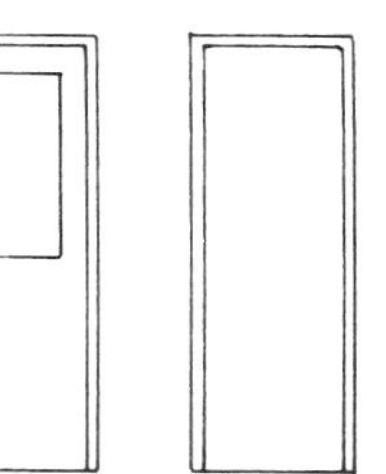
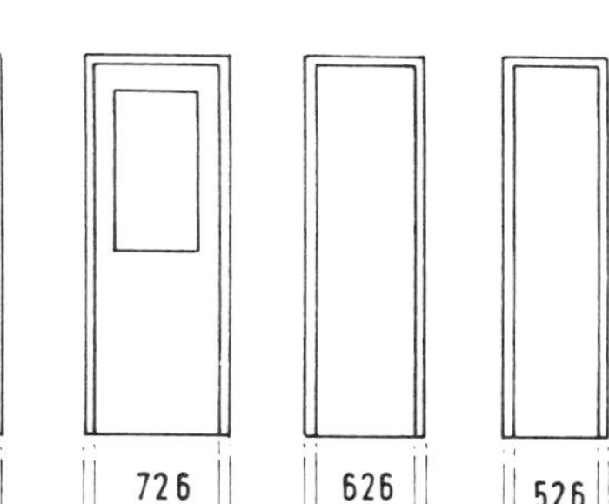
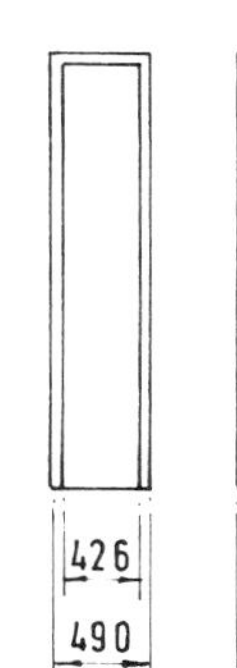
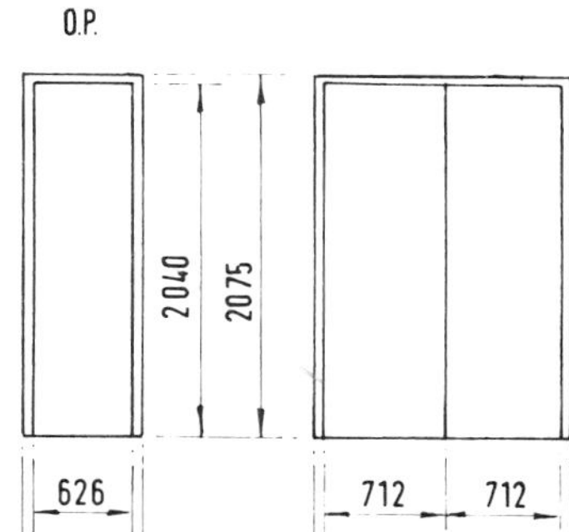
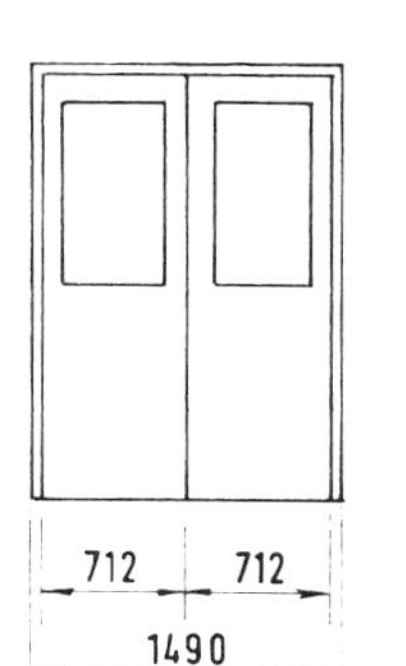
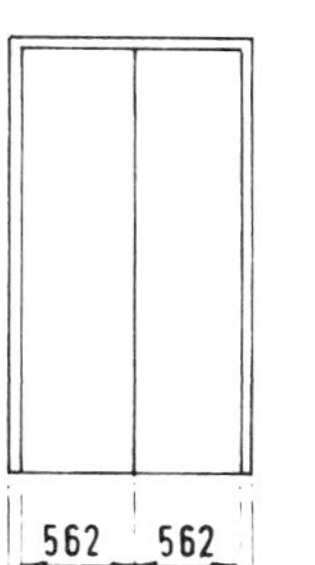
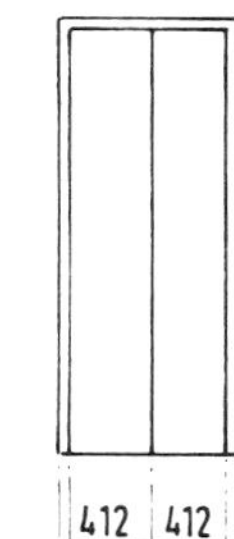
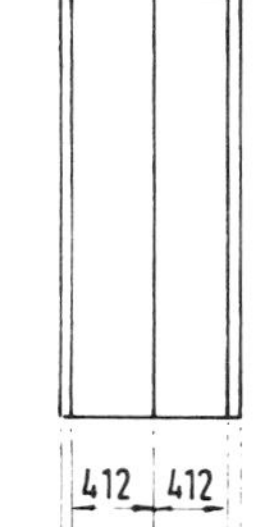

FRAME DEPTH. (mm)	FRAME & DOOR DETAILS.	O.P. DOOR.
	DRG. N°	DRG. N°
66	D. 3251.	D. 3253.

NOTE.— Job architect to specify the following on the door schedule:

a. Frame and door details drg. no. from table.
b. Height, width and depth of door frame.
c. Height, width, thickness and facing of door.
d. Door glass panel and beads (890; 790 and 1490 doorsets only) if required. see D. 3255.

WITH FANLIGHT.

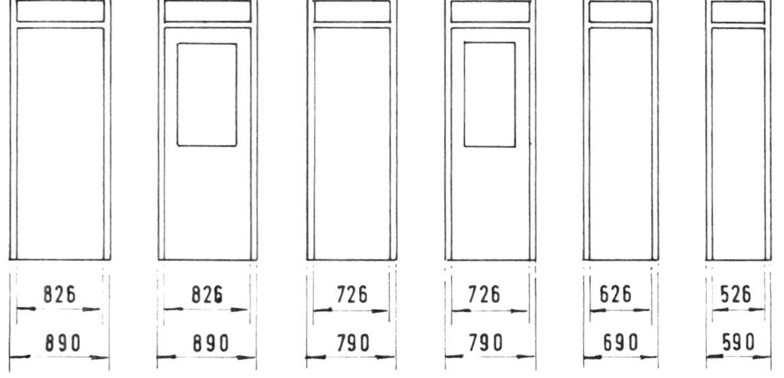
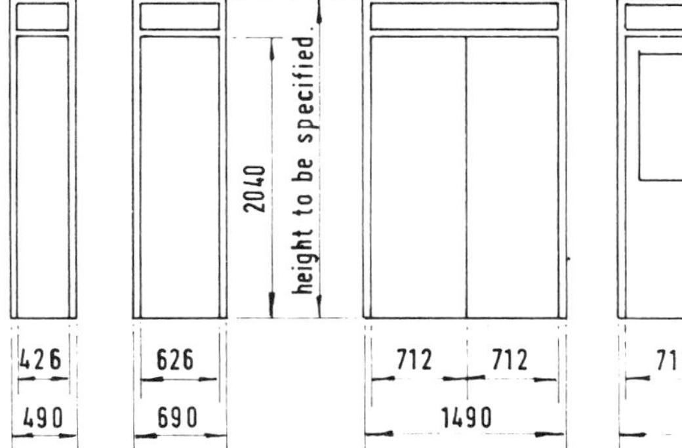
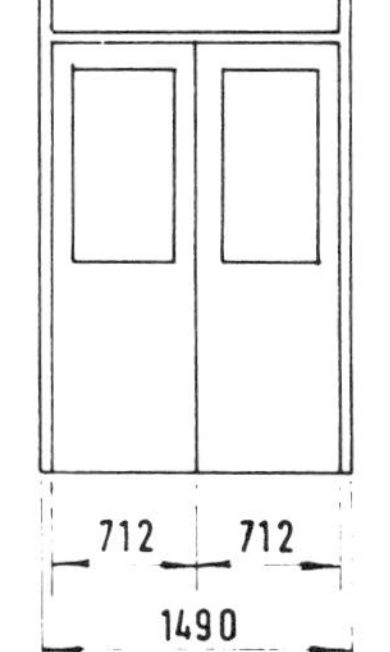
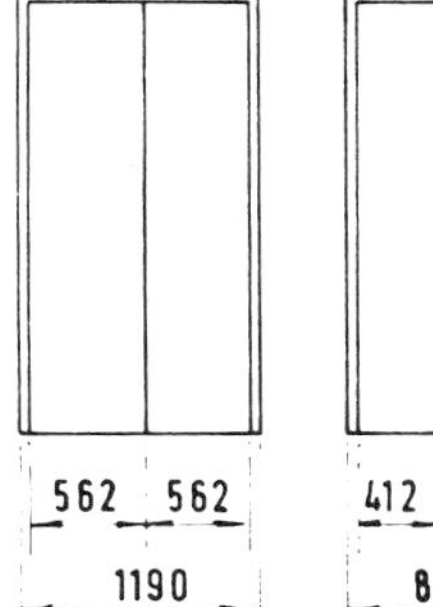

FRAME DEPTH. (mm)	FRAME & DOOR DETAILS.	O.P. DOOR.
	DRG. N°	DRG. N°
66	D. 3252.	D. 3254.

NOTE. Job architect to specify the following on the door schedule:

a. Frame and door details drg. no. from table.
b. Height, width and depth of door.
c. Fanlight panel (see doorset detail drawing.)
d. Height, width, thickness and facing of door.
e. Door glass panel and beads (890; 790 and 1490 doorsets only) if required see D. 3255.

GLC ILEA

Department of Architecture and Civic Design
County Hall SE1 7PB
Architect Sir Roger Walters KBE ARIBA FI Struct/E

References following notes are clause numbers from G.L.C. preambles to bills of quantities

Doors (not frames) are direct supply items.

All doors are 40mm thick and plywood or hardboard faced.

O.P. doors to be used in O.P. sanitary spaces.

For reference to relevant building-in details see notes on doorset detail D. 3251 or D. 3252.

All dimensions are worksizes.

Structural openings as shown on working drawings.

Departmental Standard Drawing

title

INTERNAL NORMAL FLUSH DOORSET RANGE.

scale 1 : 50.

GP | drawing no D. 2051. | rev

210678 00-010379

bldg type | space use | element [22] | feature | material | key

WITHOUT FANLIGHT

O.P.

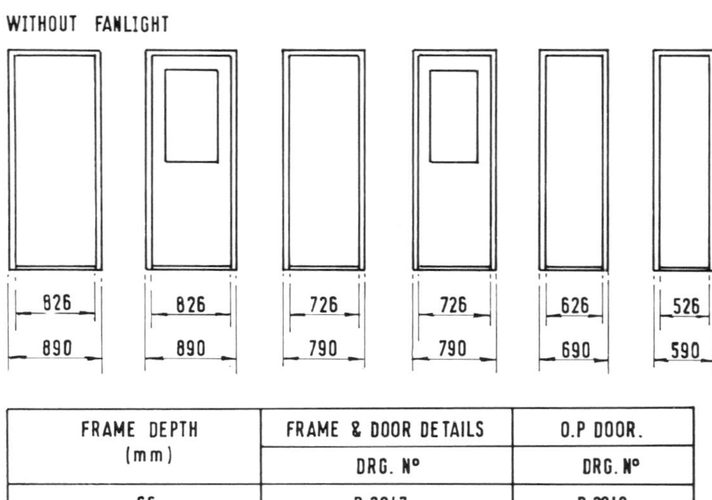

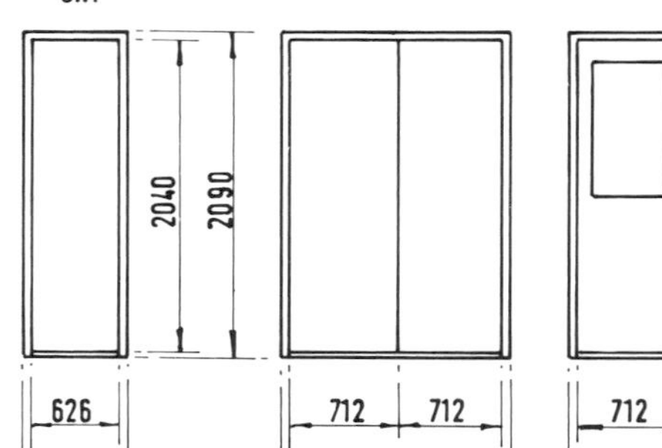

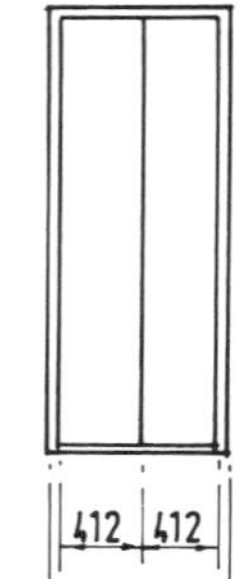

FRAME DEPTH (mm)	FRAME & DOOR DETAILS	O.P DOOR.
	DRG. N°	DRG. N°
66	D.3247	D.3249

NOTE: Job architect to specify the following on the door schedule:

a. Frame and door details drg. no. from table.
b. Height, width and depth of door frame.
c. Height, width, thickness and facing of door.
d. Door glass panel and beads (890, 790 and 1490 doorsets only) if required; see D.3255.

WITH FANLIGHT

O.P.

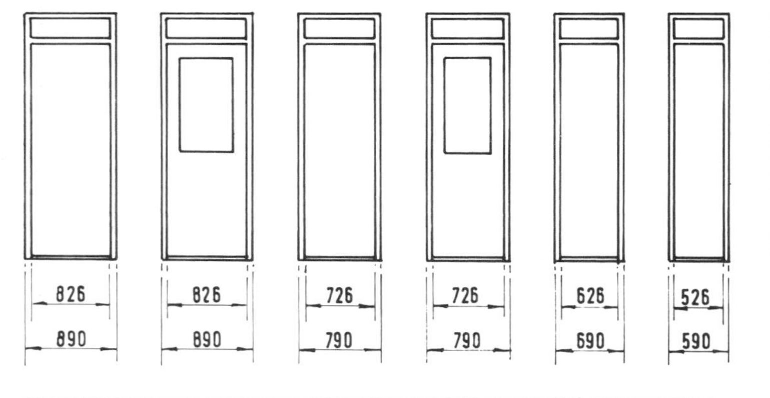

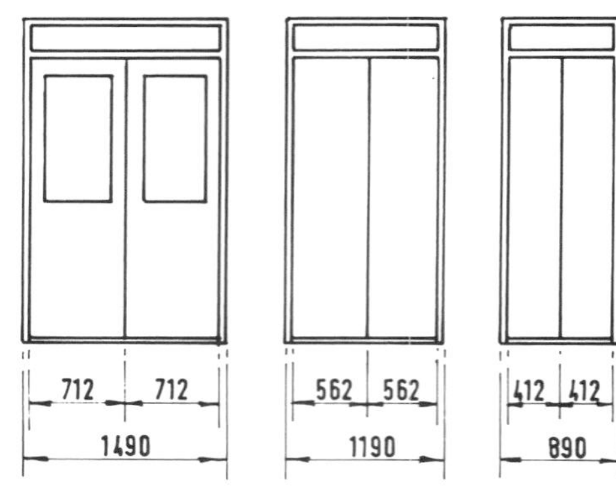

FRAME DEPTH (mm)	FRAME & DOOR DETAILS	O.P.DOOR.
	DRG N°	DRG N°
66	D.3248	D.3250

NOTE: Job architect to specify the following on the door schedule:

a. Frame and door details drg.no. from table.
b. Height, width and depth of door.
c Fanlight panel (see doorset detail drawing.)
d. Height, width, thickness and facing of door.
e. Door glass panel and beads (890, 790 and 1490 doorsets only) if required; see D.3255.

GLC ILEA

Department of Architecture and Civic Design
County Hall SE1 7PB
Architect F B Pooley CBE

References following notes are clause numbers from G.L.C. preambles to bills of quantities

Doors (not frames) are direct supply items.

All doors are 40mm thick and plywood or hardboard faced.

O.P doors to be used in O.P sanitary spaces.

For reference to relevant building-in details see notes on doorset detail D.3247 or D.3248.

All dimensions are work sizes.

Structural openings as shown on working drawings.

Departmental Standard Drawing

title

INTERNAL NORMAL FLUSH DOORSET RANGE.
WITH THRESHOLD.

scale 1 : 50

	drawing no	rev
GP	D.2053.	

22

270180

WITHOUT FANLIGHT.

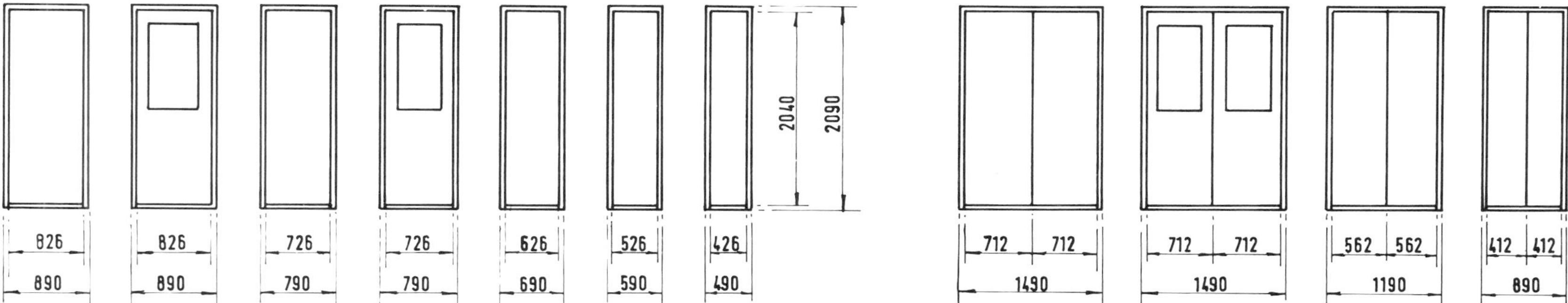

FRAME DEPTH (mm)	FRAME & DOOR DETAILS. DRG N°
81	D.3266

NOTE: Job architect to specify the following on the door schedule:

a. Doorset detail drg no. from table.
b. Height, width and depth of door frame.
c. Height, width, thickness and facing of door.
d. Door glass panel and beads (790, 890 and 1490 doorsets only) if required; see drg D.3263 detail X.1 or X.2.

WITH FANLIGHT.

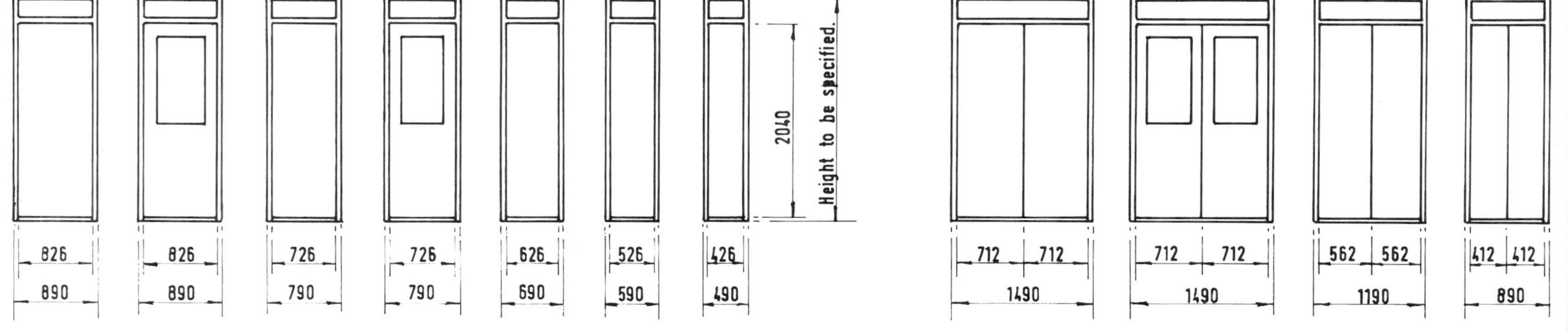

FRAME DEPTH. (mm)	FRAME & DOOR DETAILS. DRG N°
81	D.3267

NOTE: Job architect to specify the following on the door schedule:

a. Doorset detail drg no. from table.
b. Height, width and depth of door frame.
c. Fanlight panel (see doorset detail drawing.)
d. Height, width, thickness and facing of door.
e. Door glass panel and beads (790, 890 and 1490 doorsets only) if required; see drg D.3263 detail X1 or X2.

GLC ILEA

Department of Architecture and Civic Design
County Hall SE1 7PB
Architect F B Pooley CBE

References following notes are clause numbers from G.L.C. preambles to bills of quantities

All doors are 44 mm thick and plywood or hardboard faced.

For reference to relevant building in details see notes on doorset detail D.3266 or D.3267.

All dimensions are work sizes.

Brick openings as shown on working drawings.

08Z010 - ■

bldgtype | spaceuse | element [22] | feature | material | key

Departmental Standard Drawing

title
INTERNAL 1/2 HOUR FIRE FLUSH DOORSET RANGE.
WITH THRESHOLD.

scale
1 : 50

GP | drawing no D.2054 | rev

GLC ILEA

Department of Architecture and Civic Design
County Hall SE1 7PB
Architect Sir Roger Walters
KBE ARIBA FI Struct/E

References following notes are clause numbers from G.L.C. preambles to bills of quantities

All doors are 44 mm thick and plywood or hardboard faced.
For reference to relevant building-in details see notes on doorset detail. D. 3261 or D. 3262.
All dimensions are work sizes.
Brick openings as shown on working drawings.

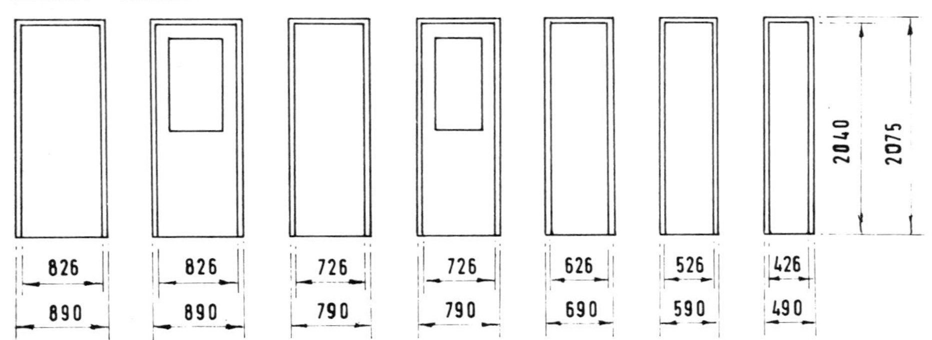

712 712
1490
712 712
1490
562 562
1190
412 412
890

FRAME DEPTH. (mm)	FRAME & DOOR DETAILS.
	DRG N°
81	D. 3261.

NOTE.— Job architect to specify the following on the door schedule:

a. Doorset detail drg no. from table.
b. Height, width and depth of door frame.
c. Height, width, thickness and facing of door.
d. Door glass panel and beads (790, 890 and 1490 doorsets only) if required see drg D.3263 detail X.1 or X.2.

WITH FANLIGHT.

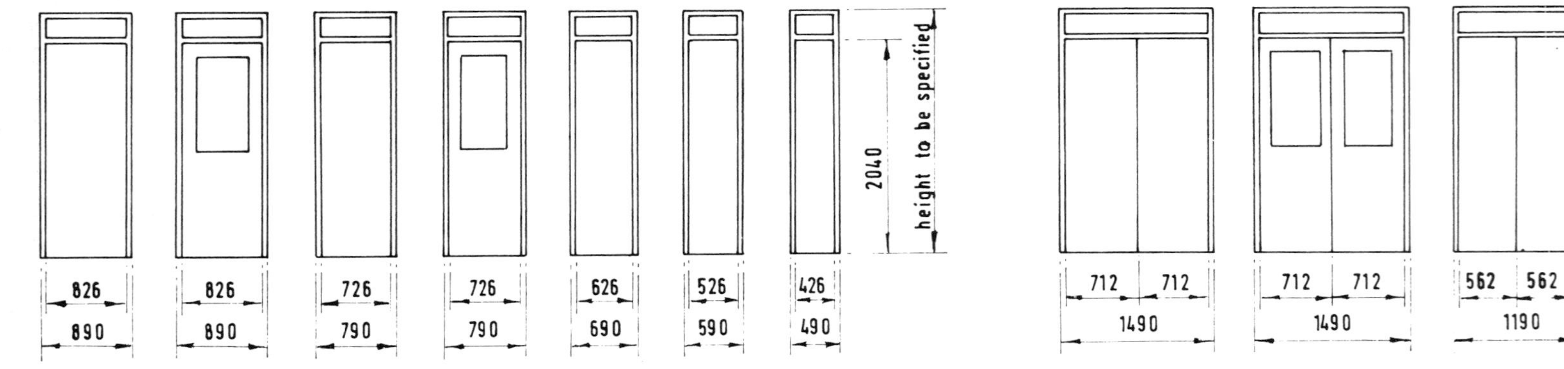

712 712
1490
712 712
1490
562 562
1190
412 412
890

FRAME DEPTH. (mm)	FRAME & DOOR DETAILS.
	DRG N°
81	D. 3262

NOTE.— Job architect to specify the following on the door schedule:

a. Doorset detail drg no. from table.
b. Height, width and depth of door frame.
c. Fanlight panel. (see doorset detail drawing.)
d. Height, width, thickness and facing of door.
e. Door glass panel and beads (890, 790 and 1490 doorsets only) if required see drg D.3263 detail X1 or X2.

Departmental Standard Drawing

title
INTERNAL 1/2 HOUR FIRE FLUSH DOORSET RANGE.

scale
1 : 50.

GP | drawing no D.2061. | rev

22

170578 -010379

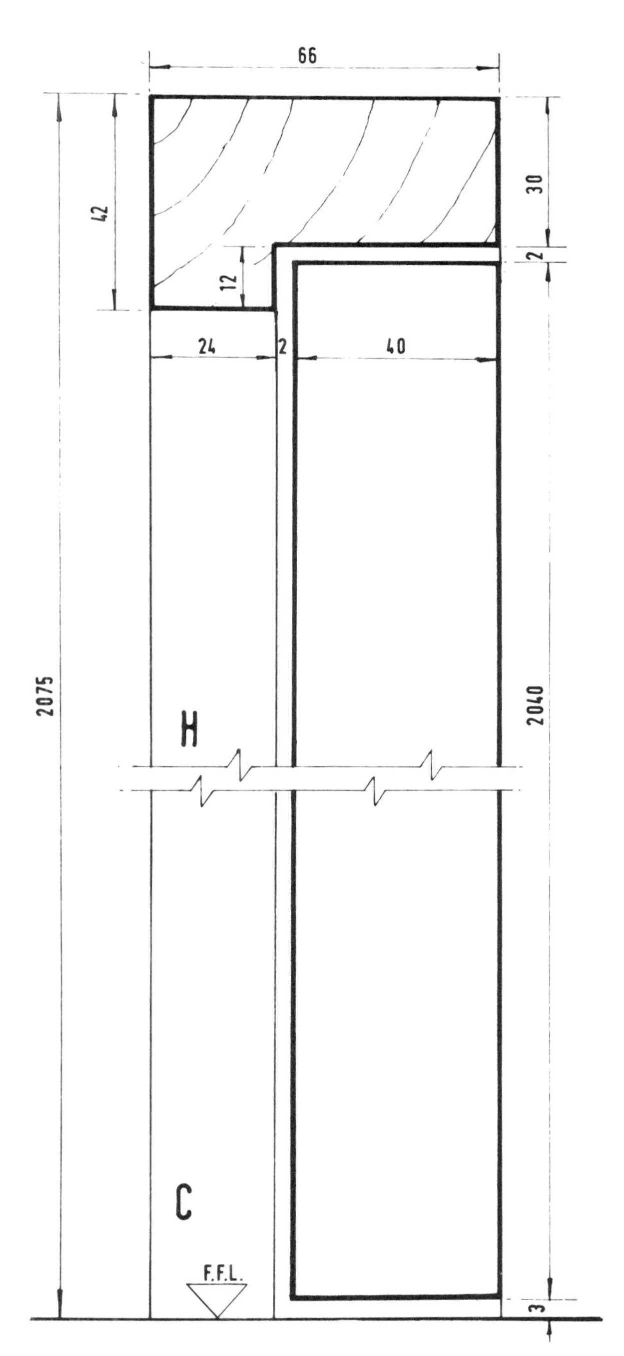

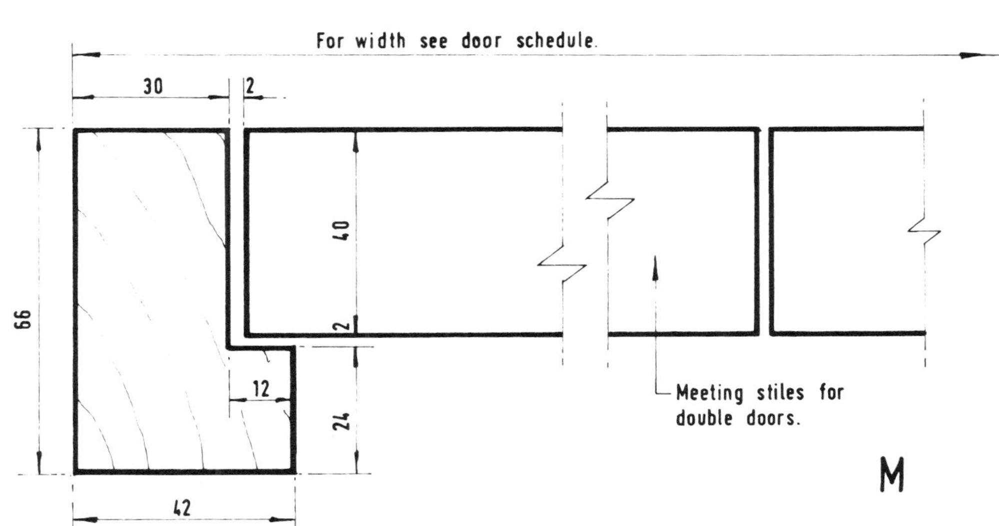

M

GLC ILEA

Department of Architecture and Civic Design
County Hall SE1 7PB
Architect Sir Roger Walters
KBE ARIBA FI Struct/E

References following notes are clause numbers from G.L.C. preambles to bills of quantities

To be read in conjunction with door schedule and job layouts.

Building-in details.

a. 50mm DRY PARTITION.
see D.5370; D.5371; D.5365.

b. 75mm DRY PARTITION.
see D.5371; D.5372; D.5365.

c. SOLID WALL.
see D.5373; D.5374.

For positioning of ironmongery see D.3264.

Doors only are direct supply items.

220678 - 010379

bldg type | space use | element 22 | feature | material | key

Departmental Standard Drawing

title
INTERNAL NORMAL FLUSH DOORSET DETAILS.
WITHOUT FANLIGHT.

scale
1 : 1.

GP | drawing no D. 3251. | rev

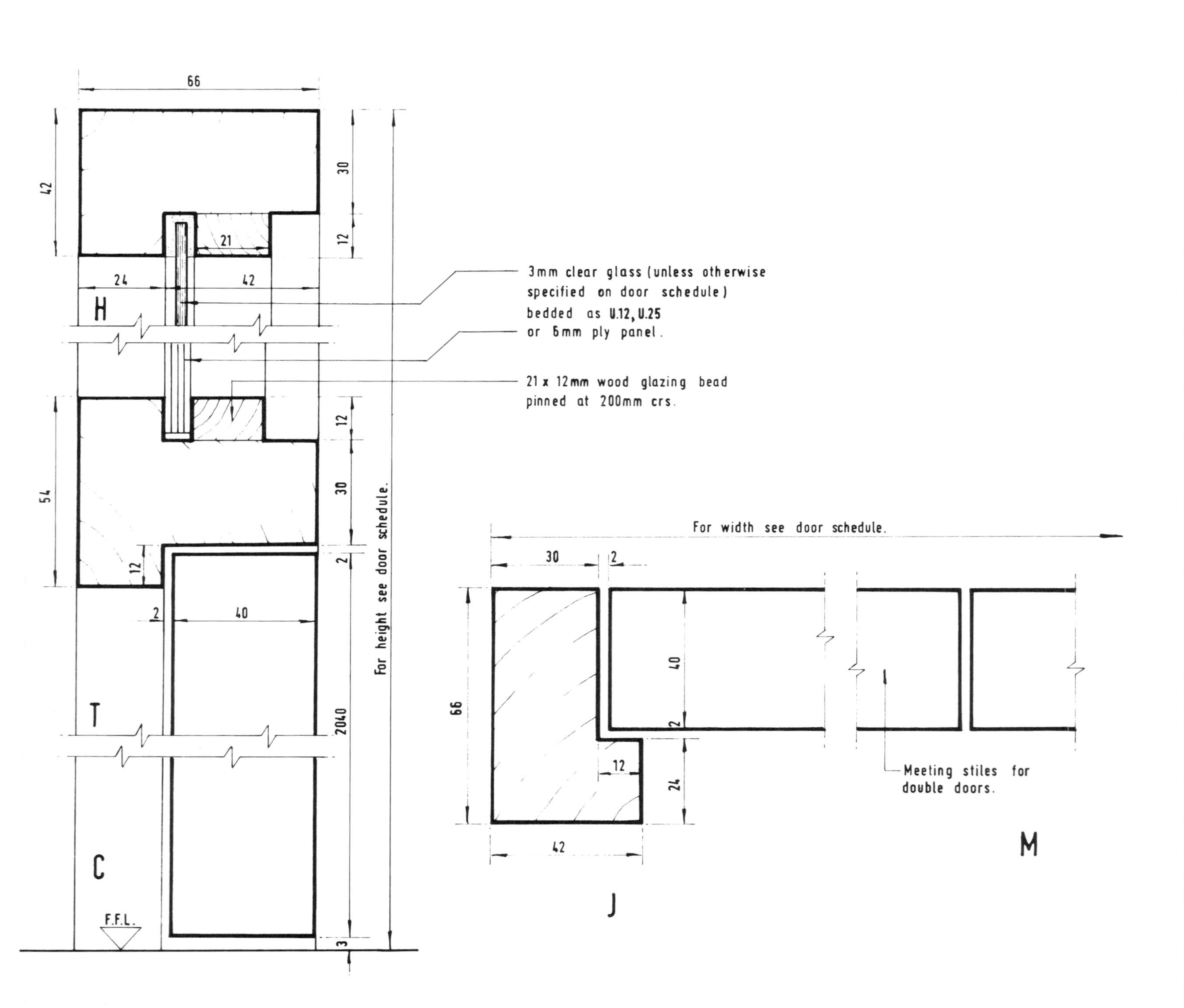

GLC ILEA

Department of Architecture and Civic Design
County Hall SE1 7PB
Architect Sir Roger Walters KBE ARIBA FI Struct/E

References following notes are clause numbers from G.L.C. preambles to bills of quantities

To be read in conjunction with door schedule and job layouts.

Building-in details.

a <u>50mm DRY PARTITION</u>. see D.5370; D.5371. J.5365.

b. <u>75mm DRY PARTITION</u>. see D.5372, D.5371, D.5365.

c. <u>SOLID WALL</u>. see D.5373, D.5374.

For positioning of ironmongery see D.3264.

Doors only are direct supply items.

Departmental Standard Drawing

title

INTERNAL NORMAL FLUSH DOORSET DETAIL.
WITH FANLIGHT.

scale

1 : 1.

	drawing no	rev
GP	D.3252.	

22

66

30

2

40

2040

2075

H

C

Trimmed on site to clear carpet.

F.F.L.

3

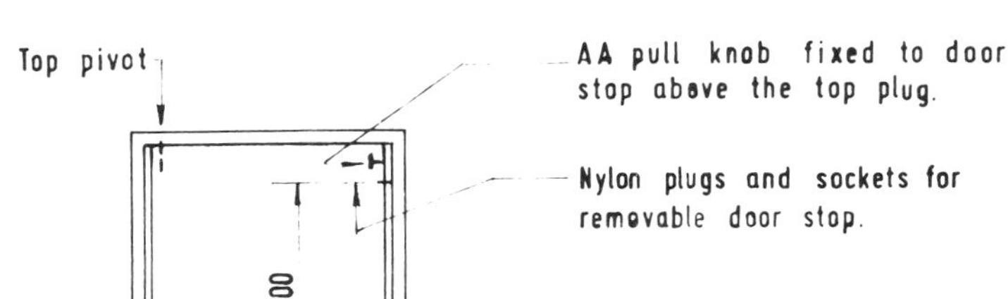

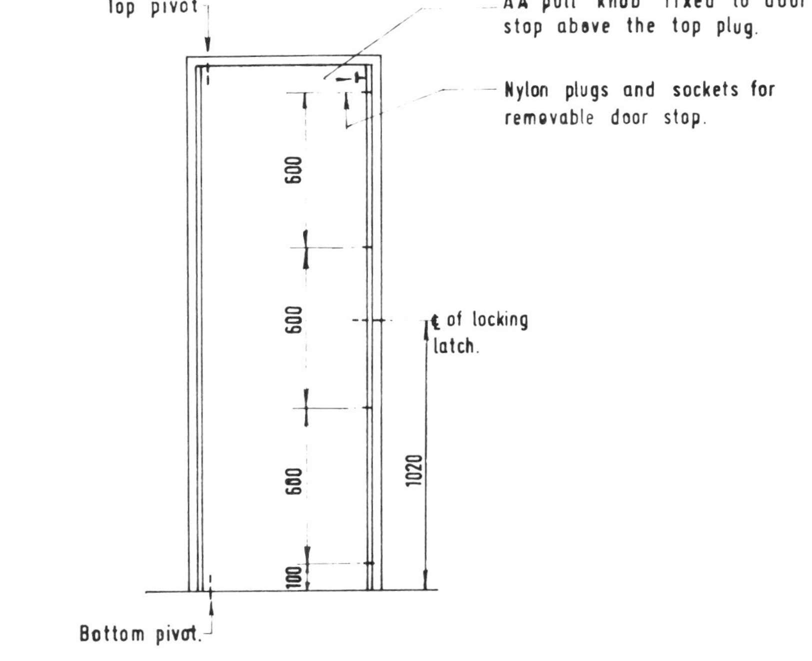

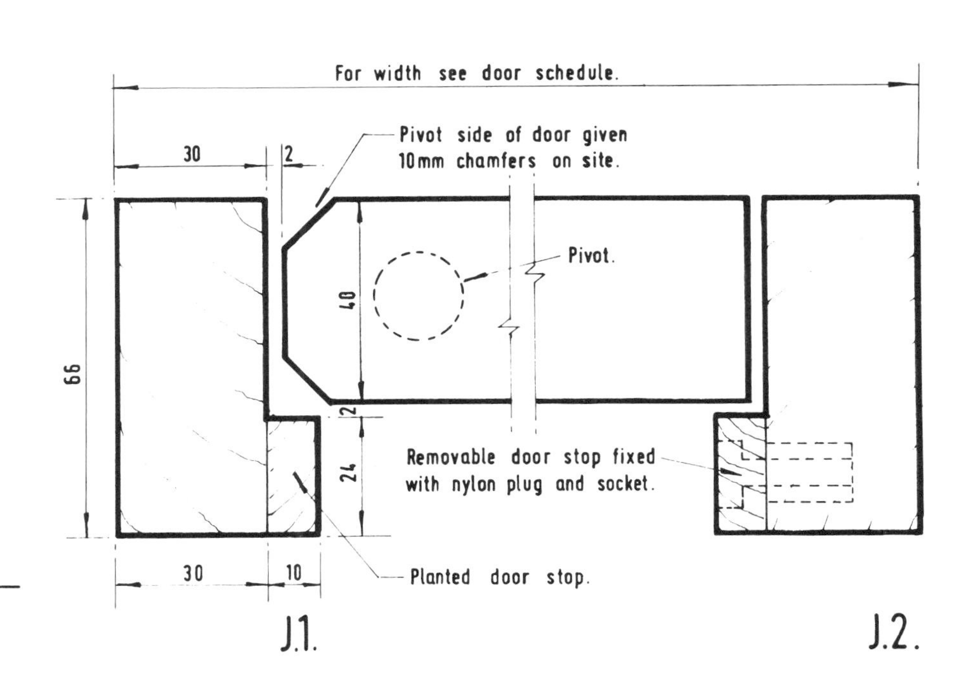

GLC ILEA

Department of Architecture and Civic Design
County Hall SE1 7PB
Architect Sir Roger Walters KBE ARIBA FI Struct/E

References following notes are clause numbers from G.L.C. preambles to bills of quantities

To be read in conjunction with door schedule and job layouts.

Building-in details.

a. 50mm DRY PARTITION. see D.5370, D.5371, D.5365.

b. 75mm DRY PARTITION. see D.5372, D.5371, D.5365.

c. SOLID WALL. see D.5373 D.5374.

For details of door pivot set see D. 3010.

For description of ironmongery see N.S.I. set F.

Doors only are direct supply items.

Departmental Standard Drawing

title

INTERNAL NORMAL FLUSH DOORSET DETAIL O.P SANITARY SPACES.

WITHOUT FANLIGHT.

scale

1 : 1. 1 : 20.

	drawing no	rev
GP	D.3253.	

feature

material

key

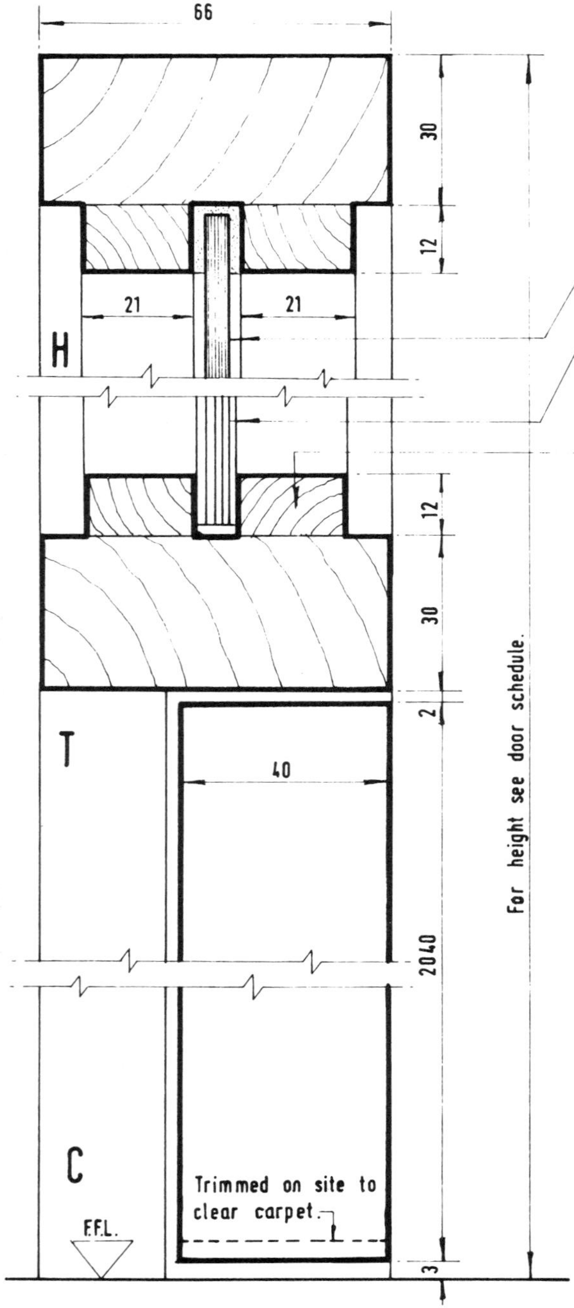

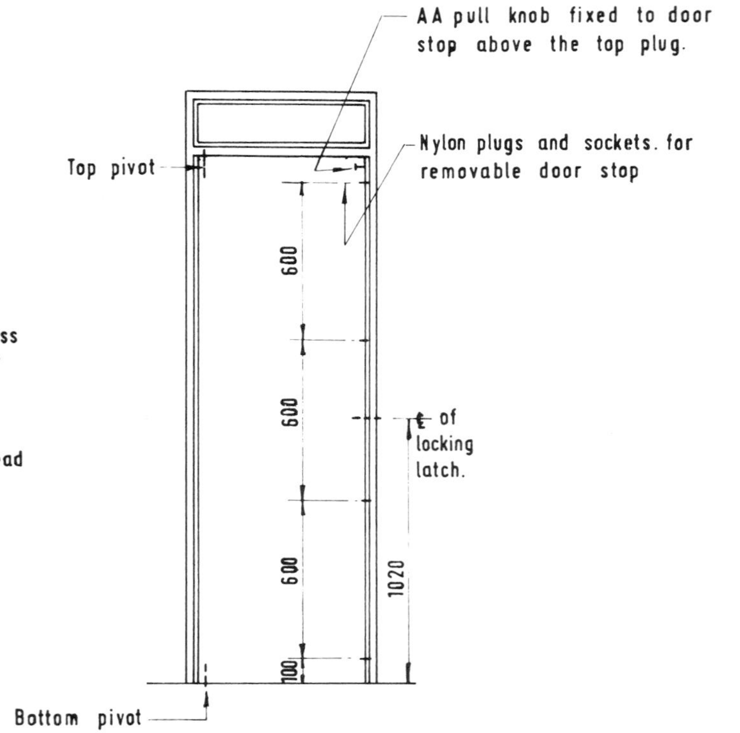

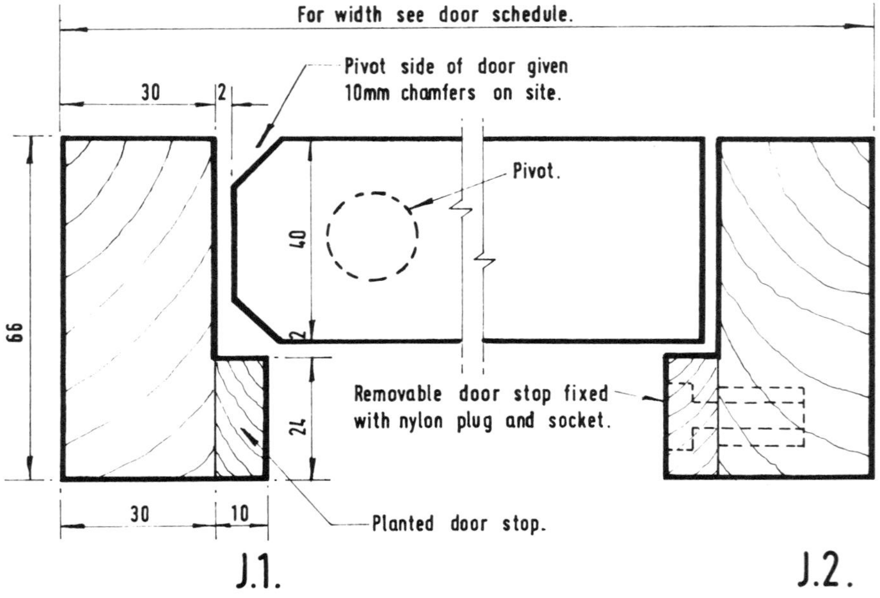

GLC ILEA

Department of Architecture and Civic Design
County Hall SE1 7PB
Architect Sir Roger Walters KBE ARIBA FI Struct/E

References following notes are clause numbers from G.L.C. preambles to bills of quantities

To be read in conjunction with door schedule and job layouts.

Building-in details.

a. 50mm DRY PARTITION. see D.5370; D.5371. D.5365.

b. 75mm DRY PARTITION. see D.5372; D.5371; D.5365.

c. SOLID WALL. see D.5373; D.5374.

For details of door pivot set see D.3010.

For description of ironmongery see N.S.I. set F.

Doors only are direct supply items.

Departmental Standard Drawing

title
INTERNAL NORMAL FLUSH DOORSET DETAIL. O.P. SANITARY SPACES. WITH FANLIGHT.

scale 1:1. 1:20.

GP | drawing no D.3254. | rev

66
30
12
21
21
H
3mm clear glass bedded as U.12; U.25 or
6mm plywood panel (unless otherwise specified on door schedule.)
21 x 12mm wood glazing bead pinned at 200mm crs.
12
30
2
T
40
For height see door schedule.
2040
C
Trimmed on site to clear carpet.
F.F.L.
3

AA pull knob fixed to door stop above the top plug.
Top pivot
Nylon plugs and sockets. for removable door stop
600
600
℄ of locking latch.
600
1020
100
Bottom pivot

For width see door schedule.
30
2
Pivot side of door given 10mm chamfers on site.
Pivot.
40
2
66
24
Removable door stop fixed with nylon plug and socket.
30
10
Planted door stop.
J.1.
J.2.

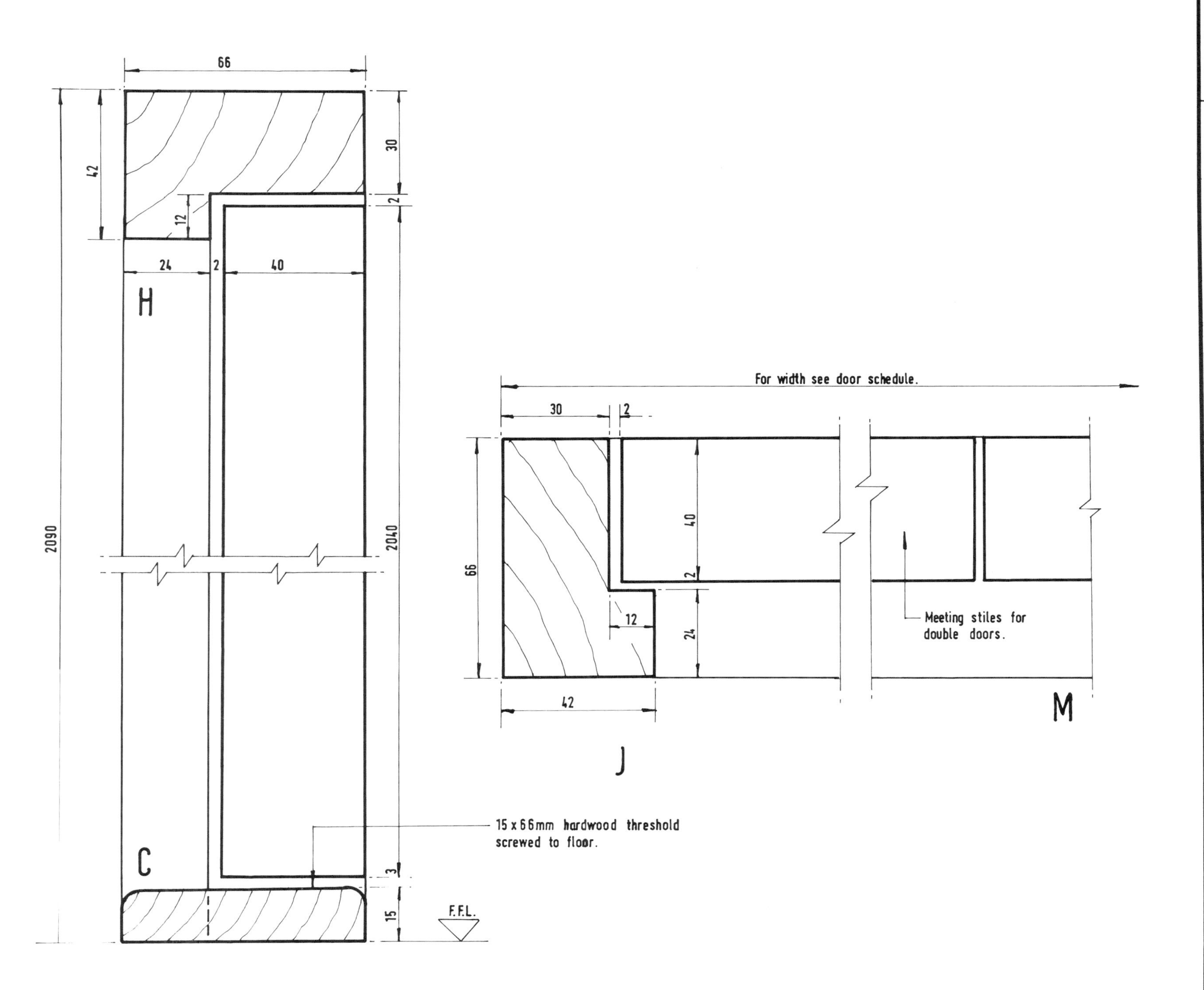

GLC ILEA

Department of Architecture
and Civic Design
County Hall SE1 7PB
Architect F B Pooley CBE

References following notes are clause numbers from G.L.C. preambles to bills of quantities

To be read in conjunction with door schedule and job layouts.

Building-in details.

a. 50mm DRY PARTITION.
see D.5370, D.5371, D.5365.

b. 75mm DRY PARTITION.
see D.5371, D.5372, D.5365.

c. SOLID WALL.
see D.5373, D.5374.

For positioning of ironmongery see D.3264.

Doors only are direct supply items.

Departmental Standard Drawing

title
INTERNAL NORMAL FLUSH DOORSET DETAILS.
WITHOUT FANLIGHT.
WITH THRESHOLD.

scale
1 : 1

	drawing no	rev
GP	D.3247	

0070~0280 | bldg type | space use | element [22] | feature | material | key

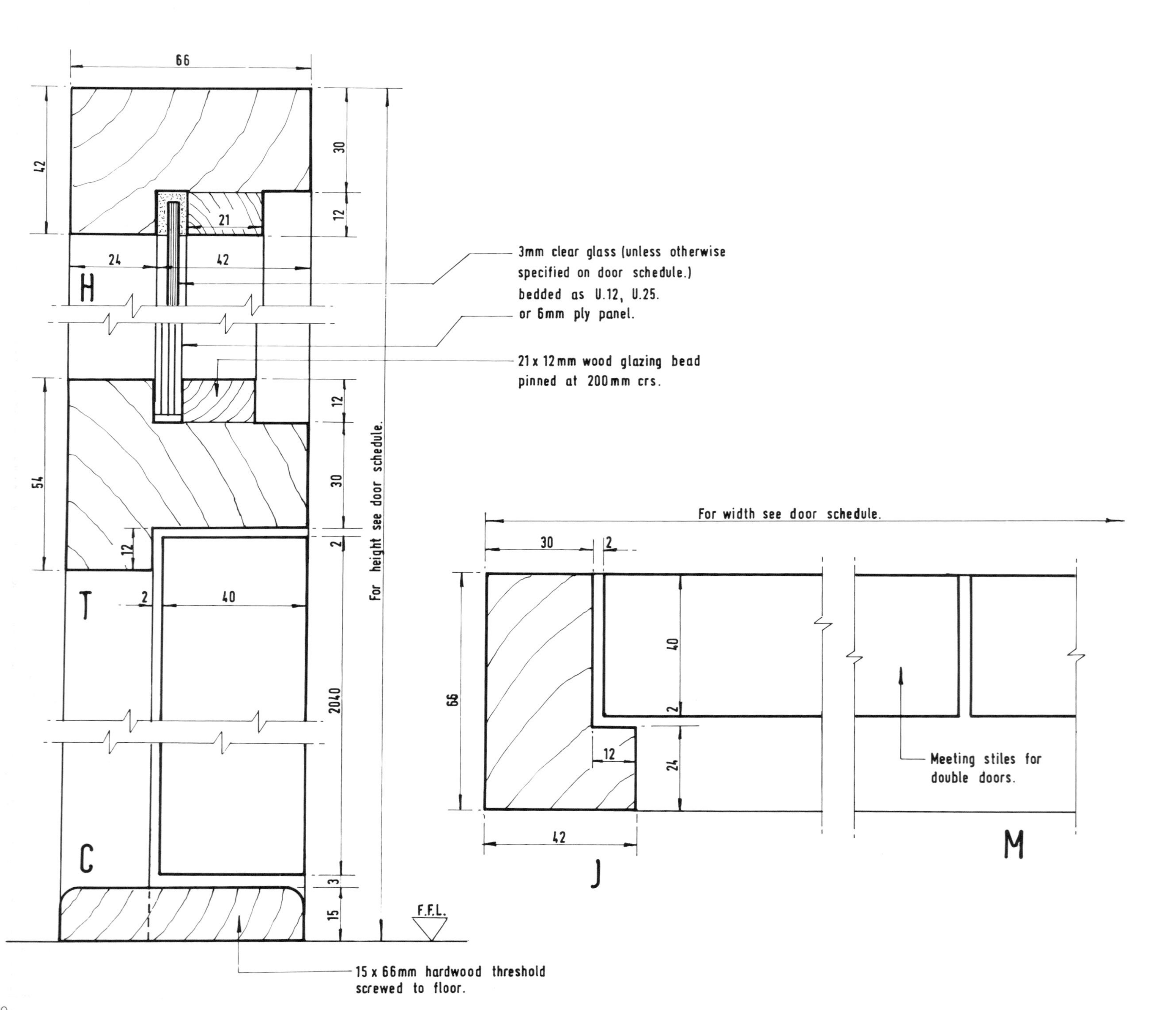

GLC ILEA

Department of Architecture and Civic Design
County Hall SE1 7PB
Architect F B Pooley CBE

References following notes are clause numbers from G.L.C. preambles to bills of quantities

To be read in conjunction with door schedule and job layouts.

Building - in details.

a. 50mm DRY PARTITION. see D.5370, D.5371, D.5365.

b. 75mm DRY PARTITION. see D.5372, D.5371, D.5365.

c. SOLID WALL. see D.5373, D.5374.

For positioning of ironmongery see D.3264.

Doors only are direct supply items.

00 - 060280

bldg type | space use | element 22 | feature | material | key

Departmental Standard Drawing

title

INTERNAL NORMAL FLUSH DOORSET DETAIL.

WITH FANLIGHT
WITH THRESHOLD.

scale

1 : 1

GP	drawing no D.3248.	rev

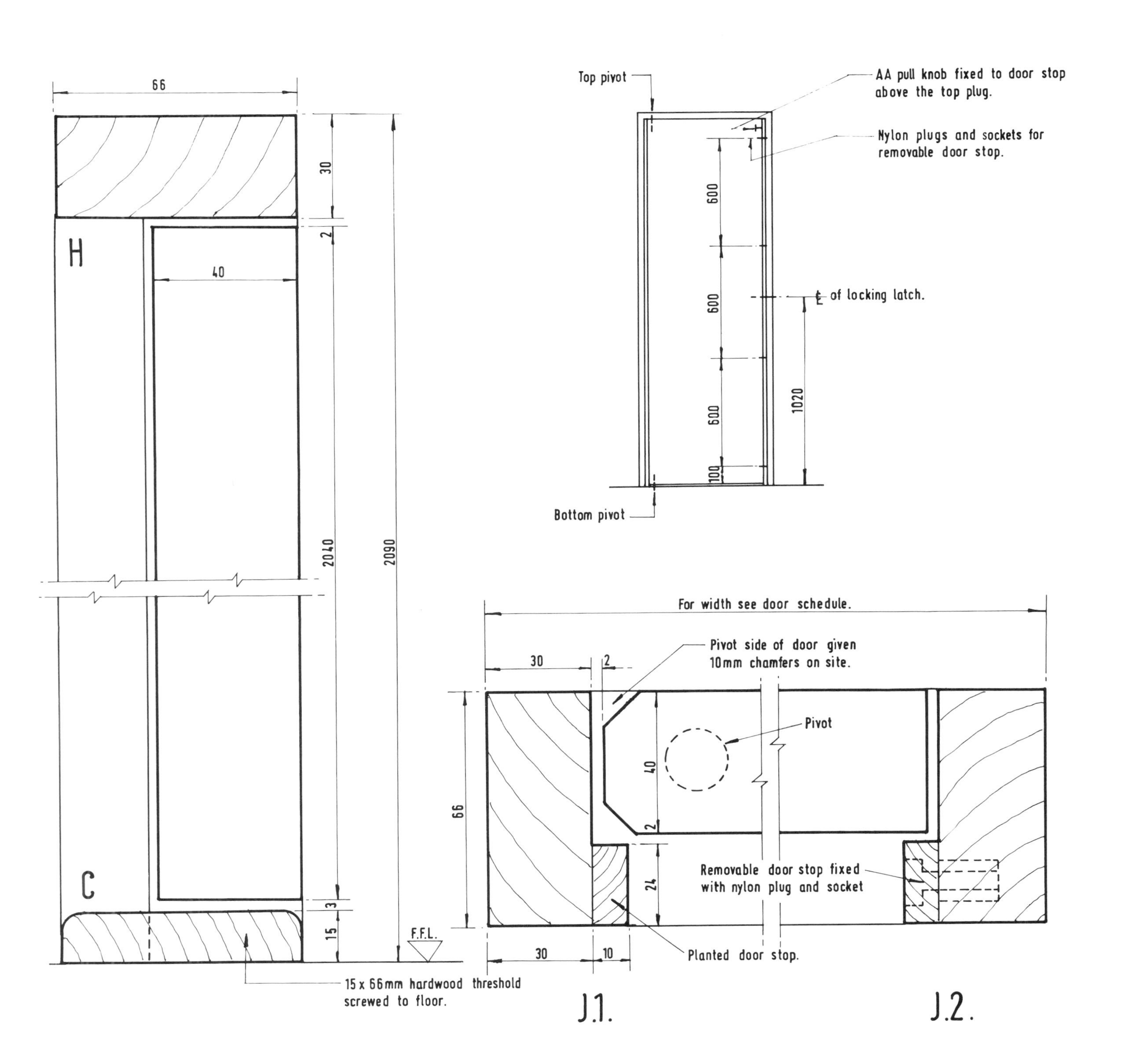

GLC ILEA

Department of Architecture and Civic Design
County Hall SE1 7PB
Architect F B Pooley CBE

References following notes are clause numbers from G.L.C. preambles to bills of quantities

To be read in conjunction with door schedule and job layouts.

Building-in details.

a. 50mm DRY PARTITION.
   see D.5370, D.5371, D.5365.

b. 75mm DRY PARTITION.
   see D.5371, D.5372, D.5365.

c. SOLID WALL.
   see D.5373, D.5374.

For details of door pivot see D.3010.

For description of ironmongery see N.S.I. set F.

Doors only are direct supply items.

080280 -

bldg type	space use	element	feature	material	key
		[22]			

Departmental Standard Drawing

title

INTERNAL NORMAL FLUSH DOORSET DETAIL.
O.P. SANITARY SPACES.
WITHOUT FANLIGHT.
WITH THRESHOLD.

scale

1 : 1

	drawing no	rev
GP	D.3249	

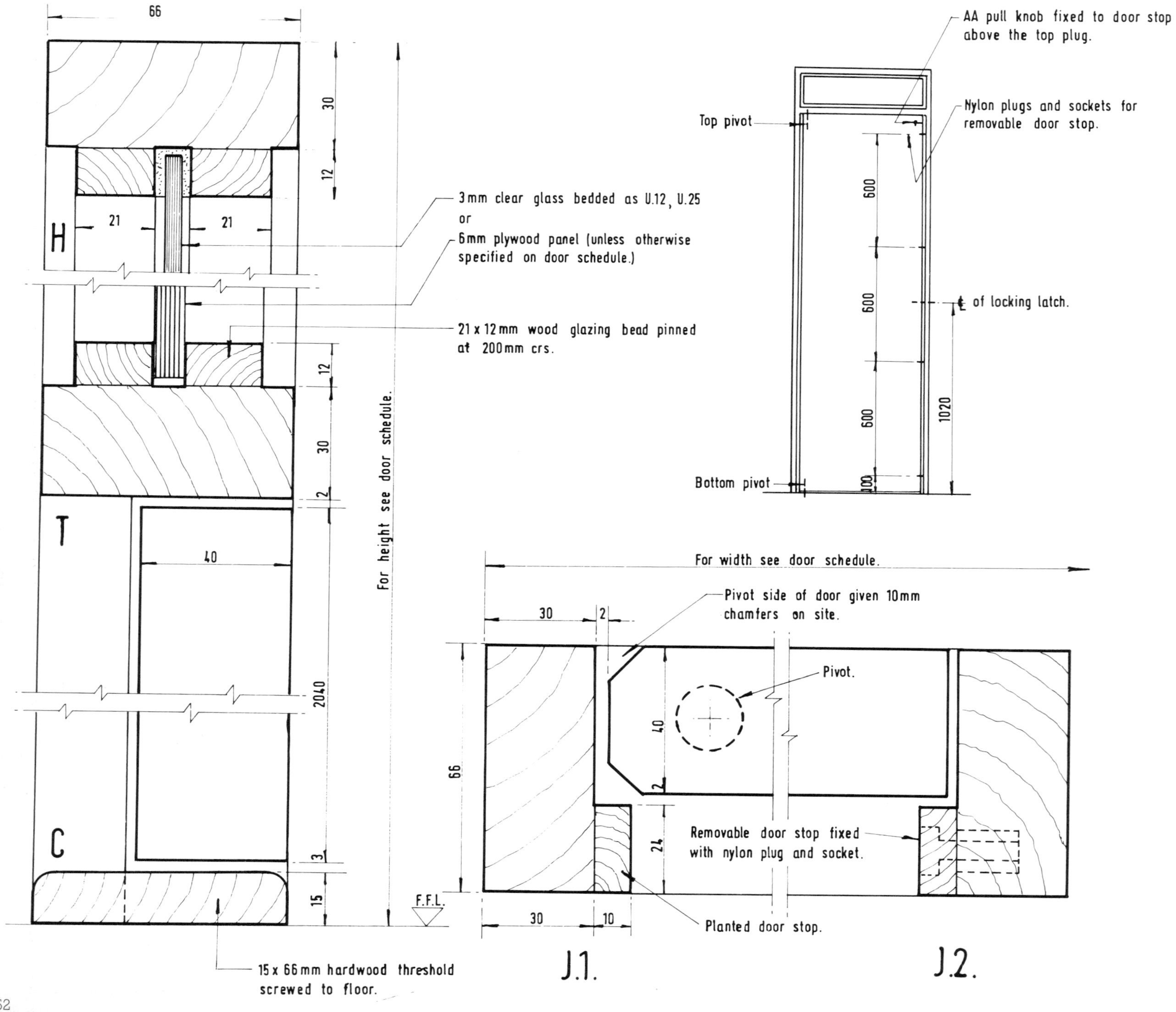

GLC ILEA

Department of Architecture and Civic Design
County Hall SE1 7PB
Architect F B Pooley CBE

References following notes are clause numbers from G.L.C. preambles to bills of quantities

To be read in conjunction with door schedule and job layouts.

Building-in details.

a. 50mm DRY PARTITION.
see D.5370, D.5371, D.5365.

b. 75mm DRY PARTITION.
see D.5371, D.5372, D.5365

c. SOLID WALL.
see D.5373, D.5374.

For details of door pivot set see D.3010.

For description of ironmongery see N.S.I. set F.

Doors only are direct supply items.

Departmental Standard Drawing

title
INTERNAL NORMAL FLUSH DOORSET DETAIL.
O.P. SANITARY SPACES.
WITH FANLIGHT.
WITH THRESHOLD.

scale 1 : 1

GP | drawing no D.3250 | rev

bldg type | space use | element 22 | feature | material | key

00 - 070280

H

T

C

66

30

12

21

21

12

30

2

40

2040

3

15

For height see door schedule.

3mm clear glass bedded as U.12, U.25
or
6mm plywood panel (unless otherwise specified on door schedule.)

21 x 12mm wood glazing bead pinned at 200mm crs.

15 x 66mm hardwood threshold screwed to floor.

F.F.L.

AA pull knob fixed to door stop above the top plug.

Nylon plugs and sockets for removable door stop.

Top pivot

Bottom pivot

600

600

600

300

1020

℄ of locking latch.

For width see door schedule.

30

2

Pivot side of door given 10mm chamfers on site.

Pivot.

40

2

66

24

Removable door stop fixed with nylon plug and socket.

30

10

Planted door stop.

J.1.

J.2.

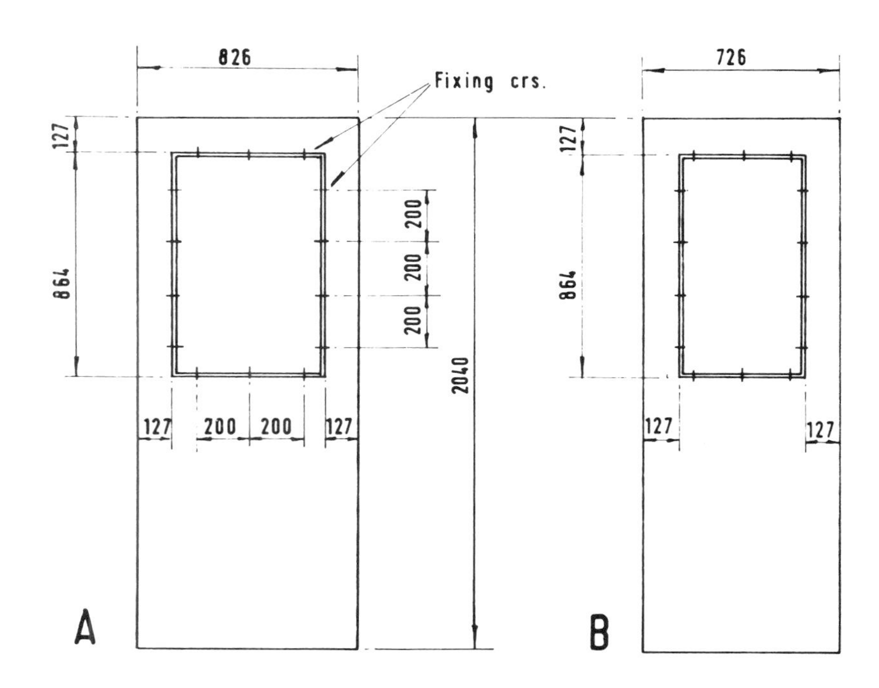
826
726
Fixing crs.
127
864
200
200
200
2040
127
200
200
127
127
127
A
B

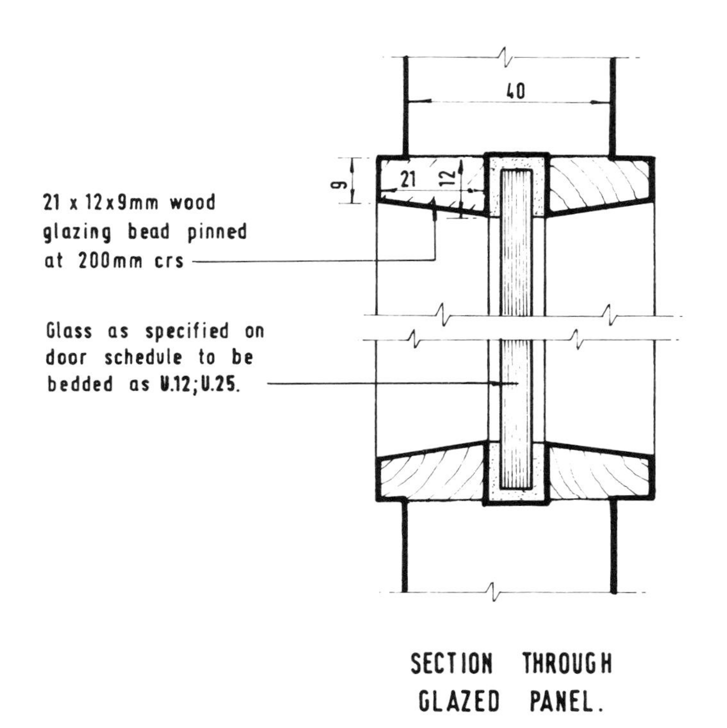
40
9
21
12
21 x 12x9mm wood
glazing bead pinned
at 200mm crs
Glass as specified on
door schedule to be
bedded as U.12;U.25.
SECTION THROUGH
GLAZED PANEL.

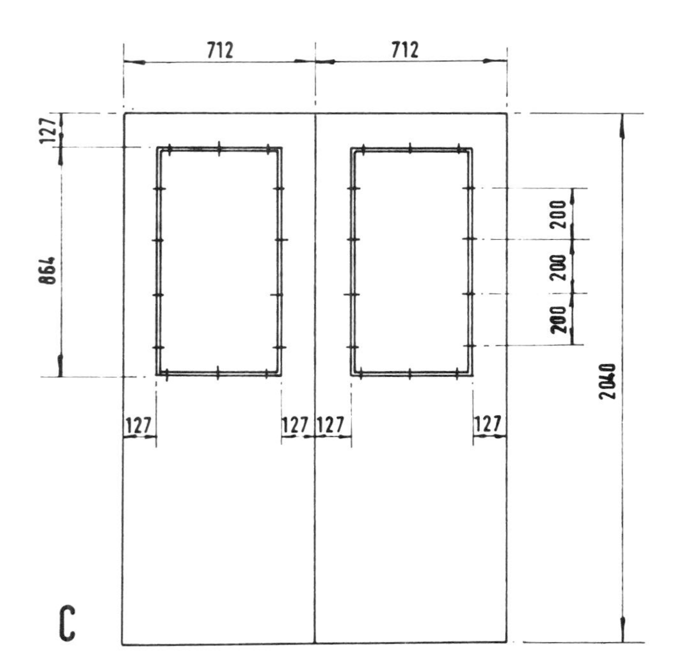
712
712
127
864
200
200
200
2040
127
127
127
127
C

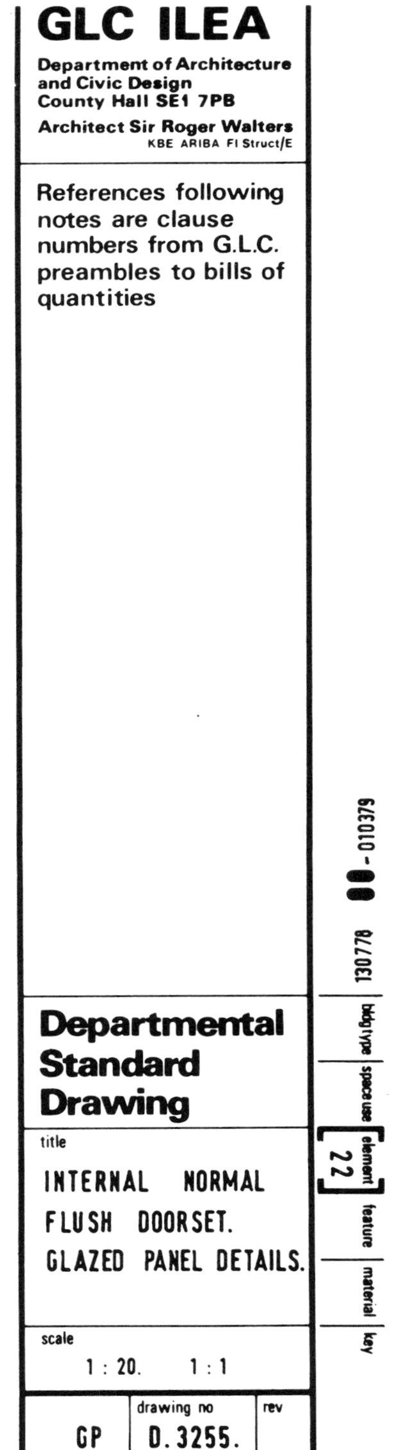
GLC ILEA
Department of Architecture
and Civic Design
County Hall SE1 7PB
Architect Sir Roger Walters
KBE ARIBA FI Struct/E
References following notes are clause numbers from G.L.C. preambles to bills of quantities
Departmental Standard Drawing
title
INTERNAL NORMAL FLUSH DOORSET. GLAZED PANEL DETAILS.
scale
1 : 20. 1 : 1
GP
drawing no
D.3255.
rev
130778
010379
bldg type
space use
element
22
feature
material
key

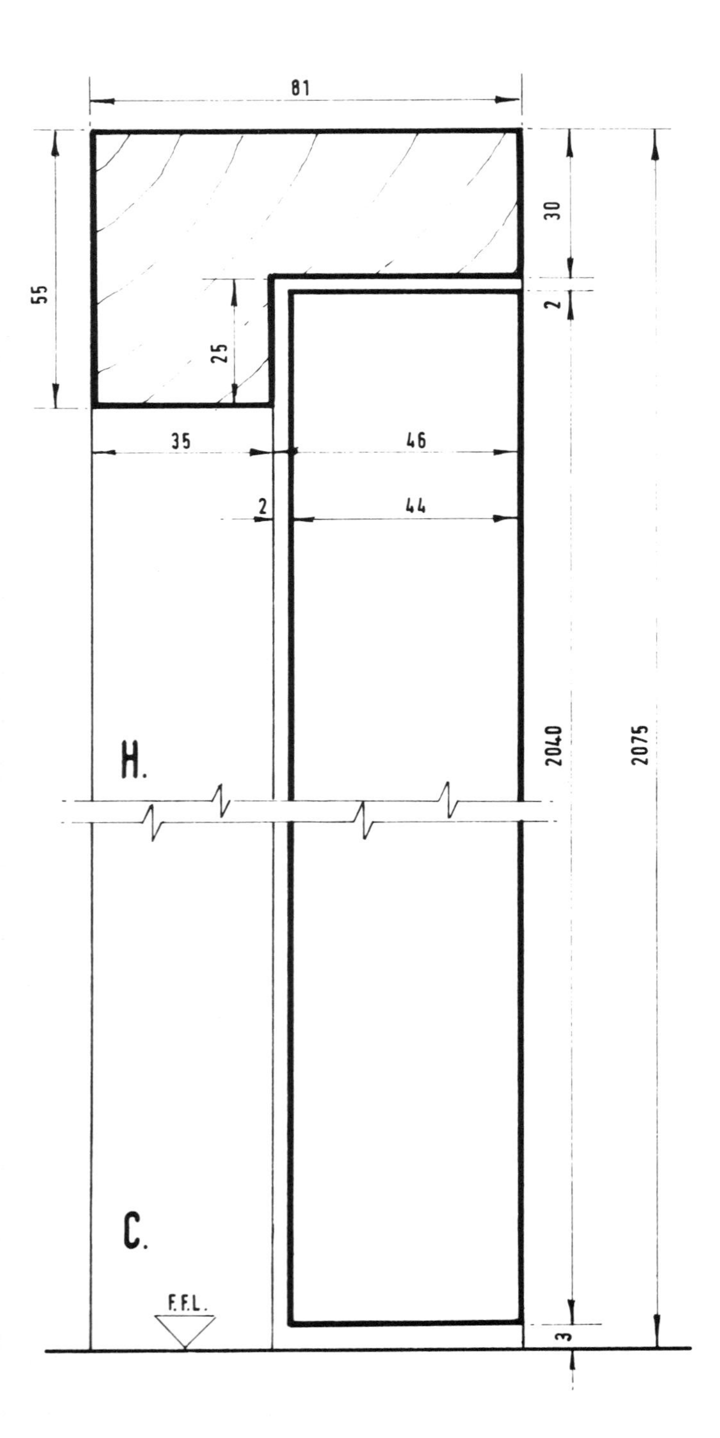

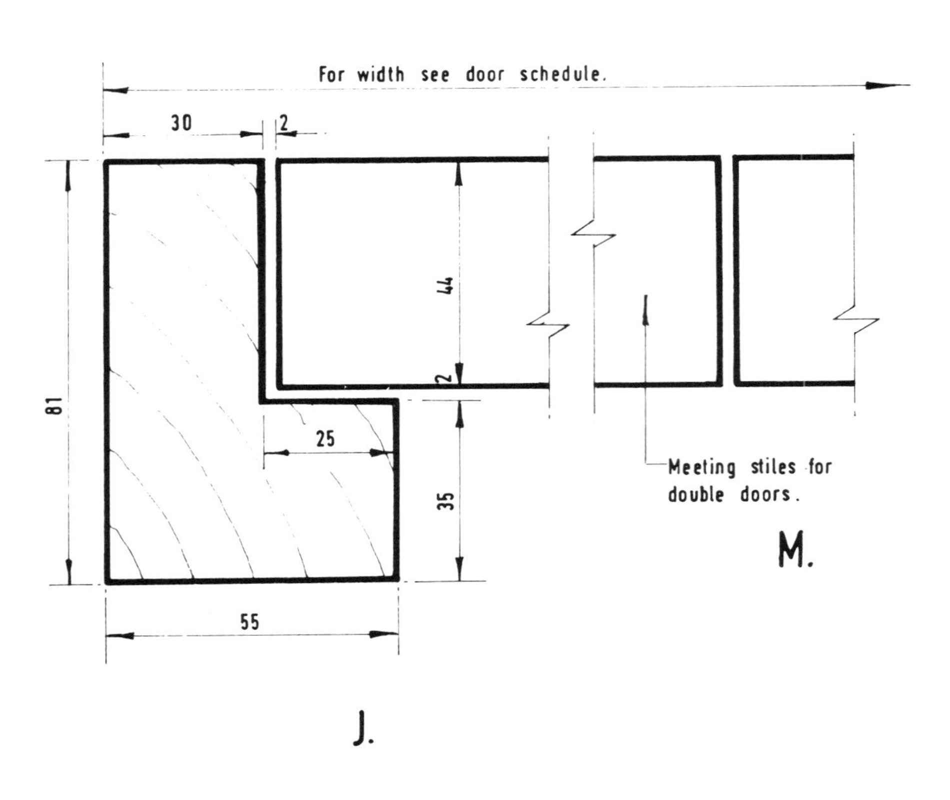

GLC ILEA

Department of Architecture and Civic Design
County Hall SE1 7PB
Architect Sir Roger Walters
KBE ARIBA FI Struct/E

References following notes are clause numbers from G.L.C. preambles to bills of quantities

To be read in conjunction with door schedule and job layouts.

Building-in details.

a. 50mm DRY PARTITION
see D.5363. D.5364. D.5365.

b. 75mm DRY PARTITION
see D.5366. D.5367. D.5365.

c. SOLID WALL
see D.5368. D.5369.

For positioning of ironmongery see D.3264.

Doors only are direct supply items.

Departmental Standard Drawing

title

INTERNAL 1/2HOUR FIRE FLUSH DOORSET DETAIL.
WITHOUT FANLIGHT.

scale
1 : 1

	drawing no	rev
GP	D.3261.	

130578. - 010379

22

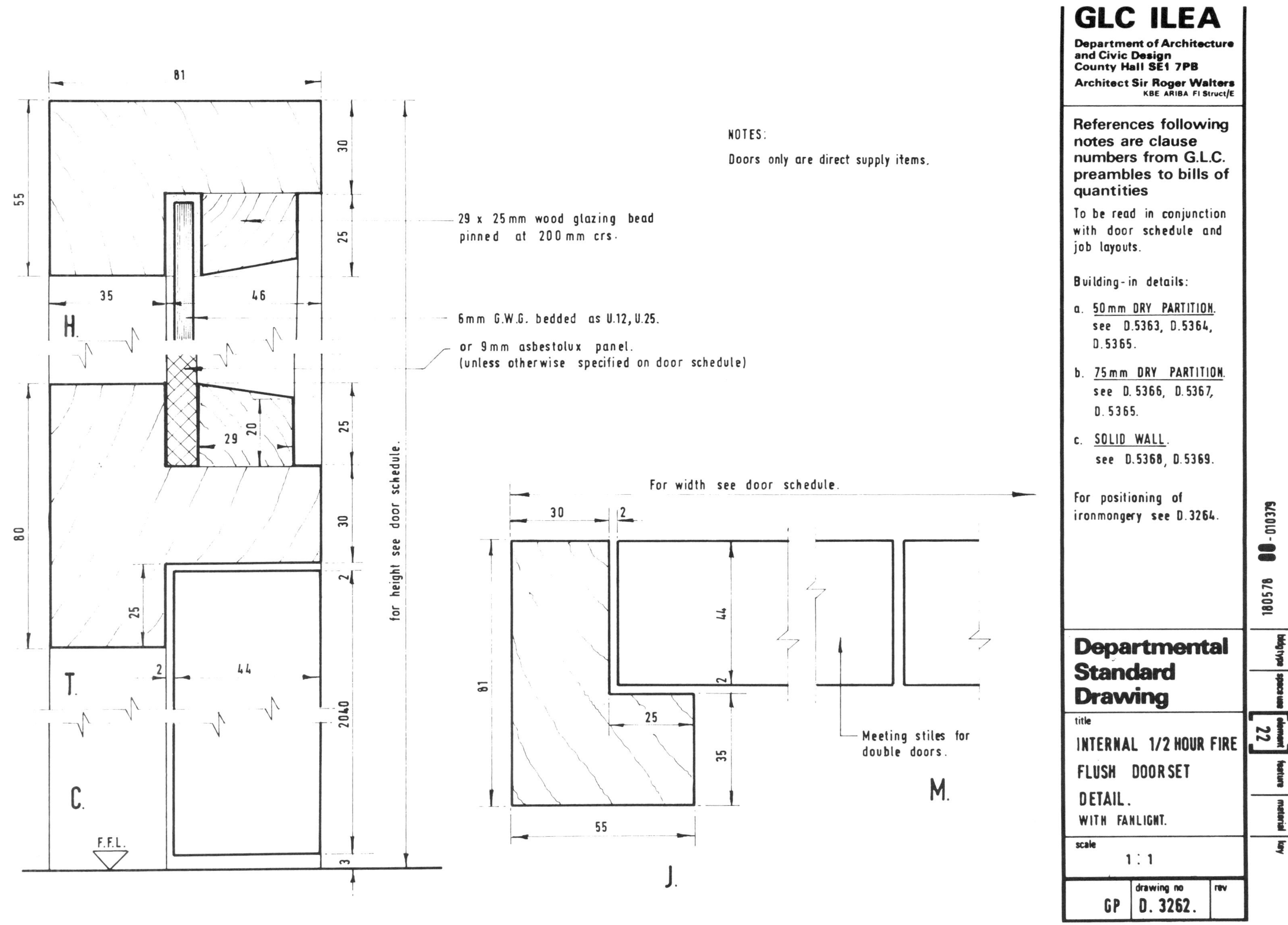
GLC ILEA
Department of Architecture
and Civic Design
County Hall SE1 7PB
Architect Sir Roger Walters
KBE ARIBA FI Struct/E
References following notes are clause numbers from G.L.C. preambles to bills of quantities
To be read in conjunction with door schedule and job layouts.
Building-in details:
a. 50mm DRY PARTITION. see D.5363, D.5364, D.5365.
b. 75mm DRY PARTITION. see D.5366, D.5367, D.5365.
c. SOLID WALL. see D.5368, D.5369.
For positioning of ironmongery see D.3264.
NOTES:
Doors only are direct supply items.
29 x 25mm wood glazing bead pinned at 200mm crs.
6mm G.W.G. bedded as U.12, U.25.
or 9mm asbestolux panel.
(unless otherwise specified on door schedule)
for height see door schedule.
For width see door schedule.
Meeting stiles for double doors.
H.
T.
C.
J.
M.
F.F.L.
81
55
35
46
30
25
80
29
20
2
44
2040
3
Departmental Standard Drawing
title
INTERNAL 1/2 HOUR FIRE FLUSH DOORSET DETAIL.
WITH FANLIGHT.
scale
1 : 1
drawing no
rev
GP
D. 3262.
180578 00-010379
22

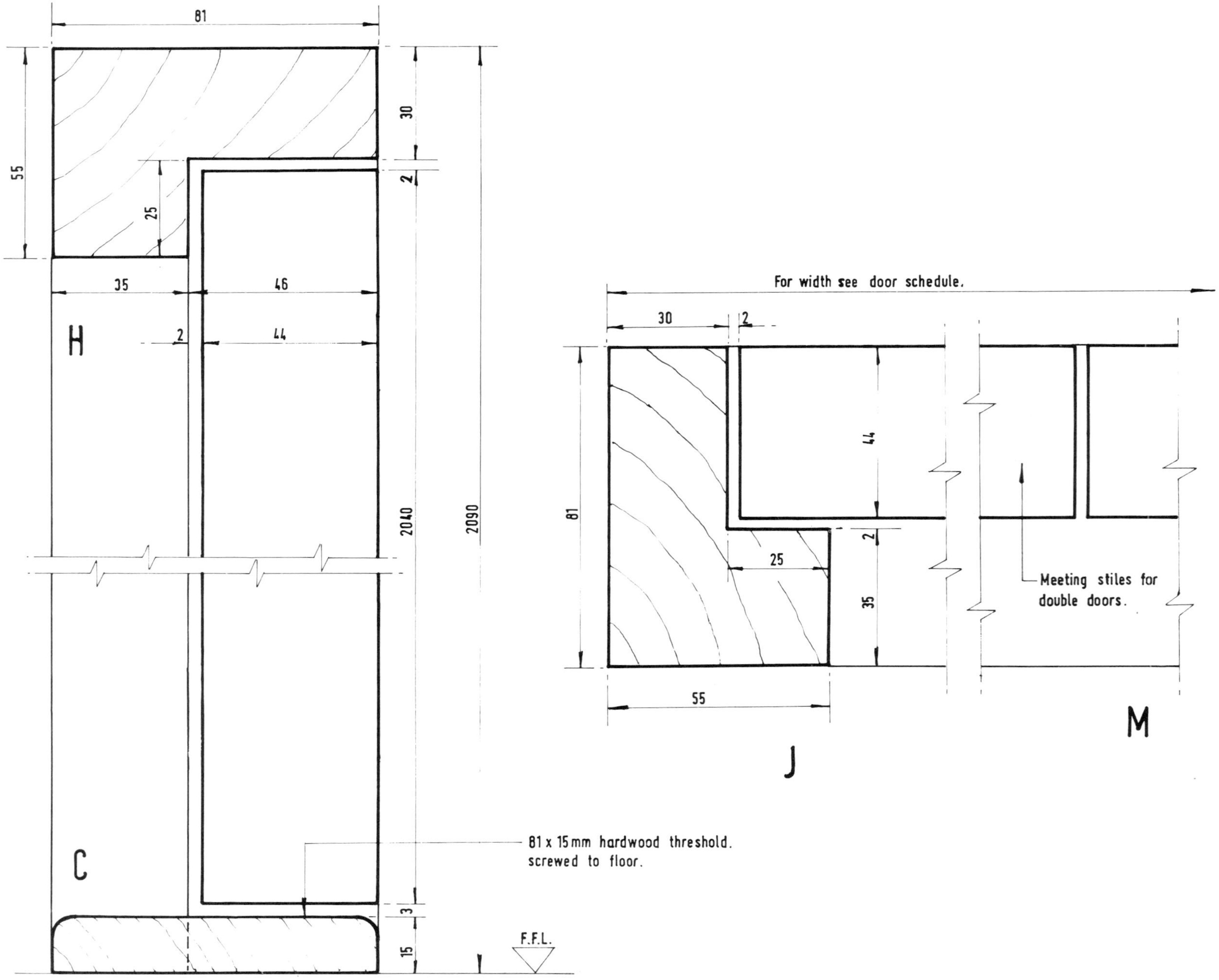

81

55

25

30

2

35

46

H

2

44

2040

2090

C

3

15

81 x 15mm hardwood threshold. screwed to floor.

F.F.L.

For width see door schedule.

30

2

81

44

2

25

35

55

Meeting stiles for double doors.

J

M

GLC ILEA

Department of Architecture and Civic Design
County Hall SE1 7PB
Architect F B Pooley CBE

References following notes are clause numbers from G.L.C. preambles to bills of quantities

To be read in conjunction with door schedule and job layouts.

Building-in details.

a. 50mm DRY PARTITION.
see D.5363, D.5364, D.5365.

b. 75mm DRY PARTITION.
see D.5366, D.5367, D.5365.

c. SOLID WALL.
see D.5368, D.5369.

For positioning of ironmongery see D.3264

Doors only are direct supply items.

290180.

bldgtype | spaceuse | element 22 | feature | material | key

Departmental Standard Drawing

title

INTERNAL 1/2 HOUR FIRE FLUSH DOORSET DETAIL.
WITHOUT FANLIGHT.
WITH THRESHOLD.

scale
1 : 1

	drawing no	rev
GP	D. 3266	

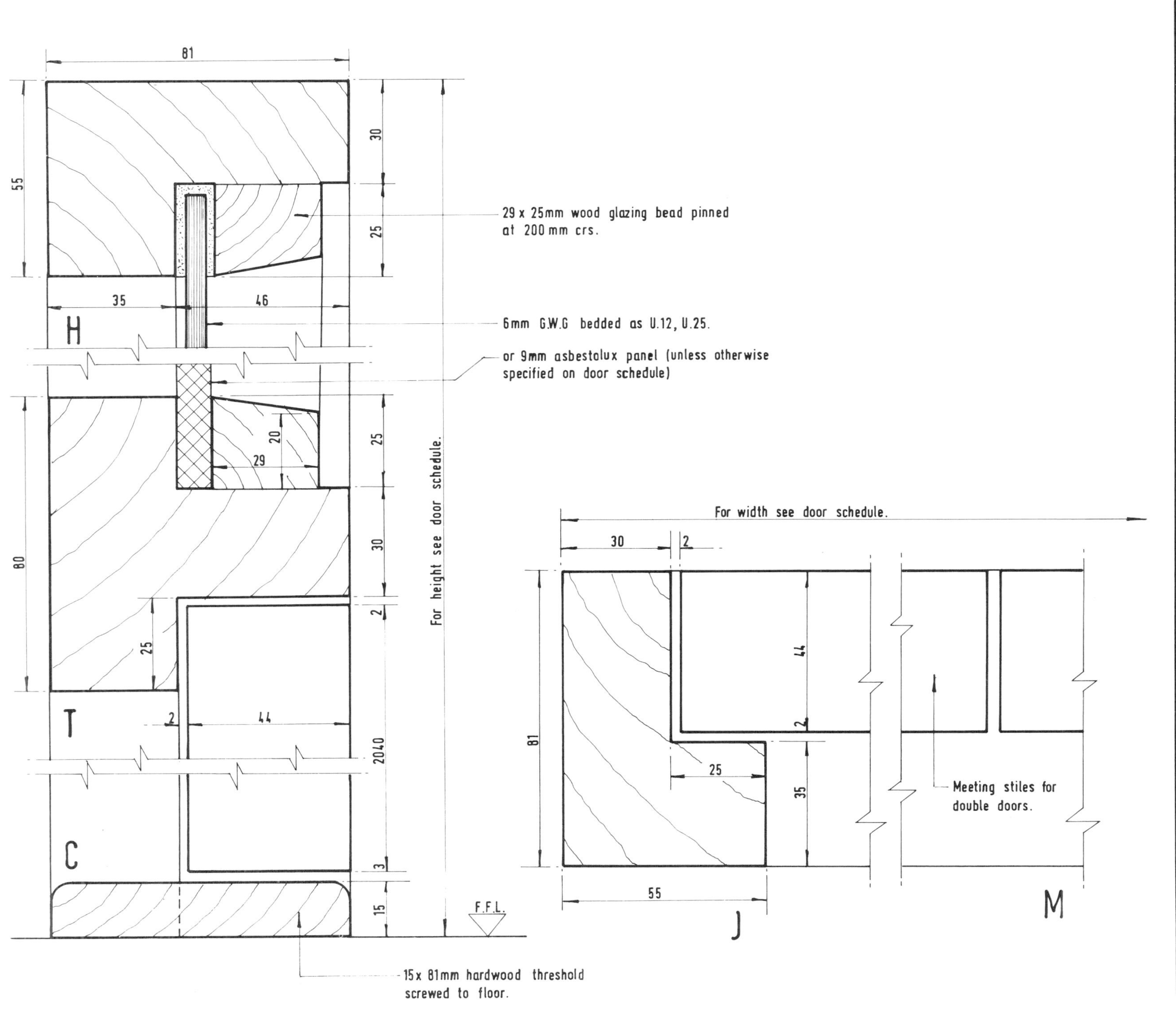

GLC ILEA

Department of Architecture and Civic Design
County Hall SE1 7PB
Architect F B Pooley CBE

References following notes are clause numbers from G.L.C. preambles to bills of quantities

To be read in conjunction with door schedule and job layouts.

Building - in details.

a. <u>50mm DRY PARTITION</u>
see D.5363, D.5364, D.5365

b. <u>75mm DRY PARTITION</u>.
see D.5366, D.5367, D.5365

c. <u>SOLID WALL</u>.
see D.5368, D.5369.

For positioning of ironmongery see D.3264.

Doors only are direct supply items.

0 - 060280

Departmental Standard Drawing

bldgtype | spaceuse | element [22] | feature | material | key

title

INTERNAL 1/2 HOUR FIRE FLUSH DOORSET DETAIL.
WITH FANLIGHT.
WITH THRESHOLD.

scale 1 : 1

	drawing no	rev
GP	D.3267.	

GLC ILEA

Department of Architecture and Civic Design
County Hall SE1 7PB
Architect Sir Roger Walters
KBE ARIBA FI Struct/E

References following notes are clause numbers from G.L.C. preambles to bills of quantities

Detail.X1. (wood beads) to be used for glass panels of max $0{\cdot}4\,m^2$

Detail.X2. (marinite beads) to be used for glass panels more than $0{\cdot}4\,m^2$ but less than $1{\cdot}2\,m^2$

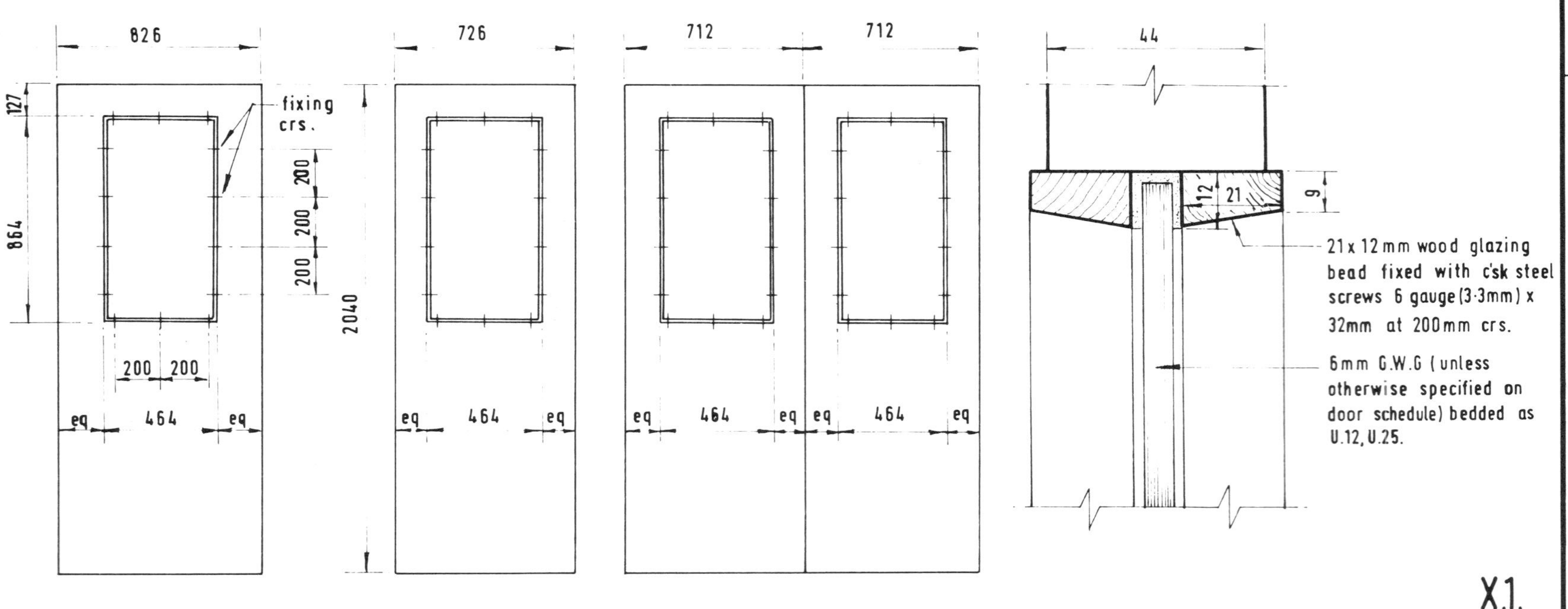

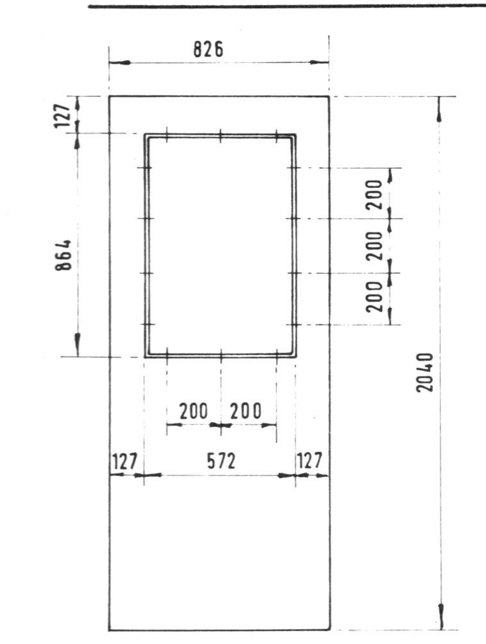

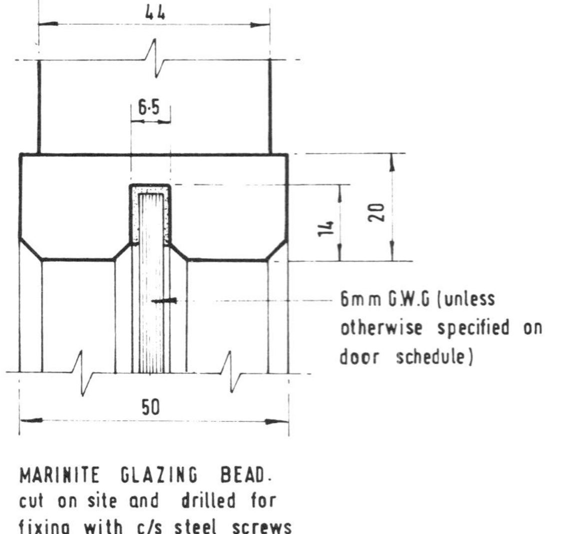

X2.

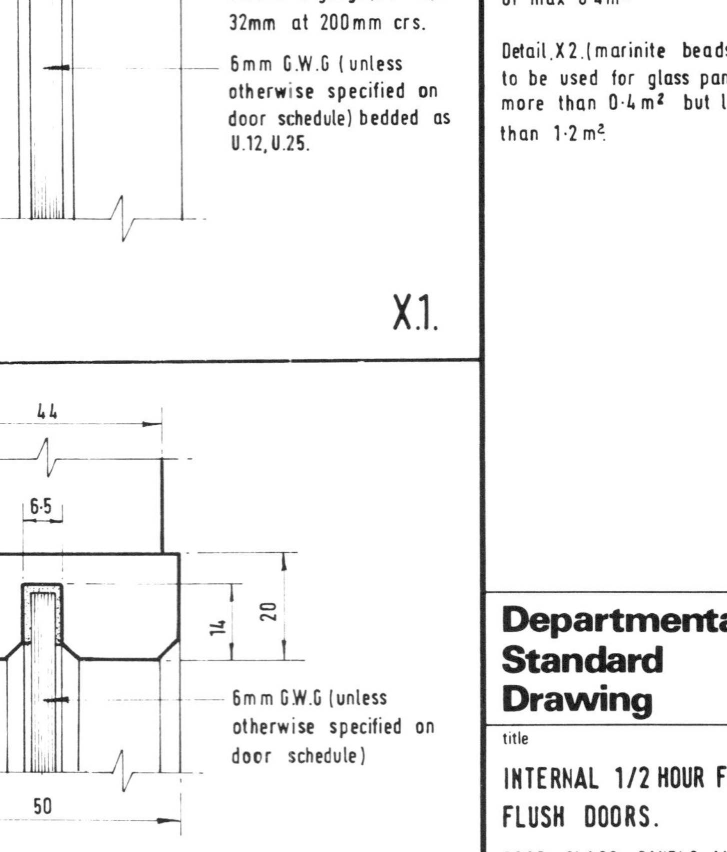

Departmental Standard Drawing

title

INTERNAL 1/2 HOUR FIRE FLUSH DOORS.

DOOR GLASS PANELS AND BEADS DETAILS.

scale 1 : 20 ; 1 : 1

GP | drawing no D. 3263. | rev

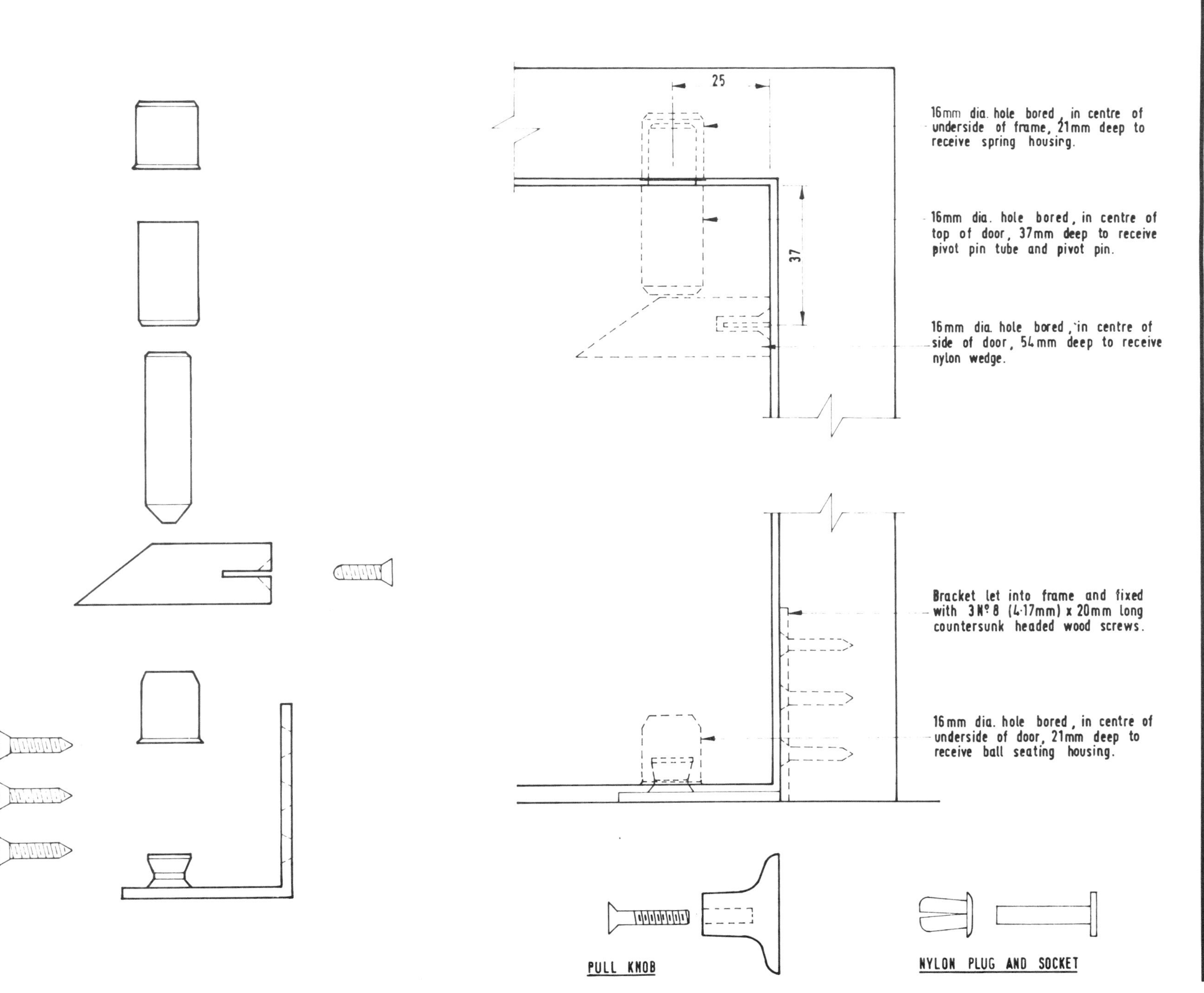

GLC ILEA
Department of Architecture and Civic Design
County Hall SE1
Architect Sir Roger Walters KBE FRIBA FIStructE

References following notes are clause numbers from G.L.C. preambles to bills of quantities.

This drawing is to be read in conjunction with all drawings of doors for O.P. sanitary spaces.

Part of ironmongery set reference F illustrated items 112 and 113.

Departmental Standard Drawing

title
INTERNAL DOORS AND FRAMES.
ASSEMBLY DETAIL OF PIVOT FOR O.P. SANITARY SPACES.

scale 1:1

drawing no D3010 rev A

bldg type 843 | space use | element [22] | feature 204 | material Xi2 | key

010379

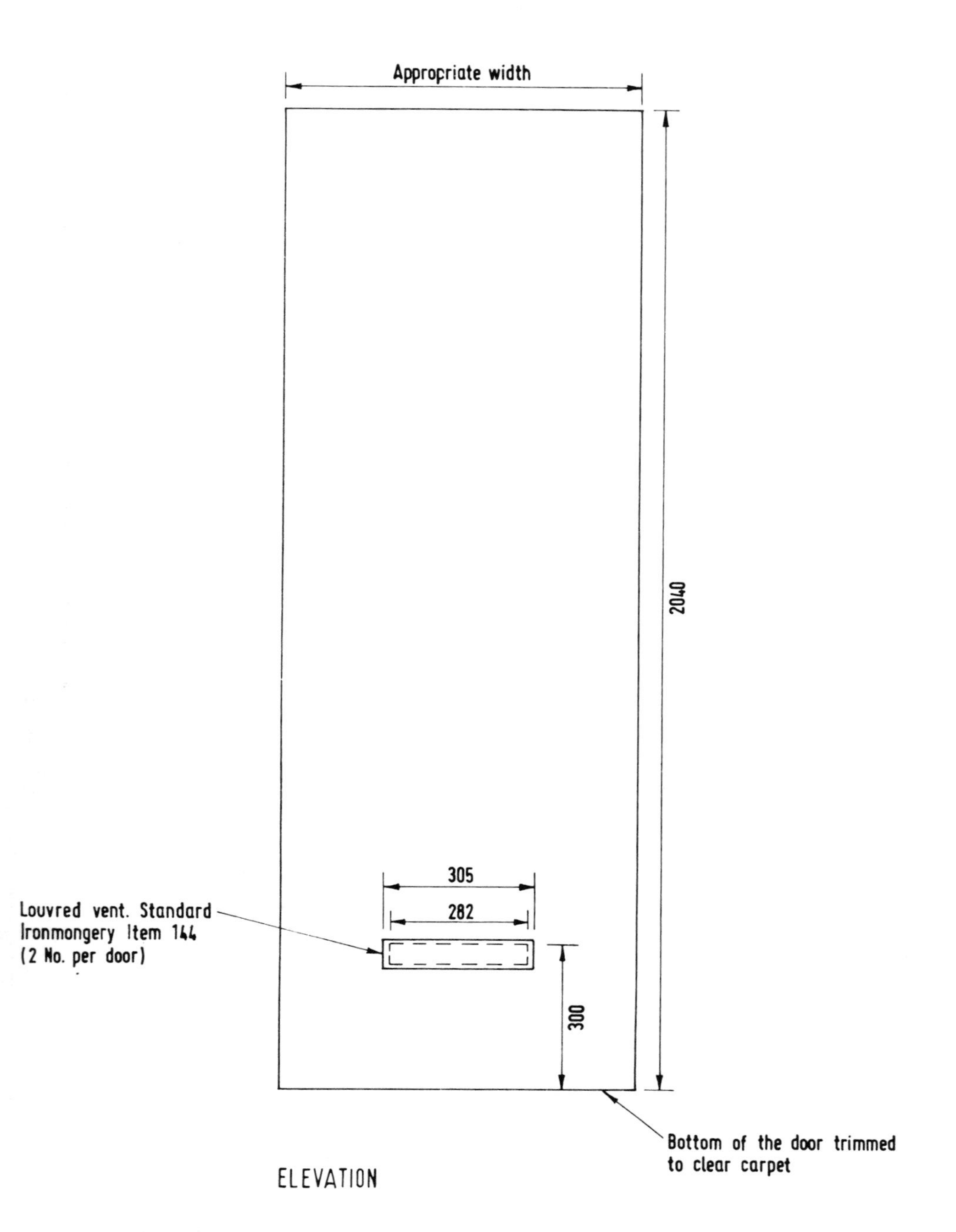

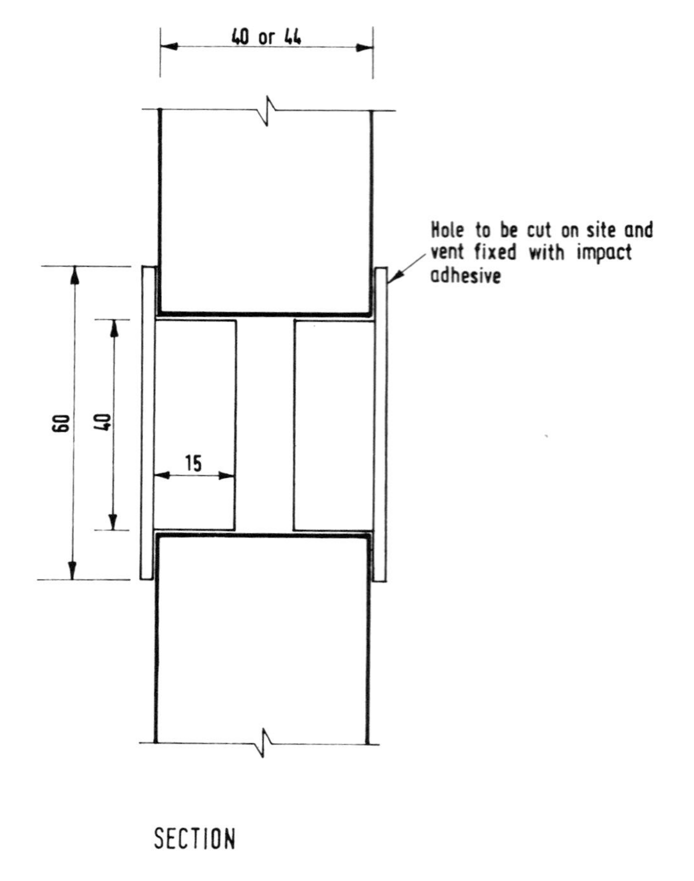

GLC ILEA

Department of Architecture
and Civic Design
County Hall SE1 7PB

Architect Sir Roger Walters
KBE ARIBA FIStructE

References following notes are clause numbers from G.L.C. preambles to bills of quantities

Departmental Standard Drawing

title

LOUVRED VENT TO DOOR - FOR BATHROOM WITHOUT NATURAL VENTILATION.

scale 1:10 & 1:1

drawing no D5110

rev

bldg type | space use | element 22 | feature 204 | material Xi2 | key

010379

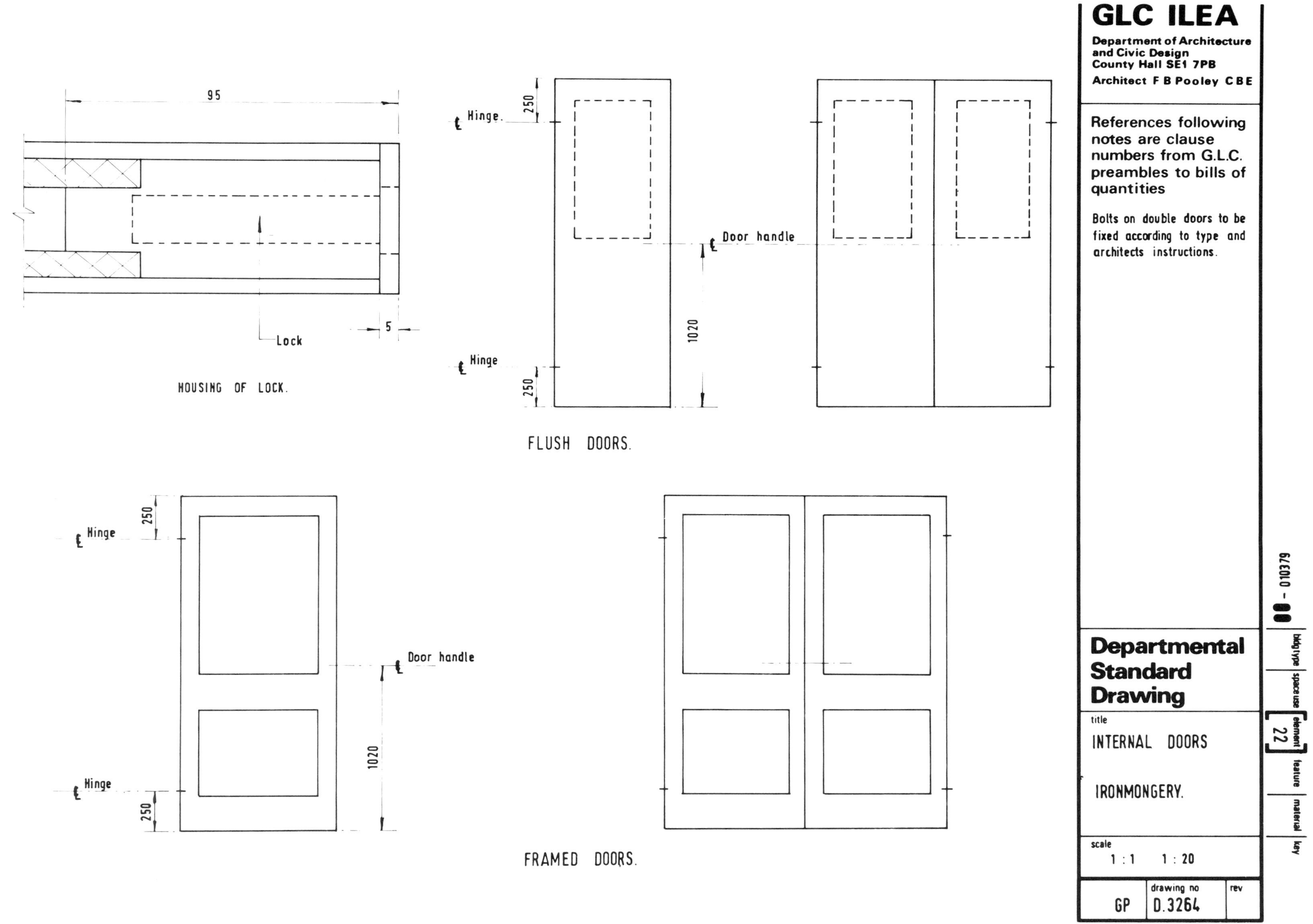
95
Lock
5
HOUSING OF LOCK.
Hinge.
250
Door handle
1020
Hinge
250
FLUSH DOORS.
Hinge
250
Door handle
1020
Hinge
250
FRAMED DOORS.
GLC ILEA
Department of Architecture and Civic Design
County Hall SE1 7PB
Architect F B Pooley CBE
References following notes are clause numbers from G.L.C. preambles to bills of quantities
Bolts on double doors to be fixed according to type and architects instructions.
Departmental Standard Drawing
title
INTERNAL DOORS
IRONMONGERY.
scale
1 : 1 1 : 20
GP
drawing no
D.3264
rev
00 - 010379
bldg type
space use
element
22
feature
material
key

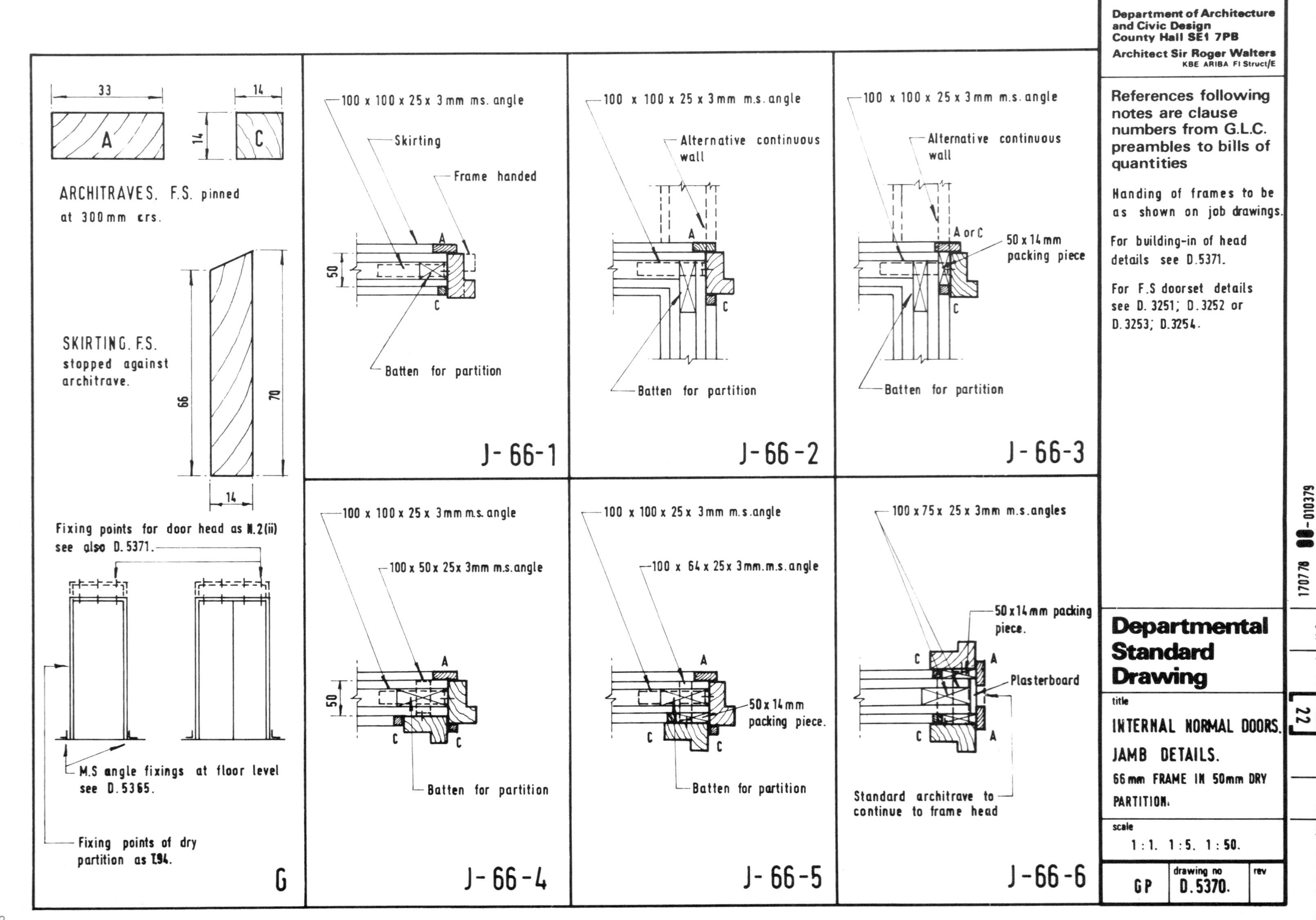
GLC ILEA
Department of Architecture and Civic Design
County Hall SE1 7PB
Architect Sir Roger Walters
KBE ARIBA FI Struct/E
References following notes are clause numbers from G.L.C. preambles to bills of quantities
Handing of frames to be as shown on job drawings.
For building-in of head details see D.5371.
For F.S doorset details see D. 3251; D. 3252 or D. 3253; D. 3254.
33
14
A
C
ARCHITRAVES. F.S. pinned at 300mm crs.
SKIRTING. F.S. stopped against architrave.
66
70
Fixing points for door head as N.2(ii) see also D. 5371.
M.S angle fixings at floor level see D. 5365.
Fixing points of dry partition as T.94.
G
100 x 100 x 25 x 3mm ms. angle
Skirting
Frame handed
50
Batten for partition
J-66-1
100 x 100 x 25 x 3mm m.s. angle
Alternative continuous wall
J-66-2
A or C
50 x 14mm packing piece
J-66-3
100 x 100 x 25 x 3mm m.s. angle
100 x 50 x 25x 3mm m.s.angle
J-66-4
100 x 64 x 25 x 3mm.m.s. angle
50 x 14mm packing piece.
J-66-5
100 x 75 x 25 x 3mm m.s.angles
50 x 14mm packing piece.
Plasterboard
Standard architrave to continue to frame head
J-66-6
Departmental Standard Drawing
title
INTERNAL NORMAL DOORS. JAMB DETAILS. 66mm FRAME IN 50mm DRY PARTITION.
scale
1:1. 1:5. 1:50.
GP
drawing no
D.5370.
rev
170778
22

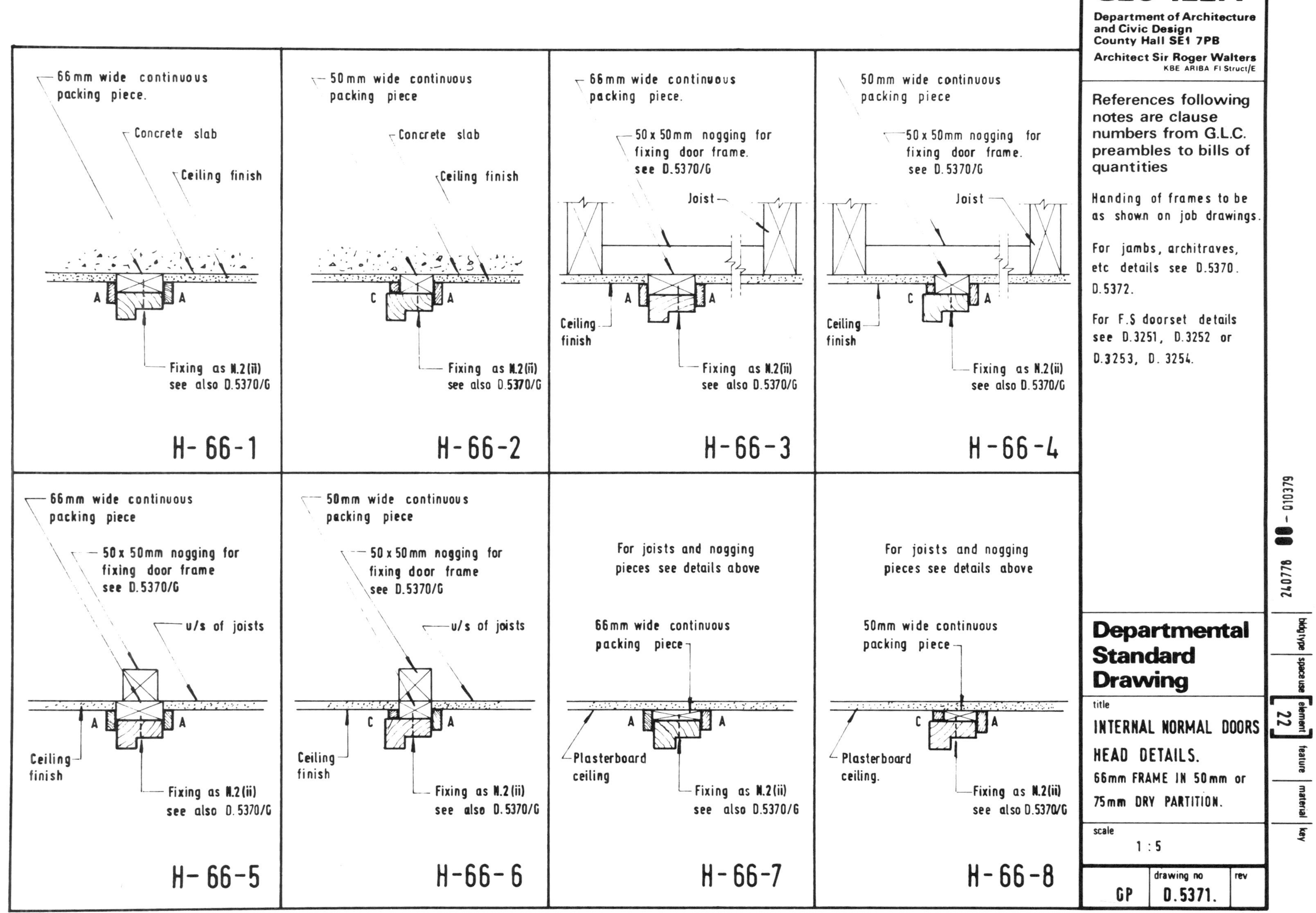

GLC ILEA
Department of Architecture and Civic Design
County Hall SE1 7PB
Architect Sir Roger Walters
KBE ARIBA FI Struct/E
References following notes are clause numbers from G.L.C. preambles to bills of quantities
Handing of frames to be as shown on job drawings.
For jambs, architraves, etc details see D.5370. D.5372.
For F.S doorset details see D.3251, D.3252 or D.3253, D. 3254.
66mm wide continuous packing piece.
Concrete slab
Ceiling finish
A
Fixing as N.2(ii) see also D.5370/G
H-66-1
50mm wide continuous packing piece
Concrete slab
Ceiling finish
C
A
Fixing as N.2(ii) see also D.5370/G
H-66-2
66mm wide continuous packing piece.
50 x 50mm nogging for fixing door frame. see D.5370/G
Joist
Ceiling finish
A
Fixing as N.2(ii) see also D.5370/G
H-66-3
50mm wide continuous packing piece
50 x 50mm nogging for fixing door frame. see D.5370/G
Joist
Ceiling finish
C
A
Fixing as N.2(ii) see also D.5370/G
H-66-4
66mm wide continuous packing piece
50 x 50mm nogging for fixing door frame see D.5370/G
u/s of joists
Ceiling finish
A
Fixing as N.2(ii) see also D.5370/G
H-66-5
50mm wide continuous packing piece
50 x 50mm nogging for fixing door frame see D.5370/G
u/s of joists
Ceiling finish
C
A
Fixing as N.2(ii) see also D.5370/G
H-66-6
For joists and nogging pieces see details above
66mm wide continuous packing piece
Plasterboard ceiling
A
Fixing as N.2(ii) see also D.5370/G
H-66-7
For joists and nogging pieces see details above
50mm wide continuous packing piece
Plasterboard ceiling.
C
A
Fixing as N.2(ii) see also D.5370/G
H-66-8
240778 - 010379
Departmental Standard Drawing
title
INTERNAL NORMAL DOORS HEAD DETAILS.
66mm FRAME IN 50mm or 75mm DRY PARTITION.
scale
1 : 5
bldg type
space use
element
22
feature
material
key
GP
drawing no
D.5371.
rev

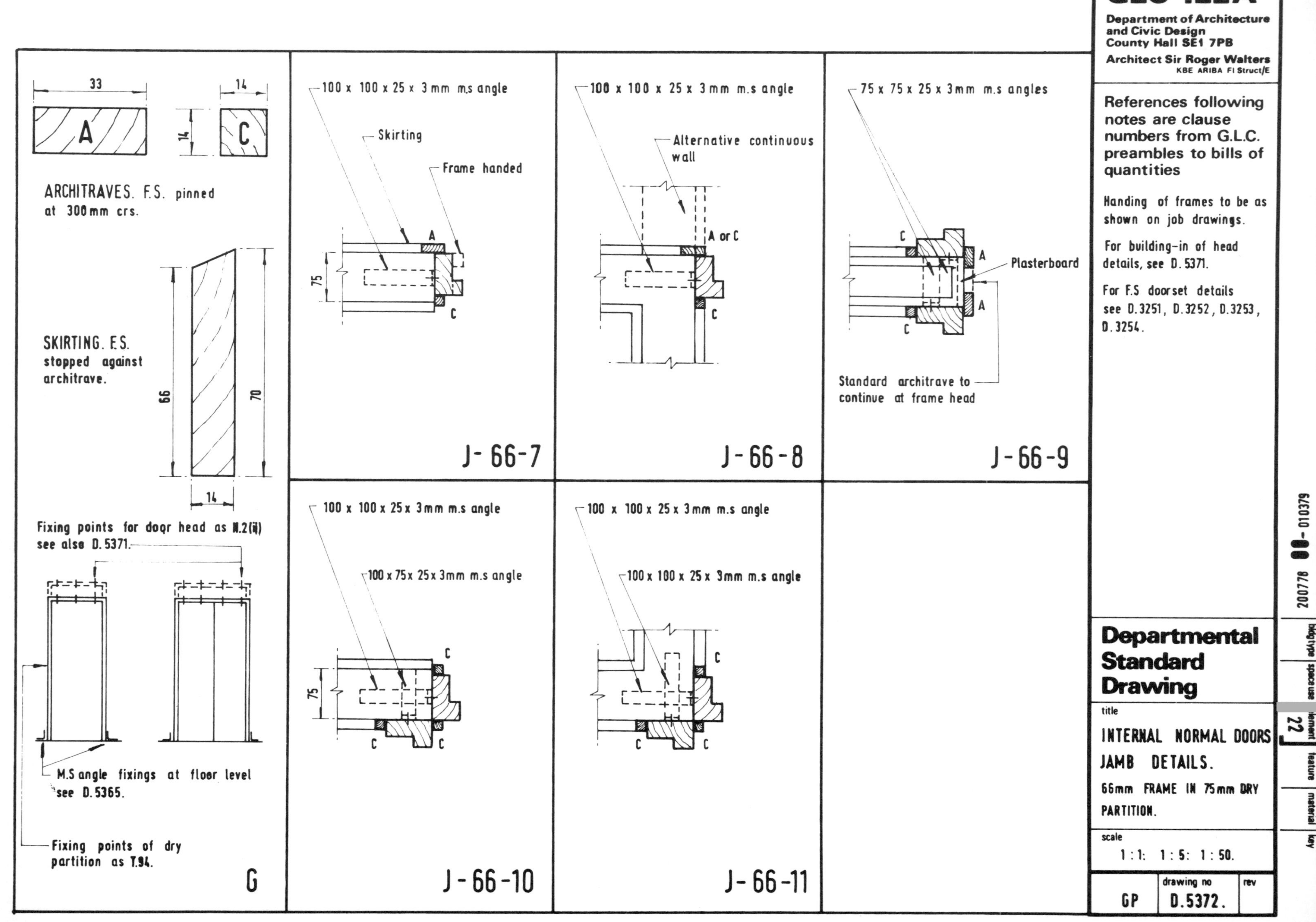
GLC ILEA
Department of Architecture and Civic Design
County Hall SE1 7PB
Architect Sir Roger Walters KBE ARIBA FI Struct/E
References following notes are clause numbers from G.L.C. preambles to bills of quantities
Handing of frames to be as shown on job drawings.
For building-in of head details, see D.5371.
For F.S doorset details see D.3251, D.3252, D.3253, D.3254.
ARCHITRAVES. F.S. pinned at 300mm crs.
SKIRTING. F.S. stopped against architrave.
Fixing points for door head as M.2(ii) see also D.5371.
M.S angle fixings at floor level see D.5365.
Fixing points of dry partition as T.94.
G
100 x 100 x 25 x 3mm m.s angle
Skirting
Frame handed
J-66-7
Alternative continuous wall
A or C
J-66-8
75 x 75 x 25 x 3mm m.s angles
Plasterboard
Standard architrave to continue at frame head
J-66-9
100 x 75 x 25 x 3mm m.s angle
J-66-10
100 x 100 x 25 x 3mm m.s angle
J-66-11
Departmental Standard Drawing
title
INTERNAL NORMAL DOORS JAMB DETAILS.
66mm FRAME IN 75mm DRY PARTITION.
scale
1:1: 1:5: 1:50.
drawing no
GP D.5372.
rev
200778 - 010379
bldg type
space use
element 22
feature
material
key

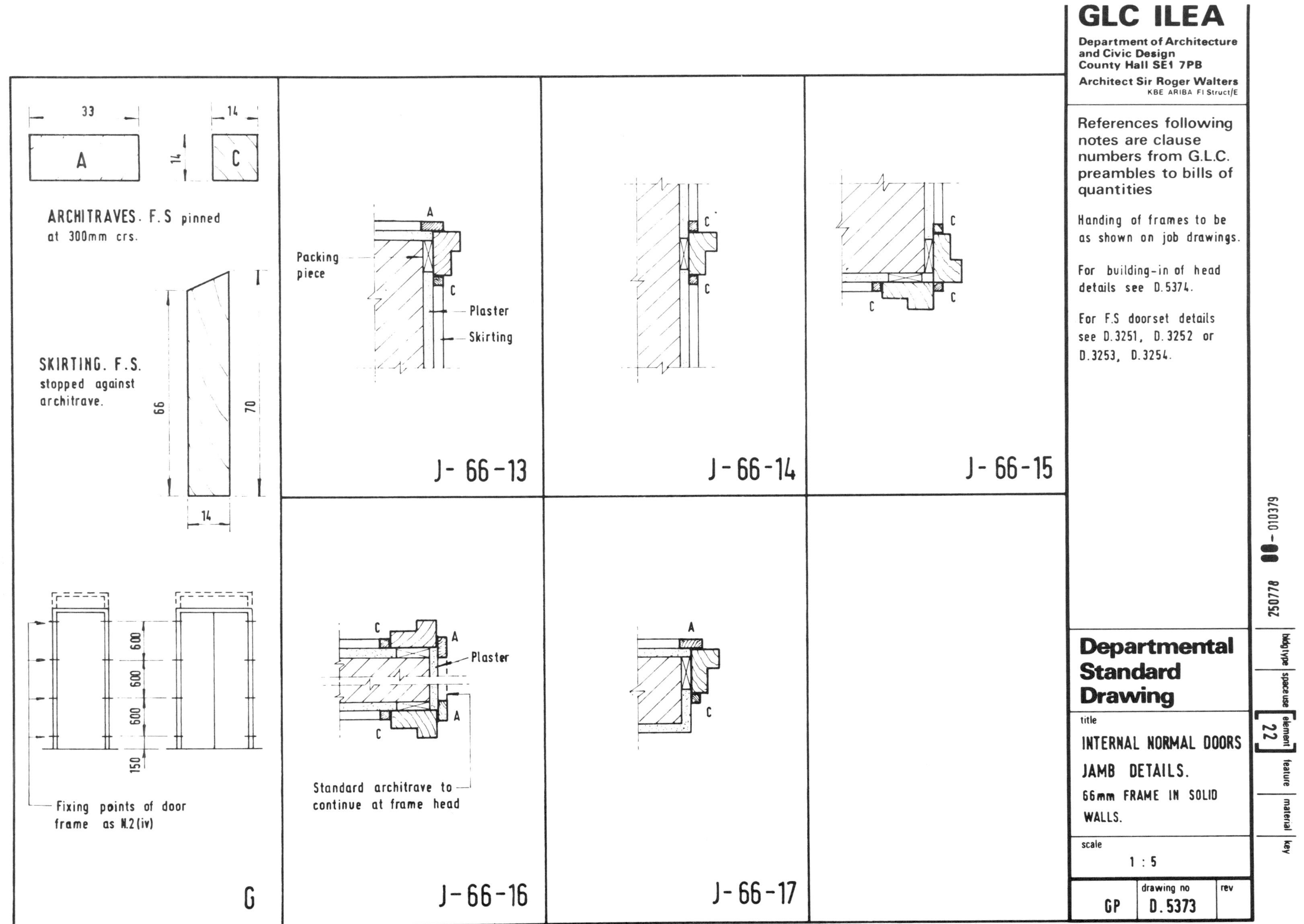
GLC ILEA
Department of Architecture and Civic Design
County Hall SE1 7PB
Architect Sir Roger Walters
KBE ARIBA FI Struct/E
References following notes are clause numbers from G.L.C. preambles to bills of quantities
Handing of frames to be as shown on job drawings.
For building-in of head details see D.5374.
For F.S doorset details see D.3251, D.3252 or D.3253, D.3254.
33
14
A
C
ARCHITRAVES. F.S pinned at 300mm crs.
SKIRTING. F.S. stopped against architrave.
66
70
Fixing points of door frame as N.2(iv)
600
150
G
Packing piece
Plaster
Skirting
J-66-13
J-66-14
J-66-15
Standard architrave to continue at frame head
J-66-16
J-66-17
250778
010379
Departmental Standard Drawing
title
INTERNAL NORMAL DOORS
JAMB DETAILS.
66mm FRAME IN SOLID WALLS.
scale
1 : 5
GP
drawing no
D.5373
rev
bldg type
space use
element
22
feature
material
key

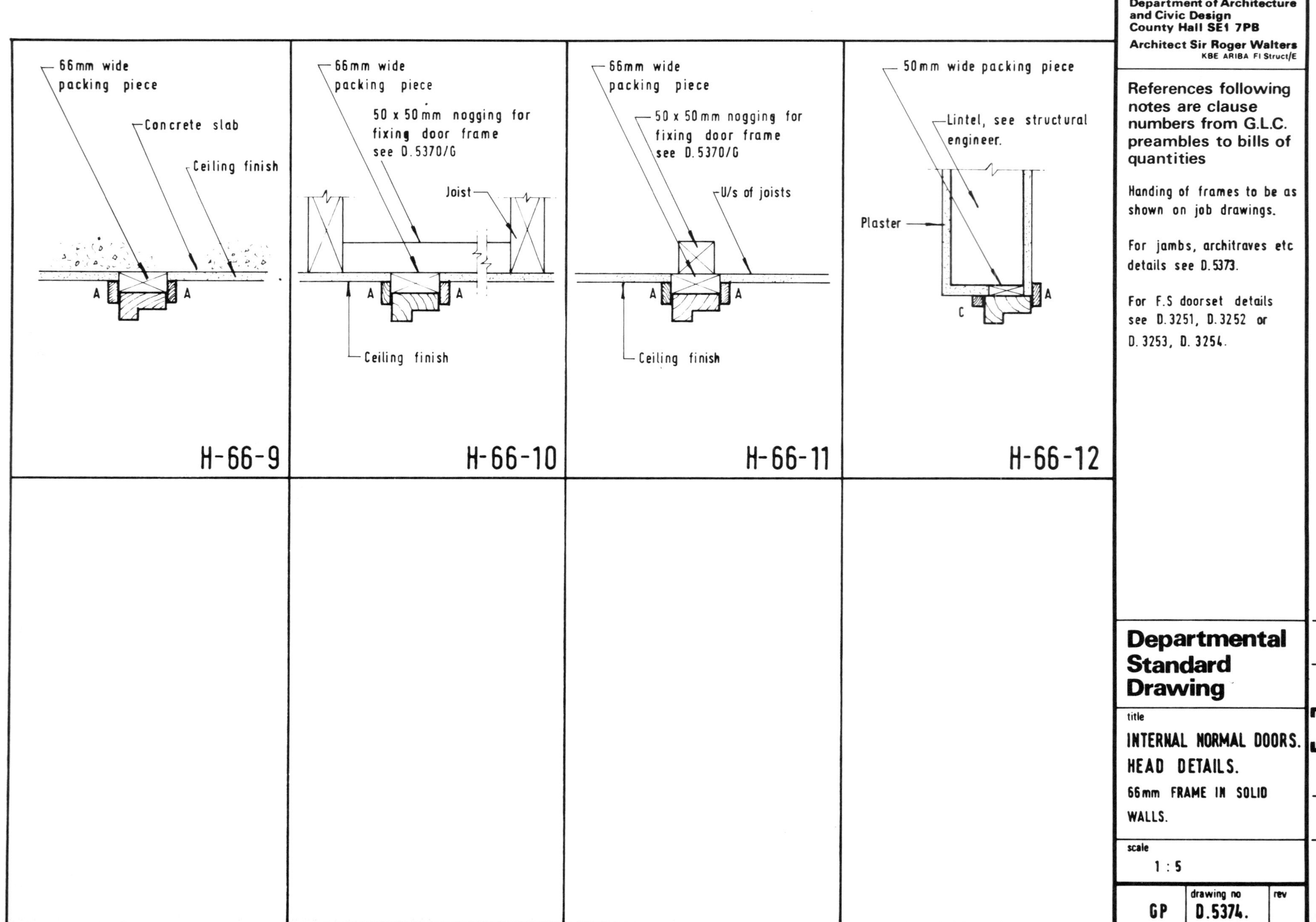
66mm wide
packing piece
Concrete slab
Ceiling finish
A
A
H-66-9
66mm wide
packing piece
50 x 50mm nogging for
fixing door frame
see D.5370/G
Joist
A
A
Ceiling finish
H-66-10
66mm wide
packing piece
50 x 50mm nogging for
fixing door frame
see D.5370/G
U/s of joists
A
A
Ceiling finish
H-66-11
50mm wide packing piece
Lintel, see structural
engineer.
Plaster
A
C
H-66-12
GLC ILEA
Department of Architecture
and Civic Design
County Hall SE1 7PB
Architect Sir Roger Walters
KBE ARIBA FI Struct/E
References following
notes are clause
numbers from G.L.C.
preambles to bills of
quantities
Handing of frames to be as
shown on job drawings.
For jambs, architraves etc
details see D.5373.
For F.S doorset details
see D.3251, D.3252 or
D.3253, D.3254.
Departmental
Standard
Drawing
title
INTERNAL NORMAL DOORS.
HEAD DETAILS.
66mm FRAME IN SOLID
WALLS.
scale
1 : 5
GP
drawing no
D.5374.
rev
260778
010379
22

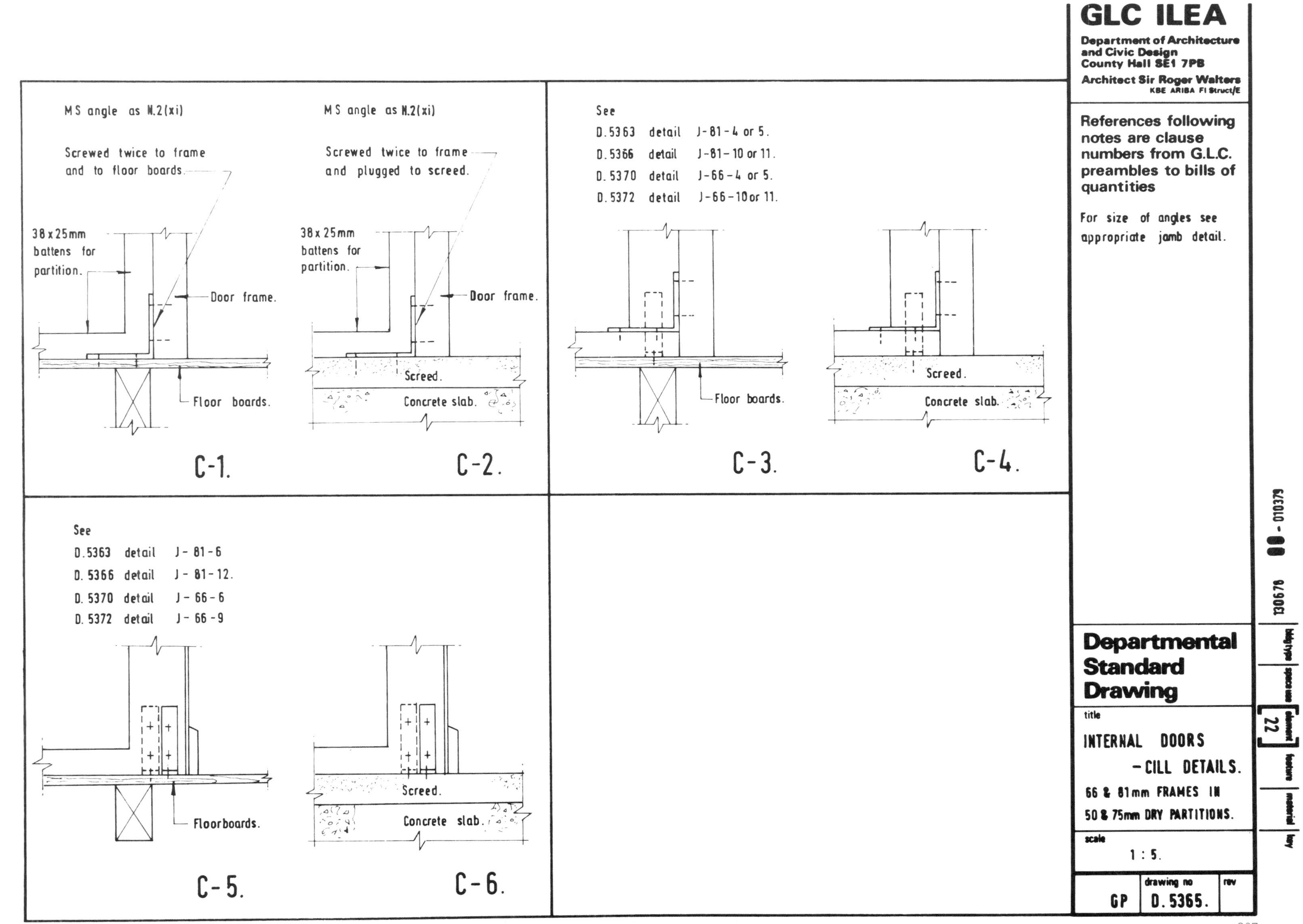
GLC ILEA
Department of Architecture and Civic Design
County Hall SE1 7PB
Architect Sir Roger Walters KBE ARIBA FI Struct/E
References following notes are clause numbers from G.L.C. preambles to bills of quantities
For size of angles see appropriate jamb detail.
MS angle as N.2(xi)
Screwed twice to frame and to floor boards.
38 x 25mm battens for partition.
Door frame.
Floor boards.
C-1.
MS angle as N.2(xi)
Screwed twice to frame and plugged to screed.
38 x 25mm battens for partition.
Door frame.
Screed.
Concrete slab.
C-2.
See
D.5363 detail J-81-4 or 5.
D.5366 detail J-81-10 or 11.
D.5370 detail J-66-4 or 5.
D.5372 detail J-66-10 or 11.
Floor boards.
C-3.
Screed.
Concrete slab.
C-4.
See
D.5363 detail J-81-6
D.5366 detail J-81-12.
D.5370 detail J-66-6
D.5372 detail J-66-9
Floorboards.
C-5.
Screed.
Concrete slab.
C-6.
130678 00-010379
Departmental Standard Drawing
title
INTERNAL DOORS
-CILL DETAILS.
66 & 81mm FRAMES IN
50 & 75mm DRY PARTITIONS.
scale
1 : 5.
bldg type
spaces use
element
22
feature
material
key
GP
drawing no
D.5365.
rev

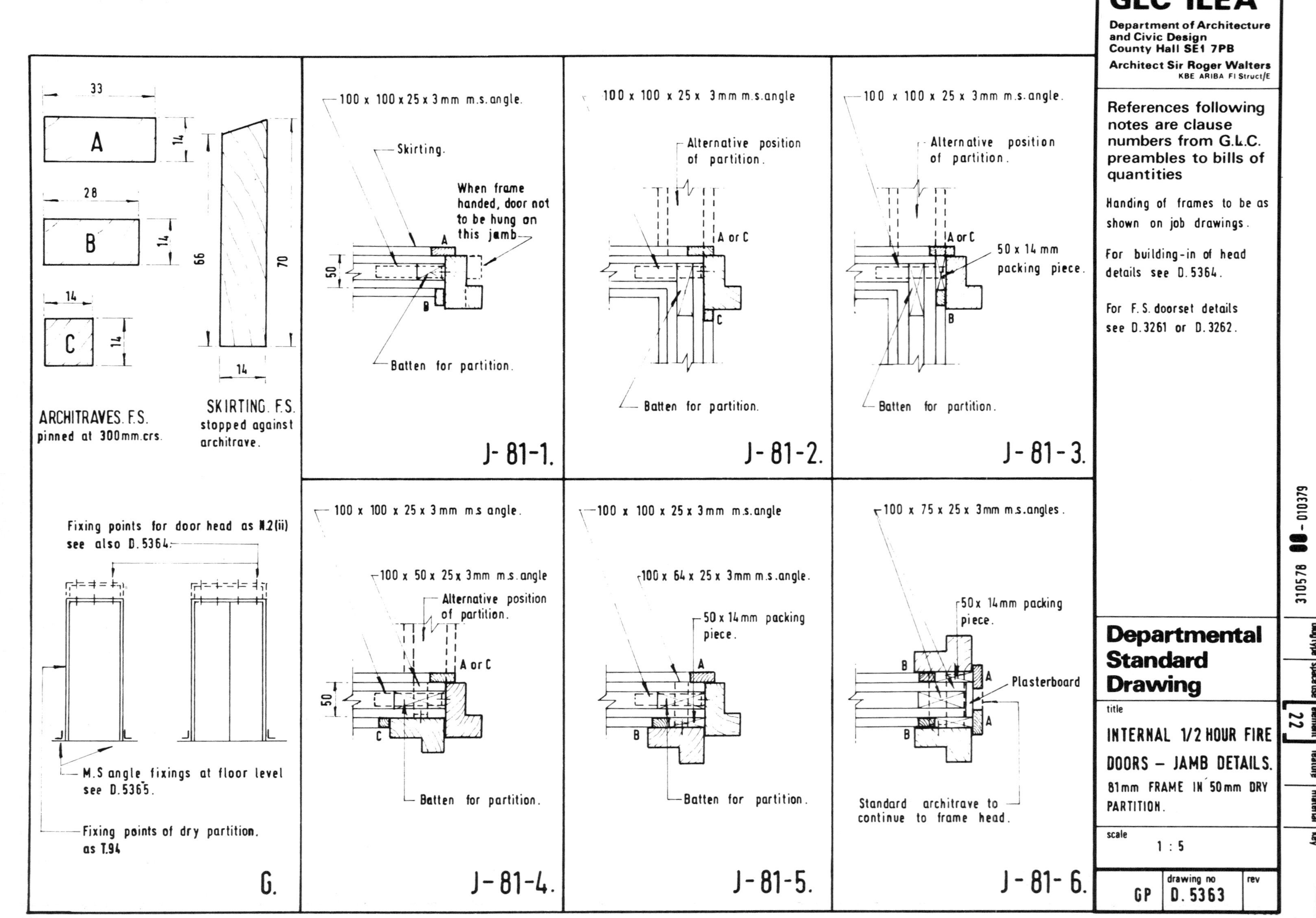
GLC ILEA
Department of Architecture and Civic Design
County Hall SE1 7PB
Architect Sir Roger Walters
KBE ARIBA FI Struct/E
References following notes are clause numbers from G.L.C. preambles to bills of quantities
Handing of frames to be as shown on job drawings.
For building-in of head details see D.5364.
For F.S. doorset details see D.3261 or D.3262.
Departmental Standard Drawing
title
INTERNAL 1/2 HOUR FIRE DOORS – JAMB DETAILS.
81mm FRAME IN 50mm DRY PARTITION.
scale
1 : 5
GP
drawing no
D. 5363
rev
310578 - 010379
bldg type
space use
element
22
feature
material
key
ARCHITRAVES. F.S.
pinned at 300mm.crs.
SKIRTING. F.S.
stopped against architrave.
A
B
C
33
28
14
66
70
100 x 100 x 25 x 3mm m.s.angle.
Skirting.
When frame handed, door not to be hung on this jamb
Batten for partition.
J-81-1.
Alternative position of partition.
A or C
J-81-2.
50 x 14 mm packing piece.
J-81-3.
Fixing points for door head as N.2(ii) see also D.5364.
M.S angle fixings at floor level see D.5365.
Fixing points of dry partition. as T.94
G.
100 x 50 x 25 x 3mm m.s.angle
J-81-4.
100 x 64 x 25 x 3mm m.s.angle.
50 x 14mm packing piece.
J-81-5.
100 x 75 x 25 x 3mm m.s.angles.
Plasterboard
Standard architrave to continue to frame head.
J-81-6.

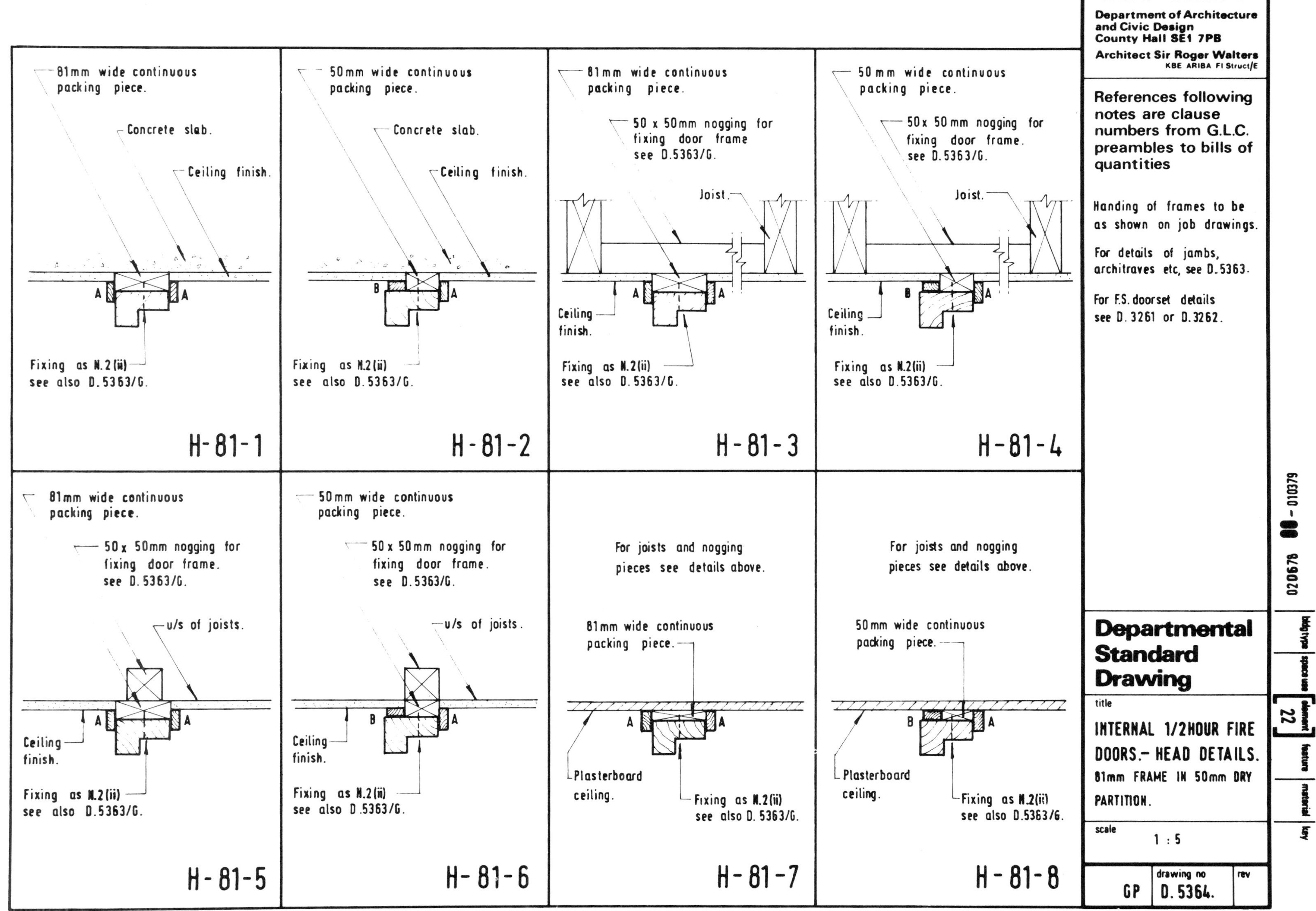
GLC ILEA
Department of Architecture and Civic Design
County Hall SE1 7PB
Architect Sir Roger Walters
KBE ARIBA FI Struct/E
References following notes are clause numbers from G.L.C. preambles to bills of quantities
Handing of frames to be as shown on job drawings.
For details of jambs, architraves etc, see D.5363.
For F.S. doorset details see D.3261 or D.3262.
81mm wide continuous packing piece.
Concrete slab.
Ceiling finish.
A
A
Fixing as N.2(ii) see also D.5363/G.
H-81-1
50mm wide continuous packing piece.
Concrete slab.
Ceiling finish.
B
A
Fixing as N.2(ii) see also D.5363/G.
H-81-2
81mm wide continuous packing piece.
50 x 50mm nogging for fixing door frame see D.5363/G.
Joist.
Ceiling finish.
A
A
Fixing as N.2(ii) see also D.5363/G.
H-81-3
50mm wide continuous packing piece.
50x 50mm nogging for fixing door frame. see D.5363/G.
Joist.
Ceiling finish.
B
A
Fixing as N.2(ii) see also D.5363/G.
H-81-4
81mm wide continuous packing piece.
50x 50mm nogging for fixing door frame. see D.5363/G.
u/s of joists.
Ceiling finish.
A
A
Fixing as N.2(ii) see also D.5363/G.
H-81-5
50mm wide continuous packing piece.
50x 50mm nogging for fixing door frame. see D.5363/G.
u/s of joists.
Ceiling finish.
B
A
Fixing as N.2(ii) see also D.5363/G.
H-81-6
For joists and nogging pieces see details above.
81mm wide continuous packing piece.
A
A
Plasterboard ceiling.
Fixing as N.2(ii) see also D.5363/G.
H-81-7
For joists and nogging pieces see details above.
50mm wide continuous packing piece.
B
A
Plasterboard ceiling.
Fixing as N.2(ii) see also D.5363/G.
H-81-8
020678 08 - 010379
Departmental Standard Drawing
title
INTERNAL 1/2HOUR FIRE DOORS.- HEAD DETAILS. 81mm FRAME IN 50mm DRY PARTITION.
scale
1 : 5
GP
drawing no
D.5364.
rev
bldg type
space use
element
22
feature
material
key

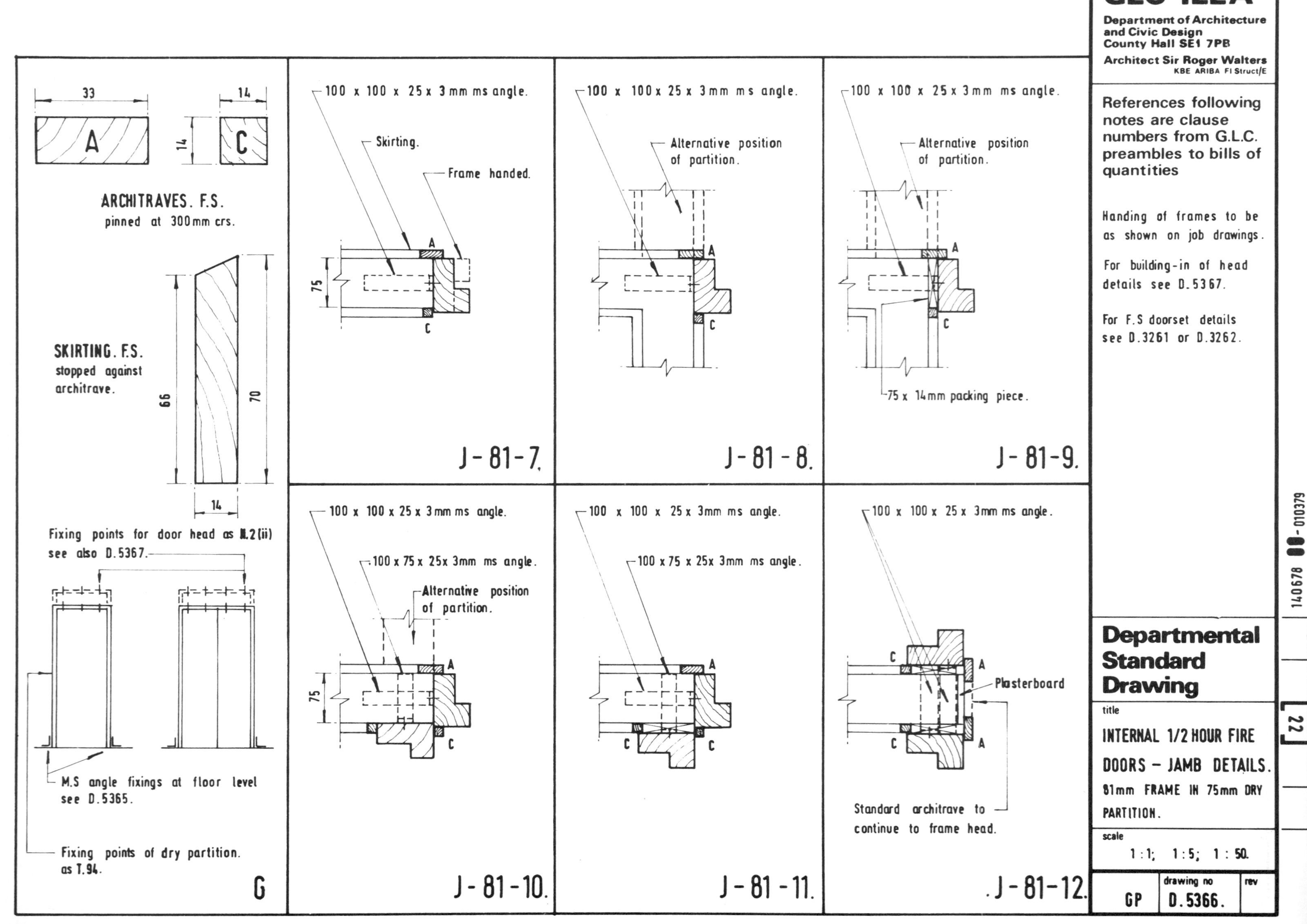
GLC ILEA
Department of Architecture and Civic Design
County Hall SE1 7PB
Architect Sir Roger Walters
KBE ARIBA FI Struct/E
References following notes are clause numbers from G.L.C. preambles to bills of quantities
Handing of frames to be as shown on job drawings.
For building-in of head details see D.5367.
For F.S doorset details see D.3261 or D.3262.
33
14
A
C
ARCHITRAVES. F.S.
pinned at 300mm crs.
SKIRTING. F.S.
stopped against architrave.
66
70
Fixing points for door head as M.2(ii) see also D.5367.
M.S angle fixings at floor level see D.5365.
Fixing points of dry partition. as T.94.
G
100 x 100 x 25 x 3mm ms angle.
Skirting.
Frame handed.
75
J-81-7.
Alternative position of partition.
J-81-8.
75 x 14mm packing piece.
J-81-9.
100 x 75 x 25x 3mm ms angle.
J-81-10.
J-81-11.
Plasterboard
Standard architrave to continue to frame head.
J-81-12.
Departmental Standard Drawing
title
INTERNAL 1/2 HOUR FIRE DOORS – JAMB DETAILS.
81mm FRAME IN 75mm DRY PARTITION.
scale
1:1; 1:5; 1:50.
GP
drawing no
D.5366.
rev
22
140678 - 010379

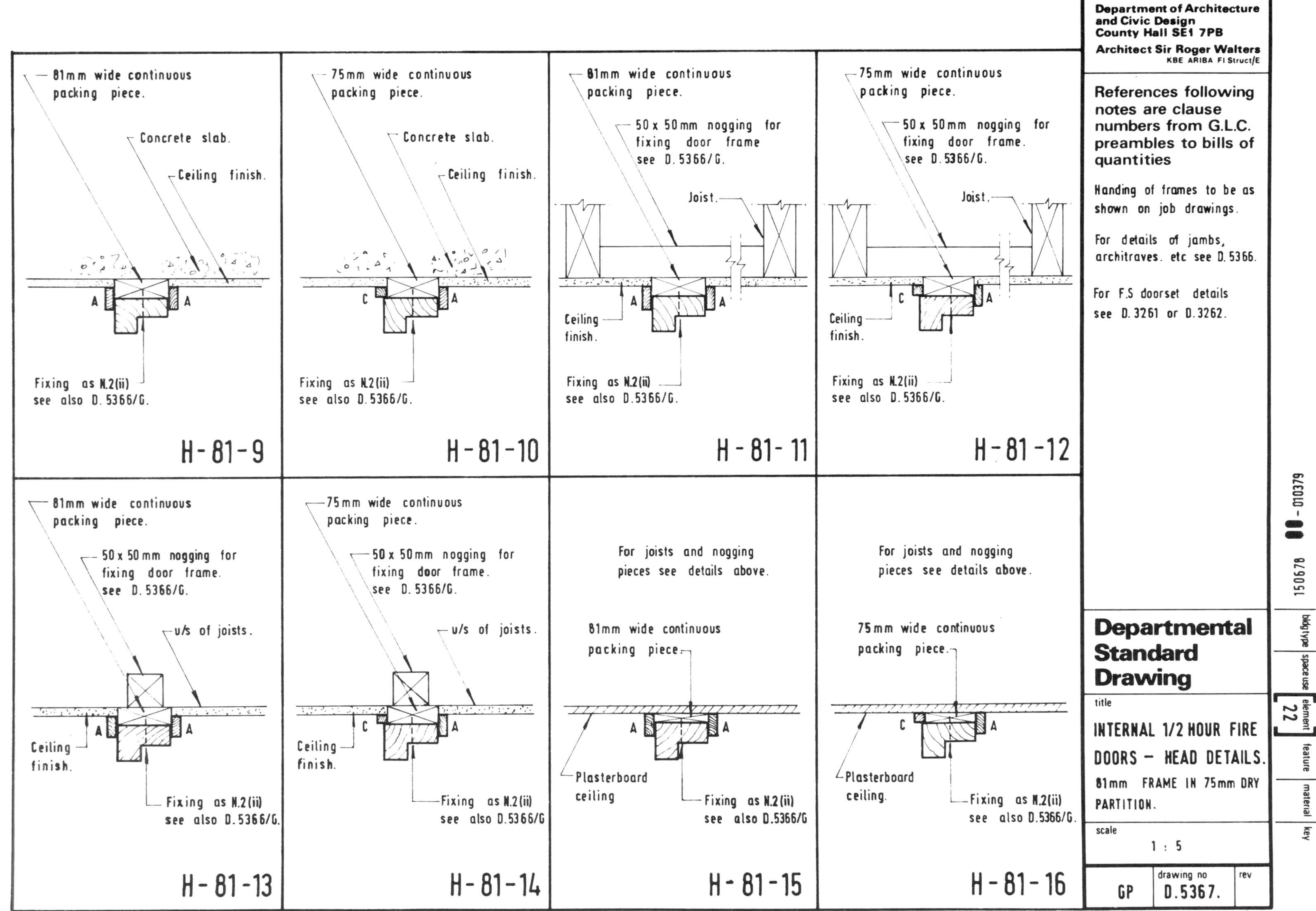
GLC ILEA
Department of Architecture and Civic Design County Hall SE1 7PB
Architect Sir Roger Walters KBE ARIBA FI Struct/E
References following notes are clause numbers from G.L.C. preambles to bills of quantities
Handing of frames to be as shown on job drawings.
For details of jambs, architraves. etc see D. 5366.
For F.S doorset details see D. 3261 or D. 3262.
81mm wide continuous packing piece.
Concrete slab.
Ceiling finish.
A
Fixing as N.2(ii) see also D. 5366/G.
H-81-9
75mm wide continuous packing piece.
Concrete slab.
Ceiling finish.
C
A
Fixing as N.2(ii) see also D. 5366/G.
H-81-10
81mm wide continuous packing piece.
50 x 50mm nogging for fixing door frame see D. 5366/G.
Joist.
Ceiling finish.
Fixing as N.2(ii) see also D. 5366/G.
H-81-11
75mm wide continuous packing piece.
50 x 50mm nogging for fixing door frame. see D. 5366/G.
Joist.
Ceiling finish.
Fixing as N.2(ii) see also D. 5366/G.
H-81-12
81mm wide continuous packing piece.
50 x 50mm nogging for fixing door frame. see D. 5366/G.
u/s of joists.
Ceiling finish.
Fixing as N.2(ii) see also D.5366/G.
H-81-13
75mm wide continuous packing piece.
50 x 50mm nogging for fixing door frame. see D. 5366/G.
u/s of joists.
Ceiling finish.
Fixing as N.2(ii) see also D.5366/G
H-81-14
For joists and nogging pieces see details above.
81mm wide continuous packing piece.
Plasterboard ceiling
Fixing as N.2(ii) see also D.5366/G
H-81-15
For joists and nogging pieces see details above.
75mm wide continuous packing piece.
Plasterboard ceiling.
Fixing as N.2(ii) see also D.5366/G.
H-81-16
150678 ■■ - 010379
bldg type
spaceuse
element 22
feature
material
key
Departmental Standard Drawing
title
INTERNAL 1/2 HOUR FIRE DOORS — HEAD DETAILS.
81mm FRAME IN 75mm DRY PARTITION.
scale
1 : 5
GP
drawing no
D.5367.
rev

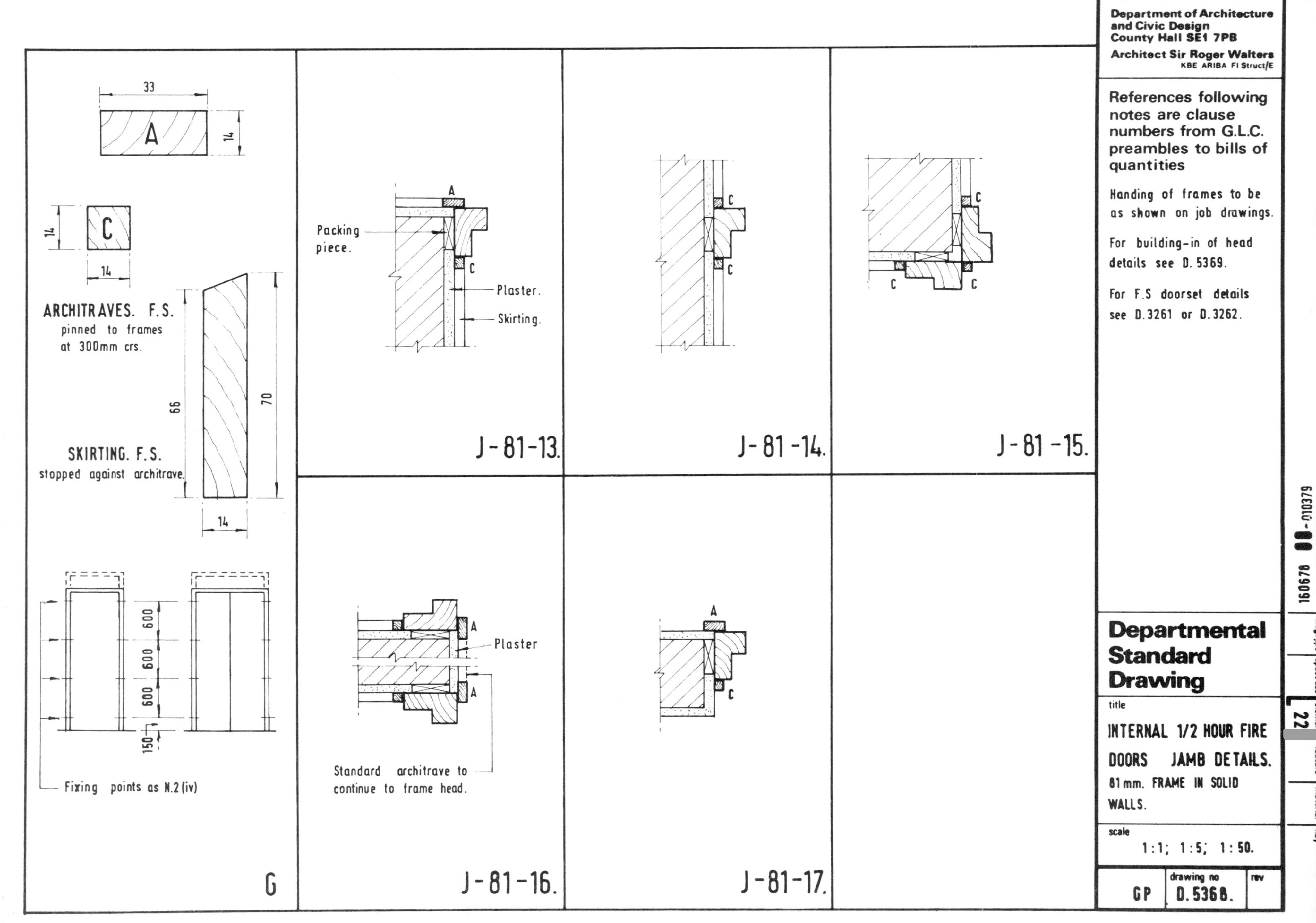
GLC ILEA
Department of Architecture and Civic Design
County Hall SE1 7PB
Architect Sir Roger Walters
KBE ARIBA FI Struct/E
References following notes are clause numbers from G.L.C. preambles to bills of quantities
Handing of frames to be as shown on job drawings.
For building-in of head details see D.5369.
For F.S doorset details see D.3261 or D.3262.
Departmental Standard Drawing
title
INTERNAL 1/2 HOUR FIRE DOORS JAMB DETAILS.
81mm. FRAME IN SOLID WALLS.
scale
1:1; 1:5; 1:50.
GP
drawing no
D.5368.
rev
33
A
14
C
14
14
ARCHITRAVES. F.S.
pinned to frames at 300mm crs.
66
70
SKIRTING. F.S.
stopped against architrave.
14
600
600
600
150
Fixing points as N.2 (iv)
G
Packing piece.
Plaster.
Skirting.
J-81-13.
J-81-14.
J-81-15.
Plaster
Standard architrave to continue to frame head.
J-81-16.
J-81-17.
160678
22

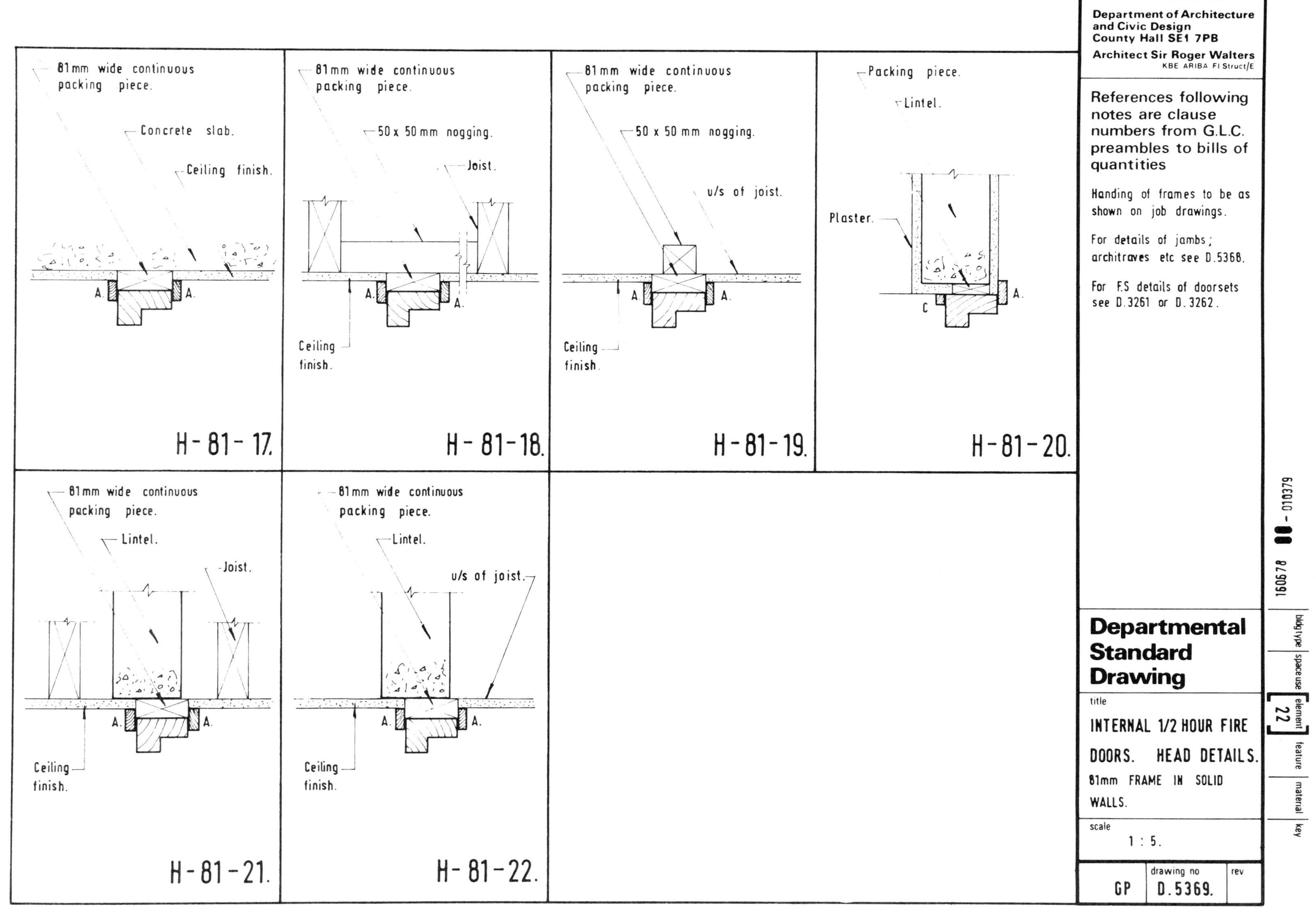

GLC ILEA
Department of Architecture and Civic Design
County Hall SE1 7PB
Architect Sir Roger Walters
KBE ARIBA FI Struct/E
References following notes are clause numbers from G.L.C. preambles to bills of quantities
Handing of frames to be as shown on job drawings.
For details of jambs; architraves etc see D.5368.
For F.S details of doorsets see D.3261 or D.3262.
81mm wide continuous packing piece.
Concrete slab.
Ceiling finish.
A.
H-81-17.
50 x 50 mm nogging.
Joist.
Ceiling finish.
H-81-18.
u/s of joist.
H-81-19.
Packing piece.
Lintel.
Plaster.
C
H-81-20.
Lintel.
Joist.
H-81-21.
H-81-22.
160678 00 - 010379
bldg type
space use
element
22
feature
material
key
Departmental Standard Drawing
title
INTERNAL 1/2 HOUR FIRE DOORS. HEAD DETAILS.
81mm FRAME IN SOLID WALLS.
scale
1 : 5.
GP
drawing no
D.5369.
rev

			DOORSET.															
LOCATION.			FRAME.				DOOR.		BUILDING – IN DETAILS.			IRONMONGERY CODES G.L.C STANDARD LIST.				REMARKS
DOOR Nº	DOOR POSITION.	FRAME & DOOR DETAILS DRG NOS	HEIGHT (mm)	WIDTH (mm)	DEPTH (mm)	FAN-LIGHT	HEIGHT x WIDTH x THICKNESS (mm) TYPE {HARDBOARD PLY FRAMED	GLASS PANEL & BEADS DRG NO	HEADS & THRESHOLD (if required)	JAMB (hinged)	JAMB (locked)	LOCK or LATCH	HINGES	OTHER		

GLC ILEA
DEPARTMENT OF ARCHITECTURE AND CIVIC DESIGN
County Hall SE1 7PB

Architect Sir Roger Walters KBE FRIBA FIStructE

drawn	checked	section

telephone 01-633

revisions	date

job

title
DOOR SCHEDULE.

scale	date

block	storey	section	room

job no.	drawing no.
GP	D. 6010.

110578. - 010379

[22]

2 Partitions

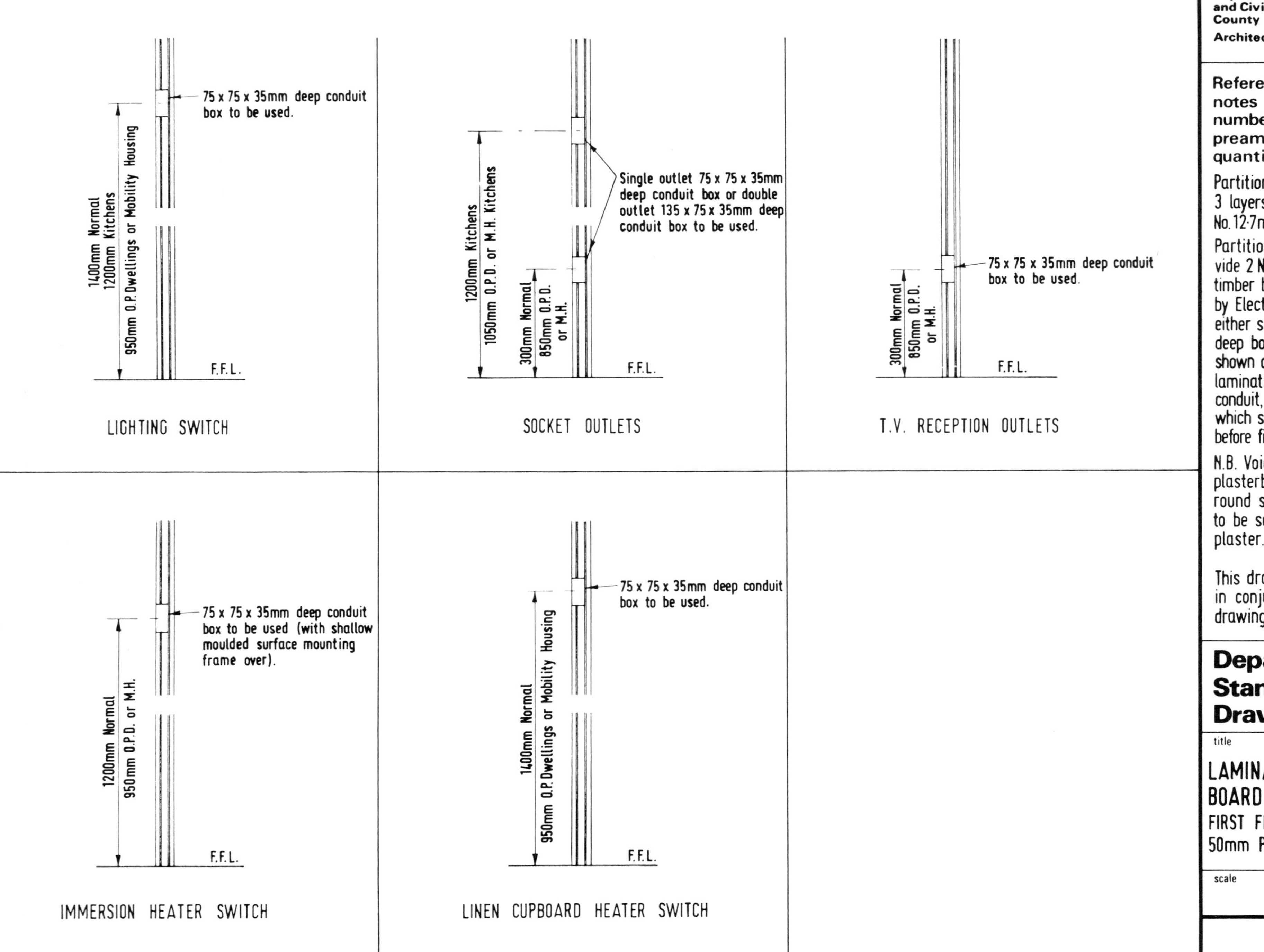

GLC ILEA
Department of Architecture and Civic Design
County Hall SE1 7PB
Architect Sir Roger Walters KBE ARIBA FI Struct/E

References following notes are clause numbers from G.L.C. preambles to bills of quantities

Partition is constructed of 3 layers of plasterboard-2 No. 12·7mm with 19mm core.

Partition Contractor to provide 2 No. 150 x 25 x 25mm timber battens to be fixed by Electrical Contractor on either side of each 35mm deep box except where shown otherwise. Middle lamination to be cut around conduit, battens and box, which shall be plastered in before fixing final lamination.

N.B. Voids in laminated plasterboard partitions round sanitary spaces to be solidly filled with plaster.

This drawing to be read in conjunction with job drawings.

Departmental Standard Drawing

title

LAMINATED PLASTERBOARD PARTITION.
FIRST FIXING DETAILS.
50mm PARTITION.

scale 1 : 10

drawing no D5247 rev A

22

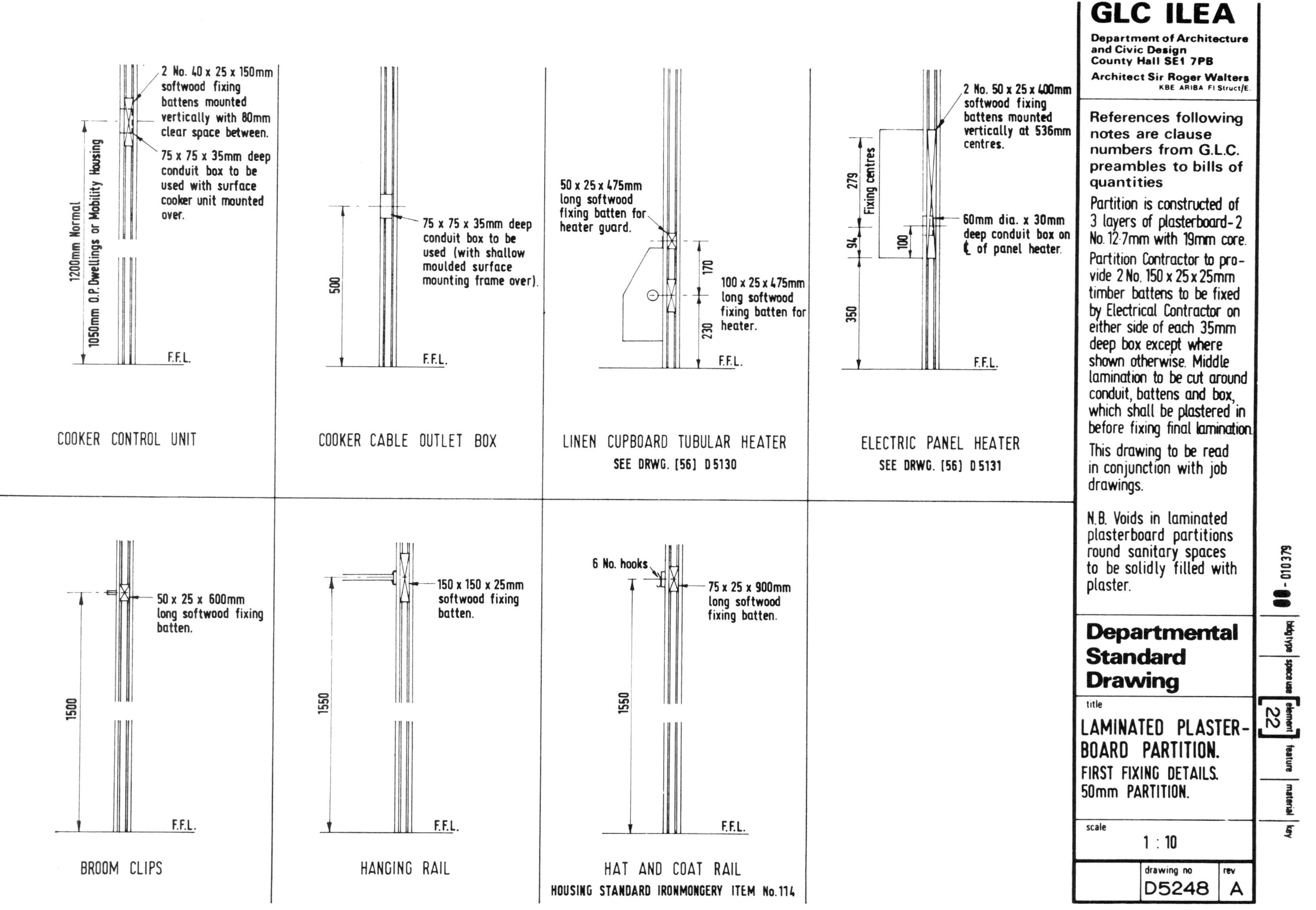
GLC ILEA
Department of Architecture and Civic Design
County Hall SE1 7PB
Architect Sir Roger Walters KBE ARIBA FI Struct/E.
References following notes are clause numbers from G.L.C. preambles to bills of quantities
Partition is constructed of 3 layers of plasterboard - 2 No. 12·7mm with 19mm core.
Partition Contractor to provide 2 No. 150 x 25 x 25mm timber battens to be fixed by Electrical Contractor on either side of each 35mm deep box except where shown otherwise. Middle lamination to be cut around conduit, battens and box, which shall be plastered in before fixing final lamination.
This drawing to be read in conjunction with job drawings.
N.B. Voids in laminated plasterboard partitions round sanitary spaces to be solidly filled with plaster.
Departmental Standard Drawing
title
LAMINATED PLASTERBOARD PARTITION.
FIRST FIXING DETAILS.
50mm PARTITION.
scale
1 : 10
drawing no
D5248
rev
A
bldg type
space use
element
22
feature
material
key
010379
2 No. 40 x 25 x 150mm softwood fixing battens mounted vertically with 80mm clear space between.
75 x 75 x 35mm deep conduit box to be used with surface cooker unit mounted over.
1200mm Normal
1050mm O.P. Dwellings or Mobility Housing
F.F.L.
COOKER CONTROL UNIT
75 x 75 x 35mm deep conduit box to be used (with shallow moulded surface mounting frame over).
500
F.F.L.
COOKER CABLE OUTLET BOX
50 x 25 x 475mm long softwood fixing batten for heater guard.
100 x 25 x 475mm long softwood fixing batten for heater.
170
230
F.F.L.
LINEN CUPBOARD TUBULAR HEATER
SEE DRWG. [56] D5130
2 No. 50 x 25 x 400mm softwood fixing battens mounted vertically at 536mm centres.
60mm dia. x 30mm deep conduit box on ℄ of panel heater.
Fixing centres
279
94
100
350
F.F.L.
ELECTRIC PANEL HEATER
SEE DRWG. [56] D5131
50 x 25 x 600mm long softwood fixing batten.
1500
F.F.L.
BROOM CLIPS
150 x 150 x 25mm softwood fixing batten.
1550
F.F.L.
HANGING RAIL
6 No. hooks
75 x 25 x 900mm long softwood fixing batten.
1550
F.F.L.
HAT AND COAT RAIL
HOUSING STANDARD IRONMONGERY ITEM No. 114

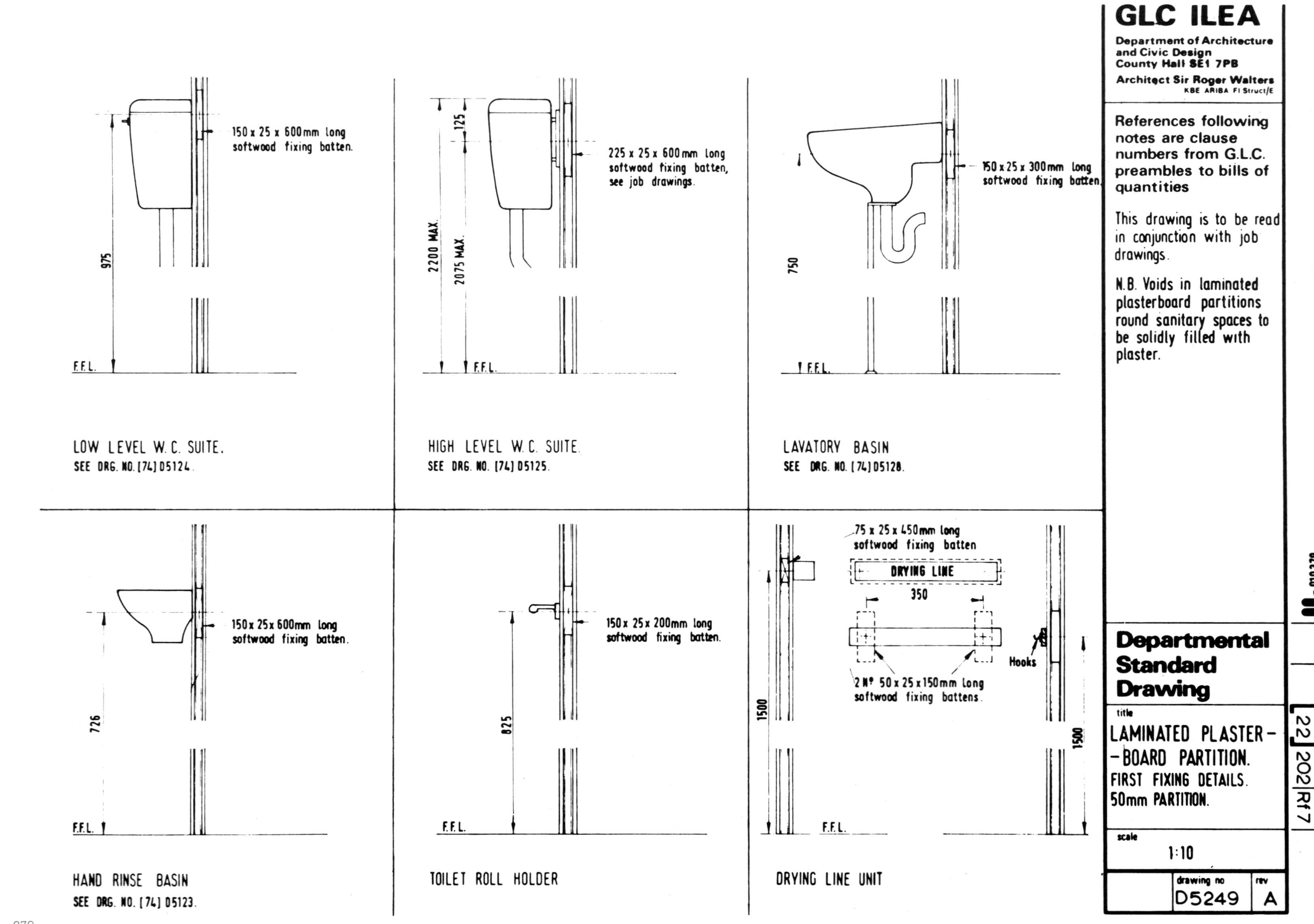
GLC ILEA
Department of Architecture and Civic Design
County Hall SE1 7PB
Architect Sir Roger Walters
KBE ARIBA FI Struct/E
References following notes are clause numbers from G.L.C. preambles to bills of quantities
This drawing is to be read in conjunction with job drawings.
N.B. Voids in laminated plasterboard partitions round sanitary spaces to be solidly filled with plaster.
150 x 25 x 600mm long softwood fixing batten.
975
F.F.L.
LOW LEVEL W.C. SUITE.
SEE DRG. NO. [74] D5124.
125
225 x 25 x 600mm long softwood fixing batten, see job drawings.
2200 MAX.
2075 MAX.
F.F.L.
HIGH LEVEL W.C. SUITE.
SEE DRG. NO. [74] D5125.
150 x 25 x 300mm long softwood fixing batten.
750
F.F.L.
LAVATORY BASIN
SEE DRG. NO. [74] D5128.
150 x 25 x 600mm long softwood fixing batten.
726
F.F.L.
HAND RINSE BASIN
SEE DRG. NO. [74] D5123.
150 x 25 x 200mm long softwood fixing batten.
825
F.F.L.
TOILET ROLL HOLDER
75 x 25 x 450mm long softwood fixing batten
DRYING LINE
350
2 Nº 50 x 25 x 150mm long softwood fixing battens.
Hooks
1500
1500
F.F.L.
DRYING LINE UNIT
Departmental Standard Drawing
title
LAMINATED PLASTER-BOARD PARTITION.
FIRST FIXING DETAILS.
50mm PARTITION.
scale
1:10
drawing no
D5249
rev
A
[22] 202 Rf7

3 Ceiling finishes

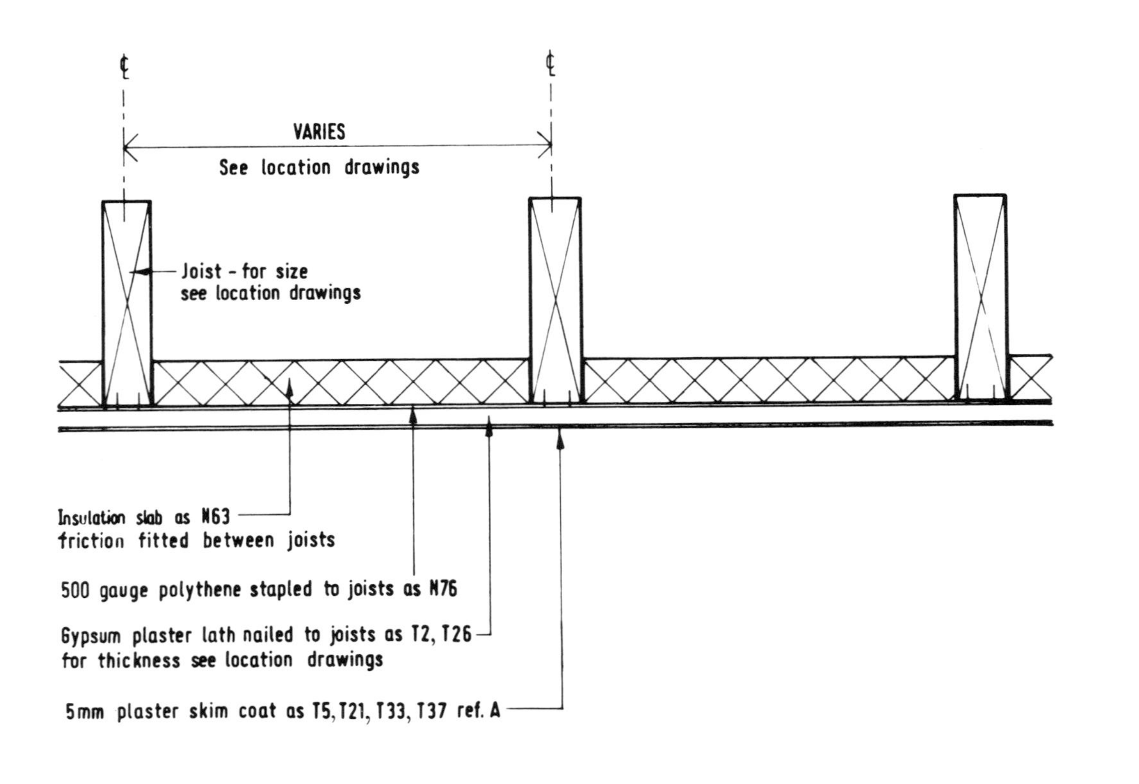

GLC ILEA

Department of Architecture and Civic Design
County Hall SE1

Architect Sir Roger Walters KBE FRIBA FI Struct E

References following notes are clause numbers from G.L.C. preambles to bills of quantities

Departmental Standard Drawing

title

INSULATED CEILING.
TIMBER ROOF.
(PLASTER LATH).

scale 1:5

drawing no D5080 rev. B

(45) 350 Rf7 B1

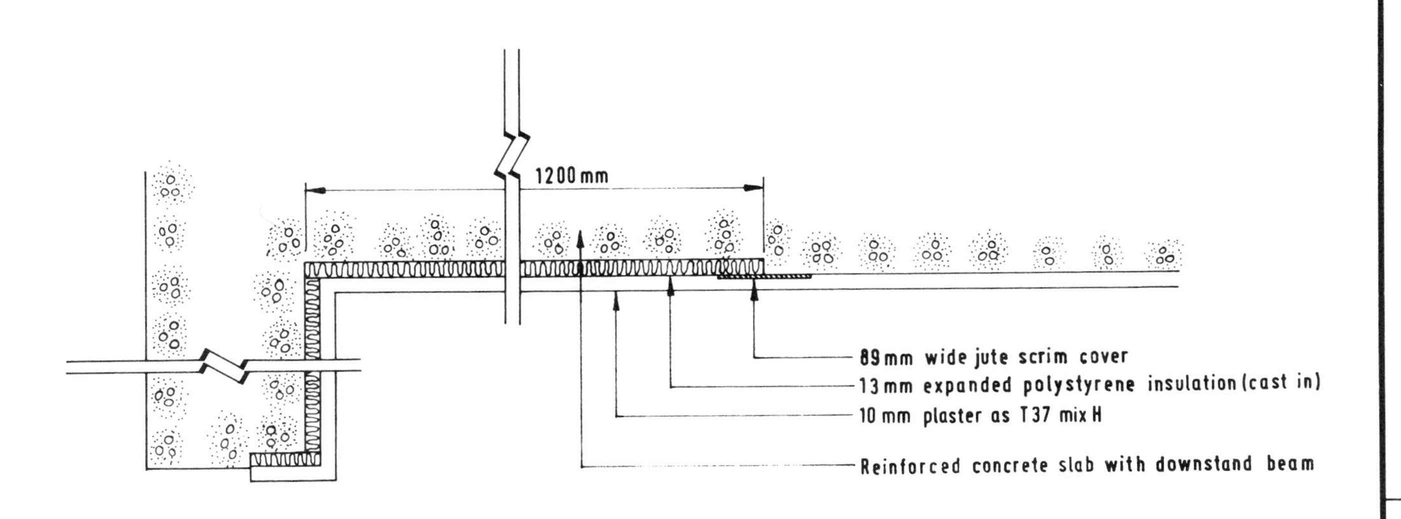

GLC ILEA
Department of Architecture and Civic Design
County Hall SE1
Architect Sir Roger Walters KBE FRIBA FI StructE

References following notes are clause numbers from G.L.C. preambles to bills of quantities.

Departmental Standard Drawing

title
COLD BRIDGE
INSULATION TO CEILING

scale 1:5

drawing no D5047A

bldg type 8 | space use | element [45] | feature 350 | material Rn7 | key A

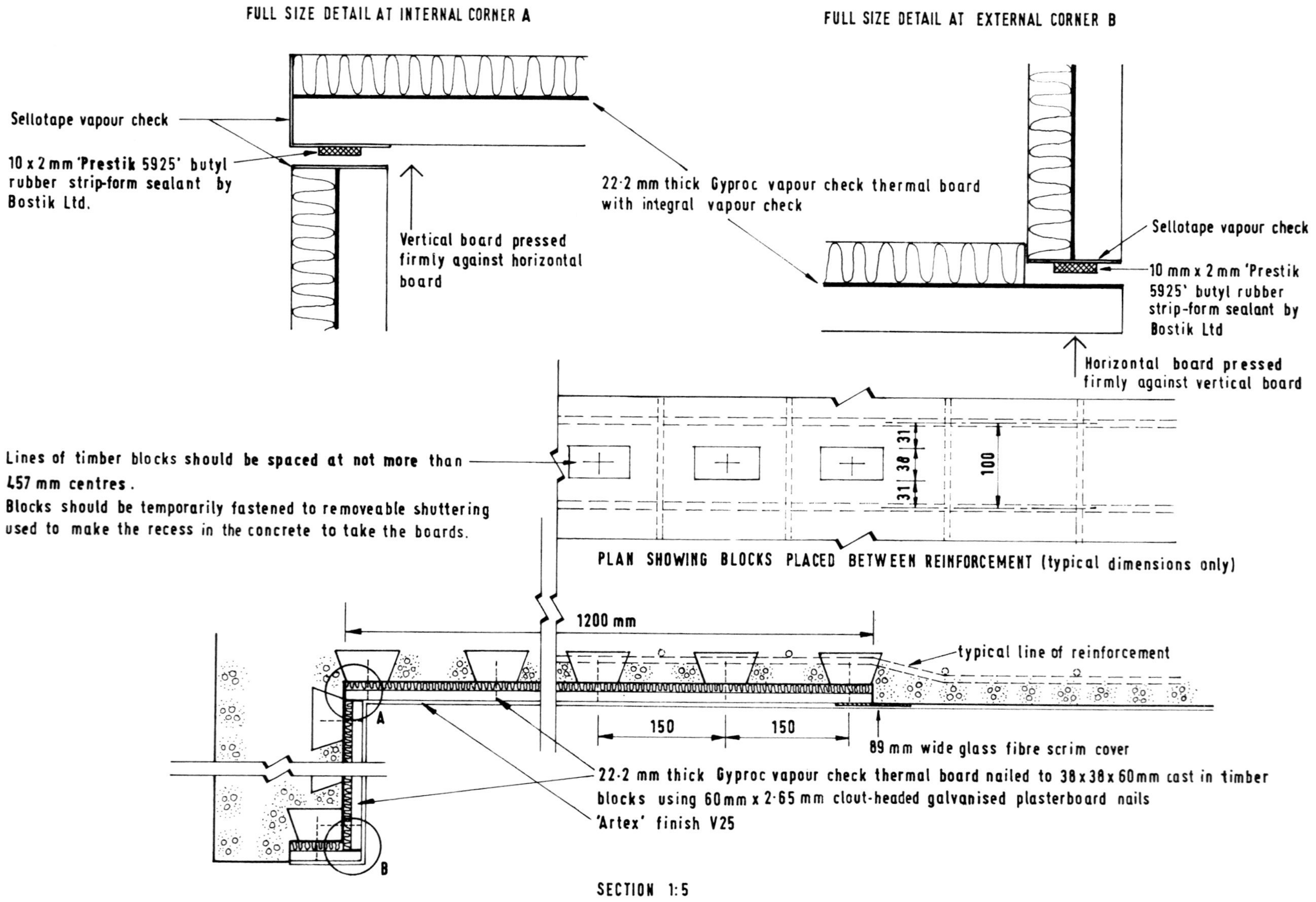

GLC ILEA

Department of Architecture and Civic Design
County Hall SE1
Architect Sir Roger Walters KBE FRIBA FI StructE

References following notes are clause numbers from G.L.C. preambles to bills of quantities.

This drawing to be read in conjunction with relevant job drawings.

Structural engineer should be consulted with regard to placing of blocks in relation to reinforcement.

Care should be taken that the structure is adequately dried out before applying the boards.

FULL SIZE DETAIL AT INTERNAL CORNER A

Sellotape vapour check

10 x 2 mm 'Prestik 5925' butyl rubber strip-form sealant by Bostik Ltd.

Vertical board pressed firmly against horizontal board

22·2 mm thick Gyproc vapour check thermal board with integral vapour check

FULL SIZE DETAIL AT EXTERNAL CORNER B

Sellotape vapour check

10 mm x 2 mm 'Prestik 5925' butyl rubber strip-form sealant by Bostik Ltd

Horizontal board pressed firmly against vertical board

Lines of timber blocks should be spaced at not more than 457 mm centres.
Blocks should be temporarily fastened to removeable shuttering used to make the recess in the concrete to take the boards.

31 38 31 100

PLAN SHOWING BLOCKS PLACED BETWEEN REINFORCEMENT (typical dimensions only)

1200 mm

typical line of reinforcement

150 150

89 mm wide glass fibre scrim cover

22·2 mm thick Gyproc vapour check thermal board nailed to 38 x 38 x 60mm cast in timber blocks using 60mm x 2·65 mm clout-headed galvanised plasterboard nails

'Artex' finish V25

A

B

SECTION 1:5

Departmental Standard Drawing

title
COLD BRIDGE INSULATION
ARTEX FINISH

scale
1:5 and F.S.

drawing no
D5048

bldg type 8 | space use | element 45 | feature 350 | material Rf7 | key C

00 - 01079

4 Trap doors and ladders

5077 Lift motor room single trapdoor
5079 Lift motor room double trapdoors
5078 Trapdoor ladder
4080 Trapdoor ladder—details
4081 Trapdoor ladder—details

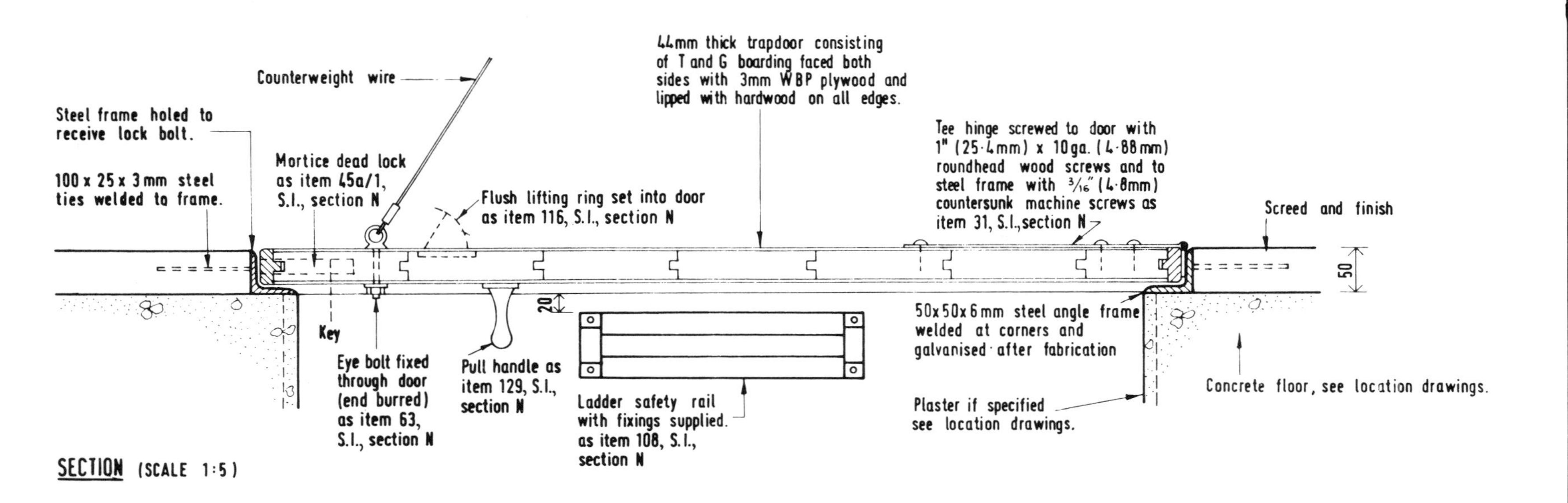

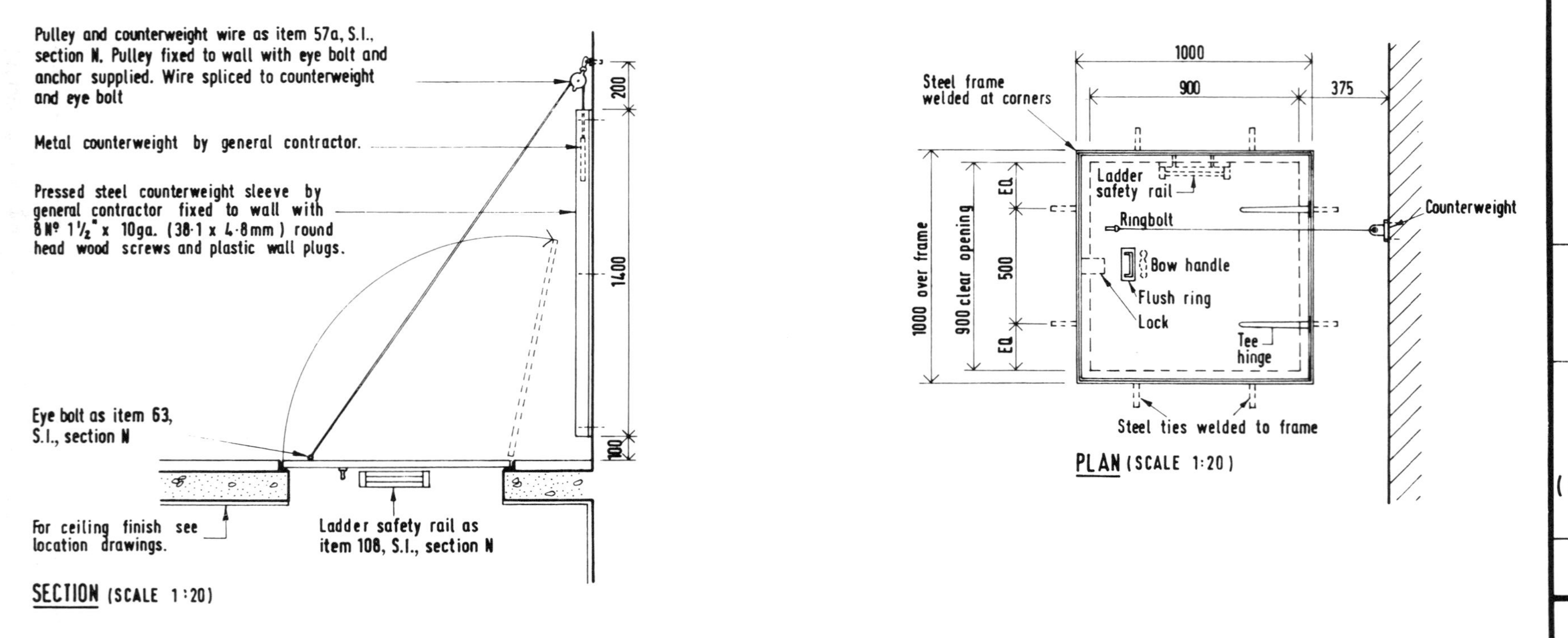

GLC ILEA

Department of Architecture and Civic Design
County Hall SE1
Architect Sir Roger Walters KBE FRIBA FI StructE

References following notes are clause numbers from G.L.C. preambles to bills of quantities.

Standard ironmongery set consisting of items 31, 45a/1, 57a, 63, 108, 116 & 129

This trapdoor must not be used as a means of escape

For ladder details see drwgs. [23] D.4080, D.4081 & D.5078

Departmental Standard Drawing

title

LIFT MOTOR ROOM TRAPDOOR
SINGLE DOOR
(PERSONNEL ACCESS ONLY)

scale

AS STATED

drawing no	rev
D5077	E

[23] 165 Xi2 A

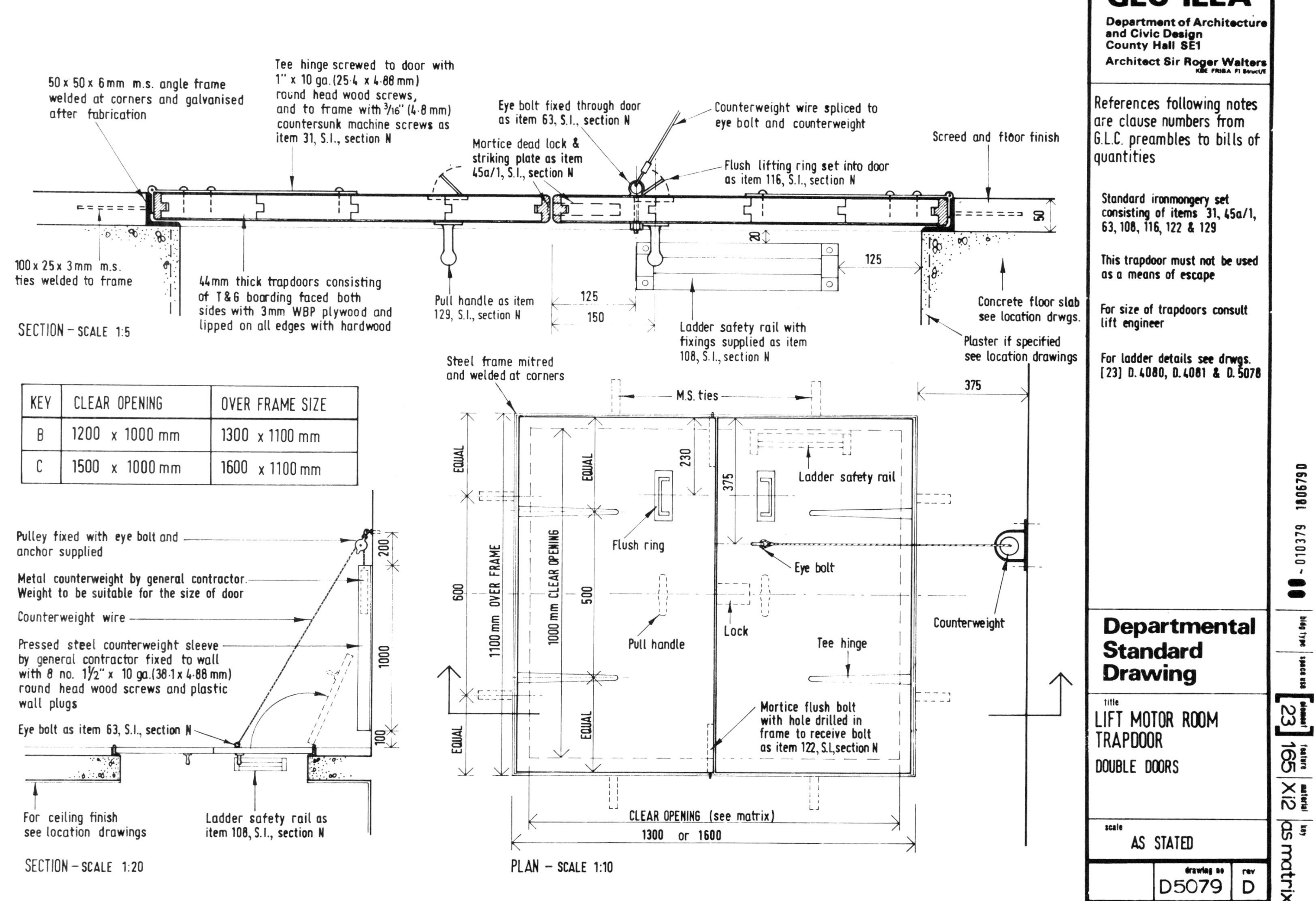

KEY	CLEAR OPENING	OVER FRAME SIZE
B	1200 x 1000 mm	1300 x 1100 mm
C	1500 x 1000 mm	1600 x 1100 mm

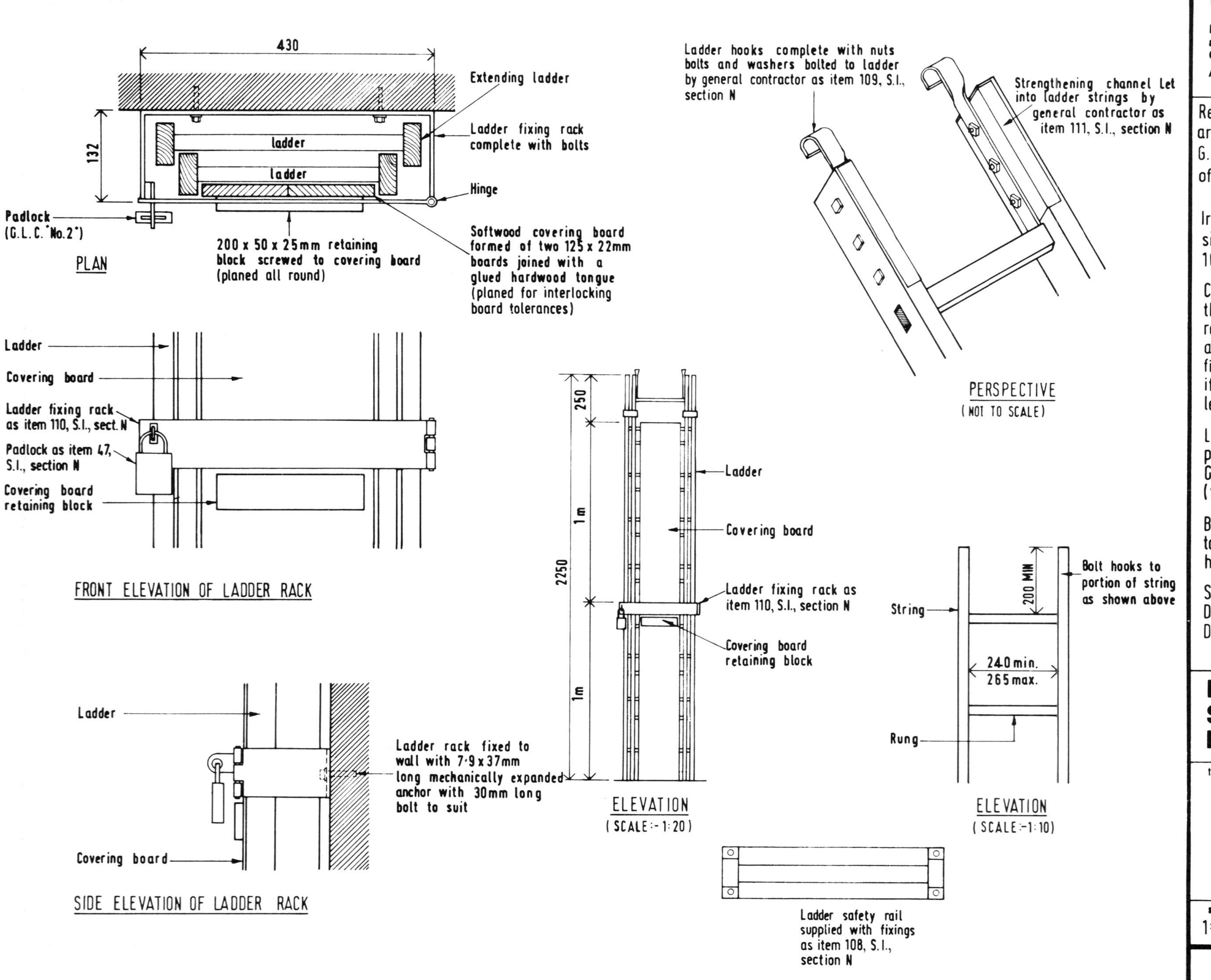

GLC ILEA

Department of Architecture and Civic Design
County Hall SE1
Architect Sir Roger Walters KBE FRIBA FI StructE

References following notes are clause numbers from G.L.C. preambles to bills of quantities.

Ironmongery set consisting of items 108, 109, 110, 47, 111.

Contractor should ensure that ladders have the required length of string above the top rung for fixing hooks and trimmed if necessary to total length shown.

Ladder safety rail provided in 2 parts. Galvanised backplate (first fixing).

Brackets and rail fixed to backplate prior to handover.

See also drwgs. [23] D.4080, D4081, D.5077 & D.5079

Departmental Standard Drawing

title

TRAPDOOR LADDER

scale

1:5 UNLESS STATED

drawing no D5078 rev E

bldg type | space use | element [23] | feature 165 | material Xi2 | key C

010379 180679E

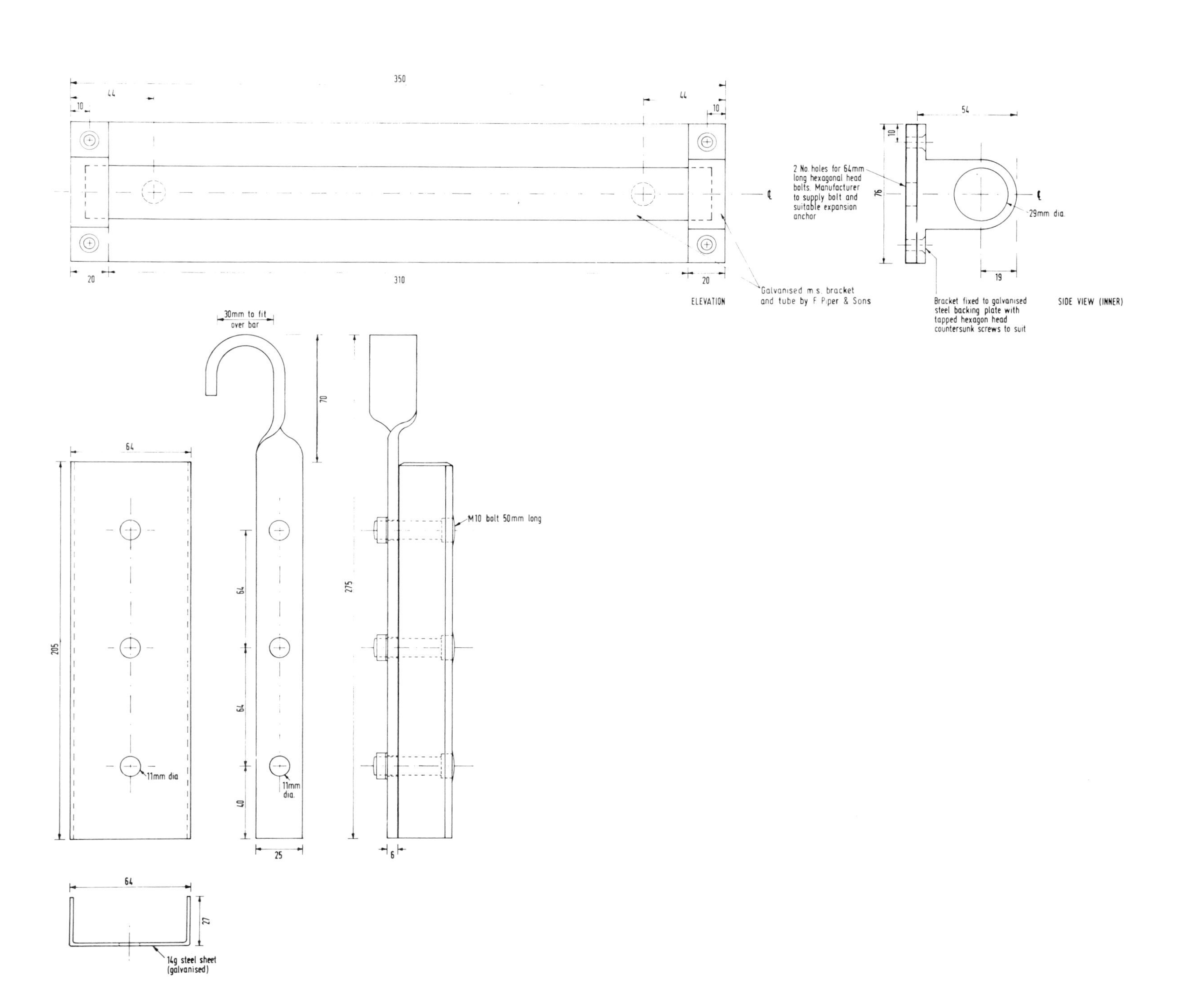

GLC ILEA

Department of Architecture and Civic Design
County Hall SE1

Architect Sir Roger Walters
KBE FRIBA FI Struct/E

1. Manufacturer to supply all parts including fixing bolts and screws and to obtain rail and brackets from F. Piper & Sons.

2. Rail and brackets will be fixed on site to backplate with screws as specified (to be provided)

3. All parts to be hot dipped galvanised after manufacture to B.S. 729

4. See also drwgs. [23] D.4081, D.5077, D.5078 & D.5079.

Departmental Standard Drawing

title

TRAP DOOR LADDER SAFETY RAIL.

STANDARD IRONMONGERY ITEMS 108, 109, 111.

scale 1 : 1

drawing no. D 4080 B

bldg type | space use | element 23 | feature 165 | material Xh2 | key

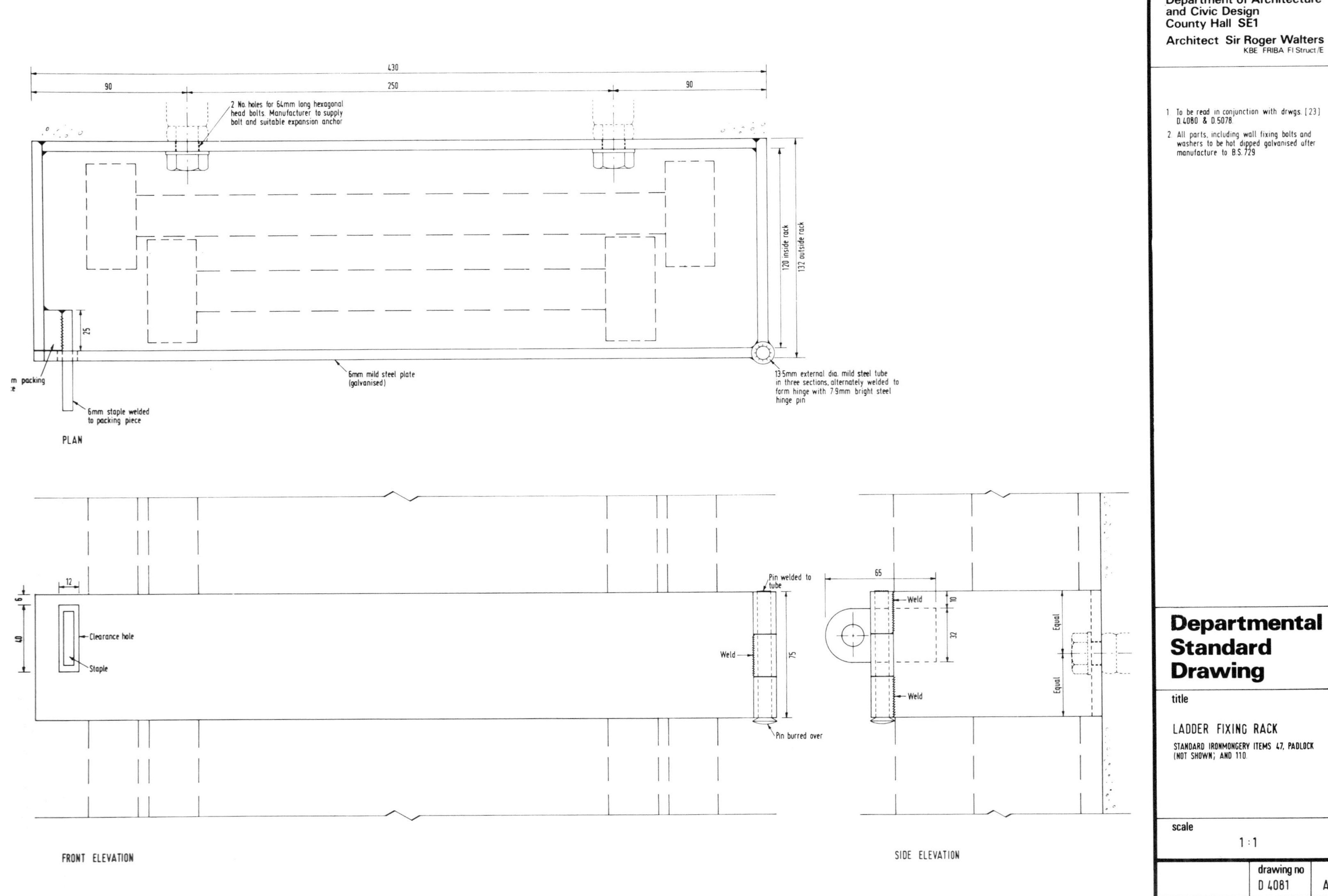
GLC ILEA
Department of Architecture and Civic Design
County Hall SE1
Architect Sir Roger Walters
KBE FRIBA FI Struct/E
1. To be read in conjunction with drwgs. [23] D.4080 & D.5078.
2. All parts, including wall fixing bolts and washers to be hot dipped galvanised after manufacture to B.S. 729
430
90
250
90
2 No. holes for 64mm long hexagonal head bolts. Manufacturer to supply bolt and suitable expansion anchor
120 inside rack
132 outside rack
25
6mm mild steel plate (galvanised)
13.5mm external dia. mild steel tube in three sections, alternately welded to form hinge with 7.9mm bright steel hinge pin
6mm staple welded to packing piece
PLAN
12
6
40
Clearance hole
Staple
Pin welded to tube
Weld
75
Pin burred over
FRONT ELEVATION
65
Weld
10
32
Equal
Equal
Weld
SIDE ELEVATION
Departmental Standard Drawing
title
LADDER FIXING RACK
STANDARD IRONMONGERY ITEMS 47, PADLOCK (NOT SHOWN), AND 110.
scale
1:1
drawing no
D 4081
A
23
165
Xh2

5 Hatches to roof spaces

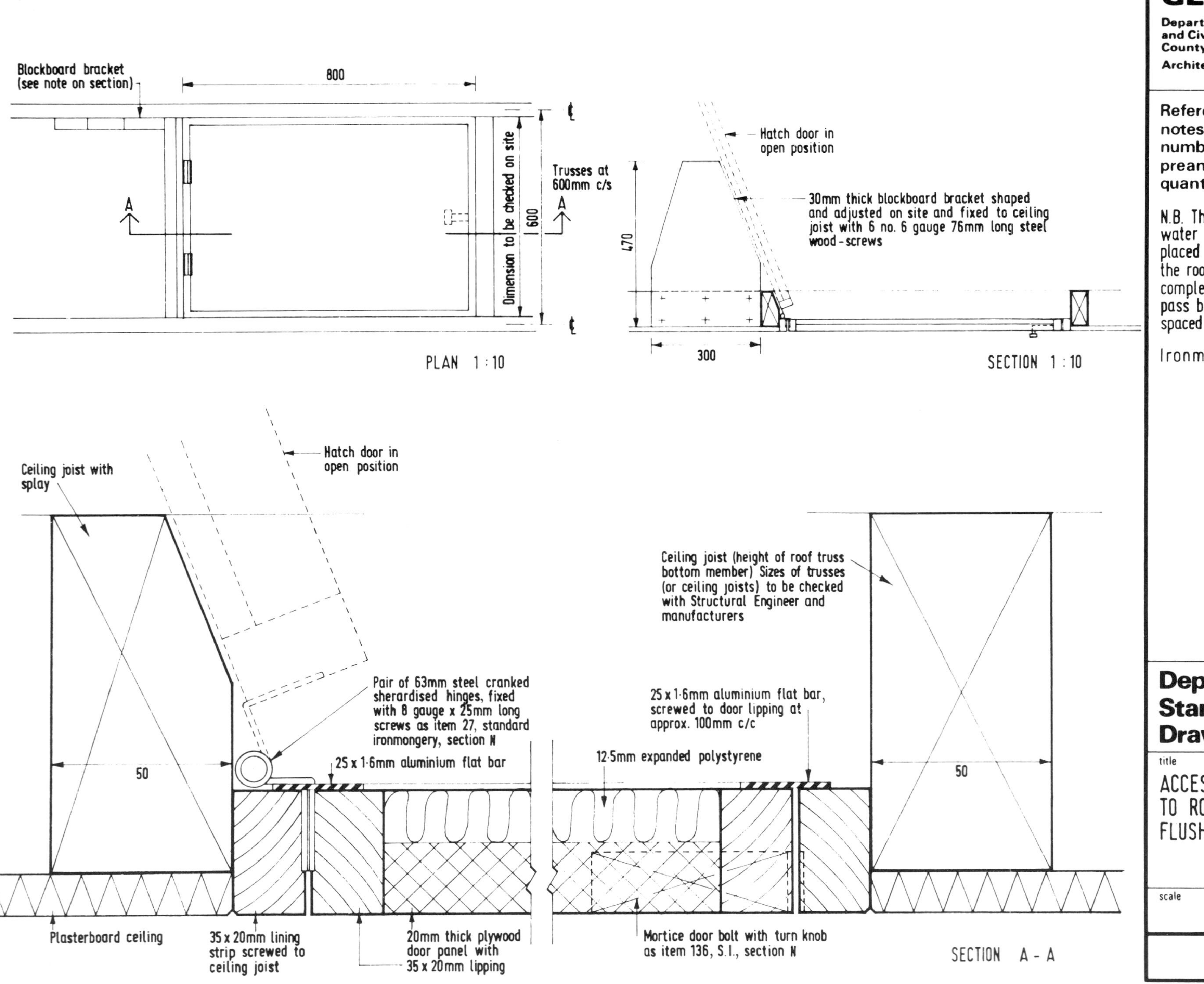

GLC ILEA

Department of Architecture and Civic Design
County Hall SE1 7PB
Architect Sir Roger Walters
KBE ARIBA FI Struct/E

References following notes are clause numbers from G.L.C. preambles to bills of quantities

N.B. The standard cold water cistern should be placed in roof space before the roof structure is complete as it will not pass between roof trusses spaced at 600mm.

Ironmongery set ZZ

Departmental Standard Drawing

title
ACCESS HATCH DOOR TO ROOF SPACE. FLUSH WITH CEILING

scale
1 : 10 & 1 : 1

drawing no	rev
D 5243	A

8 | 27 | 165 | Xi2 | F
010379

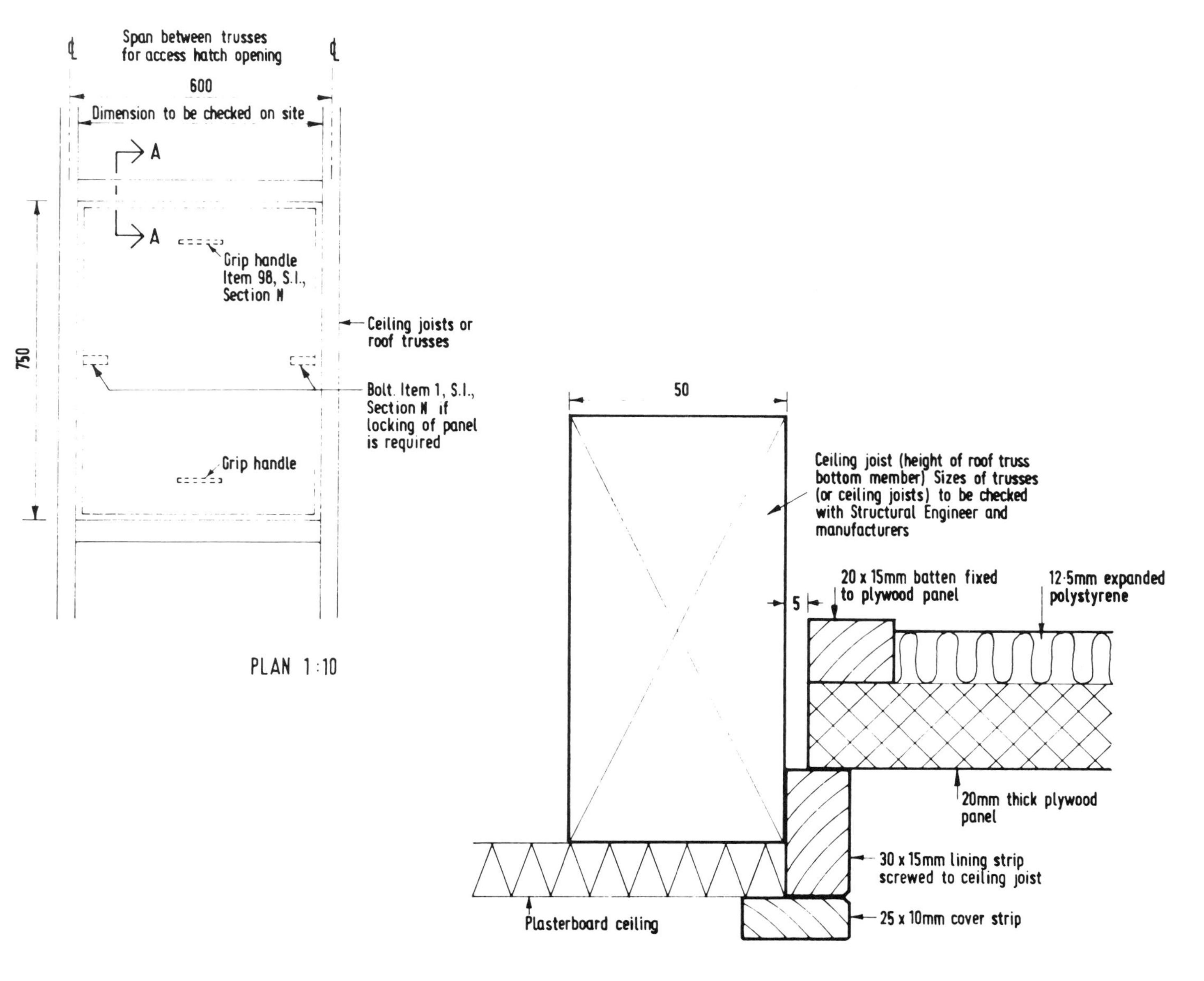

GLC ILEA

Department of Architecture and Civic Design
County Hall SE1 7PB
Architect Sir Roger Walters KBE ARIBA FI Struct/E

References following notes are clause numbers from G.L.C. preambles to bills of quantities

N.B. The standard cold water cistern should be placed in roof space before the roof structure is complete as it will not pass between roof trusses spaced at 600mm

Ironmongery set Z

Departmental Standard Drawing

title
ACCESS HATCH TO ROOF SPACE. (REMOVABLE PANEL)

scale 1:10 & 1:1

drawing no D5244 rev A

bldg type 8 | space use | element [27] | feature 165 | material Xi2 | key G

00 - 010379

6
Stairs

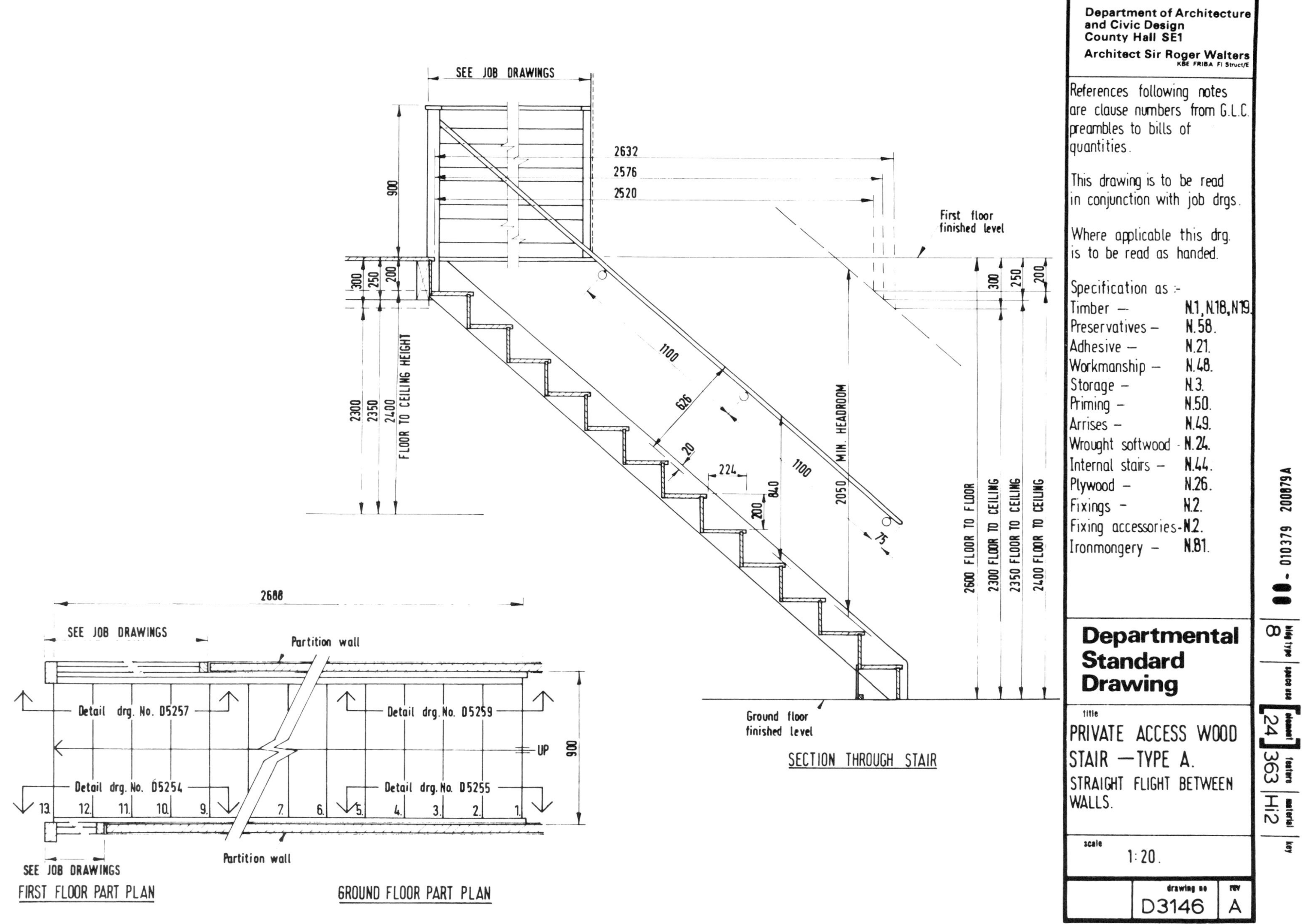
GLC ILEA
Department of Architecture and Civic Design
County Hall SE1
Architect Sir Roger Walters KBE FRIBA FI Struct/E
References following notes are clause numbers from G.L.C. preambles to bills of quantities.
This drawing is to be read in conjunction with job drgs.
Where applicable this drg. is to be read as handed.
Specification as :-
Timber — N.1, N.18, N.19.
Preservatives — N.58.
Adhesive — N.21.
Workmanship — N.48.
Storage — N.3.
Priming — N.50.
Arrises — N.49.
Wrought softwood - N.24.
Internal stairs — N.44.
Plywood — N.26.
Fixings — N.2.
Fixing accessories - N.2.
Ironmongery — N.81.
Departmental Standard Drawing
title
PRIVATE ACCESS WOOD STAIR — TYPE A.
STRAIGHT FLIGHT BETWEEN WALLS.
scale
1:20.
drawing no
D3146
rev
A
SEE JOB DRAWINGS
2632
2576
2520
900
First floor finished level
1100
626
20
224
840
200
1100
75
MIN. HEADROOM
2050
300
250
200
2300
2350
2400
FLOOR TO CEILING HEIGHT
2600 FLOOR TO FLOOR
2300 FLOOR TO CEILING
2350 FLOOR TO CEILING
2400 FLOOR TO CEILING
Ground floor finished level
SECTION THROUGH STAIR
2688
Partition wall
Detail drg. No. D5257
Detail drg. No. D5259
Detail drg. No. D5254
Detail drg. No. D5255
UP
13
12
11
10
9
7
6
5
4
3
2
1
SEE JOB DRAWINGS
FIRST FLOOR PART PLAN
GROUND FLOOR PART PLAN
8
24
363
Hi2
bldg type
space use
element
feature
material
key
0 - 010379 200879A

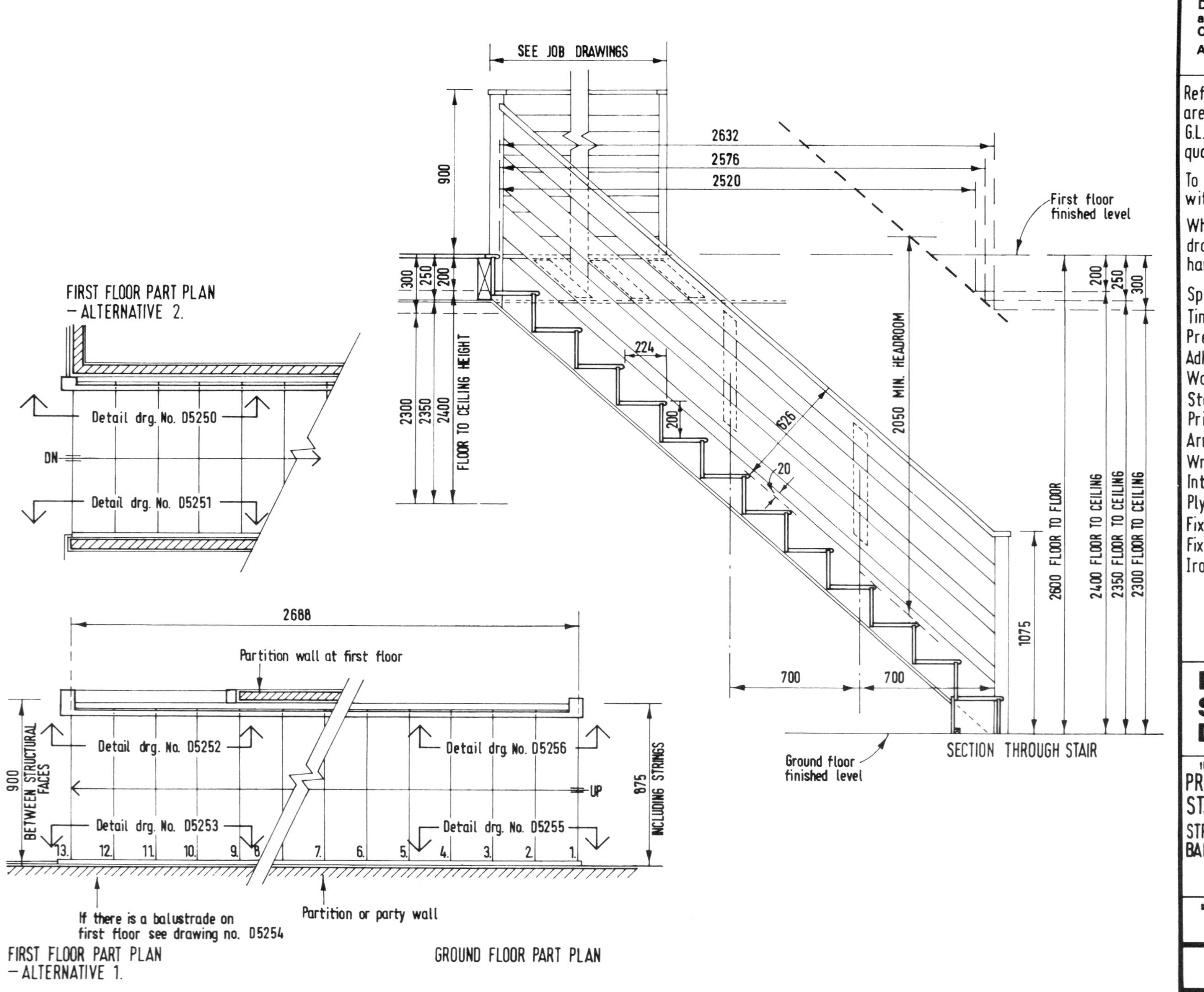

GLC ILEA

Department of Architecture and Civic Design
County Hall SE1
Architect Sir Roger Walters KBE FRIBA FI StructE

References following notes are clause numbers from G.L.C. preambles to bills of quantities

To be read in conjunction with job drawings

Where applicable this drawing to be read as handed

Specification as:

Timber –	N.1, 18, 19.
Preservatives –	N.58.
Adhesive –	N.21.
Workmanship –	N.48.
Storage –	N.3.
Priming –	N.50.
Arrises –	N.49.
Wrought softwood	N.24.
Internal stairs –	N.44.
Plywood –	N.26.
Fixings –	N.2.
Fixing accessories	N.2.
Ironmongery –	N.81.

Departmental Standard Drawing

title

PRIVATE ACCESS WOOD STAIR – TYPE B

STRAIGHT FLIGHT WITH BALUSTRADE

scale 1:20

drawing no D3147 rev

8 | 24 | 363 | H12

00 - 010379

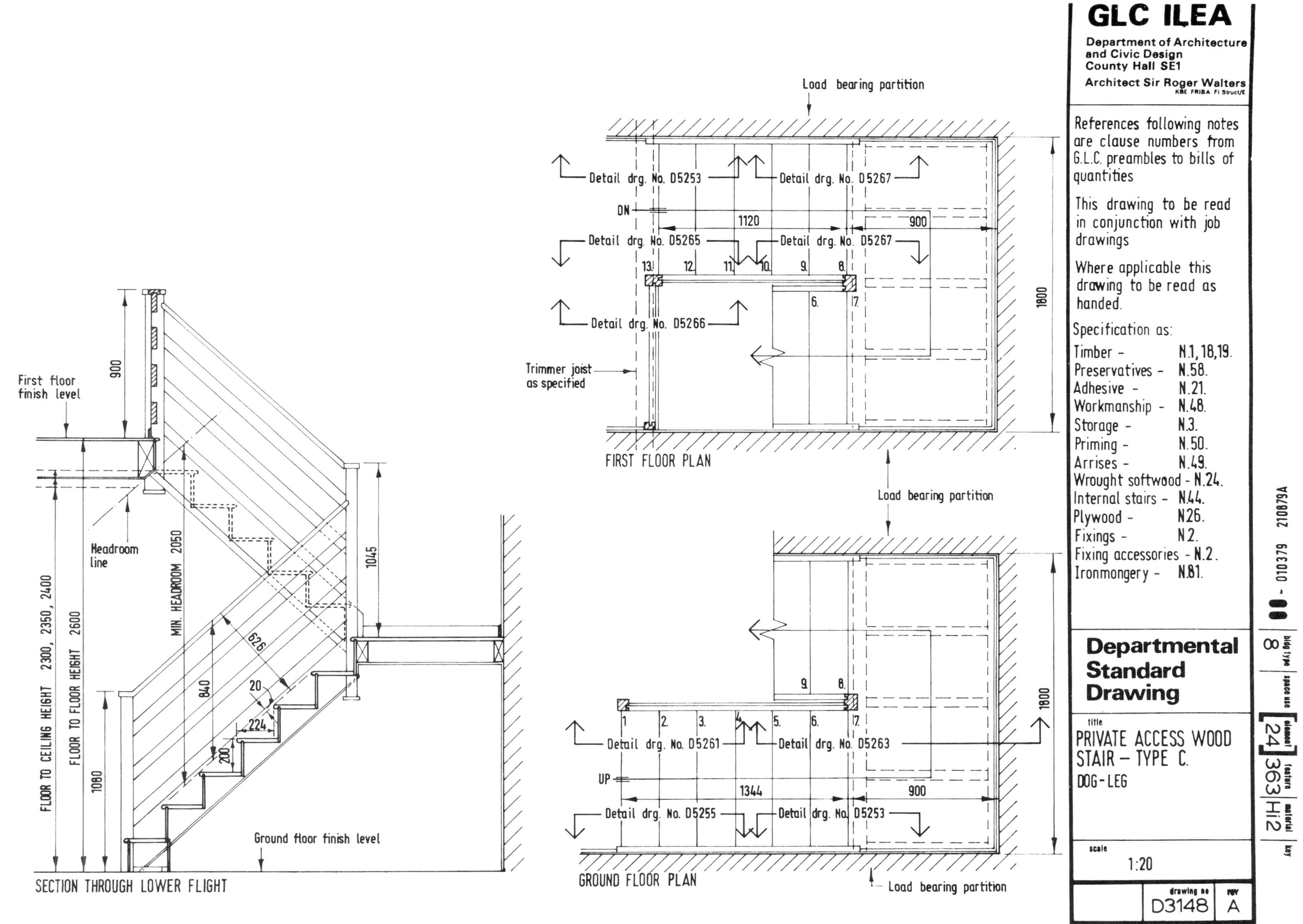
GLC ILEA
Department of Architecture and Civic Design
County Hall SE1
Architect Sir Roger Walters
KBE FRIBA FI StructE
References following notes are clause numbers from G.L.C. preambles to bills of quantities
This drawing to be read in conjunction with job drawings
Where applicable this drawing to be read as handed.
Specification as:
Timber - N.1, 18, 19.
Preservatives - N.58.
Adhesive - N.21.
Workmanship - N.48.
Storage - N.3.
Priming - N.50.
Arrises - N.49.
Wrought softwood - N.24.
Internal stairs - N.44.
Plywood - N26.
Fixings - N2.
Fixing accessories - N.2.
Ironmongery - N.81.
Departmental Standard Drawing
title
PRIVATE ACCESS WOOD STAIR – TYPE C.
DOG-LEG
scale
1:20
drawing no
D3148
rev
A
210879A
010379
bldg type 8
element 24
feature 363
material Hi2
key
Load bearing partition
Detail drg. No. D5253
Detail drg. No. D5267
DN
1120
900
Detail drg. No. D5265
Detail drg. No. D5267
13 12 11 10 9 8
6. 7.
Detail drg. No. D5266
Trimmer joist as specified
1800
FIRST FLOOR PLAN
Load bearing partition
9 8
1 2 3 4 5 6 7
Detail drg. No. D5261
Detail drg. No. D5263
UP
1344
900
Detail drg. No. D5255
Detail drg. No. D5253
1800
GROUND FLOOR PLAN
Load bearing partition
First floor finish level
900
Headroom line
MIN. HEADROOM 2050
1045
626
840
20
224
200
FLOOR TO CEILING HEIGHT 2300, 2350, 2400
FLOOR TO FLOOR HEIGHT 2600
1080
Ground floor finish level
SECTION THROUGH LOWER FLIGHT

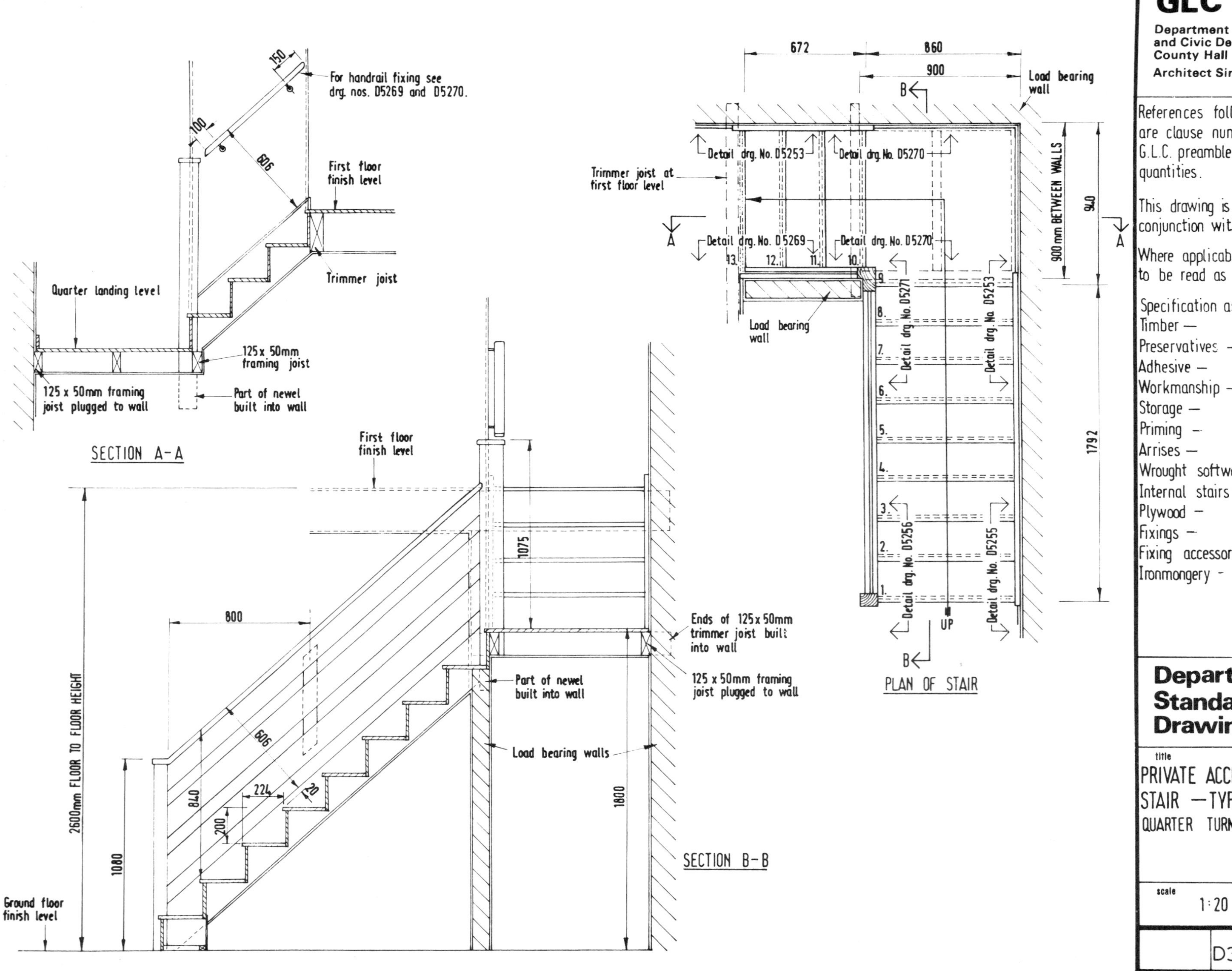

GLC ILEA

Department of Architecture and Civic Design
County Hall SE1
Architect Sir Roger Walters
KBE FRIBA FI Struct/E

References following notes are clause numbers from G.L.C. preambles to bills of quantities.

This drawing is to be read in conjunction with job drgs.

Where applicable this drg. is to be read as handed.

Specification as :–

Timber –	N.1, 18, 19.
Preservatives –	N.58.
Adhesive –	N.21.
Workmanship –	N.48.
Storage –	N.3.
Priming –	N.50.
Arrises –	N.49.
Wrought softwood –	N.24.
Internal stairs –	N.44.
Plywood –	N.26.
Fixings –	N.2.
Fixing accessories –	N.2.
Ironmongery –	N.81.

Departmental Standard Drawing

title
PRIVATE ACCESS WOOD STAIR – TYPE D.
QUARTER TURN.

scale 1:20

drawing no D3149 rev. A

210879A 010379

8 bldg type | space use | 24 element | 363 feature | Hi2 material | key

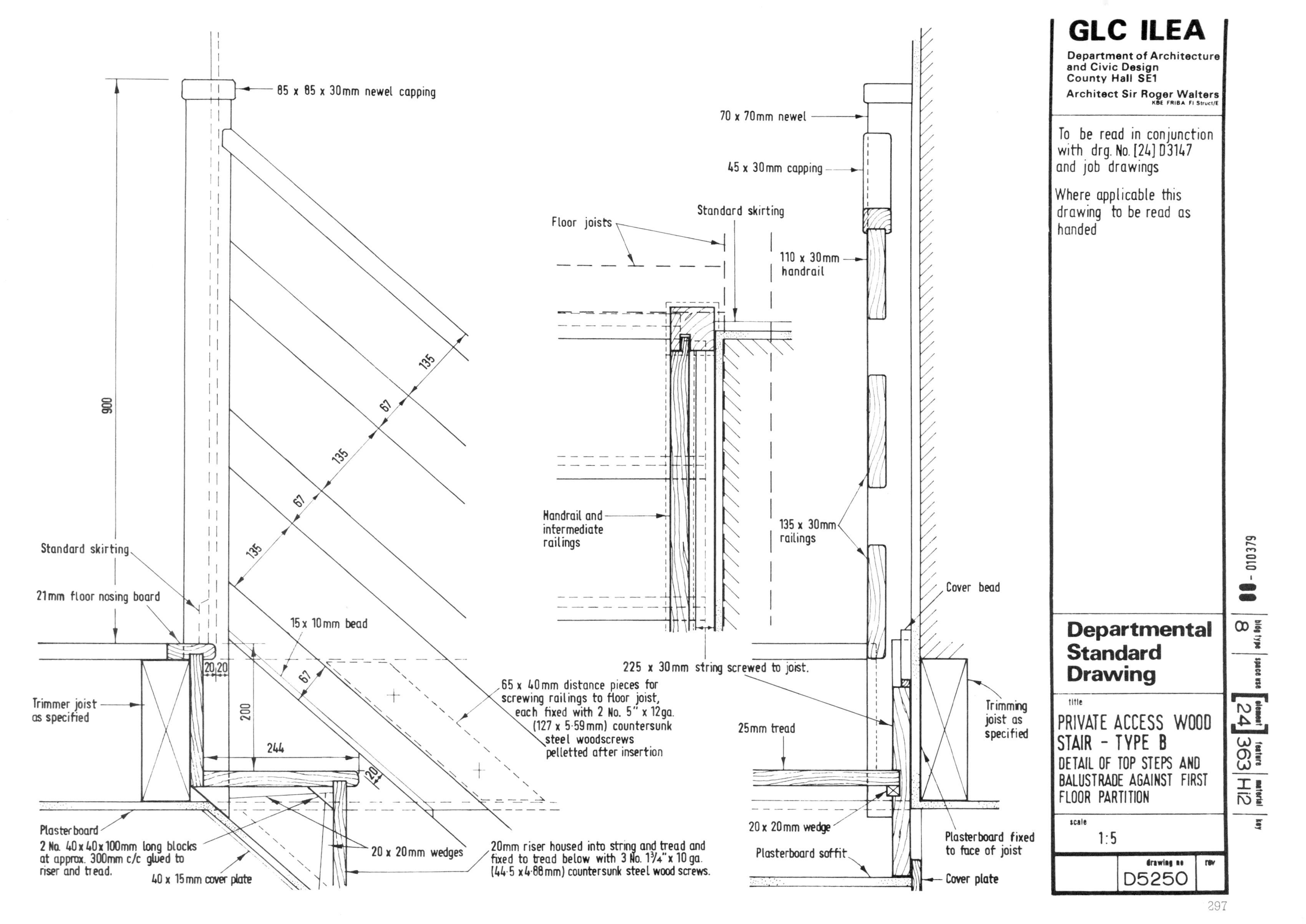
85 x 85 x 30mm newel capping
900
135
67
135
67
135
Standard skirting
21mm floor nosing board
15 x 10mm bead
20 20
67
Trimmer joist as specified
200
244
20
Plasterboard
2 No. 40 x 40 x 100mm long blocks at approx. 300mm c/c glued to riser and tread.
40 x 15mm cover plate
20 x 20mm wedges
20mm riser housed into string and tread and fixed to tread below with 3 No. 1¾" x 10 ga. (44·5 x 4·88mm) countersunk steel wood screws.
65 x 40mm distance pieces for screwing railings to floor joist, each fixed with 2 No. 5" x 12ga. (127 x 5·59mm) countersunk steel woodscrews pelletted after insertion
Floor joists
Standard skirting
Handrail and intermediate railings
225 x 30mm string screwed to joist.
70 x 70mm newel
45 x 30mm capping
110 x 30mm handrail
135 x 30mm railings
Cover bead
25mm tread
Trimming joist as specified
20 x 20mm wedge
Plasterboard soffit
Plasterboard fixed to face of joist
Cover plate
GLC ILEA
Department of Architecture and Civic Design
County Hall SE1
Architect Sir Roger Walters KBE FRIBA FI Struct/E
To be read in conjunction with drg. No. [24] D3147 and job drawings
Where applicable this drawing to be read as handed
Departmental Standard Drawing
title
PRIVATE ACCESS WOOD STAIR - TYPE B
DETAIL OF TOP STEPS AND BALUSTRADE AGAINST FIRST FLOOR PARTITION
scale
1:5
drawing no
rev
D5250
010379
8
bldg type
space use
[24]
element
363
feature
Hi2
material
key

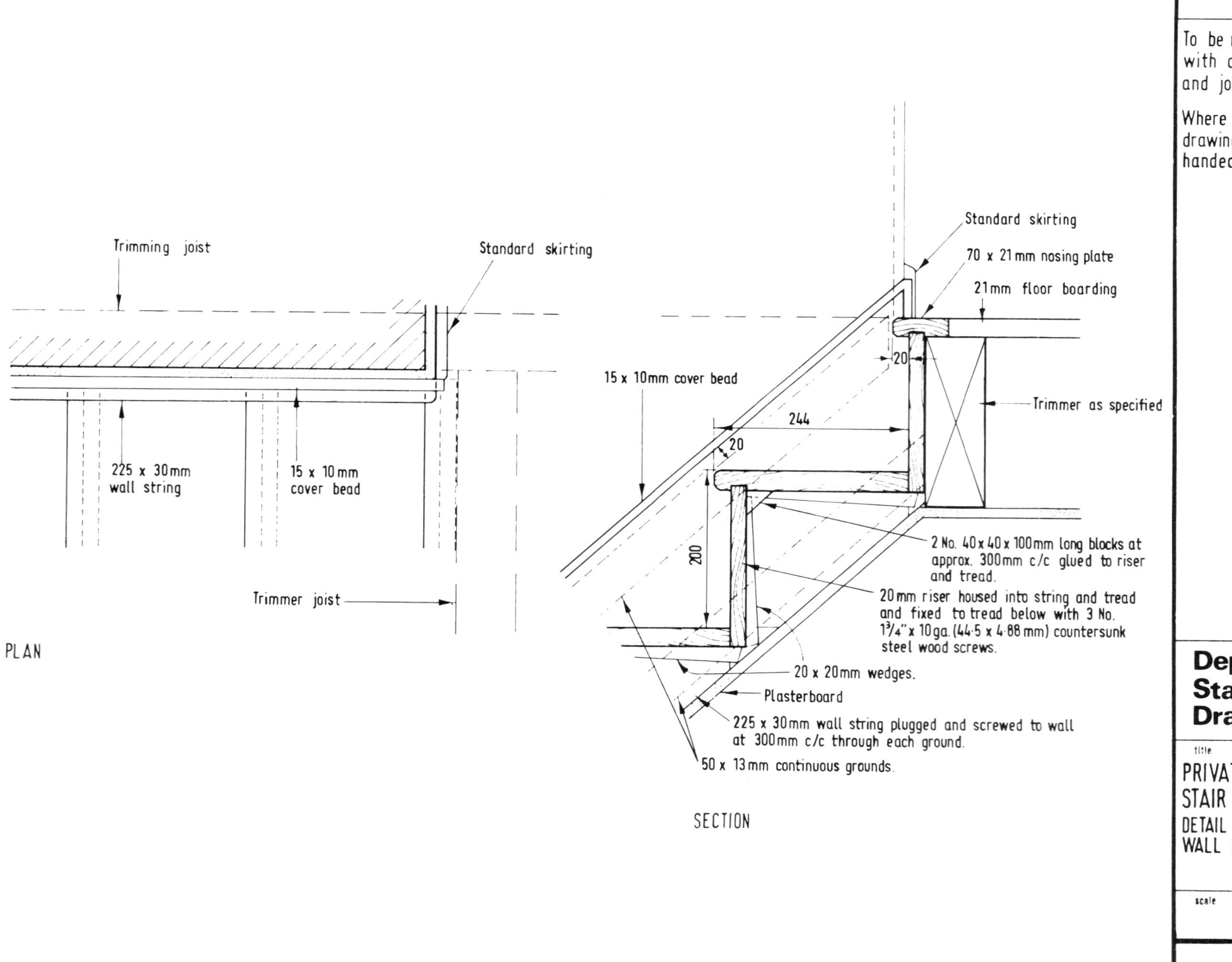

GLC ILEA

Department of Architecture and Civic Design
County Hall SE1
Architect Sir Roger Walters KBE FRIBA FI StructE

To be read in conjunction with drg. No. [24] D3147 and job drawings.

Where applicable this drawing to be read as handed.

Departmental Standard Drawing

title

PRIVATE ACCESS WOOD STAIR – TYPE B
DETAIL OF TOP STEPS AND WALL STRING

scale 1:5

drawing no D5251 rev

bldg type 8 | space use | element [24] | feature 363 | material Hi2 | key

00379

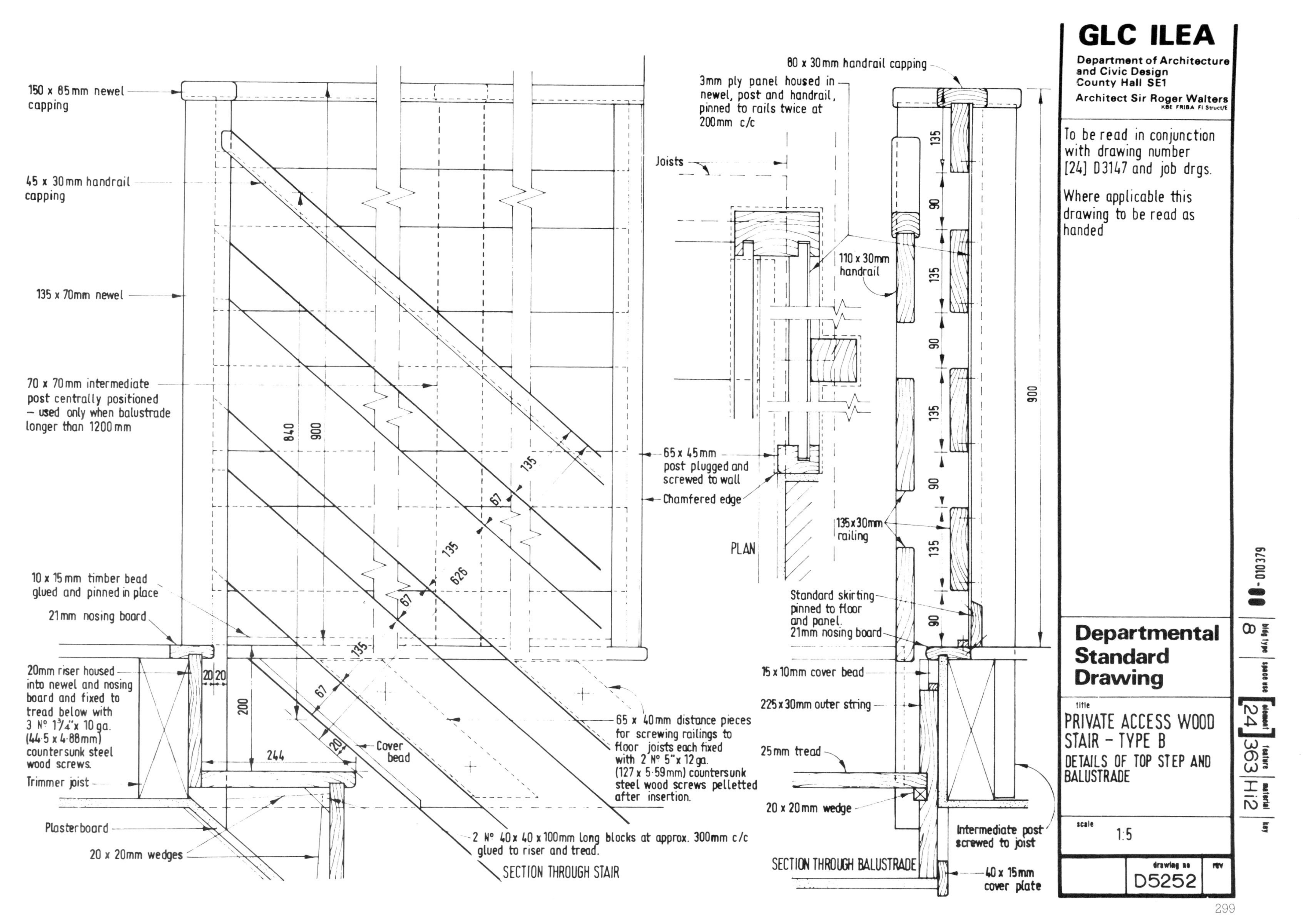
GLC ILEA
Department of Architecture and Civic Design
County Hall SE1
Architect Sir Roger Walters
KBE FRIBA FI StructE
To be read in conjunction with drawing number [24] D3147 and job drgs.
Where applicable this drawing to be read as handed
150 x 85mm newel capping
45 x 30mm handrail capping
135 x 70mm newel
70 x 70mm intermediate post centrally positioned – used only when balustrade longer than 1200mm
10 x 15mm timber bead glued and pinned in place
21mm nosing board
20mm riser housed into newel and nosing board and fixed to tread below with 3 Nº 1¾"x 10 ga. (44·5 x 4·88mm) countersunk steel wood screws.
Trimmer joist
Plasterboard
20 x 20mm wedges
Cover bead
2 Nº 40x 40 x 100mm long blocks at approx. 300mm c/c glued to riser and tread.
SECTION THROUGH STAIR
65 x 45mm post plugged and screwed to wall
Chamfered edge
65 x 40mm distance pieces for screwing railings to floor joists each fixed with 2 Nº 5"x 12ga. (127 x 5·59mm) countersunk steel wood screws pelletted after insertion.
80 x 30mm handrail capping
3mm ply panel housed in newel, post and handrail, pinned to rails twice at 200mm c/c
Joists
110 x 30mm handrail
PLAN
135x30mm railing
Standard skirting pinned to floor and panel.
21mm nosing board
15 x 10mm cover bead
225 x 30mm outer string
25mm tread
20 x 20mm wedge
Intermediate post screwed to joist
40 x 15mm cover plate
SECTION THROUGH BALUSTRADE
Departmental Standard Drawing
title
PRIVATE ACCESS WOOD STAIR – TYPE B
DETAILS OF TOP STEP AND BALUSTRADE
scale 1:5
drawing no D5252
rev
8 [24] 363 Hi2
00379

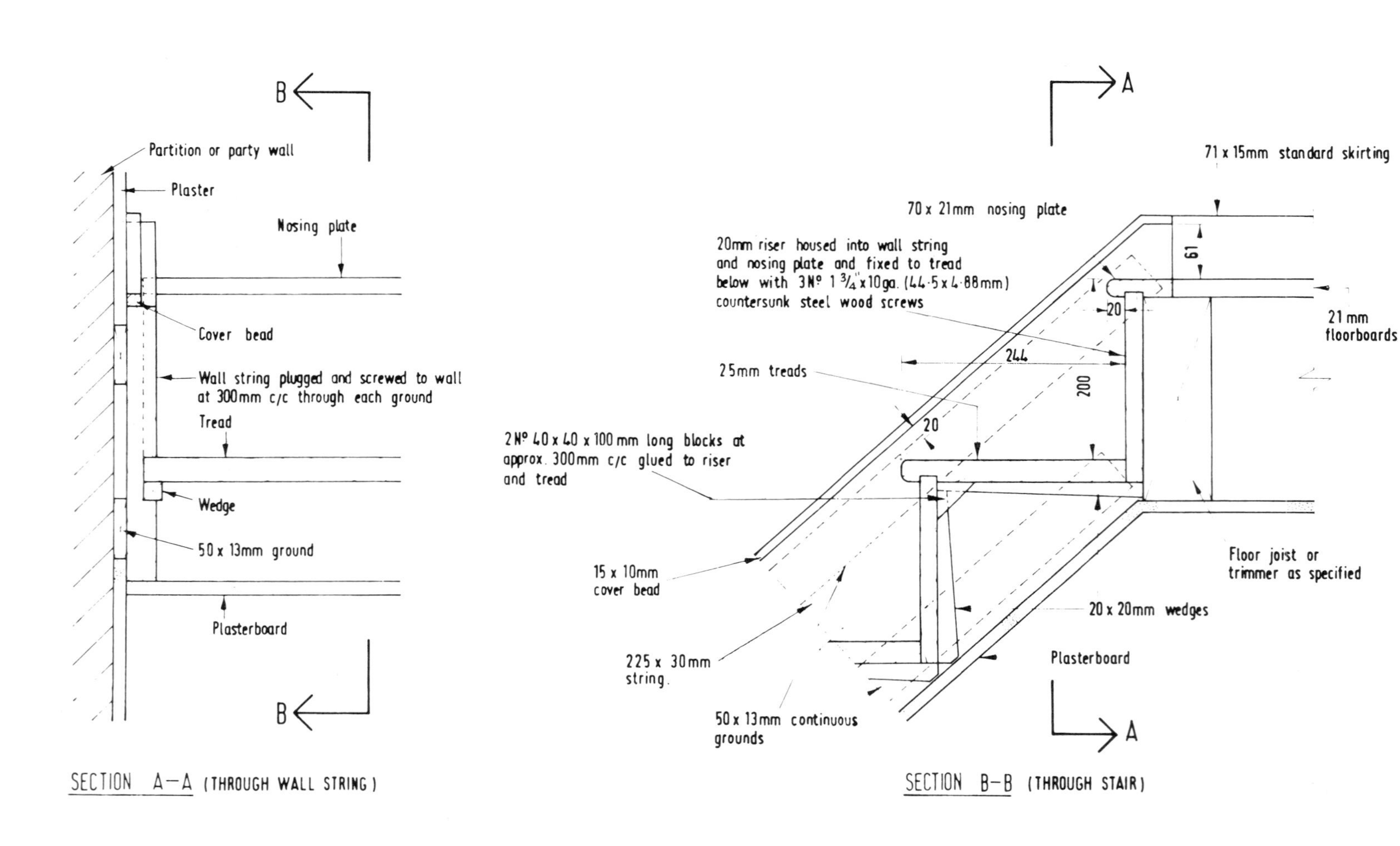

GLC ILEA

Department of Architecture and Civic Design
County Hall SE1
Architect Sir Roger Walters KBE FRIBA FI StructE

This drawing is to be read in conjunction with drawing number [24] D3147, D3148 or D3149 and with job drawings.

Where applicable this drawing is to be read as handed

Departmental Standard Drawing

title

PRIVATE ACCESS WOOD STAIR – TYPE B, C & D
DETAIL OF TOP STEP AND WALL STRING.
ALSO HALF-LANDING

scale 1:5

drawing no D5253 rev A

8 | [24] 363 | Hi2

010379 230879A

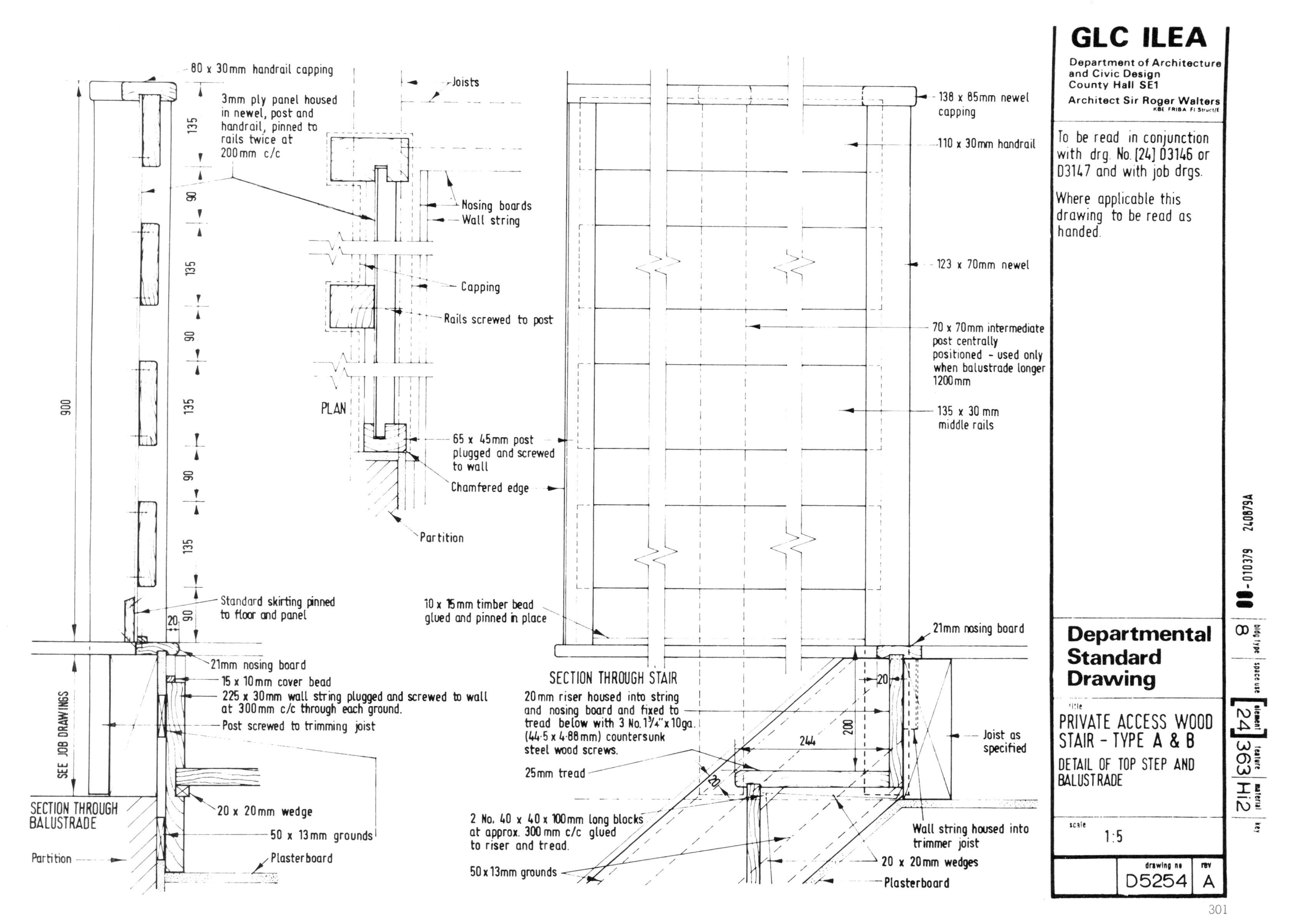
80 x 30mm handrail capping
3mm ply panel housed in newel, post and handrail, pinned to rails twice at 200mm c/c
Joists
Nosing boards
Wall string
Capping
Rails screwed to post
PLAN
65 x 45mm post plugged and screwed to wall
Chamfered edge
Partition
900
135
90
135
90
135
90
135
90
20
Standard skirting pinned to floor and panel
21mm nosing board
15 x 10mm cover bead
225 x 30mm wall string plugged and screwed to wall at 300mm c/c through each ground.
Post screwed to trimming joist
SEE JOB DRAWINGS
SECTION THROUGH BALUSTRADE
20 x 20mm wedge
50 x 13mm grounds
Partition
Plasterboard
138 x 85mm newel capping
110 x 30mm handrail
123 x 70mm newel
70 x 70mm intermediate post centrally positioned - used only when balustrade longer 1200mm
135 x 30 mm middle rails
10 x 15mm timber bead glued and pinned in place
21mm nosing board
SECTION THROUGH STAIR
20mm riser housed into string and nosing board and fixed to tread below with 3 No. 1¾" x 10ga. (44·5 x 4·88mm) countersunk steel wood screws.
25mm tread
2 No. 40 x 40 x 100mm long blocks at approx. 300mm c/c glued to riser and tread.
50x13mm grounds
20
200
244
20
Joist as specified
Wall string housed into trimmer joist
20 x 20mm wedges
Plasterboard
GLC ILEA
Department of Architecture and Civic Design
County Hall SE1
Architect Sir Roger Walters KBE FRIBA FI Struct/E
To be read in conjunction with drg. No. [24] D3146 or D3147 and with job drgs.
Where applicable this drawing to be read as handed.
Departmental Standard Drawing
title
PRIVATE ACCESS WOOD STAIR - TYPE A & B
DETAIL OF TOP STEP AND BALUSTRADE
scale
1:5
drawing no
D5254
rev
A
8
[24]
363
Hi2
bldg type
space use
element
feature
material
key
010379
240879A

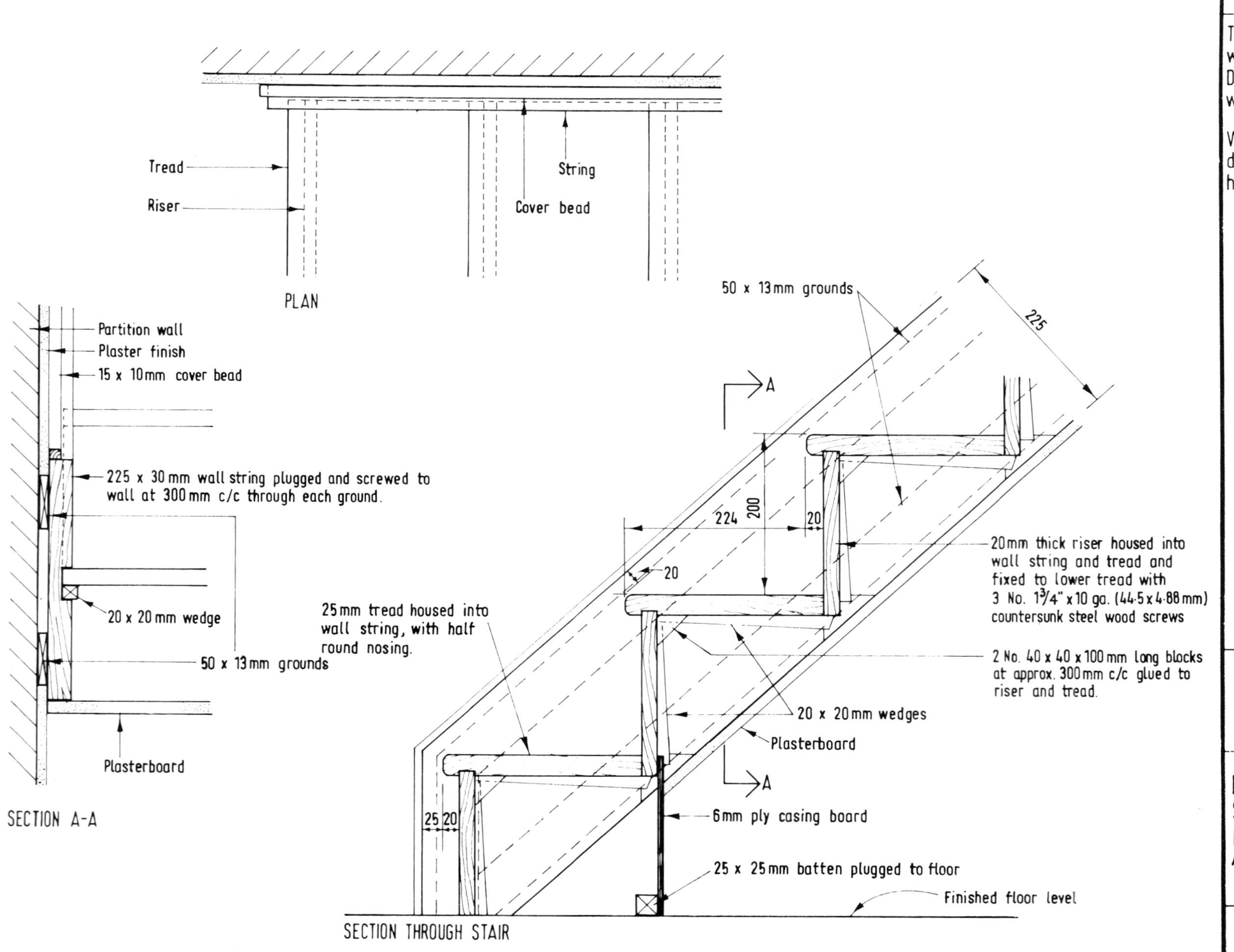

GLC ILEA

Department of Architecture and Civic Design
County Hall SE1
Architect Sir Roger Walters
KBE FRIBA FI StructE

To be read in conjunction with drg. No. [24] D3146, D.3147, D.3148 or D.3149 and with job drawings.

Where applicable this drawing to be read as handed.

010379 200879 A

bldg type 8 | space use | element [24] | feature 363 | material Hi2 | key

Departmental Standard Drawing

title

PRIVATE ACCESS WOOD STAIR – TYPE A, B, C & D
DETAIL OF BOTTOM STEPS AND WALL STRING

scale 1:5

drawing no D5255 | rev A

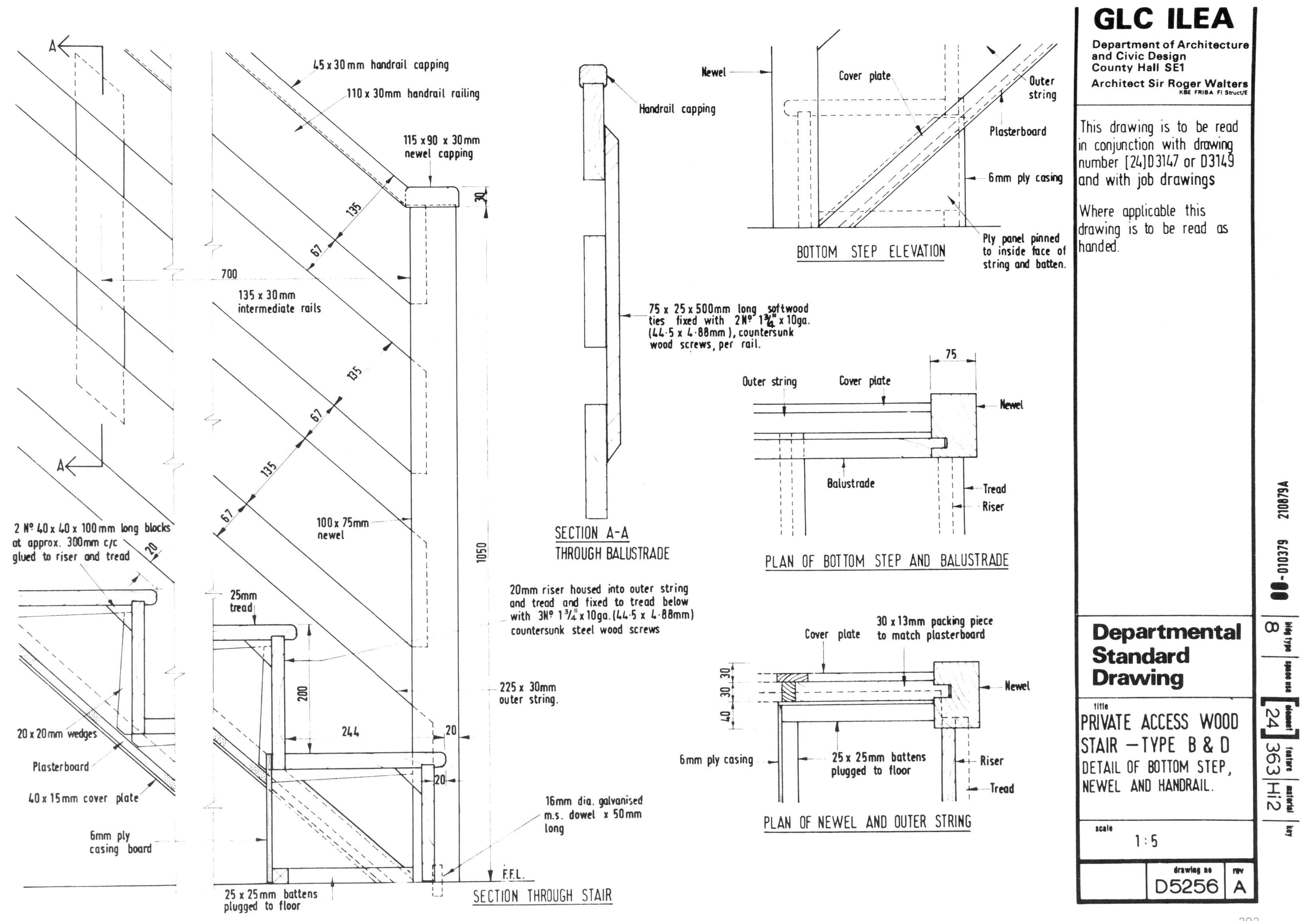

GLC ILEA
Department of Architecture and Civic Design
County Hall SE1
Architect Sir Roger Walters KBE FRIBA FI Struct/E
This drawing is to be read in conjunction with drawing number [24]D3147 or D3149 and with job drawings
Where applicable this drawing is to be read as handed.
Departmental Standard Drawing
title
PRIVATE ACCESS WOOD STAIR – TYPE B & D
DETAIL OF BOTTOM STEP, NEWEL AND HANDRAIL.
scale
1:5
drawing no
D5256
rev
A
8
[24]
363
Hi2
00-010379
210879A
45 x 30 mm handrail capping
110 x 30mm handrail railing
115 x 90 x 30mm newel capping
135 x 30mm intermediate rails
100 x 75mm newel
2 Nº 40 x 40 x 100mm long blocks at approx. 300mm c/c glued to riser and tread
25mm tread
20 x 20mm wedges
Plasterboard
40 x 15mm cover plate
6mm ply casing board
25 x 25mm battens plugged to floor
20mm riser housed into outer string and tread and fixed to tread below with 3Nº 1¾" x 10ga. (44·5 x 4·88mm) countersunk steel wood screws
225 x 30mm outer string.
16mm dia. galvanised m.s. dowel x 50mm long
F.F.L.
SECTION THROUGH STAIR
Handrail capping
75 x 25 x 500mm long softwood ties fixed with 2Nº 1¾" x 10ga. (44·5 x 4·88mm), countersunk wood screws, per rail.
SECTION A-A THROUGH BALUSTRADE
Newel
Cover plate
Outer string
Plasterboard
6mm ply casing
Ply panel pinned to inside face of string and batten.
BOTTOM STEP ELEVATION
Outer string
Cover plate
Newel
Balustrade
Tread
Riser
PLAN OF BOTTOM STEP AND BALUSTRADE
Cover plate
30 x 13mm packing piece to match plasterboard
Newel
6mm ply casing
25 x 25mm battens plugged to floor
Riser
Tread
PLAN OF NEWEL AND OUTER STRING

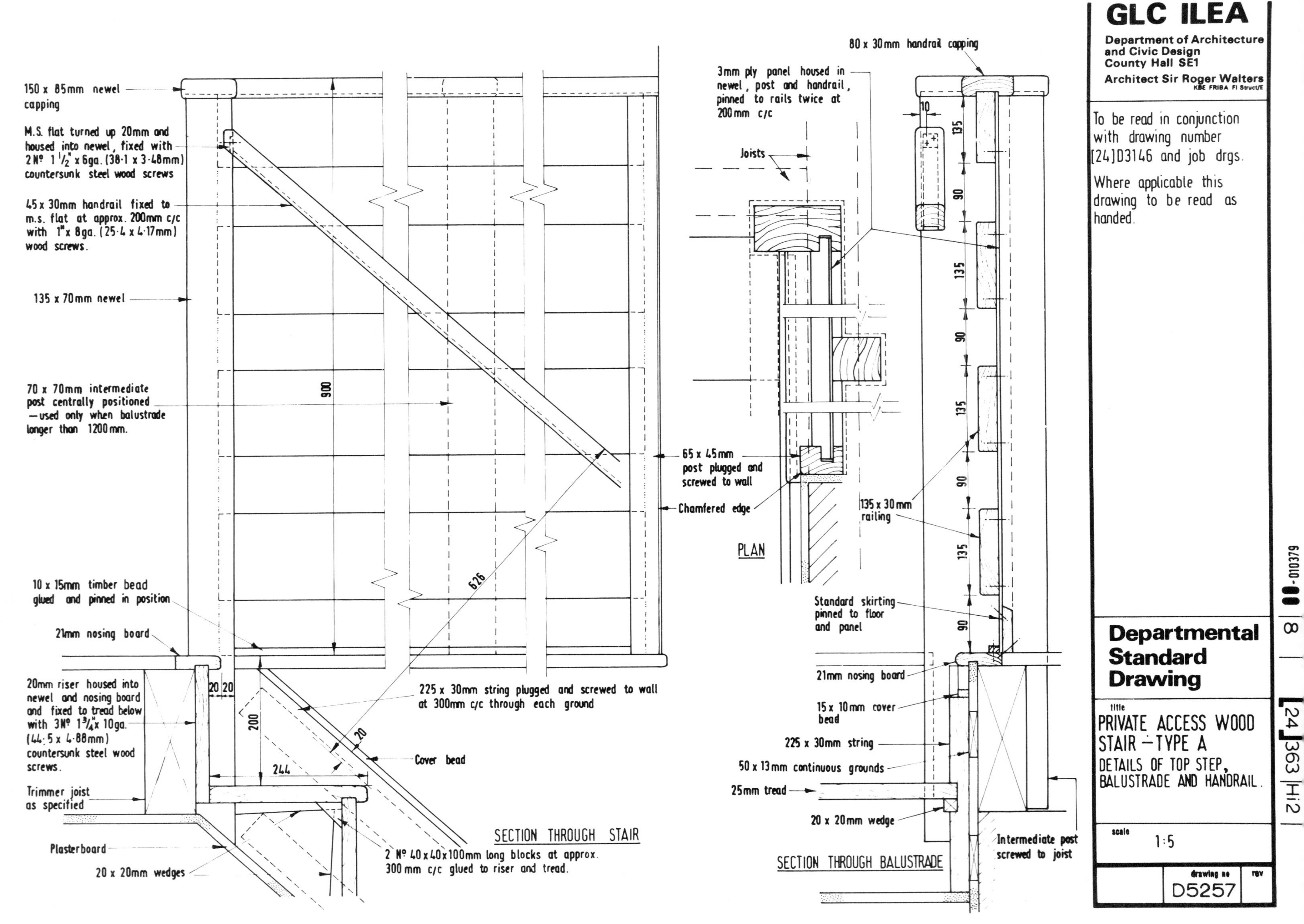
GLC ILEA
Department of Architecture and Civic Design
County Hall SE1
Architect Sir Roger Walters KBE FRIBA FI Struct/E
To be read in conjunction with drawing number [24]D3146 and job drgs.
Where applicable this drawing to be read as handed.
Departmental Standard Drawing
title
PRIVATE ACCESS WOOD STAIR – TYPE A
DETAILS OF TOP STEP, BALUSTRADE AND HANDRAIL.
scale 1:5
drawing no D5257
rev
[24]363 Hi2 | 8 |
150 x 85mm newel capping
M.S. flat turned up 20mm and housed into newel, fixed with 2 Nº 1 1/2" x 6ga. (38·1 x 3·48mm) countersunk steel wood screws
45 x 30mm handrail fixed to m.s. flat at approx. 200mm c/c with 1" x 8ga. (25·4 x 4·17mm) wood screws.
135 x 70mm newel
70 x 70mm intermediate post centrally positioned —used only when balustrade longer than 1200mm.
10 x 15mm timber bead glued and pinned in position
21mm nosing board
20mm riser housed into newel and nosing board and fixed to tread below with 3 Nº 1 3/4" x 10ga. (44·5 x 4·88mm) countersunk steel wood screws.
Trimmer joist as specified
Plasterboard
20 x 20mm wedges
900
626
20 20
200
244
20
225 x 30mm string plugged and screwed to wall at 300mm c/c through each ground
Cover bead
2 Nº 40 x 40 x 100mm long blocks at approx. 300mm c/c glued to riser and tread.
SECTION THROUGH STAIR
3mm ply panel housed in newel, post and handrail, pinned to rails twice at 200mm c/c
Joists
65 x 45mm post plugged and screwed to wall
Chamfered edge
PLAN
80 x 30mm handrail capping
10
135
90
135
90
135
90
135
90
135 x 30mm railing
Standard skirting pinned to floor and panel
21mm nosing board
15 x 10mm cover bead
225 x 30mm string
50 x 13mm continuous grounds
25mm tread
20 x 20mm wedge
Intermediate post screwed to joist
SECTION THROUGH BALUSTRADE

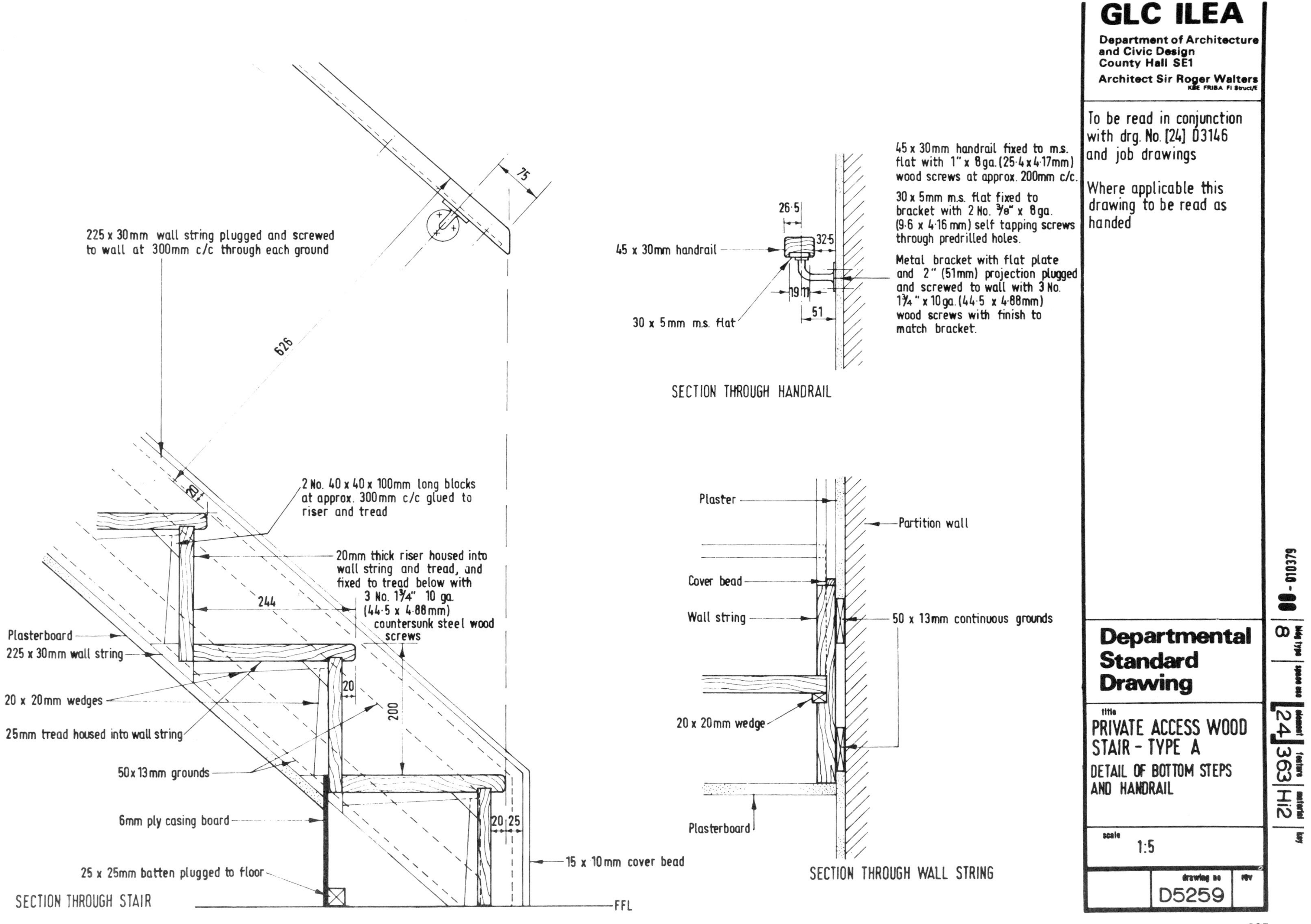
GLC ILEA
Department of Architecture and Civic Design
County Hall SE1
Architect Sir Roger Walters KBE FRIBA FI Struct/E
To be read in conjunction with drg. No. [24] D3146 and job drawings
Where applicable this drawing to be read as handed
45 x 30mm handrail fixed to m.s. flat with 1" x 8 ga. (25·4 x 4·17mm) wood screws at approx. 200mm c/c.
30 x 5mm m.s. flat fixed to bracket with 2 No. 3/8" x 8 ga. (9·6 x 4·16 mm) self tapping screws through predrilled holes.
Metal bracket with flat plate and 2" (51mm) projection plugged and screwed to wall with 3 No. 1¾" x 10 ga. (44·5 x 4·88mm) wood screws with finish to match bracket.
26·5
32·5
45 x 30mm handrail
19
11
51
30 x 5mm m.s. flat
SECTION THROUGH HANDRAIL
225 x 30mm wall string plugged and screwed to wall at 300mm c/c through each ground
75
626
20
2 No. 40 x 40 x 100mm long blocks at approx. 300mm c/c glued to riser and tread
20mm thick riser housed into wall string and tread, and fixed to tread below with 3 No. 1¾" 10 ga. (44·5 x 4·88mm) countersunk steel wood screws
244
Plasterboard
225 x 30mm wall string
20 x 20mm wedges
25mm tread housed into wall string
50x13mm grounds
6mm ply casing board
25 x 25mm batten plugged to floor
20
200
20
25
15 x 10mm cover bead
FFL
SECTION THROUGH STAIR
Plaster
Partition wall
Cover bead
Wall string
50 x 13mm continuous grounds
20 x 20mm wedge
Plasterboard
SECTION THROUGH WALL STRING
Departmental Standard Drawing
title
PRIVATE ACCESS WOOD STAIR - TYPE A
DETAIL OF BOTTOM STEPS AND HANDRAIL
scale
1:5
drawing no
rev
D5259
8
24
363
Hi2
bldg type
space use
element
feature
material
key
0010-03769

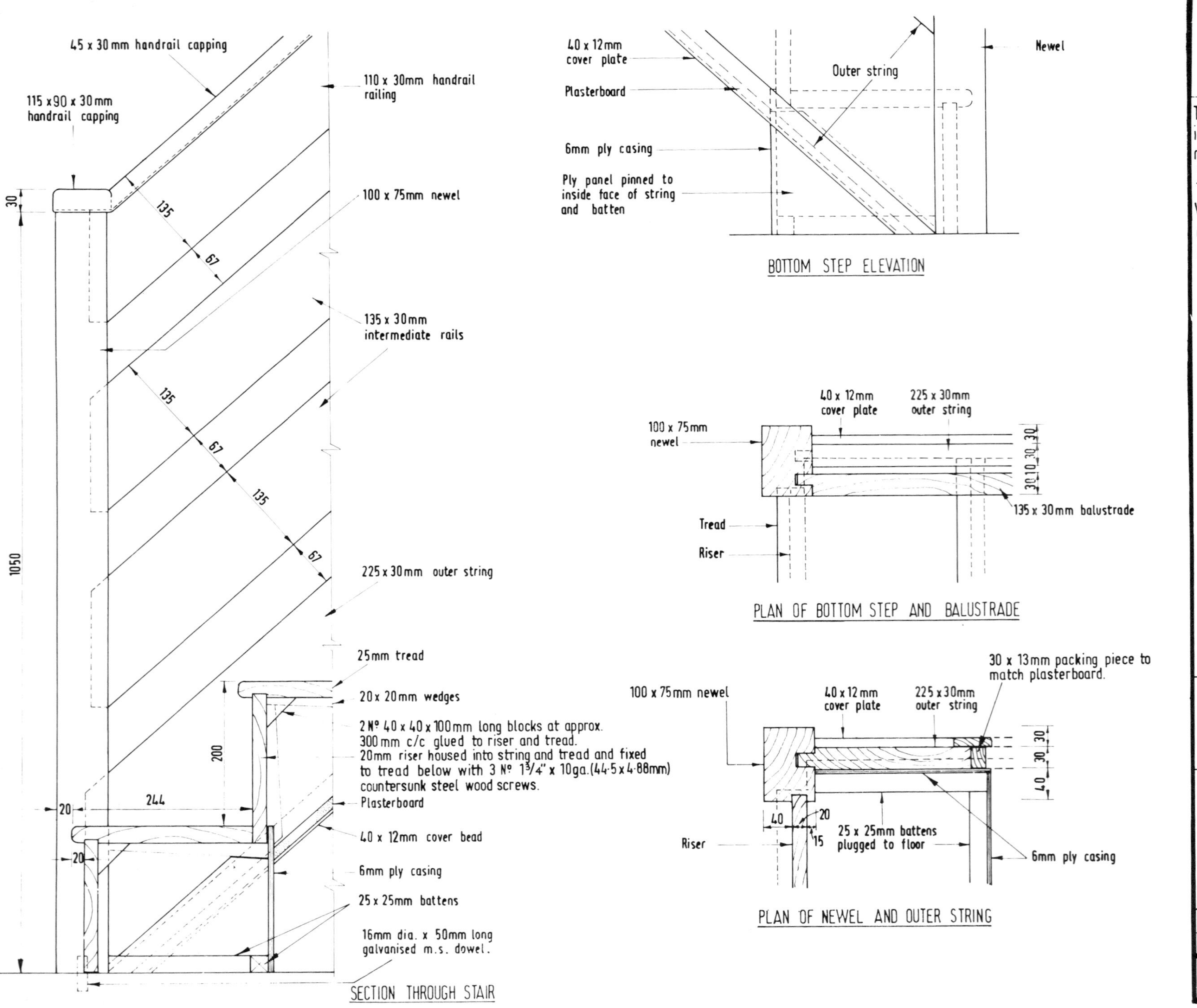

GLC ILEA

Department of Architecture and Civic Design
County Hall SE1
Architect Sir Roger Walters KBE FRIBA FI StructE

This drawing is to be read in conjunction with drawing number [24] D 3148 and job drawings.

Where applicable this drawing is to be read as handed.

Departmental Standard Drawing

title
PRIVATE ACCESS WOOD STAIR — TYPE C.
DETAILS OF BOTTOM STEP NEWEL AND HANDRAIL.

scale 1 : 5

drawing no D5261

rev

8 | [24] 363 | Hi2

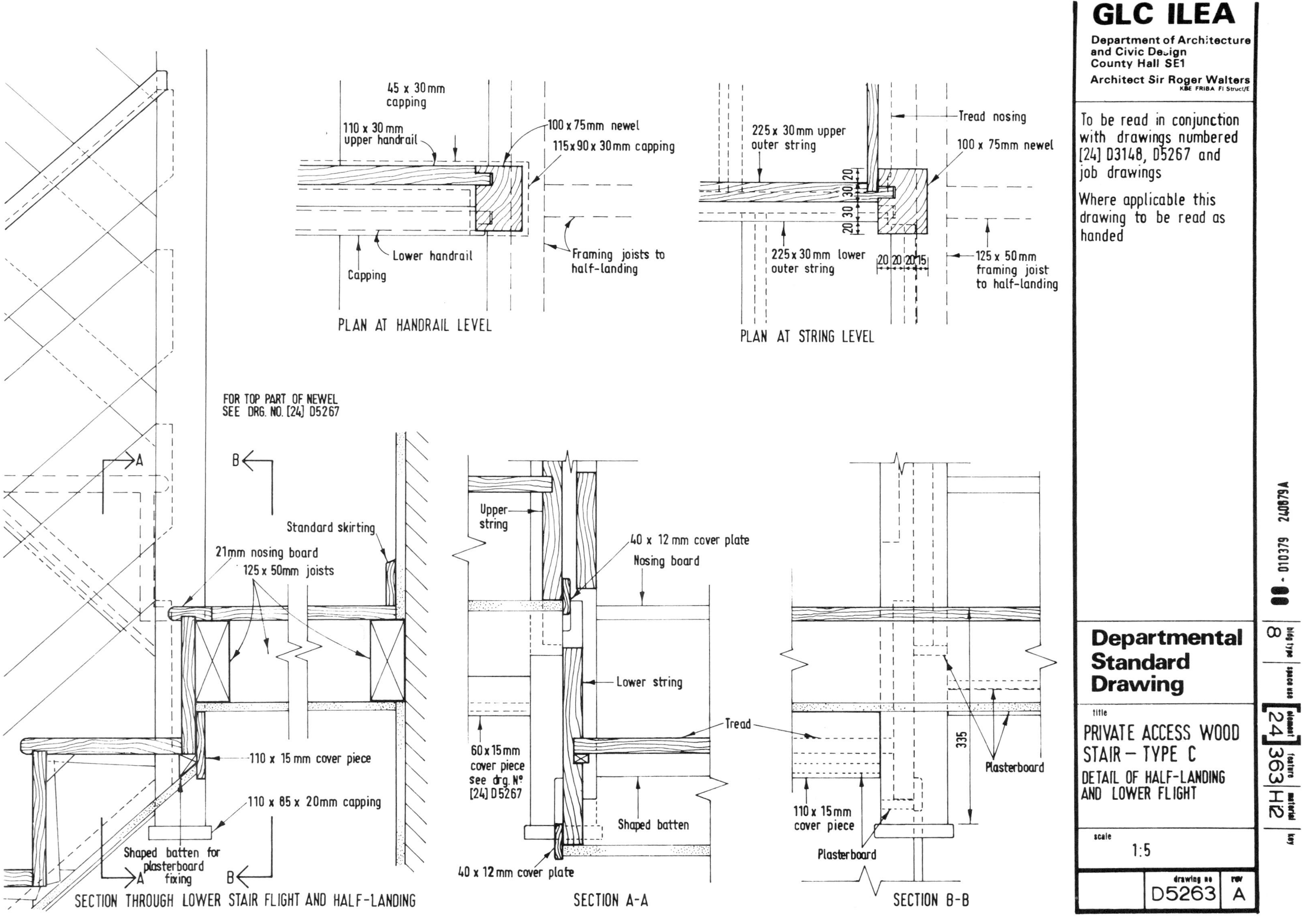
GLC ILEA
Department of Architecture and Civic Design
County Hall SE1
Architect Sir Roger Walters
KBE FRIBA FI StructE
To be read in conjunction with drawings numbered [24] D3148, D5267 and job drawings
Where applicable this drawing to be read as handed
45 x 30mm capping
110 x 30 mm upper handrail
100 x 75mm newel
115 x 90 x 30mm capping
Lower handrail
Capping
Framing joists to half-landing
PLAN AT HANDRAIL LEVEL
225 x 30mm upper outer string
Tread nosing
100 x 75mm newel
225 x 30mm lower outer string
125 x 50mm framing joist to half-landing
PLAN AT STRING LEVEL
FOR TOP PART OF NEWEL SEE DRG. NO. [24] D5267
Standard skirting
21mm nosing board
125 x 50mm joists
110 x 15 mm cover piece
110 x 85 x 20mm capping
Shaped batten for plasterboard fixing
SECTION THROUGH LOWER STAIR FLIGHT AND HALF-LANDING
Upper string
40 x 12 mm cover plate
Nosing board
Lower string
Tread
60 x 15mm cover piece see drg. Nº [24] D5267
Shaped batten
40 x 12 mm cover plate
SECTION A-A
335
Plasterboard
110 x 15mm cover piece
Plasterboard
SECTION B-B
Departmental Standard Drawing
title
PRIVATE ACCESS WOOD STAIR – TYPE C
DETAIL OF HALF-LANDING AND LOWER FLIGHT
scale
1:5
drawing no
D5263
rev
A
8
[24]
363
H2
010379 240879A

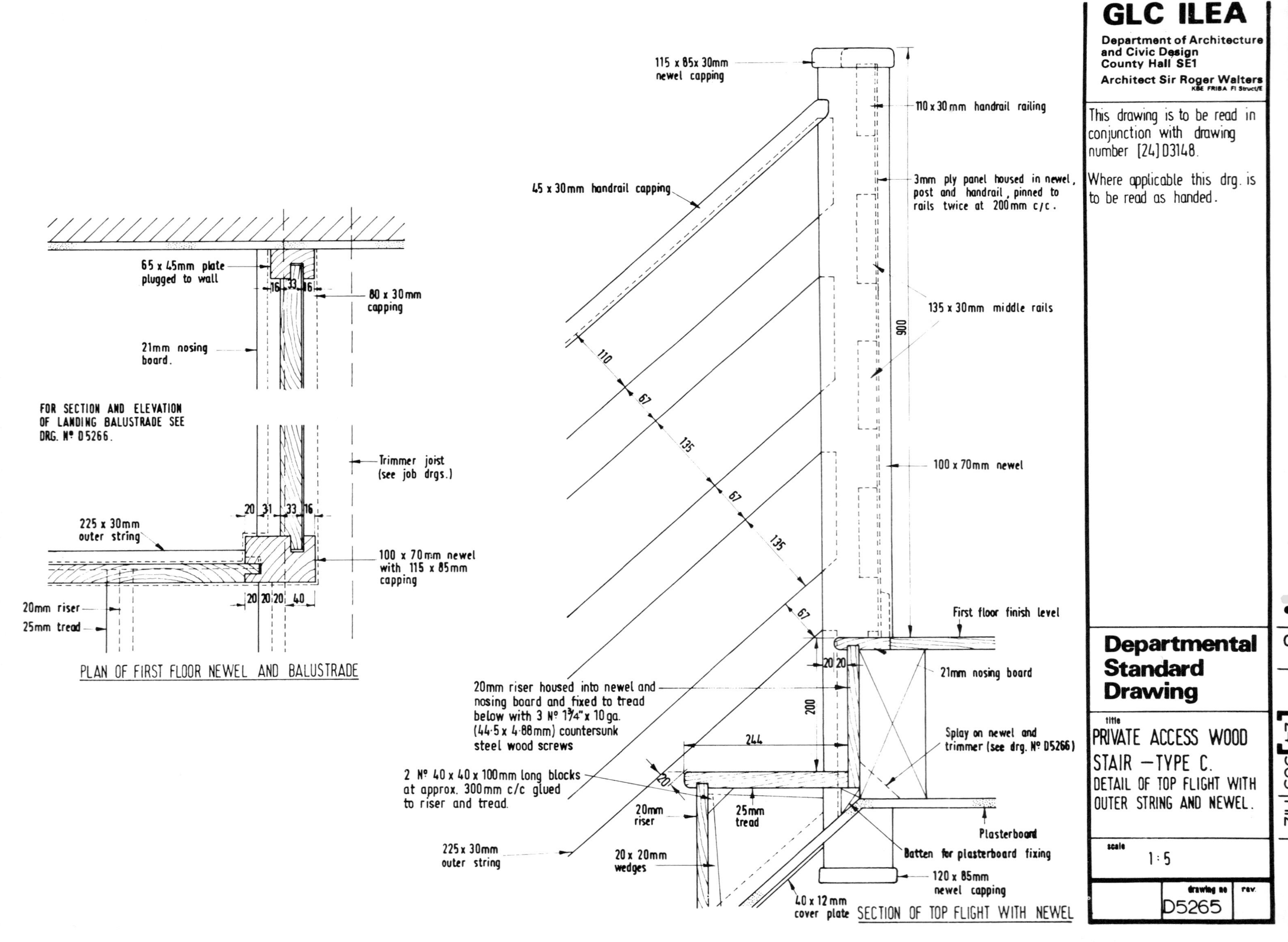
115 x 85x 30mm newel capping
110 x 30 mm handrail railing
45 x 30mm handrail capping
3mm ply panel housed in newel, post and handrail, pinned to rails twice at 200mm c/c.
135 x 30mm middle rails
900
110
67
135
67
135
67
100 x 70mm newel
First floor finish level
21mm nosing board
20 20
20mm riser housed into newel and nosing board and fixed to tread below with 3 Nº 1¾" x 10ga. (44·5 x 4·88mm) countersunk steel wood screws
200
244
Splay on newel and trimmer (see drg. Nº D5266)
2 Nº 40 x 40 x 100mm long blocks at approx. 300mm c/c glued to riser and tread.
20
20mm riser
25mm tread
Plasterboard
Batten for plasterboard fixing
225 x 30mm outer string
20 x 20mm wedges
120 x 85mm newel capping
40 x 12mm cover plate
SECTION OF TOP FLIGHT WITH NEWEL
65 x 45mm plate plugged to wall
16 33 16
80 x 30mm capping
21mm nosing board.
FOR SECTION AND ELEVATION OF LANDING BALUSTRADE SEE DRG. Nº D5266.
Trimmer joist (see job drgs.)
20 31 33 16
225 x 30mm outer string
100 x 70mm newel with 115 x 85mm capping
20 20 20 40
20mm riser
25mm tread
PLAN OF FIRST FLOOR NEWEL AND BALUSTRADE
GLC ILEA
Department of Architecture and Civic Design County Hall SE1
Architect Sir Roger Walters KBE FRIBA FI StructE
This drawing is to be read in conjunction with drawing number [24] D3148.
Where applicable this drg. is to be read as handed.
Departmental Standard Drawing
title
PRIVATE ACCESS WOOD STAIR – TYPE C.
DETAIL OF TOP FLIGHT WITH OUTER STRING AND NEWEL.
scale
1 : 5
drawing no
D5265
rev.
8 | [24] 363 | Hi2 |

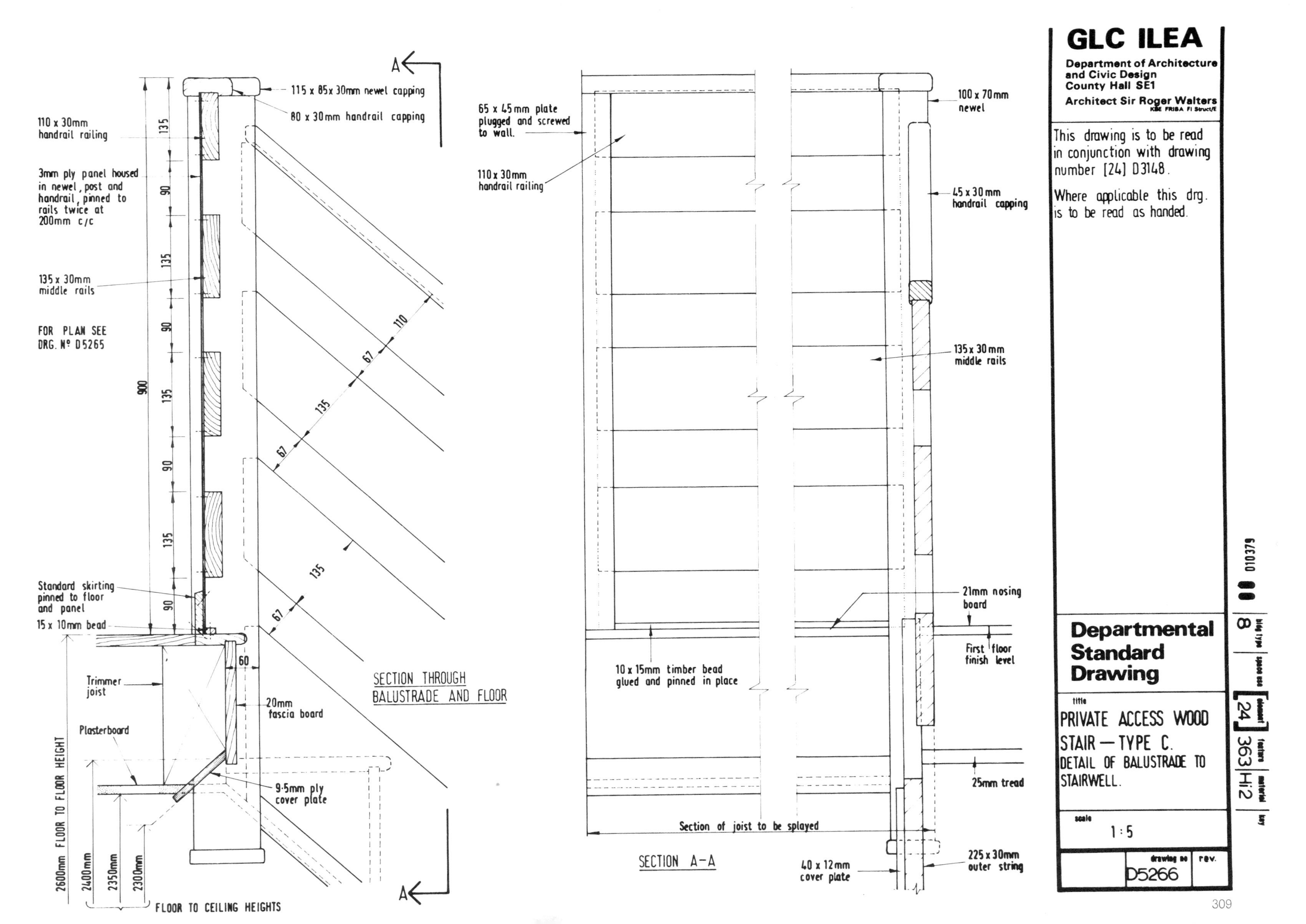
GLC ILEA
Department of Architecture and Civic Design
County Hall SE1
Architect Sir Roger Walters KBE FRIBA FI Struct/E
This drawing is to be read in conjunction with drawing number [24] D3148.
Where applicable this drg. is to be read as handed.
Departmental Standard Drawing
title
PRIVATE ACCESS WOOD STAIR — TYPE C.
DETAIL OF BALUSTRADE TO STAIRWELL.
scale
1:5
drawing no
D5266
rev.
8
24
363
Hi2
010379
115 x 85 x 30mm newel capping
80 x 30mm handrail capping
110 x 30mm handrail railing
3mm ply panel housed in newel, post and handrail, pinned to rails twice at 200mm c/c
135 x 30mm middle rails
FOR PLAN SEE DRG. Nº D5265
Standard skirting pinned to floor and panel
15 x 10mm bead
Trimmer joist
Plasterboard
20mm fascia board
9·5mm ply cover plate
2600mm FLOOR TO FLOOR HEIGHT
2400mm
2350mm
2300mm
FLOOR TO CEILING HEIGHTS
SECTION THROUGH BALUSTRADE AND FLOOR
65 x 45mm plate plugged and screwed to wall.
110 x 30mm handrail railing
100 x 70mm newel
45 x 30mm handrail capping
135 x 30mm middle rails
21mm nosing board
First floor finish level
10 x 15mm timber bead glued and pinned in place
25mm tread
Section of joist to be splayed
SECTION A-A
40 x 12mm cover plate
225 x 30mm outer string

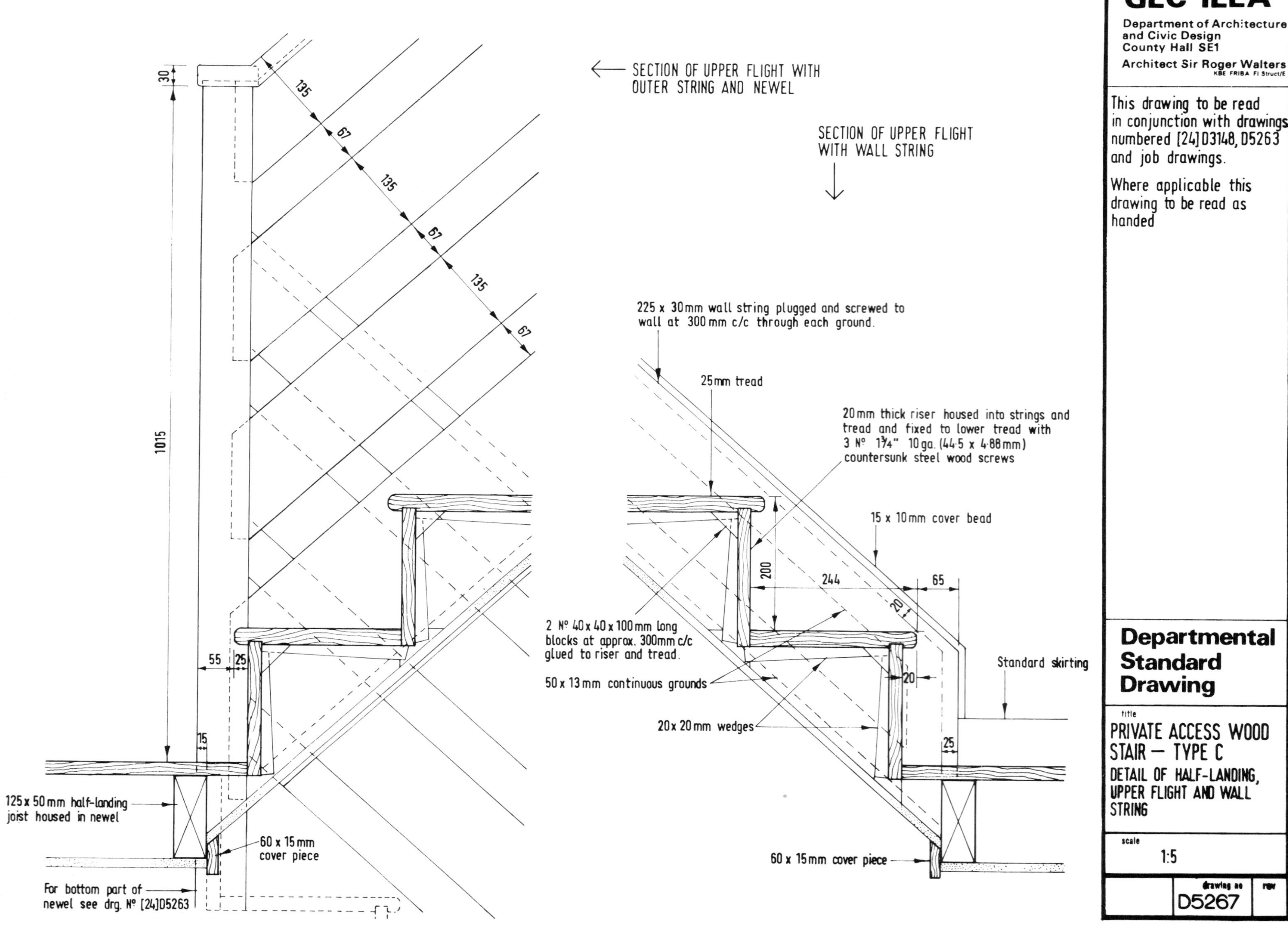

SECTION OF UPPER FLIGHT WITH OUTER STRING AND NEWEL
SECTION OF UPPER FLIGHT WITH WALL STRING
30
1015
135
67
135
67
135
67
55
25
15
125 x 50 mm half-landing joist housed in newel
60 x 15 mm cover piece
For bottom part of newel see drg. Nº [24]D5263
225 x 30mm wall string plugged and screwed to wall at 300 mm c/c through each ground.
25mm tread
20mm thick riser housed into strings and tread and fixed to lower tread with 3 Nº 1¾" 10ga. (44·5 x 4·88mm) countersunk steel wood screws
15 x 10mm cover bead
200
244
65
20
20
2 Nº 40 x 40 x 100mm long blocks at approx. 300mm c/c glued to riser and tread.
50 x 13mm continuous grounds
20 x 20mm wedges
Standard skirting
25
60 x 15mm cover piece
GLC ILEA
Department of Architecture and Civic Design
County Hall SE1
Architect Sir Roger Walters
KBE FRIBA FI Struct/E
This drawing to be read in conjunction with drawings numbered [24]D3148, D5263 and job drawings.
Where applicable this drawing to be read as handed
Departmental Standard Drawing
title
PRIVATE ACCESS WOOD STAIR — TYPE C
DETAIL OF HALF-LANDING, UPPER FLIGHT AND WALL STRING
scale
1:5
drawing no
rev
D5267
8
24 363 Hi2

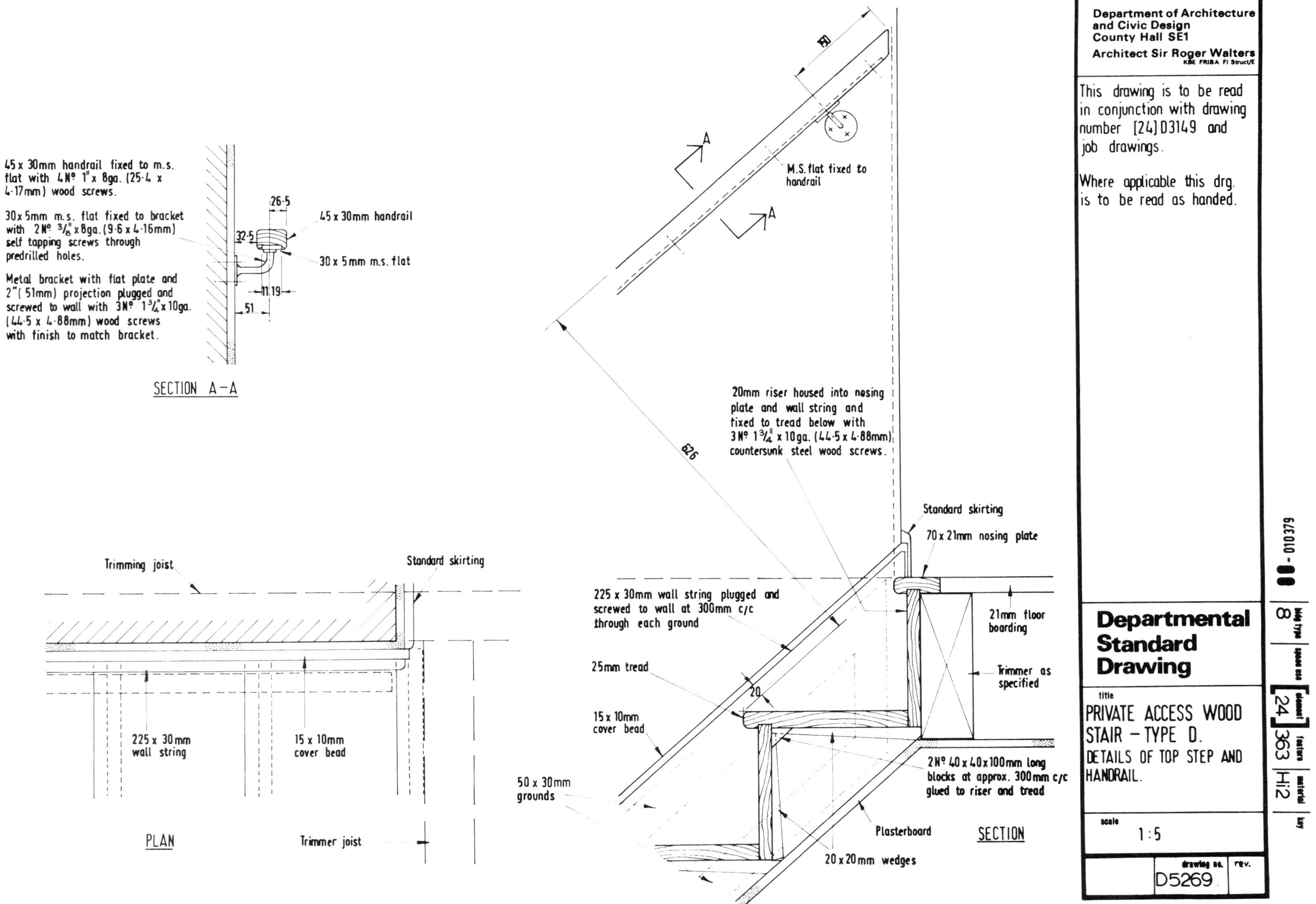
GLC ILEA
Department of Architecture and Civic Design
County Hall SE1
Architect Sir Roger Walters KBE FRIBA FI StructE
This drawing is to be read in conjunction with drawing number [24] D3149 and job drawings.
Where applicable this drg. is to be read as handed.
45 x 30mm handrail fixed to m.s. flat with 4 Nº 1" x 8ga. (25·4 x 4·17mm) wood screws.
30 x 5mm m.s. flat fixed to bracket with 2 Nº 3/8" x 8ga. (9·6 x 4·16mm) self tapping screws through predrilled holes.
Metal bracket with flat plate and 2" (51mm) projection plugged and screwed to wall with 3 Nº 1 3/4" x 10ga. (44·5 x 4·88mm) wood screws with finish to match bracket.
26·5
32·5
11.19
51
45 x 30mm handrail
30 x 5mm m.s. flat
SECTION A–A
M.S. flat fixed to handrail
A
A
50
626
20mm riser housed into nosing plate and wall string and fixed to tread below with 3 Nº 1 3/4" x 10ga. (44·5 x 4·88mm) countersunk steel wood screws.
Standard skirting
70 x 21mm nosing plate
21mm floor boarding
Trimmer as specified
225 x 30mm wall string plugged and screwed to wall at 300mm c/c through each ground
25mm tread
20
15 x 10mm cover bead
50 x 30mm grounds
2 Nº 40 x 40 x 100mm long blocks at approx. 300mm c/c glued to riser and tread
Plasterboard
20 x 20mm wedges
SECTION
Trimming joist
Standard skirting
225 x 30mm wall string
15 x 10mm cover bead
PLAN
Trimmer joist
Departmental Standard Drawing
title
PRIVATE ACCESS WOOD STAIR – TYPE D.
DETAILS OF TOP STEP AND HANDRAIL.
scale
1:5
drawing no.
D5269
rev.
010379
8
[24] 363 Hi2

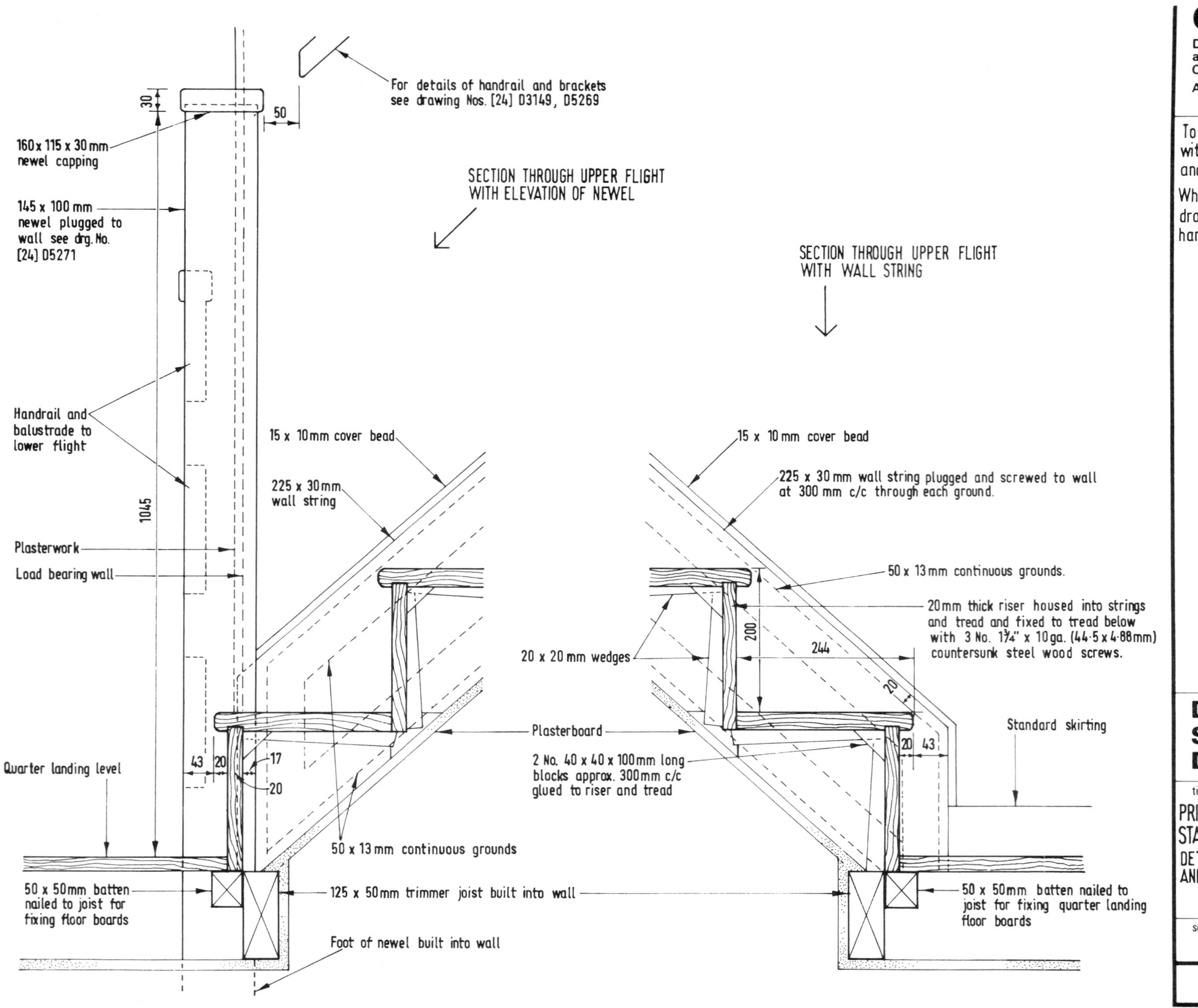

GLC ILEA

Department of Architecture and Civic Design
County Hall SE1
Architect Sir Roger Walters KBE FRIBA FI Struct E

To be read in conjunction with drg. No. [24] D3149 and job drawings.

Where applicable this drawing to be read as handed.

Departmental Standard Drawing

title

PRIVATE ACCESS WOOD STAIR – TYPE D

DETAIL OF QUARTER LANDING AND UPPER FLIGHT

scale 1: 5

drawing no D5270 | rev

8 | [24] | 363 | Hi2

010379

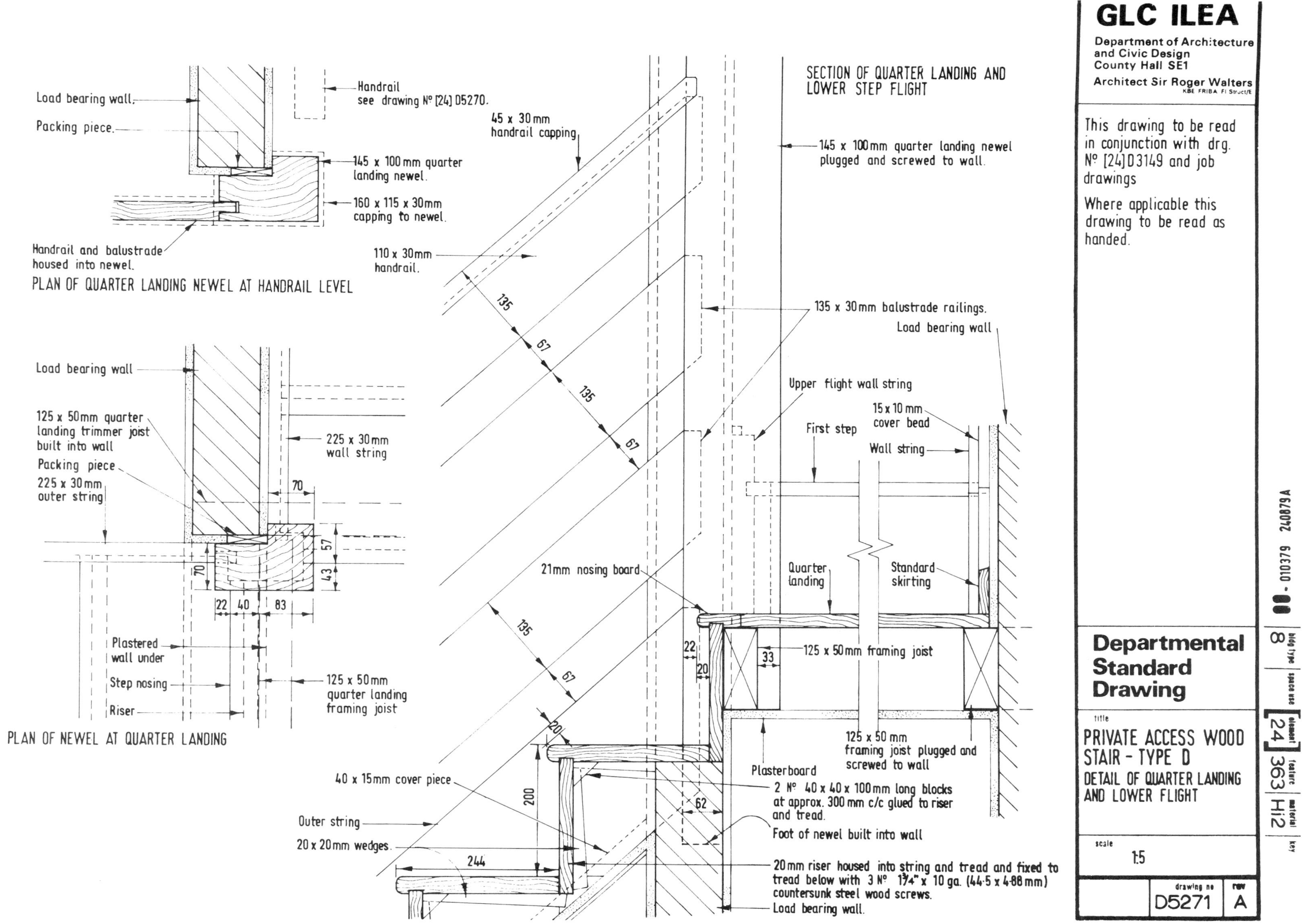
Load bearing wall
Packing piece
Handrail
see drawing Nº [24] D5270.
145 x 100 mm quarter
landing newel.
160 x 115 x 30mm
capping to newel.
Handrail and balustrade
housed into newel.
PLAN OF QUARTER LANDING NEWEL AT HANDRAIL LEVEL
45 x 30 mm
handrail capping
110 x 30mm
handrail.
SECTION OF QUARTER LANDING AND
LOWER STEP FLIGHT
145 x 100mm quarter landing newel
plugged and screwed to wall.
135 x 30mm balustrade railings.
Load bearing wall
Upper flight wall string
15 x 10 mm
cover bead
First step
Wall string
Load bearing wall
125 x 50mm quarter
landing trimmer joist
built into wall
Packing piece
225 x 30mm
outer string
225 x 30mm
wall string
70
57
43
70
22
40
83
Plastered
wall under
Step nosing
Riser
125 x 50mm
quarter landing
framing joist
PLAN OF NEWEL AT QUARTER LANDING
135
67
135
67
135
67
20
21mm nosing board
Quarter
landing
Standard
skirting
22
20
33
125 x 50mm framing joist
125 x 50 mm
framing joist plugged and
screwed to wall
Plasterboard
2 Nº 40 x 40 x 100mm long blocks
at approx. 300 mm c/c glued to riser
and tread.
Foot of newel built into wall
40 x 15mm cover piece
Outer string
20 x 20mm wedges.
200
62
244
20mm riser housed into string and tread and fixed to
tread below with 3 Nº 1¾" x 10 ga. (44·5 x 4·88 mm)
countersunk steel wood screws.
Load bearing wall.
GLC ILEA
Department of Architecture
and Civic Design
County Hall SE1
Architect Sir Roger Walters
KBE FRIBA FI StructE
This drawing to be read
in conjunction with drg.
Nº [24] D3149 and job
drawings
Where applicable this
drawing to be read as
handed.
Departmental
Standard
Drawing
title
PRIVATE ACCESS WOOD
STAIR - TYPE D
DETAIL OF QUARTER LANDING
AND LOWER FLIGHT
scale
1:5
drawing no
D5271
rev
A
8
bldg type
space use
[24]
element
363
feature
Hi2
material
key
010379 240879A

7
Mat wells

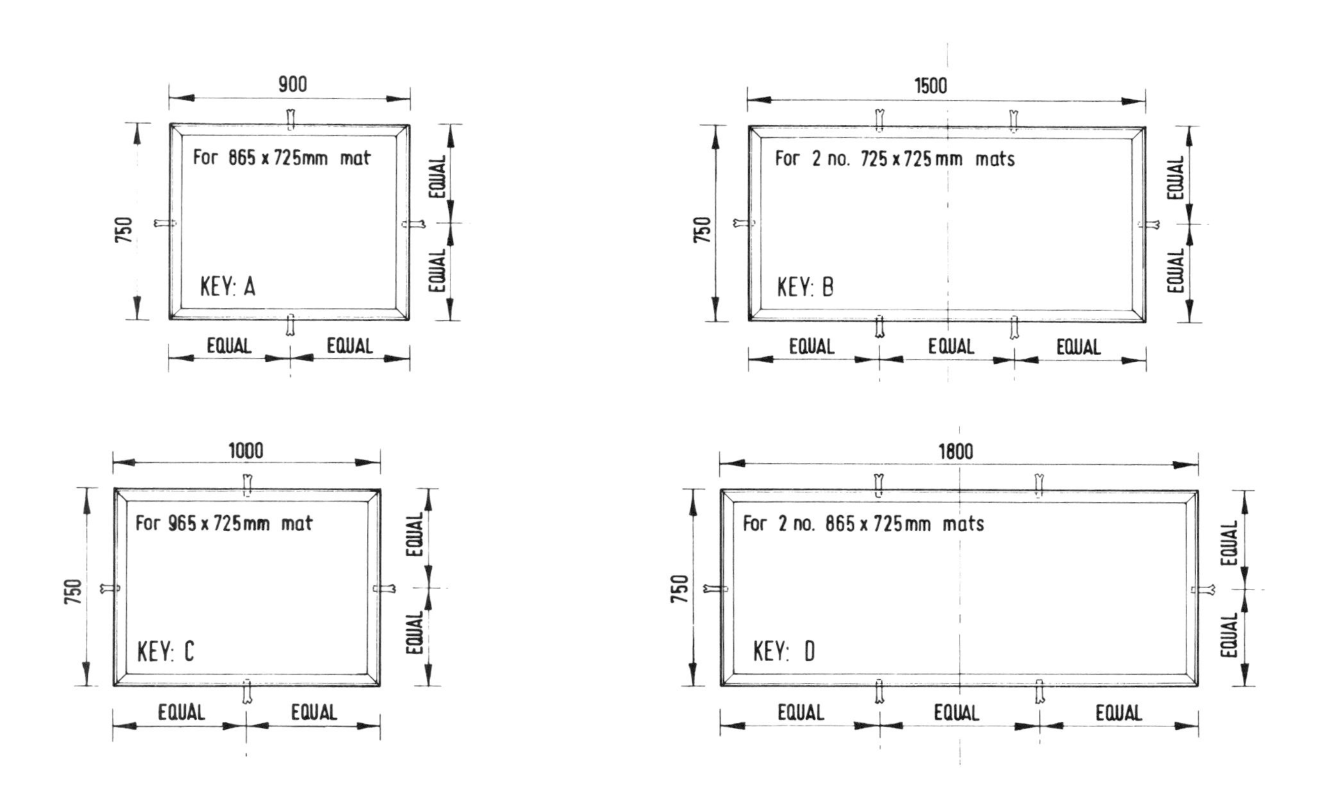

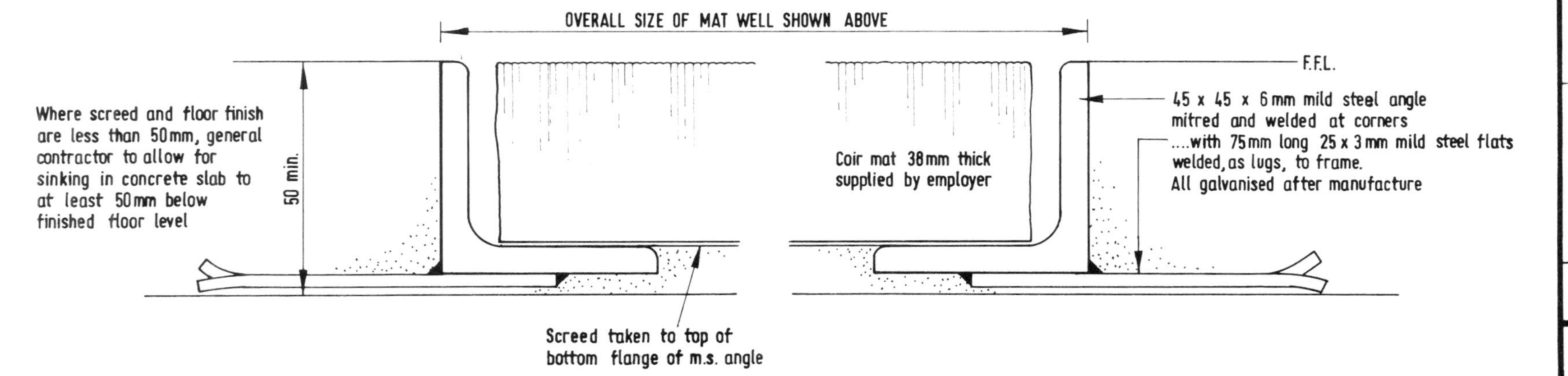

GLC ILEA
Department of Architecture and Civic Design
County Hall SE1
Architect Sir Roger Walters KBE FRIBA FI StructE

Mat sizes specially made to order, from Supplies Department.

Departmental Standard Drawing

title
MAT WELLS
MODULAR MAT WELLS FOR COIR MATS

scale
1:1 & 1:20

drawing no
D3160

bldg type | space use | element [43] | feature 370 | material Xh2 | key as drawing

010379

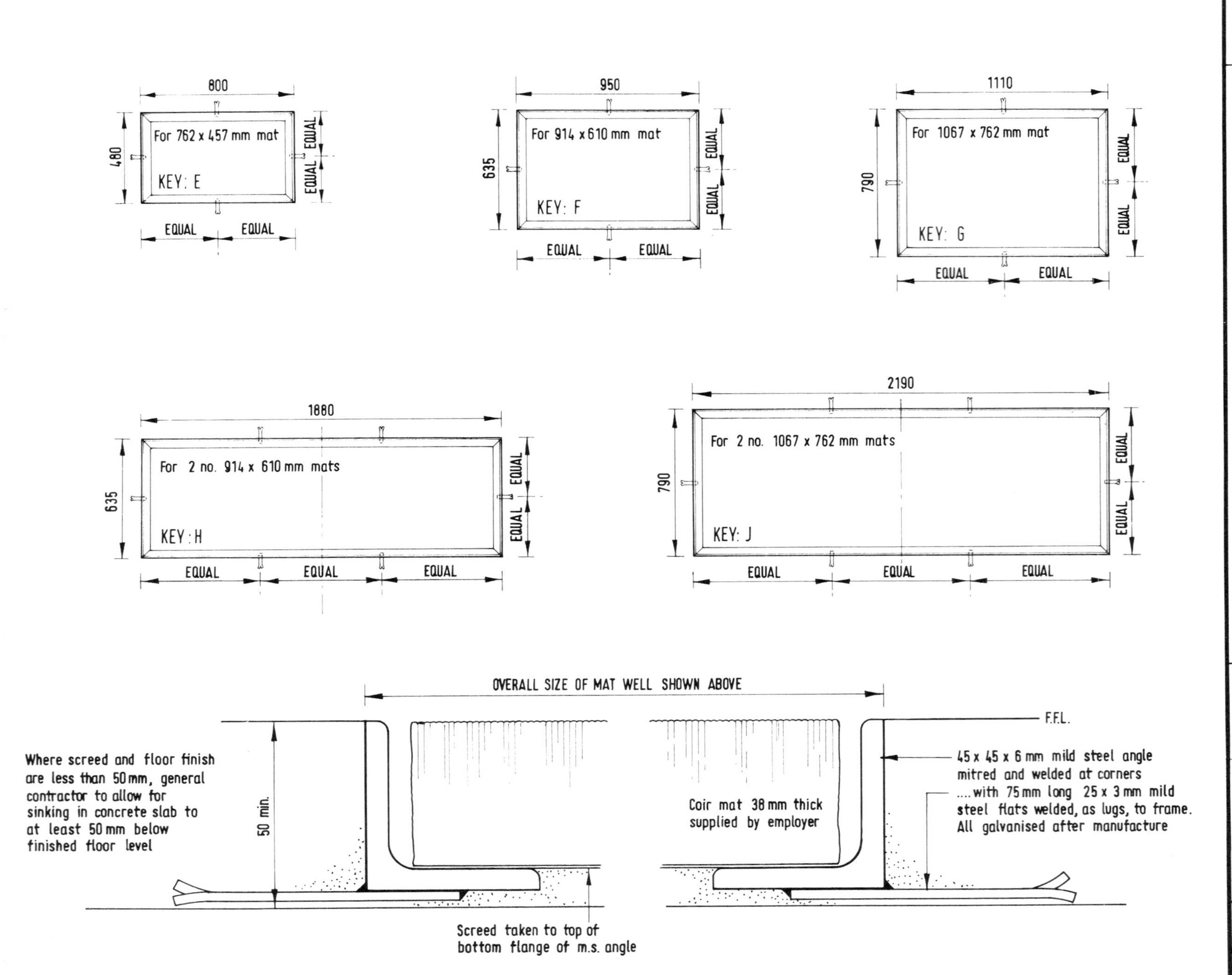

GLC ILEA

Department of Architecture
and Civic Design
County Hall SE1

Architect Sir Roger Walters
KBE FRIBA FI StructE

Departmental Standard Drawing

title

MAT WELLS
METRIC MAT WELLS FOR COIR MATS

scale

1:1 & 1:20

drawing no

D3161

bldg type	space use	element	feature	material	key
		43	370	Xh2	as drawing

010379

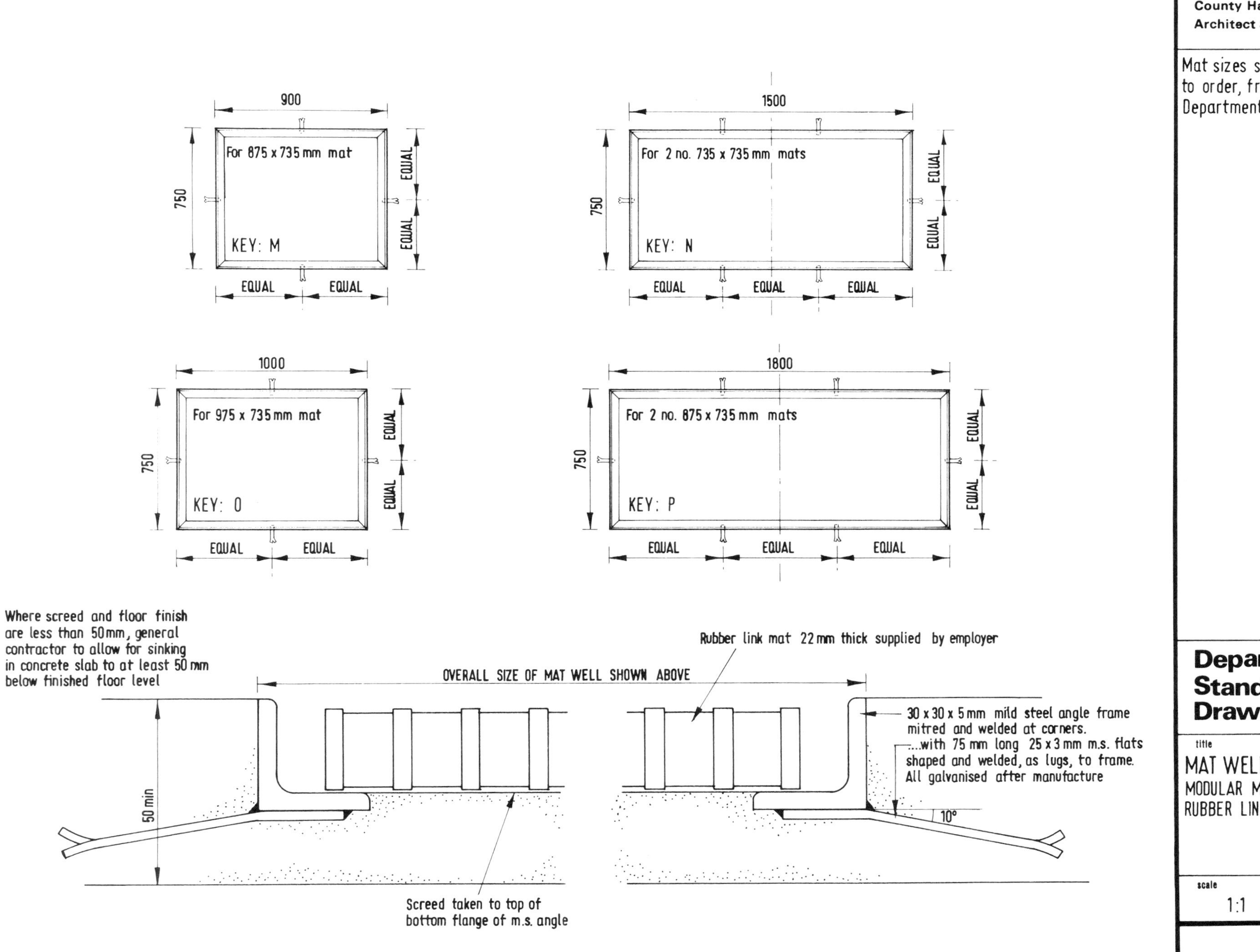

GLC ILEA

Department of Architecture and Civic Design
County Hall SE1
Architect Sir Roger Walters
KBE FRIBA FI Struct/E

Mat sizes specially made to order, from Supplies Department

Departmental Standard Drawing

title
MAT WELLS
MODULAR MAT WELLS FOR RUBBER LINK MATS

scale
1:1 & 1:20

drawing no
D3162

010379

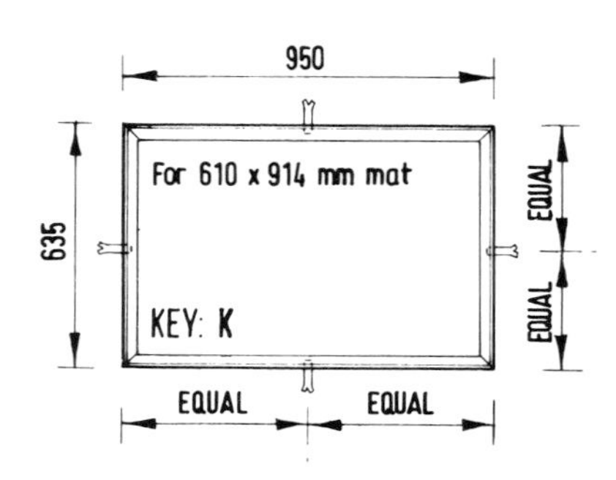

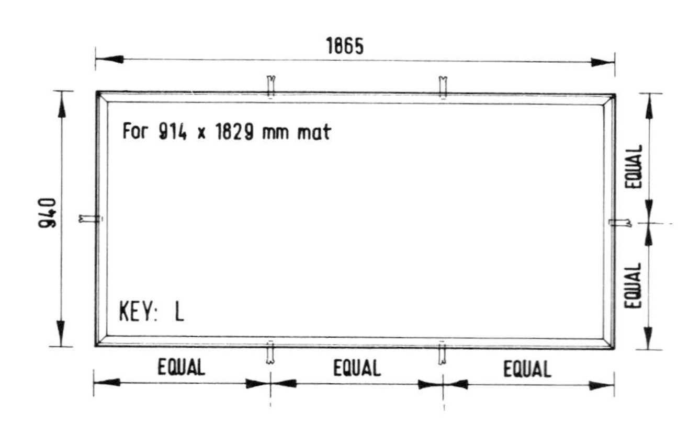

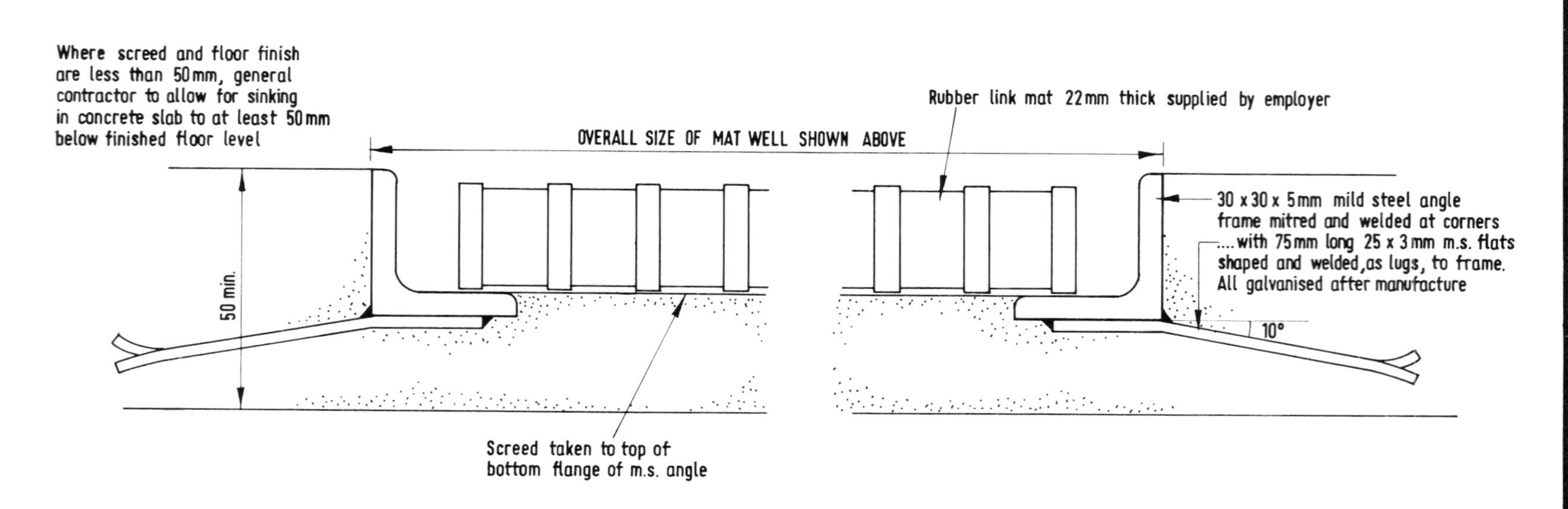

GLC ILEA

Department of Architecture and Civic Design
County Hall SE1
Architect Sir Roger Walters KBE FRIBA FI StructE

914 x 1829 mm mat specially made to order, from Supplies Dept.

Departmental Standard Drawing

title
MAT WELLS
METRIC MAT WELLS FOR RUBBER LINK MATS

scale
1:1 & 1:20

drawing no
D3163

bldg type | space use | element | feature | material | key
[43] 370 Xh2 as drawing

010379

Fittings and Services

Contents

Guidance notes

Drinking water cisterns

When the top of the cistern does not exceed 1372mm above floor level, an access platform is not required; but the cistern should be raised 150mm above the floor level for pipes and connections. In all cases where an access platform is provided, the distance from the top of the platform to the top of the cistern shall not exceed 1219mm—see figures **1, 2** and **3** for recommended dimensions.

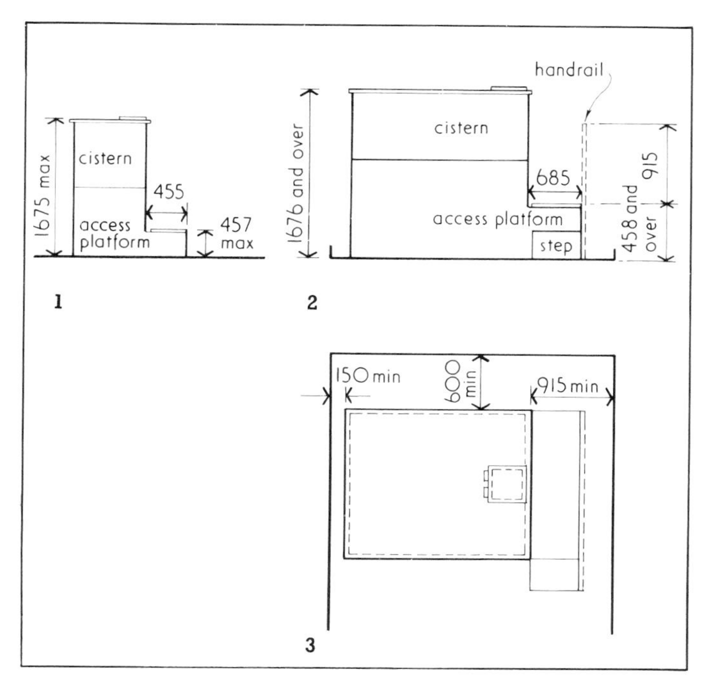

1 *to* **3** *When top of cistern does not exceed 1372 mm above floor level, no access platform is required; but the cistern should be raised 150 mm above floor level for pipes and connection. When top of cistern does exceed 1372 mm, access platform is required, such that the distance from the top of the platform to the top of the cistern does not exceed 1219 mm. Minimum cistern height is 787 mm. Cistern size should be obtained from Mechanical Engineers to establish whether provision of a platform is required. Headroom above cistern must be not less than 914 mm.*

1 *Size of platform up to 457 mm in height.*

2 *Size of platform over 457 in height, with step and guard rail.*

3 *Minimum clearances required around cistern.*

Cradling bolts and wall anchors: Layout principles

Inroduction

Cradle bolts are large galvanised steel eyebolts (a direct supply item) built into the structure of roofs. Cradling poles are lashed to these bolts in order to:—

1 Suspend cradles for the maintenance of the face of the building.

2 Haul material and equipment required for maintenance purposes to the roof.

Stainless steel wall sockets are designed to be built in flush with the face of a wall. Tubular steel adaptors are fixed into the sockets in order to:—

1 Enable maintenance staging to be tied to the structure of the building.

2 Restrain the suspension cables of cradles, which otherwise may swing dangerously.

Ladder ties, provided at first floor level, consist of Hilti toothless anchors fixed into the brickwork and ring bolts to suit. The sockets and anchors are to be included in the building contract. The Job Architect need not concern himself with the adaptors and ring bolts which will be held by the Director of Housing.

The diagrammatic section and roof plan (diagram **1**) show the cradle bolt to which the inner end of the jib pole is fixed and in addition a second row of bolts placed 1.2m in from the face of the building. These provide anchorage points for the struts supporting the jib poles. When cradling bolts are put into a timber flat roof, the roof structure, adequate in other respects, may fail due to the upward pull on the bolts. Therefore it must always be checked by the Structural Engineer against this eventuality.

It is a policy of the Director of Housing to provide these maintenance aids on all new work as shown in table I

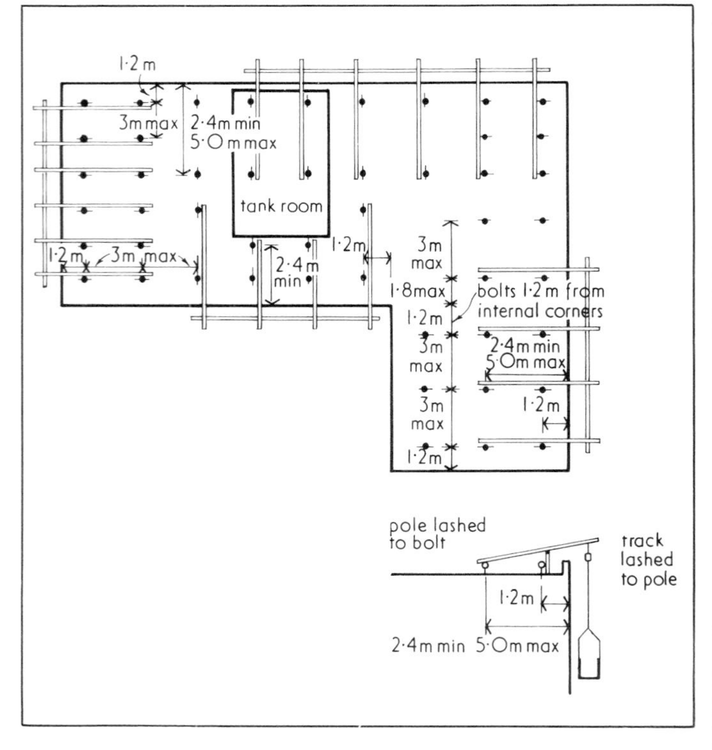

1 *Diagrammatic roof plan and section, showing spacing of cradle bolts on roof.*

Table I Schedule showing provision and spacing of scaffolding sockets and ladder ties.

Type	Diagram	Provision
Maisonette blocks, access balconies	3·3–6·3m eaves gl	Ladder ties provided at first floor level. Sockets to be provided at every upper floor level of each maisonette.
Two-storey blocks: ladders	eaves 2nd gl	Provide line of ladder ties at first floor level.
Three-storey blocks: scaffolding Four-storey blocks: scaffolding	eaves 2nd gl	Provide line of ladder ties at first floor level. Provide line of sockets as shown; or if extensive glazing prohibits wall sockets then provide roof anchors only.
Five-storey blocks: scaffolding and winch cranes	eaves 2nd gl	Provide line of ladder ties at first floor level. Provide sockets on second floor and under eaves. If extensive glazing prohibits wall sockets then provide roof anchors only.
Six to seven storey blocks: winch cradles	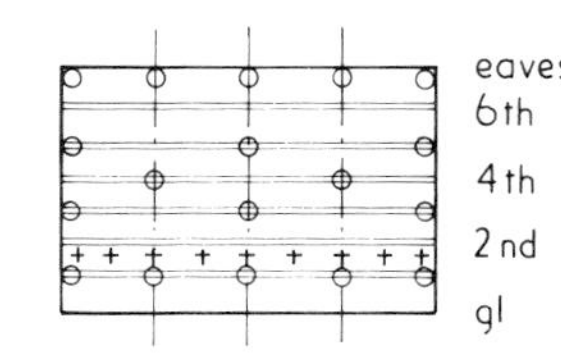	Provide line of ladder ties at first floor. *Walls with windows:* Provide sockets at every other floor (above second floor level); alternatively, eg first vertical line 1, 3, 5 under eaves; second vertical line 2, 4 under eaves; third 1, 3, 5 under eaves. *Walls without windows:* As above but for cradle wires include a line of sockets extending from second floor level to eaves, at each end of elevation. Sockets and ring bolts should be set out so that there are always sockets below the eaves, and ring bolts at first floor level at extreme ends of wall.
Eight storey blocks and over: powered cradles only	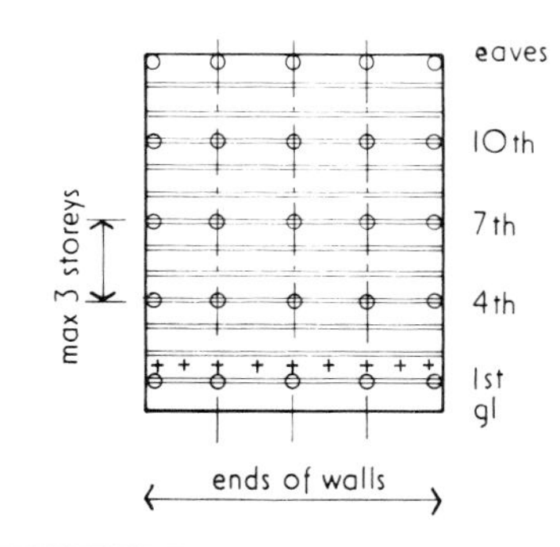	Provide line of ladder ties at first floor level. Provision of 15 amp socket outlets behind parapet walls at 6.1m intervals. Minimum 2 sockets up to 15.2m; maximum 4 sockets for blocks over 15.2m. Each vertical anchor wire fastened to sockets at least every third floor level and under eaves.

○ Scaffolding sockets spaced at 3.3 to 6.3 metres.

\+ Ladder ties fixed at equal intervals between bays at a maximum of 2 metre centres, positioned in brickwork under cills or alternatively at floor slab level.

Refuse chutes

Standard drawings D5050 to D5054 illustrate the details of refuse chutes manufactured by *Spun Concrete Ltd* (figure **1**), and *True Flue Ltd* (figure **2**). Both refuse chutes are designed to receive the standard GLC hopper door (a Direct Supply item) and cut-off unit.

Internal diameter of refuse chute is 457mm. Standard chute length is 2.44m. Shorter units are made to conform to varying floor heights and also for ease of handling where access is restricted. Note that the *Spun Concrete* unit is a separate part; while the *True Flue* hopper is integral with the floor height unit.

Restraining units should be used where refuse chutes run throughout two storeys (but no more) with no support of the spreader unit at intermediate floor. Structural engineer should be consulted about construction of refuse chute, restraining unit, and support of spreader unit on floor slab.

Refuse chutes can be freestanding as on drawings D5051 and D5056, or enclosed by a tiled brick wall as on drawings D5050 and D5055. The minimum size of the tiled panel around the hopper to be 200mm above and below hopper, and 100mm on the side; and the wall surface should be easily cleanable.

Where it is necessary or desirable to terminate the chute below the topmost floor, the chute must be ventilated by an asbestos cement vent pipe carried up through the roof (figure **3**).

In those boroughs where bulk trailers are provided, and if the size of the refuse chamber prevents the chute being placed directly over the opening of the trailer, then a 'cranked' cut-off unit should be used (figure **4**). These boroughs include Tower Hamlets, Lewisham, and Southwark.

When the ground floor of the block is planned as flats, a special refuse hopper has to be provided. It should be separate from the chute, and positioned at the first half landing level. The GLC Director of Housing requests that tenants should not walk more than a half floor level to the nearest hopper. Care must be taken to adhere to the minimum height for the hopper as shown on drawing D3156. The refuse chamber has to be of sufficient size to accommodate a separate container (1 per 5 flats) for this hopper. See figure **5.**

Job architects should consult their Division/Branch notes and the Building Regulations with regard to the design of refuse chutes, hoppers and refuse chambers.

Dry risers

Standard drawings D5090 to D5092 illustrate dry riser details.

Dry rising mains should be installed in buildings exceeding 18m in height; and should be positioned within ventilated lobbies of lobby approach staircases, or in staircase enclosures. Buildings above 61m in height should normally be equipped with wet rising mains, and the London Fire Brigade should be consulted in this connection.

The diameter of dry rising mains should be 100mm where riser is provided with only one outlet on each floor; and 150mm where riser is provided with two outlets on each floor.

Inlet boxes should be provided in external walls with due regard to position of street hydrants and within 18m from access for Fire Brigade appliances.

Outlets should be provided at each floor above the first floor (in maisonettes on every entrance floor above ground floor) in proportion of one outlet to each 930m^2 of floor area (the furthest point being no more than 60m from the outlet); and on roof. When two outlets per floor are allowed on one riser, diameter of riser should be 150mm.

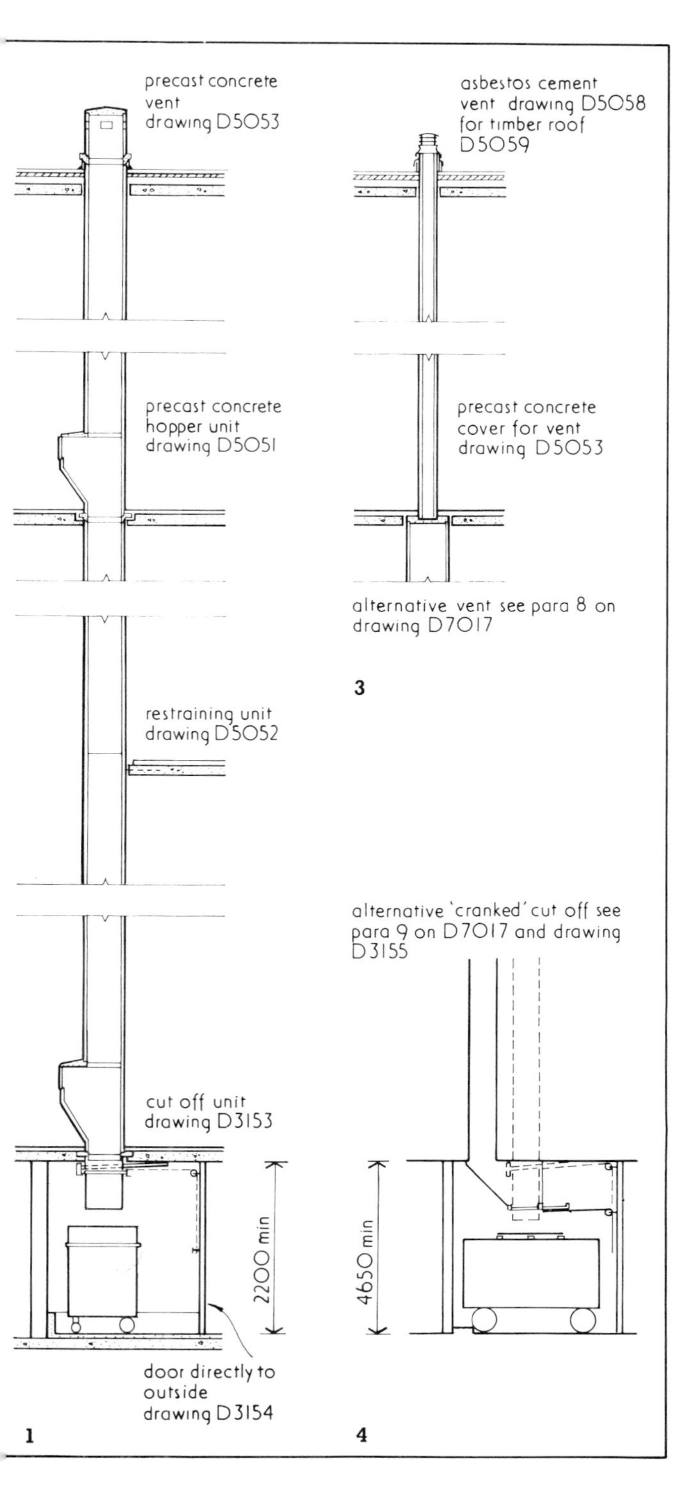

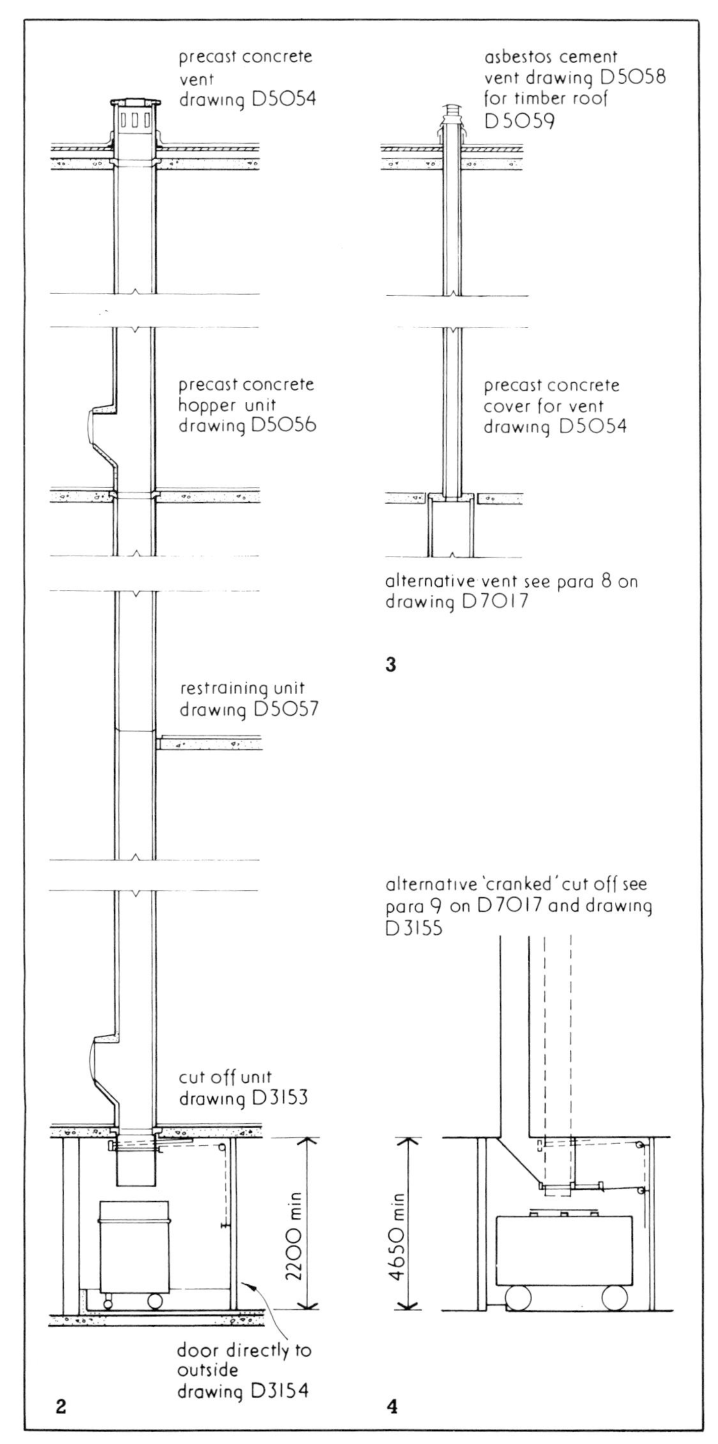

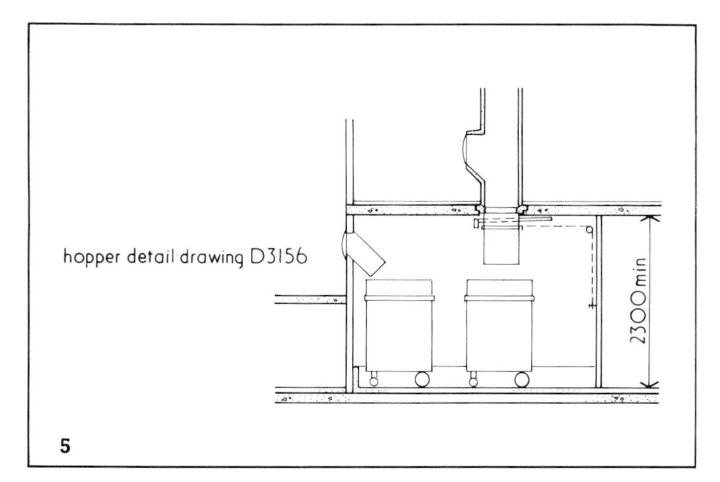

1 *Refuse chute diagram for Spun Concrete Ltd units.*

2 *Refuse chute diagram for True Flue Ltd units.*

3 *Vent pipe for refuse chutes which are terminated below topmost floor.*

4 *Cranked cut-off units.*

5 *Special refuse hopper for buildings in which ground floor consists of flats, thus necessitating hopper at first half landing level.*

For further information see CP 3 Chapter IV, 1971, *Precautions against Fire:*

Part 1 Flats and Maisonettes;
Part 2 Shops and Department Stores;
Part 3 Office Buildings.

See also GLC London Fire Brigade FP/GEN/22 (Rev 1).

Figures **1** and **2** below show the assembly as a whole in schematic form, and should be read in conjunction with drawings D5090 to D5092.

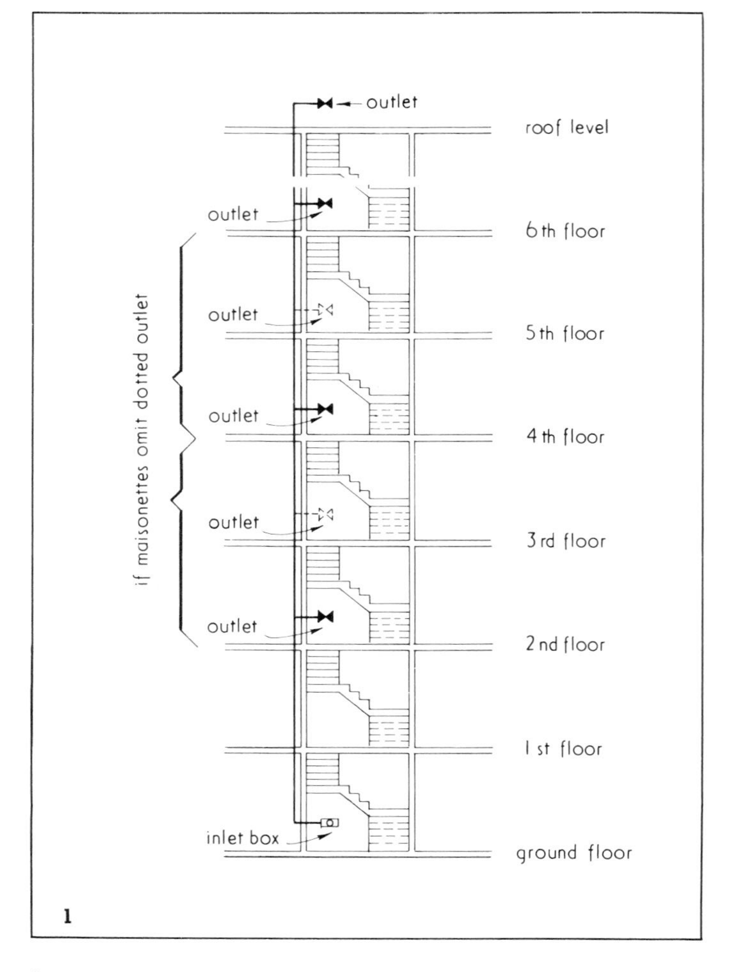

1 *Key diagram*

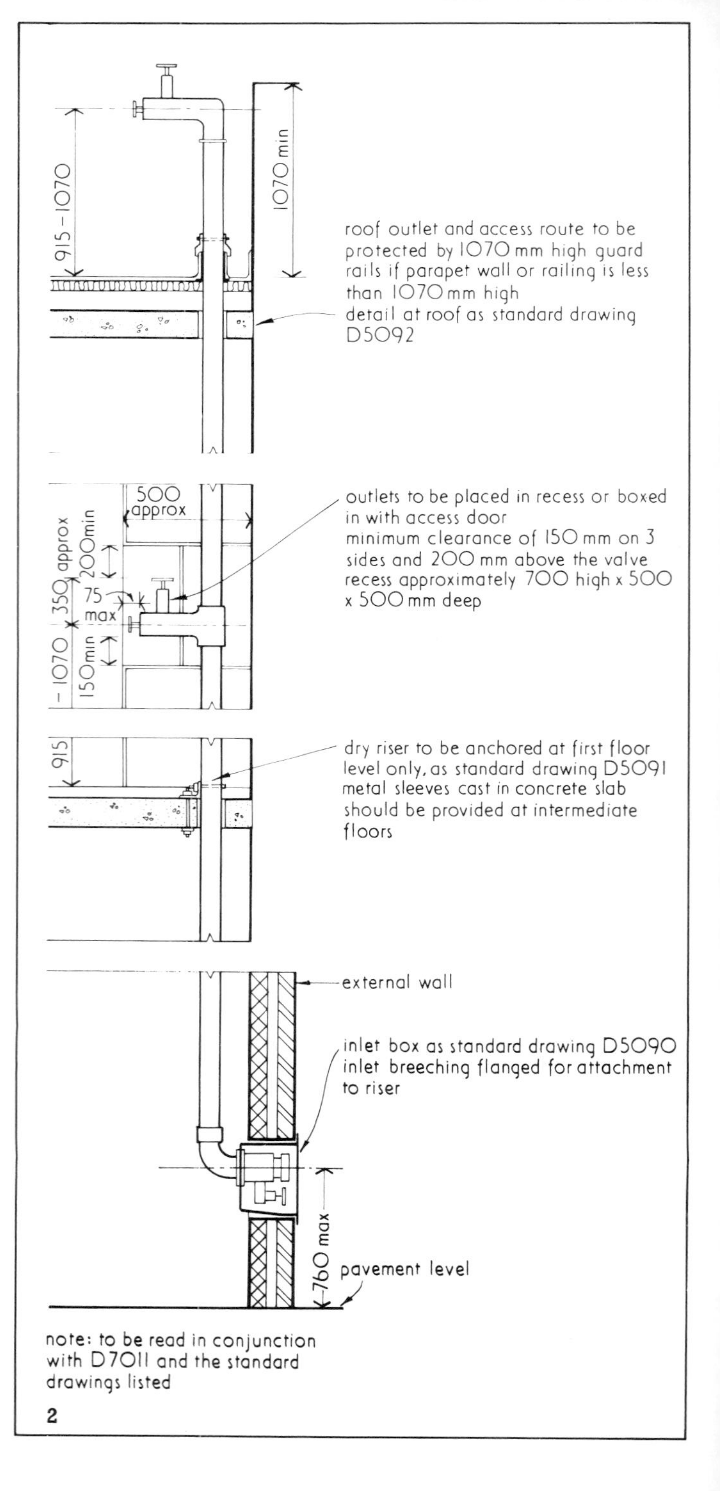

2 *Dry riser assembly shown in schematic form.*

1 Sanitaryware

5128 Washbasin (Royalex)
5119 Washbasin support
5123 Washbasin (Eldon)
3171 Sink
5124 WC low level
5125 WC high level
5121 Pull handle for old peoples' sanitary spaces
3138 Dribbler

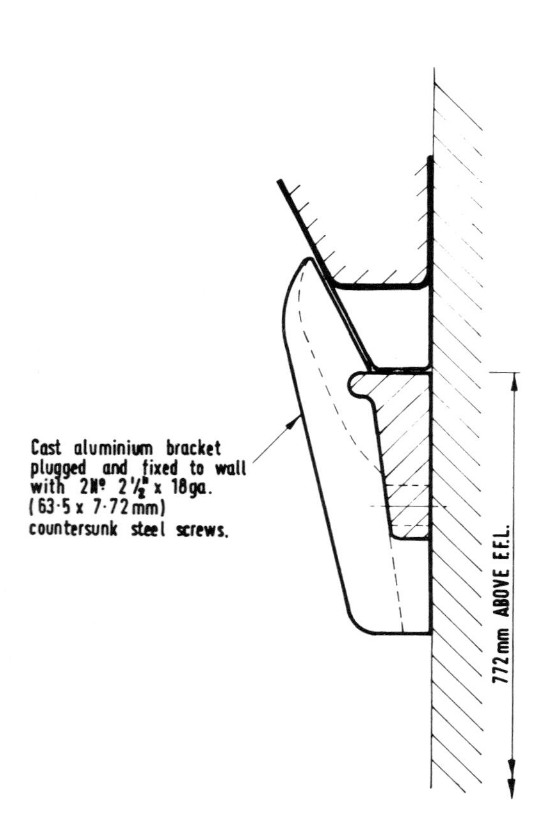

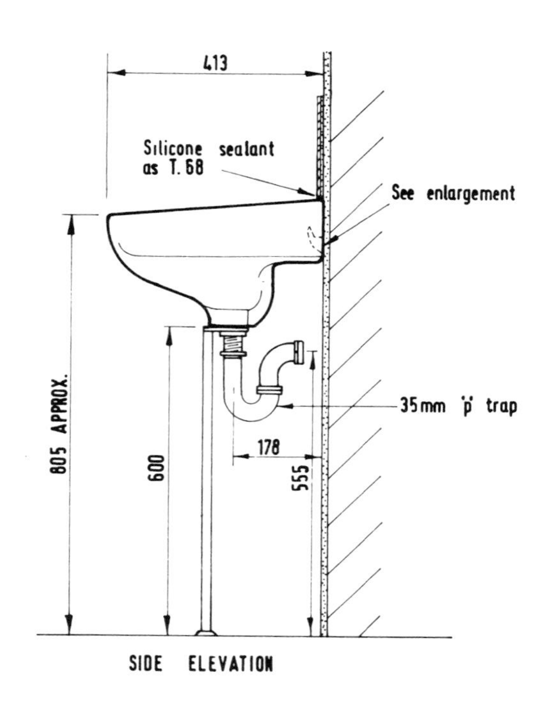

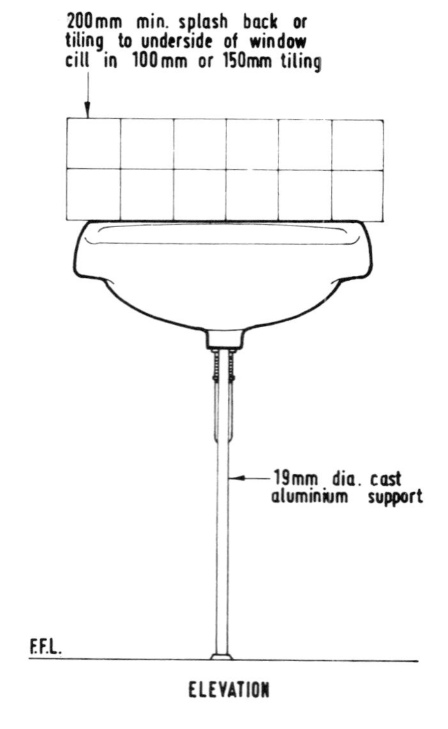

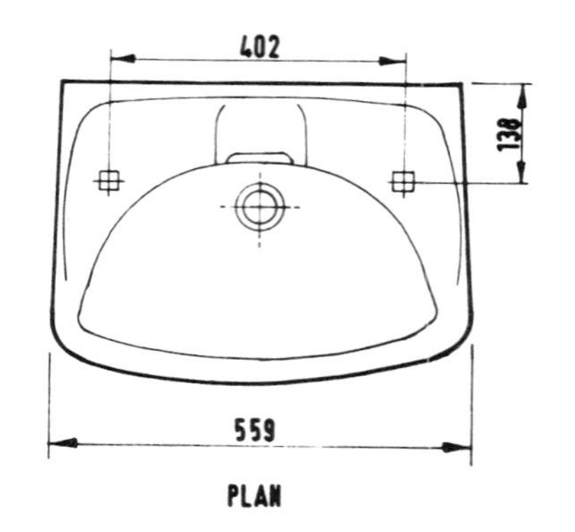

GLC ILEA

Department of Architecture and Civic Design
County Hall SE1

Architect Sir Roger Walters
KBE FRIBA FI.Struct.E

References following notes are clause numbers from G.L.C. preambles to bills of quantities.

The whole assembly is supplied by employer.

Dimensions are for guidance only. Setting out dimensions should be taken from samples on site.

Departmental Standard Drawing

title
LAVATORY BASIN
FOR DOMESTIC USE.
(ARMITAGE-SHANKS "ROYALEX")

scale
1:10 and 1:1

drawing no
D5128 A

bldg type	space use	element	feature	material	key
8		74	503	Xg2	C

00 - 010379

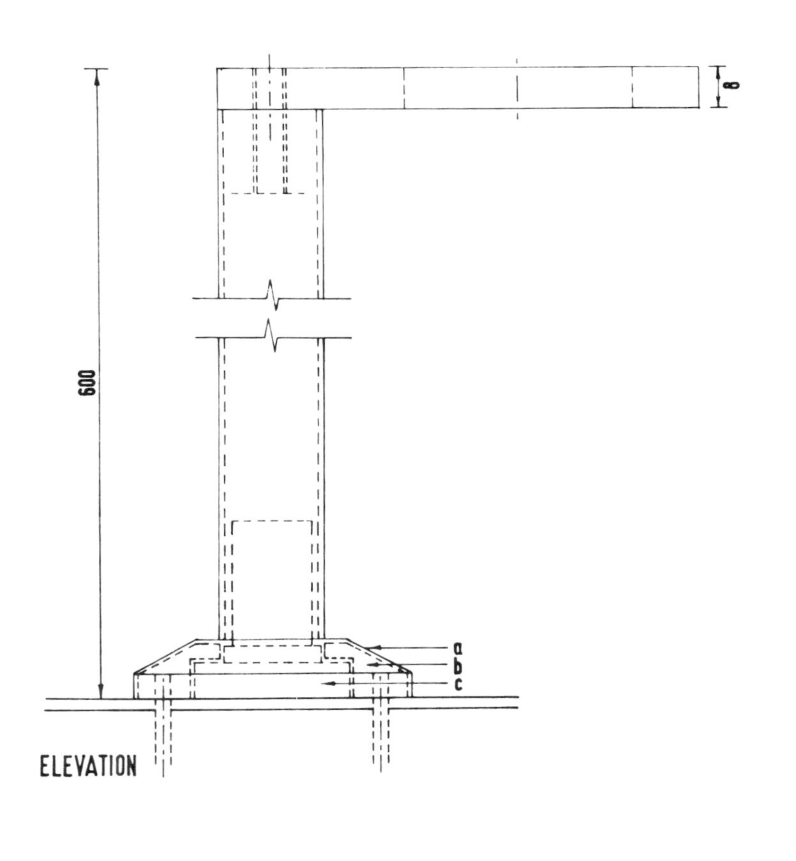

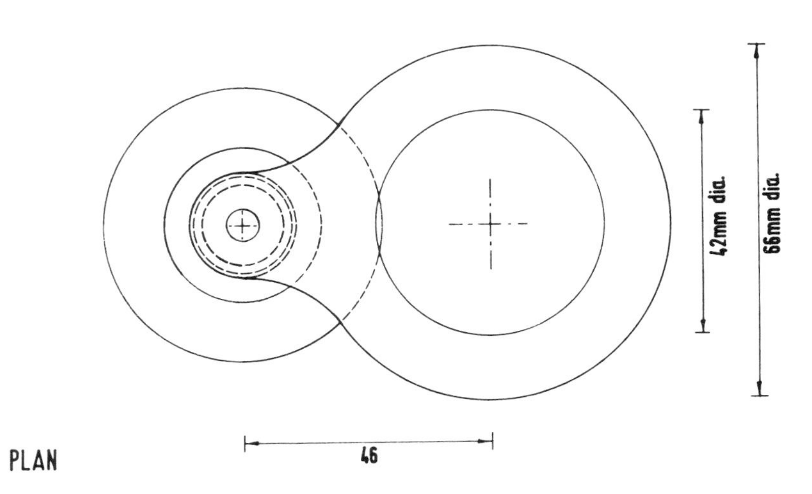

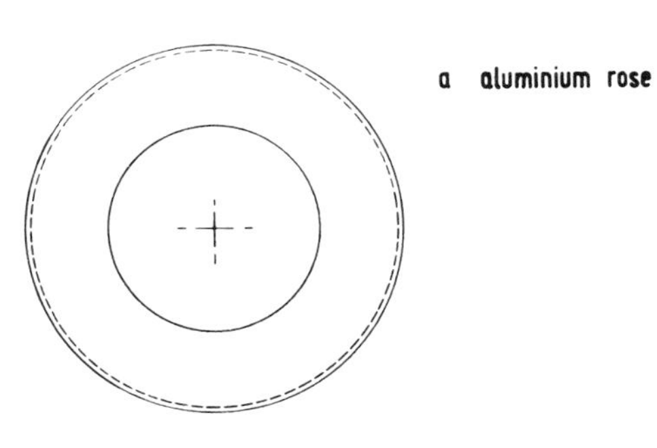

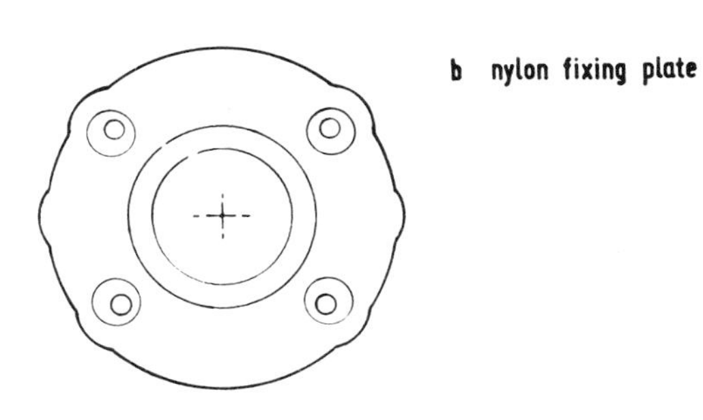

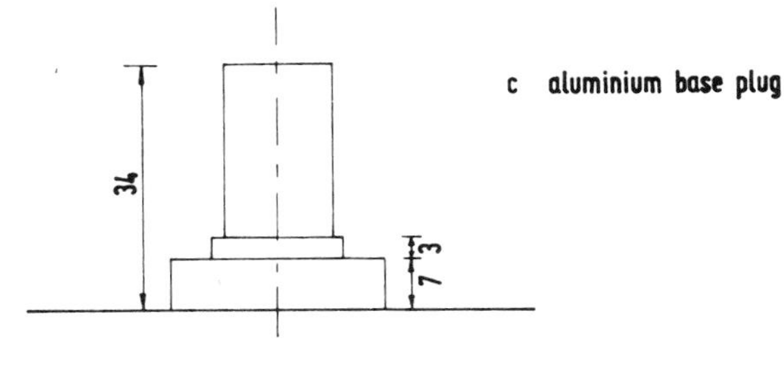

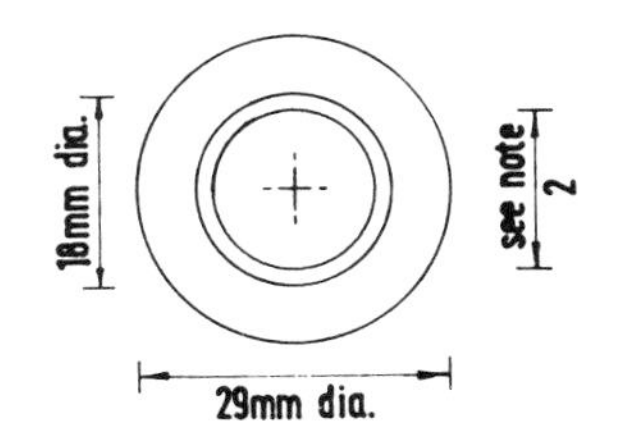

GLC ILEA

Department of Architecture and Civic Design
County Hall SE1 7PB
Architect Sir Roger Walters
KBE ARIBA FI Struct/E

References following notes are clause numbers from G.L.C. preambles to bills of quantities

1. Whole assembly to be supplied by the employer
2. Aluminium base plug to be a tight fit in tube leg
3. On timber floors the support to be screwed with 4 No. 4g 25·4mm long aluminium countersunk head wood screws
4. On concrete floors rawlplugs to be inserted into screed
5. Floor finish to be carried right through
6. For details of basin see [74] D5128

010379

Departmental Standard Drawing

title
WASHBASIN SUPPORT BASE

scale 1 : 1

drawing no D5119 | rev

bldg type 8 | space use | element [74] | feature 503 | material Xh4 | key A

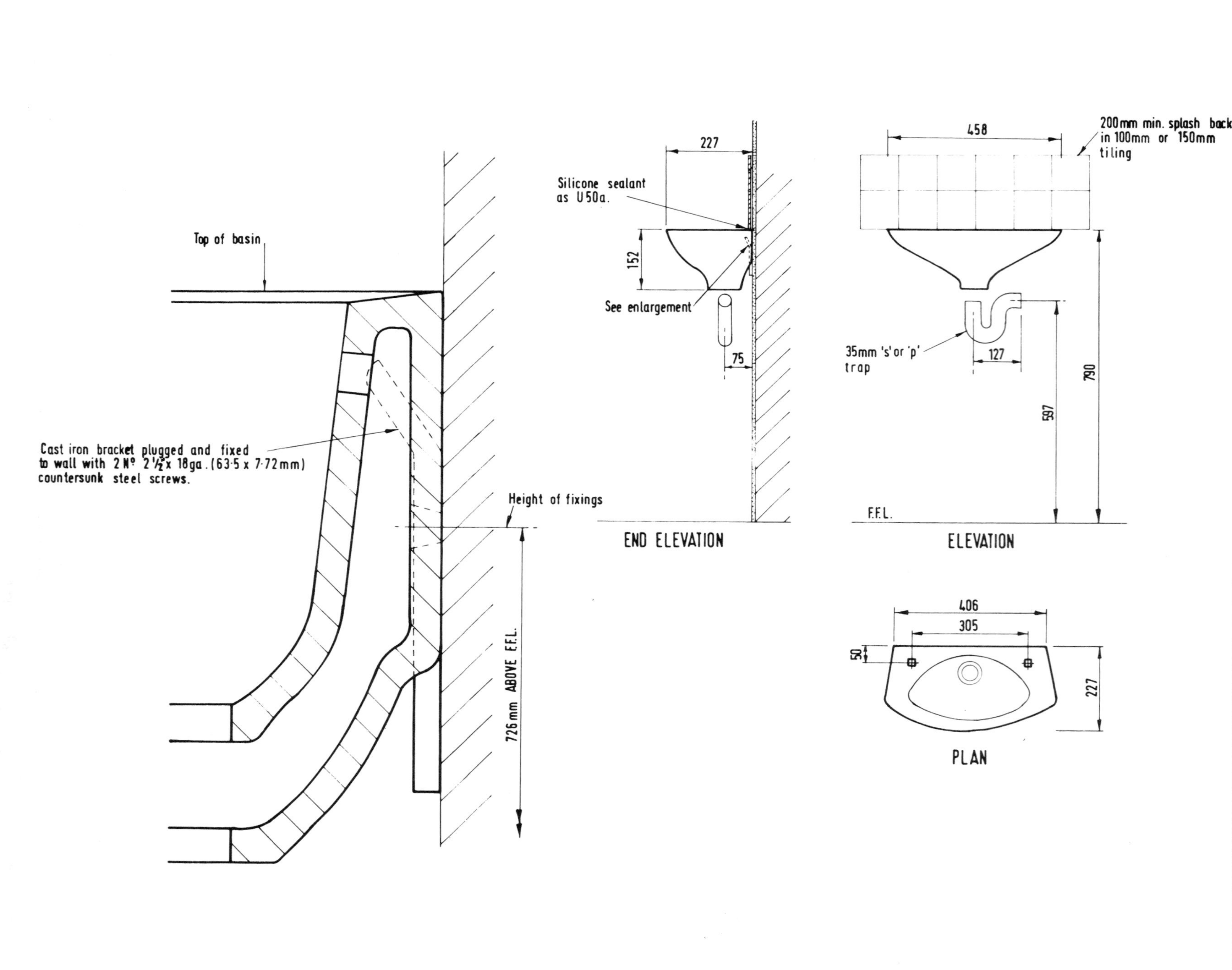

GLC ILEA

Department of Architecture and Civic Design
County Hall SE1
Architect Sir Roger Walters KBE FRIBA FI StructE

References following notes are clause numbers from G.L.C. preambles to bills of quantities.

The whole assembly is supplied by employer.

Dimensions are for guidance only. Setting out dimensions should be taken from samples on site.

Departmental Standard Drawing

title
LAVATORY BASIN
HAND RINSE BASIN FOR DOMESTIC USE.
ARMITAGE-SHANKS "ELDON"

scale
1:1 and 1:10

drawing no
D5123 B

bldg type: 8
space use:
element: 74
feature: 503
material: Xg2
key: A

010379

GLC ILEA

Department of Architecture
and Civic Design
County Hall SE1 7PB
Architect Sir Roger Walters
KBE ARIBA FI Struct/E

References following notes are clause numbers from G.L.C. preambles to bills of quantities

Dimensions are for guidance only. Setting out dimensions must be taken from samples on site.

Left hand drainer shown. Right hand alternative available.

Sink cupboard unit as specified by job architect.

Two-piece traps may be rotated at either joint to obtain a convenient position for the outlet.

50mm long earth bonding tag is welded to rear of bowl.

Taps, waste, trap and stainless steel sink supplied by employer.

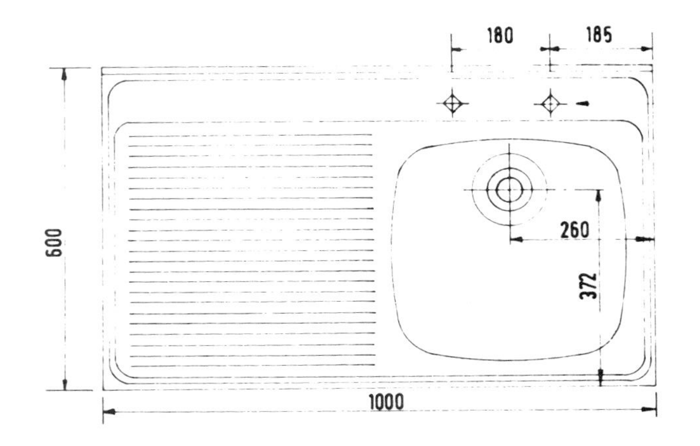

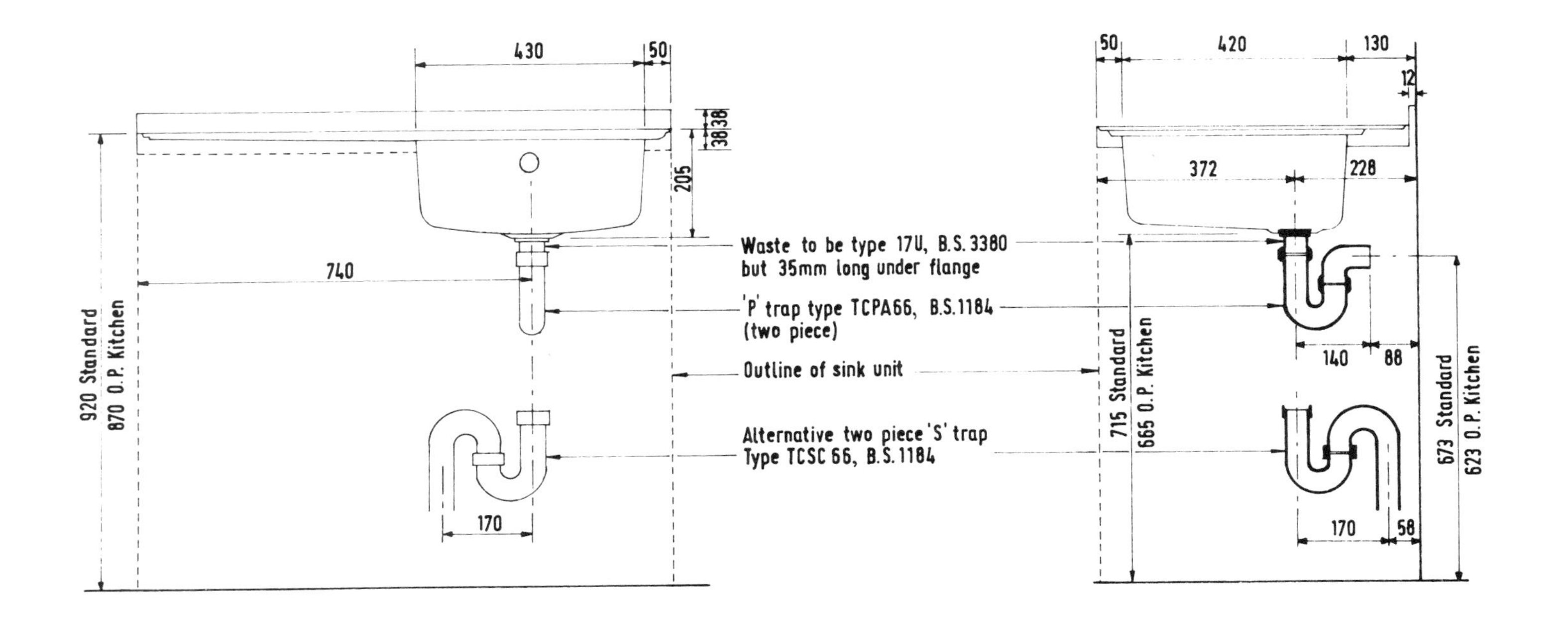

Departmental Standard Drawing

title

DOMESTIC SINK

CARRON 'SILVER DOVE'

scale 1 : 10

drawing no D3171 | rev A

8- bldg type | space use | [73] element | 505 feature | Xh3 material | A key

010379

GLC ILEA

Department of Architecture
and Civic Design
County Hall SE1
Architect Sir Roger Walters
KBE FRIBA FI StructE

References following notes are clause numbers from G.L.C. preambles to bills of quantities.

Whole assembly consisting of "LYNX" W.W.P., flush pipe and seat by SHIRES, W.C. pan MAGNIA by ARMITAGE SHANKS supplied by employer.

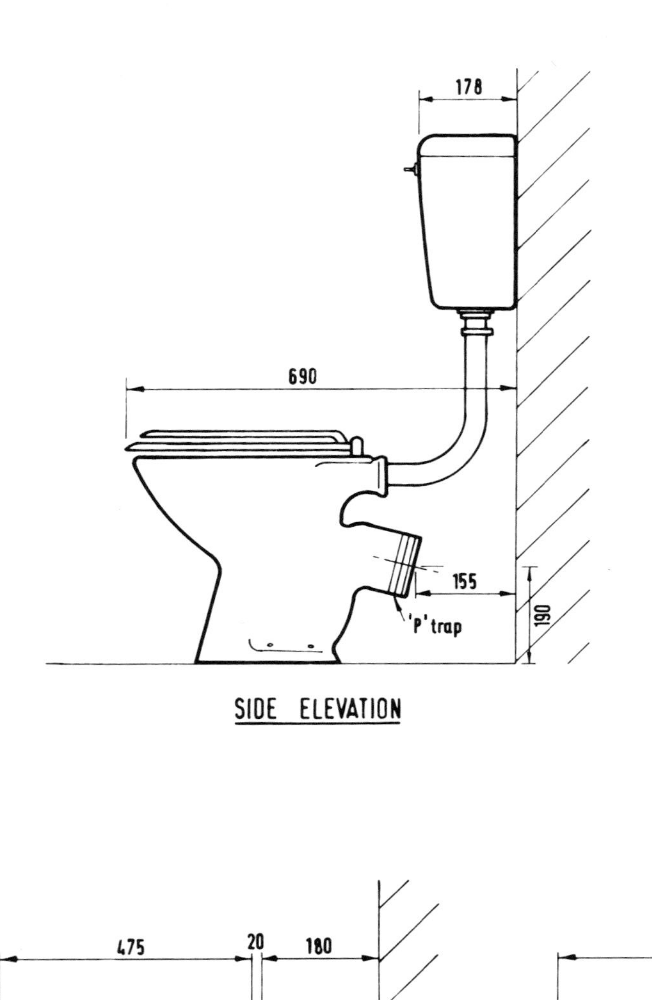

SIDE ELEVATION

KEY A1

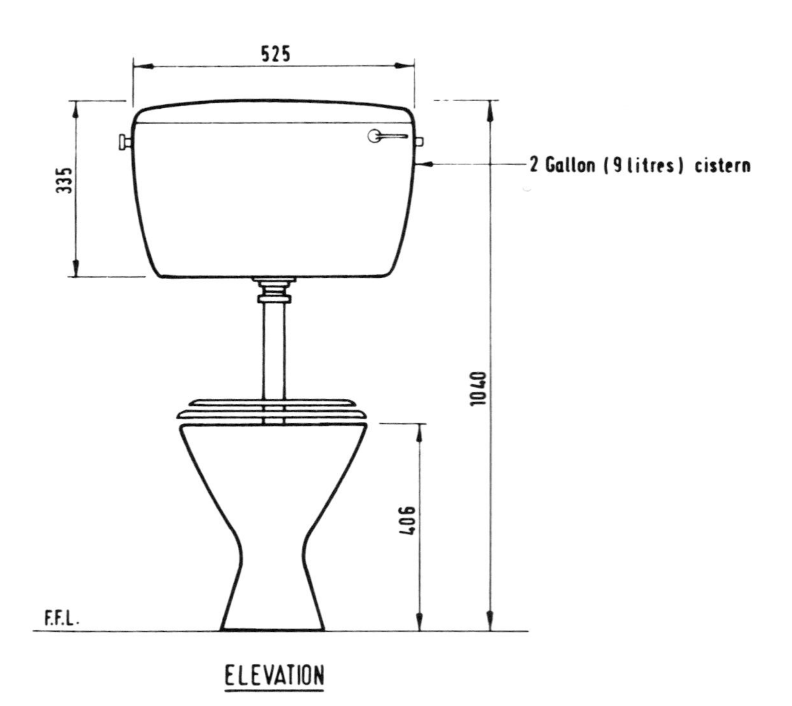

ELEVATION

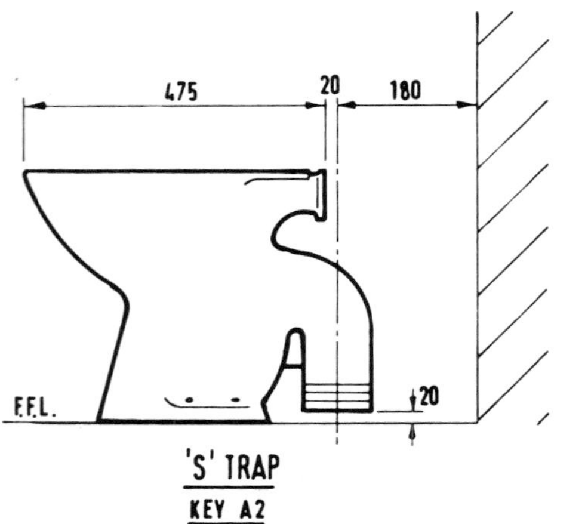

'S' TRAP

KEY A2

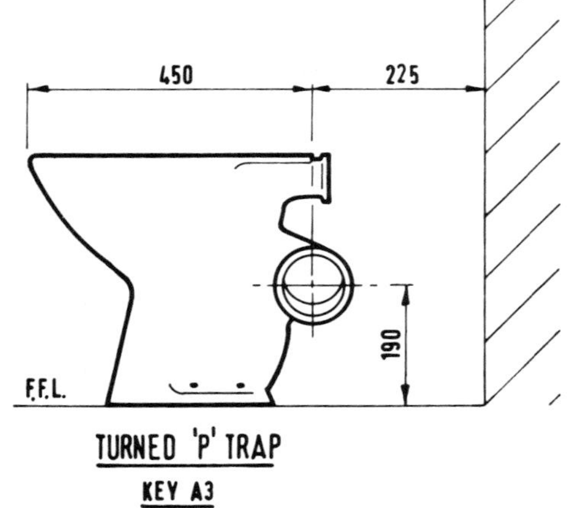

TURNED 'P' TRAP

KEY A3

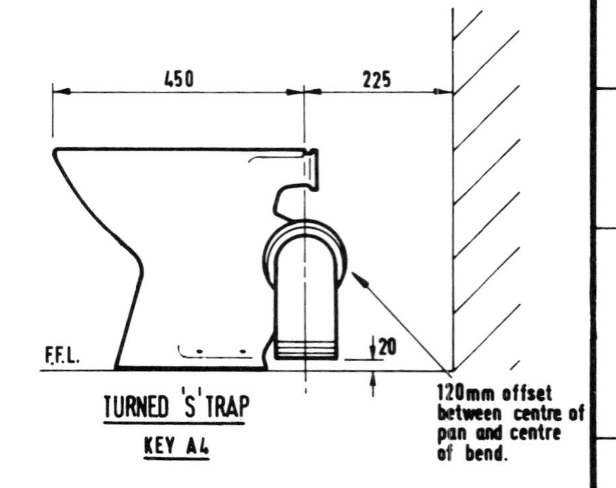

TURNED 'S' TRAP

KEY A4

Departmental Standard Drawing

title

LOW LEVEL W.C. SUITE

scale 1:10

drawing no D5124 B

bldg type 8 | space use | element 74 | feature 501 | material Xg2 | key as drawing

0/0376 - 80

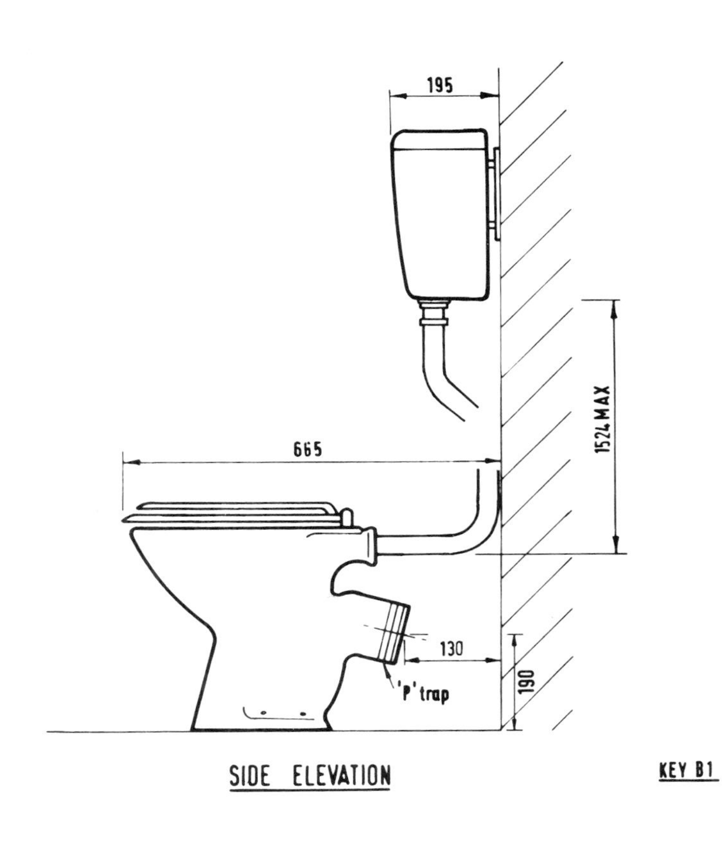

KEY B1

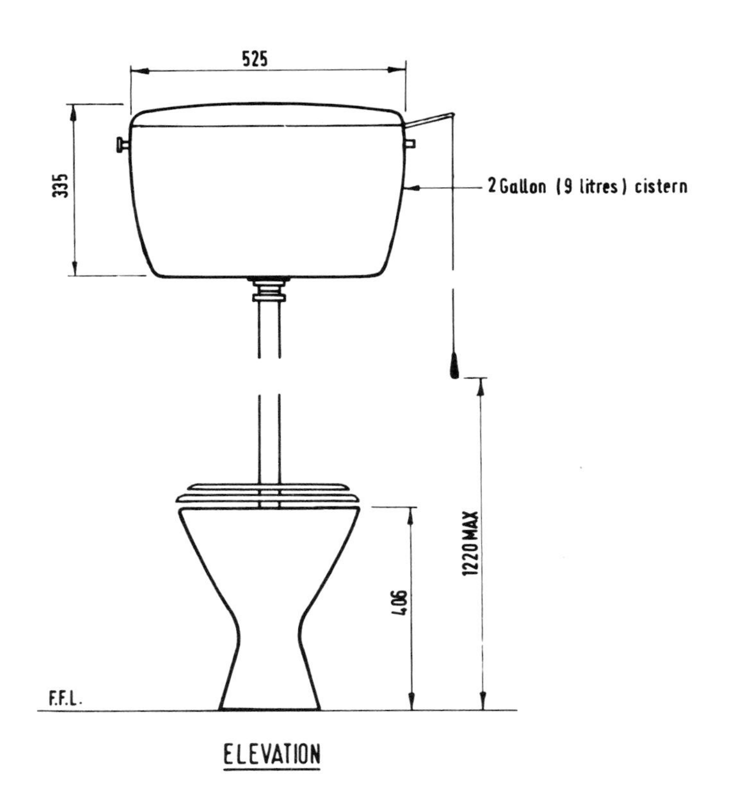

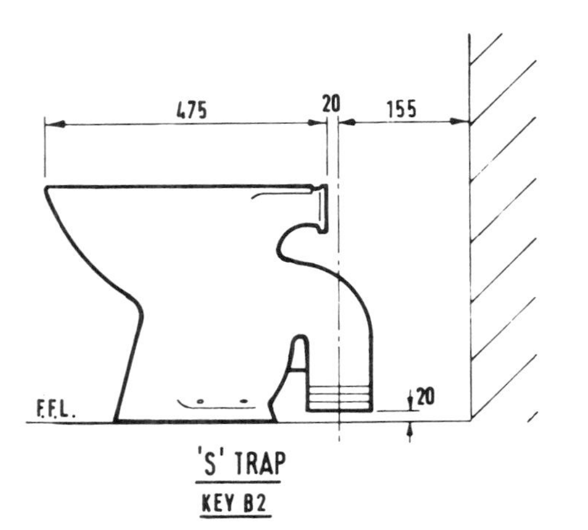

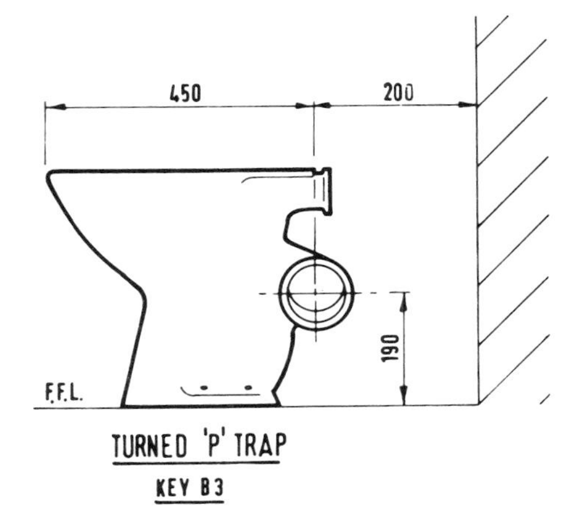

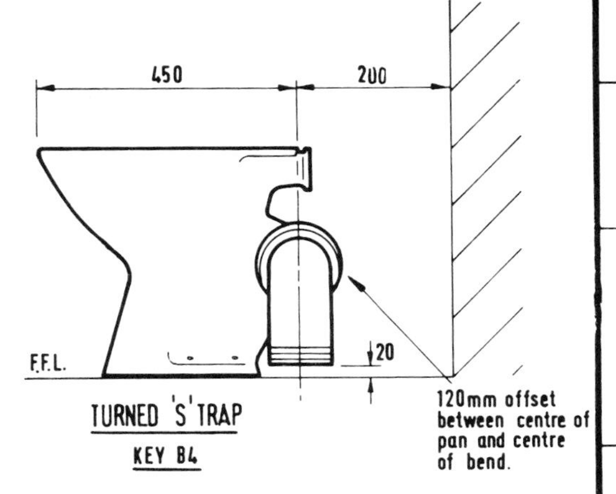

GLC ILEA

Department of Architecture and Civic Design
County Hall SE1
Architect Sir Roger Walters KBE FRIBA FI Struct/E

References following notes are clause numbers from G.L.C. preambles to bills of quantities.

Whole assembly consisting of "LYNX" W.W.P., flush pipe and seat by SHIRES, W.C. pan MAGNIA by ARMITAGE SHANKS supplied by employer.

For alternative side wall fixing suitable flush pipes to be ordered.

N.B. Shires standard flush pipe to be cut by 20mm to achieve distance from the wall as stated.

Departmental Standard Drawing

title

HIGH LEVEL
W.C. SUITE

scale

1:10

drawing no

D5125 B

010379

bldg type 8 | space use | element [74] | feature 501 | material Xg2 | key as drawing

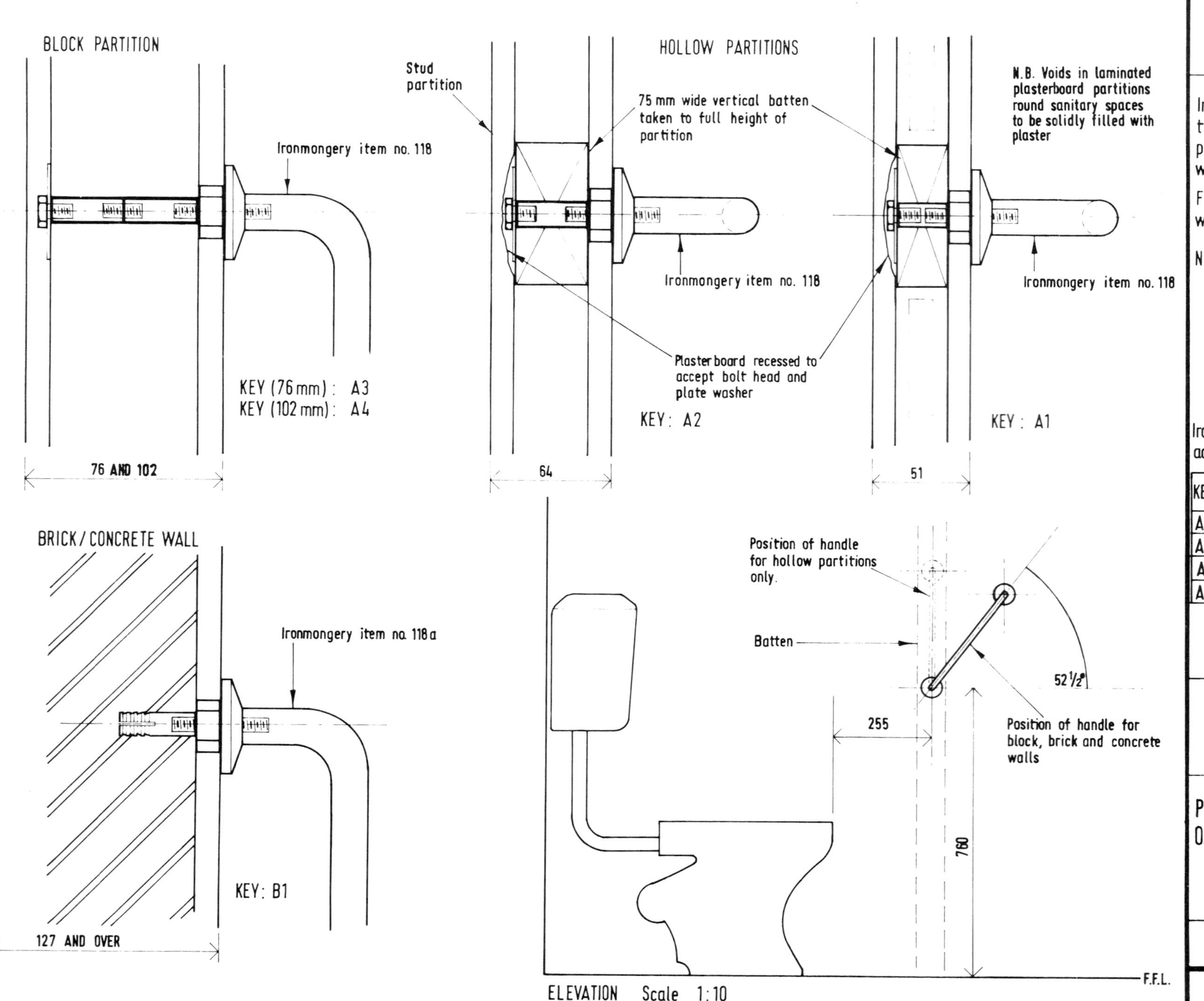

GLC ILEA

Department of Architecture and Civic Design
County Hall SE1
Architect Sir Roger Walters KBE FRIBA FI StructE

Ironmongery item no. 118 : thickness and type of partition must be specified when ordering

Fixing instructions supplied with handle

Note:
Bolts 1st fixing
Handle 2nd fixing

Ironmongery item no. 118 adaptor requirements:

KEY	ADAPTOR BUSHES 24mm	36mm	STUDS
A1	2	–	–
A2	–	2	–
A3	4	–	2
A4	–	4	2

Departmental Standard Drawing

title
PULL HANDLE FOR O.P. SANITARY SPACE

scale
1:2 AND 1:10

drawing no
D5121 B

bldg type 843 | space use | element 74 | feature 501 | material Xh2 | key as drawing

010379 -

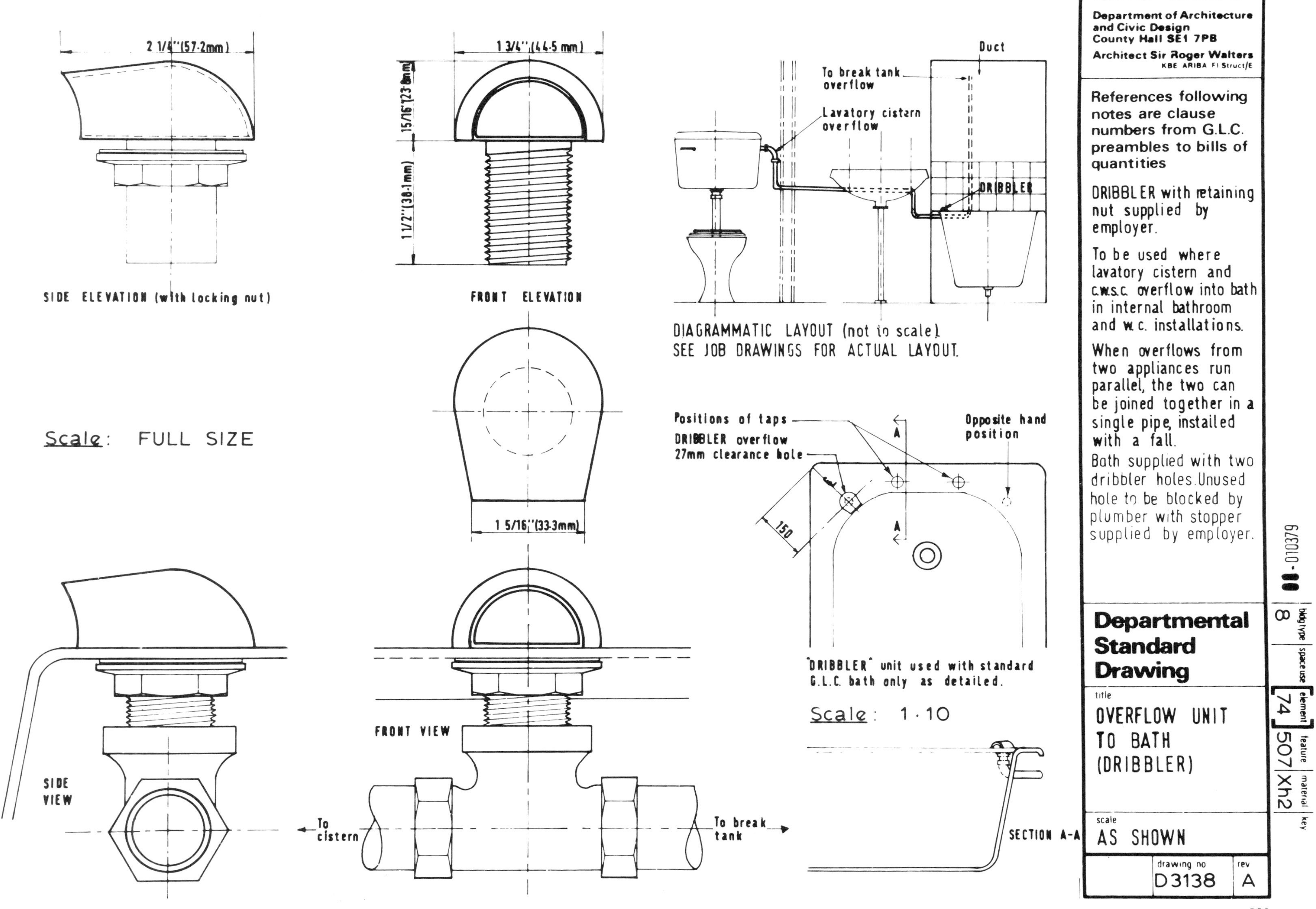
2 1/4"(57·2mm)
SIDE ELEVATION (with locking nut)
1 3/4"(44·5 mm)
15/16"(23·8mm)
1 1/2"(38·1mm)
FRONT ELEVATION
Scale: FULL SIZE
1 5/16"(33·3mm)
SIDE VIEW
FRONT VIEW
To cistern
To break tank
Duct
To break tank overflow
Lavatory cistern overflow
DRIBBLER
DIAGRAMMATIC LAYOUT (not to scale).
SEE JOB DRAWINGS FOR ACTUAL LAYOUT.
Positions of taps
DRIBBLER overflow 27mm clearance hole
Opposite hand position
A
A
150
"DRIBBLER" unit used with standard G.L.C. bath only as detailed.
Scale: 1 · 10
SECTION A-A
GLC ILEA
Department of Architecture and Civic Design
County Hall SE1 7PB
Architect Sir Roger Walters KBE ARIBA FI Struct/E
References following notes are clause numbers from G.L.C. preambles to bills of quantities
DRIBBLER with retaining nut supplied by employer.
To be used where lavatory cistern and c.w.s.c. overflow into bath in internal bathroom and w.c. installations.
When overflows from two appliances run parallel, the two can be joined together in a single pipe, installed with a fall.
Both supplied with two dribbler holes. Unused hole to be blocked by plumber with stopper supplied by employer.
Departmental Standard Drawing
title
OVERFLOW UNIT TO BATH (DRIBBLER)
scale
AS SHOWN
drawing no
D3138
rev
A
8
bldg type
space use
74
element
507
feature
Xh2
material
key
010379

2 Water tanks

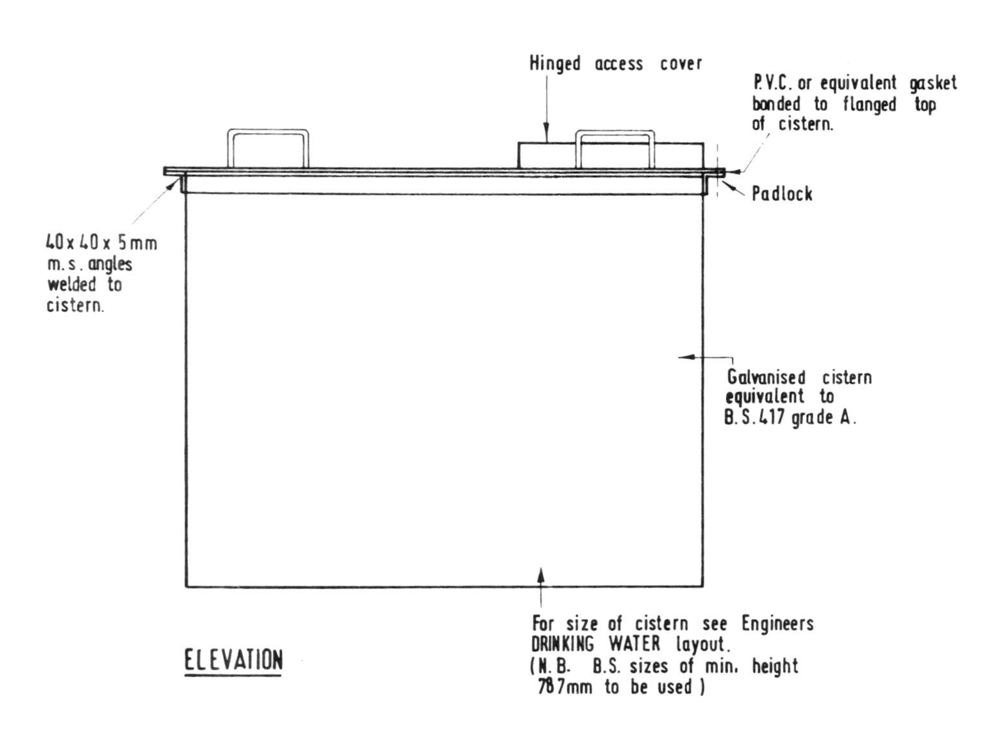

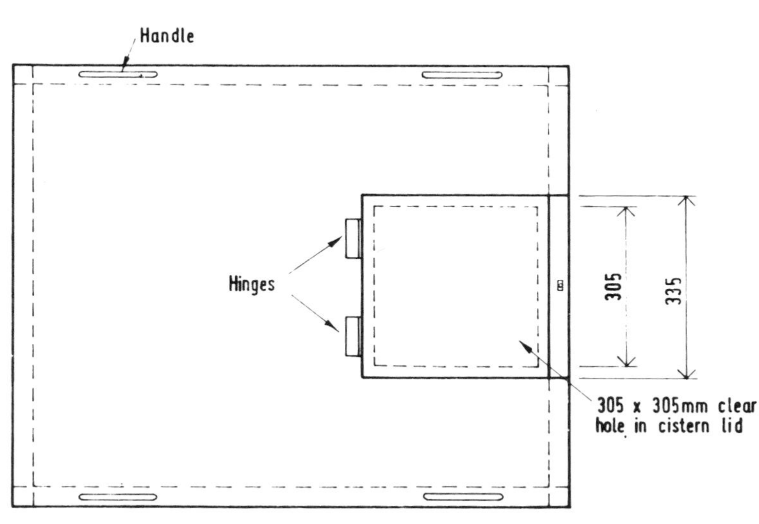

GLC ILEA

Department of Architecture and Civic Design
County Hall SE1
Architect Sir Roger Walters KBE FRIBA FI StructE

References following notes are clause numbers from G.L.C. preambles to bills of quantities.

Cistern to be painted internally with 2 coats of black bituminous paint to B.S. 3416 type 2, and insulated with 25mm thick expanded polystyrene.

The following notice must be signwritten both on the door and the side of the tank in 25mm high capitals.
DRINKING WATER NO UNAUTHORISED ACCESS.

Padlock, direct supply item, ironmongery item number 47.

This drawing is to be read in conjunction with drg. number (53) D4040.

Departmental Standard Drawing

title
DRINKING WATER STORAGE CISTERNS

scale 1:10.

drawing no D3164.

[53] 531 Xh2

000379

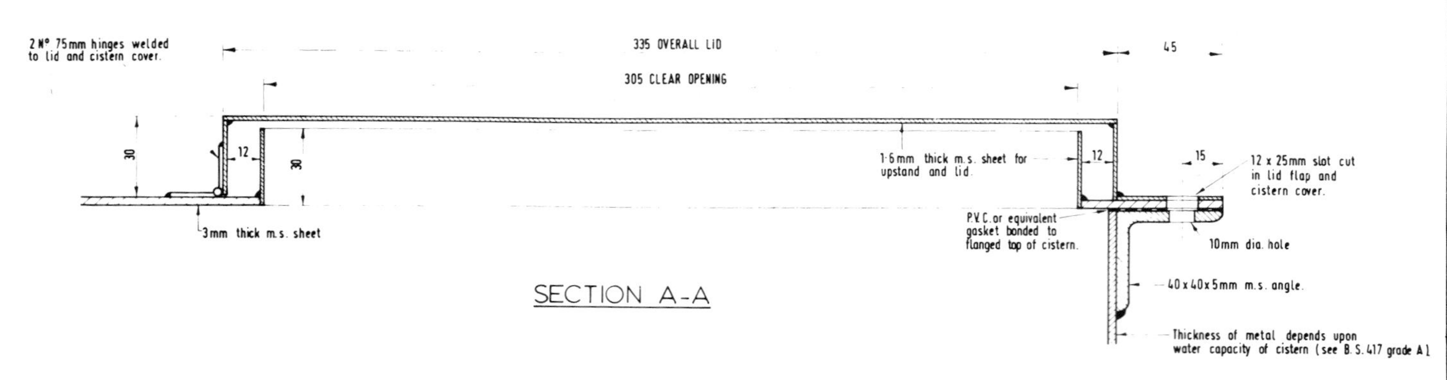

SECTION A-A

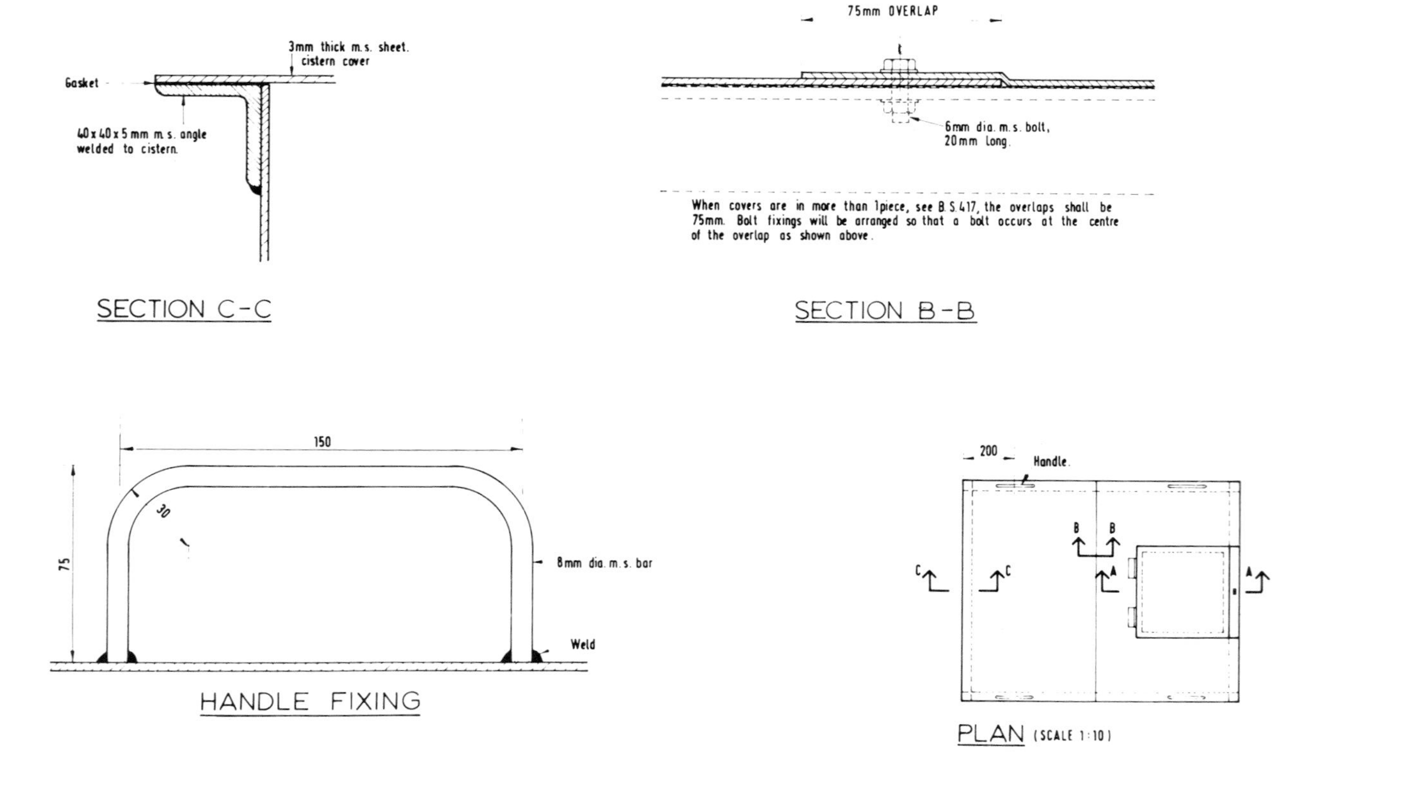

SECTION C-C

SECTION B-B

HANDLE FIXING

PLAN (SCALE 1:10)

3 Storage cupboards

- 5343 Linen cupboard with HW cylinder
- 5345 Cupboard—CW cistern and HW cylinder, 900mm door
- 5346 Cupboard—CW cistern and HW cylinder, 800mm door
- 5348 Linen cupboard 900mm door
- 5349 Linen cupboard 1500mm double doors
- 3165 Broom rack
- 3166 Hoops rack
- 3167 Sports equipment shelves
- 3168 Box files shelf
- 3169 Double shelving unit
- 3170 High shelving unit

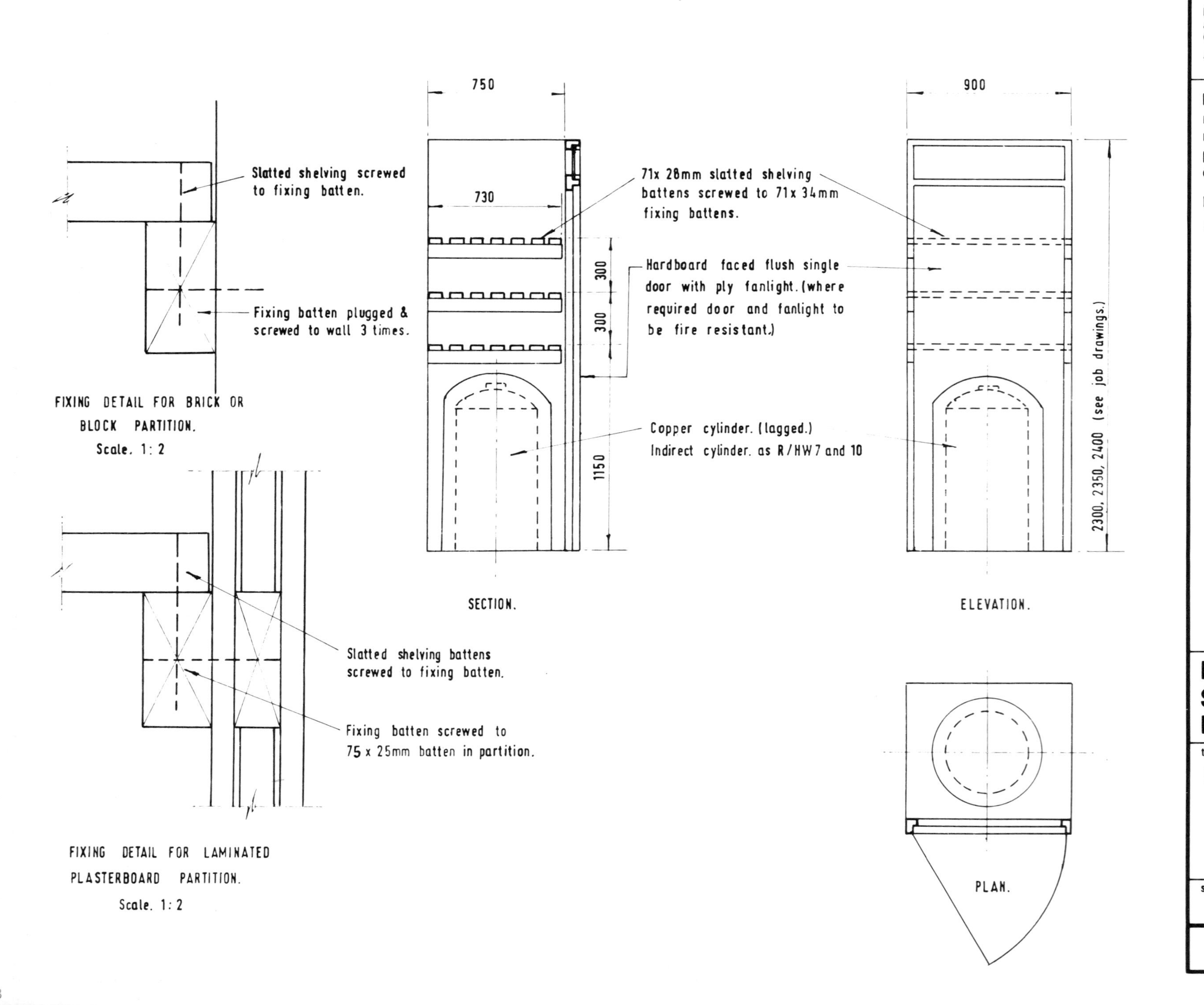

GLC ILEA

Department of Architecture and Civic Design
County Hall SE1 7PB

Architect Sir Roger Walters
KBE ARIBA FI Struct/E

References following notes are clause numbers from G.L.C. preambles to bills of quantities

Linen storage capacity of 0·4 m³ for dwelling up to 5 persons.

Departmental Standard Drawing

title
LINEN CUPBOARD with H.W. CYLINDER.

scale
1:2 & 1:20

drawing no
D.5343.

rev

bldg type 8– | space use | element 76 | feature 852 | material Hi | key B.2.

00 - 010379

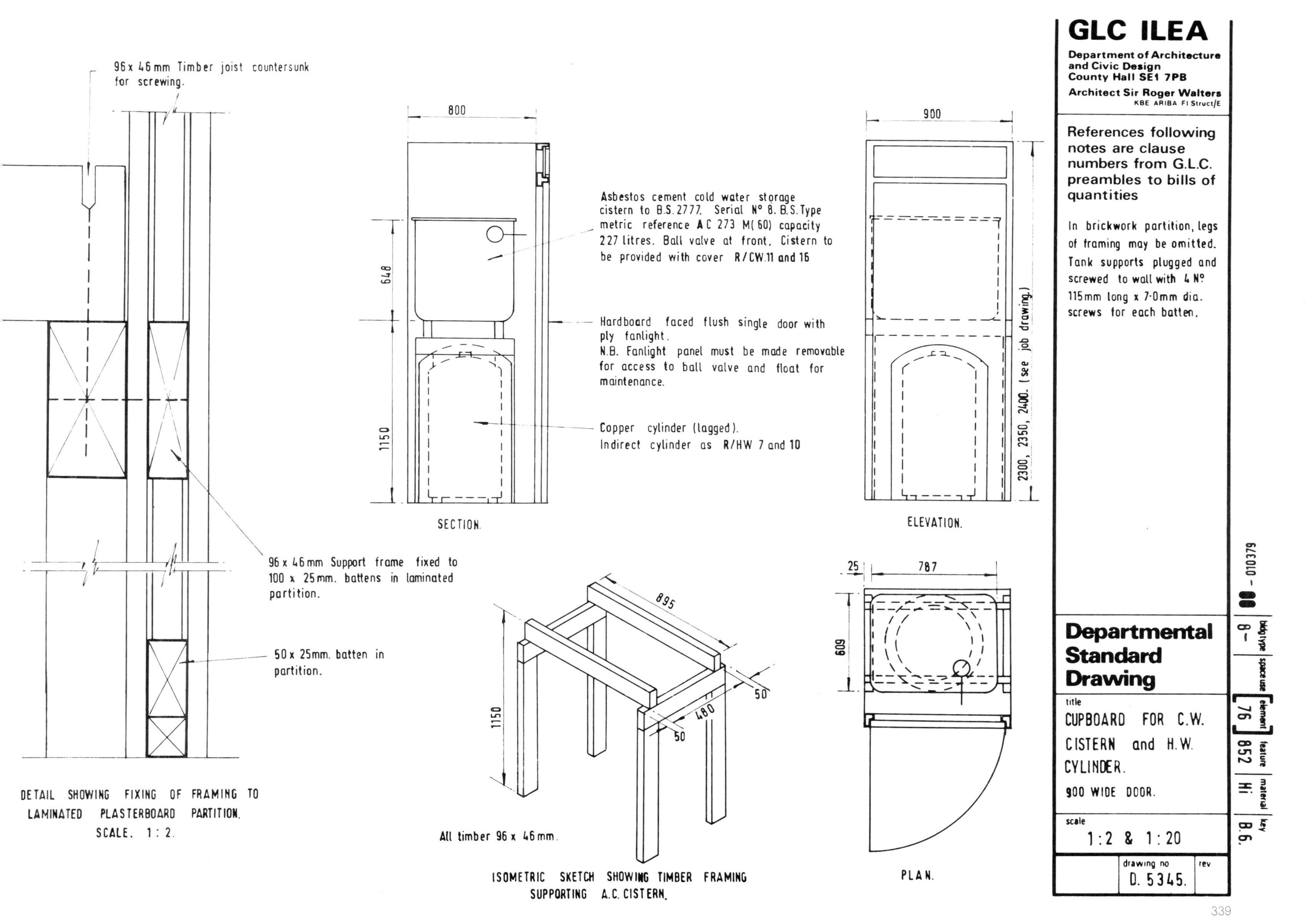

GLC ILEA
Department of Architecture and Civic Design
County Hall SE1 7PB
Architect Sir Roger Walters KBE ARIBA FI Struct/E
References following notes are clause numbers from G.L.C. preambles to bills of quantities
In brickwork partition, legs of framing may be omitted. Tank supports plugged and screwed to wall with 4 N° 115mm long x 7·0mm dia. screws for each batten.
96 x 46 mm Timber joist countersunk for screwing.
800
648
1150
Asbestos cement cold water storage cistern to B.S. 2777. Serial N° 8. B.S. Type metric reference AC 273 M(60) capacity 227 litres. Ball valve at front. Cistern to be provided with cover R/CW.11 and 16
Hardboard faced flush single door with ply fanlight.
N.B. Fanlight panel must be made removable for access to ball valve and float for maintenance.
Copper cylinder (lagged).
Indirect cylinder as R/HW 7 and 10
SECTION.
900
2300, 2350, 2400. (see job drawing)
ELEVATION.
96 x 46 mm Support frame fixed to 100 x 25 mm. battens in laminated partition.
50 x 25mm. batten in partition.
DETAIL SHOWING FIXING OF FRAMING TO LAMINATED PLASTERBOARD PARTITION. SCALE. 1 : 2.
895
1150
50
480
50
All timber 96 x 46 mm.
ISOMETRIC SKETCH SHOWING TIMBER FRAMING SUPPORTING A.C. CISTERN.
25
787
609
PLAN.
Departmental Standard Drawing
title
CUPBOARD FOR C.W. CISTERN and H.W. CYLINDER.
900 WIDE DOOR.
scale
1:2 & 1:20
drawing no
D. 5345.
rev
8-
bldg type
space use
76
element
852
feature
Hi
material
B.6.
key
010379

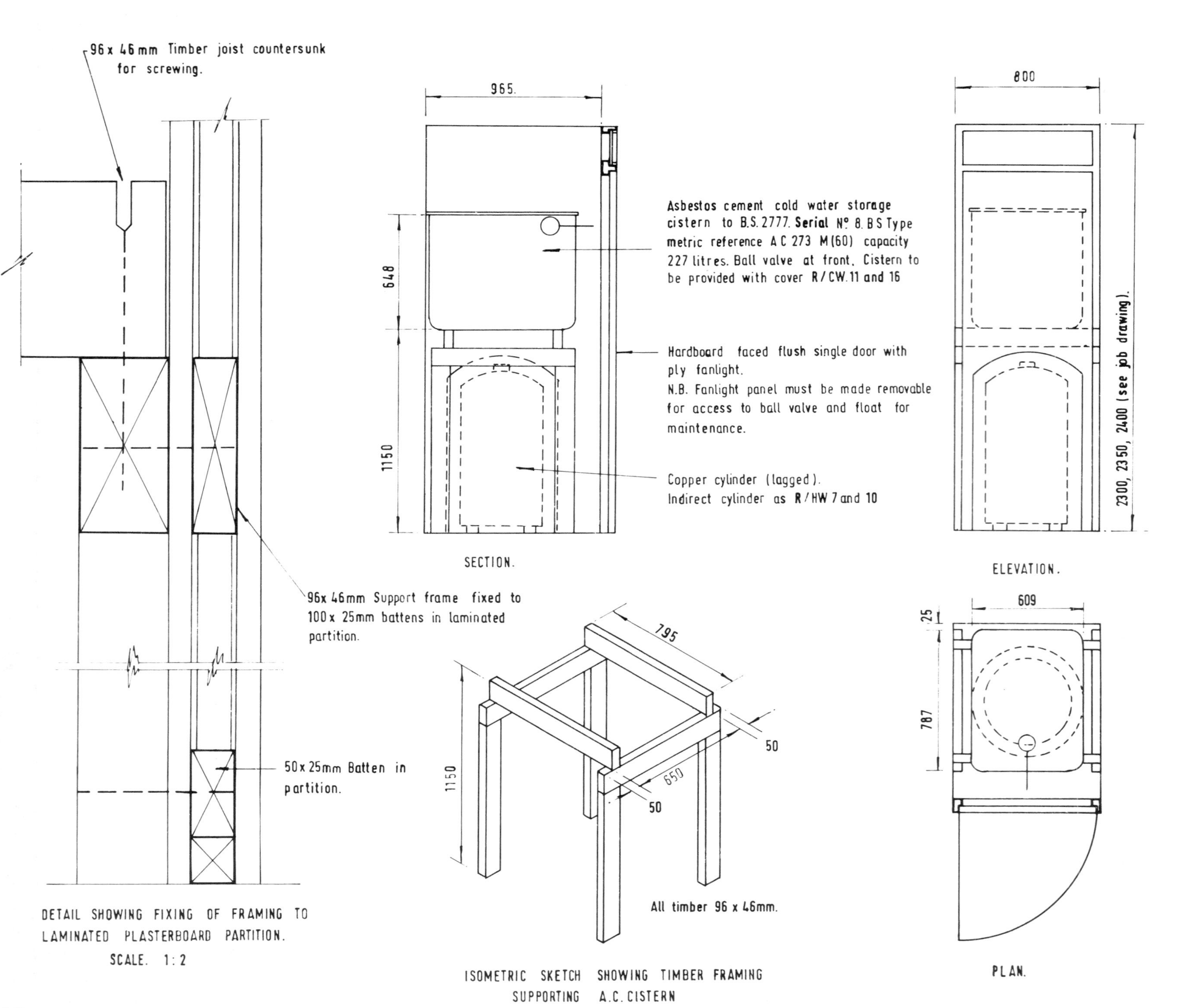

GLC ILEA

Department of Architecture and Civic Design
County Hall SE1 7PB
Architect Sir Roger Walters
KBE ARIBA FI Struct/E

References following notes are clause numbers from G.L.C. preambles to bills of quantities

In brickwork partition, legs of framing may be omitted.
Tank supports plugged and screwed to wall with 4 Nº 115mm long x 7·0mm dia. screws for each batten.

Departmental Standard Drawing

title
CUPBOARD FOR C.W. CISTERN and H.W. CYLINDER.
800mm WIDE DOOR.

scale
1:2 & 1:20.

drawing no
D. 5346.

rev

8 — | 76 | 852 | Hi | B.7. | 00 - 010379

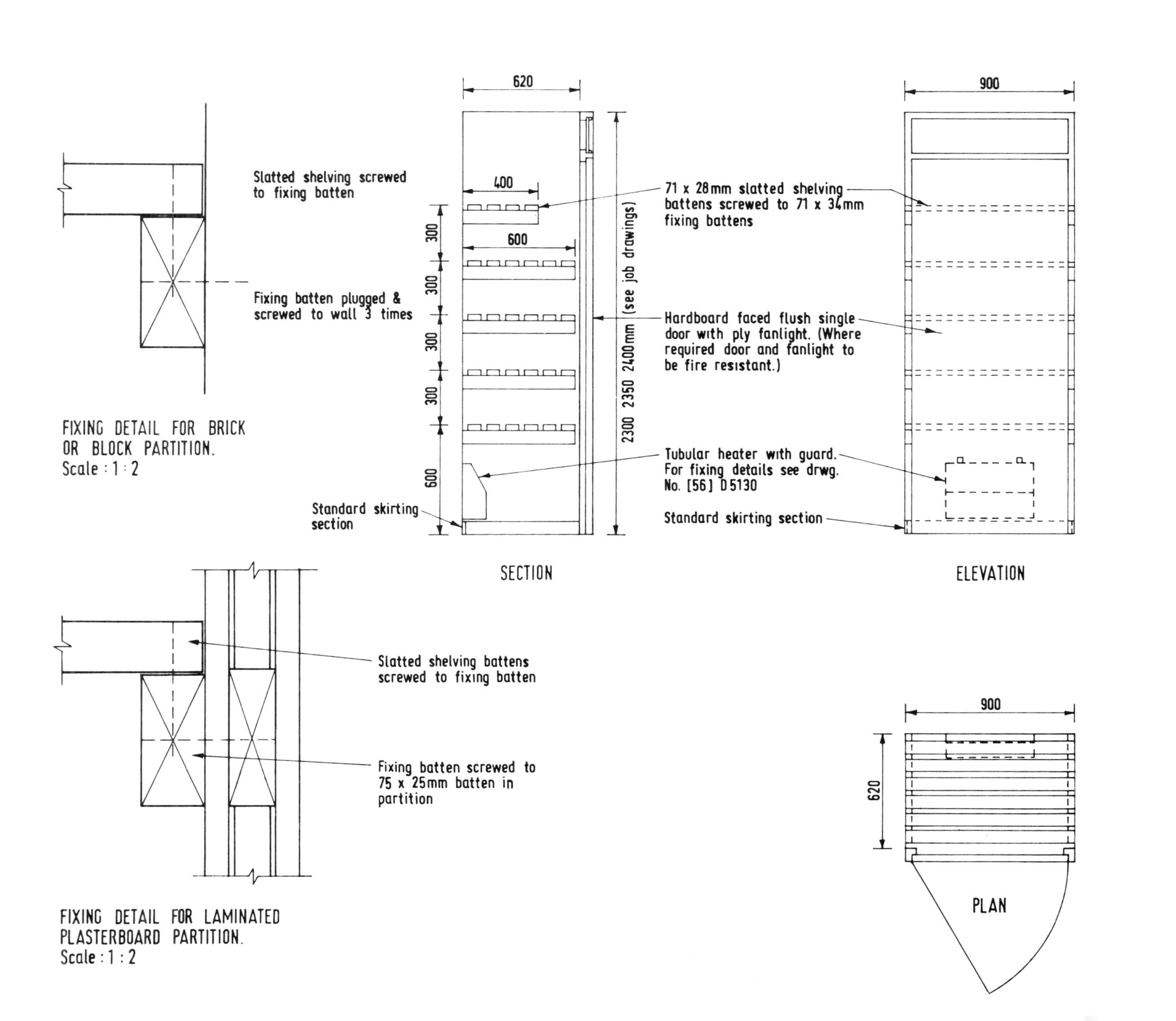
620
400
600
300
300
300
300
600
Slatted shelving screwed
to fixing batten
Fixing batten plugged &
screwed to wall 3 times
FIXING DETAIL FOR BRICK
OR BLOCK PARTITION.
Scale : 1 : 2
Standard skirting
section
2300 2350 2400mm (see job drawings)
71 x 28mm slatted shelving
battens screwed to 71 x 34mm
fixing battens
Hardboard faced flush single
door with ply fanlight. (Where
required door and fanlight to
be fire resistant.)
Tubular heater with guard.
For fixing details see drwg.
No. [56] D5130
Standard skirting section
900
SECTION
ELEVATION
Slatted shelving battens
screwed to fixing batten
Fixing batten screwed to
75 x 25mm batten in
partition
FIXING DETAIL FOR LAMINATED
PLASTERBOARD PARTITION.
Scale : 1 : 2
900
620
PLAN

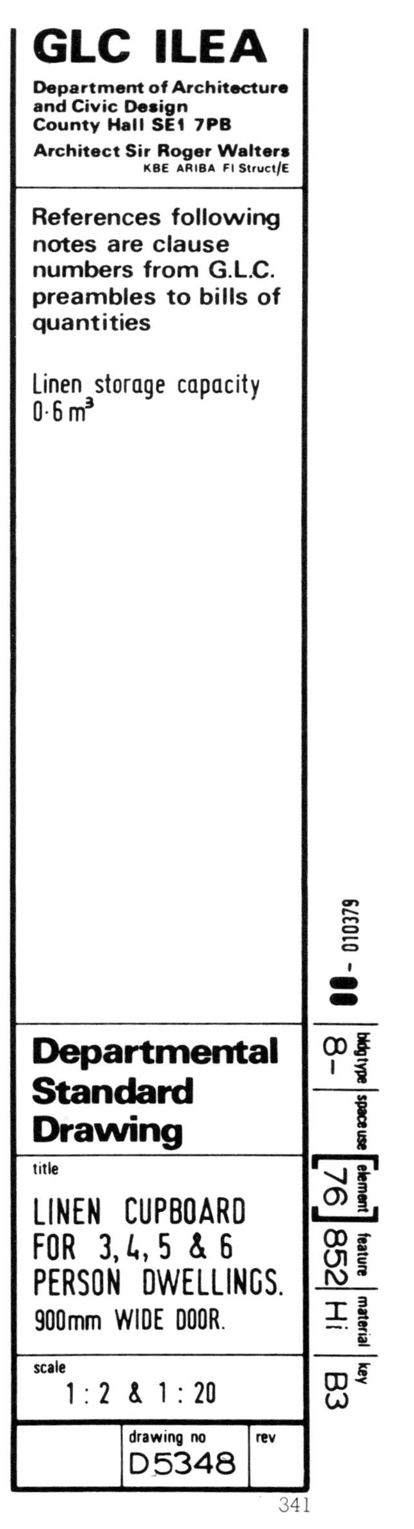
GLC ILEA
Department of Architecture
and Civic Design
County Hall SE1 7PB
Architect Sir Roger Walters
KBE ARIBA FI Struct/E
References following
notes are clause
numbers from G.L.C.
preambles to bills of
quantities
Linen storage capacity
0·6 m³
Departmental
Standard
Drawing
title
LINEN CUPBOARD
FOR 3, 4, 5 & 6
PERSON DWELLINGS.
900mm WIDE DOOR.
scale
1 : 2 & 1 : 20
drawing no
D5348
rev
8-
[76]
852
Hi
B3
010379

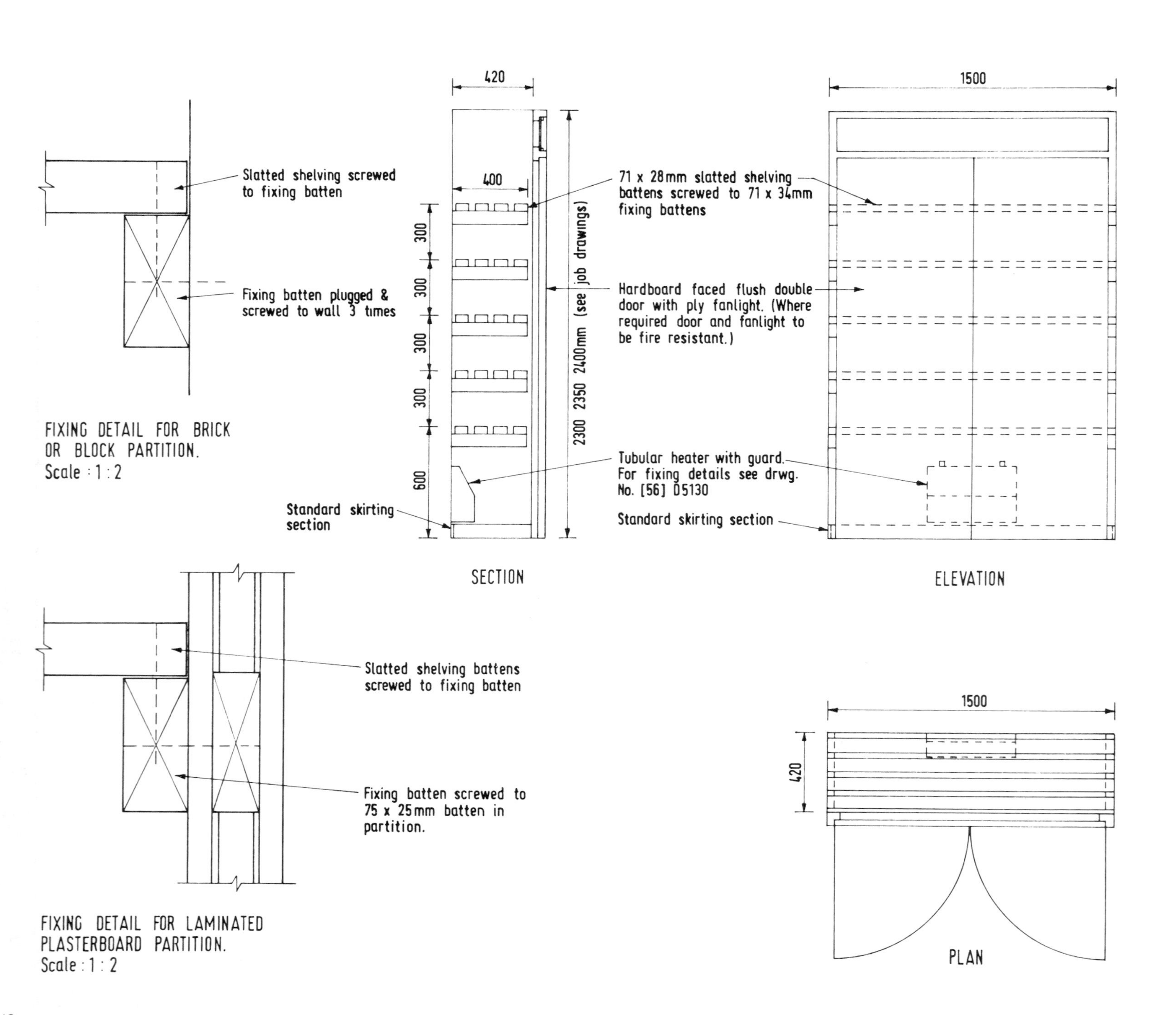

GLC ILEA

Department of Architecture and Civic Design
County Hall SE1 7PB
Architect Sir Roger Walters
KBE ARIBA FI Struct/E

References following notes are clause numbers from G.L.C. preambles to bills of quantities

Linen storage capacity 0·6 m³

Departmental Standard Drawing

title

LINEN CUPBOARD FOR 3, 4, 5 & 6 PERSON DWELLINGS.

1500mm WIDE DOUBLE DOOR.

scale

1 : 2 & 1 : 20

drawing no D5349 rev

010379

bldg type	space use	element	feature	material	key
8-		76	852	Hi	B4

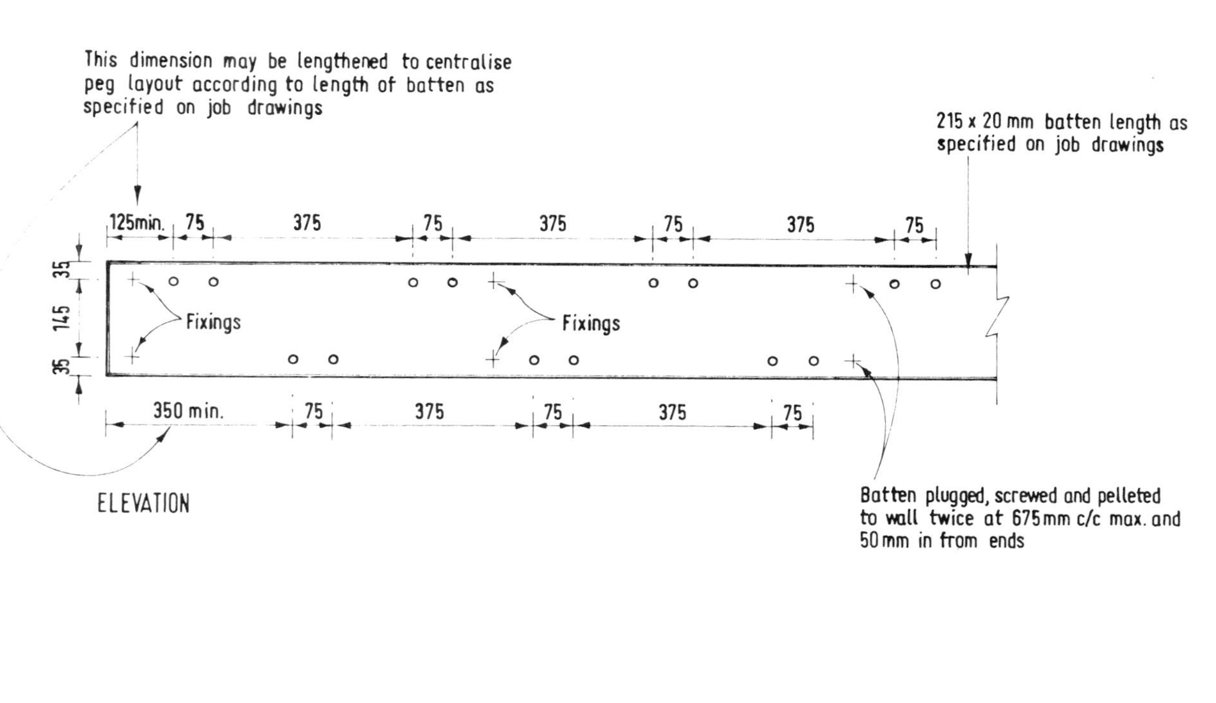
This dimension may be lengthened to centralise peg layout according to length of batten as specified on job drawings
215 x 20 mm batten length as specified on job drawings
125min.
75
375
35
145
Fixings
350 min.
ELEVATION
Batten plugged, screwed and pelleted to wall twice at 675mm c/c max. and 50mm in from ends

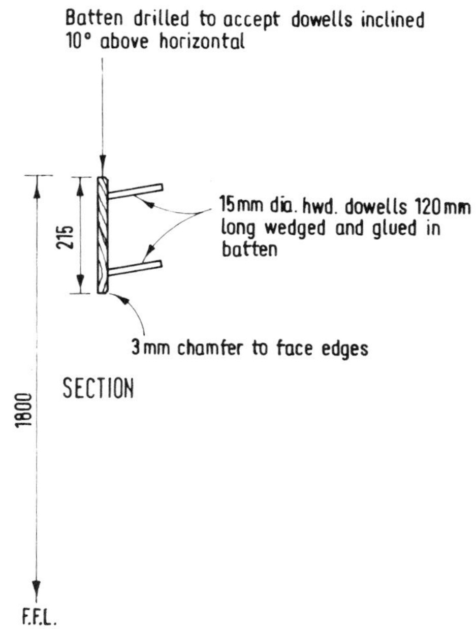
Batten drilled to accept dowells inclined 10° above horizontal
215
15mm dia. hwd. dowells 120mm long wedged and glued in batten
3mm chamfer to face edges
SECTION
1800
F.F.L.

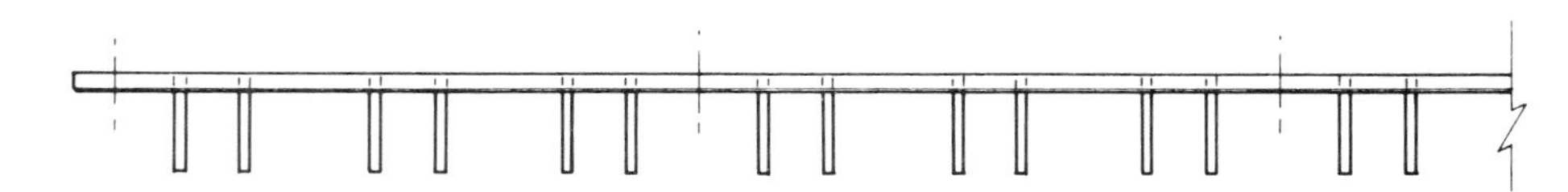

PLAN

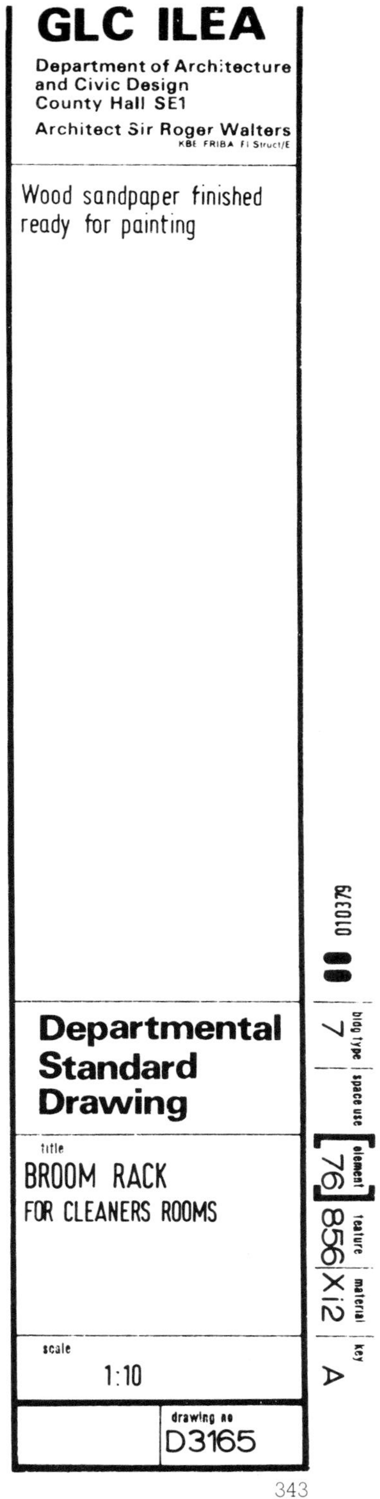
GLC ILEA
Department of Architecture and Civic Design
County Hall SE1
Architect Sir Roger Walters
KBE FRIBA FI StructE
Wood sandpaper finished ready for painting
010379
Departmental Standard Drawing
title
BROOM RACK
FOR CLEANERS ROOMS
bldg type 7
space use
element 76
feature 856
material Xi2
key A
scale
1:10
drawing no
D3165

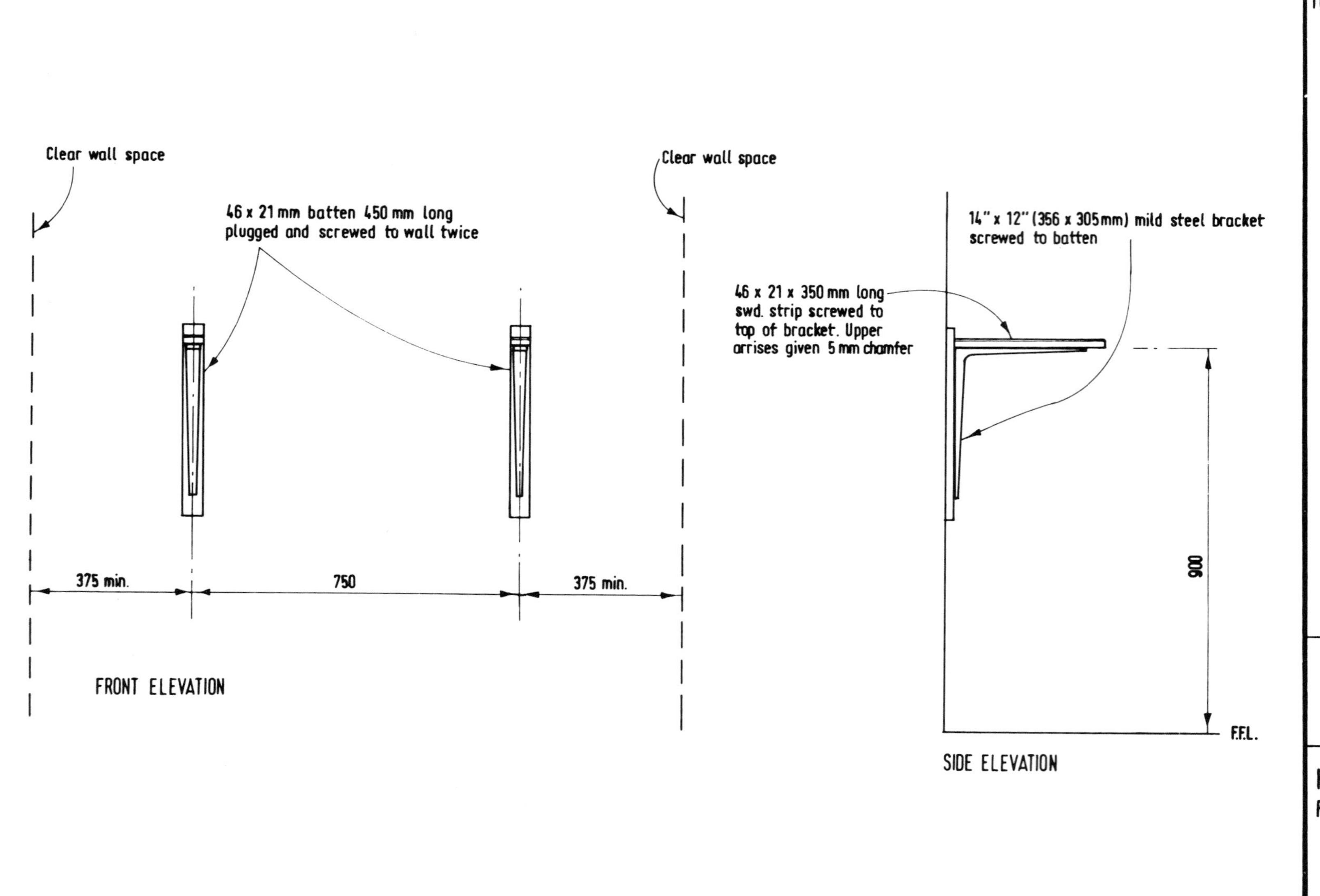
Clear wall space
Clear wall space
46 x 21 mm batten 450 mm long
plugged and screwed to wall twice
375 min.
750
375 min.
FRONT ELEVATION
14" x 12" (356 x 305mm) mild steel bracket
screwed to batten
46 x 21 x 350 mm long
swd. strip screwed to
top of bracket. Upper
arrises given 5 mm chamfer
900
F.F.L.
SIDE ELEVATION

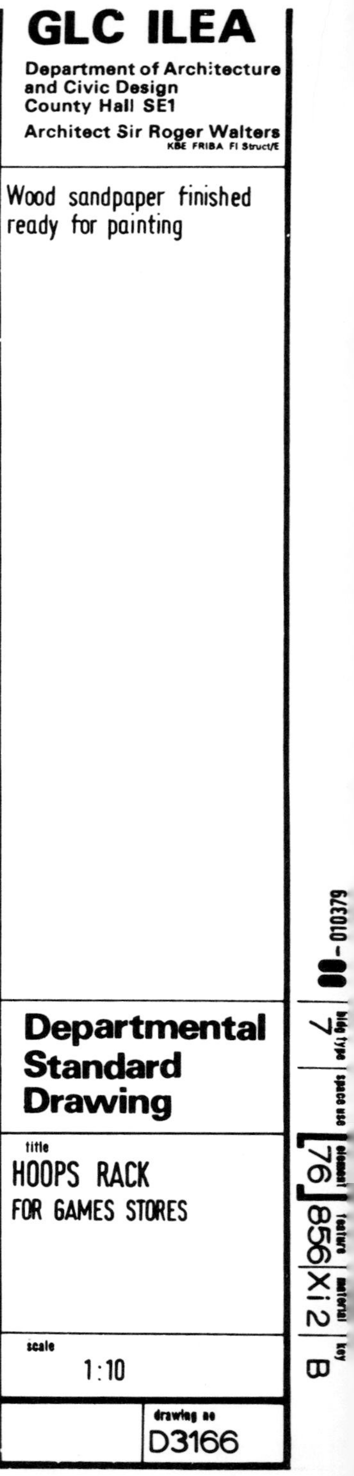
GLC ILEA
Department of Architecture
and Civic Design
County Hall SE1
Architect Sir Roger Walters
KBE FRIBA FI StructE
Wood sandpaper finished
ready for painting
Departmental
Standard
Drawing
title
HOOPS RACK
FOR GAMES STORES
scale
1:10
drawing no
D3166
bldg type
7
space use
element
76
feature
856
material
Xi2
key
B
00-010379

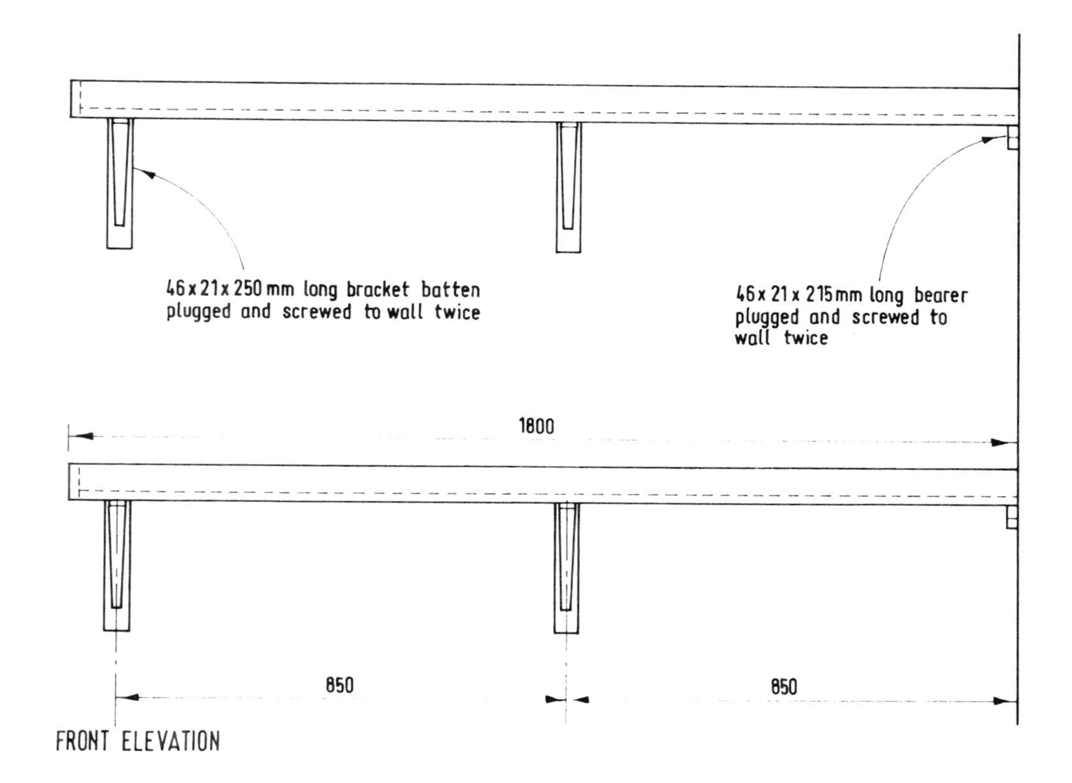
46 x 21 x 250 mm long bracket batten plugged and screwed to wall twice
46 x 21 x 215 mm long bearer plugged and screwed to wall twice
1800
850
850
FRONT ELEVATION

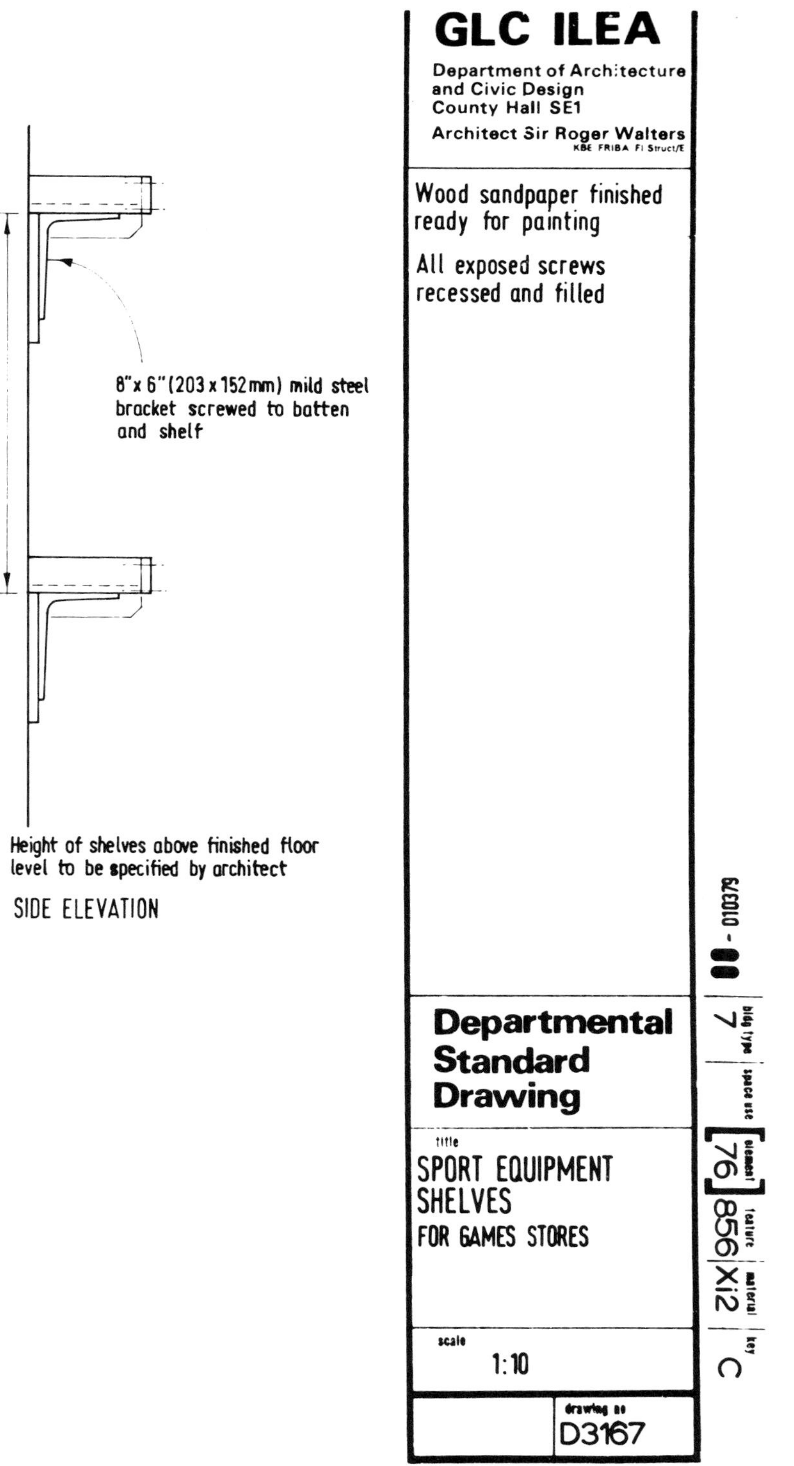
740
8" x 6" (203 x 152 mm) mild steel bracket screwed to batten and shelf
Height of shelves above finished floor level to be specified by architect
SIDE ELEVATION
GLC ILEA
Department of Architecture and Civic Design
County Hall SE1
Architect Sir Roger Walters
KBE FRIBA FI StructE
Wood sandpaper finished ready for painting
All exposed screws recessed and filled
Departmental Standard Drawing
title
SPORT EQUIPMENT SHELVES
FOR GAMES STORES
scale
1:10
drawing no
D3167
bldg type
7
space use
element
76
feature
856
material
Xi2
key
C

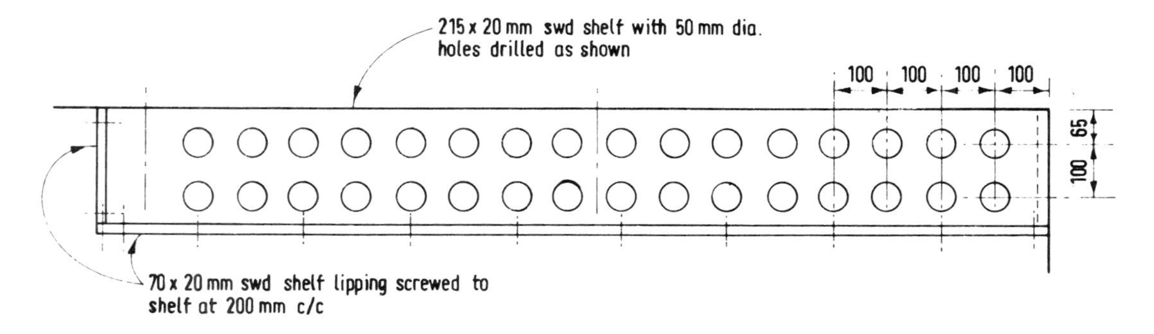
215 x 20 mm swd shelf with 50 mm dia. holes drilled as shown
100
100
100
100
65
100
70 x 20 mm swd shelf lipping screwed to shelf at 200 mm c/c
PLAN

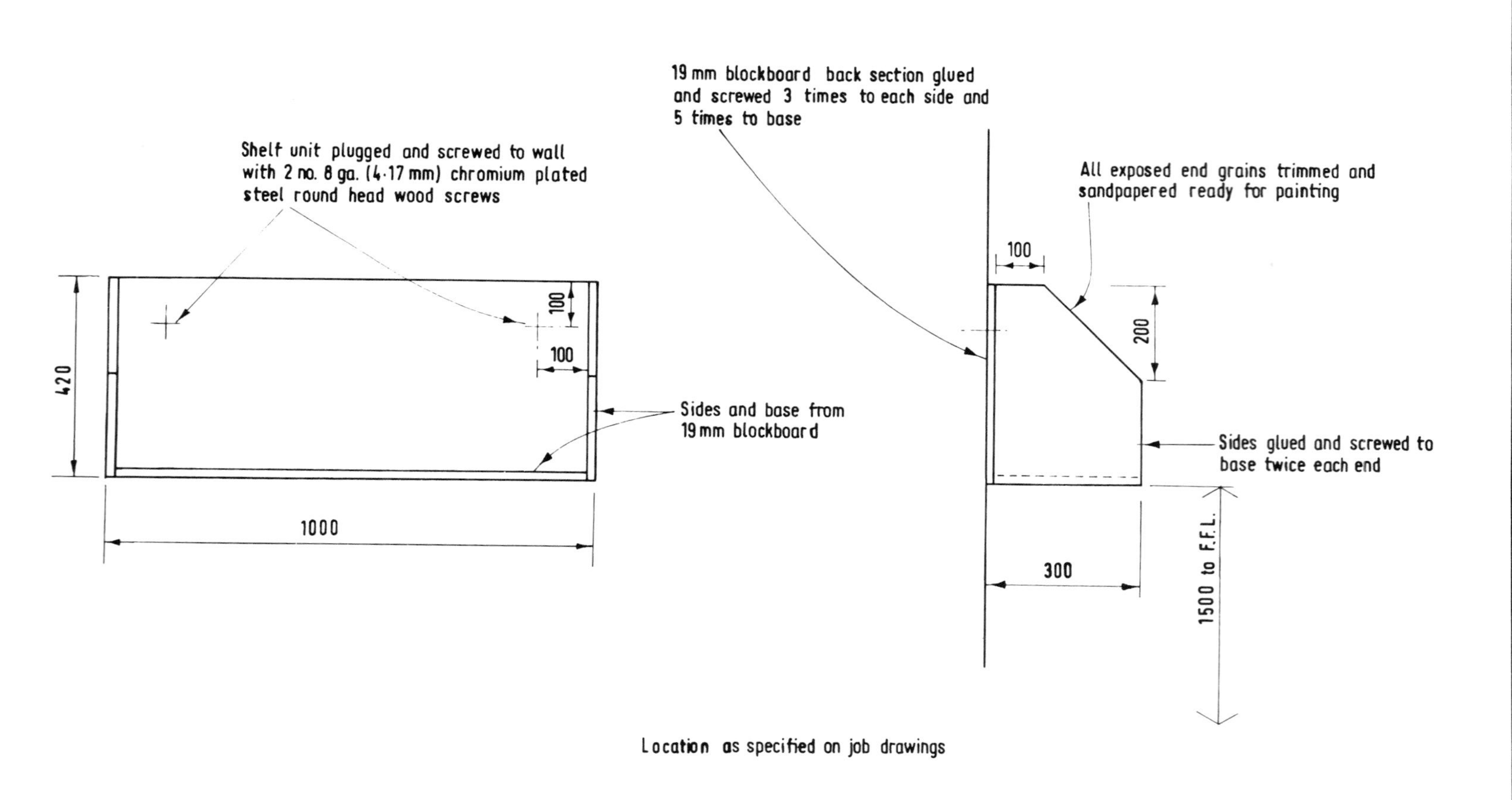
Shelf unit plugged and screwed to wall
with 2 no. 8 ga. (4·17 mm) chromium plated
steel round head wood screws
19 mm blockboard back section glued
and screwed 3 times to each side and
5 times to base
All exposed end grains trimmed and
sandpapered ready for painting
420
100
100
Sides and base from
19 mm blockboard
1000
100
200
Sides glued and screwed to
base twice each end
300
1500 to F.F.L.
Location as specified on job drawings

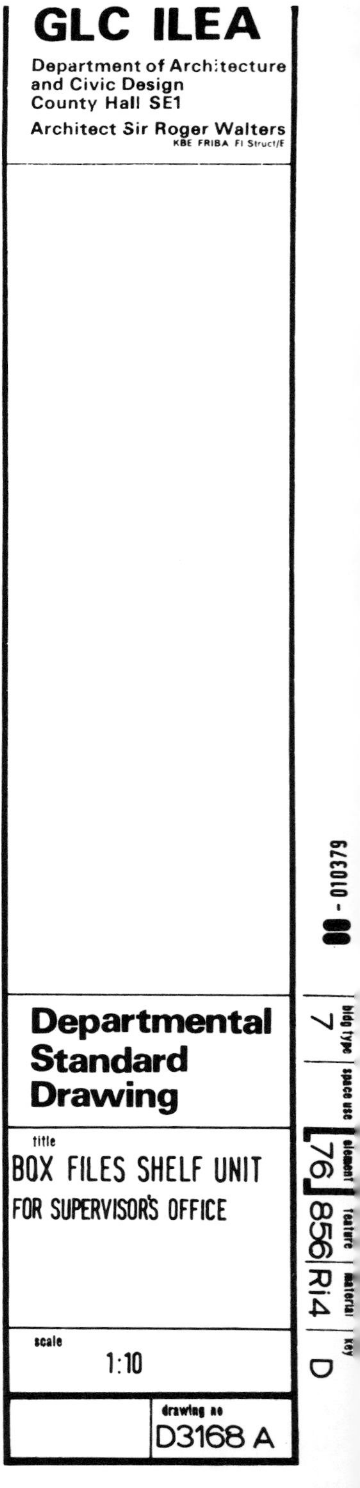
GLC ILEA
Department of Architecture
and Civic Design
County Hall SE1
Architect Sir Roger Walters
KBE FRIBA FI StructE
Departmental
Standard
Drawing
title
BOX FILES SHELF UNIT
FOR SUPERVISOR'S OFFICE
scale
1:10
drawing no
D3168 A
bldg type 7
element 76
feature 856
material Ri4
key D
010379

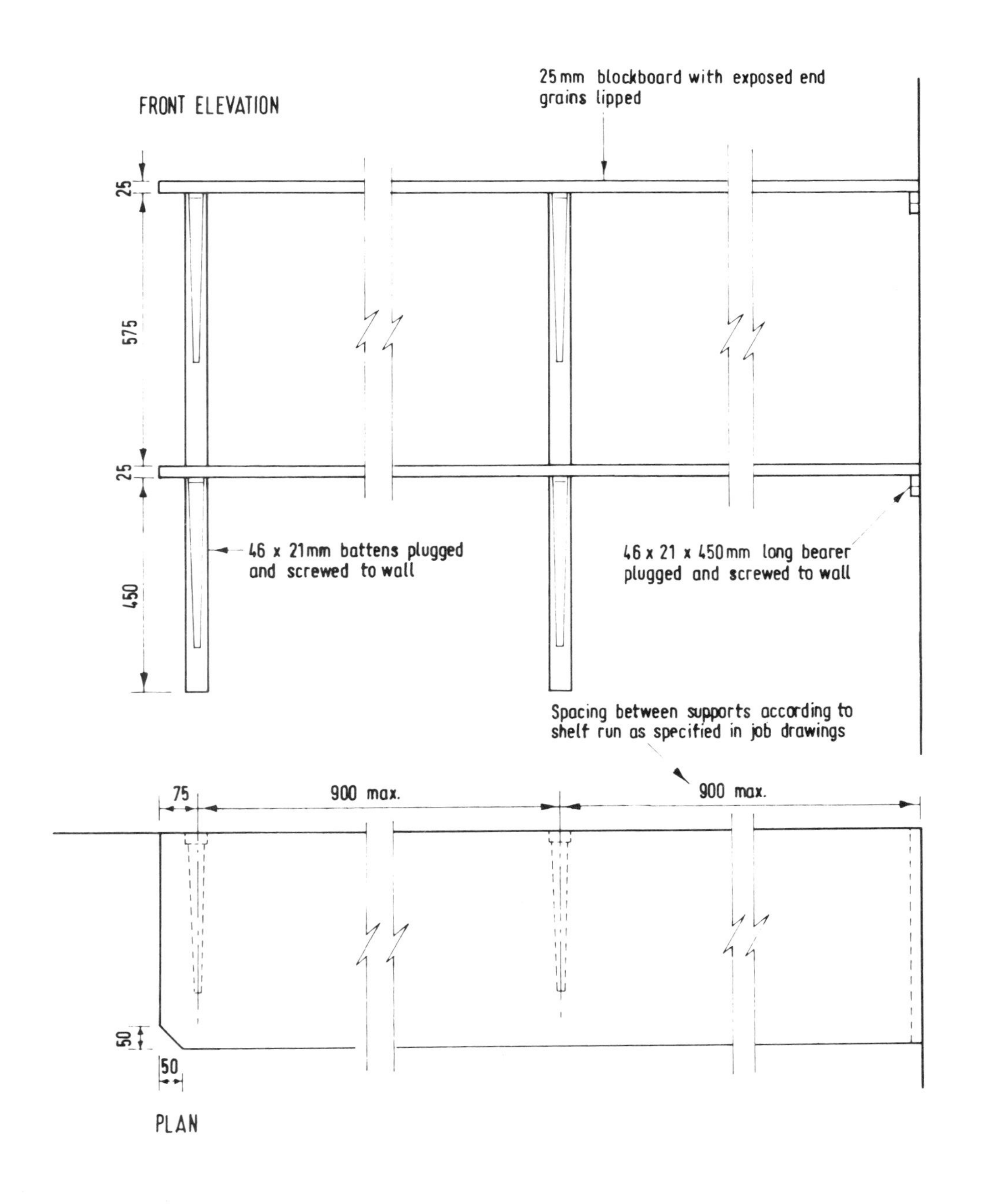

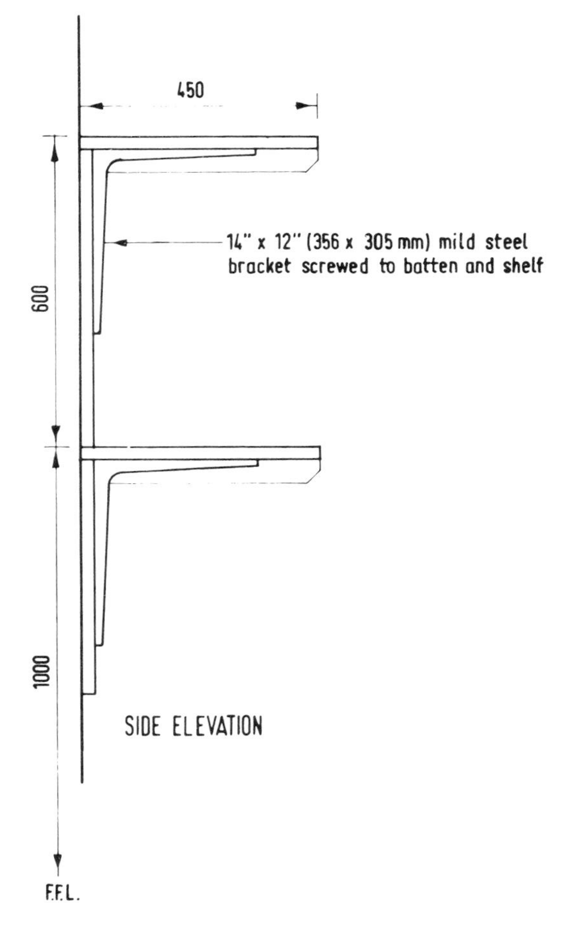

GLC ILEA

Department of Architecture and Civic Design
County Hall SE1
Architect Sir Roger Walters KBE FRIBA FI StructE

Wood sandpaper finished ready for painting

Departmental Standard Drawing

title

DOUBLE SHELF UNIT
FOR PLAY CENTRE STORE
AND GAME STORE

scale 1:10

drawing no D3169

bldg type 7 | space use | element (76) | feature 856 | material Ri4 | key E

00 - 010379

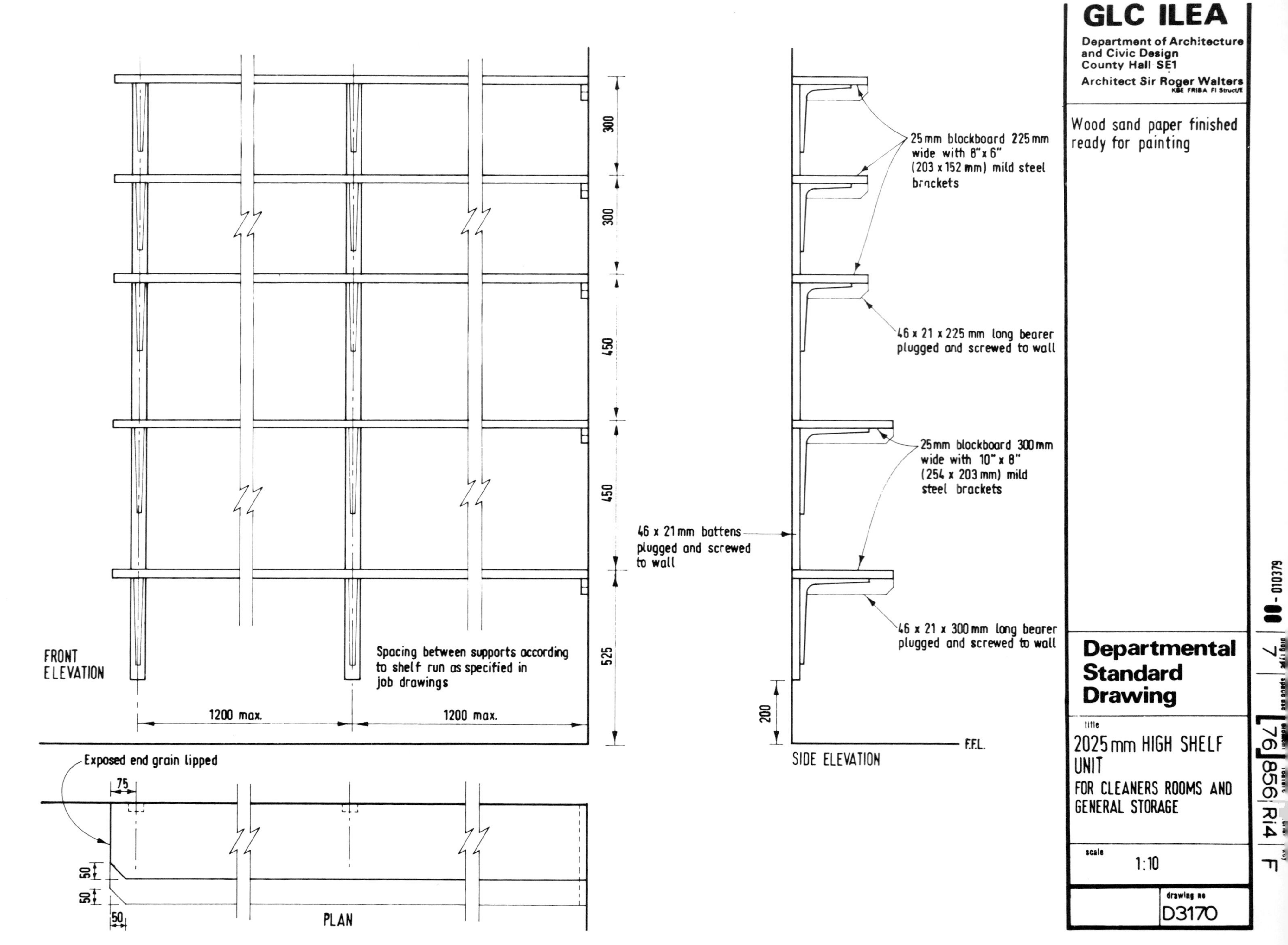
GLC ILEA
Department of Architecture and Civic Design
County Hall SE1
Architect Sir Roger Walters
KBE FRIBA FI StructE
Wood sand paper finished ready for painting
25 mm blockboard 225 mm wide with 8" x 6" (203 x 152 mm) mild steel brackets
46 x 21 x 225 mm long bearer plugged and screwed to wall
25 mm blockboard 300 mm wide with 10" x 8" (254 x 203 mm) mild steel brackets
46 x 21 x 300 mm long bearer plugged and screwed to wall
46 x 21 mm battens plugged and screwed to wall
300
300
450
450
525
200
F.F.L.
SIDE ELEVATION
FRONT ELEVATION
Spacing between supports according to shelf run as specified in job drawings
1200 max.
1200 max.
Exposed end grain lipped
75
50
50
50
PLAN
Departmental Standard Drawing
title
2025 mm HIGH SHELF UNIT
FOR CLEANERS ROOMS AND GENERAL STORAGE
scale
1:10
drawing no
D3170
7
76
856
Ri4
F
00 - 010379

4 Electric heaters

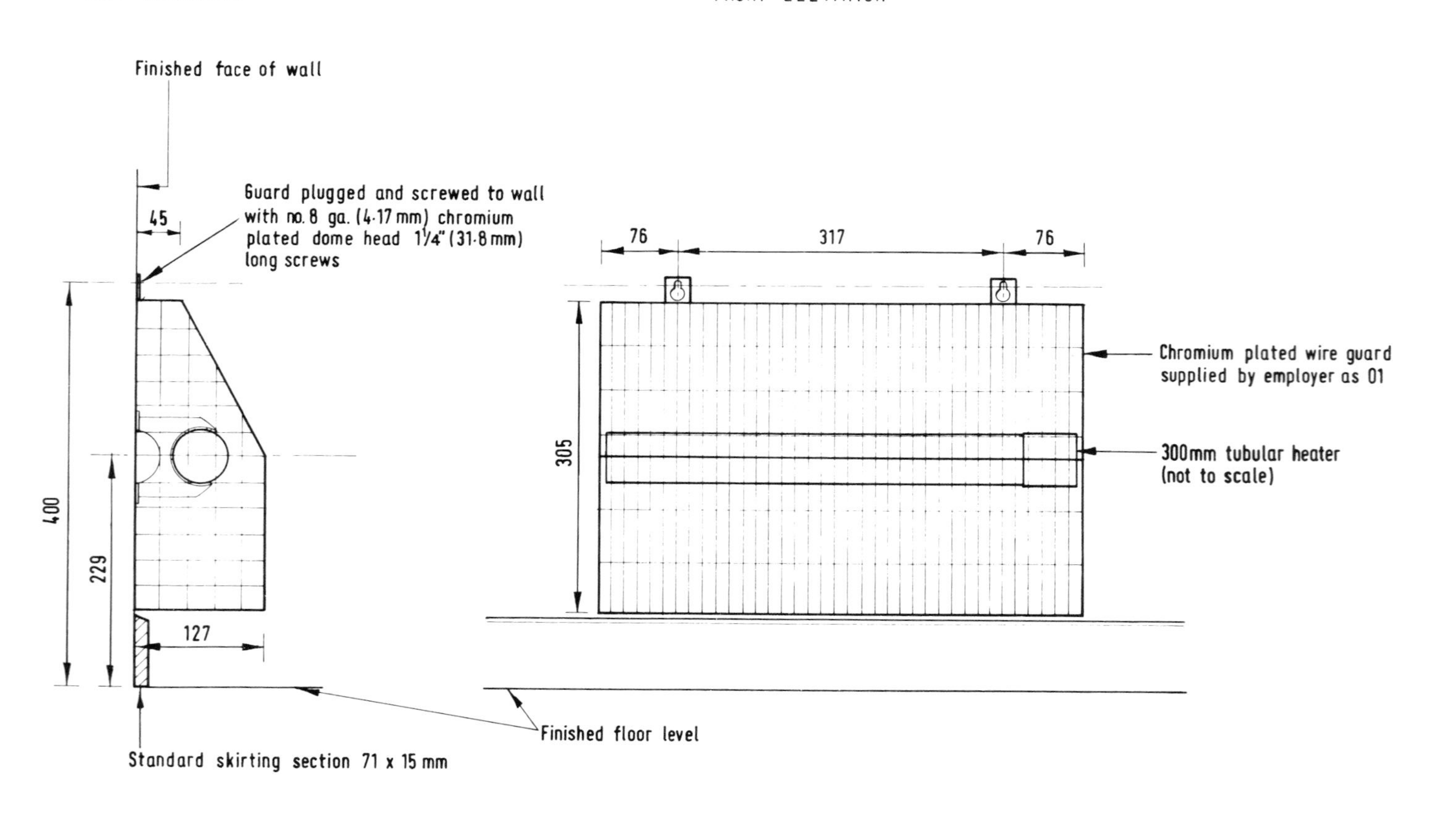

GLC ILEA

Department of Architecture
and Civic Design
County Hall SE1
Architect Sir Roger Walters

References following notes are clause numbers from G.L.C. preambles to bills of quantities

Departmental Standard Drawing

title
LINEN CUPBOARD TUBULAR HEATER GUARD
FIXING DETAILS

scale 1:5

drawing no D5130 rev A

bldg type 8 – | space use | element (56) | feature 532 | material Xh2 | key 1

00 - 010379

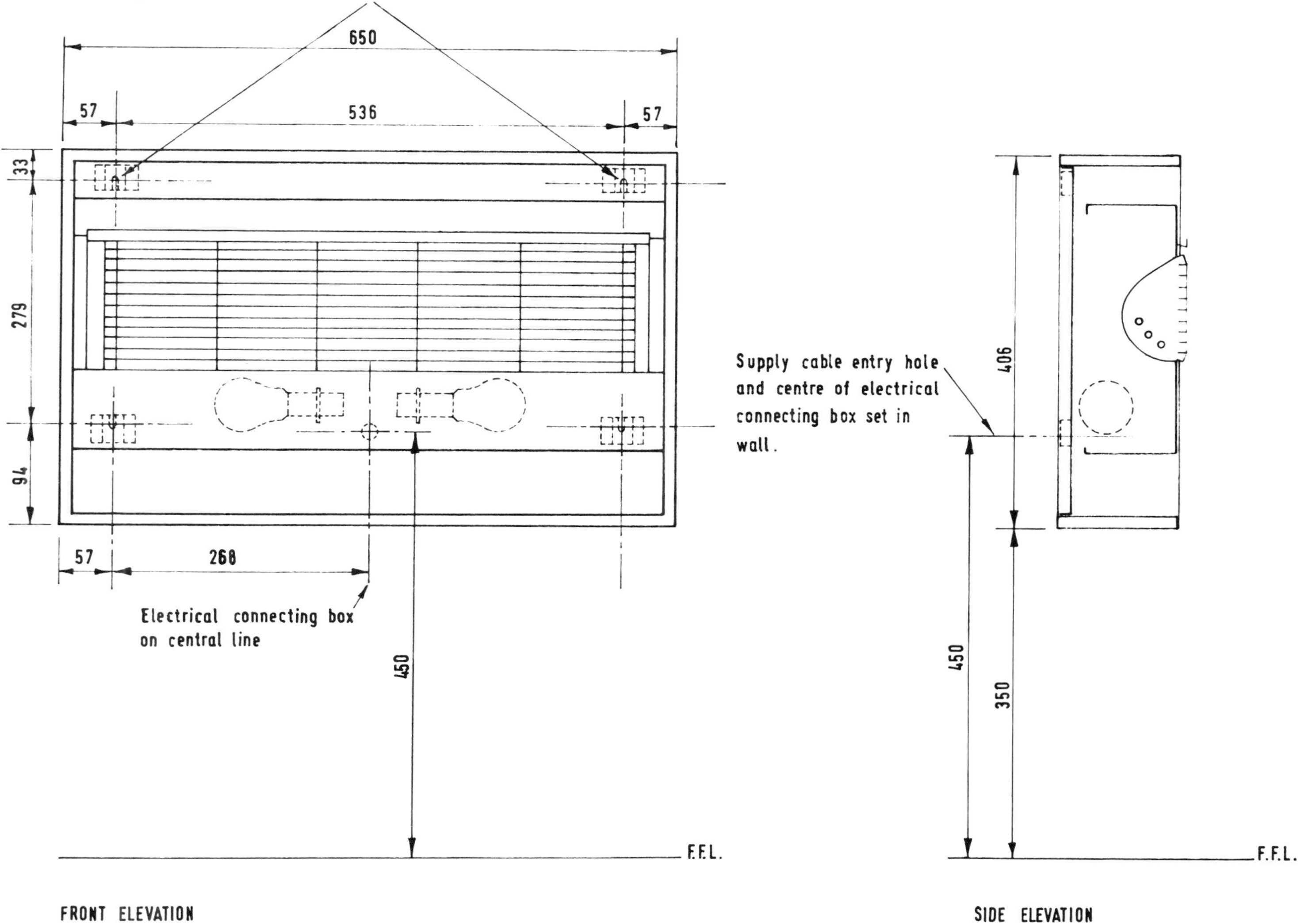

GLC ILEA

Department of Architecture and Civic Design
County Hall SE1
Architect Sir Roger Walters KBE FRIBA FI StructE

References following notes are clause numbers from G.L.C. preambles to bills of quantities.

Direct supply item.

No separate fire surround required.

Power 2·25 kw.

00 - 010379

bldg type 8 | space use | element [56] | feature 532 | material Xh2 | key 2

Departmental Standard Drawing

title

ELECTRIC PANEL HEATER

scale

1:5

drawing no

D5131A

5
Consumers' control units

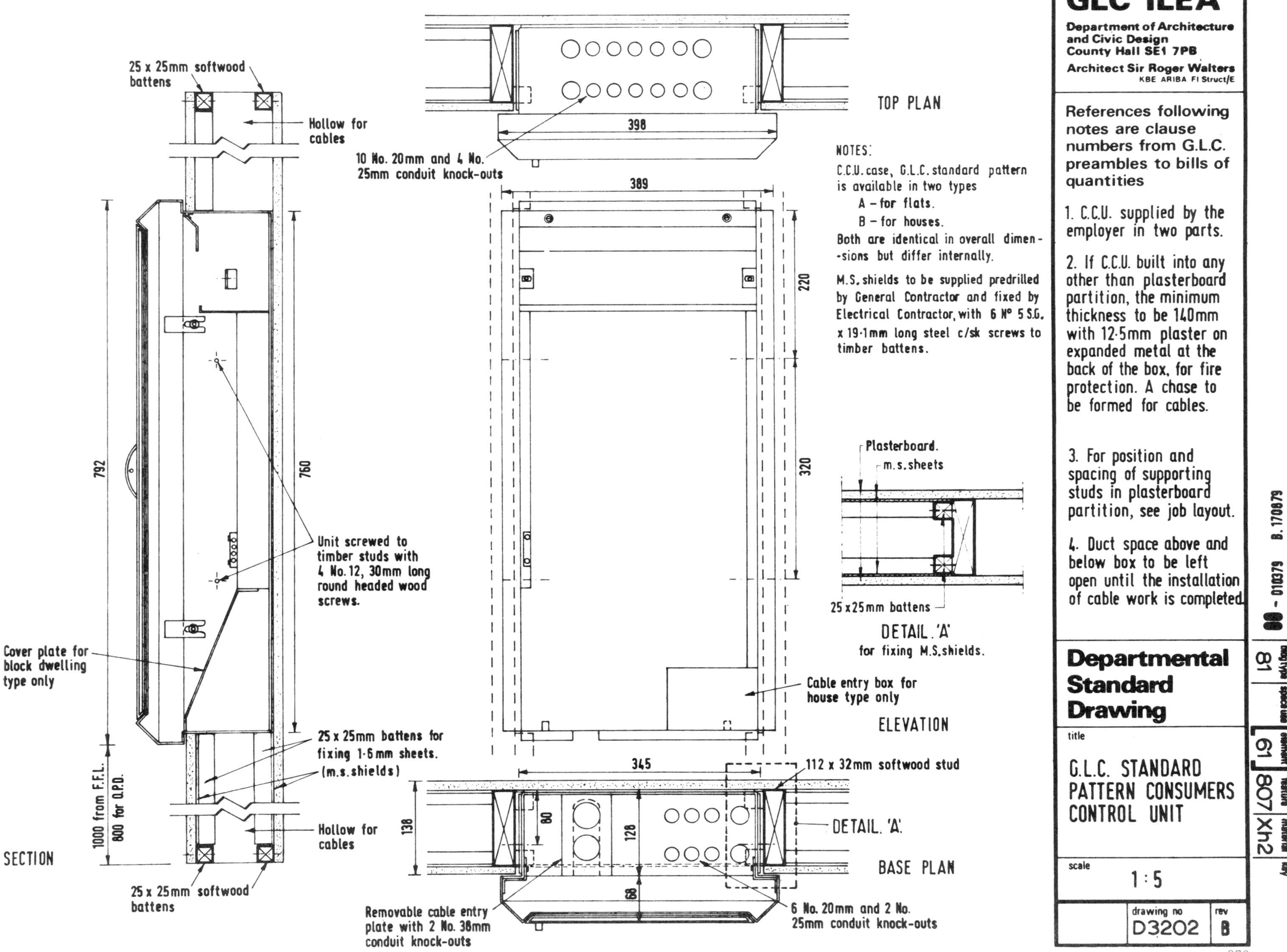

GLC ILEA
Department of Architecture and Civic Design
County Hall SE1 7PB
Architect Sir Roger Walters
KBE ARIBA FI Struct/E
References following notes are clause numbers from G.L.C. preambles to bills of quantities
1. C.C.U. supplied by the employer in two parts.
2. If C.C.U. built into any other than plasterboard partition, the minimum thickness to be 140mm with 12·5mm plaster on expanded metal at the back of the box, for fire protection. A chase to be formed for cables.
3. For position and spacing of supporting studs in plasterboard partition, see job layout.
4. Duct space above and below box to be left open until the installation of cable work is completed.
Departmental Standard Drawing
title
G.L.C. STANDARD PATTERN CONSUMERS CONTROL UNIT
scale
1 : 5
drawing no
D3202
rev
B
81
61
807
Xh2
TOP PLAN
NOTES:
C.C.U. case, G.L.C. standard pattern is available in two types
A – for flats.
B – for houses.
Both are identical in overall dimen- -sions but differ internally.
M.S. shields to be supplied predrilled by General Contractor and fixed by Electrical Contractor, with 6 Nº 5 S.G. x 19·1mm long steel c/sk screws to timber battens.
25 x 25mm softwood battens
Hollow for cables
10 No. 20mm and 4 No. 25mm conduit knock-outs
398
389
220
320
792
760
Unit screwed to timber studs with 4 No. 12, 30mm long round headed wood screws.
Cover plate for block dwelling type only
25 x 25mm battens for fixing 1·6mm sheets. (m.s. shields)
1000 from F.F.L.
800 for O.P.D.
Hollow for cables
SECTION
25 x 25mm softwood battens
Plasterboard.
m.s. sheets
25 x 25mm battens
DETAIL. 'A'
for fixing M.S. shields.
Cable entry box for house type only
ELEVATION
345
112 x 32mm softwood stud
138
80
128
98
DETAIL. 'A'
BASE PLAN
Removable cable entry plate with 2 No. 38mm conduit knock-outs
6 No. 20mm and 2 No. 25mm conduit knock-outs

6 Television

5202 Equipment case
5203 Free standing case in brick enclosure
5204 External access unit
5205 Aerial mast internally mounted
5206 Aerial mast externally mounted
5207 Aerial tube tower
5208 Aerial tower and equipment brick enclosures
5209 Aerial tower and equipment brick enclosure details
5245 External access box
4062 External access box—details ; Sheet 1, 2, 3
4063 External access box—details ; Sheet 1, 2, 3

WALL MOUNTED INSTALLATION.
[Electrical intake cupboard].

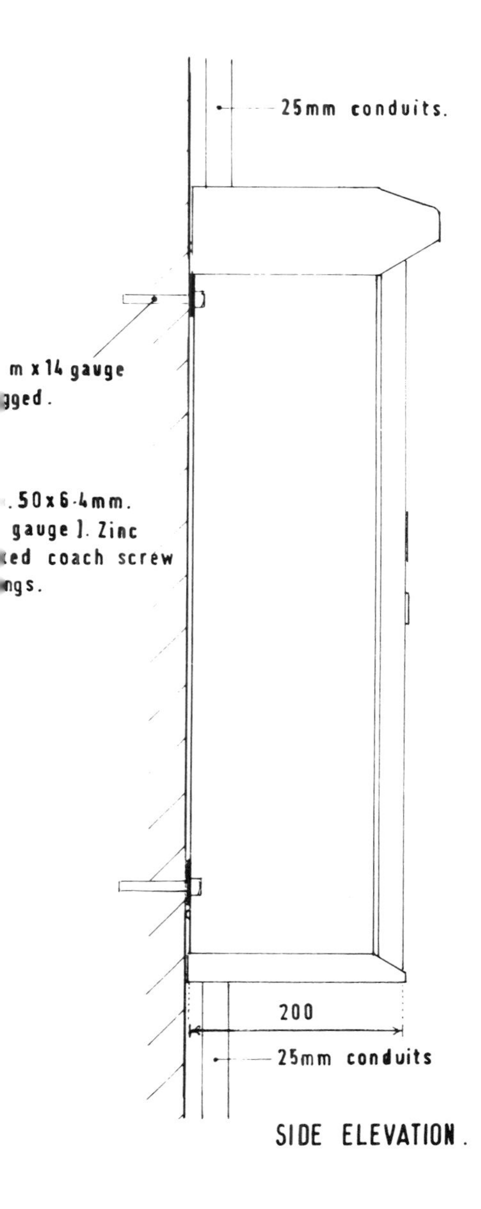

SIDE ELEVATION.

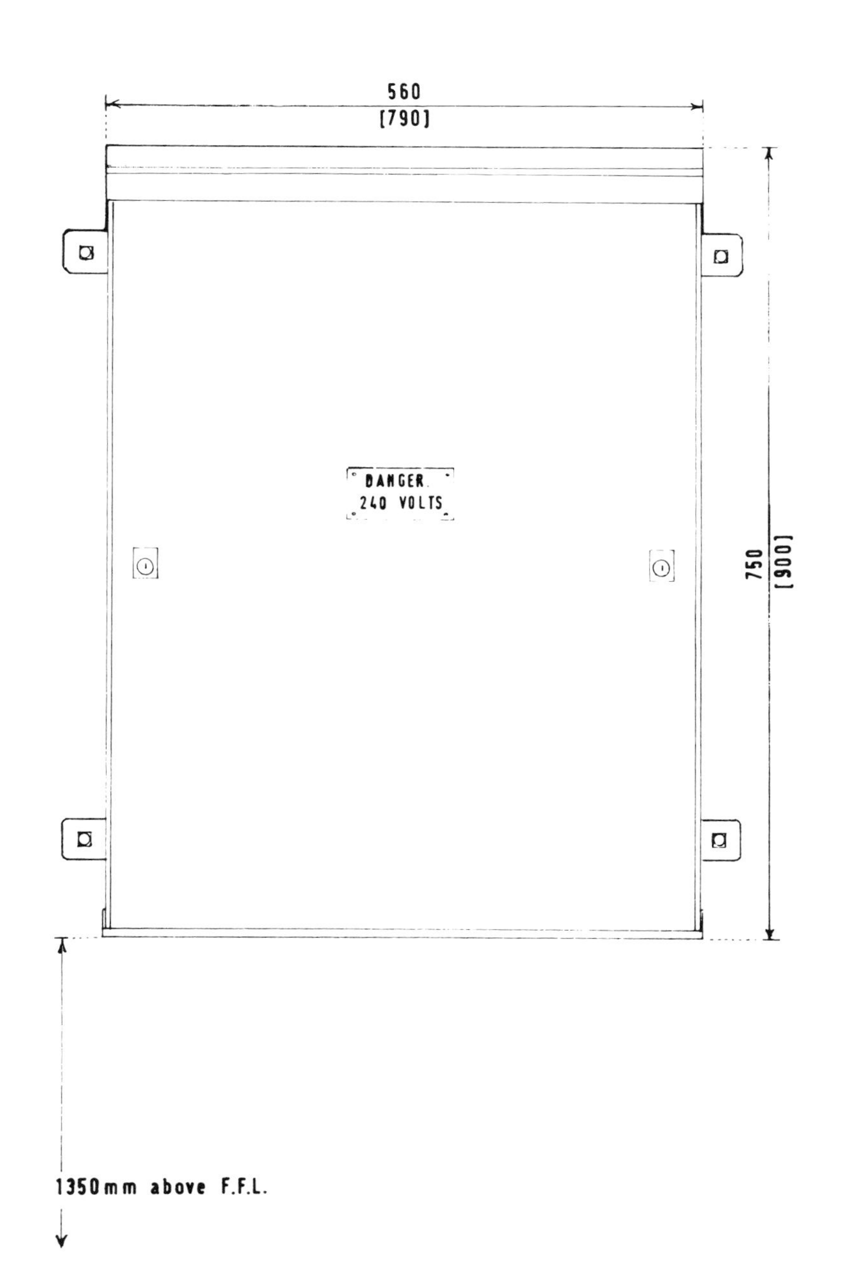

GLC ILEA

Department of Architecture and Civic Design
County Hall SE1
Architect Sir Roger Walters KBE FRIBA FI StructE

1. This dwg to be read in conjunction with system layout.
2. Dimensions for large size equipment case shown in brackets - 790 x 900.
3. For manufacturers details see dwg. D4061.
4. See job dwgs. for wall construction details.

Departmental Standard Drawing

title
COMMUNAL AERIAL SYSTEM.
EQUIPMENT CASE. WALL FIXED.

scale 1:5

AR/ME/ES/R. Ref.113.

drawing no D5202

00 - 00379

bldg type | space use | element [64] | feature 481 | material Xh2 | key

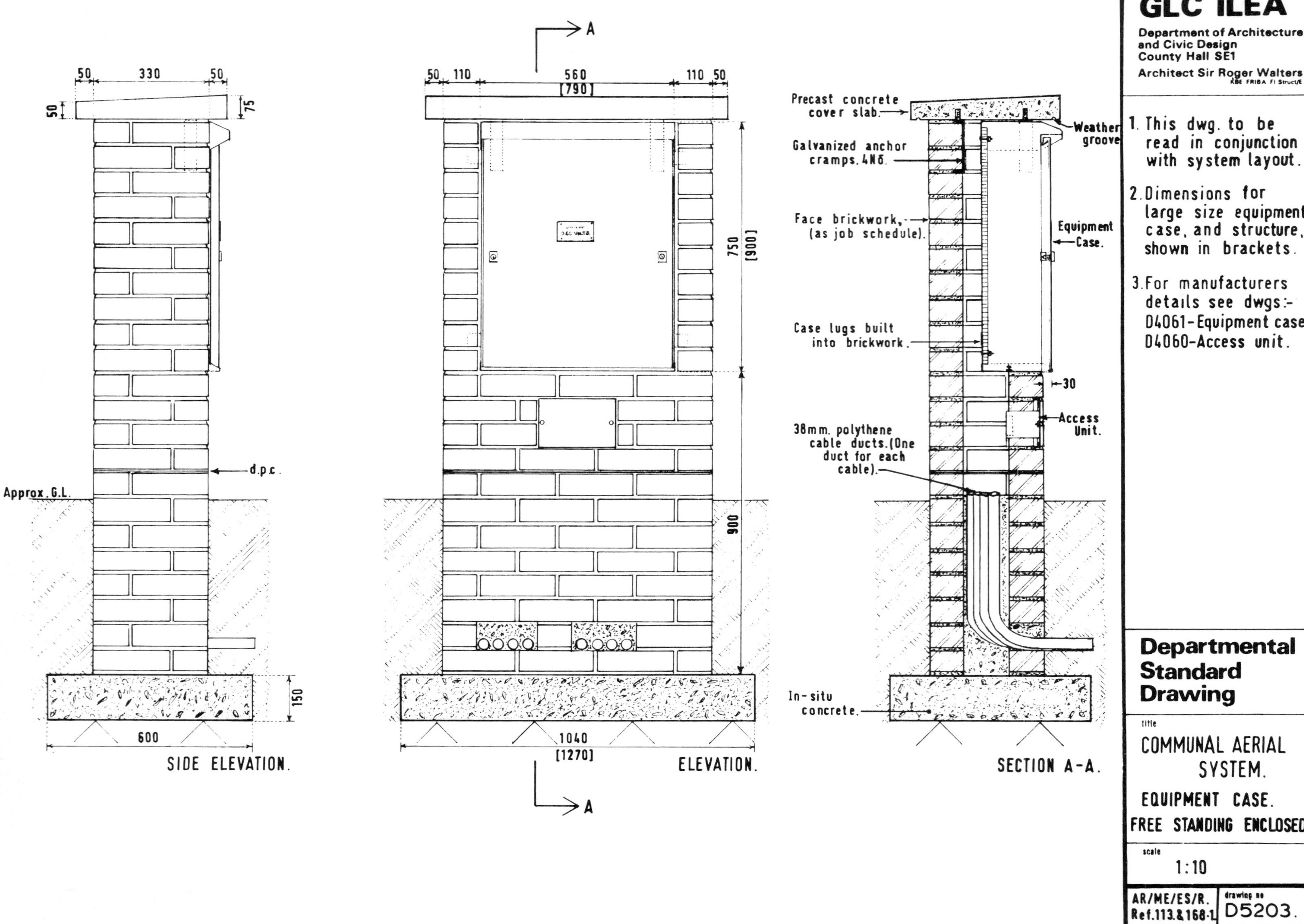
GLC ILEA
Department of Architecture and Civic Design
County Hall SE1
Architect Sir Roger Walters
1. This dwg. to be read in conjunction with system layout.
2. Dimensions for large size equipment case, and structure, shown in brackets.
3. For manufacturers details see dwgs:- D4061-Equipment case. D4060-Access unit.
Departmental Standard Drawing
title
COMMUNAL AERIAL SYSTEM.
EQUIPMENT CASE.
FREE STANDING ENCLOSED.
scale
1:10
AR/ME/ES/R. Ref.113.&168-1.
drawing no
D5203.
Precast concrete cover slab.
Galvanized anchor cramps. 4No.
Face brickwork, (as job schedule).
Case lugs built into brickwork.
38mm. polythene cable ducts. (One duct for each cable).
In-situ concrete.
Weather groove
Equipment Case.
Access Unit.
d.p.c.
Approx. G.L.
SIDE ELEVATION.
ELEVATION.
SECTION A-A.
64 481 Xh2

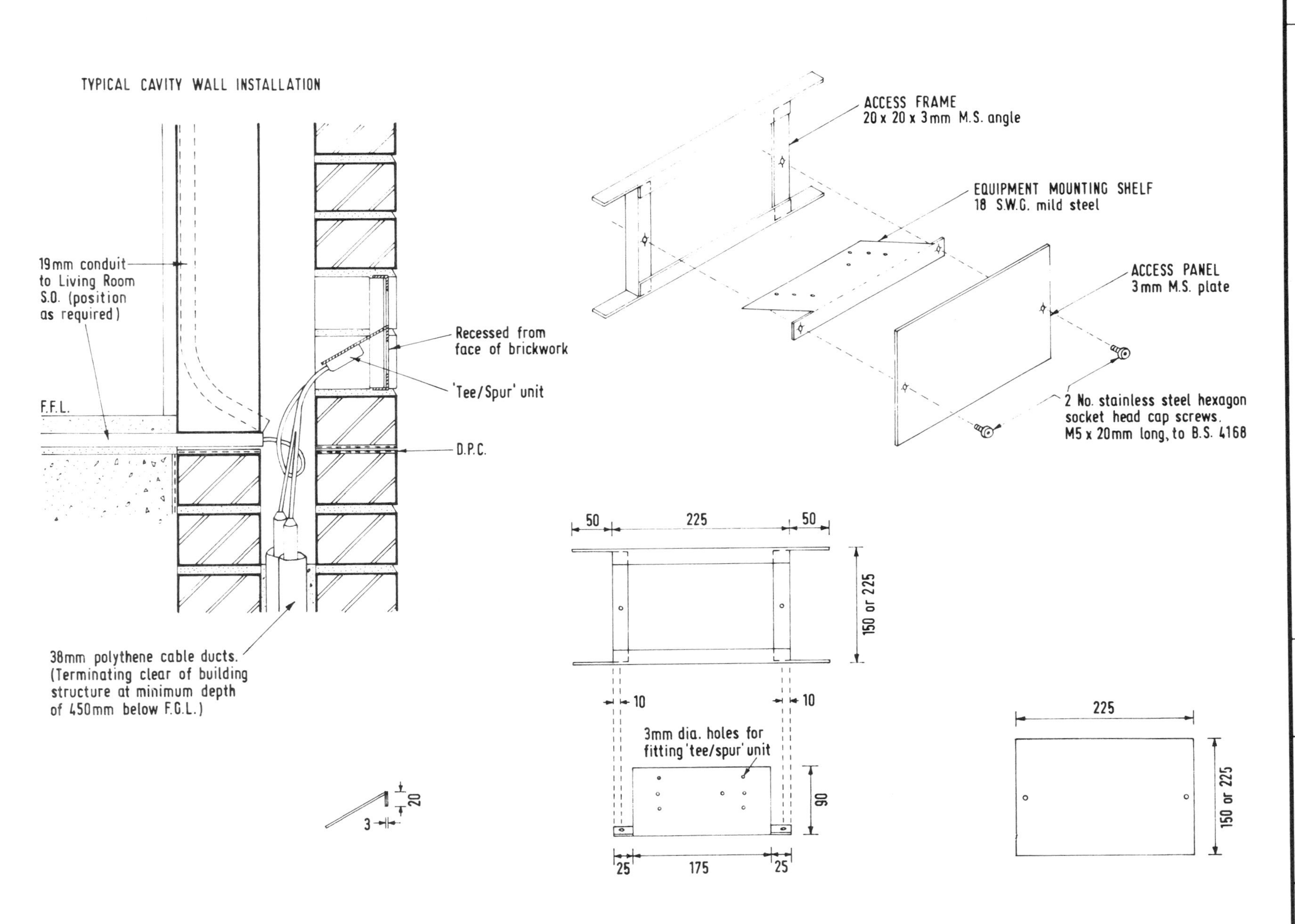

GLC ILEA

Department of Architecture and Civic Design
County Hall SE1 7PB
Architect Sir Roger Walters
KBE ARIBA FI Struct/E

References following notes are clause numbers from G.L.C. preambles to bills of quantities

1. Frames and panel hot dipped galvanised after manufacture, to B.S. 729.
2. For manufacturers details, see drwgs. D4062A & D4063.
3. This drwg. to be read in conjunction with system layout.
4. See job drwgs. for cavity wall inner skin, floor and wall finishes etc.
5. Equipment Mounting Shelf is supplied only by special request.
6. A plasticized finish in various colours is available on request.

Departmental Standard Drawing

title

U/V.H.F. COMMUNAL AERIAL SYSTEM.
EXTERNAL ACCESS COMPOSITE UNIT.

scale 1 : 5

AR/ME/ES/R Ref. 168·1 | drawing no D5204 | rev A

010379

bldg type | space use | element [64] | feature 481 | material Xh2 | key

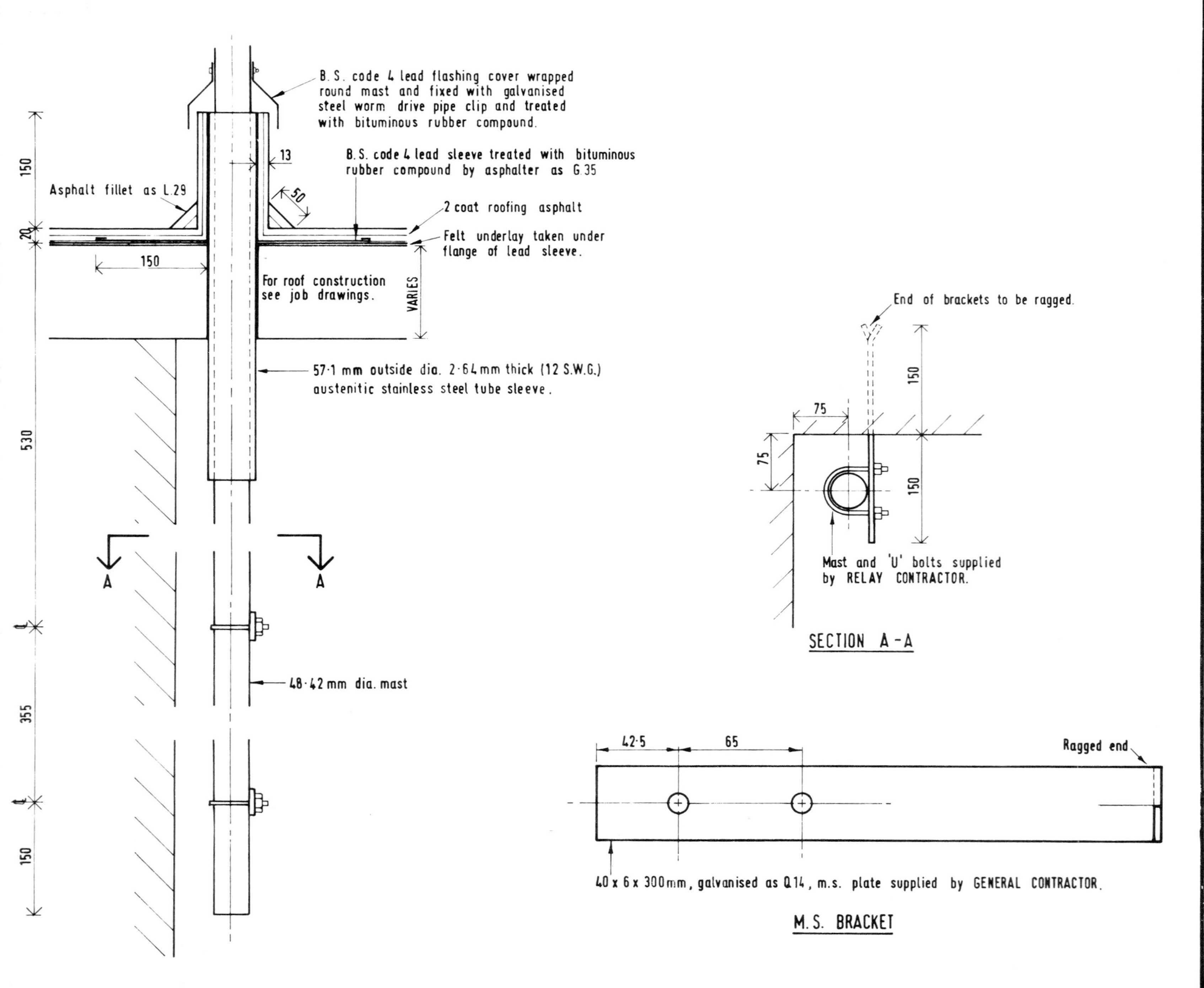

GLC ILEA

Department of Architecture and Civic Design
County Hall SE1
Architect Sir Roger Walters
KBE FRIBA F.Struct/E

References following notes are clause numbers from G.L.C. preambles to bills of quantities.

Departmental Standard Drawing

title
COMMUNAL AERIAL SYSTEM
U/V.H.F. AERIAL MAST INTERNALLY MOUNTED

scale
1:5 and 1:2.

ME/ES/R 1066

drawing no
D5205

[64] 481 Xh4 A

010379

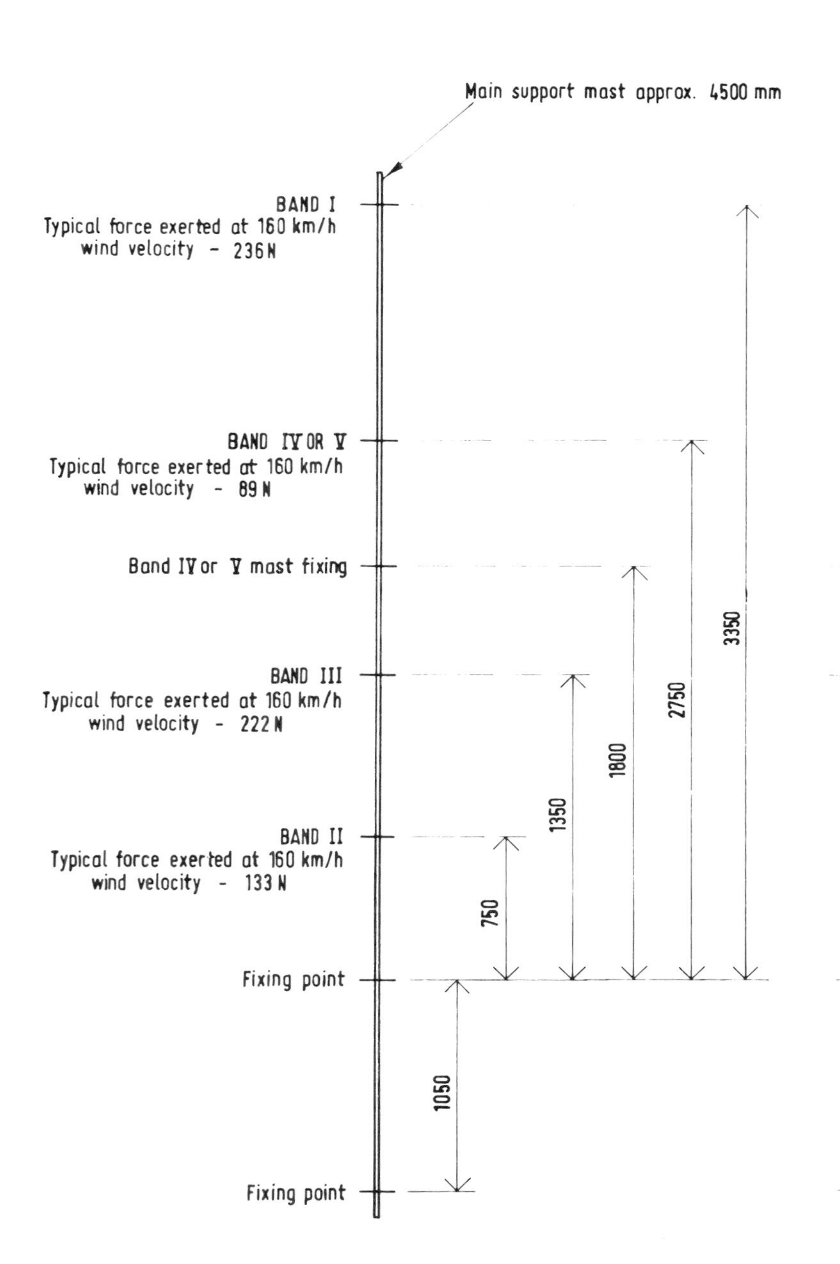
Subject to arrays being fitted in order shown below and at heights above top support bracket as indicated – total turning moment approx. 1·45 kN m
Main support mast approx. 4500 mm
BAND I
Typical force exerted at 160 km/h wind velocity – 236 N
BAND IV OR V
Typical force exerted at 160 km/h wind velocity – 89 N
Band IV or V mast fixing
BAND III
Typical force exerted at 160 km/h wind velocity – 222 N
BAND II
Typical force exerted at 160 km/h wind velocity – 133 N
Fixing point
Fixing point
3350
2750
1800
1350
750
1050

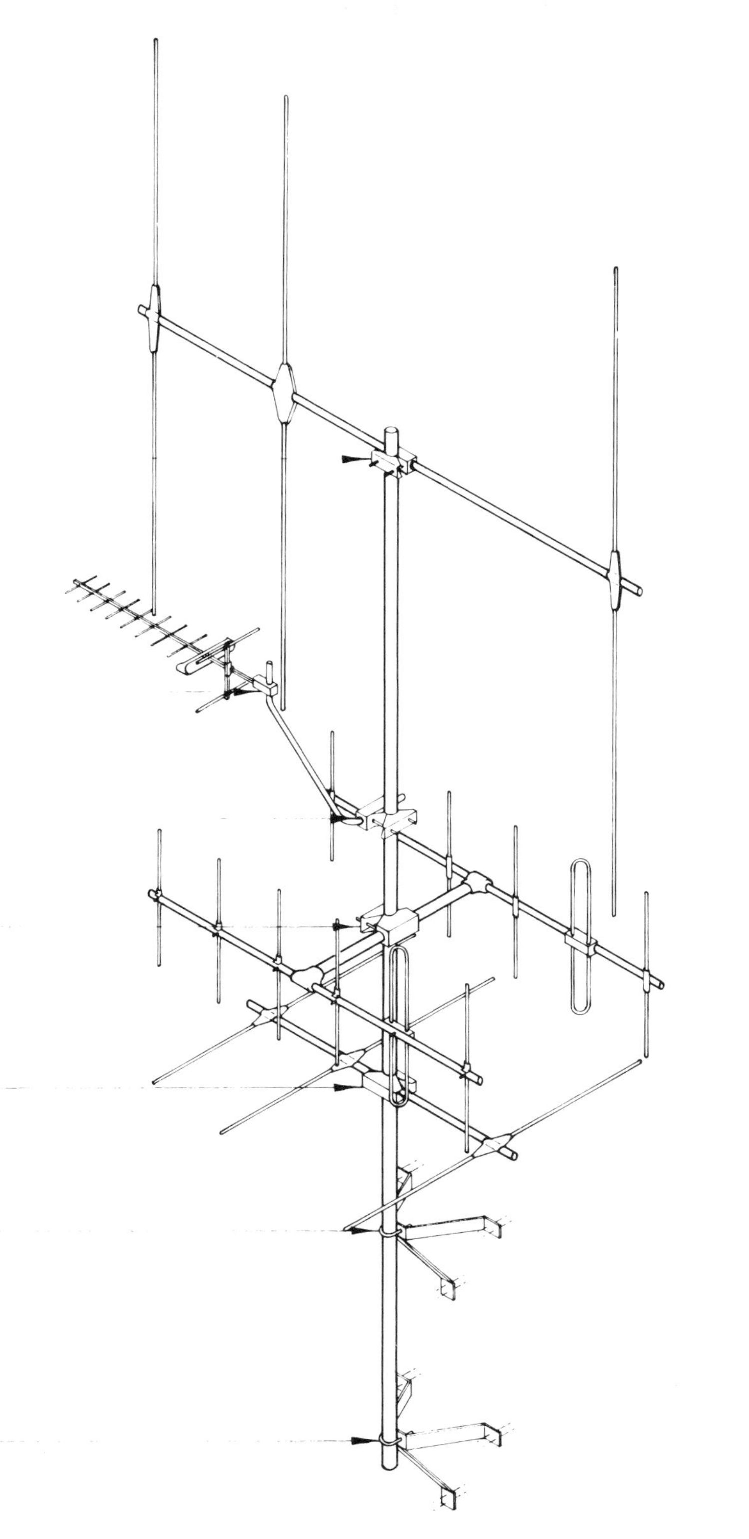

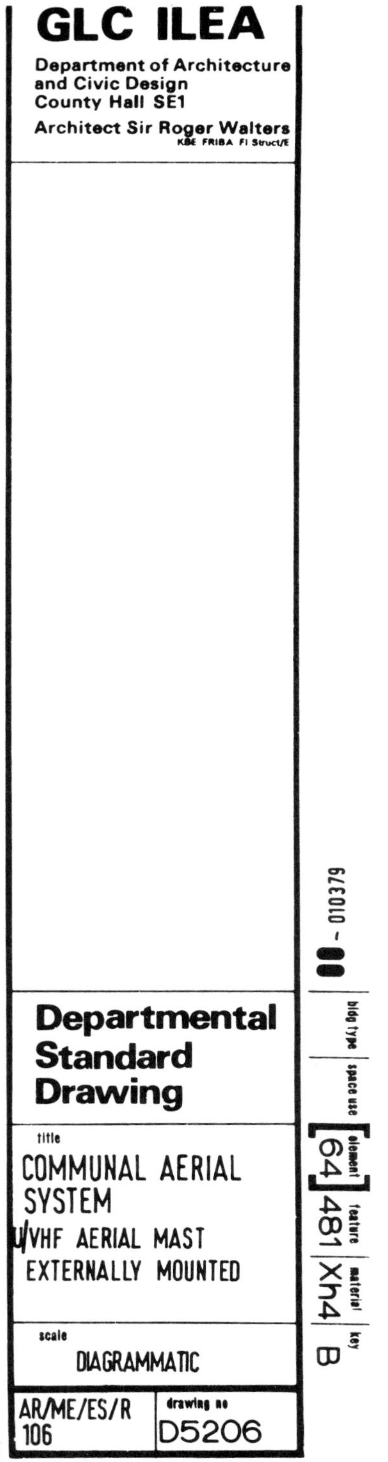
GLC ILEA
Department of Architecture and Civic Design
County Hall SE1
Architect Sir Roger Walters
KBE FRIBA FI StructE
Departmental Standard Drawing
title
COMMUNAL AERIAL SYSTEM
U/VHF AERIAL MAST EXTERNALLY MOUNTED
scale
DIAGRAMMATIC
AR/ME/ES/R 106
drawing no
D5206
00 - 010379
bldg type
space use
element
64
feature
481
material
Xh4
key
B

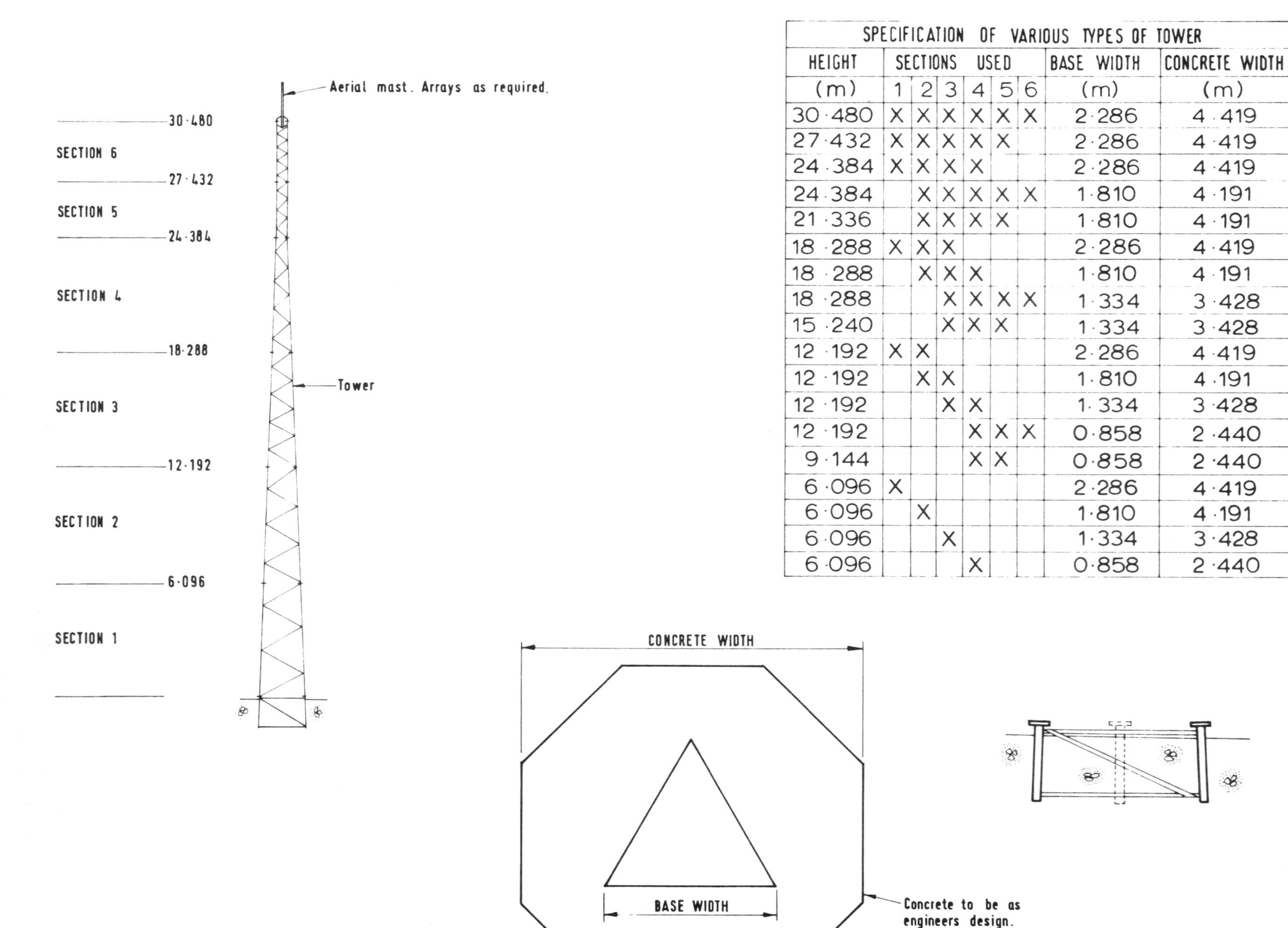

SPECIFICATION OF VARIOUS TYPES OF TOWER

HEIGHT (m)	SECTIONS USED 1	2	3	4	5	6	BASE WIDTH (m)	CONCRETE WIDTH (m)
30·480	X	X	X	X	X	X	2·286	4·419
27·432	X	X	X	X	X		2·286	4·419
24·384	X	X	X	X			2·286	4·419
24·384		X	X	X	X	X	1·810	4·191
21·336		X	X	X	X		1·810	4·191
18·288	X	X	X				2·286	4·419
18·288		X	X	X			1·810	4·191
18·288			X	X	X	X	1·334	3·428
15·240			X	X	X		1·334	3·428
12·192	X	X					2·286	4·419
12·192		X	X				1·810	4·191
12·192			X	X			1·334	3·428
12·192				X	X	X	0·858	2·440
9·144				X	X		0·858	2·440
6·096	X						2·286	4·419
6·096		X					1·810	4·191
6·096			X				1·334	3·428
6·096				X			0·858	2·440

GLC ILEA

Department of Architecture and Civic Design
County Hall SE1
Architect Sir Roger Walters KBE FRIBA FIStructE

References following notes are clause numbers from G.L.C. preambles to bills of quantities.

All metal parts to be hot dipped galvanised as R6d.

Departmental Standard Drawing

title
COMMUNAL AERIAL SYSTEM
U/V.H.F. AERIAL TUBE TOWER

scale
1:200 and 1:50.

ME/ES/R 173

drawing no
D5207

[64] 481 Xh2

00-010379

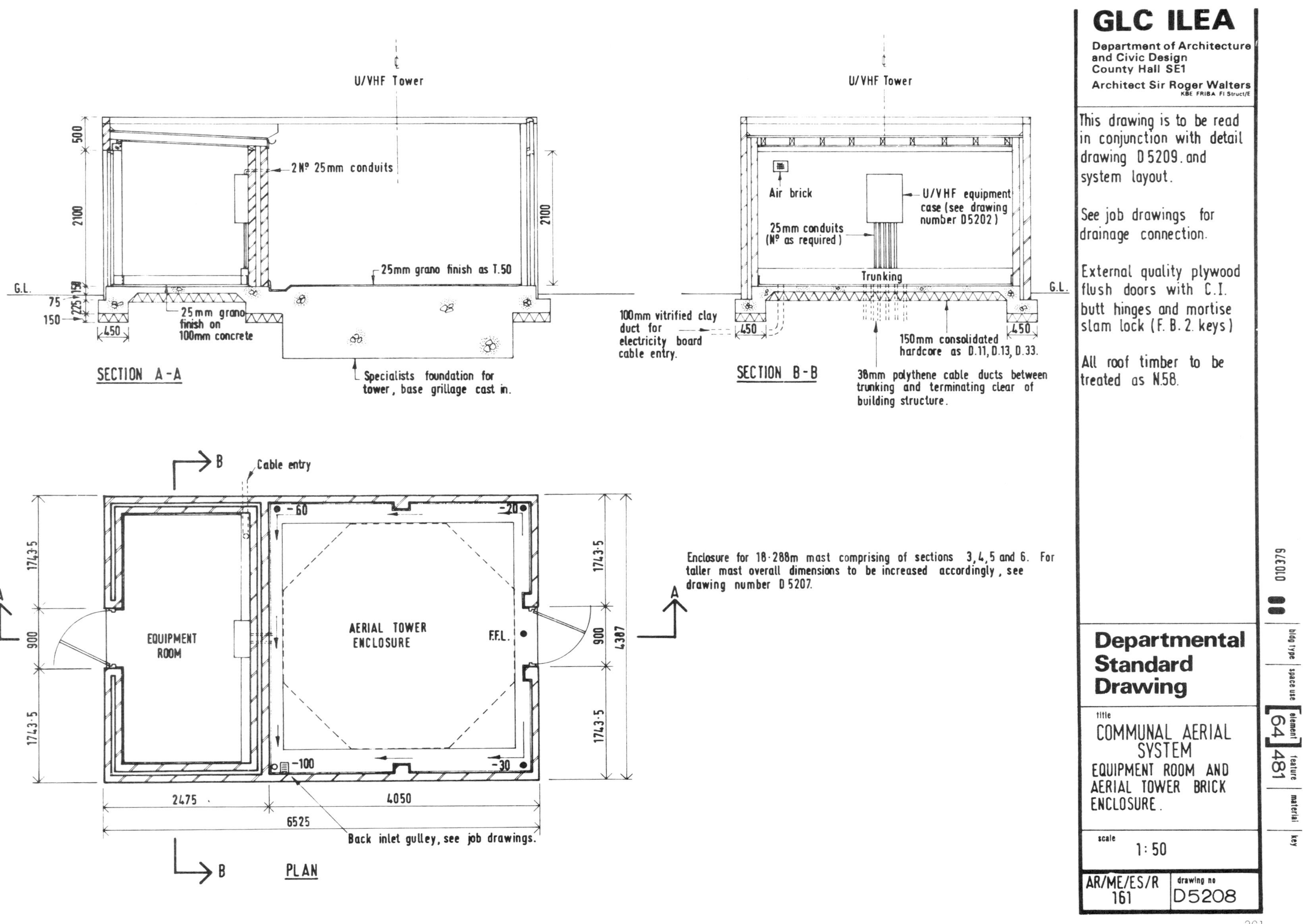

U/VHF Tower
2Nº 25mm conduits
25mm grano finish as T.50
G.L.
25mm grano finish on 100mm concrete
SECTION A-A
Specialists foundation for tower, base grillage cast in.
Air brick
U/VHF equipment case (see drawing number D5202)
25mm conduits (Nº as required)
Trunking
100mm vitrified clay duct for electricity board cable entry.
150mm consolidated hardcore as D.11, D.13, D.33.
SECTION B-B
38mm polythene cable ducts between trunking and terminating clear of building structure.
Cable entry
EQUIPMENT ROOM
AERIAL TOWER ENCLOSURE
F.F.L.
Back inlet gulley, see job drawings.
PLAN
Enclosure for 18·288m mast comprising of sections 3, 4, 5 and 6. For taller mast overall dimensions to be increased accordingly, see drawing number D 5207.
GLC ILEA
Department of Architecture and Civic Design
County Hall SE1
Architect Sir Roger Walters KBE FRIBA FI Struct/E
This drawing is to be read in conjunction with detail drawing D5209. and system layout.
See job drawings for drainage connection.
External quality plywood flush doors with C.I. butt hinges and mortise slam lock (F.B.2. keys)
All roof timber to be treated as N.58.
Departmental Standard Drawing
title
COMMUNAL AERIAL SYSTEM
EQUIPMENT ROOM AND AERIAL TOWER BRICK ENCLOSURE.
scale 1:50
AR/ME/ES/R 161
drawing no D5208

Department of Architecture
and Civic Design
County Hall SE1
Architect Sir Roger Walters
KBE FRIBA FI Struct/E

This drawing is to be read in conjunction with drg. number D5208 and job drawings.

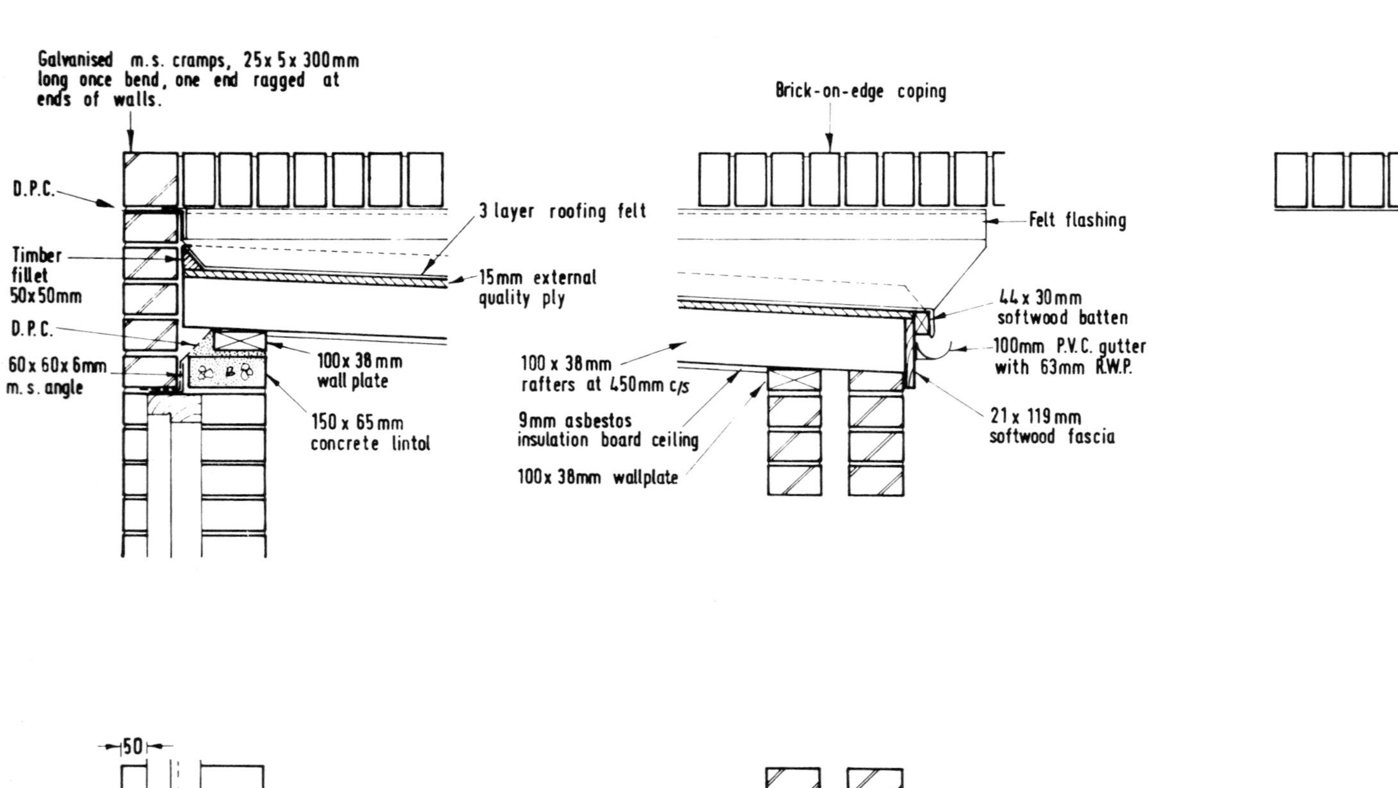

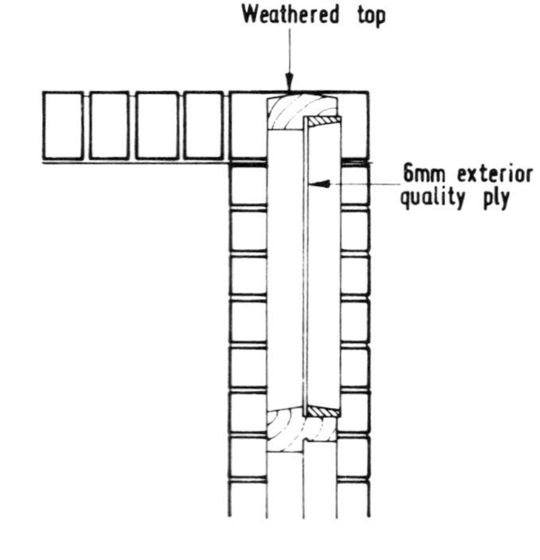

50
D.P.C.
G.L.
75mm grano skirting
25mm grano screed on 100mm concrete
150 mm consolidated hardcore as D.11, D.13, D.33.
D.P.C.
Gutter (laid to fall)
100

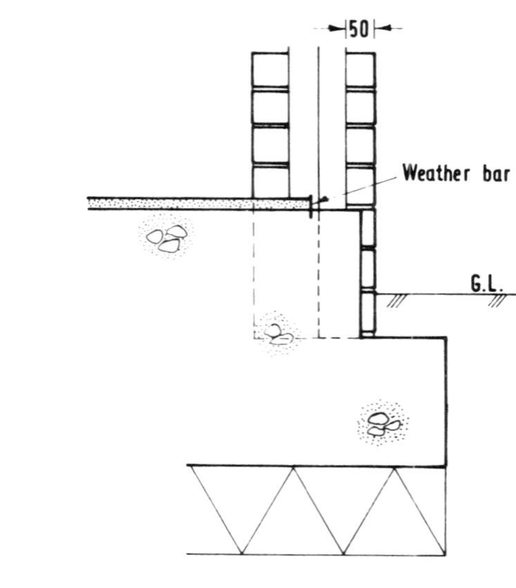

Departmental Standard Drawing

title
COMMUNAL AERIAL SYSTEM
EQUIPMENT ROOM AND AERIAL TOWER BRICK ENCLOSURE SECTIONAL DETAILS.

scale
1 : 10

AR/ME/ES/R 161

drawing no
D5209

010379
bldg type | space use | element [64] | feature 481 | material | key

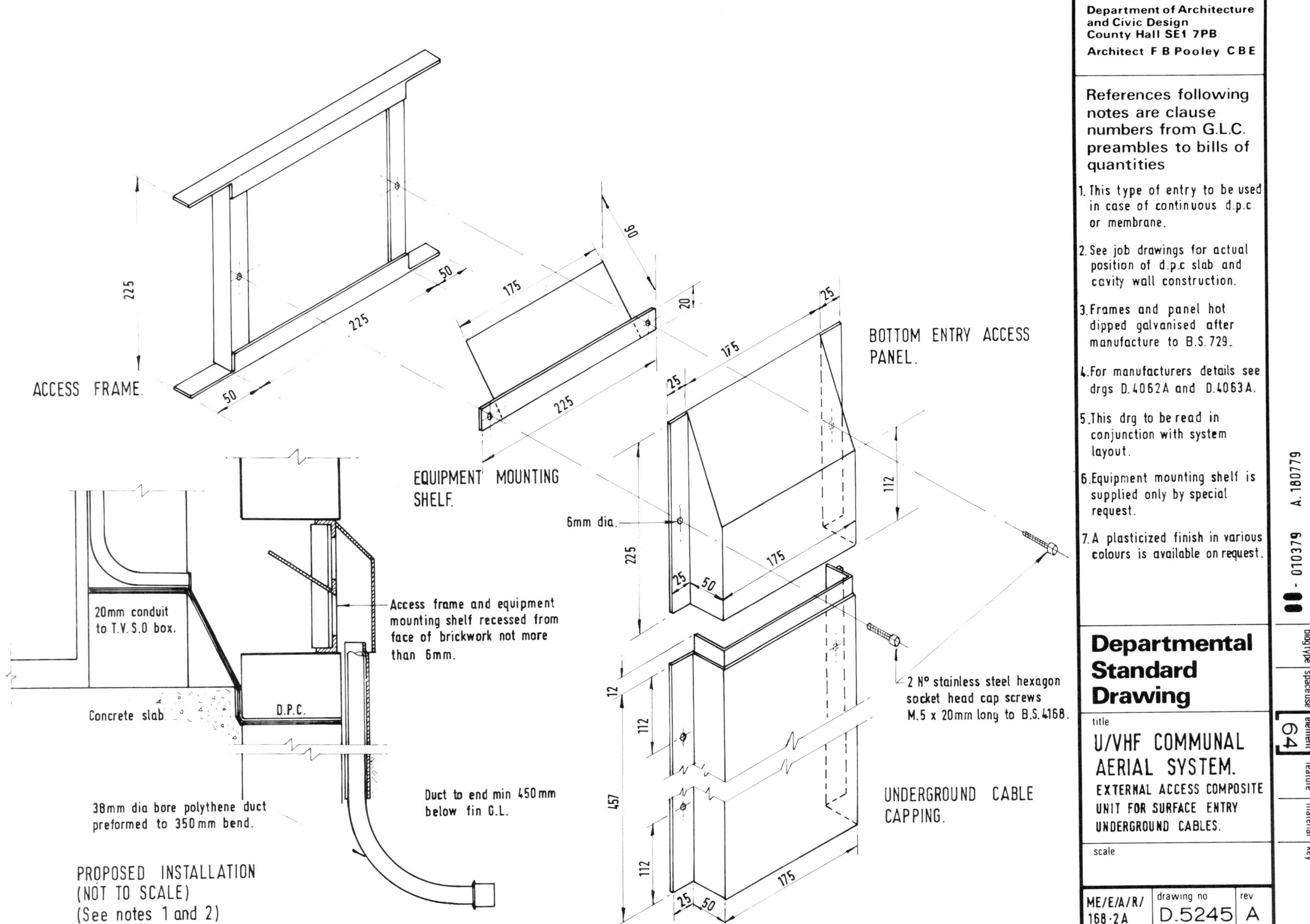
GLC ILEA
Department of Architecture
and Civic Design
County Hall SE1 7PB
Architect F B Pooley C B E
References following notes are clause numbers from G.L.C. preambles to bills of quantities
1. This type of entry to be used in case of continuous d.p.c or membrane.
2. See job drawings for actual position of d.p.c slab and cavity wall construction.
3. Frames and panel hot dipped galvanised after manufacture to B.S. 729.
4. For manufacturers details see drgs D.4062A and D.4063A.
5. This drg to be read in conjunction with system layout.
6. Equipment mounting shelf is supplied only by special request.
7. A plasticized finish in various colours is available on request.
Departmental Standard Drawing
title
U/VHF COMMUNAL AERIAL SYSTEM.
EXTERNAL ACCESS COMPOSITE UNIT FOR SURFACE ENTRY UNDERGROUND CABLES.
scale
ME/E/A/R/ 168·2A
drawing no D.5245
rev A
A. 180779
010379
bldg type
space use
element 64
feature
material
key
ACCESS FRAME.
EQUIPMENT MOUNTING SHELF.
BOTTOM ENTRY ACCESS PANEL.
UNDERGROUND CABLE CAPPING.
6mm dia.
2 N° stainless steel hexagon socket head cap screws M.5 x 20mm long to B.S. 4168.
20mm conduit to T.V.S.O box.
Concrete slab.
D.P.C.
Access frame and equipment mounting shelf recessed from face of brickwork not more than 6mm.
38mm dia bore polythene duct preformed to 350mm bend.
Duct to end min 450mm below fin G.L.
PROPOSED INSTALLATION
(NOT TO SCALE)
(See notes 1 and 2)
225
50
90
175
20
25
112
12
457

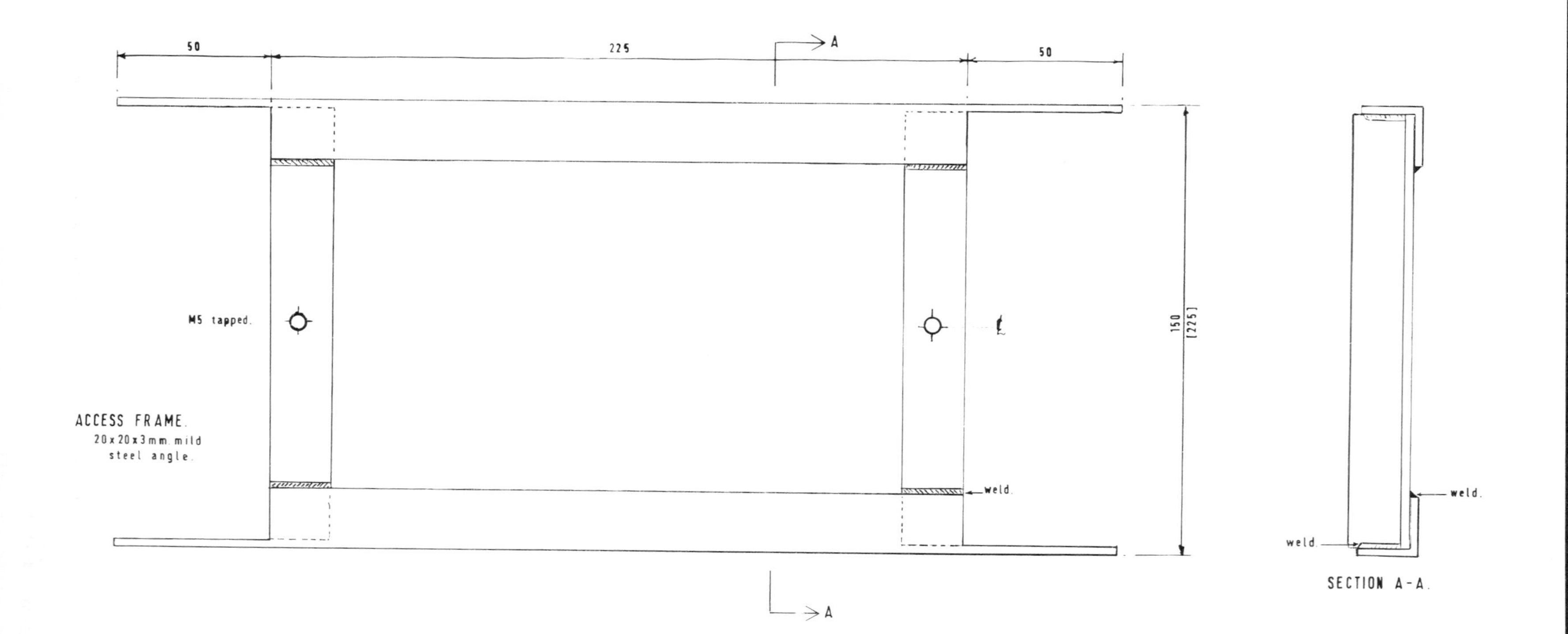

GLC ILEA

Department of Architecture
and Civic Design
County Hall SE1 7PB
Architect F B Pooley CBE

References following notes are clause numbers from G.L.C. preambles to bills of quantities

1. Frames and panel hot dipped galvanised after manufacture to BS.729.
2. Alternate sizes to access frame and panel, shown in brackets, for use as specified
3. 2 Nº M5 x 20mm stainless steel hexagon socket head cap screws for panel/frame fixing to BS.4168.
4. Equipment Mounting Shelf is supplied only by special request.
5. A plasticized finish in various colours is available on request.

Departmental Standard Drawing

title

COMMUNAL AERIAL SYSTEM

EXTERNAL ACCESS COMPOSITE UNIT.

[ALTERNATIVE EQUIPMENT MOUNTING FRAME/SHELF]

scale

Sheet.1	drawing no D.4062	rev A

010379

bldg type | space use | element 64 | feature | material | key

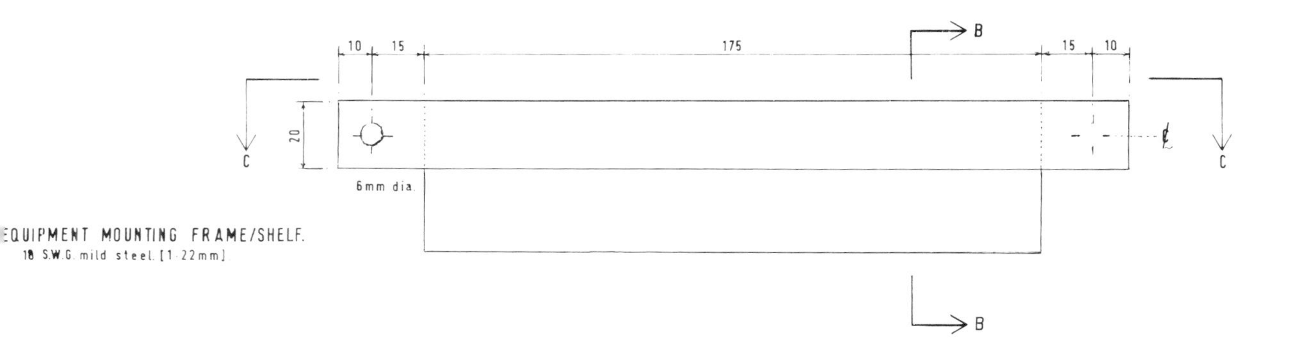

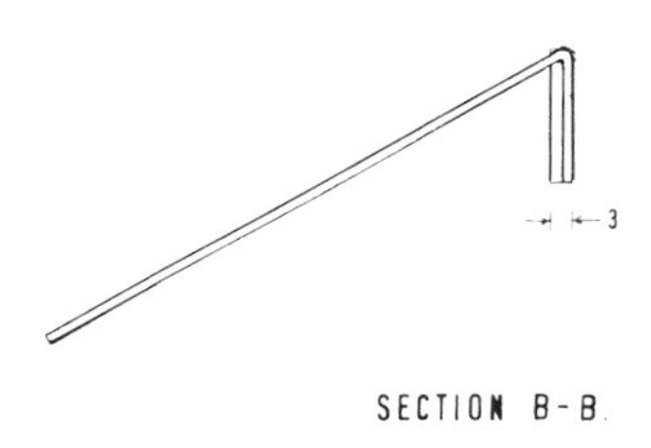

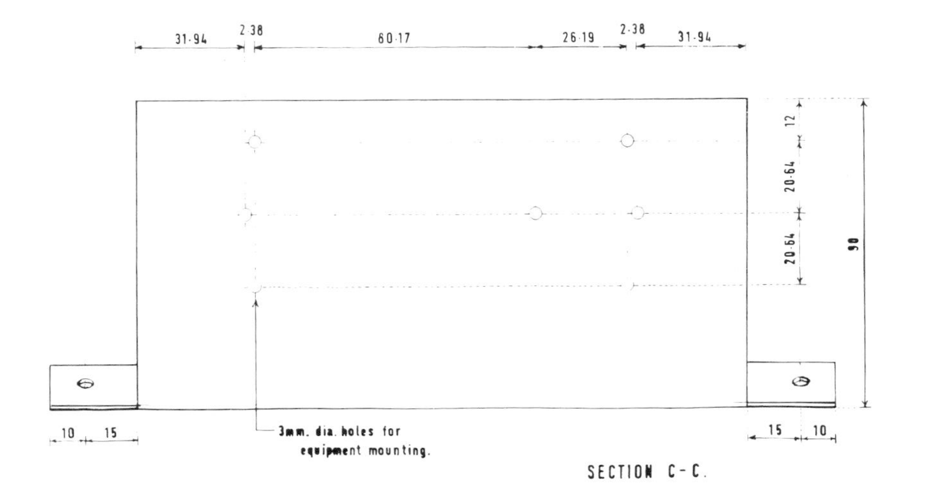

GLC ILEA

Department of Architecture and Civic Design
County Hall SE1 7PB
Architect F B Pooley CBE

References following notes are clause numbers from G.L.C. preambles to bills of quantities

For notes see Sheet.1.

Departmental Standard Drawing

title
COMMUNAL AERIAL SYSTEM
EXTERNAL ACCESS COMPOSITE UNIT.
[ALTERNATIVE EQUIPMENT MOUNTING FRAME/SHELF]

scale

	drawing no	rev
Sheet2	D.4062	A

010379

bldgtype | spaceuse | element [64] | feature | material | key

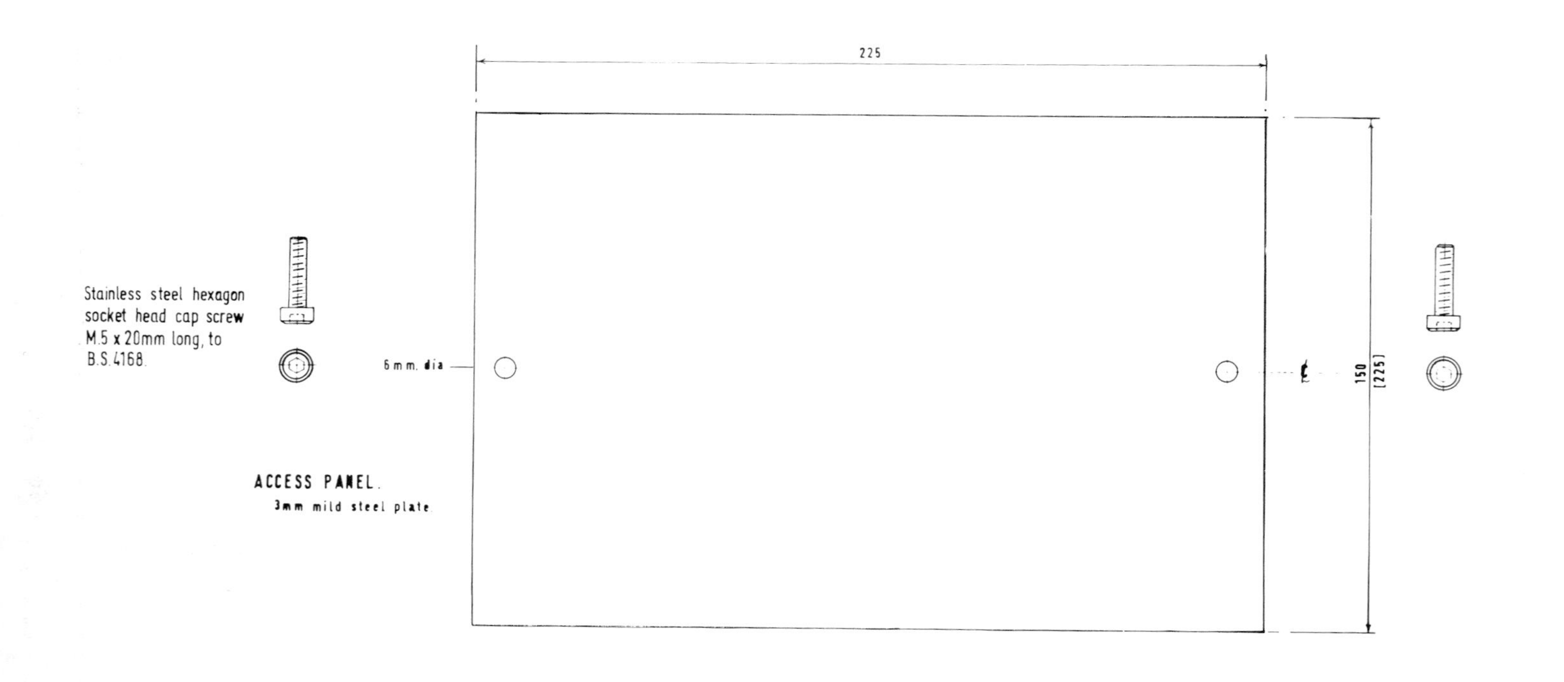

GLC ILEA

Department of Architecture and Civic Design
County Hall SE1 7PB
Architect F B Pooley CBE

References following notes are clause numbers from G.L.C. preambles to bills of quantities

For notes see Sheet.1.

Departmental Standard Drawing

title

COMMUNAL AERIAL SYSTEM
EXTERNAL ACCESS COMPOSITE UNIT.
[ALTERNATIVE EQUIPMENT MOUNTING FRAME/SHELF]

scale

	drawing no	rev
Sheet.3	D.4062	A

00 - 010379

bldg type | space use | element 64 | feature | material | key

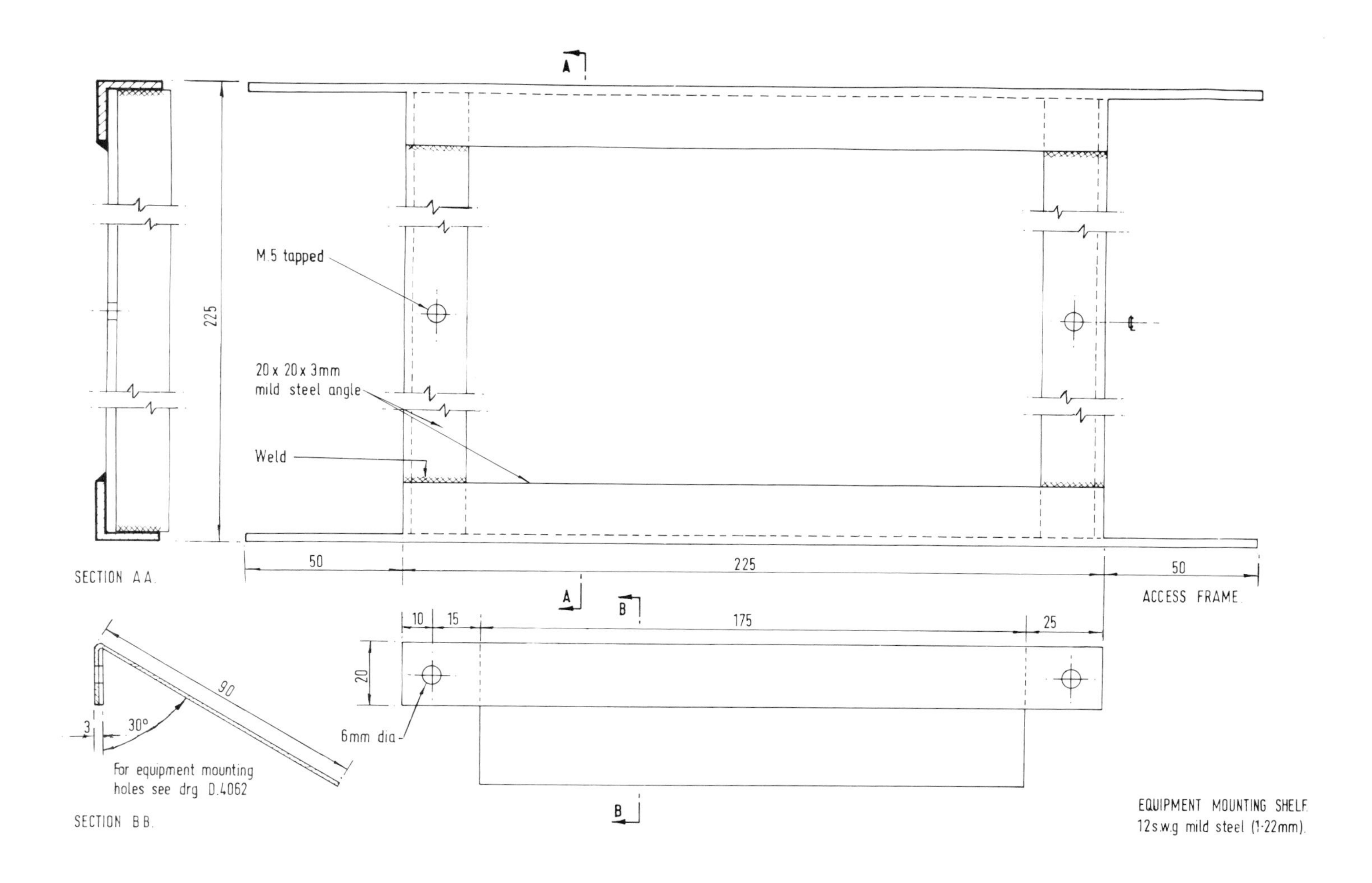

GLC ILEA

Department of Architecture and Civic Design
County Hall SE1 7PB
Architect F B Pooley C B E

References following notes are clause numbers from G.L.C. preambles to bills of quantities

1. Frames and panel hot dipped galvanised after manufacture to BS.729.
2. N.B. for equipment mounting holes see drwg D.4062A.
3. Equipment Mounting Shelf is supplied only by special request.
4. A plasticized finish in various colours is available on request.

Departmental Standard Drawing

title

U/V.H.F. COMMUNAL AERIAL SYSTEM.

EXTERNAL ACCESS COMPOSITE UNIT FOR SURFACE ENTRY UNDERGROUND CABLES.

scale

Sheet.1. drawing no D.4063 rev

bldg type | spaceuse | element [64] | feature | material | key

00-010379

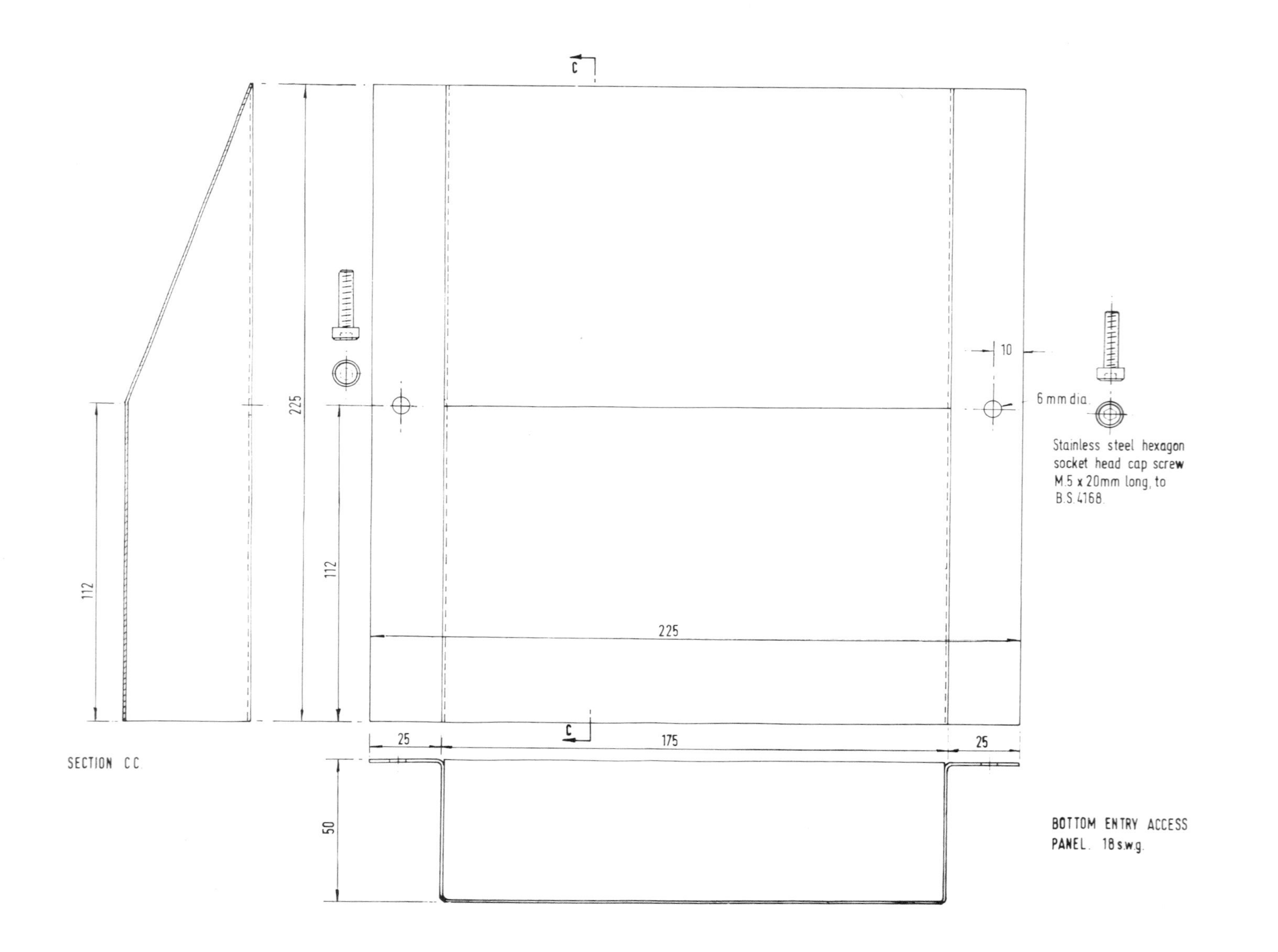

GLC ILEA

Department of Architecture and Civic Design
County Hall SE1 7PB
Architect F B Pooley CBE

References following notes are clause numbers from G.L.C. preambles to bills of quantities

For notes see Sheet.1.

Departmental Standard Drawing

title
U/V.H.F. COMMUNAL AERIAL SYSTEM.
EXTERNAL ACCESS COMPOSITE UNIT FOR SURFACE ENTRY UNDERGROUND CABLES.

scale

	drawing no	rev
Sheet 2	D.4063	

64

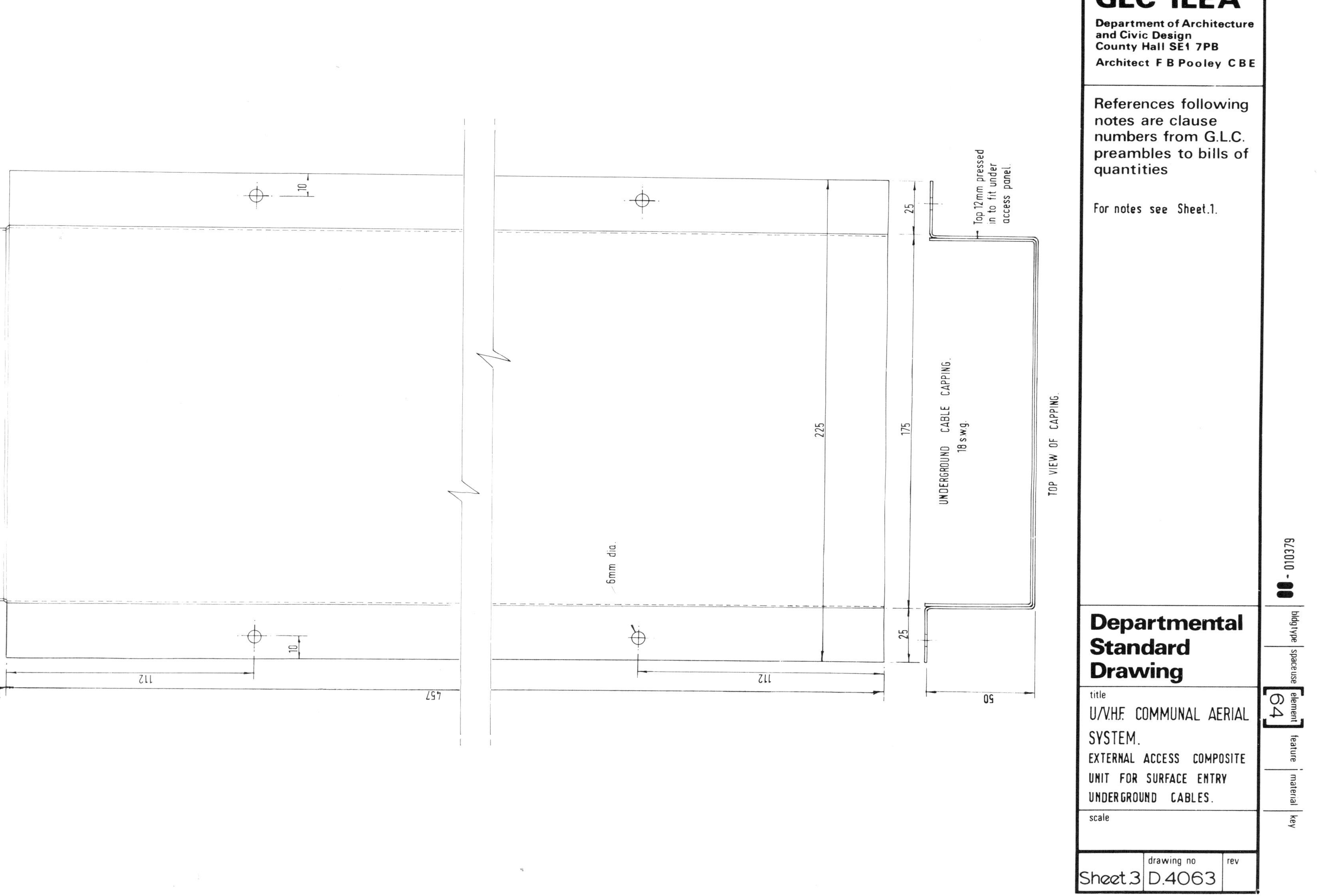

GLC ILEA

Department of Architecture and Civic Design
County Hall SE1 7PB
Architect F B Pooley C B E

References following notes are clause numbers from G.L.C. preambles to bills of quantities

For notes see Sheet.1.

Departmental Standard Drawing

title

U/V.H.F. COMMUNAL AERIAL SYSTEM.

EXTERNAL ACCESS COMPOSITE UNIT FOR SURFACE ENTRY UNDERGROUND CABLES.

scale

Sheet 3	drawing no D.4063	rev

bldgtype | spaceuse | element [64] | feature | material | key

00 - 010379

7
Cradle bolts

5062 Timber roof fixing
5326 Concrete roof fixing
5067 Anchor for ladder tie rings

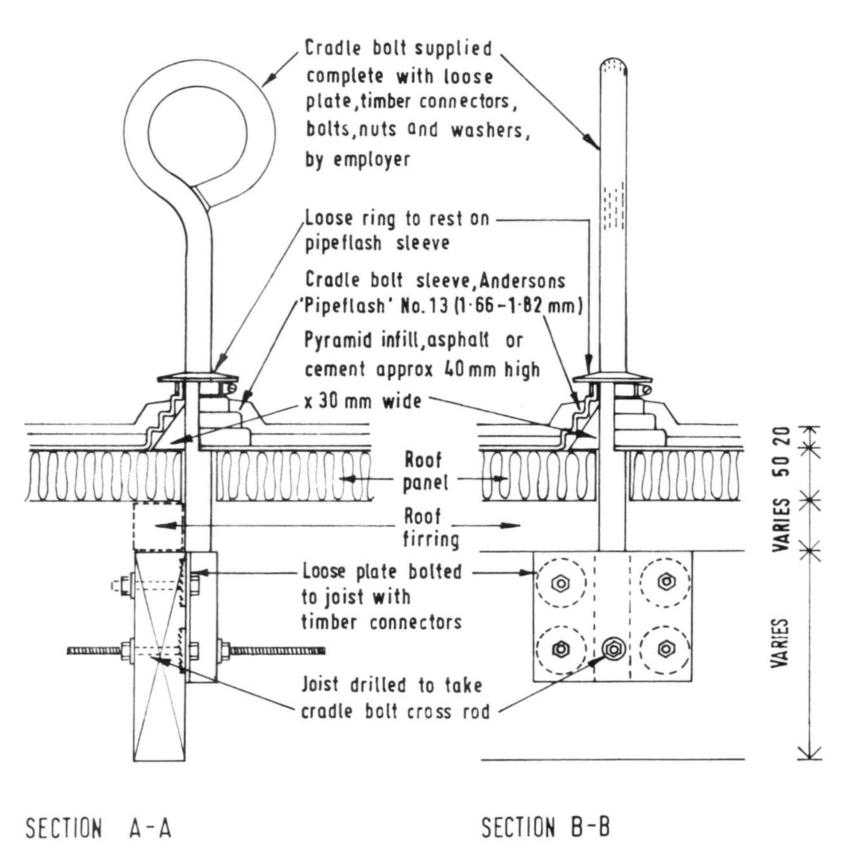

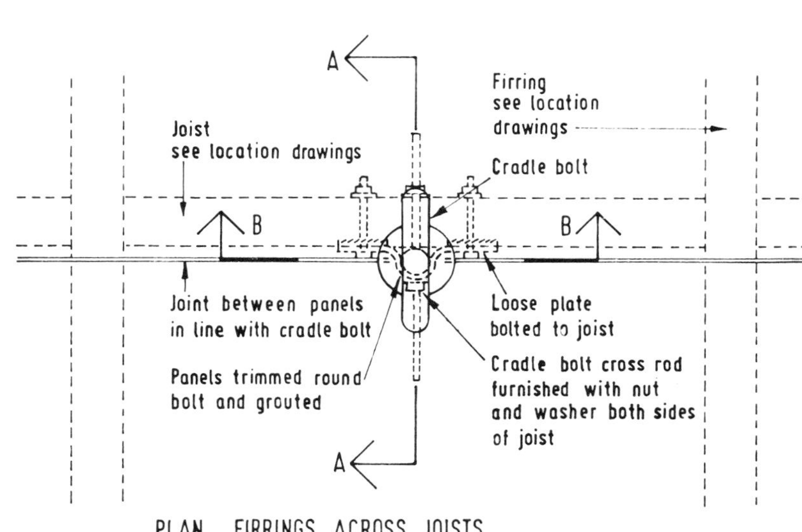

PLAN FIRRINGS ACROSS JOISTS
ASPHALT AND FELT UNDERLAY AND PIPEFLASH OMITTED
KEY B(A)

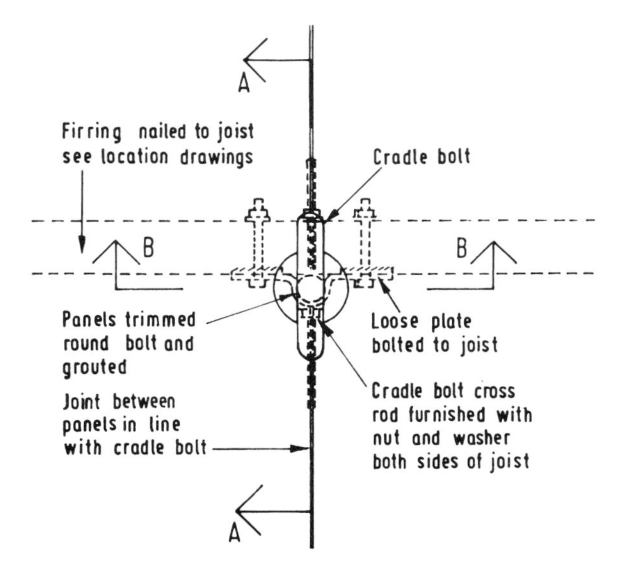

PLAN FIRRINGS ALONG JOISTS
ASPHALT AND FELT UNDERLAY AND PIPEFLASH OMITTED
KEY C(A)

GLC ILEA

Department of Architecture and Civic Design
County Hall SE1 7PB
Architect Sir Roger Walters KBE ARIBA FI Struct/E

References following notes are clause numbers from G.L.C. preambles to bills of quantities

For full description of roof finish see drawing number [47] D5020 or D5040
Bolts to be tested after fixing as BW/T1

Departmental Standard Drawing

title
CRADLING BOLT
DRY INSULATING ROOFING SYSTEM
TIMBER ROOF

scale 1:5

drawing no D5062 rev B

bldg type | space use | element [66] | feature 662 | material Xh2 | key as plans

010379

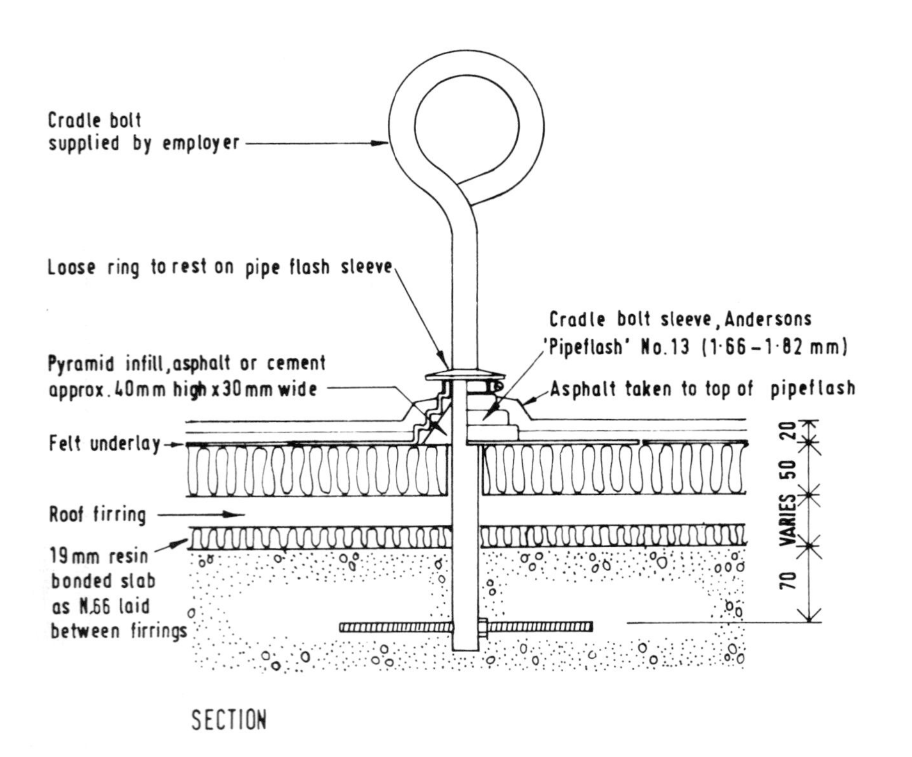

SECTION

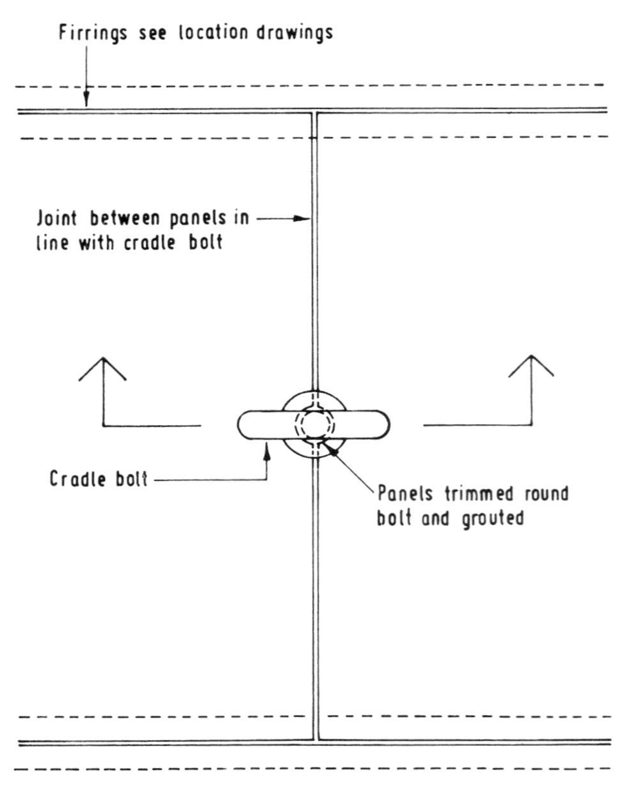

PLAN (Asphalt and felt underlay and pipeflash omitted)

GLC ILEA

Department of Architecture
and Civic Design
County Hall SE1 7PB

Architect Sir Roger Walters
KBE ARIBA FI Struct/E

References following notes are clause numbers from G.L.C. preambles to bills of quantities

For full description of roof finish see drawing number [47] D5306

Bolts to be tested after fixing as BW/T1

THERMAL INSULATION
0·6 W/m^2 deg C.

Departmental Standard Drawing

title
CRADLING BOLT
DRY INSULATING ROOFING SYSTEM
CONCRETE ROOF

scale 1·5

drawing no D5326 rev A

bldg type | space use | element | feature | material | key
[66] 662 Xh2 E(A)

010379

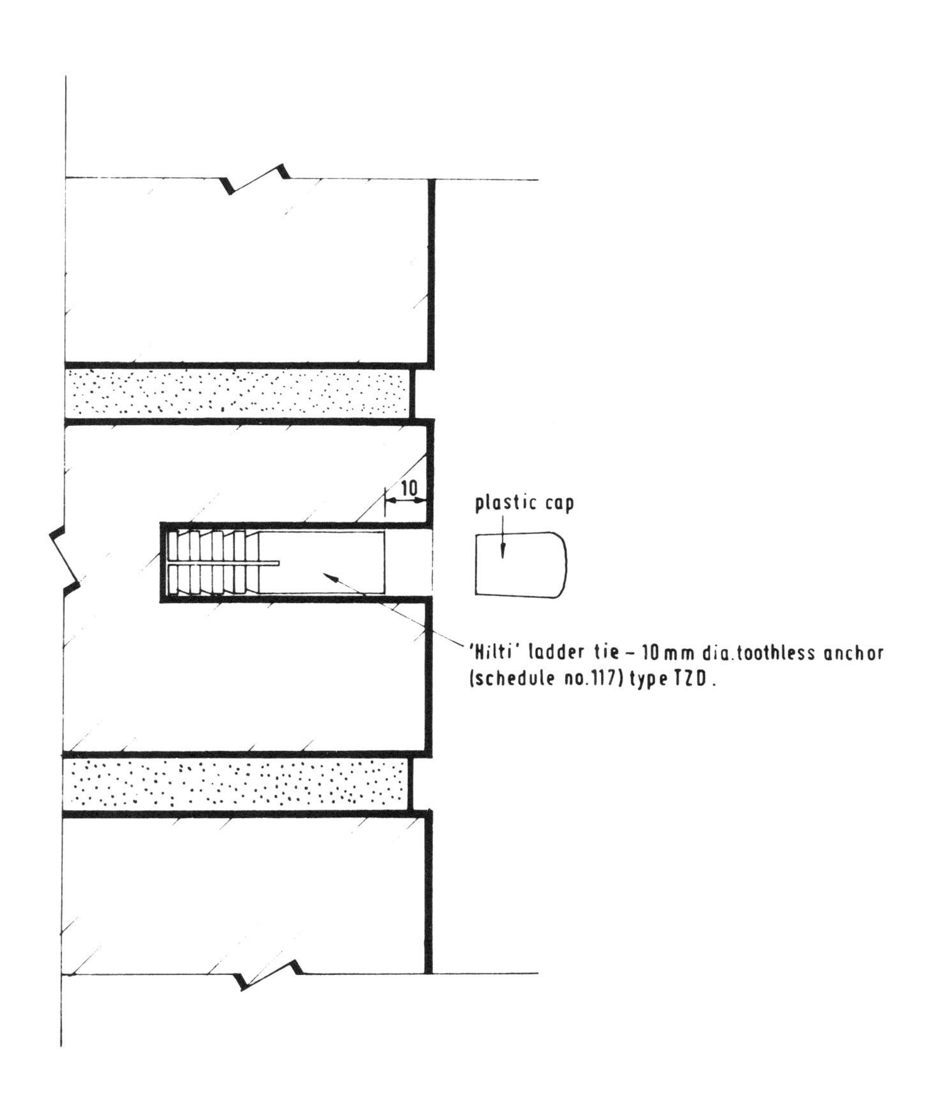

GLC ILEA

Department of Architecture and Civic Design
County Hall SE1
Architect Sir Roger Walters KBE FRIBA FI StructE

'Hilti' ladder tie – 10 mm dia. toothless anchor (schedule 117) type TZD, and 10 mm ring bolt to suit and also plastic cap, all supplied by employer. (NB. Ring bolts held by Director of Housing)

Departmental Standard Drawing

title
ANCHOR FOR LADDER TIE RINGS

scale
FULL SIZE

drawing no
D5067

[66] 662 Xh3 F

00-010379

8 Ducts

5350 Vertical duct
5351 Horizontal duct
5352 Horizontal duct at floor level
5353 Vertical duct (removable casing)
5354 Horizontal duct (removable casing)

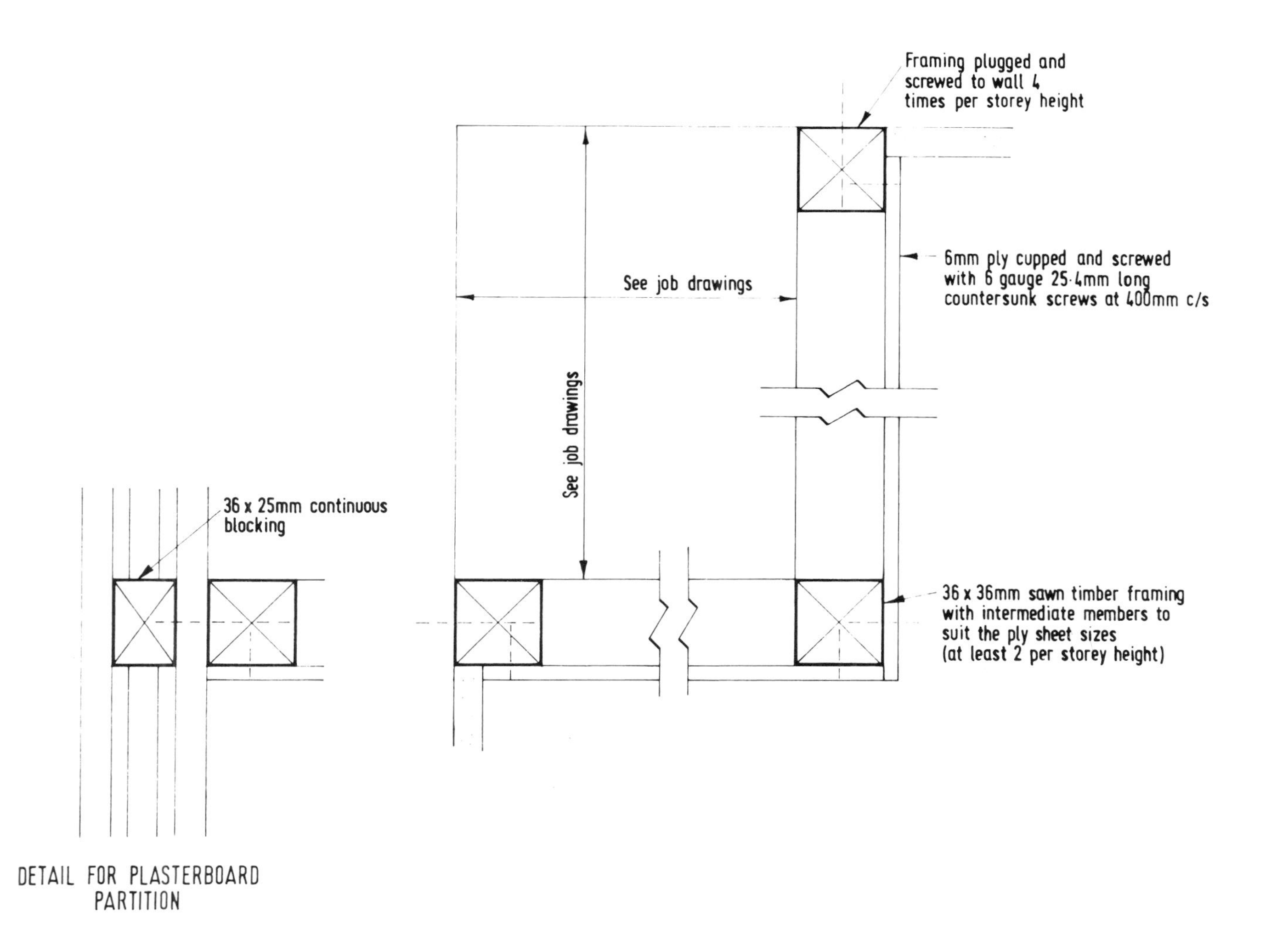

GLC ILEA

Department of Architecture and Civic Design
County Hall SE1 7PB
Architect Sir Roger Walters
KBE ARIBA FI Struct/E

References following notes are clause numbers from G.L.C. preambles to bills of quantities

All timber sawn softwood

Departmental Standard Drawing

title
CASING FOR VERTICAL DUCT
(NOT SUITABLE FOR GAS PIPES)
LIMITED ACCESS ONLY

scale 1 : 2

drawing no D5350 | rev

bldg type | spaceuse | element [22] | feature 659 | material Xi2 | key A

00 - 010379

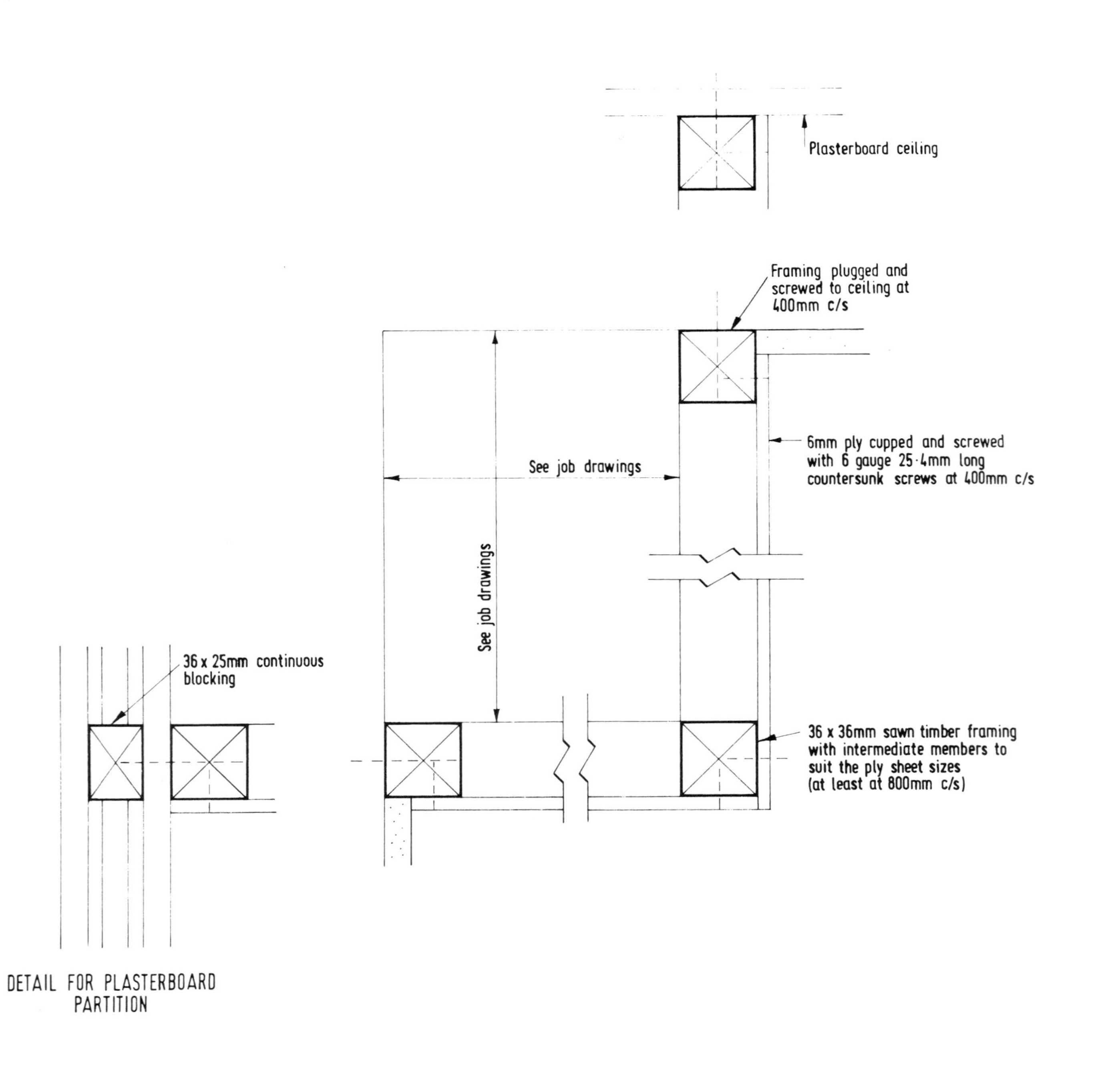

GLC ILEA

Department of Architecture and Civic Design
County Hall SE1 7PB
Architect Sir Roger Walters
KBE ARIBA FI Struct/E

References following notes are clause numbers from G.L.C. preambles to bills of quantities

All timber sawn softwood

Departmental Standard Drawing

title
CASING FOR HORIZONTAL DUCT
(NOT SUITABLE FOR GAS PIPES)
LIMITED ACCESS ONLY

scale
1 : 2

drawing no
D5351

rev

22 | 659 | Xi2 | B

010379

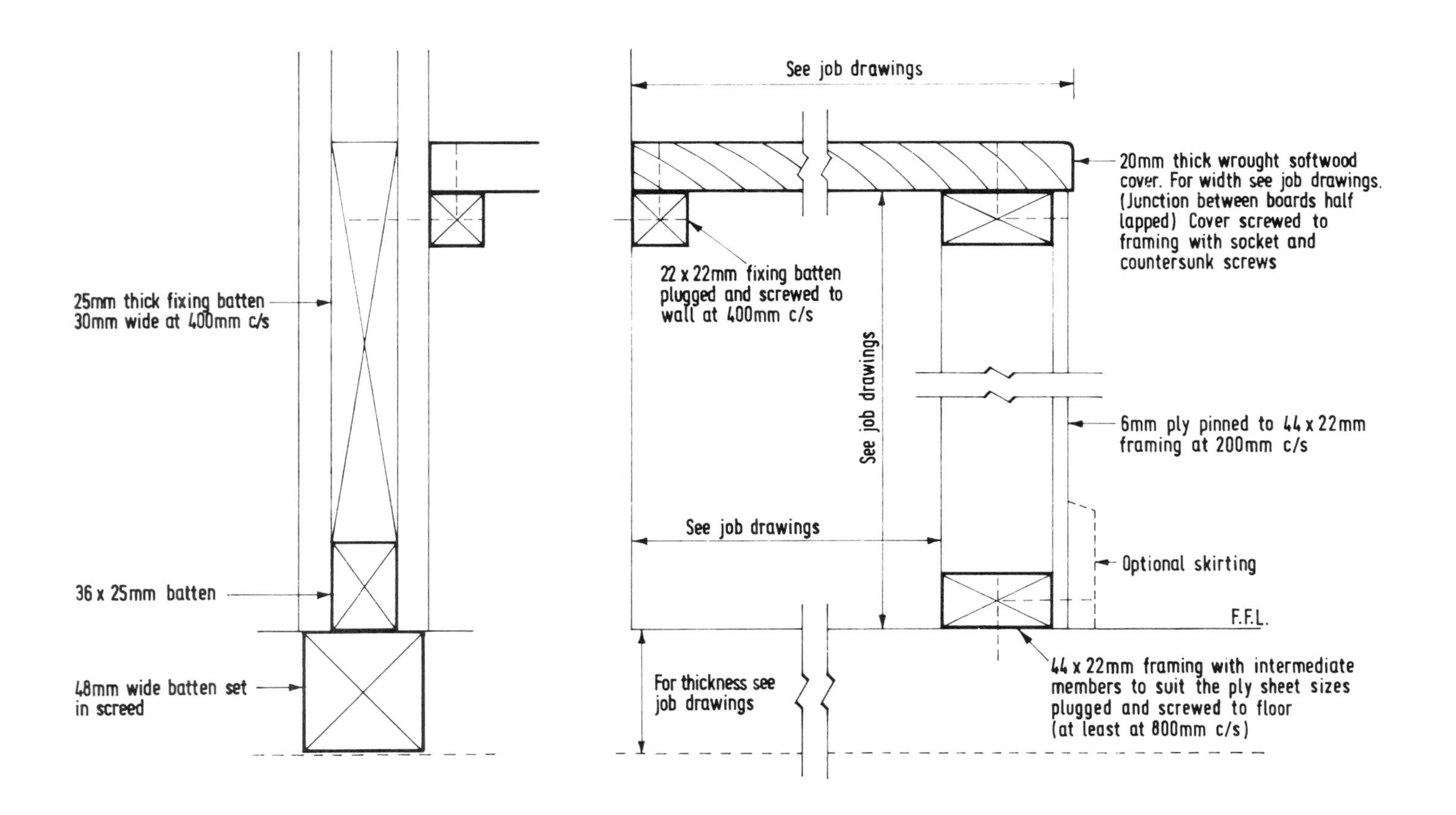

GLC ILEA

Department of Architecture
and Civic Design
County Hall SE1 7PB
Architect Sir Roger Walters
KBE ARIBA FI Struct/E

References following notes are clause numbers from G.L.C. preambles to bills of quantities

Framing timber sawn softwood

Departmental Standard Drawing

title

CASING FOR HORIZONTAL DUCT AT FLOOR LEVEL.
(NOT SUITABLE FOR GAS PIPES)

scale

1 : 2

drawing no	rev
D5352	

0 - 010379

bldg type	space use	element	feature	material	key
		[22]	659	Xi2	C

GLC ILEA

Department of Architecture and Civic Design
County Hall SE1 7PB
Architect Sir Roger Walters
KBE ARIBA FI Struct/E

References following notes are clause numbers from G.L.C. preambles to bills of quantities

All timber sawn softwood

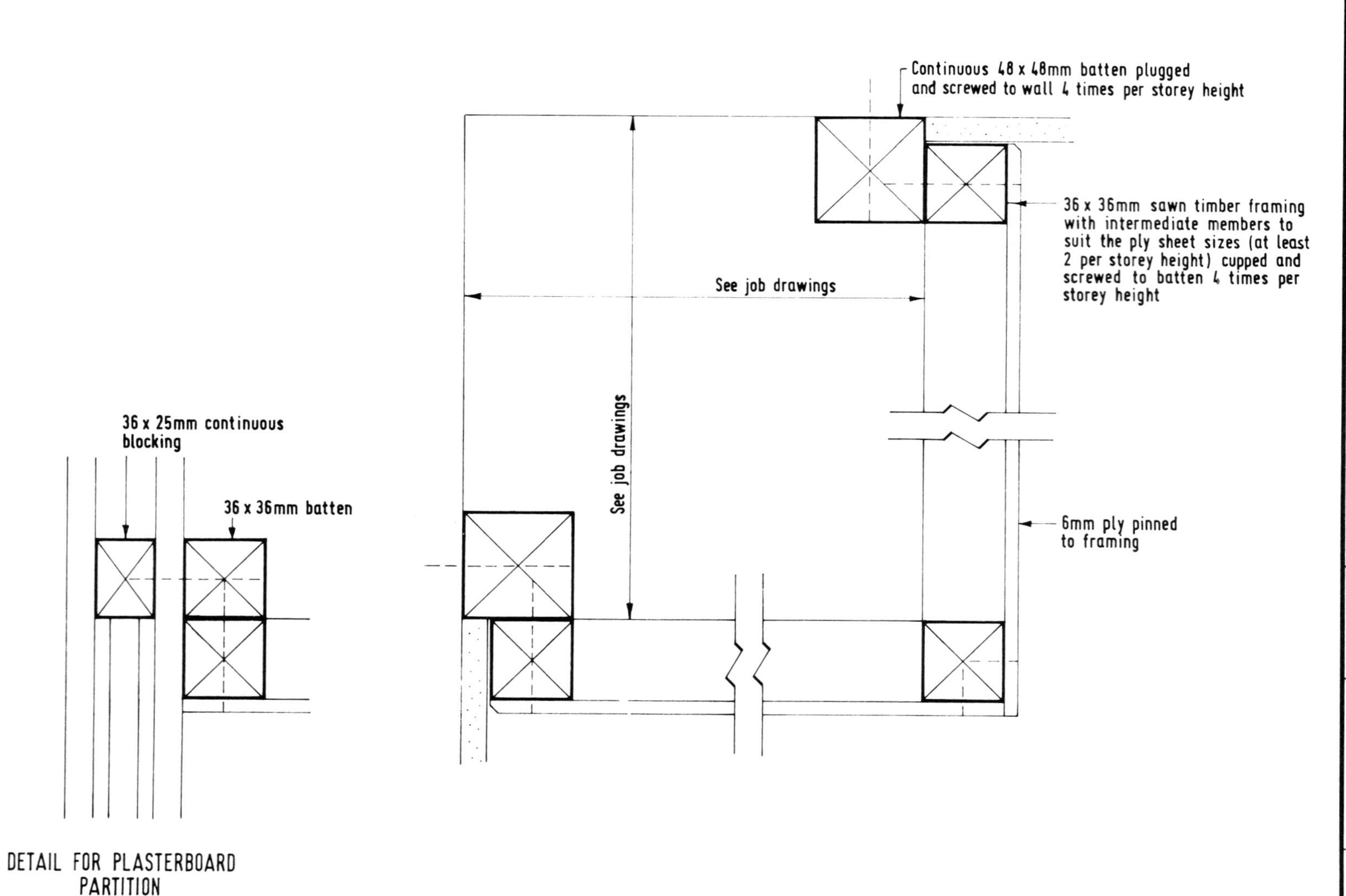

DETAIL FOR PLASTERBOARD PARTITION

Departmental Standard Drawing

title
REMOVABLE CASING FOR VERTICAL DUCT (NOT SUITABLE FOR GAS PIPES)

scale 1 : 2

drawing no D5353 | rev

bldgtype | spaceuse | element (22) | feature 659 | material Xi2 | key D

OI0379 - II

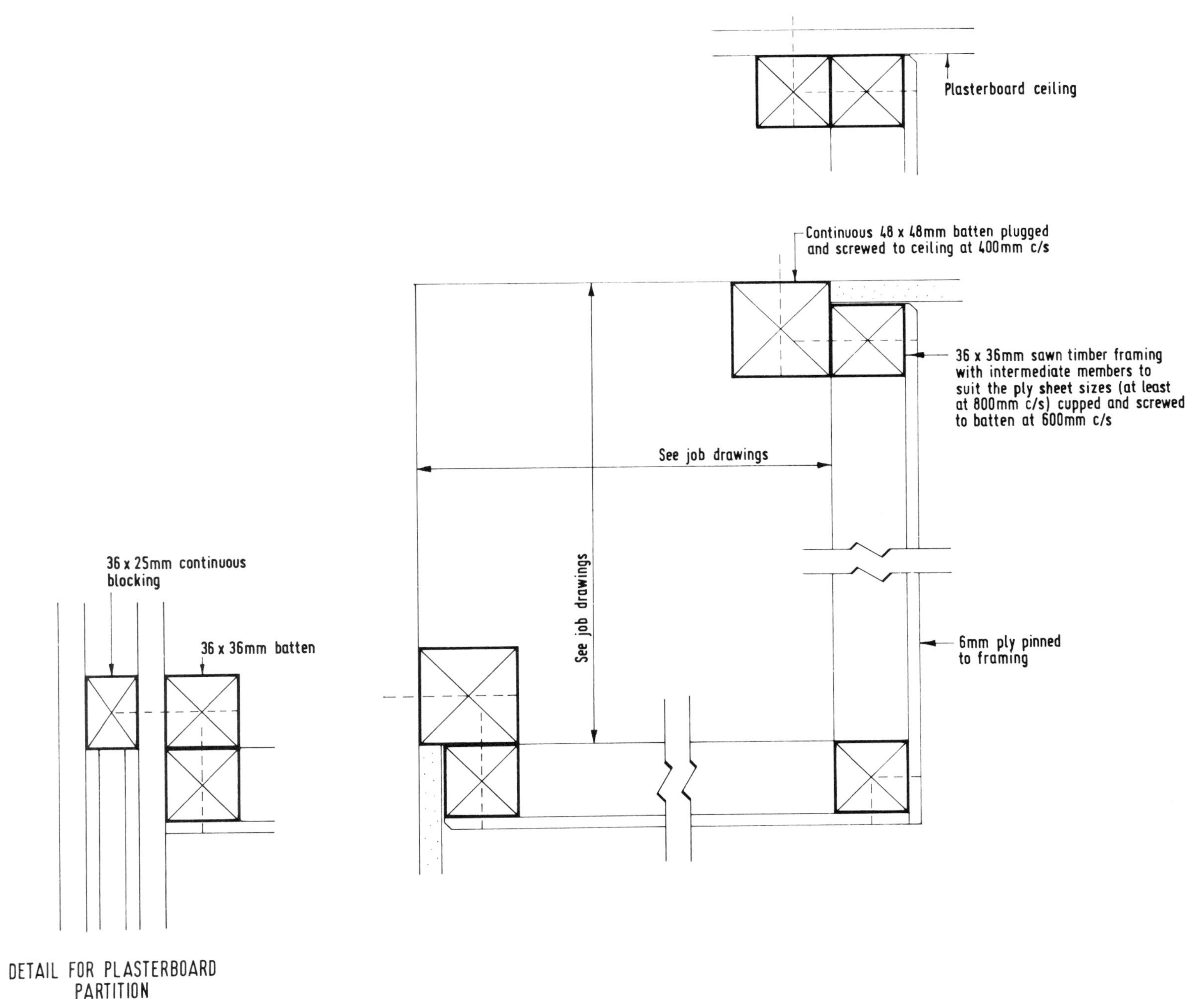

GLC ILEA

Department of Architecture and Civic Design
County Hall SE1 7PB
Architect Sir Roger Walters
KBE ARIBA FI Struct/E

References following notes are clause numbers from G.L.C. preambles to bills of quantities

All timber sawn softwood

Departmental Standard Drawing

title
REMOVABLE CASING FOR HORIZONTAL DUCT
(NOT SUITABLE FOR GAS PIPES)

scale
1 : 2

bldg type	space use	element	feature	material	key
		22	659	Xi2	E

drawing no: D5354
rev

9 Refuse disposal

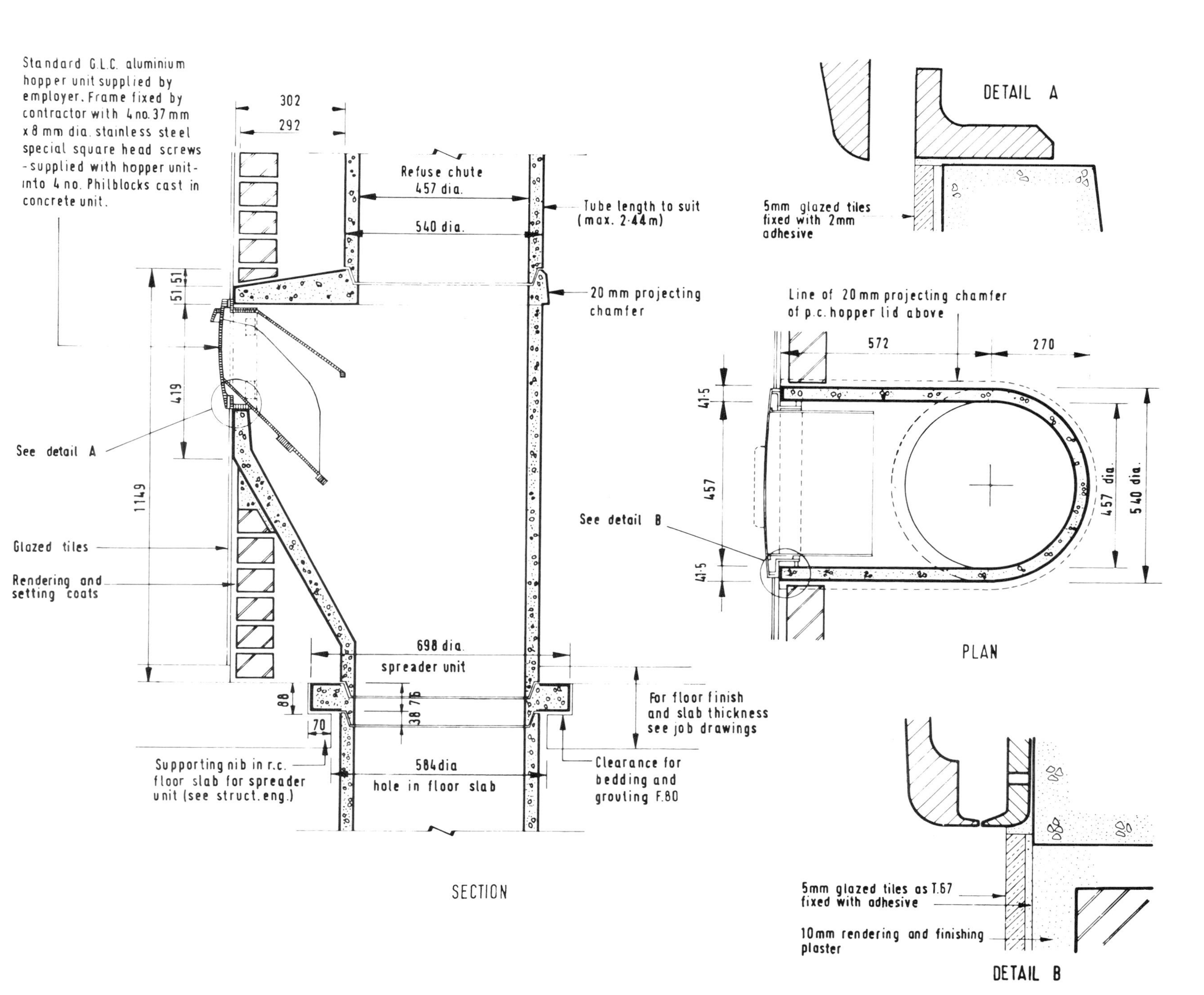

GLC ILEA

Department of Architecture and Civic Design
County Hall SE1
Architect Sir Roger Walters KBE FRIBA FI StructE

References following notes are clause numbers from G.L.C. preambles to bills of quantities

Refuse chute concrete units shown supplied by
Spun Concrete Ltd.
Rye Harbour,
Sussex.

Departmental Standard Drawing

title
REFUSE CHUTE
PRECAST CONCRETE UNITS
TILED FACING WALL

scale 1:10 & 1:1

drawing no D5050

bldg type | space use [51] | element [51] | feature 721 | material Xf2 | key A5

010379 - 00

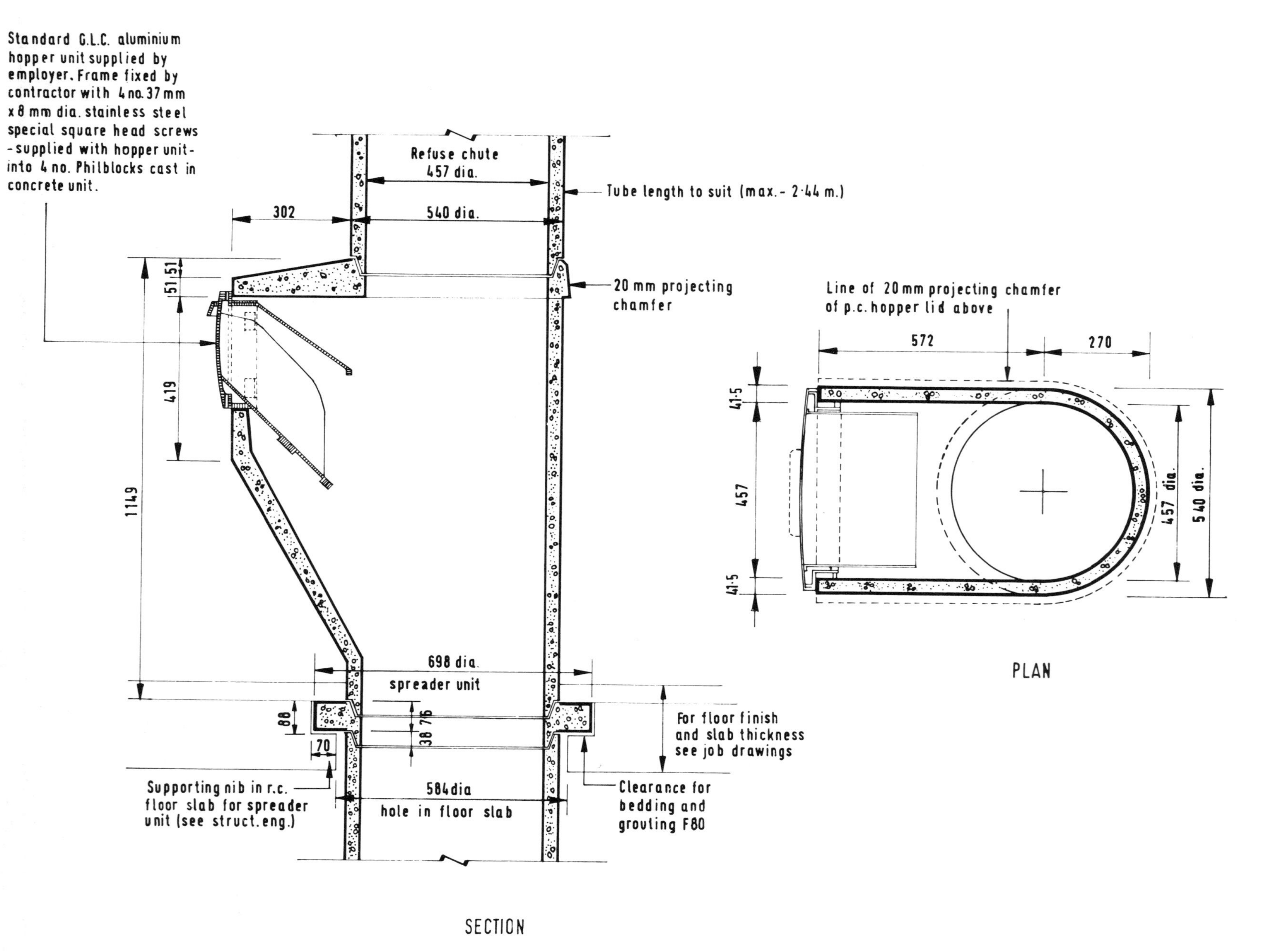

GLC ILEA

Department of Architecture and Civic Design
County Hall SE1
Architect Sir Roger Walters
KBE FRIBA FI StructE

References following notes are clause numbers from G.L.C. preambles to bills of quantities

Refuse chute concrete units shown supplied by
Spun Concrete Ltd.
Rye Harbour,
Sussex.

6/23 - 010379

Departmental Standard Drawing

title
REFUSE CHUTE
PRECAST CONCRETE UNITS

bldg type	space use	element	feature	material	key
		51	721	Xf2	A1

scale
1:10

drawing no
D 5051

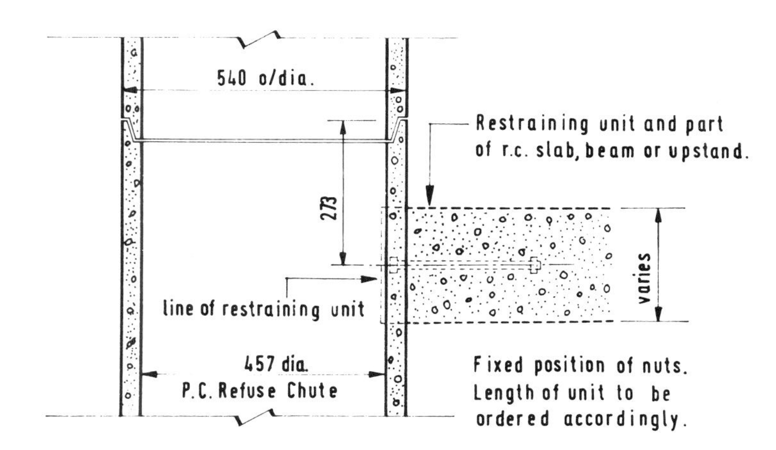

SECTION

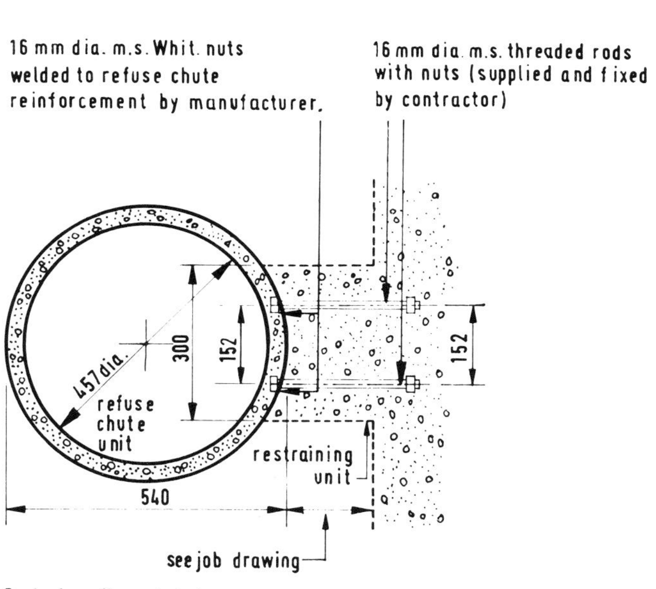

PLAN

GLC ILEA

Department of Architecture and Civic Design
County Hall SE1
Architect Sir Roger Walters KBE FRIBA FI StructE

References following notes are clause numbers from G.L.C. preambles to bills of quantities

Refuse chute units shown supplied by:

Spun Concrete Ltd.
Rye Harbour,
Sussex.

Departmental Standard Drawing

title

REFUSE CHUTE
CONCRETE RESTRAINING UNIT

scale 1:10

drawing no D5052

bldg type | space use | element [51] | feature 721 | material Xf2 | key A2

00 - 010379

GLC ILEA

Department of Architecture
and Civic Design
County Hall SE1
Architect Sir Roger Walters
KBE FRIBA FI StructE

References following notes are clause numbers from G.L.C. preambles to bills of quantities

P.C. refuse chute concrete units shown supplied by
Spun Concrete Ltd.
Rye Harbour,
Sussex.

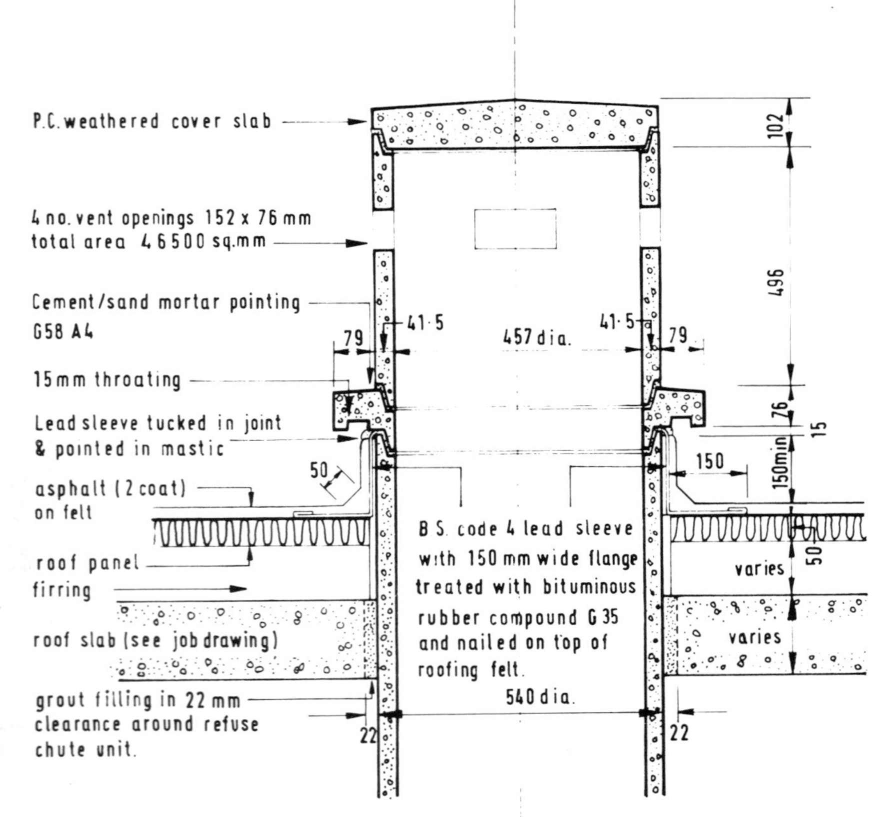

Key A3

D.S.'s advice to be sought for pipe enclosure on top floor to achieve 1 hour fire resistance

For asbestos-cement vent terminal at roof level see drawing no. D5058 (concrete roof) D5059 (timber roof)

Cement/sand mortar G58 A4

Firmly caulked asbestos string

Special cover

150 mm dia. asbestos-cement vent pipe and socket, heavy quality, to B.S. 835

Floor finish & slab as job drawing

100

Grout filling in 22 mm clearance around refuse chute unit

457 dia

540 dia

P.c. refuse chute unit

22

22

Key A4

Departmental Standard Drawing

title

ASBESTOS-CEMENT AND P.C. VENT UNITS FOR REFUSE CHUTE

scale

1:10

drawing no

D5053B

010379 00

(51) 721 Xf2 as drawing

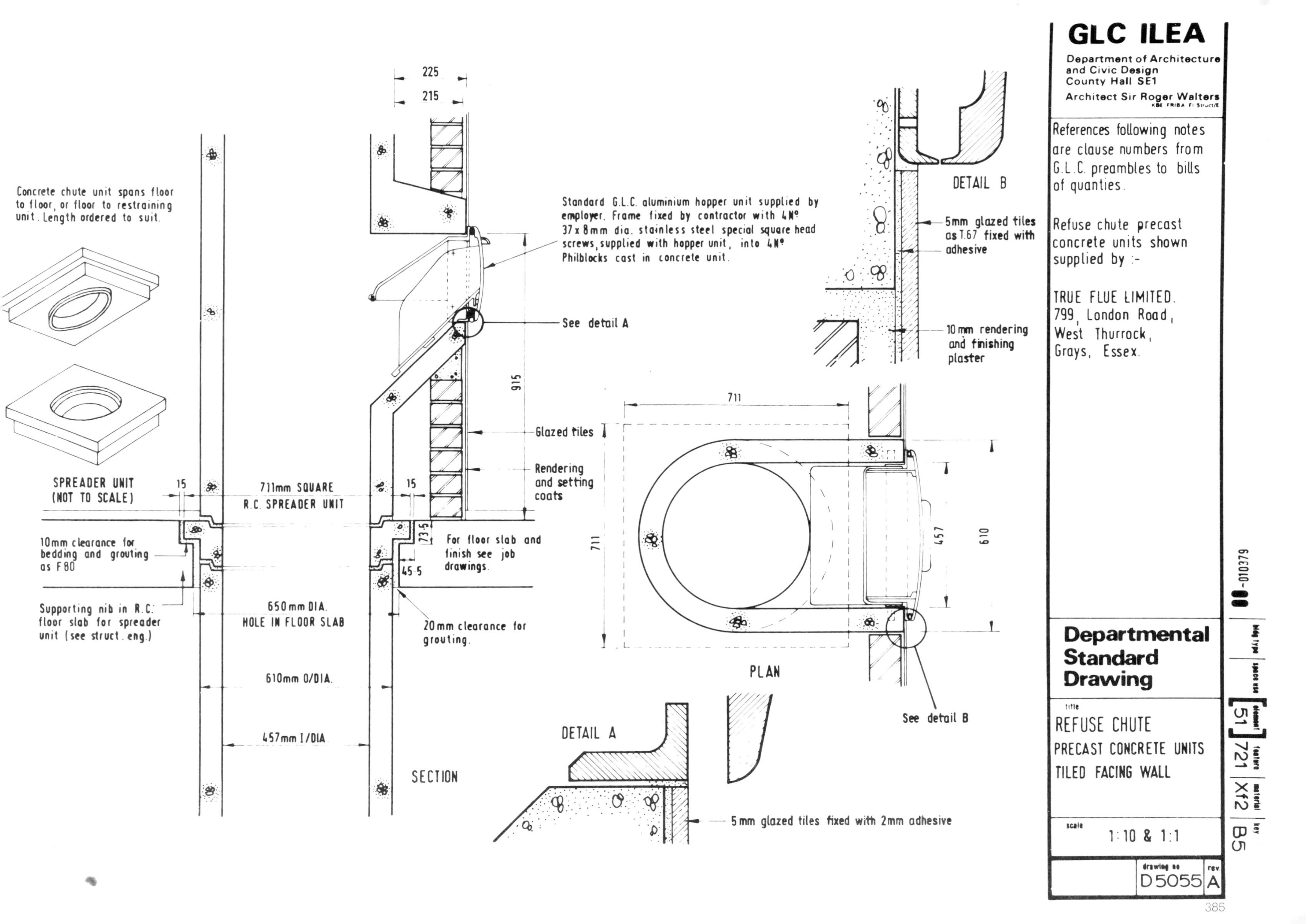
GLC ILEA
Department of Architecture
and Civic Design
County Hall SE1
Architect Sir Roger Walters
KBE FRIBA FI Struct/E
References following notes are clause numbers from G.L.C. preambles to bills of quanties.
Refuse chute precast concrete units shown supplied by :-
TRUE FLUE LIMITED.
799, London Road,
West Thurrock,
Grays, Essex.
Departmental Standard Drawing
title
REFUSE CHUTE
PRECAST CONCRETE UNITS
TILED FACING WALL
scale
1:10 & 1:1
drawing no
D5055
rev
A
51
721
Xf2
B5
010379
Concrete chute unit spans floor to floor, or floor to restraining unit. Length ordered to suit.
SPREADER UNIT
(NOT TO SCALE)
225
215
Standard G.L.C. aluminium hopper unit supplied by employer. Frame fixed by contractor with 4 Nº 37 x 8mm dia. stainless steel special square head screws, supplied with hopper unit, into 4 Nº Philblocks cast in concrete unit.
See detail A
915
Glazed tiles
Rendering and setting coats
15
711mm SQUARE
R.C. SPREADER UNIT
15
73.5
45.5
For floor slab and finish see job drawings.
10mm clearance for bedding and grouting as F80
Supporting nib in R.C. floor slab for spreader unit (see struct. eng.)
650mm DIA.
HOLE IN FLOOR SLAB
20mm clearance for grouting.
610mm O/DIA.
457mm I/DIA.
SECTION
DETAIL B
5mm glazed tiles as T.67 fixed with adhesive
10mm rendering and finishing plaster
711
711
457
610
PLAN
See detail B
DETAIL A
5mm glazed tiles fixed with 2mm adhesive

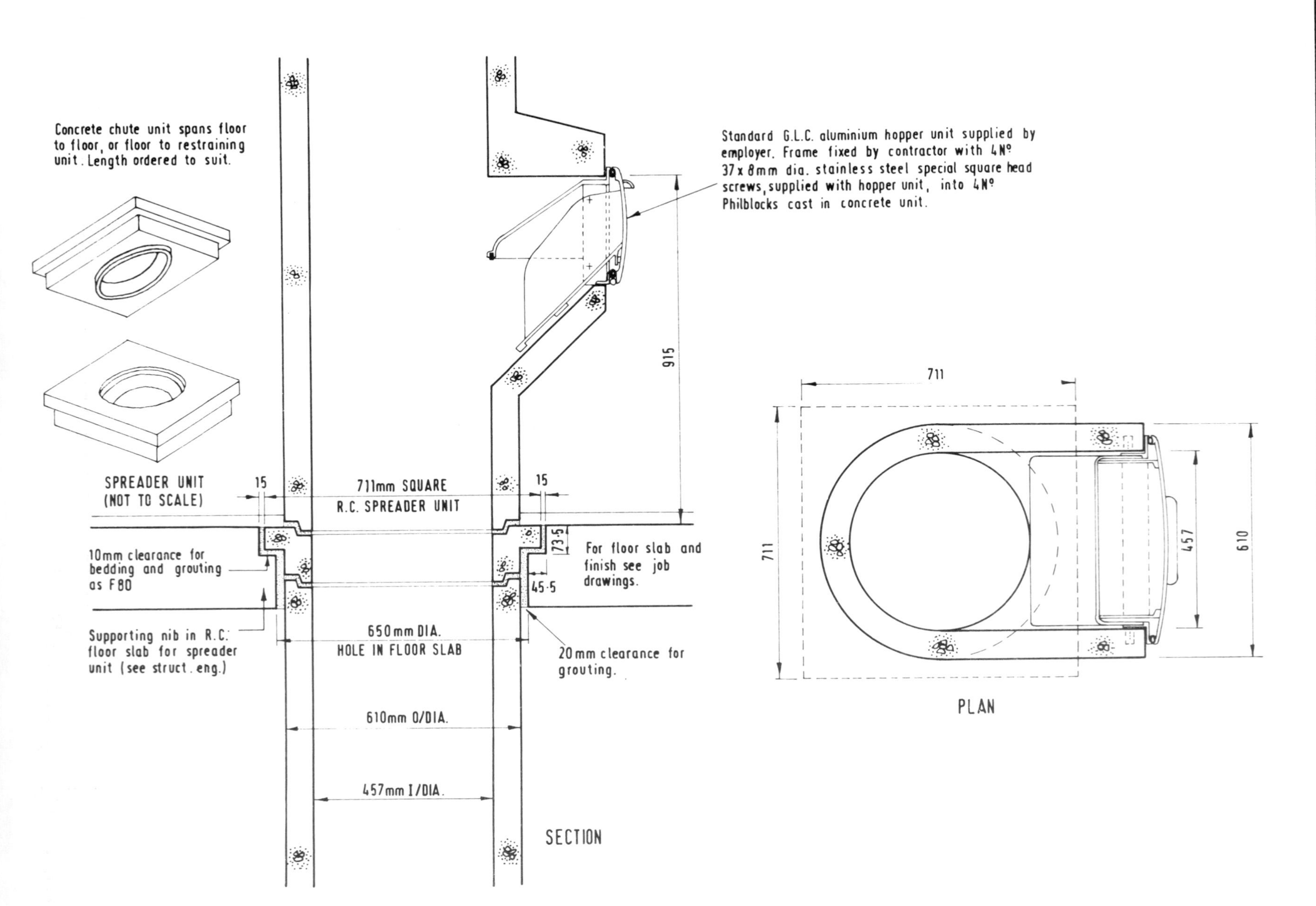

GLC ILEA

Department of Architecture and Civic Design
County Hall SE1
Architect Sir Roger Walters
KBE FRIBA FI StructE

References following notes are clause numbers from G.L.C. preambles to bills of quanties.

Refuse chute precast concrete units shown supplied by :-

TRUE FLUE LIMITED.
799, London Road,
West Thurrock,
Grays, Essex.

Departmental Standard Drawing

title
REFUSE CHUTE
PRECAST CONCRETE UNITS

scale
1:10

drawing no D5056 rev. A

[51] 721 Xf2 B1

010379

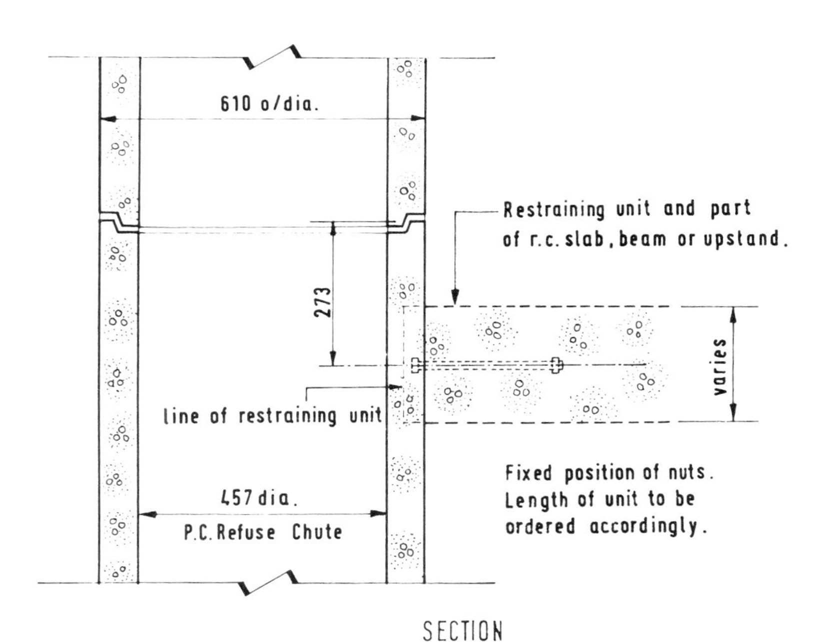

SECTION

16 mm dia. m.s. Whit. nuts welded to refuse chute reinforcement by manufacturer.

16 mm dia. m.s. threaded rods with nuts (supplied and fixed by contractor)

457 dia.

300

refuse chute unit

152

restraining unit

610 dia.

see job drawing

Part of r.c. floor slab, beam or upstand, determined by structural engineer, to be cast simultaneously with restraining unit.

PLAN

GLC ILEA

Department of Architecture
and Civic Design
County Hall SE1

Architect Sir Roger Walters
KBE FRIBA FI StructE

References following notes are clause numbers from G.L.C. preambles to bills of quantities

Refuse chute units shown supplied by:

TRUE FLUE LIMITED
799, London Road,
West Thurrock,
Grays, Essex,

Departmental Standard Drawing

title

REFUSE CHUTE
CONCRETE RESTRAINING UNIT

scale 1:10

drawing no D5057

00 - 010379

bldg type | space use | element [51] | feature 721 | material Xf2 | key B2

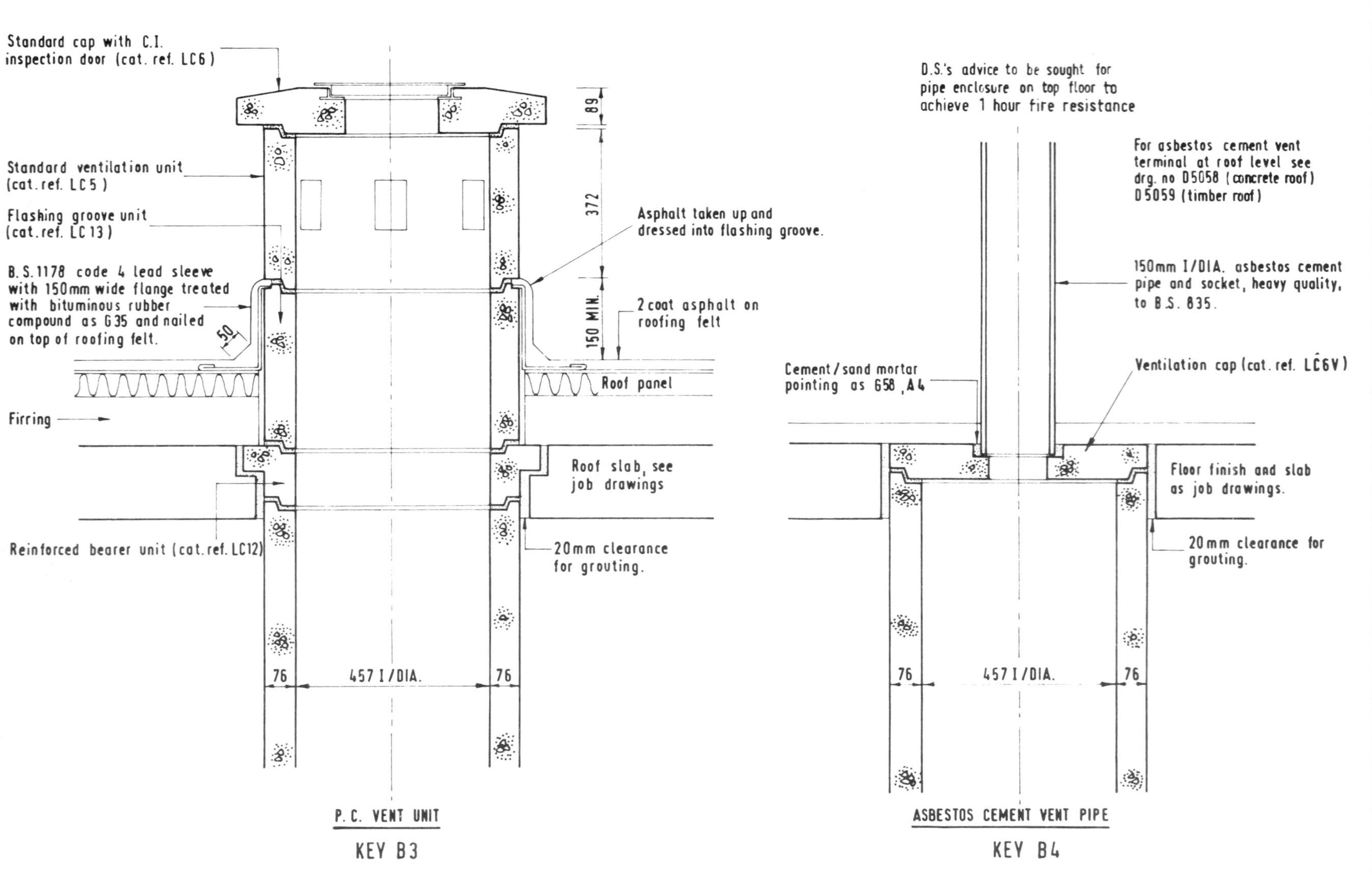

GLC ILEA

Department of Architecture and Civic Design
County Hall SE1
Architect Sir Roger Walters KBE FRIBA FI StructE

References following notes are clause numbers from G.L.C. preambles to bills of quantities.

Refuse chute precast concrete units shown supplied by :-

TRUE FLUE LIMITED.
799, London Road,
West Thurrock,
Grays, Essex.

Departmental Standard Drawing

title

REFUSE CHUTE
PRECAST CONCRETE AND ASBESTOS CEMENT VENT UNITS.

scale 1:10

drawing no D5054B

00 - 01B379 | [51] 721 | Xf2 | as drawing

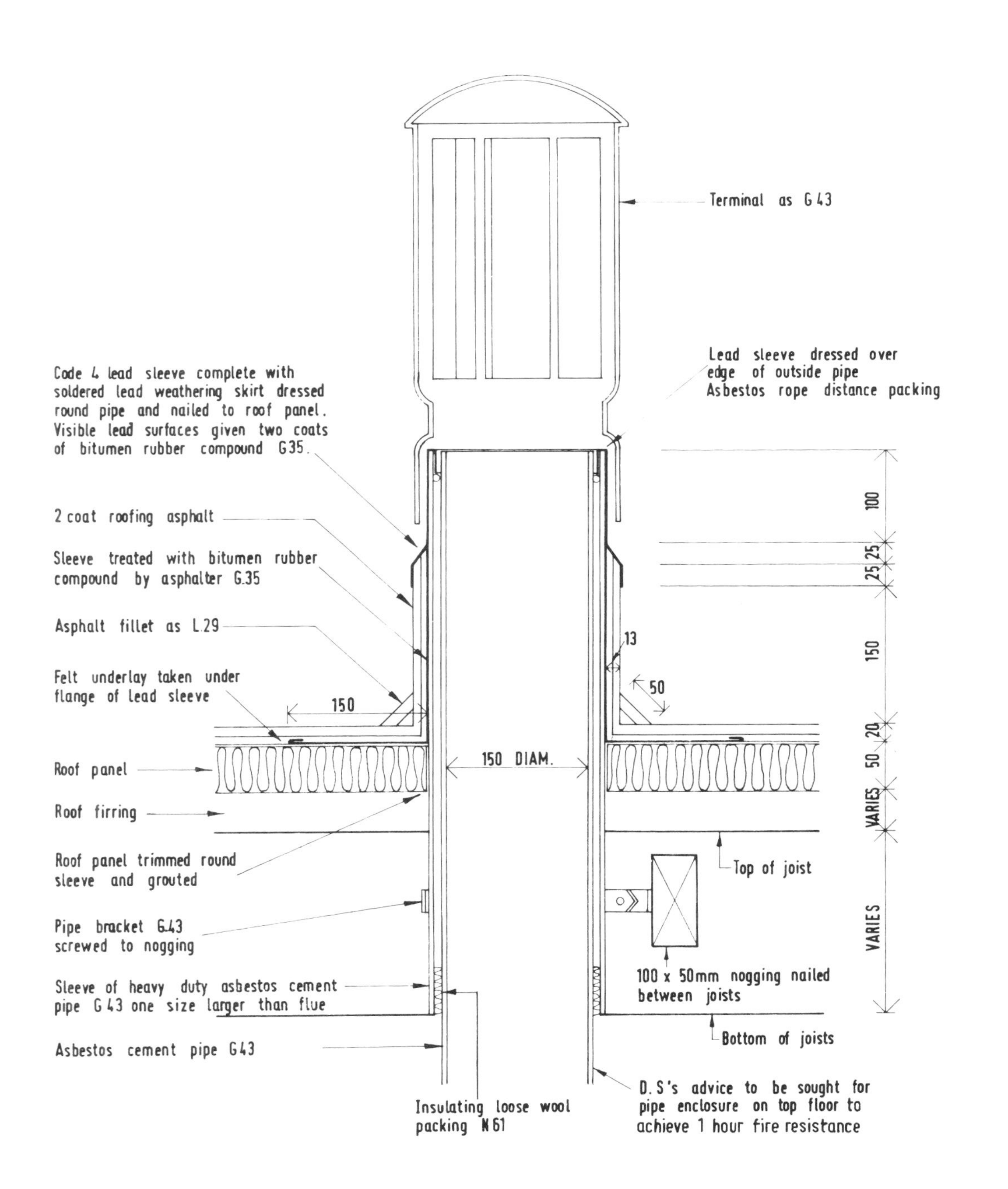

GLC ILEA

Department of Architecture and Civic Design
County Hall SE1
Architect Sir Roger Walters
KBE FRIBA FI StructE

References following notes are clause numbers from G.L.C. preambles to bills of quantities.

For full description of roof finish see drawing number [47] D5000.

This drawing is to be read with [51]D5053 or D5054.

Departmental Standard Drawing

title
ASBESTOS CEMENT VENT PIPE FOR REFUSE CHUTE

TIMBER ROOF.

scale 1:5

drawing no D5059A

bldg type | space use | element [51] | feature 721 | material Xf6 | key B

010379

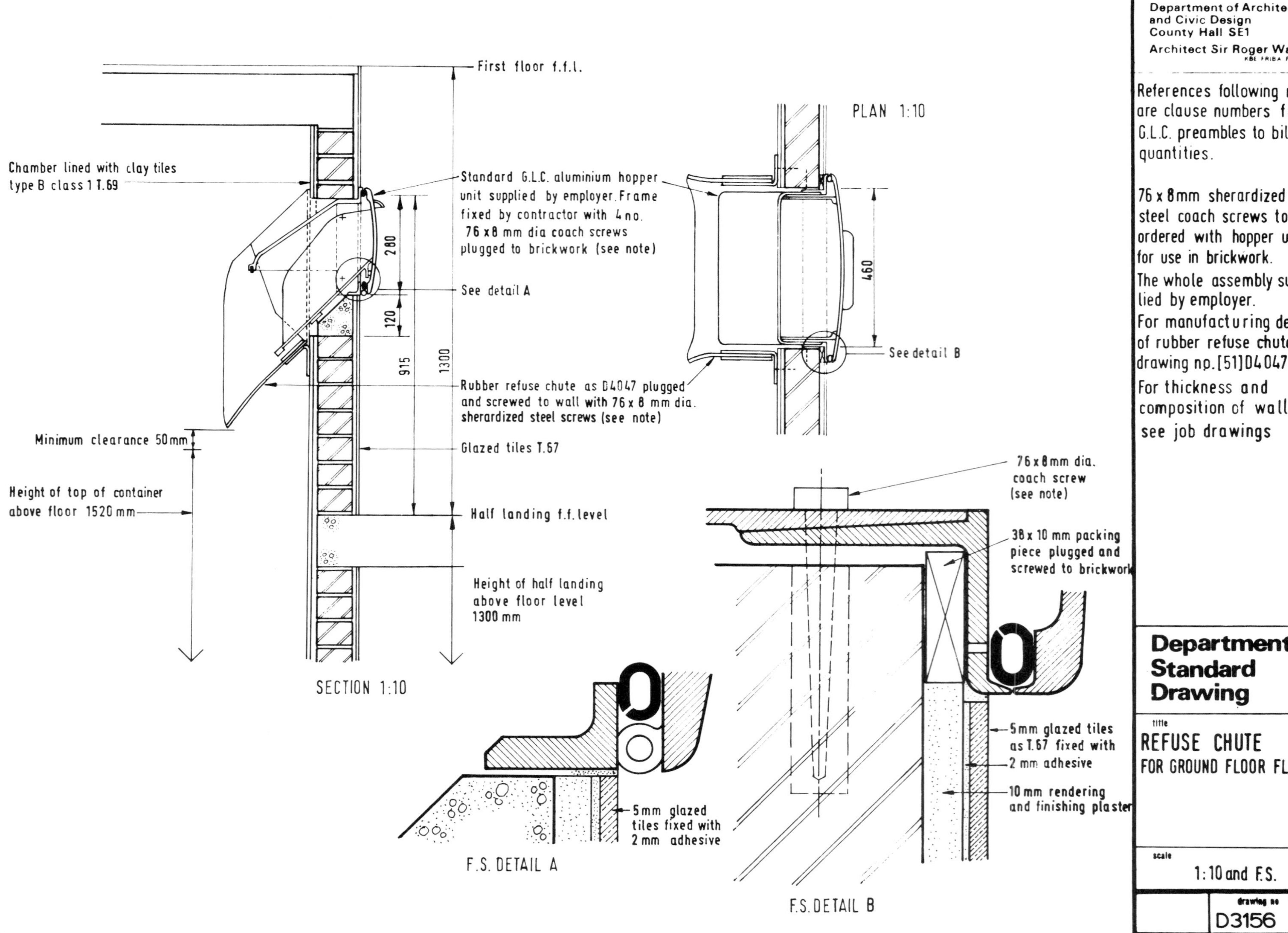

GLC ILEA
Department of Architecture and Civic Design
County Hall SE1
Architect Sir Roger Walters
References following notes are clause numbers from G.L.C. preambles to bills of quantities.
76 x 8mm sherardized steel coach screws to be ordered with hopper unit for use in brickwork.
The whole assembly supplied by employer.
For manufacturing details of rubber refuse chute see drawing no.[51]D4047.
For thickness and composition of wall see job drawings
Departmental Standard Drawing
title
REFUSE CHUTE
FOR GROUND FLOOR FLATS
scale
1:10 and F.S.
drawing no
D3156
rev
C
[51] 721 Xh4 C
First floor f.f.l.
Chamber lined with clay tiles type B class 1 T.69
Standard G.L.C. aluminium hopper unit supplied by employer. Frame fixed by contractor with 4 no. 76 x 8 mm dia coach screws plugged to brickwork (see note)
See detail A
280
120
915
1300
Rubber refuse chute as D4047 plugged and screwed to wall with 76 x 8 mm dia. sherardized steel screws (see note)
Minimum clearance 50mm
Glazed tiles T.67
Height of top of container above floor 1520 mm
Half landing f.f. level
Height of half landing above floor level 1300 mm
SECTION 1:10
PLAN 1:10
460
See detail B
76 x 8mm dia. coach screw (see note)
38 x 10 mm packing piece plugged and screwed to brickwork
5mm glazed tiles as T.67 fixed with 2 mm adhesive
10 mm rendering and finishing plaster
F.S. DETAIL B
5mm glazed tiles fixed with 2 mm adhesive
F.S. DETAIL A

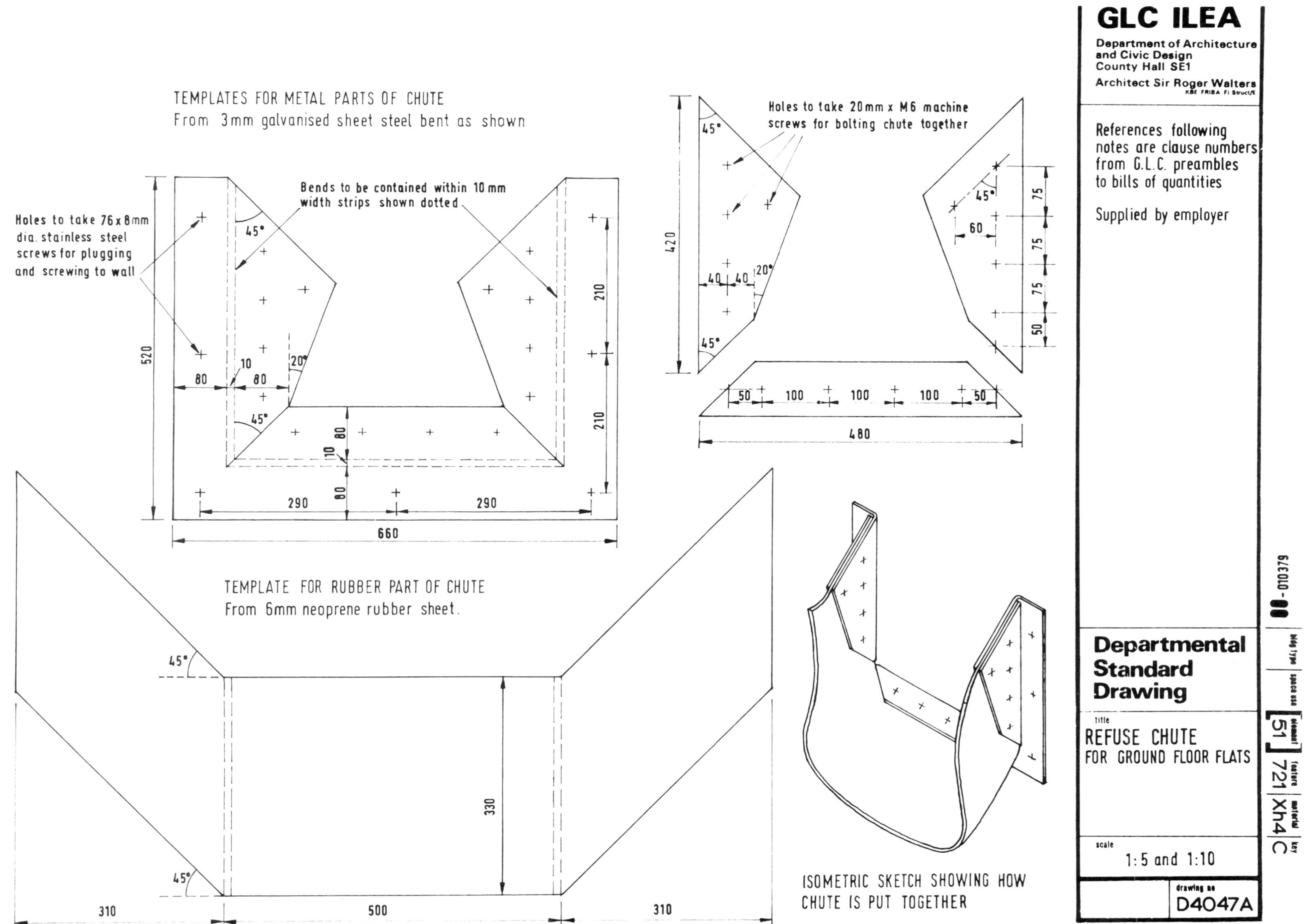

GLC ILEA
Department of Architecture and Civic Design
County Hall SE1
Architect Sir Roger Walters
KBE FRIBA FI StructE
References following notes are clause numbers from G.L.C. preambles to bills of quantities
Supplied by employer
TEMPLATES FOR METAL PARTS OF CHUTE
From 3mm galvanised sheet steel bent as shown
Holes to take 76 x 8mm dia. stainless steel screws for plugging and screwing to wall
Bends to be contained within 10 mm width strips shown dotted
Holes to take 20mm x M6 machine screws for bolting chute together
TEMPLATE FOR RUBBER PART OF CHUTE
From 6mm neoprene rubber sheet.
ISOMETRIC SKETCH SHOWING HOW CHUTE IS PUT TOGETHER
Departmental Standard Drawing
title
REFUSE CHUTE
FOR GROUND FLOOR FLATS
scale
1:5 and 1:10
drawing no
D4047A
00-010379
bldg type
space use
element
[51]
feature
721
material
Xh4
key
C

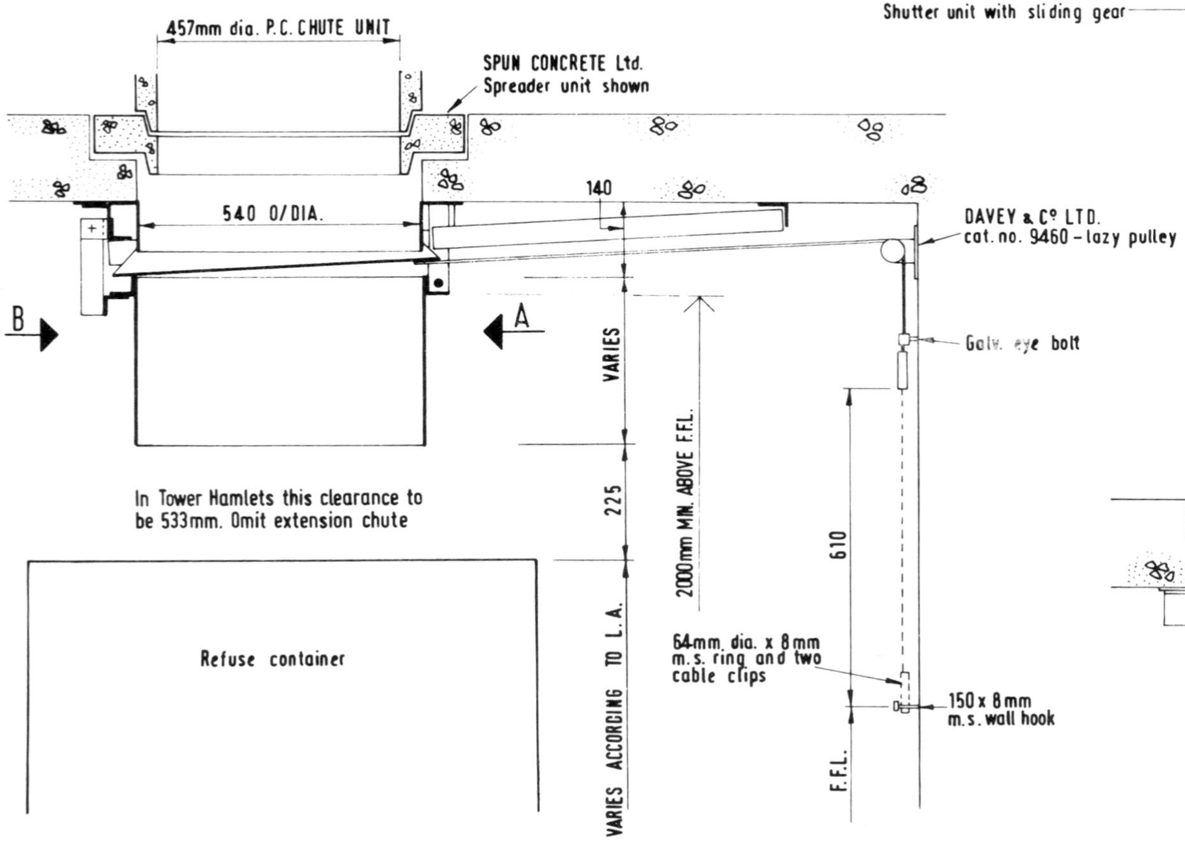

SECTION

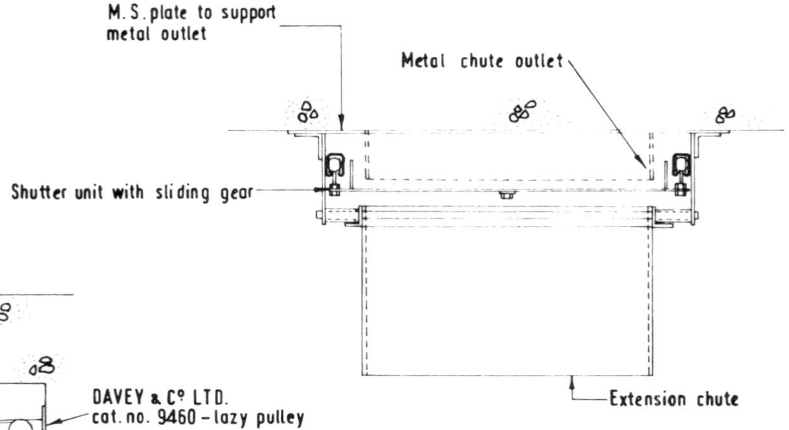

ELEVATION A

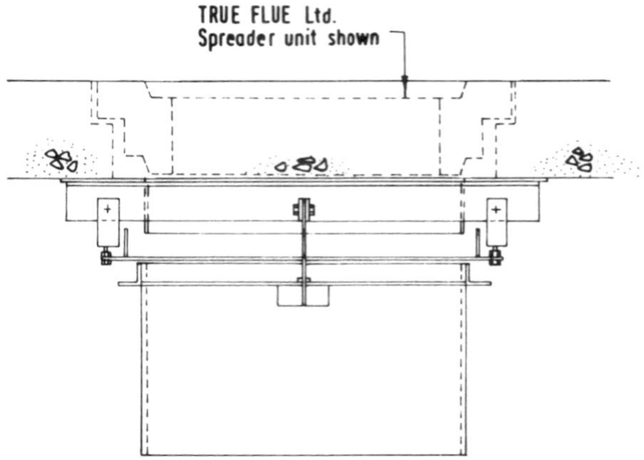

ELEVATION B

GLC ILEA

Department of Architecture
and Civic Design
County Hall SE1
Architect Sir Roger Walters
KBE FRIBA FI Struct/E

References following notes are clause numbers from G.L.C. preambles to bills of quantities.

This drawing is to be read in conjunction with drg. numbers D 4052, D 4053.

All steel parts to be galvanised mild steel.

Galv. m.s. cut-off to be supplied by contractor.

Steel wire and pulley system are standard iron-mongery items.

Departmental Standard Drawing

title

REFUSE CHUTE
CUT OFF UNIT

scale
1:10

drawing no: D3153 rev. A

010379

drg type | space use | element | feature | material | key
[51] 721 | Xh2 | A

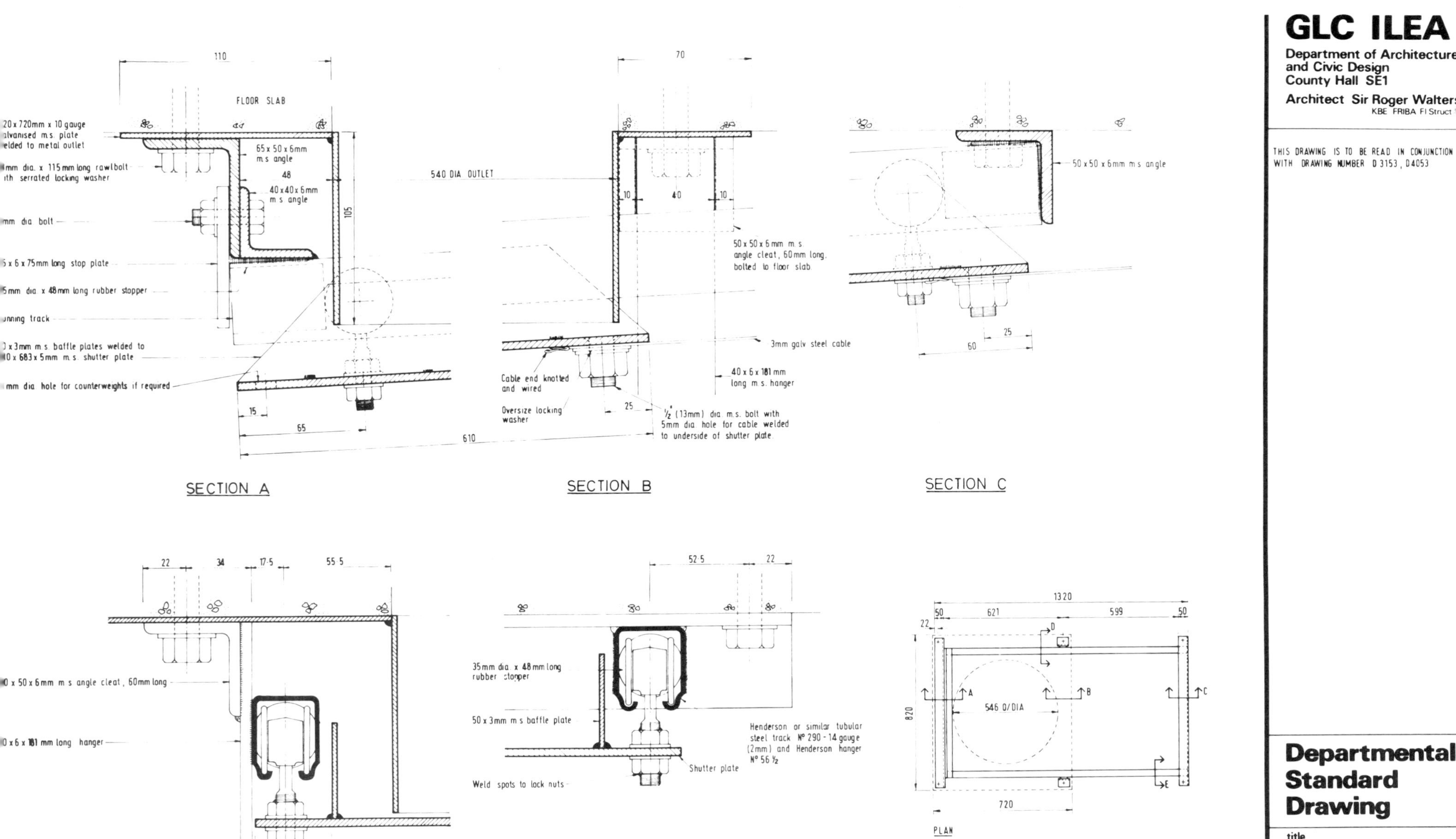
FLOOR SLAB
20 x 720mm x 10 gauge
alvanised m.s. plate
elded to metal outlet
mm dia. x 115mm long rawlbolt
ith serrated locking washer
mm dia bolt
5 x 6 x 75mm long stop plate
5mm dia x 48mm long rubber stopper
unning track
) x 3mm m.s. baffle plates welded to
0 x 683 x 5mm m.s. shutter plate
mm dia hole for counterweights if required
65 x 50 x 6mm m.s. angle
40 x 40 x 6mm m.s. angle
540 DIA OUTLET
SECTION A
50 x 50 x 6mm m.s. angle cleat, 60mm long, bolted to floor slab
3mm galv steel cable
40 x 6 x 181 mm long m.s. hanger
Cable end knotted and wired
Oversize locking washer
½" (13mm) dia m.s. bolt with 5mm dia hole for cable welded to underside of shutter plate
SECTION B
50 x 50 x 6mm m.s. angle
SECTION C
0 x 50 x 6mm m.s. angle cleat, 60mm long
0 x 6 x 181 mm long hanger
SECTION D
35mm dia x 48mm long rubber stopper
50 x 3mm m.s. baffle plate
Weld spots to lock nuts
Henderson or similar tubular steel track Nº 290 - 14 gauge (2mm) and Henderson hanger Nº 56 ½
Shutter plate
SECTION E
546 O/DIA
PLAN
SHUTTER PLATE

GLC ILEA
Department of Architecture and Civic Design
County Hall SE1
Architect Sir Roger Walters
KBE FRIBA FI Struct E
THIS DRAWING IS TO BE READ IN CONJUNCTION WITH DRAWING NUMBER D 3153, D 4053
Departmental Standard Drawing
title
REFUSE CHUTE
CUT OFF UNIT
FULL SIZE DETAILS
scale
1:1 and 1:10
drawing no
D 4052A
bldg type
space use
element 51
feature 721
material Xh2
key A

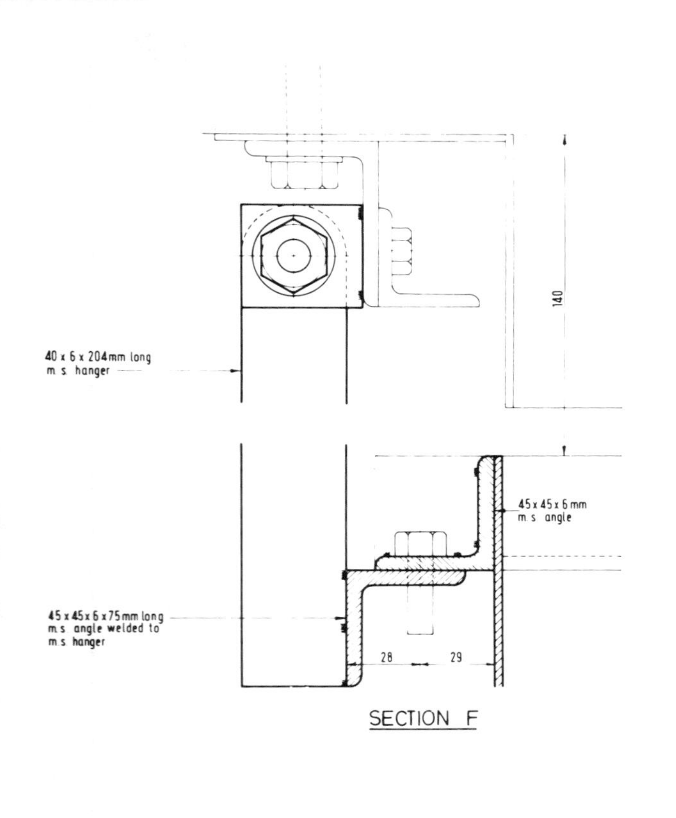

SECTION F

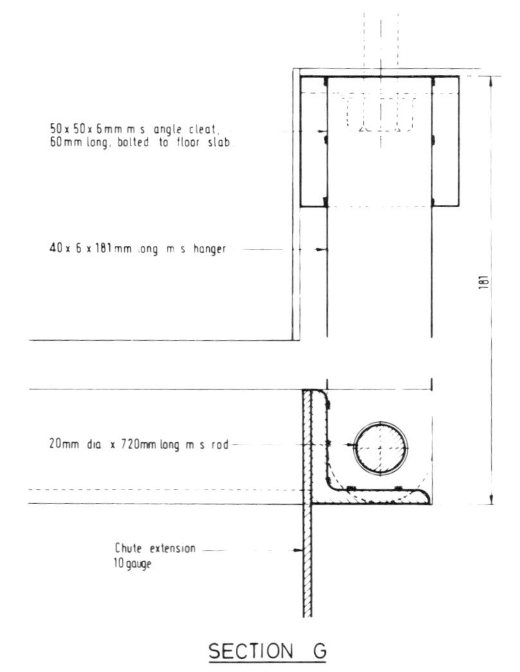

SECTION G

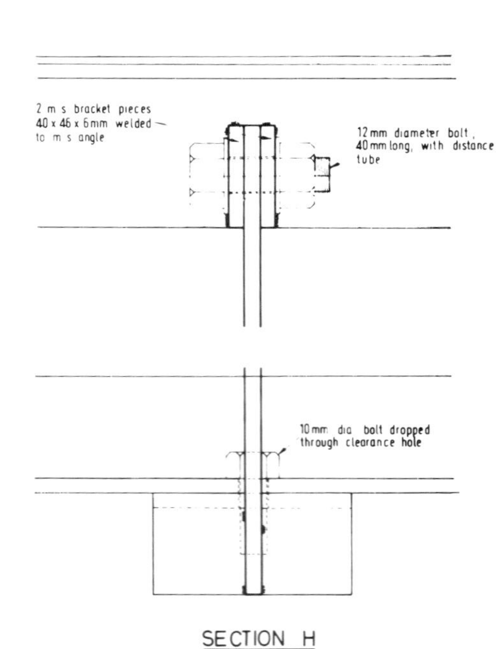

SECTION H

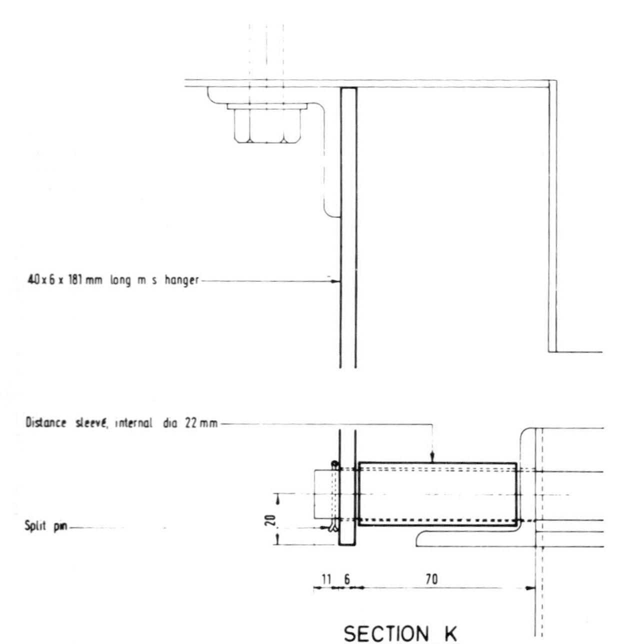

SECTION K

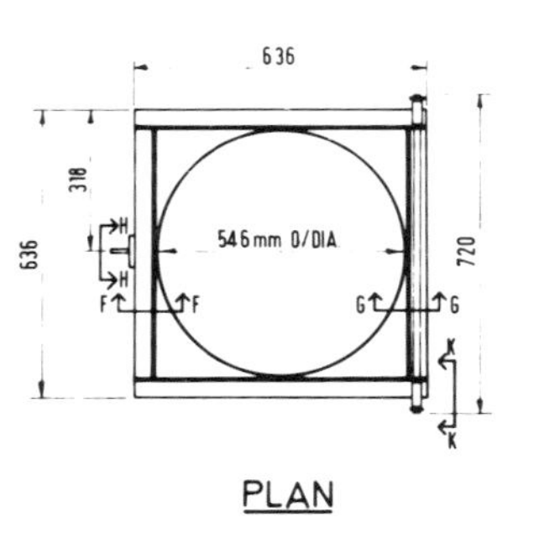

PLAN

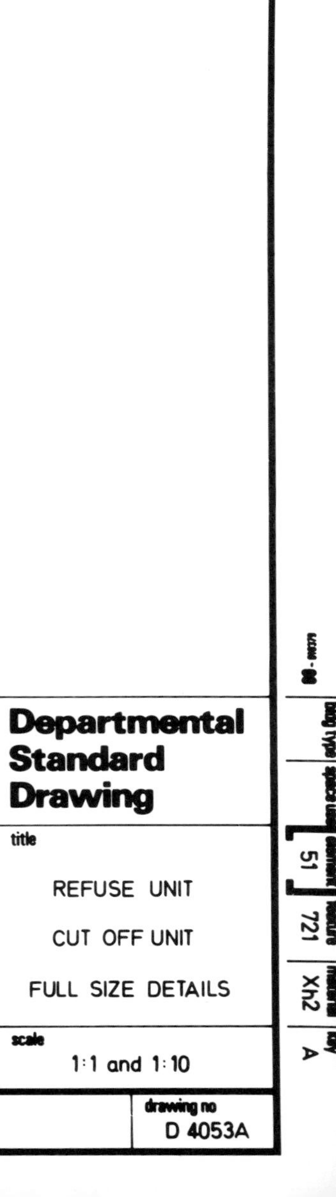

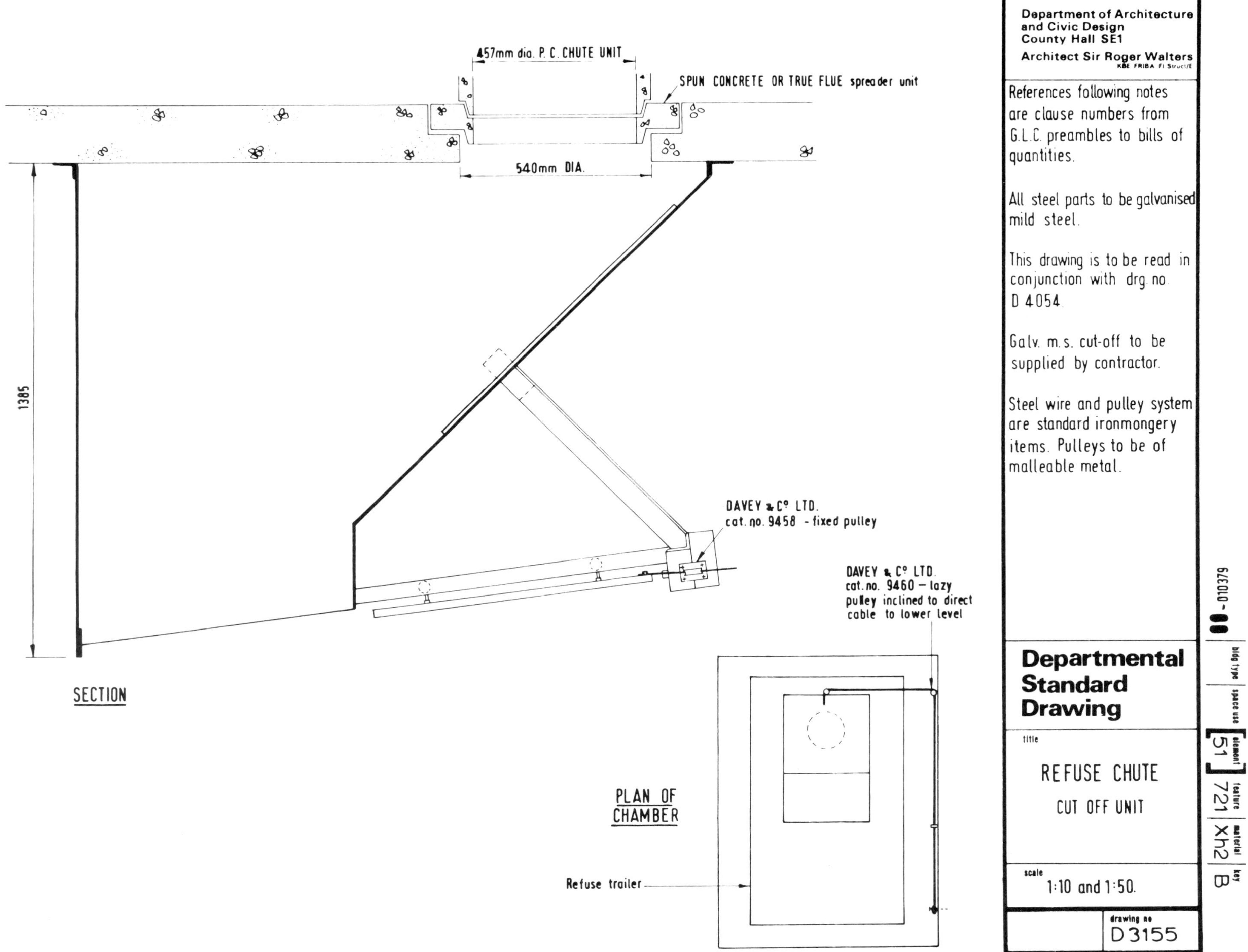

GLC ILEA
Department of Architecture
and Civic Design
County Hall SE1
Architect Sir Roger Walters
KBE FRIBA FI StructE

References following notes are clause numbers from G.L.C. preambles to bills of quantities.

All steel parts to be galvanised mild steel.

This drawing is to be read in conjunction with drg. no. D 4054.

Galv. m.s. cut-off to be supplied by contractor.

Steel wire and pulley system are standard ironmongery items. Pulleys to be of malleable metal.

Departmental Standard Drawing

title

REFUSE CHUTE

CUT OFF UNIT

scale 1:10 and 1:50.

drawing no D3155

00-010379

bldg type | space use | element [51] | feature 721 | material Xh2 | key B

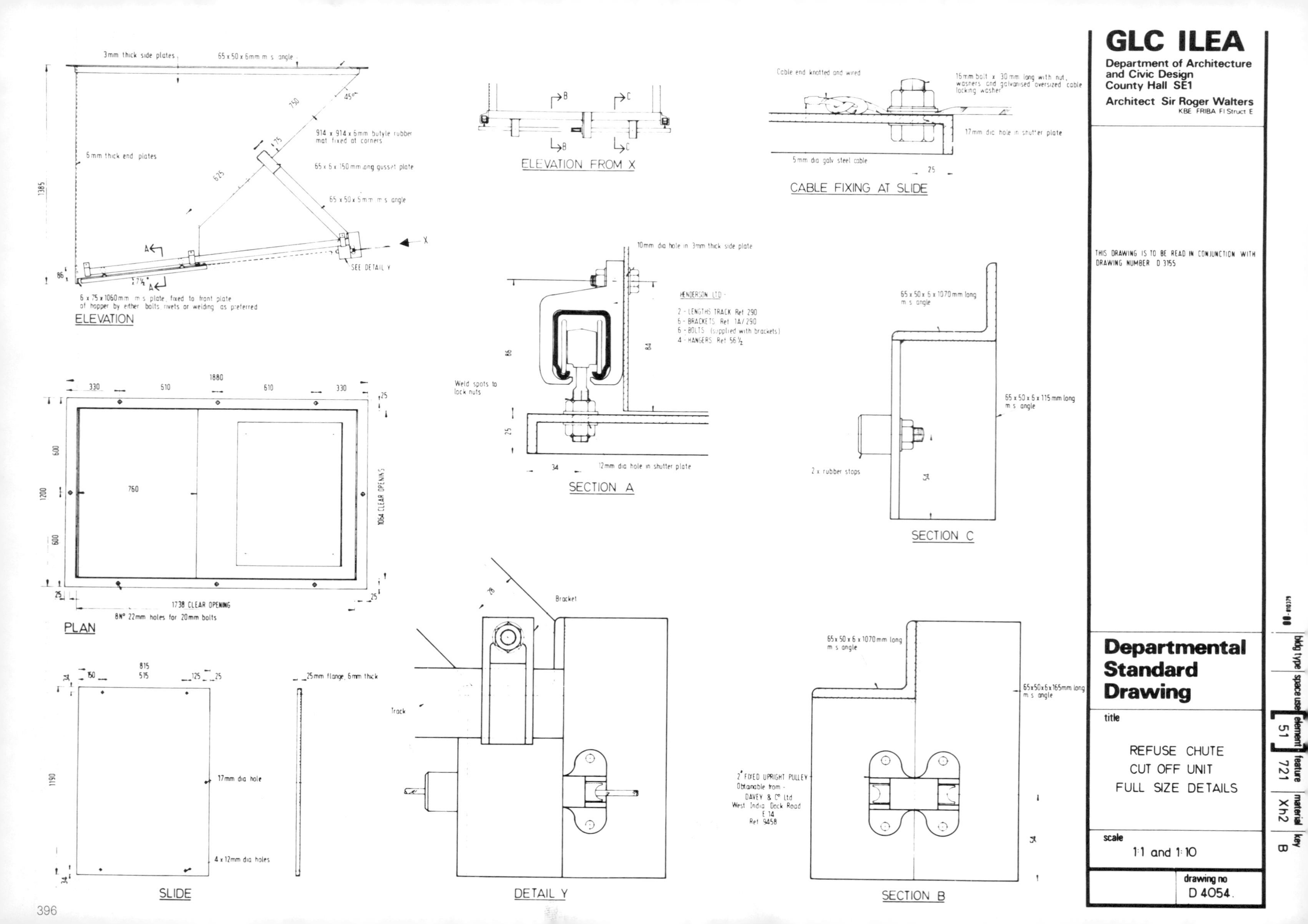
GLC ILEA
Department of Architecture and Civic Design
County Hall SE1
Architect Sir Roger Walters
KBE FRIBA FI Struct E
THIS DRAWING IS TO BE READ IN CONJUNCTION WITH DRAWING NUMBER D 3155
Departmental Standard Drawing
title
REFUSE CHUTE CUT OFF UNIT FULL SIZE DETAILS
scale
1:1 and 1:10
drawing no
D 4054.
bldg type
space use
element 51
feature 721
material Xh2
key B
3mm thick side plates
65 x 50 x 6mm m s angle
914 x 914 x 6mm butyle rubber mat fixed at corners
6mm thick end plates
65 x 6 x 150 mm long gusset plate
65 x 50 x 5mm m s angle
SEE DETAIL Y
6 x 75 x 1060mm m s plate, fixed to front plate of hopper by either bolts rivets or welding as preferred
ELEVATION
ELEVATION FROM X
Cable end knotted and wired
16mm bolt x 30mm long with nut, washers and galvanised oversized cable locking washer
17mm dia hole in shutter plate
5mm dia galv steel cable
CABLE FIXING AT SLIDE
10mm dia hole in 3mm thick side plate
HENDERSON LTD -
2 - LENGTHS TRACK Ref 290
6 - BRACKETS Ref 1A/290
6 - BOLTS (supplied with brackets)
4 - HANGERS Ref 56½
Weld spots to lock nuts
12mm dia hole in shutter plate
SECTION A
65 x 50 x 6 x 1070mm long m s angle
65 x 50 x 6 x 115 mm long m s angle
2 x rubber stops
SECTION C
1064 CLEAR OPENING
1738 CLEAR OPENING
8N° 22mm holes for 20mm bolts
PLAN
25mm flange, 6mm thick
17mm dia hole
4 x 12mm dia holes
SLIDE
Bracket
Track
DETAIL Y
65 x 50 x 6 x 1070mm long m s angle
65x50x6x165mm long m s angle
2" FIXED UPRIGHT PULLEY
Obtainable from -
DAVEY & C° Ltd
West India Dock Road
E 14
Ref 9458
SECTION B

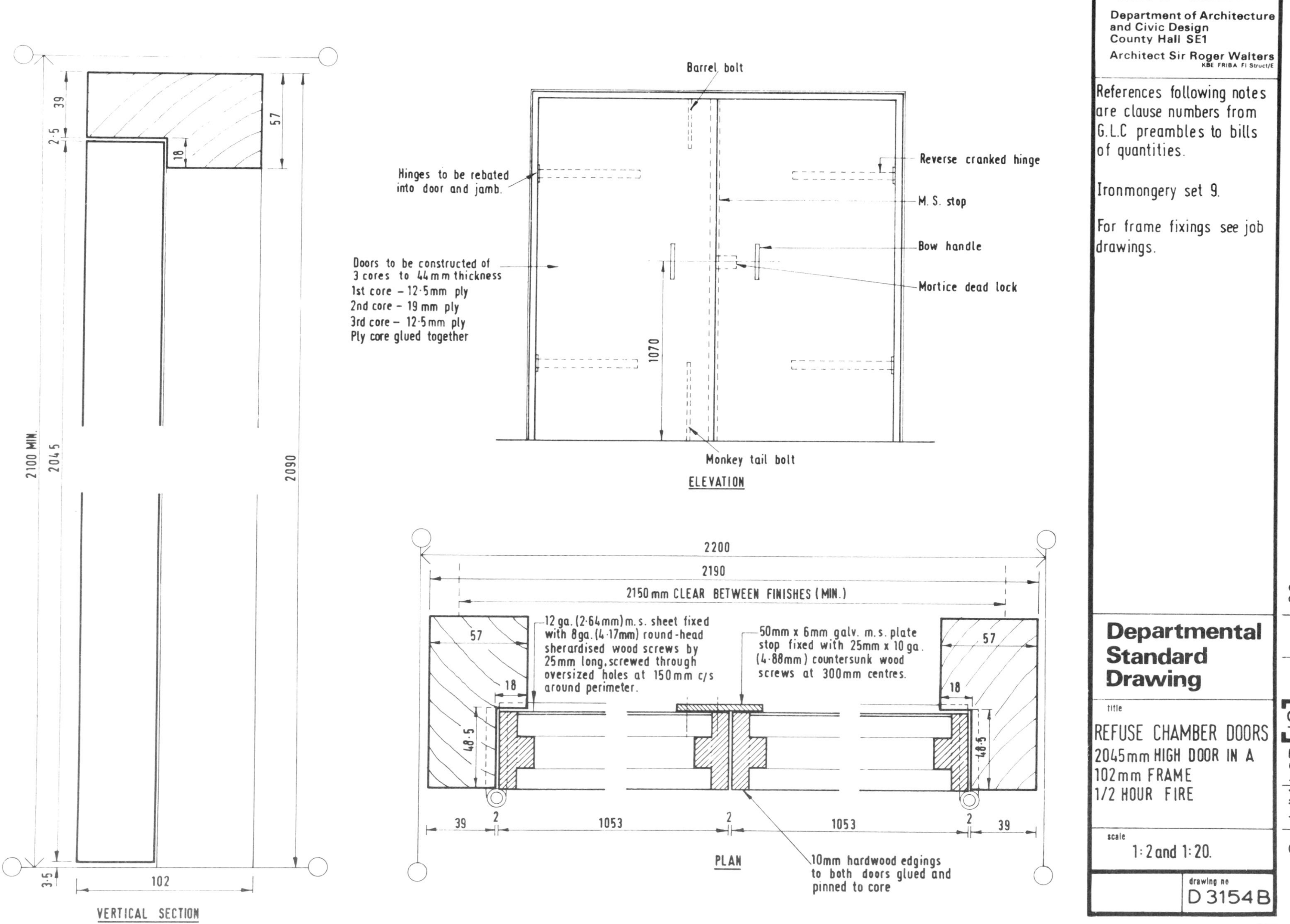
GLC ILEA
Department of Architecture and Civic Design
County Hall SE1
Architect Sir Roger Walters KBE FRIBA FI StructE
References following notes are clause numbers from G.L.C preambles to bills of quantities.
Ironmongery set 9.
For frame fixings see job drawings.
Departmental Standard Drawing
title
REFUSE CHAMBER DOORS
2045mm HIGH DOOR IN A 102mm FRAME
1/2 HOUR FIRE
scale
1:2 and 1:20.
drawing no
D 3154 B
bldg type
space use
element
feature
material
key
[51] 204 Xi4 C
010379
Barrel bolt
Hinges to be rebated into door and jamb.
Reverse cranked hinge
M. S. stop
Bow handle
Mortice dead lock
Doors to be constructed of 3 cores to 44mm thickness
1st core – 12·5mm ply
2nd core – 19 mm ply
3rd core – 12·5mm ply
Ply core glued together
1070
Monkey tail bolt
ELEVATION
39
2·5
18
57
2100 MIN.
2045
2090
3·5
102
VERTICAL SECTION
2200
2190
2150mm CLEAR BETWEEN FINISHES (MIN.)
12 ga. (2·64mm) m.s. sheet fixed with 8ga. (4·17mm) round-head sherardised wood screws by 25mm long, screwed through oversized holes at 150mm c/s around perimeter.
50mm x 6mm galv. m.s. plate stop fixed with 25mm x 10 ga. (4·88mm) countersunk wood screws at 300mm centres.
57
18
48·5
39
2
1053
2
1053
2
39
PLAN
10mm hardwood edgings to both doors glued and pinned to core

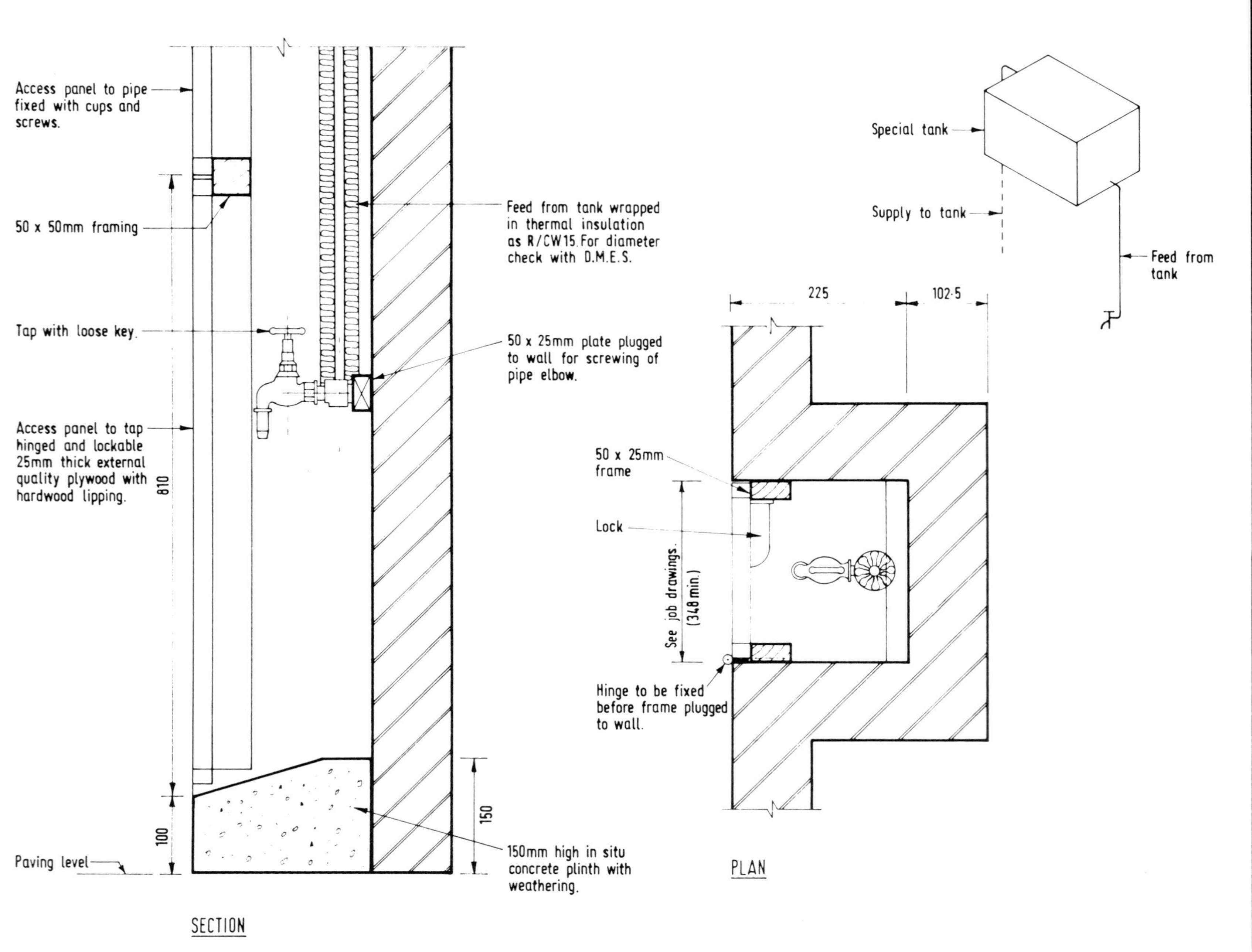

GLC ILEA

Department of Architecture and Civic Design
County Hall SE1 7PB
Architect Sir Roger Walters
KBE ARIBA FI Struct/E

References following notes are clause numbers from G.L.C. preambles to bills of quantities

Ironmongery.

(1) Pair of steel cranked hinges as item 143

(2) Steel rim night latch as item 39. Number of keys to be specified by job architect.

To be read in conjunction with Water Engineer's job layout.

Departmental Standard Drawing

title

STANDPIPE HOUSING FOR REFUSE CHAMBER.

scale

1 : 5

drawing no D5089

rev A

bldg type 8- | space use | element [51] | feature 721 | material | key

010379

10
Fire fighting

3200 Fire fighting equipment panel
3201 Hose reel in recess
5090 Dry rising main—inlet box
5091 Dry rising main—pipe fixing at First Floor
5092 Dry rising main—pipe fixing at Roof Level

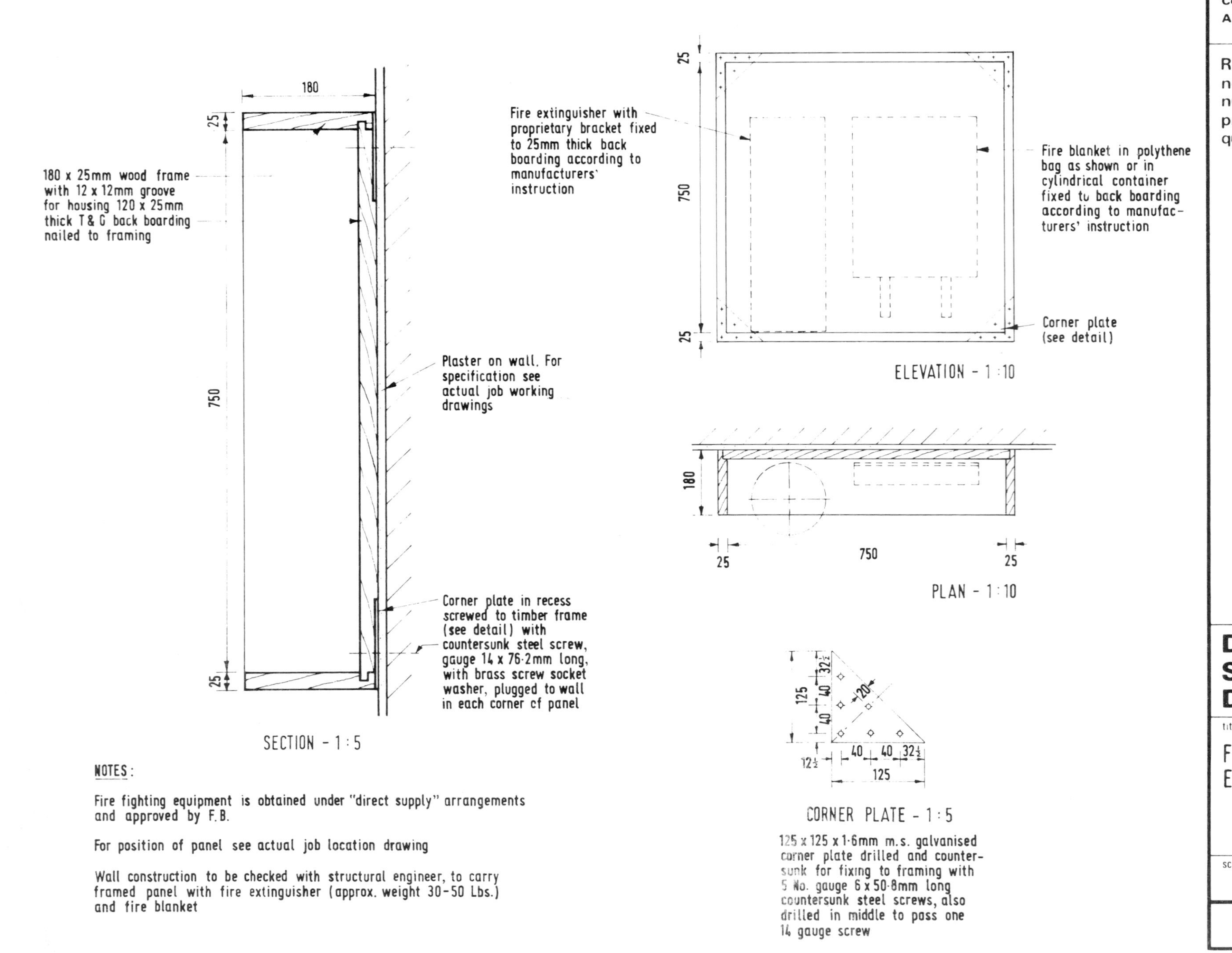

GLC ILEA

Department of Architecture and Civic Design
County Hall SE1 7PB
Architect Sir Roger Walters
KBE ARIBA FI Struct/E

References following notes are clause numbers from G.L.C. preambles to bills of quantities

Departmental Standard Drawing

title

FIRE FIGHTING EQUIPMENT PANEL

scale

1 : 5 & 1 : 10

drawing no D3200

rev

010379

bldg type 7-
space use
element 68
feature 441
material Xi2
key

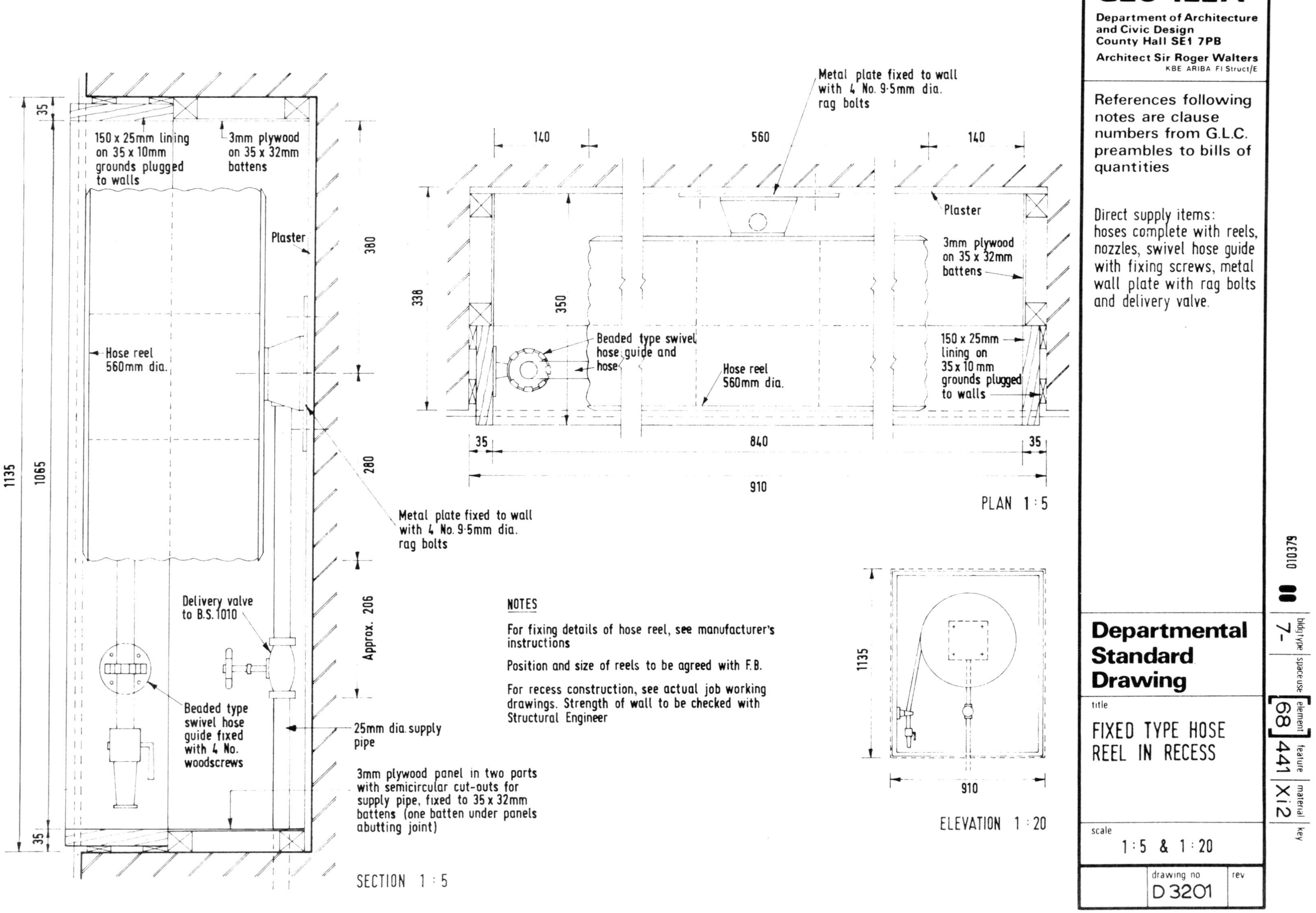

GLC ILEA
Department of Architecture and Civic Design
County Hall SE1 7PB
Architect Sir Roger Walters
KBE ARIBA FI Struct/E
References following notes are clause numbers from G.L.C. preambles to bills of quantities
Direct supply items: hoses complete with reels, nozzles, swivel hose guide with fixing screws, metal wall plate with rag bolts and delivery valve.
150 x 25mm lining on 35 x 10mm grounds plugged to walls
3mm plywood on 35 x 32mm battens
Plaster
Hose reel 560mm dia.
Metal plate fixed to wall with 4 No. 9·5mm dia. rag bolts
Delivery valve to B.S. 1010
Beaded type swivel hose guide fixed with 4 No. woodscrews
25mm dia. supply pipe
3mm plywood panel in two parts with semicircular cut-outs for supply pipe, fixed to 35 x 32mm battens (one batten under panels abutting joint)
Approx. 206
380
280
1135
1065
35
SECTION 1 : 5
140
560
140
338
350
Beaded type swivel hose guide and hose
Hose reel 560mm dia.
3mm plywood on 35 x 32mm battens
150 x 25mm lining on 35 x 10 mm grounds plugged to walls
35
840
35
910
PLAN 1 : 5
NOTES
For fixing details of hose reel, see manufacturer's instructions
Position and size of reels to be agreed with F.B.
For recess construction, see actual job working drawings. Strength of wall to be checked with Structural Engineer
1135
910
ELEVATION 1 : 20
Departmental Standard Drawing
title
FIXED TYPE HOSE REEL IN RECESS
scale
1 : 5 & 1 : 20
drawing no
D 3201
rev
bldg type 7-
space use
element 68
feature 441
material Xi2
key
010379

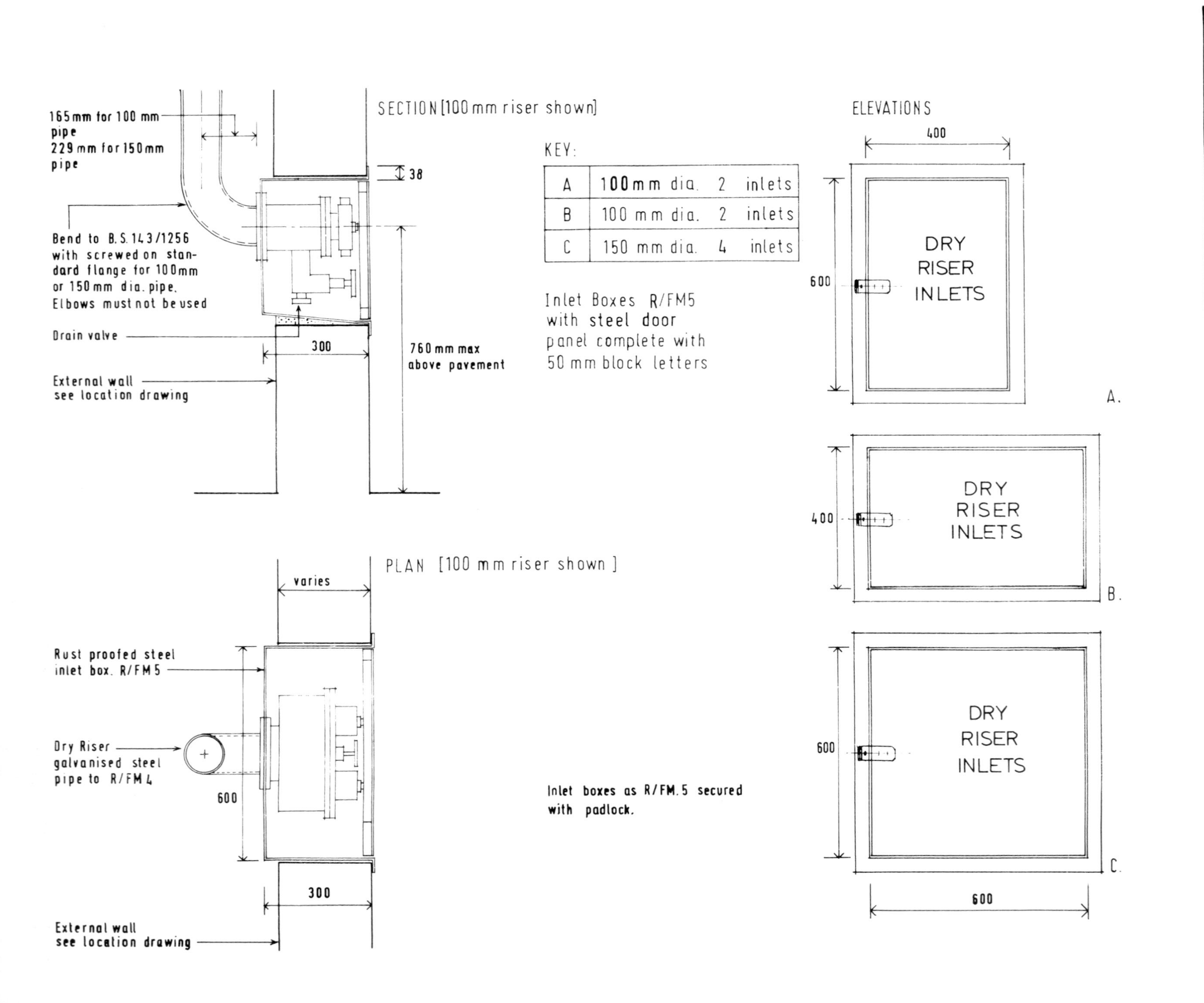

GLC ILEA

Department of Architecture and Civic Design
County Hall SE1
Architect Sir Roger Walters KBE FRIBA FI StructE

References following notes are clause numbers from GLC preambles to bills of quantities

Departmental Standard Drawing

title
DRY RISING MAIN
INLET BOX

scale 1:10

drawing no D5090 rev B.

[53] 742 | Xh2 | as matrix

010379

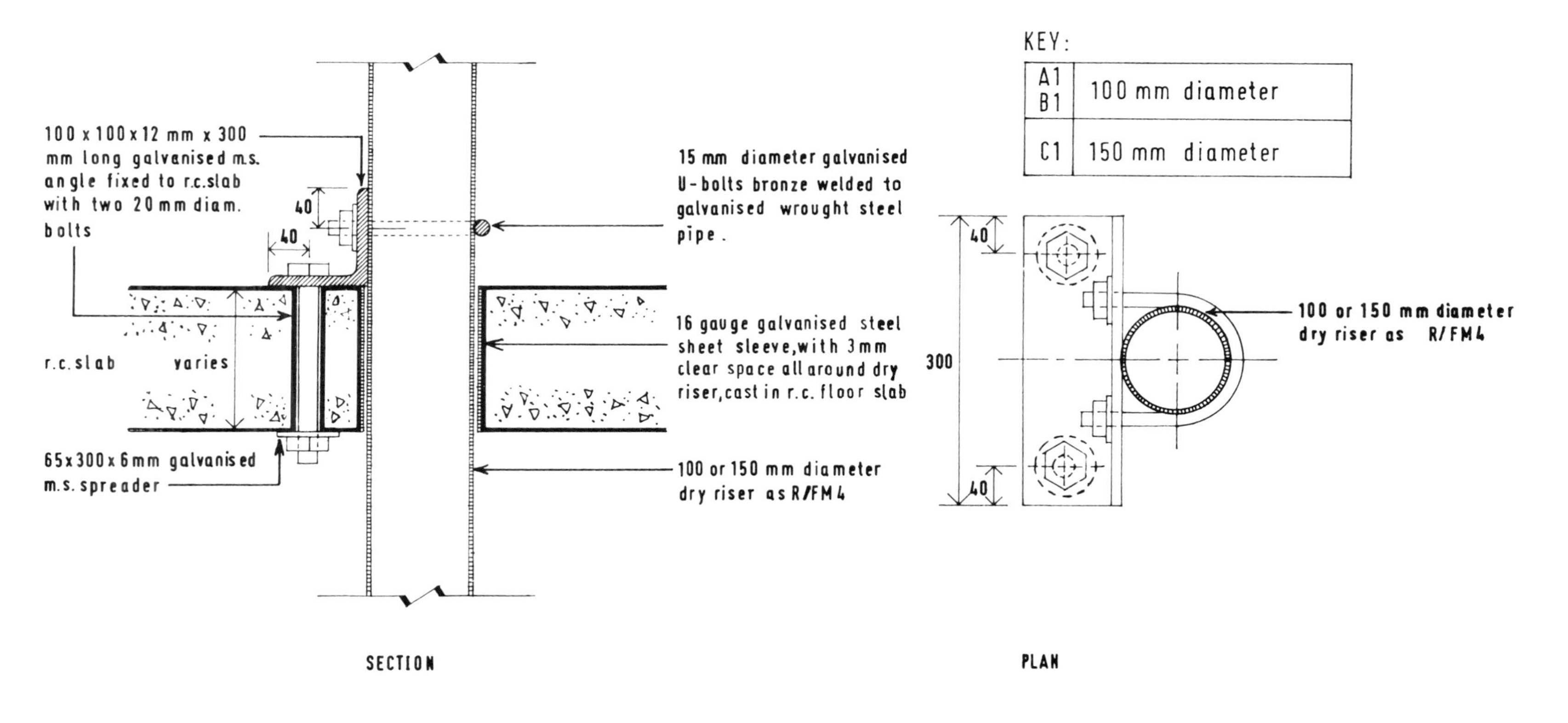

GLC ILEA

Department of Architecture
and Civic Design
County Hall SE1
Architect Sir Roger Walters
KBE FRIBA FI Struct/E

References following notes are clause numbers from GLC preambles to bills of quantities

Departmental Standard Drawing

title

DRY RISING MAIN.
DETAIL OF SUPPORT
AT FIRST FLOOR LEVEL

scale 1:5

drawing no D5091

00 - 010379

[53] 742 Xh2 as matrix

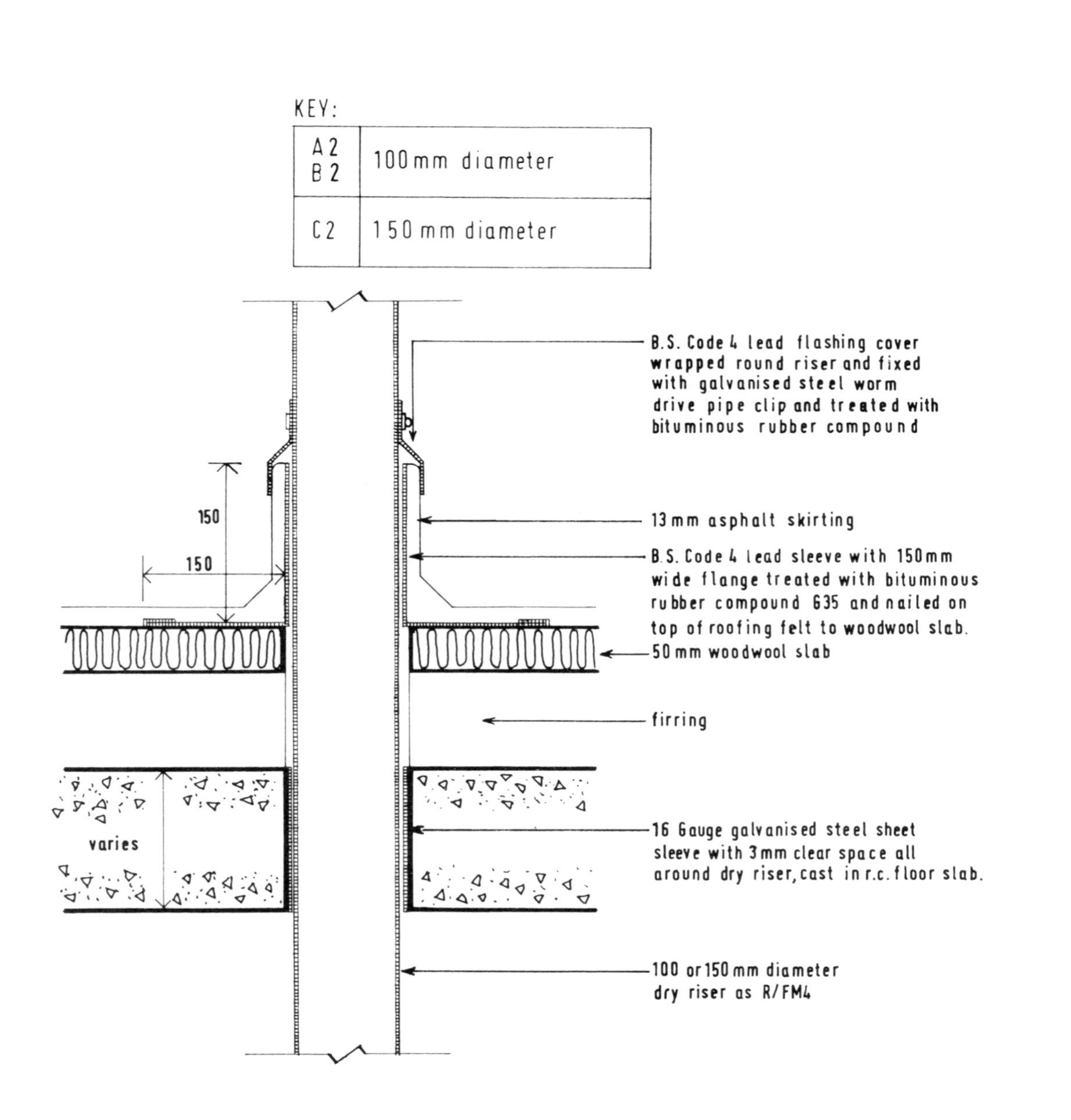

GLC ILEA

Department of Architecture and Civic Design
County Hall SE1
Architect Sir Roger Walters KBE FRIBA FI StructE

References following notes are clause numbers from GLC preambles to bills of quantities

Departmental Standard Drawing

title
DRY RISING MAIN.
DETAIL AT ROOF LEVEL.
[R.C. SLAB]

scale
1:5

drawing no
D5092

53 | 742 | Xh2 | as matrix

010379

11 Sound attenuators

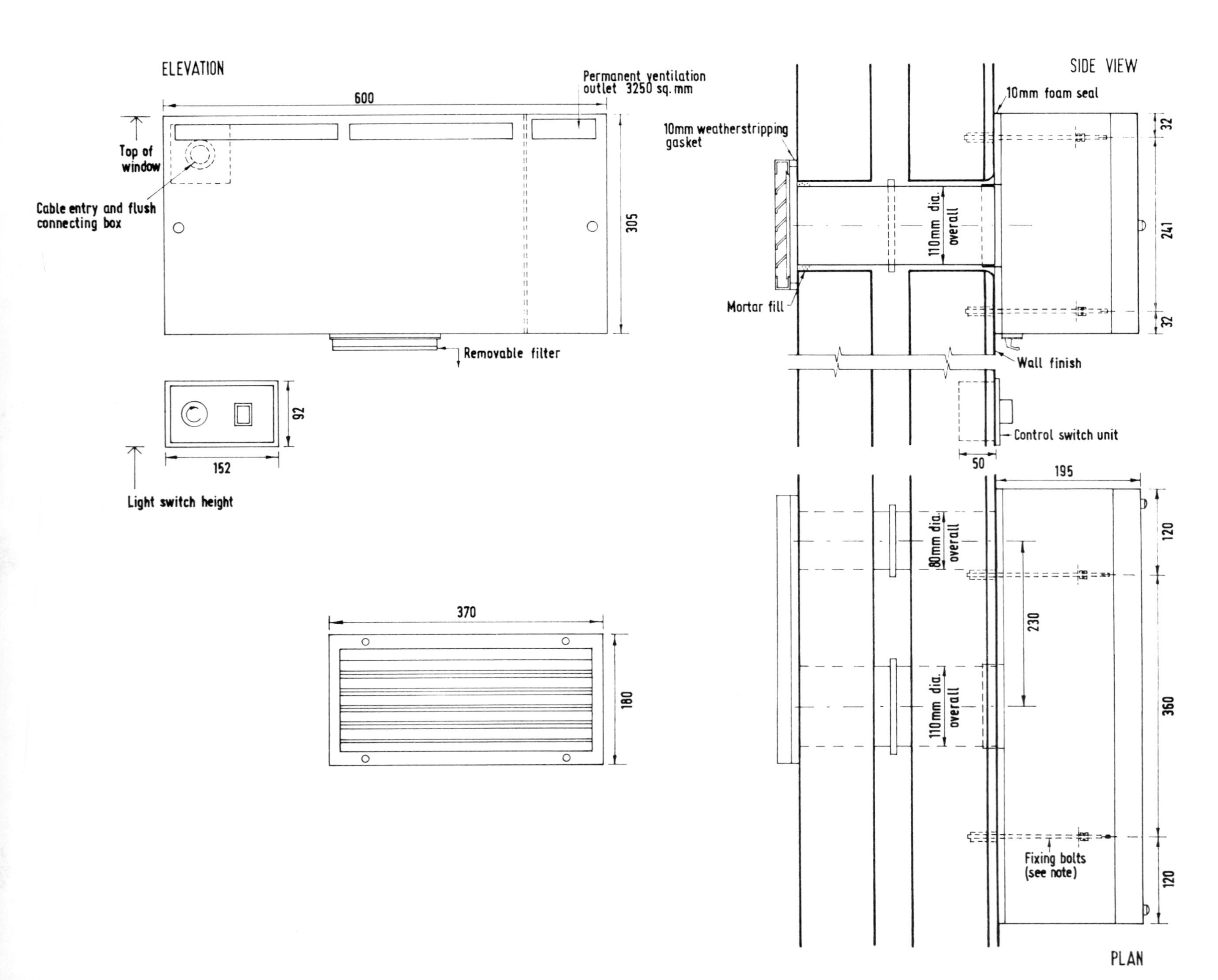

GLC ILEA

Department of Architecture and Civic Design
County Hall SE1 7PB
Architect Sir Roger Walters
KBE ARIBA FI Struct/E

References following notes are clause numbers from G.L.C. preambles to bills of quantities

Unit mounted at high level, with remote control switch unit mounted at light switch level under or adjacent to unit.

Unit supplied complete with fixing bars and sockets, electric control box, duct and external grille which can be delivered separately if required earlier on site.
Mounting-insulated block walls. 4 undersize holes: 15/32 dia. drill size, drilled in wall from template marked on carton by Hilti expanding sockets. Sockets expanded by 8 turns of threaded bars from take-up point of socket in block. Unit mounted onto threaded bars in position on wall. Nuts tightened inside case with cover removed. For hollow panel mounting. UNI-FIX Fastbrolly Screw Anchors, ref. SA11 with same threaded bars and nuts.

Departmental Standard Drawing

title
SOUND ATTENUATOR UNITS. G.L.C. BONAVENT HORIZONTALLY FIXED.
ACCADIAIR LTD.
MODEL REF. AV113.

scale
1 : 5

drawing no	rev
D 3144	A

(57) 698 Xh2 A

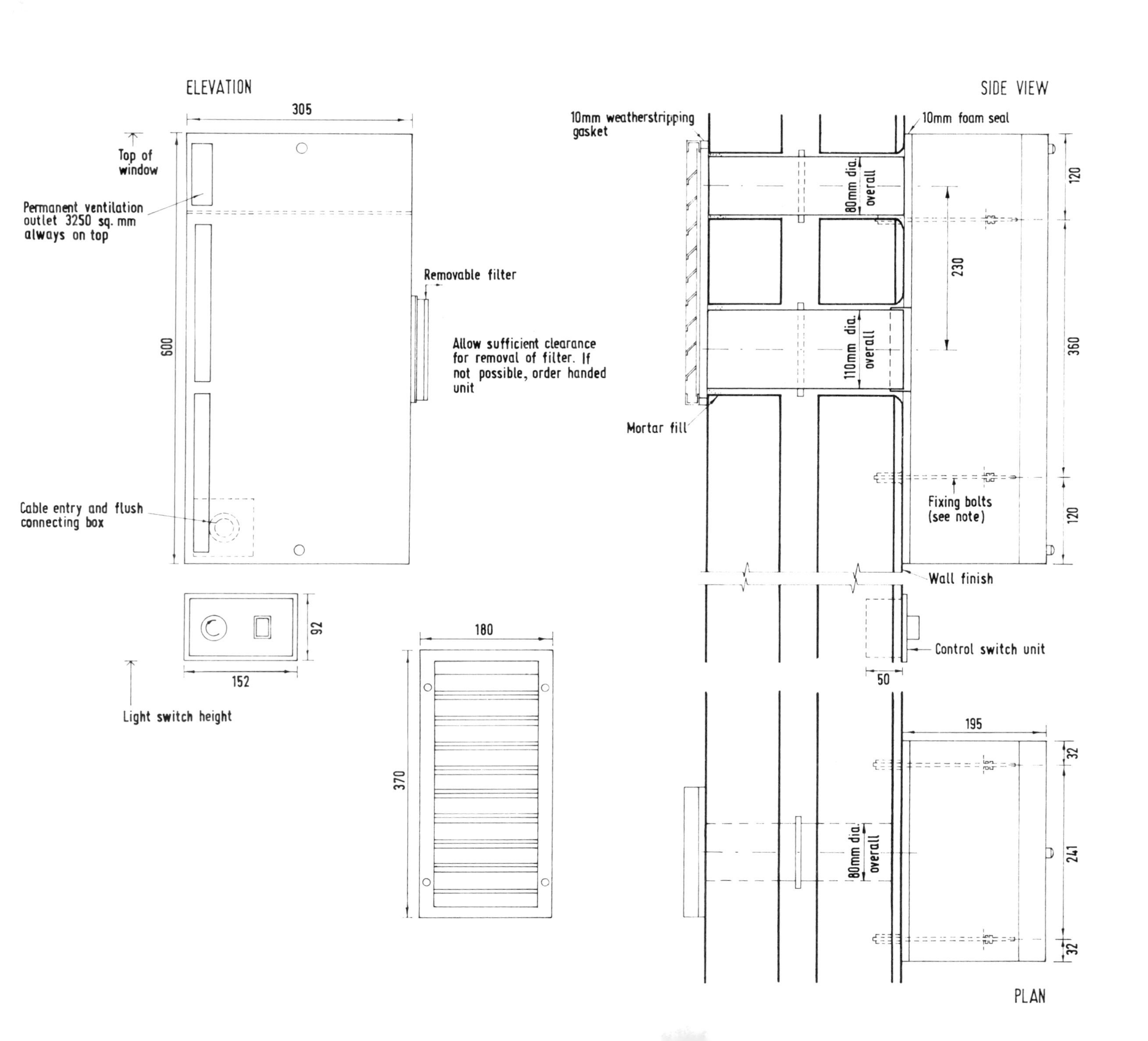

GLC ILEA

Department of Architecture and Civic Design
County Hall SE1 7PB
Architect Sir Roger Walters
KBE ARIBA FI Struct/E

References following notes are clause numbers from G.L.C. preambles to bills of quantities

Unit mounted at high level, with remote control switch unit mounted at light switch level under or adjacent to unit.

Unit supplied complete with fixing bars and sockets, electric control box, duct and external grille which can be delivered separately if required earlier on site.
Mounting-insulated block walls. 4 undersize holes: 15/32 dia. drill size, drilled in wall from template marked on carton by Hilti expanding sockets. Sockets expanded by 8 turns of threaded bars from take-up point of socket in block. Unit mounted onto threaded bars in position on wall. Nuts tightened inside case with cover removed. For hollow panel mounting. UNI-FIX Fastbrolly Screw Anchors, ref. SA11 with same threaded bars and nuts.

Departmental Standard Drawing

title
SOUND ATTENUATOR UNITS. G.L.C. BONAVENT VERTICALLY FIXED.
ACCADIAIR LTD.
MODEL REF. AV113.

scale 1 : 5

drawing no. D 3145 rev. A

010379

filing type | staircase | element [57] | feature 698 | material Xh2 | key B

12 Letter boxes

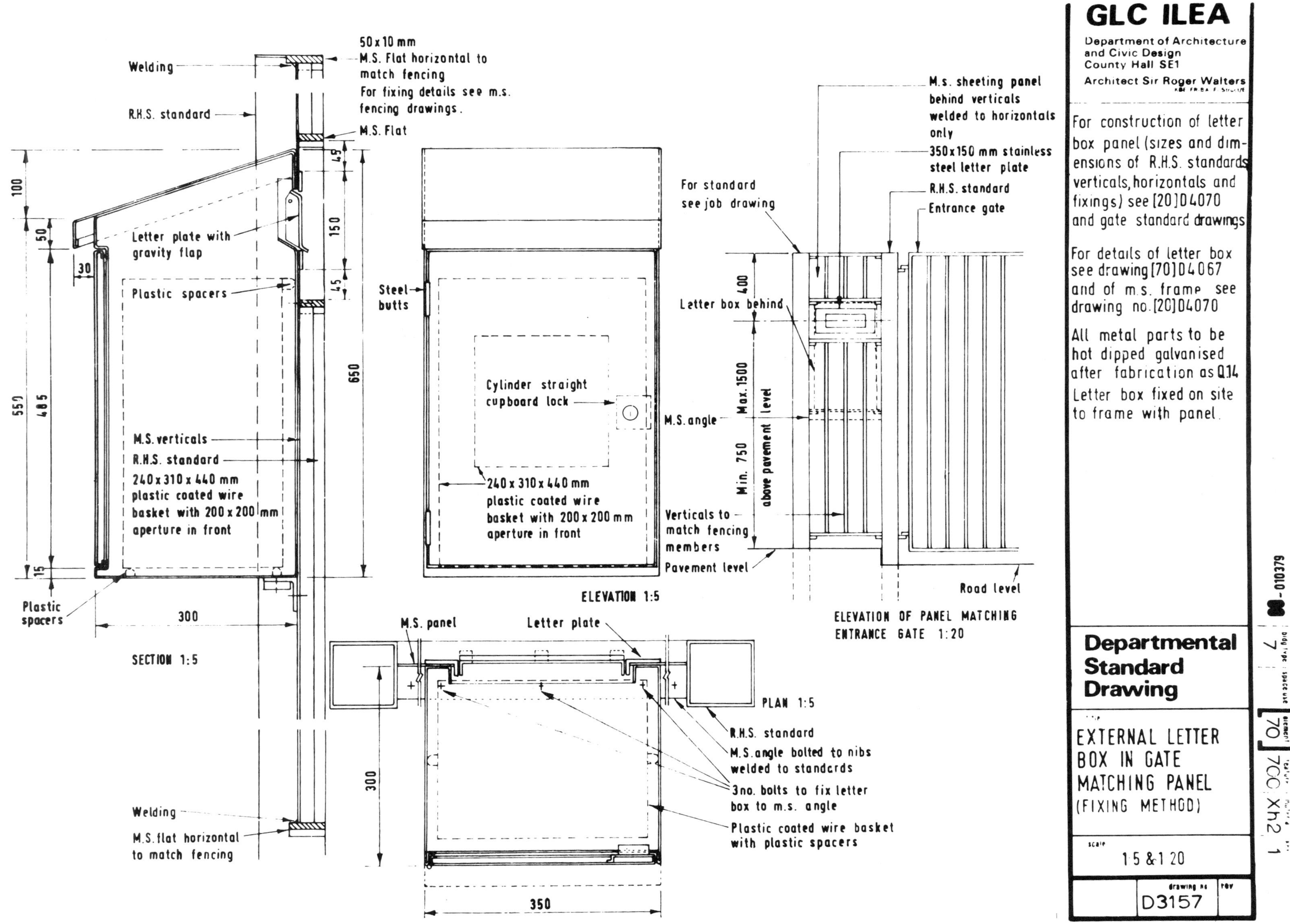
50 x 10 mm
M.S. Flat horizontal to match fencing
For fixing details see m.s. fencing drawings.
Welding
R.H.S. standard
M.S. Flat
Letter plate with gravity flap
Plastic spacers
M.S. verticals
R.H.S. standard
240 x 310 x 440 mm plastic coated wire basket with 200 x 200 mm aperture in front
Plastic spacers
300
SECTION 1:5
Welding
M.S. flat horizontal to match fencing
Steel butts
Cylinder straight cupboard lock
240 x 310 x 440 mm plastic coated wire basket with 200 x 200 mm aperture in front
ELEVATION 1:5
M.S. panel
Letter plate
PLAN 1:5
R.H.S. standard
M.S. angle bolted to nibs welded to standards
3 no. bolts to fix letter box to m.s. angle
Plastic coated wire basket with plastic spacers
350
M.s. sheeting panel behind verticals welded to horizontals only
350 x 150 mm stainless steel letter plate
R.H.S. standard
Entrance gate
For standard see job drawing
Letter box behind
M.S. angle
Max. 1500
Min. 750 above pavement level
Verticals to match fencing members
Pavement level
Road level
ELEVATION OF PANEL MATCHING ENTRANCE GATE 1:20
GLC ILEA
Department of Architecture and Civic Design
County Hall SE1
Architect Sir Roger Walters
For construction of letter box panel (sizes and dimensions of R.H.S. standards verticals, horizontals and fixings) see [20]04070 and gate standard drawings
For details of letter box see drawing [70]04067 and of m.s. frame see drawing no. [20]04070
All metal parts to be hot dipped galvanised after fabrication as Q14
Letter box fixed on site to frame with panel.
Departmental Standard Drawing
EXTERNAL LETTER BOX IN GATE MATCHING PANEL (FIXING METHOD)
scale 1:5 & 1:20
drawing no D3157
rev
7
[70]
700 Xh2 1
010379

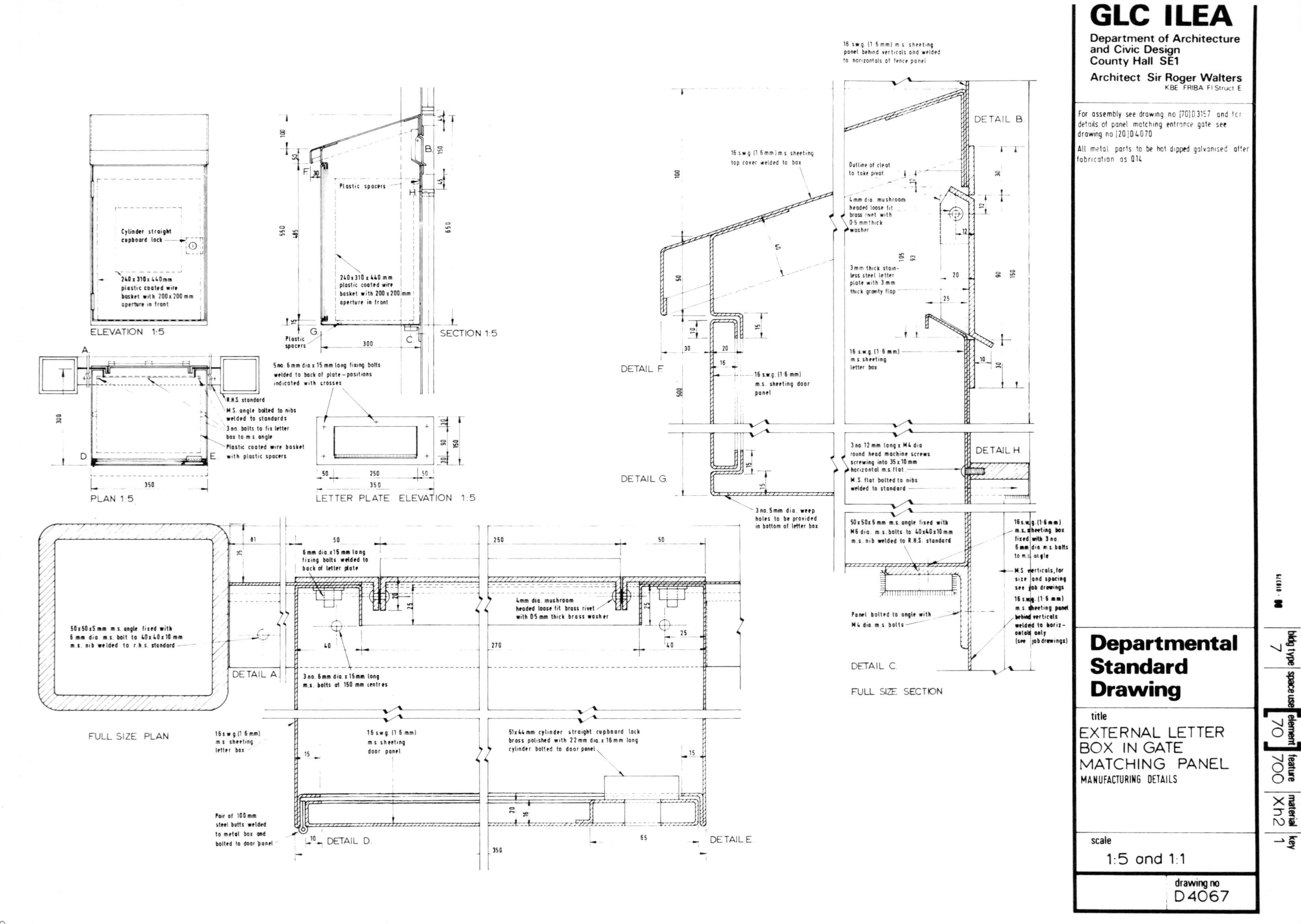
GLC ILEA
Department of Architecture and Civic Design
County Hall SE1
Architect Sir Roger Walters
KBE FRIBA FI Struct E
For assembly see drawing no [70]D3157 and for details of panel matching entrance gate see drawing no [20]D4070
All metal parts to be hot dipped galvanised after fabrication as Q14
Departmental Standard Drawing
title
EXTERNAL LETTER BOX IN GATE MATCHING PANEL
MANUFACTURING DETAILS
scale
1:5 and 1:1
drawing no
D4067
bldg type 7
space use
element [70]
feature 700
material Xh2
key 1
ELEVATION 1:5
Cylinder straight cupboard lock
240 x 310 x 440mm plastic coated wire basket with 200 x 200 mm aperture in front
SECTION 1:5
Plastic spacers
PLAN 1:5
R.H.S. standard
M.S. angle bolted to nibs welded to standards
3 no. bolts to fix letter box to m.s. angle
Plastic coated wire basket with plastic spacers
5 no. 6mm dia x 15 mm long fixing bolts welded to back of plate – positions indicated with crosses
LETTER PLATE ELEVATION 1:5
16 s.w.g. (1.6 mm) m.s. sheeting panel behind verticals and welded to horizontals of fence panel
16 s.w.g. (1.6 mm) m.s. sheeting top cover welded to box
DETAIL B
Outline of cleat to take pivot
4mm dia. mushroom headed loose fit brass rivet with 0.5 mm thick washer
3mm thick stainless steel letter plate with 3 mm thick gravity flap
16 s.w.g. (1.6 mm) m.s. sheeting letter box
DETAIL F
16 s.w.g. (1.6 mm) m.s. sheeting door panel
DETAIL G
3 no. 5mm dia. weep holes to be provided in bottom of letter box
3 no. 12 mm long x M4 dia round head machine screws screwing into 35 x 10 mm horizontal m.s. flat
M.S. flat bolted to nibs welded to standard
DETAIL H
50 x 50 x 5 mm m.s. angle fixed with M6 dia. m.s. bolts to 40 x 40 x 10 mm m.s. nib welded to R.H.S. standard
16 s.w.g. (1.6 mm) m.s. sheeting box fixed with 3 no. 6 mm dia. m.s. bolts to m.s. angle
M.S. verticals, for size and spacing see job drawings
16 s.w.g. (1.6 mm) m.s. sheeting panel behind verticals welded to horizontals only (see job drawings)
Panel bolted to angle with M4 dia. m.s. bolts
DETAIL C
FULL SIZE SECTION
50 x 50 x 5 mm m.s. angle fixed with 6 mm dia. m.s. bolt to 40 x 40 x 10 mm m.s. nib welded to r.h.s. standard
DETAIL A
FULL SIZE PLAN
6mm dia. x 15 mm long fixing bolts welded to back of letter plate
4mm dia. mushroom headed loose fit brass rivet with 0.5 mm thick brass washer
3 no. 6mm dia. x 15mm long m.s. bolts at 150 mm centres
16 s.w.g. (1.6 mm) m.s. sheeting letter box
16 s.w.g. (1.6 mm) m.s. sheeting door panel
51 x 44 mm cylinder straight cupboard lock brass polished with 22 mm dia. x 16 mm long cylinder bolted to door panel
Pair of 100 mm steel butts welded to metal box and bolted to door panel
DETAIL D
DETAIL E

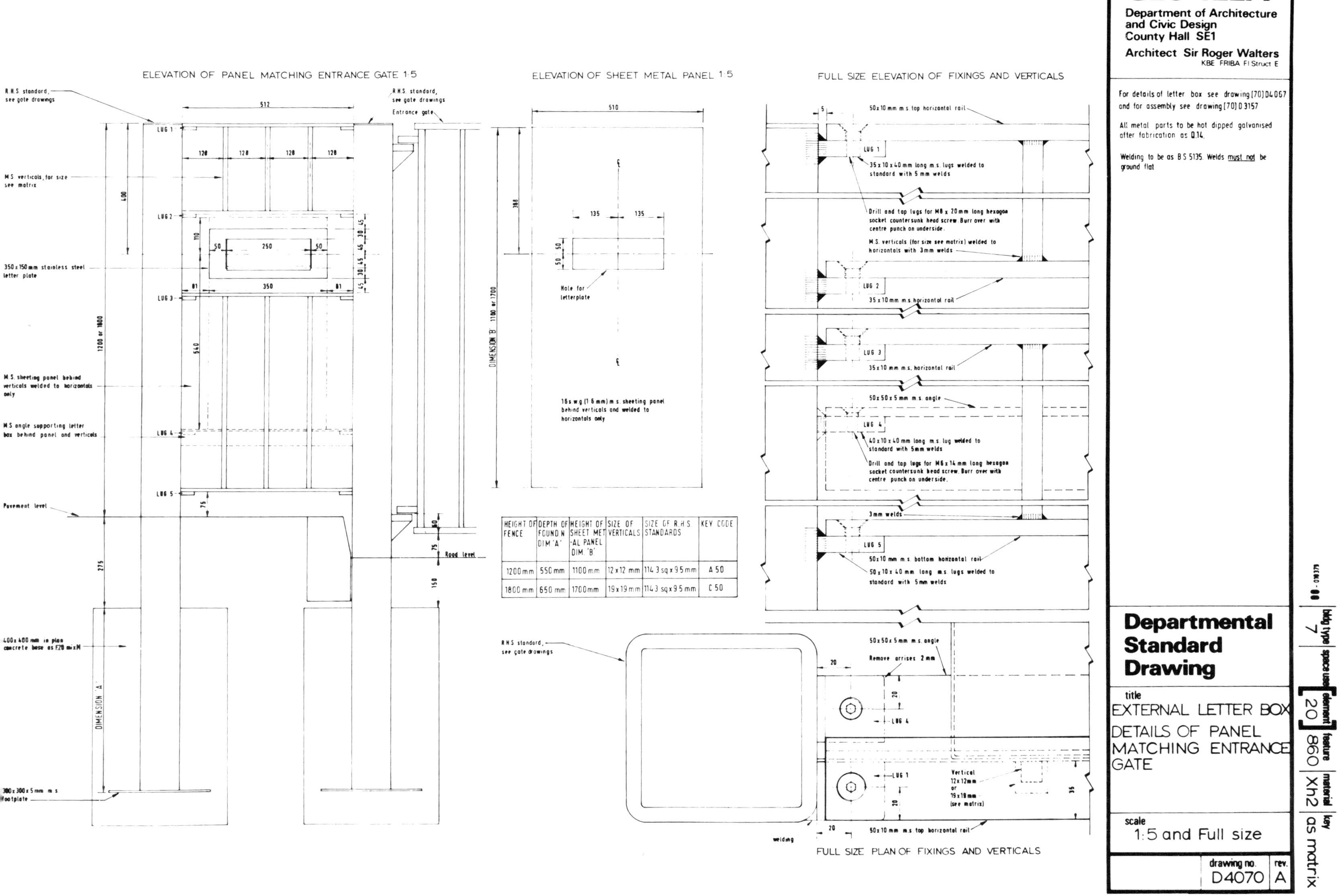

HEIGHT OF FENCE	DEPTH OF FOUND.N DIM 'A'	HEIGHT OF SHEET MET-AL PANEL DIM. 'B'	SIZE OF VERTICALS	SIZE OF R.H.S. STANDARDS	KEY CODE
1200mm	550mm	1100mm	12 x 12 mm	114.3 sq x 9.5mm	A 50
1800mm	650mm	1700mm	19 x 19mm	114.3 sq x 9.5mm	C 50

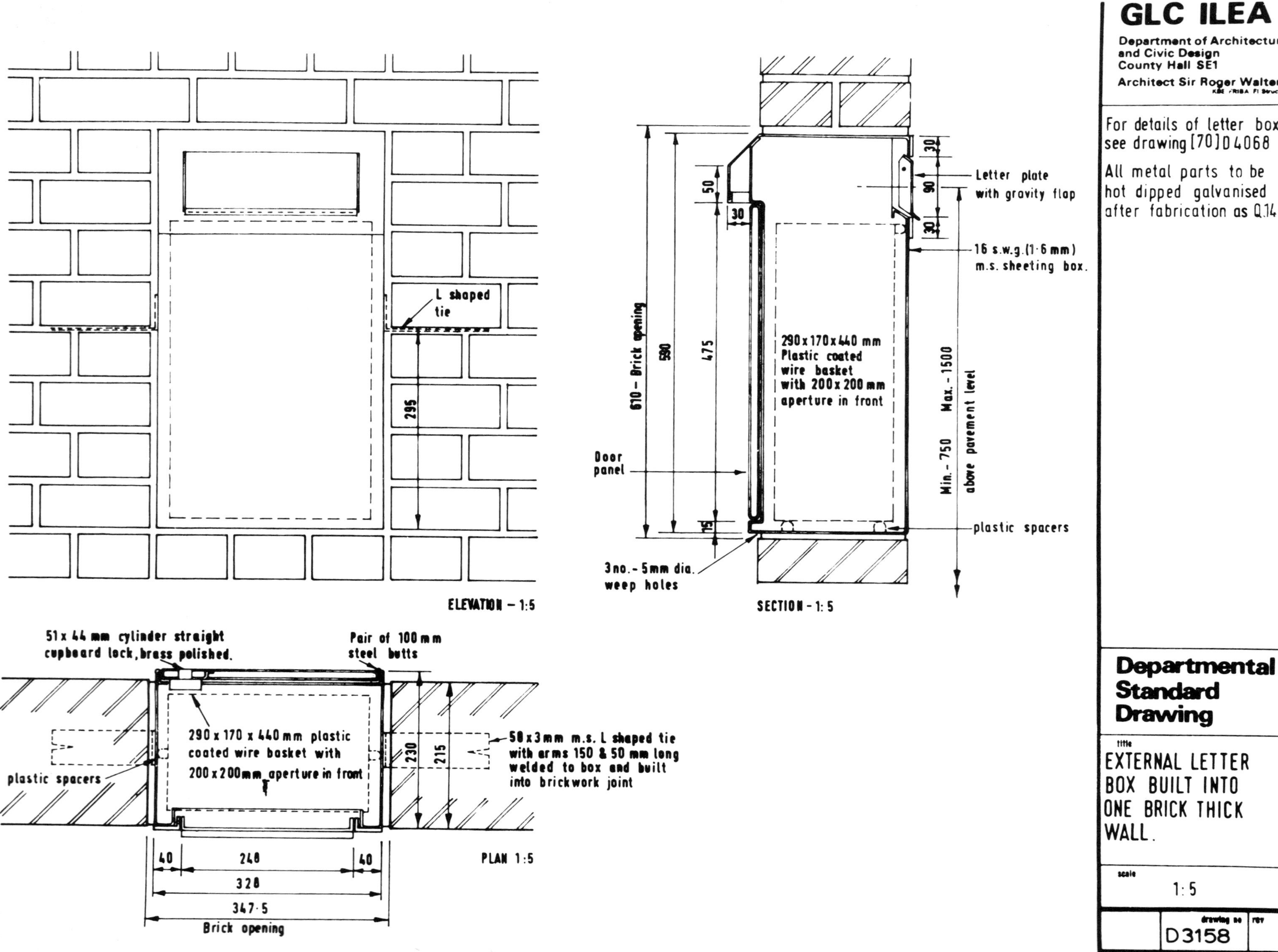
GLC ILEA
Department of Architecture and Civic Design
County Hall SE1
Architect Sir Roger Walters
For details of letter box see drawing [70] D 4068
All metal parts to be hot dipped galvanised after fabrication as Q.14
L shaped tie
295
ELEVATION – 1:5
610 – Brick opening
590
475
50
30
15
Door panel
3 no. - 5 mm dia. weep holes
290 x 170 x 440 mm Plastic coated wire basket with 200 x 200 mm aperture in front
Letter plate with gravity flap
30
90
30
16 s.w.g. (1·6 mm) m.s. sheeting box.
Min. - 750 Max. - 1500 above pavement level
plastic spacers
SECTION - 1:5
51 x 44 mm cylinder straight cupboard lock, brass polished.
Pair of 100 mm steel butts
290 x 170 x 440 mm plastic coated wire basket with 200 x 200 mm aperture in front
50 x 3 mm m.s. L shaped tie with arms 150 & 50 mm long welded to box and built into brickwork joint
230
215
plastic spacers
40
248
40
328
347·5
Brick opening
PLAN 1:5
Departmental Standard Drawing
title
EXTERNAL LETTER BOX BUILT INTO ONE BRICK THICK WALL.
scale
1:5
drawing no
rev
D3158
bldg type 7
space use
element [70]
feature 700
material Xh2
key 2
010379

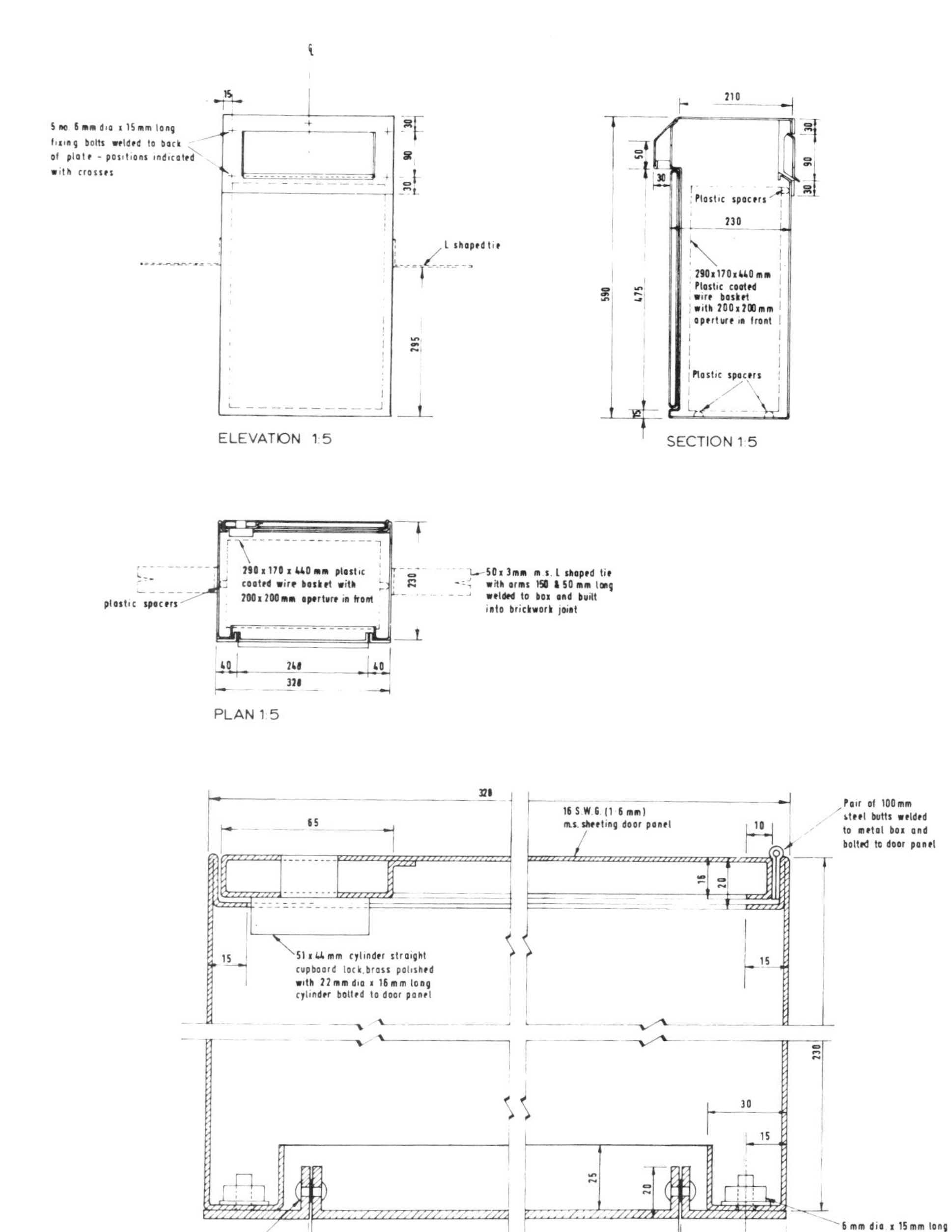

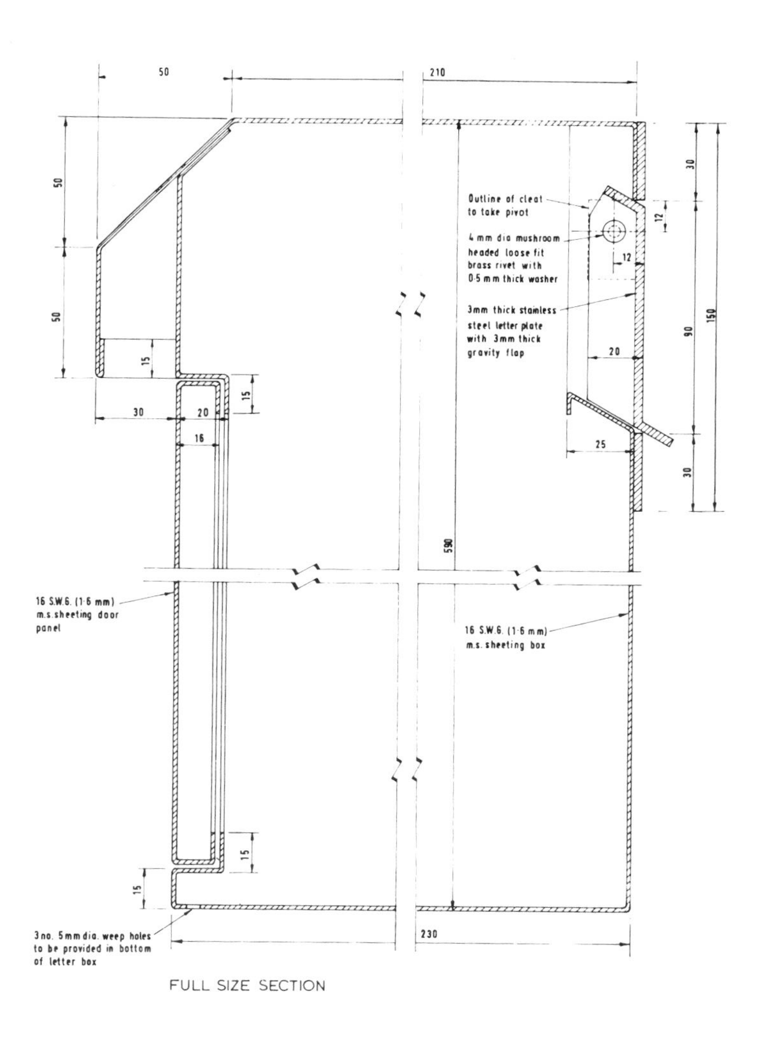

GLC ILEA

Department of Architecture and Civic Design
County Hall SE1

Architect Sir Roger Walters
KBE FRIBA FI Struct E

For building in details see drawing no [70] D 3158

All metal parts to be hot dipped galvanised after fabrication as Q.14

Departmental Standard Drawing

title
EXTERNAL LETTER BOX
BUILT INTO ONE BRICK THICK WALL
MANUFACTURING DETAILS

scale
1:5 and 1:1

drawing no
D 4068

bldg type	space use	element	feature	material	key
7		[70]	700	Xh2	2

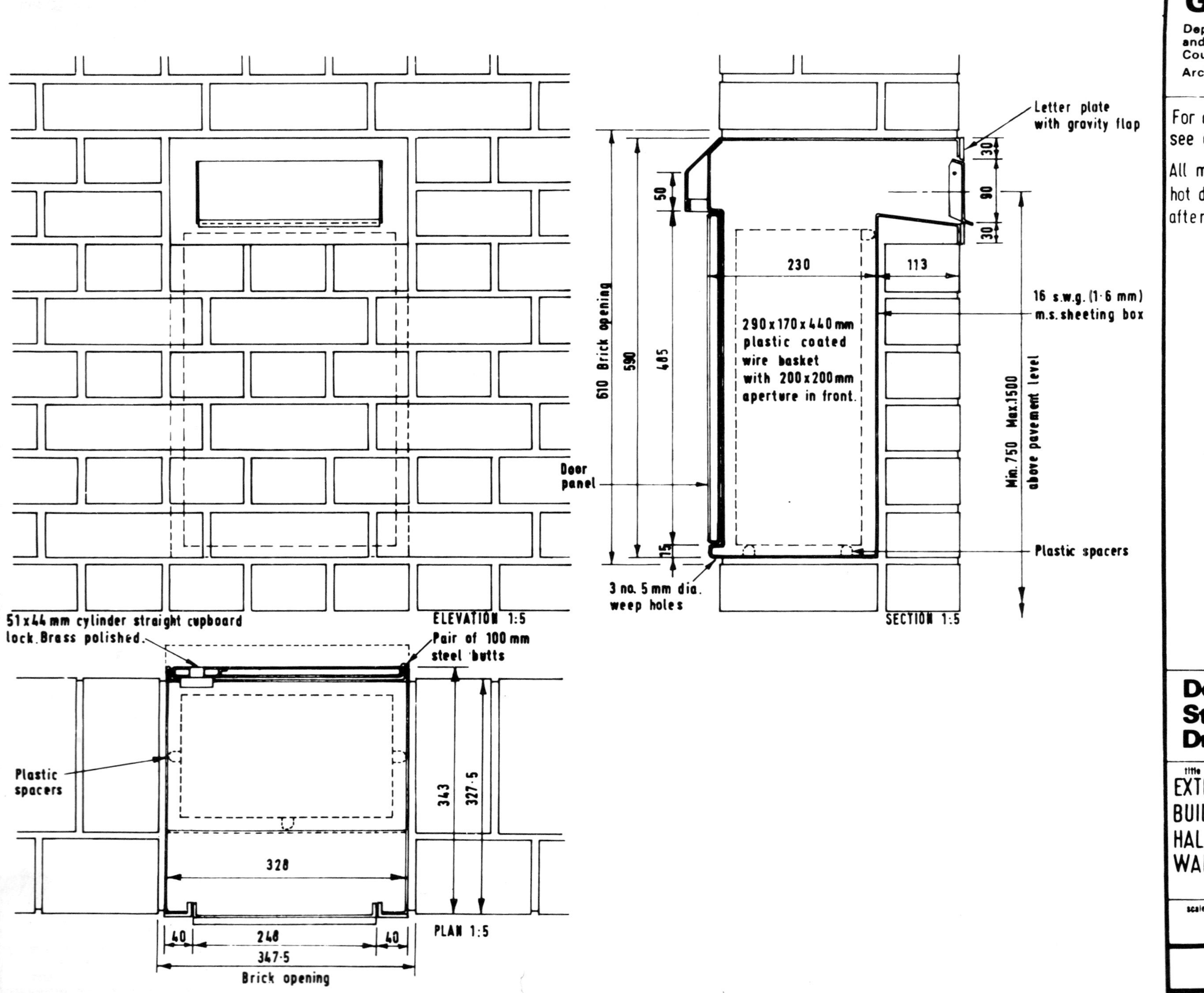

GLC ILEA

Department of Architecture
and Civic Design
County Hall SE1
Architect Sir Roger Walters
KBE FRIBA FI StructE

For details of letter box see drawing (70)04069

All metal parts to be hot dipped galvanised after fabrication as Q.14

Departmental Standard Drawing

title
EXTERNAL LETTER BOX BUILT INTO ONE AND HALF BRICK THICK WALL.

scale
1:5

drawing no D3159 | rev

bldg type 7 | space use | element (70 | feature 700 | material Xh2 | key 3

00 - 010379

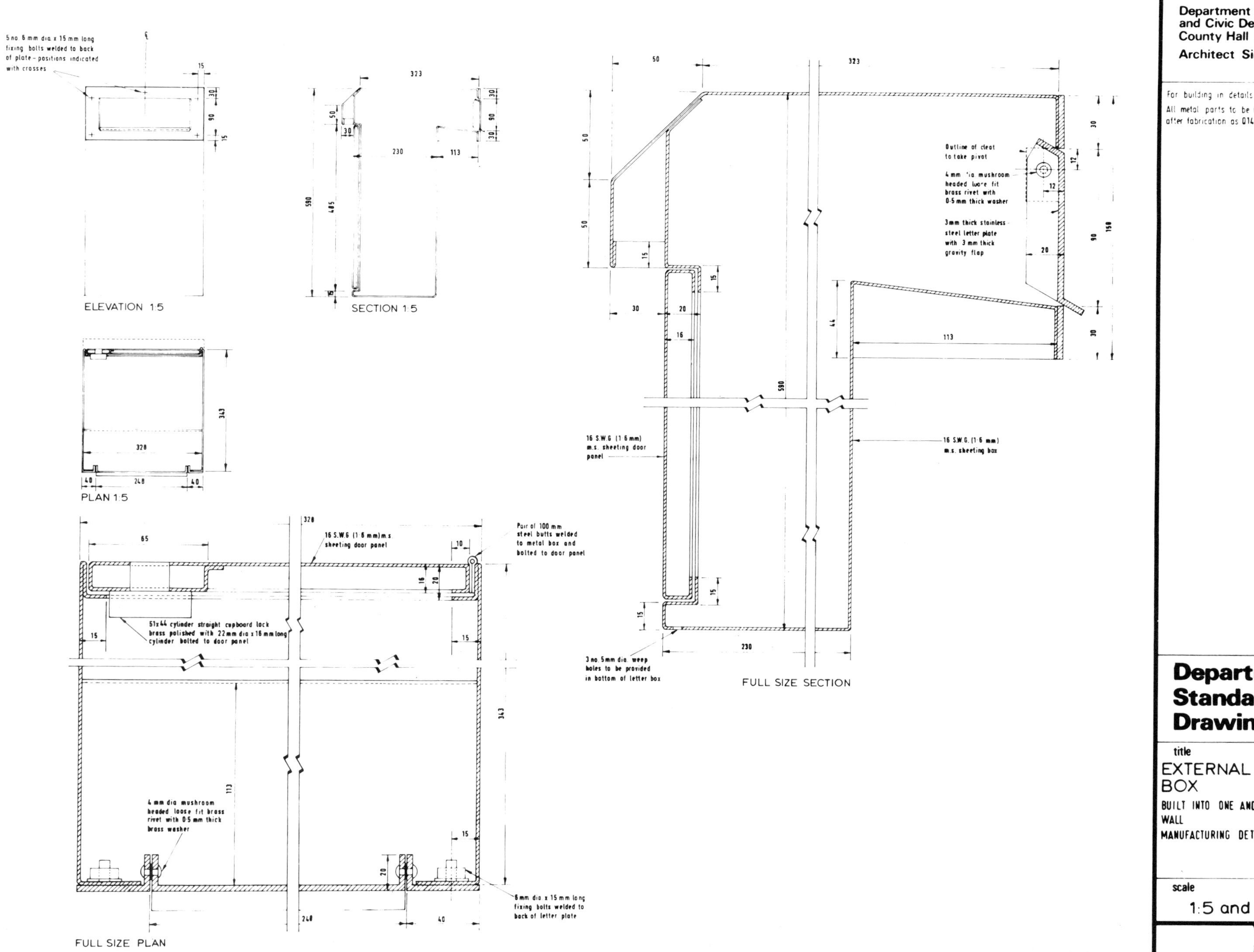

GLC ILEA

Department of Architecture and Civic Design
County Hall SE1
Architect Sir Roger Walters
KBE FRIBA FI Struct E

For building in details see drawing no [70] D3155
All metal parts to be hot dipped galvanised after fabrication as 014

Departmental Standard Drawing

title
EXTERNAL LETTER BOX
BUILT INTO ONE AND HALF BRICK THICK WALL
MANUFACTURING DETAILS

scale
1:5 and 1:1

drawing no
D4069

bldg type	space use	element	feature	material	key
7		[70]	700	Xh2	3

Credits

Produced in the Department of Architecture and Civic Design, Greater London Council.

Architect to the Council
F B Pooley, CBE

Technical Policy Architect
Malcolme Gordon

Technical Information Group
Roger Cass
J Max-Jarzabek
Z F Janik
D R Thomas
S A Higgs
A A J Izzi
G Noak

Drawing Selection Panel
R Apsey
R Garton
F Hand
M Hohmann
K Lyall
K Nicholson
Ms J Price
G Stewart

Graphics and Book Design
John Beake

Editorial control by David Atwell, Departmental Information Officer, to whom any enquiries regarding the contents of this book should be addressed.